*WORLDWIDE PRAISE for **A World at Arms***

United States

"...the prose is clear, the detail arresting and the arguments carefully deployed...This is a tour de force, classical diplomatic history at its best. Mr. Weinberg's global view of the war pays dividends again and again."

– David Reynolds, *The New York Times Book Review*

"Mr. Weinberg has provided a masterful study that captures the global sweep, carnage and ultimate triumph of this war. It is a book to read, ponder and then reread. Quite simply, *A World at Arms* had now taken its place as the one-volume history of the Second World War."

– Calvin L. Christman, *Dallas Morning News*

"This brilliant and exhaustively researched masterwork is simply the best book to date on World War II."

– *Detroit Free Press*

United Kingdom

"Splendid and truly encyclopedic...A vast public of many nationalities needs to know what happened to the world between 1939 and 1945. Intelligent, learned, methodical, patient and lucid, Mr. Weinberg's book may well stand for the next twenty years as the most important instrument available to serve this need."

– *The Economist*

"There can be no better book to turn to than this for an explanation of the whole war...there seems to be nothing about which Gerhard Weinberg is not an expert...the text is a masterpiece of clear, level-headed explanation, remarkably free of the sound of any axe-grinding."

– *The Sunday Telegraph*

"This is a monumental work incorporating the major secondary literature, of which there is now a huge amount, as well as original research. No doubt it will remain one of the standard reference works on the Second World War, a tribute to Gerhard Weinberg's industry and perseverance."

– John A. S. Grenville, *The Times Higher Education Supplement*

Ireland

"This work by a German refugee of the time is a refreshing and stimulating perspective from which to review the war as a whole."

– Eoghan Corry, *Irish Press*

Germany

"Fifty years after World War II, which decisively marked the face of this century, there is now a marvelous, all-embracing complete account of it from a global perspective, which is without parallel. Weinberg always tries to grasp all aspects of the global conflict and to fit them into a comprehensive treatment. Whether dealing with the fighting on land, sea, or in the air, espionage or reconnaissance, psychological warfare or weapons systems – with each new invention often leading to a counter-weapon – nothing is left out. Furthermore, he tries to assign the individual aspects their proper weight, an especially difficult undertaking. He has been successful in this over and over again."

– Hans-Adolf Jacobsen, *Das Parlament*

Japan

"...a global history of the war deserving the attention of serious scholars and amateur historians alike...a well-researched clearly written book that will provide new insights to most readers."

– Ken Belson, *The Daily Yomiuri*

Australia

"Let it be said loud and clear. Any reader with the remotest interest in modern history needs to be alerted to the existence of this book. Weinberg's *A World at Arms*...is an extraordinary achievement."

– Trevor Wilson, *The Sydney Review*

"Professor Weinberg has achieved probably the most succinct, yet all-embracing, account of World War II...Not only has he achieved what he set out to accomplish, but he has done it in a manner both absorbing and eminently readable. It is one of the great war histories of the century."

– Frank Cranson, *Canberra Times*

Sweden

"This is a huge and highly educated history of World War II on all of its fronts."

– Jan Sandström, *Arvika*

The North and Central Atlantic

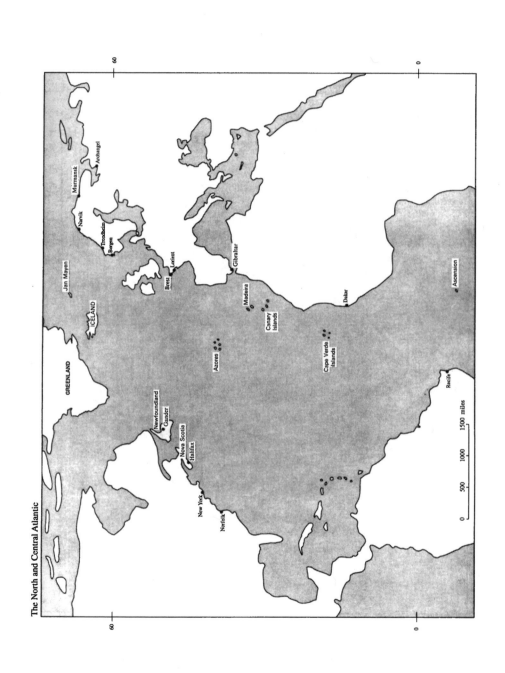

The Pacific

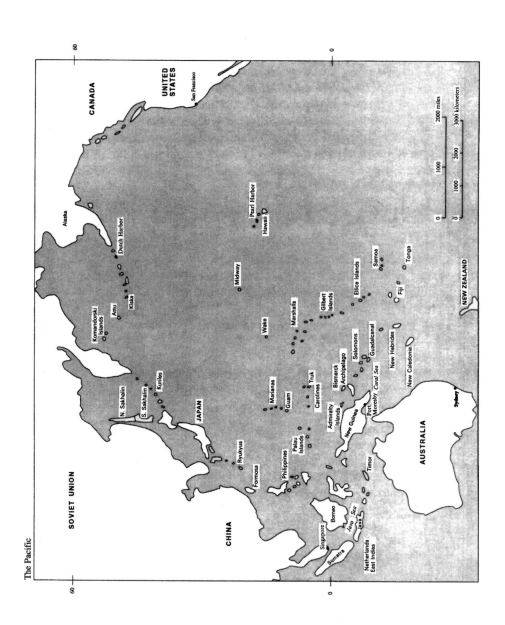

GERHARD L. WEINBERG

A WORLD AT ARMS

A GLOBAL HISTORY OF
WORLD WAR II

Second Edition

CAMBRIDGE
UNIVERSITY PRESS

CAMBRIDGE UNIVERSITY PRESS
Cambridge, New York, Melbourne, Madrid, Cape Town, Singapore, São Paulo

Cambridge University Press
40 West 20th Street, New York, NY 10011-4211, USA

www.cambridge.org
Information on this title: www.cambridge.org/9780521853163

First published 1994
Second edition first published 2005

Printed in the United States of America

A catalog record for this publication is available from the British Library.

Library of Congress Cataloging in Publication Data

A world at arms : a global history of World War II 2nd ed. / Gerhard L. Weinberg.
p. cm.
Includes bibliographical references and index.
ISBN 0-521-85316-8 – ISBN 0-521-61826-6 (pb.)
1. World War, 1939–1945. I. Weinberg, Gerhard L.
D743 .W424 2005
941.54 22   2005041954

ISBN-13   978-0-521-85316-3 hardback
ISBN-10   0-521-85316-8 hardback

ISBN-13   978-0-521-61826-7 paperback
ISBN-10   0-521-61826-6 paperback

FOR JANET

CONTENTS

MAPS

PREFACE TO THE NEW EDITION

In the decade since this book was published, kind readers have followed the request in the original Preface to send me corrections. I am most grateful to those who have taken the trouble to call to my attention errors that it has been possible to correct in subsequent printings. Reviewers of the book have been very kind to it. In the intervening decade, there have been important new materials made accessible to scholars and there has, in addition, been a continuous outpouring of scholarly works dealing with the greatest war of which we know. While there may be an opportunity to revise the book as a whole, in the meantime this is a good interval at which to point to some areas where either changes will be needed or new studies have reinforced the interpretation previously offered.

Certainly the original thesis that Germany deliberately initiated World War II on September 1, 1939, by a procedure that drew on Adolf Hitler's "lesson" of Munich, namely that he would not be cheated of war again as had happened in 1938, has been confirmed by the detailed examination of the immediate origins of the war.[1] An analysis of Soviet procedure in dealing with the German army in the 1939 Polish campaign by promptly and courteously returning all German prisoners of war captured by the Poles makes for an extraordinary contrast with the opposite handling of British and American prisoners held by the Germans in 1944–45.[2]

The description of the German decision to attack the Soviet Union has been confirmed by the new materials that have surfaced from both German and Soviet archives as a result of the effort of some to convert the German invasion into a sort of preventive move designed to forestall a planned invasion

---

[1] Stefan Kley, *Hitler, Ribbentrop und die Entfesselung des Zweiten Weltkriegs* (Paderborn: Schöningh, 1996).

[2] Compare the account in Sergej Slutsch, "Die deutsch-sowjetischen Beziehungen im Polenfeldzug und die Frage des Eintritts der UdSSR in den Zweiten Weltkrieg," in Bianka Pietrow-Ennker (ed.), *Präventivkrieg? Der deutsche Angriff auf die Sowjetunion* (Frankfurt/M: Fischer, 2000), with the one in John Nichol and Tony Rennell, *The Last Escape: The Untold Story of Allied Prisoners of War in Europe 1944–45* (New York: Viking, 2002).

by the Soviets invented by the advocates of this interpretation. From the German side we now have the project of the German army's chief of staff, General Franz Halder, for an invasion of the Soviet Union still in the fall of 1940 with orders and preparations starting on June 3, even before the armistice with France.[3] When Hitler decided on July 31 that the fall of 1940 would not allow for enough time to prepare and carry through the invasion, but that preparations for an invasion in 1941 should start, the general staff was already working on that. If there had been any concern about a Soviet invasion, why the willingness to wait?

From the Soviet archives there is plenty of confirming evidence for Stalin's desperate efforts to join the Tripartite Pact and his refusal – even hours after the German invasion – to credit the obvious signs of German intentions.[4] It is now known that Stalin not only received a summary of the German invasion plan from the government of the United States but even earlier from his own intelligence service, but that he refused to believe either warning and forbade his military advisors to take action against the German concentrations in the spring of 1941. As for the offensive projects imagined for him, it is difficult to square such concepts with the Soviet decision that the railways in the newly acquired Eastern portion of Poland were to be changed to the Russian wide railway gauge over seven years.

A subject that has needlessly cluttered the bookshelves has been the continued inability of some scholars to recognize that the critical issue was not whether the Germans could seize Moscow – or some other specific place – but whether the Soviet government, like that of Alexander I in 1812, could retain control of the unoccupied portions of the country and mobilize its human and material resources. Neither the Tsarist government of Nicholas II nor the Provisional Government of Alexander Kerensky had been able to do that, even though the Germans had not advanced in 1917 as far as they did in 1941 and 1942. As I pointed out in my book, the Soviet regime was fully prepared to carry on the war if Moscow were captured by the Germans. We now know of preparations for the demolition of important buildings in the capital if it actually fell.[5]

The accessibility of some, but by no means all, Soviet records has certainly enriched our understanding of the whole course of the fighting on the Eastern Front. Not only the defeat of the Soviet offensive on the central portion of the

[3] Carl Dirks and Karl-Heinz Janssen (eds.), "Plan Otto," *Die Zeit*, September 19, 1997, p. 16. I am grateful to Mr. Janssen and to Mr. John V. Hunter III for sending me copies of this article.
[4] See the book edited by Bianka Pietrov-Ennker cited in note 2 and Gerd R. Ueberschär and Lev A. Bezymenskij (eds.), *Der deutsche Angriff auf die Sowjetunion 1941: Die Kontroverse um die Präventivkriegsthese* (Darmstadt: Primus, 1998).
[5] Benjamin B. Fischer, "Preparing to Blow Up the Bolshoi Theater," *International Intelligence History Study Group Newsletter* 7, No. 2 (Winter 1999): 8–10; also published in *Center for the Study of Intelligence Bulletin* No. 10 (Winter 2000): 11–12.

front in the winter of 1942–43 (Operation "Mars") but many other aspects of the bitter combat in that theater have been illuminated by the books of David Glantz and others.[6] We now also have a much more reliable account of the enormous Soviet military casualties as well as a careful study of German military deaths.[7]

Two aspects of the war in the East need a further look: one on the basis of a reevaluation of events long known and the other on the basis of very important new information. The point that, like most authors, I have not stressed sufficiently is the general strategic significance for the course of the war on the Eastern Front as well as elsewhere of the success of the British in crushing the pro-Axis revolt in Iraq in May 1941 and the subsequent conquest of Syria from its Vichy French defenders. Had it been possible for the Germans to establish firm bases in either or both locations – as they very much hoped and as both Rashid Ali al-Gaylani in Iraq and the Vichy French authorities in Syria were quite willing to provide – the implications for subsequent developments would have been enormous. Could the Red Army have held in the Caucasus in 1942 with a German base in their rear and also in a position to cut the supply route through Iran? Would the Japanese have grasped the possibility of a meeting with their European ally in reality as opposed to the theoretical speculations on this subject?

An entirely different aspect of the war in the East has come to light with the declassification in 1996 of the British intercepts of reports by units of the German Order Police (Ordnungspolizei) on large-scale shooting of Jews in newly occupied portions of the Soviet Union in the summer of 1941. It turns out that essentially from the beginning of the campaign in the East, these units, containing about fifteen thousand men, were tasked with killing Jews in the same general areas in which until recently it had been believed that it was the Einsatzgruppen, the murder squads, that did all or most of the killing. Some had assumed that the approximately two thousand five hundred men of these latter units could hardly have been charged with killing the hundreds of thousands of Jews in the newly occupied Soviet territories, even with the assistance of pogroms by the local population that the Germans hoped for. Now that we know that close to twenty thousand men were engaged in the mass killing from the summer of 1941 on, the likelihood that they were so instructed before the invasion is far more likely – and the evidence was so read by the British government in the fall of 1941.[8] This fits with the information

---

[6] David M. Glantz, *Zhukov's Greatest Defeat: The Red Army's Epic Disaster in Operation Mars, 1942* (Lawrence: University Press of Kansas, 1999), and other books by the same author.

[7] G. F. Krivosheev (ed.), *Soviet Casualties and Combat Losses in the Twentieth Century* (London: Greenhill, 1997); Rüdiger Overmans, *Deutsche militärischen Verluste im Zweiten Weltkrieg* (Munich: Oldenbourg, 1999).

[8] Richard Breitman, *Official Secrets: What the Nazis Planned, What the British and Americans Knew* (New York: Hill & Wang, 1998).

in the even more recently released early interrogations of Otto Ohlendorf, the head of one of the murder squads.[9] This last is one of the mass of documents declassified as a result of the work of the Interagency Working Group established to implement the Nazi War Crimes Disclosure and Imperial Japanese Government Records laws of 1998 and 2000.[10] Additional information on aspects of the war can be expected to emerge as scholars mine these newly accessible materials.

Recent years have seen other important works on the systematic killing of Jews using both newly accessible materials and the essential recognition of the centrality of this aim to the German conduct of the war. While some of these works have added to the understanding of the German army's role in what has come to be called the Holocaust, others have traced the process of German decision making or the involvement of local collaborators in the murder program.[11] It is safe to assume that there will be considerable further work by scholars on this facet of wartime developments.[12]

The fighting in North Africa continues to draw the attention of both scholars and the public, but beyond adding detail and local color, new works have not altered our understanding of the course of events. The relationship of that campaign to the survival of the Jewish community in the British Mandate of Palestine is never considered. That Erwin Rommel was given by Hitler an estate stolen from the local Jewish community is mentioned but never related to the expectation that his conquest of Palestine was to enable the Germans to kill all Jews there before turning the area over to Italy. Similarly, the significance of control of the Indian Ocean for the ability of the British Eighth Army to be reinforced and supplied remains as absent from the new literature as it was from the old.[13] Of importance for an understanding of subsequent events in the Mediterranean and Southeast Europe is a newly located document on Hitler's reaction to the Axis defeat in Tunisia in May 1943.[14] It sheds light on both Hitler's concern about the situation in Italy and his early interest in

---

[9] The newly released material is cited in Hilary C. Earl, "Accidental Justice: The Trial of Otto Ohlendorf and the Einsatzgruppen Leaders in Nuremberg, Germany, 1948–1958," PhD diss., University of Toronto, 2002.

[10] See the pieces by professional historians prepared for the IWG and published in Richard Breitman et al., *U.S. Intelligence and the Nazis* (New York: Cambridge University Press, 2005).

[11] Donald M. McKale, *Hitler's Shadow War: The Holocaust and World War II* (New York: Cooper Square, 2002); Christopher R. Browning, *The Origins of the Final Solution: The Evolution of Nazi Jewish Policy, September 1939–March 1942* (Lincoln: University of Nebraska Press, 2004); Martin Dean, *Collaboration in the Holocaust: Crimes of the Local Police in Belorussia and Ukraine, 1941–44* (London: Macmillan, 2000); Walter Manoschek, *"Serbien ist judenfrei": Militärische Besatzungspolitik und Judenvernichtung in Serbien 1941/42* (Munich: Oldenbourg, 1993).

[12] Shlomo Aronson, *Hitler, the Allies, and the Jews* (New York: Cambridge University Press, 2004).

[13] An example is John Bierman and Colin Smith, *The Battle of Alamein: Turning Point, World War II* (New York: Viking, 2002).

[14] Kapitän zur See Rolf Junge an Grossadmiral Karl Dönitz, May 15, 1943, Bundesarchi/ Militärarchiv Freiburg, RM 7/260, f. 197, kindly provided to me by Professor Bernd Wegner.

a German military occupation of Hungary, an operation that would actually come ten months later in March 1944.

The war in Europe in 1944 has certainly attracted much attention from scholars. The question whether the Red Army's halt before Warsaw during the Polish uprising there was a deliberate choice to enable the Germans to crush forces loyal to the Polish Government-in-Exile or the result of unrelated military and logistical developments at the front will continue to agitate people interested in those dramatic events. Since the Red Army crossed the Vistula both above and below Warsaw, and since Stalin refused landing rights to British and American planes trying to bring supplies to the Poles fighting in the city's streets, I remain convinced of the former interpretation.

The publication of the diary of Georgi Dimitrov, a close associate of Stalin's, provides new insights into that leader's thinking about many aspects of events during the war. We thus see Stalin suspicious about Yugoslav Marshal Tito's negotiations with the Germans.[15] This is especially ironic in view of the ongoing argument about Churchill's shifting of support to Tito being or not being influenced by a Soviet mole in the British SOE intelligence organization.

The fighting in the West in 1944 has been the subject of much study in England and the United States even though it was on a far smaller scale than the struggle in the East. Recent work on the Normandy invasion certainly adds to our understanding of that key event, but it hardly alters the general picture.[16] An exception may be the successful American defeat of the German counter-offensive at Mortain, which owed less to signals intelligence than has previously been believed.[17] The attention devoted to the siege of Bastogne and the role of the 101st Airborne Division in that fight has unjustifiably overshadowed the critical part that the 7th Armored Division played in the defense of St. Vith at the northern front of the German offensive, but no one has managed to minimize Field Marshal Montgomery's foolishness in his public claiming of success when it was actually his failure to drive into the German bulge from the North that enabled so much of the attacking force to avoid encirclement. The German winter offensive further south, Operation Northern Wind (Nordwind), has begun to receive more attention but is still not properly fitted into the broader picture. An interesting aspect of all these battles is that, contrary to much literature claiming some sort of superiority

---

[15] Ivo Banac (ed.), *The Diary of Georgi Dimitrov 1933–1949* (New Haven, Conn.: Yale University Press, 2003), pp. 267–68.

[16] Adrian R. Lewis, *Omaha Beach: A Flawed Victory* (Chapel Hill: University of North Carolina Press, 2001); Russell R. Hart, *Clash of Arms: How the Allies Won in Normandy* (Boulder, Colo.: Lynne Rienner, 2001).

[17] Mark J. Reardon, *Victory at Mortain: Stopping Hitler's Panzer Counteroffensive* (Lawrence: University Press of Kansas, 2002).

for the fighting ability of the German army, in many cases American infantry in inferior numbers and without adequate armored support held and then defeated the German units they faced.

The war at sea continues to receive the attention it deserves, but in this case also details improve our understanding but do not appear to call for any major revisions. The point that has been too frequently overlooked is that the enormous resource allocation by the Germans to the construction of hundreds of submarines created a significant drain on Germany's ability to produce the tanks and guns that its forces fighting on the Eastern Front so desperately needed. The air war has recently attracted much attention in Germany because of the way it enables some to imagine the German people as victims in the war. Rather than recognize the foolishness of insisting on building an air force in violation of treaty and law in a world without heavy bombers, those in the glass house who threw bombs as well as stones claimed astonishment when others shifted from dropping leaflets to also dropping bombs. This story may not be accurate but it is telling: A few German soldiers entered the Paris studio of Pablo Picasso in the summer of 1940 and saw there some of his preliminary sketches for his famous picture "The Bombing of Guernica." One of the soldiers asked, "So you did this?" and Picasso answered, "No, you did."

Two aspects of the air war have received important new studies. Tami Davis Biddle has looked into the way in which the theory and practice of strategic bombing developed in the years between the two wars and during the conflict itself.[18] The very large and important role of German anti-aircraft defenses from the prewar period into the last days of fighting is brought out in a book by Edward Westermann.[19] On the German last-minute recruitment of kids and the elderly into a sort of home guard militia, the Volkssturm, as well as the preparations for a largely failed underground movement in occupied Germany, there are now excellent studies.[20] In this connection, we can also see more clearly how the Western Allies came to believe in a serious German effort to hold out for a considerable period of time in a southern redoubt and why General Eisenhower was influenced by that possibility.[21]

---

[18] Tami Davis Biddle, *Rhetoric and Reality in Air Warfare: The Evolution of British and American Ideas about Strategic Bombing, 1914–1945* (Princeton, N.J.: Princeton University Press, 2002).

[19] Edward B. Westermann, *Flak: German Anti-Aircraft Defenses. 1914–1945* (Lawrence: University Press of Kansas, 2001).

[20] David K. Yelton, *Hitler's Volkssturm: The Nazi Militia and the Fall of Germany, 1944–1945* (Lawrence: University Press of Kansas, 2002); Perry Biddiscombe, *Werwolf! The History of the National Socialist Guerilla Movement, 1944–1946* (Toronto: University of Toronto Press, 1998).

[21] Timothy Naftali, "Creating the Myth of the Alpenfestung: Allied Intelligence and the Collapse of the Nazi Police State," in Günter Bischof and Anton Pelinka (eds.), *Contemporary Austrian Studies*, Vol. 5, *Austrian Historical Memory and National Identity* (New Brunswick, N.J.: Transaction Publishers, 1997), pp. 203–46.

The Japanese attack on Pearl Harbor continues to attract conspiracy theorists without producing a shred of evidence – an obvious sign for the theorists that the conspiracy was diabolically clever. The critical point that has escaped all too many observers is the connection between two factors for which the evidence has long been available. On the one hand there are the records declassified in the 1970s that show how the intercepts of German messages to their submarines in the Atlantic were utilized to avoid incidents – when they could as easily have been utilized to create incidents on an almost daily basis. On the other hand, there is the enormous amount of time that President Roosevelt personally invested in the endless negotiations with Japan. It was clearly his hope that if the Japanese government could be stalled until those in Tokyo could see the Germans losing rather than winning, they would stay out of jumping into a wider war on the losing side. The converse of this tactic – which came within two weeks of working – has been illuminated by new information on the German side. It has become clear that one reason Hitler drove the German army forward on the Eastern Front toward Moscow in late November–early December 1941 was precisely because he was afraid that the Japanese – whom he had been urging forward for months – might not take the plunge.[22] In this context it is easier to understand the enthusiasm that Hitler expressed to Joseph Goebbels, as revealed by the newly published portions of the latter's diary, about Japan's action as well as Hitler's own immediate order to initiate hostilities with the United States.[23]

On the immediately following events of the war in the Pacific there is what might be called a developing consensus on some issues. The refusal to allow the bombers, sent to the Philippines in the hope of deterring a Japanese attack, to fly missions against the Japanese as soon as Manila heard of the attack on Pearl Harbor as well as the prior shift of the defensive plans for Luzon from Bataan to the beaches are both seen as serious errors of judgment by General Douglas MacArthur. On the other hand, his role in stabilizing the situation in Australia in 1942 by his arrival there when the country was seriously concerned about a Japanese invasion, as well as his role in pushing hard for the allocation of American resources to the defense of Australia and America's route to it, can increasingly be seen as both positive and significant. This point was especially important when some of Australia's own forces were retained in the Mediterranean theater and in effect had to

---

[22] Notes by General Walter Scherff published in Marianne Feuersenger, *Im Vorzimmer der Macht: Aufzeichnungen aus dem Wehrmachtführungsstab und Führerhauptquartier, 1940–1945* (Munich: Herbig, 1999), p. 110. See also Donald M. Goldstein and Katherine V. Dillon (eds.), *The Pearl Harbor Papers: Inside the Japanese Plans* (Dulles, Va.: Brassey's, 2000); and Henry C. Clausen and Bruce Lee, *Pearl Harbor: Final Judgement* (New York: Crown, 1992).

[23] Elke Fröhlich (ed.), *Die Tagebücher von Joseph Goebbels*, Teil II, Band 2, *Oktober–Dezember 1941* (Munich: Saur, 1996).

be replaced by units from the United States. There are certainly new studies of several of MacArthur's campaigns as well as of the fighting on and around Guadalcanal, but these generally add detail rather than revise the existing picture.[24]

It has long been evident that by regularly underestimating Japanese strength at points to be attacked, MacArthur's chief of intelligence, General Charles Willoughby, provided stiff competition for the head of German military intelligence on the Eastern Front from 1942 to 1945, General Reinhard Gehlen, for the title of stupidest intelligence chief of World War II. A very careful analysis of the intelligence operation supporting the second avenue of attack toward Tokyo, that of Admiral Chester Nimitz across the Central Pacific, reveals where and when that intelligence succeeded and when it fell short.[25] It thus becomes easier to understand why the assaults on the Marshall Islands, Guam, and Tinian were substantially less difficult than those on Saipan, Peleliu, Iwo Jima, and Okinawa turned out to be.

Our understanding of the long fight for Burma has been enriched by a fine study of the way in which the Indian Army rebuilt itself after the initial disasters in that exceptionally difficult theater of war.[26] None of the works that deal with the Indian collaborator with Japan, Subhas Chandra Bose, or his Indian National Army has engaged either Bose's reaction to German mass killing of Sinti and Roma (Gypsies) because their ancestors came from India or the reaction of the soldiers in his army to the sex slaves kidnapped in Japanese-occupied lands and held in enclosures attached to the camps in which they were being trained to follow their Japanese comrades in the occupation of India.

Recent studies certainly enrich our understanding of the naval battle in the Philippines in October 1944. One of these underlines the extraordinary achievement of the destroyer and escort carrier crews in defending the American landing on Leyte while Admiral Halsey was away chasing Japanese decoys.[27] Detailed examinations of the fight on Iwo Jima and events on the

---

[24] William H. Bartsch, *December 8, 1941: MacArthur's Pearl Harbor* (College Station: Texas A&M Press, 2003); Harry Gailey, *MacArthur Strikes Back: Decision at Buna, New Guinea 1942–1943* (Novato, Calif.: Presidio, 2000), and other works by the same author; Thomas E. Griffith, Jr., *MacArthur's Airman: General George C. Kenney and the War in the Southwest Pacific* (Lawrence: University Press of Kansas, 1998); Stephen R. Taaffe, *MacArthur's Jungle War: The 1944 New Guinea Campaign* (Lawrence: University Press of Kansas, 1998); Richard B. Frank, *Guadalcanal: The Definitive Account of the Landmark Battle* (New York: Penguin, 1992).

[25] Jeffrey M. Moore, *Spies for Nimitz: Joint Military Intelligence in the Pacific War* (Annapolis, Md.: Naval Institute Press, 2004).

[26] Daniel P. Marston, *Phoenix from the Ashes: The Indian Army in the Burma Campaign* (Westport, Conn.: Praeger, 2003).

[27] James D. Hornfischer, *The Last Stand of the Tin Can Sailors: The Extraordinary World War II Story of the U.S. Navy's Finest Hour* (New York: Bantam, 2004). Important for the war in the Pacific in general, Carl Boyd and Akihiko Yoshida, *The Japanese Submarine Force and World War II* (Annapolis, Md.: Naval Institute Press, 1995).

nearby island of Chichi Jima serve to underline the fierce nature of the struggle for and about those islands in early 1945.[28]

Considerable quantities of printer's ink have been lavished on the final stage of the war in the Pacific. A series of serious and careful analyses of the plans for the invasion of Japan reinforce the views of those who have held that shocking Japan into surrender by the dropping of two atomic bombs saved both vast numbers of American lives and even larger numbers of Japanese lives that would have been lost in the battles that the Japanese army leadership hoped would discourage the United States from insisting on an occupation and trials of war criminals.[29] Two aspects of the war that even these studies have not taken sufficiently into account belong in this context. One is that in addition to the approximately seven hundred thousand American casualties anticipated in Operation Olympic, the landing on Kyushu, there would have been very large numbers of casualties from the sending of American troops through a battlefield drenched by the fallout of the atomic bombs that were to be dropped in tactical support of the landing at a time when this aspect of atomic weapons was not yet understood.[30] The other factor that is generally neglected in the literature is that of the fighting elsewhere in the Pacific, on the mainland of China, and in Southeast Asia. Tunnel vision concentrated on the atomic bombs has led to the screening out of the continued fighting in the Philippines, the planned landings on Java and Malaya, and at numerous other places where Allied forces were engaged in fierce fighting with the Japanese. Similarly absent from most books on the end of the war in East Asia is any discussion of the fate of the great numbers of Allied prisoners of war whose murder had been ordered by Japanese headquarters in Tokyo.

There is now additional information on the home fronts of the major belligerents. We have a better insight into the way in which the Soviets mobilized their resources for the great conflict, and it is now apparent that Germany drew more women into the war effort than has hitherto been believed. On the other hand, there is still neither a comprehensive study of the hundreds of thousands of women who served in the Red Army nor any analysis of German records to determine to what extent the order to kill all captured women soldiers was actually carried out.

---

[28] Derrick Wright, *The Battle for Iwo Jima 1945* (Thrupp, Stroud, UK: Sutton, 1999); Chester G. Hearn, *Sorties into Hell: The Hidden War on Chichi Jima* (Westport, Conn.: Praeger, 2003).

[29] John R. Skates, *The Invasion of Japan: Alternative to the Bomb* (Columbia: University of South Carolina Press, 1994); Thomas B. Allen and Norman Polmar, *Code-Name Downfall: The Secret Plan to Invade Japan – and Why Truman Dropped the Bomb* (New York: Simon & Schuster, 1995); Richard B. Frank, *Downfall: The End of the Imperial Japanese Empire* (New York: Random House, 1999).

[30] Edward J. Drea, *In the Service of the Emperor: Essays on the Imperial Japanese Army* (Lincoln: University of Nebraska Press, 1998), chap. 11.

The issues of collaboration and resistance in areas occupied for some time by the Germans, Italians, and Japanese, issues that were heavily loaded with emotions, myths, and deliberate distortions for decades, are beginning to be examined in a more objective manner. It is probably safe to predict that future decades will see increasingly balanced treatments of these sensitive matters. This is also the situation in regard to the confiscation, sale, and resale of works of art and other assets taken not only from Jews but also from non-Jewish individuals and museums during hostilities and occupation. The social changes that were hastened or retarded by the war are also likely to see further exploration.

Records on intelligence operations of the belligerents are slowly being declassified, but there is still a long way to go. This is especially true for the intelligence, counter-intelligence, and code-breaking operations of the Soviets.[31] Since the relevant records in all the archives are on paper that is deteriorating and will disintegrate entirely before many more years pass, one can only hope that they will be opened and microfilmed before they disappear forever. The process of deterioration that is tied to the quality of wartime paper threatens to cut off those who still guard them from their own history. For this reason, every step toward additional openings should be welcomed by people who are interested in the war that shook the world and its inhabitants on an unprecedented scale.*

Gerhard L. Weinberg
October 2004

---

[31] Robert W. Stephan, *Stalin's Secret War: Soviet Counterintelligence against the Nazis, 1941–1945* (Lawrence: University Press of Kansas, 2004), is a good start in this difficult field.

* There are, of course, large numbers of useful and important works that have been published in the last twelve years but are not cited here.

PREFACE TO THE FIRST EDITION

When you go home
Tell them of us, and say:
For your tomorrow,
We gave our today.

This text is inscribed on a memorial to British soldiers who were killed
in one of the most desperate but least known battles of World War II:
the fighting around the town of Kohima in eastern India not far from
the border with Burma, from which a Japanese army had set out to
march to Delhi in 1944. At Kohima, Indian and English soldiers had
defeated a Japanese force which was followed by some Indians who
believed that the Japanese treated the people of their colonial empire,
such as the Koreans, far better than the British treated theirs. The leader
of those Indians who believed that a victory of Japan and Germany
over Britain, the United States, and the Soviet Union was greatly to be
desired was a man named Subhas Chandra Bose. He had fled from
India to Germany across the Soviet Union during the period of the
Nazi-Soviet Non-Aggression Pact and had had an opportunity to see
for himself in Europe how kindly the Germans were disposed toward
those they conquered until, in 1943, the Germans sent him by submarine
to the Indian Ocean where he had transferred to a Japanese submarine
for the rest of the trip to East Asia.

This series of inter-related events may serve to illustrate why it has
seemed to me to be appropriate to try to write an account of World War
II which looks at it in a global perspective. For the origins of that vast
conflict, I believed it both appropriate and possible to pursue a theme
which might serve to tie the whole complicated story together; it
appeared convincing to me that the foreign policy of Hitler's Germany
provided such a theme. I stated in the preface of the first of my two
volumes on that subject:

Whatever the conflicting ambitions, rivalries and ideologies of the world's powers in the 1920s and 1930s, it is safe to assert that, with the solitary exception of Germany, no European nation considered another world war as a conceivable answer to whatever problems confronted it. Local wars and conflicts, specific aggressive moves or attempts at subversion, miscalculations leading to hostilities - all these were conceivable, and most of them occurred. But without German initiative another world-wide holocaust was inconceivable to contemporaries in all countries and is unimaginable retrospectively for the historian. Accordingly, the course of German foreign policy provides the obvious organizing principle for any account of the origins of World War II.

But once the Germans initiated hostilities in September, 1939, the conflict took a course of its own. German initiatives dominated its early stages, but even then not always in the way that its architects had anticipated. In the summer of 1940 the European war was already taking on forms far different from those confidently planned in Berlin. And the entrance of Japan into the wider conflict, though ardently desired and long urged by the Germans, dramatically altered the dimensions and nature of the war. Certainly the Japanese would never have expanded the war with China which they had been waging since 1937 into a portion of the wider conflict had it not been for the great German victories in the West in 1940. Without those victories, the East Asian fighting, however terrible for those involved and especially for the vast numbers of Chinese killed in it, would have remained an isolated war like that Japan and China had fought in 1894-95. But once Japan decided that the opportunity for the seizure of an enormous empire in Southeast Asia had come, none of the participants could operate in the world-wide conflagration as it preferred; all had to adjust to the necessities – even the terrors – of the moment.

It is in the face of the resulting complexity of the struggle that it seems to me impossible to draw out a single unifying theme. On the other hand, too many of the existing accounts treat the war either from quite parochial perspectives or by dealing with different geographical areas as if one were an appendage of another. It is the special and peculiar characteristic of the upheaval which shook the world between 1939 and 1945 that dramatic events were taking place *simultaneously* in different portions of the globe; decision makers faced enormous varieties of decisions at one and the same time, and repercussions in areas far distant from those of any specific crisis or issue before them had constantly to be kept in mind.

It is with this global point of view that I have tried to review the war as a whole with special emphasis on the inter-relationships between the various theaters and the choices faced by those in positions of leadership.

That has meant that the bloody details of fighting, of the seemingly endless struggle for control of the seas, and the interminable tedium of war broken by moments of sheer terror, may all appear to have been sanitized or at least obscured. If such is the effect, it was not the intent. But there are far more books which convincingly convey the immediacy of the fighting than those that survey the broader picture.

A further special problem appears to me to affect much of the literature on the war. It is too frequently forgotten that those who had choices and decisions to make were affected by memories of the *preceding* war of 1914-18, not by the Cold War, the Vietnam conflict, or other issues through which we look back on World War II. They did not know, as we do, how the war would come out. They had their hopes – and fears – but none of the certainty that retrospective analysis all too often imposes on situations in which there were alternatives to consider, all of them fraught with risks difficult to assess at the time.

The effort to present the war in a global perspective, looking forward rather than backward, and to do so at least in part on the basis of extensive research in the archives, has been challenging. It could not possibly have been accomplished without a great deal of help. The National Endowment for the Humanities awarded me a fellowship which enabled me to initiate the research for this book, and the Rockefeller Foundation Conference and Study Center at Bellagio provided the opportunity to review the findings of that initial foray into the archives. Those forays had been substantially assisted by earlier fellowships of the Guggenheim Foundation and the American Council of Learned Societies. Archivists at the National Archives in Washington as well as the National Records Center in Suitland, the Franklin D. Roosevelt Presidential Library at Hyde Park, the U.S. army's Center for Military History, the Public Record Office at Kew on the outskirts of London, the Imperial War Museum Library and the Liddell Hart Centre for Military Archives at King's College in London, the German Foreign Ministry Archive in Bonn, the German Federal Archive in Koblenz and its Military Archive in Freiburg, the Institute for Contemporary History in Munich, and the Center for Research on the History of National Socialism in Hamburg were invariably courteous and helpful to what must have seemed to them an extremely demanding, presistent, and at times difficult customer. The William R. Kenan, Jr. Charitable Trust has made much of the research travel possible and has been helpful in innumerable other ways.

The Houghton Library at Harvard allowed access to the William Phillips papers; the papers of Jay Pierrepont Moffat were made accessible by his widow, Mrs. Albert Lévitt. Many scholars have enlightened me by discussion and by providing specific information; I would especially like to thank Josef Anderle, Richard Breitman, Michael Gannon, the late Louis Morton, Richard Soloway, Stephen Schuker and Robert Wolfe. Work on the War Documentation Project of Columbia University and, later, the American Historical Association's project for microfilming captured German documents afforded me an unequalled opportunity to familiarize myself with masses of German archival material.

Crown copyrighted quotations from the collections at the Public Record Office are used with the kind permission of the Controller of Her Majesty's Stationery Office. The Trustees of the Liddell Hart Centre for Military Archives have agreed to my quoting from the papers of Lord Ismay and of Lord Alanbrooke in their custody.

When I began work on this book in 1978, my late wife Wilma was already fighting the cancer which took her life; she not only insisted I go forward with this project but spent many hours copying portions of documents for me in Freiburg. At a very difficult time in my life, a new light came into it. While I was resuming the writing of this book, the lovely lady to whom this book is dedicated came to share in the travails of its completion. And her mother, Lois Kabler, transformed hundreds of pages of my hieroglyphs into the word processor; surely a mother-in-law story to warm the heart. An extraordinary copyeditor, Margaret Sharman, has caught numerous slips. It is my hope that readers will take the trouble to call errors to my attention so that they might be corrected in any future edition. Many have been kind enough to do so, and it has been possible to make corrections in this printing. All remaining mistakes are, of course, my responsibility.

ABBREVIATIONS

AA Auswärtiges Amt. The German Foreign Ministry: used to designate the archive of the Foreign Ministry in Bonn. Followed in the citation by the section of the archive, title and number of the volume, and a frame number stamped on the document if these are provided.

ADAP Akten zur Deutschen auswärtigen Politik 1918–1945. The German language edition of documents mainly from the German Foreign Ministry files, cited by series letter, volume number, and document number.

BA *Bundesarchiv.* The German Federal Archive in Koblenz. Followed in the citation by the collection and folder designations.

BA/MA *Bundesarchiv/Militärarchiv.* The Military Archive Branch in Freiburg of the German Federal Archive. Followed in the citation by the collection and folder number. All "N" citations are from collections of private papers deposited in the archive.

Bd. *Band.* Volume number of a series in the German Foreign Ministry archive.

CEH Central European History

DRuZW Das Deutsche Reich und der Zweite Weltkrieg. The German official history of World War II being published by the Military History Research Office in Freiburg.

f. Folio(s), used for pagination on a document in an archive, frequently helpful when a group of documents has been bound together and then given folio numbers by archivists.

FDRL Franklin D. Roosevelt Library, Hyde Park, N.Y.

fr. Frame, indicates frame number either on microfilm or stamped on a document prior to microfilming.

FRUS Foreign Relations of the United States. The main series of U.S.

documents published by the Department of State; the volumes are cited by year, and volume number for that year or special title.

GPO Government Printing Office, used where the U.S. Government Printing Office is either the publisher or distributor of a book. This includes books which were originally issued by the historical offices of the U.S. army and air force.

Hamburg, Research Center Forschungsstelle für die Geschichte des Nationalsozialismus in Hamburg. A research institute in Hamburg with some archival holdings, cited by the system used there.

HMSO His/Her Majesty's Stationery Office, the British government's official printing office.

Hung. Docs. Hungarian Documents. The set published by the Hungarian government and containing, in addition to the texts in Magyar, a summary of each document in German.

Imperial War Museum A museum and research library in London.

IMT International Military Tribunal.

IMTFE International Military Tribunal for the Far East.

Institut für Zeitgeschichte Institute for Contemporary History, Munich.

JCH Journal of Contemporary History

JMH Journal of Modern History

KTB Halder Hans-Adolf Jacobsen (ed.), *Generaloberst Halder, Kriegstage-b uch*, 3 vols. (Stuttgart:/Kohlhammer, 1962-64). War Diary of General Halder.

KTB OKW Kriegstagebuch des Oberkommandos der Wehrmacht, War diary of the high command of the armed forces.

KTB Skl Kriegstagebuch der Seekriegsleitung. Diary of the high command of the navy. Citations are followed by the Part number (almost always A), the volume number, and the date. Cited from the originals in Freiburg, these volumes are currently being published, but the references as given here can be used to locate material in both.

MGM Militärgeschichtliche Mitteilungen. This important journal is published by the German Military History Research Office in Freiburg.

MR Map Room. A section of the Roosevelt Library.

NA National Archives. The main American depository. The records cited are from the main building in downtown Washington and the National Records Center in Suitland, Maryland, but many are likely to be moved to the Archives II building located in College Park, Maryland.

To avoid confusion, location as between the two existing buildings is not given.

OF Official File. A segment of the files at the Roosevelt Library.

PRO Public Record Office. The main British depository. All those cited are located in the new building in Kew. The letters and first number following PRO constitute the "Class" of the file and are followed, after a slash, by the folder number.

PSF President's Secretary's File. A segment of the files at the Roosevelt Library.

RG Record Group. The designation of major segments of the holdings of the U.S. National Archives.

St.S. Staatssekretär. State-Secretary, used in designating citations from that part of the German Foreign Ministry archive called the Büro Staatssekretär.

TMWC Trial of the Major War Criminals before the International Military Tribunal, 42 vols. (Nürnberg: The Tribunal, 1946-48).

USSBS United States Strategic Bombing Survey. Used for the author of publications emanating from this agency.

U.St.S. Unterstaatssekretär. Special title of the head of the political division of the German Foreign Ministry, used for a section of the records of the AA.

VjZ Vierteljahrshefte für Zeitgeschichte. Major journal published by the Institute for Contemporary History in Munich.

ZS Zeugenschrifttum. Depositions by witnesses, a collection at the Institute for Contemporary History.

ZSg. Zeitgeschichtssammlung. Collection on recent history. A designation for several collections of papers at the German Federal Archive.

INTRODUCTION

Although this book contains a chapter on the background of World War II, it defines that war as beginning in 1939 in Europe. While some have argued that the war was merely a continuation of World War I after a temporary interruption created by the armistice of 1918, and that the whole period from 1914 to 1945 should be seen as the age of a new European civil war, a Thirty-one Years War if you will, such a perspective ignores not only the very different origins and nature of the prior conflict but obscures instead of illuminating the special character of the second one. If an important by-product of both wars was the weakening of Europe and its hold on the world, the *intentions* of the belligerents were fundamentally different. It is true that these changed somewhat in the course of each of these lengthy struggles, but a basic differentiation remains.

In World War I, the two sides were fighting over their relative roles in the world, roles defined by possible shifts in boundaries, colonial possessions, and military and naval power. It is true that the Austro–Hungarian empire anticipated the elimination of Serbia's independent status, and Germany very quickly came to the conclusion that Belgium would never regain its independence, but beyond this expected disappearance of two of the smaller states which had emerged from larger constructions during the nineteenth century, the other powers—and most especially the major ones—were all expected to survive, even if trimmed by the winners. In this sense, the war, however costly and destructive in its *methods*, was still quite traditional in its aims.

It is also true that the fighting itself, with its unprecedented casualties, its incredible costs, the appearance of such new weapons as poison gas, airplanes, tanks, and submarines, as well as vast shifts in world economic patterns, ended up completely transforming the pre-war world and doing so in ways that none of the belligerents had anticipated. The effects on winners and losers alike were colossal, and the pre-war world could not be revived even if some made valiant and sometimes counter-productive efforts to do so. But neither side had either intended or preferred the massive changes which resulted from the ability of the modern state to utilize the social and mechanical technologies developed in the preceding two centuries to draw vast human and material resources out of their respective societies and employ them—and thereby use them up—in the cauldron of battle.

In World War II, all this was very different indeed. The *intent* was different from the start. A total reordering of the globe was at stake from the very beginning, and the leadership on both sides recognized this. The German dictator Adolf Hitler had himself explicitly asserted on May 23, 1939, that the war he intended would be not for the Free City of Danzig but for living space in the East; his Foreign Minister similarly assured Italy's Foreign Minister that it was war, not Danzig, that Germany wanted. When Germany had conquered Poland and offered a temporary peace to Britain and France, those countries responded by making it clear, as British Prime Minister Neville Chamberlain explained, that there could be no agreement with a German government led by Hitler, a man who had regularly broken his promises. If Chamberlain, who has often been derided for allegedly not grasping the true nature of the National Socialist challenge, saw the issues so clearly, the historian decades later ought not to close his or her eyes to the reality of a very different war. This was, in fact, a struggle not only for control of territory and resources but about who would live and control the resources of the globe and which peoples would vanish entirely because they were believed inferior or undesirable by the victors.

It was in this way that the two wars which originated in Europe differed greatly from each other even if separated by only two decades, and it was also in this way that the European war which began in 1939 differed from those initiated by Japan in China in 1931 and 1937 and the one waged by Italy against Ethiopia in 1935–36. However grim for the participants, and especially for the Chinese and Ethiopians, those wars, too, belonged in a prior framework. Both the first and the second stages of Japan's aggression against China were a resumption of a pattern of imperial expansion which Japan had initiated in the last decade of the nineteenth century. Designed to expand its resource and power base at the expense of China, these efforts looked to the expansion of Japanese power, not the disappearance of China—to say nothing of the total disappearance of the Chinese.

Similarly, Italy's invasion and occupation of Ethiopia was the last of a series of European wars for the control of portions of the African continent, a colonial war in the tradition of earlier seizures of African territory by the Spanish and Portuguese, British and French, Dutch and Belgians, Germans and the Italians themselves. It is for this reason that the account of war offered in this work begins with the German attack on Poland, not the prior fighting in East Asia or Africa. Those other struggles would become merged with the one that began on September 1, 1939, but they had begun quite independently of it and would have remained both separate and different had not Germany launched a new type of war which came to absorb them.

The focus of this book, therefore, is on the war initiated by Germany in September 1939. It attempts to cover it until the defeat of Germany and those who became its associates, and since these came to include Japan, until that country's surrender in 1945 as well. The fighting of that war ranged and raged over all the oceans, including even the Arctic ones, and touched every continent. Although most of the combat occurred in Europe, Asia, and Africa, such Australian cities as Darwin were repeatedly bombed and the Western Hemisphere was subjected not only to Japanese invasion in the north but to a silent assault by thousands of balloons carrying incendiaries and explosives to the western parts of Canada and the United States. It was, therefore, a war which reached further around the globe than any which had ever preceded it.

Furthermore, the extent of destruction was very much greater, and spread over vastly larger areas, than in any prior war, while the loss of life was at least twice that of the war of 1914–18. Contemporaries of that earlier struggle were so impressed by its destructiveness of both life and property, as well as by the vast lands and populations it engulfed, that they had quite early come to call it "The Great War," a name by which its survivors recalled it when they did not instead refer to it as "The World War." Both by comparison with that terrible event, and when set against all other wars of which we have any knowledge, the second world-wide conflagration of this century surely deserves to be called "The Greatest War." Only an all-out nuclear war could ever be yet greater, and there would presumably be no historian left alive to record it — to say nothing of any records for a reconstruction of its course.

The account offered here is designed to try to illuminate the war in all its major aspects and theaters, with particular attention to the major decisions and choices made by the participants. There has, therefore, been little room for the details of combat on land and in the struggles for control of the skies and the seas. The emphasis is on the why? rather than the how? of war. If some incidents, like the fight over Madagascar or the campaign in Burma, receive more attention here than might be expected, this is precisely because they have been neglected in most broader surveys of the war. A deliberate attempt has been made to allot to the terrible fighting on the Eastern Front the attention it deserves in the framework of the war as a whole; and if the resulting account is still not as lengthy and detailed as the role of that front in the over-all picture of the war merits, it is still very much more extensive than in other Western surveys.

Similarly, an effort has been made to integrate the use of intelligence into the narrative of policies and operations and to try to relate the events in widely separated parts of the globe to each other. This has meant some rapid shifting of geographic focus within individual chapters, but the processes of a world-wide conflict do not always lend themselves to easy dissection into conveniently separated narratives. It has, nevertheless, seemed useful to draw together in special chapters discussion of the evolution of new weapons and procedures during the whole war, and to survey the fate of the belligerents in the throes of hostilities. A certain amount of duplication is inevitable between the two thematic chapters and the chronological account, but it may be found helpful to have some material both integrated into the record of the war and that of nations and their weapons.

Certain peculiarities of the text call for explanation. I have decided to use the old rather than the new spelling of Chinese personal and place names; all contemporary maps and records use them, and the substitution of the spelling introduced in the 1970s will only lead to useless searching in much of the existing literature. For Japanese names, the Japanese sequence, which places the family name first, is used at all times except only where the title of a book or article includes it in the reverse order. All translations, unless otherwise indicated, are my own. There is a certain arbitrariness in the utilization of place names which have changed as a result of territorial and other changes stemming from the war. As a general rule, the names used at the time will be found in this book; that is certainly in no way to be taken as a reflection on the propriety of subsequent boundaries. References to "England" may in some cases be interpreted as meaning the whole of Britain.

Two types of annotations have been separately marked and printed. Those which relate directly to the text and should be read with it have been marked by letters in the text and are located at the bottom of the page. Notes which are of a more technical nature are marked with numerals and are printed at the end of the book. These contain references to archival documents, discussion of and references to secondary literature, and they occasionally deal with controversial issues of interpretation and other related questions. For both footnotes and endnotes there is a list of abbreviations and special terms on pp. xvii–xix.

It has not seemed either sensible or useful to include a detailed biblio-graphy, which would necessarily provide literally thousands of items. Anyone who works on World War II will be inclined to believe that the prophet Koheleth in asserting that "of making many books there is no end" must have been looking ahead to that event. All works directly cited in the notes have been provided with full citations the first time they appear. The bibliographic essay is designed to provide the interes-ted reader with some of the most important works, in some instances with my comments. Such a listing cannot possibly be exhaustive; it may, however, both point to relevant literature and provide additional refer-ences through the bibliographies contained in most of the books concerned.

It has, similarly, seemed to me pointless to append a list of the thou-sands of archival folders and rolls of microfilm which have been scrutin-ized in the preparation of this book. Specific archival references will be found in the notes wherever this is appropriate, and a very short discus-sion of the archives is included in the bibliographic essay. Only those who have themselves toiled in the vast and often confusing records of the war can have a sense of the extent to which the scholar is dependent on the "kindness of strangers." I can attest for the benefit of any readers, who may be tempted by reading this account to work in the records themselves, that those strangers quickly become valued friends.

1

———— • ————

FROM ONE WAR TO ANOTHER

When a German warship opened fire on the Polish garrison in the special area reserved for them within the Free City of Gdansk (Danzig)—and German troops and airplanes attacked Poland—a terrible conflict began that was quickly called "The Second World War." This name implies some relationship to the great prior conflict of 1914–18. At the beginning of September 1939, when German actions started this new war, however, there was already fighting in two other areas of the globe. Since the Japanese had struck in northern China in July 1937, there had been hostilities between the two East Asian nations; that war had reached something of a stalemate by the fall of 1939, but no end to it was in sight. In addition, since May 1939, Japanese and Russian troops were engaged in bitter fighting on the border of their respective puppet states in a conflict called after its location the Nomonhan Incident by the Japanese and the Khalkhin-gol Incident by the Russians. Diplomatic relations between the Soviet Union and Japan continued even while their forces clashed, and a cease-fire in this struggle on September 16, 1939, followed upon Japan's defeat in battle. The continuing East Asian conflict between Japan and China would, however, have remained isolated, like the war those two nations had fought in 1894–95, had not events in Europe led Japan to join the hostilities begun there. It is thus entirely appropriate to think of the Second World War as having been initiated by Germany and eventually embroiling the whole globe. How did this come about? Was not one world war enough?

The war which ended with the armistice of November 11, 1918, had been horrendous in its impact on the participants. In more than four years of bloodshed and destruction, vast portions of Europe had been wrecked and the domestic institutions of the continent transformed. The capacity of the modern state for mass mobilization had drawn human and material resources out of each belligerent to an extent no one had previously imagined possible, and these human and material resources had been consumed in the furnace of war. The other portions of the globe had become involved either because they had joined one side or because their colonial status had sucked them in; while the few remaining neutrals saw their trade and their very structures dramatically affected by the great upheaval all around them.

That struggle, which was generally referred to then as "The World War" to distinguish it from the localized or smaller conflicts of preceding decades, was the great formative experience of those who survived it: they would thereafter look at the world through the framework of the lessons they believed that war had taught them. This was as much the case for the victors as for the defeated; and the framing of peace in 1919, the conduct of policy in the two following decades, and the direction of the new war were all the work of individuals who saw and measured new choices by reference to choices made or not made in the great war just concluded.

The peace settlement of 1919 was complicated by a series of compromises primarily among the victors and secondarily between the victors and the defeated. Four major factors in the situation affected these compromises. First, the unanticipated suddenness of the German defeat—coming a year earlier than expected, *after* German victories over the Allies in East, Southeast, and South Europe, and *before* the Allies had invaded Germany herself—meant that there were substantial limits on the choices of the victors and no clear recognition of total military defeat in Germany.

The troops of the victors were not in occupation of all or almost all of Europe, as the Allies had once anticipated, and this limitation on the authority of the victors became ever more significant as the pressures for demobilization in the victorious countries pushed all before them after the years of sacrifice and suffering. This situation meant that in many parts of Europe, especially in eastern and Southeastern Europe, local elements could take the initiative into their own hands. Since Russia had been defeated by the Central Powers, who were in turn defeated by the Western Allies, there was a unique situation in Eastern Europe: the great empires which had contended with each other in prior centuries were on this occasion *all* defeated, and the smaller powers and peoples of the area had their one opportunity to try to assert their own will, and at times to do so in defiance of the victors writing the peace treaties in the far-away suburbs of Paris.

This same circumstance, the early and unanticipated German defeat, left the people of that country dazed by events. A succession of great victories had led the Germans to anticipate possible total victory; the bitter, drawn-out fighting and the deprivations imposed on Germany's home front had led some Germans in the latter part of the war to fear or to hope for a compromise of some sort; but almost no one expected a total defeat. The decision of Germany's military leaders to call for an end to the fighting in September 1918 rather than risk a collapse at the front meant that the guns stopped firing when the war maps still showed German troops deep inside the territory of Germany's enemies. The shock of being told that the war was lost almost immediately produced a collapse of the German home front and the disappearance of its dynasties and institutions; and this in turn made the country practically totally defenseless.

The turmoil of a few weeks in the country that had had the most solid home front during the war of all the European belligerents would later be transposed in malice aforethought by some and in subjective honesty by others with the defeat at the front which had actually preceded and caused it.[a] The stab-in-the-back legend thus created—the false claim that action at home had caused defeat in battle—would have a large number of fateful effects subsequently, but the immediate result of the German military collapse would be that the victors became more concerned that there should be a government of some sort in Germany to accept the terms of peace than about possible German rejection of whatever was proposed. The victors were indeed prepared to march in and occupy the country if the peace treaty were rejected, but that contingency was correctly believed unlikely to arise.

The second major factor at work in the peace settlement was the desperate fear of German might. The very fact that it had taken most of the world to crush Germany and her allies and then only in a long, bitter, and costly struggle, with Allied defeat averted by the narrowest of margins, suggested that the German state at the center of the continent, newly formed less than half a century earlier, was extraordinarily dangerous to the welfare, even existence, of others. The fact that the victors were meeting in the French capital, which had been threatened by German capture a year earlier and still bore the marks of shelling, guaranteed that no one would forget how narrow the margin of victory had been. Furthermore, the German introduction into combat of what seemed to many people at the time the most horrendous of the new weapons and methods of warfare

---

[a] Such a reversal of events close in time even by those who lived through them is not as uncommon as one might think. An example from American history would be the frequently expressed belief that at the Yalta Conference of February 1945 areas had been turned over to the Soviet Union, when in fact those areas had been liberated or occupied by the Red Army in the preceding months.

only accentuated concern about a continuing menace from that nation. The bombing of cities from the air, unrestricted submarine warfare, and the use of poison gas certainly looked to the victors as innovations the world owed to German genius but might well have done without.

This mixture of fear and hate combined with loathing for Germany's invasion of Belgium, her despicable conduct in that country, and her wanton destruction of French territory as it was evacuated, to suggest the wisdom, indeed the imperative need, for measures to limit German power in the future if other nations were to survive the German experiment of nationhood. Such measures were, however, halted short of eliminating that experiment by a fundamental assumption and principle of the peacemakers, the third of the conditioning elements of the peace settlement. This was the belief that Europe should be organized on the principle of nationality, and that violations of this principle had had a large part in bringing on the war. If one started from this belief—perhaps it would be better to say basic assumption—then certain highly significant implications for any peace settlement would necessarily follow. The first and by far the most important was that there would continue to be a German nation.

As can be seen by any analysis of even the harshest terms proposed by anyone before or during 1919, the continued existence of a German state, however truncated or restricted, was taken for granted by all.[1] The experience of World War II would call this assumption in question, and one major facet of the war aims discussion among the allies who fought against Germany in that second conflict revolved precisely around this issue, but such was not the case in 1919. Although the process of German unification under Prussian leadership had been accompanied by the disappearance of several states which had existed for centuries, and although German war aims in the conflict just over had always included the end at least of Belgium's existence as a really independent state,[2] not one among the victorious leaders assembled in Paris advocated such a fate for Germany. What arguments there were all revolved around the extent of and the methods for weakening or restraining Germany. This focus of emphasis on the modalities of a continued German state would subsequently blind the Germans to possible alternatives to the peace treaty they were obliged to sign, as effectively as it would conceal from critics of the settlement its single most portentous feature.

The second major implication of the acceptance of some form of the national principle as a basic assumption underlying the settlement was the rejection of any thought of imposing on the smaller nationalities of Central and Eastern Europe some over-arching multinational structure, be it a revised form of the old Austro–Hungarian empire or a federation newly devised for the occasion. Such an imposition of unity would have required the use of force by the victors, just as division could have been imposed on Germany only by force; but in both cases the assumptions of the victors were consonant with their perception of what was practical. The voluminous records of the deliberations at Paris contain no discussion of an enforced new multinational structure for Central and Southeast Europe, just as they reveal no parallel to the World War II debates about the need for some sort of division of Germany. The new states emerging out of the ruins of the German, Ottoman, Austrian, and Russian empires would have to develop their own independent structures or federative polities as best they could, a process hampered by their national rivalries and great power interference, and terminated—at least for years—by a new war out of which, unlike World War I, a victor in their part of the world would emerge to dominate the area.

The fourth major factor conditioning the peace settlement was the sense shared in some way by all alike that the war had changed the world, and that these changes had to be accommodated to the national interests of the victors—as the leading powers among the victors perceived them—and combined with some new machinery to try to prevent any recurrence of the disaster they had all been through. The changes which were most dramatically obvious at Paris were certain presences and absences. The two countries which had carried the major shares of the burden of fighting on the main front, France and Great Britain, were of course prominently represented at Paris, and so were the other European victors like Italy and Belgium. But while the United States had on occasion played some role in the consideration of European powers before 1914, her participation in the peace conference, as in the war itself, was so different from her presence at the Algeciras Conference on Morocco in 1906, to mention one example from the immediate pre-war period, that it was a difference in kind rather than degree.

The military and financial role of the United States in the war had made her into a world power; and while the ending of the war a year earlier than anticipated had kept that role from being as overwhelming as it would have become a year later, there was here an entirely new factor on the world stage. Joined to the realities of American power were three additional elements enhancing the United States' position. The United States itself had been strengthened, not weakened, by the events of the war; its industrial and actual or potential military power could be expected to become even greater into the distant future; and the articulation by President Woodrow Wilson of American ideals, projected onto the world scene by his oratory, made many look to him and his views as harbingers of a new world order.

Another new power present at Paris was Japan. Though clearly not as important in the war or as likely to play a major role in European affairs, Japan shared with the United States the characteristic of having been strengthened rather than weakened by the war. Furthermore, if the representatives of the United States, like those of Canada, Australia, South Africa and New Zealand, were non-Europeans participating in the settlement of European issues, these were all individuals of European ancestry. The inclusion of Japan among the great powers brought onto the scene a people who had adapted European material and social technology to their own cultural and political traditions; but who were, who saw themselves, and who were seen by others, as basically non-Western. When as a result of the peace settlement a portion of eastern Germany came to be under the control of the reborn country of Lithuania in order to provide that nation with a good port on the Baltic Sea at Memel (Klaipeda), certain restrictions were placed on the Lithuanian government to protect the rights of the Germans living in that area. Japan was one of the powers designated as monitors for this arrangement.[3] It would be difficult to imagine a more conspicuous reversal from the days when German citizens enjoyed extra-territorial rights in Japan to the time when Germans in the Memel territory had to look, among other places, to Tokyo for the protection of their own rights under Lithuanian rule.

One power was as conspicuous by the novelty of its absence as the United States and Japan were by their presence: Russia. One of the original allies in the war against Germany had withdrawn from the conflict. The Tsarist government had been overthrown by revolution early in 1917, and the successor regime which had continued in the war against Germany had in turn itself been overthrown in November of that year by the Bolsheviks, who had then pulled Russia out of the war.[a] Preferring to consolidate their hold on whatever portions of the country a settlement with Germany would leave them—a decision made easier for them by their belief in the imminence of world-wide revolutionary upheaval and their own prior support from the German government— the Bolsheviks in March 1918 signed a peace treaty dictated by Germany.

This dramatic breach in the alliance against the Central Powers had a host of implications. Inside Russia, it meant a breach between the Bolsheviks and their only internal political allies; from then on they would rule whatever they controlled as a one-party state. Externally it

---

[a] The Russians changed from the Julian to the Gregorian calendar after the revolutions of 1917. By the calendar in effect in Russia at the time, the first revolution took place in February and the second in October; the adoption of the new calendar meant that the first would fall into March and the second into November.

meant the release of German troops for use on other fronts, primarily in the West, in Germany's last great bid for total victory in the war. For the Western Powers it meant a challenge to their domestic institutions, but more immediately it threatened them with utter defeat at Germany's hands. To revive the dispersion of forces imposed on Germany by an Eastern Front, the Western Allies supported those internal Russian enemies of the Bolsheviks who were willing to have Russia return to the war, but these efforts failed. The Western Allies barely held on in the West and then defeated Germany as well as the other Central Powers by themselves. They thereby incidentally saved the Bolsheviks from the fate that a victorious Germany intended for them, but they had no intention of inviting them to the peace conference. Whatever the outcome of the internal upheavals still shaking Russia during the proceedings in Paris, that country would be present in the thoughts of the conferees as an object of hopes and fears, not as a participant.

Two additional novel features of the situation in Paris require comment. One has already been mentioned: the presence of representatives from Canada, Australia, South Africa and New Zealand and, though not with the same status, of India. Here was a first internationally visible sign of one of the major results of World War I, the breakup of the European colonial empires into independent political entities. The "British Dominions," as they were then called, had earned their independence and their right to participate in the proceedings on their own by their share in the fighting. This share was the converse of the declining ability of the mother country to provide by itself the military forces required for victory. For the future, this meant that only with the assured support of these extra-European ex-colonies now turned independent could the European settlement of 1919 be upheld and defended—a matter of crucial importance in 1938 and 1939. It is not an accident of history, though a fact frequently overlooked, that at the turning of the tide in North Africa in 1942 the majority of the "British" forces engaged came not from the United Kingdom but from Britain's allies, that is, from Australia, New Zealand, India, and South Africa; from what by then was called the "British Commonwealth."

The other novel feature was the general belief that the prevention of any new calamity like the war just concluded required the establishment of new international institutions. The fact that the first part of each of the peace treaties with the defeated was the text of the Covenant of the League of Nations, and that similarly included in the peace settlement were provisions for the establishment of the International Labor Organization and of the World Court, reflected the perception that making peace at the end of such a terrible conflict required more than drawing new boundaries, arranging for compensations, and imposing other limitations on the defeated. A general additional attempt should be made so to order international affairs as to preclude a repetition of what had just taken place.

These idealistic aspirations—with some justice one might call them the only truly realistic conclusions drawn from the war—were almost certain to be shattered by the other terms of any peace settlement. As the human and material costs of the war had mounted, only the hopes for a better world to follow had sustained much of the enormous effort required of the participants. But the very escalation of sacrifice supported by rising expectations of a new and improved world in the postwar era practically guaranteed disillusionment. How could a world in which over thirty million had lost their lives or their health in combat, in which millions had been uprooted, and in which the ingenuity of advanced industrial societies had for years concentrated on the maximum destruction of the material resources of mankind, be so much improved over the by then shadowy pre-war world, now surrounded with a halo of memory conferred by the intervening horrors?

The higher the hopes raised, the swifter and surer the disappointment. Nothing, measured against the lives lost and suffering endured, was likely to look worth the sacrifices made. And that an even worse fate might have been averted by victory seemed little consolation, especially as with the passage of time the fear of defeat, once so acute, faded from people's minds, but the empty places in the family circle remained conspicuously empty. That under such circumstances most of the disappointment, disillusionment, and disgust born of the war and its aftermath should focus in the first instance not on the war but on the peace settlement should not occasion great surprise.

The terms of the peace imposed on the defeated included, along with the provisions for new international organizations, primarily territorial, military, and financial terms. The territorial arrangement provided for substantial transfers to the victors, with Serbia gaining enormously at the expense of Austria–Hungary and becoming under the name of Yugoslavia a multinational state of its own, Romania gaining at the expense of Hungary and Bulgaria, as well as regaining territory it had lost to Russia in 1878, a new state called Czechoslovakia being formed out of portions of Austria–Hungary, Italy gaining some land also at Austria–Hungary's expense, and Greece being awarded what had been Bulgaria's coast on the Aegean Sea. Germany had to return part of northern Schlesvig to Denmark after a plebiscite, turn over small pieces of land to Belgium, and return Alsace and Lorraine to France.

More traumatic for the Germans for reasons to be examined sub-sequently was the return to a revived Poland of substantial portions of the territory Prussia had taken from her in the partitions of 1772 and 1793, together with a part of the Silesian lands Prussia had taken from Austria earlier in the eighteenth century. Danzig, the main port of Poland on the Baltic and also grabbed by Prussia in 1793, was not returned to the Poles in spite of the promise of a "free and secure access to the sea" in President Wilson's famous Fourteen Points and sought after initial rejection by Germany as the basis for the peace. The city's over-whelmingly German population led the peacemakers to a compromise: the establishment of a free city whose internal affairs would under inter-national supervision be democratic—and hence controlled by Ger-mans—but whose foreign policy and trade affairs would be subject to Polish control.

A small part of eastern Germany was to be under Lithuania as already mentioned, the Saar area with its coal mines was to be under French control for fifteen years, and all of Germany's colonies were taken from her. These last were, like portions of the collapsed Ottoman empire, placed into a newly devised category of "mandates," territories under the control of various of the victors but not included in their territory or colonies and instead being prepared for self-government at some future time.[a]

The military provisions of the treaties imposed severe limits on the size of the armed forces of the defeated, prohibited certain weapons and activities entirely, provided for the demilitarization of German territory west of the Rhine river plus a strip east of it, and instituted a temporary military occupation of the Rhineland to assure adherence to the peace treaty.

The economic provisions of the treaties were drawn to impose on the defeated all the war costs of Belgium together with those costs of the war of the other allies which were still to come, primarily the reconstruc-tion of damage caused by the war and the payments to survivors of those killed in the conflict. These impositions were called "reparations" to distinguish them from the punitive payments, usually called "indemnit-ies," exacted by the victor from the vanquished after prior wars, such as those exacted from France by Germany after the Franco-Prussian War of 1870–71 or by Japan from China after their war in 1894–95.

[a] It is the former status of German Southwest Africa as a C-Class mandate of the then Union of South Africa which made what is now known as Namibia an issue of international concern (with the United States' role due to Germany's cession of sovereignty over her colonies to the victors to be assigned by them to mandatory powers).

Since the economies of Germany's European enemies had been damaged much more by the war than her own, this arrangement, if implemented, would have operated at least to some extent to off-set the relative strengthening of the German economy as a result of the war. But this was not to be.

The terms of the peace settlement were attacked vehemently by the Germans at the time and subsequently, and these attacks came to coincide with the general disillusionment about the new world which had emerged from the war and the peace among the former allies. There was a popular delusion, widespread at the time, sedulously fostered in the 1920s and 1930s by German propaganda, generally believed then and remaining the staple pabulum of history textbooks today, that Germany had been most terribly crushed by the peace settlement, that all manner of horrendous things had been done to her, and that a wide variety of onerous burdens and restrictions imposed upon her by the peace had weakened her into the indefinite future. On the basis of this view, a whole series of modifications was made in the settlement, all without exception in favor of Germany. The occupation was ended earlier than the peace treaty indicated, the commissions to supervise disarmament were withdrawn, the reparations payments were reduced and eventually cancelled, and the trials of war criminals were left to the Germans with predictable results, to mention only some of the most significant changes made. If at the end of this process, Germany—a bare quarter of a century after the armistice of 1918—controlled most of Europe and had come within a hair's breadth of conquering the globe, there was obviously something wrong about the picture generally accepted then and later.

The adoption of the national principle as the basis for the peace settlement meant that the most recently created European major power, Germany, would survive the war, her population second in Europe only to Russia's and her industrial and economic potential less affected than that of her European enemies, since it had been on the back of their, not Germany's, economies that the war had been fought out. Though weakened by the war, Germany had been weakened less than her European enemies, and she had thus emerged relatively stronger potentially in 1919 than she had been in 1913. The same national principle, added to war-weariness, which had restrained the victors from using their armies to keep the new Germany apart, had equally restrained them from using their armies to refurbish the old or create some new larger structure in Central and Southeast Europe. The very portion of the peace treaty that all Germans found most obnoxious, the revival of

Poland, protected Germany from her potentially most powerful and dangerous adversary, Russia. The various arguments over the details of the new boundaries between Hungary and Romania, between Poland and Czechoslovakia, between Bulgaria and Greece, between Austria and Yugoslavia, all only underline two facts of supreme importance: that Germany was now actually or potentially infinitely more powerful than any of her eastern and Southeastern European neighbors, and that there was practically no likelihood of those neighbors ever joining together against Germany.

The modifications introduced into the peace settlement reinforced rather than mitigated the stronger relative position of Germany. The prime example of this was the reparations question. The Germans shook off the reparations payments by simple refusal to pay, by destroying their own currency—in part to demonstrate inability to pay—and by more than off-setting what payments were made through borrowing abroad, followed by repudiation of most of these loans in the 1930s.[a]

This process and the international public discussion of it fed an illusion of fateful significance. Because Germany did not pay reparations, it came to be widely believed that no or almost no reparations were paid at all. This, of course, is nonsense. All the reparations were paid: the devastated towns were rebuilt, the orchards replanted, the mines pumped out and all the pensions to survivors were paid (with some still being paid). The bill was simply shifted to other shoulders, primarily the very countries that had seen their economies suffer most from the war. This shifting of the burden of repair costs from the less damaged German economy to the more damaged economies of others thus served to redouble rather than off-set the impact of the war itself. Only when a realistic perspective is restored to an examination of the peace settlement, its nature, its impact, and its modifications, can one begin to understand how a period of supposed German enfeeblement could culminate within less than two decades in a Europe, even a world, again terrified of German might.

The governments and peoples of the post-war era were not only preoccupied with the real and imagined defects of the peace settlement but also by what they thought were the lessons of the war. There was a great deal of discussion and concern about the causes of the Great War, primarily because it was seen as a horrendous disaster whose causes and origins ought to be examined from the perspective of avoiding any repetition. If military leaders are often castigated for preparing to fight

---

[a] Recent work on reparations by such scholars as Sally Marks, Stephen Schuker, and Mark Trachtenberg has begun to displace the traditional picture.

the last war, civilians can be castigated with equal justice for trying to avoid it. In both cases, there is a measure of value in circumspectly drawn lessons of limited application, but the conceptualization is inherently faulty even if understandable. One can no more avoid a war one has already been in than one can refight a conflict that is over; but as the recurrent discussion in the United States of not getting into another Vietnam should remind one, these obvious truths rarely prevent anyone from trying.

Certainly American policy in the post-1919 years came to be dominated by beliefs about how the United States had become involved in the war and might accordingly take steps to avoid a repetition. Americans tend to express their beliefs in their laws. The various neutrality laws were deliberately designed to preclude any repeat performance of what many thought a mistaken entrance into an unnecessary war; and it is possible that if enacted in the first rather than the fourth decade of this century, they would indeed have had that effect. By the 1930s, however, the decision of 1917 was beyond recall. It could in fact be argued that, combined with a voluntary reduction of the American army to about the level imposed on Germany by the peace treaty, the measures taken to keep the United States out of war merely encouraged Adolf Hitler and thus helped precipitate another war. In any case, the view that America had made a mistake in allowing itself to become embroiled in what came to be perceived as a quarrel not of vital interest to this country largely determined American policy. And that view certainly precluded any American commitment to uphold that war's outcome.

The new leaders of the Soviet Union had not waited until the armistice of November 1918 to decide that the war was not for them. They had withdrawn in March. Though rescued by the victory of the Western Powers over Germany from the most onerous provisions the Germans had imposed on them in the peace treaty they had signed that month, the Bolshevik leaders never abandoned the view that they had been wise to pull out of the war on whatever terms they could obtain. The whole conflict had been an inherent and necessary concomitant of a capitalistic world, of which they neither had nor wanted any part. By definition, such horrors would continue to be an inherent and necessary concomitant of any capitalist world that survived, a view which suggested the desirability of neutrality in any repetition whenever and wherever it might come. Given the weakness of the new regime, caution was clearly indicated lest the capitalist powers join together to attack the Soviet Union rather than fighting each other. The essentially defensive posture of the Soviet Union was obscured by the world-wide antics of the Comintern, the international organization of Communist Parties which had agreed to subservience to Moscow; but as the largely self-created Russian war scare of 1926–27 could have led one to predict, the appearance of real dangers in East Asia from 1931 and in Europe from 1933 produced the most cautious responses from the Soviet Union: a combination of concessions to potential attackers with encouragement for others to fight them.

If the great powers on the periphery of Europe moved toward isolation and neutrality on the basis of their view of the war, what about the European powers themselves? The Italians alone had been divided over the prospect of entering the conflict; its costs destroyed their economic, social, and political system. If the new regime Benito Mussolini installed in 1922 on the ruins of the old glorified war as a sign of vitality and repudiated pacifism as a form of decay, the lesson drawn from the terrible battles against Austria on the Isonzo river—in which the Italians fought far better than popular imagination often allows—was that the tremendous material and technical preparations needed for modern war were simply beyond the contemporary capacity of the country.[a] This was almost certainly a correct perception, but, given the ideology of Fascism with its emphasis on the moral benefits of war, it did not lead to the conclusion that an Italy without a big stick had best speak very, very softly. On the contrary, the new regime drew the opposite conclusion.[4] Noisy eloquence and rabid journalism might be substituted for serious preparations for war, a procedure that was harmless enough if no one took any of it seriously, but a certain road to disaster once some outside and Mussolini inside the country came to believe that the "eight million bayonets" of the Duce's imagination actually existed.

France had borne the greatest burden of the war, including the highest proportion of both casualties and destruction. Triumphant only in association with powerful allies, terrified of her own isolated weakness, France looked apprehensively rather than confidently upon the post-war world. For her leaders the war had only reinforced the twin conclusions drawn from the war of 1870–71: France needed allies, and a war with Germany was likely to be fought out on French soil. The lessons drawn from these conclusions were, however, contradictory. If France needed allies and if these allies were to be of any help against Germany, then the French would have to be willing to come actively to the aid of those allies if they in turn were threatened. On the other hand, if another war on French soil were to be avoided, then an even more elaborate system of border defenses than that of the pre-1914 period would be needed,

---

[a] This generalization does not preclude either technical advances in design and engineering of advanced weapons or planning for mechanized warfare in abstract terms; what was absent was the capacity to translate either into the massive actual forces required by modern war.

with victory coming as it had in 1914–18 by again halting any German attacks, only this time at the border rather than in the middle of France's richest provinces.

That this strategy promised catastrophe for any continental allies of France was so obvious that it was for years ignored outside France as much as in Paris. Even those like the Socialist leader Léon Blum, who objected to military alliances in the belief that the existence of such alliances had contributed to the outbreak of the last war, never suggested any alternative national strategy. The spectacle of a France essentially without a coherent policy can be understood only with reference to the weakness of what had once been Europe's leading power and to the mental debility of a military leadership, which apparently hoped to off-set its 30 percent underestimation of German front-line strength in 1914 by a 300 percent over-estimate of German front-line strength in the 1930s.[5]

As for French diplomacy in the immediate post-war years, it fastened on the hope of rescuing what could be rescued from the shambles made by the United States and Britain of the peace settlement by their refusal to honor the bargain made with France over the Rhineland, when they had promised a defensive alliance to dissuade France from detaching the Rhineland permanently from Germany. Here too domestic developments, in this case of a fiscal and social nature,[6] prevented adherence to a coherent and determined foreign policy, so that Paris reaped all the disadvantages and none of the advantages of firmness toward Germany. Facing the memory of the Great War, perhaps it would be better to say paralyzed by that memory, France resigned herself to an era of drift and despair.

In Britain there were also two lessons drawn from the war, one from its origins and one from its conduct. The lesson of its origins was believed to be that a quarrel in an obscure corner of Europe—obscure needless to say only from the perspective of London—had led to a general catastrophe. This was taken to mean that if any problem anywhere in Europe were not solved peacefully, even if at some sacrifice to those involved, it could lead to a war that was most likely to become once again a general war, drawing in England as well as most other nations. If the lesson of 1914 was that war in Europe could not be localized, then local wars obviously had to be kept from starting in the first place; and from this view came the concept of peaceful change as a means of resolving local issues likely to precipitate local wars that would in any case become general once again.

The other lesson drawn from the conduct of war was that England's unprecedented creation of a huge continental army, however necessary at the time, must under no circumstances become a precedent for the future. Even those who claimed that Field Marshal Haig had started with a strategic concept in his great campaign of 1917 — and there were and are those who dispute that contention — generally agreed that the British could, should, and would never again go to Passchendaele, the scene of slaughter that symbolized the bloody horror of the trenches. Great Britain, like the United States, would dismantle her armed forces, and in particular reduce her army also to about the size specified for Germany by the peace treaty. Distaste for the past constricted any realistic concept of the future. If war ever came again, Britain would return to her earlier pattern of subsidizing continental allies and providing substantial but limited land forces, while relying on blockade pressure and the strategic possibilities afforded by sea power to throttle any continental enemy.

If Austria–Hungary had dissolved under the impact of war and defeat, Germany had been and continued to be held together by nationalistic sentiments and the exertions of those political parties and leaders who in pre-war Germany had been denounced as the alleged enemies of the state. Within the country, discussion of the war and its lessons was heavily concentrated on the supposed failure to implement the "Schlieffen Plan" for victory fully as a cause of German defeat in the first Battle of the Marne in 1914, and on the imaginary stab-in-the-back by the home front as the cause of defeat in 1918. Although an excellent case can be made that Count Alfred von Schlieffen should have been committed to a mental institution for his plan to employ non-existent army units, whose creation he opposed, rather than celebrated as a military genius; and an even better case can be made for the position that Germany's home front was the most solid and the least disaffected of any European great power during the war, all the speculations of a contrary nature made in Germany were of purely theoretical significance for foreign policy at that time since only a flood of harmless, even if utterly misleading, books and articles resulted from them during the 1920s. Policy was determined in that decade by men who recognized that Germany could not risk another general war, and that only a localized war that was absolutely certain to remain localized could ever be contemplated; and this qualification meant that in practice Germany could not go to war under any then foreseeable circumstances.

All this would change when Adolf Hitler came to power in 1933 because his deductions from the war differed in important respects from those of others. War had been an intended and even a preferred part of National Socialist policy from the beginning, not so much out of a preference for fighting for its own sake, but from the entirely accurate conviction that the aim of German expansion could be secured only by war.

Germany was to seize the agricultural land needed to feed its population, a population that would grow further as it obtained such land, and which would accordingly expand its needs and its lands into the indefinite future. This crude Social Darwinism, in which racial groups fought for land which could provide the means of subsistence, expelling or exterminating but never assimilating other groups, was derived from a view of history as deterministic as that of Marx, but substituting race for class as the key to understanding.[7] Its application had internal as well as external implications.

The Jews were seen as the most immediate threat to racial purity inside Germany, and as the main motor of resistance outside the country. A policy of extreme anti-Semitism would accordingly be a central concern of the government in peace first and in war later. Furthermore, a key internal need was the urgency of increasing the birthrate of the allegedly better and reducing the birthrate of the supposedly inferior racial stocks within the German population, measures that required a dictatorial regime, which alone could in addition prepare for, and hope to succeed in, the wars a racial policy called for in external affairs. Measured by the criterion of feeding a growing German population with the products of its own agricultural land, the boundaries Germany had once had were almost as useless as those of the 1920s; and thus a revision of the Versailles Peace Treaty of 1919 could be only a propaganda excuse and never a goal of German policy. The vast reaches of additional land to be obtained would never be granted peacefully, and war was therefore both necessary and inevitable.

The bulk of the land to be conquered was in Russia, which, by what Hitler considered a stroke of particularly good fortune for Germany, had been taken over by what he believed to be a group of Jewish Bolsheviks who were incapable of organizing the — in any case inferior — largely Slavic population for effective resistance. The real obstacles to German expansion lay elsewhere. Germany was in the middle of Europe and would have to establish a completely secure position there before heading East. France was the closest main enemy and Czechoslovakia the closest minor one. The sequence of wars would therefore be Czechoslovakia first, France second, then the drive East, and thereafter elsewhere. In the decade 1924–34 Hitler had thought that a war with England could be postponed until after the one with Russia, but events early in his rule disabused him of this illusion; and by 1935 he was convinced of the opposite and making preparations accordingly.

But belief in the necessity for a series of new wars immediately raised the memory of the last, and it is in this regard that Hitler's deductions from that conflict become significant. If the last war had started with an unforeseen incident in the Balkans, and in what he considered the wrong year at that, his wars would start at times of his choosing and accordingly with incidents of his creation.[a] If the last war had spread from a corner of Europe to the whole globe, drowning Germany in a flood of enemies, Germany would so arrange the circumstances of its wars that they could be fought in isolation, one at a time, against enemies of its choice and with victory in each facilitating victory in the next. If it had been the long drawn out enfeeblement of Germany under the impact of blockade on the home front and a stalemated battle of attrition in the trenches that had brought on collapse at home and then defeat at the front, the alternative was to establish a firm dictatorship at home where privations would be kept to a minimum, and to fight the wars in such a fashion as to preclude stalemate and obviate the impact of any blockade. Such procedures would enable Germany to eat the European and eventually the world artichoke from the inside, leaf by leaf, strengthened by each meal for the next, until world peace would be attained, when, to quote his views as one of his associates, Rudolf Hess, summarized them in 1927: "one power, the racially best one, has attained complete and uncontested supremacy."[8]

The early stages of Hitler's program would be enormously facilitated by the great gap between the realities of power produced by the peace settlement and the widespread illusions which have been described. Many thought that Germany's grievances should perhaps be met by concessions, but in any case there was little immediate recognition of danger. The very idea that anyone could even think of starting another European war after the experience of 1914–18 was inconceivable to most, and Hitler shrewdly recognized the reluctance of others to interfere with his moves. He would take the first steps under the pretense of satisfying German grievances and thereby strengthen both his international and his domestic position.

The domestic consolidation of power with a dictatorship based on a one-party state as in the Soviet Union and Italy—which Hitler had held up as models for Germany before 1933[9]—proceeded with great rapidity in 1933 and 1934.[10] The establishment of political and cultural controls was essentially completed in those first years, though their effectiveness would increase with time; while the economic controls were imposed

[a] It is indicative of the extent to which memory of World War I dominated Hitler's thinking about plans for the future that at one stage his plans for the annexation of Austria included a German-arranged assassination of either the German ambassador or the military attaché in that country, and that similarly, the German-arranged assassination of the German Minister to Czechoslovakia was thought of as an appropriate pretext for the attack on Czechoslovakia—both concepts obviously inspired by the role of the assassination of the Austrian Archduke Francis Ferdinand in precipitating World War I. In both instances other projects replaced these first thoughts.

more slowly, primarily in the years 1934–36. Both processes were assisted by the political, economic, and social effects of massive government spending, which greatly speeded up the economic recovery that had begun before the National Socialists came to power. Included in the spending program was a major buildup of the armed forces, which took many off the unemployment roll directly by putting them in uniforms and others by employing them both in the armaments factories and in construction projects for headquarters, army bases, air force landing fields, and naval shipyards. A huge rearmament program had always been intended by the National Socialists; now it seemed to provide temporary economic and hence domestic political advantages as well. Coming at a time when other countries were more inclined to reduce their military expenditures under the impact of the depression and the pressure of pacifist sentiments, the German armament program would change the balance of currently available military power rather quickly.

Germany disregarded, first in secret and then in the open, those restrictions imposed on her by the peace settlement. Before 1933 there had been relatively minor violations, some of the more significant being assisted by the Soviet Union, where German officers could keep up with developments in air, armored, and chemical warfare in exchange for training Red Army officers. Now the new government's big rearmament drive, creation of a large air force, reintroduction of conscription, and initiation of a huge naval building program, broke all prior dimensions and restraints. These steps were, to judge by all available evidence, enormously popular in Germany; whether the reaction they necessarily evoked abroad makes them the "successes" which they are still frequently called is a question not often examined with sufficient care.

In any case, the world was left in little doubt that a new Germany would adopt new policies. Germany left the League of Nations, repudiated all controls on her army and air force, and planned from the beginning to disregard the limitations on her navy which she nominally accepted in a 1935 agreement with England. In 1936 Hitler took advantage of Italy's breach with the Western Powers over the invasion of Ethiopia to break the provisions of both the Peace Treaty and the Locarno Treaty of 1925, which called for the demilitarization of the Rhineland in exchange for guarantees against a repetition of the French 1923 occupation of the key Ruhr industrial region. An attempt in 1934 to overthrow the Austrian government had failed;[11] but the German rapprochement with Italy, reinforced by joint intervention on the Nationalist side in the Spanish civil war, opened up the possibility of a takeover of Austria, combining pressure from the inside with military threats from the outside.

In the world of the 1930s it was by no means easy to decide what to do in the face of the German menace. The international institution created in the peace settlement, the League of Nations, had been crippled at birth by the absence of the United States and the exclusion of Russia as well as the defeated powers. When confronted by its first serious test in Japan's 1931 seizure of Manchuria, it failed over a problem inherent in the concept of collective security, recurring monotonously in the 1930s, and of continuing difficulty today. In a world of separate states, the theory of averting the danger of war by the threat of universal or at least large-scale collective action requires for its implementation that in practice countries be willing to go to war if necessary over specific issues that might be, or at least appear to be, of only marginal significance to them. Not only does this require all involved to maintain substantial forces at all times, but it also makes every little war into a very big one. No power was prepared to do so over Manchuria.[12] Hitler's strategy of fighting a series of isolated wars would confront the powers with the same dilemma: the responsibility for converting his carefully delimited conflicts into a world war would be left to others— others who were peacefully inclined and who had begun their rearmament after and in response to Germany's.

Under these circumstances the United States and the Soviet Union held to their isolationist stance. Insofar as they modified these positions, it tended to be in opposite directions. The American President, Franklin D. Roosevelt, increasingly thought that the Western Powers should be strengthened so that they could resist Germany and thus hopefully avert war from the United States. The most tangible expression of this approach had been an effort to assist in the building up of the French air force, that is, to help out in an area where the Western Powers were clearly especially weak and in which the use of American industrial capacity could benefit defence capabilities on both sides of the Atlantic.[13] By 1939 Roosevelt's policy culminated in attempts to revise the neutrality laws so that the United States could at least sell weapons to countries resisting Hitler, and in urging the Soviet Union to align herself with the Western Powers lest a Germany triumphant in Western Europe reach out to dominate the globe.[14] If the first of these policies foundered on Congressional opposition, the second reached the Soviet dictator Josef Stalin when he had already decided that the way for the Soviet Union to avoid war was neither to join the anti-Hitler coalition nor remain neutral, but rather to nudge Hitler into war against others by promising to assist him.

The fact that Soviet archives for those years are only now beginning to be opened a little, necessarily makes discussion of Soviet policy somewhat speculative. There are, however, some things which are known from materials published by the Soviet Union itself, from the archives of other nations, and from the open record of Soviet actions. It is known from Soviet and other publications that through espionage agents and other intelligence sources Moscow knew that Germany had refused to ally herself with Japan against Russia (as Tokyo wanted), and that Tokyo in turn had declined German efforts to secure an alliance with Japan against the Western Powers. Similarly, the Soviet government was informed of the German plan to secure either the subservience or the defeat of Poland.[15] Finally, the fact that the Soviet Union had a spy in the code section of the British Foreign Office until his arrest in September 1939 suggests that, either by direct access to British documents or the reading of British codes, Moscow was fully informed on British policy.[16]

Under these circumstances, the knowledge that Germany intended to attack Poland—and thereafter the Western Powers—and was looking for allies in these ventures, while Britain and France could either fight Germany alongside Poland or after Poland was conquered, reopened for Stalin the possibility of an agreement with Hitler, something he had repeatedly but unsuccessfully attempted to obtain in prior years.[17] Now Hitler might be interested, and his interest could be stimulated if public negotiations by the Soviet Union with Britain and France ran parallel to secret talks with the Germans. As Stalin would himself explain his view in July 1940: "the U.S.S.R. had wanted to change the old equilibrium . . . but that England and France had wanted to preserve it. Germany had also wanted to make a change in the equilibrium, and this common desire to get rid of the old equilibrium had created the basis for the rapprochement with Germany."[18]

By steadily raising their demands on the British and French as earlier Soviet demands were met, the Soviets could use negotiations with the Western Powers to insure that Germany would pay a high price for Soviet cooperation, a project realized in the secret agreements between Germany and the Soviet Union of August 23, 1939, which partitioned Eastern Europe between them.[19] Whether Stalin was wise to encourage and subsequently assist Germany, or whether the British, French, and American perception, that Germany could be held back from war or alternatively defeated in war only by a great coalition, was the sounder view, would be determined by events.[a]

[a] Sometimes the secret British–German contacts of 1939 are cited as a parallel to the German–Soviet negotiations. When compared, they reveal a fundamental and characteristic difference.

The Italian government observed German moves toward war with a mixture of admiration and apprehension. Determined to expand Italy's role in the world by the acquisition of control of the Mediterranean and as much of Southeast Europe, North Africa, and the Near East as possible, Mussolini was favorably impressed by the German threat to the positions of Britain and France, the two powers most obviously blocking his path. He was at least equally impressed by the signs of military and industrial might as well as of public unity which he had seen during his own trip to Germany in September 1937.

At the same time, there were two nagging causes of apprehension. There was always the possibility that Germany might move before Italy was ready, a concern which affected Italy's last-minute maneuvers in the crises of both 1938 and 1939. Unprepared to cope with any serious offensive against Italy by Britain and France, her leaders were all too aware of another lesson of World War I: what had happened to Germany's Austrian ally in 1914 when German concentration on the Western Front had exposed an unassisted Austria to disaster on the Eastern Front.

A second apprehension took the form of rivalry between the two. Would Germany secure gains out of all proportion to those falling to Italy? In 1939 the timing of Italy's decision to end the independence of Albania in April was undoubtedly influenced by Germany's seizure of most of what was left of Czechoslovakia in March. This pattern would subsequently be repeated.

The recognition by Mussolini in 1939 that a long and major war would certainly develop out of a German attack on Poland led him to listen to those of his advisors, especially his son-in-law and Foreign Minister, Count Galeazzo Ciano, who argued that Italy was not ready for war and had no obligation to join Germany. Later events would bring a shift in these assessments.

Mussolini's pride, however, left him reluctant to temper public and private expressions of sympathy for Germany by cautions appropriate to Italy's unreadiness for war. This reluctance was reinforced by the desire to prevent the recurrence of German reproaches about Italy's alleged unreliability as an ally stemming from Rome's joining the Allies in World

The British specified that any Anglo-German agreement was possible only if Germany first demonstrated her good faith by taking a step back from her breach of the Munich agreement, that is, by freeing Czechoslovakia, and second, if she refrained from attacking Poland. The Soviets, on the other hand, specified that agreement would come if Germany agreed for the Soviet Union to secure large parts of Poland, all of Latvia, Estonia, and Finland, as well as a large part of Romania. The Soviet Union alone outside the Axis accepted the disappearance of Czechoslovakia and anticipated the disappearance of other countries; the British hoped to reverse the whole process of making independent countries disappear.

War I, rather than maintaining her pre-war alliance with Germany and Austria–Hungary. The Italian unwillingness to reveal to Berlin that the verbal cheering from Rome would not be translated into military participation in war on Germany's side would have the effect of surprising Hitler when he sounded the trumpet for battle–only to discover that Mussolini anticipated some years of peacetime concerts.

The first time this happened had been in 1938 when, at the last-minute, Mussolini's urging of a peaceful settlement on Hitler had been a major factor in the latter's last-minute reversal of a choice for war.[20] That Italian reversal—as it seemed to Hitler—would make Hitler change his approach to the initiation of war as well as his reaction to a repetition of Italy's last-minute reservations. The way for the 1938 reversal had been prepared by British policy, and Italian reluctance in 1939 would also be greatly influenced by Rome's understanding of British determination.

The British, threatened like Russia in both East Asia and Europe, concentrated their attention, like the Russians and later the Americans, on what was perceived as the more dangerous threat in Europe. While beginning to rearm, their belief that a war anywhere would eventually involve them led the London government to try for local peaceful solutions of specific issues or, as an alternative procedure capable of simultaneous implementation, to secure a general settlement with Germany in which economic and colonial concessions would be exchanged for German acceptance of the essentials of the status quo in Central and Eastern Europe. Hitler invariably rejected out of hand all British efforts at a general settlement, in fact he would never allow them to become the subject of serious discussion, precisely because it was the status quo that he intended to destroy.[21] As for the British alternative hope of securing the peaceful resolution of specific issues, this would be realized only once, to Hitler's great disgust and everlasting regret.

In 1938 Hitler thought that he had with great care laid the groundwork for the first of his wars. Czechoslovakia would be destroyed in a war started over an incident ordered from Berlin, with the victim isolated politically by propaganda about the alleged grievances of the Sudeten Germans living in that country, isolated militarily by the deterrent effect on France of Germany's western fortifications, and isolated diplomatically through the active participation of Hungary and Poland and the passive participation of Italy and Japan on Germany's side. Once tricked into negotiations by British Prime Minister Neville Chamberlain, Hitler tried desperately to extricate himself; but then at the last moment funked at war when confronted by the doubts of his own people and advisors, the warning of war with England and France, the reluctance of Mussolini, and the hesitation of Hungary. Reluctantly he settled for his ostensible aims rather than his real ambition; that is to say, he took the portions of Czechoslovakia adjacent to Germany and inhabited predominantly by Germans, but he refrained from the war to destroy Czechoslovakia and seize most of the country as he had originally intended.

While others thought of the Munich agreement of 1938 as a sign of German triumph and as a symbol of weak-kneed acquiescence in aggression, Hitler looked on it as a terrible disappointment then and as the greatest error of his career later.[22] He had been cheated of war and, after destroying what was left of Czechoslovakia anyway, he would move toward war in a manner calculated to preclude what he considered the disappointing outcome of 1938.

The war for which in the winter of 1938–39 Hitler prepared Germany and sought appropriate relationships with other powers was one against Britain and France. They had threatened him in 1938, and they would in any case have to be defeated before Germany could safely turn to that conquest of the Soviet Union which would provide her with vast space for the settlement of her people. The preparations for this war were internal as well as external.[23] Internally, the government began a major effort to remedy what seemed to be a reluctance of the population at the prospect of war itself, a reluctance all too obvious in 1938. Hitler attributed this in part to his own regime's propaganda stress on the peaceful objectives of German policy, a propaganda designed to lull fears at home and abroad in the early years of National Socialist rule but now in need of reversal lest it undermine the resolution of the German public. The main organs of mass communications would have to be orchestrated to arouse war fever in the country.[24]

In addition, the anticipated war with the Western Powers required a substantial acceleration of the German armaments program. Since it was increasingly obvious that France was most reluctant to fight at all and that the backbone of Western resistance to Germany would come from Great Britain, it would be those portions of the German military machine most specifically needed for use against the latter country that would be given added emphasis at this time. In this framework of priorities, it will be easier to understand why it was precisely at this time that special orders were given for a great buildup of the German air force, with particular emphasis on the new two-engined dive bomber, the Junker-88, designed with England in mind.[25] Similarly, in January 1939 the highest priority in the allocations of scarce raw materials and labor was assigned to the naval construction program.

Whether or not either these internal preparations or the external ones still to be discussed could be completed quickly, Hitler already thought of himself under great time pressure. Both material and personal considerations made him think of war not only as an essential tool for the conquests he intended, but as preferable sooner rather than later. The material consideration was simple. Once Germany had by her rapid rearmament gained a headstart over her neighbors, the sooner she struck, the greater the chances for success. The longer war was postponed, the more likely it would be that rearmament programs inaugurated by others in response to the menace from Germany could catch up with and surpass that of the Third Reich. Lacking within her original borders the economic resources for the repeated replacement of one set of weapons by more modern ones, Germany could either strike while she still had an advantage over others or see the balance of strength shift in favor of her potential adversaries. The very advantage of Germany's headstart would become a disadvantage as other powers brought into production on their greater economic bases more recently developed and more numerous weapons. Germany would therefore have to strike before such a situation developed, a point which Hitler had repeatedly explained to his associates, and which indeed represents an essentially accurate assessment of the situation if Germany were to have even the slightest hope of succeeding in even a portion of the preposterously ambitious schemes of conquest Hitler intended.

The personal element was Hitler's fear of an early death for himself or, alternatively, the preference for leading Germany into war while he was still vigorous rather than aging. Identifying Germany's fate and future with his personal life and his role in its history, Hitler preferred to lead the country into war himself, lest his successors lack the will to do so. He also thought of his age as a factor of importance; it is impossible to ignore his repeated extraordinary assertions in 1938 that he preferred to go to war at the age of forty-nine and in 1939 that he would rather lead his nation at the age of fifty than go to war when fifty-five or sixty years old.[26] In this regard one enters a realm yet to be seriously and reliably explored by psychohistorians, but one can no more overlook references to his personal role and age in the final war crisis of 1939 than the fact that his earlier decision to begin his first war against Czechoslovakia in 1938 was taken in early May of that year—a few days after fear of cancer had induced him to write his last will.[27]

Here, too, one must accept a certain tragic accuracy in Hitler's perception; whether any other German leader would indeed have taken the plunge is surely doubtful, and the very warnings Hitler received from a few of his advisors can only have reinforced his belief in his personal role as the one man able, willing, and even eager to lead Germany and drag the world into war. Under these circumstances, what counted in 1939 was that the propaganda effort and the new program to redouble the armament effort had been launched, not the degree to which they were in reality falling short of their objectives, or required far more time for their completion than Hitler's personal clock allowed.

In foreign affairs, German preparations for the war against Britain and France moved along two parallel lines. Certain major powers were to be brought in as allies, while minor powers on Germany's eastern border were to be induced to accept a position sufficiently subservient to Germany to assure the latter of a quiet Eastern Front when the attack was launched in the West. Both lines of policy were pursued simultaneously, and in both Germany had, or appeared to have, a success and a failure.

The major powers scheduled to be Germany's allies were Italy and Japan. With their navies helping to make up for the deficiency in the naval armaments she needed for war with England and France but had not yet remedied herself, and with their strategic position threatening British and French colonies and communications in the Mediterranean, the Near East, Africa, and East Asia, the two adherents to the proposed new Triple Alliance could either assist Germany directly in war with the Western Powers or at the very least force a major diversion of strength on the latter. In lengthy negotiations, the Germans succeeded in persuading the Italians to accept an offensive and defensive alliance, signed in May of 1939; but in even lengthier negotiations the Japanese balked at the prospect.

The government in Tokyo was divided on the proper course to follow, but even those who favored an alliance with Germany wanted one directed against the Soviet Union, not one against the Western Powers. There had been fighting with the Soviets in the preceding year and there was further fighting in 1939. Not only those in the government inclined toward an aggressive policy toward Russia, but even those who favored a more restrained attitude thought that a closer alignment, with Germany and Italy directed against Russia, could help Japan either to fight the Soviet Union or to make that country more amenable in negotiated settlements of outstanding differences between Moscow and Tokyo. But almost no one among the contending factions at that time wanted to risk war with Britain and France, especially because of the real possibility that such a conflict meant war with the United States as well. In spite of strong urgings from the Germans, who were vigorously supported in this regard by the Japanese ambassadors in Berlin and Rome, the Japanese government simply would not agree to an alliance against Britain and France.

From the perspective of Berlin, the interest of Japan in an anti-Soviet instead of an anti-British and anti-French alliance was utterly silly. At a future time of her own choosing, Germany would seize what she wanted from the Soviet Union, an operation Hitler thought of as simple to carry out once he had cleared his Western Front by crushing Britain and France. It made no sense at all to drive the Russians into supporting Germany's main and immediate enemies by joining with Japan in an anti-Soviet alliance. If the Japanese did not want to join with Germany in an alliance directed against the West, that was a reflection of their short-sightedness and their unsuitability as an ally in the immediate situation. A possible substitute for Japan in Hitler's perception could in fact be provided by the Soviet Union itself. He had earlier regularly rejected Soviet suggestions for closer relations, but now that country could be helpful because it might both replace Japan in threatening Britain and in addition assist in dealing with the portion of his other foreign policy preparation for war which was not working out quite the way he had hoped.

In order to consider an attack in the West safe, Hitler wanted his eastern border buffered during that attack by the subordination of Germany's eastern neighbors to her. Czechoslovakia had been effectively subordinated; three other countries bordered Germany on the east: Poland, Lithuania, and Hungary.

It was obvious to the German government that Lithuania would do out of fear whatever Germany wanted, and at a time chosen by Berlin; that portion of Hitler's program was accordingly entirely subordinated to his assessment of appropriate tactics in regard to Poland.[28] Germany annexed the portion of Lithuania which Germany had lost in 1919 and did so under circumstances designed to put maximum pressure on Poland; thereafter she intended to annex all of Lithuania by agreement with the Soviet Union—only to trade most of it and later sell the rest to Moscow during the war.

The Hungarians had annoyed Hitler by refusing in 1938 to join in an attack on Czechoslovakia because they were certain that such an attack would lead to a general war, and a losing one at that. Their continued interest in sharing in any partition of Czechoslovakia and their fear of the implications for their own ambitions of better relations between Germany and Romania led to a reorientation in Hungarian policy in the winter of 1938–39. Accompanied by major personnel changes in the government, this reorientation made the Hungarian government completely dependent on Germany; the reluctant partner became, or at least became for the time being, a dependable subordinate.[29]

The symbolic gesture of obeisance to Germany made by Hungary—but refused by Poland—was adherence to the Anti-Comintern Pact. Originally devised by Joachim von Ribbentrop and Japanese military attaché General Oshima Hiroshi as a means of tying Japan to Germany, and accompanied by a whole series of self-contradicting secret agreements,[30] this pact had become for the Germans a sort of performance bond to be exacted as a test of distance from the Western Powers and subordination to herself. It was, of course, known in Berlin that the Hungarian, like the Polish leaders of the time, were vehemently, even violently, anti-Communist; adherence to a German-sponsored Anti-Comintern Pact could not make them any more so. It could however be recognized as a sign of willingness to take orders from Berlin—and it was so regarded at the time.

The leaders of Poland, however, saw themselves as the guardians of her regained independence. They had repeatedly, and at times by extraordinary and disturbing gestures during the 1920s and 1930s, made clear their insistence that Poland would not compromise either her independence or her right to be consulted about issues they saw as directly affecting that independence.[31] When the Germans in the winter of 1938–39 demanded from Poland territorial and transport concessions, concessions they had earlier promised not to ask for, and also insisted that Poland adhere to the Anti-Comintern Pact, the Warsaw government was willing to consider some compromises on the first two points, but it flatly refused the ritual of obeisance.

For five months, from late October 1938 to late March 1939, the Berlin authorities hoped for and tried to obtain Polish surrender by alternating offers and threats, promises and pressure. The Warsaw government was for obvious reasons interested in a peaceful settlement by negotiations on problems in German–Polish relations, but unwilling to acquiesce in a voluntary relinquishment of the country's independent and sovereign status. As this was precisely the key point for the German government, Hitler decided, and so informed his associates, that the sequence of German steps would have to be altered. First Poland would be destroyed by war, and then Germany could safely attack in the West. If the Western Powers came in on Poland's side right away, then a wider war would come sooner rather than later; but since a war with the West would come anyway, and since an attack in the West without a prior crushing of Poland would involve leaving large German forces to guard against Poland, it was preferable to run the risk of general war now.

In the context of this revised concept for 1939, the immediate focus of military planning would be on an attack on Poland delivered in the fall of 1939, with enough time to defeat that country before the autumn rains softened the generally unpaved roads and runways. Lithuania and the newly created puppet state of Slovakia would be invited to join in the attack on Poland from the north and the south; and, if they were agreeable, they would be rewarded with suitable pieces of the conquered state. Italy would be invited to join; and if Japan turned out to be too cautious or too stupid to do likewise, then the Soviet Union was an obvious new partner.

Since Germany's attack on Poland was from Berlin's perspective the necessary preliminary to an attack on Britain and France—with the Soviet Union's turn coming later—an agreement with Moscow would isolate Poland and either discourage the British and French from joining the obviously doomed Poles or alternatively break any Allied blockade of Germany even before it could be imposed. Under these circumstances Berlin welcomed and reciprocated hints of agreement from Moscow and developed an economic and political agreement with the Soviet Union while moving towards a war against Poland.

This would be the lovely little war of which Hitler felt he had been cheated in 1938. Propaganda about the poor persecuted Germans in Poland would consolidate opinion in Germany and isolate Poland from Britain and France the way similar propaganda—sometimes using identical stories—had been utilized in 1938. Germany's allies and supporters in other countries would either deter the Western Powers from aiding Poland or assist in the conflict.

If in these respects the pattern of 1938 was to be repeated, in others it was deliberately changed. In 1938 Germany had been involved in negotiations practically the whole year and at the last moment had not been able to break out of them into hostilities. This time there would be no negotiations with Poland after the Poles had declined German demands for subservience on March 26.[32] As the Germans stepped up their propaganda campaign, they prepared with meticulous care the incidents which would be staged to justify the attack on Poland. Unlike 1938 when this project had been entrusted first to the German army and later to recruits from the German minority in Czechoslovakia, this time the show would be arranged by the German security service itself and staged on German soil, not inside the country to be attacked. To avoid the risk of becoming entangled in last-minute diplomatic negotiations, the German ambassadors in London and Warsaw were recalled from their posts and not allowed to return to them in the final critical weeks. Demands on Poland designed to influence public opinion inside Germany for war and outside Germany against it were formulated, but Hitler would take no chance on these demands being either accepted or made the basis of new negotiations. He personally instructed his

Foreign Minister not to let them out of his hands; the demands were to be produced after war had started as a justification to the German public at home and any gullible souls abroad for the German attack. As Hitler explained to his generals on August 22, his only worry was that at the last minute some S.O.B. — the German term used was *Schweinehund* — would come along and try to deprive him of war by compromise.[33]

When Hitler provided the leaders of Germany's armed forces with this insight into his evaluation of what had gone wrong in 1938 and what he therefore intended to avoid in 1939, he knew that there would be an agreement with the Soviet Union. Such an agreement would divide Eastern Europe between the Third Reich and Russia, and would either discourage the Western Powers from intervening in support of an isolated Poland, or dramatically weaken all their hopes of blockading Germany and of obliging her to disperse her armed forces among several fronts if they went to war all the same. He could count on the reassuring effect this situation would have on his generals, and he could also count on their vehement anti-Polish attitudes to produce a considerable degree of enthusiasm for a war against Poland.[a]

There were, as we now know, a few skeptics in the German armed forces intelligence service, but all they could do was to leak an account of Hitler's comments to the British.[34] The vast majority of Germany's military leaders were either enthusiastic or acquiescent. In the first days of World War I, there had been a sense of national unity in Germany transcending all divisions of class, party, and religion; something the Germans called a *Burgfrieden*, a peace inside a castle under siege. This time, in the last moments before the launching of World War II, all that the regime needed was such a *Burgfrieden* among the holders of military authority; they were the only ones who could conceivably threaten the government and its policy. With war to be waged against Poland, and with what looked like a successful avoidance of the dreaded two-front war, the military were for the most part prepared to follow Hitler into the abyss. To Hitler it all looked much better than 1938; to most of his generals, it also looked better than 1914.

Almost as soon as the German Foreign Minister began talking with Stalin on August 23, it became obvious to Hitler that agreement with the Soviet Union would certainly be attained. Partitioning Poland between Germany and the Soviet Union presented no difficulties. In the area of the Baltic States, von Ribbentrop had been instructed to suggest the river Dvina as a new border between the two partners, an arrangement

---

[a] Hitler's temporary rapprochement with Poland had certainly not been popular in German government circles where an anti-Polish line was always preferred — and with great fervor.

which would have left Estonia to the Soviet Union and Lithuania to Germany, while dividing Latvia between them. Stalin wanted all of Latvia; and von Ribbentrop, who had received instructions from Hitler to make extensive concessions in the negotiations, was inclined to agree. His telegram from Moscow asking for Hitler's approval on this point— an approval that was promptly given—showed Hitler that a treaty with the Soviet Union was assured. Without waiting for the final signing, to say nothing of von Ribbentrop's personal report, Hitler on August 23 ordered war to begin with the attack on Poland on August 26.

As the German military machine moved into position for the invasion of Poland, and while the civilian agencies of the German government made their last moves to be ready for the other steps timed to coincide with the beginning of hostilities, Hitler planned his final diplomatic moves. He met with Foreign Minister von Ribbentrop on the latter's return from Moscow on the 24th and together the two appear to have worked out in detail the steps to be taken that day and the next, the last hours before war.[35] Mussolini was informed of what was coming by a telephone call to Ciano in the night of August 24–25, and a detailed letter was delivered to him on the 25th. The favorable situation created by the Nazi–Soviet Pact was described and the imminence of hostilities to crush Poland was announced—but with no reference to the fact that war had already been ordered for the next day. Hitler called on Italy to fulfill her obligations under the terms of the alliance, the "Pact of Steel" signed in May, and he apparently assumed that, under what looked like most favorable circumstances for the Axis, Mussolini would surely join in promptly.[a]

Japan certainly could not be expected to come in on Germany's side; on the contrary, the government in Tokyo—which imagined itself to be involved in negotiations with Germany for an alliance *against* the Soviet Union—toppled under the political shock of the Nazi–Soviet Pact even as it ordered a protest in Berlin against what looked to Tokyo like an outrageous violation of the Japanese–German Anti-Comintern Pact.

While Japan, still engaged in actual hostilities with Russia at the time, was not expected by Berlin to be of assistance in ending the German– Polish dispute in a manner suitable to Germany, the Soviet Union natur- ally was. On August 25, therefore, Germany urgently asked for the appointment of a new Soviet ambassador to Berlin and the prompt

[a] It must be recalled that one important factor that had restrained Italy in 1938 was no longer present. In the preceding year, the still continuing Spanish civil war opened up the possibility that a general war in Europe would lead to French and British intervention in Spain with dire effects for the substantial Italian contingent fighting with the Nationalists. The victory of Franco's nationalists in the spring of 1939 had ended this assignment; from the perspective of Rome, there was no longer an expeditionary force hostage to the situation in Spain.

dispatch of a Soviet military representative to help coordinate the forthcoming campaigns against Poland. The newly formed and loudly trumpeted association of the Soviet Union with Germany was seen as a means of forestalling Western intervention on behalf of Poland, and Berlin was accordingly interested in publicly visible signs of the new alignment.

Simultaneously with the notification to Italy and the invitation to Moscow, the German diplomatic staging actions of August 25 included special messages to the smaller countries of Western Europe: Holland, Belgium, Luxembourg, and Switzerland. All were to be promised German respect for their neutrality and threatened with war and destruction if any of them failed to protect Germany's rear by abandoning neutrality in favor of the Western Powers. The German government, as will be shown, intended to end the existence of all four countries, but at the moment when Germany was about to attack the first of the many nations it had promised to leave in peace, more promises were cheap and might be useful.

On the same day special efforts were also made to discourage Britain and France from siding with Poland; Hitler still hoped that the war with the Western Powers could be started at a time of his own selection after Poland had been crushed. If during the time needed for the Polish campaign London and Paris could be preoccupied with the hope of new agreements, the possibility of any danger to Germany in the West could be obviated until she was ready to strike herself. On the day before war was to begin, therefore, Hitler sent new messages to London and Paris, anticipating that these would be received and discussed by the governments there on the following morning—at the same time as they learned of the German invasion of Poland a few hours earlier.

On the entirely correct assumption that the French would not move without the certainty of British support, the more elaborate German message was sent to London. Pointing out to the British government that his new treaty with Russia meant both that there would be no real Eastern Front since "Russia and Germany would never again take up arms against each other," and that there would be no possibility of an effective blockade of a Germany that could now draw on the raw materials of the Soviet Union, Hitler promised that, after the German–Polish dispute had been settled, he would send an alliance offer to London. Instead of war with Germany under circumstances far less favorable to the Western Powers than in 1914, he offered the prospect of Germany's defending the British empire against any enemy, a promise of no territorial demands in the West, moderation in colonial demands, and an agreement on the limitation of armaments. Just as in March 1936 the breach of the Locarno Treaty of 1925, the only defensive alliance

Germany ever had with England, had been accompanied by a vast array of German promises and offers which could be debated while German troops marched West to remilitarize and refortify the Rhineland — and all of which were broken or withdrawn once they had served this purpose — so now a lengthy list of tempting bait was to be dangled before British eyes as German troops marched eastwards into Poland. Between the dispatch of this offer and the arrangement for the message to Paris, Hitler gave the final go-ahead for the attack on Poland at 4:30 a.m. the following morning, August 26.

Hoping to discourage the French from honoring their alliance with Poland, Hitler next saw the French ambassador to Germany and asked him to inform Edouard Daladier, the Prime Minister of France, that Germany did not want war with France and had no claims on her, but that the situation in German–Polish relations was intolerable. If France wanted a war with Germany that would be unfortunate, but it would be their choice. With the Soviet Union already aligned on Germany's side, with Britain, as Hitler hoped, deflected by his offer, the French Cabinet would have his kind words in front of it as its members debated what to do the following morning. The strong pacifist sentiments known to exist in France might well keep the French from going to war while Germany secured its Eastern Front for the turn against the West. All seemed ready for war as German troops moved toward the border, ration books were ready for issue to the civilian population, and the concentration camp inmates who were to be murdered wearing Polish uniforms were prepared for the staged incidents that would prove to Germany and the world that it was the Poles who had begun hostilities.

Two developments which became known in Berlin in the afternoon of August 25 caused Hitler to consider a minor alteration in the stage management of Germany's initiation of hostilities. These two developments shed considerable light on the policies of other powers, while Hitler's response to these underlines his continued overwhelming preference for war as opposed to any peaceful settlement. The German government learned that Italy was not willing to join in and that Great Britain had just signed an alliance treaty with Poland. The first news item is revealing about Italian, the second about British, policy.

In Rome, the news of the forthcoming signing of a Nazi–Soviet Pact had for a very short time been seen as possibly creating a situation in which Germany could fight Poland in an isolated war. Under such happy circumstances, Italy could follow her own inclinations and German advice by attacking Yugoslavia, that country on the other side of the Adriatic which Italy had long hoped to destroy and which was now outflanked by the earlier Italian seizure of Albania. Ciano first and then

Mussolini, however, returned quickly to the firm belief that Britain and France would fight alongside Poland regardless of Soviet actions, and they tried to convince their German ally of this view. In any case, they were now confronted by a German request for an unequivocal answer.

The Italian government had the option of promising full support in what its leaders were certain would be a general war, and one in which the first blows of the Western Powers were almost certain to hit them. And they would be moving under circumstances they had not foreseen: Germany had kept its intentions secret from them until the last moment, intentions about which the Germans were not giving them the full details even now. Alternatively they could explain that they were not yet ready and could come in only after making up the deficiencies in their preparations. Mussolini followed the advice of most of those around him and reluctantly informed Hitler that Italy could not yet commit herself to entering the war. Having anticipated the full support of Mussolini, Hitler was astounded by Italy's decision, news of which reached him right after his meeting with the French ambassador and about the time he learned of the signing of the Anglo–Polish alliance.

The British government had reached its basic decision in the early weeks of 1939 when rumors of a forthcoming attack on Holland had produced a decision to fight Germany if she attacked any nation which resisted. It had subsequently turned out that the information pointing to an imminent attack in the West was incorrect, and the next German move had instead been the destruction of Czechoslovakia's independence. That country, stripped of its military defenses by the territorial concessions made to Germany in 1938 and demoralized by its abandonment by the Western Powers, had not resisted the final German onslaught; but Germany's breach of the Munich agreement showed that the alleged German concern about the fate of her minorities abroad was fakery designed to obscure the actual aim of subduing *non*-Germans.

The subsequent British policy in the face of possible German moves against Romania and Poland, therefore, was one characterized by three consistent themes. In the first place, with the previously accepted assumption that a war started anywhere in Europe was, like that of 1914, certain to spread to the whole continent, it made little difference whether Germany first attacked in the West or in the East; Britain would be involved anyway. In view of this, it might well be wise to reverse the diplomatic strategy followed in 1938, when a firm warning to Germany had been postponed in the hope that uncertainty of British support might make for maximum concessions by Czechoslovakia, while the possibility of British intervention might persuade the Germans to accept such concessions rather than risk a general war. Now the British government would announce its position early rather than late, hoping that firmness would deter Germany, reassure her victims, and rally others to their side. This shift in approach was in large part due to the second characteristic of London's view of the situation in 1939.

German propaganda in 1938 about the real or imagined grievances of the over three million people of German descent in Czechoslovakia had had a substantial impact on the British government, the British public, and the positions of the governments in the British Commonwealth. It was generally known in government circles in London that the Germans living in Poland might well have something to complain about—in fact that they had been treated more harshly than those in Czechoslovakia and that Poland should be urged to restrain such harsh treatment—but all this was now seen as obviously a manipulated pretext for German policies aiming at the domination of all of Europe. Only one German step could reverse that view: a restoration of independence to Czechoslovakia. And that was as permanent and clear a British pre-condition for any new agreement with Germany as it was a step that the German government was under no circumstances prepared to take.[a]

The third characteristic of the British perception was that the firm public posture, which took the specific form of an announcement at the end of March 1939 that Britain would go to war alongside Poland if that country were attacked by Germany and defended herself, had to be accompanied by measures to attract other allies to Britain's side. The most obvious ally was France, herself threatened by the rising might of Germany and tied to Poland by an alliance of many years. The utter panic in Paris on September 12 and 13, 1938, when a British statement that England would fight if Germany invaded Czechoslovakia showed that the French could no longer hide behind Britain's alleged unwillingness to fight, had at that time triggered Chamberlain's first trip to Germany;[36] it suggested that in future crises London would be well advised to be most considerate of French concerns. It is in this context that one should see the reversal of Britain's neglect of her ground forces, and in particular the introduction of the first peacetime conscription law in the spring of 1939.[37] France could not be expected to fight together with England unless she could anticipate a British army fighting on the continent beside her own.

---

[a] The restoration of Czechoslovakia, if it had come to war in 1938, like that of Poland in 1939, was always discussed in London in terms of the World War I fate of Serbia: overrun by Germany during the fighting, it had been restored as a result of military victory by the Allies on other fronts.

Furthermore, the new posture of early firm public opposition to any new German aggression might rally other allies. It became increasingly evident that not only New Zealand but also Australia and Canada were reversing their neutralist positions of 1938; it is a revealing coincidence that on August 25, 1939, MacKenzie King, the Prime Minister of Canada who had met Hitler in 1937, warned the latter that Canada would join England if it came to war.[38] Even the Union of South Africa was shifting toward a position more favorable to siding with England, though in the event only a change in the government there would bring a divided country into the war by a narrow margin. Even the return of port facilities vital to the protection of British commerce had made no impact on the Irish Free State's determination to remain neutral, and new issues would come to the fore there during the war; but at first London did hope that there would be support elsewhere for a firm front against further German moves.

The signing of a formal treaty between England and Poland, whose terms had been worked out in the spring of 1939, had been postponed pending an agreement between the Western Powers and the Soviet Union, it being assumed that the treaty with Poland would be subordinate to that with Russia. No one in the British government or military circles had any faith in the Soviet Union's ability to mount offensive operations into Central Europe, a view much laughed at in retrospect but perhaps not quite so inaccurate as often assumed. That the Red army in 1944–45 could move into Central Europe vast armored forces supported by an enormous array of American trucks is hardly proof that such operations were a plausible contingency in 1939. Obviously the Soviet leadership did not think so: Stalin's repeated efforts at a rapprochement with Germany suggest that his assessment of the situation was not so different from London's view, that Russia could provide supplies and support to Poland as well as defend herself against attack but was not in a position to launch offensive operations across the zone of poor communications of eastern Poland. It was precisely for such support of Poland that Britain and France hoped; and as the Soviet Union steadily raised its demand during the 1939 negotiations, the Western Powers wanted at least to restrain Moscow from siding with Germany. As has already been mentioned, these hopes were dashed; but Russia's aligning herself with Germany did not alter the fundamental perception of the London government that Germany had to be confronted, preferably with allies to disperse German strength, but if necessary without them.

The United States government had obtained accurate information on the Nazi–Soviet negotiations, primarily from a member of the German embassy staff in Moscow. For obvious reasons, that information was kept a carefully guarded secret in Washington; but as the signing of a German–Soviet agreement looked increasingly likely—as opposed to the one between the Soviet Union and the Western Powers Roosevelt had urged on Stalin—Washington did tip off the London government. There, because of incompetence or Soviet infiltration in the Foreign Office Communications Department, the relevant telegram was not deciphered for days, so that the British government was taken by surprise when the forthcoming trip of von Ribbentrop to Moscow for the signing of a Nazi–Soviet Non-Aggression Pact was announced.[39]

The British government, however, saw in this development no fundamental change in the basic situation: Germany would be more dangerous, not less so, as a result of finding a new friend. To make certain that no one in the German or Italian government drew false conclusions about British policy from this spectacular event, messages were promptly sent to Berlin and Rome making it clear that there would be no change in the British commitment to fight alongside Poland if Germany attacked that country. It was these messages which in Rome contributed to the realization that a general as opposed to a local East European war would indeed be brought on by a German move East and hence to the Italian refusal to participate. In Berlin such messages had led Hitler to believe it worth trying to make one more attempt to detach England from Poland by the promise of an alliance offer.

It was to underline the point made in Chamberlain's letter of August 22 to Hitler that Germany should have no doubt whatever about England's willingness to go to war—with a reference to the alleged German uncertainty about British policy in 1914—that London now moved quickly to sign the alliance with Poland. Once it had become obvious that there could be no British alliance with the Soviet Union, there was no point in holding up action on the other one; and last-minute drafting changes were made as quickly as possible. This meant that the text was ready for signing on August 25, and an announcement of the signature was made public at 5:35 p.m. that day. Hitler received the news, therefore, *after* he had sent the British ambassador off to London with his new promises and *after* the final order to attack on the following morning had already been given.

The German dictator had been surprised to learn of Italy's unreadiness to participate and England's renewed expression of resolution implied in the freshly signed alliance. Hoping to try once more to separate the Western Powers from Poland, he asked his military leaders whether it was feasible to stop the military machine already set in motion or if it were already too late. He was quite willing to go to war the next

day if his advisors believed that it was no longer possible to call back
the troops. They, however, told him that counter-orders could still reach
all the units in time, and such orders were thereupon issued. Some
incidents involving German border crossings took place, so that it was
obvious to careful observers that war had been intended for the 26th,
but the faked provocations involving concentration camp inmates as well
as the massive invasion forces were halted in time.[40]

Hitler had originally set his military advisors the target date of September 1 for the war; he had then moved the date up to August 26
because he wanted to begin as early as possible. He now explained to
his naturally somewhat confused army Commander-in-Chief that the
attack on Poland would take place on September 1 after all and that he
might wait one more day, but that September 2 was the latest possible
date;[41] thereafter problems with the weather would in Hitler's view have
prevented a single brief campaign against Poland. The intervening days
were now available for renewed diplomatic moves to separate Britain
and France from Poland, though in the end Hitler did not use all the
days available by his own assessment of the situation. As soon as it
became clear to him that the Western Powers would indeed intervene,
he ordered the attack for the morning of September 1. Since he wanted
the war to start as early as possible, he could see no point in waiting even
the one day his own timetable allowed; a small but revealing indication of
his order of priorities.

The agitated discussions of the last days of peace need not be reviewed
here. They only confirmed the picture already obvious by August 25 —
if not earlier. Italy was not prepared to join Germany, and Hitler's
expression of willingness to fight England and France if they supported
Poland in no way reassured Mussolini; that was precisely what he was
worried about. The Polish government was no more willing to sign
away its independence now than earlier, and there was no disposition in
London to urge them to do so. A fairly negotiated settlement of outstanding difficulties was desired by both Warsaw and London; but the
fact that the British government would not pass on to the Poles a German
demand for the immediate appearance of a Polish negotiator until *after*
the German deadline for his appearance had passed showed that there
was no interest for capitulation in either capital. The French government
was understandably shaken and disappointed about the Soviet Union's
aligning herself with Germany, but the Daladier government was
resigned to war; the French Foreign Minister still had hopes of a last-
minute compromise, but he was by this time rather isolated in the
Cabinet.

No appeals from prospective neutrals could move Hitler. He not only would not put off war for one day, he was in such a hurry that he gave the orders to begin hostilities hours earlier than the German military timetable required.[42] To justify war in the eyes of the German public, he shared in the preparation of demands on Poland that might sound reasonable to his people—and that he ordered withheld until after they were no longer valid. He would not again run the "danger" of having his ostensible demands agreed to, or made the basis for real negotiations, or be met with counter-offers. Now that there was no longer any chance of splitting the Western Powers from Poland, his focus of attention was on the German home front in the coming war, a reflection of his belief that it had been the collapse there which had produced defeat in the preceding great conflict. When von Ribbentrop refused to give a copy of the German demands to the British Ambassador at midnight of August 30–31, the two almost came to blows. Ambassador Henderson, who had long advocated concessions to Germany, recognized that here was a deliberately conceived alibi the German government had prepared for a war it was determined to start. No wonder Henderson was angry; von Ribbentrop on the other hand could see war ahead and went home beaming.[43]

On the morning of September 1 the German offensive into Poland began. When Hitler spoke to the Reichstag, Germany's one-party parliament, that day, he blamed the breakdown of negotiations—in which he had refused to participate—on Poland; recounted the incidents along the border—which he had ordered staged the preceding night; and contrasted these evil deeds of others with the great generosity of his own demands—which he had carefully withheld until they had lapsed. To the thunderous applause of the representatives of the German people, he announced that Germany was once more at war.[44]

Almost every nation eventually participated in the new war, some as victims of attack, some as eager attackers themselves, some at the last moment in order to participate in the post-war world organization. A flood of blood and disaster of unprecedented magnitude had been let loose on the world. If the details of military operations and the localities of combat were often vastly different from those of World War I, the fearful anticipation that a new war would be as horrendous or quite likely even worse than the last proved all too accurate. There would be, however, no agitated discussion this time, as there had been after the crisis of 1914, of the question of who was responsible for the outbreak of war. It was all too clear that Germany had taken the initiative and that others had tried, perhaps too much, but certainly very hard, to avert another great conflict. There would be no second "war guilt" debate.

Some of the developments in the great upheaval which changed the world were initiated and directed by Hitler's Germany, but many flowed from the initiatives and reactions of other countries. The concept Hitler wanted to implement, of a succession of wars, each started on his own initiative against victims of his choosing, each isolated from the other, but victory in each one facilitating a German victory in the next, fell short of realization from the very beginning when England and France declared war in support of Poland. The failure of the French to mount an offensive in the West in September 1939 almost enabled him to return to his original concept. Germany attacked in the West in 1940 very much the way Hitler had intended after crushing Poland in an isolated war; and his agreement with the Soviet Union enabled him to conduct the campaign in the West with all his forces on one front for the last time in the whole war. But then his thrust was halted by England and soon thereafter the dimensions of the conflict were increasingly out of his control. Even as he marched his armies to their destruction at the hands of the Red Army by invading the Soviet Union, the United States loomed ever more menacing on the horizon. Japan's advance in East Asia, urged insistently by Germany as a means of defeating Britain and diverting the United States from Europe, only contributed to the eventual arrival of American troops on German soil.

A critical element in Hitler's inability to adjust to the altering world balance around him was the fact that he had set out to change it dramatically himself and was prepared for his country and its people to perish in the attempt rather than turn back. Though some may consider him insane for attempting to implement the doctrine of *Lebensraum*, of living space, it was the essence of his policies at all times. Even the reality of internal German migration *westward* did not deter Hitler from attempting to lay the foundation for an external migration *eastward*. On February 1, 1939, he had felt obliged to issue an edict to try to reverse the process of migration within the existing borders which was denuding Germany's eastern provinces of their "Germanic" population.[45] But even such a grudgingly admitted engagement of current reality was not allowed to intrude upon his vision of long-term policy aims. As Hitler explained to his military commanders on May 23, 1939, the object of war was not Danzig but the expansion of Germany's *Lebensraum*.[46]

The concept of revising the peace settlement of 1919 in Germany's favor, which he had ridiculed in his writings, remained for him a foolish and rejected alternative even as he used it in his propaganda. In mid-October 1939, at a time when Germany and the Soviet Union were urging the Western Powers to make peace on the basis of an acceptance of what Germany and Russia had done to Poland, the Swedish explorer Sven Hedin, a great admirer of Germany, visited Hitler. The Führer explained that peace would be possible only if the British gave up "the foolish idea of a restoration of Czechoslovakia."[47] The vital point dividing him from the Western Powers was not that of Germany taking over areas inhabited by Germans or people of German descent but rather the seizure by Germany of lands hitherto inhabited by *other* peoples who were to be enslaved or exterminated and replaced by Germans. Under the diplomatic and geographic circumstances of the time, the Czechs were the first and the Poles the second of these peoples, but it was the process which was both the key point in Hitler's program and the galvanizing element in making his attack on Poland the occasion for a war wider than he preferred at that moment.

It was precisely because Hitler understood that his aims could be realized only by war that he plunged forward. Because he was always peculiarly conscious of his own mortality, and because he recognized that the limited material resources of the Germany he controlled in peacetime would assure him a headstart in armaments for only a few years before other nations caught up, he was in a hurry to start the first of his wars at the earliest possible moment according to his assessment of the diplomatic and military situation. Given the strides beginning to be made by the rearmament England and France had initiated in response to the new menace from Germany, one must concede a certain mad logic to his belief that time was running against his cherished goals.

Because of his preference for war, Hitler conducted policy in 1939 under the personal trauma of Munich. He had shrunk from war then—and thereafter attributed such cowardice to everyone else around him—and he would not be cheated once again of the war he had always intended. Just as his anger at having been deprived of war in 1938 made him all the more determined to have it in 1939, so his postponement of the attack on Poland on August 25 left him all the firmer in an almost hysterical fixation to attack a few days later. He would not back off again; his tirade to the would-be Swedish intermediary Birger Dahlerus on September 1, in which he declared himself ready to fight England for ten years if necessary,[48] reflects the views of a dictator who had once balked before the great risk, had then tried to minimize its scope, and was now under no circumstances willing to pull back a second time. Without war, his whole program and his whole life made no sense to him. The war he started would destroy both.

There is a grim irony in the fact that most of the precautions Hitler took to make certain that there would be no diplomatic settlement of the 1939 crisis, no new Munich, were quite unnecessary. Not having agreed to the Munich treaty in good faith, he could never understand how anybody else could have; and hence, although he recognized how deeply the Western Powers were chagrined by his destruction of that settlement, he never comprehended that their policies were now based on different assumptions. When French Prime Minister Daladier declined Mussolini's suggestion of a conference, he stated that he would rather resign than attend a second "Munich."[49] Chamberlain was similarly determined that there would be no new Munich; and even had he wanted one, the British Parliament would never have allowed it after the German seizure of Czechoslovakia on March 15, 1939. Certainly no one in London was interested in exploring a new grab-bag of promises of future good behavior from a German dictator who had broken most of his earlier ones, was in the process of breaking some more of them, and was now offering to protect the British empire against his Italian ally, his Japanese Anti-Comintern Pact partner, and against his newly found Soviet friend.

The Poles were certain to fight for their independence. If the relatively conciliatory Polish Foreign Minister Josef Beck, the architect on the Polish side of the earlier rapprochement with Germany, was unwilling to accept subordination to Berlin, other Polish leaders were even less likely to consider submission a serious alternative for their country. The tragi-comedy of midnight, August 30–31, was entirely unnecessary, however revealing for participants and historians; the possibility of having his ostensible demands granted, to which Hitler had succumbed in 1938, simply did not exist in 1939. Had von Ribbentrop handed the demands to Henderson officially, Hitler would still have had his war.

Similarly, the great propaganda operations were hardly any more effective or necessary than the last-minute diplomatic moves. It was not necessary to persuade the German public of the need to fight Poland, and it was practically impossible to persuade them of the need to fight England and France. As for the outside world, all the reports of atrocities and incidents dreamed up by the fertile imagination of Germany's propaganda minister or secret police chief were unlikely to convince anyone who had lived through German use of similar tactics a year earlier. Perhaps all this noise was necessary for Hitler's self-induced excitement over the situation on Germany's eastern border, steeling him against doubts that might otherwise have assailed a man who on occasion shifted tactics and procedures. Few others were affected; but the great tragedy of 1939 was that no one else needed to be affected. Hitler alone made the key decision, though those who had contributed toward the creation of that situation in so important and powerful a country as Germany, as well as those who carried it out without hesitation, have their share of the responsibility for that decision and its terrible results for the world.

2

———— • ————

FROM THE GERMAN AND SOVIET INVASIONS OF POLAND TO THE GERMAN ATTACK IN THE WEST:
September 1, 1939 to May 10, 1940

The German plan for the invasion of Poland had been developed since the spring of 1939 and was greatly assisted by the very favorable geographical position Germany had always had, a position further improved by the territorial changes of early 1939. It was the intention of the Germans to combine surprise coups to seize special objectives at, or even before, the moment of attack with a sudden overwhelming attack on two fronts carried forward by the mass of the German army supported by most of the German air force.[1] As Hitler had emphasized to his military leaders on August 22, it was Poland as a people that was to be destroyed; and therefore from the beginning it was assumed that massive slaughter of Poles and particularly the extermination of their political and cultural elite would both accompany and follow the campaign designed to destroy Poland's regained independence. The possibility of some kind of subordinate puppet government in a portion of occupied Poland was temporarily left open, but any such concept would be dropped quickly: German policy made collaboration impossible for self-respecting Poles and any individuals still so inclined were turned away by the Germans in any case.

The planned surprise coups for the most part failed; even the peacetime sending of a warship with a landing party into Danzig could not force the quick surrender of the minute Polish garrison there, and the attempted seizure of the strategically important railway bridge over the Vistula at Tszew (Dirschau) was thwarted as Polish engineers blew up the great span.[2] A portion of Poland's navy succeeded in escaping the German effort to destroy it, but the major land offensives were crushingly effective.

The Polish government had faced four problems in contemplation of any German attacks, and all were probably insoluble under the circumstances. In the first place, until 1939 the assumption had been that the

1934 agreement with Germany made it safe to confine military planning to the contingency of a renewal of the conflict with the Soviet Union, a conflict ended by the Peace Treaty of Riga of 1921, which had left to Poland substantial territory that had belonged to her before the partitions of the eighteenth century, but that the Soviet government was likely to want to recover. As German demands on Poland in the winter of 1938–39 made it increasingly evident that the more immediate danger was from the West, not the East, Polish military planning had to prepare for a new threat, but in this it was affected by three other great difficulties.

First, there was the absence of modern military equipment, with no prospect of Poland either producing it herself or obtaining it by purchase. Germany's headstart in rearmament made it impossible for Poland to buy—even had she had the necessary cash or credits—modern weapons elsewhere, while her own industries were not yet up to the production of the planes, tanks and artillery that would be needed to hold off a German attack. A second great difficulty lay in the puzzle of precisely what to defend against any German invasion. A concentration of Polish forces would expose most portions of the country to quick occupation; any attempt to defend the major industrial and population centers, on the other hand, practically guaranteed defeat at whichever points the Germans chose to attack with what would be overwhelming local superiority. The Polish general staff opted, on the whole, for the latter, broader defense strategy, with precisely the results that could be anticipated.

The final element in the Polish dilemma was that of timing: if Poland mobilized her forces as the danger in 1939 appeared more urgent, she would both damage her own fragile economy by the withdrawal of skilled labor from industry and simultaneously provide the Germans with propaganda opportunities for blaming Poland as responsible for the increase in tensions and the outbreak of any war that occurred. Alternatively, the government in Warsaw could postpone mobilization until the last moment, thereby keeping the economy functioning normally and warding off any blame for war, but the country would risk being caught by a German attack when not yet fully mobilized and prepared.

The Polish government opted for the latter alternative, and this option also would have the effect that could be anticipated. It meant that militarily the armed forces of the country were caught in the middle of mobilization and could be defeated all the more quickly; but the choice must be seen in its political and historical context. The years since 1914 had seen a vast public debate and an enormous controversial literature about the causes of the Great War and the responsibility for its outbreak. We have already seen how Hitler had concluded that the way to deal with this question was to pick the time for an attack, fake an incident at the appropriate moment, and concoct a reasonable sounding set of demands to release to the public after war had started in order to consolidate the German home front and place the blame on the others. The Polish government, in part still hoping to avoid war altogether, in part at the urging of the Western Allies, took the opposite course of trying to avoid incidents and postponing mobilization, the sequence of mobilizations in 1914 having been a major element in the debate about the outbreak of that conflict.[3]

As already mentioned, the inclination to postpone mobilization was reinforced by advice to this effect from London and Paris. If such advice was heeded in Warsaw—to its own ultimate great cost—the political context in which Poland found herself was of the greatest importance. Only the firm support of Great Britain and France for Poland offered any real hope of either deterring Germany from attacking her at all or, alternatively, defeating Germany if the Third Reich did attack. Like Serbia or Belgium in World War I, a Poland battered and even largely occupied might recover her independence—and perhaps even enlarge her territories—within a victorious Allied coalition; but only if, first, there was such a coalition, second, if it were clear to all that the attack on her was unprovoked, and third, if she had done whatever was possible with her limited means to contribute to the cause by fighting in her own defense.

It was, therefore, essential that Poland be seen as the victim of unprovoked aggression by the governments and public of Britain and France, and the diplomacy of Polish Foreign Minister Josef Beck as well as the military posture of the Polish government have to be seen as designed to achieve such a situation. That meant restraint in the face of German provocation, a restraint which created the desired impression in London and Paris and which, as we now know, also greatly annoyed the Germans, who were desperate for politically plausible pretexts to inaugurate hostilities.[4]

At the same time, the Polish government would do what it could to defend against attack and contribute to the cause of an Allied victory over Germany. In July of 1939 the Polish code-breaking experts with the approval of their government turned over to the French and British duplicates of Polish reproductions of the German enigma machine used for encoding radio messages. By this step and related ones Poland made a major contribution to the whole Allied war effort, which has tended to be obscured by the excessive award of credit to themselves in French and British accounts of what came to be known as the "ultra" secret.[5] The Polish armed forces would certainly fight as hard as they could, even in seemingly impossible situations.

There was some hope in Warsaw, more reasonable at the time than might appear in retrospect, that, with a French offensive in the West, which they had been promised in May 1939, forcing the Germans to divert substantial forces to their Western border, it would be possible for the Polish army to hold out in at least portions of the eastern parts of the country through the winter. Developments which will be reviewed subsequently dashed both hopes: the French did not attack in the West as they had promised, and the Soviet Union broke its non-aggression pact with Warsaw and invaded Poland from the east. Under these circumstances, Polish forces would be defeated in their home country, but many members escaped across the borders of Hungary and Romania and joined others already in the West to form new military units. Later augmented by men released from Soviet camps, these units participated in the war until Allied victory in 1945.

But these developments were shrouded in a distant and desperate future as German forces struck on September 1.[6] In the first days of the campaign, the German air force swept the skies clear of what few modern planes the Polish air force could deploy and thereafter devoted all its strength to supporting the invasion by the German army. In the north, units of the German 4th Army quickly covered the fifty miles separating Pomerania from East Prussia. While the 3rd Army lunged southeastward from East Prussia to reach first the Narev and then the Bug river in order to cut behind Warsaw and the Polish forces defending the central portions of the country, larger German forces struck northeastwards from Silesia and through German-occupied sections of Slovakia as the German 8th, 10th, and 14th Armies cut their way through the defending Polish forces into the heart of the country.

The first week of fighting saw the German invaders ripping open the main Polish defenses; during the second week the major Polish forces were surrounded or pushed back as German units fought in the outskirts of Warsaw. Polish counter-attacks as well as the break-out attempts of surrounded or almost surrounded Polish units repeatedly caused local defeats or delays for the Germans, while some of the isolated Polish garrisons fought on bravely in the face of overwhelming odds. Polish units in and around Warsaw resisted fiercely and effectively, but the signs of defeat were all too obvious. The Polish government had to evacuate the capital and would eventually cross the border into Romania; but even before this final step, the mechanism of control over the armed forces of the state was in terrible disarray, a disarray not only due to the speed of the German advance and the evacuation of the capital but also to the bombing of the Polish transportation system with its few, often single-track, railways. At the time when Poland was supposed to receive the relief of a French offensive in the West, which had been promised for the fifteenth day after French mobilization at the latest, she instead found herself invaded by the Soviet Union from the east.

The Soviet and French policies behind these developments deserve and will receive separate description; here they must first be seen in the role they played in the crushing of Polish resistance. From the German point of view, the most rapid possible defeat of Poland was seen as enormously important. Certainly concern over the deteriorating weather in the late fall was a major element in this, but this was by no means the only factor. From the military perspective, the quicker the victory, the less likely effective support of or supplies to Poland could be provided by anyone. The quicker the German victory the more likely a return to the original concept of separating the attack on Poland from the attacks in the West for which it was to provide a quiet Eastern Front. But even if speedy victory did not serve that purpose, it would in any case enable the German government to redeploy its forces to the Western Front in case of any dangerous developments there. This desire for speed not only influenced the German conduct of military operations, but must be seen as a major factor in German diplomatic maneuvers during the first days of the war. Berlin made a concerted effort to enlist as many allies as possible in the attack on Poland, hoping thereby to hasten the victory and perhaps isolate the campaign in the East by a new temporary settlement from the war in the West for which additional preparation would be useful.

The Germans not only used the territory of the puppet state of Slovakia[7] as a base for attacking Poland from the south but urged the regime installed there to take a formal part in the war. The government of Joseph Tiso agreed to go beyond the use of its territories to an active role for its German-drilled soldiers in the attack on Poland, a policy rewarded by Germany with some 300 square miles of Poland, much of which had once been included in Czechoslovakia and were in the part of Poland allocated to Germany by the Nazi–Soviet Pact—a shrewd German move designed both to speed up the campaign and to give Slovakia a vested interest in whatever new arrangements Germany might wish to establish in the defeated country.[8]

The destruction of Czechoslovakia in March 1939 had not only brought German domination of Slovakia but had also assured Hungary a common border with Poland, when Budapest had been instructed by the government in Berlin to occupy the eastern extremity of Czechoslovakia, Ruthenia or the Carpatho-Ukraine.[9] Here too the Germans tried hard in September 1939 to bring another ally into the war on Poland. They asked the Hungarian government to allow German troops and supplies to move across Hungarian territory, dangling pieces of Poland in front of their eyes as bait.[10] The government in Budapest had territorial claims on Romania, not Poland, and had long looked on Poland as a potential ally in the future, as Magyars and Poles had considered each other friends in the past. They were at this time also very much concerned that joining Germany would mean war with Britain and France as well as Poland. To the annoyance of Germany, Hungary remained neutral, and by permitting numerous Poles to escape across its territory hardly endeared itself to Berlin; but there was at the moment little the German government could do but growl.

Another potential but equally unwilling ally in the war on Poland was less fortunate. In the hope of making the Polish cause look utterly futile, the Germans tried hard to secure the participation of Lithuania in the conflict. Here they thought themselves in an especially good bargaining position. Although once joined by a personal union into one dynastically united state, Lithuania and Poland in the years of their new independence since 1918 had been anything but friends. The two countries both claimed the city of Vilna and the territory surrounding it; and since Vilna had long been the capital of Lithuania in prior centuries, its inclusion in Poland as well as the deliberate bullying of the smaller by the larger country, especially in 1938, seemed to open up the possibility of recruiting Lithuania as a German ally. Furthermore, in their secret prewar negotiation with the Soviet Union, the Germans had not only secured Soviet agreement to the incorporation of Lithuania into the German sphere of influence but also to its expansion by Vilna (Vilnius) and adjacent territory out of the part of Poland otherwise scheduled for inclusion in the Soviet sphere. The government of Lithuania, however, refused to attack its neighbor, hoping to remain neutral and reluctant to join a Nazi Germany at war with Britain and France. The German government was extremely annoyed; and in this case, unlike that of Hungary, would soon find a way of punishing the Lithuanians for dragging their feet when Berlin sounded the trumpet. By the end of September, Lithuania had been traded to the Soviet Union for an added portion of Poland.[11]

From the very beginning, the ally most sought by Berlin in the attack on Poland was of course the Soviet Union. First Prussia and then the new Germany of 1871 had looked to Russia as a partner in the reduction, then the elimination and thereafter the suppression of any new independent Poland. Its revival at the end of World War I had altered the current details but not the fundamental perceptions of policy toward Poland in Berlin and Moscow. No substantial elements in either government ever recognized the possibility that a sovereign Poland, however unpleasant that country's revival might be, provided each with a measure of protection against the other while itself unable to threaten either, once both had recovered from the upheavals of the revolutionary period 1918–23. Hatred of Poland was a major factor in bringing Weimar Germany and the Soviet Union together.[12] It influenced both the policies of Nazi Germany and Soviet Russia toward each other as well as their conduct in Poland once they had again divided it between themselves.

In the early years of National Socialist rule in Germany the government had, at the personal insistence of Hitler and against the preference of his diplomatic and military advisors, put the anti-Polish line in abeyance while pursuing other aims. Precisely because Hitler's long-term aims were so vastly greater than could be satisfied at the expense of Poland, he was more willing to make tactical concessions in German–Polish relations for a short time. During that time, a Germany which had no common border with the Soviet Union and had temporarily shelved the anti-Polish line could easily wave off the approaches for a rapprochement with Moscow which Stalin made periodically.[13] Once the Poles had refused to subordinate themselves to Germany so that the latter could feel safe in attacking in the West, however, this situation changed. Now the Soviet Union was again a plausible ally against Poland, and the hints of a possible alignment emanating from Moscow had accordingly met with a very different reception in 1939.

The implications for the conduct of war of the Nazi–Soviet Pact of August 23, 1939, with its secret provisions for dividing Poland and other parts of Eastern Europe between the two powers, require additional examination at this point. The German desire for speed in the operations against Poland meant that the earlier Soviet intervention into the fighting came, the better it would be. The original dividing line agreed upon on August 23 would bring the Red Army to the east bank of the Vistula in the suburbs of Warsaw, and since the *distance* Soviet forces would have to move to the demarcation line was greater than that which faced the Germans, an early Soviet start could only be welcomed in Berlin. While most Polish forces faced the Germans, the road and railway networks in the area to be occupied by the Soviet were worse, a transportation problem accentuated by the change of railway gage at the Polish–Soviet frontier.

Under these circumstances, the German government began urging the Soviet Union to move into Poland in the first days of hostilities and repeated this request ever more insistently thereafter. Berlin stressed the speed of the German advance and the rapid collapse of Polish resistance as well as the problems created by the retreat of Polish formations eastward. The Germans pointed out that they would either have to pursue Polish forces further and further into the area allocated to the Soviet Union or see new regimes established there. Surely the Russian government would wish to move quickly into the territory it was scheduled to obtain.[14]

From the perspective of Moscow the situation did not look quite so simple. The evidence suggests that the Soviet government anticipated neither the rapid German initial advance nor the subsequent holding out of Polish forces in the Warsaw area; the former misjudgement led them to think they had more time to prepare than was actually the case, while the latter appears to have reinforced Stalin's concern about any Polish survival in a rump state should one be created.

The Soviet leader's initial inclination to delay an invasion of Poland from the east was reinforced by several considerations. In the first place, there was the need to mobilize Soviet armed forces for the attack; a process which would take some time, especially since some of the forces to be employed came from the interior portions of the U.S.S.R. [15] and some had to be brought from the Far East.[16] Secondly, Stalin appears to have placed considerable emphasis on so arranging the timing of the attack as to make it plausible domestically and externally as a measure for the recovery of lands in large part previously included in Russia at a time when the Polish state had effectively ceased to exist, rather than as an act of aggression imitating and joining the German one. Finally, the fighting between Soviet and Japanese troops on the border of their respective puppet states was still in progress, though a decisive Soviet victory there had come with an offensive on August 20. The Soviet government indicated to Tokyo that it wanted to settle the incident on August 22 (the day before von Ribbentrop's arrival in Moscow).[17]

As interested in avoiding war on two fronts as the Germans—though more careful and successful at this than Hitler—Stalin wanted to make certain that the situation in East Asia was under control before launching military operations in Europe. This aim was assisted not only by the victory of Soviet troops in late August but by a combination of two additional factors. First, the signing of the Nazi–Soviet Pact—which had opened up the possibility of invading Poland in concert with Germany in the first place—had quite literally collapsed the government in Tokyo. Imagining themselves engaged in negotiations with Germany for an alliance *against* the Soviet Union, the leaders of Japan learned to their consternation that their prospective European ally had signed a non-aggression pact with the very power against which they were fighting a losing battle and had hoped to secure German pressure. The government in Tokyo resigned and the new Prime Minister there had difficulty even finding a suitable Foreign Minister for some time and had to hold on to both positions for a month. That under these circumstances the Japanese ambassador in Moscow was instructed to negotiate an armistice on terms which in effect accepted the Soviet claims in the border dispute should not be surprising, and that the Germans in their eagerness for a quick Soviet move in Europe should do their best to facilitate an agreement between their pre-war and their new-found friend should also be easy to understand.

A second element facilitating a Soviet–Japanese agreement was that, just as the Tokyo government was eager to end the disastrous fighting at Nomonhan (Khalkhin-gol), Stalin's own sense of urgency about the European situation as the speed of the German advance became obvious led him to refrain from further possible offensive operations in the border fighting and instead agree to a settlement which the Japanese government could accept without extreme humiliation.[18] The Soviet–Japanese armistice agreement of September 15 provided for a cease-fire on the following day; but well before the agreement was reached, at least by September 9, it must have been obvious to the Moscow authorities that the conflict in East Asia was about to end and all attention could be concentrated on her western border.[19]

It was in this context that the Soviet government withdrew its ambassador to Poland as well as most of the embassy personnel on September 11, the same day that the Soviet press reported on the collapse of Polish resistance.[20] Although in fact some Polish resistance was to continue for another three weeks, it must have looked to Stalin that any substantial further delay entailed two equally great risks: there might be a German–Polish armistice which would leave the Soviet Union entering a war already concluded, on the one hand, or German advances into the depths—not just the fringes—of the part of Poland allocated to Russia, which might in turn encourage the Germans to demand a shift of the partition line in their favor, on the other.[21] Moving up the timetable as much as possible, the Soviet leader notified the Germans that the Red Army would attack on September 17, excusing the violation of the Soviet Union's treaties with Poland by declaring that state to have ceased to exist. The day before, on September 16, the Soviet government had recognized the puppet state of Slovakia, thus giving public notice of its belief—unique outside the Axis—that Czechoslovakia had also ended its legal existence.[22]

The political implications of these Soviet actions, and simultaneous ones in the Baltic and Balkan areas, will be examined later; here it is important to record the immediate meaning of the Soviet invasion for Poland. The advancing Red Army eliminated any prospect of Polish forces taking advantage of the temporary check of German forces before

Warsaw to organize continued resistance in the communications-poor forests and swamps of eastern Poland; it also quickly forced the Polish government and remaining soldiers to cross the border into Romania and Lithuania (and to a lesser extent Hungary) before Soviet occupation closed off the last escape routes. Several hundred thousand Polish soldiers came to be Russian prisoners of war—a subject we will have sad occasion to return to—and would be followed into exile in the interior of the U.S.S.R. by hundreds of thousands of other Poles deported from their homes once the Soviet-occupied territories had been annexed to the Soviet Union.[23]

Under these circumstances, the Soviet intervention had the military effect hopefully anticipated by the Germans. They could coordinate the last stages of the campaign with the Red Army in a process that involved some technical problems but none that proved insurmountable.[24] The failure to inform the advancing German units of the terms of the planned eventual partition lines caused some confusion, but in a few days in the period September 20–26 the German troops pulled back to the line agreed upon on August 23. They left all Polish forces east of that line to the tender mercies of the Red Army while themselves concentrating on crushing the remaining centers of Polish resistance. By the end of the month, this process was essentially completed. At this time in the war the Germans were enthusiastic advocates of unconditional surrender, which was required of the Warsaw garrison. Other remaining isolated centers of Polish resistance were also beaten down in the last days of September and the first days of October.[25] The fighting in Poland had ended. A million Polish soldiers had been captured by the Germans and Russians; over 100,000 had died; something over 200,000 had fled across the borders. The whole country was once again occupied by foreign troops who would install new systems of terror—one animated by racial and the other by class ideology.

The victors' losses were far smaller.[26] The German casualties of about 45,000 would affect her subsequent campaigns and military buildup only minimally,[27] while the Soviet casualties of 2,600 barely justified Stalin's proud assertion of December 1939 that the friendship of Germany and the Soviet Union had been "cemented with blood."[28] More important was the question whether they could turn their joint victory over Poland into wider and more lasting gains either in the immediately affected territories of Eastern Europe or in the broader realm of international affairs.

The German government had left open the possibility of some minimal rump-Poland from the beginning, but as will be seen, dropped this idea as soon as the Soviet Union indicated that it would be happier without such a contraption.[a] Given the relative insignificance of Polish territory in the framework of Hitler's broader ambitions and aims, it is easy to understand why the attack on Poland was not preceded by the kind of extensive and detailed planning for administrative and economic measures, running parallel with the precise preparations for military operations that were to characterize the preliminaries for the invasion of the Soviet Union during 1940–41.[29] Big pieces of Poland were annexed to Germany; and in line with Hitler's insistent denunciation of any and all attempts to regain the German borders of the pre-Versailles Treaty era, the new lines had nothing in common with Germany's borders of 1914.[30] The Poles living in these areas would be driven out. Here would be demonstrated the alternative procedure for relating people to boundaries which the Germans were determined to substitute for that followed at the end of World War I. At that time, an effort had been made to adjust state boundaries to population with plebiscites in areas of uncertainty and the possibility of "option," or transfer to the other state with one's property, a last resort meant for those who did not wish to live within the state into which new boundaries placed them. All this was now to be reversed. Under the new system, the victor would set the boundary wherever he thought appropriate at the moment and any people he did not want on one side of the border would be shoved, preferably without their property, to the other. Instead of fitting boundaries to people, the victor would fit the people to new boundaries – a procedure heralded in the German–Italian agreements for the transfer of Germans from the South Tyrol, [31] but first applied radically to Poles in the territories newly annexed to Germany. Like so many German innovations, this one too ended up being applied to them; but its first desperate victims were those Poles driven out of their homes to wander in the winter of 1939–40 in search of new homes.

But where could they go? While the vast stretches of Poland directly annexed to Germany were to be emptied of Poles to be replaced by German settlers, all preferably without any of the Catholic religious institutions once so strong in the area,[32] a substantial portion of central Poland was placed into a special category of exploited territory called the "General Government" under the direction of the National Socialist Hans Frank. By a redrawing of the August 23 partition line which will

---

[a] It is at times asserted that the German abandonment of the idea of a rump-Poland was caused by the refusal of the Allies to arrange peace with Germany after the German victory in Poland. This interpretation cannot be fitted into the chronology. Hitler's September 19 speech in Danzig already forshadowed the positive German response to the Soviet suggestion of that date that there be no Polish state at all. The German views of September 19 and 20 can hardly be interpreted as a response to Chamberlain's speech of October 12 (which is discussed subsequently).

be examined in the context of German–Soviet relations, this structure came to include, after September 28, 1939, an additional portion of central Poland previously allocated to the Soviet Union. After July 17, 1941, still more of southeast Poland, under Soviet control from 1939–41 but seized by the German army in the first stage of the invasion of Russia, would also be added to it.[33] In this whole area the Germans, beginning in September 1939, experimented with the most extreme of their concepts for ruling occupied territories and subject peoples: forced deliveries of food, mass executions of the political, cultural and religious elite, random slaughter of civilians, massive levies of forced labor, new settlement and resettlement projects according to the latest brain waves of various officials, and, beginning in the winter of 1941–42, the wholesale murder of Polish and Central and Western European Jews. Before setting out on this whole program, Hitler had described his intentions in broad and candid terms and had tried to reassure any doubters among his military commanders by reminding them that the uproar caused by the massacres of the Armenians earlier in the century had quietened down with time.[34]

What would have happened subsequently had Germany won the war is too awful to envisage; her loss of it meant that the application of such policies was halted, and, in addition, the role Germans had played in Eastern Europe in preceding centuries came to an abrupt end. In an earlier age, German settlement and expansion had meant conflict accompanied by some economic development and some cultural advances; now it meant conflict leading only to economic exploitation, the elimination of cultural life, and death and destruction on an unprecedented scale. Hans Frank, the man Hitler put in charge of this area, never appreciated the irony in his design to have the Government General settled by Germans and then called the Gau (or district) of the Vandals, named thus for that fine group of Germanic people which he believed maligned by anti-German propaganda, and who in his imagination had first brought the blessings of Germanic culture to this portion of the globe.[35]

More will be said about Poland in Chapters 9 and 13, but here we must return to the events of September 1939 as German and Soviet forces completed the occupation of the country. The original partition plans of the two governments had cut the major area of Polish settlement at the Vistula river and had left open the question of some form of a rump-Polish state. From the German point of view, which looked toward an attack in the West as the necessary prerequisite for a subsequent invasion of Russia, the Polish question was always of a subordinate tactical nature. From the perspective of the Soviet Union, however, the question looked very different. While hating the Poles about as much as the Germans, the Soviet leaders as devout adherents of what they generally called Marxism–Leninism considered what they labelled the Second Imperialist War a struggle over markets and investments between nations of monopoly capitalism. There was no room in their thinking then or later for the idea that Hitler's agrarian expansionist concepts of a racial Social Darwinism might be the well-spring of German policy, not merely a propaganda device to delude the German masses. A new settlement in Eastern Europe, once it had been worked out with the German government, might therefore be lasting, not temporary, and could establish the framework from within which the Soviet Union would observe the capitalist world for decades to come.

From this perspective, the events of mid-September 1939 suggested to Stalin that some rearrangements in the deal with Germany might be in order. The Western Powers had not only declared war on Germany but gave every sign of continuing to fight. If they did make peace with Germany after all, then it would be best to collect all that the secret agreement with Germany promised her and to do so quickly lest peace break out before the booty had been collected. But if the war indeed continued, there would be great advantage to the Soviet Union in leaving the major nominal cause of that continuance— the Polish question—to the Germans. The fact that even after the initial German victories the Polish forces in central Poland continued to fight bravely, and that this caused the German army to have to continue for a while fighting Poles within the portion of the country assigned to the Soviet Union, can only have reminded Stalin of the extent to which national sentiments animated a large part of the Polish population. Both considerations pointed in the same direction from Soviet perspective: no Polish rump state and fewer Poles on the Soviet side of the new border. Stalin informed the Germans on September 19 that he had now concluded that it would be better not to allow any kind of Polish state [36]—a proposal the Germans promptly accepted—and on September 25 personally suggested a highly significant alteration in the boundary between the Soviet and the German lines of influence as agreed on August 23.[37]

The Germans themselves had some ideas on small adjustments in the new border, in particular at the southern end, where they would greatly have liked to obtain the Polish oil fields across the agreed line at Borislav-Drogobic. The Soviet leaders would make additional concessions on oil shipments to Germany, and they even agreed to give the Germans a small additional piece of Poland at the other end of the border by letting them have the Suwalki area, which included a lovely forest for the disappointed German Foreign Minister to hunt in; but they were insistent on retaining the San river line and thus the oil fields as provided in the secret protocol of August 23.[38] On the other hand, in the middle portion of the new border they themselves proposed a major change. They would turn over to the Germans a substantial portion of central Poland between the Vistula and Bug rivers in exchange for the Lithuanian state, which the two powers had previously agreed to enlarge by the Vilna area.

From the Soviet point of view, such a shift would bring the Germans substantially further east in the central part of their common border while pushing them further west at the northern end. It would leave the Soviet Union with very large stretches of east Poland in which, however, the non-Polish portion of the population—the Belorussians and the Ukrainians—constituted a majority. It would place all three Baltic States within the Soviet sphere, something Stalin might have preferred from the beginning. If that had been his preference, he could not easily insist on it in the August negotiations, in which the Germans had originally proposed dividing them in such a fashion that each would get all of one and half of the middle one by dividing Latvia at the Dvina river. The Germans had agreed to cede all of Latvia to the Soviet Union at that time, but if Stalin wanted Lithuania already then, he clearly found it wiser to postpone asking for it. Now he offered a large part of Poland in exchange.

From the German point of view, the advantages of such a trade were not as obvious. The Germans were planning to take control of the enlarged Lithuania along lines that, as far as can be determined, would have been somewhat similar at the beginning to those governing Germany's relations with the puppet state of Slovakia.[39] Whether it would suit her diplomatically to do so right away—as the Soviets were doing with Estonia and Latvia—was unclear. The possibility of additional territories for German settlement directly adjacent to East Prussia was more attractive than the geographically more remote portion of Poland being offered; on the other hand, the latter was considered considerably better agricultural land. The possibility of friction with the Soviet Union in regard to Polish questions if the central area of Polish population remained divided between the two countries had to be weighed against the disadvantage of appearing to the outside world as the primary element in the subjection of Poland. Hitler authorized von Ribbentrop to agree to the trade, possibly influenced by the recalcitrant attitude of the Lithuanians when they had been asked to join the attack on Poland.[40]

In the negotiations on this question during his second trip to Moscow, von Ribbentrop secured a small piece of Poland on the right bank of the Bug river in order to straighten out the line created by the rivers, as well as a piece of Lithuania to round out the Suwalki area—territories Stalin could afford to give up as he was getting back the Vilna portion of east Poland previously scheduled to go to Germany when it took Lithuania. Before the other portions of the series of new German–Soviet agreements of September 28 are discussed, it should be noted that the new German–Soviet border would not only include all three Baltic States in the Soviet sphere but have major implications for the subsequent fate of Poland, its relations with the Soviet Union, and the latter's relations with the rest of the world.

The other agreements worked out by the German and Soviet governments at the end of September 1939 reflected their joint interest in supporting each other's desire for a rearrangement of Eastern Europe in accord with the preference of Berlin and Moscow but without regard for those of either the smaller countries of the area or the Western Powers as the basis for their friendship with each other. They promised to suppress any and all attempts of the Poles to regain their independence. The good relations the two powers would have with each other were to be cemented by population exchanges at the new boundary between them; and, in accordance with this principle, those of German descent in the Baltic States which were now all in the Soviet sphere were to be allowed to move to Germany (which could then settle them in portions of Poland to replace dispossessed or murdered Poles).[41] New economic arrangements were to be worked out and these would be designed to assist Germany if her war with the Western Powers continued. But the two new joint masters of Eastern Europe called upon the West to withdraw from the war, accepting the end of the independence of Poland, Czechoslovakia, and the Baltic States as Germany and the Soviet Union had just arranged and agreed.[42]

Both proceeded to move forward with this program, rearranging Eastern Europe to suit their preference and launching a combined propaganda campaign calling on the British and French to make peace on that basis. While the Germans took steps to rearrange the enormous portions of Poland they had seized, the Soviet government consolidated its hold on eastern Poland, pressured the Baltic States into accepting Soviet military and diplomatic control, and began a diplomatic campaign of pressure on Romania, Bulgaria, and Finland to extend Soviet territory and influence in those directions in accord with the German–Soviet agreements.[43]

While the two powers reordered the affairs of Eastern Europe and waited to see whether their call for a return to peace under the newly changed circumstances would be rewarded by a favorable answer, their relationship with each other could proceed on several levels. They worked out a series of new economic agreements in further detailed negotiations, not only to implement their prior economic treaty of August 19 and the special oil delivery and railway transit agreements growing out of the discussions of the Borislav-Drogobic oil fields,[44] but going far beyond such relatively minor matters to a massive exchange of Soviet raw materials for German manufactured products, technical designs and equipment, and other specialized items. The formal new economic treaty was not signed until February 11, 1940, and in the intervening weeks there had to be extended and at times rather difficult further negotiations, conducted for the most part in Moscow and with the repeated personal involvement of Stalin. When signed, it provided the economic basis with which Germany could be confident of her ability to attack in the West—there would be enough oil for her tanks, enough manganese for her steel industry, and enough grain for her soldiers and workers.[45] And in regard to those products which the Soviet Union could not supply from her own resources, she would assist Germany by purchasing them for her elsewhere in the world or transporting them across Soviet territory to Germany if the latter purchased them herself.[46]

Even while the economic relations of the two powers were being worked out, the Soviet Union supplemented its political support of the combined peace propaganda campaign—in which the Comintern played a prominent part—with direct assistance to Germany in the naval sphere. An extensive series of measures supported German naval warfare against the Western Powers; it included the provision of a special naval base at Western Litsa Bay near the major Soviet port of Murmansk, the use of other Soviet ports, and, eventually making possible the movement of a German auxiliary cruiser around Siberia into the northern Pacific to prey on Allied shipping.[47] Simultaneously, the Soviet government rebuffed the slightest gestures which might imply better relations with the Western Powers; the long-term advocate of better British–Soviet relations, Sir Stafford Cripps, could not even get a visa to visit the country.[48]

In return, the Soviets demanded, and within limits the Germans agreed to assist in, the building up of Soviet naval power on which Stalin personally and repeatedly insisted. Before the war, the Soviet leader had looked primarily to the United States for technical and construction help in the development of a Soviet blue-water navy. He had sought and obtained some naval supplies, especially for submarines, from the Third

Reich,[49] but he had tried unsuccessfully to have a battleship built in the United States and had made other attempts at receiving American assistance for a modernized and enlarged fleet.[50] Now he turned to Germany, which found it expedient to use naval equipment, naval plans, and even an uncompleted cruiser as part payment for raw materials delivered by the Soviet Union.

Here too the contrasting perspectives of Hitler and Stalin are revealed. The Soviet leader was willing to help Germany fight its current war with the Western Powers while looking to the long-term buildup of Soviet power, in this instance in the naval field, in a world torn by war only among the capitalist powers. Hitler, on the other hand, wanted whatever assistance he could get to win the war with the West, which he had always considered the great and difficult prerequisite for unlimited territorial expansion eastwards. He was confident that any improvements the Russians could make in their navy in the interim would make no difference in the outcome of Germany's big move east when it came.[51] If the Soviets would trade oil for the engineering plans of the German battleship *Bismarck*, he was certain of accomplishing his aims long before the Soviets could build their version of the *Bismarck* or even complete the unfinished cruiser *Lützow*.[52] What counted was the immediate situation in the West.

THE WAR IN THE WEST AND AT SEA

What was the situation in the West? There the Germans were formally at war with Great Britain and France. The two Western Powers were committed to defending Poland against unprovoked attack, France by a long-standing treaty of alliance, England by a promise publicly made at the end of March and confirmed by the alliance signed in late August of 1939. When the news of the German invasion of Poland reached London and Paris early on the morning of September 1, decisions had to be made promptly in both capitals. Because these decisions were based on contradictory advice from their respective military advisors, the two governments found it difficult to harmonize their immediate diplomatic steps.[53]

The London government was from the beginning insistent on a withdrawal of German forces from Poland if general war were still to be averted; the French government, because of some residual inner divisions, was not quite as clear. Since the Italians attempted some last-minute efforts at restoring peace and the Germans hoped that the news of quick and substantial military victories might yet discourage Britain and France from honoring their pledges to Poland, there was another day's delay in implementing the decision for war. The British military advisors were telling their government to move with speed from any ultimatum to a formal declaration of war because of their concern about a possible German surprise air attack in the interval. This concept of a possible knock-out blow on London from the air being struck by waves of German planes at the height of a crisis—something on the order of a Pearl Harbor attack on England's most important city—had haunted British military thinking in prior years.

The French government was hearing opposite advice from its military advisors. They were concerned about air or land attacks interfering with French mobilization, and therefore wanted a maximum amount of time in order to complete as much of the mobilization process as possible before any declaration of war. Here was a divergence between the prospective allies at the very beginning of a war that was certain to strain both, one especially hard to resolve in a situation where Chamberlain faced a parliament overwhelmingly determined to move quickly—but which could hardly be enlightened about the divergent military advice received in London and Paris. Under these circumstances, the British moved ahead of the French but not so much as to make it too obvious that they were pulling a still partially reluctant French government behind them. At the last minute the expiration time of the French ultimatum to Germany was moved up twelve hours so that, although still a few hours after the British, the two declarations of war on Germany came on the same date: September 3, 1939.

It was of enormous importance for the conduct of the war which began that day, that the cumulative experience of others with Germany in prior years was to bring in on the side of London and Paris allies who came to share a significant portion of the war's burden. Australia, New Zealand, and a few days later Canada declared war on Germany. In the Union of South Africa (as it was then called), the government in power did not wish to join in. There was a bitter parliamentary fight; a new government under Jan C. Smuts replaced that of James B. M. Hertzog; and that Dominion also declared war on Germany on September 6.[a]

The British-controlled government of India declared war on Germany without consulting the representatives of the major Indian political parties, a step that was to have important repercussions subsequently. The Irish Free State, on the other hand, refused to join the other Dominions

[a] Some of the opponents of war with Germany sympathized with National Socialism, and the leaders of this faction would take over the government in Pretoria in 1948, dominating the government of what was to become the Republic of South Africa thereafter. On the role of the new Prime Minister who took South Africa into war in the September 1939 crisis, see Kenneth Ingham, *Jan Christian Smuts: The Conscience of a South African* (New York: St. Martin's, 1986), pp. 205–7.

and proclaimed its neutrality. In some relatively minor areas of military affairs, the Irish Free State would make supportive gestures, preferably in secret, to assist Britain,[54] but on major issues—such as Britain's use for anti-submarine warfare of the treaty ports which had originally been reserved for the Royal Navy and had only recently been turned over to full control from Dublin—the Prime Minister of Ireland, Eamon de Valera, would resist all pleas from London.[55] Here was a subject reopened repeatedly during the war; de Valera never budged, and this, too, had repercussions not only during World War II but into the rest of the century.

How was a war against Germany to be fought? Having begun their rearmament program long after Germany, the British and French believed themselves behind in armaments, especially in the air and on land. Their basic strategy, therefore, was to remain on the defensive in the first stages of war. If Germany could be held in check, Britain and France could continue to build up their air forces, France could hopefully purchase additional planes in the United States to make up for deficiencies in its own air force, while the British could move forward seriously with the buildup of a substantial army, conscription having been introduced earlier in 1939. As this program went forward, the naval forces of the Allies would destroy German and protect Allied shipping. Furthermore, a reading of World War I which included the belief that the blockade had made a great contribution to victory in 1918 suggested that in spite of major changes—such as the opening of a huge hole in any blockade by the German–Soviet Pact—blockade might once again play such a role.

This misperception, as we now know it to have been, was reinforced by another perception which was even more removed from reality. It was widely believed, and continued to be believed until well into the war, that Germany's economy was severely strained and operating at full or near-full capacity, so that any substantial interference with that economy was likely to have serious repercussions on her capacity to fight. The building up of Allied forces while Germany was assumed to have already reached a pitch of military and economic efficiency was expected to open up the prospect for Allied offensive operations after an initial period of defensive fighting.

The staff talks of the British and French in the spring of 1939, which examined the contingencies then facing the two powers, had considered a war started by Germany and Italy as the most likely one, with their enemies looking at the time element from the opposite point of view, that is, looking to early victory from successful early offensives mounted at a time of Axis military superiority, in order to avoid the likely shifting of the military balance over time as the strength of the Allies increased. The conclusions drawn by the British and French from this have been aptly summarized in the British official history as pointing to the following view of war:

> first a mainly defensive phase directed towards maintaining as far as possible the integrity of the two empires but during which no opportunity should be lost to achieve, without undue cost, successes against Italy calculated to reduce her will to fight; then a second phase directed towards holding Germany and dealing decisively with Italy; then the final objective, the defeat of Germany.[56]

How long would such a war take? On September 6 the Secretary of State for War in the War Cabinet in London asserted that it should be assumed that the war would last "at least five years."[57]

A problem which this set of assumptions and the conclusions drawn from them did not address directly was the situation to be faced by Poland, the country both Britain and France had pledged themselves to assist if attacked.[a] The assumption throughout was that Poland in World War II, like Serbia in World War I, would be overrun during hostilities but restored to independence after an Allied victory. Neither Western Power expected that the Soviet Union, if so inclined, could do much to assist Poland against Germany except by providing some supplies (though able to do a considerable amount to defend *herself* if attacked). There is no evidence that an immediate offensive into Germany if she attacked Poland was ever considered. Theoretically such a move could be seen as dangerous to Germany and highly advantageous for the Allies. German forces would be busy in the East and weakest in the West. But there was no substantial British army available to participate in such an operation, and the French government and military leaders were united in their refusal to contemplate offensive operations on the Western Front by themselves.

Without any willingness of Belgium to participate in such an operation, any offensive would have had to be launched at precisely that portion of the German border best covered by the defenses of the Westwall, as the Germans called what the Allies referred to as the Siegfried line. Though in reality nowhere near as strong as the French believed, or pretended to believe, the Westwall looked to the hesitant French military leadership of the time like an insurmountable obstacle, or one which could be broken into only at the cost of casualty levels that the country could not afford. Even in 1936, long before the construction of fortification in the Rhineland, the French

---

[a] The British did make sure that Poland's gold would be safe from German seizure; something they had failed to do in the case of Czechoslovakia.

Commander-in-Chief, General Maurice Gamelin, had believed that the French army could not break through the Rhineland;[58] he could hardly be more optimistic now. Any questioning of the efficacy of the Westwall would have implied questioning the strength of France's own elaborate defensive fortification system, the Maginot Line, and no one was prepared to make the mental effort and face the political and military implication of such dangerous thoughts.[59] And with a military doctrine which dispersed the French armored forces as supporting elements among the infantry units, there was perhaps some truth to the view that, if the French army did move after it had completed mobilization, there would in any case not have been time for its slow advance to make itself felt before the bulk of the German army could be returned to the Western Front from its victory in Poland. Even without such thoughts, however speculative, the French military leaders saw the prospect of victory *not* in an early offensive but in a successful defensive, followed only after lengthy preparation by an offensive of their own. That was how they had won in 1918; it was their only recipe for victory in the future.

In spite of this defensive military policy, which in effect wrote off any smaller Eastern allies of France, to be overrun before an offensive was mounted against Germany, the French in negotiations with the Polish Minister of War in May 1939 had promised a major offensive in the West at the latest on the fifteenth day of mobilization, after they had started bombing Germany immediately on the outbreak of war and begun limited local offensives on the third day after announcing mobilization.[60] The origins and purposes of this deception remain to be explained, but all available evidence shows that there was never any intention of implementing the central portion of these promises — a major offensive starting on the fifteenth day of mobilization — and the man who would have had to command it, General Alphonse Georges, in fact asserted that he would resign if ordered to carry it out.[61]

The French military would wait for the buildup of a substantial British army, a process guaranteed to last a year or two, and would hope that the increasing strength of the Western Allies might induce the Belgians to side with them and permit an eventual invasion of Germany across their territory, an even more remote contingency. The meaning of such a policy, whatever explanations for it were offered later, was that only nominal French actions in the West would occur while Poland was overrun. The focus of concern was a successful defense of France against a German offensive, whenever it came.

That left the possibility of using the British and French air forces to bomb Germany; but here too there were doubts in both governments, doubts which reinforced each other. As Nicholas Bethell has put it, "Both sides were relieved by the other's reluctance to act."[62] In spite of the obvious and public evidence of German bombing of civilian targets in Poland, the British and French both still insisted on restraining their air forces by strict limitation in target selection to the purely military. [a] Furthermore, there was great concern that an air offensive might simply lead to extensive German retaliatory raids, which neither the British nor the French believed themselves prepared to meet.[63] The British plans for bombing German industrial targets in the Ruhr area were met not only by concern over civilian casualties which would inevitably result, but by French fears for their own industry, still without adequate defense. As for the French air force, it was neither prepared for nor inclined to offensive operations of any kind; it would merely support the ground operations of French forces—and of these, as we have seen, none were under way.[64] Aside from unsuccessful attempts to attack German warships from the air [65]—*the* purely military target for bombers by its very nature—the air effort over Germany in the first months of war illuminated the political perceptions rather than the military intentions of the Allies. British planes dropped millions of leaflets over Germany explaining the causes of the war and calling on the German people to end it. Unwilling or unable to believe that a population assumed to be cultured and civilized could support its government in the terrible course Germany had undertaken, the Allies still hoped that an internal upheaval might end the conflict. This assumption confused Germany's enemies for a long time, and only the endlessly dedicated support Hitler received from the country eventually dispelled illusions which did credit to the sentiments if not to the insight of those who held them.[66]

Other than in Poland itself, the war began in earnest in September 1939 only at sea. Two German pocket-battleships and sixteen submarines had been sent into the Atlantic before the German initiation of hostilities so that they might begin to attack Allied shipping immediately. When war started, the German naval construction program had to be curtailed for the time being; the big battleships *Bismarck* and *Tirpitz* as well as the heavy cruiser *Prinz Eugen* were to be completed, and work was also continued on one of the two aircraft carriers; but work on the super-battleships which were designed to provide Germany with a major

---

[a] The record of the extended discussion of this subject in the British Cabinet meeting of October 14, 1939, is highly instructive. There were still to be restraints on bombing because of concern over civilian casualties. The Germans were to be left the dubious honor of starting with the bombing of cities (in the face of evidence that they had already done so in Poland), but the British would do the same if the Germans began general bombing or invaded neutral Belgium. War Cabinet 47(39), PRO, CAB 65/3, ff. 123–27.

surface fleet had to be postponed for the time being.[a] Available resources, insofar as they were allocated to the navy at all, were concentrated on submarines, destroyers, and smaller warships.

After a brief initial period of restraint to see whether the Western Powers, and especially France, were seriously going to become involved in military activities against Germany, the German navy began its attack on Allied shipping.[67] Even in the cautious first days, the liner *Athenia* was sunk with large loss of life; but the German government, which preferred to postpone war with the United States, pretended that this sinking was a British provocation; and Admiral Raeder, the Commander-in-Chief of the navy, was careful to maintain this fiction after talking to the captain of the German submarine which had fired the torpedo.[68] With mines laid off the British coast, submarines in the waters around Great Britain, the pocket-battleships in the Atlantic and Indian Oceans, and a little later auxiliary cruisers disguised as merchant ships, the Germans did what they could to interrupt Allied shipping. They also tried to support these efforts by using their only two then available battleships for diversionary operations closer to home. The penetration of the great British naval base at Scapa Flow and the sinking of the battleship *Royal Oak* by a German submarine (U-47) on October 14, 1939, was a serious blow for the British but certainly could not balance the uneven strength in capital ships.

The German efforts did indeed have a substantial impact with the sinking of several hundred thousand tons of Allied shipping, but on balance it must be noted that the greater strength of the Allies at sea gave them an advantage the Germans could not yet overcome. The convoy system for protecting Allied shipping was initiated on the most threatened routes almost immediately—instead of after great delay as in World War I—and reduced losses. One of the pocket-battleships was forced into naval action off the coast of Argentina and Uruguay and subsequently scuttled by the Germans themselves. Although a substantial portion of the crew of the *Graf Spee* eventually returned to Germany with the assistance of the Soviet Union,[69] the morale effect in both Britain and Germany of the spectacular developments surrounding what was called the "Battle of the River Plate" was clearly in favor of the

---

[a] Admiral Raeder thought that England had gone to war in 1939 for fear of a deteriorating naval situation later when the German navy had completed its construction program. ("Gedanken des Oberbefehlshabers der Kriegsmarine zum Kriegsausbruch 3.9.1939," 3 September 1939, BA/MA, RM 6/71.) Like most German, but unlike most Japanese, naval officers, Raeder considered only Germany's construction plans and their implementation while ignoring the naval construction programs of other powers. This curious form of blindness—there is no reference to the fact that Great Britain and the United States had begun substantial naval building programs in the 1930s and that the ships being built would some day be completed—awaits investigation.

Allies.[70] Not as obvious to the public, but perhaps more significant in the long run, was the way in which confusion over strategy and organization in the German navy produced the sacking of first one fleet commander and subsequently his successor by Raeder.[71]

Three critical aspects of the war at sea which would remain characteristic features of the whole struggle were already becoming evident in the first months of the war. The first was the fact that the British navy had greatly underestimated the extent to which German submarines could operate successfully against Allied shipping, in spite of techniques of anti-submarine warfare developed during World War I, so that the small number of German submarines at sea in the first year of the war could have a major impact. In this, the Germans were aided by the fact that they had developed a submarine type which operated effectively in the Atlantic in spite of its relatively slow speed, its need to spend as much time as possible on the surface, and the use of a torpedo model which well into the war was as likely to malfunction as to explode as it was supposed to.[72] Far into the war, in fact until mid-1943, the German navy was also assisted in its attacks on Allied shipping by information derived from broken British codes, at first less important ones, but in 1940–43 the Royal Navy Code 3 used for the convoys.[73]

On the other hand, unknown to the Germans, the British, using the basic information supplied by Polish cryptologists, were beginning to work on the German naval codes as well as on improving their radio direction finders. The Commander-in-Chief of the German navy, Admiral Raeder, on January 23, 1940, warned Admiral Dönitz, the commander of German submarines, about restricting the use of radios by submarines to reduce the danger from radio locators, but the latter could see no great danger—on this issue he would remain stubbornly ignorant until after Germany's defeat.[74]

A second element of the conflict at sea was the restriction imposed on the Germans by the absence of any effective naval air arm. This is a long and complicated story, the origins of which are even now not entirely clear, but the key fact was that the German navy never had its own air reconnaissance system and had to depend on the very intermittent and eventually non-existent willingness or ability of the German air force to provide such support. In practice, this meant that German submarines had to find the convoys themselves, by no means an easy task and one that would subsequently lead them into great difficulties.

The third factor evident in the first months of naval war was the extraordinary willingness of British naval ships to run whatever risks seemed appropriate to fight it out regardless of losses in specific engagements. They were spared the disaster which would surely have followed had the pet project of Winston Churchill as First Lord of the Admiralty been implemented in the fall of 1939. As yet unaware of the danger of sending surface warships into seas dominated by enemy air forces, he was urging that British navy units move into the Baltic Sea in the face of German control of the skies there.[75] When it came to actions in reality, as opposed to imagination, however, the Royal Navy showed daring and skill. The destruction of the *Graf Spee* by British cruisers she outclassed was only the first spectacular instance. Another would follow soon after, and one closely related to that example.

The *Graf Spee* while busy sinking ships had been supplied by a German naval auxiliary, the *Altmark* (which had been sent out for this purpose as early as August 5, 1939)[76] and to which she transferred the crews captured from those ships. The *Altmark* was then to take these as prisoners back to Germany. While illegally taking her prisoners through Norwegian waters, the *Altmark* was boarded by a British destroyer which freed the 300 prisoners on February 16, 1940, while allowing the ship itself to continue.[77] The Royal Navy had not lost its spirit, as many subsequent events confirmed.[78]

If protection of Allied shipping against German submarines and surface ships was the major defensive function of Allied naval power, its offensive role was its participation in the blockade of Germany. The mythology of World War I included belief in the efficacy of the blockade as a decisive weapon in the Allied success against the Central Powers. Scholarship questioning this view did not appear until long after World War II; and in the pre-war years the British government assumed that blockade would again become a major element in the Allied arsenal in any new war against Germany. In the event, the measures initiated in 1939 and strengthened in the following years did have some effect on Germany, but their impact was greatly reduced by the availability of supplies provided by or across the Soviet Union until June 1941, by the German conquest of Western Europe from the spring of 1940 on, by pre-war German stockpiling of critical supplies, and by changes in German industrial procedures which reduced dependence on imported raw materials. First British and later United States purchases of scarce materials in neutral countries, especially Spain, Portugal and Turkey, had their effect, primarily in the last year of World War II, but there is no evidence to suggest that the measures of what was termed "economic warfare" actually played a major role in Allied victory.[79]

It was in fact as a part of their effort to throttle the German war economy that the British and French governments in the winter of 1939–40 gave serious consideration to the occupation of Sweden and aerial bombardment of the Caucasus oil fields during the Russo-Finnish War.

Some aspects of this will be discussed in connection with the review of that conflict, but it should be noted here that the root of these projects was to be found in the hope of depriving Germany of iron ore from Sweden and oil from the Soviet Union. In the case of the former, the massive shipments of high-grade ores to Germany were believed then and continued to be thought later to be essential to Germany's armaments industry. Recent research has shown these calculations to have been somewhat exaggerated—Germany had alternatives available to her—but at the time it was widely believed that an Allied occupation of the key mines in northern Sweden, attendant on the sending of assistance to Finland in her defense against Soviet invasion, would have the effect of crippling armaments production in the Third Reich.[80]

Similarly, bombing Soviet oil fields in the Caucasus, especially those at Baku, was seen as a way of making it impossible for the Soviet Union to provide Germany with the oil supplies so important to her war effort. Pushed very heavily by the French government, this project was delayed and eventually turned down by the British government which saw it as certain to bring a war with Russia but unlikely to end either the war with Germany or the newly initiated one against the Soviet Union. Both this and the Scandinavian project reveal more about the anxiety of the French government to transfer hostilities from Western Europe to practically anywhere else on the globe with little attention to the likely implications and about the greater realism of the British leaders of the time, especially Prime Minister Neville Chamberlain and Foreign Secretary Lord Halifax, than about any real prospects of defeating Germany by measures in the economic field.[81]

THE NEUTRALS

If these were the initial moves of the major belligerents, how did the new war look to other powers? Italy had allied herself formally with Germany in May of 1939 by treaty.[82] Her understanding had, however, been that several more years of peace would precede the joint war against France and Britain for which the "Pact of Steel" was designed. Moving forward at his own speed rather than Rome's, Hitler had disregarded the warnings from Italy and had plunged into war. The Italians had not only stood aside but had tipped off the Western Powers of their intention to do so. They had been angry with the Germans for disregarding what they perceived as Italy's need for additional preparation, and had been alarmed at the possibility that if they joined in they would be exposed to defeats from French and British attacks launched against them while Germany concentrated her forces on Poland. They saw themselves exposed in 1939 to the fate which had befallen Austria–Hungary in 1914 when Russian armies destroyed the cream of the Dual Monarchy's forces in Galicia while Germany concentrated on what was supposed to be a quick victory over France. Italy's Foreign Minister, Count Galeazzo Ciano, was especially annoyed with the Germans and reinforced as much as he could the inclination of Mussolini to refrain from entering the war on Germany's side. The Italian fear of an Allied attack on them was by no means unwarranted. The vulnerability of Italy was as obvious to London and Paris as it was to Rome—all three overestimating Italian strength about equally—but the Western Powers were not about to take advantage of their superiority by attacking a neutral Italy.[83]

For a short time in late September the Italians thought that perhaps the Germans could be persuaded to give up a large portion of the Polish territory they had occupied, make peace with a Polish government, and thus restore something akin to the situation preceding the outbreak of war. That, in turn, might have provided the Italian government the year of peace they wanted to prepare themselves for war with the Western Powers. Count Ciano learned very quickly, however, during his visit to Germany on October 1st that the Germans were under no circumstances going to give up anything. Hitler became as hysterical over suggestions of restoring an independent Poland when urged in that direction by Ciano as he rejected all ideas of a revived Czechoslovakia. Hitler explained that he did not expect peace with the West—a subject to which we will return—but was prepared to fight to victory. Rejoicing in his victory and his fine relations with the Soviet Union, he was not about to draw back.[84]

Mussolini also toyed briefly with the idea of organizing a Balkan bloc to mediate peace, but quickly drew back as it became clear that this might separate him permanently from Germany. His basic policy was and remained an alignment with Hitler and entrance into the war as soon as possible. He could see no alternative way for Italy to attain the imperial ambitions he craved for her. If the Allies won—as he sometimes feared and as Ciano expected—they would hem in Italy's position permanently. If Germany won without Italian help, Italy would not only get nothing for herself but could in fact end up under German domination, something Mussolini feared. Whatever the hopes and fears of Ciano or the Italian military, the Vatican or the royal family, to say nothing of the Italian population, Mussolini would steer a course toward war. Only the details of timing and intervening issues of the day-to-day conduct of government remained to be settled.[85]

The Italian government during the period of "non-belligerence," as they called it in preference to the pacific sounding term "neutrality," cooperated minimally with the Germans in the economic sphere. Here the Italians were in a quandary. The very preparation they wanted to make for war with the West entailed imports which might be made subject to blockade. Simultaneously, the Germans alone would and could supply the coal Italy needed, a hold on Italy reinforced by Germany's conquest of Poland's coal mines which had been supplying Italy since the British General Strike of 1926 had interrupted coal shipments from Britain. Whatever the details and the arguments over shipments, purchases, and blockade measures, the basic position of Mussolini never changed. [86]

The same thing was true of the continuing troubles over the long-promised evacuation of Germans from the South Tyrol. The Italians repeatedly and pointedly contrasted the rapidity and apparent smoothness with which German people were evacuated from the Baltic States and other areas coming under Soviet control with the interminable delay in moving Germans out of the South Tyrol.[87] But while they complained and fretted, they could never see themselves breaking over this issue with the Germans, who shrewdly pointed out to them that it was in part to provide settlement space for these very people that she could not abandon her schemes for massive population shifts in Poland. And the Italians themselves, or at least the authorities on the spot, were by no means certain that any massive emigration of the sort the German government was planning, as a part of its population transfer program, would be such a wonderful thing for them: who would cultivate the alpine farms abandoned by those who left for Germany?

There were plenty of occasions for friction since Italians and Germans heartily disliked one another, and this gave rise to any number of incidents, including a German-deciphered warning by the Italians to Holland and Belgium that they were about to be invaded.[88] All the same, Mussolini would not break with Hitler, Hitler would not break with Mussolini, and no person or group in either country could force a major shift in policy.[89]

Mussolini was especially concerned about the possibility that the Soviet Union might displace Italy as Germany's most important ally and did what he could to deflect what he perceived to be a real danger to Italy's position in a Europe in which Germany would, in his judgement, always be the most powerful country. This was the underlying reason for his willingness to tolerate and even share in Ciano's use of the opportunity provided by the Russo-Finnish war to endanger Italian–Soviet relations which had generally been excellent since the early 1920s.[90] The Germans did their best to patch up the quarrel between their old and their new-found friend,[91] but Mussolini need not have worried; Hitler had no intention of letting his satisfaction over Soviet support in the current war against the Western Powers interfere with his long-term aims for expansion in the East. On the very day that the Soviet–Finnish war was ending, Mussolini would commit himself to entering the war against Britain and France on Germany's side.

The other European power closely aligned with Germany, Spain, had made no secret of its interest in remaining outside the war, at least for the time being. The civil war there had ended with the triumph of Francisco Franco's Nationalists only a few months earlier, and the country was in no condition to undertake any great adventures. Not only was a period of reconstruction after three years of warfare necessary, but Spain was dependent upon imports of food and petroleum products, with both subject to interruption by Allied blockade. The economic needs of Spain, in fact, led to important trade agreements with France in January and with England in March of 1940. The Germans were not only obviously unable to provide Spain with any goods the latter needed; but their insistence in the months between the end of the civil war and the beginning of World War II on repayment by Spain for the aid provided during the fighting soured opinion in government circles in Madrid.[92] And certainly the Spanish dictator, who had just been urged most insistently by Berlin to join the Anti-Comintern Pact,[93] was not enthused by Germany's signing up with the Soviet Union.[94] Nevertheless the Spanish government thought of itself as favoring Germany and was, as will be shown, willing to assist the German war effort. In the long run, there was always the hope that a German victory might bring the return of Gibraltar to Spanish control.[95]

The German government was not surprised by Spain's neutrality in 1939. They had been angered by Franco's early announcement of neutrality in 1938, but they expected nothing else this time. Already in January 1939 Hitler had explained to Propaganda Minister Joseph Goebbels that Spain could do no more than remain neutral.[96] The Germans had, however, long been planning to use neutral Spanish and other territory for their naval war against the Western Powers. The German navy had taken preliminary steps in this direction already in 1938; in January 1939 they drew lessons for the future.[97] A study of this subject remains to be written; understandably the Germans—and presumably the Spaniards— did not leave massive records of these clandestine activities, but enough has already come to light to provide some sense of what was going on.[98] From the beginning of the war into its last days, the Germans maintained a massive intelligence operation inside Spain, often with Spain's assistance. In addition to using this, especially to observe traffic through the Straits of Gibraltar, the Germans relied on Spanish harbors to repair and refuel their submarines. This had been a key part of their pre-war plans for "using" Spain's neutrality, and it would long be an important feature of the German conduct of submarine warfare. If usually not as publicly conspicuous as presented in the movie, "Das Boot," it was still a highly effective way for the Spanish government to show where its real sympathies lay.[99]

A number of other European neutrals were of particular importance to Germany. Sweden, as already mentioned, provided the German economy with a substantial proportion of her high-grade iron ore. In spite of German efforts to exploit her domestic ores, especially through the new works of the Four-Year Plan, Germany imported enormous quantities of ores from Sweden, which in 1939 and 1940 provided 40 percent of her total iron supply (measured by Fe content).[100] Although the proportions dropped thereafter to about 25 percent because of German conquests in Western and Eastern Europe, the contribution of Swedish ores to a central segment of Germany's war economy is obvious. In recent years there has been a controversy in the scholarly literature about the extent to which Germany could or could not have managed without these imports from Sweden, an argument revolving around the provocatively formulated question: "Could Sweden have stopped the Second World War?" and eventually answered with a qualified "no" on the grounds that the German economy had other reserves and possible alternatives.[101]

Whatever the final judgement on this question, there was no doubt in anybody's mind at the time. The Germans believed the supplies were essential to them; the Swedes were entirely willing to sell Germany what she wanted;[102] the Germans could never be certain whether or not the Swedes would blow up the mines if Germany tried to seize them;[103] and the Allies always considered the ore supplies from Sweden an essential element in the German war effort. The enormous contribution Sweden thereby made to Germany's industry was heightened by two further aspects of these deliveries; the ores were of very high iron content and hence required far less processing effort and material than any alternative ores, and the Swedish merchant marine provided delivery service to German ports.[104]

From the beginning of the war, therefore, the German government was interested in maximum exploitation of the Swedish economy for her own purposes and could always postpone the risk of Sweden's destroying the mines until the Third Reich had attained its anticipated victory and could then terminate the independence of Sweden without having to worry.[105] In the interim, the Swedes could make lots of money and the German government would, when appropriate, be careful of Swedish susceptibilities.[106] After the conquest of Norway and Denmark, the Germans would feel able to pressure Sweden into greater concessions, but to begin with all they wanted was the iron needed for their war effort.[107]

If Sweden had been providing much of Germany's iron ore, Turkey was important to Germany for its deliveries of chrome. The complicated diplomatic negotiations of Turkey with Germany, the Soviet Union, Great Britain and France in the summer and fall of 1939 had eventually led to an alliance of Turkey with the Western Powers on October 19, 1939. The combined pressure of Germany and the Soviet Union on Ankara had not succeeded in preventing this Turkish step; in fact, their cooperation looked especially dangerous to the Turks, who had previously counted on Soviet support against Germany's Balkan ambitions. As long as Turkey could believe in the strength of the Western Powers, she could allow a situation in the economic sphere to continue in which the absence of agreement with Germany meant no chrome deliveries by Turkey and no arms delivered by Germany. For a while Britain regained her economic position in Turkey, which also looked more kindly upon a France which had just ceded a piece of the mandate of Syria to her.[108] The German victory in the West in the spring of 1940 would open a new chapter in Turkey's position in the war. She had remained neutral up to that point; the price of neutrality would change thereafter.[109]

Economically important to the German war effort in Southeast Europe were the countries of Yugoslavia and, even more, Romania. Yugoslavia was potentially a major supplier of copper; Romania of oil. Both countries preferred to remain neutral and tried to resist German pressure; both made some concessions. In the case of Yugoslavia, as long as France was still considered strong and Italy remained neutral, the government in Belgrade could maintain a degree of independence. It promised to send some copper to Germany in exchange for arms deliveries promised by Germany earlier but not yet supplied and now deliberately held up. Pushed by both sides of the developing conflict, the government, led by the Regent Prince Paul, certainly preferred a victory by Britain and France but was reluctant to defy Germany, tried to use the establishment of diplomatic and economic relations with the Soviet Union as a counterweight, and made some concessions on trade. It was made known, however, that Yugoslavia would fight if attacked, and Belgrade encouraged the French and British to open a Balkan front against Germany by landing forces at Salonika as they had done in World War I. Nothing came of these projects; the main worry in Belgrade continued to be the likelihood of an attack by Italy.[110]

For all the belligerents, Romania was of enormous importance because it was, after the Soviet Union, the major petroleum producing country in Europe. The Germans had been trying hard for some time to secure as large a proportion of Romania's oil exports for themselves as possible while the British and French, whose nationals owned a large stake in the Romanian oil industry, had begun to fight back. In the fall of 1939 and the following winter this silent struggle over Romania's oil went forward, complicated by Soviet, Hungarian, and Bulgarian territorial ambitions on portions of Romania's territory and Britain's (unsuccessful) efforts to sabotage the oil fields as well as the transportation system used to deliver oil to Germany.

As long as the situation in Western Europe remained essentially unchanged, the Romanians could get by with minimal trade concessions to the Germans, designed in part to reduce German complaints about Romania's allowing numerous Poles to flee into and eventually across her territory.[111] They would trade some oil for weapons; they would allow the Western Powers to use their ownership powers in the oil fields to restrict exports to Germany; and they could hold on to their territory because the Soviet Union became embroiled elsewhere — as a result of its attack on Finland — while Hungary and Bulgaria were restrained by fear of becoming involved in the war. Once France was defeated, all this would change.[112]

Outside Europe, the most important powers in 1939 were undoubtedly Japan and the United States. Japan was at the time already deeply involved in hostilities with China. After seizing the northern provinces of that country in 1931 and organizing them into the puppet state of Manchukuo, Japan had tried to protect its rich loot and to expand its influence in China by a series of interventions, particularly in the rest of northern China. These steps had not surprisingly produced a rising tide of anti-Japanese sentiments in China, which in turn led the Japanese to embroil themselves even more deeply into Chinese affairs. When this tendency to interfere in China was combined with a degree of internal confusion and incoherence within the Japanese government that made the Chinese warlords of the time look well organized, new trouble was almost certain to follow.

An incident near the Liukiachow Bridge at Peking in July 1937 became the occasion for hostilities between steadily increasing Japanese forces and the Nationalist regime of Chiang Kai-shek. Although the Japanese built up their forces in China slowly and the Nationalists — in part trained by German officers — fought hard, the Chinese were unable to hold the Japanese back. Sometimes with the approval of all the authorities in Tokyo and sometimes without, the Japanese army pushed forward. Various efforts to mediate the conflict failed. The most promising of these, that by Germany, which preferred for her East Asian friends to confront the Western Powers rather than each other, foundered on the steadily escalating demands of the Japanese and the insistence on these demands by the civilians in Tokyo, led by Prime Minister Konoe Fumimaro, when for once the Japanese military were more agreeable to a settlement.[113]

The war between Japan and China ground on. Ever larger forces were committed by the Japanese who also tried hard and violently to end all Western influence in and support of China. As the war continued, the Japanese conquest of much of China weakened the Nationalist government and provided the Chinese Communists with a great opportunity to increase their influence.[114] The authorities in Tokyo, however, had their attention focused on the Nationalists. They tried to end their war with the latter by a variety of generally self-contradictory policies. They periodically mounted new military offensives; they at times tried to negotiate with Chiang through various intermediaries; they hoped to pressure other countries into cutting off any supplies to the Nationalists; and they attempted to split the Nationalists by creating an alternative Nationalist regime under Wang Ching-wei, a defector from Chiang's movement who had occupied prominent positions in the Nationalist Party.

The Japanese military advances were far too limited to accomplish the intended purpose. It was not until 1944 that, as will be discussed subsequently, the Japanese launched offensives that were comprehensive enough to crush Chiang's armies—but by that time only the Chinese Communists could benefit since Japan was being defeated by the United States. The soundings for a compromise of some sort with Chiang, of which the first began in November 1939, were never carried forward with any real coherence.[115] A comprehensive study of them remains to be written, [116] but their only real effect was to strengthen Chiang's hand in extorting aid from the United States by always projecting the possibility of an accommodation with Japan as an available alternative to the policy of continued resistance.

The Japanese hopes of obliging Chiang to give in by cutting off his foreign sources of supply were first implemented by seizure of most Chinese ports. Pressure on France to restrict use of the railway crossing northern French Indo-China into China, what was known as the Yunan railway, came next. Later on, the territory that railway crossed would itself be occupied by Japanese troops and there would be pressure on the British to close the road which ran from the end of the railway at Lashio in northern Burma (and the Irrawaddy river at Bhamo) to Chungking, the Nationalist capital. The other route across which supplies reached the Nationalists was a long land route, which ran from the

Soviet Turk-Sib railway at and north of Alma Ata in Central Asia across Sinkiang and Inner Mongolia to Chungking, a distance of over 3000 miles, but of enormous symbolic if not equivalent practical importance.[117] The Japanese government, which saw this supply route as both substantially and psychologically very important for the Nationalists, periodically tried to include its closing as an aspect of improved Japanese–Soviet relations whenever they pursued that line of policy.[118]

Finally, they hoped either to arrange a substitute for Chiang or to frighten him into agreement by establishing a new government for China under Wang Ching-wei. This project the Japanese themselves undermined by imposing on Wang conditions so onerous as to make him an obvious puppet of Japan rather than a credible alternative to Chiang.[119]

At the time Germany began the war in Europe, the Japanese were in the last stages of being defeated by the Soviet Union in bitter and bloody fighting on the border of Manchuria and Outer Mongolia in what was called the Nomonhan (Khalkhin-gol) Incident.[120] This fighting and its settlement by an armistice on September 15 has already been discussed in the context of Soviet policy; what needs to be stressed here are some ramifications of this crushing defeat for Japanese policy then and in the following years. It made some within the Japanese military yearn for revenge, but it led many of them to rethink their plans for the future.[121] The Soviet Union was clearly a formidable power, and now that it was relieved by agreement with Germany of any immediate danger in Europe, all the more able to develop its military potential in East Asia. This suggested to many in Tokyo that a reorientation of Japanese policy might well be desirable. The navy had long looked southwards rather than northwards for expansion; the army now began to do an about face as well. The Japanese would protest formally—and rather sheepishly—against Germany's violation of the secret protocol to the Anti-Comintern Pact by signing the Nazi–Soviet Pact,[122] but the new policy being developed in Tokyo could draw a benefit from the surprising turn of events. Since Germany now had such good relations with Moscow, she could assist Japan in improving relations with the Soviet Union.[123] A Japanese–Soviet rapprochement might conceivably be used to put pressure on Nationalist China, but it would in any case facilitate a Japanese move southward.[a] This meant potentially a clash with the Western Powers, and since the Germans had long been urging precisely such a course on Tokyo, the Japanese could feel confident of German support.

---

[a] The Japanese government formally adopted a policy line calling for a settlement of outstanding issues with the Soviet Union and possibly a non-aggression pact on December 28, 1939; see Hosoya in James W. Morley (ed.), *Fateful Choice* (New York: Columbia Univ. Press, 1980), pp. 27–8, 36–7.

And although on occasion Hitler would self-righteously explain that Germany could crush Britain all by herself, on most occasions then and until December 1941 he urged Japan to attack southwards, particularly against Great Britain, which he saw as Germany's most dangerous and determined enemy.[124] Such a course, however, meant for the Japanese the real possibility of a clash with the United States and for this they did not consider themselves ready. The Japanese navy had long contemplated the possibility of war with the United States and developed plans for such a contingency.[125] The construction program of the Japanese navy was geared to this contingency; in fact the huge super-battleships planned since the fall of 1934 were specifically designed to outclass American ships and, once they had appeared in action, confront the United States government with the dilemma of building equal ships, which would be too wide to pass through the Panama Canal and would be restricted to one ocean, or to continue building inferior ships.[126] But the advocates of moving forward were not yet in control in Japan.[127] The new government of Abe Noboyuki insisted on neutrality in the European war and held to that line until its fall in January 1940; but, as the most careful recent analysis of this period shows, no really pro-Western course could be followed.[128] Approaches were made to the United States primarily because she had given the required notice in July 1939 that the Japanese–American trade agreement would lapse. The hope in Washington had been that such a step, by which the commercial treaty would expire in late January 1940, might restrain Japan.[129] The United States' policy of limited aid to China, particularly in the financial field, was clearly designed for the same purpose, as well as to make it more difficult for Japan to obtain complete control of China and then turn her attention in other directions.[130] Minimal Japanese gestures toward the United States in the fall of 1939 indicate that this was not an entirely hopeless idea; but because continued advance in China remained basic to Japanese policy—and it was precisely on this point that the United States expected at least some concessions from Tokyo—nothing came of these efforts.[131]

The Japanese had some quite realistic views on such subjects as Soviet strength and the likelihood of the European war lasting for several years.[132] They were, furthermore, not prepared to cut off their ties with the Polish government and maintained diplomatic relations with it.[133] They would for a while be very cautious in their economic dealings with Germany; in fact, they were quite willing to take advantage of the Third Reich's desperate need for soybeans from Manchuria to drive a hard bargain.[134] Such tactics would continually introduce friction into

German–Japanese relations throughout the war. In the early part of the conflict, there were particularly aggravating difficulties as the Japanese refused to help the Germans as much as the latter hoped and expected in arranging for the shipment of rubber and other important goods to the railheads of the Transsiberian railway for dispatch to Germany. The Japanese measures had the effect of reducing the extent to which Germany, with the approval and assistance of the Soviet Union, could benefit from this gap in the blockade.[135]

There were, however, elements in Japan pushing for a vastly more adventurous policy. Led by such individuals as Shiratori Toshio, until the fall of 1939 Japanese ambassador in Rome, they looked forward to a full alliance with Germany, hoping to end the war in China by partitioning it with the Soviet Union (and incidentally turning over to the Soviet Union those districts of China controlled by the Communists), and heading for war with Britain, France, and the United States.[136] As yet these elements were restrained by others, first in the Abe government and then in that of his successor, Yonai Mitsumasa, but any turn of the war in Europe favoring the Germans would enable them to carry the day.[137]

The United States had played a major part in the outcome of World War I. Its munitions and other supplies had helped the Allies conduct the war; its soldiers and credits had played a key role in halting the final German offensive in the summer of 1918 and in turning the desperate situation of Britain and France of the spring and summer of that year into victory in the fall.[138] In the same post-war years as more and more Germans convinced themselves that they had been defeated by a stab in the back, with America's role in deciding the issue of war being a legend, increasing numbers of Americans became persuaded that entry into the conflict had been a terrible mistake. German belief in the stab-in-the-back legend — with its implication for underrating the importance of American involvement in the war — would lead to a grotesque underestimation of United States military potential, a subject which will be reexamined repeatedly.[139] The Americans, on the other hand, had tried to insulate themselves against war by neutrality legislation.

When World War II began in September 1939, those who had urged American support of the peace settlement of 1919, and, in particular, believed that the United States should join the League of Nations, could now point to the accuracy of their prophecies that only a full share in the maintenance of world order could prevent another war. Their advice had been ignored — and here was the second world war within a generation. This argument, that American abstention from an active role in maintaining the peace settlement of 1919 had contributed heavily to making the second war possible, would eventually come to be accepted by a large proportion of the American electorate and lead them and a majority in both political parties to approve of a very different policy in the post-World War II era. But this acceptance of a "lesson" from the past came slowly and did not become a dominant strain in American thinking for some time.[140]

The initial reaction of both the leadership and the public in the United States to the outbreak of war in Europe was essentially similar and uniform. The overwhelming majority blamed Germany for starting the war; the overwhelming majority hoped that Britain and France would win; the overwhelming majority wanted to stay out of the war.[141] The near unanimity on these three basic issues did not extend, however, to two other subsidiary but in practice critical matters: the real prospects of the Allies and the policy to be followed by the United States toward them.

There were those in the United States who thought it made no difference who won, but for many, the prospect of the victory of the Allies was not only the preferred but the most likely outcome of the conflict. As German victory in Poland was followed by a quiet winter, more of the public began to doubt the ability of Britain and France to defeat her; and their doubt, not surprisingly, increased with German victories in Scandinavia and the West in the spring of 1940. President Roosevelt's views on this subject appear to have been somewhat different—and in retrospect a great deal more far-sighted—than those of many others. He certainly always hoped for an Allied victory over Germany, but he was very skeptical of Western power. In the years before the war, he had been very conscious of the deficiency in French air power and had attempted to assist her air rearmament.[142] While the weakness of French air power was generally recognized at the time, that of the French army was not perceived by most. It was widely assumed that the army which had played the predominant part among the Allies in World War I, and one of whose marshals had led them to victory in 1918, remained the strongest in the world—and if not the strongest, certainly powerful enough to withstand any attack on France.

There is substantial evidence to show that Roosevelt did not share this optimistic assessment of French military strength. He had regularly read with care the reports of his two ambassadors to France in the 1930s, Jesse I. Strauss and William C. Bullitt. Both had excellent contacts in France, both were clear-sighted observers, and both were extremely dubious about French strength.[143] The picture they conveyed of a nation divided and diffident, terrified of war and uncertain about the course to follow in the face of its approach, was not always accurate in its details but sound in its general import. The enormous literature on Franklin

Roosevelt as yet contains no studies which systematically examine the evidence on his views of either France or Germany, the two major continental nations whose languages he knew, but one thing seems to be clear. Perhaps because of his own predilection for naval matters he appears never to have been affected by the aura of strength surrounding the French army in the inter-war years. Certainly his warning to Stalin in the summer of 1939, that the Soviet Union would be well advised to align itself with the Western Powers rather than Hitler because a German victory in Western Europe would menace all other nations, implied a perception of German strength and French military weakness and a belief in the possibility of a German victory over France on land, which few shared in the pre-war world. On the other hand, as would become apparent in the terrible crisis of the summer of 1940, President Roosevelt would think it likely that first Britain and subsequently the Soviet Union could hold out when most thought otherwise.

These perceptions of the President must be kept in mind in assessing and understanding the practical steps Roosevelt urged on Congress and the American people. He believed that Nazi Germany and its allies threatened the whole world, including the Western Hemisphere, and he very much hoped to keep the United States out of the war. Unlike Stalin, who believed that the best way to avert war from the Soviet Union was to help the Germans fight the Western Powers, Roosevelt thought that the most likely prospect for continual avoidance of war was to assist Britain and France in defeating Germany. Because he believed, correctly as we now know, that the Western Powers were deficient in weapons of war, he considered the prohibition on the sale of weapons to them in the neutrality laws a bonus for the early rearmament of the aggressors and a major handicap for the Allies. He would, therefore, try again to have the neutrality laws changed.

Roosevelt hoped that this could be done on a non-partisan or bi-partisan basis, and in the initial stages tried to involve the 1936 Republican Presidential and Vice-Presidential candidates, Alfred Landon and Frank Knox, in the process.[144] In the Congress, however, a bitter debate, largely though not entirely on partisan lines, ensued. The issue divided the country. What came to be a standard pattern over the next two years emerged. On the one side were those who believed that, both to stay out of war and to assist Britain and France, neutrality law revision was in the country's interest. A few took this side because they expected or wanted the United States to join the Allies. Against this position were those, generally called isolationists and later strongly identified with the America First Committee, who believed that the best way to stay out of the war was to do nothing to assist Britain and France or to help them to help themselves; and some took this side because they thought that it might be just as well if Germany won or at least that it made little difference to the United States if she did so.[145]

In the weeks before the outbreak of war, the isolationists had won on the issue of allowing others to buy arms in the United States, when Roosevelt had proposed it as a way of warning Germany that American arsenals would be open to those certain to control the seas if Germany started a war. Now that the Germans had started it, the isolationists lost. After a lengthy and bitter struggle, during which Roosevelt, as he put it, was "walking on eggs,"[146] the Congress approved what had come to be called "cash and carry" early in November; the President signed the bill on November 4.[147]

The Germans, who were watching this struggle with great interest,[148] were no more in agreement among themselves than the Americans, only in Germany there was a dictator who decided on policy. The navy could hardly wait to bring the United States into the war by repeating its World War I procedure. On October 10, at the same meeting that he advocated a German seizure of bases in Norway, Admiral Raeder urged on Hitler a completely ruthless submarine campaign to throttle England, if necessary at risk of war with the United States.[149] The head of the navy could see no way for Germany to crush England except to destroy her seaborne commerce, whatever the risk of other complications, a repetition of the German navy leadership's argument of 1916 unaffected by the experience of 1917–18.[150] Though at first sounding agreeable, Hitler in fact set limits to the projects of his naval Commander-in-Chief.

Hitler's view of the United States was based on an assessment that this was a weak country, incapable because of its racial mixture and feeble democratic government of organizing and maintaining strong military forces.[151] The antagonism of Americans, both in government and among the public, toward Germany was therefore no cause for worry. Certain that Allied victory in World War I was the result of Germany's having been stabbed in the back by the home front, he was never interested in the American military effort in that conflict or any possible renewal of it. He had long assumed that Germany would have to fight the United States after conquering Eurasia, and he had begun preparations toward that end both in airplane and naval construction.[152] The outbreak of war in Europe in 1939, however, forced a temporary postponement in the program to construct a big navy of huge battleships and numerous other surface ships. Although it is not clear when Hitler learned the facts, the project for building planes which could reach the American east coast was also not going well.

Under these circumstances, Hitler preferred to defer war with the

United States, not because he was greatly worried about that prospect, but because he saw no reason to rush into premature hostilities when he had not completed his blue-water navy, and the navy actually at his disposal did not yet have the number of submarines which might really seal off the British Isles. Nothing that had happened in 1939 changed his basic views of the United States. When he saw the German military attaché to Washington in February 1939, the only topic on which he queried the latter was the alleged Jewish ancestry of President Roosevelt.[153] He had dismissed Roosevelt's peace appeal of April 1939 with derision; the very fact that in September the United States had proclaimed its neutrality showed what incompetents the Americans were, as, in his judgement, strong and determined nations took sides and acted in wartime.[154] Not surprisingly, Hitler preferred the Soviet Union's policy of assisting Germany while neutral to the Americans' inclination to assist Britain and France while neutral; and it hardly needs to be pointed out that Germany was as eager to have neutrals like the Soviet Union and Spain provide assistance to her as she was to denounce as violations of international law any actions by a neutral that aided her opponents. Such antics, however, shed no light on German policy which was guided by entirely different considerations.

One of the elements in Hitler's low assessment of the United States' military potential was, reasonably enough, the weakness of the American army and the near total absence of any air force. When the war started, there were 190,000 men in the American army with no real divisions, corps, or armies as yet; most of the equipment was of World War I vintage and wearing out.[155] The air force was too small even to provide the Germans with target practice. Roosevelt, whose view of American military potential was informed by an entirely different perspective from Hitler's on the role of the United States in helping the Allies defeat Germany in World War I,[156] had been trying to build up forces since before the war. He had begun the rebuilding of the navy in the 1930s; authorized in 1934, the battleship *North Carolina* was begun in October 1937; additional new battleships as well as other vessels would follow.[157] Although it has been observed quite correctly that the President, who had been the second man in the Navy Department under President Wilson and was an avid sailor and collector of ship models, always kept a special place in his heart for the navy, the major push he actually made in the drive to rearm the country concerned the air.[158] It was his hope after the obvious signs of German unhappiness with the Munich agreement that a massive program of air rearmament might impress the German government in an earlier version of what would later be called "deterrence," somewhat the way the fear of German air superiority—

real or imagined—had cowed Britain and France in the 1938 crisis. Given the near absence of any substantial American military aircraft industry, foreign orders for military planes obviously would be of great help in building up that vital element in any future American armaments program. Finally, Britain and France could not be expected to continue to invest in the American aircraft industry if they were not allowed to purchase its products precisely when they most needed them. Although for domestic political reasons the President never stressed this aspect of neutrality law revision in public, there can be little question that the matter was very much in his mind. Gearing up American military production facilities was going to be a huge task, and any and all help would speed the process.[159]

The other area of immediate concern to the administration in Washington was the situation in Central and South America. There was worry about the large German element in several Latin American countries, about German ships—and their crews—stranded by the outbreak of war in Latin American ports, and about the attitude of several of the governments in the area toward Germany and the Western Allies. In Central and South America there was a reciprocal concern. All preferred to stay out of the war, some were also worried about German activities at home, and a few either had or hoped to have better relations, especially trade relations, with Germany. A conference held in Panama beginning on September 23, 1939,[160] affirmed the neutrality of the hemisphere. The most spectacular action of the conference was its unanimous endorsement of a neutral war zone reaching far out into the Atlantic, but perhaps of greater substantive significance was the extent to which the nations of the area were prepared to work together under United States leadership. This novel development was, to some extent, a result of Roosevelt's Good Neighbor Policy toward those countries—vigorously implemented by Secretary of State Cordell Hull and Under Secretary Sumner Welles [161]—combined with fears of Germany, particularly in countries with substantial minorities of German settlers.[162] Insofar as Germany had established some significant positions for herself in the economic life of several Latin American countries, the beginning of war in 1939 created a new situation: the Latin Americans could neither market their products in Germany nor draw on German industry for imports. In this regard, much would depend upon the length and outcome of the war; in the meantime, the South American countries had to look elsewhere for markets and supplies.[163]

An important issue on which Roosevelt himself changed tactics during the first month of World War II was that of the possibility of a peace settlement between the Western Powers and Germany after the initial defeat of Poland. Convinced that any such settlement on the heels of a German military triumph could only lead to even greater dangers later, Roosevelt refrained from giving any encouragement to such steps in the fall of 1939.[164] He did not directly discourage several Americans who made private efforts in this direction, but he used those efforts—as he had often done with private persons in the past—to inform himself about the situation in Germany.[165] The British government, in any case, was advised to pay no attention to these busybodies.[166] The President himself was primarily worried that during the period of peace soundings, which are reviewed below, the defeatist views of his ambassador in London, Joseph P. Kennedy, might be mistaken for his own, when in fact he thought of the ambassador as a "pain in the neck."[167]

Early in 1940, the increasingly close cooperation of Germany and the Soviet Union led him to be concerned that the Germans might launch an offensive in the West before France and Great Britain were adequately prepared to resist it and that Germany and the Soviet Union could then be joined by Italy. It was under these circumstances that he authorized Under Secretary of State Welles to make his famous tour of European capitals, a tour which revealed that the positions of the belligerents were irreconcilable, but in no way delayed the German offensive which by that time, as will be discussed, had been postponed for entirely different reasons. This tactical shift on Roosevelt's part, however, marked no change in his basic views or in American policy; and as the brief review of the peace soundings of the winter 1939–40 will show, there were in reality no prospects of peace anyway.[168]

PEACE SOUNDINGS

Since Hitler had wanted to clear his eastern border preparatory to launching the great German offensive in the West, which he saw as the necessary prerequisite for a vast but easy seizure of living space in the East, he would have been quite happy to have Britain and France acquiesce in the conquest of Poland peacefully and await their turn to be attacked. The Commander-in-Chief of the German air force, Hermann Göring, was also in charge of large segments of the German economy. He wanted more time for economic preparations he considered important and was similarly interested in a respite in open hostilities. In view of these perceptions and aims, Hitler and Göring launched some peace feelers, Hitler in public, Göring in private. Hitler in speeches pointed to the fate of Poland and explained there was now nothing to fight over.[169] Göring sent out feelers through Birger Dahlerus, the Swedish intermediary he had used before, and through other channels as well.[170]

Hitler was most doubtful that peace would be restored, and because he had no intention of making the slightest concessions to obtain it, he was simultaneously ordering preparations for a major offensive in the West to be launched a few weeks after the end of fighting in Poland, most likely in early or mid-November.[171] Many of the key figures in the German military thought this a highly risky venture likely to produce either a defeat or a bitter stalemate of the sort all of them had seen at first hand in World War I; some of them recoiled at the plan to invade the neutral Low Countries; and a small number had doubts about the National Socialist regime as a whole. Supported by and in some contact with a few officials of the German foreign ministry, they too launched a series of peace soundings as did some foreign ministry officials on their own. Though under way in the same months as the ones of Hitler and Göring, these were, of course, not sanctioned by the Führer. Most in fact assumed his displacement. For this reason they will be examined separately at the end of this discussion.[172]

Other countries were also interested in having formal hostilities ended. During von Ribbentrop's second visit to Moscow, the German and Soviet governments had agreed that now that Poland had disappeared peace was in order. In support of German policy and in accord with Stalin's perception of Soviet interests, the Soviet Union and the Communist Parties around the world now launched a vocal campaign for peace.[173] Stalin had made clear his belief that the disappearance of Poland and Czechoslovakia from the map of Europe was entirely appropriate; a peace which ratified the existing situation in Eastern Europe would imply Western recognition of Soviet as well as German gains. If the war continued, that meant from his point of view that the capitalist powers would tear each other up to the benefit of the Soviet Union.

The Italians for a while also thought peace could be to their advantage. Since they wanted additional time to prepare for war with Britain and France, a restoration of peace would both provide that time and mitigate Mussolini's embarrassment at not having been able to join Hitler in the war immediately. The Italians, however, recognized from the start that only major and real German concessions offered the slightest hope of having any peace proposal taken seriously by the Western Powers. They quickly learned that there was no prospect of such concessions and therefore equally quickly gave up their attempts.[174] The Hungarians for a short time also tried their hand at getting contacts for peace negotiations,[175] the Belgian and Dutch rulers appealed for peace when a German invasion looked likely,[176] and individuals from other neutral countries, like the Norwegian Bishop Eivind Berggrav, made personal attempts at diplomacy.[177] Because the German government was not about to take any steps backward from their prior advances—which had been designed to be the bases for subsequent further advances—nothing could come from such efforts.

Central to any possible peace under the circumstances of the time was the policy of France and Great Britain. There is some evidence that French Foreign Minister Georges Bonnet might have been willing to consider negotiations, but he was in any case soon removed from office by Prime Minister Edouard Daladier, who took over that portfolio himself on September 13. While the latter supported a variety of schemes designed to divert hostilities to other portions of Europe, preferably at a distance from France herself, he was a determined man who was not going to negotiate a peace with Hitler's Germany on the basis of accepting Germany's conquests. The detailed record is not entirely clear as yet, but insofar as it is, it shows a complete unwillingness to negotiate with Germany unless that country evacuated Poland, restored Czechoslovakia, and withdrew from Austria. Whether or not British belief that the French would this time insist on a dismemberment of Germany was correct, there was certainly no chance that the French government would give serious consideration to terms other than ones which the Germans were certain to reject.[178]

The British Cabinet began to worry about the impact on public opinion in England and elsewhere of any German peace offensive as early as September 9. Their first concern was that all be reassured that Britain would fight on. Far from exhibiting any interest in negotiations with the German government of the day, Prime Minister Neville Chamberlain asserted that "it was clear that the essential preliminary to any settlement of European problems was the destruction of Hitlerism."[179] The complete loss of any possible trust in the Hitler regime as a result of the violation of the Munich agreement by the latter had manifested itself in the summer of 1939 in British insistence that Germany take a step backward, that is, restore independence to Czechoslovakia, before there could be any new Anglo-German agreement.[180] Now that Germany had attacked Poland, the British government would insist not only on the evacuation of Poland and a restored Czechoslovakia but an entirely different government in Germany. Experience had taught the British that agreements with Hitler were not worth the paper on which they were written. In view of these perceptions, any agreement with the existing government in Berlin would be seen in London as counter-productive, or likely to strengthen the Hitler regime instead of displacing it as the British thought essential.

The discussion in London, as well as the consultations of London with Paris in the following weeks, accordingly revolved around making these points clear and explicit while simultaneously trying to reassure the Germans that, if they displaced the Nazi regime and restored the independence of Poland and Czechoslovakia, they might look forward to a satisfactory existence in a peaceful Europe. In a series of discussions within the government, these points were clarified.[181] Poland had to be evacuated by the Germans; although the question of what to do about the portions of Poland occupied by the Soviet Union was left open, the fact that the redrawing of the boundary at the second von Ribbentrop–Stalin meeting had left most of the ethnic Poles on the German side of the line was recognized.[182] While the British government was not pre-pared to commit itself on the details of the borders and internal structure of Czechoslovakia, there was no argument over the central issue: the Germans would be required to agree to the restoration of that country's full independence. Unlike the Soviet Union, Britain and France had never recognized the de jure disappearance of Czechoslovakia; they con-tinued to recognize the ambassadors of the Prague government.[183]

On these points there was no disagreement between London and Paris.[184] The Austrian question, however, was not so easily disposed of. From the available evidence it appears that the French government was insistent on a fully independent Austria under any circumstances. The British, on the other hand, took the position that a genuine plebiscite should be held there, thereby implying a willingness to accept either possible verdict of the Austrian voters.[185] This was an issue in no need of great debate at the time; it would be faced long after the fall of France and by a different anti-German coalition.[186]

In the discussions in London, it was understood that this line of calling for a return to earlier borders and replacing the Hitler regime would make Britain Hitler's key enemy, to be pounded by air and all other possible means, and that the German government would do its best— or worst—to crush England from the occupied Low Countries before turning East.[187] But there appeared to be few alternatives. When first approached by individuals purporting to represent opposition elements in Germany, the British government authorized contacts by its agents in the Netherlands, only to have the project blow up in their faces. The Germans arranged the kidnapping of the British intelligence officers by the SS, which had engineered the whole scheme. This affair is generally referred to as the Venlo Incident after the Dutch town where the kidnap-ping, and the murder of a Dutch officer, took place on November 9, 1939. It put a shadow over all subsequent contacts between the British and those Germans claiming to be opposed to the Hitler regime; but, as will be discussed below, the London government still tried that route much of the winter.[188]

The fundamental issue, however, remained the same from the beginning to the end. In commenting on one of the earliest of the approaches from Dahlerus, British Foreign Secretary Lord Halifax had stated on September 19: "I can conceive of no peace offer which the German government are likely in present circumstances to make that could be considered by H. M. Government or the French Government."[189] As the Cabinet contemplated a possible German offer on October 7 and 9, there was agreement that the chief war aim was the elimination of Hitler plus the restoration of Poland and Czechoslovakia, and disarmament, and that no reliance could be placed on the word of the present German government.[190] The public position presented in Chamberlain's speech of October 12 had been worked out with great care; the Dominions and the French had been consulted; and the participation of Winston Churchill, then First Lord of the Admiralty, would leave Chamberlain's successor pleased with the result and considering it appropriate for his own government.[191] In full public view Chamberlain explained that Hitler's proposal that Britain and France accept what Germany had done was impossible for Britain to agree to. For Britain, there was no alternative to fighting on until the European countries which had lost their independence had had it returned to them, the Hitler regime had been removed, and such restrictions had been imposed on Germany as would prevent her from attempting to conquer Europe and dominate the world a third time.[192]

The reaction of the German government to the responses they received from London and Paris to their public and private peace soundings was as negative as Britain and France had expected. The Germans were not about to evacuate Poland, to say nothing of restoring independence to Czechoslovakia. As for Poland, it had been to assure a quiet Eastern Front in preparation for attacking in the West that Hitler had invaded that country in the first place; he was not about to allow an independent nation there again. Time and again he asserted that the Polish question was entirely for Germany and the Soviet Union to settle according to their preferences; he was certainly not prepared to consider any British interest in the fate of that country's ally.[a]

Suggestions that Czechoslovakia should regain her independence

---

[a] Many historians have attributed to Hitler a supposed interest in agreement with England; they never contrast his care to accommodate the interests of Italy, Japan, Turkey, the Soviet Union, and others when he wanted agreement with those countries with his refusal ever to consider interests expressed by the London government. See also Gerhard L. Weinberg, "Hitler and England, 1933–1945: Pretense and Reality," *German Studies Review*, 8 (1988), 299–309.

aroused him to even greater anger. Since he had never taken seriously the fate of the over three million people of German descent living in that country, whom he had used as a propaganda pretext for destroying Czechoslovakia, he could not understand that anyone else had. The British insistence on reversing his breach of the Munich agreement as a prerequisite for restoring the German government's international credibility was, therefore, completely beyond his comprehension. If his own and Göring's soundings could sow doubt and confusion in the enemy camp, that was just fine. As for concessions he would make none.[193] As he told Goebbels on October 14, he was pleased that the talk of peace was over and that all could now be concentrated on the war against England.[194]

Not everyone in Germany shared Hitler's enthusiasm for continued war, and, as previously mentioned, elements in the German military made approaches to the British government through diplomatic and other channels. It was the hope of those involved in these soundings that with some assurances from the Western Powers not to take advantage of any change of government in Germany, the military leaders who had doubts about Hitler's insistence on an offensive in the West could be encouraged to launch a coup to displace him, perhaps at first by Göring, and then by a non-Nazi.[195] The most promising of these approaches was made by German high command intelligence(Abwehr) to Rome and involved Pope Pius XII, who took the matter up with the British Minister to the Vatican.[196] Another contact was made in behalf of the former German ambassador to Italy, Ulrich von Hassell, by a man who, unknown to von Hassell, turned out to be a rather dubious character.[197]

Since the British, as we have seen, looked to the elimination of the Hitler regime as a major war aim, they were naturally interested in these soundings, though several factors made them suspicious. The intermediaries all too often wanted to retain all or most of the very gains Hitler had made, and thus the Germans these intermediaries represented looked little better from the outside than the government they expected to displace. There was always the shadow of Venlo, something not likely to be dispelled easily when there were serious doubts about von Hassell's intermediary. Most important, there was no sign that the opponents of the regime in the army would ever muster the courage to move; and, as is well known, they did not do so until years later. Although the British, therefore, made clear to their interlocutors London's interest in seeing a new government in Germany and in making peace with such a government on a basis that would assure Germany a fair place in a peaceful Europe, they would commit themselves no further. The implication was that Germany would have to disgorge its loot and could count on the maintenance of its independence. Beyond that London would and could not go until those in Germany who were always about to strike against the Nazi regime actually did so.

In November 1939 a German by the name of Johann Georg Elser, working entirely by himself, did carry out a daring and well-conceived plan to blow up Hitler when he gave his annual speech to the party faithful in Munich on the anniversary of the failed coup attempt of 1923. Because Hitler left early for a military conference in Berlin, he was not killed when the bomb exploded. Elser was killed in 1945.[198] The German military leaders, on the other hand, were unwilling to take any action against the Führer. Instead, they prepared and subsequently carried out attacks on a whole series of neutral countries, thereby hopelessly undermining any credibility they or their civilian associates had in Allied capitals whenever the question of contacts between opposition elements within Germany and the Allies came up later. The war continued.

EARLY DEVELOPMENTS ON THE HOME FRONT

Inside each of the major belligerent powers, the first dislocation of war caused local problems and dissatisfactions. In Britain and France the absence of serious fighting on land in the West and the failure of the anticipated massive German air raids to take place gave an unreal atmosphere to the situation. The description of the conflict as a "phony war" mirrored a sense of confusion which, in the absence of clear and determined leadership at the top, led to internal divisiveness rather than sustained effort. In Germany, too, there was considerable dissatisfaction, along with a sense of triumph over the quick victory in battle against the hated Poles. But there was also the beginning of a major intensification of the National Socialist revolution.

The racialist core of National Socialist ideology had been apparent from the beginning, and the first measures of implementation had come in the first months of Nazi rule in 1933. One aspect of this had been the persecution of the Jews, an immensely popular program of discriminating against Germany's Jewish citizens—less than 1 percent of the population. Over the years from 1933–39, these measures had been made increasingly stringent, ruthless and violent; designed to drive Jews out of the country after the stealing of their property, this process had attained about half of the former and most of the latter goal by September 1939. More dramatic and extreme measures were yet to come: in his speech of January 30, 1939, Hitler announced to the Reichstag and the world that in any new war the Jews of Europe would be exterminated.[199] When he started the war in September, large numbers of Polish

Jews were killed by German soldiers, police, and special SS murder squads, but the systematic extermination program was still to come. Hitler would begin that with segments of his own "Aryan" people.

The racialist measures aimed at the over 99 percent of Germans who were not Jewish had also begun in 1933 with encouragement for early marriage and numerous progeny on the one hand and compulsory steril- ization for those allegedly afflicted with hereditary diseases on the other. In this field, also, there were additional steps in the years after 1933, but it was in this regard that a major radicalization occurred soon after the outbreak of war. For years the government had propagated the idea that the incurable should be killed, not cared for. In July 1939, with war planned for that year, the initiation of such a program was advanced for the near future. Now, under the cover of war, action was taken to imple- ment a program of mass murder. Ordered by a secret written decree of Hitler in October, which was back-dated to September 1, the day Ger- many began the war, the program, usually referred to under the euphem- istic term of "euthanasia," provided for the first German effort at sys- tematically identifying a group of people, shipping them to institutions designed and equipped for murdering them, killing those so identified and shipped, and then disposing of the bodies.

With the cooperation of important segments of the SS and the German medical profession, thousands of Germans were taken out of hospitals, mental institutions, and old peoples' homes, transferred to a small number of what can only be called murder factories, and killed and cremated there. By August 1941, one of these factories, that at Hadamar, held a special party for its employees to celebrate the crema- tion of the ten thousandth body.[200]

Several aspects of this horrendous process merit special attention. Unlike other atrocities before and after 1939, these measures involved not random but systematic violence, not occasional murder but the sys- tematic, bureaucratic selection of categories of people to be killed as a matter of routine. While engaged in this operation, the Germans developed both practical experience with procedures and a corps of individuals with a set of attitudes civilized societies do not need but German racial policies required: individuals who would murder others not in isolated incidents but day in and day out, from morning to lunch- time, from early afternoon until it was time to go home for dinner. Most of the techniques of identification, transportation, murder, and disposal of corpses which came to be the hallmark of what was called the "New Order" of Nazi-controlled Europe were experimented with and first perfected in this program. Others had held that charity begins at home; in Hitler's Germany, it was systematic mass murder.

There was still one other way in which this program was distinctive. It provoked criticism and resistance within Germany. Some institutions refused to surrender their patients for murder; in a few instances, there were riots when the buses came to remove patients to what all assumed was certain death; and there was general unease, stimulated not only by the families of the victims—who quickly became suspicious—but by clergymen like Bishop Clemens August von Galen of Münster who denounced the murder program in public in August, 1941.[201] In the face of such protests, and the (well-founded) rumors that this was the intended fate of the war wounded, the government temporarily halted major portions of the program. It continued on a somewhat lesser scale throughout the war, especially the killing of babies born with supposedly serious handicaps and elderly cripples who were deliberately starved to death, but at least some of the intended victims were safe until German victory when their turn was to come. By August 1941, over 100,000 had been killed, and the regime had a solid core of experts in bureaucratic mass murder for whom it would very quickly find other employment.

In the same days that the monstrous war on the ill and the aged was begun inside Germany, the German government also took the organizational steps to implement the regime of terror, deportation, and murder it intended for occupied Poland. The general nature of that system has already been sketched; the point which should be noted in this context is that in October 1939 the military administration of occupied Poland was terminated.[202] As Hitler explained to Goebbels, the German military were too soft for him.[203] Others would carry out the horrors he intended with fewer objections and more enthusiasm.[204]

The other country whose independence the Germans had ended and were so insistent must never be revived was Czechoslovakia. The large portions of that country annexed by Germany after the Munich agreement were integrated into Germany; similarly, the pieces annexed by Hungary in 1938 and 1939 were subjected to a policy of Magyarization. The western and central parts remaining had been declared a protectorate of Germany when occupied in March 1939, while the eastern part was awarded nominal independence under the name of Slovakia.

In the protectorate, German policy looked toward the removal of those Czechs who either could not or would not be Germanized. In the meantime, they would be allowed to collaborate by working hard for the German war effort under their own administration, which in turn was supervised by an enormous German administrative and police apparatus.[205] The local Czech administration was secretly in touch with both the Czech leaders in exile and a minimal underground movement. They relieved the Germans of the need for even more administrators as long as the exigencies of war led the Germans to postpone the fate ultimately in store for the bulk of the population. The concentration of the German mania for murder and resettlement on Poland left the far smaller Czech population under less pressure for the time being. A complicated racial census, somewhat similar to one also being conducted in occupied Poland, pointed the way to the future when other priorities were not so pressing in German eyes. With the beginning of World War II, the German police operating under Karl H. Frank were given even greater independence of the nominal administrative head, Constantin von Neurath, so that there could be no prospect of restraint from the latter if any danger threatened. When the Czechs tried to celebrate their "Fourth of July" equivalent, October 28, the situation quickly led to student demonstrations followed by massive German repression. The universities were closed, a number of students were shot, more than two thousand were sent to concentration camps, and more terror threatened. Thereafter, the situation was relatively quiet. The Czechs could go back to working for the German war effort.[206] What Germans were available for settling Slavic areas would for now be sent to Poland.

As for the Slovak puppet government, it had already shown its good behavior by joining in the war against Poland. For this it was rewarded by its new allies: the Germans gave Slovakia pieces of Poland and the Soviets accorded the state formal recognition. Slovakia could serve at least until the German victory in the West in 1940 as a sort of model for other countries in Southeast Europe: here was the proof of how well Germany treated those who did as they were told.[207] Germany even took the trouble to negotiate its periodic demands with them; their leaders were treated with respect; and their President, Monsignor Tiso, could have his birthday greetings to Stalin published in Pravda. What more could any state of Southeastern Europe possibly want?

As also already mentioned, the Soviet Union was moving forward to secure the loot it had been promised in its secret bargain with Germany. As soon as she attacked Poland, she began insisting that Estonia and Latvia — both assigned to her sphere of interest by the Nazi–Soviet secret protocol of August 23 — sign pacts of mutual assistance allowing the stationing of Soviet troops at designated points in the country. Under threats and pressure, Estonia signed on September 29 and Latvia on October 5.[208]

In their invasion of Poland the Russians moved troops into that portion of eastern Poland around Vilna which they had previously agreed with Germany should be added to Lithuania as a part of Germany's share of Eastern Europe. The exchange of Lithuania for central Poland in the German–Soviet negotiations, culminating in von

Ribbentrop's second trip to Moscow on September 28, meant that Stalin was now free to pressure the Lithuanian government into an analogous mutual assistance pact. In fact, he could hold out the cession of Vilna, long desired by Lithuanians anxious to reclaim the historic capital of the country, as an inducement for the treaty signed on October 10. The Soviets also told the Lithuanians about the strip of territory that they were to lose to Germany,[209] thus removing any Lithuanian inclination to throw in their lot with that country. They also promised the Germans not to station troops in that strip in southwest Lithuania which had been promised to Germany when they occupied the whole country as both Germany and the Soviet Union anticipated. There is simply no evidence on the subject of why the two powers did not move to a "permanent" partition and occupation of Lithuania in the fall of 1939 as they had done with Poland.[210] This issue would come back to haunt both Moscow and Berlin in 1940.

THE SOVIET–FINNISH WAR

Simultaneously with these moves into Poland and the three Baltic States, the Soviet Union also began to apply pressure on Romania, Bulgaria, and Turkey, the countries south of Poland in which she wished to expand her influence under the umbrella of the agreement with Germany. In regard to Romania, the first designs of Stalin were territorial. In 1878 the Russians had insisted on Romania's ceding Bessarabia to them, although Romania had fought hard alongside Russia in the war against the Ottoman empire which preceded the new settlement. At the end of World War I, the Romanians had reclaimed the lost province, but the Soviet Union had always refused to recognize the new border; this was the only one of the post-1917 borders of Russia which the Soviet government had never recognized.[211]

Since the majority of the population in the area between the Pruth and Dniestr rivers was non-Slavic by everybody's reckoning, one can only conclude that the major factor motivating Soviet policy toward the area before as during Stalin's rule was strategic. The annexation of Bessarabia would not only bring the Soviet Union to the mouth of the Danube. It would bring her so close to Bulgaria — especially if that country could reclaim some of its territory lost to Romania — that any Soviet–Bulgarian tie would practically choke off Romania from the Black Sea and come close to providing the Soviet Union with a direct route overland to the Straits at Istanbul. Whether in 1939 Stalin already had territorial ambitions in this direction, going beyond Bessarabia to other portions of Romania, as became clear in 1940, is not known, but might be revealed as the archives of the former Soviet Union are opened. In any case, the development of Soviet pressure for territorial concessions by Romania to Russia, in terms then still publicly referred to only as Bessarabia, began in late 1939.[212]

At the same time, the Moscow government was initiating steps to establish itself in Bulgaria. It urged Bulgaria to sign a mutual assistance pact, though the terms initially proposed did not provide for the stationing of Soviet troops in the country, presumably because, unlike the Baltic States, Bulgaria had no common border with the Soviet Union.[a] There was, from the perspective of Bulgaria, always the possibility of gaining territory from Romania in conjunction with Russia's territorial demands on that country, as well as a remnant of Bulgarian friendship for Russia harking back to the time when the latter had aided her in attaining her independence from the Ottoman empire. Nevertheless, the government in Sofia was reluctant to commit itself to a pact of mutual assistance with Moscow. There was always the possibility that any "assisters" would not leave. A non-aggression and friendship treaty was suggested by the Bulgarians instead.[213]

Still another country was being urged to sign a pact of mutual assistance by Moscow at the same time: Turkey. Here too there was reluctance. If Romania, Bulgaria and Turkey were all spared greater pressure in the last months of 1939, this was certainly not due to German influence. Turkey signed with Britain and France as we have already seen. In the secret negotiations in Moscow, Germany had agreed to the Soviet demand for Bessarabia and had promised to disinterest itself politically in the rest of the area. Von Ribbentrop had been authorized to sign over to the Soviet Union everything all the way to the Straits, but Stalin had not thought to ask for that much.[214] What saved Romania and Bulgaria for a while was the outcome of the simultaneous Soviet pressure on Finland.

The Soviet Union had repeatedly discussed with the Finnish government in 1938 and 1939 the possibility of territorial adjustments in favor of the Soviet Union which would, it was asserted, facilitate the defense of Leningrad. No settlement had been reached in these talks.[215] Now that the Soviets had assured themselves of German agreement that Finland, like East Poland and first two and subsequently all three Baltic States, was in their sphere, Moscow moved in regard to Finland at the same time as the Baltic States.[216] In both cases, negotiators were summoned to Moscow to receive the Soviet demands. Like those placed

---

[a] It is true that *before* the war, Lithuania did not have a common border with the Soviet Union either, but this changed as soon as Russian troops occupied eastern Poland.

before the others, these included a demand for a pact of mutual assistance, but in other respects there were important differences. Only one, not several, military bases in Finland was demanded; in addition, the Russians demanded a substantial territorial concession in the Karelian area north of Leningrad and the western part of the Rybachi peninsula in the north but offered substantial territory in eastern Karelia to Finland in exchange.

In the negotiations which followed during the rest of October and the first days of November 1939, the Finns slightly enlarged their original offer of territorial concessions to the Soviets, while the Soviets agreed to drop the demand for a treaty of mutual assistance and somewhat reduced their territorial demands.[217] The Soviet leaders clearly expected an agreement to be reached, and the Finnish negotiators also thought it possible. When the talks were broken off without agreement, however, on November 9, the Finns may have thought that new negotiations might be possible, but the Soviets quickly moved in other directions. As early as November 13 the Moscow government was taking steps to organize a puppet government of Finnish Communist exiles, and military preparations appear to have been begun about the same time, although there had been internal discussion of a possible war with Finland as early as the summer of 1939.[218] While the negotiations were in progress, Molotov had included an account of Soviet demands in his speech of October 31, hailing the agreement with Germany, welcoming the territorial acquisitions from Poland, and calling on Britain and France to end their war against Germany.[219] The Soviet government had engaged itself in public; it expected prompt agreement; it was not about to let the opportunity slip by.

In a carefully orchestrated sequence, an incident was arranged by Moscow and blamed on the Finns on November 26; on November 29 diplomatic relations with Finland were broken off; the Red Army attacked Finland on November 30; on December 1 a puppet government of Finnish Communists under the leadership of Otto W. Kuusinen was established, nominally in the little town of Terijoki just occupied by the Red Army; and on December 2 the Soviet government signed with this new government a treaty of mutual assistance and friendship, which provided for a border between the two countries along the lines proposed by Stalin in the Moscow negotiations.[a] New appeals for peace negotiations

---

[a] The Kuusinen government also began to set up its own military force. The whole project looks in retrospect like a rehearsal for what was later done by the Soviet Union in regard to Poland: a new regime established in Lublin with its own military force under General Berling. The big differences are two: the Red Army did not occupy Finland but did occupy Poland; and the Kuusinen government was to get its compensation for yielding territory from the Soviet Union itself, while Poland was to get its compensation from Germany.

from the government in Helsinki were turned away by Moscow with reference to the fact that the real government of Finland was not at war with the Soviet Union; only the Kuusinen government counted, and it enjoyed excellent relations with its neighbor.

What the hopes and intentions of Stalin at this time were is not known. Were the original demands the first step to the annexation of Finland? Was the attack accompanied by the establishment of the Kuusinen government designed with the same aim in mind? Or was the Soviet leader really trying to improve Soviet security, and, if so, did he really believe this was the way to do it? There is no way to know. The later annexation of the Baltic States, the nature of the Kuusinen government, and the basic thrust of the Nazi–Soviet Pact all point to the intent of eventual annexation. It is possible, however, that Stalin was not at first certain on that aim himself. Assuredly he expected the Finns to concede what he demanded; and when they refused, he may well have changed his own goals, that is, substituted immediate annexation for a more limited rearrangement, whatever was to follow later.

The argument that he wanted to prevent Britain from using Finland as a base, repeatedly voiced by Stalin and Molotov, hardly fits with the return to the Finns of Petsamo—the port through which the British could contact Finland—at the end of the war. The argument that all this was designed against Germany is even sillier: this was the same period when he had just offered the Germans a closer approach to Moscow by ceding central Poland. Whatever Soviet aims at the beginning of the attack on Finland, there can be no doubt that a quick and decisive victory with very little fighting was anticipated.

Stalin was evidently deluded by his own ideology and the dated and misleading assessments of Finnish Communist exiles into believing that a few blasts on the trumpets from Moscow, accompanied by some air raids on the Finnish capital and a substantial display of force on the border, would suffice to install the Kuusinen regime in Helsinki and bring the walls of Finnish resistance tumbling down.[220] In this estimation, he was to be horrendously mistaken.

Soviet troops not properly prepared for warfare in the Arctic weather and terrain of much of the front, untrained for serious combat, and led for the most part by the terrified incompetents who had succeeded the officers killed or deported in the purges, launched major offensives on the Karelian Isthmus, north of Lake Ladoga, at central Finland, and at Petsamo in the north.[221] Only the landing force at Petsamo succeeded in seizing the town and nickel mines and advancing some distance southward in the portion of Finland previously demilitarized by agreement with Russia. On the Karelian Isthmus, the main Soviet offensive was halted by the Finns, fighting from field fortifications called the Mannerheim Line after their Commander-in-Chief. The attacks into Finland between Lake Ladoga and Petsamo were either stalled or crushed by Finnish resistance with enormous Soviet casualties. The bitter fighting, clearly going against the Russians, created an international situation no one had anticipated and produced a new series of policies which had their own repercussions.

The real Finnish government while mobilizing its resources hoped to restart negotiations, but it is doubtful whether, even if the Soviet Union had been willing to negotiate in December and January, it could have accepted the terms likely to be offered in the face of a public opinion jubilant over the early victories and unheeding of the danger ahead. Some Swedes came to help their neighbor, but the Swedish government was not about to become involved in war with anyone if it could possibly help it. The Finns repeatedly tried to obtain diplomatic support from Germany; but Berlin had promised Finland to the Soviet Union and, far from being prepared to help the Finns, was willing to aid the Soviet Union, both to repay Soviet favors in the ongoing war against Britain and France and to assist in a swift Russian victory. The fighting was of no use to Germany; it threatened to reduce the availability of Soviet supplies to herself, and opened the possibility of an Allied intervention in Scandinavia which could threaten her own iron supplies from Sweden. The Germans refused to sell weapons to Finland, tried to keep what few weapons the Finns could order in Italy from getting there, and left the Swedes worried about a possible German invasion if they came to Finland's assistance.[222]

The Finns, who had relied on Soviet adherence to their mutual treaties, also appealed to the League of Nations. There they received a lot of sympathy but very little practical help. The expulsion of the Soviet Union from the League in no way assisted the Finns but undoubtedly made the Soviet leadership even more dubious about such international organizations in the future than they had been before they had reluctantly joined the League in 1934.[223]

More significant potentially, and possibly more influential in its impact on Soviet policy, was the matter of British and French assistance to Finland. There was, as has already been mentioned, a considerable amount of discussion in and between the governments of the Western Powers about using the opportunity, which appeared to be created by the Russo-Finnish war, to strike indirectly at Germany by helping Finland. Any aid to Finland, even of a purely material sort, which prolonged that war would reduce the aid the Soviet Union could provide to Hitler. Western intervention in the form of troops could come effectively only through Norway and Sweden and would simultaneously cut Germany off from the Swedish iron mines. Since the involvement of Allied troops on the Finnish front meant war with Russia, the bombing of Soviet oil fields in the Caucasus would both aid that effort and deprive the Germans of petroleum supplies from Russia.

These projects were debated endlessly with no decision to go forward reached, but the debates shed light on British and French views of the war and by themselves probably influenced Soviet policy because their nature, if not all of their details, became known at the time. The French were very much more enthusiastic about these schemes than the British, a reflection of their greater interest in keeping the fighting as far as possible from France, which had been so devastated in World War I. It may also be that the antics of the large Communist Party of France which, faithfully in pursuit of the latest instruction from Moscow was now calling for the immediate end of the war against Germany,[224] made those in the government see Germany and the Soviet Union more completely aligned than they really were.

The British government, on the other hand, was most skeptical.[225] This appears in part to have been due to a slightly more realistic assessment of the risks.[a] As for the British Communist Party, it, of course, was also parrotting the line about the desirability of an immediate peace with Hitler, but its numerical insignificance eliminated it as a serious concern. The British government, both because of general principles and out of concern for American public opinion, was also much more reluctant than the French to violate the neutrality of Norway and Sweden, a step that increasingly appeared to be an unavoidable concomitant of any effective assistance to Finland.

Whatever the abstract sympathies Norwegian and Swedish governments might have for fellow Scandinavians in their hour of peril, they were not about to do anything which exposed them to the risks of hostilities with either Germany or the Soviet Union. The Swedes, as will be evident later, would go very far to accommodate Germany: they would allow hundreds of thousands of German troops to move across their territory to and from different parts of Norway and they would permit tens of thousands to move across to attack the Soviet Union. This was from their point of view at a time and under circumstances without any

---

[a] Chamberlain was most cautious at his meeting with Daladier on December 19. He wanted no expeditionary force planned and was primarily worried about the possibility that all of Scandinavia might come under German–Soviet control with vast implications for the situation in the Atlantic.

major risk of retaliation from either Britain or Russia. If they allowed British and French troops across to Finland in 1940, however, certainly Germany and possibly Russia would take military action against them. The Western Powers, therefore, could move only if they were willing to fight Norway and Sweden, and this they were not prepared to do. Even before these issues were sorted out, new Soviet policies had altered the whole situation.

When the second as well as the initial set of Soviet offensives failed, Stalin made a number of changes in policy and approach. Massive reinforcements from all over the Soviet Union were moved to the Finnish front, particularly the Karelian Isthmus, to make a major offensive feasible. That offensive was designed to crush Finnish resistance, penetrate the Mannerheim line, and force the Finns to give up the fighting. As soon as the preparations for the great offensive were well under way, Stalin in effect dropped the Kuusinen regime and agreed to negotiate once again with what had, to his great surprise, turned out to be the real government of Finland.[226] As the Red Army clawed its way through the Finnish defenses, the Finns decided that further resistance was hopeless and, with Sweden acting as intermediary, negotiated for peace.

The Soviet demands now went considerably beyond what they had asked earlier and, it would appear, became slightly greater during the very process of negotiations, perhaps because the military situation continued to shift in Russia's favor.[227] Stalin insisted on a substantially enlarged transfer of territory in the south, a major cession in central Finland, and on an area larger than that specified the preceding October to be leased at Hangö for a Soviet base. While in the north the Soviets did not extend their territorial demands beyond the western portion of the Rybachi peninsula already specified earlier, and agreed to evacuate the Petsamo area and to its return to Finland, there was now to be no territorial compensation for the Finns. The Finnish government saw no alternative to accepting what it considered a very harsh peace. They had fought hard and lost; they had no real prospects of effective aid; and though they had retained their independence, their position for defending it in the future was geographically weaker than before. There may, however, be other elements in the picture which relate to the shift in Soviet policy of January 1940.

There is no way of knowing for certain why and in what direction Stalin revised his approach early in 1940, but the following is suggested as the most likely explanation in view of the known facts and subsequent Soviet policy. With Soviet prestige clearly engaged, Stalin was determined to win the war and to commit whatever resources were needed for that purpose. But in line with the cautious approach he had earlier followed toward Japan in the Nomonhan incident, victory in battle should pave the way for a prompt settlement the other side could accept[228] rather than extended further fighting. That fighting limited the ability of the Soviet Union to push forward in the Balkans and had all sorts of attendant risks—in this case, possible war with Britain and France and even complications with the United States, which repeatedly protested against the Soviet invasion.[229] A quick settlement could be reached only by abandoning Kuusinen's crew and dealing with the government in control in Helsinki. While such a settlement gave the Soviet Union substantially more than had been asked before the fighting began, it would leave the Finns their independence, at least for the time being.[a]

It seems to me that it is in this context that one must see the return of the occupied territory around Petsamo to Finland. That area not only contained valuable nickel deposits and provided Finland with its only outlet to the Arctic Ocean but it also constituted a territorial buffer between the Soviet Union and Norway.[230] All the evidence available to Moscow pointed to a possible conflict between the Germans and the Western Powers in Scandinavia; here was the simplest way to isolate the Soviet Union from any such conflict: she would have no border with either Sweden or Norway. The just defeated Finns could serve to keep any new complications in Scandinavia away from the Soviet Union. As for Finland's ultimate fate, that could be decided later.

Stalin had miscalculated and some 200,000 Soviet soldiers—along with 25,000 Finns—had paid with their lives, but he had drawn new conclusions from the experience. On the other hand, by driving the Finns into implacable hostility, Stalin had left Leningrad, Murmansk, the Soviet Union's ice-free port, as well as the Murmansk railway, in even greater danger than before; but this was a miscalculation he did not understand at the time.

The peace treaty between the Soviet Union and Finland was agreed to in the night of March 12–13, 1940, and accepted by a stunned Finnish parliament on the 15th. In the following days the Red Army occupied the areas allotted to the Soviet Union and drew back to the new border in the north. Although here again clarity will not be attained for years, another major decision of fateful importance was made by Stalin in those days and should, in my judgement, be seen in connection with his concern over isolating the Soviet Union even more tightly from the continuing war between Germany and the Western Powers.

The systematic shooting of almost all Polish officers, reserve officers

---

[a] It should be noted that the Soviets allowed the Finns living in the transferred territory to leave—as practically all promptly did—according to rules similar to those agreed to for the Germans in the Baltic States, and they also arranged for a full exchange of prisoners of war.

and other specialists captured by the Red Army in 1939 has generally been referred to as the Katyn forest massacre from the location near Smolensk where a substantial proportion of their bodies was found, and is discussed in the literature in connection with that grisly discovery in the spring of 1943. While the repercussions of the discovery will be examined in the context of other developments of 1943, the point that must be remembered is that the camps in which the victims had been held were dissolved in March and the men killed early in April of 1940 (obviously with no anticipation that the corpses would be found).[231] The decision to dissolve these camps and murder the inmates simultaneously at different geographical locations in the Soviet Union was made by Stalin and confirmed by the Politburo on March 5, 1940.[232]

It has been suggested that the motive for this terrible step was to reassure the Germans as to the reality of Soviet anti-Polish policy. This explanation is completely unconvincing in view of the care with which the Soviet regime kept the massacre secret from the very German government it was supposed to impress. Besides, nothing the Soviet Union was doing in east Poland would or could lead the Germans to believe that Stalin had suddenly become a great friend of Poland.

A more likely explanation is that, like the rapid and in Soviet (though not Finnish) eyes moderate settlement with Finland, this step should be seen as looking to a future in which there might possibly again be a Poland on the Soviet Union's western border. Since he intended to keep the eastern portion of the country in any case, Stalin could be certain that any revived Poland would be unfriendly. Under those circumstances, depriving it of a large proportion of its military and technical elite would also make it weaker. Before the spring campaign weather arrived in Western and Central Europe, the Soviet Union would isolate and protect itself even further from whatever might happen in what it called the Second Imperialist War. As the Secretary of the Soviet embassy in Rome explained in early March, the Soviet–Finnish peace would make clear to the Italians that for them as well as Germany and the Soviet Union the real enemy was Great Britain. "One must ardently hope that the world war will begin in earnest as soon as possible."[233]

GERMAN PLANS FOR THE WEST

The Germans had hoped to launch the war "in earnest" long before. Hitler had been anticipating a war against the Western Powers for years. As he began to think of that war as an imminent possibility rather than a prospect for the distant future, he had formed some very specific ideas of how it would be waged. Two inter-related aspects appeared in his formulations relatively early. One was that Germany would invade the Low Countries, both Holland and Belgium and not only Belgium as in World War I. The other one, clearly related to this concept, was that the key enemy in the West was not France—as most of his military advisors believed—but England, and that the control of the Low Countries was particularly important for Germany so that she could strike at England from bases there as well as in northern France. He explained these views to his military leaders on May 28, 1938,[234] and again on May 23, 1939.[235] The army would seize the area, which the German air force could then utilize for what Hitler called the "death blow" at England. The instrument with which this death blow was to be struck was the JU-88, the two-engined "wonder bomber."[236] On August 31, 1939, Hitler ordered a dramatic increase in JU-88 production, and again on September 6, before leaving Berlin for the front in Poland, ordered special priority for the JU-88 program.[237] Simultaneously he ordered a speed-up in preparation for gas warfare.[238] Both the JU-88 and the gas-warfare programs ran into many difficulties; they are mentioned here as signs that the German allocation of resources and priorities was geared to a perception of concentrating on blows against England from bases in Holland and Belgium (as well as northern France), which would be seized by a violation of the neutrality of the Low Countries, a plan held to consistently from pre-war times into the early days of the invasion of Poland. The new bases in the Low Countries and France would, of course, also be available for the German navy's war against British shipping.

In the first days of the war, as German forces invaded Poland, the army necessarily confined itself to a defensive posture in the West, but this was only to protect German territory against any French offensive. The intention always was to move forces from the East to the West as quickly as possible, and by September 8 Hitler was already discussing a forthcoming German offensive in the West.[239] He explained his ideas to the Commanders-in-Chief of the army, navy and air force on September 27 and ordered planning for the offensive to go forward.[240] He was thinking of an attack in late October or early November; in other words, just as soon as forces could possibly be moved West and prepared for a new operation and in any case before winter weather made an attack that was expected to be heavily dependent on air strikes impossible.

Two aspects of these plans as Hitler saw them, and as his military advisors developed them, deserve attention. As for the specifics of these early plans, they aimed precisely at the goals Hitler had been talking about at least since May of 1938. The offensive was to concentrate on striking into the Low Countries and into northern France to defeat the enemy forces there and seize the basis for further operations, primarily against England. Though sometimes referred to as repetition of the pre-World War I Schlieffen plan, it was in reality nothing of the sort, sharing only its insistence on violating the neutrality of the Low Countries. The new plan was not the vast encircling movement into *France* that a mentally unbalanced Chief of the German General Staff had once envisioned as the best way to protect Austria–Hungary against a Russian attack, regardless of whether it also brought England into the war. Instead this was a thrust westward with a primary emphasis on defeating *England* by seizing bases in the Low Countries and northern France for air and naval use against Great Britain. The defeat of the French forces likely to be met during this operation would be an essential by-product of the campaign but not its main objective.[241] The initial German planning for the attack in the West has to be understood from this perspective.

The other important aspect to be noted is the opposition Hitler's planned attack evoked among some German military leaders. A few were opposed to having Germany once again attack a neutral country, to say nothing of several neutrals. Many believed that it made more sense to await a French offensive — if it ever came. Others hoped that the existing stalemate in the West without serious fighting might lead to peace talks. Most were much less confident than Hitler about the ability of German forces to defeat the French and instead anticipated a costly stalemate, as had happened in World War I.[242] Finally there was a small number who thought that rather than going along with this descent into the abyss of total war it would be preferable to overthrow the National Socialist regime.[243]

We have already seen how this combination of views affected some attempts to contact the Western Allies, in the hope of obtaining assurances that might encourage more of the wavering generals to join the tiny number of resolute individuals willing to risk a coup attempt. Nothing came of any of this, primarily because the key figures in the German military hierarchy were unwilling to act. The central question was always whether the Commander-in-Chief of the army, then General, later Field Marshal, Walther von Brauchitsch, could be moved to action against Hitler. A man entirely lacking in moral courage, he had been bought by Hitler quite literally in 1938,[244] and there was no way to provide him with a backbone implant. When officers horrified by the atrocities being committed by Germans in Poland mobilized the senior living German soldier, the aged Field Marshal August von Mackensen of World War I fame, to appeal to von Brauchitsch to put a halt to the horrors, the latter responded that he would talk things over with Himmler![245] That was also his recipe for dealing with the crisis of confidence created within the German army by Himmler's published summons to the men of the SS to beget lots of children, inside and outside marriage.[246] It should not surprise anyone that his minimal protest to Hitler on November 5, 1939, about the intended offensive in the West was quickly overborne by an angry and self-confident Führer.[247] If there was any atrocity or violation of a neutral in World War II that von Brauchitsch stopped or even tried to stop prior to his dismissal in December 1941, no record of it has been found.

The army Chief of Staff, General Franz Halder, at times pondered taking action against Hitler but never did; of the three Army Group commanders one, Ritter von Leeb, was willing to move at that time, but, however skeptical, neither of the others, von Bock or von Rundstedt, would act. Eventually each would be cowed and bribed into line.

The Commander-in-Chief of the German navy was at this point, as always, in full agreement on major issues with Hitler. Since, like Hitler, he saw England rather than France as Germany's main enemy, he welcomed the proposed acquisition of bases for the navy, especially in northern France, and would only, as will be discussed below, press on Hitler in early October an extension of German offensive operations into Norway in order to obtain naval bases on that side of England as well. Göring, the air force Commander-in-Chief, had some doubts about the offensive in the West, but neither then nor at any other time would even think of defying his beloved Führer.

The fact that there was considerable doubt among the military about the planned offensive was known to Hitler, and he devoted considerable time and effort to counteracting it. In a memorandum dated October 9 (though written earlier) and in a talk to some 200 German high-ranking officers on November 23 he explained his own reasoning at great length.[248] He set forth the basic assumptions underlying his policy. He had always intended to go to war, and it was therefore critical to select the proper moment. This was it. If Germany were to conquer the living space she needed and avoid destruction at the hands of her enemies, which he asserted was their goal, she must move now. Time was not an ally because Britain and France would build up their forces, the Soviet Union might not always be friendly, Italy might not always be helpful, and the United States might not always be neutral. A defensive posture would be far too dangerous. Now that Germany could take the initiative and do so on one front, she should move as quickly as possible, allowing no opportunity for a compromise but striking into the Low Countries to provide a base for the continuing struggle with Germany's main enemy in the West: Britain.[a] Germany, he was confident, would win — otherwise all would be lost.

Hitler had reinforced his own certainty by these arguments, even if he had not persuaded all in his audience. First plans and orders were issued with a target date in early November; it was in connection with the necessary reviewing of these orders that Hitler left the annual celebration of the failed coup attempt of 1923 early on the evening of November 9 and thus narrowly escaped the assassination scheme of Elser. The weather, however, repeatedly forced postponement; the Germans needed clear weather to take full advantage of their air force.

The successive postponements eventually pushed the offensive back six months from the original date in November 1939 to May 1940, but those postponements themselves had a whole series of repercussions. In the first place, they obviously provided the Germans with added time to assimilate the lessons of the Polish campaign in regard to troop training as well as to make up for equipment losses and repairs. As will be shown in the following chapter, their enemies did not put this half-year interval to equally good use. Secondly, the German intention to attack repeatedly leaked out, at times because of Allied intelligence; at least once through an Italian warning to the Dutch and Belgians;[249] once by the accidental landing of a German plane carrying relevant operational orders which were not all completely destroyed; and repeatedly by the deliberate warnings given out by a key opponent of the National Socialist regime in German central military intelligence, Colonel Hans Oster.[250] The very repetition of warnings and alerts followed by new warnings and alerts, however, eventually had the effect of obscuring the significance of the final warnings in May of 1940; it was hard to credit the fact that the warnings had been accurate when each — until the last one — had been followed by postponement.

A third aspect of the postponements was a twofold reorientation in the German military planning for the offensive in the West. One of these, more in detail than in broad concept, affected the role of Holland in the invasion plans. A shift from inclination toward a partial to a complete occupation of that country was accompanied by increasing emphasis on the use of airborne troops, the latter also being given an enhanced role in the seizure of key spots controlling river crossings in Belgium.[251] More significant was a shift in the general operational concept of the offensive. Increasingly the main thrust was changed from the northern to the southern Army Group participating in the offensive into

---

[a] As Hitler told Goebbels on December 11, 1939: "I want to beat England whatever it costs." Goebbels, *Tagebücher*, 12 Dec. 1939, Vol. 3: 663.

the Low Countries (while the third held the front along the old German–French border).

This shift involved more than a reassignment of specific divisions from one point or higher command to another. Rather it meant a slow but basic change in both the goal of the offensive and the means to attain it. Instead of a thrust into the Low Countries and northern France to provide a basis for future operations against Britain and France, the new plan was designed to destroy so large a proportion of the French and British forces on the continent as to end the war in the West at one blow. The attack by the Army Group on the northern section was now intended to draw out and engage whatever French and British forces joined the Dutch and Belgians in defense of their countries, while a carefully planned and hopefully in the initial stages concealed armored thrust further south, through the Ardennes, drove to the coast like a scythe, cutting off the French and British forces that had moved north-ward to meet the German invasion. The destruction of these, however, would both open all of France to German conquest and provide bases on the Atlantic as well as the Channel coast for naval and air warfare against England if she remained in the war.

This reorientation in goals and operational plans was the result of combining the thinking of Hitler and one of his generals, Erich von Manstein, with the ambitions of the Commander-in-Chief of the Army Group now to have the key role (von Rundstedt) and the armored com-manders who would spearhead the attack. The very fact that both the Low Countries and the Western Allies had learned some details of the *earlier* German plan now served to make them even more vulnerable to the *later* one, because it suggested that a massive Allied advance might halt the main German push when in fact it would draw them more deeply into a trap.

Simultaneously, it should be noted, the increasing prospect of the new plan's real possibility of success reduced whatever inclination to oppose Hitler and his offensive project had existed among the German military leaders. The few who still had their reservations either withdrew into silence or were transferred to unimportant assignments.[a]

---

[a] As late as February 19, 1940, one of the higher officers in the German naval command, Heinz Assmann, wrote a memorandum arguing that as long as Germany kept the United States neutral and refrained from an attack through Holland and Belgium she could not lose, but any attack into the Low Countries would probably lead to war with the United States. Recognizing—as few Germans did—that the Treaty of Versailles had left Germany a united and relatively strong country, he warned that if Germany lost this time, she could not expect a second Versailles Treaty. "Entwurf: Beurteilung der Kriegslage (19. Februar 1940)" BA/MA, III M 502/4.

THE GERMAN CONQUEST OF NORWAY AND DENMARK

Closely related to the intended offensive in the West, and given a major impetus by the original German plan for an operation limited to the seizure of the Low Countries and portions of northern France, was the German project for seizing Norway and, as a subsidiary portion of that seizure, also occupying Denmark. Both because there was some discussion among the Western Allies about an operation in Scandinavia and because the central figure in the German plan, Admiral Raeder, was tried for his role in the invasion of Norway after the war at Nürnberg, especially eloquent lies were told about this project by him and those who wanted to defend him.[252] In order to understand the origins and purpose of the German attack northwards, however, it is necessary to disregard the fairy tales put forward afterwards and to examine the operation in the terms in which it was seen at the time.

The concept of the German navy's needing bases in Norway for a war with England in order to break out of the confines of the North Sea goes back decades before World War II.[253] The German naval leadership of World War II was entirely familiar with this idea and began discussing its application under the current circumstances right after the war started.[254] In early October 1939, there was extensive discussion and correspondence in naval circles about the need for bases for the naval war against England. Bases near Murmansk, on the Norwegian coast— with Trondheim as a favorite—and on the French Atlantic coast all figured in the discussion. The doubts of the army Chief of Staff, General Halder, that the German army could reach the French Atlantic coast, and the developing original plan for an offensive westwards which did *not* look toward a prompt occupation of Brittany and the coast south of that peninsula, combined in early October, 1939, to concentrate naval attention on Norway.[255] It was under these circumstances that Raeder raised the question of obtaining bases in Norway with Hitler on October 10, 1939.

Raeder argued that the more brutally Germany waged the war at sea, the sooner the whole war would be over. The possibility of conflict with the United States should not be allowed to hinder the war at sea—if the war lasted a long time, the United States would join in anyway. The Soviet offer of a base near Murmansk would be investigated, but a base in Norway, preferably at Trondheim, was especially desirable.[256] While

The key figure in planning for a coup in the high command of the army, Helmuth Groscurth, was relieved of his post by General Halder on February 1, 1940 (Helmut Krausnick and Harold C. Deutsch (eds.), *Helmuth Groscurth: Tagebücher eines Abwehroffiziers 1938–1940* [Stuttgart: Deutsche Verlags-Anstalt, 1970], pp. 84, 246–48, 323).

the protection of Germany's steel imports from Sweden would later be brought in as an added argument for the occupation of Norway—in the winter, when the Gulf of Bothnia was frozen, the ore was routed by train to the Norwegian port of Narvik and then by boat down the coast— the original concept was an offensive one aimed at England. Once Hitler's attention had been focused on Norway and orders extracted from him to prepare an invasion of that country, the leaders of the German navy could afterwards pretend to have been acting only in accordance with orders from above.[257]

As the project for an occupation of Norway developed in the following months, several aspects of it acquired ever greater significance. Once inaugurated, these preparations looked not to a temporary military action as a wartime expedient but to the permanent incorporation of Norway into a greater German empire: the country was never to regain its independence.[258] In making their preparations, the Germans took advantage of internal Norwegian support, led and symbolized by the man who would give his name to the concept of selling your own country to the tender mercies of another, Vidkun Quisling. This leader of Norwegian sympathizers with National Socialism had long been in touch with and in part financed by the foreign policy office of the Nazi Party under Alfred Rosenberg. He was now put in touch with Admiral Raeder, the key advocate of a German occupation of his country. Quisling urged the Germans to move quickly and, as former War Minister of Norway, did what he could to provide them with tactical military information that might assist them in seizing Norway as easily as possible. A man who combined enormous vanity, cupidity, and stupidity, he would earn his keep and his reputation.[259]

Quisling's role as a traitor to his country turned out to be a mixed blessing for his German paymasters. He was so unpopular in Norway that German sponsorship of him undoubtedly hardened the resolve of most Norwegians against the invader, but at one place he could be of help: at Narvik. This was a key point in the whole German operation; it was furthest from Germany, most exposed, and most difficult for the navy to reach. The commander of the garrison there happened to be a Quisling supporter, and in the event he would promptly surrender to the German invaders.[260] These were to be brought primarily on ten fast destroyers, which could not venture that distance without assurance of maintenance and refueling. These would be provided, in turn, by Germany's other supporter in the daring strike into Arctic waters: the Soviet Union. A special maintenance and supply ship, the tanker *Jan Wellem* had previously been dispatched to "Basis Nord," the German naval base at Zapadnaya Litsa Bay near Murmansk; and as soon as the invasion of

Norway was scheduled for April 9, the ship was ordered from there to Narvik where she met and refuelled the German destroyers. After the Royal Navy had destroyed the German warships at Narvik, the *Jan Wellem* was scuttled, but she had by then played her part in facilitating the conquest of Norway.[261]

The dramatic events at Narvik, of which only a few have just been mentioned, show how the German plan called for a combined operation in which the whole navy was committed to the support of the army in a campaign which had been developed in response to that navy's pressure. Given the location of Norway in relation to German military power, the planning staff in Berlin came to the conclusion that Denmark had to be seized at the same time, and all planning took this into account. The promises to respect Denmark's neutrality were to be violated, along with those to the Norwegians; it was hoped that the Danes might be overawed so quickly that no serious fighting would be required. At the appropriate moment, Berlin would publish "proofs" that the invasion of the two countries was everybody's fault but Germany's.[262] Those who had prepared an analogous volume to show that the outbreak of war in 1939 was the fault of Poland and Britain had time for this project before getting out the next set of pretexts for the invasions of Holland, Belgium, and Luxembourg. They would get lots more practice, even if few outside Germany believed them.

As the approaching end of the Russo-Finnish War suggested that there was no likelihood of any Allied intervention in Scandinavia, some German officers began to have their doubts about the planned operation against Norway and Denmark. Even in the navy there seem to have been last-minute reservations, perhaps reinforced by the knowledge that the changes made in the meantime in the German plans for an offensive in the West now promised access to the better bases on the French coast they had hoped for but had not been promised in the fall. These doubts were reinforced by the German Minister to Norway, who was confident that Norway would maintain her neutrality and that the Allies would not violate it. Raeder still believed in the operation, as he told Hitler on March 26. Hitler had made up his mind and would not draw back. As he explained to the commanders of the forthcoming operation at a final conference on April 1, the very daring quality of the invasion would assure success. The war with England was the essential key to Germany's future access to the oceans, and the opportunity of fighting on one front must be seized. France was weak; the German air force superior to the British and French air forces combined; Italy was getting ready to join Germany's side; and relations with the Soviet Union as good as Germany could possibly want. Now was the time to move.[263]

The official German directive for the invasion had been given on March 1, 1940.[264] In the first days of April the German ships were loaded with troops and supplies, while the air force got ready for its role in the attack. The First Lord of the Admiralty in London, Winston Churchill, had long urged British action in Scandinavia and on March 14 had expressed to Foreign Secretary Lord Halifax his dismay at the victory for Germany implicit in the end of the Russo-Finnish war while the Western Allies only waited on events.[265] The British would try by mines to force German ore transports from Narvik into open waters, but there was to be no Allied invasion. When, however, the naval attaché sent warnings from Copenhagen that German warships were headed for Norway, Churchill disregarded them, so that the British, like the Norwegians and Danes themselves, were surprised when Germany struck.[266] German officers had been sent to Oslo and Copenhagen ahead of time, traveling in civilian clothes, and there could meet the landing forces as they arrived.[267]

The German forces moving into Denmark over land and also arriving at key points by sea quickly overpowered local resistance and overawed the Danish government. Within the day, Denmark had surrendered; and the Germans now controlled the exits from the Baltic Sea, the agricultural resources of Denmark, and a key stage on the sea and air route to Norway.

The Norwegian operation, on the other hand, did not go so easily. In view of Germany's inferiority at sea, the only hope for success was seen as surprise. A series of separate but simultaneous landings would take place at the key centers of Norwegian population and port facilities, scattered over enormous distances because of the geography of the country.[268] These landings were both so far apart from each other and, especially at Narvik and Trondheim, at such a great distance from German bases that only fast warships could carry the assault troops. This, in turn, meant that the number of soldiers in the initial assault wave had to be quite small, and that it would greatly help if the surprised Norwegians could be persuaded to surrender rather than to fight.

Confusion within the German forces and some effective resistance by the forts defending the Norwegian capital, however, did more than lead to the sinking of Germany's newest heavy cruiser, the *Bluecher*, by an ancient gun bought from Krupp and torpedoes purchased from pre-World War I Austria.[269] It gave the Norwegian government time to evacuate the capital and Quisling an opportunity to make his role public. That combination settled it: the government would not give in and the people would not submit to the eccentric from the fringes of Norwegian politics who had sold out his country. The Germans' dropping Quisling and appointing the Nazi district chief (*Gauleiter*) Josef Terboven from Germany in his place could not undo the damage; on the contrary, it only revealed to the Norwegians where a German victory would leave them.

If military victory at Oslo was accompanied by political defeat and naval losses, the rest of the campaign followed an extraordinarily similar pattern. Everywhere German surprise and initiative triumphed over the unprepared, inadequate, and poorly armed Norwegian forces. Having quickly seized the main ports and airfields, the Germans were in an excellent position to strike back at the British, French and Polish forces which landed north and south of Trondheim, at Namsos and Andalsnes, to assist the Norwegians. If the German command structure was confused, that of the Allies was chaotic and further hampered by examples of that gross incompetence on the part of British generals, which would continue to bedevil the British army, at least into the summer of 1942.[a] The control of airports in Norway, secured in the first days by the Germans, allowed them to demonstrate dramatically and quickly early in the war the critical importance of land-based airpower as dominant over seapower and landing forces without their own land-based air force. The German units moving from Oslo and Trondheim toward each other joined, while the British, French and Polish troops in central Norway had to be evacuated.

In this portion of the campaign the Germans, though winning on land and in the air, had suffered substantial damage to their naval forces. In the far north, at Narvik, it was even worse. The ten destroyers—half of the German navy's modern ships of this type—which had carried the landing force to Narvik were all destroyed as a result of two attacks into the fjords around Narvik by the British navy. Many of their crew members joined the troops which tried to hold the town against an Allied landing force, but the ships were gone. As it was, the Allies took Narvik at the end of May in an extraordinarily dilatory campaign, only to evacuate it because in the meantime the German offensive in the West made it seem advisable to pull all Allied forces out of Norway. The difficult situation of the German troops, a situation which had caused Hitler to panic at one point, was redeemed by the victory in the West; the naval losses could not be made good so quickly.

---

[a] Just one example was the assertion of the British commander at Namsos that the route to the north was impassable; the Germans would move across almost 90 miles of it in four days (Earl F. Ziemke, *The Northern Theater of Operations, 1940–1945* (Washington: GPO, 1960) pp. 90, 96–97). The British loss of an aircraft carrier, the *Glorious*, to a surprise surface attack when it did not have any of its planes out scouting and no lookout aloft suggests that the Royal Navy was also capable of some extraordinary ineptitude (the most recent account in David Kahn, *Seizing the Enigma: The Race to Break the German U-Boat Codes, 1939–1943* [Boston: Houghton Mifflin, 1991], pp. 122–23).

These were, furthermore, increased by the extraordinary reaction of the German naval command to the signs of victory in the West as well as in Norway. All the evidence available suggests that Raeder completely lost his head over what he, like so many Germans, saw as the prospect of imminent victory in the whole war. Forgetting his and the navy's own prior emphasis on the *French* ports as the best base for Atlantic operations, and fearful that the war might end before he could demonstrate to Hitler's satisfaction the great value of a battleship navy, he ordered the two available battleships into operations off the Norwegian coasts in late May and June 1940. Both the *Scharnhorst* (only just repaired from earlier damage in the Norwegian operation) and *Gneisenau* were torpedoed by British submarines in these prestige maneuvers; they would not be ready for operations in the Atlantic again until the end of December. And in the process another German admiral was canned by Raeder, while his successor was covered with reproaches.[270]

At the end of the campaign, the Germans, who had employed practically their whole navy in the operation, had lost most of their larger surface ships, at least for some time. On July 1, 1940, the German navy could deploy for action one heavy and two light cruisers together with no more than four destroyers! All the other ships of destroyer size or larger had been sunk or damaged.[271] As they faced the prospect of mounting an invasion of England in the critical summer and fall of 1940, they had to do so practically without a surface fleet. Neville Chamberlain was often mocked for his comment on April 4, 1940, that Hitler "missed the bus" by not launching a big offensive earlier.[272] The Norwegian campaign which followed a few days later was often held up as a sign that it was the Allies, not the Germans, who had missed it. The German strategic dilemma of the summer of 1940, which will be examined in the next chapter, may suggest that the answer is by no means so obvious.

What was obvious, however, was that the Allies had suffered a visible defeat under circumstances in which by the views of the ordinary person they should have won. The end of the Russo-Finnish war in Soviet victory and without Allied intervention had led to the fall of the Daladier government in France in March; the Norwegian campaign would end the government of Neville Chamberlain. The debate in the House of Commons in early May was bitter; an accumulation of dissatisfaction, disappointment, personal animosity and partisanship washed over the government in spite of the defense Chamberlain and Churchill put up. The government's majority dropped substantially as many Conservatives voted against it and even more abstained. Knowing that the other parties would not serve under his leadership—he had asked them at the outbreak of war only to be refused—Chamberlain promptly decided to resign. The new German offensive in the West, just launched, made a national coalition government essential. His own expectation and that of most others was that Lord Halifax would succeed him, but Halifax himself did not want to take the position of Prime Minister. Churchill was the obvious choice under these circumstances, and the other parties as well as Neville Chamberlain and Halifax agreed to serve under him.[a] The new leadership will be examined in the context in which it came to power in May of 1940; its succession was occasioned by the allied debacle in Norway.

There would be several further occasions when the British were called upon at the last minute to rescue some country unexpectedly invaded by the Axis powers, and when they had held off Allied assistance until too late in the vain hope that neutrality provided some protection against attack. In all such cases there would again be considerable criticism in London of the British government—rather than of the poor judgement of Germany's most recent victim—but never again would the ensuing disasters bring down the government.

If the Norwegians lost their independence, the British their government, and the Germans most of their surface fleet—at least for the time being—what did the invaders gain? The most tangible immediate benefit was the assurance of iron ore from Sweden. Not only did control of Norway mean that the Germans could ship iron ore to Narvik by train and from Narvik to Germany in winter, but combined with the occupation of Denmark the occupation of Norway provided a strong position to extort from Sweden almost anything the Third Reich wanted. Already during the fighting the Swedes had allowed German specialists and supplies to travel across Sweden to aid in the fighting at Narvik. Now the Swedes would feel obliged to agree to a whole series of concessions to Germany. Not only would iron ore be delivered in vast quantities, everything possible would be done to assure supplies for German war industry including draft deferments for those Swedes working in the mines. Vast numbers of German soldiers would be allowed to travel on Swedish trains, hundreds of thousands by the end of the war, as Swedish "neutrality" was modified to accommodate German demands. The German navy could order warships built in Swedish yards, and the Swedish economy would

---

[a] In order to understand the preference of many at the time for Lord Halifax over Churchill, one must recall that Churchill was then not on good terms with either Conservatives or Labourites. He had broken with the former on one of the few issues on which the latter shared the view Churchill rejected: more self-government for India. This situation was personified in 1940 by the other key figures. Clement Attlee, the leader of the Labour Party, has served on the Statutory Commission which has prepared the original draft of the Government of India Act that Churchill opposed; Lord Halifax had been the Viceroy of India whose conciliatory attitude toward Gandhi had infuriated Churchill.

operate on rations set in Berlin.[273] It was, and remained, easier for the Germans to exploit Sweden in this fashion for her own war effort than to run the risks and costs of occupation. If Germany won the war, as she confidently expected, then Sweden's independence would follow that of Denmark's and Norway's into the trashcan; if she lost, Sweden could reorient her policy once again, as she in fact began to do in 1943–44 once this looked safe.

The Germans could also begin the process of incorporating Norway as well as Denmark into their new empire. The first steps along these lines were taken during the war; others would follow after victory. Here were some real Germanic types who could add their numbers and skills to those fine Nordic Aryans who had brought them into a greater fold. In the thousand-year Reich there would be plenty of time and opportunity to integrate the people along with the splendid scenery; in the meantime those so inclined could be recruited into the special Germanic formations of the SS which Himmler was developing. A special unit, eventually a full division, would be recruited from these Nordics.

A more substantial benefit in the war was assumed to be attained by the acquisition of those bases on the Norwegian coast which the German navy had long sought. In the short run, this meant opportunities for German submarines and surface ships to use Norwegian ports in the war on British shipping. In the intermediate time period — the later stages of the war — bases for ships and planes in Norway would be of enormous assistance in attacking Allied efforts to supply the Soviet Union by the Arctic route, a subject to be reviewed in its context later. Finally, in the long run, Trondheim was to become a German city, joined by a four-lane highway to the German heartland, and offering a permanent base for Germany's blue-water navy in its world-wide role.[274] This project was being built on as late as 1943, but by that time another aspect of the commitment to Norway was becoming apparent: it called for ever greater investment of German troops and materiel, most of both being held there until the surrender of 1945.

The Soviet Union had isolated herself from the campaign in Norway by restoring Petsamo to Finland at the end of the Russo-Finnish war. She happily congratulated the Germans on their victory, a victory assisted by the Soviet provision of a naval base for the key supply ship to Narvik. Whether Stalin was as clever as he thought himself in assisting the Germans to drive the Allies out of Northern Europe, just as he would soon help the Germans drive them out of Western Europe, is another matter.

The American government and public were shocked by the invasion of Denmark and Norway. This dramatic ending of the "phony war" immediately occupied the headlines and the news reels. Once again Germany had attacked, in this instance two countries which obviously had done nothing against her. The speed of events and the inability of the Allies to stop Germany were ominous. The alarm as well as the revulsion caused by this step were accentuated by a factor which, as far as the evidence shows, had been ignored by the Germans. Greenland was under Danish sovereignty, and if not visible from Berlin was highly visible from Washington. Steps were taken to develop direct relations with that great island and later to include it in the Western Hemisphere neutrality zone. In Washington as well as in London there was also great concern about the fate of Iceland, tied as it was to the Danish crown and strategically located in the North Atlantic.[275]

The Allied inability to halt the Germans in Norway reinforced Roosevelt's already dim view of their military power at the same time as the American public began to obtain a clearer view of what the concept of "neutrality" meant to the leaders of Germany. Even before the campaign in Norway ended early in June, there would be further dramatic evidence on both counts: the military weakness of the Allies and the attitude of the Germans toward neutral countries.

3

———— • ————

THE WORLD TURNED UPSIDE DOWN

GERMANY WINS IN THE WEST

Early in the morning of May 10, 1940, Germany invaded Holland and
Belgium, having infiltrated troops into Luxembourg the night before.
These neutrals would be rewarded for their prior shielding of Germany
in the West by the swift destruction of their independence. But that
destruction was incidental to a broader aim. The purpose of the German
invasion was to crush the French and British forces on the continent so
that Germany would have quiet in the West while conquering living
space from the Soviet Union in the East. The three neutrals in the West
were to provide the avenue for victory over France and a coastal base
for defeating England, while the great neutral in the East, the Soviet
Union, both enabled Germany to concentrate her forces on one major
front and helped supply these forces with the materials Germany needed
in taking this preliminary step for the subsequent campaign in the East.

As already described, the German plan had changed from an initial
one for a limited offensive in the north to a subsequent one for an attack
toward the Channel coast through Luxembourg, Belgium and northern
France.[1] Disagreements over strategy and weather problems had led to
twenty-nine postponements. These postponements, however, had some
major advantages for the Germans. They utilized the seven months' lull
in the fighting to make good the losses and take into account the lessons
of the Polish campaign. Because some details of the original German
campaign plans came to the attention of the Western Allies when a
German plane, carrying an officer with relevant documents he could not
destroy quickly enough, made a forced landing in Belgium, the Allies
were misled into disregarding the signs of a reorientation of the direction
of the main German thrust. They were, therefore, inclined to fall all
the more completely into the trap created by the second and actually
implemented campaign plan. Finally, the repeated leaks of Germany's
intention to invade, several of them deliberately arranged by Hans Oster,

a key figure in the internal opposition to Hitler, left the immediate victims of attack doubtful about crediting the last warning in the series.[2]

The Allies had observed the smashing blows which broke Poland's armies so quickly, but they had learned little from these events. Chamberlain recognized the impact of the new warfare, but the British army had been provided the necessary resources to begin rebuilding so recently that there was little chance to profit from the disaster in the East.[3] The French also had some idea of how the quick blows and rapid exploitation of the German armored divisions supported by the German air force might interfere with their own process of deliberate and methodical campaigning, but similarly did little or nothing to alter the scattering of armor and the dependence on stale tactics.[4]

Recognizing that the Germans would again strike in the West through neutral territory in order to by-pass the French fortifications on the Franco-German border, the famed Maginot Line, the French and British had to choose between disregarding the neutrality of Belgium and Holland by advancing into them before Germany struck, abandoning those countries to their fate when invaded while trying to hold the Germans on a longer and more dangerous front on the Franco-Belgian border, or pushing their own forces into the Low Countries to assist the latter once the Germans had launched their attack. For political reasons, the Allies rejected the first of these possibilities. They would not try to move before the Axis, a policy the British subsequently abandoned in dealing with the French fleet and the important island of Madagascar in the Indian Ocean. The second approach—abandoning the Low Countries to their fate—appeared to be doubly disadvantageous. Such a strategy would write off what armed forces Belgium and Holland might muster, particularly the Belgian army which was correctly thought to be a substantial force and was in fact larger than the army Britain had been able to send to the continent in the first part of the war. Furthermore, holding the Belgian–French border would mean both fighting closer to key centers of French population and industry and defending a line longer than one that might be attained if French and British forces pushed forward at least into Belgium.

Under these circumstances, the Allies settled on a plan to advance into the Low Countries once these were attacked, in the hope of halting the Germans on a front that covered much of Belgium and perhaps a small part of Holland.[5] This project was thus designed to assist the neutrals victimized by German aggression and simultaneously to include their defensive capabilities into the general military power of the Allies. It suffered from two major defects, one obvious from the start, the other apparent only once the fighting began. The shortcoming evident at the time, never adequately remedied, and contributing greatly to the Allied defeat, was the refusal of Holland and Belgium to coordinate their defensive plans fully with France and Britain. Fearful of arousing the ire of the Germans, the two neutrals allowed some secret contacts and exchange of information with the Western Powers, but never agreed to the development of fully coordinated plans with appropriate preparation to implement them when Germany struck. On the contrary, in both countries the highest officers in the army were replaced by men less inclined to cooperate with France and Britain. The Dutch thereupon decided on a withdrawal plan guaranteed to isolate them from any assistance by land, and the Belgians—whose military forces were far more substantial—also refused to work out a coherent defensive strategy with their only conceivable protectors. Whether, in the face of such attitudes, it made sense for France and Britain to plan a commitment of their best equipped forces to a move forward into countries unwilling to coordinate their own efforts with those whom they planned to ask for help, raises a question of great complexity which had arisen in Norway; it reflects the redoubling of an advantage unscrupulous attackers have over cautious countries which hope to avoid war by avoiding measures thought likely to provoke the attacker—the same advantage Germany had enjoyed and exploited in the face of the delayed Polish mobilization.

The second defect of the Allied plan, which became evident only in the course of the fighting, was closely related to the first. If the French and British forces were to move effectively into the Low Countries in order to assist them in stemming a German onrush, these forces would have to be relatively mobile and well equipped. In other words, the best and most mobile units of the French army and practically the whole British Expeditionary Force would be committed in the face of a German attack which turned out to be aimed differently from Allied expectations, thereby playing unwittingly into Germany's hands by assuring that it would be the most mobile and effective units that were cut off by the German thrust across the Ardennes to the coast. Under these circumstances, defeat in the initial battle would mean *not* a new line of defense further back than the Allies had hoped to hold, but disaster. This last point was made doubly sure by the faulty strategy of the French supreme commander, General Gamelin, who both insisted, against the advice of his generals, that the main French reserve, the French 7th Army, be assigned to the rush into Holland at the extreme left flank, and also that half of the total French forces available be assigned to the Maginot Line, so that there were no readily available reserves of any kind.

The German attack which began on May 10 can most easily be described by a review which goes from north to south. In the north, the attack on Holland included the use of German troops in Dutch uniforms, a substantial employment of paratroopers which, however, failed to seize on the first day the centers of population and government at which they were aimed, and an essentially unopposed movement by substantial German forces across the border. The retreat of the Dutch army was, as already mentioned, directed away from, rather than toward, the advancing forces of the Allies, with the result that it was quickly completely cut off by the Germans. Before the Dutch army surrendered on May 15, two events occurred which would affect the subsequent course of the war.

In the first place, the Queen and her government left Holland for England so that thereafter a Dutch government-in-exile would continue on the side of the Allies, a matter of considerable importance, given the strategic location of the Dutch colonial empire in South America and Southeast Asia and the large size of the Dutch merchant fleet. Secondly, the invasion itself (along with that of Belgium and Luxembourg) opened up the whole question of restraints on warfare in the modern world. The Dutch had not been involved in World War I and had greatly helped German citizens in the difficult times after their defeat of 1918. To show their gratitude, the Germans carried out a ruthless bombing attack on the city of Rotterdam on May 14, destroying the old city core and killing hundreds of civilians in a deliberate move designed to terrorize the Dutch into surrender.

The German air force had destroyed the city of Guernica during the Spanish civil war in April of 1937 by an attack etched into the world's consciousness by Pablo Picasso's famous painting. The Luftwaffe had repeated this approach in the bombing of Warsaw and other Polish cities, but these were events and places distant from the consciousness of Allied leaders in the West. The latter had imposed the strictest constraints on their own bombers, but they had already considered the possibility of reducing these if the Germans broke the neutrality of the Low Countries.[6] Now the Germans had done so in the most flagrant way and had used their air force in an obviously deliberate assault on civilian targets. The restraints on Allied bombing policy were lifted thereafter, and German cities eventually reaped the whirlwind sowed by the Luftwaffe. Ironically the first major air raid on a German city occurred when German planes by mistake bombed

Freiburg in southwest Germany on May 10, 1940; and the German government claimed this proved first that the French and later that the British had begun with the bombing of civilian targets![7] A special monument in central Rotterdam commemorates those who died in this air attack designed to cow the civilian population, but those who set the world on fire would see their own roofs burn.

In the same hours and days that the storm broke over Holland, the Germans attacked a Belgium they had promised to respect for the second time in the century. Paratroopers and glider troops seized key river crossings and the forts guarding the critical routes into central Belgium. In World War I, the Germans in an especially notorious incident had burned down the library of the University of Louvain; rebuilt in the inter-war years, it was again set on fire, this time by German artillery.[8] Belgian units fought bravely against the invaders, but coordination with the arriving French and British armies was abysmal. The Belgian government, still imagining that it could earn points from the Germans, complained about British troops moving through the "open" city of Brussels, a symbol of attitudes that had vanished by the time British soldiers returned in 1944.[9]

As the German assault pushed forward into Belgium and the French front was pierced further south, the Belgian military leaders, and especially King Leopold, began to reconsider their position. The King in particular was unwilling to follow the example either of Belgian King Albert in 1914 or of the Queen of the Netherlands in 1940. Rather than leave the country, against the advice of his government he remained there as a prisoner while the Belgian army surrendered unconditionally to Germany on May 28.[10] This action was in part the result of a calamitous French defeat further south, but contributed to the deepening Allied disaster and greatly complicated the situation of the Belgian government, which now moved into exile. That government would, as will be shown, waver briefly in the summer but eventually remain in the war, controlling the Belgian Congo with its great mineral resources, particularly copper and uranium. King Leopold remained a German prisoner and abdicated in 1951.

The decisive German thrust, however, came not in the north where the advancing German forces were soon engaging the French and British units which had hurried forward to join the Belgians and the Dutch, but through Luxembourg and southern Belgium into northern France over roads through the Ardennes. The thin screen of French forces holding this sector was quickly pierced, and already on May 13 the first German spearheads had crossed the Meuse river. The

German armored units pushing forward rapidly from these crossings threatened to cut off the whole Allied northern flank. Although some of the French units engaged in this encounter fought bravely, the initial German breakthrough was never seriously threatened, or even halted, before it reached the Channel coast in the night of May 20–21, ten days after the initial attack had been launched and one week after the crossing of the Meuse 150 miles away. How could such a victory be won so quickly?

Several factors combined to enable the Germans to win not only quickly but relatively easily. The shrewd and daring handling of the concentrated German armored formations, effectively supported at critical moments by the tactical employment of the German air force, gave the major impetus to this victory; but two critical errors of the French command contributed immensely to the inability of the Allies to cope with the breakthrough once they had discovered what was really happening.

In the first place, the French Commander-in-Chief, General Maurice Gamelin, had left such large forces in and behind the Maginot Line and deployed such substantial elements at the far left flank for a useless dash into Holland that there was no substantial reserve force available to push either into the gap or against the flanks of the German spearhead. Unlike World War I, when time and again initial breakthroughs had been contained by moving reserves to hold a new front, there were no such forces available in time on this occasion. That left the other possibility, used in the prior conflict to supplement the use of reserves: the redeployment of units already in the front elsewhere. Exploiting this possibility was vitiated by the second great mistake of Gamelin, a mistake to which, it should be noted, the allies of France contributed.

In spite of the terrible experience of 1918, when the absence of unity of command had almost led to the defeat of the Western Allies, no effective, functioning, Allied command structure existed in 1939–40. In fact, the French had not even organized their own command system so that it could work with minimal efficiency. There is no need to go into the rivalries and confusions affecting the French command, especially the unclarified relationship of Gamelin to the key field commander, General Alphonse Georges, or the equally confused command relations below Georges. The key point is that there was no time for the leisurely sorting out of incompetents, no opportunity to bring forward new ideas, no clear vision of needed measures, no ruthless will to impose order upon the chaos of demoralized headquarters. That under these circumstances some of the

French units broke in battle is not nearly as astonishing as the fact that so many of them fought so well. In World War I it had been said, with at least some degree of justice, that the British soldiers fought like lions but were led by donkeys. In the first stage of World War II, this description best characterized the French.[11]

None of this should be taken to imply that British leadership was especially inspired. Already during the winter, what can only be called a conspiracy of generals, War Office and Foreign Office civilians, together with court circles, had caused the dismissal of the Secretary of State for War, Leslie Hore-Belisha, one of the few driving persons in the Cabinet, in retaliation for his shaking up a British military establishment at least as torpid as the French.[12] The commander of the British Expeditionary Force, Lord Gort, was an extraordinarily brave man, but he became almost paralyzed by the first signs of Allied defeat. Many of his key subordinates rose to critical commands later in the war; he himself would be assigned to govern first Gibraltar and then Malta, where a steady hand but no wider responsibilities were involved.

The French and British air forces were unable to destroy the bridges critical to the German advance, but that inability reflected a lack of both interest in and *real* training for ground support operations, a problem that would bedevil Allied air forces for years into the war. The two Allied air forces fought well but with diminished strength and from inadequate or distant bases as the land battle raged.[a] Much was made at the time and in some of the post-war literature about the refusal of the British to employ their last reserves of fighters in the campaign, but nothing suggests that adding to the inadequately based and supported air forces would have accomplished much beyond robbing the British of the planes they would need so desperately to cover the evacuation from Dunkirk, soon to be discussed, and to defend the home island against the Nazi onslaught thereafter—both operations carried out from home bases.

The efforts of the French and British to cut off the German

---

[a] The French had ordered large numbers of planes from the U.S. only to have assembly shifted from Brest in Brittany to Casablanca with resultant delays. The main beneficiaries of the French orders came to be the British who took over their orders in the U.S., but 40 American fighters ended up on the French aircraft carrier *Béarn*, which spent the war at Martinique in the West Indies. See John M. Haight, Jr., *American Aid to France, 1938–1940* (New York: Atheneum, 1970), chap. 9. There is a useful survey of the air war in the Western campaign using recently opened French archives in Lee Kennet, "German Air Superiority in the *Westfeldzug*, 1940," in F.X.J. Homer and Larry Wilcox (eds.), *Germany and Europe in the Era of the Two World Wars: Essays in Honor of Oron James Hale* (Charlottesville: Univ. Press of Virginia, 1986), pp. 141–55. Key documents on the British air effort in PRO, AIR 8/287.

armored spearhead by attacking from north and south before German infantry could catch up with their own advancing armor failed. Neither push had the strength and the two pushes never had the coordination necessary for real hope of success. The process of coordination was complicated not only by an incoherent command structure in the north but also by a change in leadership at the center of the French military. Earlier, the French government of Edouard Daladier had fallen on March 20, in part because of the collapse of all French hopes tied to the cause of Finland when the latter had made peace with the Soviet Union on March 13. The British ambassador to Paris, Sir Eric Phipps, wrote sadly to Lord Halifax that with Daladier there had fallen a leader all out for victory and in his opinion the only French politician of complete integrity.[13]

The new Prime Minister, Paul Reynaud, was thought to be both more flamboyant and activist, a man who had the reputation of being a strong anti-Nazi, and who signed an agreement with Britain that neither would make a separate peace with Germany. Though strong in intention, he would be wavering in implementation, and there is substantial evidence that under the influence of his mistress, Madame de Portes, his resolution weakened in June.[14] He had been about to fire General Gamelin when the German invasion of the Low Countries became known and refrained from doing so under those circumstances. A few day later, however, as the dimensions of the disaster became clearer, he replaced Gamelin with General Maxime Weygand—who had first to fly back from Syria—and simultaneously he himself took over the Ministries of National Defense and War from Daladier. It fell to Weygand to try to stem the German onrush, but in the event he could neither coordinate the needed counter-attack quickly enough nor reinvigorate the reeling French forces.[15]

It was argued at the time and provided a useful excuse for many that a "fifth column" of subversives played a major role in the speedy German advance and Allied collapse. There can be no doubt that the confusion caused by German soldiers in Dutch uniforms on the one hand and the anti-war propaganda conducted by the French Communists on the other made their contribution to weakening the resistance to German might, but the basic factor was surely that a poorly led and badly coordinated Allied force was pierced at a critical point by concentrated German armor and was never able to regain even its balance, to say nothing of the initiative.

The immediate problem facing the Allies was what to do in the north and south as their forces were separated from each other by the German thrust to the coast, while the Germans had to decide how best to deal with the two enemy forces remaining in the field. The interaction of the answers the two sides gave to these questions determined the course of the rest of the campaign. In the north, the British decided that Allied inability to break through the tier of German forces separating them from the south required an effort to evacuate as much of the cut-off army as possible while preparing a renewed buildup of British forces alongside the French in the south. The War Cabinet in London first learned of the German break-through across the Meuse on May 14;[16] in subsequent days they followed the situation with increasing anxiety. As it became clear that communication with the south could not be regained, a desperate effort was made to withdraw the British Expeditionary Forces to the coast and evacuate by sea. This possibility had been first canvassed as early as May 19; it was put off in favor of a last attempt to break through to the south, became inevitable once the Belgians capitulated on May 28. but had looked like the most plausible course already by May 25. The real question was, would it be possible to stage a fighting retreat to the coast and ship out the troops—presumably without their equipment—alongside French forces fighting with them?

At first it looked as if Great Britain would lose practically its whole army including the professional officers who would be needed for the rebuilding of any substantial new land force. The stubborn fighting of the British and French troops, however, slowed down the Germans even as British naval, merchant, and small private ships began to lift soldiers off the piers and beaches near Dunkirk. The evacuation of the majority of the British—about 220,000—and a substantial number of French soldiers—about 120,000—was unwittingly assisted by the German decision on how to deal with the divided forces of the Allies.[17]

On May 24 Hitler and General Gerd von Rundstedt, the Com-mander-in-Chief of the German Army Group whose forces had made the great breakthrough, agreed that the armored forces moving north be halted so that they could be repaired and refurbished for the advance southward against the new front Weygand was building up.[18] The first thought also was that the soggy, canal-crossed terrain of Flanders was inappropriate for tanks, many of them worn down by the prior movement and fighting. The destruction of the cut-off Allied forces could more easily be left to the German air force, which threw itself into this task with abandon.[19] In practice, however, poor weather delayed Luftwaffe employment, and then the Royal Air

Force—here based on its home airports—was able to intervene effectively in the battle. The German air force initially believed that it was succeeding in its efforts,[20] but this proved to be an erroneous assessment. A renewed push north by the Germans ordered on May 26 meant a second reversal in direction for the German armor and could not be immediately implemented. Hitler was confident that few of the British would escape[21]—the later suggestion that he hoped that the British might be encouraged to make peace by being allowed to get away is a fabrication—but his confidence was misplaced. A check was administered to the German air force which lost heavily in the fighting over the beaches;[22] the political import of the Dunkirk evacuation will be examined subsequently.

The French, who had effectively lost a large proportion of their best units in the north, now attempted to establish and maintain a new defensive line across France. Weygand's sole hope was that his weakened forces could hold the Germans until reinforcements were available to strengthen his lines; reinforcements which could only come from the evacuated northern units once they had been refitted in England. For a few days in early June this might have appeared to be the direction of developments. The renewed German offensive, launched on June 5, was briefly held; while General Brooke, the evacuated former commander of the British II Corps, had been ordered to France via Cherbourg to organize and command a new British Expeditionary Force, which would combine those British and Canadian forces previously south of the German breakthrough with units to be returned to the continent from the United Kingdom.[23]

All this was, however, a play with shadows. In severe fighting, the Germans broke through the French front, overwhelming whatever resistance some French units still put up. On June 14 German troops entered Paris; on the same day they broke into the Maginot Line. The French army was in a rapid process of disintegration, and General Brooke, instead of commanding a new British Expeditionary Force, was organizing a second evacuation of British troops. As German units raced rather than slogged through France, the real question was whether or not the French government would fight on from the French empire and whether or not the British would fight on from the home islands if possible or from the British empire if necessary?

The superficial appearance of a war ending in German victory moved other countries to act, or begin to act, even before these questions had been definitely answered. Italy had stood aside in the fall of 1939, and the Italian government had toyed with the idea of helping negotiate a compromise peace for a moment after the defeat of Poland. But then, in spite of irritation over the German–Soviet agreement and the resulting German support of Russia in the latter's attack on Finland, Mussolini had returned to his basically pro-German policy. On March 18 Hitler and Mussolini held a meeting at the Brenner Pass near the border, in which they reconfirmed their friendship and explained their respective policies to each other. Hitler pointed out that he had moved in the fall of 1939 since waiting would only have provided Britain and France more time to rearm; Mussolini set forth the situation of Italy which made it impossible for her to sustain a long war. He would be ready to enter in three to four months but only if the German offensive in the West was successful.[24] Hitler returned to Germany enthusiastic about Mussolini,[25] and, anticipating a great victory for the planned German offensive, now assumed that Italy would join the attack on France. In the interim, he kept Mussolini informed about the invasion of Denmark and Norway, had his ambassadors in Rome and Moscow work on repairing the rift in Italian–Soviet relations (with Soviet encouragement),[26] and made sure that there were no Italian missteps in the Balkans which might cause difficulties there at a time when Germany had her forces concentrated for the offensive in the West.[27]

As that offensive got under way, Hitler kept an increasingly enthusiastic Mussolini up to date about the progress of operations. In a conversation that took place between Germany's Scandinavian and Western offensives Mussolini had rejected as absurd the notion that a German victory in Europe might subject Italy to German hegemony,[28] and he now turned aside all approaches and appeals from France, England and the United States to stay out of the war.[29] In view of his contempt for the democracies, the Italian leader could not conceive of any extended hostilities once the main French forces had been defeated by Germany. Accordingly he planned to enter the war formally as soon as this issue was clear but *without* making sure that his military leaders had made any plans and preparations for action.[30] Italy accordingly joined the war formally on June 10 but made no serious moves to attack French or British positions anywhere, an omission that was to prove costly indeed for Italy and her German ally.[31] Until the string of Italian defeats began in the late summer of 1940, the only memorable aspect of her entrance into the war was the famous comment of President Roosevelt: "The hand that held the dagger has struck it into the back of its neighbor."[32]

Mussolini was not the only carrier of daggers in the spring of 1940. The leader of Spain, Francisco Franco, had, like Mussolini, stood aside in the fall of 1939. Given the weakening of Spain by the terrible civil war which had ended only a few months before the outbreak of World War II, as well as the country's dependence on imported food and oil, it was understandable that Franco was exceedingly cautious, but caution in no way affected his appetite. Spain had wanted to recover Gibraltar from the British ever since its capture in 1704, but the Franco regime—with its military roots in Spain's North African empire—also looked forward to an enormous expansion of that empire at the expense of the French. The Spanish ruler's appetite even extended to portions of French Africa which had been German before World War I! All such dreams obviously could be realized only with German assistance and in the event of a total Franco-British defeat.[33]

In view of this combination of almost unlimited ambition with extremely limited resources and capabilities for their attainment, the Spanish leader followed a policy combining caution with bravado. He would cautiously assist the Germans by relatively riskless measures until the latter had won the war;[34] then with great bravado he would offer to join them provided he were promised both the assistance he needed and the loot he coveted. Until German troops actually appeared on the Spanish–French border, caution still prevailed over bravado; even the entrance of Italy into the war on June 10 did not induce Franco to follow suit. Unlike Mussolini, he preferred to have clear assurances from the Germans *before* taking the plunge.

The Spanish government warded off approaches from Britain and France—except for signs of possible surrender from the latter which were promptly passed on to Berlin. Spain also notified her demands in a general way through a press campaign that called for Gibraltar, all of Morocco, and the expansion of Spain's colony on the Guinea coast (Spanish Guinea or Rio Muni, now Equatorial Guinea).[35] Only the international zone of Tangier was actually occupied by Spanish troops on June 14 in a move unlikely to call forth dangerous complications under the circumstances.[36] But as Franco began to edge closer to war, the two firm assurances he received from Hitler were not yet enough. On June 10 Hitler promised to support Spain's claim to Gibraltar and asserted that Germany merely had economic interests in Morocco.[37] The former promise required Spain's going to war with England, if it were to be implemented; a step Franco would take only if there were greater loot to be had.[38] As for the second commitment, the Germans themselves would break it in a manner that gravely affronted the Spanish dictator. For a few weeks, the issue was still open as Spain hesitated on the brink.[39]

The Soviet Union had watched the development of the war with great care, had joined in the attack on Poland, and obtained the right to station troops in the Baltic States, but had then attacked Finland and become involved in far more serious and prolonged hostilities than anticipated. This sobering experience had made Stalin extremely cautious. The push forward in the Balkans was shelved temporarily, a steady stream of supplies was provided to Germany,[40] and the war with Finland was brought to a quick and victorious end. That war, however, left the city of Leningrad and the important port of Murmansk in greater danger than ever because now, instead of a neutral Finland which had rejected German pre-war treaty offers, there was now a Finland likely to ally herself with Germany or England to try to regain the territory lost in the March peace settlement.[41]

Under these circumstances, Stalin had been most careful to keep Germany and England out of any role in Soviet relations with Finland, using Sweden as intermediary. The German invasion of Norway was hailed by Moscow which had assisted the key German operation at Narvik.[42] Now there was no further possibility of Scandinavian complications involving the Soviet Union in a war with the Western Powers, and Germany's triumph in Norway also reduced the potential of difficulties from the British nickel-mining concession in the Petsamo area. We do not as yet know much about Soviet prior knowledge of the German plans for the offensive in the West, but the almost total denuding of Germany's eastern areas of military units can hardly have remained unnoticed. Whatever apprehensions remained were removed by the German attack of May 10; if the invasion of Norway had caused a sigh of relief in Moscow, the strike at the West was welcomed with enthusiasm.[43]

Once Germany and the Western Powers were fully engaged in major hostilities in Western Europe, the Soviet Union could resume its advance in the Baltic and Balkans without concern over either of the warring sides being able to interfere. To make sure that there was no trouble in East Asia while new steps in Europe were under way, a border settlement was worked out with the Japanese, culminating in an agreement signed on June 9. This was designed both to prepare for "positive action on our western border," as a Soviet document put it, and to encourage Japan to move south and provoke western, especially American, resistance, the latter greatly hoped for in Moscow as long as United States–Soviet relations were not harmed by too close a Soviet–Japanese alignment. While this condition could be met by looking toward the eventual signing of a neutrality pact with Japan rather than a non-aggression treaty, the "positive action" on the western border of the Soviet Union was already under way.[44]

By late May, the Soviet government was moving to implement new policies apparently decided upon as soon as the extent of Germany's victory in the West was evident. The first major troop movements to the Romanian border were being reported by May 21, and the first steps looking toward the annexation of the Baltic States were taken on May 25, with Lithuania, the country between Germany and the other two Baltic States, being dealt with first. New pressures on Finland followed soon after, and the Soviet Union also explored the possibility of utilizing its recently improved relations with Italy for further Balkan expansion.[45]

In the middle of June, after a series of ultimata, the Red Army occupied all three Baltic States, ending the independence of their peoples and arranging for their subsequent formal incorporation into the Soviet Union as Soviet Socialist Republics. The broader political framework for this had been provided in the secret agreements with Germany; but since the Red Army occupied all of Lithuania, including the small portion that was to have been taken by Germany, this left a tricky problem for future resolution. Germany's considerable economic interests in the Baltic States could be accommodated by Moscow easily enough, and the remaining people of German cultural background were allowed to leave. Moving on the Romanian and Finnish portions of the Soviet Union's western border was to prove a bit more complicated.

The earlier Soviet pressure on Romania had been relaxed during Moscow's pre-occupation with the war against Finland. In the winter months, there was a tug-of-war between the Germans and the Western Powers over petroleum deliveries from that country to Germany and Italy,[46] but Germany had the stronger hand. She could offer the Romanians arms either produced by themselves or captured from Poland; she might conceivably offer some protection against Soviet demands; and she had an obvious interest in the maintenance of an independent Romania able and willing to produce and sell oil to Germany.[47] The British and French, on the other hand, had no arms to sell, made it clear that their guarantee of 1939 did not apply against the Soviet Union,[48] and were more interested in wrecking the Romanian oil wells than in maintaining their productivity. The German victories in Western Europe in May 1940 quickly ended whatever doubts still existed in Bucharest: Germany was the obvious country to lean on. The only question was whether a reorientation of Romanian policy toward Berlin could be implemented quickly enough.

Since the Germans had promised support for Soviet claims to Bessarabia and consistently maintained that they had only economic interest in the whole area, they urged the Romanians to satisfy Soviet demands. The Romanians, however, were reluctant to take the initiative, not only because they still hoped to hold on to at least parts of Bessarabia but also because they feared that territorial concessions to the Soviet Union would immediately precipitate territorial demands from their Bulgarian and Hungarian neighbors. The initiative was taken by the Soviet Union which, in view of Germany's well-understood reliance on Romanian oil, notified Berlin of the forthcoming Soviet demands. These were to be presented in a manner calculated to be doubly shocking. Stalin demanded not only the whole of Bessarabia but in addition called for the cession of the Bukovina, a rich area previously never under Russian control.[a] Furthermore, the demand on Romania was in ultimatum form, less than two days being allowed for a response, with an invasion to be launched forthwith if Soviet demands were not complied with. If peace did break out in Western Europe, Stalin wanted to be certain that the borders of the Soviet Union had first been pushed forward as far as possible.

The Germans persuaded Moscow to limit Soviet demands to the northern portion of the Bukovina and, together with the Italians, strongly urged the Romanian government to accept the Soviet ultimatum. Blaming the Romanians for the situation in which they found themselves, the Germans saw Romania's political position as of more interest to Italy, [49] and were primarily concerned about any possibility of fighting which might endanger the productivity of the oil fields. Pressed on all sides and with no hope of support, the Romanians, who at one time appear to have seriously contemplated following the Finnish example of 1939 by fighting if the Soviets demanded more than the 1856 border, decided to give in and turn over the areas demanded by the Soviet Union. In very quick marches, the Red Army seized the territories ceded and later went on to occupy a few islands in the Danube as well. The real analogy to Finland would be that of driving Romania fully into German arms.[50]

Beyond Romania lay Bulgaria, a country which the Soviet Union

---

[a] There have been attempts to explain Soviet policy in 1939–40 as one of reclaiming the 1914 border of Russia, but neither in the Polish nor the Romanian situation did Stalin pay attention to that line. The advocates of this explanation merely reveal their ignorance of European historical geography.

had approached in the fall of 1939, but where there had also been a lull in Soviet pressure because of the Russo-Finnish war. The Germans left open their own policy toward Bulgaria if the Soviet Union demanded bases there but did not see the issue as pressing during the winter of 1939–40.[51] The Bulgarians hoped to take advantage of the obvious shifting in the European situation in the early summer of 1940 but were exercising some caution.[52] They most wanted to regain an outlet on the Aegean Sea, having lost the last portion of it after World War I; their second demand was the return of the southern Dobruja from Romania; and finally they hoped to gain portions of southern Yugoslavia. The Bulgarians preferred to resolve all this peacefully—a rather unlikely speculation—but were in any case told by the Germans that this was something they should work out with the Italians.[53]

From the perspective of the Soviet Union, however, it all looked rather different. If Bulgaria obtained *all* of the Dobruja from Romania—and it should be noted that in his conversations about Soviet agreement to Bulgarian aspirations Molotov regularly referred to the Dobruja, *not* the southern Dobruja as others did—then the Soviet Union would have a common border with Bulgaria once Bessarabia had been annexed. Simultaneous Soviet support for Bulgaria's access to the Aegean Sea would open the possibility for the Soviet Union to obtain bases on both the Black Sea and Aegean coasts of Bulgaria and thus to have bases on both sides of Turkey's European territory.[54]

These aspirations and others apparently put forward at about the same time looking toward territorial concessions on the Turkish–Soviet border, as well as calling for alterations in the terms of the convention governing the Straits into the Black Sea,[55] would, however, be blocked by German policy changes in the summer of 1940. The policy changes, to be discussed later in this chapter, also altered the role of Romania in German plans, simultaneously and similarly changing the role of Finland.

Like Romania, Finland made an effort to improve relations with Germany in the hope of obtaining support in case of Soviet moves analogous to those then being made in the Baltic States. But at first, here as in the case of Romania, the initial German reactions were only in the economic sphere, with interest focused on displacing the British controlling share of the nickel mines in the Petsamo area. As Soviet pressure on Finland revived in June 1940, the Finns stalled and simultaneously tried to appease Germany by withdrawing from the League of Nations, recognizing the puppet state of Slovakia, and accommodating the Germans on the question of nickel supplies.[56]

It is not yet clear—and will not be until relevant Soviet archives are accessible—whether the Soviet moves on Finnish diplomatic issues and domestic politics in June, July, and August of 1940 were designed as steps toward the incorporation of Finland into the Soviet Union, as Molotov subsequently described Soviet intentions in his conversation with Hitler on November 13, 1940.[57] Here, as in the case of Romania, the Germans at first concentrated exclusively on an economic issue—nickel in this case as it had been oil in the other.[58] Very soon, however, here too a fundamental change in German policy produced an entirely different situation with immediate ramifications for basic political rather than economic questions. That big shift was the German decision to attack the Soviet Union, a decision involving a dramatic revision of German policy toward both Finland and Romania, which now became prospective allies for German offensive plans. This revision in turn would have major immediate implications for German relations in the fall of 1940 with the powers involved: the Soviet Union and Italy. Before this whole complex of issues can be examined, however, it is necessary to turn back to the situation in the West and the choices made there by the French, British, and American governments.

NEW CHOICES IN FRANCE, BRITAIN, AND THE UNITED STATES

The German breaching of Weygand's new defensive line and the subsequent capture of Paris produced a major crisis in the French government. As in 1914, the government moved to Bordeaux, but unlike 1914, defeatism rather than resolution characterized many of its members. Two major differences can be seen in the longer perspective which now separates us from those two occasions. The first is the purely military one. A week after the German advance of 1914 had forced the French government to move to Bordeaux, the Allied victory in the first Battle of the Marne had given the French renewed confidence in their ability to recover from great initial defeats. In 1940, on the other hand, the days following the government's leaving Paris not only saw the capital itself seized by German troops but obvious signs that the Germans could occupy all of France's European territory; and that therefore any continuation of the war would necessarily have to be conducted from North Africa and the other French territories around the globe, using the French fleet, whatever troops were stationed and could be raised overseas or could still be evacuated, and alongside her British ally.

Such a prospect involved a second factor in which the situation would prove very different from 1914. It required a grim determination to fight on, and it was this which was most lacking.[59] There were those inside the government and those soon to join it who believed that this was an impossible and even an undesirable prospect, and who thought that there might be a place for a defeated France in a German-controlled Europe. They would under no circumstances fight on against the Germans and Italians. When British planes began to bomb Italy from French bases, they had trucks driven onto the runway.[60] In the remaining years of World War II, these men were prepared to see French forces fighting against the British, the Americans and other Frenchmen, but not against the Germans, Italians, or Japanese. Although the Germans themselves invariably rejected their approaches, as will become evident, they themselves banked on a German victory and hoped for some crumbs from Hitler's table. In this approach, a few were motivated by a sense of inevitability, more by opposition to the values of the Third Republic, most by disdain if not hatred for the British, and all by a sense of the futility of further fighting against Hitler—if the great French army could not halt the Germans, then no one could.[61]

This element was led by two men who from 1940 to 1945 symbolized a regime which came to be called after the resort which served as the seat of the new government, Vichy.[62] The famous World War I military leader, Marshal Philippe Pétain, and the Third Republic politician, Pierre Laval, formed a new Cabinet which persuaded the French Assembly to grant them full powers and which tried to extricate France from the war. In this endeavor they were opposed by a tiny number of Frenchmen of whom Charles de Gaulle, a junior general who left France for England and urged a continuation of the fight against Germany on the day after the French request for an armistice, came to be the symbol and eventual leader. The new Vichy government leaders were not deterred by their treaty promise to England not to make a separate peace with Germany, and they in fact believed that the British were likely themselves to make such a deal.

The negotiations for that French treaty with England had contributed to the development of a radical and novel idea: a permanent direct association of the two countries in some kind of a merged combined state. Originally it had been contemplated that such a union would grow out of their wartime association.[63] In the great military crisis of May–June 1940 it was suggested that this step be taken immediately; De Gaulle in particular urged the British government to take it to assist Reynaud in keeping France in the war. The British Cabinet approved the proposed union, but the French government never considered the idea seriously although it grew in part out of their own initiative.[64] A deal with a winning Hitler looked more promising than union with a losing Britain; the same day, June 16, on which the British government accepted the idea of union with France, Reynaud was replaced as Prime Minister by Pétain, who promptly asked for an armistice.

The French were encouraged to take this route in June 1940 by the shrewd maneuvering of the Germans, who saw the possible danger to themselves of continued French resistance very much more clearly than many of those now coming to power in France.[65] The Pétain government, which asked for an armistice through Spain as intermediary on June 17, was confronted by a German government which adopted a policy that combined continued rapid military advances with the offering of terms that were extremely harsh but which left open the prospect of a minimal unoccupied France. Since Hitler knew that in the absence of a German navy he could not readily seize the French colonial empire by force, and also wanted to make sure that the French navy did not join the British, he offered terms which a French government might accept.[66] He would not for now demand the French colonies—which might otherwise fight on—or the French navy—which might sail to British ports insofar as it was not already there.[67] He would, however, insist on occupation of the majority of the country, including its whole Channel and Atlantic coasts, and enormous payments which made the post-World War I reparation demands look like small change.

Hitler also insisted that the French agree to an armistice with Italy before a German–French armistice could take effect. In order to get the French to agree to this procedure and make it work, he persuaded Mussolini to limit Italian demands lest the French continue in the war or the French colonies Italy might want see that demand as a signal to defect from the homeland and join Britain. The singularly inglorious record of the Italians in what little fighting they had done on the Franco-Italian border facilitated German policy; Mussolini felt in no position to ask for what he really wanted in the way of either European or African territory.[68] He had hoped and still hoped to obtain Nice, Savoy, and Corsica in Europe, Tunisia, French Somaliland and bases on the coast of Algeria and Morocco in Africa, Syria in the Middle East, and the

French fleet; but for now he had to restrict himself to a minimal occupation zone and some demilitarization in the French colonial empire. The two armistice agreements, the Franco-German and the Franco-Italian ones, accordingly both went into effect on the night of June 24–25.[69]

In France itself and in most of the French colonial empire the war appeared to be over. The encroachments of Germany and Japan which prejudged any future settlement were only just beginning; the key point in the eyes of the Vichy leaders was to reverse the trend toward a more democratic society which had characterized pre-war France and had, in their judgement, weakened it. Perhaps the French island of Martinique in the West Indies most clearly symbolized the new system: authority was vested in a military man—in this case an admiral, all the nation's problems were blamed on the Third Republic, the officials hated Britain, the United States and de Gaulle with approximately equal vehemence. Above all, the time seemed finally to have arrived to reverse the verdict of French society on the Dreyfus case, that watershed in the recent history of the country in which equality had triumphed.[70]

At one point it looked as if others might follow the French example. The King of Belgium had remained in the country and had tried to keep the Cabinet there as well. The latter had originally left to stand by the Allies, but in late June made some attempts to contact the Germans, return to Belgium, and work out an accommodation with the Third Reich. At first the Berlin authorities observed the soundings of the Cabinet of Prime Minister Hubert Pierlot with restraint, but by the end of June Hitler had decided that all such approaches should be rejected. He had other ideas for the future of Belgium, which were likely to be hindered rather than helped by the presence of a Belgian government.[71] There are some hints in the surviving records that the Grand Duchess of Luxembourg may also have thought of returning home in some accommodation with Germany; here too the German government was determined not to be obstructed in its annexationist ambitions.[72]

Similar rejection greeted private and entirely unofficial sounding from individual Poles. A strongly pro-German Polish professor, Wladislaw Studnicki, had already been waved off in late 1939; when he tried again early in 1940, the Germans had him put in a sanatorium.[73] A more serious approach came in July 1940 from former Under Secretary of State in the Polish Foreign Ministry, Count Jan Szembek, and a former Polish military attaché in Romania, Colonel Jan Kowalewski, both clearly operating without the authorization of the Polish government-in-exile; but the Germans rejected all such approaches.[74] If there was one thing

Berlin did not want it was anything that might restrain their murderous activities in occupied Poland.

What the German government wanted was a temporary truce in the West, ending hostilities there, so that it could turn to the conquest of living space in the East. That meant not bargaining with Belgians and Poles but getting England to follow the example of France by acknowledging the totality of German victory and Allied defeat. It was exactly this, however, that the British government refused to do. Certain portions of the British official record for the critical period May–July 1940 remain closed, and it is possible that when these are opened the details of our knowledge of British policy will change; but it would appear that much of the closed material concerns the antics of the Duke of Windsor—which will be reviewed presently—and that the currently available information is entirely adequate for an understanding of the basic evolution of policy in London.[75]

As the collapsing situation in France became apparent to London, the possibility of Britain's having to fight on by herself rose as the one clear image out of the fog of confusion and disaster on the continent. Having begun to face the possibility of a French collapse on May 17, the Cabinet received on May 25 a full report from the Chiefs of Staff Committee on "British strategy in a certain eventuality," the latter phrase a polite circumlocution for France's defection.[76] While asserting that Britain could continue to fight only if she had the support of the United States, the British Chiefs of Staff argued that the way to victory would be in combining bombing of Germany and German-controlled Europe with a blockade as vigorous as Britain could make it and the raising of revolts against the Germans as their hold was weakened by bombing and blockade. Here was the outline for Britain's strategy for victory, a strategy Churchill made his own with that combination of enthusiasm, determination, and inventiveness that was peculiarly his.

For a few days, primarily May 26 and 27, the Cabinet canvassed the possibility of considering any reasonable terms which preserved the independence of the United Kingdom that Hitler might offer; but it was not expected that such an offer would really be made, and even the concept that any proposals from Germany could be looked at was dropped in the immediately following days. I read the evidence as showing that only until it became obvious, as it did by May 28 and 29, that substantial numbers of the British Expeditionary Force could be extricated from the disaster on the continent, was there any willingness even to think about the possibility of peace. As evacuation became a reality, and it thus appeared possible to organize some defense of the home islands, all thought of a compromise vanished.[77] And in this resolve, the overwhelming majority of the population was clearly behind the government.

Very quickly the emphasis shifted. A major effort was made to try to insist with the French on conditions for relieving them from their treaty promise not to make a separate peace. While most of these conditions were not met, the emphasis in them was on practical measures to assist Britain in continuing the war or at least not hindering her.[78] In these last-minute salvage operations, special attention was given to the fate of gold reserves, a subject on which the British were very sensitive in view of Germany's having gotten a large part of Czechoslovakia's gold.[79] British success in protecting the gold of her allies was limited—the Vichy authorities would transport the Belgian gold reserves from Dakar in French West Africa back to the continent for delivery to the Nazis. But the British government moved quickly and decisively on its own assets. As early as May 21 it decided to act against the contingency of German occupation of the British Isles. In late June and early July Britain's gold, foreign exchange reserves and negotiable foreign securities were shipped to Canada; within a few weeks over five billion dollars worth of bullion, bonds, and other securities crossed the Atlantic in a battleship, two cruisers and three passenger ships for deposit in vaults in Toronto and Montreal. The British war effort could now be financed from North America if necessary.[80]

By that time, the government was concentrating fully on its new strategy for continuing the struggle. With the leaders of the Conservative, Labour, and National Liberal parties all in the Cabinet, only David Lloyd George, the Liberal leader and World War I Prime Minister, remained outside. A major effort was made to include him, too, in spite of the initial reluctance of many to serve with him. But Lloyd George refused. In his country's most dire crisis, he did not respond to Churchill's plea. Chamberlain suggested that perhaps Lloyd George saw himself playing the role of the British Pétain, a speculation which Churchill thought likely.[81] It seems more plausible, however, that Lloyd George saw himself as the British Laval; the role of Pétain would be played by another person who favored a prompt peace with Germany: the Duke of Windsor.

Since his abdication in 1936, the Duke had lived mainly in France. He, and even more his wife, had displayed strong pro-German sentiments which were enthusiastically reciprocated by Hitler. Although the evidence is not entirely clear, there seems to have been a German agent in the Duke's immediate entourage, with or without the Duke's knowledge, and during the first months of the war important information passed from his blabbering through that agent to the Germans.[82] In late June the couple went to Madrid where the British ambassador, Sir Samuel Hoare, who had his hands full trying to restrain Franco from entering the war, tried to get him off the continent as quickly as possible.[83] The Germans on the other hand wanted him to stay in Spain.[84]

From the perspective of Berlin, here was the perfect prospective puppet.[85] It would be all to the good if he remained accessible in Madrid as a possible replacement for the King of England, and with the option of calling on someone willing to make peace on German terms—like Lloyd George—who could take the place of Churchill as Prime Minister.[86] The British government, however, pressured the Duke first to move to Portugal and then to accept an appointment as governor of the Bahamas, a position suitably remote and—at least for the Germans—inaccessible.[87] After an inordinate amount of waffling on the part of the Duke and Duchess and some melodramatic projects by German intelligence at the very least to keep them in Portugal, and preferably to move them back to Spain, the couple finally left for the Duke's new post a month after he had accepted it. By that time, the air attack on Great Britain had begun in a major way, and George VI soon showed by his presence in the bombed Buckingham Palace and tours of devastated areas of London that there were more important things for a King to worry about than the furnishings of a Paris apartment, which still preoccupied the Duke.

If one asks, what does this tragicomedy mean, three points deserve to be made. The least significant is that concerning the Duke himself. The evidence is clear that he seriously considered working with the Germans and, in fact, remained in contact with them for some time *after* going to the Bahamas. But he did finally follow the call to the new post and the advice of his old friend, Sir Walter Monckton, whom Churchill had sent to Lisbon to keep him from doing anything obviously foolish. More important is the light this episode sheds on British and German policy in the summer of 1940. It shows a British government determined to remove the possibility of any confusion about its continuing in the war; Churchill, who had once isolated himself in British politics by defending Edward VIII in the abdication crisis, now took the lead in pressuring the Duke into the equivalent of exile.[88] The German maneuvers, on the other hand, while giving evidence of a completely unrealistic assessment of the situation in England, do show the extent of Berlin's casting about for any possible handle to use to obtain an end to hostilities in the West.[89]

While the Germans were still imagining that they had won the war which had begun on September 1, 1939, and were making preparation for future wars in both East and West, to be reviewed subsequently, the British, who had no intention of giving up, were beginning to implement the strategy they believed necessary for eventual victory: to defend themselves, to bomb and blockade Germany and German-controlled areas, and to raise revolts against the Germans wherever possible.[90] The first necessity, clearly, was to defend the home islands if at all possible. That meant that the navy had to be in a position to defend the United Kingdom and protect the supply routes to it. In view of the almost complete absence of effective German surface naval forces in the summer of 1940, the navy could expect to be successful if it were protected against the German air force and could cope with enemy submarines. The first condition was, as we shall see, met by the Royal Air Force; the second was increasingly dependent on assistance from the United States, an issue that will also be examined. The Royal Air Force had acquitted itself well in the earlier fighting in spite of incurring heavy losses. It would now be put to another stern test of battle, and it is important to point out that it entered that battle with airplanes and the critical radar screen which had been ordered in the years when Chamberlain led the British rearmament effort. Finally, the army had to be rebuilt after the disaster on the continent so that it could cope with a German invasion.

Most critical, in the eyes of those in charge in London, were several immediate complications in each of these areas. Britain's naval situation would be catastrophically injured if the Germans were to gain control of the French navy. Concern over this question was agitating the British government by June 11, and the sailing of French warships to British ports had been Britain's absolute condition for relieving France from its promise not to make a separate peace. The French instead had agreed to armistice terms which provided for their fleet to go to metropolitan French ports, there to be demilitarized under Axis control. This opened up the possibility of their being seized by the Germans and not only replacing German losses, but, together with the Italian fleet, giving them superiority over the British. This was seen as an intolerable risk by the British government. The alternative of relying on the promises of the French naval commander, Admiral Darlan, never to let the ships fall into German hands, looked equally dangerous to Churchill, though many British naval and political leaders were prepared to accept this alternative, especially after the French battleship *Richelieu* left Dakar for France and had to be chased back by the British. The idea of tying up large parts of the British navy in watching the ships of its former ally as the Germans were preparing to invade England looked like a recipe for certain disaster. On July 3, 1940, British warships attacked the French at

Mers-el-Kebir in North Africa when the French refused to sail to British ports, demobilize, or sail to the French West Indies. Many French ships elsewhere were seized or immobilized. However distasteful this attack on an erstwhile ally, those who preferred keeping their new agreement with Germany to observing their prior treaty commitment to Britain could hardly expect greater consideration from the latter.[91]

In commenting on this sad episode in his speech of July 14, 1940, Churchill added to a general report on the war and the future of France when she would again be freed, the assertion that "we are prepared to proceed to all extremities, to endure them and to enforce them" in the continuing war against Germany.[92] That was a reference not only to the action against the French fleet which had, of course, taken place in full public view, but also the prospective battle against any invading German army. On June 15 the Chief of the Imperial General Staff, Sir John Dill, had argued for the use of poison gas against any German forces which succeeded in getting ashore and could not be immediately repulsed. After initial objections from some, Churchill obtained the agreement of the Cabinet for such use of gas on June 30.[93] This decision on the "extremities" to which the British were prepared to resort was, ironically, assumed by the Germans in their own plans for the invasion,[94] but is barely reflected in post-war accounts since those involved preferred to veil the issue in discreet silence. In any case, the Germans, though planning to land their troops with gas masks, did not have them for the thousands of horses which were to be included in the first assault waves.[95]

The British were prepared to use gas on German invaders not only if they came ashore in England, but also if they secured a lodging in Ireland.[96] As the collapse of France brought Germany to the open Atlantic Ocean, the neutrality of the Irish Free State both made the British navy's task in the Battle of the Atlantic more difficult by closing some of the nearby ports to save shipping, and simultaneously seemed to invite German invasion to a place where — as in the other recently invaded neutrals — resistance would be minimal. Furthermore, there were those in Ireland, primarily the Irish Republican Army (IRA), who preferred control of all of Ireland by the Germans to partition with the northern portion, Ulster, still a part of the United Kingdom.[97] Opposed to the government in Dublin as well as that in London, they believed, like some extreme nationalist groups in other parts of the world, that if only the Axis triumphed over the Allies all would be well for their cause. These movements never comprehended that if Germany and Italy, subsequently in alliance with Japan, could conquer Great Britain, as well as its later allies the Soviet Union and the United States, it was hardly likely that they themselves could maintain their peoples' independence against the victors.

It was precisely this point, however, which was understood by Eamon de Valera, the leader of the Irish Free State, who wanted his country to stay out of the war but preferred for England rather than Germany to win. Facing a very difficult internal situation, where a radical opposition wanted to work with the Germans to overthrow his government as well as the British administration in Ulster, and where that radical support had contacts reaching into his own government—including the general commanding one of the two Irish divisions—de Valera resisted all approaches from London.[98] In June of 1940 those approaches included an offer to negotiate an end to partition. Since the end of partition would mean, in effect, that all of Ireland would be in the war on Britain's side, de Valera refused. He asserted that Ireland would fight whomever invaded first, Germany or Britain, and ask the other for assistance; but he authorized preliminary arrangements for such assistance only with the British.[99] He passed up an opportunity for Irish unity in the summer of 1940 and again in December 1941; formal neutrality looked to him like the most practical policy for his people. The defeat of the Germans and the restraint of the Allies left Ireland both neutrality and partition.[100] The German bombing of Belfast in April of 1941 and of Dublin the following month greatly affected public opinion in the Irish Free State and probably made it easier for de Valera to make some practical concession first to the British and later also the Americans in the conduct of the war; but from his perspective, it would always remain their war.[101]

At home, the British, having decided to continue fighting before Hitler recognized that this was indeed their policy, proceeded to prepare to meet a German invasion which they anticipated he would launch even before Hitler himself recognized its necessity. The critical issue was no longer military manpower but equipment. By mid-June, there were rifles for all the one and half million regulars but not yet for the newly organized local Defense Volunteers, subsequently called the Home Guard. These were about to be loaded in the United States.[102] Heavy weapons and armored vehicles were the great need—the British Expeditionary Force had left most of its modern equipment in France. But some was coming out of the factories and some was about to arrive from the United States, at least in a trickle. The Prime Minister, who also held the new position of Minister of Defense, watched the process carefully and urged progress with zeal.[103] All would attempt to fight; Churchill's assertion, "you can always take one with you," characterized the attitude of many.[a] If worse came to worse, gas would be used on established beachheads; and while the army fought as best it could, a guerilla organization readied in secret was to operate in any portions of the United Kingdom which the Germans might overrun.[104] Beaches were mined, bridges prepared for demolition, and a variety of devices, some more and some less outlandish, was tried out. Thousands of people thought possibly dangerous were hurriedly interned.[105] Whatever the efficacy of these preparations, in retrospect they illuminate the grim determination of large numbers; at the time they took people's minds off recent disasters.

If the country could not be defended successfully, there was the possibility of doing what the Polish, Norwegian, Belgian, and Dutch governments had done and which the British had so strongly urged on the French: evacuation overseas to continue the war from Canada. This was not much discussed at the time and has left few traces in the available documentation, hardly a surprising situation given the negative impact on morale any such discussion would surely have had. In any case, the financial preparations for that contingency were secretly under way. It is understandable that continuation of the war even if the British Isles were occupied by the Germans was mentioned as a possibility to Spain, the country which was correctly thought most unlikely to join England's enemies if the war were prolonged for years.[106]

Whatever preparations could be made to meet any invasion attempt, the critical question was increasingly seen to be the ability of Britain to defend herself against the German air force. As Hitler had long seen, and as anyone looking at a map of Europe could tell, bases for the German air force in the Low Countries and northern France made it far easier to attack Great Britain, simultaneously interposing additional obstacles to any British air attack on the cities of Germany which were in any case far from British air bases.[b] Could Germany utilize her numerical advantage in the air and the proximity of her airfields to much of England to destroy the British air force and either cow or bomb or invade the country out of the war? Could the British, using their fighters and their radar screen, blunt the German assault sufficiently so that the Germans either would not risk invasion or do so under circumstances in which the odds no longer favored them?

The air battles over Dunkirk had provided a foretaste of what was to come, and though the Royal Air Force had checked the Luftwaffe, it

---

[a] As a boy in England at the time, I recall this comment being repeated by our school teachers in regard to the hunting rifles lent them by the headmaster for their service in the Home Guard.

[b] The Germans could also strike at Britain by air from bases in Norway, but distance as well as weather and supply problems combined to make this a lesser threat.

too had suffered heavy losses there as well as in the preceding and subsequent battles over the continent. Now there was considerable preliminary skirmishing as the German government faced the implications of at least some continuation of hostilities, reorganized and reorientated the Luftwaffe toward operations primarily against England rather than France, and began to test the British defenses.[107] The Commander-in-Chief of the German air force, Hermann Göring, was confident that his planes could crush the Royal Air Force in about five weeks; most of the German air force high command shared these optimistic expectations. The formations, ground support system, and the aircraft industry of Britain would all be attacked.[108]

In the event, British defenses were sorely tried but successful. In preliminary skirmishes during June, July, and the first weeks of August, both sides suffered heavy losses. When the Germans stepped up the pace in mid-August, losses on both sides increased; but the British were more successful in replacing their losses, in part because British fighter production was by this time higher than Germany's. It was, in any case, becoming evident that the British were indeed holding on and that the attacks were not even close to their aim. The concentration of Luftwaffe attacks on the airport and radar control facilities inflicted great damage and strained the resources of Fighter Command, but in the battle of attrition that was developing, the British were at the very least holding their own.

At the end of August, the Germans changed their air strategy. It had originally been their intention to wait with a massive terror bombing of London until the invasion was to be launched. What slight evidence we have suggests that Hitler originally thought of a "Rotterdam"-type operation which would cause the people of London to flee the city and block the roads just as German troops were about to land.[109] When a large number of German airplanes bombed London on August 24, the British replied with attacks on Berlin.[110] Though on a small scale, the British air raid, and the ones which followed when the weather allowed, led Hitler to order mass bombing of London to begin forthwith. Always sensitive to attitudes on the home front—given his belief in the stab-in-the-back as reality, not legend—he announced that London would be destroyed.[111] Early in September, the Luftwaffe shifted from attacking the sector stations of the Royal Air Force to a massive series of attacks on London.[112]

The attacks on the British capital and other cities, though causing great damage and numerous casualties, exposed the Luftwaffe to great losses while allowing the RAF to rebuild its support system. When, in response to the heavy losses in daylight raids the Germans shifted to night bombing, their losses dropped, but so did their effectiveness.[113] The British fighter defenses had held in daytime and though they were at that time essentially ineffective at night, this made no difference to the prospect of invasion which would have had to come in daylight. Only if the British public broke could such air raids accomplish their main objective. The panic Berlin expected did not occur. In the face of a resolute British public—buoyed up by then by the obvious inability of the Germans to launch an invasion—the Blitz, as it was called, failed.[a] Rallied by a united government, the people suffered but held firm. A few in the government, but certainly not the public, knew that British air power was being assisted by the first important decrypts of German air force machine code messages, decodes which also helped them understand and begin to counter the new German beacon system designed to help the bombers find target cities.[114]

The British government had begun to work out its offensive projects for winning the war long before it became obvious in the fall of 1940 that their defense against the German onslaught would be successful. As previously described, it would combine a massive bombing of a block-aded German-occupied Europe with efforts to stir up revolts against Nazi rule until the whole system came crashing down. There was here an analysis based on a British version of the German stab-in-the-back legend; Germany had been throttled, not defeated in World War I, and the resistance forces might now play the part originally to have been played by the French army: to hold and wear down the Germans until bombing, blockade and revolts brought them down without the massive armies the British did not have. Whether or not such a strategy would in fact have been effective will never be known, but the decisions made in London to implement it had their impact on the course and nature of the War.

Recognition of the fact that Britain by herself could never field the size of army needed to defeat the German army was behind the development of the British strategy and the allocation of resources to its implementation. The Special Operations Executive, the SOE, was organized in the summer of 1940 in order, as Churchill put it, "to set Europe ablaze." In the following years, it sent agents into occupied Europe, attempted to arrange arms deliveries to resistance forces, and in every other way tried to make life difficult for the German occupiers.[115] Local revolts were expected to increase over time; and eventually the disruption created by bombing, revolts, and the impact of blockade would make it possible for small British units to assist the conquered people of Europe

---

[a] The victor of the Battle of Britain, Air Chief Marshal Sir Hugh Dowding, was promptly dismissed. The subject awaits a full scholarly investigation.

in regaining their independence. British faith in the possibilities of European resistance organizations seems preposterously exaggerated in retrospect, but few then realized how solid a hold the Germans would acquire.

Even the Germans themselves might be expected to share in the process of revolt. The British government had by the summer of 1940 given up on those internal opponents of Hitler who had so often expressed their opposition before the war and in the winter of 1939–40. All they had done, it seemed, was whisper conspiracy and then carry out Hitler's policies of invading neutrals with enthusiasm and efficiency. Churchill, it must be remembered, had been in the government which received the messages that if Great Britain would promise to allow Germany to keep Hitler's loot—or at least most of it—the military would topple him. He would hark back to that experience when approaches from German opponents of Hitler reached London in later years. It was in this context that the British turned for a while to the rather unlikely idea of getting the dissident Nazi Otto Strasser to raise a revolt within Germany against both Hitler and the old elites cooperating with him; nothing came of it all, but it reflects the thinking of a government that hoped someday to find successor regimes in all of Nationalist Socialist controlled Europe.[116]

While the imposition of Nazi rule was believed likely to create conditions for anti-German revolts in the occupied areas, those conditions would be further exacerbated not only by the sabotage SOE would hopefully organize, but also by the impact of the blockade and bombing. Enforcement of economic warfare measures was believed likely to strain the German war economy and the situation in German-occupied Europe to a vastly greater extent than turned out to be the case, in part because of the basic misassessment of the German economy previously referred to. There was, furthermore, an even more hopelessly inaccurate perception of what could be accomplished by bombing. Not until 1942 was some degree of realism injected into the assessment of the possible effectiveness of bomber operations against Germany; but what must be recognized, if the subsequent course of the war in Europe is to be understood, is that in the summer of 1940 and for considerable time thereafter the bombing offensive looked like and in fact was the only practical way for Britain to strike at the Germans. The German invasion preparations could be and were interfered with by attacks on the port facilities from which any invasion might be launched as well as on the ships being gathered there for the purpose. But beyond that essentially defensive project lay the offensive one of attacking German and German-controlled industries and cities. And that meant a major commitment of material and human resources to the building up of Bomber

Command, the British strategic air force. The impetus given to this program by Churchill in the summer of 1940 helped define the British effort until the end of the war.

In the midst of these preparations to defend themselves against invasion and destroy German control of Europe by blockade, bombing, subversion, and the eventual return of small contingents of troops, the British government was not interested in checking out some vague peace soundings coming out of Germany. Churchill was willing to use the theoretical possibility of any successor government handing the British fleet over to Germany as a means of pressuring the United States into providing more aid to stave off a German victory,[117] and some in the British diplomatic service suggested a somewhat similar scare tactic of warning of a possible Anglo-German peace to awaken the Soviet Union to the dangers facing them in their continued support of Germany.[118] The record shows, however, that the government was not interested in exploring any possibilities of a negotiated peace, the assumption being that no terms offered by Germany would be acceptable — and that any acceptable terms could not be trusted.[119]

By the time Hitler made a public gesture, suggesting on July 19 that England should call off the war, the government in London had long passed beyond considering such possibilities, and it was left to Lord Halifax to reply with a public rejection.[120] Hitler's assertions in his speech that the Allies had been about to invade Holland and Belgium, that the British had bombed Freiburg, and that they should now simply leave him with his conquests were not likely to inspire confidence in a government which knew that he was lying.[121] Hitler made fun of the British government's intention to continue the war from Canada if necessary, noting that the British population would then be left behind to face the harsh realities of war. He refrained from explaining his government's intention of deporting the male population aged 17–45 to the continent, but people and government in England had some understanding of the nature of Hitler's "generosity" without needing to have it spelled out.[122]

In holding on, the British looked for support to the United States. They would need weapons made in the United States, and they faced the early exhaustion of the financial resources needed to pay for them,[123] a process necessarily speeded up both by London's taking over the French contracts in America and any increasing deliveries of American arms. The United States was neutral, though most of its people were sympathetic to the Allied cause. There was some talk of improving German–American relations again on both sides in early 1940, but nothing came of the idea of returning the ambassadors who had been recalled in November 1938, when the

United States reacted against the anti-Jewish violence in Germany.[124] The ideological differences were too great.

Hitler continued to think the United States as of no importance, a view reinforced by the German military attaché in the United States, General Friedrich von Bötticher, whose misassessments of America reinforced Hitler's own.[125] For Hitler, as for all who believed that Germany had been defeated in World War I because of the stab-in-the-back by the German home front, it was America's military role in assuring Allied victory which was the legend. To cite only one example from the spring of 1940, Hitler was quite certain that the United States could never reach the production goals for airplanes set by the President, production goals which were to be surpassed two years later.[126]

A critical question which the Americans faced in 1940 was the Presidential election scheduled for that year. Roosevelt was inclined not to run; he preferred to return to Hyde Park, and the traditions of the country were strongly against any third-term candidacy. His neighbor, close associate, and Secretary of the Treasury, Henry Morgenthau, was certain that the President would not run and did not change his mind until May or June under the impact of the German conquests in northern and Western Europe.[127] Roosevelt wavered literally until the last moment;[128] he appears to have veered reluctantly but steadily in the direction of running again. Modifying his own traditional exuberant partisanship, he tried to create something of a coalition government. Simultaneously with his breach of the "no third term" tradition, he broke with the established party context for the highest offices. He tried to get Alf Landon, his Republican opponent in the last election, to join the government; and when that failed, on June 19 took Frank Knox, the Republican vice-Presidential candidate of 1936, into the Cabinet as Secretary of the Navy. At the same time he recruited the last Republican Secretary of State, Henry Stimson, to be Secretary of War (who in turn secured another Republican, Robert Patterson, as Assistant Secretary); and soon after Roosevelt brought in an additional prominent Republican, William Donovan, for special assignments which would eventuate in his heading the Office of Strategic Services.[129] It was hardly a coalition government like the one the British had formed six weeks earlier, but it was the closest thing to it in the history of the United States before or since.

These unprecedented developments did not, of course, end the political struggle in the United States during an election year. The German government intervened into that struggle in a way and to an extent that was also probably unprecedented. In addition to sending espionage and sabotage agents on a scale large enough to cause trouble in German–American relations but never remotely adequate either for the collection of much intelligence or the carrying out of substantial sabotage, the German government tried very hard to sway the election.[130] Many of the details of this major intervention by a foreign power into the American electoral process remain unclear – the recipients of German money as well as their German paymasters were understandably reticent – but there is enough evidence to show that the effort was on a vast scale.[131] The hope clearly was that Roosevelt's defeat would facilitate lulling the American people while Germany consolidated her hold on much of the rest of the world and, as will be discussed presently, prepared for war against the United States. The invasion of a string of neutrals, however, served to undermine the work of German and isolationist propagandists in the spring and summer; dramatic reports to the American public on the bombing of British cities in the fall and winter had similar effects. As German actions had propelled Roosevelt into running once more, so they contributed to the decision of the majority of American voters in returning him to office.

From that office, the President could see dangers on the outside and the stark remains of apathy on the inside.[132] Roosevelt had lived in Germany for years in his youth and recalled those experiences as he watched developments in 1940.[133] The assault on one neutral country after another suggested that there was no limit to German ambitions; the defeat of France and the threatening defeat of England opened up the darkest prospects. From the French colonial empire in Africa – now open to penetration by the Axis – there seemed to be a major threat to Latin America, especially those countries with large numbers of settlers from Germany.[134] Suppose Germany began to seize islands in the Atlantic as she had seized Norway? A new framework of measures would be needed for the defense of the Western Hemisphere.[135] But what to defend with?

The armed forces of the United States had been neglected in the 1920s and reduced further in the 1930s. There had been some new naval construction ordered over the objections of the isolationists, but otherwise the picture was grim. What efforts the administration made to increase preparedness were met by skepticism in the Congress – on April 3, 1940, the House Appropriations Committee cut the armed forces budget by almost 10 percent, eliminating two-thirds of the 166 planes to be ordered![136] When the Germans struck in the West, the United States army could field fewer than a third the number of divisions Belgium put in the field; there were all of 150 fighters and 50 heavy bombers in the army air force.[137] Under the impact of the German blows, the country began to wake up. Army Chief-of-Staff George C. Marshall enlisted Morgenthau's help for building up a major army with a President inclined to look toward the navy, his old favorite, and for a vast increase in aircraft production.[138] The Congress now hastened to vote enormous sums of money as soon as they were asked for. The army and the army air force were both now to be built up. As long as it was assumed that the country need face only one possible major enemy at a time, a one-ocean navy which could be moved when necessary from the Atlantic to the Pacific via the Panama Canal would do; with the collapse of Britain seen as possible, the country would need a "two-ocean navy," since dangers could be simultaneous. In July the bill to create such a navy easily passed the Congress.[139] Signed by the President on July 19, it authorized the construction of 1,325,000 tons of warships. By far the largest such increase in the country's history, this meant roughly doubling the nation's fleet, and with modern ships at that.

Ironically, that naval buildup confronted Japan with a dilemma it chose to resolve by going to war with the United States. In the 1920s the extremist elements in Japan had been upset over the Washington Naval limitation Treaty of 1922 which restricted the number of Japanese capital ships to three-fifths that of the United States. What they failed to realize until after they had insisted on the abrogation of those limits was that they operated to restrict *American* construction far more. Once the United States decided to build, it could easily outbuild Japan not 5 to 3 but, if the Congress and President agreed it was necessary, 10 to 3 or 20 to 3 or 30 to 3. From the summer of 1940 on, the Japanese had to reckon with the fact that the fleet being built by the United States would some day be completed, that their own limited and strained resources precluded any prospect of matching such a building program, and that they would be left hopelessly behind. If therefore they did not turn to the offensive against the United States soon, their opportunity to do so was certain to vanish.

The long-term implications of the American naval buildup for Japan will be reviewed subsequently; here, in discussing the early months of 1940 it must be noted that the United States was very conscious of its vulnerability at the time and tried hard to discourage the Japanese from adventures. The President repeatedly restrained those in the administration who wanted to take a harder line with Japan. As he made clear to Cordell Hull in December 1939 as the expiration of the Japanese–United States trade agreement approached, Japan should not be pushed too hard.[140] He hoped to provide Japan with incentives for restraint, letting the treaty expire in January and planning only the most limited—and practically insignificant—restrictions on Japanese purchases of critical materials in the United States when the six months termination period ended in July.[141] Japan was on notice: the United States would end its most important commitment in East Asia, control of the Philippines, in 1946 in accordance with legislation passed and signed years before,[142] but Japan had best be cautious in the interim and would have no choice thereafter. It would all look very different from Tokyo, especially to those who kept their eyes and minds closed.

More immediate to Roosevelt's concern than these distant prospects was the rapidly developing situation in Western Europe. And it was to enable the United States to devote attention to it that he had insisted on a cautious position toward Japan. Since the preceding October, the President had been receiving periodic comments and reports from Winston Churchill, then still First Lord of the Admiralty. This contact, known to and approved by the Cabinet in London,[143] was expanded after Churchill became Prime Minister in May. It would provide a major avenue of direct communication between the two leaders until Roosevelt's death in 1945, and it came to play a significant role in the development of Anglo-American relations. In the critical days of 1940, it was supplemented by daily and occasionally twice daily secret reports which Churchill had the British ambassador in Washington, Lord Lothian, hand to the President beginning on May 19. On May 25 the ambassador by mistake left the original British embassy document at the White House along with the President's copy. It now rests among the papers at Hyde Park, mute testimony to the anxiety of days when the whole world seemed to be collapsing. Five days later, Lord Lothian added to that day's report the handwritten postscript that he had just heard that up to 5:30 that morning 180,000 troops had been evacuated from Dunkirk. On July 4, the ambassador's handwritten addition noted "that Winston Churchill has taken the action in regard to the French fleet which we discussed and you approved."[144]

In the midst of the crisis created by the German victories, the United States found herself temporarily cut off from her own diplomatic service by the discovery that diplomatic codes had been compromised by a massive leak in the London embassy. Tyler Kent, a code clerk there, had taken some 1500 coded telegrams as well as duplicate keys to the code and index rooms and had apparently made these available to individuals in a spy ring run by Italy, penetrated by the Soviet Union, and also connected to the Germans. Kent claimed that his actions were motivated by a desire to keep the United States out of war.

All the details and implications of this security disaster have not yet been clarified; it is clear that American codes had been compromised, certainly to the Italians and Soviets and probably also to the Germans, that a British Member of Parliament, Captain Ramsey, was involved in the affair, and that numerous members of the spy ring went to jail. President Roosevelt had Kent's diplomatic immunity lifted, ordered more careful FBI supervision of isolationists in the United States, and reduced his reliance on State Department communications.[145] The hemorrhage of American secrets was only partly plugged; high-ranking officers in Washington who disapproved of the President's policies provided secret information to one of his key domestic isolationist opponents, Senator Burton K. Wheeler, to show that there was no danger to the United States in June 1940, and in December 1941 would leak the American victory program. British officers had once given Churchill inside information on the British and German air force which he could use in Parliament to urge rearmament; analogous steps taken in the United States were designed with the opposite purpose in mind.

The most immediate and difficult problem facing Roosevelt was whether and how much to assist Britain in the critical summer months. The United States was itself desperately short of weapons and warships; did it make sense to sell weapons which might be lost as quickly as the planes sent to France and to transfer ships which might be sunk in a hopeless cause or, worse still, end up in German hands, perhaps manned by the crews of German destroyers lost in the Norwegian campaign? Was not the first priority the rebuilding of America's own forces and, in view of the dangers perceived there, the defense of Latin America? Here was a series of conundrums as fateful as they were difficult to resolve. Complicating their resolution were the political angles. What would the American people — as voters — say about a President who overruled his military advisors to send weapons to a losing cause, thus leaving American troops stripped of arms to face a hostile world? How could warships be legally transferred to a warring power in the face of the needs of America's own navy, a strong contingent of isolationist opponents in the Congress, and a public that had for years been subjected to a barrage of attacks on the President asserting that he had dictatorial tendencies?

With a combination of caution, daring, and political shrewdness, Roosevelt threaded his way through these complications.[146] He decided that some World War I weapons should be sent to England; the first large shipment began to move on June 24.[147] Some had been shipped earlier and more would follow. Clearly such weapons could help arm the Home Guard and replace at least a fraction of the artillery the British army had lost on the continent.[148] It would encourage the British to hold out—a subject on which there was as yet not great confidence in Washington—but without inordinate cost to American defense. The provision of destroyers to the British navy was a far more difficult matter. The British desperately needed these both to protect shipping and to relieve warships to cope with any invasion attempt. Churchill repeatedly asked for over-age United States World War I destroyers to be turned over, and Lord Lothian reinforced this pressure.[149]

But could destroyers be spared, could they be legally transferred, and would they not perhaps fall into German hands? The British attack on the French fleet was certainly in part calculated to show the Americans that England intended to fight on. The President also insisted on assurances from London against Washington's greatest nightmare: that the British fleet might be handed over to Germany. The legal barriers to a destroyer transfer, which weighed heavily with the President,[150] were dealt with by a double approach. There appeared, at least to some, to be a legitimate procedure and, far more important, the destroyers came to be traded for bases instead. Lord Lothian early saw the necessity for Britain making naval bases in its Western Hemisphere possessions available to the United States on a 99–year lease basis; and a reluctant Churchill eventually came around on this point, solving British susceptibilities by turning over two bases as a free gift in addition to the five exchanged for 50 destroyers.[151] Furthermore, the whole transfer was closely associated with an agreement for joint defense between Canada and the United States, a subject on which United States opinion was more willing to be receptive.[152] As Roosevelt saw these issues being resolved in a way that involved great political risks at home but with a Britain appearing to have at least some chance of holding on, agreement was reached and the destroyers reactivated for transfer.[153]

This exchange had symbolic as well as practical significance. As the destroyers (and some smaller ships) began to join the British navy, and as American forces began to develop the new bases, the two powers were obviously and publicly associated in a common defense. Clearly the American government was now gambling on Britain's survival, had put aside all thoughts of urging a compromise peace,[154] and would build up its own defences alongside a program of support for Great Britain.

It is not a coincidence that the public controversy in the United States over the destroyers for bases deal was immediately followed by an even more heated debate over the proposal for the country's first peacetime draft. In the fall of 1940 the United States began a first serious effort to build up its military forces, a project that took years to implement, but the great German victories had provided the impetus for starting it. The United States–Canadian agreement made it clear that if the British government ever did have to move to Canada, there at least it could count on United States support against the Axis. Already in July 1940, President Roosevelt had also initiated the development of a chain of airfields which would make it possible to fly airplanes from the United States to Latin America and later across the South Atlantic to connect with the Takoradi air route from the British Gold Coast (now Ghana) to Egypt and the theater of war in the Eastern Mediterranean.[155] The President had ordered an investigation of the possibility of developing atomic weapons in the fall of 1939; that program would not acquire the Belgian stocks of uranium until September 1942 (using Canadian ore in the interim), but the uranium itself was already stored in the United States.[156] A whole host of new initiatives was under way; they would take years to become effective, but the critical decisions date to the summer of 1940.

The American supplies that were beginning to move across the Atlantic in slowly greater volume had to be paid for out of Britain's dwindling financial resources and carried on ocean routes threatened by German submarines. Here were problems for the future; but the present looked faintly better for Britain. The United States could see the cliffs of Dover as important to its defense. In the great wars against continental opponents of the past—the Spain of Phillip II, the France of Louis XIV and of Napoleon—the British had fought by combining a substantial navy with small land forces and extensive financial support for continental allies. In World War I, Britain fielded a huge land army in addition to providing a big navy, a large air force, and massive financing of her allies. Now there were no continental allies, there was no large army, and her financial resources were not even adequate for her own war effort. It would remain to be seen whether the United States would do financially for Britain what the latter had so often done for her own allies in past conflicts.

If the support of the United States was increasingly a possibility but of only remote effectiveness, what about a revived France—or French colonial empire—and the Soviet Union? General de Gaulle tried to rally Frenchmen, especially in the French colonial empire, to the continued war. He was, however, greatly hindered in this endeavor by three factors over which he had no control. The first was his own status in the eyes of other Frenchmen. Unlike Marshal Pétain, who was then a revered leader with an established reputation, de Gaulle was as yet a practically unknown officer who had held neither high command nor high civilian office. His name later became a household word, but when he broadcast in the name of a French National Committee on June 23, that was decidedly not the case. He was, or put on the air of being, certain of his destiny; few others were. Secondly, the defeatist attitudes of most Frenchmen were, if anything, reinforced by the very step the British government took ten days later to prevent the French fleet from being handed over to or seized by the Germans. The same action which reassured the Americans that the British were in the war to stay was not likely to encourage Frenchmen to join them.

Finally, the authorities in the French colonial territories were not only traditionally anti-British in their orientation, but they had acquired the *idée fixe* that the British only hoped to seize parts of the French colonial empire for themselves. This fear, not held by the officials in the Dutch and Belgian colonial empires, restrained most from siding with what they perceived as the main enemy of France overseas, an attitude reinforced by the restraint Germany imposed on Italy in the 1940 armistice negotiations. It is hardly a coincidence that the one portion of the French colonial empire in which a serious movement for a break with Vichy and a return to the war developed in 1940 was that part where the local officials had good reason to expect a German claim to the land.

Before World War I, a major German colonial possession had been the Cameroons in West Africa. After the war, a slice had been turned over as a mandate to the adjacent British colony of Nigeria, but the bulk had been assigned as a mandate to France. The French, however, had turned over to their other colonies in French Equatorial Africa those portions of the mandated territory which had been ceded to Germany as part of the settlement of the second Morocco crisis of 1911, and these parts had thereupon been reincorporated into the colonies of Chad, Gabon and the French Congo. It was in all these areas that concern—entirely justified as will be shown—about a return of German control contributed to a revolt against Vichy in late August. In a few days, officials supporting de Gaulle took over not only Chad, whose governor was sympathetic to de Gaulle, but Cameroons and the French Congo as well.[157]

An attempt in September by a joint British–Free French expedition to seize the critical port of Dakar in French West Africa as a part of an effort to obtain the defection of all or most of that area failed miserably. While the British came to blame the Free French for this disaster, the level of confusion and incompetence was sufficiently high for all participants to have a major share. The fiasco revealed a number of things: that the British were only making the barest beginnings of knowing how to launch offensive operations of the most minimal sort; that the Free French had little support among the French forces in West Africa; and that in obedience to Pétain, most officers were prepared to lead their men in fighting the British and other Frenchmen, but *not* the

Germans. This dramatic rebuff to British hopes was at least partially off-set by a further Free French success in the face of the most extreme British reluctance: from their newly acquired bases in French Equatorial Africa they completed their control of that area by the occupation of Gabon in October and November of 1940.[158]

Free French control of French Equatorial Africa had symbolic and practical impact on the further evolution of World War II. Symbolically it provided de Gaulle with a substantial territorial base and thus a sign of status. It could not yet elevate the French National Committee to the status of a government-in-exile like those of Poland, Norway, Belgium and Holland, to which Czechoslovakia was added on July 21, but it made the whole concept of a continuing fight of some kind alongside but independent of England plausible.

Fort Lamy (now called Ndjamena), the capital of Chad, was not only the symbolic center of a reviving French alternative to the regime in Vichy, but it was also a very important place on the map of Africa. The Takoradi route for air reinforcements to the Middle East, which has already been mentioned and which grew in importance in 1941 and 1942, crossed Chad with airplanes stopping at Fort Lamy on their way from Nigeria to the great supply center of Khartoum in the Sudan. At times thereafter the Germans and the Vichy French would discuss ways of recovering the areas lost to de Gaulle, but nothing substantial ever came of those talks. Hitler as well as the Vichy authorities were eager to recover the colonies which had turned to de Gaulle; but the Vichy authorities lacked the competence and Hitler the confidence in them to release sufficient French forces for such operations to make a successful effort.[159]

Furthermore, the possibility that other portions of French Africa might follow the example of the equatorial colonies and join de Gaulle thereafter restrained Germany in its dealings with Spain and Italy—any promises to either could leak out and inspire further defections that Germany could not prevent. The whole of French North and West Africa was at risk, and Hitler would look to these issues with some concern throughout the fall of 1940 and the following winter. The actual presence of a French regime under de Gaulle in control of African territories thus had a meaningful impact on the war. It was a long road from Fort Lamy, Douala, Brazzaville, and Libreville to Paris; but then, one had to start somewhere.

NEW CHOICES IN MOSCOW

Whatever the eventual role of Free French forces, they could hardly affect the situation in 1940, and their armament in any case depended on American supplies at some distant date because the African territories coming under de Gaulle's control contained neither stores of weapons nor munition factories. The situation of the Soviet Union was entirely different. It had a large army, which could be expected to be assimilating the lessons of the war with Finland, and it was thought by some in London unlikely to be overjoyed by the rapid German victory in the West.

Under these circumstances, the British government tried to persuade the Soviet leadership to shift from a pro-German to a pro-British stance in the conflict. Consideration was given to the possibility of recognizing the Soviet territorial gains in Eastern Europe as a way of seeing in them a barrier to German expansion, a view Churchill had expressed in the fall of 1939.[160] To explore this issue, the British government sent Sir Stafford Cripps to Moscow. Long strongly pro-Soviet in his views, Sir Stafford had visited the Soviet Union early in 1940 where he had met Molotov and other Soviet officials. Originally sent to negotiate a trade agreement, he was made ambassador when the Soviet Union insisted that any talks be at the ambassadorial level. Optimistic to begin with, Cripps quickly became disillusioned in Moscow, and only a personal letter from Churchill to Stalin provided an opportunity for him to take his case for better Anglo-Soviet relations to the Soviet leader. In the process, he learned from Stalin that it had been the desire to destroy the European equilibrium which had brought him together with Hitler, and that the Soviet Union had no interest in restoring the pre-war situation. Stalin professed to see no danger threatening the Soviet Union from Germany.[161]

The Soviet leader may well have been surprised at the speed with which the Germans had won in the West once he had made it possible for them to concentrate all their forces on one front, and there is evidence that he found it advisable to take some lessons from the military experience of the German campaign in France. The earlier dismantling of larger Soviet armored formations was now reversed.[162] But he not only gave the Germans a full and accurate account of his talks with Sir Stafford,[163] he provided them with far more substantial assistance. In the summer of 1940, he ordered Soviet ice breakers to make it possible for a German auxiliary cruiser to pass through the Arctic waters north of Siberia, so that it could engage in sinking British ships in the Pacific Ocean.[164] Long before this auxiliary cruiser reached the Pacific, the Soviet government was also doing its best to accelerate the shipment of important supplies to Germany both from its own stocks and from East Asia across the Transsiberian railway.[165]

The Soviet government thought itself entitled to German support for its steps in the Baltic States and Romania as long as it respected Germany's interest in Romanian oil. As for its commitment that a portion of Lithuania was to fall to Germany when that country's independence was terminated, Moscow recognized the obligation but then asked the Germans to agree to compensation for it rather than reopen the question of borders.[166] Having been promised Finland in the secret protocol of August 23, 1939, Stalin also appears to have assumed at first that he could pressure that country into new concessions. Similarly, the Soviet Union asked for territorial concessions from Turkey and made less extreme but still extensive demands of Iran.[167]

Soviet policy toward two other powers in the summer of 1940 needs to be described briefly before any effort is made to provide a general interpretation of Stalin's perception of the new world created by the great German victory. Once full diplomatic relations between the Soviet Union and Italy had been restored by an exchange of ambassadors, the Soviets tried to work out an accommodation with Italy over their respective interests in the Balkans.[168] Having been assured, in the secret agreements of August 23, 1939, that Germany had no political interests in Southeast Europe, Moscow understandably sought agreement to its own aspirations in this area from Italy. As the Italians saw Germany triumphant in North and West Europe while telling them to hold back on Italian hopes for gains in North Africa at the expense of France, they turned to Southeast Europe as the only possible alternative direction for Italian expansion. It therefore looked for a while as if these Soviet–Italian soundings would lead to an accord. They would be aborted by a German veto which derived from new German decisions still to be reviewed and which was effective because Italy's weakness made it impossible for Mussolini to act without German consent.

Simultaneously with the Soviet attempt to work out an accommodation with Italy, there was a somewhat similar effort to work out an agreement with Japan.[169] Because the Japanese, as we shall see, drew from the German victory in the West the conclusion that this was the time for them to move south and seize control of as much of Southeast Asia as possible, there was a somewhat similar evolution toward an agreement with the Soviet Union in Tokyo. The subsequent development of these negotiations and their successful conclusion in the neutrality pact of April 1941 will be discussed in a later chapter; what is important here is the point that the Soviet Union in the summer of 1940 thought it useful to explore the possibility of improving its relations and adjusting its aspirations with Italy while simultaneously freeing Japan from concern about her back door, so that she could move toward a violent confrontation with Britain and any powers aligned with the latter in Southeast

Asia, most especially the United States.[170] That in this situation an alignment with London was the last thing on Stalin's mind ought to be
obvious to the subsequent observer even if it took a long time for Sir
Stafford Cripps to grasp it at the time.[171]

What did all this imply for Soviet relations with Germany? The consolidation of Soviet control over the Baltic States, the push for a somewhat if not entirely similar control over Finland, and the thrust into the
Balkans show a determination in Moscow to reap whatever advantages
might be obtained fairly easily from the support it had given Germany.
From the perspective of Moscow, Germany had certainly profited
immensely from the German–Soviet deal; analogous accommodations
with Italy and Japan might be equally fruitful for both parties to such
arrangements. It may well have looked to Stalin that both Rome and
Tokyo would see how effectively Berlin had taken advantage of his
cooperating with Hitler in destroying the European equilibrium, and
there is solid evidence that, with or without reference to the example of
August 1939, Rome and Tokyo showed real reciprocal interest.

As for the Germans, in Soviet eyes they had not only demonstrated
their military prowess but had opened up for themselves—and with
Soviet backing—enormous possibilities for further expansion. If one seriously believed in the analysis of National Socialism then current in the
Soviet Union and among many Marxists elsewhere, which argued that
Fascism was the handmaiden of monopoly capitalism in the struggle for
markets, investments and control of raw materials abroad while
repressing the working class at home, the Germans now certainly had
every incentive to look toward the colonial empires and trade and investment connections of their defeated enemies in the West. The Germans
could now inherit from the Netherlands, Belgium, and France and even
the British, whom at this time the Soviets expected Germany to defeat
in short order if the London government did not fall in with the idea of
making a quick peace with Germany, as Moscow and Communist Parties
around the world were urging even more loudly than Berlin. As the
Soviet ambassador to London, Ivan Maisky, explained during the Battle
of Britain, the British placed the German airplane losses on one side
and their own on the other, while he placed both in one column and
added them up.[172]

Under these circumstances, from the perspective of Moscow, Germany had every incentive to maintain its good relations with the Soviet
Union—which had opened such marvellous opportunities for her—and
might in fact be willing to make even more far-reaching new arrangements for the division of yet greater spoils. Until new German–Soviet

negotiations for such happy prospects could be initiated, as they were in the fall of 1940 at least in Moscow's view of things, the best thing to do was to remain on good terms with the Third Reich. It is in this context that the accommodating attitude of the Soviet Union toward German economic and naval requests in the summer of 1940 should, I believe, be understood. All was well with German–Soviet relations and should be kept that way, and similar blessings as those derived from the prior German–Soviet agreement might now be attained by deals with Italy and Japan. Thereafter or simultaneously, a further agreement might be worked out with a Germany whose current wishes and needs should be met as far as possible. The new situation on the continent—Czecho-slovakia disappeared, Poland, Norway, Denmark, the Low Countries and France all conquered—seemed fine to Moscow. Throughout the world the Communist Parties in the Comintern called for peace; Britain in particular should accept the new situation and end hostilities.[173]

On July 17, 1940, Sir Orme Sargent, then Deputy Under-Secretary of State in the British Foreign Office, summarized his own and the Foreign Office view that the Germans and Soviets were likely to continue to cooperate though in a competitive way. The Soviet Union, like Germany, saw Britain as the ultimate enemy and would not side with her in a situation where intervention was extremely risky, while threatening Germany with closer Soviet–British relations might strengthen the Soviet bargaining position.[174] All this was quite sensible as far as it went. This analysis, however, completely overlooked exactly the same critical element which was also missing from the Soviet one. Absent from the perspective of both traditional diplomacy and Marxist–Leninist analysis was the basic reality of National Socialist ideology: the insistence on the conquest of living space for German agricultural settlers in Eastern Europe, meaning primarily the rich lands of the southern U.S.S.R. Whether or not it made sense from the perspective of traditional diplo-macy, which attributed somewhat similar even if exaggerated perspect-ives to Hitler, or whether it fit the stereotypical Marxist perception of Hitler as the tool of monopoly capitalists, the reality as we shall see was that the racial agrarian expansionism of National Socialism was a decisive motive force—*not* a propaganda gimmick—and produced German pol-icies which neither London nor Moscow understood then, and which the Soviet Union never grasped at all. Both powers would make policy and military choices in the following months on the basis of a major misassessment of German intentions.

As we will see, the British made their choices in late 1940 and early 1941 on the assumption that they still faced invasion, while the Soviets made theirs on the assumption that they did not. Before the German decisions of the summer of 1940 can be examined, however, it is necessary to look more closely at the reaction of the Japanese to the German victory in Western Europe, a reaction already referred to in connection with Soviet–Japanese relations.

NEW CHOICES IN JAPAN

For the Japanese, a high priority was their continued war with China. In November, the Nationalists had launched a winter offensive using units rehabilitated since the defeats suffered earlier in an attempt to drive back the Japanese. These operations proved very costly to Chiang Kai-shek's forces which were neither strong enough nor sufficiently equipped. After taking heavy losses, the Nationalists returned to a holding action; the Japanese held much of the coast and important inland cities, and the Chinese Communists concentrated on building up guerilla forces.[175] While maintaining their position on the mainland, the Japanese tried to prop up the puppet regime of Wang Ching-wei and toyed from time to time with schemes for negotiating with Chiang;[176] but their emphasis shifted in new directions, in part because of the stalemate in China, in part because of the dramatic German victories in Western Europe.

The Yonai government had followed the war situation in Europe with caution and had been unwilling to extend itself to help the Germans. On the contrary, Berlin had found the Japanese reluctant to help them import critical raw materials from East Asia and occasionally contrasted that reluctance with the greater cooperativeness of the Soviet Union.[177] The German offensive of May 1940 changed the situation dramatically in three ways: it raised the question of the future of the Dutch East Indies once Holland was invaded and overrun, it suggested that there might be a way for Japan to gain control of French Indo-China once metropolitan France was defeated by Germany, and it appeared to open the door to the British possessions in South and Southeast Asia, because a Britain fighting for its life in Europe could hardly defend its position in Asia.

Furthermore, a Japanese advance into Southeast Asia could—in the eyes of the Japanese—contribute to ending the war in China by cutting off the supplies Chiang was getting by railway across northern French Indo-China and by road from northern Burma. The Japanese estimated in June 1940 that 41 percent of the outside supplies reaching Chiang came through the port of Haiphong in French Indo-China, 31 percent on the Burma road, 19 percent by coastal waters, and 2 percent over the land route from the Soviet Union.[178] Accurate or not, these figures help explain how Tokyo saw the connection between a push southwards and the on-going war in China.

Already, during the winter, the military and naval authorities in Tokyo had begun their preparations for a move south. In mid-November, a new 4th Fleet for the South Seas was organized directly under Imperial Headquarters.[179] Japanese navy insistence on converting the island of Hainan into a Japanese naval base during negotiations with the puppet regime of Wang during November and December illuminates the priority given to the southern push.[180] In April, even before the German invasion of Holland, the Japanese navy called for the occupation of the Dutch East Indies and obtained a public Foreign Ministry statement of concern over the islands' fate in the European war.[181] The German invasion of Holland on May 10 immediately aroused concern in Tokyo either that the British and French might try a preventive occupation of the islands—as they did with the Dutch West Indies—or that Berlin might decide to take them over itself. The 4th Fleet was sent south so that it could seize the Dutch East Indies if so ordered, while every effort was made to persuade the Germans to leave Japan a free hand there. Though hardly enthusiastic about the rapid but belated conversion of Japan to a stance more favorable to Germany, Berlin complied with the request on May 20.[182] By then, everything was beginning to move into new channels in Tokyo.

The day after the Germans struck in the West a draft neutrality treaty between Japan and the Soviet Union was prepared in Tokyo; after discussion within the government there, it was handed to the Soviet government on July 2. If Japan was heading south, it needed peace at its back door.[183] In the period May 15–21, 1940, while the discussion of a treaty proposal was still taking place in government circles, the Japanese navy held its only major map exercise before December 7, 1941. War with the United States, Great Britain and the Netherlands, a seizure of the Dutch East Indies, and an invasion of Malaya were all part of the program. The oil of the Dutch East Indies would be needed for the war, but there would still be transportation problems even after that conquest and only enough for a year's fighting to attain victory.[184] The picture was clear enough for those who cared to look, but few were willing to do so. By this time, Admiral Yamamoto Isoroku had already begun thinking of a surprise attack on the United States fleet in Pearl Harbor as a way to start the war and shield the drive south from American interference.[185] As yet a different strategy for conducting war against the United States still dominated Japanese naval planning, but the impetus for actually going to war would be given that summer in Tokyo.

The triumph of Germany in the West brought a dramatic shift in Japanese government circles. There was enormous enthusiasm.[186] Now was the chance to pressure the French into closing the railway which carried supplies from Haiphong to Nationalist China and, soon after, to occupy the northern portion of the French possession in order to make certain of the blockade and provide a basis for further expansion. Furthermore, now was the opportunity to threaten the British that dire consequences would follow if the latter did not stop shipments from Hong Kong and close the Burma Road.[187]

The French caved in quickly, first closing the railway and then accepting Japanese occupation of northern Indo-China. Vichy France was willing to fight the British and Free French for Dakar and French West Africa but not the Japanese for Hanoi and northern French Indo-China. Faced by the Japanese demands and threats, the London authorities debated the dangerous choices before them: could they afford to antagonize Japan when mortally threatened at home; was not supplying Chiang Kai-shek one way of tying down Japan lest she fling herself directly on British territories in Asia and the South Pacific; was there any hope of American support if Japan took drastic steps? The policy which emerged was a three-months closure of the Burma Road beginning July 18, 1940. This might keep Japan quiet for a while; and by the end of that period Britain would hopefully have warded off the immediate German onslaught and have obtained greater and more obvious support from the United States—both hopes which were realized and resulted in a refusal to maintain the closure.[188]

During the days of policy debate in London, an even more important and fateful debate was under way in Tokyo. From within the army, the navy, and the diplomatic service there came strong pressures for an alliance with Germany, an attack southwards against the British, Dutch, and Americans, as well as a settlement with the Soviet Union to shield the move from the outside, and, at the same time, a new consolidation at home to provide a base inside the country for these new policies.[189] Here seemed to be the great opportunity for Japan to realize the fondest and most extravagant hopes of empire. With Germany about to defeat Britain after crushing France and the Netherlands, Japan could seize whatever she wanted, and if that also meant war with the United States, so be it. The anticipated completion of the new United States navy would end Japanese prospects of such expansion; the time to move was now.[190] The Yonai government could at the last moment substitute a diplomatic for a military approach to the Dutch East Indies,[191] but then that government was pushed aside. Emperor Hirohito, apprehensive about the possibility of war, reminded his advisors that their confident prediction of a quick settlement in China had proved sadly mistaken.[192] But the Emperor would be confronted with a new government unanimously determined on a new foreign and domestic policy, a situation in which he could only give way.

The new Prime Minister, Konoe Fumimaro, knew that his policies would not be agreeable to the Emperor. He assumed that when he took office on July 14, 1940, Hirohito would ask him to respect the constitution, avoid upheavals in the business world, and cooperate with Britain and the United States—but on all of these he himself preferred to go in new directions.[193] The man who had been Prime Minister at the beginning of the war against China four years earlier and who had pushed through the decision of January 1938 not to negotiate with Chiang Kai-shek,[194] had helped to force out the Yonai government to pursue a whole set of goals: he wanted to obtain an alliance with the Axis, still hoped to crush China, intended to launch a push to the south, and preferred to install a "new political structure" designed to transform the political system of Japan by drawing the whole population into a cohesive whole controlled by the Cabinet.[195]

In order to make certain that all members of the government were for once in agreement on the steps to be taken, Konoe held a special conference in his home. The new structure at home and the new policy abroad which combined a German alliance with a push south and agreement with the Soviet Union won the concurrence of the army and navy along with the civilian leadership represented by Konoe and his new Foreign Minister, Matsuoka Yosuke. The new course called for war with Britain and the Netherlands to seize their colonies (as well as Portugal's). Konoe still hoped to avoid war with the United States, but included a willingness to have such a war rather than abandon the great push south. He called for negotiations with Germany for an alliance and with the Soviet Union for a neutrality pact, and inaugurated the organization of the Imperial Rule Assistance Association inside Japan as a new mass mobilization of the people behind these policies. At the end of ten days of discussion, all this was officially approved at the Liaison Conference of July 27, 1940.[196]

It was assumed in these internal discussions that a Japanese push into Indo-China and especially into southern Indo-China would, because the latter pointed to new adventures against Britain and the Dutch rather than continuing the old one against China, most likely provoke the United States into economic sanctions, which in turn would lead Japan to go to war with the United States.[197] Japan needed American oil to fight the United States, and its leaders simultaneously wanted the oil and expected that their moves looking toward war with the United States would lead to its being cut off. No wonder that their confused solution to this self-imposed conundrum was to rely on using footholds that the Japanese imagined Germany and Italy had in South America "to carry out its future policies toward the United States."[198]

In the crisis created by the simultaneous threat of an invasion of Britain by the Germans and a move south by the Japanese, the governments in London and Washington decided that discretion was the better part of valor. They could place some limits on exports to Japan, but the extraordinarily confused discussions in both capitals did not and perhaps could not result in more determined policies.[199] Japan could continue to purchase American oil to stockpile for war against the United States. The minimal sanctions neither encouraged nor discouraged the Japanese. They moved forward into north Indo-China and began negotiations with Germany and Italy for a Tripartite Pact. A central figure in these steps to implement the policies agreed on during the preceding weeks was the new Foreign Minister, a bombastic and unstable individual who, because he had lived as a young man in the United States, imagined that he understood that country, and was at least for a time just the man to implement the foreign policy lines Konoe wanted: alliance with Germany and Italy, alignment with the Soviet Union, and now expansion southward as Japan had once pushed into Manchuria where Matsuoka had first made his mark.[200] As already mentioned, he found the French complaisant and the British doubtful. The Germans, once they overcame their initial hesitations growing out of past grievances, however, were enthusiastic. The new expansionist policy of Japan seemed to fit perfectly with Berlin's own new choices.

NEW CHOICES IN GERMANY

The new choices made by Germany in the summer of 1940 were perhaps more personally and directly those of Hitler than at almost any other time in his twelve years as Chancellor. The triumph in the West in its speed, apparent ease and completeness, was not only in dramatic contrast with the years of bloody slogging on the Western Front in World War I; but, as most inside the circles of Germany's leadership knew, was the product of Hitler's insistence on an offensive in the face of the doubts and hesitations of many. That its impact on the United States would doom the Third Reich to ultimate defeat was entirely beyond the comprehension of the public and the elite of Germany—the great victory over the armies of Germany's enemies elevated Hitler to an unchallengeable pinnacle of popularity and power.[201]

In this situation, Hitler's views of what to do with victory set the tone. As regards France, it meant a tactical and temporary reticence in regard to her colonies and navy in order to make a quick armistice with a remaining French government feasible, otherwise there was a risk of defection of French colonies threatened by German, Italian or Spanish colonial demands, or continued fighting by the French navy and forces in North Africa on England's side—both contingencies likely to encourage England to remain at war.[202] On the other hand, as Hitler never trusted the French, he would reject all efforts at a long-term accommodation with a new French government.[203] The efforts at collaboration in general originated from the French side and were made by those who visualized a place for their version of France in the Nazi New Order; Hitler consistently rejected these approaches, a point which became more obvious as the relations between the occupiers and the occupied developed in subsequent years.[204]

England, Hitler assumed, would acknowledge defeat and accept its ejection from any say in continental affairs. If, as became increasingly obvious, she refused to do so, heavy blows by bombing and, if needed, an invasion would bring the people—if not their government—to their senses. As previously explained, there were even hopes that an alternative government in London with a returned Edward VIII as King and Lloyd George as Prime Minister—both admiring visitors of Hitler's—might accept the junior role the Führer intended Britain to assume while he completed his immediate land conquests and prepared for those further conquests which required a huge navy.

Preparations were made for a direct attack on the United Kingdom, with a struggle for air control seen as the necessary prerequisite for invasion. Those preparations, which included the drawing up of an extensive arrest list, the appointment of a secret police chief—who would subsequently command one of the murder squads on the Eastern Front—and the establishment of internment camps on the mainland to which all adult males between the ages of 17 and 45 were to be deported, reflect an attitude of harsh hostility rather than the gracious feelings for Britain some historians ascribe to Hitler.[205]

While these direct measures against England were under way, Hitler did what he could to encourage his Italian ally to strike at the key British positions in the Near East. In June and July of 1940 he strongly urged the Italians to seize Egypt and other British-held areas in the Mediterranean and, in order to cut the lifeline of the British empire, offered German long-range planes to mine the Suez Canal from Italian bases on the island of Rhodes.[206] The Italian military leaders, who combined extreme reticence with incompetence, did not move for months, and German planes could not begin mining the Suez Canal until the following year. The fact that the first Italian–British naval engagement, that of July 9, ended badly for the Italians in spite of their having superiority in ships and the decoded text of the British orders, was to have a key long-term effect in reinforcing the inferiority complex of the Italian naval command.[207] The World War II joke that the Royal Navy lived on rum and the American navy on whiskey, but the Italians stuck to port, could be applied to Italy's admirals—though certainly not its ordinary sailors—practically from the beginning of hostilities. The concept of striking at the basis of British power by an assault on her position in the Eastern Mediterranean, however, must be accepted as an essentially realistic one, even if the attempted execution at the time of greatest opportunity for the Axis was missed by the Italians.[208] Hitler's great admiration for Mussolini misled him for a few months in the summer of 1940; he was soon awakened to the reality of Italy's war-making capabilities.

If Italy was to occupy Northeast Africa, Germany herself would acquire a vast colonial empire in Central Africa.[209] That empire was to include the former German colonies of Togo and Cameroons in West Africa as well as German East Africa, now to be joined into a huge contiguous Central African domain stretching from the South Atlantic to the Indian Ocean and rounded out by the inclusion of the British colony of Nigeria, the French colonies of Dahomey and French Equatorial Africa, the Belgian Congo, Uganda, the southern half of Kenya, and perhaps the northern portion of the Portuguese colonies of Angola and Mozambique.[210] Former German Southwest Africa (now Namibia) might either be reclaimed from the Union of South Africa in exchange for the British protectorates of Bechuanaland (Botswana), Swaziland and Basutoland (Lesotho),[211] or, alternatively, it might be left to the Union in connection with the partitioning of the Portuguese colonial empire in Africa. In either case, Germany expected to enjoy good relations with a South African state ruled in this vision by the extreme nationalist elements among those Afrikaaners who had opposed the Union's entrance into the war in 1939 and who were and remained devoted admirers of both National Socialist ideology and its German practitioners. In the 1948 elections the devotees of Nazi ideas indeed took over power in South Africa—power they wielded for decades thereafter—but of the other German colonial dreams there remain only endless files of their preparations, containing everything from strict laws against inter-racial sex to proof coins for a new currency.[212]

Another major alteration in the African colonial picture planned by the Germans was related to their projected reorganization of Europe.

That reorganization, about which more will be said shortly, was not to be limited to boundaries and economies, it was also to affect the population of the continent. First priority in the demographic restructuring of Europe was to be the removal of the Jewish population to the island of Madagascar in the Indian Ocean.[213] This island, then a portion of the French colonial empire, now the independent state of Malagasy, was to be ceded by France to Germany and its French settlers evacuated—the millions of local inhabitants were evidently expected to vanish.[a] The three to four million Jews living in the portions of Europe then controlled from Berlin would be shipped there, to be supervised by a police governor under Heinrich Himmler. Preparations for this scheme went forward in the Reich Security Main Office and the German Foreign Ministry with Hitler's approval in the summer of 1940, but the refusal of Britain to leave the war made this project as impossible of realization as that for a German colonial empire in Central Africa.[214]

Hitler had considered the removal and possible killing of Jews as a part of the war as much as the killing of the mentally ill, the elderly, and others he and many other Germans considered unworthy of life. He had tried to include the murder of vast numbers of Jews in the initial stages of the war in Poland but had run into difficulties with the military. He had then removed the military from control of occupied Poland but had postponed further action.[215] As it became obvious in the summer of 1940 that there was no immediate prospect of acquiring Madagascar as a sort of super-concentration camp for the Jews, the same project that Hitler turned to in those same weeks of the summer, the invasion of the Soviet Union, would provide a new opportunity for ending the existence of Jews in Europe as he had publicly threatened to do before he began the War.[216]

If the Jews were to disappear physically as human beings, numerous European countries were to vanish from the map as independent entities. Norway, Holland, Belgium and Luxembourg were to be absorbed by Germany,[217] Denmark could be expected to follow once Germany had won the war, and France would survive as a tiny and impotent dependency.[218] But that was not all. The German victory in the West looked like the opportunity for Germany to end the independence of some other countries as well. Since revision of the World War I peace settlement had always been a pretence, not an aim, for National Socialist policy, this looked like the right time to end the existence of another country which had been neutral in that conflict: Switzerland.

---

[a] According to the official *German* statistical annual, the *Statistische Jahrbuch für das Deutsche Reich 1941/42*, there were almost 3,800,000 inhabitants of whom about 25,000 were assumed to be French settlers.

There had been periodic instances of friction in the relations between the Third Reich and the small neutral, but the basic issue was always the existence of the latter, a small democratic state on a continent Germany intended to transform. At 1:35 a.m. on June 25, 1940, the armistice between Germany and France went into effect; a few hours later orders went out of the high command of the German army to prepare an invasion of Switzerland. In the following weeks, these plans were worked out in considerable detail, and the prospective Commander-in-Chief of the invading forces, Ritter von Leeb, who would be one of the horde promoted to the rank of Field Marshal by Hitler on July 19, personally reconnoitered the terrain.[219] The plan was to crush Swiss resistance quickly and then partition the country with Italy, Germany taking the northern four-fifths and Italy the remaining area south of a line running from Lake Geneva east.[220] Originally code-named operation "Green," the project was renamed "Christmas Tree" when the former name was applied to the planned invasion of Ireland; it was never launched as more important projects came to the fore in German planning.[221] The end of Switzerland, that pimple on the face of Europe as Hitler described it in August 1942,[222] would have to wait until Germany had defeated her European enemies.[223]

The other neutral immediately affected by the German victories of the spring of 1940 was Sweden. The German invasion of Norway, combined with the quick occupation of Denmark, dramatically altered the situation of Sweden. Now it not only controlled iron ore resources important to the German war effort but was itself practically surrounded by German forces. In the early stages of the operations in Norway, the Germans still exercised some caution in their treatment of the Swedes. They wanted no Swedish aid for the beleaguered Norwegians but, instead, to utilize the Swedish railway system themselves in order to send reinforcements to the isolated German garrison in Narvik and to evacuate the naval crews stranded there by the sinking of their ships.[224] Swedish suggestions that they themselves might occupy Narvik were turned aside; the last thing the Germans wanted was for Sweden to have its own free outlet to the Arctic Ocean.[225] Once the Germans were in control of all of Norway, they could press upon the Swedish government that view of neutrality which best suited Berlin.

German troops and supplies would cross Swedish territory practically at will; the Swedish economy would be reoriented toward Germany; and Swedish ship yards would build merchant ships and warships for the Third Reich.[226] The kind of cooperation Sweden had refused to Finland as well as to the Western Powers in the winter of 1939–40 was now accorded to the Third Reich. The key difference was the assumption in

Stockholm that refusing the democracies might bring unkind words but refusing the Germans meant more substantial dangers. In the face of German pressure, Stockholm capitulated on practically all matters; and the Germans could draw on the resources and transportation system of the country for their own war effort as long as they seemed to be winning. If they won, Sweden's nominal independence would go the way of Norway's; if they appeared to be losing, the Swedes might begin to reassert their rights.[227] German public pronouncements of their intentions to dominate the European economy and exploit all of it—including Sweden's—for their own purposes, like Minister of Economics Walter Funk's declaration of July 25, 1940, might evoke criticism in the Swedish press, but there was no substantial resistance from Stockholm until the tide of war had been turned by the exertions of others.[228]

German plans for a newly ordered Europe were being discussed in Berlin in the summer of 1940, and were accompanied by the squabbling of government and party agencies on the one hand and the grasping cupidity of German business and industrial concerns on the other; both characteristics of the internal situation of the Third Reich. Every agency had plans and every firm had hopes. Whatever the details, Germany would control everything. There would certainly be no general peace conference—Germany would impose her will in bilateral negotiations.[229] What international organizations remained were to be replaced by new ones of German devising; the International Labor Organization, for example, by an International Central Labor Office with headquarters in Berlin.[230] Italy was still seen as entitled to a special role, especially in North Africa and the Near East,[231] but the German capital would certainly be the center around which all would revolve. And such smaller satellites like the puppet state of Slovakia would have to march in lockstep with Berlin now that it was no longer necessary to treat them leniently as models of how nicely Germany could behave.[232]

The great problem for the future was the fact that the Germans had been obliged by the outbreak of war in 1939 to postpone construction of the navy needed for the war which Hitler expected to wage against the United States. The first of the battleships designed with the British navy in mind, the *Bismarck* and the *Tirpitz*, were being completed; but work on the super-battleships which were expected to outclass anything the United States might build had been halted in September 1939. Knowing that the completion of these enormous ships took years, Hitler was eager to have work on them resumed as soon as possible. On July 11, 1940, the orders to do so were agreed upon between him and the Commander-in-Chief of the navy. At a time when Hitler still had some hope that Britain might pull out of the war, he was looking forward to the contest ahead when a great blue-water navy would enable him to defeat the United States with England either conquered or allied with *either* of the two major contestants. Nothing more clearly illuminates the world-wide ambitions of the Third Reich than the decision to press forward with a vast program for constructing battleships, aircraft carriers, and other warships at a time when the war that began in September 1939 was believed to be over. Unlike some post-war German apologists and many non-German historians, Hitler recognized, and acted on the recognition, that a pre-condition for any successful war with the United States was not the selection of American beaches on which to land but the building of a navy that could project German power across the Atlantic.[233]

For the immediate conduct of submarine warfare against British shipping, the ability to use bases on the French Atlantic coast, especially Lorient, was an immediate and enormous advantage; and the Italian offer to supplement the German effort in this regard by stationing a substantial fleet of Italian submarines at Bordeaux was happily accepted.[234] But the anticipated German naval bases for future transatlantic operations involved more grandiose plans. A huge base was to be built at Trondheim in German-annexed Norway. Not merely repair and naval construction facilities would be provided there but a whole German city with at least a quarter of a million inhabitants, joined by a four-lane highway and colossal bridges directly to Germany. This enormous project—on which German workers were hard at work until March 1943— was however to be only one, if perhaps the biggest, of the bases for Germany's world-class fleet.[235]

Not only would the Germans expand the bases on the French coast at St. Nazaire and Lorient but they would hold on to the British Channel Islands which were occupied in the summer of 1940.[236] In internal affairs, this portion of the United Kingdom could eventually serve as a model for the sort of Britain Germany expected to see in the world: its Jews evacuated and murdered, the islands themselves furnished with an example of that marvellous institution of the National Socialist state, the great concentration camp fully equipped with reusable coffins and all the rest. And there was to be a major naval base. Furthermore, there would be a series of bases outside Europe to enable the German fleet to protect the routes to the country's revived and enlarged colonial empire as well as assist in the projection of its naval power across the Atlantic.

The navy proposed and Hitler very much made his own a series of projects for bases on and off the coast of Northwest Africa.[237] Included in these plans were bases to be constructed and owned by Germany not only in formerly French colonial possessions, especially the French protectorate of Morocco, but also on Portuguese and Spanish territory, in particular the Spanish Canary Islands.[238] This project, to which the German government clung rigidly in the summer and fall of 1940, is especially illuminating for our understanding of the priorities of Berlin, since the Germans sacrificed the possibility of Spanish participation in the war to it.[a]

Unlike Mussolini, who had jumped into the war at what he believed was the last minute but without prior assurances from Berlin about the realization of Italian aspirations in the forthcoming peace settlement, Spanish leader Francisco Franco had cautiously reversed the sequence. He was ready to enter the war on Germany's side, but he first wanted assurances about both the conduct of hostilities and the satisfaction of Spanish war aims. As already explained, he had told the Germans of his desire to join them in the war but had specified both the supplies he needed and the colonial expansion he wanted.[239]

The German response to Franco's offer to join in was far more tentative than later efforts from Berlin to entice Spain into the war might lead one to expect. The initial Spanish list of demands was sent to Berlin on June 19; but the response sent a week later was clearly a stalling one.[240] As some have recognized, the Germans, not the Spaniards, were holding back.[241] One contributing factor may have been the belief in Berlin at that time that the war with England was about over and Spain's help was not needed. Moreover, the extravagance of Franco's expansionist aims may well have astonished the Germans; certainly his idea of expanding Spanish Equatorial Africa (Rio Muni, now known as Equatorial Guinea) at the expense of the former and soon to be reclaimed German colony of Cameroon did not win him any friends in Berlin. When the Germans subsequently dangled colonial bait in front of the Spanish dictator to obtain his participation in the war, they always took care to evade this last request. But there was a third element which may well have contributed to the initial German reticence and which would constitute a critical element in all subsequent approaches to Franco.

When at the invitation of the Germans at the end of August formal negotiations for Spain's entrance into the war began, the Germans insisted that while Spain would certainly get Gibraltar and an expansion of Spanish Sahara (Rio de Oro) southward, French Morocco would go to Spain subject to the siting of German naval bases there, and, in

---

[a] It should be noted that the British government was making contingency plans to occupy the Cape Verde Islands and the Azores if the Germans moved into Spain and Portugal. See Smyth, *British Policy and Franco's Spain*, pp 139–54; C 8361/75/41, PRO, FO 371/24511; C 7429/13/41, FO 371/24515.

addition, the Germans would obtain a base in the Spanish Canaries. These latter demands were fiercely opposed by Franco as well as by his negotiator, Serrano Suñer, when the latter visited Berlin in September. Whatever else Franco hoped for and wanted, he saw himself as a Spanish nationalist; he would not accept territory in Morocco subject to German interference and he was under no circumstances about to yield a base on Spanish territory in the Canary Islands to Germany or any other country. The fact that the Germans were willing to forgo Spain's participation in the war rather than abandon their plans for naval bases on and off the coast of Northwest Africa surely demonstrates the centrality of this latter issue to Hitler as he looked forward to naval war with the United States.[242]

For years Hitler had been calling for an airplane capable of bombing the United States, and work on such a plane had been under way since 1937.[243] The realization of this project, however, was still not imminent in 1940, and the Germans could only push forward with it in the hope that by the time the planes were ready, refueling in the Portuguese Azores would be possible and would increase the possible bomb load. The prerequisites for war with the United States were being worked on, but it was obvious that they would take time to complete. While the preparations went forward, a project which was thought to be much simpler and capable of completion long before the huge blue-water navy and swarms of four-engined bombers had been built was to be carried out by Germany's victorious army: the invasion of the Soviet Union and the defeat of that country so that huge portions of it could be annexed and settled by German farmers, and the area's metal and oil resources harnessed to the subsequent campaign against the United States.

The whole project of crushing France and England had, after all, been undertaken only as a necessary preliminary, in Hitler's eye, to the attack in the East which would enable Germany to take the living space, the *Lebensraum*, he believed she needed. And it is too often forgotten in retrospect that in his view the campaign in the West was always expected to be the harder one. If in World War I Germany had struggled unsuccessfully in the West though victorious in the East, the fortunate willingness of the Soviet Union to assist her in winning in the West this time could make it all the easier to win in the East against inferior Slavs ruled by incompetent Jews, as Hitler believed.

Hitler's pressure for launching the great offensive in the West already in the fall of 1939 was in part due to his eagerness to get to the offensive eastwards as quickly as possible, originally in the spring or summer of 1940.[244] Circumstances previously mentioned led to a postponement of the attack in the West into the spring of 1940, a postponement which enhanced rather than dampened his desire to get to the next operation as quickly as possible. Moreover, the appearance of the Red Army in eastern Poland in September–October 1939 and the initial setbacks suffered by the Soviet Union in the Russo-Finnish war only served to reinforce Hitler's belief that the Soviet Union was incapable of defending itself.[245]

In view of this background it should not be surprising that already in mid and late May of 1940, as soon as it became clear that the German offensive in the West was going forward as quickly and successfully as Hitler could possibly hope, he began to turn his thoughts to the attack on the Soviet Union. He was beginning to discuss this project with his military associates in late May, and in June had them starting on the first preparations of plans for such an operation.[246] Initially conceived of as an offensive to be launched in the fall of 1940, the campaign was expected to last only a few weeks. If the mighty French army, which had stopped the Germans in the last war, could be crushed in six weeks and the British driven ignominiously from the continent, then victory in the East would take hardly any time at all. The concept of a "one-front" war always meant one *land* front to Hitler, so that the question of whether or not England remained in the war after the defeat of France was initially irrelevant to the timing of an attack in the East.[247]

During the latter part of July, the preliminary discussion of the new offensive coincided with the recognition that Britain would not withdraw from the war. Far from discouraging Hitler, this had the opposite effect of making him all the more determined to attack the Soviet Union. In his eyes, the British were staying in the war in expectation of the Soviet Union and United States replacing France as Britain's continental ally, something he assumed the English invariably needed. The quick destruction of the Soviet Union would not only remove one of these two hopes but would indirectly eliminate the other as well. Once Japan was reassured by the German attack on the Soviet Union against any threat to her home islands from the Pacific territories of Russia, she could strike southwards into the areas she had long coveted, and such an action would necessarily draw American attention and resources into the Pacific. The destruction of Russia, accordingly, would serve as an indirect means of forcing Britain out of the war as well as opening up the agricultural land and raw materials of the Soviet Union for German settlement and exploitation.[248]

In those same days, however, as the indirect fight against England was added to the original aims of the invasion of Russia, Hitler came to the conclusion that the attack in the East had best be launched in the early summer of 1941 rather than in the fall of 1940. Influenced it would seem by the arguments of his immediate military advisors that the transfer of German forces from the West to the East, their refitting for new operations, and the needed logistical preparations in an area of underdeveloped transportation facilities meant risking that the short campaign could not be completed victoriously before the onset of winter, Hitler had decided by the end of July that it made more sense to wait until the following year when the whole operation could be completed in one blow.[249]

Three aspects of this decision deserve additional attention. In the first place, the turn to an invasion of the Soviet Union which Hitler had communicated to his key advisors by July 31 could, of course, have been revoked by him; and since some of those in the National Socialist leadership had doubts about the decision to attack Russia, such a reversal would have met with a good deal of support within military and government circles in Germany. But quite aside from the fact that there is not the slightest evidence that Hitler ever seriously considered reversing himself on this issue, it is important to note that the decision had a whole series of immediate repercussions on German policy. As will be shown in the balance of this chapter, military and diplomatic policy was immediately and in some instances dramatically affected by the new direction embodied in the decision to attack Russia. In fact, many of the changes in German actions in the summer and fall of 1940 can only be understood if they are seen in the context of this great new plan.

Secondly, even as the preparations for the invasion of England went forward, the German belief, shared by Hitler and his associates,[250] that the Soviet Union was incapable of any effective defense, made the planned land operation in the East, in which the spectacularly victorious German army which had just smashed France would crush a Red Army that had had great difficulty defeating Finland, look very much *easier* than the risky attack across the Channel with a Royal Air Force still in the air, the British navy likely to risk all in defense of home waters, and a slowly recovering land army waiting on the far shore. When asked in August of 1944 why he had not invaded England in 1940, Hitler said he would have liked to but lacked the means. Pointing to the fact that the British and Americans had needed two years to prepare for an invasion across the same waters, he explained that he had only enough ships to get the first wave ashore and no ability to send supplies because of the British navy and also no guarantee from the air force.[251] By comparison with the risks of an invasion across the Channel, the move on land looked much more certain, and Hitler did not wish to endanger the steady sequence of victories which so enhanced his prestige and the fear which Germany inspired.

The third point which must be stressed is that both of the foregoing factors were self-reinforcing. The diplomatic steps Germany took to prepare for war with the Soviet Union would sooner or later alert and annoy the latter and thus make a prolongation of good relations with her more difficult. And, with the passage of time, the risks of invading England would grow greater: some of the German warships damaged in the Norwegian campaign would be repaired by late 1940, but by then the weather precluded a cross-Channel operation in 1940, while in 1941 Britain would have had even more time to prepare her defenses. And by that time, the fixation on loot and blood in the East was, as we shall see, so strong that any reorientation was practically inconceivable.[252]

The conclusions drawn from the new orientation of German policy in the military sphere were curiously ambivalent. On the one hand, the shift of large numbers of troops from the West to the East began with the transfer of the German 18th Army in late July.[253] Massive further redeployments were ordered in July and September. Simultaneously, the communication and supply difficulties, which had played a key role in the deferral of an attack from the fall of 1940 to the spring of 1941, were to be remedied by a program ordered on August 9 under the cover name of "Buildup East" (*Aufbau Ost*).[254] There was much discussion of alternative plans for the intended attack on Russia; in fact, there was a cavalier disregard for security in the way numerous officers were simultaneously working on operational plans. A certain lackadaisical quality was also characteristic of the general mobilization and equipment plans for the new stage of the war.

As early as February 9, 1940, Göring had ordered development stopped on new weapons not likely to be finished in 1940 or promising results in 1941.[255] While massive increases in the production of poison gas were ordered as of June 1, 1940,[256] and the furloughing of soldiers from divisions to be demobilized in the summer of 1940 was arranged so as to enable those units to be reactivated on short notice, the increases in the size of the German army structure ordered at that time were not accompanied by any massive arms buildup.[257] The number of armored units was to be increased but without any substantial acceleration in the production of tanks, and there was similarly no big buildup of the air force, which was in any case fully engaged in the war against England. And some priority had to be given to the navy and air force for that fight.[258] Certainly as the prospect of fighting in the East approached, there was some frantic last-minute effort at further buildup, but the basic belief that the Soviet Union was weak and could be hammered to bits by a few well-aimed German blows dominated the preparations as it helped inspire the decision for the attack in the East.[259]

The limited industrial resources of Germany at their relatively low level of mobilization were not, however, capable of coping simultaneously with the preparations for the new land campaign in the East and the construction of the great battleship navy. Once again—as in September 1939—these projects had to be postponed. Victory over the Soviet Union would release the necessary resources for a resumption of construction on the big ships; in the interim, Germany would concentrate at sea on the blockade of Great Britain by submarines and airplanes.

The postponement of fleet building, in turn, had immediate implications for Germany's direct and indirect relations with the United States. In the direct sense, it meant that the German submarines were instructed to be careful of incidents with the United States, and Hitler ordered restraint on a navy ever eager to strike at American shipping. Simultaneously, in the indirect sense the position and role of Japan with its great navy became more important in German eyes. As already mentioned, Hitler anticipated that an attack on the Soviet Union would help propel Japan forward in Asia, thus tying up the United States in the Pacific in the years that Germany was still building her own surface navy. Between the decision to attack Russia and the implementation of that decision, however, there were now the intervening months to consider.

It was in this context that lining up Japan with the Axis came to be seen as increasingly important, a process which met the interests of the new leadership which had come to power in Tokyo in the days of decision in Berlin. The Tripartite Pact of Germany, Italy and Japan was not signed until September 27, but the new impetus from Berlin, in spite of earlier German unhappiness with Japan, needs to be seen in the context of the decisions of late July. Furthermore, the slow dawning on Germany's leaders of the realization that England was not going to give in operated to reinforce the policy choice previously made. A Japanese attack on Britain's possessions in Southeast Asia, particularly on Singapore, could not help but assist Germany's own fight against the United Kingdom.

There were implications of the decision to attack the Soviet Union for German policy at points far closer to home than Southeast Asia. Both were discussed at the conference of July 31, 1940, at which Hitler explained his decision to launch an invasion of Russia in 1941. As Hitler saw it, Finland would make a useful ally at the northern end of the prospective Eastern Front and Romania could serve as a southern anchor. New policies toward both powers were adopted in the immediate aftermath of the decision for war in the East, but the very different circumstances of the two meant that the details and ramifications of German policies toward them differed in detail. Although these policy changes and their repercussions occurred simultaneously, it will be easier if they are summarized separately, first as regards Finland and then for Romania.

Finland had been assigned to the Soviet Union in the German–Soviet agreement of August 1939, and the German government had respected this arrangement during the Soviet–Finnish war. Had the Soviet Union occupied the whole country either in that war or when it annexed the Baltic States in June 1940, Berlin would presumably have accepted such action. As late as May 20, 1940, in any case, the German government still held to its prior policy; Hitler rejected arms deliveries to Finland even though these were important ways of compensating that country for the copper and nickel Germany wanted from it.[260] In the following weeks, however, policy began to change; and in the July 31 conference Hitler assumed that Finland would fight the Soviet Union alongside Germany.[261] Germany began to send weapons to Finland, at first secretly through a semi-official arms dealer who had earlier played a similar role in supplying Franco during the Spanish civil war, and later more openly. In addition, the Germans made their interest in the British-owned nickel mines in northern Finland near Petsamo increasingly obvious and, by September, were signing agreements with Finland for the transit of German air force personnel and troops across that country to northern Norway.[262]

The Finns were by early July hearing from their contacts in Germany about the discussion of a war against the Soviet Union there; they very much wanted German support against the pressures for new concessions coming from Moscow; and they were entering upon the slippery slope which brought them back into the war. That the Soviet Union observed this massive intervention by Germany into the sphere officially assigned to her with a combination of anger and suspicion was hardly surprising. With Soviet assistance the Germans had conquered Poland, Norway, Denmark, France and the Low Countries; what more did they want? And why did they now need Finnish nickel when they had just won a great victory over their enemies in the West without it? The issue would dominate the next major German–Soviet negotiations as a touchstone of German intentions in Soviet eyes.

Romania, the country at the other end of the front of any prospective attack on the Soviet Union, might, in German eyes, be sympathetic for the same reason as Finland: both had recently lost territory to the Soviet Union and both could hope to reclaim that territory only in alliance with the Third Reich. That in both instances it had been Germany which had enabled the Soviet Union to seize the areas in question was ironic but irrelevant. The situation of Romania was, however, different from that of Finland in three very important respects. In the first place, Romania was a major source of oil, vastly more important to Germany than Finland's nickel. While Hitler at one point in 1940 claimed that Germany could do without this oil,[263] the reality is that she did need it and Hitler conducted his military policy accordingly.

Secondly, unlike Finland with its stable democratic order, Romania was torn by periodic internal rivalries which repeatedly threatened to break into violent struggles affecting the cohesion of the state. From the German point of view, stability was the key prerequisite for effectiveness in the war; and Berlin therefore left the Finns to keep their democracy for the time being while propping up the regime of Romania against internal dissidents, even when these were the Iron Guardists who were much more sympathetic to National Socialism and maintained clandestine ties to various German agencies, especially in Himmler's SS empire.

Finally, and most urgently, Romania was in the throes of being pressured by her Hungarian and Bulgarian neighbors into giving up to them territory she had acquired at the end of World War I. The Hungarians, encouraged from Moscow,[264] were especially eager to seize what they could and appeared willing to go to war if Romania would not yield peacefully. Hitler had, of course, not only encouraged the Soviet Union to make its own territorial claims on Romania and had urged the Romanians to grant them, but he had seen the cessions as the just punishment for a Romania which had compromised itself.[265] He originally thought the Soviet actions pointing toward the Bosporus as primarily of concern to Italy;[266] Romania, he expected, would have to concede territory to Hungary and Bulgaria as well as the Soviet Union.

As the Romanian–Hungarian negotiations appeared likely to eventuate in a war, however, Hitler became very concerned. Great pressure was put on the Hungarians to refrain from war.[267] Once hostilities began, there was no way to anticipate the outcome. In the process the Romanian oil wells might be destroyed or seized by the Soviet Union. Neither idea fit in with his plans; and at the same meeting of July 31 in which he explained to his military advisors his intention of attacking the Soviet Union the following year with Finland and Romania as allies, he also explained that he intended to settle the dispute between Hungary and Romania himself and then to give Romania a guarantee.

Several important effects flowed from the implementation of this decision to involve a reduced but German-guaranteed Romania in the intended German operation against Russia. The Romanians and Bulgarians came to an agreement in direct negotiations at Craiova, an agreement that was reaffirmed after World War II and defines the border between the two countries today. The Hungarian–Romanian conversations, on the other hand, did not produce an agreement, so the German and Italian governments jointly drew a new border in the Vienna arbitration of August 30. They awarded a substantial portion of Transylvania to Hungary; not enough to satisfy Hungary but too much for Romania to become reconciled to.[a] The Axis partners then guaranteed the new borders of Romania, a step certain to annoy the Soviet Union who saw this guarantee as directed against herself.[268]

While in German eyes the promised defense of Romania was indeed directed against the Soviet Union, it was as a part of the planned invasion of the country—not as some special protection for Romania—that the guarantee must be understood. The Germans intended to occupy Romania, during August prepared to send military units there, and did dispatch the first ones in September 1940 so that they could prepare for the attack on Russia the following year.[269] When the Soviets, however, first demanded and then seized some Romanian islands in the Kilia channel of the Danube in October, Berlin declared itself disinterested.[270] These pieces of "guaranteed" Romania were obviously not needed for Germany's future operations.

If the Soviet reaction to Germany's assertion of predominance in the Balkans was a displeased growl, Italy reacted rather more vehemently. In the summer of 1940, Mussolini had hoped to be able to pull off a quick invasion of Yugoslavia and Greece. When the Italians checked about their plans with the Germans in early August, however, they received a prompt and firm veto. The Germans, who had just decided to settle the Hungarian–Romanian dispute in order to keep the Balkans quiet until they could use them as a basis for attacking the Soviet Union, certainly did not want Italy to initiate an upheaval in that portion of Europe.[271]

The German argument to Rome for holding back was not, however, honest. Instead of taking Mussolini into their confidence—probably for fear of immediate leaks from Rome—they merely stressed the supreme importance of keeping the Balkans quiet. When the Italians a few weeks later learned from the newspapers that German troops had been sent to Romania, they were livid. To Mussolini and Ciano it looked as if Germany had held them back so that Germany could move forward without regard for Italian interests in Southeast Europe. They accordingly decided that the next time Italy wanted to act in that part of Europe, they would tell the Germans afterwards and not beforehand. The Italian

---

[a] After World War II Romania received the ceded territory back; the nationality conflicts in the area continue to agitate both nations.

adventure in Greece has to be seen in this context as one more outgrowth of Germany's decision to move East.

Finally, the decision to attack the Soviet Union in the spring of 1941 also meant that there were several months available during which Germany could try to work out some new combinations in Western Europe if Britain did not leave the war. The German government would make a number of such efforts in the fall of 1940, and these will be described in the next chapter; but it must always be remembered that all these projects in the West, as well as the ones in the Mediterranean which grew out of Italy's disasters in Greece and North Africa, were carried forward by the Germans under a self-imposed deadline. The clock was running for the next big land operation—to the East.[272]

The spectacular events of April to September 1940 not only brought Germany temporary control of Central and West Europe but set the framework for the balance of the war. The British decided to fight on and to emphasize bombing as their main military contribution to the defeat of Germany. The United States began to confront the danger ahead and to build up the military and naval power needed in a world vastly more dangerous than its people had ever imagined, and quite possibly under a leader who would need an unprecedented third term to do so. The Japanese decided that their opportunity to seize Southeast Asia had come and that they would go to war with the United States rather than abandon that project. The Soviet Union hoped that peace would now be made while she reaped the benefits still to be gotten from her deal with Berlin. The German government still looked forward to its long-term ambition of world naval power but decided to realize its aims of seizing vast lands from the Soviet Union in the immediate future. The next five years of war would see the decisions made in the last months of its first year carried out.

4

———— • ————

THE EXPANDING CONFLICT, 1940–1941

The months immediately following the great decisions of the summer of 1940 look like a time filled by a series of unrelated and unconnected events, ranging from diplomatic travels by Hitler as far as the border of Spain on the one side of the globe to a conflict between Thailand and French Indo-China on the other. In between there were struggles in the Balkans and Near East, anxious diplomatic activities by the Soviet Union, new initiatives by the United States, and fighting on and below the surface of the oceans. The time from the summer of 1940 to the summer of 1941 in Europe and from the summer of 1940 to the end of 1941 in the Pacific can best be understood if it is seen as the first working out of the choices made in July and August of 1940—as these implementations interact with each other and as they were affected by the independent initiatives of others, especially Italy.

GERMANY HEADS EAST

One of the most fateful of those decisions of the summer of 1940, and one which drew others in its train, was the German decision to attack the Soviet Union. This project not only entailed a number of preparations by Germany but also established a time limit for other German initiatives. As will be seen, German moves in regard to Spain, Southeast Europe and the Mediterranean were very much affected by the recognition in Berlin that forces would be needed for the attack on the Soviet Union in the spring of 1941 and that major troop commitments elsewhere had to be brought to a conclusion by that time.[1] Over and over again Hitler stressed the need to concentrate the nation's striking forces for a particular blow, and the diversion of power over several theaters of war in the latter part of the War reflects the loss of German initiative in the conflict.

The military planning itself had begun in the summer of 1940. By the end of July, the decision had been made to attack in the spring of

1941 rather than in the fall of 1940. This new schedule made it possible for the Germans to develop the physical preparation of the logistic basis on the ground in the eastern reaches of German-occupied Europe as well as the theoretical preparations in the staffs of the army, the air force, the over-all high command, and eventually the navy over a period of several months. The physical effort ordered in August consisted of improving the railway and communication system in an area of limited rail and road networks and of building up supply stocks for the forthcoming operation.[a] Since it was assumed that the whole campaign would be completed in the summer and early fall of 1941, no preparations were made for winter fighting—a lack that cost the Germans dearly when the fighting went very differently from their expectations.

The staff planning consisted of a number of alternative proposals, developed to some extent independently in the summer and fall of 1940 by different headquarters, eventually molded together primarily in the army general staff with considerable influence from Hitler personally, and issued in a general directive on December 18, 1940, with more detailed implementing military orders following in January of 1941.[2] Not entirely resolved in these plans were the main directions of offensives between the initial attack and the assumed final positions; there was, however, no argument over two concepts. These were that heavy initial blows would be struck in such a fashion as to cut off and destroy large Soviet forces in the area closest to the border in order to preclude their retreating to new lines in any systematic trading of space for time, and that the goal was a line roughly from Archangel on the Arctic Ocean in the north to Astrakhan on the Caspian Sea in the south. The experience, mobility, aggressiveness, and excellence of staff and equipment of the Germans were assumed to be sufficiently superior to the Red Army and air force to make it possible to complete this operation in two or three months. It was assumed that the Soviet system would collapse under the German hammer blows; and, as will be discussed subsequently, the Germans were so certain of victory in this, the easier of their campaigns as compared with the prior one in the West, that much attention in the staffs would be given in the weeks immediately before the attack to those operations which were to ensue upon its successful conclusion.

In 1940, the Germans had won quickly over France and had then needed weeks to gear up staff work for the invasion of England; they did not want to be caught short like that again. In retrospect, this loss

---

[a] This massive buildup made the Germans especially anxious in the spring of 1941 to avoid having Soviet boundary and other commissions travelling around in the area immediately to the west of the border.

of momentum looked most serious to the Germans, and they were deter-mined that this time they would be all set for the next operations. To the post-war observer, this pre-occupation with planning for the steps to follow the quick victory over the Soviet Union may appear ludicrous, but it must be understood as one of the lessons drawn by the Germans from their difficulties in following up on the great victory over France.

The perception of a weak Soviet Union could not be remedied by accurate intelligence. The Germans had very little, and they would not be dissuaded by those whose estimates of Soviet strength were more perceptive, primarily because the prejudices against Slavic peoples were reinforced by the euphoria of victory in the West. Having practically no agents inside the Soviet Union, except for those actually working for Moscow and feeding them disinformation,[3] the Germans could add to their knowledge only by two other methods: signals intelligence and overflight. Their signals intelligence never penetrated higher-level Soviet codes and therefore, although useful for tactical details, never provided any major insights (with neither of these conditions changing after 1941). The Germans began a substantial program of aerial reconnaissance over the Soviet Union in October 1940, but this, too, was primarily of tactical significance.[4] In general, assumptions were not affected by understand-ing in spite of the simultaneously obvious errors in the German assump-tions about a British collapse under bombing. They quickly forgot that the Red Army had learned fast from its early defeats at the hands of the Finns;[5] it was now assumed that they would or could not learn from defeats inflicted by Germans.

A second area of preparation was the economic one. The invasion was, after all, designed to seize vast agricultural land for future settlement by German farmers. That involved the eventual displacement of those currently living in the area to be occupied, but in the interim there was the prospect of endless loot and ruthless exploitation. At the Nazi Party rally on September 12, 1936, Hitler had asserted that the ores of the Urals, the forests of Siberia, and the wheat fields of the Ukraine could provide all Germans with a life of plenty.[6] Here was the opportunity to translate these dreams into reality. The seizure of food would cause famine in the rest of Russia, but the death of millions of Russians from starvation was perceived as an advantage, not a disaster.[a] The mines of the Don and Donets basins and the forests of northern Russia would

---

[a] Note that Hitler also held that the German casualties would be fewer than the number of workers tied up in the synthetics industries; that one group of Germans was alive and the other dead or wounded was evidently not important to him (Weinberg, *Germany and the Soviet Union*, p. 165, n 31). If that was his attitude toward the allegedly superior Germans, his view of the so-called sub-humans may be easier to understand. See also *Das Deutsche Reich und der Zweite Weltkrieg*, 4: 989.

serve as fine substitutes for the riches of the Urals and Siberia of which Hitler had spoken earlier.

The extensive preparations for organized looting and exploitation of the areas to be seized point to the special character of the campaign in the East. It is, of course, correct that as a by-product of their conquest of Holland, Belgium, and France, the Germans stripped those countries and harnessed their economies to their own war effort while extracting enormous sums on the pretext that these were occupation costs, all this on a scale which showed that the post-World War I reparations charges imposed on Germany had been small change. But although a final accounting—if an accurate one can ever be developed—might well show that the economic benefits extracted by the Germans from the rapidly over-run and basically wealthy Western economies were in reality considerably greater than those taken from the more heavily war-ravaged and in part less wealthy occupied portions of the U.S.S.R., the intention was clearly different. The economic exploitation of the territory to be seized in the East was from the beginning a critical element in the whole German perception of the campaign against the U.S.S.R., formed a major part of the preparations for that campaign, assumed permanent German control of most of European Russia, and provides an important key to any understanding of the different type of warfare the Germans from the very beginning intended to wage in the East.

The attack on Poland was in some ways a rehearsal for the invasion of Russia. In that case also Hitler had made it clear to his military associates that destroying the life of the Poles as a people, not breaking the strength of the Polish army, was the aim of German policy. At that time, there had still been some reluctance among the military leaders to become involved in mass murder; and, in any case, the focus of attention had shifted to the great campaign ahead in the West. Now all this was changed. The war in the West was, or at least appeared to be, over, and almost all restraints were cast aside. As Hitler explained in ever greater detail, especially in a speech to military leaders on March 30, 1941, the new campaign would differ from the prior ones, that a war of extermination was at hand, and that a massive demographic revolution was about to begin in Eastern Europe. His views were met with understanding, agreement, and support. A minute number had reservations, and one of these, Admiral Canaris, the chief of intelligence, had the courage to voice them, but most either went along with or showed their support for such schemes by putting all their considerable energies into developing careful plans for their implementation.[7]

In post-World War II Germany, a steady stream of military memoirs on the book market and perjury in court proceedings obscured these sad truths for some time, but recent publications based on research in the archives instead of post-war fabrications have provided a more accurate picture—and have not surprisingly been met by vocal hostility from some.[8] It is now beyond doubt that the orders and procedures worked out in detail before the invasion and calling for the killing of several categories of prisoners of war, including Jewish soldiers and all political officers captured, were very widely carried out and that the assumption was that the huge masses of Russian prisoners that the German army expected to capture would be allowed to die of hunger and disease. The application of these terrible policies, as well as their import for the victims and for the Soviet Union, will be reviewed later; what has to be noted at this point is the inclusion of such ideas in the planning of the invasion.[9]

Furthermore, it was also anticipated that the mass murder of those in mental institutions and old peoples' homes, by this time in high gear inside Germany, would be extended to include those found in the areas newly overrun. Here was one of the "benefits" of German culture that was to be spread with German military control. In the early months of 1941 opposition to the killings in German institutions was beginning to make itself heard and felt; those who could be released from their active role in this terrible endeavor in the summer of 1941 would soon find employment for their by now well-developed talents in Eastern Europe.

Although even now all the details are not entirely clear—in part because much was not committed to writing, in part because some of those involved at the time were dead by the end of the war or, if alive, found it expedient to lie about the past—it can be taken as fully proven that before the invasion of the U.S.S.R., and as an integral part of the planning for that invasion, the German government also made new decisions in regard to the treatment of Jews.[10] The prior conquest of large parts of Poland and of Western Europe had vastly increased the number of Jews under German control; in fact, these conquests had added more than ten times as many as had succeeded in emigrating from Germany in the pre-war years. The project for moving the approximately four million Jews of German-dominated Europe to a dubious fate on the island of Madagascar had been rendered impractical by the continued resistance of Britain. Now, following a mere trickle of emigration across neutral Spain and Russia, there would be a further massive increase in the number of Jews under Germany's control as her armies swept eastward across portions of pre-war Poland, the Baltic States and the western U.S.S.R., areas with a very large Jewish population.

While the shooting of certain categories among the prisoners of war the Germans expected to capture would be left to the army, and it was also to be the army's function to deal ruthlessly with any real or imagined obstruction by the civilian population—with those shooting civilians promised amnesty in advance—the sorting out of those categories of peaceful civilians who were to be killed would be assigned to special murder commandos, called *Einsatzgruppen*, a term perhaps best translated as Special Employment Units. First established in connection with the occupation of Austria, the Sudetenland and Czechoslovakia, they had acquired considerable practice in mass murder during the invasion of Poland.[11] Drawing on this experience and calling on individuals throughout the SS apparatus, new and expanded units of this type would accompany the German armies as they invaded the Soviet Union. They were instructed to kill Jews, Communists, and other categories of civilians once the invasion had begun, following upon and assisted by the regular army. In addition, they would shoot those prisoners of war who fell in the proscribed categories but had not been killed immediately upon capture.[12]

Whether by the time Hitler instructed Himmler to establish these units in March 1941 he had already decided that, after the Jews in the newly occupied areas had been killed this process would immediately be extended to all other Jews in areas under German control, is not known at this time. But since Hitler expected to win, not lose, the war, there was no urgent need at that moment to decide the matter of timing. Victory would make possible the killing of all Jews at a time that suited German convenience, and timing could well be influenced by the reaction inside and outside the Third Reich to the first stupendous massacres. Two points are beyond dispute and essential for an understanding of what followed. First, that in this planned operation of mass murder, the systematic killing of Jews, as opposed to expulsion, forced conversion, or random cruelty, was decided upon for the first time in history and with immediately planned and then implemented measures. Second, this program of mass killing was from the beginning a major portion of the whole ideological war planned for the East with its intended demographic revolution.[13]

The plans and preparations for the attack on Russia which have been discussed so far were of an essentially theoretical kind until June 1941. A small but growing number of people knew about them, and as they learned, they reacted. A few reacted negatively, warning against the initiation of war on another front while the fighting against England was still under way and in some instances calling in question the whole idea of a war against the Soviet Union. Most of Hitler's immediate military advisors were reassured by the postponement of invasion from the fall of 1940 until the spring of 1941. The head of the German navy, Admiral

Raeder, believed that the war against Britain should have priority and, on the basis of the navy's experience with the Soviet Union, argued that Germany would do better to cooperate with her.[14] There is some evidence that Göring voiced doubts,[15] and there is a detailed letter from the long-time Minister of Finance, Schwerin von Krosigk, arguing against war with Russia.[16] Members of the German embassy in Moscow were horrified to hear of the idea and pooled their objections in a memorandum for the German army Chief of Staff,[17] while the ambassador later personally argued with Hitler against the attack.[18] The second man in the Foreign Ministry, State Secretary Ernst von Weizsäcker, wrote out his objections,[19] and Foreign Minister von Ribbentrop himself at first expressed doubts.

None of these arguments made any difference to Hitler, primarily it would seem because they could not engage the critical point in the whole project: the decision grew not out of either some possibly remediable circumstance of the moment, or a sense of being threatened, but out of purposeful determination. This was what had in general always been intended, as a central project of the whole system, and without it the National Socialist experiment made no sense.

Others were pleased rather than alarmed when they learned of the intended attack. Alfred Rosenberg was happy to receive from Hitler the commission to plan for the occupation which he would head, in title if not always in reality. And when the SS officer Hans Prützmann learned of his forthcoming appointment to head up the police in the Ukraine, he was able to celebrate his new position well ahead of time at a special farewell dinner in the circle of his Hamburg associates.[20]

Those in charge of Germany's army had to make some adjustments in their planning. The expected reduction in the size of the military forces was reversed; instead of decreasing from about 140 to 120 divisions, the army was now to be increased first to 180 and, by August 21, 1940, to a more likely 200.[21] Many of the new units were, however, equipped with captured weapons; and though there was some modernization (particularly the replacement of old smaller tanks by newer medium tanks), the army which was to attack the Soviet Union in 1941 was not appreciably greater than the one which had attacked in the West in 1940. Two factors contributed to this situation. First, German underestimation of Soviet defensive power combined with a reluctance to impose total mobilization on the German economy to hold down both production and recruitment levels. Secondly, the need to station at least a quarter of Germany's army in the West, in Southeast Europe and in the Mediterranean theater meant that whatever increases were arranged for in the year between the two campaigns were tied down elsewhere.

At least in a small way, the army was now to begin fighting a multi-front instead of a one-front war.

If these factors meant that Germany attacked the Soviet Union with an army of essentially the same size as that of May 1940, the air force deployed for the new offensive was actually smaller.[22] Because of heavy losses during the Battle of Britain and then the bombing of England in the winter of 1940–41, the diversions of air force units to the Mediterranean following on the Italian military disasters, and the need to maintain a substantial number of fighters to defend German-controlled Europe against British air raids, the German air force attacked the Soviet Union with two-thirds of a force which was already somewhat smaller than that unleashed against the West the year before. While no one could realistically expect the air forces of such allies as Finland, Romania and Hungary—to say nothing of the seventy Italian planes—to add a great deal of power to the new offensive, the German air force command nevertheless assumed that by the fall of 1941 the campaign in the East would have been completed, and the main thrust of the air offensive could once again be turned on England.[23]

The expectation of an attack on the Soviet Union also had internal economic repercussions. On the one hand, the emphasis in German war production would have to be on the army after all; priority for the navy and air force again had to be postponed. In the eyes of the German economic and business leaders of the time, whatever might be the temporary disadvantages of such a policy seemed to be offset by the economic gains and business profits anticipated from the rapid seizure of Soviet property and resources.[24] On the other hand, it had to be assumed that the invasion would at least for a while interrupt the welcome flow of critical war supplies from and across the Soviet Union. Obviously there would be no voluntary deliveries from Russia and no transshipment of goods purchased in South and Southeast and East Asia across the Russian railway network.[25] Since the Germans knew when they were intending to attack, they could adjust their own delivery schedule to avoid most payment by delay until after the invasion; the Soviet regime's effort to appease the Germans, as we will see, would provide massive deliveries of many Soviet products and extra transshipment of such critical items as natural rubber from East Asia in the months immediately preceding the attack.[a]

Most of the preparations hitherto discussed gave few or no immediately obvious and visible clues of the new German policy to outside

[a] The shipment of rubber was especially important because a small proportion of natural rubber was still needed in the process of making "Buna," the German synthetic rubber, from coal.

observers. Some actions, however, could not be easily hidden; pretended reasons for them could be advanced—and some of these are still accepted by a few scholars—but the steps themselves were apparent to contemporaries. The Germans quickly began to fortify the northern coast of Norway and to move troops and equipment through Finland to get there.[26] The major change in German policy toward Finland was discussed in the preceding chapter, and during the fall of 1940 it became increasingly obvious that Germany was delivering arms to that country, developing new ties with it, and generally including it in the German sphere of military, diplomatic and economic influence.[27] Although an outside observer would not necessarily conclude that detailed military planning for joint German–Finnish operations against the Soviet Union was under way at least from December 1940 on,[28] one did not need inside information on these general staff contacts to see that Germany was not treating Finland as a portion of the sphere allocated to the Soviet Union as had been the case a year before.[29] The Germans anticipated a major role for Finland in the offensives to be launched in central Finland against the railway from Murmansk as well as from southern Finland towards Leningrad, a role which would earn Finns major territorial gains at Soviet expense; but in the far north the Germans expected to provide the spearhead forces in an offensive toward Murmansk themselves.[30] Moving these forces into position for that operation involved getting the cooperation of Sweden, and, in the final stages of the deployment there, the Swedish government permitted a full German division to cross the country on its way to the front.[31]

At the other end of the intended front, Romania was the key country; like Finland it had lost territory to the Soviet Union with German approval and like Finland it was now to recover it and more in alliance with the Third Reich. The German shift looking toward this new development has already been discussed; in late 1940 and early 1941 the preparations here too went forward. In military affairs this meant a buildup of German forces and, in addition, assistance on a limited scale in the modernization of Romania's own military.[32] This process would be temporarily affected by the events in Greece, which were themselves the product of Germany's sending troops into Romania, but, regardless of such details, the planning for an attack on the Soviet Union from the south proceeded even as Germany pushed for control and expansion of Romanian oil production.[33] The Romanians were eventually informed and directly involved in this planning process which was also affected by two other factors in German–Romanian relations, both new and both critical in the subsequent evolution of that relationship.

Hitler met the new leader of Romania, Marshal Ion Antonescu, and was greatly impressed by him; no other leader Hitler met other than Mussolini ever received such consistently favorable comments from the German dictator.[34] Hitler even mustered the patience to listen to Antonescu's lengthy disquisitions on the glorious history of Romania and the perfidy of the Hungarians — a curious reversal for a man who was more accustomed to regaling visitors with tirades of his own.[35] Closely related to the developing personal tie between Hitler and Antonescu, but surely also influenced by the German desire for an effectively functioning military alliance with a competent leadership in this key satellite, was the suspension of German support for the Iron Guard hotheads in Romania's internal affairs. Various ties of German intelligence and party agencies to the Iron Guard remained; but when the Guard attempted a coup in January 1941, the German government stood squarely behind Antonescu. The Germans tried to keep him from shooting too many of their spiritual kinsmen after the coup failed — as they had once frowned on King Carol's shooting of Iron Guard leaders — but they bet on what they saw as the strong man of Romanian politics.[36] Like the leaders of Finland, he too could look forward to territorial expansion at the expense of the Soviet Union.[37]

The other country on the southern flank of the planned attack on the Soviet Union was Turkey, which both controlled the Straits connecting the Black Sea with the Mediterranean and had a common border with the Soviet Union in fairly close proximity to the latter's Caucasus oil fields. Turkey was nominally an ally of Great Britain and France, but hoped to keep its prior good economic relations with Germany and its generally good relations with the Soviet Union while staying out of the war — though perhaps picking up a few pieces of territory. In the years before the outbreak of war in 1939 their careful balancing acts had gained the Turks a piece of the French mandate of Syria; there was always the hope of more. In addition, there might be ways to pick up bits of Greece and/or a few islands in the Aegean. The main assets of Turkey in such efforts were her strategic location, her hardy army, and the mineral resource of chromium, a critical ingredient for the making of steel alloys, which Germany in particular had great difficulty in obtaining from anywhere else.[38]

As they contemplated war against the Soviet Union, the Germans reversed their earlier willingness to allow Russia control of the Straits — something they had been prepared to offer Stalin in 1939 — and instead hoped at least to neutralize Turkey temporarily until they could either get her to join them in the war or, alternatively, invade the Middle East across her themselves after the defeat of the Soviet Union. In the months before their attack on the Soviet Union, therefore, the Germans worked to deflect Soviet aspirations from the Straits and to maintain and even improve their own relationship with Ankara. In this endeavor they largely succeeded. By June 1941 they had assured themselves of Turkey's benevolent neutrality in the coming campaign, even though the Turks had not always been as cooperative as the Germans had wanted in their efforts to dislodge Great Britain from the Middle East in the interim.[a]

It should be easy to understand that, during the months that the Germans were getting ready to attack the Soviet Union, they did not want their Italian ally to work out any new spheres of influence agreements with Russia which might encourage the latter to move forward in the Balkans. As mentioned in the preceding chapter, the Germans now reversed their earlier attempts to improve Italian–Soviet relations when that improvement threatened to go beyond a return of ambassadors to serious negotiations for an accommodation of Italian and Soviet interests in Southeast Europe. Unwilling to let the Italians know until the last moment that they were about to invade Russia, the Germans had to restrain Mussolini's hopes of an agreement with Moscow throughout the winter of 1940–41. The Russians clearly wanted to work around the new difficulties they seemed to be having with Germany by dealing with Italy—a repeat performance of British diplomacy of 1937–39—but the Germans vetoed such projects and could make their veto stick.[39]

Like Italy, two other prospective allies of Germany against the Soviet Union were only informed by Berlin in the last days before the attack. Hungary had to be told both because of the need to transport troops and supplies across her territory to Romania and because of her own common border with the Soviet Union.[40] The puppet state of Slovakia did not border on the Soviet Union but was also important for transportation and communication purposes; her leadership was tipped off at the last moment. Italy, too, was provided with no advance information.[41] None of this was publicly conspicuous or even very significant at a time when the changes in German policy toward Finland and Romania showed Moscow that Germany appeared to be heading in new directions.

The new German policies toward Finland and Romania were both met with unconcealed Soviet grumbling. Finland was supposed to be in the Soviet sphere, and arms deliveries to that country—to say nothing of the presence of German troops—obviously violated the Soviet–German agreements.[42] Protestations of innocence were not believed in Moscow; here was a clear sign of a new German policy. The guarantee of

---

[a] The refusal of Turkey to assist Germany as much as Berlin would have liked during the Near East campaigns of May and June 1941 is discussed below.

Romania, followed soon after by a military mission and the dispatch of German troops, were also seen as unfriendly acts by the Soviet Union, especially as they appeared to be designed to block off Soviet aspirations for bases in Bulgaria and Turkey.[43] These departures from the prior course of German–Soviet relations obviously required explaining.

Although these developments suggested trouble ahead, the Russians certainly did not want such trouble and showed themselves cooperative. They enabled a German auxiliary cruiser to travel around Siberia by the northern sea route so that it could enter the Pacific and prey on Allied shipping there.[44] Some supplies were sent for it across Siberia by train; but by the time the ship was to return to Germany, it had to be ordered to go via the Indian Ocean and Atlantic, since the Germans were about to attack the Soviet Union.[45] In the economic sphere there was also continued cooperation from the Russians who provided massive deliveries of critical raw materials; what problems there were came from Germany's failure to make the promised deliveries designed as repayment.[46] The Soviets were understandably annoyed that the Germans refused to deliver weapons of the very type they were able to send to Finland, made some trouble, but continued to aid the German war economy.[47] That aid included providing transit facilities to Iran and East Asia.[48] And the Soviets were always happy to assist the Germans in stirring up trouble for the British in Asia, making it possible for Subhas Chandra Bose, the extreme Indian Nationalist leader who was speculating on an Axis victory, to get to Germany from Afghanistan where he had fled from India.[49]

Since the Soviets had themselves crossed the lines established in the German–Soviet agreement of 1939 when they seized all of Lithuania, much attention was lavished by Moscow on settling this issue to Berlin's satisfaction. The southwest corner of Lithuania had been promised to Germany in a secret agreement of September 1939, but the Red Army had occupied it as part of the full Soviet occupation of Lithuania in July 1940. The Soviets now offered to purchase this piece from Germany. Though acknowledging the German claim to the area, they were extremely reluctant to change boundaries once these had been set, and offered the Germans half of what Russia had been paid by the United States for Alaska in 1867.[50] The Germans agreed in principle to sell their claim but stalled the negotiations and asked for vastly more. Figuring that they would conquer it in the early hours of their invasion of the Soviet Union—as in fact they did—the Germans decided to make the issue as uncomfortable and expensive as possible for the Russians in the meantime; a settlement finally being reached for the total price of Alaska ($7\frac{1}{2}$ million gold dollars) in January of 1941.[51]

The Soviet concessions to Germany in the last stages of these negotiations must be seen in the context of other concessions made simultaneously by Moscow in new German–Soviet economic talks, concessions designed by Moscow to assist in moving forward the broader political issues discussed between the two countries since September of 1940. The Germans had told the Russians about their Tripartite Pact with Italy and Japan at the last moment and had pointed out that this treaty was open to Soviet adhesion. Molotov was subsequently invited to Berlin to discuss this project, with a visit of von Ribbentrop to Moscow to follow. Molotov was to talk over the current problems in German–Soviet relations as well as the possibility of joining the Axis powers.[52]

In anticipation of this trip, the two sides made very different preparations. Though collecting material for the talks, including a draft treaty for the Soviet Union to join the Tripartite Pact,[53] the Germans quietly went forward with their preparations to attack the Soviet Union. As the relevant order of Hitler put it:

> Political conversations designed to clarify the attitude of Russia in the immediate future have been started. Regardless of the outcome of these conversations, all preparations for the East previously ordered orally are to be continued. [Written] directives on that will follow as soon as the basic elements of the army's plan for the operation have been submitted to me and approved by me.[54]

There was, in other words, no German expectation of a new long-term agreement with Russia; war was intended, and only the details of relations in the intervening months would be explored.

The Soviet government went at this matter very differently. Evidently anticipating a new general agreement with the Germans, an agreement bringing up to date the prior ones of August and September 1939, and one that would insure continued fruitful cooperation between them against Great Britain, the leadership in Moscow attempted a replay of their 1939 tactic of pretending to negotiate with Great Britain in the hope of extracting greater concessions from Germany. In the spring of 1940 they had requested trade negotiations with the British, and in the summer they had insisted on Sir Stafford Cripps being made ambassador if he were to be received for any such negotiations.[55] Unlike the French, who had been almost exuberant in their attempts to shift the theater of war from Western Europe and involve the Western Powers in hostilities with Russia,[56] the British had held back. Repeatedly Chamberlain and Halifax had resisted pressure for actions against the Soviet Union, had stalled the French projects, and had insisted on maintaining diplomatic relations with Moscow.[57] The failure of the effort of Cripps to interest the Soviet Union in the dangers posed by German domination of Western and Central Europe has already been recounted.[58] As Cripps explained to London, fear of Germany dominated Soviet policy, but the conclusion drawn by Moscow was the need to remain on good terms with her and under no circumstances to provoke Berlin by alignment with London.[59]

There did follow some negotiations looking toward a trade agreement and a possible political agreement as well, but the Soviet government was careful both to avoid coming to any agreement—the British never received an answer to their approach—and to leak information on the fact that negotiations were taking place. They evidently hoped that once again the publicly ventilated possibility of a Soviet alignment with the West might facilitate agreement with Germany, but they would find that they had miscalculated badly.[60] Unlike 1939, this time, as in the years *before* 1939, the Germans were not interested, having already made very different decisions about their relationship with Russia. In view of Soviet efforts to come to a new agreement with the Germans, all the British could do to sour the Berlin visit of the Soviet Foreign Minister, who could not find the time to receive their ambassador, was to bomb the German capital while Molotov was visiting there.[61]

The talks Molotov had with Hitler and other German leaders covered a great deal of ground, even if some conversations had to be held in an air raid shelter.[62] The Germans reviewed the progress of the war and expressed their desire for the Soviet Union to join in a general southward advance in which Germany and Italy would divide Africa between them, the Soviet Union would head for the Indian Ocean and Persian Gulf,[63] while Japan would take over South and Southeast Asia. Molotov agreed in principle to joining the Tripartite Pact but wanted the details clarified. In particular, he made it clear that the Soviet Union intended to annex Finland and expected the Germans to adhere to their prior agreement to such a step. Furthermore, he argued for real and immediate Soviet advances toward the Straits and thus to the Mediterranean rather than the vague route to the Indian Ocean. As subsequent events would show, the Soviet government believed that the differences between Soviet and German proposals could be worked out; but the refusal of the Germans to promise that they would abide by their prior policy on Finland should have opened eyes in Moscow.

The Finnish question, in fact, was the one which took up more time than any other. One wonders whether Molotov ever asked himself why the Germans, who did not need the Petsamo nickel mines in 1939 when about to go to war with Britain and France, were so certain they needed them now? Even more extraordinary was the insistence of Hitler that the war with Great Britain had already been won, but that in case of new troubles between the Soviet Union and Finland, the British or the United States might station an air force in Finland! In any case, the Germans made it clear that they would not stand for the Soviet Union to carry out its intention of annexing Finland and that they would block any further Soviet advance in Southeast Europe. We know now that these German positions were designed to protect the flanks of their attacks on Russia the following spring; apparently Molotov, however much annoyed by German views, did not grasp their real import.

Shortly after Molotov's return to Moscow, the Soviet government took steps toward what it appears to have assumed would be a new settlement with Germany. Simultaneously Moscow moved on three fronts. A revised protocol for Russia to join the Tripartite Pact was sent to Berlin on November 25. Obviously meant as a serious offer, it reflected previously expressed Soviet aspirations and contained nothing that the Germans would have objected to the year before: a mutual assistance pact between the Soviet Union and Bulgaria, bases at the Straits, Finland to be left to the Russians with German interest in the nickel and forest products there to be protected, and the abandonment of Japan's special concessions in northern Sakhalin, concessions Japan would not need once she acquired the rich resources of Southeast Asia.[64] On the same day, the Soviet government proposed a mutual assistance pact to Bulgaria with both powers expected to join the Tripartite Pact.[65] Finally, at the same time the Soviets made massive economic offers to the Germans, showing themselves willing to make major sacrifices in Soviet–German economic relations to demonstrate to Berlin the potential value of good relations with Moscow.[66]

Since the Soviet government had worked out this program with care and repeatedly urged the Germans to respond to their proposals, one must assume that they thought it a reasonable basis for a new agreement. They clearly anticipated that the war between Germany and Great Britain would last for some time yet and wanted the Germans to concentrate on that while the Soviet Union strengthened its position in Eastern Europe. The Tripartite Pact which Moscow offered to join included a commitment to fight alongside Germany, Italy and Japan if any of these countries became involved in war with the United States, and thus could easily bring the Soviet Union into war with the two Western Powers. Stalin evidently thought this an appropriate risk to run, especially since he would be in such mighty company—company which in any case was located between the Soviet Union and the Western Powers on the major European and Asiatic fronts. If the French and, to a far lesser extent, the British had been reckless in their willingness to risk war with the

Soviet Union in the winter of 1939–40, the Soviets were prepared to return the favor with compound interest in the winter of 1940–41 in the form of a willingness to fight the United States and Great Britain.

The Germans, however, were completely uninterested in having the Soviet Union join the Tripartite Pact and never replied to the Soviet offer in spite of reminders. They encouraged the Bulgarians to reject the approach from Moscow and went forward with their own plans to send troops into Bulgaria for an invasion of Greece that will be reviewed subsequently. There was only one facet of the Soviet move that Germany was happy to respond to positively, and that was the offer of a new economic agreement on terms highly favorable to the Germans. After a good deal of bargaining, complicated by German refusal to supply some of the materials the Soviet Union wanted as well as large arrears in German payments and the need to settle the argument over compensation for the piece of Lithuania, a new agreement was finally signed on January 10, 1941.[67] Molotov, who apparently hoped that as in 1939 Soviet economic concessions would pave the way to a political agreement with Germany, asked on January 17 whether such an agreement could now be worked out and expressed astonishment at the absence of any answer to the Soviet offer to join the Tripartite Pact.[68] He never got one.

Given the German decision to attack the Soviet Union, it should be easy to understand why Berlin never replied to the political proposals but was happy to sign a new trade agreement. If the Soviet Union would help supply the German war economy until the day of the invasion, that was certainly all to the good. If, on the other hand, there were detailed political negotiations on sensitive subjects on which German strategic interest connected with that invasion precluded German agreement to Soviet wishes, there was a real possibility that the Russians might hold back on the promised deliveries and transit shipments from East Asia which the Germans so desperately wanted. From Berlin's perspective, gathering in the goods while keeping their diplomatic mouths shut was clearly the smartest policy.

This pattern continued for the remaining period until June 22, 1941. The Soviets were unhappy about Germany's occupying Bulgaria and steadily expanding its influence in the Balkans. They were equally displeased about the obvious way in which Finland moved more and more into the German orbit. But because many of these moves looked to the Soviet Union as if they were primarily directed against Great Britain— and that was particularly the case when the Germans destroyed the pro-British regimes of Yugoslavia and Greece in April 1941—they could continue to imagine that their pact with Germany served their own interests. Since they did not see these moves as preparing the flanks for a forthcoming attack on themselves, they stood by for the third time in a year as the Germans cleared continental Europe of Allied forces.[69]

Strangely enough, at the end of the process of helping Germany conquer Northern, Western, and Southern Europe, the Russians found themselves on the continent with Germany by themselves. This dangerous prospect was unfolding for the Soviet Union in the spring of 1941.[70] Whatever they did or did not believe of the reports from their agents in Europe, from the warnings they received from the British, from the Americans, and from their agents in Japan, it was certainly obvious that Germany was building up very large military forces in Eastern Europe. Whether designed to threaten or to attack, this buildup suggested the danger of war. Terrified of the prospect, the Soviet government now tried desperately to reassure the Germans by placating gestures.

In a series of moves Moscow attempted to pacify Germany. They not only stopped pressuring Finland but even promised to deliver extra wheat to that country.[71] They gave in to the Germans on border delimitation issues.[72] They withdrew their diplomatic recognition of the Belgian, Norwegian, Yugoslav and Greek governments-in-exile and recognized the anti-British government established by Rashid Ali al-Gaylani in Iraq.[73] Of greater practical importance than these political gestures was the massive increase in economic deliveries. Extra trains were run in such numbers that the Germans had a hard time shipping the vast quantities of supplies received from the border stations where the train gage changed. Though thrilled to obtain these supplies—especially the extra transshipments of rubber from East Asia—the Germans reciprocated by deliberately stalling on their own return deliveries. If the Soviets would run trains across the border until minutes before the attack, that was fine with the Germans but had no impact on their policy.[74]

That policy was also unaffected by other steps the Soviet Union took. The Russians allowed a German commission to take a good look at their aircraft industry, but the report of the greatly impressed commission was simply not believed.[75] The neutrality treaty with Japan signed in April might show the Germans that they could not count on Japan to join in an attack on the Soviet Union. In a number of demonstrative gestures, Stalin tried to show his own great personal interest in continued good relations with Germany.[76] In a speech to the graduates of Soviet military academies on May 5, the day before he took over the formal leadership of the government, Stalin appears to have set forth in some detail and quite frankly the relative strengths and capabilities of Soviet and German military powers, showing the need for Russia to take German superiority into account while continuing to build up its own defenses.[77]

Stalin evidently anticipated German demands and wanted to prepare both the Soviet public and leadership for the concessions he expected to have to make to obtain a new agreement.[78] He appears not to have recognized that Hitler had as a rule found it preferable to attack at a time of his own choosing and without preliminary negotiations; instead Stalin assumed a period of discussion and negotiations. There is some evidence suggesting that he was prepared to make not only further economic offers but to give up all or part of Lithuania—a not unreasonable anticipation of German demands had any been intended.[79] Certainly there were no plans for a Soviet preventive attack into the German buildup; the Germans never considered such Soviet action likely; they found no evidence of such a project after the invasion; and they were assured by their own military observers in the Soviet Union before June 22 that there were no signs of aggressive intentions.[80]

Stalin appears to have believed in the basic Marxist perception of National Socialism as a tool of German monopoly capitalism with a central rivalry for markets, raw materials, and investment opportunities with other capitalist states. There would be no sense in attacking Russia in this perception if all Germany needed from her would be made available. The very precision of warnings from others as well as his own agents and even from within the German embassy staff in Moscow appears to have convinced him that this was all provocations and plants, designed by the Germans to provoke him or by the Allies to involve him in war with Germany on their side. It all made him all the more determined to hold back, and hence the German attack would come as a complete and shattering surprise.[81]

In the final days before the attack, Hitler gave more attention to the British than to the Soviet reaction to his intended move. At times he thought the British might quit fighting;[82] at other times he thought they might take advantage of the situation to try to reconquer the Channel Islands, which he planned to keep permanently and now ordered fortified more heavily to cope with any British landing attempt.[83] In a pep talk to his army and navy leaders on June 14, he insisted that there was no alternative to an attack on the Soviet Union now, that the figures on Soviet strength were of no importance, and that Germany had to be ready to deal with the United States subsequently.[84] As recent research has shown, weather and general logistic issues, not the Balkan campaign of spring 1941, led Hitler to set the date for the attack at June 22.[85] In the last days before the invasion, his big worry—as in August 1939— was the possibility that his prospective enemy might approach Germany with a big offer at the last minute and thus create propaganda difficulties for the German home front. Neither he nor the German Foreign Minister was to be accessible to the Soviet ambassador in Berlin, and the Germans were greatly relieved that the latter had only routine questions to ask at a time when Molotov's attempt to reopen talks could be evaded easily by the German ambassador in Moscow.[86]

The substantive worries in German headquarters in the final weeks before the attack concerned preparations for the operations which were to follow upon the anticipated swift victory over the Soviet Union. The resources of German industry were to be shifted from the army to the air force and navy for the war against Great Britain and also against the United States. A big program of landing ship construction was to be carried out in the fall of 1941 for an invasion of England in 1942.[87] In the meantime, German forces were to strike across Turkey, Egypt and the Caucasus into the Near East. There they would control the key oil resources and gain access to the Indian Ocean.[88] The big battleship navy could then be built to deal with the United States, while the air force would batter England. Hitler was so enthusiastic and eager about these prospects that to the consternation of the army leadership he ordered the first major shift of production from the army to the air force on June 20, 1941.[89] Like the Soviet Union, Germany was in for a big surprise.

Early in the morning of June 22, 1941, German forces struck across the border of the Soviet Union while the German air force attacked Russia's planes on the ground. Everywhere the Germans achieved tactical surprise; at first Moscow could not believe the reports from the frontier and thought these were provocations. In a few hours it became evident to the most determined dreamers in the Soviet capital that this was for real, that they had waited in vain for Germany to make demands, and that they were now in a battle for their lives. The Red Army already knew.

THE MEDITERRANEAN

Before the vast and grim battles on the Eastern Front can be examined, other developments which had occurred since the summer of 1940 must be reviewed: the German projects during the period of their preparations to attack Russia, the Italian disasters of the fall and winter of 1940 and the German rescue efforts, the ongoing war in the Atlantic and the increasing United States involvement in it, and finally the decision of Japan to expand the war in East Asia.

While moving forward with plans and preparations for the invasion of the Soviet Union scheduled for the early summer of 1941, the German government tried to use the intervening months to put together a combination against Great Britain that might assist in striking at that country even as German bombers pounded its cities, and German surface ships and submarines destroyed its shipping. For a short time in the fall of 1940, the German government toyed with the idea of lining up France and Spain into an anti-British alliance.

The Germans thought for a while, and argued among themselves endlessly, that it might be possible to engage France in the struggle against England by promising minimal concessions in occupied France and territorial compensation at the expense of Great Britain for colonial concessions France would have to make to Germany, Italy, and Spain. In the process, German leaders repeatedly discussed such projects with the Vichy French, and on one occasion Hitler himself met with Pétain.

Nothing came of these projects for several reasons. Although some elements in the German navy, diplomatic service, and army favored an accommodation with France, Hitler himself always remained skeptical. He was reluctant to make any concessions, always suspicious of the French, including those most inclined to go with Germany, and forever looking for evidence that the French were really as awful as he had always believed. The December 13, 1940, dismissal of Laval by Pétain confirmed all his prejudices, and if there had ever been a real opportunity for an accommodation, there was none thereafter. There was, furthermore, now a little reluctance on the French side. It was increasingly obvious in the fall of 1940 and thereafter that the quick defeat of Great Britain, a defeat of which the Vichy leaders were perhaps even more certain than the Germans, was not about to take place. Though American aid to Britain was clearly as yet a trickle, there was every reason to believe that it would grow; and whatever those in charge of the French government thought of England, they did not want to get into an open war with the United States. The fact that the Germans, instead of making concessions which might strengthen the position of French advocates of an accommodation, went out of their way to antagonize the French public, placed the would-be collaborators in an impossible position. The German annexation of Alsace-Lorraine followed by large-scale expulsions of inhabitants loyal to France across the new border was guaranteed to sour the atmosphere. Hardly had the uproar over this outrage begun to dim than the Germans began deporting German Jews and dumping them in France as well. On top of all this, there were the chicaneries of the occupation, the imposition of enormous financial exactions, and the retention of almost all the French prisoners of war.

The longer all these processes lasted, the less the possibility of a new start.[90]

The Spaniards had initially shown some enthusiasm for joining the war on Germany's side only to meet with disinterest at first.[91] In the face of strong British efforts to discourage their entrance,[92] they had held to their preference for going to war for some time.[93] By the time the Germans began to be interested in bringing them in to strike added blows at England, however, some Spaniards were beginning to have doubts. These doubts were strongly reinforced by German demands for bases not only in the area of French Morocco that Spain wanted for herself but in the Spanish Canaries. Whatever Franco might have been willing to concede in regard to his aspirations for former French colonies, he was absolutely unwilling to consider giving up one of the Spanish Canary Islands as the Germans insisted, to say nothing of trading Spanish Guinea or the island of Fernando Po to the Germans.[94]

The most pro-Axis of his associates, Serrano Suñer, came back from his talks with German leaders in September 1940 very much disillusioned,[95] and at the same time the desperate economic situation inside Spain was hardly conducive to military experiments. In mid-October Franco dropped his Foreign Minister, the somewhat Anglophile Juan Beigbeder Atienza, and replaced him with Suñer, but from all evidence he did this in order the more readily to carry out Beigbeder's policy of keeping out of the war unless the Germans completely changed their approach.[96] As became clear to Franco when he met Hitler at Hendaye on the border of Spain and occupied France, the Germans still wanted Spanish bases, were not inclined to agree to all of Spain's colonial demands, and—of increasing importance as the British blockade kept Spain on short rations—were not in a position to supply Spain in a long war.[97]

All the detailed and complicated German plans for an assault on Gibraltar and for subsequent deployment into Northwest Africa turned out to be in vain.[98] The repeated German demands that Spain enter the war on their side were met with evasions and postponements from the Spanish side and the Spanish refusal was passed on to the British.[99] The new policy of Spain could not be changed by pleadings from Rome; in fact, the Italian defeats of the winter of 1940–41 probably reinforced Franco's disinclination to enter the conflict. He would try to keep the Germans from becoming so angry as to invade Spain by extending his prior support of German submarine warfare to the refueling of German surface ships,[100] but no messages from Berlin could make him take the step to open war on the Axis side without assurances of colonial booty, material supplies, and an abandonment of German demands for Spanish bases.[101]

Franco was still enormously impressed by the great German victory in the West and could not see a real prospect for Britain to win,[102] but he also doubted that Germany would win as quickly as Hitler and von Ribbentrop kept telling him. Spain was in no condition for a long war, but she would fight any country that attacked her.[103]

The Germans for now gave up on Spain. They were extremely concerned that promises of concessions of French colonial possessions to Spain would leak out and precipitate the defection of those colonies from Vichy to de Gaulle. Berlin was in fact pushing for Vichy reconquest of the territories which had already defected to the Free French leader and could hardly expect much to come of the reconquest plans if such areas were subsequently to be turned over to other powers.[104] Moreover, in anticipation of the planned invasion of the Soviet Union, Berlin thought a British landing on the Iberian peninsula possible—a concern similar to the German worry about British operations toward the Channel Islands and Norway—and intended to launch an invasion of Spain on their own at the first sign of such a diversionary operation by the British.[105] Hitler had only unpleasant thoughts and nasty comments about Franco Spain as he turned his attention to the Eastern campaign; the possibility that Germany's own demand for Spanish territory to use against the United States and for Germany's colonial empire might have affected the views of a proud nationalist never occurred to him.

The German project for a harmonized alignment of France, Spain, and Italy against Britain in the West was not only limited in time by the need to move forces east for the attack on the U.S.S.R., but it was hampered and eventually aborted in part because of the new step Italy took in reaction to a portion of the German preparations for that invasion. The Germans had very firmly told the Italian government in August 1940 that they wanted the Balkans kept quiet and that Italy was not to move against Yugoslavia and Greece.[106] Hardly had the Italians reconciled themselves to this restriction than they learned of German troops being sent into Romania. Since the Germans had not informed the Italians that this, like the delivery of arms to Finland, was an outcome of their decision to go to war with the Soviet Union, it was not surprisingly read in Rome as part of a new German forward strategy in the Balkans. Italy was to keep quiet while Germany took over Southeast Europe.

This was not the reason Italy had gone to war as Germany's ally: to restrain her demands on France so that the latter could be brought out of the war, and to restrain her own advances in the Balkans so that the Germans could take over there. Mussolini was very angry to hear of the German move into Romania a few days after his meeting with Hitler on October 4;[107] as he explained to Ciano on October 12: "Hitler always faces me with a *fait accompli*. This time I am going to pay him back in his own coin. He will find out from the papers that I have occupied Greece. In this way the equilibrium will be re-established."[108]

The Italians had already declined German offers of armored units in North Africa to help them with their operation into Egypt.[109] They would move forward in Egypt on their own, that is, whenever the Italian commander on the spot could get around to carrying out Mussolini's orders. Now they would try to launch an invasion of Greece without proper preparations or adequate forces, in fact right after partially demobilizing their own army. Both operations briefly appeared to the Italians like a way to secure some spectacular victories of their own at a time when the Germans had been able neither to make peace with England, nor to invade the island, nor to knock it out by air attacks.[110]

In a series of incredibly confused conferences the Italian military leaders heard Mussolini explain his decision to attack Greece on or about October 26 and argued over various unlikely schemes for implementing this project. Simultaneously it became clear that the army in North Africa was, as usual, not ready to move forward. The Germans were not told officially about the invasion of Greece until the last moment, and the contradictory indications they received ahead of time were in any case no basis for decisive action which might seriously offend their Italian ally, at a time when Hitler still hoped to work out some accommodation of Italy with France and Spain. Whether or not he had given Mussolini a green light the last time they met on October 4, when the two met again at Florence on October 28 he could only put a good face on the situation created by that morning's Italian attack. Anger came later.[111]

The Italian attack concentrated on a push south in the Albanian–Greek coastal sector, an effort to cut the only significant east–west road across northern Greece at the central portion of the front, and a minimal holding attack at the Macedonian end of the border. The Greeks had been alerted by prior press polemics and diplomatic pressures and hence had begun to move up forces to meet an anticipated invasion.[112] Bulgaria's refusal to join in the attack on Greece—perhaps out of concern that Turkey might then join in—meant that the Greek leadership could move troops from Thrace to Macedonia to aid in stemming the Italians.[113]

After initial advances the Italian forces in the coastal sector were held, those on the offensive in the middle were cut off and destroyed, while those at the north eastern end were quickly pushed back. Within a week it was clear on both sides that the Italian forces had suffered a serious set-back in spite of having control of the air and alone fielding armored vehicles. A Greek counter-offensive began on November 14 and quickly threw Italian forces back into Albania. The front then stabilized approximately thirty miles inside Albania with Italian counter-offensives held by the Greeks, and further Greek attacks in January and February 1941 making only smaller advances; both sides were exhausted.

The Greek forces had better artillery and were assisted after the first days by some British air force support—about which more later—but these cannot be assigned a major role in the outcome. It also will not do to point to the terrible weather and terrain since these were the same for both sides. Certainly terrain and weather conditions kept the Greeks from exploiting their victories into clearing the Italians out of Albania altogether, as they would quite possibly have made it difficult for the Italians to exploit a victory in the initial battles had they won any, but the actual events were decided by the determined and brave fighting of the Greeks on the one hand and the almost incredible incompetence of the Italian planning, preparations, and leadership on the other. Anyone who has seen the terrain over which Italian troops fought in World War I will recognize that they are entirely capable of fighting bravely under the most difficult circumstances; but in an army where intelligence and rank were distributed in inverse proportions, nothing but utter disaster could be expected. Twice the top commander on the Italian side was relieved, but all to no avail. Two decades of Fascist rule had left Italy with an army dramatically more poorly led, and equipped, and trained than that of 1915.

As if these set-backs were not sufficient, the British navy carried out a previously planned assault by torpedo-carrying planes from an aircraft carrier on the Italian fleet at Taranto in the night of November 12–13. Three battleships were hit, one of them beyond repair.[114] Furthermore, the British were building up their forces in Egypt for a counter-attack there.

The Italians had halted after their initial advance to Sidi Barrani and had for months argued about the next step toward Alexandria: an offensive to seize the railhead eighty miles to the east at Mersa Matruth.[115] Every few weeks the Italian commander, Marshal Rudolfo Graziani, had either promised to move or received orders to do so. He was still contemplating either his navel or the sand dunes when the British struck.

In spite of the danger of invasion of the home islands, the British had sent significant reinforcements to Egypt.[116] Though nothing like the forces subsequently engaged in the North African campaign, the extra tanks, planes, and troops—the last primarily from India and Australia—added to the units defending Egypt enabled the British commander, General Sir Archibald Wavell, to launch an offensive on December 9. Surprising and overwhelming the Italians, the attacking forces quickly destroyed the armored and infantry units in the Sidi Barrani area; in a few days the British disposed of three Italian divisions and pushed almost sixty miles to the Egyptian–Libyan border, where the Italians attempted to make a stand.

After a two-week pause to bring up supplies, the British struck again on January 3, 1941. In a series of moves, alternating infantry assaults with daring thrusts by armored spearheads, the British in the following four weeks destroyed whatever remained of the Italian 10th Army after Sidi Barrani. The Italian garrisons at Bardia, Tobruk, and Derna were routed or captured. In two months the Italians lost not only their toehold in Egypt but the whole of Cyrenaica. The British took 115,000 prisoners; and for the time being removed the threat to Egypt and redoubled the blow to Mussolini's prestige—or what was left of it after the prior Italian defeat at the hands of Greek troops.[117]

Other international and internal Italian repercussions of these disasters will be dealt with shortly, but there was one immediate military one of great strategic importance in the war as a whole. Italian forces in East Africa had occupied British Somaliland and a border post in the Sudan; thereafter they had very unwisely shifted to a defensive posture at a time of Great Britain's weakness. The isolation of Italian East Africa was increased and made almost absolute when the concentration of Italian air transportation efforts on re-supplying the faltering forces in Albania ended even this tenuous link with the distant garrison. Now, in February 1941, the British counter-attacked from Kenya, and then landed on the coast of both British Somaliland and Eritrea while an expedition under Orde Wingate headed for Addis Ababa, the capital of Ethiopia, from the Sudan. In short order the main Italian forces were defeated, the remainder surrounded at isolated points in the interior, and the Ethiopian ruler Haile Selassie returned to his throne.[118]

Over 100,000 more Italian soldiers had become prisoners of war; the conquest of Ethiopia, Mussolini's proudest accomplishment, had been undone; for the first time, a country occupied by the Axis had been liberated. There were two implications of great import for the continuing war. The United States government could claim that the Red Sea was no longer a war zone and thus open to American shipping; as of April 11, President Roosevelt so announced. United States ships could now go to Suez to carry supplies directly to the British forces there and relieve the pressure on British shipping. Furthermore, the removal of

Italy from Northeast Africa cleared the western shore of the Indian Ocean, a matter of major significance when Japan entered the war later and there were Axis hopes of cutting the Allied lifelines through those critical waters.

The humiliating set-backs suffered by Italy's armed forces on the Greek front in November, accompanied by the Taranto raid, and soon followed by the collapse in North Africa, shook the Fascist system in Italy. Here were unmistakable signs of incompetence on the one hand and a war obviously about to last a long time on the other. If anyone in Italy had doubts on either score, the remobilization now ordered, a dramatic tightening of the rationing of basic foodstuffs on December 1, and the British naval bombardment of Genoa on February 8,[119] enlightened them.

There was great disaffection which Mussolini could not divert from himself by firing Marshal Pietro Badoglio, the Chief of the General Staff, instead of his son-in-law Ciano whom many Italians blamed for pushing Italy into the Greek adventure.[120] The public relations stunt of sending all Cabinet members aged 45 or under to the front in Albania in January entertained rather than reassured the people at home, even as it alienated those associates of Mussolini who found their pleasant berths in Rome replaced by distinctly uncomfortable tents in the frozen highlands of Albania.[121] Since neither the King nor the church nor the military leadership could or would act against the regime, the police and the activist elements in the Fascist Party—with considerable use of their traditional means of persuasion, clubs and castor oil—managed to hold the discontent of the people in check. A major appeal by Churchill on December 23,[122] by pointing out that it was "one man alone" who had brought the Italians into this disastrous situation, clearly suggested a way out, but practically no one was prepared to take it.[123] Mussolini's dreams of great power status had turned into a mirage by the light of shell-fire at the front,[124] and the regime would have to be rescued from its Balkan folly and North African calamity by Germany. The price of German rescue was the end of Italy's independence; won in the nineteenth century, it could be reestablished only by the Allies.[a]

The Germans would have had no serious objections to the Italian invasion of Greece had it been as promptly successful as their own

---

[a] There is surely some symbolic significance in the fact that the most voluminous secret file of the German embassy in Rome (Quirinal) is the one on the "purchase" in Italy of art objects for Hitler and Göring. See Bonn, Pol. Archiv, Botschaft Rom (Quir.) Geheim 527/40 in 44/4. British consideration in December 1940 of possible armistice terms for Italy, if these were asked for, already include reference to a quick German occupation of the country (see PRO, FO 371, R 9066/6840/22).

invasion of Norway, and they had themselves repeatedly urged the Italians forward in the North African theater. Militarily, success in these two endeavors could only help German war plans at the time. Italian control of Greece would seal off the Balkans from the south during the invasion of the Soviet Union. An Italian conquest of Egypt, for which the Germans offered an armored division, would strike a very hard blow at Britain and simultaneously free Axis forces to threaten Vichy-controlled Northwest Africa on the one hand and assist in the reconquest of the French colonies in Equatorial Africa from de Gaulle on the other. From the perspective of Hitler's own political and ideological views, there would similarly have been advantages. He viewed the Mediterranean as Italy's destined *Lebensraum* (living space), and his repeated reassurances to Mussolini on this point were by all available evidence sincerely meant. The German navy, which saw the problems of the Mediterranean and North Africa in very different terms—as a major theater of war for the defeat of Great Britain—was never able to convert Hitler to its view.[125] As for the oil resources of the Middle East, these could nourish Italy's fleet and air force while the oil wells of the Caucasus would supplement those of Romania in supplying Germany's on a scale even more lavish than could be attained by trade with Russia.

The reality of Italian defeats, by contrast with the possibility of Italian victories, opened up a series of dangers from the perspective of Berlin. The defeat in Greece could lead to the opening of a real Balkan front in the war—an intolerable situation for a Germany which wanted to concentrate its land and air forces for an attack on Russia—and, possibly even more dangerous, might result in the stationing of British planes on Greek air bases from which they could attack the Romanian oil fields.[126] It must be remembered that the enormous difficulties of air attacks on distant oil fields were not understood by either side at this time; it was assumed on both sides that even small air raids could bring about vast fire and destruction.

An Italian defeat in North Africa which led to the British occupation of all of Libya would open the Mediterranean to British shipping, Italy itself to attack from the south, and quite possibly to the defection of the Vichy-controlled French colonies in North and West Africa. Moreover, the blows to the prestige of the Fascist regime from such disasters, accompanied by the apparently unavoidable loss of Italian East Africa, could easily lead to the complete collapse of the whole system Mussolini had established, and this was recognized at the time; it is not hindsight from 1943.[127]

In view of these facts, the Germans moved promptly to assist their ally. Whatever the doubts and sarcastic comments of some German officials and officers, Hitler himself was absolutely determined to take action to save his friend. He might at times dictate military strategy and priorities to Mussolini, but he was always careful to try to do so in a manner calculated to offend Mussolini minimally because he recognized then, as he had repeatedly stressed earlier, that only Mussolini assured Italy's loyalty to the Axis.[a]

In the immediate situation in Albania, the Germans provided transport planes in December to assist the Italian air force in ferrying troops and supplies to a land poorly provided with docking, unloading, and internal transportation facilities.[128] The Germans had originally planned to send dive bombers to Italy and Sicily to participate in attacks on British ships in the Mediterranean; upon the first great British victories in Egypt and at the Egyptian–Libyan border, the German air force speeded up its dispatch of the 10th Air Corps from Norway to support the Italian forces and attack British naval and merchant ships. By mid-January the Luftwaffe was flying numerous missions primarily from bases in Sicily.[129] This immediately altered the situation in the Central Mediterranean; it was from this time on that Malta came under serious bombardment.[b] Moreover, in mid-January the Germans began bombing and mining the Suez Canal—as Hitler had wanted to do for half a year—with massive effect on all British operations in the Mediterranean theater.[130]

As the Italian situation in Albania and North Africa deteriorated further, the Germans had to examine the possibility of sending troops as well as planes. The idea of sending a corps with two mountain divisions to Albania was eventually dropped for two reasons: the Italian forces appeared no longer in danger of being completely driven into the sea by the Greeks and the logistical situation in Albania simply could not accommodate two German divisions. Since Hitler was unwilling to send anything less than enough for a real push, nothing came of the alternative which Mussolini would have preferred: the sending of only one German division to strengthen the Italian defense.[131] The Italian troops in Albania, totally unsuccessful in their efforts at resuming the offensive, had to await the results of a German attack on Greece from an entirely

---

[a] It deserves to be noted that Hitler was *not* prepared to take advantage of the difficult situation of Italy to work out an agreement with Vichy France. Now that Mussolini was desperate for such an agreement, and Hitler could no longer assert that Italy's demands and interests interfered with a German–French accommodation, it became clear that it was Hitler's fundamental opposition to the French which precluded an agreement on *any* terms. See Admiral Weichold, "Schicksalskampf der Achse im Mittelmeer 1940–1943," Part I, pp. 228–29, BA/MA, Nachlass Weichold, N 316/1. On Hitler's continued high opinion of Mussolini, see Jochmann, *Hitler, Monologe*, 21/22 July 1941, p. 43.

[b] On January 11, 1941, and again later, the Germans severely damaged the aircraft carrier *Illustrious* which had launched the Taranto raid and now had to be withdrawn from the Mediterranean.

different direction. The British reaction to this German strategy would not only collapse before it but contribute decisively to the success of the German rescue operation in North Africa.

The Italians, who had earlier proudly refused the German offer of an armored division to help them in the conquest of Egypt, were forced by their December and January defeats to ask the Germans for help. Originally a small blocking force of barely division strength was considered; it would do in North Africa what Mussolini had hoped a German mountain division might do in Albania.[a] By the time preparations for this project were under way, the situation of Italian forces in North Africa had deteriorated dramatically. The British victory at Beda From in early February, which led to the destruction of the rest of Italy's 10th Army, seemed to both Germans and Italians to open the way for a complete British occupation of Libya. Only a larger German force could, it was believed, keep the British from doing to the Italians in North Africa what the Greeks were evidently too exhausted to do to them in Albania. We now know that even before Beda Fromm, the British had decided to halt their North African offensive; but the Germans were taking no chances.[132] On February 12 the new commander of a larger German force, requested by the Italians and sent under conditions largely set by the Germans, arrived in Tripoli. This was General Erwin Rommel, whose decisions and forces, soon designated the German Afrika Corps, would change the war in the Mediterranean.

SOUTHEAST EUROPE

The main German relief expedition for Italy was, however, to attack Greece through Bulgaria from Romania. The weather in the mountains near the Greek–Bulgarian border made such an offensive impossible before the spring of 1941, and the Italians would have to hang on in Albania until then as best they could. Bringing up sufficient forces and equipment for such an operation would occupy the intervening months since such forces had to be shipped across Hungary, built up in Romania, and then launched across Bulgaria into Greece. But in Hungary, Romania, and Bulgaria there were land transportation facilities directly accessible to the Germans, unlike the Albanian front reachable only by water across the Adriatic from Italy and then across unpaved mountain trails within the Italian colony itself.

The fact that at the last moment bridges across the Danube between

[a] Hitler was originally willing to send such a small force called a *Sperrverband* or blocking unit, to North Africa because he did not at that time contemplate an offensive there as he did against Greece. Occupying Greece and holding in North Africa looked like the way to sustain Mussolini while he was preparing the attack on the Soviet Union.

Romania and Bulgaria would have to be constructed by German engineers in practice meant that the assembly in Romania would be shielded against any interference from the south in the unlikely contingency of Bulgaria and Turkey joining the British and Greeks. What may look at first like the long way around was the best from the perspective of Berlin. This route had the added advantages of increasing German strength in Romania, ensuring the cooperation of Bulgaria, which would be suitably rewarded by a slice of Greece, isolating Yugoslavia completely, and making it most unlikely that Turkey could intervene. In a play on the names of three countries, a joke of the time had suggested that when Hitler got hungry, he would have turkey with plenty of grease. Here was the opportunity.

It was an opportunity that the Germans were determined not to miss. Hardly had the Italian offensive on Greece which began on October 28 stalled, than the Germans on November 1 began to consider a drive through Bulgaria to the Aegean. In the following months the project grew until it encompassed a complete occupation of Greece. By November 4 the Yugoslav government was beginning to indicate quietly to the Germans that they would be willing to join in the attack on Greece if they could be promised the Aegean port of Salonika, thus freeing them from dependence on the Italian-controlled Adriatic.[133] Simultaneously, there began a series of secret soundings in which the Greeks tried to obtain German mediation for a cease-fire and new peace which could spare them from being overrun.

The soundings from Yugoslavia were welcomed by Berlin and led to lengthy negotiations which culminated in Yugoslavia's eventually adhering to the Tripartite Pact on March 25, 1941; and when the government which had taken this step was overthrown in a coup two days later, Hitler immediately decided to invade and conquer Yugoslavia along with Greece.[134] As for the peace feelers from the latter, Berlin was not interested. No amount of assurances from Athens and no volume of evidence that the country was not becoming a base for British troops or long-range bombers could turn Hitler from his determination to occupy all of Greece.[135] There were to be no even slightly loose ends left on the flanks of his forthcoming attack in the East.

The British had considered various schemes to try to create a front in the Balkans to divert Italian and possibly also German forces from the Western Front earlier in the war.[136] Like the schemes to sabotage the Romanian oil fields, all this came to naught as Germany drew Romania into its fold and cast its shadow over Hungary, Yugoslavia, and Bulgaria after its victory in Western Europe. The Italian attack on Greece with its quickly obvious set-backs appeared to offer the British an opportunity along with an obligation. The obligation was to try to provide some substance to the guarantee the British had given to Greece when Italy occupied Albania; the opportunity was the possibility of creating on the continent of Europe a Balkan front based on Greece and supplied from North Africa and possibly drawing on those other Southeast European countries also menaced by the Axis: Yugoslavia, Turkey, and possibly Bulgaria. And from that base, there might be the possibility of raids on the Romanian oil fields.

Whatever these tempting visions, there were some realities that could not be disregarded and other realities which when disregarded would prove fatal for British designs. In the first instance, the British only sent some air force units to Greece to assist the Greek forces fighting on the Albanian front. In the face of initial Italian domination of the air, this was of considerable help, even though numerically the British forces were never large. In November 1940, the British commander in the Middle East, General Sir Archibald Wavell, was husbanding all his resources and carefully collecting reinforcements for his planned offensive against the Italians in the following month. He could spare little equipment to remedy the desperate shortages of the Greek army, he had no ground forces to send there, and in early November made it clear that none would be dispatched.[137]

In the following weeks, the British began to inch their way into an army venture in Greece even as their troops chased the Italians over miles of North African desert. In December some paratroops were sent to Crete to replace a Greek army division being sent to the Albanian front—here was a first diversion from the African campaign which temporarily aided the Greeks but otherwise did little good because the British did almost nothing to get the island ready for defense.[138] In an astonishing imitation of Italian incompetence, the British had hardly improved those defenses by the time they were getting ready to meet a German landing half a year later!

The Greeks did not want British troops on the mainland because they feared such a presence would serve to provoke a German attack; they did not recognize that it made no difference to Berlin whether the British presence was real or potential. The death of the Greek dictator, Ioannis Metaxas, on January 29, 1941, removed what was probably the last obstacle to a British reversal of policy. Always a realist as well as a patriot, Metaxas might have saved the British from a futile gesture which helped the Greeks little and cost the Allied cause much.[139]

As it became clear that the Germans would attack Greece through Bulgaria, the Greeks looked at British aid differently and the British revised their own priorities. Having moved the bulk of their forces and essentially all their supplies to the Albanian front, the Greeks were now interested in British land forces to help defend themselves against a German invasion. The authorities in London, encouraged by excessively optimistic reports from Wavell as well as from the new British Foreign Secretary Anthony Eden and the Chief of Imperial General Staff Field Marshal Sir John Dill, who were in Greece in late February, ordered the land flank in central Libya held while troops and supplies were switched to Greece.[140]

This diversion of effort from completing the conquest of Libya to aiding the Greeks against Germany left the Italians with essentially all of Tripolitania as a base for the Germans who would then hold on in North Africa and repeatedly threaten Egypt for more than two additional years. It was done in part to honor the political promises given to the Greeks, but it was also in part due to a complete disregard of the military and political realities in Southeast Europe. The military realities were the ability of the Germans to bring massive power to bear on an operation there over land supply routes, and a complete inability of the British to bring even remotely equivalent forces to the same theater. The bravery of the British navy could get British troops to Greece and, when necessary, evacuate them (though without their equipment).

The Royal Navy could also protect the British troops against the Italian navy. This was shown dramatically in the naval battle off Cape Matapan on March 28 when, in part because of their ability to read German code machines,[a] in part because of the superiority of British radar, the Royal Navy sank three Italian heavy cruisers and two destroyers when the Italian navy tried to interfere with British convoys to Greece without effective German air support.[141] The operation had been launched by the Italian navy under great German pressure; its failure contributed to subsequent greater reluctance in the Italian naval command to risk their ships and hardly increased their eagerness to defer to German wishes.

The British, however, regardless of naval successes, simply did not have the land and air forces in the Mediterranean to hold against the

[a] There is some irony in the fact that key Italian Admiralty cypher books were generally not broken by the British whose signals intelligence came from the reading of German air force enigma code machines and those enigma machines the Germans had either given or sold to their ally for greater security. The British read important Italian *diplomatic* codes; but the Germans who also read these did not want to tell Rome, presumably on the assumption that no one else could do what they themselves had only been able to accomplish with great difficulty. There is an unconsciously humorous record of these matters in documents in the files of the State Secretary in the German Foreign Ministry on Italy; Woermann for Ribbentrop, "U.St.S.Pol. Nr. 256gRs," 1 April 1941, and "Nr. 261gRs," 3 April 1941 (AA, St.S., "Italien," Bd. 4, fr. B001669–70, B 001673); Memorandum by Weizsäcker, "St.S. Nr. 293," 2 May 1941, and Woermann for Ribbentrop, "U.St.S.Pol. Nr. 422gRs," 15 May 1941 (St.S., "Italien," Bd. 5, fr. B000847, B000894–95).

German offensive into Greece. The successful transport of troops, therefore, only assured the loss of their equipment together with many of the soldiers as well as the confidence of the Australian government, many of whose troops were involved, in the judgement of the British military.

Integrally related to the military miscalculation was an equally serious but more easily understandable political one. The British hoped that they could weld together a general alignment in Southeast Europe against Germany and that this would in particular include Turkey as well as Yugoslavia and possibly Bulgaria. The Bulgarians had decided by the end of 1940 that they would side with Germany. Incapable of recognizing in the face of his belief in Germany and his hopes for territorial gain at the expense of Greece that in the long war ahead Bulgaria's interest lay in opposing rather than cooperating with the Third Reich, King Boris led his country onto the road to disaster.[142] It is indicative of his limited perspective that he thought the American effort to reinforce the British attempt to create an alignment against Germany through the mission of Colonel William J. Donovan to be silly.[143] The ruler who would absolutely insist later that year on declaring war against the United States was perhaps not as shrewd as many thought him.

The Turks were terrified of the Germans and the Russians on the one hand and hoped for territorial gains from Greece on the other. In spite of endless efforts, projects, schemes, and hopes on the part of the British, they were not about to join any front against Germany until the Germans themselves invaded Turkey, something the Germans naturally promised they would never do and something they equally naturally planned for the moment it was safe for them to do so, namely after they had conquered the rest of the Balkans and defeated Russia. Until that moment, Germany would exchange limited amounts of equipment for much needed chrome and sweet-talk the Turks far more persuasively than the British.[144] In offering portions of Greece to Bulgaria and Yugoslavia, the Germans were careful to exclude that portion of Greece bordering on Turkey. Here was bait to dangle before Ankara's eyes, and in the event the Turks would receive a minimal slice of Greece so that they could control the route of an important stretch of railway.[145]

As for Yugoslavia, here too there was no realistic prospect of action against Germany and Italy by a weak regime governing a divided country of feuding nationalities and which coveted a piece of Greece for itself. It is correct that here too British diplomatic efforts had some American support,[146] but it was surely unrealistic—given the past record of both Yugoslavia itself and Britain's and the United States' obvious inability to provide substantial deliveries of weapons—to expect Yugoslavia to take the only step likely to be useful: a quick invasion of Albania from the north to throw the Italians out of that colony entirely and join up with Greek forces. The coup in Belgrade on March 27 appeared to give some retroactive validity to earlier British efforts, but by then it was entirely too late. Undoubtedly the British gestures of defiance, both the diplomatic and the military ones, encouraged the spirits of those opposed to the Axis in a grim time. Unlike the Soviet Union, which was still begging to join Hitler,[147] the British at least tried to help his victims. They—like the victims—would pay heavily.

On the day of the coup in Yugoslavia, Hitler, as already mentioned, immediately decided to attack that country as well as Greece. He knew and was reassured by German diplomats that Yugoslavia had no intention of helping Greece; it was simply that many in Belgrade objected to joining the Axis and assisting an attack on their own southern neighbor which was certain to put them completely in Germany's power. But the German leader felt relieved not to have to make even for a moment the concessions he had promised[148] and was positively enthusiastic about the opportunity to crush Yugoslavia at a time when German forces were in any case concentrated for an operation in Southeast Europe.[149]

Plans for the invasion of Yugoslavia were made to coincide with the attack on Greece, scheduled for Sunday, April 6, 1941. Hitler wanted to make this a real spectacular: the opening would be a surprise massive bombing of Belgrade in the hope that what had worked at Rotterdam (but was not working in these same nights in Glasgow, Coventry, Birmingham, and Bristol), might terrorize the population of Yugoslavia and paralyze its government.[a] If the latter purpose was accomplished to a considerable extent, the former, as subsequent developments showed, was not. Even unleashing the band of extreme Croatian nationalists, the Ustasha, out of the sewers of Europe to slaughter anybody and everybody they and the Germans did not like would prove incapable of "pacifying" a country which remained a center of resistance to Axis rule until 1945;[150] but the formal resistance of the Yugoslav army was broken in a few days. German columns moved quickly to cut through and eventually round up an army that was too spread out to retreat southwards as it had in the fall of 1915.[151]

As in the case of the attack on Poland in 1939 and on France in 1940, Hitler summoned the vultures to speed up the destruction of his prey. The Italians, who had long cast hostile and covetous eyes on the South

---

[a] It should be noted that the German Minister to Yugoslavia, now recalled to Berlin, warned against this step (*German Documents*, D, XII, No. 259). Ribbentrop insisted on Gert Feine remaining as chargé in Belgrade, where the German legation was destroyed in the raid but he survived (IfZ, ZS 891).

Slav state, and who had been kept from attacking it the preceding year only by a timely German veto, hastened to repeat against Yugoslavia what they had unsuccessfully tried to do against France.[152] With Yugoslavia falling apart, Italy could look forward to a substantial share of the booty, though necessarily deferring to Germany in the allocation of territory.

Hungary had refused German proposals to join in the war against Poland in 1939; such a declination did not recur. For years Berlin had been urging the leaders of Hungary to give up their demands on Yugoslavia, make their peace with that country, and turn revisionist aspirations in other directions. A reluctant Hungarian government had finally adopted such a course and had signed a treaty of "permanent peace and eternal friendship" with Yugoslavia on December 10, 1940. Now they were both to provide a base for German troops to attack Yugoslavia and to join in themselves.[153] The government in Budapest decided to enter the war on Germany's side and proceeded to do so in the face of the protesting suicide of Prime Minister Pal Teleki.[154] Hungary obtained a portion of the territories it had hoped to acquire, but having hitched itself to the German war chariot would find the traces difficult to slip. Bulgaria was also invited to help itself to appropriate slices of Yugoslavia and happily did so.[155]

The delighted victors divided the stricken country among themselves. Germany annexed a large area in the north and held the old core of Serbia under military administration. The Italians received a substantial piece in the northwest, much of the coast, and an addition to their Albanian colony. A puppet state of Croatia was created which at one time Hitler thought to place under Hungarian influence, then agreed to put under Italian control, and eventually tried to have the Germans direct themselves. Hungary received a share in the northeast and Bulgaria in the south.[156] Within this welter of conflicting claims, massive population transfers were begun immediately,[157] and confusion between arming, supporting, and opposing various elements in the new rivalry between Germany and Italy in Croatia was also well started by May of 1941.[158] The bloodbath that was World War II Yugoslavia had begun, not ended, with the few days of fighting that preceded the unconditional surrender of April 17.

On the same day that German planes opened the attack on Yugoslavia by the bombing of Belgrade, German troops invaded Greece. Temporarily held at the Greek–Bulgarian border, they quickly sliced behind these forces through the southeast corner of Yugoslavia to seize Salonika, cut off the Greek units to the east and thus obtain their surrender. Driving rapidly through the southwestern corner of Yugoslavia, the

Germans both separated the Greek forces in central Macedonia from the English units moving up to help them and broke into the rear of the main Greek army facing the Italians in Albania. The Greek army in Macedonia had to capitulate like that in the east; soon after the one on the Albanian front followed suit. The King of Greece, like the King of Yugoslavia, had to leave the country. Years of desperate hunger, oppression and resistance, civil war and endless suffering awaited the Greeks like their hapless northern neighbor.

The three British divisions, one Australian and one from New Zealand (plus an English armored brigade), were able to retreat to the coast of Attica from which most of the men were evacuated by April 29, five days after the final capitulation of Greece. While 218,000 Greek and 12,000 British soldiers followed 344,000 Yugoslav soldiers into German prisoner of war cages, the equipment of still another British expeditionary force had had to be destroyed or left behind for the Germans. Some 250 German soldiers had lost their lives in this campaign; once again quick and ruthless action by one side and division and indecision on the other had made possible a dramatic German victory at very low immediate cost.

In this fighting, German air superiority had played as significant a role as it had in the Blitzkrieg in Norway and Western Europe. The failure of the Allies was also due to the inability of the British to send to Greece the size forces and the quantities of supplies which they had anticipated providing. One of two important contributing factors in this has already been mentioned. Time and again German bombs and mines had closed the Suez Canal to shipping, a critical point ignored in many accounts.[159] The other was the offensive Rommel launched as soon as he had even a minimal force gathered in North Africa.

The combination of a British deliberate halt in order to send forces to Greece and the beginnings of German intervention temporarily stabilized something resembling a front near El Agheila. As soon as Rommel had his first advance detachments in place, he wanted to attack before the British could bring in reinforcements and while they were busy in Southeast Europe. In conferences with Hitler and others in Germany on March 20 and 21 and with Mussolini and other Italian leaders on the following days he tried but failed to receive orders or even permission to attack. None of that restrained him. Rather than wait for the armored division scheduled to arrive in May, he decided to attack with the segments of the 5th Light Division already on the spot. Beginning his offensive on March 31, he drove his forces forward, relying heavily on the Italian units which were really not under his command, and in less than two weeks chased the British out of Cyrenaica.

This visually dramatic event opened the possibility of a new attack on

Egypt, this time with German forces alongside Italian ones. King Farouk of Egypt secretly contacted the Germans to explain his hopes for a German occupation of his country.[160] The dangerous situation forced the British to reduce the strength of their expeditionary force destined for Greece. Wavell had to keep one of the Australian divisions scheduled to be shipped there in Egypt, redivert other resources to the desert, and press for the East African campaign to be finished promptly so that the units there would also be available for the North African campaign (from which some of them had come). The spectacular advance also catapulted Rommel into the public limelight and Hitler's favor, and led some elements in Egypt to look to Germany for support; both King Farouk himself and some nationalist officers imagined that a German victory would help them.

On the other hand, the quick drive with limited resources made it impossible for Rommel to accomplish any greater purpose. As his forces advanced, the British pushed added strength into the advanced port of Tobruk and held it against the Germans. Unable to advance into Egypt without taking Tobruk and thereby opening both the land route along the coast and the harbor for supplies, and also being unable to concentrate all his forces on one push, Rommel insisted on a series of poorly planned and executed attacks on the Tobruk perimeter. These failed in bloody fighting from April 11–18; a subsequent limited British attack on the Germans at the Libyan–Egyptian border was warded off successfully, but a renewed German–Italian effort to seize Tobruk at the end of April also failed. Major reinforcements could not be sent to Rommel because German planning assumed that the main effort would be against the Soviet Union in 1941; a push into the Near East was to follow, not precede, the victory over Russia confidently expected by Berlin for the fall of 1941.

In spite of heroic efforts of the British to reinforce their army in Egypt with tanks and planes sent at great risk directly through the Mediterranean (rather than the safer but very much longer route around the Cape of Good Hope) in the second week of May, the new offensive "Battleaxe" in mid-June could not dislodge Rommel from the border area and relieve the siege of Tobruk. There will always be arguments over the causes of the British defeat in this battle, a defeat which led to the relief of General Wavell; but there can be no doubt about certain important contributing factors. The need for the British command in the Middle East to direct forces barely recovered from the disaster in Greece and the subsequent even bloodier defeat on Crete to campaigns first in Iraq and then in Syria—all of which will be discussed shortly—dramatically reduced the strength available for operations in the western desert. A second factor was one which the British did not remedy for a very long time: faulty tactics in armored warfare which failed to take account of the strength of German anti-tank fire—especially the famous 8.8 cm anti-aircraft gun which could be and often was used in ground fighting. A third factor was a curious converse of the German command situation. While Rommel was wont to attack in spite of restraint from above and scant supplies on the spot, the British commanders in the field often found themselves harried into premature offensives by the ever-aggressive Churchill, who was as likely to disregard logistics as Rommel. And as the later Chief of the Imperial General Staff General Brooke so often and so eloquently lamented in his diary, the British higher officer corps was singularly lacking in talent, his explanation being that those who would have done best had been killed in World War I.[161]

In any case, the rapid reconquest of Cyrenaica, coming in the same days as the German invasion of Yugoslavia and Greece, dramatically altered not only the military situation in the Mediterranean but also saved for the time being the Fascist regime in Italy. No one was fooled by the insistence of Mussolini on a second surrender ceremony in Greece in which the Italians could join their German rescuers in lording it over the Greeks. Ironically the Germans proceeded to loot Greece of everything not nailed down and much that was and then turned most of the starving country over to the Italians to occupy and look after, so that in the end the Italians found themselves feeling sorry for the very people whom they had precipitated into the war. But the Italian public was quieted for a while.

Perhaps most important in all this was the postponement of an Allied victory in North Africa which would expose Italy to bombing and invasion. At one point in the flush of victory in the winter of 1940–41 the British had begun to make plans for such operations. These now had to go back into the drawer for a year. A few air raids were flown by the Royal Air Force against Italian cities, but the interminable debate over the bombing of Rome did not as yet have much real substance to it.[162] Mussolini had been reprieved.[163] Hitler believed that Mussolini had gotten about as much out of the Italians as possible,[164] and that once Germany had crushed the Soviet Union there would be such vast German forces relieved for duty elsewhere that there would be no need to worry about the future course of events in the Mediterranean theater.

THE MIDDLE EAST

The German priority on plans for the campaign against the Soviet Union was especially obvious in the weeks immediately following upon the completion of the campaign on the Greek mainland and Rommel's reconquest of Cyrenaica, both effectively accomplished by mid-April. What looked for a moment like an opportunity for Germany to strike into the Middle East was in fact a process of closing down operations in that area so that German attention and resources could be assigned elsewhere.

On April 2, 1941, just before the German move into Yugoslavia and Greece, the pro-Axis elements in Iraq staged a coup which brought to power Rashid Ali al-Gaylani who hated the British and, like the IRA in Ireland and Bose in India, hoped that a German victory over Britain would solve the world's and especially his country's problems. For months Rashid Ali's supporters in and out of the Iraqi government had been in touch with the Axis powers and expecting their victory; now looked like an ideal time to move. The British, who faced Rommel's first offensive in Libya and were trying to move forces to Greece, had no troops to spare in the Middle East but began moving soldiers from India against the possibility of the new Iraqi government siding openly with the Axis. Indian troops landed at the base at Basra which was critical for the whole Middle East supply situation, and other soldiers began to reinforce the airfield at Habbaniya, some 55 miles west of Baghdad. The government of Rashid Ali protested, sought help from Germany and Italy, and surrounded the airfield. On May 2 hostilities started.[165]

Inspired by desperation, the British moved quickly. In a few days, their soldiers cleared the immediate area around Habbaniya airfield, received reinforcements trucked as well as flown in from Palestine, and began an advance on Baghdad. Defeating the disintegrating Iraqi army along the way, they reached the outskirts of Baghdad on May 30. Key Iraqi leaders thereupon fled to Iran and those left behind surrendered. Rashid Ali himself eventually went to Germany, where he would spend the rest of the war hoping to return to Baghdad with German assistance.

That assistance had been rather scanty during the time when it might have been most effective. Given the internal dissension within the Iraqi military and the incompetence of its leadership, even greater help might not have made much difference, but there was in reality little that the Germans could do quickly. The same factor which made it so difficult for the British to send substantial forces — and which may have encouraged the Iraqi plotters to strike — also restrained the Germans. At the beginning of their campaign in Yugoslavia and Greece, they naturally wanted to concentrate on the immediate tasks at hand. From Berlin's perspective, Rashid Ali had moved a month too soon, and throughout April the Germans urged caution even as they tried to figure out ways to help. There were other problems, and these quickly surfaced as the German victories in the Balkan campaign enabled them to take some steps to give effect to their desire to help their new ally.

Since Turkey was reluctant to help transport supplies or troops,[166] the Germans had to fly via the Italian island of Rhodes not only warplanes to intervene in the fighting but all supplies they could send across French Syria. They could also arrange to get some French military supplies already in Syria transported overland to Iraq,[167] but this, as well as using air bases in the French mandate, required negotiations with Vichy and possible concessions to the latter. The Vichy leaders and their subordinates on the spot were willing to help — as has been explained, they would fight the British and other Frenchmen but not against Germans — but all such arrangements took time. There ensued new but inconclusive German–French negotiations. Darlan was prepared to provide assistance, but Hitler was as usual reluctant to make concessions to the French.[168] The Germans did what they could under the circumstances, and by mid-May the first planes were participating in the fighting over Iraq; but the minimal forces and supplies sent made little difference in the outcome. In the planning of German strategy, Iraq (like Egypt) came *after*, not before, the campaign in the East, and it was assumed that a pro-Axis government under Rashid Ali would return to Baghdad in the wake of German tanks in the late fall of 1941.

Whatever efforts Germany might make were further complicated by the position and ambitions of Italy. The Germans at least nominally recognized Italy's political hegemony in the Arab world.[169] Most of the communications between the regime of Rashid Ali and Berlin had to go at first through the Italian legation in Baghdad because Italy, not Germany, had full diplomatic relations with Iraq.[170] Since the British could read the Italian diplomatic code, they knew of Rashid Ali's appeals to Germany and Italy from his first days in power. Furthermore, this Italian diplomatic presence reflected Italy's imperial ambitions in the Middle East, ambitions to which Germany at least in theory deferred — but about which many Iraqis had their doubts. They may not have understood the nature of National Socialist Germany and that country's attitude toward the independence of people it considered "inferior," but they did have a clear idea that Mussolini saw himself as an empire-builder in the Mediterranean and Near East. And how all this could be harmonized with Axis dependence on the French, whose colonial rule in Syria was hardly popular with Arab nationalists, was beyond anyone's resolution. Under these circumstances, it was probably easier for Rashid Ali to devise great plans for a German protectorate over Iraq in the capital of the Third Reich.[171]

The collapse of the pro-Axis regime in Baghdad, under circumstances which showed that for the moment Germany was not in a position to support an analogous coup and anti-British policy in Afghanistan, operated to restrain those elements within that country and among Afghan exiles in Europe who also thought that the triumph of Hitler would aid their cause. Like Rashid Ali, they too would have to await the moment when German forces could come effectively into the Near East.[172]

The very days that the fighting in Iraq was nearing its climax were also the days when the Germans won a spectacular but costly victory on Crete. The British had first sent forces there in the preceding November, but most of those who would defend the island were troops evacuated in late April from Greece. Not certain at first that Crete should and could be defended at all in the face of German air superiority, the British finally decided to try to do so. Placed in command was the New Zealander General Bernard C. Freyberg, a World War I hero whose support by Churchill and the New Zealand government could assure him reinforcements (and the removal of some non-combatants) but not the needed air support which was simply unavailable. The British could read German air force signals and therefore had a clear picture of what was brewing; they would let Freyberg and his men fight it out, a choice difficult to fault since the New Zealanders almost made it.[173]

The Germans had been thinking about a possible seizure of Crete for some time, Hitler having originally offered on October 28, 1940, to assist the Italian invasion of Greece from Albania by landing German airborne forces there. Mussolini, who still thought of himself as waging an independent and parallel war, declined this offer just as he refused a German armored division for North Africa. Italy would prove equally incapable in both theaters. The Germans became alarmed over the possibility of British use of airfields in Crete to bomb the Romanian oil fields, and of a naval base at Suda Bay on the north coast of the island to interrupt the tanker traffic from Romania to Italy which provided much of Italy's oil supply. The possibility of including the seizure of Crete as part of the German campaign in the Balkans was therefore present from the early planning of that venture.

If a decision to seize Crete was not taken until quite late in the spring of 1941, this was in part due to the competition of another target for a German airborne landing: Malta. The British-held island in the Central Mediterranean had not been seized by the Italians in the first days of war and was repeatedly reinforced by British convoys and by planes flown from aircraft carriers approaching within range. As a British naval and air base, it obviously lay across Italian and German supply routes to North Africa. If the British ever did clear the Axis out of North Africa, it would provide an excellent base for attacks on Sicily and the Italian mainland. In Axis hands, the island could not only protect the route to North Africa and the coast of Sicily but block the Central Mediterranean to the British navy.

The obvious way to seize Malta was by the sort of airborne landing which the Germans had tried out in Holland and Belgium in May of 1940, though the terrain and the walls dividing fields on the island made the use of gliders impractical and required dependence on parachutists. The high command of the armed forces (OKW) argued strongly for giving the seizure of Malta priority over Crete, but the navy argued for the reverse; Crete should be tried first to provide a basis for further offensive operations in the Eastern Mediterranean.[174]

In late April 1941, the German airborne forces expert, General Kurt Student, reinforced what appears to have been Hitler's own inclination to seize Crete. In this decision, several factors appear to have played a role. The German air force commander, Göring, favored the project. The parachutists had, in Hitler's eyes, proved their worth not only in the West but in the effort to seize the bridge over the Corinth Canal during the Greek campaign on April 25.[175] Although his reasoning on this point may well have been faulty, the possibilities of air attacks on the Romanian oil fields from Crete appear to have weighed heavily. Turkey could be expected to take notice and either assist or remain quiet. Finally, the project has to be seen as an extension, but also as the final step, of the German effort to secure firmly and finally the southern flank of Eastern Europe before the attack on Russia. And certainly in the details of planning the landing on Crete, code-named operation "Mercury" (*Merkur*), the timetable and other details were dominated by the need to move quickly and then shift the forces engaged to their assignments for the Russian campaign.[176]

For this invasion the Germans expected to have and did have the control of the air which the RAF had kept them from obtaining over England. Over 1200 German planes were to participate in the operation. Initially parachute and glider troops were to seize two airports and other footholds; then transport planes and a motley array of small boats would bring in reinforcements. While the British had extremely accurate knowledge of German intentions as a result of their break into German codes, the Germans grossly underestimated the strength of the British defenses on the island. On May 20 the first waves of German planes dropped parachutists and gliders on the northwestern part of Crete. In bitter fighting the New Zealand, British, and Greek troops inflicted heavy casualties on the invaders; but the New Zealand brigade commander during the night ordered his troops to pull back from Maleme airport, which the Germans seized in part during the night and in part with the forces of their second wave the following day. Although very heavy fighting continued for several days, and the British navy destroyed one convoy of ships carrying reinforcements and turned back another, German possession of an airport sealed the outcome. Once an attempted New Zealand counter-attack on May 22 had failed to recapture Maleme field, a steady stream of German transport planes could bring in reinforcements and supplies while the German air force kept the British navy confined to night-time missions. On May 26 Freyberg requested and received approval to evacuate his troops, and the remaining days of fighting on the island covered the evacuation which ended on June 1.

At the end of the fighting, the British evacuated 16,000 men and lost an equal number, three-quarters of them prisoners captured in the last days of battle. Several thousand Greek soldiers were killed or captured. Right after the end of the fighting, Student ordered a massive destruction of Cretan villages and the slaughter of unnumbered civilians, allegedly as reprisals.[177] The large-scale massacres of civilians which became the single most outstanding characteristics of German occupation in Southeast Europe in World War II began on the island that Hitler had marked out as the concluding episode in the campaign.

The most serious losses suffered by the British in this campaign were, however, at sea. The attempts of the Royal Navy to supply, assist, and eventually evacuate the garrison on Crete cost dearly. Two British battleships, an aircraft carrier and other warships were damaged, while three cruisers and six destroyers were sunk. It was once again obvious that warships could not operate in waters dominated by an enemy's land-based planes, and British planning for future operations in the Mediterranean had to be accommodated to this hard reality.

German losses had been extraordinarily heavy. Several hundred planes had been destroyed or damaged, and the 4000 killed and 2500 wounded vastly outnumbered the casualties of the whole Yugoslavian and Greek campaigns. More important in the long run than the numbers themselves was the fact that this wrecked the German airborne forces for the time being and put an end to Hitler's willingness to use them in that capacity forever after, even when they were reformed and increased later in the war. No large-scale airborne assault was ever attempted again by the Germans in World War II—it was the Allies who would carry out airborne operations.

The unsuccessful defense of Crete successfully defended Malta; the Germans had had the resources and the will to try once, and after their experience with Freyberg's troops on Crete they would never try again. As for the eastern Mediterranean possibilities theoretically opened up by the German seizure of Crete, these remained theoretical for two reasons. In the practical and the strategic sense, Crete was a dead-end for the Axis. Practically, the next step would have been Cyprus, but another airborne assault as this would have had to be was out of the question. Not only had the German airborne forces been mauled beyond recall for the time being, but Cyprus was at that time out of fighter range from Rhodes, the nearest Axis stronghold. And from the strategic point of view, the Russian theater had immediate priority; thereafter German forces could march and drive into the Near East. The Cretan experience only reinforced the belief of most Germans and especially Hitler that marching and driving was a great deal better than trying to swim or jump.

The reluctance of the Germans to make any moves into the Near East beyond Crete was quickly reinforced by developments in Syria. There had been a few Free French supporters in Syria but the elements who stuck with Vichy were in full control under Commissioner Henri Dentz. The enormous danger which this situation posed for Great Britain was dramatically exposed by Vichy support for the pro-Axis elements in Iraq—the same Frenchmen who could not fight the Germans had found weapons to deliver to Rashid Ali—as well as by the permission granted to German warplanes to land on Syrian airfields. The new figure in control of French politics under Pétain after the ouster of Laval was Admiral François Darlan, who hoped to be allowed to join Germany as an ally in the war against Britain, exchanging support for Germany in North Africa and the Near East for concessions from Berlin. He would be rebuffed by the Germans as already mentioned, but this the British did not know at the time. What they did know at least in part was that this Vichy leader hated them more than any other, was willing to support Rommel from Tunisia and was also prepared to provide the Germans a strong foothold in the Near East from which to bomb the critical oil refineries at Abadan or move against the Suez Canal through Palestine from the north.[178]

Under these circumstances, the British decided that, come what may, it was necessary to shift Syria from Vichy French to Free French control. The forces available were inadequate, but a hastily put together combination of Australian, British, Free French, and Indian troops—the last fresh from victory in Italian East Africa—struck into the Syrian and Lebanese mandates from the south on June 8. The Free French and the British both publicly announced their support for independent status for the mandates while the British commander also drew on forces released by the surrender of Rashid Ali to strike into Syria from the southeast as well as the east.[179]

The Vichy French forces fought bitterly but in vain. The Germans were now so fixated on the coming invasion of the Soviet Union that almost the only help they provided was to allow the French to move troops and supplies from North Africa to Syria and by train from France to Salonika where they were stopped by the British blockade. A stalemate before Damascus was avoided when the failure of "Battleaxe," Wavell's offensive in the western desert, released further British forces after June 17. On June 21 the Syrian capital fell. Dentz now concentrated his remaining strength on the defense of Beirut. In bitter battles, the British approached the city and took it on July 10. On the following day, Dentz asked for an armistice. The hard-fought campaign was over. With Turkey refusing to allow train transit of troops and supplies, British control of the sea held down reinforcements to Dentz at a time when Germany was no longer willing to risk substantial numbers of planes after the losses on Crete and just before the attack on Russia.

The armistice was signed, perhaps appropriately, on July 14. De Gaulle took over in Syria. Thereafter he could and would quarrel endlessly with Great Britain as well as Syrian nationalists over the policies to be followed in the mandates, but the Axis hopes were shut out. If they could not defeat the Soviet Union, where they were already locked in bloody battle by the time the fighting in Syria ended, there would be no base for Germany at the center of the Near East.

The turning of Syria over to the Free French did relieve the Germans of having to be concerned about French susceptibilities in promising pieces of Syria to Turkey if that should prove desirable and in proclaiming their support of Arab nationalist demands.[180] This was a subject about which they had agonized a good deal before and continued to debate among themselves and with the Italians for some time yet. They at times hoped that with the help of Haj Amin al-Husayni, the former Mufti of Jerusalem, they could get uprisings going against the British. However, while al-Husayni was all in favor of defeating Great Britain and thrilled by German persecution and subsequent killing of the Jews, there was never anything practical he could do to help install the Axis in the Near East; and until after the anticipated victory over Russia, there was little the Germans could do to install al-Husayni in Jerusalem. Years later he could recruit some Muslims in occupied Yugoslavia to participate in anti-partisan warfare and the massacres of civilians so beloved by the Germans, but how this activity furthered the aims of Arab nationalism was never very clear. He and Hitler could exchange compliments but little else.[181]

If the Near East was too far, India was even farther. Like al-Husayni and Rashid Ali, Bose hoped that a German victory in the war would bring independence to his country—a speculation which reflects very poorly on the intelligence of a man who spent considerable time in Germany and had plenty of opportunity to observe the way in which the Germans treated peoples who had come under their control. Like the refugees from Jerusalem and Baghdad, he would spend a good deal of time in Berlin and Rome, collecting subsidies and arguing for German proclamations of support for his cause. It is difficult to believe, but there were still those who thought Hitler's word when given in public and in written form might prove useful outside the toilet. The Germans themselves, not surprisingly, shared this view and debated the subject throughout the war. As will become clear subsequently, Bose was eventually shipped off to Japan,[182] while al-Husayni and Rashid Ali remained in Europe to feud with each other and share in the arguments between and within the governments in Rome and Berlin.

If the British campaign in Syria which closed a major path for the Axis into the Near East had been assisted by the transfer of forces after the "Battleaxe" campaign in North Africa as well as the fighting in East Africa, the conclusion of the fighting in Syria in turn freed units for a return to Egypt and their concentration there for a renewed offensive against Rommel. Under insistent pressure from London, the new British commander, General Claude Auchinleck, built up his army for what came to be known as operation "Crusader." The British, now finally able to concentrate their Near Eastern strength on *one* front, would strike in the Western Desert where Rommel could get no major reinforcements at a time when Germany concentrated on the Eastern Front. With the British holding on to Tobruk, Rommel would have had to attack there first before heading east into Egypt again. Before he could launch such an offensive, Auchinleck began his on November 18, 1941.[183]

The British offensive involved English, New Zealand, South African and Indian units and, for the first time, included 300 American tanks, some 40 percent of those employed.[184] In rapidly moving warfare, the German and Italian armored units at first held their own. British numerical superiority began to tell even as the New Zealand division attacks near the coast reached the Tobruk perimeter. There followed German counter-attacks which briefly isolated them alongside the Tobruk garrison, but then new British attacks and a rather foolish raid by Rommel himself toward the Egyptian border left the Axis forces so weakened that retreat was clearly necessary. Although Auchinleck replaced the commander of the British army on the spot, his replacement was no more able to concentrate the British armor in a decisive blow. The German and Italian forces near the Egyptian border were not evacuated or ordered to break out and hence had to capitulate in January, but

Rommel was able to pull the bulk of his forces out of Cyrenaica and return to El Agheila. This time there would be no Beda Fromm victory cutting off the retreating Axis forces as in the preceding year. German armor and anti-tank guns were still superior both in quality and in their handling.[185] Rommel was back where he had started ten months earlier. What did it all mean?

The Germans and Italians, with the latter fighting far harder and more effectively than before, suffered almost 40,000 casualties, roughly double those of the British. For the first time in the war, the British had succeeded in administering a defeat to the German army. They still had a great deal to learn, as the campaign which followed showed all too dramatically, but they had made a start.[186] Similarly, the Germans had made a start at abandoning forces cut off by Allied advances rather than evacuating them or ordering a break-out attempt, a major contributing factor in the capture of thousands of German soldiers.

More important was the way in which this first major Allied offensive against the Germans in World War II interacted with other fronts of that world-wide conflict. In the summer of 1940, when Britain was fighting for its life, the Soviet Union had provided the Germans with oil. In the winter of 1941–42, as the Soviet Union was fighting to defend its capital, the British North African offensive forced the Germans to shift from the Eastern Front to the Mediterranean their 2nd Air Force fleet (*Luftflotte* 2) because the 10th Air Corps (*Fliegerkorps* X) which had been sent a year earlier—itself weakened by transfers to the Eastern Front—was no longer sufficient to the most urgent needs of the Mediterranean theater.[187]

Equally dramatic was the effect of the North African situation on the war at sea. The Axis supply situation in North Africa became desperate as more and more ships were sunk by the British, in part because the Italians at German insistence had adopted German enigma code machines which the British could read from the summer of 1941 on.[a] Hitler again worried, and probably with good reason, that a complete defeat in North Africa would lead to a collapse of the Mussolini regime. To help out, not only the 2nd Air fleet but also large numbers of German submarines were diverted to the Mediterranean—a point illustrated by the famous movie "Das Boot"—with serious consequences for the Battle

---

[a] There is a file in the records of the German embassy in Rome (Quir.), Geheim 89 (1941), entitled "Vorführung der Chiffriermaschine "Enigma"" (Demonstration of the "Enigma" Code Machine). It deals with the request of the Technical and Commercial School in Rome of March 13, 1941, for the loan of an enigma machine regularly offered for sale in Italy so that it could be shown at an exhibition. Included is a sales brochure in Italian, appropriately illustrated, that had been printed in Berlin. The Germans refused to provide a sample machine with the claim that it was not available for loan or sale!

of the Atlantic.[188] The leaders of the German navy had long argued that the Mediterranean was a critical theater in the German war against Great Britain; now they had to commit forces to that theater at precisely the time they least wanted to: when they were finally about to get the war against the United States for which they had been pleading for two years.

WAR IN THE WEST

Once it had become clear that the Germans were not about to try an invasion of England in the fall of 1940,[189] the newspaper and newsreel accounts of the war between Germany and Great Britain were dominated for months by the bombing of English cities. Night after night German planes, occasionally assisted by Italian ones, dropped bombs, mines, and incendiary bombs on the major cities of the country; pictures of fires raging around St. Paul's Cathedral and of Londoners sleeping in the subway corridors caught the attention of the world.

Occasionally smaller numbers of British planes struck at German cities; for the first time on December 12, 1940, the British attacked an entire city, Mannheim, in retaliation for a German raid on a city, Coventry, in this case.[190] It was an approach to bombing that came to be more important later. In Churchill's eyes, it was always an option once the Germans had dropped all pretence of aiming at military targets,[191] but it did not come to dominate British air strategy until an attempt to concentrate on oil targets in the first months of 1941 had failed. Here was a target system correctly believed to be critical to the German war effort; the problem was that, with the technology of the time, the targets could not be readily located, and if they could be located, they could not be hit.[192] Over the course of the summer of 1941, it became increasingly obvious that because of the strength of German fighter defenses, the RAF not only had to bomb at night—a discovery the Germans had earlier also made—but also because of technical inadequacy was incapable of hitting specific targets in darkness. That meant either abandoning offensive action against Germany entirely or bombing industrial cities as a whole. The British government, which had earlier been drawn by German initiatives to abandon the restrictive bombing policy with which it started the war, naturally opted for the latter.[193] Subsequent developments in the new British alliance with the Soviet Union, the self-perpetuating process of resource commitment, and the real needs of the war would all reinforce this choice. Many in Germany received an opportunity to rethink the question of whether the rebuilding of an air force in the face of treaty commitments not to do so was in reality the great success some had thought it; but since almost no one has taken advantage of that opportunity even as this is written, one must assume that few did so at the time.

Although not as spectacularly reported upon as the bombing raids, the German attempt to throttle England's lifeline by attacks on Allied shipping was considerably more effective and dangerous. Important factors in the German war against the oceanic supply routes of the United Kingdom were surface warships, both regular navy and auxiliary cruisers operating as commerce raiders, long-distance airplanes, especially the famous Condor (Focke-Wulf 200), mines put out by German ships and planes, and air force attacks on British shipping in port. By far the most important component in this effort, however, was the submarine campaign. Month in and month out in the war's longest battle, the U-Boats and the Allies fought the Battle of the Atlantic.[194]

The German navy's program for the construction of greater numbers of submarines was still in its infancy. Furthermore, there was no more a solution in 1941 to its endless controversy with the air force for greater assignment of planes to aerial reconnaissance than earlier or later in the war.[195] On the subject especially dear to the navy's heart, the freedom to sink any and all ships at the risk of provoking an American entrance into the war, Hitler was also as reluctant in 1941 as in 1940. Until he had defeated the Soviet Union and could turn back to the construction of a huge navy, he preferred to postpone war with the United States. This issue of possible incidents between Germany and the United States in the Atlantic will be examined further shortly, but there was still another problem for the Germans in the war at sea on which Hitler came to differ with Admiral Raeder, the Commander-in-Chief of the German navy. This was the surface fight employing battleships and cruisers.

Raeder wanted the big ships to participate in the war against British shipping to demonstrate their usefulness to Germany and to preclude the deterioration of morale and discipline in idleness which had affected the surface fleet in World War I. In this he ran into trouble with Hitler for two reasons. Hitler's skepticism was repeatedly strengthened by the fate of the big ships in action. The designs for the engines of Germany's navy turned out to be very poor; the ships were subject to repeated breakdowns and long repair periods. In addition, their fate in combat action proved as risky as could have been expected. On April 6, 1941, the battleship *Gneisenau* was hit by a British aerial torpedo. A few days later it was further badly damaged by British bombers while in port at Brest. The following month, the new battleship *Bismarck*, accompanied by the heavy cruiser *Prinz Eugen*, headed out into the Atlantic, was spotted, sank the British battle cruiser *Hood* and damaged the battleship *Prince of Wales*, but was itself sunk on May 27.[196] The next major surface ship to try for an Atlantic operation, the pocket battleship *Lützow*, was torpedoed on June 13. In this, British code-breaking played a key role,[197] a point also to be reviewed.

With these and other German setbacks, Hitler returned to a point he had raised before and on which he would insist the following fall: the British might attempt a landing in Norway to relieve the pressure on the Soviet Union in the war he began against that country on June 22. Therefore, the big surface ships still available should be concentrated there to assist in Norway's defense, and he also directed that even the large warships at Brest be transferred there. Whatever the uproar in Britain provoked by their successful dash through the English Channel in February 1942 — and the uproar in German government circles when the two battleships *Scharnhorst* and *Gneisenau* both ran into British mines — Germany's Atlantic campaign with surface ships was effectively over.[198]

The submarines, on the other hand, were sinking more shipping than the British could build, especially in the first half of 1941.[199] In the second half of the year, the situation turned temporarily in favor of the British, and not only because Churchill concentrated his attention and pressure on it.[200] The German transfer of submarines to Norway and the Mediterranean late in the year contributed substantially to this result, but a very significant factor was the ability of the British admiralty to route convoys around the waiting U-Boats because in those months it could read the relevant German navy codes, sometimes on a daily basis.[201]

The mortal threat of the submarines to Britain's survival was always there, but it did not keep the British from continuing those measures they had developed earlier in order to pursue the war against the Third Reich. The bombing offensive has already been mentioned. The blockade of Germany was still important in British eyes, and their control of the sea helped them deny its use to Germany as well as to protect their own shipping. They were naturally very concerned about the leak in the blockade by which goods went across the Soviet Union by land and then into German-controlled Europe.[202] They also continued to look to the Special Operations Executive (SOE) to try to undermine German power in Europe by revolts, but after the Soviet Union was attacked came to prefer that resistance forces in East Europe be armed by the latter, an expectation that would produce all sorts of problems in the case of

Poland.[203] Furthermore, they hoped to increase the French colonial territory shifting to de Gaulle. There was considerable discussion of projects to help de Gaulle seize the islands of Réunion and Madagascar in the Indian Ocean—a project Churchill strongly favored—and of the same possibility for French Somaliland (Djibouti).[204] And, as has already been recounted, in June 1941 British and Free French forces began a successful campaign to take Syria and the Lebanon away from Vichy.

Under these circumstances, it should be easy to understand that the British government was no more interested in suing for peace in 1941 than in 1940. The soundings which the British on occasion believed they were getting were rejected out of hand.[205] Churchill directed on January 20, 1941, that any contacts be met with "absolute silence";[206] it should be noted that the German government gave similar directions for the treatment of any soundings from the Churchill government.[207] Nothing changed in the British attitude after the German attack on the Soviet Union. In view of the belief of many that either during the fighting in the East or afterwards, if the Germans defeated the Soviet Union, a new "peace offensive" might be launched from Berlin, Foreign Secretary Anthony Eden in a speech at Leeds on July 5 emphatically stated in public that the British were not about to negotiate with Hitler at any time on any subject.[208] When in August 1941 they received a feeler from someone claiming to represent the opposition to Hitler inside Germany who suggested that peace could be made on the basis of Germany getting her pre-World War I colonies back and holding on to Alsace-Lorraine, her 1914 borders in the East, Austria, and the Sudetenland, the officials in the Foreign Office could only shake their heads.[209] Churchill terminated this type of foolishness on September 10, 1941, with a reiteration of a policy of "absolute silence." Both the United States and the Soviet Union would be disturbed by any other policy. "I am absolutely opposed to the slightest contact."[210]

By that time, another person who had planned to contact the British had been incarcerated for the first four months of what would be many decades behind bars. Hitler's deputy head of the Nazi Party Rudolf Hess had arrived in Scotland by parachute on May 10, imagining that he could talk the British into making peace on German terms. After assuring themselves that this unexpected visitor was indeed the Deputy Führer as he claimed, the British locked him up for the rest of the war, making clear their intention of trying him as a war criminal once the war was over. There was, understandably, an uproar in the German government; the public announcement that the second man in the state was mentally unbalanced was not exactly reassuring. Hitler was furious but hardly in a position to do anything about his old friend's strange action (except for dismissing some of Hess's associates). In spite of various speculations and the suspicions of the Russians, nothing was planned and nothing ever came of this startling adventure.[211] The real war went on.

THE UNITED STATES AND THE WAR

That real war increasingly involved the United States. The destroyer for bases deal and the increasing delivery of goods to England in the fall of 1940 had shown the direction in which things were moving. The reelection of Roosevelt meant that there would be continuity in this regard, but in fact the Republican candidate, Wendell Willkie, had indicated that he too supported aid to Britain.[212]

There was considerable difference of opinion in Germany as to how to react to the American support of Britain. The navy always favored drastic action, primarily because of faith in unrestricted submarine warfare, at the risk of war.[213] Göring, the head of the air force, took a similar position. As he said when warned about American potential: "What does the USA amount to anyway?"[214] The German ambassador to the United States, in Germany since November 1938, on the other hand, tried to explain that it made a great difference whether the United States was at war or not and that those in Germany who took the view that the United States was already doing all it could and that hence it did not matter if it entered the war formally were very badly mistaken.[215]

Hitler took an entirely different tack from all his advisors on this issue. Since by this time he had already decided to attack the Soviet Union, he assumed and repeatedly assured his associates that this step would free Japan to move south, thereby drawing American power into the Pacific. This aspect of German policy will be reviewed in the context of the analysis of Japan's policy leading to the Pacific War, but it must always be kept in mind in assessing Hitler's orders to the German navy in the second half of 1940 and the first half of 1941. Since he planned to attack the Soviet Union and to defeat that country quickly, he would first get America diverted to the Pacific and subsequently be enabled to shift resources to naval construction to deal with the United States directly. In the interim, it made no sense to him to provoke the United States into open hostilities by incidents attendant upon what he believed would be a relatively small increment in U-Boat and surface raider sinkings.[216] He learned from a study he ordered the navy to undertake that a surprise attack by submarines on the American fleet in American harbors was not practically feasible;[217] if that sort of blow was not possible, it made more sense to wait. If an under-water "Pearl Harbor attack" could not be mounted, it would be better to postpone hostilities with the United States until either Germany acquired an ally with a large navy or had time to build one of its own.

The converse of this policy of restraints imposed on the existing German navy was a double one. In the diplomatic field, it meant, as we shall see, urging Japan forward in the Pacific, if necessary with the promise to go to war against the United States alongside Japan if that was what the Japanese believed they needed to do. In the military field, it meant returning from emphasis on the army to emphasis on naval construction and on the air force just as soon as the war in the East seemed to be going as well as Hitler confidently anticipated. It is in this context that one must understand why the moment he (quite incorrectly) believed that the campaign in Russia was going well, Hitler ordered the big program of battleship, aircraft carrier, and cruiser construction resumed.[218] That program had to be set aside in the fall of 1941, as had been necessary in the fall of 1940, when the fighting went very differently from the way Hitler had expected. The failure of the German navy to cancel one of the contracts led to the delivery in *June 1944* of four completed battleship engines.[219] Promptly scrapped, these relics of earlier dreams show how seriously the Germans had held at one time to their plans for fighting the American navy.

The American President hoped to avoid open warfare with Germany altogether. He urged his people to aid Great Britain, and he devised and proposed, as we shall see, a whole variety of ways to do just that and to make sure that the aid actually reached its destination; but he hoped until literally the last minute that the United States could stay out of the war. There has been almost as much argument about Roosevelt's foreign policy in 1940–41 among historians as there was among contemporaries. Several types of recently available sources confirm dramatically the reliability of a number of long-known statements made by Roosevelt at the time but not always taken as accurate indications of his views.

On August 22, 1940, when trying to get the support of the chairman of the Senate Naval Affairs Committee for the destroyers for bases deal, Roosevelt engaged the argument that such a step might lead to war with Germany because of retaliatory acts by the latter. He argued that if the Germans wanted to go to war with the United States, they would always find an excuse to do so, but that the United States would not fight unless attacked.[220] At the end of the year, when explaining his policy in detail to the American high commissioner in the Philippines, he stressed the global aspects of the aid to Britain policy but again asserted that the country could and should stay out of the war in both Europe and the Far East unless herself attacked.[221] When recordings of press conferences made in the White House in the fall of 1940 became available recently, and it turned out that a machine had been inadvertently left turned on, extraordinarily similar remarks by Roosevelt in private conversation came to light. On October 4 and on October 8, he explained to political and administrative associates that the United States would not enter the war unless the Germans or Japanese actually attacked; even their considering themselves at war with the United States would not suffice.[222] We know that in practice he would follow that approach in December 1941 towards Hungary, Romania, and Bulgaria, trying unsuccessfully for half a year to persuade those countries that they might find it wiser to withdraw their declarations of war on the United States.[223]

The picture of Roosevelt trying and hoping to avoid war has been reinforced by what we now know about the breaking of German codes. Although the Americans told the British of their successes in breaking the major Japanese diplomatic code already in September 1940,[224] and provided them with a machine for reading such messages themselves in January 1941,[225] the British did not reciprocate with information on their breaking of German enigma machine codes until April 1941.[226] Thereafter cooperation became more and more extensive. For the rest of 1941, the knowledge of German naval dispositions gained from the reading of naval messages was regularly and carefully utilized to *avoid* incidents, when it could very easily have been used to *provoke* them.[227] The famous Presidential order to shoot at German submarines on sight, thus, was more to frighten them off than to provoke them. Aware of German orders to submarines to avoid incidents, the President could push forward with his program of aid to Britain knowing that at worst there might be isolated incidents in the Atlantic.[228]

The general assumption of many that countries are either at war or at peace with each other was not shared by Roosevelt, who knew that the American navy had originated in the quasi-war with France at the turn of the eighteenth to the nineteenth century and that more recently Japan and the Soviet Union had engaged in bloody encounters at specific points in East Asia while continuing to have diplomatic relations and without entering into general hostilities with each other. Some of Roosevelt's advisors did think the United States should or would have to enter the war to assure the defeat of Hitler, but there is no evidence that the

President himself abandoned his hope that the United States could stay out. He had been proved right in his belief that Britain could hold on in 1940—against the view of many;[229] he would be proved right in his expectation that the Soviet Union could hold on in 1941—again against the view of many. In a way he would be proved right on the question of formal American entrance into the war. We now have his comments on October 8, 1940; "the time may be coming when the Germans and the Japs [sic] will do some fool thing that would put us in. That's the only real danger of our getting in..."[230]

Lord Lothian, the British ambassador to the United States, was one of the few who understood the desire of Roosevelt to help England within the limits of the politically and legally feasible but to stay out of the war if at all possible. As Britain's ability to pay for supplies was nearing its end, he persuaded a reluctant Churchill to lay the financial facts openly before the President, and Lothian himself in public exposed the fact that England was running out of money.[231] Out of this approach came Roosevelt's call for the Lend-Lease program, a massive system of Congressional appropriations for the purpose of providing assistance to Britain in wartime which was subsequently extended to other countries.[232] Following great pressure by Roosevelt, Hull, and Secretary of the Treasury Henry Morgenthau—the administration's key figure on the issue—for Britain to come up with as much gold and dollars from the sale of investments as possible,[233] and a very noisy debate in the public arena as well as in Congress, the bill, cleverly labelled H.R. 1776 to reassure House Majority Leader John McCormack's Irish constituents, became law on March 11, 1941. The first appropriation of seven billion dollars had been voted before the month was out.

Passage of this legislation in intense and widely reported debate signalled the American public's belief that the threat posed by Germany was great enough to merit drastic American support of Germany's enemies. Most still hoped to stay out of hostilities, but by contrast with the identical Soviet hopes of those months, the way to realize that hope was seen to be the massive shipment of supplies to Hitler's enemies rather than to Hitler. Simultaneously, this process assisted in the more efficient and effective building up of America's own rearmament program.

The administration also took other steps to deal with the dangerous world situation. Relations with Britain were improved when Ambassador Joseph P. Kennedy, who did not have the confidence of either the Churchill government or President Roosevelt, was replaced by John Winant who was trusted by both.[234] Earlier, the sudden death of Lord Lothian, the British ambassador in Washington, had led to the appointment of

Lord Halifax, who proved to be in his own way as successful as his predecessor.[235] Perhaps even more important was the evolution of personal ties between Roosevelt and Churchill, first through Harry Hopkins whom Roosevelt sent to London in January 1941[236] and then when they met in person at Placentia Bay in August.[237] Still alarmed about the security of its codes, the United States took new steps to tighten up in this field.[238] Internal security was also enhanced by the closing of German and Italian consulates in the United States and the confiscation of German and Italian ships in American harbors.[239] By pressure on Vichy, exerted through a most distinguished ambassador, Admiral Leahy, when General Pershing had to decline, the Roosevelt administration tried to restrain the policy of collaborating with Germany.[240] The special Takoradi air route across Africa, already alluded to, was built up with direct American participation.[241] In April 1941, the United States signed an agreement with the Danish Minister in Washington on the joint defense of Greenland which allowed American bases there, maintained Danish sovereignty, and caused hysterics in Berlin.[242]

Perhaps of greatest long-term importance was the elaboration of new or revised contingency war plans, both within the United States government and jointly with the British, the Canadians, and eventually the Dutch and Australians. In lengthy and repeated discussions, high-ranking American and British officers came together to work out the strategic dispositions which they would follow if the initiative of Germany or later also of Japan precipitated the United States into the war.[243] These plans, fitted together with American ones, came to set a priority on defeating Germany first while holding Japan in check as well as possible, preferably without war at all, with major offensives against Japan if she did go to war to follow upon Germany's defeat. President Roosevelt never officially approved these contingency plans, but he knew of them, allowed American officers to work on them, and authorized the strictly American planning to be guided by the framework they provided. He did not agree to projects for sending American warships to Singapore as the British suggested, but he was prepared to cooperate in other ways.[244]

Of these, the most significant was the increased use of the American navy to protect shipping in the Atlantic. In February 1941, the force in the Atlantic attained fleet status and its commander, Ernest J. King, became vice admiral. In view of his later role, it is important to recall that King's first major assignment in the war was in cooperation with the British. That cooperation came to include the repair of British warships in United States ports, a matter of special urgency in 1941.[245] The American aircraft carrier *Yorktown* and several destroyers, followed by three battleships, were transferred from the Pacific to the Atlantic; it appears that only the personal arguments of the Commander-in-Chief Pacific Fleet Admiral Kimmel, persuaded Roosevelt not to order additional transfers.[246]

The British disasters in the Mediterranean in the spring of 1941 led to anguished debates in Washington as to what to do.[247] The most important new step to aid Britain that the United States took was the result of Roosevelt's shift in favor of sending American troops to Iceland to replace the British garrison there, a step he had earlier refrained from taking in the face of a request from Iceland.[248] The Americans, furthermore, drew for themselves the conclusion that part of the British military trouble had been caused by their divided command structure, with a resulting American emphasis on the power of theater commanders.[249] In the immediate situation, they worried about what would happen if the Germans were now to seize the Spanish and Portuguese islands in the Atlantic the way they had taken Crete and thereby shift the battle in that theater decisively to their advantage.[250] The Germans, however, moved east, not west, with the result that the new puzzle facing Washington was whether to extend aid to the Soviet Union and how to divide the scarce available supplies between the British and the Soviets while still building up America's own military power.

The American military thought in the final days before the German attack on the Soviet Union that this might indeed happen but that the Russians might well hold out if they staged a fighting retreat. Unlike the Germans, who had failed to understand the relevant evidence, the Americans had a real appreciation for the quality of Soviet armor.[251] Economically, American intelligence correctly estimated, the Germans would not only lose the Transsiberian route's access to East Asia but would do less well from any occupied territory than they were doing already by trade with Russia. There could be a respite for England but encouragement for Japan to move south.

The President quickly determined to send the Soviet Union whatever help could be provided; the fact that he placed his closest confidant, Harry Hopkins, in charge of this endeavor testifies to the importance he attached to it. Hopkins was sent to Moscow to get the whole project moving and took along Colonel Philip Faymonville, a strong believer in the ability of the Red Army to hold out, to handle aid at the Russian end.[252] Knowing of popular opposition to aid to the Soviet Union, Roosevelt worked hard to try to have people see that this dictatorship was less threatening than the immediate menace of the German dictatorship, and he was especially concerned about calming the widespread concern over the lack of religious freedom in the Soviet Union.[253] There were great worries and enormous difficulties, some growing out of the fact that there had been such vast differences between United States and Soviet policies in the preceding years.[254] The Moscow conferences of early August 1941 produced an agreement on major shipments of military supplies in the face of the preference of United States and British military leaders who preferred to keep what weapons were coming off the assembly lines for their own forces.[255] In the face of the German advances in the East, which if victorious would then free them for a renewed push in the Atlantic, Roosevelt pressed his associates to get the materials moving.[256] In a way, he understood better than many contemporaries and most subsequent observers the anti-American component in Hitler's planning and hoped to preclude its success by making the German search for victory in the East as hard as possible.[257] Difficulties in the production process and the problem of reconciling United States and British needs with those of the Soviet Union kept down actual shipments in 1941, but the fall of that year saw the beginnings of a vast flow.[258]

All the measures advocated by the administration were accompanied by bitter public controversy. The extension of the term of those drafted into the army was carried by only one vote in the House of Representatives in August 1941;[259] and Secretary of War Stimson, when asked whether the army was now large enough for defense, had to explain that it was almost as large as the Belgian and Dutch armies combined in May 1940.[260] Hidden from public view at the time but of fateful import eventually was Roosevelt's decision of October 9, 1941, in the presence of Vice-President Henry Wallace and on the advice of Vannevar Bush, to move forward in a substantial way with the effort to make an atomic bomb and to place this vast new scientific and industrial project under the control of the army.[261]

The American government's greatest concern was that the advance of Japan in Asia would threaten both itself and the British and thereby simultaneously aid Germany and possibly precipitate the United States into war. In the fall of 1940 and the winter of 1940–41 the United States government, under the prodding of Chiang Kai-shek and with Henry Morgenthau as the main advocate of assistance, took new steps to provide credits to China. The hope was that such support would restrain Chiang from making a settlement with the Japanese, because such a settlement would release Japanese forces for adventures elsewhere. It was not a coincidence that on November 30, 1940, the same day that the Japanese recognized the puppet government of Wang Ching-wei, Roosevelt announced plans for a one hundred million dollar credit for

Chiang, and Hull explained that the United States recognized only his government.[262]

In February–March 1941 Laughlin Currie was in China on a special mission for the President. His recommendations that the United States should strengthen Chiang, urge reform on him, try to prevent civil war in China and look to China as a great power in the war and in the future, either fitted in with Roosevelt's own views or influenced them; these certainly came to be the main points of the President's and hence United States policy in regard to China thereafter.[263] The hope was that a stronger China could contain and restrain Japan;[264] whether that would be possible depended on other factors as well.

All through 1940 and 1941 the Roosevelt administration tried to find ways to hold off Japan while the United States rearmed itself, aided Britain, and, after the German invasion of the Soviet Union, aided the latter. Concentrating primary attention on the Atlantic and the dangers there, the administration hoped to restrain Japan, possibly pry her loose from the Tripartite Pact, and figure out ways to keep her from expanding the war she had already started in China. The assistance provided to the Chinese Nationalists was one element in this policy. The end of the US–Japan trade agreement, which left the Japanese guessing as to the next American step, was another.[265] Roosevelt did not want to take steps which might drive Japan to take radical action,[266] but he was being pushed by a public opinion which objected to the United States selling Japan the materials it needed for the war against China; on this subject the same people who objected to aid for Britain for fear of war were among the most vociferous advocates of a forward policy in East Asia.[267]

JAPAN STRIKES

The hope of the administration that some accommodation could be reached with Japan which would restrain the latter by a combination of patient negotiations, continued American rearmament, and a passive stance in the Pacific, was dashed by the insistence of the Japanese government on a sweeping offensive in Southeast Asia; but for months there at least appeared to be a prospect of success. That prospect turned out to be a deliberately manufactured illusion created by a few private individuals, who pretended to the Americans that a project they had concocted had the approval of some elements in Japan, at the same time pretending to the Japanese that it had American approval—when in reality neither assertion was true.[268] That this fakery could go on for so long and be the focus of months of anguished diplomatic talks can be explained only by two factors, both of which shed more light on the 1941 situation than any detailed reviews of those negotiations themselves. On the Japanese side, the ambassador to the United States, Nomura Kichisaburo, really wanted peace with the United States. The Americans correctly believed this to be the case, and since several of the key figures in Washington, including the President and Secretary of State, knew and respected him, they did their best to accommodate him. Nomura, however, was not an experienced and skilful diplomat, frequently failed to inform his government accurately, and never recognized that the whole negotiating project was a fraud perpetuated with the best of motives but the poorest judgement by private persons. The hopeless confusion within the Japanese government, in which some elements did indeed still want peace with the United States, only confirmed Nomura's mistaken impressions.[269]

On the American side, the hope that some way of avoiding war with Japan could still be found encouraged the President and Secretary of State to meet time and again with the Japanese ambassador, and later the special envoy sent to assist him, as well as to tolerate the interference of private persons and irregular channels. It was their hope, furthermore, that the negotiations themselves might enable them to win enough time to rearm to such an extent that eventually the Japanese would give up any projects of new conquests altogether. In this regard, the two-ocean navy program looked to the distant future; for the time immediately ahead, the anticipated delivery of the new B-17 Flying Fortress 4–engine bomber was thought to be a possible deterrent. Quite exaggerated expectations were attached to the small numbers of these planes becoming available in 1941 and 1942, and it was seriously believed that their presence in the Philippines would make it possible to deter a Japanese attack southward—by the implied threat of fire-bombing the cities of Japan—or, if worse came to worse, to defend those islands effectively. Since all prior American planning had been based on the assumption that the islands in the Western Pacific could not be defended in the years before they were to attain independence anyway, this new concept showed how greatly illusions about small numbers of planes affected thinking in Washington in 1941.[270]

The astonishment Roosevelt wanted to have conveyed to Japanese Foreign Minister Matsuoka, whom he thought mentally disturbed, about the latter's failure to visit Washington on his tour of Europe in 1941, reflects the President's concern about keeping talks active early that year.[271] The draft agreement of April 9, 1941, about which such long talks followed for the rest of the year was, as Robert Butow has shown, concocted by Iwakuro Hideo of the Japanese embassy in Washington and Father James M. Drought without any authority from either the Tokyo or the Washington government.[272]

What necessarily complicates any understanding of the highly complex negotiations which followed is, on the one hand, that those in Japan who, like Matsuoka, wanted the negotiations to fail, interfered with those who had been misled into thinking the project actually had come from the United States government.[273] On the other hand, when Nomura failed to carry out his instructions from Tokyo or did not report quite accurately on his talks, the Washington authorities knew of this from their reading of "Magic," the decrypts of Japan's diplomatic messages.

It must, however, be noted that if the Japanese government had figured out that the project under discussion, with its extensive concessions to their position on such issues as the situation of troops in China, the end of United States aid to Chiang, a negotiated peace between Japan and Chiang, and Japan's position in the Tripartite Pact, did *not* represent the official position of the United States government at all, they would very likely have broken off the talks much earlier. They would have saved themselves all the arguments with the Germans which will be mentioned subsequently, because it would have become obvious to Tokyo early in 1941 that their own unwillingness to forego any of their major objectives meant that they would have to fight for them, and then the sooner the better from their point of view.

It was for this reason that the Japanese were pushing forward in East Asia even as they promised restraint to Britain and the United States. Having made their basic decision in the summer of 1940, most arguments in Tokyo thereafter were about details. There was a recognition of deficiencies in economic strength but this in no way restrained the authorities.[274] In the face of the unanimous contrary opinion of their naval attachés in the Western Hemisphere, the navy went along with a policy directed toward war with the United States.[275] In spite of Japanese complaints, their own steps breaking the promises made to Britain gave the latter a perfect case for reopening the Burma Road at the end of the temporary closing period.[276] The Japanese authorities encouraged Thailand to reclaim parts of French Indo-China, a process which led to fighting between the Thais and Vichy France but left both under greater Japanese influence as the Germans restricted French reinforcements.[277] While inside Japan the Konoe government moved forward with its program of trying to establish a new political order, a program which led to the creation of the Imperial Rule Assistance Association, Japan's would-be single party,[278] the new line in foreign policy was pushed forward vigorously.

In September 1940 the government decided to ally itself with Germany. Now was the time to move in an alignment with Germany to seize all of Southeast Asia, quite possibly adding Burma and India and the islands of the South Pacific. If that meant war with the United States, so be it. Even the navy, at one time reluctant, was now prepared to go along; because of the American naval building program, "now is the most advantageous time for Japan to start a war."[279] Certainly the Japanese struck a tough bargain with Berlin. They made the German negotiators promise them that Japan could decide for itself whether to join in war with the United States and that the former German colonies in the Pacific under British, Australian, and New Zealand's control would be added to those they had already acquired, a concession the German diplomats kept from their own government![280] But the advocates of war against the United States now pushed all before them. In the Imperial Conference on September 19 it was argued that Japan had all the materials, including oil, that it needed for the war with China. And if a long war with the United States had to be fought, Prime Minister Konoe claimed that all would be well. Japan could solve the China problem and get Germany's help for better relations with the Soviet Union.[281] At the Privy Council on September 26, the navy minister explained that the navy was getting ready for a long war with the United States.[282] All seemed to be ready for the big push south.

Negotiations to take over the Netherlands East Indies had already been started in late August and were now moved forward. But although the Japanese were able to order a great deal of oil, they did not get anywhere with their project of a political treaty binding the Netherlands East Indies to Japan. The Dutch naturally looked on Japan's joining with their German enemy in the Tripartite Pact most unfavorably, and they simply strung out the negotiations, feeding the Japanese delegation until the Dutch authorities on the spot were "rather short of eatable birds nests."[283]

If the Dutch were delaying, the French were not. In the very days of September 1940 that Vichy French forces fought against the British and Free French at Dakar, they agreed to the Japanese demands for the occupation of Northern Indo-China.[284] In the following weeks, the Japanese also made another effort to come to an agreement with Chiang Kai-shek, trying both direct contact and pressure on Chiang via Germany, but nothing came of the attempt. The Japanese were not only hopelessly confused among themselves as to how to go about this and how to harmonize approaches to Chiang with their plan to recognize the puppet government of Wang Ching-wei, but their demands for Japanese long-term control of large parts of China (including Hainan) were unacceptable to Chiang. If there was any chance of agreement, now as before and later, the chaos of conflicting ambitions in Tokyo could be depended on to wreck it.[285]

Not recognizing either that the Germans had suffered a serious check in their effort to defeat England[286] or that they had already decided to attack the Soviet Union, the Japanese decided to improve their relations with the Soviet Union, either directly through a Japanese–Soviet pact or by getting the Soviets to join the Tripartite Pact. Either would clear the Japanese rear of danger when they moved south against the British, Dutch and Americans, and Tokyo worked long and hard on this project. Because the negotiations for Soviet adhesion to the Tripartite Pact were aborted by the Germans, the Japanese worked all the harder on a direct agreement with Russia; and, as previously mentioned, were able to obtain a neutrality treaty with the Soviet Union in April 1941.[287]

That treaty omitted the more far-reaching demands both sides had raised during the preceding year of talks but assured each of the neutrality of the other in case it were involved in war with other countries. Since the Soviet Union had been unable to join the Tripartite Pact as it would have preferred, this at least assured her of a quiet frontier in East Asia if German–Soviet relations deteriorated; conceivably, it might also lead to better relations. Furthermore, facilitating Japan's move south would embroil Japan with other powers in 1941 as facilitating Germany's aggression had done in 1939. From the perspective of Tokyo, an agreement with the Soviet Union might put pressure on the United States, would strike a blow at the Chinese Nationalists since it violated the 1937 Chinese–Soviet Treaty, would clear the way for a move south by securing Japan's northern flank, and strengthen Matsuoka's own position in Japan.[288] In any case, for the 1941 campaign season, both the Soviet Union and Japan could consider themselves safe from each other. Both followed the advice of the Japanese ambassador in Moscow who had advised his government that "carpe diem should be our motto now."[289]

From the perspective of Berlin, a major advantage of the Japanese–Soviet pact was the relief it provided Japan on its northern flank and the encouragement this would give the hitherto reluctant Japanese to move south.[290] For months, the Germans had weighed the advantages of Japan's attacking the British in Southeast Asia, even if that also meant war with the United States. Each time they looked at the prospect, it looked better to them. Time and again the Japanese had shown their caution to be both excessive and at Germany's expense. There were innumerable German grievances over the failure of the Japanese to assist

Germany in moving raw materials she needed from East and Southeast Asia.[291] Unfavorable comparisons were made between what the United States was doing for Britain and what Japan was doing for its German ally. Over and over the Germans urged the Japanese to strike at Singapore: the way to destroy the British empire was to attack it while it was vulnerable, and that time was obviously now.[292] To reassure the Japanese that such a move would not be dangerous for them, they provided Tokyo with one of their great intelligence scoops of the war: the capture in November, 1940, of a British Cabinet report which showed that Britain could not and would not send major fleet units to East Asia in case of a Japanese attack.[293]

From time to time, the Japanese would point out to the Germans that Japan would be ready to move in 1946, the year when the last United States forces were scheduled to leave the Philippines, to which the Germans responded by pointing out that by that time the war in Europe would be over and the American fleet doubled.[294] Perhaps more important was the German assurance that if Japan could move against Singapore only if she struck the United States at the same time, then she could count on Germany to join her.

This was a point von Ribbentrop had already made in 1939.[295] A detailed examination of the issue by the German naval attaché in Tokyo seemed to show that this would be a good bargain for Germany; Japan as an open ally would more than offset the disadvantages of converting the United States from a tacit to an open enemy of Germany.[296] Here is a key point which most analysts of the situation have overlooked and which has led them to puzzle endlessly and needlessly over Germany's declaration of war on the United States in December 1941. Hitler had long intended to fight the United States. He had tried to begin air and naval preparations for this in the late 1930s. These had been aborted by the outbreak of war in 1939, but on each occasion thereafter, when it looked as if the campaign immediately at hand was over, he had returned to the big blue-water navy program. It was always his belief that Germany needed a big navy to tackle the United States that made him want to postpone war and avoid incidents with the United States; when the right time came he was confident that he would find a good excuse — he always had with other countries.

But if the Japanese, who had hung back so long, took the plunge, then the naval deficit would automatically disappear. He had thought of removing that discrepancy by a German sneak under-water attack on the United States navy in port. Told by his navy that this was impossible, there was the obvious alternative of Japan providing a navy for his side of the war; that the Japanese would do from above the water what he had hoped to do from underneath was not known to him beforehand, but that made no difference. The key point was that Japan's joining openly on the Axis side would provide a big navy right away, not after years of building, and hence remove the main objection to going to war with the United States now rather than later. It was therefore entirely in accord with his perception of the issues that he promised Matsuoka on April 4 that if Japan believed that the only way for her to do what the Germans thought they should do, namely attack the British, was also to go to war at the same time with the United States, they could move in the knowledge that Germany would immediately join them.[297] This policy was fully understood in German headquarters and would be voiced repeatedly thereafter.[298]

Because they held this point of view, the Germans were seriously alarmed by what they learned of a possible Japanese–United States accommodation growing out of the negotiations between the two countries. The dangerous converse of tension in the Pacific leading to war and the tying up of the United States fleet there was the possibility of a United States–Japanese agreement freeing the United States fleet for even greater employment in the Atlantic. Like the immediately involved negotiators in Washington and Tokyo, the Germans did not understand that this was all shadow-boxing about an unofficial proposal neither side had originated, and the German government did what it could to discourage any agreement from the sidelines. (Had the Germans actually wanted to avoid a war with the United States, an opposite policy would, of course have been followed by Berlin.) Especially in May 1941, when there appeared to be a slight possibility that something would come of the talks, the Germans were seriously worried.[299]

What could the Germans do to prevent any agreement that would be, they thought, so detrimental to them? They could try to make faithfulness to Germany and Italy appear as attractive as possible to Japan. The early months of 1941 therefore saw a series of directives and moves to assist Japan with intelligence, details on their own weapons, and other practical aspects of warfare.[300] Since the Germans would not tell the Japanese that they were about to attack the Soviet Union, and only gave them hints that things were not going well in German–Soviet relations — hints which some in Japan understood — the next major German move had to come after the attack had been launched.[301]

Hitler had originally *not* wanted Japan to participate in the war against Russia. His view was that Japan, already involved in a conflict with China, could best help by attacking to the south; in fact, he repeatedly explained that making this possible for Japan was a major benefit Germany would derive from attacking the Soviet Union.[302] Only if Japan decided *not* to attack in the south was there a German interest in having her attack the Soviet Union instead. Such an action would bring Japan into the war by the back-door because it would commit her to open hostilities against one of the countries with which Germany was fighting. The Germans were confident of finishing off the Soviet Union on their own—it was precisely when they were most certain of quick victory in the East that Hitler urged Japan to join in the fray. By getting her committed in this fashion, however, the Germans would circumvent the effects of any Japanese–United States agreement, which would necessarily presuppose Japan's abandoning a move south.[303] This effort to draw Japan into the war by the back-door proved both futile and unnecessary. The reaction in Tokyo to the German attack on the Soviet Union was quite different from what the Germans had expected. Even before the German invasion the Japanese had already decided to enter the war through the front door, and the German action and alternative proposal only led them, after brief consideration, to adhere all the more firmly to their prior decision for war against Great Britain, the Netherlands, and the United States.

The definitive Japanese decision to shift from concentrating on war with China to war against the Western Powers came in early June 1941. The hinge of decision was the shift from occupying *northern* French Indo-China, which was part of the war against China because that country could then be blockaded more effectively, to occupying *southern* Indo-China, which pointed in the opposite direction, that is, to war against the British and Dutch to the south and against the Americans in the Philippines and on the Pacific flank of the southern advance. Pressure to take this step had been building in Japanese government and military circles for months.[304] A Liaison Conference on December 12, 1940, had considered the move but without examining the danger and repercussions.[305] On May 22, 1941, the issues were again discussed; Foreign Minister Matsuoka spoke so extravagantly that the minutes record Navy Minister Oikawa Koshiro asking whether he was sane.[306] In early June, 1941, the issue came into final focus. The Liaison Conferences of June 12 and 16 decided in favor of the move into South Indo-China, first with diplomatic pressure and then with troops, and in the clear recognition that this move was looking toward war not only with the British and Netherlands but also with the United States.[307]

Hardly had this been agreed to when the German invasion of the Soviet Union reopened the issue for at least one key figure, Matsuoka. He now suddenly reversed his earlier advocacy of a push south, shielded by the pact with the Soviet Union which he had himself brought home in triumph two months before, and insisted instead that the sequence of wars should be reversed. Japan should now strike against the Soviet Union first and then head south. In a few anxious days in Tokyo, these issues were debated in a series of conferences in which the original choice for war with Britain, the Netherlands, and the United States was reaffirmed. There was no time to build up the needed forces in Manchuria for a push into the Soviet Far Eastern provinces since the troops in China had to remain there. An attack on the Soviet Union could therefore be made only if it were obvious that that country was in a state of total collapse. Army and navy leaders agreed with Prime Minister Konoe Fumimaro that priority had to be given to the war against Britain and the United States. The way to reaffirm this was to have the Cabinet resign and then reform without Matsuoka. There would be no attack on Russia; South Indo-China would be occupied; and Japan anticipated going to war with Britain, the Netherlands, and the United States.[308]

There were those in the Japanese government who opposed the suicidal policy of going to war alongside Germany. The ambassador to Germany, Kurusu, had warned his government about the way the war was really going on February 14, 1941;[309] he had been replaced by General Oshima who could not wait for Japan to get in. The ambassador to the United States, Nomura Kichisaburo, warned Matsuoka's replacement, Toyoda Teiijiro, on July 19 about aligning Japan with a country "in which a popped up revolutionary tries a great adventure."[310] In the Liaison Conferences, only Minister of Commerce and Industry Kobayashi Ichizo pointed to the likelihood of a Japanese defeat because Japan lacked the resources for a great war (he had obviously done more in the Netherlands East Indies than eat birds' nests; he had learned something).[311] The Lord Privy Seal, Marquis Kido Koichi made the same point in detail to Konoe on August 7, also stressing a point so obvious that others had overlooked it to Japan's vast disadvantage: if Japan seized the Netherlands East Indies and got into a war with the United States, the oil from the wells in the Indies, after these had been repaired, would still have to be shipped to Japan, which would then be vulnerable to blockade by submarines and planes.[312] The self-evident point that conquest would not move the oil wells from Borneo or Sumatra to the Japanese home islands (any more that it would move the rubber plantations or tin mines there) had apparently not occurred to anyone else in Tokyo; it was not about to hold them back now. The Japanese navy, hitherto skeptical, was pushing for war with the United States, preferably soon, and took this view well *before* there was any American oil embargo. The Japanese naval attaché in Washington, who was well informed and warned against this policy, was disregarded like all the others.

It was decided that the conversations with the United States would continue, but even during these negotiations the occupation of South Indo-China went forward.[313] The talks with the French began on July 12 and were concluded on July 22; the Vichy authorities had just fought long and hard for Syria but agreed to the Japanese occupation without firing a shot. Now the Japanese military could prepare the next steps, which would be the use of force against Britain, the Netherlands East Indies, and the United States, in earnest.[314] While those preparations, which will be reviewed below, were in progress, there could still be talks in Washington in case the United States was prepared to give in on everything. As the Chief of the Bureau of Military Affairs explained it, "Japan must be guaranteed freedom of control in the Greater Far East sphere, both in relation to its security and defense and in relation to future expansion."[315] If the Americans would accept all prior Japanese conquests and also help her future expansion, they might be allowed to live in peace.

The American government observed these developments with great anxiety. The shipping war in the Atlantic was drawing more and more attention, and now there would need to be aid to the Soviet Union as well as Britain. The fact that the Tokyo government had decided not to attack the Soviet Union was known in Washington by July 3.[316] The key issue now was whether Japan, as Washington feared, would move south. Japanese diplomats alternately denied and affirmed that the Japanese were about to move into South Indo-China, and the American government made a last-ditch effort to urge them not to. Washington tried both the stick and the carrot; the Japanese were warned of the dangerous repercussions of such a move, and Roosevelt personally promised economic commitments if they agreed to neutralize the area.[317] The Japanese government was uninterested then as it was subsequently in receiving oil from the United States and its other potential victims if such deliveries were at the cost of giving up the South Indo-China base for attacking them. They had long thought it likely that there would be a complete embargo on petroleum.[318] This possibility was now raised in the administration in Washington. The President did not want to do this as he was concerned that such a measure would push the Japanese even further forward when freezing their assets and controlling their oil purchases on a continuing basis might restrain them more effectively. The application of the July 1941 freezing order by the Foreign Funds Control Committee made it into an embargo in effect, and thereby kept the Japanese from buying oil to stockpile for an attack on the United States.[319] Roosevelt still hoped that the new proposals he was making to

Nomura would get the Japanese to hold back, but he proved to be mistaken.[320]

Against the possibility that Japan was still determined to go ahead, the American government tried yet another way to get them to reconsider. United States contingency planning for any war in the Pacific with Japan, the so-called Orange Plan, had always pre-supposed that it would be impossible to defend the Philippines, an assumption reinforced by the Tydings-McDuffy Act of 1936, which called for independence for the islands in 1944 and the withdrawal of the last American forces in 1946. Only following a defeat of Japan in a war brought across the Pacific by the United States navy could the islands be freed from Japanese occupation. Former U.S. army Chief of Staff General Douglas MacArthur had gone to the Philippines to help the Commonwealth government begin to build up its own defense for the day of independence. Now, on July 26, 1941, MacArthur was recalled to active duty and the United States War Department began to build up his forces, especially with the supposedly so useful B-17s in order to deter a Japanese attack. Perhaps the time gained by negotiations between Washington and Tokyo could be used to strengthen the islands to such an extent as to make a Japanese attack on them appear too risky and a Japanese move south which avoided them as also too dangerous in the eyes of policy makers in Japan.[321]

All these projects, including the continuing negotiations in Washington, made no real difference because those in Tokyo had already decided to go to war. There would be all sorts of talks, including a project for Konoe to meet Roosevelt in person,[322] but on the central issues the Japanese had made up their minds. They did not intend to attack the Soviet Union, and the continuing fighting on the Eastern Front served to reinforce this determination. Perhaps on the basis of their own prior bloody defeats at the hands of the Red Army, perhaps depressed by a spectacular Soviet sabotage operation in Manchuria on August 2, 1941,[323] the Japanese recognized quite early that the Soviet Union would not collapse.[324] From this, they drew two conclusions: that they themselves had best move south while the Soviet Union was still pre-occupied with fighting the Germans, and that it would be a good idea if the Germans thought seriously of making peace with the Soviet Union so that both Germany and Japan could concentrate their forces on fighting their most important and most dangerous enemies, Britain and the United States.[325] The Germans neither then nor in subsequent years listened to this Japanese advice, but its thrust was always clear: war against the Western Powers had the highest priority in Tokyo. What the Japanese wanted and received from Moscow was an assurance that her enemies, in particular the United States, would not be allowed bases in the Far Eastern portion of the Soviet Union.[326]

Reviewing the situation in a series of meetings between August 16 and September 6, 1941, the Japanese decided to go forward with war. They would seize Southeast Asia, talking with the United States but going to war with her if she did not give in on all points. The sooner war came once the Japanese army and navy were ready, the better. Germany and Italy were likely to come in on Japan's side while the Soviet Union could not move against her when engaged in bitter fighting with Germany. The expectation was that in the early stages of war Japan would win great victories and that there would then be a stalemate and a new peace acknowledging her gains. All the key figures, including the Prime Minister, the army and the navy, were in agreement. Only Emperor Hirohito had doubts, but in the face of unanimous advice, he could only assent.[327]

Because of the insistence of the United States government on continuing negotiations and the desire of the Japanese ambassador in the United States (who was not informed about his government's intention) to do so also, the authorities in Tokyo had to reexamine the issues several times in October and November, always coming back to the same conclusion: now was the time to fight. In the process, Konoe became tired of the discussion of a policy he had himself launched and was replaced by War Minister Tojo Hideki, but there was no inclination within the government to reverse the course for war.[328] The new Foreign Minister, Togo Shigenori, and Finance Minister Kaya Okinori had doubts but were overridden by the others. The Japanese would demand control of Southeast Asia, the end of American aid to Chiang Kai-shek and guarantee of American oil deliveries with more demands to come if these were accepted. War would come in early December, and once the Western Powers had been defeated, Japan would attack the Soviet Union. Germany and Italy would be asked to join in. With all at the end of the discussions again in agreement, the Emperor's plaintive asking of questions (probably inspired by Kido), such as how could Japan justify invading Thailand and how would Japan cope with airplane and submarine attacks on oil transports, were brushed aside. The course was set for war.[329]

The Japanese in mid-November wrapped up the last details of their political plans. Germany and Italy would be notified just before war started and requested to join in, with the proviso that if Japan were asked to join Germany's war on the Soviet Union, she would decline. Thailand would be occupied and all foreign concessions in China seized.

The Japanese would meet European Axis forces in the Indian Ocean, crush Britain, arrange a German–Soviet separate peace, and after defeating the United States offer to sell her rubber and tin as an inducement to get her to accept Japan's dominance of East and Southeast Asia and the Pacific.[330] There was only one possible fly in the ointment. The United States might at the last moment make an offer that some in the Japanese government might wish to accept. Like the Germans, the Japanese did not intend to be cheated of war.

This explains the way in which the Japanese government, which wanted war, reacted to the last proposal discussed by their diplomats in Washington with the American government, where *both* parties to the talks wanted peace. The idea was to return to the situation before the Japanese move into South Indo-China in July 1941. The Japanese would pull out their troops from South Indo-China and the Americans would resume selling oil. In other words, the Japanese would abandon their push south and could purchase what materials they needed. This was under no circumstances acceptable to the government in Tokyo, whose interest was in buying oil to stockpile for war against the Western Powers, a war which they intended to launch in part from South Indo-China. The emissaries in Washington—Kurusu had been sent to assist Nomura—were immediately told that this idea was absolutely out.[331] If there was one thing the Japanese government did not want at this time it was a settlement which delayed or otherwise interfered with the rush to war.

The Japanese had decided to provide a public explanation by making extensive demands on the United States which they expected to be refused and which could be increased if accepted. A lengthy memorandum was therefore sent to Washington following on earlier such demands. In between, they received and disregarded a restatement of the American position (which they afterwards for propaganda purposes called an ultimatum). All this was shadow-boxing. The Japanese government had decided on war; had kept this fact from their own diplomats in Washington so that these could appear to be negotiating in good faith; and instructed them to present a lengthy note in time for Japan to initiate hostilities.[332] Like the war plan as a whole, this small portion miscarried.

The timing issue was of interest for Japan because of a major change made in October 1941 in their plan for the war in the Pacific. Their concept of war had for decades assumed two inter-related projects. There would be a series of assaults in the south designed to seize as rapidly as possible as much of Southeast Asia as they could. It was always believed that the American navy on the Pacific flank of this advance would come either to the relief of the Philippines or to assault Japan or to cut the Japanese line of communication to the newly conquered southern empire. This fleet was to be harried on the way across the Pacific by Japanese submarines and possibly also destroyers and so weakened that when it met the battle fleet in a great sea battle Japan would win. The Japanese therefore built up a large fleet of submarines designed and trained for action against warships and a battleship navy including several super-battleships designed for a slugging match in the open sea.

Once the Japanese government had decided in July 1940 that this was the time to move south, preparations for war with the United States in immediate reality rather than distant speculation began. In September and October of 1940, the navy took its first big steps in this direction, and on November 15, 1940, came the comprehensive order for its mobilization.[333] The Flag Officers' code was changed on December 1 and not broken by the United States until after Pearl Harbor.[334] Ten days later the Cabinet approved a new materials program which for the first time gave priority to the navy over the army.[335] All army and navy war plans discussions in early 1941 assumed that war would be against Britain, the United States, and the Dutch,[336] a perception of the coming war generally shared in the Japanese government: by the end of January 1941 the Minister of Finance authorized the printing of occupation currency for the Philippines, British Malaya, and the Dutch East Indies.[337]

All these plans assumed war with the United States according to the naval strategy long believed appropriate. There now came into this picture an alternative approach proposed by Admiral Yamamoto Isoroku, the Commander-in-Chief of the Combined Fleet. He took the decision of the government to move south as a decision to fight the United States.[338] As early as March or April of 1940 he had begun to talk about an attack on the American fleet at Pearl Harbor as an alternative to the established strategy of harassing that fleet and then meeting it as it came across the Pacific.[339] In December 1940, he appears to have concluded that this was a far better procedure,[340] perhaps influenced by the British success against the Italian fleet at harbor in Taranto the month before. On January 7, 1941, he explained to Navy Minister Admiral Oikawa that a surprise attack by carrier-borne planes on the American fleet at harbor would destroy it, and thus American morale. Similar surprise attacks would precede landings in the Philippines and Singapore. If such an operation against Pearl Harbor were not mounted, the United States might burn Japan's cities as a result of air attacks of its own.[341]

Over the following months, Yamamoto and his staff developed the details of this project and carried out war games employing it rather than the traditional strategy. In heated arguments, Yamamoto and his assistants tried to convert the navy leadership to his concept, which required split-second timing with all the other operations geared to the surprise Sunday attack on Pearl Harbor scheduled and worked out ahead of time. Only by threatening to resign at key points in October 1941, when war had already long been decided upon and the Admiralty staff did not want to lose its most important fleet commander just before the start of hostilities, could Yamamoto get his way. On October 20, the Chief of the Admiralty Staff finally consented. All was now geared to Yamamoto's plan for an attack on December 7/8.[342]

There were several conceptual difficulties with this project. In the basic sense, it ran counter to Japan's over-all strategy for the war. If surprise were attained, it was more likely to arouse the United States to fight a long war than break morale and enable Japan to secure American agreement to a new situation in East Asia. At one of the key planning meetings, Rear Admiral Onishi Takijiro pointed out that while a war which began with an attack in the south might be ended in a compromise, an attack on Pearl Harbor would destroy any hope for a compromise settlement.[343] There was a further basic flaw: the project assumed that there was a threat to the flank of the Japanese advance south which needed to be dealt with by either the old or the new strategy, when in reality there was no such threat, and the Japanese had simple ways of knowing it. The fleet in Pearl Harbor did not have the tankers and other supply ships it would need for an attack across the Pacific; something the excellent Japanese spy network operating out of the consulate in Honolulu knew perfectly well. The knowledge of this by the Americans in Pearl Harbor contributed to their discounting the risk of a Japanese attack.[344] Furthermore, as already mentioned, a large portion of the American fleet had been transferred from Pearl Harbor to the Atlantic. In spite of their knowledge of these publicly conspicuous transfers, Yamamoto persisted with what has to be considered a manic single-mindedness. In the Japanese navy war game conducted in September 1941, the aircraft carrier *Yorktown*, which had left for the Atlantic the preceding April, was "sunk" in Pearl Harbor![345]

Since Yamamoto's idea involved an attack in a shallow port on a Sunday, it had two other implications that were easily predictable and closely related to the rebuilding of the American navy in any longer war. In the shallow harbor the ships would be grounded, not sunk, and could therefore most likely be raised and eventually repaired and returned to service. The Japanese knew of the shallow water and especially altered their aerial torpedoes to run at minimal depth; the last shipment of the modified torpedoes being delivered on November 17, just before the fleet sailed.[346] In addition, most of the American crew members were likely to survive, either being on shore leave at the time of the raid or rescued as the ships were grounded in port. In both of these respects, any action in open seas, as anticipated by the earlier plan, would have had very different results. Neither strategic nor practical considerations, however, held back Yamamoto, who thought only of tactical success.[347] In the Pearl Harbor planning, some thought was given to a landing to seize the islands but ruled out; landing forces were needed for the southern push.[348]

The day before the attack on Pearl Harbor, the Chief of Staff of the Combined fleet, Rear Admiral Ugaki Matome, wrote in his diary: "When we concluded the Tripartite Alliance and moved into Indochina, we had already burned the bridges behind us in our march toward the anticipated war with the United States and Great Britain."[349] Having established the need for a big navy by pointing to the United States as the enemy to fight, the Japanese navy could hardly say it was unable to fight. It had pushed for war, and itself set the framework for starting it.[350]

On December 7 in the early morning six Japanese aircraft carriers launched an attack on the United States Pacific fleet which, as was the custom of its commander, Admiral Kimmel, was at anchor in Pearl Harbor. Attacking in two waves, the Japanese planes, which arrived undetected, dropped bombs and torpedoes which blew up the battleship *Arizona* and grounded seven others, sank or damaged ten other ships, and destroyed or damaged most of the army's planes on the ground. The Japanese lost several small submarines and a few planes. Over 2400 Americans were dead and another 1100 wounded. The two American aircraft carriers still with the Pacific fleet were out at sea and thus escaped; the Japanese aircraft carriers returned unscathed to Japan.

Soon after, Japanese forces invaded Thailand, beginning what they called freeing Asia from European control by seizing Southeast Asia's only independent country. Landings on the Malay coast would prepare for the seizure of Singapore. On the day after the attack on Pearl Harbor, they surprised MacArthur in the Philippines as effectively as they had Kimmel and his army associate, General Short, in Hawaii, and soon followed this operation with landings on the Luzon coast. Its flank shielded by the elimination of the American fleet, the Japanese southern advance was on.

It had been a fixation on the unfolding of the preparations for this advance that had mesmerized Washington. The leakage by an air force officer of the American program for building up and deploying forces if the country were drawn into the war to the *Chicago Tribune* in early December caused a flurry in Washington but extraordinarily little reaction in either Germany or Japan.[351] The major question agitating the administration was: If the Japanese by-passed the American Far Eastern possessions and attacked the British and Dutch, what should the United States do?[352] As more and more details poured into Washington about what looked like an imminent attack in the south, the administration saw little sense in further negotiations with Japan, and a meeting was scheduled for the afternoon of December 7 in the White House to consider the problem.[353] By the time they met, the President and the military and civilian leaders knew of the attack, and Hull had already given the Japanese diplomats, who were as surprised as the Americans, a piece of his mind. The following morning the President asked for and Congress voted a declaration of war. When half a year later Hull asked the President about a plan to publish a compilation of American documents on United States–Japanese relations 1931–41, including many statements and meetings of Roosevelt's, and worried whether the President wanted it all published in full, Roosevelt told him to "cover it all."[354]

Immediately after the attack, all sorts of speculations grew up about the causes for the surprise, and some found it—and still find it—expedient to invent various explanations suggesting the government knew of or even invited the attack beforehand. Whatever the results of confusion in the administration, the key point was the unwillingness of the navy and army commanders in Hawaii to credit the Japanese with the skill and daring to pull off precisely what in staff courses and field exercises they had been told for years was the most likely Japanese way of starting hostilities. Then, as occasionally later, Americans assumed that the Japanese had to be manipulated and favored by others, that they could not keep a secret or maintain radio silence.[355] If it is any consolation, the British were afflicted with the identical concomitant of racist thinking. Eden noted on April 23, 1941, that the Chief of the Air Staff, Sir Charles Portal, had recently told him that he rated the Japanese air force below the Italian one.[356] The British like the Americans had some hard lessons to learn.

In reality, the Pearl Harbor attack proved a strategic and tactical disaster for Japan, though the Japanese did not recognize this. The ships were for the most part raised; by the end of December, two of the battleships Yamamoto had imagined sunk were on their way to the West Coast for repairs. All but the *Arizona* returned to service, and several played a key role, as we will see, in a great American naval victory in October 1944.[357] Most of the crew members survived to man the rebuilding American navy. These tactical factors were outgrowths of the basic strategic miscalculation. As anyone familiar with American reactions to the explosion on the *Maine* or the sinking of the *Lusitania* could have predicted, an unprovoked attack in peacetime was guaranteed to unite the American people for war until Japan surrendered, thus destroying in the first minutes of war Japan's basic strategy. The hope that the American people would never expend the blood and treasure needed to reconquer from Japan all sorts of islands—most of which they had never heard of—so that these could be returned to others or made independent, became completely unrealistic with the attack on Pearl Harbor. The attainment of surprise guaranteed defeat, not victory, for Japan.

Others were eager to join Japan in war with the United States. The Germans and Italians had been asked by Japan to join in and enthusiastically agreed.[358] Mussolini had already promised to join in on December 3 and now did so,[359] an extraordinary situation given Italy's string of defeats.[360] Hitler had repeatedly urged the Japanese to move against Britain and was positively ecstatic that they had acted at last.[361] The idea of a Sunday morning air attack in peacetime was especially attractive to him. He had started his campaign against Yugoslavia that way a few months earlier; here was an ally after his own heart. Now there would be a navy of battleships and aircraft carriers to deal with the Americans.[a] His own navy had been straining at the leash for years and could now sink ships in the North Atlantic to its heart's content. Since the Japanese had not told Hitler precisely when they planned to move, he had just returned to East Prussia from the southern end of the Eastern Front, where he had dealt with a crisis caused by a Soviet counter-offensive, when the news of Pearl Harbor reached him. It would take a few days to organize the proper ceremonies in Berlin on December 11, but that did not have to hold up the open hostilities he was eager to begin. In the night of December 8–9, at the earliest possible moment, orders were given to sink the ships of the United States and a string of countries in the Western Hemisphere.[362] Two days later Hitler told an enthusiastic Reichstag the good news of war with America.[363] Those who really believed that Germany had lost World War I because of a stab-in-the-back, not defeat at the front, were certain that it was American military power which was the legend. For once the unanimity in the Reichstag mirrored near unanimity in the government of the Third Reich. The German government's only worry was that the Americans might get their formal declaration of war in before they could deliver one themselves; they would get their way.[364]

President Roosevelt asked for and obtained declarations of war against Germany and Italy from Congress in response to the German and Italian

---

[a] Hitler considered the Japanese fleet superior to that of the United States. See *Goebbels Tagebücher*, 1 February 1941, 4: 486.

declarations, steps which those countries had followed up by a treaty with Japan promising never to sign a separate peace.[365] When Romania, Hungary, and Bulgaria also declared war on the United States, the President tried to get these declarations withdrawn. Perhaps the peoples of those countries could live quite happily without having a war with the United States. But the effort to persuade them of this truth failed, and in June the Congress reciprocated.[366] The whole world was indeed aflame.

5

THE EASTERN FRONT AND A CHANGING WAR, JUNE TO DECEMBER, 1941

INVASION

When Germany and her allies invaded the Soviet Union on June 22, 1941, the war changed in several ways. One change that not everybody recognized right away but that is certainly clear in retrospect is that from that date until the end of the war in Europe in May, 1945, the majority of the fighting of the whole war took place on the Eastern Front: more people fought and died there than on all the other fronts of the war around the globe put together. This was due to three factors which will be the theme of much of the rest of this account of the conflict: the massive size of the forces engaged, the nature of the fighting which made it unlikely that the two sides would return to peaceful relations, and the ability of Germany's enemies to stick together and thereby insure Germany's eventual defeat.

The attack on the Soviet Union was launched in the early hours of June 22 and was a total surprise. There had been a last-minute alert to Soviet units on some sectors of the front, but orders generally were to hold fire in case this was all a German provocation. The German air force, using about 60 percent of its total strength, employed over 2700 war planes; in carefully planned strikes that morning it destroyed a large portion of the Soviet air force on the ground, damaged its forward fields, and shot down most of the Red Air Force planes that got into the air.[1] The combination of surprise with experience in prior campaigns enabled the German air force to destroy over 4000 Soviet planes in the first week of the campaign. The resulting near total German control of the air did not last long, but it was in effect in the early months of fighting and greatly facilitated the advance of Germany's ground forces.

The German army with over three million men together with more than half a million soldiers of countries allied with Germany (and over 600,000 horses) attacked according to plans that had been carefully worked out in the preceding months.[a] In the far north, German mountain divisions struck across the Finnish–Soviet border in the hope of seizing Murmansk and the Kola peninsula. On the rest of the Finnish front, the Finnish army with attached German units would attack a few days later to cut the railway from the Soviet Union's important port at Murmansk south, as well as striking on both sides of Lake Ladoga toward Leningrad and that city's connections with the interior of the country. At the southernmost end of the land front, the German 11th together with the Romanian 3rd and 4th Armies attacked soon after across the Pruth river into Bessarabia.

The main attacks were launched on June 22 by three German Army Groups, North, Center and South.[b] In the first days, German Army Group North with three armies struck into the Baltic States, overrunning Lithuania in a few days, crossing the river Dvina at several places, and controlling most of Latvia by the end of the first week of July. On the Central front, essentially the part of the border between the Baltic States and the Prijpet Marshes, Army Group Center with four armies crashed through the Soviet forces facing them and seized the eastern Polish territories annexed by the Soviet Union in 1939 in the first two weeks of fighting. Army Group South with three armies in addition to the 11th drove across the southern part of the pre-war Polish territories into the pre-1939 Ukrainian Soviet Socialist Republic.

The striking element in these rapid advances was not the large areas overrun so much as the huge Soviet forces enveloped and destroyed by rapid armored thrusts followed by an experienced and effectively fighting infantry. The Germans very much wanted to destroy as much of the Red Army as close to the border as possible, hoping that such terrific initial blows would topple the whole Soviet structure. The one thing they did not want was a long campaign with a need to drive the Russians back slowly and frontally for hundreds, even thousands, of miles. To some extent, the German concept worked on the central portion of the front where in two large encirclement battles over 300,000 Russian soldiers were captured, but in both north and south, Soviet troops were pushed back rather than cut off. Soviet losses in dead and wounded men, in equipment and transport, were huge.

These dramatic victories gave the German leadership at the very top the impression that they had accomplished what they had set out to do, that is, to destroy Soviet military power with one hard blow. Recognizing

---

[a] It is generally overlooked that the German army of World War II relied primarily on horses for transport, *not* vehicles. A preliminary survey in R. L. Di Nardo and Austin Bay, "Horse-Drawn Transport in the German Army," *JCH* 23, (1988), 129–42.

[b] The units attacking from Romania were under Army Group South, but for easier comprehension of the campaign are referred to separately.

but not understanding the implications of the determined fight most Red Army men put up, whether surrounded or being driven back, the Germans believed they had won the critical battle. On July 3, the German Army Chief of Staff, General Franz Halder, wrote in his diary: "On the whole, one can say that the assignment of smashing the mass of the Russian Army before the Dvina and Dnepr [rivers] has been fulfilled...It is probably not too much to say when I assert that the campaign against Russia has been won within two weeks."[2] On the same day, he replied to congratulations for his birthday (June 30) with the comment that the "Russians lost this war in the first eight days."[3]

This impression of victory was heightened by the events of the first two weeks of July. In further great encirclement battles Army Group Center, now increased to five armies, swept into central Russia, grabbed another 300,000 prisoners even as it seized the cities of Orsha and Smolensk on the road to Moscow, and already striking beyond Smolensk on both sides of that route. Simultaneously Army Group North rushed into Estonia and the outer defences of Leningrad, while Army Group South headed for Kiev and the rich agricultural and industrial areas in the Dnepr bend area of the Ukraine. It certainly looked to the German leadership as if little but mopping up remained to be done. To the German troops in the field who faced continued fighting, the brave resistance of the Red Army, the continued appearance of new formations, and the steady wear and tear on their own vehicles and equipment, things did not always look so rosy; but those at the top still believed that all was going well.

The whole German offensive had been predicated on the assumption that this campaign would be a short one. No replacements were available or planned for either personnel or equipment after the first weeks, and no one was worried about this situation.[4] One of the astonishing features of the detailed situation maps kept by the Germans is the absence of substantial numbers of formations in reserve, a characteristic of these maps that would hold true from the first to the last days of the campaign in the East. The air force expected to be back fighting the British after two months in the East; most of the anti-aircraft guns were at home or in the West in any case.[5] During July Hitler and many German leaders believed that their gamble had paid off.[6]

For a short time it looked as if the war in the East had been won and that the Germans could do whatever they wanted, both in the occupied Soviet Union and in the rest of Europe, while implementing prior planning for the next steps in the war against England. Hitler explained to his associates that the new border of Germany would be at the Urals, and whenever there appeared to be a revival of danger beyond that line,

German forces would drive further East. The bulk of the urban population in European Russia was to be starved to death, as would the captured Red Army soldiers, a subject on which Hitler, his economic experts, and the military were all in agreement.[7] At a meeting with Alfred Rosenberg, the new Minister for the Occupied Eastern Territories, Hans Lammers, the head of the state chancellery, Field Marshal Keitel, the head of the OKW, Göring, and Martin Bormann, Hess's former chief assistant and now replacement as head of the Nazi Party Chancellery, Hitler explained on July 16 how he expected to exploit the newly won empire for Germany's benefit. No rights would be allowed any remaining local population, least of all the possibility of bearing arms. Bits of the occupied territory might go to Germany's allies, but some of these, especially Finland, would be absorbed by Germany anyway. The Germans would never give up their conquests; all local inhabitants who looked doubtful would be shot. There was considerable discussion of personnel questions—who was to be appointed to run which section of the occupied territory—but the key point was that all policy and personnel were to aim in the direction of exploitation for Germany's benefit and German settlement in the conquered lands.[8]

What all this certainly did *not* mean was freedom for any of the peoples now or soon to be under German control. Individuals from the Baltic States and some Ukrainians, who imagined that the Germans might be willing to help them gain or regain their independence, had already been rebuffed in the preceding days.[9] The Germans had no intention of "freeing" anybody. On the contrary, the Baltic States and the Ukraine, as well as other portions of the occupied territories, were to be settled by Germans, and it is no coincidence that much of the serious resettlement planning, sometimes referred to under the heading of "General Plan for the East" (*Generalplan Ost*) was first developed in July of 1941.[10] Closely related to this is Hitler's decision of late July to resettle Germans from Southeastern Europe and other more distant places, presumably also in the East.[11]

In those same days of late July, as victory seemed certain, Hitler also appears to have given instructions, most likely verbally, for the extension of the program for killing the Jews in the occupied Soviet territories and among the POWs to all the Jews of German-controlled Europe. This whole program is discussed later in this chapter, but the decision to inaugurate the second stage of the murder program has to be seen in the context of other decisions made in July 1941. The mass murder of Jews in the newly conquered territories had started in the first days of the invasion and was by this time claiming thousands of lives daily. There had been little objection; now was the time to expand the project. On

July 22 Hitler spoke of getting all the Jews out of every European country and predicted that Hungary would be the last to surrender its Jews.[12] On July 31, 1941, the head of the Reich Security Main Office (RSHA), Reinhard Heydrich, obtained from Göring a commission to plan and carry out the final solution of the Jewish question in German-controlled Europe, a commission phrased so that he could use it to obtain the assistance of those German agencies and offices which, unlike the murder squads already busy shooting civilians and prisoners, were not under his control.[13] Major new steps in this endeavor would soon follow, the first being the development of gas vans which began in August.[14]

If these were the plans for the newly seized lands and those believed about to fall into German hands, what about the war against Great Britain? Here too the euphoria of July brought new decisions. On July 14 Hitler ordered the armaments program reoriented toward the air force and the navy, with their planned employment to include both the direct attacks on England and its shipping in the Atlantic as well as the British position in the Middle East.[15] This had been the intention before the attack on Russia was launched; now seemed to be the time to begin implementing the projects designed to follow victory in the East. As in the summer of 1940, when victory in the West was thought to have been attained, so now once again the plans for the great battleship and aircraft carrier navy were reactivated. The immense surface fleet for which the contracts were now reactivated would be fed by the oil from conquered Russian wells; the tools for the expected war against the United States could now be forged and sustained. For a short time all looked rosy.

By the time these new projects were being started or at least contemplated in late July, however, the realities of the situation at the front were beginning to dawn on a few in the German hierarchy. In spite of the enormous losses in men and equipment suffered by the Russians, there was clearly both a continuing front and a steady, if not yet massive, stream of new formations and replacements. Furthermore, the men of the Red Army were fighting hard; there were local counter-attacks; and there were signs of revival from the Red Air Force, which the Germans had misassessed both as to its frontline strength and its replacement capabilities.[16] The Soviet system was clearly holding together, and as word spread of the killing of all captured political officers of the Red Army, of the slaughter of numerous other prisoners of war and the horrendous mistreatment of the rest, of the murder of tens of thousands of civilians—Jews, party officials, people in mental institutions, and anybody who looked unpleasant—the fate which awaited those who fell under German control began to become increasingly obvious to Soviet citizens on both sides of the front. From World War I there had remained a residue of memory that the German army fought hard but generally treated prisoners and civilians decently; it was now obvious that there had been a dramatic change.

The earliest signs of an awakening can be detected in the second half of July.[17] By the first week of August it was beginning to be recognized that the Caucasus and Murmansk would probably not be reached in 1941 and that the campaign could be expected to continue into the following year.[18] The German units had to be refurbished, and during the ensuing pause of late July and August, decisions had to be made as to the direction of the next offensives in the East. The very fact that such decisions as to priorities for further major offensive operations were necessary showed that the original German plan to bring about the collapse of the Soviet Union by stupendous initial blows had failed. If anyone still had doubts on that score, the heavy Soviet counter-attacks on the Central front removed them. On July 20, 1941, the Germans had captured the town of Yelnya, 25 miles southeast of Smolensk; on September 5 the Red Army drove them out as part of one of the first Soviet local victories in the war.[19]

The Germans now had to decide whether to resume the offensive on the Central front or in the south and north. The very fact that they could not repeat the earlier simultaneous offensives in all three sectors shows the weakening of German assault strength, or the lengthening of the front as one moves further east, and the obvious existence of continued Soviet resistance. The relatively more effective defense of the Red Army or the less spectacular offensive success of the Germans on the southern portion of the front gave the arguments over what to do next a peculiar twist for the Germans. If they pushed ahead in the center toward Moscow, they risked very serious dangers on the southern flank of such a thrust, dangers which they lacked the reserves to meet. If they took advantage of the further advance in the center in order to cut in behind the Soviet forces holding them back in the south, they would lose time on the Central front.

The argument went forward at the time as vehemently as it has among historians since; the dispute in my judgement ignores the fact that the German assault on the Soviet Union had failed to attain its objective and that at this point they could win further tactical successes on one or another of the front segments but had already lost whatever chance they might theoretically have had to defeat the Soviet Union.[a] Furthermore, as a careful analysis of the transportation and supply problems has

---

[a] There is an interesting repetition here of the situation on the Western Front in the spring of 1918. Once the initial German offensive there had failed to win the war for them, they could strike additional blows—and did so—but had already lost whatever opportunity for victory they might have had.

conclusively shown, the Germans were simply incapable of immediately resuming the offensive on the central portion of the front after they had reached the geographical limits of the truck supply system on which their initial advance depended. Whatever they planned to do next, they first had to repair the railways so that these could bear the burden of logistical support for operations further east.[20] After some hesitation, Hitler decided to transfer some of the forces from Army Group Center to assist the attacks toward Leningrad in the north while others were to be detached for an assault into the rear of the Soviet forces defending Kiev in the south.[21] And soon after, on September 11, Hitler saw himself obliged to reverse priorities in war production again: the army and the anti-aircraft defenses had to be put on top once more so that the German army could carry on in the East and the home front be defended against British air attacks. The navy and air force, the main means for the offensive against Britain, would have to wait.[22]

The renewed drive toward Leningrad scored considerable gains, including a narrow foothold on Lake Ladoga from the south, thus cutting off land communications to the city and inaugurating a long and bitter siege. Hitler had ordered a halt on the approaches to Leningrad itself because in 1941, unlike 1942, he did not want German troops engaged in large-scale house to house fighting in big cities. Furthermore, he had decided earlier that both Leningrad and Moscow should be razed to the ground, their population killed or driven into wasteland further east.[23] These bloodthirsty designs, understood in broad outlines if unknown in detail at the time, now recoiled upon the Germans as the Russians defended themselves in desperation.[24]

FIGHTING IN THE FALL AND WINTER

An important aspect of the German drive in the north had been the hope of making land contact with Finnish forces moving southward on both sides of Lake Ladoga. Here, too, things worked out very differently from German—and Finnish—expectations. Soviet forces were pushed back, and the Finns quickly recovered the territory they had been required to cede to Russia in the peace treaty of March, 1940, but thereafter the Finnish offensives stalled, never to be effectively resumed in the war. Several factors were responsible for this crucial and permanent shift at the northern end of the Eastern Front. Determined Soviet resistance assisted by the employment of Red Army reserves eventually stabilized the front. In the far north, the German attack toward Murmansk was halted, ironically at the same point, Zapadnaya Litsa Bay, at which the Soviets during their earlier alignment with Germany had provided the German navy with a secret base to use against the Allies. In the central portion of the northern front, the combined German–Finnish forces were stopped by the Red Army short of Kandalaksha and the railway from Murmansk. In neither sector could the invaders ever make a decisive advance against Soviet forces which had obviously learned the lessons of the earlier Russo-Finnish war.

In the southern portion of the Finnish front, the Finns were eventually blocked by a combination of military and political factors. The primary military factor was that the continuing resistance of the Red Army drained the reserves of a country small in population and still recovering from the earlier conflict. By late August, 1941, the Finns were experiencing very serious difficulties in maintaining the strength of their frontline units.[25] The new German push of September 1941 southeast of Leningrad inspired the Finns to a new effort which brought them to and even at points across the Svir river, but there the advance was stopped never to be resumed; and although this advance did cut the direct railway to Murmansk, it left open the railway connection into the interior of Russia which branched off at Belomorsk.

A political factor also restrained the Finns as they approached the border they had had before the Russian attack of 1939. They came under increasing pressure from Britain and the United States to stop at that old border. There were elements within Finland which favored such a halt; and in their hour of peril in October–November 1941, the Soviets through the United States offered to return to that border if Finland would make peace. The euphoria caused by the same German victories which produced this Soviet offer misled the Finns into disregarding it and continuing in the war for expansionist objectives in eastern Karelia and in the far north. The British thereupon declared war on Finland, while, in fear that the United States would do the same, the Finns refrained from even further offensives.[26] They had managed to secure the worst of all the alternatives; they were at war with the Soviet Union and Great Britain; they had not cut the Murmansk railway; and they had missed their one chance to get out of the war cheaply before the German disaster of December near Moscow altered the whole picture.[27]

Although overshadowed by developments further south still to be reviewed, there was one last German offensive on the northern segment of the front. In October and November, the German Army Group North which had cut off Leningrad (and also a smaller Red Army-held enclave to the West) made one last effort to strike eastward to Tikhvin and beyond in the hope of joining up with Finnish forces east of Lake

Ladoga. This final gasp of German offensive strength sputtered out in the December snows as the Russians held fast after initial retreats. The Germans were incapable of pushing beyond Tikhvin, and the resulting salient almost invited attack.

The major German operation on the southern part of the main front in the East involved the use of armored formations of which one, previously with Army Group Center, drove southward to meet another armored assault northward across the Dnepr river at Kremenchug. Meeting about 150 miles east of Kiev, these operations in September 1941 led to the destruction of huge Soviet forces; the Germans took over 600,000 prisoners and captured thousands of guns; but once again the Soviet leadership was able to build up a new front.[a] Like the German Army Group North, that in the south could and did win more local victories, taking most of the Crimea and occupying much of the central and eastern Ukraine, including the great city of Kharkov, and also advancing along the north shore of the Sea of Azov. This advance culminated in the seizure of Rostov at the mouth of the Don river on November 21, but here, as in the north, German offensive strength was at an end. In the following days, the Red Army's counter-attacks not only stopped the invaders but drove them out of Rostov, and thus doomed all German hopes of cutting off the Soviet Union's ability to transport oil from the Caucasus oil fields to her armies and factories—to say nothing of seizing these oil fields for the Third Reich. Even before the German attack toward Moscow had been halted and crushed, their formations at the southern as well as the northern ends of the front were blocked and in the south already in retreat.

The units sent to assist the German Army Groups in their September offensives in the north and south returned to the Central front for a renewed attack in October. The supplies needed for a renewal of the attack in the center had now been brought forward. In two great armored breakthrough and envelopment operations, the Germans tore up the major Soviet forces on that front, capturing another 600,000 prisoners and moving within 50 miles of Moscow. As German announcers proclaimed final victory,[28] and the Soviet government evacuated most agencies from the capital to Kuibyshev, there was a temporary panic in Moscow.[29] But once again Red Army reserves, reformed units, and scratch formations held a new front with grim determination, even as German offensive strength waned because of lost or worn out equipment, heavy casualties, and a degree of exhaustion among the soldiers still fighting—which many at the highest levels of the German command

[a] It is about this campaign in particular that we may expect new information as a result of a more open approach to history in the former U.S.S.R.

structure did not comprehend. They had now to decide whether to make one more bid for Moscow or to halt and try again the following year.

Once again the very fact that the Germans faced this choice reflects the extent to which their effort to crush the Soviet Union in one great campaign had failed. All the fighting in the last months of the year was predicated on the assumption that there would be another year of war in the East and that the question now was what was the best position for the German forces to be in as they anticipated the 1942 campaign, with the expectation of shifting resources to the air force and the navy *thereafter* so that England could be defeated.[30]

There was some sentiment among the German military leadership that it would be best to hold the positions attained in late October and early November, straighten out the lines some, and try to use a defensive posture to remedy the very strained supply situation and provide some rest to the exhausted troops. Others, including Hitler himself as well as the Commander-in-Chief of the army, Field Marshal von Brauchitsch and Chief of Staff General Halder, thought that one last push might win them Moscow, and with it better winter quarters for the German forces. Such a local victory would also disrupt the Soviet railway and command system, would mean that the Russians would lose Moscow's industrial facilities, and strike a major psychological blow. The now available evidence makes it clear that General Halder was the most influential and extreme advocate of a renewed offensive.[31]

A number of additional factors contributed to the decision. The existing front line was not advantageous for the defense and, as already mentioned, the real state of the German combat units was simply not understood by many at the top of the command structure. Perhaps most importantly, not only were the continued fighting capacity of the Red Army and the slowly reviving Red Air Force grossly underestimated, but German intelligence was, as before and for the rest of the war, very much in error in its broader assessment of Soviet strength.[32] The Germans had no real concept of the rate at which the Soviet Union had been mobilizing new forces to introduce into the battle, and they were so far off in their view of Soviet power as to assert early in December that the Red Army had neither the ability nor the intention of launching any significant counter-offensive of its own.[33]

The Soviet Western Front (the Soviet term for an Army Group) held the Germans in bitter fighting north, west, and south of Moscow. During subsequent months Hitler himself in conversations with the representatives of other countries, and after the war German generals in their apologias, attributed their defeat in 1941 in large part to the weather. Already in the preceding year, they had often attributed their defeat in the Battle of Britain to the bad weather over England; now they explained defeat in the East as due first to mud and then to snow and cold temperatures. A moment's more careful reflection shows how ridiculous this line of argument generally is. Just as the occurrence of rain over England is hardly a great secret—and curiously enough affects British fliers very much the way it affects others—so there is a winter in the Soviet Union every year. Not only is winter not some extraordinary occasion which the Russians arrange to have in years when they are invaded, but it is as cold—just as the mud and later the snow are as deep—for Russian forces as they are for invaders. In certain limited situations, the weather may indeed favor one side or the other. Bad weather, for example, usually assists the defenders; but if the Red Army was on the defensive in November, it was the Germans who were on the defensive after the first week of December. What needs to be understood is that the Germans were at the end of their offensive strength, that they had not mobilized their society as thoroughly for war as the Soviet Union, and that the Soviet leadership not only remained in effective control of the unoccupied portions of the country but mustered its human and materiel resources for a devastating blow at the invaders. Before the background of that blow can be recounted, a word has to be said about the allies of Germany other than Finland in the early fighting on the Eastern Front.

The first plans of German officers for the attack on Russia made no provision for troops of other countries to participate—they assumed that the Germans who had just won in the West could finish off the Soviet Union in short order and by themselves. Hitler, while just as sure that this could be done quickly, had from the beginning counted on the participation of Finnish and Romanian troops at the northern and southern ends of the front.[34] He had assumed that the Finns and Romanians would wish to reconquer the territories which they had lost to the Soviet Union—with German approval at the time—and he was prepared to reward them with additional lands beyond the old borders if their military contribution were sufficiently enthusiastic and substantial. The coordination with Finland has already been discussed while that with Romania has been mentioned in connection with the operations at the southern end of the front. Joint planning for these operations had proceeded in the winter of 1940–41, and the Romanian leader, Marshal Ion Antonescu, showed himself more than willing to participate.[35]

Two Romanian armies took part in the initial assault. With the help of the Germans, they quickly pushed the Russians out of the areas ceded to the Soviet Union the year before, but as they attempted to seize the great port city of Odessa discovered that they had not joined a simple victory march. The Russians halted the Romanians, drove them back in counter-attacks, and, in accordance with a decision reached on October 1, evacuated the by now isolated city on October 16 without the Romanians realizing it until it had been completed.[36] As a reward for their contribution, the Romanians received from the Germans not only the territory lost in 1940 but a substantial additional area between the Dnestr and Bug rivers, officially called "Transnistria," to administer and perhaps eventually incorporate into the country.[37] The cost of the fighting, however, had been far higher than anyone in Bukarest had originally thought likely;[38] and as the war on the southern part of the front continued after the German defeat at Rostov in November, the Romanians would see the price rise steadily.

One special problem for the Romanians was their hatred for the Hungarians, who had received a portion of Transylvania the preceding year, a portion the Romanians hoped to get back, while Hungary looked forward to someday seizing the rest. It was this friction which threatened to explode into open hostilities at any moment that led Antonescu to ask that Romanian and Hungarian troops always be kept separated on the front.[39] How had the bitter enemies suddenly become extremely unlikely and reluctant allies?

The Germans were always glad to use Hungarian territory to transfer their troops to Romania, both for the attack on Greece and for the invasion of the Soviet Union, but Hungarian hesitation about joining Berlin in hostilities during the international crises of 1938 and 1939 had left Hitler doubtful about active Hungarian participation in the Eastern campaign. Hungarian Regent Miklós Horthy was, however, prepared to consider going to war with the Soviet Union, and his Chief of Staff, Henryk Werth, was an enthusiastic advocate of war on the side of Germany.[40] It was in the latter that the Germans confided on June 19,[41] but the actual entrance of Hungary into the campaign was to be attended by circumstances as spectacular in their own way as the suicide of Prime Minister Teleki when the Hungarians had attacked Yugoslavia less than three months earlier. While the Soviet government attempted to maintain peaceful relations with Hungary, a number of that country's leaders pushed for war, partly because they believed an action on Germany's side was wise in any case, and partly because they feared that the participation of their Romanian and Slovak rivals in the campaign could leave a neutral Hungary in an impossible position after the anticipated German victory. Opponents of war were worried about a break with the Western Powers, feared the Germans, and could see no advantage to Hungary in war against a country with which she had no quarrel. The issue was resolved on June 27 when the advocates of war utilized a still not clarified bombing incident on June 26 to take the nation into war. Two or three airplanes, which may have been Russian planes with navigation errors, German ones sent as a provocation, or German ones with Slovak pilots scoring off their Hungarian "friends" while on a mission to or from the front, dropped bombs on Kassa (Kosice), causing damage and casualties. Without waiting for a clarification of what had really happened—a clarification that might have been possible at the time—the government rushed into the conflict.[42]

A Hungarian battle group and a so-called "Rapid Corps" participated in the campaign until mid-November when the heavy casualties incurred in the fighting, the hopelessly obsolete character of its equipment, and the general lack of enthusiasm for war against the Soviet Union inside Hungary made the withdrawal of almost all Hungarian forces from the front necessary in both Hungarian and German eyes.[43] Realizing that the war was far more serious than anticipated, some Hungarian military leaders by August were urging a comprehensive mobilization and the dispatch of vastly greater forces.[44] Over this issue Werth was dismissed in September,[45] but the problem would come back to haunt the government in Budapest. In the meantime Hitler, in line with his generosity in handing out pieces of another country's territory which he did not immediately want for Germany, promised Horthy some snippets of Poland, a prospect never realized even temporarily, like Romania's "Transnistria" experiment.[46]

It has already been mentioned that Slovakia's joining in the war had contributed to the eagerness of some Hungarian officials not to be left out of the anticipated victory. Having shown their attitude by joining Germany in the war on Poland in 1939, the puppet state of Slovakia was now given the opportunity to repeat this performance by going to war with the one country outside the Axis which had legally recognized its so-called independence. Slovakia joined the attack on Russia and sent a small expeditionary force to the southern section of the front in the hope of eventually securing German support for recovering bits of Hungary ceded to that country in 1938 to add to the pieces of Poland obtained in reward for their 1939 action.[47]

Considerably more significant than the participation of Slovakia would be that of Italy. The Germans had kept their intentions secret longer from the Italians than any of their other allies for fear of an immediate leak from Rome. As soon as he heard of the German attack, Mussolini was determined to join in. Having been thrashed by the Greeks and the British, he was evidently eager for more.[48] An army corps was ordered to the Russian front on Mussolini's initiative and without any German request; the Duce's only worry as he explained to the Council of Ministers on July 5 was that they might not arrive in time to share in the fighting![49] Three divisions, some 60,000 men, were sent as an Italian Expeditionary Corps (CSIR) to the southern section of the Eastern Front where they had plenty of opportunity to fight.[50]

Mussolini personally joined Hitler in reviewing some of these troops when he visited his headquarters at the end of August. He hoped that Italian participation in what he recognized was the main project of the whole war for Hitler would assure his country a significant role in the peace settlement, which he expected to be dominated by the Germans. Quickly recognizing that the campaign would last far longer than the Germans—or he himself—had anticipated, he soon offered additional forces for the coming year and saw this offer accepted. While thus showing some insight into the reality of the campaign, he had no sense for the realities of his own country and the situation of his soldiers. They fought hard under difficult conditions with wretched equipment, impossible supply lines reaching all the way back to Italy, and no goal even remotely visible as they quickly lost their initial enthusiasm. The eagerness with which Mussolini squandered the lives of his soldiers only contributed to the further weakening of the Fascist regime at home.

It was ironically in part to ward off Italian aspirations at domination over the Axis puppet state of Croatia established on the ruins of pre-war Yugoslavia that the government of that new creation offered to send troops to the Eastern Front. Such a contingent might increase German interest in the slaughterhouse the Ustasha, the extreme Croatian nationalist organization, was organizing,[51] provide them with German equipment, and also serve as protection against Italy. The Germans accepted this unsolicited offer of cannon fodder for a front where the members of the Croatian regiment fought and died with few ever noticing this drop in the sea of blood.[52]

Minimal groups of volunteers were recruited elsewhere, especially in France,[53] but a full division, called the Blue Division and carried on German rolls as the 250th, was sent by Franco's Spain. Seen as an outlet for Spanish anti-Bolshevik enthusiasm, a form of repayment to Germany for her aid in the Spanish civil war, and as a reinsurance against German demands for entering the war, the division came to include some 45,000 Spanish volunteers. Some of them may have been either amused or aghast when greeted by a German air force band playing the wrong national anthem—that of their Republican civil war opponents—but they soon found little amusement in the desperate fighting on the northern section of the Eastern Front where they were committed.[54] In subsequent years, the division would be at the center of controversies within Spain and between Spain and the British and

Americans, but until 1944 Spanish soldiers fought hard alongside Germans on the approaches to Leningrad.[55]

The Germans had wanted the participation of Finland and Romania. Sweden and Turkey would have been welcomed but both declined suggestions that they participate.[56] The other partners to the fighting were accepted without initial enthusiasm. The disasters suffered by the German army in the winter of 1941–42 greatly increased Berlin's interest in and pressure for enlarged contributions by her allies and satellites for the heavy fighting expected in 1942; it is to these disasters inflicted by a resurgent Red Army that we must now turn.

THE FIRST SOVIET OFFENSIVE

The big Soviet counter-offensive of December 1941 came at the end of a series of military defeats which in their size and extent have no known parallel in the history of warfare. If the Germans had miscalculated their Soviet victims, the Soviet leadership had made different but equally enormous miscalculations. If German leaders had imagined the Russians to be inferior Slavs directed by incompetent Jewish Bolsheviks who could neither organize nor lead effective fighting forces, Stalin had been similarly blinded by his own ideological preconceptions. Looking toward the conquest of markets and investments as the tools of monopoly capitalism, the Germans certainly had plenty of prospects for booty elsewhere, especially after their speedy victory over the other capitalist countries of the West. Hitler might drive a harder bargain now that he was at a peak of strength; and since the Germans had not responded to the Soviet offer to join the Tripartite Pact, they obviously wanted even more than the Soviet Union had promised in the new economic treaty of January 1941 or offered in the spring months of 1941; but in Soviet eyes they had no reason to risk a two-front war.

Only this set of views, combined with a recognition of the horrendous danger in which Soviet policy had placed the country now isolated in a Europe from which it had helped Germany drive all others, can explain the determination with which Stalin rejected all warnings of German plans for an attack and insisted into the early hours of the invasion that the Red Army hold its fire and not allow the Germans to stage a provocation. For months the American government, which had early received inside information on the German plans, had been trying to warn the Soviet Union of what was coming, and in considerable detail. For months Soviet intelligence and diplomatic sources had been providing analogous warning. In the spring, Churchill had tried to caution the Russians, and although British Ambassador Sir Stafford Cripps botched delivery of the key message, clear indications had come from London. In the last hours before the attack several deserters from the German army revealed the imminence of invasion. Nothing could shake the Soviet leader. In spite of the recent record of German attacks on neutrals without prior demands or warnings, he was certain that in this case Hitler would act differently.[57]

The disaster which overtook the Red Army and air force on June 22 was compounded by three other factors. In the first place, the purges had decimated the officer corps of army, navy, and air force. In the spring and summer of 1940, as the Russians evaluated first their own war against Finland and then the great German victories in the West, some 4000 officers who had survived in labor camps or disgrace were returned to duty and many others were rapidly promoted. But there was little time to train the officers who had replaced those slaughtered in prior years, and the whole procedure was not likely to induce self-confidence in the officers' corps. The new models of airplanes and of tanks, primarily the T-34 and KV-1, were just beginning to come off the assembly lines and there had been practically no time for their effective integration into the army.

The second contributing factor was a faulty set of defense plans which played directly into the hands of the Germans. Not only had defense in depth and preparations for partisan warfare been neglected because these were seen to be defeatist, but the major defensive field works and positions along the 1939 border of the Soviet Union had been denuded for a concentration of Soviet forces in the newly acquired territories. Spread over these areas without adequate communications and supplies or new field positions, the Red Army was positioned in a manner and in locations best suited for the German plan to cut through, surround, and destroy the forces facing them. The annexations, ironically, contributed to the initial defeats rather than assisting in the defense of the country.[58]

The third factor grows out of the combination of the one just mentioned with the incapacity of Stalin to react quickly and reasonably to the German onslaught in the early hours of June 22, 1941. Unable or unwilling to believe what was happening, Moscow provided no useful orders or guidance to its desperately fighting forces on that crucial day. It took until noon for the government to announce to its people that war had started, and the orders given that day culminated in the evening in a directive which completely unrealistically called for a large series of counter-offensives to drive back the German army immediately. This meant that Soviet armored forces were committed to combat in hasty and ill-prepared battles in which heavy losses accomplished little (with a minimal exception in the south) except to weaken the Red Army's ability to develop a coherent defensive strategy.[59]

Soviet resistance continued in spite of frightful losses in the first six weeks of fighting. With a repeatedly reorganized command structure, generally referred to as the Stavka from the first word in its Russian names, Stalin tried to rally his forces by a combination of exhortation to the public and the army with ruthlessness and improvisation toward the command structure. Unlike the French, the Russians were not completely demoralized by the initial German victories; orderly if rushed movements of forces to the front or reluctantly ordered pull-backs began to replace confusion. In spite of great losses in casualties and prisoners, Soviet forces, often supported by literally tens of thousands of civilians, hastily threw together new defensive positions and regrouped even when these in turn were pierced. In the process they steadily inflicted losses on the Germans, who could ill afford them, and gave them some real shocks with their heavy tanks, which the Germans could not yet match with a comparable tank of their own and which were almost invulnerable to most anti-tank guns as well. The greater success of the Soviet southern front in holding the Germans combined with the massive sending of reinforcements in stabilizing the center in July and early August.

Refusing to listen to Marshal Georgi K. Zhukov's warning of a German push to encircle the Red Army in the Ukraine, Stalin replaced him on July 29 with the ailing Boris Shaposhnikov as Chief of the General Staff with General Vasilevsky as deputy. The catastrophic defeat around Kiev in the south followed, but in the north a combination of Soviet generalship and tenacity with German hesitation in view of Hitler's plans to destroy Leningrad physically made it possible to hold the German onrush there in September. On the Central front, however, the resumption of German offensives in early October destroyed the laboriously rebuilt Soviet defenses and seemed to open the road to Moscow. By mid-October, as much of the government was evacuated from the capital, the Red Army with 2.3 million men had reached its smallest size in World War II,[60] and weapons, especially the new tanks as well as the excellent katyusha multiple rocket launchers, were in short supply. Experienced officers were now so scarce that more were released from labor camps, and increasingly the numbered armies were reorganized to direct smaller numbers of divisions directly without corps staffs at all.

Much of the industrial and agricultural capacity of the country had been lost to the German occupiers. The available supply of workers and potential soldiers had also been drastically reduced as a result of the

German occupation of so much of the country. But the Russians not only held on grimly before Moscow right after driving the Germans out of Tikhvin in the north and Rostov in the south, they were preparing a substantial counter-offensive against the German army which was heaving itself forward at the end of its offensive strength, had no substantial reserves whatever, and believed that the Soviet Union too had no further reserves which might be thrown into battle. Not since their belief that an invincible air force could quickly crush England in the late summer of 1940 had the Germans been so wrong in their understanding of the situation.

The Soviet Union was in a position to launch a major counter-offensive for several reasons. The holding of a front, whatever the difficulties and the costs, was obviously the most important one. Secondly, in the territory not occupied by the Germans, the control system of the Soviet state functioned, if not efficiently, certainly effectively—a point of special importance by contrast both with what had happened to the Tsarist regime and the Provisional Government in World War I and with what the Germans had confidently expected to happen in World War II. In the third place, the Soviet Union had initiated major industrial development in the Urals and portions of Central Asia and Siberia during the 1930s; and while these were by no means able to make up for the losses at the front and the loss of industrial capacity in the West, they did provide a substantial base for continued industrial production. Furthermore, there were certain industrial areas in the European U.S.S.R. either still functioning without German interference, as in the Gorki and Stalingrad areas, or in spite of German bombing and shelling, as around Moscow and even in Leningrad. In addition, a massive program of evacuating industrial equipment along with technical specialists had rescued substantial industrial capacity from destruction or seizure, and was now leading to the reestablishment of the evacuated plants in secure areas, frequently in the vicinity of other factories.[61] The remaining capacity of the Soviet Union to produce the needed weapons and other equipment was therefore far greater than the Germans had ever imagined, even if there were still desperate shortages only slowly beginning to be remedied.

Two additional factors contributed to the survival and revival of Soviet military power in the last critical months of 1941. The decision of Japan to strike south against Britain, the Netherlands, and the United States, rather than north against the Soviet Union which was discussed in the preceding chapter, came to be known in Moscow. Much credit for this has been accorded to Richard Sorge, a Soviet spy in Japan whose informants had apprised him of the Japanese choice long before the police arrest of October 18, 1941, ended his career in Soviet intelligence.[62] In view of Stalin's reluctance to believe agent reports about the imminence of a German invasion, it is by no means clear what role the messages from Tokyo played in the decisions reached in Moscow, but it is doubtful that a retrospective recognition of the accuracy of the Sorge ring's warnings before the German attack lent added credibility to its subsequent assertions that the Japanese had decided not to attack the Soviet Union.

Only blown espionage networks make the news, and there may well have been other ways in which Japanese preparations to strike in the south came to Soviet attention in the period July–September 1941. Furthermore, it was surely clear to Soviet intelligence that there simply was no massive Japanese building up of troops and supplies in Manchuria, an obvious necessity for Japan if it had planned to attack the Soviet Union, in view of the earlier defeats she had suffered at Soviet hands. Whatever the cause, the decision was made in Moscow in early October to begin a major replacement of Soviet units in the Far East by newly raised, less well equipped and trained divisions. The last stages of the defense of Moscow already saw the first Siberian divisions in action, but more were on the way and could be included in the planned Soviet counter-offensives. At the same time that these soldiers, many of them battle hardened in prior fighting against the Japanese, were now available for employment against the tiring Germans, replacements sent to the Far East kept the paper strength of the Red Army there high enough to discourage any Japanese change of mind.

If Japan's turn to an offensive against the Western Powers relieved Soviet need for large numbers of high-quality units in East Asia, the very countries against which Japan was moving—especially Britain and the United States—were already trying to assist the Soviet Union. They had tried unsuccessfully to alert the Russian government about the danger it faced; until the last moment, these warnings were dismissed as transparent efforts to embroil the Soviet Union with Germany. Here, too, we may never know whether the accuracy which these warnings acquired in retrospect in any way affected Stalin's subsequent evaluation of information he received from the West; but whatever the answer to that puzzle, there can be no doubt that he looked quickly and anxiously for help from that quarter.

Since Soviet policy had long been influenced by the belief that all the capitalist powers, especially those in the West, were merely awaiting a suitable opportunity to gang up on the Soviet Union, there may well have been concern in the first days of the German attack that Britain might now make peace with Germany with the United States standing aside cheering on the invaders.[a] The presence of Rudolf Hess in British custody appears to have fed such Soviet suspicions or at least provided a suitable public explanation for their being maintained in the face of all the evidence. In any case, there were no voices in the British government for a reversal of policy; ironically the only open advocates of peace with Germany had been the same Communist sympathizers who now switched to the most vociferous advocacy of assistance to the Soviet Union in its fight against Germany.

Churchill immediately declared in public the solidarity of Great Britain with the latest victim of German aggression.[63] As intelligence reports had made it more and more obvious to the British that a German attack on the Soviet Union was imminent, the authorities in London in the two weeks before the invasion had considered both the policy to follow in that contingency and how best to implement it. Ambassador Cripps had left Moscow certain that the Soviet Union would give in to whatever the Germans wanted and originally did not expect ever to return.[64] The Cabinet, however, thought it likely the Russians would fight and wanted a military mission to Russia prepared and ready to go to coordinate aid to the Soviet Union, while the Royal Air Force began preparations to take action to try to prevent the Germans moving air units to the East.[65]

Whatever the skepticism of many in the British military and government about Soviet military capabilities, it was obviously in Britain's interest to help the Soviet Union maintain an Eastern Front as long as possible.[66] What aid could be sent would be sent, and the special military mission under General Mason-MacFarlane, once Britain's military attaché in Berlin, was appointed to Moscow on June 24.[67] At the beginning of his mission, the general was not only optimistic about the prospects for cooperation—an attitude which experiences in the Soviet Union would soon alter—but he was also firm in the belief that the Russians would hold on and hold out in spite of great difficulties; and in this view, first expressed after his arrival in Moscow and a reception by Stalin, in a letter to General Brooke on July 14, 1941, he never wavered.[68] The aggravating incidents which later also bedeviled American military representatives to the Soviet Union were not allowed to interfere with the fundamental need to work together; as Brooke put it, "don't press the Russians too hard in their agony."[69]

At a time when Britain itself was hard pressed, there was no prospect

[a] The British ambassador to the Soviet Union, Sir Stafford Cripps, may have inadvertently aggravated Soviet suspicions by repeatedly—in direct violation of his instructions—warning the Soviets that their attitude could affect British reactions to German peace offers. Graham Ross (ed.), *The Foreign Office and the Kremlin: British Documents on Anglo-Soviet Relations, 1941–1945* (Cambridge: Cambridge Univ. Press, 1984), pp. 10–11, and doc. 2.

of major landing attacks on German-controlled Europe, so there were really only three ways in which the British could help the Soviet Union in the last half of 1941. They could and did increase the bombing of targets in Western Europe and in Germany, thereby forcing the Germans to keep a substantial portion of their fighter planes, and most of their anti-aircraft guns, away from the Eastern Front.[70] They devised a program of delivering weapons and other supplies to the Soviet Union, a process seriously begun in mid-July [71] and carried forward in spite of endless friction with and complaints from the recipients.[72] A convoy of supply ships left Iceland for Murmansk on August 21, the first of forty which made the perilous journey during the war through the deadly seas where German submarines, planes and mines sank almost a hundred of the eight hundred ships to try the route.[73] A possible alternative route for supplies would be across Iran; and the British and Russians agreed to occupy that country for the duration of the war. Beginning on August 25, Soviet and British troops made sure that there would be no repetition of the pro-Axis activities which had flared up in neighboring Iraq; and the ports, railway, and truck routes across the country came to carry a small portion of British aid and eventually almost a quarter of American aid for the Soviet war effort.[74]

A third and more immediate form of British action was the renewed British offensive in the Mediterranean theater. After the failure of "Battleaxe" in the summer, the British struck again on November 18, 1941. Operation "Crusader" forced back Rommel, relieved Tobruk, and pushed further forward. Churchill had hoped to have this offensive launched sooner and had been as upset as Stalin about the delay, but the commander on the spot had felt unable to move sooner. Now the British army struck hard.[75] The impact of this on the Eastern Front was that the Germans, unable to spare land forces from the fighting there, decided to transfer a whole air fleet under Field Marshal Kesselring from the Eastern Front to the Mediterranean in the critical days of early December 1941 (along with numerous submarines). The earlier British defence against the German air force had already cost the latter heavily; she began the war in the East with 200 *fewer* bombers than she had had on May 10, 1940.[76] In such ways the British repaid the Russians for the diversion of German bombers to the East in the summer and winter of 1941; in any case, it was certainly a different procedure from the Soviet Union's sending supplies to Germany in the summer months of 1940 when the English were fighting for *their* survival.

On the political front, the Soviet Union and Great Britain had signed an agreement in Moscow on July 12, 1941.[77] Requested by Stalin as a sign of cooperation, it provided for mutual assistance and an understanding not to negotiate or conclude an armistice or peace except by mutual consent. Soviet insistence on such an agreement presumably reflected their suspicion of Great Britain, though there is no evidence that either party to it ever ceased to have its doubt about the loyalty of the other if attractive alternatives were thought to be available. In any case, the Soviet leadership soon after the signing of the agreement demanded dramatic steps to relieve the pressure on the Eastern Front by landings on the French and Norwegian coasts. The British had no prospects of being able to carry out the former and only the slightest of bringing off the latter operation; it is not known when and whether Stalin understood this situation and whether the demands were in fact a form of bargaining to obtain supplies and political concessions from a power incapable of helping in other ways. The chorus of demands that would continue for years began in July, and it influenced first the British and American supply plans and then the British political posture in the last months of 1941.

Before these matters can be examined, the role of still another country must be reviewed because of its central position in the wartime calculations and post-war expectations of all the major belligerents: Poland.

In the crisis faced by the Soviet Union in the summer of 1941, Stalin appears to have been willing at least for a short time to make some concessions to the government of the pre-war Polish state—which he had earlier asserted no longer existed—as represented by the Polish government-in-exile operating out of London. An agreement signed with it on July 30, 1941, implied full Soviet recognition of that government, declared that the Soviet–German treaties of 1939 about Poland were invalid, and provided for the release of Polish prisoners in the Soviet Union who could then join a new Polish army.[78] Both sides to this shotgun wedding were reluctant; the Soviet Union would apparently have preferred to set up a subservient new Polish regime of its own,[79] while many in the Polish government-in-exile wanted a positive affirmation of the 1939 border. Both sides were pushed by the British and to a lesser extent by the Americans, but most of all by the Germans. Stalin may well have figured that if the Soviet Union defeated Germany he would be in full control of Eastern Europe, while if the Germans did win, it all made no difference. Furthermore, he knew all too well that any rebuilt army would be without experienced and trained officers. The Polish leader, General Wladislaw Sikorski, on the other hand, appears to have been motivated especially strongly by the hope that the raising of a new Polish army out of the Poles incarcerated and exiled in the

Soviet Union would not only alleviate the fate of these individuals but would open up the possibility of a Polish army fighting on the *Eastern Front* in alliance with the Red Army but under its own government as the Germans were eventually driven back. It all turned out very differently, and the first step toward a new Soviet–Polish relationship was to be the last. But for a short time a most difficult problem which threatened to separate the Soviet Union from its major present and potential allies was greatly alleviated. Polish prisoners began to be released, and for a while even the strongly anti-Soviet Polish ambassador in Washington, Jan Ciechanowski, acknowledged that "the Soviet government is legally fulfilling all its engagements."[80]

It was precisely in the United States that there was at first some diffidence about extending aid to the Soviet Union. The American public was still upset over the Soviet invasion of Poland and attack on Finland in 1939, and the United States refused to recognize the incorporation of the Baltic States into the Soviet Union in 1940. At a time when the attempts of their government to provide secret information to Moscow about the forthcoming German invasion had fallen on deaf ears, the American public remained vehemently anti-Communist in its orientation. The German attack appeared to relieve Britain, which Americans were increasingly inclined to assist; but while most preferred for the Russians to defeat the invaders, there was strong opposition to helping them directly. This opposition derived not only from doubts about the Soviet system and reluctance to divert more supplies from the British, but also a belief among many of Roosevelt's advisors that the Soviet Union would in any case not be able to hold out and resist effectively for long. In addition, the isolationist opponents of the administration now saw their own position vindicated.

President Roosevelt saw these issues differently. Contrary to the views of many of his advisors, he did *not* expect that the Soviet Union would collapse quickly; he was being urged by Churchill to act on this belief by helping the Soviet Union; and he was strongly reinforced in that opinion by Joseph E. Davies, an old friend from the years of the Wilson administration, whom he had sent to Moscow as ambassador from early 1937 to the summer of 1938. The President soon saw his confidence in the possibility of continued Soviet resistance bolstered by the reports of his personal confidant and emissary Harry Hopkins, whom he sent to see Stalin in late July.

As a careful politician who knew that he had to move cautiously on this difficult issue the President worked publicly and privately toward a program of aid to Hitler's latest victim, doing what he could to remove domestic resistance to such a policy by special emphasis to the most sensitive point: that of freedom of worship in the Soviet Union. It took several months of careful coaxing to obtain a basis of public support for his policy, but the point which needs to be understood is that he was steering the country in this direction from the first day of the German attack on June 22, 1941.[81] Once the Japanese attack on Pearl Harbor and the German and Italian declarations of war on the United States had drawn the country into the conflict, these issues would become less difficult on the American domestic scene. In the meantime, Roosevelt's preference was encapsulated in his note on a memorandum from Hopkins on plans to ship airplanes to Russia, "OK but say to them from me; Hurry, Hurry, Hurry! F.D.R."[82]

Even before the tiny trickle of American aid to the Soviet Union could become a substantial source of supplies for the Russian army and economy, the Germans and Japanese began to be concerned about the delivery of such aid across the Pacific to Vladivostok and other Soviet ports and bases.[83] This was a subject on which they could never reach agreement because the Japanese decision to head south and go to war with Britain, the Netherlands, and the United States was predicated on their respecting the neutrality treaty with the Soviet Union, which might otherwise allow the United States to use Soviet bases for air attacks on the home islands of Japan. It would be a source of constant friction between the Tripartite Pact partners that about half of the volume of American aid to the Soviet Union could be shipped quite literally under the noses of the Japanese while the German army bled to death on the Eastern Front. Roosevelt with his perspective on global interrelationships would be gravely concerned about the possibility of Japan switching to a defensive posture in the Pacific in the spring of 1942 and turning against the Soviet Union, with a resulting need for the United States to find ways to tie down the Japanese by attacks while developing new supply routes to the Soviet Union; but as will become apparent in the following chapter, this danger, if it ever existed, was obviated by developments in the Pacific War in 1942. It should, however, be noted that the converse would also remain a permanent feature of the Pacific War: the Soviet government until 1945 maintained its refusal of bases to the United States and thereby prevented massive air attacks on the Japanese home islands from a "second front" in the Soviet Far East. Similarly, the dangers on the front with Germany obliged the Soviet Union to tread carefully in its relations with Nationalist China, and a case can be made for the argument that Chiang was able to reassert authority in Sinkiang and thereby retain it for China because of the German–Soviet conflict.[84]

Long before the Japanese had brought the United States into the war, the question of how the Western Powers could best help the Soviet Union in its travail had become the focus of complicated negotiations between the new partners. In early July 1941 Hopkins, who was in London in behalf of Roosevelt for conferences on supplies for the British at home and in the Middle East, went on to Moscow for several meetings with Stalin. On Roosevelt's instructions, he discussed the aid requirements of the Russians and simultaneously received the clear impression of an effectively working system likely to continue in the war. The broader view of Russian determination and ability to continue the fight reinforced Roosevelt's beliefs; the discussion of aid requirements led to a joint British–United States mission to Moscow in late September.[85]

The activities of this mission, led by Lord Beaverbrook for the British and Averell Harriman for the Americans, essentially set the tone for the aid the Western Powers provided to the Soviet Union until the end of the War. With the British at this point taking the lead, agreements were reached on substantial schedules of weapons and supplies to be delivered to the Russians. Since there was no prospect of any early invasion of Europe from the West, it appeared essential to help Russia keep fighting in the East with whatever could be sent, even if this meant—as it certainly did for the British—cutting back on the reinforcement of other theaters, especially the areas of Southeast Asia threatened by Japan. Beaverbrook was clear in his own mind that only aid provided unconditionally and on the largest possible scale made any sense, and the Americans quickly fell in with this line.

It was argued by a few at the time and many later that conditions should have been attached to the aid provided, but this view was rejected, especially by Beaverbrook, in view not only of the need to bolster the Soviet Union at first when it was in great danger and subsequently as it carried the greatest burden of the fighting, but also because there was no alternative. Even in the darkest days of the fighting the Soviet Union was unwilling to make the slightest political concessions; Stalin was never prepared to negotiate with the Western Powers in a bargaining fashion of give-and-take as he had been with Germany and with Finland—the British and Americans might accept his demands and deliver what they could or not; but he would not make any promises in return other than to fight the Germans. And if they decided to help Russia less, it would merely mean they would have to fight Germany the more—and suffer the attendant casualties and costs—with the possibility of a separate Soviet–German peace always in the background.[86]

The prospect first of a possible Soviet collapse and thereafter of a Soviet–German peace hung over the alignment of the three great powers from June 1941 until the end of 1944. Not only the memory of Soviet action in making a separate peace which had left the Allies to face the German onslaught in the West in the latter part of World War I, but also their pact with Hitler in the first part of the Second World War was ever present in the thinking of British and American leaders—all of whom had lived to see the earlier as well as the later example of such a policy. In addition to the obvious possibility that, once the Germans had been halted, they might be amenable to some new deal with the Soviet government, there was the evidence of intercepted and decoded Japanese attempts to bring the Russians and the Germans together again. The ability of the Americans, and, through their assistance, of the British, to decipher Japanese diplomatic radio messages meant that they could follow in considerable detail the efforts of Tokyo to persuade the Germans and Russians to make peace, so that Germany could concentrate her strength on fighting against the British and, after December 1941, against the United States.

There will be repeated references to the Japanese interest in this possibility, but two aspects of that interest must be noted in its initial phase in the winter of 1941–42. In the first place, the Japanese, who very much wanted such a German–Soviet agreement, were probably more optimistic about the feasibility of their plan than the facts warranted;[87] and secondly, their constant repetition of advice to the Germans to make peace in the East always reminded the Western Powers—who were reading this advice—that if the Soviet Union and Germany were ever both simultaneously interested in actually arriving at an agreement, there was a method readily at hand for getting negotiations started.[88]

The question of whether either was actually seriously interested in such a possibility will recur at several points in the history of the war. The existing literature is necessarily in large part speculative; and the most recent serious study of the issue, though of great value, is flawed by an interpretive framework which appears to discount Soviet interest in an accommodation and to over-emphasize the interest of some elements in Germany.[89] The evidence convinces this writer that the first serious Soviet interest came after the halting of their great counteroffensive of early 1942, when the road to victory looked very difficult for Russia and, it could be assumed in Moscow, must now look more difficult for the Germans. On the German side, some of those opposed to Hitler hoped to arrange a compromise peace but had no influence on a government which remained determined to secure victory on the field of battle. Whatever the reality, however, the prospect of the possibility was always on British and American minds and contributed to the constant British preoccupation with making political and territorial concessions to the Soviet Union lest she pull out of the war.

This concern was exacerbated in the fall of 1941 by the great difficulties in allocating already scarce supplies to Russia and the inability to respond to Stalin's appeal for either a massive invasion of Western Europe or the sending of 25–30 divisions to fight alongside the Red Army on the Eastern Front. Since the Soviet leader presumably knew that these divisions did not exist—and could not get there if they did—his demand must be understood as a measure both of his desperation in the face of the German onslaught and his desire to pressure the British into doing *something*.[90] For a time Churchill seriously considered the sending of two British divisions to join the Russian southern front; but as the fighting in Libya turned into a slugging match in late November, it made more sense to employ them there in the operation, previously referred to, which diverted the 2nd German Air Fleet from the Eastern Front to the Mediterranean. Furthermore, the British government, at the personal and repeated insistence of Churchill, was providing the Soviet government with information on German plans for operations in Russia derived from the reading of German codes.[91] It is unknown whether the Soviet high command made appropriate use of this highly valuable information, but from Kim Philby, their own agent in the relevant section of British intelligence, they had every reason to know the real source and hence reliability of the information they were receiving.[92]

Stalin's continued complaints and the high level of friction in daily Soviet–British relations led the British to add to their supply, military and intelligence efforts a mission by Foreign Secretary Anthony Eden to confer with the Russians in Moscow.[93] Authorized to sign a wartime alliance together with a commitment to post-war cooperation, Eden was confronted by a demand for the recognition of the annexation of the Baltic States, the cession of not precisely defined portions of Poland, the 1941 border with Romania and Finland plus the addition of Petsamo, the partition of East Prussia between the Soviet Union and Poland, and a host of other territorial changes, along with Soviet agreement to British bases in France, Belgium, and the Netherlands. By December 16, the date of this meeting of Stalin and Eden, the world situation had greatly changed from the time when Eden's trip had been planned. The Soviets had halted the Germans and were throwing them back; the Japanese had attacked the Western Powers; and Britain, at Soviet insistence, had declared war on Finland, Hungary, and Romania. Stalin recognized, or at least temporarily recognized, that the British could no more help the Soviet Union by a second front in Europe than he could help them by opening a new front against Japan in East Asia, but he was absolutely insistent on a treaty in which the British would agree to the pre-June 1941 border of the Soviet Union.

The British, however, had committed themselves to the Americans in the Atlantic Charter in public and in diplomatic negotiations in private *not* to make any agreements on post-war borders, a position that fitted with the public posture the Soviet Union had announced on November 6[94] but was now completely contradicted by Stalin's proposal. Eden could only offer to bring the Soviet demands to the attention of his government; and in the ensuing negotiations, the vehement insistence of the United States restrained the willingness of the London government to agree with a Soviet position which was obviously so important to them and from the implementation of which—assuming victory in the war—the Western Powers could not keep them anyway.[95] Roosevelt, however, was absolutely insistent on this issue, influenced by memories of the World War I secret treaties, which in the eyes of many had contributed to the failure of the peace settlement of 1919, and by great concern for domestic United States opposition to any such actions. When, in view of their inability to mount substantial military operations in Western Europe the British began to give in anyway, they quickly discovered that this led to new Soviet demands, and the 20-year alliance treaty of May 26, 1942, finally signed contained no territorial provisions. Partly because of United States insistence on no wartime agreement on post-war borders, partly because of excessive Soviet demands once the British had agreed to Stalin's original ones, the territorial issues were left open for more difficult negotiations later. It was not a happy beginning for an alliance, made all the less happy because the one joint military project which once had appeared capable of realization, a joint attack on the Finnish port of Petsamo, had proved impossible to launch after all.[96]

On specific issues on which the Russians wanted the assistance of their allies in the West, such as the possibility of German use of poison gas, they would be quite cooperative.[97] But in general, the relationship was exceptionally difficult from the start. Having themselves helped Germany against the Western Powers earlier in the war, the Russians now often assumed that the British and later the Americans were deliberately following a somewhat similar policy. The fact that they carried such a large share of the burdens of war reinforced this view,[98] while it provoked reminders from their allies that the terrible situation of the Soviet Union was of its own making.[99] The contrast between the Soviet victories in Europe in the winter of 1941–42 and the disasters of Britain and the United States in the Pacific and Southeast Asia only heightened Soviet disdain for their allies. The insistence of the Soviets on neutrality in the

Pacific War led to Stalin's refusal for a general meeting of the major Allies in Moscow when Roosevelt proposed it in December of 1941.[100] The three powers, joined by the attacks on them of Germany and Japan, would continue to work together for victory, but only with enormous difficulty. But, whatever those difficulties, the Soviet Union could count on a measure of help for itself and none for its mortal enemies, a situation very different from that faced by the British in their hour of greatest peril.

It was in this context that the Red Army launched its counter-offensive on the Central front on December 5, surprising its allies as well as the Germans.[101] The prior and concurrent limited but successful Soviet attacks at the northern and southern ends of the front, at Tikhvin and Rostov, meant that the stretched out German forces on the Central front, exhausted and at the end of their own unsuccessful and already halted attacks toward Moscow, could not count on any substantial reinforcements from the other segments of the front. Both north and south of the capital Soviet reserve formations struck at the German pincers reaching for Moscow; and immediately afterwards, the Red Army also drove westwards between those pincers. Careful preparations and shrewd timing characterized a Soviet offensive operation directed and largely planned by Zhukov, and totally surprising the Germans. Although the balance of forces only slightly favored the Russians, their superior equipment for the weather, the fact that many of the attacking units were rested, and the exhaustion and surprise which characterized the Germans, gave the Red Army a substantial advantage. Urged on by Stalin and a sense of uplift that accompanied the largest Soviet offensive of the war to date, the Russian troops smashed the German advance units, drove at places into their rear, and, especially in the area northwest of Moscow, quickly threatened to cut off and destroy large portions of the German forces which had come closest to the city.[102]

The bitter fighting which ensued during the remaining days of 1941 was marked by several significant characteristics. First, the Red Army, in spite of some local setbacks, was able to drive into the German lines and force them back, inflicting great losses on the whole central portion of the front. Second, in this process the Germans not only suffered heavy casualties from both combat and frost but also lost vast quantities of equipment not only to Soviet artillery but also because they simply could not haul it back, in some instances having to destroy it themselves.[a] Third, there were clear signs of panic in many German units as poorly

---

[a] In this connection, the heavy German reliance on horses proved a major handicap; by this time, the surviving horses were often simply too weak to pull artillery in the deep snow. See the von Bock Diary, 16 December 1941, BA/MA, N 22/9, f. 176–78.

clad soldiers in the most wretched weather (for which they had not been equipped on the assumption that the fighting would have ended long before) faced an attacking foe who seemed likely to overwhelm them. Fourth, in spite of all these hallmarks of a great Soviet victory, the Red Army was not able to trap any large German units. Sometimes with and sometimes against the orders of Hitler, the German generals on the spot did what they could to extricate their forces as their soldiers fought desperately to hold together with some semblance of cohesion.

The victory attained by the Red Army and the disaster suffered by the German army in the first ten days after December 5 led to new decisions of far-reaching significance on both sides of the front, decisions which, in a manner neither Hitler nor Stalin could have anticipated, interacted with each other. On the German side, the possibility of the army being totally routed, driven into a demoralizing general retreat on the scale of Napoleon's catastrophe, and losing most of its equipment in the process, led Hitler to order the German Army Group Center to hold in place, risking a loss of the whole force. What reinforcements could be found would be rushed forward on whatever trains could be spared from the higher priority assigned to carting Jews to be slaughtered in the occupied territory; but with no prepared lines to fall back on and no way to salvage the heavy equipment, the German units at the front had to fight where they stood, even if the lines were broken.

Simultaneously with a series of strenuous efforts to find reinforcements, there came a whole series of changes at the top. One of the generals fired in early January, the Commander-in-Chief of the 3rd Panzer Army General Hoepner, had saved two surrounded corps and was not only replaced but was to have been tossed out of the army and deprived of his pension.[103] The laws which prevented these latter steps without a court martial enraged Hitler sufficiently that after the stabilization of the front in April he would summon the Reichstag for a session to cancel any law or regulation protecting the rights of German citizens.[104] In this one field National Socialism attained its objective of completely substituting arbitrary power for any and all restraints on government authority. But by the time Hoepner was dismissed, a whole host of other major changes had been made.

On December 19 Hitler accepted the resignation of the Commander-in-Chief of the German Army; at the same time or soon after, many others were also relieved. All three Army Group commanders and a row of army commanders were replaced. Hitler evidently intended to replace the Chief of Staff of the army, General Halder, as well, but changed his mind.[105] The position of von Brauchitsch Hitler decided to take over himself; the other positions were filled from within the army's higher ranks. Such massive replacements of high-ranking officers who had in many instances become well known in Germany because of their prior role in the war hardly helped morale at home. The news of Japan's attack and Germany's declaration of war on the United States was quickly followed by big news of victories in East Asia, but these temporary diversions now gave way to bad news from the Eastern Front, almost immediately followed by a general appeal to the population for donations of warm winter clothing, especially furs, for the troops. Here the German population could get a first really clear picture that things had gone drastically wrong.[106]

For the German troops the new orders and commanders meant a desperate struggle to hold on. A case can be made for the view that the as yet unshaken confidence of the soldiers in Hitler contributed to their rallying to him as the new Commander-in-Chief of the army and halted what might otherwise have been a collapse of morale.[107] But the new Commander-in-Chief of Army Group Center, von Kluge, could no more halt the Red Army than his predecessor could. In bitter fighting, the Germans were steadily driven back with heavy losses in men and materiel. Some reinforcements reached the front, but never as much as promised; the retreats did not shorten the lines sufficiently to make subsequent defense easier; and the temporary holding out of isolated German units did not keep the Russians from pushing forward. If by the end of January a badly battered Army Group Center survived, though in a most complicated front line, several factors contributed to this temporary stabilization as opposed to the total disaster which had repeatedly looked imminent.

One element was undoubtedly the ability of experienced German higher officers. A second was the desperate cohesion of small units caught up in a defeat but holding together for survival. A third was the narrow margin of Red Army superiority; although the Germans always reported overwhelming Russian strength, the reality was rather different. The inexperience and rigidity of Soviet officers also contributed to the Germans being able to hold on, but the most important contribution from the Soviet side was almost certainly the decision of Stalin to try for an exceedingly ambitious general counter-offensive in the hope of smashing the whole German front, instead of concentrating all available resources on the sector in the middle where the chances for a truly major further victory were probably greatest.

THE SECOND SOVIET OFFENSIVE

In mid-December, even as the German defeat before Moscow was being justifiably celebrated in Soviet public announcements, Stalin called for major offensive operations on *other* sectors of the front.[108] Now that the Red Army had retaken Tikhvin on December 9, a large-scale effort was to be mounted to relieve Leningrad and encircle a major portion of the German Army Group in the north, and in addition big drives were to be launched into the Ukraine as well as the Crimea, even as thrusts into the deep flanks of the German Army Group Center were supposed to cut it off in a huge encirclement similar to those which the Germans had so effectively carried off in the summer and fall. Success in these operations would tear the guts out of the German army and assure the rapid liberation of all the territory they had seized since June. The newly mobilized and rebuilt formations available to the Stavka were to be employed in these thrusts; it looked to Stalin as if the strained and exhausted German army could be sent reeling by hard and essentially simultaneous blows on all major segments of the front. The morale of the Soviet home front was certainly being lifted by the freeing of cities earlier taken by the Nazis.[109]

Rejecting the contrary advice of several Red Army commanders, Stalin ordered this series of offensives to begin in the first ten days of 1942. In the north, an attack by the 2nd Assault Army opened a narrow corridor through the German line along the Volkhov river. Cut off once, reconnected to the main Soviet lines, and cut off a second time, this army could not be effectively reinforced; and even sending in one of Stalin's favorite and ablest commanders, General Andrei Vlasov, who had distinguished himself in the defense of Moscow, could not save the 2nd Assault Army from later destruction. Vlasov himself would be captured in the summer and make a futile effort to establish an army out of prisoners of war to fight alongside the Germans for an independent non-Stalinist Russia.[110]

On the southern shore of the Gulf of Finland the Russians were able to open a land bridge between Leningrad and the Independent Coastal Group cut off around Oranienbaum since the preceding fall. Further south, the Red Army tore open the junction between the German Army Groups North and Center, driving deeply into the rear of the latter, and also isolating a small German force in Cholm and a larger one with almost 100,000 soldiers around Demyansk. But the Germans managed to hold both "islands" in bitter fighting and with supplies brought by the air force until in the spring both garrisons were relieved by pushes from the remaining German front. This success of sorts may well have inclined Hitler to over-estimate the possibility of air supply for an isolated force, disregarding the fact that both held far fewer troops and were much closer to German air bases than the Stalingrad pocket later in 1942.[111] In the spring of 1942, however, the holding of these areas appeared to have vindicated the tactics of the winter battle and to leave behind a projection of the front which offered at least the appearance of an opportunity to close the gap to the German Army Group Center still holding at Rzhev.[112]

Here, too, the Germans had managed to hold on to a key position, clearing the threatened connecting route south to Vyazma on the main railway and road to Smolensk. With his forces worn down by the exertions of the December counter-offensive, and deprived of the needed reinforcements by the efforts at strategic blows in the north and south, Zhukov's forces dented and drove back but could neither surround nor crack the front of the Army Group Center.[113] A massive breakthrough into the southern portion of this front by forces led by General Belov and supported by several large airdrops—the largest Soviet parachute operation of the war—still did not have the power needed to cut off the German 9th and 4th Armies as intended. Soon Belov's own forces, and the partisans associated with them, were themselves cut off and, very much like the 2nd Assault Army in the north, largely destroyed by a German operation in late May 1942.[114]

Further south the Soviets were able to seize and hold on to the vital town of Kirov, thus cutting the main north–south railway from Vyazma to Bryansk, but beyond forcing the Germans back from the southern approaches to Moscow had not been able to attain the more spectacular goals established for them by the Stavka. A drive across the Donets around Izyum designed to cut off the Germans holding Kharkov to the north, destroy the German armies (17th and 1st Panzer) to the south, and at least reach the Dnepr, was held by the Germans in a bulge. A Soviet spring offensive further north together with the bulge were destroyed in a major German operation in late May, 1942.[115] The German troops which had been forced out of Rostov were able to hold a front along the Mius river; it took some hard fighting—and the replacement of the German Army Group commander soon followed by the death of his successor—but here both sides were matched in exhaustion. On the Crimean peninsula, German efforts to complete its conquest by taking the great naval base of Sevastopol were countered by a Soviet amphibious operation across the Kerch Straits, which retook the eastern portion of the Crimea. Here, too, additional Soviet landings and offensive operations were eventually held by the Germans.[116]

A jagged front marked the failure of the German effort to defeat the Soviet Union in a quick campaign in 1941 and of the Soviet hopes of crushing the German invaders in a wide-ranging strategic offensive in the first weeks of 1942. Stalin had underestimated the resilience of the

German forces and, in trying for too much at once, had led the Red Army to a major victory but without destroying the German army.

Both sides now looked ahead to the 1942 summer campaign. Most of Stalin's senior advisors urged a defensive posture while the Soviet Union rebuilt its military power. It seemed to them to make sense to integrate into the army the weapons now coming off the assembly lines of the old and the relocated factories in greater numbers, to retrain and reorganize the army units mauled in the heavy winter fighting, and to allow the Red Air Force to rebuild its squadrons. Offensives, in their eyes, could be launched effectively in the fall, assuming that a new German summer offensive would be held.

Like his military leaders, Stalin believed that the 1942 German summer offensive would come on the Central front against Moscow. This opinion was apparently reinforced by the obvious closeness of the German lines to the Soviet capital—about 80 miles—and the desperation with which the Germans had successfully held on to Rzhev, a place with no visible importance to them except in connection with a new offensive toward Moscow. In addition, the impression that the German effort would come there was so effectively reinforced, as far as we can tell, by a carefully worked out deception operation,[117] that all signs of a very different plan for 1942 provided by both Soviet intelligence and the Western Powers were dismissed as erroneous.[118]

Unlike the military leaders, however, Stalin did not consider it wise to await the blow and ordered a series of offensive operations in the spring, hoping thereby to disrupt the German plans. Of these attacks only a small one in the far north and a large one in the Kharkov area materialized before the German summer offensive. On the Litsa river front before Murmansk, a Soviet attack in late April 1942 was halted after minimal gains and with very heavy losses.[119] In the Ukraine, Timoshenko began a major offensive toward Kharkov on May 12. Not only was this attack held by the Germans but a few days later they crushed the bulge at Izyum left from the Soviet winter counter-offensive. This double disaster cost the Red Army about half a million dead, wounded, and prisoners; it was not an auspicious way to begin the year.[120]

Most Germans still looked to the future with confidence.[121] There were exceptions. The air force's chief of construction and development, the famous flier Ernst Udet, committed suicide on November 17, 1941.[122] In the same month, the Commander-in-Chief of the replacement army, General Fritz Fromm, and the head of construction and armaments, Fritz Todt, urged Hitler to make peace,[123] while the chief of armed forces intelligence, Admiral Canaris, told Fromm on March 20, 1942, that the war could not be won.[124] But Hitler himself thought otherwise. He had recognized that the campaign in the East would continue into 1942 earlier than most.[125] Major projects were undertaken to try to rebuild the German army, though it could never regain its strength of the summer of 1941. Hundreds of thousands of German workers were transferred from industry to the army; instead of the anticipated reduction in the number of divisions—so that the air force and navy could be built up to fight England and the United States—there might have to be an increase.[126] The workers drafted from industry into the army were to be replaced by Russian prisoners of war, but, as will be discussed subsequently, most of these had either been murdered or starved to death. Hitler was very much aware of this; along with the concern lest German soldiers surrender more readily, this was one reason he rejected all efforts to have the International Red Cross look after German and Russian prisoners of war.[127] Eventually a huge slave labor program involving civilians from the occupied Eastern territories would be instituted instead. In any case, the time for a relaxed home front in Germany was over, and the armaments industry had to be geared up. The new directive on the armament program issued on January 10, 1942, marks German recognition of the fact that the whole concept of a Blitzkrieg, a lightning war, had failed.[128]

However much Hitler might press forward with mobilization of industry and manpower, and however pleased he might be with the prospect of spring coming eventually on the Eastern Front,[129] the army could not do the fighting by itself. The defeat of December 1941–January 1942 only reinforced the proclivity of the Germans to use their air force primarily in ground support operations; even more drastically than before the Luftwaffe was kept from any strategic role and hitched to tactical assistance of the army.[130] But even the air force would not be enough to enable the army to initiate another major offensive in the East. Germany's allies would have to help. The Romanians were urged to maintain and expand further the substantial forces they already had in the field, while Italy and Hungary were expected to convert their contingents into corps and eventually army strength expeditionary forces. In this project Mussolini as usual displayed more enthusiasm than judgement and the Hungarians dragged their feet as best they could; but the critical point to be noted is that it was at German insistence that massive contingents of poorly equipped and trained, and often badly led, troops were collected and sent off to play vital roles in German-planned operations which were hardly likely to arouse the enthusiasm of the soldiers, would end in death and disaster for most, and where they would thereafter provide the excuse for their own and Germany's defeat.[131]

Although the German armies on the Eastern Front had by this time begun to enroll large numbers of captured Russian soldiers as auxiliaries (called *Hilfswillige*, or *Hiwis* for short), their attempts to organize armed units made up of volunteers recruited from among Soviet citizens, whether previously captured or not, were halted by Hitler's personal order. Although a few locally activated formations existed—almost certainly without Hitler knowing about them—he prohibited the establishment of such units as a matter of principle: the Germans had come to the East to slaughter many and enslave the rest; certainly arming these people to fight alongside the Germans was not the correct way to implement such a policy.[132] That policy will be examined shortly, but first the aims and plans of the Germans for 1942 must be described briefly.

The hope of reaching the oil resources of the Caucasus, or at least denying them to the Russians by cutting the routes from there to the rest of the Soviet Union, had been dashed in 1941 by the successful resistance of the Red Army.[a] This was now to be the highest priority for 1942. The conquest of the Don basin and the Caucasus would shift the industrial and oil resources of these areas from the Russian to the German side and open up the prospect of a drive across the Caucasus into the Middle East where, perhaps assisted by other German drives through Turkey and across North Africa, they hoped to meet the Japanese advancing across the Indian Ocean from the other end. The meeting of the Axis partners, as the German and Japanese leaders assured each other, would sunder the alliance and the communications of their enemies. Here were prospects as rosy for the Germans and the Japanese as they were dangerous not only for the Russians but also for the British and the Americans.[133] Only the Western Powers early recognized the immense danger threatening them, while the Russians still anticipated a German effort to seize Moscow. But with the initiative still held by Germany and Japan, it was these powers which would establish the framework for the great battles of 1942.[134]

BEHIND THE FRONT: GERMAN PLANS AND ACTIONS

The enormous front in the East which had been opened up by the German attack in June was, as already indicated, in many ways different from earlier fighting in the war. By German design, it was not only a

---

[a] All the evidence indicates that the Germans were not originally aware of the fact that the Soviet Union had completed a railway from Baku to Astrakhan, and therefore believed that railway communications into the Caucasus could be cut by the seizure of Stalingrad.

fight to the death between huge armies but a portion of a broadly conceived, even if not yet precisely detailed, project for a complete reordering of the peoples both of the areas directly affected and of Europe as a whole. The plans to kill certain categories of prisoners of war were being implemented from the first days of the campaign, and this became with a speed difficult to credit merely a small portion of a far wider horror, the deliberate starving to death—or allowing the death by exposure and disease—of hundreds of thousands of Soviet prisoners.

By February 1942, of the 3.9 million Soviet soldiers captured up to then by the Germans, the vast majority, some 2.8 million were dead. At least a quarter million had been shot; the others had died under the horrible conditions imposed on them by the Germans.[135] Whatever fairy tales were put out by those involved in these horrors or apologists for them, careful scrutiny of the contemporary evidence makes it clear that this atrocity of vast proportions was carried out with the willing, even enthusiastic, participation of German army, police, and civilian authorities. There were indeed exceptional individuals who objected and in some instances tried to alleviate the situation, but their minute number only underlines the broad consensus between the civilian and military leadership.[a]

On the German side, this agreement on the rapid physical elimination of a large portion of the enemy population—a step without precedent in modern history—has to be seen as part of a consensus, at least temporarily, on a major portion of that extreme form of Social Darwinism which was central to National Socialism and which would have still other implications for the people of Europe. On the Russian side, this had two significant effects. In the first place, the shooting of some categories of prisoners—in part announced in German leaflets—as well as the rapid spread of knowledge of the fate of the rest, served to spur the officers and soldiers of the Red Army to even more determined resistance. This was so obvious that a number of German generals urged the end of the policy of shooting captured commissars, a point on which Hitler eventually agreed in May of 1942. The second effect of German treatment of the captured Red Army men was on the population of the occupied territories. The fate of the prisoners was in front of their eyes; any who did not see the enclosures and marches where they died or were shot by the thousands would either hear by word of mouth or see the wounded and disabled whom the Germans deliberately dumped on the countryside to die. Here was an enemy who made even Stalin's labor

---

[a] The intended fate of most Russian prisoners of war also helps explain why the Germans rejected Soviet efforts to have prisoners treated according to the relevant international conventions (Streit, *Keine Kameraden*, pp. 224–37).

camps look humane—a considerable accomplishment—and one with long-term political implications.

A German policy closely related to that of killing or letting die millions of prisoners of war was the previously discussed series of decisions about the killing of Jews.[136] Jewish POWs were frequently shot, and special murder squads (*Einsatzkommandos*) were attached to the German armies as they moved forward. These implemented the decision to kill all Jews in the area overrun by the advancing armies. When it became obvious that these massacres ran into little resistance from the military, and were in fact often assisted and even urged on by them, the heady days of victory of July seemed to provide the opportunity to extend this process both to the rest of the territory that would be occupied by the German army and to the whole of German-occupied and controlled Europe. Here was, or at least seemed to be, the opportunity to kill all Jews German power might reach.

The SS took the lead in this colossal project, obtained a legitimizing commission from Göring, and began to develop plans for its implementation.[137] On the technical side, this meant increasing recourse to new methods of slaughter either already in use elsewhere or now developed. Mass shooting always remained a significant element in the process but did not work with the speed and efficiency those in charge preferred. The gas vans based on prior projects in the so-called euthanasia program had their part, along with the people who had acquired experience in their use during that program; and the construction of large special facilities for mass murder, begun in the fall of 1941, would include big gas chambers. These, first tried out on some of the Russian prisoners of war, eventually became the preferred though by no means exclusive method of murder.

From a practical point of view, it quickly appeared best to the Germans to reverse the procedure initiated in the summer of 1941; instead of bringing the murderers to the victims, they would bring the victims to the murderers. This part of the project began with large shipments of German Jews on October 15, 1941; it is not a pure coincidence that in the presence of Himmler and Heydrich on October 21, 1941, Hitler referred to the extermination of Jews, and the mayor of the city of Hamburg alluded in his diary on the same day to the taking over of Jewish homes.[138]

From the administrative side, it became increasingly obvious to the SS that the program could not be carried out without the cooperation and continuing involvement of many German government agencies. Representatives of these agencies were summoned to a conference, originally scheduled for December 9 and then postponed to January 20.

At this meeting, generally called the Wannsee Conference after its location, the nature and implementation of the program to kill all the Jews of Europe was reviewed at length for the benefit of the agencies to be involved. The dimensions were spelled out and they included not only all Jews in German-controlled and influenced areas, but those—like the ones in England, Spain, Sweden, and Portugal—which it was assumed would soon also be under German domination.[139]

Those present understood what was to happen;[140] they had been reading the regular reports of the murder squads on their activities, including the one on the largest single slaughter, that of 33,000 at Babi Yar near Kiev.[141] The various agencies not already participating became involved hereafter; the role of the Foreign Ministry being especially important because it had the task of obtaining the Jews from territories under German influence but not total control. It was decided to begin with France from where the first transport left for Auschwitz, one of the major centers for killing, on March 27, 1942.[142] Madagascar was no longer needed, but all areas where Germany had any influence, including even Denmark, then still held up as a model of the cooperative and independent satellite, were expected to fall in line eventually.[143] German arms would, Hitler hoped, extend this program beyond Europe. As he discussed the anticipated offensive across the Caucasus into the Middle East with the Mufti on November 28, 1941, he explained that Germany's only aim in the area would be the destruction of the Jews there.[144]

Within the German army there was a high level of agreement on the propriety of this program. On the one hand, there were those who wanted to move it along even faster, while there were also some who objected. The former view was particularly obvious in Serbia, the portion of Yugoslavia under direct German military supervision, where the local German commanders were so enthusiastic about the program that they applied it locally on their own initiative.[145] On the other hand, there was in addition to the opposition of a few German officers evidently some muttering of discontent from among the army rank and file. It is this muttering that must, in this author's opinion, be adduced to explain the extraordinary phenomenon of generals ordering explanations and defenses of what was described as the "hard but just punishment of the Jewish sub-humans" to be read to their troops. German field marshals and generals were otherwise not in the habit of explaining themselves to the troops. A first order of October 10 by Field Marshal von Reichenau was distributed at the insistence of Field Marshal von Rundstedt to all armies in his Army Group South and then at von Brauchitsch's order to all units in the East. Along with repeated orders to refrain from sending home pictures of mass executions—evidently a common habit of German soldiers—these directives, which were cited in trials after the war to incriminate their authors, in addition show something of far broader significance.[146]

They illustrate a general recognition of the fact that the German army had embarked on an enterprise very different from the traditions and laws of earlier warfare, that all were involved in this project, that there were some in the ranks who did not approve of this new course; but that such dissenters could not count on any support from the leaders of the army who identified themselves with the program of mass slaughter for ideological reasons. The German soldier was to be, as the order put it, "the carrier of a merciless racial concept" ("Träger einer unerbittlichen völkischen Idee"), and whatever restrictions on conduct remained were designed to maintain discipline in the bloodbath, not to restrain it. No one said so in writing, but the very fact that a few brave officers did object must have shown all who did not that there was no turning back.

In the occupied areas of Eastern Europe, this program had its own set of repercussions. Some of the local people, moved by fear of the Germans, anti-Semitic sentiments, greed, sadistic feelings, hunger, or a combination of several of these factors, joined in the process, especially in Lithuania and portions of the Ukraine. Once they had joined, they quickly realized that they had burned their bridges behind them, had to stick with the Germans, and if they survived the war try to disappear, preferably as anti-Communist refugees in the West. A few brave people tried to help their neighbors, but the vast majority looked on uneasy and apprehensive: a system which acted this way against one group might well act similarly against another. The sample of the New Order, of the new cultural mission of Germanic peoples in Eastern Europe, did not look promising.

In the rest of the world, news of the project for the systematic killing of all of Europe's Jews did not penetrate quickly. It is generally now understood that the outlines of the project and the first major stages in implementing it were known in the West in the summer of 1942.[147] Before that time, however, extensive information about portions of the terrible events had reached the Allies and the neutrals. Though the relevant files remain closed, it is known that the British had broken the police cipher in which the reports of the murder squads beginning in July 1941 and the daily returns from the camps beginning in the spring of 1942 were sent to Berlin.[148] At least for a time, practically nothing was done with this knowledge, though it is by no means clear what could have been done.[149] Here was a problem that transcended both comprehension and remedy. At a time when the Western Allies were being defeated by the Axis in the war at sea, in North Africa, and in the Pacific, the first priority was to hold on and pull together the home front for hard times and eventual victory (which alone could keep the Germans from killing all the other Jews on earth). Public statements and threats would have to wait until they might have some measure of credibility.

Beyond the decimation of Russian prisoners of war and the killing of all the Jews, how did the Germans see the future of their new empire in the East? The policies applied by the Germans in occupied Europe are reviewed in Chapter 9, but some general things must be said here to relate the specifics already discussed to broader objectives. Moscow and Leningrad were to disappear. In addition to the Jews, the Gypsies were also to be slaughtered; and this program, like that against the Jews, was beginning to be implemented in 1941.[150] The overwhelming majority of the newly conquered population was, of course, Slavic. The mentally ill, the sick, and the elderly among them were to be killed as the regime had begun to do within Germany itself. This "benefit" of German culture was already being extended on a massive scale to the occupied portions of the U.S.S.R., and there were here none of the obstacles which slowed down that program inside Germany.[151] The bulk of the population was expected to be dramatically reduced by starvation. German estimates of the numbers run into millions as the cities in the Ukraine and the whole food-deficit area in the north were to be deprived of food, which was seized for the German army or shipped to Central Europe.[152] The surviving peasants were to work in a retained collective farm system producing food for the Germans. But what about their future?

It is in this connection that one must see the experiments initiated in 1941 for the development of measures for the mass sterilization of individuals, without the standard surgical procedures earlier developed by modern medicine, and applied on a massive scale by the German medical profession since the beginnings of National Socialist rule.[153] While the cruel experiments to develop cheap and quick techniques for mass sterilization were performed in concentration camps on Jewish as well as non-Jewish victims, it should be obvious that the intended victims of the measures, once these had been perfected, could not be the Jewish population, which was expected to have been exterminated by that time.[154] It will also not do to assume that it was anticipated that these measures were developed with the slave laborers and prisoners of war imported into Germany during the war in mind, as this whole program was assumed to be a temporary aberration. It is my opinion in the absence of evidence to the contrary, and in view of the centralization of the experiments in the hands of Himmler's SS, that the intended victims of these procedures were segments of the Slavic population of occupied Eastern Europe, whose labor could still be utilized in anticipation of their disappearance from the scene.

But then, who was to live and work in the newly conquered areas? It is here that the settlement aspect of the *Lebensraum* ideology fits in. Tens of thousands of Germanic settlers were to be established in villages and would eventually spread out over the whole area. It was in this fashion that the new lands would be Germanized. Into this area would be directed a steady stream of German settlers, augmented by Dutch, Danish, Norwegian, and Swedish recruits into the upper ranks of the Nazi racial hierarchy.[155] The very highest level would be provided by those higher ranking German officers (and other high officials who had acquired great merit in Hitler's eyes) who would be and in some instances already were assigned estates in the East as part of Hitler's large program of bribing his generals. This program has not been subjected to systematic investigation—the subject is clearly very sensitive—but enough is known about the huge sums given secretly to all the field marshals, four-star generals, and equivalent naval ranks, along with direct allocations of vast stolen estates, to show what the future held for Germany's military leaders—and for the peoples of Eastern Europe.[156]

ALLIED AND AXIS PLANS

How did Stalin and his associates see the future of Eastern Europe? It was obviously their hope that the Germans together with their allies would be driven out as rapidly as possible. In the liberated areas, the Soviet system would be reestablished to whatever extent it had not been secretly maintained by partisans and the underground. As Stalin explained to Eden in December 1941, the Soviet Union might make some minimal adjustments in its June 1941 border with Poland but expected to keep the rest of its gains from the 1939 treaty with Hitler. In addition, the northern section of East Prussia and the Finnish port of Petsamo on the Arctic Ocean were to be annexed to the Soviet Union. Any territorial aspiration beyond these frontiers of the U.S.S.R. were not mentioned as yet, and the question of what was to be the precise post-war fate of the states of Eastern Europe (other than that there would be Soviet bases in Finland and Romania) was probably at this time still unclear in Stalin's own mind. But it may be safely assumed that they would be so organized or controlled as to preclude any danger of their ever again providing a springboard, or allies, for invasion from the West.

As the Allies and the Axis looked to the continued war at the end of

1941, differing perceptions and priorities affected both groupings, though in all cases the gigantic struggle on the Eastern Front dominated everything. The British–Soviet talks and their outcome have already been reviewed. The refusal of Stalin to meet Roosevelt and Churchill meant that these two met without the Soviet leader; and having such a meeting right after the United States had been precipitated into the war was a special concern of Churchill's. He and his military advisors were very much concerned lest the Americans, in view of the focus of American public attention on the dramatic events in the Pacific, might abandon the concept of defeating Germany first in favor of concentrating on the battle against Japan. With the desperate pleas of the Russians for supplies and for a second front in Western Europe, an American turn to the Pacific would be especially dangerous. Britain and the Soviet Union both had no alternative to concentrating on Germany first, and the Soviet Union might either collapse before a new German onslaught or make a separate peace if the Western Allies did not carry a heavy share of the fighting against Germany. From December 22 to January 14 the highest British and American leaders met in Washington in what was called the Arcadia Conference.[157]

Four major decisions were agreed upon by the British and Americans.[a] First and most important, there was continued agreement on the need to defeat Germany first. In addition to the sending of United States troops to relieve British units in Iceland and Northern Ireland, there should be a landing in North Africa to preclude any German move into the area, meet the British forces advancing from Egypt, and establish a basis for further action against Germany. The raw material and shipping resources of the Western Allies would be pooled and allocated by joint agreement. There would be not only a local unified Allied command under Field Marshal Sir Archibald Wavell to meet the advancing Japanese in Southeast Asia, but a whole staff structure for the joint planning and conduct of war. This would be called the Combined Chiefs of Staff, meeting in Washington, with the British Chiefs of Staff represented by delegates in Washington when they were not present in person. And a side benefit of this structure was that it practically forced the Americans to adopt a regular format for inter-service coordination somewhat similar to the British Chiefs of Staff Committee, but called then and since the Joint Chiefs of Staff.

If the implementation of the basic strategic concepts of preparing for major blows against the Germans while trying to hold back the Japanese was to suffer a major set-back by the series of disasters to British and

---

[a] It was also at this meeting that the United Nations declaration of war aims was prepared and signed.

American forces in North Africa, the Atlantic, and Southeast Asia in the ensuing months, one decision reached almost by default as a result of the Washington meeting was to provide the glue which held the two Allies together in spite of great and repeated friction. The personal cooperation of Roosevelt and Churchill, the common aim of defeating the Axis, and the joint determination to fight on regardless of set-backs and defeats were, of course, pre-conditions for the success of the Anglo-American alliance. But given past—and continuing—suspicions, diverging strategies and perceptions, alterations in relative contributions to the common cause, and differing visions of the future, there would always be opportunities for friction which could have sundered the effective working relationship of the two powers. It was in this regard that Sir John Dill came to play a central role in the war.

Churchill had decided to replace Dill as Chief of the Imperial General Staff by General Alan Brooke because he had lost confidence in him. The Prime Minister had arranged his promotion to field marshal as a consolation prize, and planned to send him into effective military retirement as provincial governor to Bombay. He took Dill along to Washington while the new Chief of the Imperial General Staff remained in London. It quickly became apparent that Dill's personal qualities not only made him more acceptable to the Americans than most British generals but gave him the special friendship and trust of Marshall, Hopkins, and Roosevelt himself. He became first the acting and eventually in October 1942 the permanent head of the British military mission in Washington and from that position was to play a key role in maintaining the working relationship of the British and Americans until his death in November 1944.[158] The equestrian statue by his grave in Arlington National Cemetery, the only such monument in a final resting place for American soldiers, reflects the esteem in which he was held and the sense of loss he left behind.[159]

If the British and Americans had worked out a machinery for running their part of the war and the rudiments of a strategy for winning it, the Axis powers in those same weeks discussed the elements of their strategy and of military coordination but were less successful in implementing either. There was, as already explained, agreement that the way to victory lay in a meeting of the German and Japanese forces in the Middle East and Indian Ocean. The leadership in both countries, but especially that of the two navies, saw quite clearly that control of the Indian Ocean was essential to an Axis victory. This was not only an effective route for communication and exchange of goods between them. It was obviously preferable to the possible use of Japanese diplomatic pouches across the Soviet Union for mail, [160] or the hazards of a northern seaway across the Arctic Ocean around Siberia,[161] or the risks of trying to run blockade-breaking ships between Germany and Japan across oceans dominated by the Allies[162] — a shipping procedure that made the hazards of the convoys to Murmansk look simple by comparison.

Even more important than the ease of transport over an Axis-controlled Indian Ocean was the possibility of shifting the oil resources of the Middle East from the Allied to the Axis side. Along with the Japanese conquest of Southeast Asia with its rubber, tin, and oil then under way, there would be a fundamental alteration in the world situation with the Axis controlling the bulk of the basic raw materials and the Allies living on short rations. Furthermore, both China and the Soviet Union would be more effectively cut off from the outside world, China by the closing of any route for supplies from Britain and the United States, and the Soviet Union by the loss of the route across Iran. Here were the rosiest of prospects.[163]

But not only would the Germans and Japanese find their efforts to implement such a strategy held back by the resistance of their enemies, they faced other complications, many of their own making. The Axis hopes of beating Britain first, unlike the Allied ones of defeating Germany first, were hopelessly hampered by the divergence between Germany and Japan on the best way to do this. And while the Japanese ambassador to Germany could welcome the reorganization of the German high command in December 1941 because he correctly saw Hitler as the most pro-Japanese of the German leaders,[164] the fact remains that the difficulties of establishing understanding between the partners in the Tripartite Pact make the frictions between Britain and the United States and even between either and the Soviet Union look minor by comparison. In addition, as will become evident in the next chapter, the Japanese could not agree among themselves as to the direction in which best to exploit their initial victories: westwards into India, southwards into Australia, or eastwards into Hawaii and Alaska.

On only one point the leadership on both sides had an equivalent sense of certainty now that the war had become truly global. The United States and Britain, along with others, had asserted in the United Nations Declaration of January 1, 1942, approved at the Arcadia Conference, that they would fight on to victory and not make any separate armistice or peace. A couple of weeks earlier, the Germans, Japanese, and Italians had signed a similar agreement in treaty form. Certainly the Japanese, rushing from victory to victory, had no thoughts of peace. The Italians had effectively lost their independence because of Mussolini's blundering. The Germans did not see the problems on the Eastern Front, after their defeat in the Battle of Britain, as any reason to contemplate peace either in the East or, after the victory over Russia which they now confidently anticipated for 1942, in the West. In September 1941 Hitler told his companions that he would fight on for ten years rather than make peace,[165] while Foreign Minister von Ribbentrop, always in his Führer's footsteps, asserted that Germany was ready for a thirty-years war.[166]

6

HALTING THE JAPANESE ADVANCE, HALTING THE GERMAN ADVANCE; KEEPING THEM APART AND SHIFTING THE BALANCE: DECEMBER 1941 TO NOVEMBER 1942

JAPAN'S OFFENSIVE

The Japanese launching of war in East Asia was designed to secure control of the resources of Southeast Asia as rapidly as possible; the attack on the United States navy at Pearl Harbor being designed to shield the flank of this operation from American interference, as the neutrality treaty with the Soviet Union and the maintenance of substantial forces in Manchuria were to protect its rear from Soviet intervention. These were, however, subsidiary moves. The major objective was a rapid seizure of the Philippines and Malaya as a preparatory step for the conquest of the Netherlands East Indies. Combined with an occupation of Burma and the seizure of added portions of New Guinea, the Bismarck Archipelago, and the Marshall and Gilbert Islands, this new empire would assure Japan both control of the oil, rubber, and tin producing lands she coveted and a perimeter of bases from which to defend that empire against any who might try to wrest it from her.

The detailed military plans to implement this program had been carefully worked out in the fall of 1941, but while they included careful schedules for the offensive operations, they were totally deficient in two critical ways. There was no agreed plan for going forward thereafter if the planned conquest succeeded and there was no plan to go back if it failed. As the Germans had, earlier in 1941, assumed that the war on the Eastern Front would end when their armies had reached the Archangel–Astrakhan line, so the Japanese assumed that their war would end when it had reached the perimeter of their newly won empire. But there was never any prospect of this happening; had there ever been one, they had themselves eliminated it with the attack on Pearl Harbor, because the calculation that the Americans would never expend the blood and treasure to reconquer for others a whole host of islands and other places most of them had never heard of, and did not care about if they had, was invalidated by the way in which the Japanese had started war with the United States. It took them until 1945 to discover their error because, even after the tide of battle had turned against them, they invariably returned to the same fundamentally erroneous strategic concept of trying to raise the cost for the Americans to a level the latter would not pay. But there was a long and dramatic string of Japanese victories before any of these new considerations came to enter the picture.

The decision to include war with the United States as a part of the move south was related to the belief that it was simply not safe to by-pass the Philippines; and since the Japanese did not believe they could wait until the Americans left those islands in 1946, as the latter had already decided to do, those islands had to be invaded. Conquered by Japan, they would themselves provide an excellent base for the invasion of the Netherlands East Indies and a fine station along the route into the southern empire.

The Japanese planned to knock out American air and naval power in the Philippines, correctly believed to be concentrated on the large northern island of Luzon, to land two divisions on that island to seize air bases on it, and then to crush the remaining American and Filipino army units in a short campaign on Luzon, the large southern island of Mindanao and several of the other islands. The naval and air bases in the Philippines could thereafter be utilized for the invasion of the Netherlands East Indies in which, it was anticipated, many of the Japanese units involved in the Philippine operation would themselves also participate.[1]

The original American plan for the defense of the Philippines had called for a concentration on defense of Manila Bay and the withdrawal of the major United States army forces to the Bataan peninsula, with the hope that they could hold out there for half a year until a relief force from Hawaii could reach the islands. This latter part of the plan was in reality a wistful thought rather than a serious possibility; and American contingency planning for war, with its assumption that Germany constituted the greater danger and must be defeated first by the United States fighting alongside Great Britain and the Soviet Union, implied a defensive posture in East Asia, assumed the early loss of Guam and the Philippines, and looked to a victory over Japan in some distant future after the defeat of Germany.

For some time this perspective — and the anticipated total departure of Americans from the islands in 1946 — had meant that it made little sense to allocate scarce equipment and men to the doomed territory, but all this changed in two inter-related developments in the fall of 1941. The energetic and optimistic former U.S. Army Chief of Staff and now commander in the Philippines, General Douglas MacArthur, was training a Philippine army for the day of independence and thought the existing defense plan with its implicit abandonment of most of the islands, with a besieged garrison as a tiny beam of hope, a very poor project indeed. He preferred to defend the whole island of Luzon on the beaches. And he thought that a building up of the Philippine army could be combined with a second new development: the creation of an effective air force, including the new B-17 Flying Fortresses, in whose ability to deliver unescorted and devastating blows to enemy installations and landing forces not only the United States army air force but also the American government and military leaders generally had a vast faith. This faith is difficult to understand in retrospect when one recalls the really minute numbers involved: thirty-five were in the Philippines at the time that MacArthur's new plan for defending the islands was approved at his insistence in Washington.

There was indeed some hope in Washington that the building up of the army and air force in the Philippines, in addition to the stationing of a small fleet consisting primarily of submarines, might deter the Japanese from attacking at all, a hope which must be seen in connection with the simultaneous British transfer of warships to Singapore, which will be discussed in connection with the disasters there. It is, of course, theoretically possible that a longer period of building up forces might have had a deterrent effect on the Japanese; but the Japanese did not intend to wait, in part precisely because they could see the United States rearming.

The Japanese insistence that surprise at Pearl Harbor take precedence over everything else and the time differential between the Philippines and Hawaii meant that MacArthur had plenty of warning that war had started by the time the Japanese began their attack on the Philippines hours later. But on that fatal morning — December 8 on the East Asian side of the international date line — there was only confusion at his head-quarters. The confusion was accentuated then as at times subsequently by MacArthur's Chief of Staff, General Sutherland, who kept others, in this case the air commander, General Brereton, from seeing the Commander-in-Chief. The result was that some ten hours after the Pearl Harbor attack, the planes of the U.S. Far East air force were for the most part caught on the ground by Japanese attacks and more than half destroyed along with their installations.[a] This disaster, which included fighter as well as bomber aircraft, left the navy bases and repair facilities open to Japanese attack, and this in turn forced the naval commander, Admiral Hart, to pull out what was left of his units to participate in the defense of the Netherlands East Indies.[2] They had proved of little help to the Philippines, as the submarines were useless against the ships carrying and escorting the Japanese invasion forces, partly because of poor handling, partly because of defective torpedoes.[b]

The Japanese plan of attack called first for small landings on the northern shore and southeast corner of Luzon to secure air bases to cover the main landing forces that would seize Manila Bay; in addition, there were to be even smaller landings to seize Davao on Mindanao as well as the island of Jolo between Mindanao and Borneo, to cut off the Philippines from reinforcement and prepare the way for subsequent advances south. These landings all succeeded on December 10; and over the next ten days the Japanese landing detachments advanced inland while the air force destroyed most of what was left of the Far East air force and chased the United States navy's ships out of the archipelago. The main landing forces began to go ashore on the eastern coast of Lingayen Gulf north of, and at Lamon Bay south of, Manila on December 22. The Japanese 14th Army of General Homma Masaharu had one reinforced division, the 48th, for the Lingayen Gulf landing and portions of another, the 16th, for Lamon Bay. With these approximately 50,000 men the Japanese struck at a force of American and Filipino troops that was more than twice as large in nominal strength but consisted overwhelmingly of recently inducted, untrained, and often unequipped Filipinos.

In the very first days of fighting it became obvious that the defenders could not hold back the Japanese. MacArthur's beach defense plan might conceivably have worked half a year later; it guaranteed disaster in December 1941. Within two days he had decided to reverse course and fall back on the earlier plan to pull the forces into Bataan and try to hold out there. Only a portion of this plan could now be implemented. While many of the Filipino troops had fled or surrendered, others fought bravely and these, together with most of the American soldiers, staged

---

[a] It should be added that if used in an unescorted attack on Formosa, as Brereton intended, the B-17s would surely have suffered disaster anyway. But they might instead all have been used from bases on Mindanao to interfere with the invasion, as a handful eventually were. Clayton James, *The Years of MacArthur*, chap. 1, comes to very similar conclusions.

[b] Ibid., pp. 240–44. Like the Germans in 1939, the Americans went into the war in 1941 with submarine torpedoes that often either failed to explode at all or did so when nowhere near a ship. A comparative study of this phenomenon has yet to be written.

a successful fighting retreat into Bataan, forming a line across the peninsula to hold back the Japanese and deny them use of the great harbor of Manila Bay as originally intended. But the related portion of the original plan, the stocking of supplies on the peninsula to support the beleaguered garrison, could not be implemented as quickly. Many of the supplies had been moved forward to support the beach defense plan while others could no longer be transported in the confused situation because MacArthur had refused to allow a beginning of such movement in the two weeks preceding his order to switch from beach defense to the Bataan defense on December 23. By then it was too late, and the troops arriving in Bataan found themselves without adequate food, munitions, and medical supplies.

In the two weeks from December 24 to January 8, 1942, the American–Filipino forces held defensive lines long enough to avoid encirclement and also to enable the southern Luzon force fighting the Lamon Bay landing to pull back through central Luzon into Bataan. Now that many of the untrained Filipinos had fled, the rest fought hard, and the Americans learned quickly. Homma did not push his forces forward as rapidly as he might have, and the Japanese air force rested on its laurels instead of attacking the Americans crowding the roads into Bataan. American and Filipino bravery and Japanese hesitations would lead to a far longer campaign than Tokyo had imagined.

The first major Japanese attacks on the American–Filipino forces on Bataan in mid-January forced a retreat to the main defensive line across the peninsula, called the Bagoc–Orion line after towns on the western and eastern coasts of Bataan peninsula. Their attack on that line in late January was defeated by the defenders with heavy losses to the Japanese, and the attempts of the latter to land at points on the southwest coast of Bataan were also beaten off. There followed two months of stalemate during which the Japanese rebuilt their forces, the American and Filipino soldiers wasted away from hunger and disease, while the desperate efforts directed from Washington to send supplies through to the doomed garrison produced a mere trickle in the face of distance, shortages, and the Japanese.

There were during the lull of February and March the beginnings of those signs of collaboration with the Japanese which later came to be widespread, at the same time as other Filipinos began a guerilla movement; and the Philippine President, Manuel Quezon, toyed with the idea of pulling out of the war. President Roosevelt dismissed all such projects, ordered continued resistance, and directed MacArthur to leave his command post on the island of Corregidor, which dominated the Manila Bay entrance, for Australia to build up a new front and command new forces. The Philippine President was evacuated, and General Mac-Arthur, the United States High Commissioner and a group of American officers left on March 11. Before leaving, MacArthur, Sutherland, and two other American officers accepted huge sums of money from Quezon with the knowledge of Roosevelt and Marshall;[3] what would the soldiers left behind on Bataan and in the rest of the Philippines have said about this? They were already doubtful about their commander, but his boastful publicity and the prolonged resistance at a time when all else was crumbling even more rapidly would make MacArthur a great hero in the eyes of the American public.

In early April the renewed Japanese offensive quickly broke the famished and diseased American and Filipino soldiers, who had to surrender on April 9. Japanese bombardment and subsequent landing forced the surrender of the island of Corregidor by May 6; the remaining forces in the other islands had surrendered by June 9. The tens of thousands captured had before them a terrible death march in which thousands of American and Filipino soldiers died or were slaughtered;[4] years of privation in the most wretched prisoner of war camps followed. But by the time of the last surrender in the Philippines, the Pacific War had changed and the great tide of Japanese victories which had lapped around as well as over the Philippines was already being halted.

The other American holdings within reach of the Japanese had also fallen. Guam, the largest island in the Marianas, had been practically undefended and was occupied quickly. Wake Island, a key position in the central Pacific, had been defended, successfully beating off the first Japanese landing attempt with heavy losses; but a relief attempt from Hawaii was bungled, and a second Japanese assault on December 22 succeeded in overwhelming and capturing the island. The British garrison in Hong Kong was by that time also clearly headed for the POW camps.[5] They staged a five-day fighting retreat from the mainland portion of the territory to the island of Victoria, on which the Japanese unleashed a landing in the night of December 18–19. A week's bitter and bloody fighting followed, and by December 26 the surviving British, Canadian, and Indian troops had to surrender. Here, as on Wake and Bataan, a garrison with little hope of relief had fought hard and effectively against an experienced but not very capably led opponent; Malaya was different on both counts.

Unlike the Americans, who had decided to leave the Philippines long before, the British had intended to remain in Malaya into the indefinite future. They controlled certain portions including the island of Singapore as a crown colony, and had worked out a complicated system for directing the affairs of the federated and the non-federated Malay States which made up the rest of the area. Defense arrangements were fully in British hands but afflicted by a series of contradictions and complications which, but for their tragic implications, would have been considered too far-fetched for a Gilbert and Sullivan operetta.

The main defense point was the naval base at Singapore which, it was assumed, would provide—as naval bases generally should—a base for a navy to defend the area. But there was no navy and, until the last moment, none was expected. Since the navy was busy in the waters off Europe, dealing with the Germans, a series of major airfields had been constructed so that the area with its important naval base could be defended by units of the Royal Air Force. But under the pressures of war in Europe and North Africa as well as the need to send planes to the Soviet Union, the air force had not received the planes to defend and operate from the airports. So now, to keep the Japanese from seizing the airfields, the army was to defend them as well as the naval base. The army, in turn, faced the preposterous task of defending airfields and a naval base located at opposite ends of the 300-mile-long peninsula with no tanks, practically no anti-tank weapons, and the widely held assumption that the Japanese were inferior and incompetent.

The major operation planned for the contingency of war under these circumstances was a move called "Matador" into the adjacent portion of Thailand where the Japanese, it was correctly assumed, would land and from which they were expected to mount their major thrust into Malaya.[a] The unit prepared for this operation, one of the two Indian divisions, which along with one Australian division and some smaller British units constituted the defending army, was never given the order to carry out "Matador," in part because of concern over Thai neutrality and provoking the Japanese, in part because of a level of hesitation and confusion in the headquarters in Singapore at the beginning of the war which makes that in Manila look well organized.

The Japanese wanted to conquer Malaya for several reasons. It produced rubber and tin which they preferred to control themselves rather than purchase from others; it offered a fine naval base at Singapore; and it opened a route into the Netherlands East Indies and into the Indian Ocean. The occupation of southern French Indo-China in the summer of 1941 had provided them with the naval and air bases for this operation as well as the staging ground for the units that were to carry out the invasion of Malaya; in fact, that had been one of Japan's primary reasons

---

[a] This was a complete reversal of all earlier British planning which had dismissed the idea of a Japanese landing in the north and then an advance on Singapore by land as preposterous and depended upon defending Singapore against a landing from the sea. Note Rohwer and Jäckel, *Funkaufklärung*, pp. 266–68.

for occupying South Indo-China and subsequently for their refusal to consider evacuating it. Detailed plans were worked out for a series of landings in southern Thailand and northern Malaya by the Japanese 25th Army commanded by General Yamashita Tomoyuki, whose three divisions were to carry out the operation. With Japanese naval air concentrated on the Hawaii attack, army air based on French Indo-China would carry the primary burden of beating down the British air and naval forces, thereafter operating from the British-built airports in north Malaya once the landing army units had seized them.

Early in the morning of December 8 (local time and date) the Japanese began landing.[6] While their air force quickly destroyed most of the available British planes, the landing force rapidly pushed inland, overwhelming the 11th Indian Division in the west and pushing back the 10th Indian Division on the east coast. In the first few hours of fighting it became clear that the poorly directed and inadequately trained Indian divisions, bled of many of their best officers and non-commissioned officers for the building up of new formations in India, could not hold off numerically inferior but well directed and equipped Japanese advance detachments. Even as the Japanese were driving the British out of north Malaya, they ended any prospects of defense pinned on the Royal Navy.

In part in the hope of deterring any Japanese move south, the British Admiralty, overruled on this issue by an insistent Churchill, had sent the battleship *Prince of Wales* and the battlecruiser *Repulse* to Singapore, where they arrived at the beginning of December.[7] Without an attached aircraft carrier, they would be dependent for air support on the already hopelessly inadequate units of the Royal Air Force in Malaya. Hoping to surprise first the real Japanese landing at Khota Baru in north Malaya and, when discovered by Japanese reconnaissance, shifting to attack what proved to be an imaginary Japanese landing farther down the Malay coast, the British commander, Admiral Phillips, went down with both ships and hundreds of others under Japanese bombs and torpedoes on December 10. Coming on top of successful Japanese landings and air raids, this disaster for the British badly damaged both military and civilian morale in Malaya and Singapore, as it simultaneously exhilarated and spurred on the Japanese.

In the following weeks the energetic Japanese forces drove forward, out-flanking British roadblocks and periodically surrounding and destroying such strong points as the defenders clung to.[8] Steadily driven back, the Indian, Australian, and United Kingdom units also began to lose heart. This situation was not remedied by the reinforcements sent to assist them. In the mistaken belief that parts of Malaya and Singapore might still be held, air reinforcements were sent in only to be used up quickly in battle; in addition, large numbers of army units, British, Indian, and Australian, often made up of barely trained soldiers, poured into the battle through Singapore harbor. Demonstrating dramatically and sadly what would have happened if MacArthur had received the reinforcements he was calling for,[9] these additions to the defending forces served primarily to increase the eventual bag of Japanese prisoners. Sent elsewhere, they could have reinforced the new fronts being built up in Burma and Australia.

In a series of short but bloody battles in the second and third weeks of January, the Japanese broke the major British defenses in northern Johore province, the last important line that could protect the fortress.[10] The remaining British forces then retreated to the island, blew up the causeway connecting it to the mainland, and awaited the final Japanese blow. Almost no serious preparations to meet a siege had been made on the island of Singapore in the two months since fighting had begun any more than in the preceding decades of peace. When Japanese infantry assaulted across the straits, beginning in the night of February 8–9, they quickly gained footholds which they as quickly expanded.[11] Some of the defenders fought hard, but others were clearly demoralized.[12] On February 15, the British commander, General Percival, surrendered about 70,000 soldiers, many of them having only just arrived with the last reinforcing convoys.

Two days after the surrender, General Sir Archibald Wavell, who had been put in charge of all Allied forces in southern Asia, wrote the Chief of the Imperial General Staff that he would have needed one additional month of fighting on the mainland of Malaya to build up an adequate defense for the Netherlands East Indies.[13] The subsequent analysis of the greatest disaster in British military history prepared in the British War Office in 1942 suggests that underestimation of the Japanese, lack of aggressive leadership, inadequate armaments, the constant splitting of divisions and even smaller units in battle, and the piecemeal tossing of reinforcements into battle all contributed to defeat.[14] The author of the official history added a divided command structure to this list. There was certainly plenty of blame to go around, but perhaps the most important points to be stressed are that a vigorous Japanese offensive crushed a partly dispirited, poorly handled and badly trained though much larger force at a time when the major focus of the defeated had perforce to be in another theater of war against a more threatening and powerful enemy. Even the temporary checks administered to that enemy by the RAF in the West, the Red Army in the East, and the British desert army in North Africa could not provide enough relief for adequate concentration against the assaulting Japanese.

This deficiency had become ever more dramatically obvious as, even during the Japanese run of victories in the Philippines and Malaya, the forces of the Allies were being crushed at other places. Before the fall of Singapore the Japanese advance southward had begun to strike into Burma and the East Indies. The campaign in Burma will be taken up shortly. The seizure of the East Indies was begun at practically the same time but completed first. On December 15 the Japanese began landing on the island of Borneo, important both for its location and its great oil resources. Divided between the British and Dutch, the island could not be defended seriously by either as both had to concentrate what forces they had available on other assignments: the British, the defense of Singapore; the Dutch, the protection of the island of Java. In two weeks the northwestern British portion of the island with its great resources was taken over; many of the oil installations had been destroyed by the British themselves, but not so effectively as to deny them to the Japanese for long. In January Japanese forces seized key points in Dutch Borneo and completed the conquest of the island by mid-February. Here, too, the oil installations though damaged were repairable.[15]

In operations which overlapped with the latter stages of the attack on Dutch Borneo, the Japanese landed forces on the larger islands of the Netherlands East Indies: Sumatra, Celebes, and Amboina. To isolate the Allied troops on Java, and to provide a springboard toward Australia, the Japanese also landed on Timor in late February 1942. Since parts of this last island were Portuguese, there was great concern in the German government that Japanese action there could lead Portugal to offer facilities to the Allies on the Portuguese Azores, with very bad results for the German submarine campaign in the Atlantic; but while this issue produced endless diplomatic exchanges, it ended up having no significant impact on events (and neither did the lengthy holding out of a small Australian force on the island).[16]

Vastly more important than the endless diplomatic discussions about Portuguese Timor was the core issue: could the Allies defend the key island of Java against the Japanese?[17] With the Japanese holding air superiority this was primarily a question of naval power. The Allies were able to put together a collection of Dutch, United States, and British cruisers and destroyers by now under the general command of the Dutch Admiral Conrad Emil Heltfrich, who had replaced Admiral Hart as a result of a series of complicated maneuvers reflecting Allied dissension rather than cooperation. Though fighting with incredible stamina and great bravery, the Allied naval force was simply no match for the larger, more numerous, and in part more modern Japanese naval forces escorting the invasion transports for Java. In the Battle of the Java Sea, the largest surface naval battle since Jutland in 1916, the Japanese literally destroyed the Allied fleet in a series of engagements on February 27–28. Four American destroyers had been sent to Australia to refit; the other Allied ships, including five cruisers, were all sunk in this and immediately following engagements.[18] The whole action held up the Japanese landings for only one day. The main landings on Java took place on March 1, and on March 8 the remaining Dutch, British, Australian, and American soldiers on Java had to surrender.[19]

By this date, March 8, the Japanese had also attained a number of other objectives of their initial plan. They had landed on the north and east coast of New Guinea (the towns of Lae and Salamaua were seized on March 8) and, striking south from their bases in the Mariana and Caroline Islands, had moved into the Admiralty Islands, the Northern Solomons, and, perhaps most important, into the Bismarck Archipelago which included at the eastern end of the island of New Britain the best harbor and most important base in the area: Rabaul. With the easy occupation of the Gilbert Islands, this series of barely contested victories gave the Japanese the southern and southeastern anchors of their projected defense perimeter, placed them in an excellent position to threaten Australia, and did so at what looked like very little cost to themselves.[a]

March 8 was, however, not only the date of the surrender on Java; it was also the day on which Rangoon fell to the advancing Japanese 15th Army of General Ida Shogin.[20] General Wavell, while still the British commander in India and before assuming the general Allied command in Southeast Asia, had rejected Chiang Kai-shek's offer of troops to assist in the defense of Burma. Now his subordinates had wholly inadequate forces to hold the area against the advancing Japanese. Most Allied reinforcements were being poured into Malaya and Java in the hope of holding the Japanese onrush there, while the Australian division from the Middle East scheduled to bolster the defense of Burma was rerouted to Australia at the rigid insistence of the Australian government. The Australians believed, not unreasonably, that home defense must be their first priority. They were eventually persuaded in the face of the Japanese menace from the north that in their most dangerous hour, with the Japanese air force bombing Darwin in the north, a Japanese midget submarine attack inside Sydney harbor in the south,[21] and the Japanese army controlling portions of the Australian mandate of southeast New Guinea, they could safely leave their other division with the British

---

[a] The final order of January 29, 1942, for these operations had included reference to the possible seizure of Port Moresby (Morton, *Strategy*, pp. 214–15), but that was *not* originally thought necessary.

8th Army in North Africa *only* if they could depend on the United States to send forces to them. This, in part at the insistence of Churchill, in part as the most obvious way to cope with the situation, the United States agreed to do. It must be noted, however, that the diversion from the Germany First strategy implied by this decision, the role that all this would mean for General MacArthur, and the long-term implications for the defense relationship between Australia and Britain on the one hand and Australia and the United States on the other, all grew out of the desperate military situation created by the Japanese advance.

In the meantime, without adequate reinforcements and under poor military leadership, the small forces defending Burma could not hold the advancing Japanese, who pushed forward across southern Burma and by seizing Rangoon on March 8 effectively cut off the remaining British units from their main supply route by sea. What British reinforcements and belated Chinese units could still get to Burma were quite incapable of halting the Japanese drive north. A new commander, General Sir Harold Alexander, who had distinguished himself in the 1940 fighting in Belgium and would play a major role in the Mediterranean campaign later, was sent by Churchill to take charge. He could add his calmness and good sense but little else.

The Americans, at Roosevelt's insistence, were determined to find some way to keep open a supply route to China, which he believed should be treated as the great power he was certain it would become as the European colonial empires faded into history (as he was equally certain they should and would). The United States, too, sent a new commander to the area. The man who had just been designated to head up an operation named "Gymnast," an Allied invasion of Northwest Africa scheduled for the spring of 1942, Major General Joseph W. Stilwell, was appointed to this difficult post.[22] The new appointee had spent years in China and knew the language; he was a driving and efficient commander; he had the complete confidence of Marshall; and he was well known to be an impatient and frequently undiplomatic man. All these qualities would be evident and even accentuated in his years in the China–Burma–India Command where he held an assortment of titles and positions until his recall in 1944.

Alexander and Stilwell faced disaster in their new assignments. Alexander commanded the British troops which were forced steadily northwards as the Japanese drove first to Lashio, where the railway ended and the Burma road into China began, and then to the great center of Mandalay to the south and the other important railhead, Myitkyina to the north. Chinese forces helped in the defense, but no firm front could be held anywhere. By mid-May, Alexander and his able ground forces commander, General Slim, had gotten their 12,000 remaining soldiers out of Burma to add to the defense of India while Stilwell hiked out with a small band at the end of what he himself called "a hell of a beating."

The Japanese had conquered a new empire for themselves in the very short span of less than six months. In these newly conquered areas they revealed with equal speed that they had come to conquer, not liberate, the population.[23] Not only brutality toward prisoners of war—especially Filipinos—and rounded-up Westerners, but wanton rape and slaughter of the local population showed the inhabitants that the new masters retrospectively made their former colonial overlords look like beneficence personified. The ordinary people of the Philippines, Malaya, the Netherlands East Indies, and Burma were unlikely to have heard of the horrors of the rape of Nanking when rampaging Japanese soldiers murdered over 200,000 civilians, but they now received visual instruction on their own home territory. The use of military and civilian prisoners for bayonet practice and assorted other cruelties provided the people of Southeast Asia with a dramatic lesson on the new meaning of Bushido, the code of the Japanese warrior.

The leaders of political movements in the various former colonial territories had, of course, some greater familiarity with Japan's wretched record as an oppressive colonial power in Korea, Manchuria, and the other portions of China occupied by the Japanese since 1937. The fact that the Japanese in effect ended the independence of Thailand, the one country of Southeast Asia which had retained its sovereignty, also provided a clue to Tokyo's intentions.[24] There were, nevertheless, some who hoped to emulate Pu Yi, the Japanese puppet Emperor installed in Manchuria, the most prominent being the Prime Minister of Burma who cited that very example as the model he hoped to follow as Japan's chief collaborator in Burma. Unfortunately for him, his exchanges with the Japanese were intercepted and read by the Americans on whose tip the British arrested him.[25] Others gambled on the hope of gaining and maintaining independence from Japan after the latter, in alliance with Germany and Italy, had defeated Britain, the United States, and the Soviet Union; but as anyone holding to and acting on that theory was not likely to be endowed with great intelligence, such movements never assumed major proportions in any of the occupied territories. The vast majority of the local population would sit it out.

Two less tangible things had come with the rapid Japanese conquests. The first was a sense among the British and Americans that the Japanese seemed to be unbeatable. A converse of the earlier racialist attitudes of superiority toward the little Orientals, who could only imitate, who couldn't fly well because of their slanted eyes, and who were incapable of sound military organization, the new view endowed them with super-human endurance and ingenuity. The American and Australian soldiers would get over this new set of ideas as they slugged it out with the Japanese army on Guadalcanal and New Guinea in the second half of 1942; the British and Indian armies did not recover their self-confidence until the bitter battles in India and Burma in 1944.

The other new element was the converse of that just mentioned: what was called the Japanese victory disease. Unwilling to recognize that their conquests had been made possible by the earlier victories of Germany and the ongoing conflict in Europe, the Atlantic and the Mediterranean theaters of war, the Japanese not only celebrated their triumphs over the British, Americans and Dutch but assumed that these were due to the inherent superiority of the Japanese over all others, especially over the weak and decadent Europeans. The Japanese could do anything, could conquer in whatever direction they chose to strike, and most assuredly had no need to think of the compromise peace which at one time was supposed to have followed upon the initial victories they had anticipated winning, though not with such speed or little overall cost.

If these were the delusions of the victory disease, their prospect of recovering from it by confronting set-backs rather than triumphs was inhibited by a fundamental flaw in the Japanese military command struc-ture.[26] The militarists had literally shot their way into power by assassin-ating or threatening to assassinate those who stood in their way within Japan, but they had never worked out a central coordinating command structure of their own. Since direct access to the Emperor and action in his name had been the institutional key to their exercise of power, the army and the navy could carry out any specific policy only if they were in agreement. The agreed project could be put before the Emperor for the imperial sanction, a formality rather than a decision; but if they could not agree, there was no individual Commander-in-Chief—like Hitler, Stalin, Churchill, Roosevelt, or Mussolini—who could decide on one course of action and insist on adherence to that course with every expectation that all would fall into line.

There was still one further complication in Japanese planning. Not only were the army and navy often in disagreement with each other, the failure to develop plans for the future and the absence of clear and respected lines of authority within the navy led to a situation where competing personalities advocating differing strategies precluded the adoption of any coherent and clear-cut strategic plan at all. As will be shown, there were three basic competing alternative offensive strategies: the Japanese proceeded in a period of less than three months to try all three in succession, not one of them wholeheartedly, and, perhaps as a result, to suffer disaster or something very close to it in each one in turn. There were those who advocated an orientation of Japanese power into the Indian Ocean to wrest control of that sea from the British and link up with Germany in the Middle East. There were some who thought that Japan should continue to push southwards, some calling for an invasion of either northern or all of Australia, but most urging a somewhat less ambitious extension of Japanese control to the south coast of New Guinea, including the seizure of Port Moresby, to be followed by the capture of islands in the South Pacific such as Fiji[27] and New Caledonia. Such an offensive thrust would sever the communications between the United States and Australia, thereby making it impossible for the United States to use Australia as a base for attacking the southern perimeter of Japan's newly conquered empire. Finally, there were the advocates of a strike in the central Pacific which, by including the seizure of Midway and hopefully the Hawaiian islands, would, it was believed, force what was left of the United States Pacific fleet to give battle and enable the Japanese to defeat it.[28]

The first of these, the attack into the Indian Ocean, was potentially the most threatening for the Allies. A major offensive into India itself could topple British rule there at a time when the image of British power was hopelessly tarnished by a string of disasters, and the reality of that power was stretched so thinly as to call to mind the story of the Emperor without clothes. There were those in India who thought this was the time to throw off British rule, and the nationalist agitation in the country rose to a new peak in the spring and early summer of 1942.[29] A combination of the most unlikely developments prevented all the most likely contingencies from eventuating: a Japanese invasion, a major rallying of the people of India to the Allied side, a major rallying to the Axis side, or a massive uprising inside the country.

There was no major Japanese invasion in 1942 because the army leadership preferred to keep its main forces in China and in Manchuria; it was still contemplating an invasion of the U.S.S.R. if the German 1942 summer offensive led to a collapse of Soviet resistance. This fixation on the Chinese and possible Soviet theaters of war precluded any major commitment of land forces elsewhere; it set rigid limits to the size of the ground force contingents the army allocated to the whole southern expansion project, and precluded invasion not only of India but of Australia as well. Furthermore, to avoid being drawn into major land forces commitments in the Indian Ocean, the Japanese army General Staff, in spite of its theoretical advocacy of a close alignment with Germany, would not even agree to allocating the two divisions needed for an invasion of Ceylon. By the time the Japanese army was willing to order its troops into India in 1944, the war situation had changed too far for such an operation to make much difference, regardless of the result.

A rallying of the peoples of India to the Allied side was precluded by the British policy of avoiding or postponing major concessions to Indian nationalist aspirations, especially in the area of defense.[30] In spite of the efforts of Sir Stafford Cripps, sent as special envoy by the British government, and Colonel Louis Johnson, dispatched by Roosevelt to India as a symbol of United States concern about the situation there, agreement was close but never reached. Without reviewing the details of the tortuous negotiations, it is safe to argue that the key stumbling block was the British Prime Minister. Churchill had originally broken with the Conservative Party over concessions which that party wished to make to Indian self-government; he had, once returned to office and especially the office of Prime Minister, resisted all further changes on this issue. And he was not about to replace the reactionary Marquess of Linlithgow, Viceroy since 1936, with his old opponent, Sir Samuel Hoare, the man who over Churchill's body had steered the Government of India Act of 1935 through the House of Commons and who saw the future of India in very different ways from Churchill's turn of the nineteenth- to the twentieth-century perspective. It was left to Churchill's deputy as Prime Minister and successor in 1945, Clement Attlee, to adopt a different policy on Indian independence under very different circumstances.[a]

A possible rallying of articulate Indian public opinion to the side of the Axis was prevented by the split in the Indian nationalist movement and the ambivalence of Axis policy. Whatever their opposition to British rule, neither most of the leaders of the Congress Party nor the Muslim leaders looking toward a separate Muslim state were eager for Germany or Japan to replace Great Britain. Some might have been indifferent about the outcome of the war then raging, but many had great doubts about the intentions of the Germans and the Japanese, neither having acquired especially good reputations for treating subject peoples well. Furthermore, the fact that their former rival in the Congress Party, Subhas Chandra Bose had identified himself with the Axis did not endear

---

[a] It is too often forgotten that on the issue of greater self-government for India Churchill had been on the opposite side not only from his fellow Conservatives but also from the Labour Party, one of whose representatives on the Indian Statutory Commission had been Clement Attlee. This was part of the background of Labour's original preference for Lord Halifax over Churchill as Prime Minister in May 1940; Halifax had been the Viceroy in 1926–1931 and had been denounced by Churchill for meeting with Gandhi.

his sponsors to Bose's competitors inside India. But these sponsors were themselves unsure and uncertain as to what to do with him and about India.

For several months in early 1942 the Germans, Italians, and Japanese negotiated endlessly between each other and within their respective governments as to which policy to follow, what policy, if any, to announce publicly, and whether to side openly with Bose or try to develop contacts with Mahatma Gandhi and Pandit Nehru, the acknowledged leaders of the Congress Party in India. The Germans and Japanese, furthermore, were concerned about the possible greater advantages accruing to the other from the evolution of the situation in India, while there is evidence that Hitler, looking toward a victory over the Soviet Union in 1942, may have thought that some compromise peace might thereafter be imposed on Britain. In any case, neither the Japanese, who merely hoped to inspire an anti-British uprising in India, nor the Germans, who had a very low opinion of Indians in general, ever had any intention of supporting independence for India; they merely wished to use it.[31]

The Germans made publicity for Bose and, after lengthy consideration of flying him to East Asia either from Rhodes or across the northern Soviet Union, eventually shipped him in a submarine (U-180) which transferred him to a Japanese submarine in the Indian Ocean in 1943, a subject to which we will return in Chapter 11, but the possibility of any real resonance in India was by then long gone.[32]

The last of the possible prospects for India in the first half of 1942 was that of a massive uprising against a gravely weakened Britain, an uprising which might count on some sympathy from both China and the United States among Britain's allies. As Germany resumed successful offensives in North Africa and the Soviet Union in May–June 1942, it looked as if the Axis forces would soon reach India's borders from the West as well as the East. Gandhi had been restrained from calling for all foreign troops to leave India only by the arguments of Nehru and others in the Congress; in early August the Congress decided to call on the British to quit India, and soon thereafter a substantial popular uprising did begin. The security forces of the government, supported by military units spread widely over the sub-continent, were able to hold in check and then put down the widespread demonstrations. Since the overwhelming bulk of Indian army units remained loyal to the crown and unwilling to join the revolt, government authority was maintained.[33] The war went on, reaching India again in very different ways in later years.

Any shift in the position of India would not only have meant a massive loss of Allied power—to say nothing of the fate of the Indian army[34]—

but it would have severed China's last link with the possibility of American aid. The development of new supply routes to assist Chiang Kai-shek will be reviewed subsequently; the point which must be made clear at this point is that any and all such routes pre-supposed the availability of land and air bases in Assam, the northeast corner of India, to the Allies.

HALTING THE JAPANESE ADVANCE

Though the Japanese could not try an invasion of India or even a landing on Ceylon because of the refusal of the army to provide the troops, the navy could try and did try a significant offensive into the Indian Ocean. This was the obvious direction to move at a time when the British position there was weak but in the process of being reinforced. Here was a key Allied supply route, providing the main means of reinforcement for the Middle East theater and one of the routes for supplies to the Soviet Union. Finally, here was the back door to the important oil resources of the Middle East on which much of the British war effort depended.

The Japanese naval sortie, however, though involving the major aircraft carrier fleet which had struck Pearl Harbor, could only carry out some raids on Colombo, the capital, and Trincomalee, the major naval base, on Ceylon, shell some spots on the Indian coast, and sink two British cruisers, a small carrier, a destroyer, and 23 merchant ships. Though achieved without great cost to themselves, these Japanese tactical victories of the first ten days of April constituted a major strategic defeat for several reasons.[35]

First, the newly accumulated British fleet for the most part escaped destruction and was, therefore, able to provide continued protection for Allied supply shipping across the Indian Ocean. Second, the temporary character of the Japanese incursion could not long be concealed; for a while radio propaganda could pretend that the rising sun was about to shine on India and the whole Indian Ocean area, but it became obvious by the late summer that this was simply not likely. Third, the Japanese had toyed with the fairly obvious idea of seizing a base in Madagascar with the consent of Vichy France, obtained if necessary with the aid of German pressure on Vichy, pressure which would not have been needed because Laval wanted to invite Japan to occupy the island.[36] If such a base could once be established and maintained thereafter, there was the real possibility of completely cutting the Allied supply routes to Egypt, to the Soviet Union across Iran, and to India. But for almost the first time in World War II the Allies got somewhere *before* the Axis.

The enormous danger to the Allied cause from a Japanese seizure of bases on Madagascar had been evident for some time — anyone could see it from a map. De Gaulle repeatedly called attention to the need to seize the island and expressed the undoubtedly mistaken opinion that the garrison was ready to come over to the Free French side.[37] The British, especially Churchill himself, could see the danger clearly enough but did not have forces available for an expedition at a time when all available reinforcements were being sent first to increase the scale of disaster in Malaya and thereafter to try to avert disaster in Burma. And the London government had no faith in either the security of de Gaulle's headquarters or the willingness of the Vichy garrison to switch to the Allied side.[38] On the other hand, not only was Churchill very much aware of the threat,[a] the London government was also being urged to move by Prime Minister Jan Smuts of the Union of South Africa. In the face of a danger from Japan in the Indian Ocean on the outside and the agitation for a separate peace with the Axis by the extreme Afrikaaner nationalists on the inside, Smuts believed immediate action to forestall a Japanese move absolutely essential.[39]

An expedition for the island left Britain on March 23 and, with the endorsement of the United States, which had provided a task force to take the place of the British warships diverted from the Atlantic, landed on the northern tip on May 4, 1942. The original plan was to seize only the naval base at Diego Suarez; there were not enough forces available to capture the rest of the island, and even the major units sent to Diego Suarez had to go on to India as soon as the first part of the operation was completed.[40] Eventually it seemed both essential and possible to take the remainder of Madagascar, though this campaign took until November 6, as Vichy troops, in line with their prior record, fought against the British as they never fought against the Japanese or Germans.[41] The Japanese had missed their opportunity, a failure ameliorated but not remedied by the success of one of their midget submarines in torpedoing the old battleship *Ramillies* in Diego Suarez harbor.[42] Coming on top of the other British naval losses of early 1942, this was a serious blow, but it could not obscure the fact that it was the British, not the Japanese, who continued to dominate the western and central portions of the Indian Ocean.

The fourth and final way in which the Japanese foray into the Indian Ocean contributed to making this episode disastrous for Japan was the time it occupied and the wear it imposed on the central striking force of the Imperial navy, the main fleet carriers. These had now been in

---

[a] This was one time that Churchill overruled Brooke who thought the operation unnecessary. Note David Fraser, *Alanbrooke*, (New York: Atheneum, 1982), p. 253. The British official history sides with Brooke, *Grand Strategy*, 3, Part 2, pp. 489–92.

continuous action since leaving the Japanese home bases on November 26, 1941, for the assault on Pearl Harbor. By the end of the operation off Ceylon on April 10, 1942, the big carriers had to return to home waters for repairs and maintenance work as well as replacements for the casualties incurred. This meant that the whole Japanese timetable was compressed at a point in the war when the projects that had been decided upon by Imperial Headquarters required more time, not less. As will become clear in the account of the Japanese push to the south which ended at the Battle of the Coral Sea and that to the east which ended at Midway, even those most afflicted with the "victory disease" could not find a way to use the same aircraft carriers in two operations thousands of miles apart simultaneously, and therefore settled for a sequence in which the carriers employed in one operation turned out not to be available for the other. What is more, intelligent Japanese assessment of these operations had been thrown off and United States intelligence about them would be increased by the reaction to an event two days before April 20, the day the first of the Japanese carriers returned home: on April 18 the Americans had bombed Tokyo.

The origins of the great clashes which signalled the high-water mark of the Japanese tide in the Pacific and led to the first American counter-attack in the Solomon Islands go back to the aftermath of the Pearl Harbor attack. Immediately after that operation, Yamamoto had called for the development of a plan for the invasion of Hawaii as the first of three great invasion projects, Ceylon and Australia being the other two. He assumed that quick action on these as a follow up to the conquest of Southeast Asia would force the remaining United States fleet into battle. That battle the Japanese would win and thereupon make peace.[43] The call by the Allies, newly designated the United Nations as a result of the Washington Conference, for a united campaign until victory were obtained did not make any impression on Tokyo. There, while the Combined Fleet Headquarters was developing the plans to implement Yamamoto's project, the War Ministry was defining the organization of Japan's new empire. In addition to all the territory that Japan was just beginning to conquer, such as the Philippines, Hong Kong, Guam, Wake, the Gilberts, Australian New Guinea, the Bismarck, Solomon and Admiralty Islands, the world carvers there expected to cover a long list of countries, territories, and portions of countries to be included in the empire. All of Australia and New Zealand, Ceylon and much of India, all of Alaska, western Canada and the state of Washington, all of Central America plus Colombia and Ecuador, Cuba, Haiti, Jamaica and other assorted Caribbean islands would be taken over by Japan, while Macao, Hainan, and Portuguese Timor were to be purchased. Independent kingdoms under Japanese control were to be established in the East Indies (Dutch and British), in Burma (expanded at the expense of India), in Malaya, Thailand, Cambodia and Annam.[44]

Against these wild schemes, a navy project for seizing Hawaii to be followed by Ceylon, Fiji, Samoa, and New Caledonia and more advances in the south thereafter looked positively modest.[45] A Japanese submarine shelled the California coast on February 23,[46] but the more extensive projects of the navy had to be cut down in the face of the army's unwillingness to allocate troops, either for the huge expeditions the War Ministry's own schemes would have required, or for the more modest conquests pushed by the navy. This had meant a sortie into the Indian Ocean instead of an invasion of Ceylon; it also meant that an invasion of the main islands of Hawaii could not be carried out.

The navy leadership was itself divided. On the one hand were the advocates in Yamamoto's Combined Fleet Headquarters of a strike in the Central Pacific, now looking toward the seizure of Midway Island as a prerequisite for the landing on Hawaii, but making that possible by forcing the American navy, and especially its carriers, into a decisive battle. The central naval staff under Admiral Nagano Osami preferred to concentrate on securing the empire Japan was winning in the south and considered an expedition to the east much too risky. In the face of Yamamoto's threat to resign,[*] the navy staff caved in, and a Midway operation was approved, but with a smaller operation in the south as a preliminary and as a concession to both the army and the navy general staffs.[47] The developing consensus on a small operation in the south followed quickly by a larger one in the east was reinforced by American decisions and operations in both areas.

As an immediate reaction to the losses suffered at Pearl Harbor, the United States moved one carrier, the *Yorktown*, three battleships, a destroyer squadron and twelve submarines from the Atlantic, where they had been on convoy duty back to the Pacific.[48] But that was not all. The rapidity of the unfolding disasters in the Philippines and Malaya led to a more general reassessment of the situation there. It was clear to Roosevelt and Marshall that steps had to be taken to keep open a route to Australia as a base for reinforcement of the Philippines if there was to be any hope of prolonging resistance there and for liberating the islands if they fell to the Japanese. The analysis of the situation prepared by then Brigadier General Dwight Eisenhower, the officer soon to be made

---

[*] This is the procedure Yamamoto had used to obtain approval for the Pearl Harbor attack. The similarity to General Erich Ludendorff's procedure in World War I is startling. Repeatedly he too had forced the German government to adopt his projects (which turned out equally disastrously) by threatening his own and Field Marshal von Hindenburg's resignation.

Chief of the War Plans Division, calling for a buildup to defend northern Australia, put these concepts into clear focus.[49] In January 1942, the decision was made to garrison New Caledonia to secure the route to Australia,[50] well in advance of the invitation by both Germany and the Vichy French government to the Japanese to occupy the island, which had rallied to de Gaulle in the fall of 1940.[51]

As the situation in the Philippines deteriorated, it became obvious that aid could not be sent there in substantial quantities; instead the United States decided to send an army division (the 41st) to Australia on February 14, and, a week later, MacArthur was ordered there as well to take charge of the forces being built up.[52] Primarily American planes defended northern Australia against a whole series of Japanese air raids concentrating on Darwin, beginning in February 1942 and continuing into 1944.[53] In early 1942, moreover, the United States government was being forced by circumstances to alter its general plans in two other ways. First, it became clear that a vastly greater shipping construction program would be necessary: there was no point in building up a huge army if it could not be sent out and supplied, and from here on, the shipping issue more and more obviously determined the size of America's forces.[54] Secondly, reinforced by Churchill's insistence, the United States sent even more army units to Australia, thus postponing any possibility of "Gymnast," the intended landing in French Northwest Africa.[55]

The shift, including the dispatch of a second division, necessarily had repercussions on the planned buildup in Great Britain of forces for operations in Europe, thus derogating temporarily from the Europe First strategy. It was a step taken in part at the urging of the British, who were later inclined to complain about it, but it was received with enthusiasm in Australia and enabled the London government to get Canberra to leave one Australian division in the Middle East.[a] The shift also left Roosevelt all the more determined that *something* would have to be done in Europe in 1942.

The beginning of a real buildup of American ground and air forces in the South Pacific under a famous commander with great influence in Washington combined with a series of United States navy operations to remind Tokyo that the war in that region was not yet over. A series of raids in February and early March 1942 by American navy carrier task forces on Japanese and Japanese-conquered islands in the South Pacific,

---

[a] The 6th and 7th Australian Divisions were returned from the Middle East to Australia and would play key roles in the Southwest Pacific; the 8th was sent to Malaya, and the 9th remained in the Middle East until the end of 1942. Important relevant documents have been published in D.M. Horner, *Crisis of Command: Australian Generalship and the Japanese Threat 1941–43* (Canberra: Australian National University Press, 1978), pp. 41–50.

and on the landing forces off New Guinea showed the Japanese that American naval power was still very active. These operations, furthermore, beyond inflicting some losses on the Japanese, provided the American ships and planes with very important practice in the handling of carriers and their planes.[56] The need for both a further action in the south and for a way to bring the American navy to battle seemed clear to the Japanese.

These calculations were reinforced dramatically by the air raid on Tokyo. Roosevelt had been calling for a raid right after Pearl Harbor, a view combining morale considerations with a belief in the role of air power against Japan.[57] The technical problem of flying to Japan from a carrier which was itself out of the range of Japanese land-based planes was solved by the device of using land-based B-25s to fly off the carrier *Hornet* and on to China rather than back to the carrier (on which such planes could not have landed anyway). Although the American task force was spotted by Japanese picket boats and had to send its sixteen planes off at a greater distance than planned, the project worked. The Japanese were completely surprised and did not shoot down a single one of the planes, which landed in China or crashed on running out of gas, one landing in the Soviet Union where its crew was interned.[58] There was little physical damage, but the morale uplift of the raid, led by then Colonel James Doolittle, for the Allies was great. The morale blow to the Japanese was even greater. The sacred precincts of the homeland had been violated and the possibility of future violations of that kind made all too obvious. The murder of several of the American fliers who were captured and the slaughter of Chinese civilians who had helped others escape could not solve the basic problem; a new offensive to build a shield for Japan's home waters was essential and that meant an assault on Midway.[59]

The pressure of time imposed by the need to strike before the Americans added new forces to those already deployed in the Pacific now finally produced agreement on a firm schedule for a series of Japanese operations. These would be, first, an attack to seize Port Moresby and the seaplane base at Tulagi in the Solomons in May; and because of the recent appearance of American carriers in the South Pacific, this operation would have to be supported by a carrier division of two aircraft carriers. Second, in early June would come the invasion of Midway to force the United States navy into battle, a project to be accompanied by a simultaneous diversionary attack on the Aleutian Islands off Alaska in the far north. In July, with the United States fleet disposed of, there would follow a Japanese attack on Fiji, Samoa, and New Caledonia.

Assaults on Australia were to follow and there could still be an invasion of Hawaii.

In facing these Japanese threats the Americans had one resource of great value and another they hoped for but did not get. The resource they had was an increasing ability to read the Japanese naval code as a result of cryptographic work done at Pearl Harbor, Washington, the Philippines (moved to Australia), and Singapore (moved to Ceylon). Unlike the diplomatic machine code which had been broken earlier, the main naval code was just beginning to be deciphered.[60] The increased Japanese naval radio traffic, generated by the fleet units sent out in April 1942 to try to catch the American carrier group which had launched the Tokyo air raid, provided much new material for the American and British cryptographers, an important by-product of that raid.[61] The knowledge gained about Japanese plans and dispositions from cryptanalytic intelligence was essential to the proper disposition of the American navy at both Coral Sea and Midway; in turn the American naval leaders learned from this experience how valuable such intelligence could be, devoted more men and resources to it, and came to pay the most careful attention to their intelligence officers.[62]

Not so successful, with opposite long-term implications, was the American effort to increase carrier strength between the Coral Sea and Midway battles. With the resources in the Pacific strained to the limit while two American carriers were assisting the British in the Atlantic and Mediterranean, the Commander-in-Chief of the American fleet, Admiral Ernest J. King, on May 18 asked the British to provide one of the three British carriers then operating off the African coast for the Pacific. He was promptly turned down.[63] This was a serious error in spite of the concern over the Indian Ocean which motivated the refusal. King had spent much of the preceding year, at a time when the United States was still neutral, leading American warships in their operations in the Atlantic assisting Britain in its hour of peril. He never forgave the British their refusal to help in the Pacific when the situation was reversed and accepted British fleet units in the Pacific in 1944–45 only because of the insistence of President Roosevelt. Aside from a few units of the Australian navy, the Americans faced the Imperial Japanese navy in the great crisis of the Pacific War by themselves.

The Japanese were determined to seize Port Moresby to protect their southern perimeter, to control the straits between New Guinea and Australia, to threaten Australia, and, if the army ever changed its mind, to provide a base for invading that continent. The Americans, on the other hand, were equally determined to assist the Australians in holding it as an essential outpost for the defense of Australia and an equally essential springboard for any counter-attacks northwards.[a] The Japanese were therefore planning to seize it by seaborne landing, with a carrier group of two large and one light carrier providing air support. The idea that this small force could obtain control of the air over Port Moresby and shield the landings at Tulagi in the Solomons as well as near Port Moresby was ridiculous—six carriers had hit Pearl Harbor, four had been used to cover the seizure of Rabaul, and five for the attack on Ceylon. But the insistence of Yamamoto on his strike at Midway prevented the allocation of adequate forces to the Port Moresby attack.

It was between these carriers and their screening units on the one hand and the two American carriers *Yorktown* and *Lexington*, with their screens on the other, that the Battle of the Coral Sea was fought on May 3–8, 1942. The Japanese landing on Tulagi in the Solomons to seize a base there was carried out on May 3; that scheduled for Port Moresby on May 10 would never take place. After attacking the Japanese ships covering the Tulagi landing and destroying the reconnaissance planes there, the American carriers in a series of air strikes fought the Japanese carriers on May 7 and 8. In a naval battle carried out at a great distance and for this reason unlike any prior naval engagement, the airplanes sought out the ships of the other side without the ships themselves ever firing directly on each other as had been characteristic of all prior fighting at sea. The American planes sank the light carrier *Shoho* (12,000 tons) while losing the fleet carrier *Lexington*. The *Yorktown* and the Japanese fleet carrier *Shokaku* were damaged while the other Japanese fleet carrier, the *Zuikaku*, lost planes but was not damaged. The Japanese thereupon abandoned the idea of a landing at Port Moresby and decided to try to take it by an advance overland, a campaign reviewed later in this chapter. But the inter-action between the Coral Sea Battle and that at Midway as well as the latter battle itself must be reviewed first.[64]

In the first great carrier battle, the tactical advantage was clearly with the Japanese who had, in effect, traded a light carrier for one of the few American fleet carriers. But the strategic advantage was all with the Americans. The Japanese advance had been halted for the first time. The landings to seize Port Moresby had been called off and the follow-up operation to seize Nauru and Ocean Islands (between the Solomons and the Gilberts) also had to be postponed for months. The Japanese

---

[a] The very negative comments on the Australians in the diary of the Chief of the Imperial General Staff hardly seem warranted. At this time it was the Australians, not the British, who faced the real possibility of invasion. Brooke Diary, 12 May, 1942, Liddell Hart Centre, Alanbrooke Papers.

pretended in public and to their German allies that they had won a great victory,[65] and at first they may themselves have believed at least some of the tales of American battleships and aircraft carriers sunk in this battle, but the reality was very different. As the projected attack on Midway had prevented an adequate allotment of Japanese forces to the Port Moresby operation, so, reciprocally, the Port Moresby operation reduced the Japanese strength available for Midway.

The damaged *Shokaku*, which could neither launch nor recover planes, had to be returned to home base for repairs and could not return to service until July.[66] The *Zuikaku*, though not damaged, had lost a larger proportion of its planes, needed to be refitted after its prior actions, and therefore was also not immediately available for the central Pacific project. The Japanese navy simply did not have the replacement aircraft and crews available. The Americans, on the other hand, recalled the damaged *Yorktown* to Pearl Harbor and made minimum essential provisional repairs on it in three days so that it could fight again. As a result, the United States navy would be able to meet the four carriers of the Japanese with three of its own. Time pressures, over-confidence, and, as will become apparent, a ridiculous plan, hampered Yamamoto at the same time as desperate measures, excellent intelligence, and good judgement helped the Americans.

The detailed plans worked out in Yamamoto's Combined Fleet Head-quarters to implement the project he had insisted upon involved a dispersion of effort to an extraordinary extent. Though originally counting on the two fleet carriers sent to support the operation against Port Moresby, the Japanese still were neither going to concentrate their remaining eight carriers on the Midway attack nor would they wait for the undamaged *Zuikaku* to be ready to participate. Instead, the original time schedule would be adhered to and four carriers were diverted to other missions. Two carriers were to provide air support for a simultan-eous assault on Alaska, focusing on the air base at Dutch Harbor and also seizing two of the western Aleutians.

This strange project was designed with several aims. It would provide a diversion to confuse the Americans; because of its assault on American territory it might coax the American navy into battle; and finally it would provide bases for blocking any American attacks on the Kuriles and the Japanese home islands from Alaska. It ended up doing none of these things, in part because the Americans knew from their code-breaking what was coming—although Admiral Robert A. Theobald, the naval commander, refused to believe that the Japanese would do anything so silly—and there were no plans for an American northern assault on Japan. The operation did mean that, at the crucial battle, the Japanese not only did not have the superiority in carrier air that they might have had but that two carriers were too far away to return in time to the main Japanese striking force.

Furthermore, two light carriers, the *Hosho* and *Zuiho*, were also abstracted from the main attack and kept behind in the framework of the support force of battleships and cruisers which would theoretically participate in any main fleet action which might occur (presumably against battleships Yamamoto thought he had sunk at Pearl Harbor). Of the nine carriers potentially available to Yamamoto therefore, the central part of his operational plan involved only four, a force with no margin for the hazards of war. It also deserves to be noted that the four carriers could not be brought back to full strength in planes because there were not enough replacements for the losses incurred to date and many of the replacement pilots actually allocated were not fully trained.[67] The great advantage with which the Japanese had begun on December 7, 1941, was dwindling. Nevertheless, the Japanese were confident that Midway Island could be neutralized by carrier strikes and then seized with the American fleet destroyed soon after. All questions raised within the naval staffs were brushed aside; Japanese experience and superiority would suffice to cope with all contingencies.

The attack on Dutch Harbor by planes from the carriers sent to the Alaska operation on June 3 showed the Americans that their intelligence was correct. In the ensuing fighting, the Japanese inflicted some damage and suffered minor losses in planes. By the time their carriers were recalled, naturally too late to help the main force embattled at Midway, the Japanese had prepared the way for unopposed landings on the uninhabited islands of Attu and Kiska. They left without contact with the American warships in the area which Admiral Theobald, against explicit orders, had sent to the wrong position. The capture of the two islands could be and was trumpeted as a great accomplishment by Tokyo, but it could neither justify the diversion of Japanese strength from, nor off-set defeat in, the main engagement.[68]

The Japanese carriers headed for Midway followed by a landing force, both with screening warships and, at a distance, by a large naval force including the new super-battleship *Yamato* with Yamamoto himself aboard. He had decided not to assume command of the carrier strike force, which was headed by Admiral Nagumo Chuichi, nor to stay ashore; as a result he could hardly communicate with his various forces during the battle. The first task of the carriers was to launch an attack on Midway and if necessary a second one to prepare the way for the landing to seize the island, and enable the Japanese to use the airfield there themselves in the naval engagement that was expected to follow.

How Nagumo was to cope with the Midway base and the American navy if involved with both simultaneously had never been clarified, since honest answers to those officers who raised the question would have required abandonment or major modification of the whole plan.

It was, however, precisely this contingency which arose. Once the Americans had figured out the correct sequence of the intended Japanese moves in the South and Central Pacific on the basis of careful and successful signals intelligence, they collected their remaining usable three carriers in the Pacific and provided them with what screening force was available. With the two modern battleships *North Carolina* and *Washington* in the Atlantic, nothing larger than cruisers could be employed. Unknown to the Japanese, the three carriers were sent out to meet them.

On the morning of June 4 the Japanese carriers sent their first strike against Midway, but the Midway commander was determined not to be caught with his planes on the ground. The bombs dropped by Midway planes on the Japanese all missed; but the damage caused by the raid on the island, though considerable, was not considered sufficient by the Japanese to prepare the way for the landing assault. A second air attack on the island was ordered, but from here on things began to go wrong for Nagumo. He had to change the arming on the planes kept on his carriers for the second strike; he had to recover the planes returning from the first strike; and he received reconnaissance reports that there were American warships soon identified as carriers in the area and therefore once again altered the arming of his planes for this contingency. The upshot of the resulting sequence of orders was that his carriers were extremely vulnerable to attacks from the American carriers because fuel hoses, armed planes, and ammunition were all over the hangar and flight decks in incredible confusion.

The initial American waves of attacking torpedo and bombing planes were all warded off by Japanese fighters and anti-aircraft fire with great losses to the Americans and at little cost to the Japanese; but while many of the American planes failed to find the Japanese ships, those that did had attacked bravely, if without direct results, at *low* levels. This meant that when minutes later American naval dive bombers appeared above, the Japanese, who lacked radar and whose visual spotters were concentrating on the low-level action, were caught off guard and with their fighter planes unable to gain the altitude necessary to intercept. Within a few minutes, three of the four carriers were hit by bombs which tore open their decks, ignited fires, and set off great explosions among the tanked up and armed planes on and below the flight decks. Ammunition and fuel fires and explosions quickly followed; and all three carriers,

Akagi, *Kaga* and *Soryu*, were soon out of commission, two sinking that night and the third being scuttled the following day.

The planes from the *Hiryu*, the fourth Japanese carrier, attacked and damaged the *Yorktown*; but the second strike from the *Hiryu*, which was supposed to attack one of the other American carriers, struck the *Yorktown* again, not recognizing that this was the same ship. The other two American carriers remained undamaged and, using the remainder of their own planes and some of those from the *Yorktown*, hit the *Hiryu* in circumstances very similar to those which had caused such devastation on the other three carriers. In little time, the *Hiryu* too was lost. During the next two days, a Japanese submarine was able to sink the badly damaged *Yorktown*, and an American submarine attack led to a collision between two Japanese heavy cruisers of the covering force with one subsequently sunk and the other badly damaged by air attacks; but the main action was over in one long day of battle. Reluctantly Yamamoto had to call off the Midway operation—he could not pull together in time the carrier forces his own plan had scattered over the Pacific. The Americans, on the other hand, had every reason to be careful and avoid being drawn into battle with the great fleet of battleships and cruisers (as well as the other carriers) the Japanese had sent out.[69]

What was the importance and what were the implications of this battle? The most obvious implications were the losses of both sides. The American loss of the *Yorktown* was soon offset by the return of the repaired carrier *Saratoga* to the fleet at about the time the Japanese had refitted the *Zuikaku* with a new group of airplanes; but the fundamental fact was that there was no way for the Japanese to replace within a reasonable time the four carriers they had lost. The idiotic nature of Japan's insistence that the naval limitation treaty of 1922 restricted her unduly was never more dramatically illustrated: during the whole Pacific War, Japan commissioned 14 carriers of all types, the United States 104.[70] Equally important, the Japanese had great difficulty replacing the more than 300 airplanes lost—the whole complement of four carriers—and the hundreds of experienced air crews and thousands of naval crewmen who did not return.[a]

Every effort was made to keep the Japanese public from learning of the defeat, but the Emperor was told the truth.[71] An attempt was also made to mislead the Germans into thinking Japanese losses were smaller and American losses greater than the Japanese themselves knew; but the Germans eventually found out what had really happened, in part because the Japanese asked them whether they could purchase and transfer to

---

[a] Over 2000 men were lost on the carriers. While some of the aircrews were saved, the majority were either shot down or lost with the carriers.

the Pacific the uncompleted German aircraft carrier *Graf Zeppelin!*[72] The project to assault New Caledonia was dropped immediately,[73] and Yamamoto became generally more cautious hereafter.[74]

Fortunately for the Americans, this caution did not extend to the codes used by the Japanese. Neither a careful analysis of the Midway battle itself, which could have raised suspicions about code security, nor a significant hint from the Germans,[75] nor a *Chicago Tribune* story about the use at Midway of the breaking of Japanese codes by the American navy,[76] registered in Tokyo. Routine changes made in naval codes did hold up American cryptographers for a while and thus contributed to the Japanese naval victory at Savo Island on August 8, but the basic procedures remained in use — and vulnerable — until the end of the war.

A lesson the Americans might have learned, but did not, was the ineffectiveness of their land-based bombers. Unwilling or unable to recognize that a smaller number of dive bombers had sunk four carriers, they did not recognize for years that the Army and marine bombers had merely hit the ocean.[77]

More important than any of these matters was the broader impact of Midway on the war. Here was, as one scholar has put it, "the first irreversible Allied victory of the Second World War."[78] As the construction figures indicate, there was no way the Japanese could defeat the United States, but the course of the war as a whole could still have proceeded very differently. The Japanese losses and the American victory prevented a major new Japanese offensive either in the south or in the Indian Ocean and opened the way for the Americans to stage a counter-attack in the Solomon Islands,[79] which, as will be seen, pre-occupied the Japanese for the rest of 1942 and prevented them from any return to an offensive in the Indian Ocean, an operation they had hoped for and promised to the Germans. Finally, closely related to the foregoing and perhaps most important, a Japanese victory and an American defeat would certainly have forced a major reexamination of the Europe First strategy. The American victory on the other hand — ironically for Admiral King — made it possible for the United States to maintain in principle and eventually in practice a strategy that placed first emphasis on victory over Germany.[80]

The only possible resumption of the offensive to which the Japanese, as already mentioned, now turned was an overland assault to seize Port Moresby.[81] Because the new Allied command in the South Pacific was building up slowly, the Japanese were able to get first to the northern end of the land route, the Kokoda trail.[82] Landing an army contingent at Buna on July 21, they proceeded to push back the Australians across the rugged Owen Stanley Mountains and eventually covered 120 of the

150 miles toward the key base.[83] This was possible in part because the Australian units facing them were too small, MacArthur's intelligence having completely failed to recognize the threat, and in part because the air force command structure simply did not function well. Certainly in the face of a determined and energetic Japanese push, new measures were needed. The debates in Washington and Melbourne, where MacArthur's headquarters were located, and between them, had delayed a planned United States–Australian landing at Buna, so that the Japanese had arrived there first. Now all appeared to be going badly. A new air commander was sent out, and that commander, General George C. Kenney, soon brought about dramatic improvements. The air strikes he commanded helped the Australians finally halt the Japanese on September 17. By then the Japanese were themselves so weakened from losses and the horrendous terrain that they were told to halt by their headquarters, which was at this time so engrossed in the campaign for Guadalcanal that reinforcement for New Guinea had to be postponed until after Japanese victory in the Solomons — which never came.[84] From places within sight of Port Moresby the Japanese began a withdrawal back across the Kokoda trail; few ever saw home.

If the Japanese had beaten the Allies to Buna, the reverse was true at the southeastern end of New Guinea. There Australian troops with some American engineers and anti-aircraft units had been landed on June 25 at Milne Bay to begin establishing what became one of the great shipping and air bases in the South Pacific. When Japanese marines came ashore on August 25, they were met by the entrenched Allied force. In two weeks of bitter fighting the Japanese were crushed, losing over 2000 men and evacuating only a remnant by September 7.[85] For the first time in the war, a major Japanese amphibious force had been defeated ashore. The tide was turning against Japan on New Guinea even before her weary land forces had begun to trudge back over the Kokoda trail.

The follow-up to the victory at Milne Bay did not go smoothly. Unfamiliarity with the terrain problems, another intelligence failure which put Japanese strength in the Buna–Gona area at under two thousand when it was actually more than four times that large, and the inexperience of all the American and some of the Australian staffs, produced a long and bitter campaign. Heavy Allied casualties due both to Japanese weapons and disease, the sacking of both United States and Australian generals and a proclamation of victory from MacArthur's headquarters long before the campaign was over, characterized a battle that did not end in victory for the Allies until January 22, 1943. At the margins of the newly acquired Japanese empire, the forces engaged and the casualties were small by the standards of the great front in Eastern Europe, but the fighting was no less hard and the percentage of casualties as high. Of the 15,000 or so Japanese committed to this battle, almost none survived, while over 10,000 battle casualties and disabled by disease constituted about half the Allied soldiers involved. But the Allies were learning how to fight the Japanese and the terrain of New Guinea; they were paying a heavy price; but they were learning and winning. The same could be said of the better known and equally difficult battle that began before and ended after that in Papua: Guadalcanal.

THE FIRST COUNTER-OFFENSIVE: GUADALCANAL

As the Japanese advance moved apparently irresistibly forward in the first half of 1942, the Allies had tried to halt it or at least contain it by the creation of a general command for all Allied forces in the area. This structure, the American–British–Dutch–Australian (ABDA) Command under Wavell, had collapsed under the hammer blows of Japanese victories. The British had fallen back on India, and the Americans found themselves committed to the defense of Australia. For this task, they had established a new command under MacArthur, and that headquarters, soon officially denominated the Southwest Pacific, had mounted first the actual defense of Australia and then the Papuan campaign just described. But that left open the whole range of the Pacific Ocean, and here army–navy rivalry precluded a simple resolution. The navy, and especially Admirals King and Nimitz, was not about to let an army commander, least of all General MacArthur, control the deployment and employment of its main fleet in an area that was so obviously an oceanic one as the Central Pacific. On the other hand, there was no way that as assertive a general as MacArthur was going to serve under any admiral. Only divided theaters with cooperation enjoined upon them would do; and in war as in much of real life, logic turned out not to be the best guide. In spite of all the complaints, the double command system would work with the Joint Chiefs of Staff from Washington coordinating the two prongs of the defense and later offense. By putting up with lots of belly-aching and posturing from MacArthur and occasional complaints from Nimitz, the American command got the best out of both, while the Japanese were never able to concentrate their resources on coping with the one as they were time and again whipsawed between the two. The first instance of this was to be the fighting in the Solomons in the very months that the Japanese were still trying to make their way to Port Moresby.

The minimal American Pacific counter-attack that seemed feasible after Midway was itself hastened forward by the receipt of news in

Washington that the Japanese had not only seized the base at Tulagi but were beginning to construct a major air base in the northern portion of the nearby large island of Guadalcanal. As the advances of the Allies and of the Japanese had inter-acted on New Guinea, so now the Solomons operation was rushed forward, lest the Japanese so entrench themselves there as to threaten not only any United States action in the islands but open the way for further Japanese advances to cut the route to Australia.[86] Although the available resources in trained men, shipping, and air power were really not adequate, it seemed wiser to President Roosevelt and Admiral King to move quickly before the Japanese on Guadalcanal could become so strong that even a larger force would be likely to fail. The ensuing battle showed how closely the scales were balanced.

On August 7, the 1st U.S. Marine Division with some added units, escorted by much of the Pacific fleet, staged its landings on Tulagi and several small adjacent islands as well as on the north shore of Guadalcanal. The fighting on and near Tulagi was soon ended by the destruction of the Japanese forces there, but on Guadalcanal, everything turned out very differently from what either side had expected. The Japanese were completely surprised there as on Tulagi, and they did not realize for weeks either the substantial size of the American force committed or their determination to hold on. The Americans, on the other hand, not only were poorly informed about the terrain features of the island but did not anticipate the extent and continuity of the Japanese fixation on recapturing their positions.[87]

At first, all went very badly for the American landing force. As the Japanese reacted, the American carriers pulled away, leaving the marines without naval air support. The United States navy made a serious error in not immediately completing construction of the airfield, named in honor of Major Loften R. Henderson who had lost his life at Midway.[88] Henderson Field became a critical base for the Americans—as it was expected to be for the Japanese—and became the focus of marine corps aviation as of Japanese recapture attempts for months. Even more disastrous for the Americans ashore was the decision to withdraw the transports with many of the supplies not yet unloaded as well as a portion of the marine division. Most spectacular of all was the naval battle off Savo Island in the night of August 8–9, when a Japanese naval force of five heavy and two light cruisers in short order sank three American and one Australian cruisers with almost no loss or damage to themselves. The worst defeat the United States navy had ever suffered exposed the transports to attack, but the Japanese commander, Admiral Mikawa Gunichi, decided that, in the absence of clear knowledge of what other United

States naval forces were in the area, it would be best to withdraw.[a]

The marines were now isolated, but began to be reinforced first by isolated ships and small groups of planes flown into Henderson Field, later by convoys. The Japanese in turn on August 17 initiated a major effort to reinforce their small remaining land forces on Guadalcanal.[89] A long and bitter series of engagements followed as each side, determined to win the struggle, poured in additional forces. Repeatedly the Japanese sent convoys of transports and warships loaded with men to the island; repeatedly they shelled and bombed Henderson Field; repeatedly their troops assaulted the marines' positions.[90] The fighting on land, in which the marines learned under the most difficult terrain and weather conditions how to cope with the Japanese, slowly turned in favor of the Americans, who reinforced and eventually relieved the marines with army units.[b] In October the situation looked so critical to the Americans that planes and supplies were rushed in to avert disaster;[91] thereafter the issue was not in doubt.

During the six months of fighting on the island, there was a series of naval battles in the area. Japanese and American navy task forces covering reinforcing convoys clashed, with the Americans by now again often warned of the approaching danger by breaks into the Japanese codes and by "coast-watchers," civilians who lived on the islands. In addition, the warships—usually destroyers—which were utilized by both sides to rush reinforcements for the land battle to the island were attacked by the air force, submarines and, occasionally, the navy of the other side. In this fighting both sides suffered substantial losses. First the Japanese and then the Americans lost a carrier; then the Americans lost still another carrier while two Japanese carriers were damaged;[c] finally in an engagement running over several days in mid-November, the Japanese lost two battleships. In most of these engagements, both sides also lost cruisers and destroyers as the Japanese first did well and later began to suffer heavily in night engagements. The naval battle of attrition was being won by the Americans in October–November, even as the land battle turned against the Japanese.[92]

The repeated land assaults, sometimes combined with naval bombardments, had not crushed the American landing force; the Japanese navy

---

[a] The Australian cruiser sunk was the *Canberra*. The United States thereupon named one of its new cruisers for the Australian capital. Roosevelt to Knox, 6 Sept. 1942, Hyde Park, OF 18, Box 9, Dept. of Navy 1942 Sept.-Dec.

[b] The sending of the Marine Division to Australia in turn made it possible for the 9th Australian Division to remain in North Africa and participate in the battle of El Alamein rather than return to Australia. Morton, *Strategy*, pp. 340–45.

[c] This produced another instance of U.S.–British friction over an American request for a British carrier to be transferred to the Pacific. Eventually the *Victorious* was sent, but by then (March 1943) the crisis had long passed. See Roskill, *War at Sea*, 2: 229–31, 415.

was increasingly dubious about the steady losses in ships; the losses of naval and army airplanes were becoming more difficult to replace. At the end of December, 1942, the Japanese high command decided to begin an evacuation of what was left of their army on the island and, fooling the Americans into thinking that a new reinforcement offensive was about to be launched, succeeded in pulling out something over 10,000 men out of the more than 40,000 who had fought on Guadalcanal.[93] On February 7, 1943, the half-year-long battle was over. What did it all mean?

The fighting itself would be remembered by the survivors as one long nightmare; it took a full year's rehabilitation before the 1st Marine Division could again be committed to battle. On the broader canvas of war, there were broader implications. The Americans learned here as in Papua that the Japanese were hard fighters but not invincible. When the odds were reasonable, and the leadership competent, the Allies could hold and defeat the seemingly invincible Imperial army and navy. But obviously only at great cost. It would be a very long and a very tough fight. As for the Japanese, they had seen that their basic strategy of defending the perimeter of their newly won empire was evidently not working the way they had planned. The assumption had been that the Americans would be unwilling to pay the price in blood and treasure to retake islands of which they had never heard, to be returned to allies for whose colonial empires they had only disdain. Here was proof that they would; and, in the face of this, the leaders in Tokyo displayed a bankruptcy of strategic thinking.

The Americans were committed to building up forces in England and at home for an assault on Germany. The Europe First strategy meant that there was little option for the United States but to send a steady trickle of reinforcements to the South Pacific in the hope that these could avert disaster, make up for losses, and begin to push the Japanese back. It is critical to note that the October crisis and the November victory on and near Guadalcanal coincided with the final preparations for an early landing and fighting in Northwest Africa. The leaders in Tokyo, however, did have choices. Once the major outlines of battle were drawn by late August, early September, 1942, the Japanese could do one of three things. They could write off Guadalcanal and concentrate their forces elsewhere, either on New Guinea or, probably more promising, in the Indian Ocean. A second possibility open to them, as it was not for the United States, was to allocate massive reinforcements, providing sufficient superiority to crush the American forces in the Solomons. At a time when the mass of Japan's navy was intact and most of her army neither engaged nor about to be engaged elsewhere, this was

an obvious possibility. The third possible course of action—and the one
adopted—was to do by choice what the Americans were doing by necessity, and that was to keep putting more and more resources in, never
enough to overwhelm the enemy but in the end allowing only a salvage
of what could be saved. This course of action lost Japan not only tens
of thousands of men, hundreds of planes along with experienced crews,
and numerous warships, but above all it lost her the strategic initiative
for the whole second half of 1942. This meant that the opportunity to
meet her European allies by an advance into the Indian Ocean slipped
by unutilized; it was an opportunity which both Tokyo and Berlin saw
at the time and which never came again.

The Germans and Japanese were in any case finding it difficult to
cooperate; the troubles of the Western Allies with the Russians and with
each other were harmony itself compared with the frictions between the
Germans and the Japanese. The Japanese did not want any German
economic or other presence in their newly won empire, and they resisted
all efforts, whether by private firms or by government agencies, to restore
or expand German activities and interests of any kind in Southeast Asia.
Frictions, suspicions and anxieties resulted; and even Hitler's ruling that
there was to be no German interference in the economic affairs of
Southeast Asia never completely calmed the troubled waters.[94] Not unrelated to the friction over possible German economic interests in South
and Southeast Asia were the difficulties in the direct economic relations
between the Tripartite Pact partners. The practical problems of implementing any cooperative exchange between them will be reviewed in the
next chapter, but the negotiations conducted for an economic agreement
were certainly anything but friendly.[95]

Political cooperation also proved extraordinarily difficult. As already
mentioned, they went back and forth on the subject of utilizing the
Indian collaborator Subhas Chandra Bose.[96] The project for sending
him to East Asia came to be mixed up with an endless argument about
the organizing of direct flights between the European and Far Eastern
Axis partners, the thought being that Bose and others would fly East
while a special delegation of high-ranking Japanese appointed by the
Emperor and hence referred to as the Tenno-delegation could fly
West.[97] In spite of the success of one Italian plane in making the trip to
Japan and the return journey as well in July 1942, or perhaps because
there was undesirable publicity about this feat, the whole project came
to nothing.[98] One of the issues raised in the talks, however, illuminates
a key divergence between the strategies of Germany and Japan in the
war.

The Germans were at war with the Soviet Union and preparing a major new summer offensive which they believed would succeed in fatally weakening Soviet power. A flight route to East Asia across the northern reaches of the Soviet Union seemed entirely appropriate to them. Furthermore, once they had launched their summer offensive, not only von Ribbentrop but Hitler too suggested to Tokyo late in June 1942 that now was the time for Japan to attack the Soviet Union and meet the Germans in Central Asia. The Japanese, on the other hand, hoping to recover from the setbacks at Coral Sea and Midway, looked to a renewed offensive against the United States and did not feel they could take on any additional enemy. Extraordinarily sensitive to any air attacks on the home islands after the April raid on Tokyo, they were worried that any overflight of the Soviet Union on a route between Europe and East Asia might lead the Russians to permit American use of Siberian bases. They had assured themselves of Russian neutrality before attacking the United States, Britain, and the Dutch, and they were not about to do anything that might offend their powerful neighbors, least of all as they were now obviously locked into a bitter and lengthy war with America.[99]

If the obvious signs of a continuing war with the United States, which did not end after six months as the Japanese had once anticipated, kept Tokyo from giving serious thought to the German request for an attack on the Soviet Union, the fierce campaign in the Solomon Islands and the way in which it pre-occupied the Japanese for half a year also determined how that war could and could not be waged.[100] The main German interest in Japan's conduct of the war in 1942 was not the fleeting suggestion in the summer that she attack Russia but the pressure all year for a major offensive into the Indian Ocean.[101] As already mentioned, this had been Japan's great opportunity and the Allies' great worry in the first half of 1942, and the Germans kept repeating to their East Asian ally the urgency of such a step. Here was the opportunity to cut off the supply route to Russia across Iran and to the whole British North African theater. Hardly a single meeting between German and Japanese representatives in Berlin or Tokyo took place in 1942 without this topic on the agenda (and without the Allied cryptographers afterwards reading the Japanese telegraphic reports).[102] The possibility came to the fore even more in the summer of 1942 for two reasons. In the first place, there is evidence to suggest that the Japanese themselves began to focus more distinctly on this question, in part because the British action on Madagascar showed how seriously the latter regarded that threat, in part because the insistence of the Germans made a small dent in the essentially provincial perspective of many in the Japanese military and naval hierarchy.

The second and perhaps more significant reason for renewed Japanese attention to this issue was the great German triumph in North Africa in June 1942. That campaign is examined later in this chapter, but its spectacular character and the grand visions it opened up for the Germans and Japanese must be seen in the context of a global conflict. Here appeared to be an opportunity for the Germans and Japanese to collaborate and even meet, and the Japanese under these circumstances did change their attitude of the first half of the year.[103] They moved a substantial number of submarines to the western part of the Indian Ocean to interfere with the vital British supply route to Egypt (as well as to the India–Burma theater and to the Russians across Iran) and they promised to make a major effort in that direction in the fall.[104]

It was in this regard that the campaign in the Solomons proved decisive. Unable to drive the Americans out of Guadalcanal with the resources they were willing to commit to that struggle, and unwilling to give up trying, the Japanese found themselves in a battle of attrition which precluded implementation of the Indian Ocean strategy they had promised to the Germans. What is more, they found that they could not even maintain the allocation of submarines to the western Indian Ocean but had to recall these for use in the South Pacific.[105]

The long and bitter fight for Guadalcanal, which looked to many then and some since as a diversion from the Europe First strategy of the Allies, in fact had major positive implications for the European theater. In the critical months of the war in the Mediterranean, when Britain was on the ropes there, her forces could be reformed and rearmed to hold the German–Italian army on the approach to the Suez Canal on the basis of supplies sent across the Indian Ocean. Simultaneously, as the Russians battled to hold the German armies threatening to break into the Middle East across the Caucasus from the north, the supply line across Iran was also kept open. It is no coincidence that October 1942 was one of the two months during World War II that a majority of American supplies to Russia were carried across Iran.[106] By the time the Japanese decided to evacuate Guadalcanal, the tide had turned in both North Africa and the southern section of the Eastern Front. The denial to Japan of opportunity in the Indian Ocean by the Solomons campaign could not be reversed. Those who fought and died in and around the island with the strange name could not know their place in the broader contours of World War II, but these become clear once the issue is placed in the perspective of global war. As the Germans and Japanese looked to the future, they could talk about what each would do, the Germans on the Eastern Front and the Japanese in the Pacific, but their hopes for a combined victory over their enemies still looked to a meeting in the Middle East and the Indian Ocean,[107] which had been blocked for the Japanese at Midway and in the Solomons as it was blocked for the Germans in North Africa and the southern part of the Eastern Front.

THE GERMAN DRIVE INTO EGYPT AND ALLIED STRATEGY

The possibility of a German–Japanese meeting in the Near East in 1942 appeared to be a real one, because the Japanese advance and potential threat from the east was likely to meet a German thrust from the west. Since the Italian position on the Indian Ocean in the Horn of Africa had been destroyed by the British conquest of that area in the winter of 1940–41, and the British had also closed off the German attempt to build up an alternative position in the Middle East by putting down the pro-Axis government of al-Gaylani in Iraq and defeating the Vichy French forces in Syria in May and June of 1941, the Germans could return to this part of the world only by striking from what was left of Italy's colonial empire in Libya, by crossing Turkey, or by conquering Russia, with the last two closely interrelated. For a while it looked as if the first of these three avenues might work for them.

The transfer of the German 2nd Air Fleet from the Eastern Front to the Mediterranean in December 1941 and the exhaustion of the British army that had driven back Rommel's North African army enabled the Germans to establish a line holding the western part of Libya in January 1942. Rommel was assisted in this by a series of Axis naval victories in which German submarines sank the British aircraft carrier *Ark Royal* and the battleship *Barham*, even as Italian mini-submarines seriously damaged two additional battleships in the harbor of Alexandria at a time when other British warships had to be sent East to cope with Japan's entrance into the war. Furthermore, the constant bombardment of the British-held island of Malta by the German air force made it easier for the Germans and Italians to re-supply their army in North Africa almost without interference. Once again surprising the British (as well as the German and Italian high commands), Rommel struck on January 21, 1942, and quickly overran the advance British position. By the end of the month Benghazi had fallen to the Germans, but their offensive came to a temporary halt a week later because the Italians refused to participate. Both sides faced the question of what to do next.

The British were indeed planning an attack to drive the Germans back and hopefully complete the conquest of Italian North Africa. Such an operation would relieve the dangerous situation of Malta, open the Mediterranean to at least some Allied shipping, and end the threat to Egypt from Libya once and for all. Furthermore, such an operation figured largely in the broader strategic concept of the British. As will be discussed subsequently in this chapter, the civil and military authorities in London had been thinking for some time of a landing in Northwest Africa in cooperation with the Americans. Such a landing would make possible the reopening of the Mediterranean and provide a base for assaults on Europe from the south in line with a broader strategy of defeating Germany by peripheral assaults that weakened her for the final blow. The disasters in the Pacific in the winter 1941–42 had forced the abandonment of such projects in early 1942, but Churchill hoped to revive them. A victory over Rommel in the spring of 1942 might pave the way for such a project, but the inter-relation between the desert war and a possible landing in Northwest Africa would be very different indeed.

The Germans and Italians had to choose between staying in place, a renewed attack in Libya toward the Suez Canal, or an invasion of Malta to close the Central Mediterranean to the Allies and open it for themselves, so that a major sustained offensive into the Middle East could be carried out.[108] The first alternative, that of simply holding with minimal forces, was ruled out by the fact that over time the British might accumulate overwhelming force in the theater; unless the Japanese and German navies closed the supply route through the Indian Ocean to Egypt, the Allies could always replenish their forces there, even if it took a lot of time. The second and third possible courses—Malta and a direct attack into Egypt—were closely related. Having failed to seize Malta by a quick stroke in 1940, the Italians had lost their best chance. In 1941, the Germans had opted for an airborne assault on Crete rather than Malta; they had the resources for only one at that time, and Crete had appeared to be the more profitable objective. But the heavy casualties incurred in that campaign had left the German high command and most definitely Hitler himself very leery of the idea of an airborne assault on a defended island.[109] The Italians had come to think that seizing Malta was absolutely essential for continued operations in North Africa and were making preparations for an assault. Later this came to be planned as a joint German–Italian operation, code-named "Hercules," which was supposedly to be ready in July. Unwilling to wait until that time for any offensive at all, the Germans proposed and the Italians agreed on a compromise: the Axis would attack in late May and drive to the Libyan-Egyptian border; then would come "Hercules;" and finally there would be the invasion into Egypt which could be adequately supplied after the capture of Malta and could therefore be sustained all the way to the Suez Canal.[110]

The British had superiority in numbers by late May 1942 but the leadership was exhausted and ineffective, much of the equipment inferior to that of the Germans, cooperation between the land and air forces poor and, above all, the tactical dispositions which invariably stressed breaking up divisions into pockets hopelessly defective. To make things even worse for the Allies, with Italian assistance the Germans had broken the code of the United States military representative, Colonel Bonner F. Fellers, and could follow the British plans and dispositions by reading his detailed and accurate reports.[111] British intelligence did decypher enough of the relevant German radio traffic to warn Cairo of what was coming but was not believed until too late. On May 26 Rommel struck a few days ahead of the British 8th Army.[112]

The battle usually referred to as that of the Gazala line was a bitter slogging match in which the Germans and Italians crushed the British 8th Army. Over a two-week period, the British armored units were battered to pieces and their major defensive positions seized one by one. By mid-June the German units were about to cut off Tobruk for a second time and the British were preparing for a second siege. But the 1941 experience was not repeated. This time the Germans' armor quickly penetrated Tobruk's defenses, received the surrender of over 28,000 soldiers, and seized enormous stores that could keep them supplied for an advance to and even into Egypt. This spectacular German victory and British disaster had major repercussions for both Axis and Allied strategy in the war.[113]

The Axis powers could not at first agree on a course to follow. The Italians, though agreeable to an advance to the Egyptian border, wanted the Malta operation to go forward. Rommel, however, wanted to push on into Egypt right away. In this he had the support of Hitler, who had always had his doubts about the assault on Malta and now saw the opportunity to demolish the whole British position in the Middle East, in the days when the German summer offensive on the Eastern Front was, in his opinion, about to open the door to an invasion across the Caucasus from the north in a gigantic pincer. With control of Egypt dangling before Mussolini as a reachable prize, Berlin and Rome agreed to skip the "Hercules" operation and put all their resources—including those set aside for the landing on Malta—into the effort to seize Egypt.[114] They promised in public to respect the independence of Egypt while planning secretly that it would be controlled by Italy.[115] In that country, as in other parts of the Middle East, they found some who believed the promises and ignored the realities of Axis imperialism.[a] Relying on air attacks to contain the role of Malta in interfering with their supplies and on control of Crete as an alternative base for shipping supplies and reinforcements, the Axis forces stormed into Egypt, reaching within 60 miles of Alexandria by the end of June, a mere ten days after the capture of Tobruk. All appeared to be going their way, and contact with Japan looked like a realistic goal.[116]

The immediate repercussions for the Allies were grim; the long-term ones of perhaps even greater importance. The obvious need was to stem the German advance. In desperate fighting, the British 8th Army held the Axis onrush at the El Alamein position, picked because it was short and practically impossible to outflank through the Qattara Depression to the south. Assuming personal command of the battle, Field Marshal Sir Claude Auchinleck fought the German–Italian forces to a standstill but could not dislodge them from their advanced positions.[117] The July struggles ended in stalemate at the El Alamein line with both sides hoping to go on the offensive again, the Germans to drive all the way to the Canal, the British to prepare the coordination with a landing in Northwest Africa. With both Churchill and Brooke on the spot, the whole British command was now changed. Auchinleck was replaced by Alexander, who was to have commanded the British part of the Northwest African landing, while General Montgomery, who was originally to take Alexander's place in Northwest Africa, was called out to take over the 8th Army, whose newly designated commander, General William Henry E. (Strafer) Gott, was killed before he could assume command.[118]

The new team quickly put an end to the attention being lavished on elaborate withdrawal and denial plans, which included everything from retreats up the Nile and into Palestine and the evacuation of Palestine — leaving the Jews there to be slaughtered by the Germans — to the destruction of the oil fields in Saudi Arabia and elsewhere lest they fall into Axis hands ready to utilize them.[119] A new spirit began to be infused into the British forces as Alexander's calm combined with Montgomery's relentlessly driving professionalism.[120] Reinforcements and supplies were rushed to the scene by the British and Americans; some of the most critical items were even flown in.[121] The Germans and Italians could send only limited reinforcements to Rommel at a time when the fighting on the Eastern Front absorbed their energies, and the British were once again rebuilding the Malta air force.

---

[a] The Mufti and al-Gaylani naturally saw this time as their great opportunity. It was also at this time that Nasser, Sadat, and other Egyptian army officers in touch with the Germans were either arrested or sent to remote posts.

A revived 8th Army beat back what would be Rommel's last big offensive in the Battle of Alam el Halfa.[122] From August 30 to September 5 the Germans assaulted the British positions, now far more carefully prepared and forewarned by excellent intelligence. The two sides were for once evenly balanced in numbers of tanks, but the 8th Army's revived spirits, tactical surprise on the battlefield and excellent ground-air cooperation in the face of Axis superiority in aircraft numbers enabled the British to defeat the Afrika Corps. During the very days of this fighting, the first 200 new Sherman tanks from the United States arrived for the counter-offensive to drive Rommel back. Their arrival must be seen in the broader context of Allied strategy as changed by the Tobruk disaster; the decision to send them had been made in Washington on June 21, the day that news of the surrender of Tobruk was flashed to the American capital.

The Allied reaction to the Tobruk disaster must be fitted into their prior discussion of plans for the war against Germany. At the conference in Washington in December 1941–January 1942, the Americans and British had not only reviewed the disastrous situation in East Asia and the measures which might be developed to contain the Japanese flood but had reaffirmed their belief in the need to defeat Germany first, and had developed the staff structure of the Combined Chiefs of Staff and the war materials production and allocation system to implement that strategy. But all this left open the way in which Germany might best be defeated, and on this point there were very great differences of opinion between the two Western Allies.[123]

There was agreement that assisting Russia, which was carrying the main burden of the fight against Germany, was essential. There was also temporary agreement on a project to seize French Northwest Africa by a small expedition, a project that vanished quickly as the Allied rout in East Asia and the great increase in sinkings in the Atlantic[124] ruled out any such offensive operations in the spring of 1942. The greater issue then and subsequently was the basic one of direction and priorities in the assault on Germany. The earliest British plans for the defeat of Germany, already touched on in Chapter 3, contemplated a return to the continent as Germany collapsed under the weight of bombing attacks, exhaustion from blockade, and uprisings in the occupied areas. Such projects did anticipate a landing in Northwest Europe and always assumed that Antwerp, the great Belgian port, would be the main base for an assault on the Ruhr area, Germany's industrial heart.[125] These projects, however, looked to a distant future, assumed that German resistance would be near an end *before* the landing, and that the landing itself would be preceded by a long series of operations on the periphery.

Not only Soviet calls for actions that would directly and more dramatically relieve pressure on the Eastern Front, but a fundamentally different American approach called this concept into question.

The Americans argued that the way to defeat Germany was to concentrate the largest possible force as early as possible in England and strike across the Channel at the main German forces, the assumption being that such an invasion would bring about rather than follow upon the end of German resistance; and that its being prepared would tie down German forces in the West even before any landing took place. Operations on the periphery would have the effect not, as the British thought, of weakening Germany but of diverting Allied strength and, in particular, frittering away the scarce shipping resources in support of campaigns at a greater rather than a lesser distance from the major industrial and manpower base in the United States.[126] The shortest route looked best to the Americans, while the British, who had been kicked off the continent three times already by the Germans, wanted to take advantage of the naval superiority of the Western Allies to wear down the Germans at points where the Germans would be in a difficult position to bring their great land and air power to bear.

Furthermore, the British were very skeptical of American military abilities, and the Americans had their doubts about the British. Practically none of the American commanders had had any experience in the direction of large-scale military operations and their armies were only just beginning to be organized. The idea of a massive assault on Northwest Europe by as yet non-existing American units, which in practice would mean a landing by British units against whom the Germans could readily throw overwhelming force, made no sense to the British military and political leaders; and as the American forces did begin to build up, their likely performance in battle as well as the ability of their leaders looked doubtful to those in London. A disaster in Northwest Europe would not only be of no help to the Russians, it would be positively dangerous for them by enabling the Germans to concentrate on the Eastern Front for a long time, secure in the knowledge that no new operation could be launched against them in the West for months if not years. Furthermore, the strained resources of the British Isles might not be adequate for a renewed attempt; a second Dunkirk could presage utter disaster, not recovery. Operations in the Mediterranean, on the other hand, would have a real impact on the Germans by depriving them of their Italian ally, forcing them to increase garrisons in Southern Europe in addition to those already immobilized by occupation duties and the threat of invasion in the West and in Norway, and greatly reduce the effectiveness of the German campaign against Allied shipping by substituting the short Mediterranean supply route for the long route around the Cape of Good Hope.

If there were British doubts about the Americans, the latter had grave reservations about both British performance and policy. Though admiring British courage and determination, the Americans were impressed only by their performance in the air and on the seas. The steady series of defeats suffered by the United Kingdom in the war was not likely to impress Americans with British leadership abilities; and it is essential to remember that, although people were too polite to mention it, the string of disasters continued after American entrance into the war. The defeat of the British in Malaya culminating in a quick surrender there would be followed a few months later by the terrible defeats in North Africa and the surrender of Tobruk.[127] If, two years after being chased off the continent by the Germans, the British referred to themselves as an "amateur army fighting professionals," [128] there was perhaps less reason to listen to them than both British leaders at the time and historians afterwards assumed. The Americans not only believed that British interest in the Mediterranean was governed more by imperial concerns than by sound military strategy, they did not believe that the operations there were handled with great competence.[129] There were good reasons to send assistance because a complete German victory in North Africa would threaten Russia's southern flank and open the possibility of a German–Japanese junction in the Indian Ocean, but there was general agreement among American military and political leaders, especially President Roosevelt, Secretary of War Stimson, and General Marshall, that a major United States commitment in the Mediterranean would divert resources away from the primary theater and produce an endless series of minor operations with little hope of crushing Germany.[130]

In the British–American discussions of spring 1942 there was, or at least appeared to be, an evolving consensus that some action needed to be, could be, and would be undertaken in Western Europe in 1942. It has sometimes been suggested that British agreement to American pressure on this issue was merely a pretense designed to preclude a switch of American priority from Europe to the Pacific theater. It must be noted however, that in the very months that the British were actually urging the United States to send troops to the Pacific for the defense of Australia while both countries were committed to the buildup in England for an invasion of Europe code-named "Bolero," internal British documents repeatedly stressed the intention of landing in Europe in 1942 and seizing and holding a bridge-head on the continent that would draw German forces from Eastern Europe (at least air if not land units) and provide the basis for a further advance on land in 1943.[131]

In April 1942 when American military leaders went to England for critical conferences on strategy, determined to get agreement on their preference for a landing in 1942, there was, therefore, a tentative agreement for the buildup in England to make possible a landing later that year, in which the British would play the major initial role with American participation steadily increasing.[132] But there was not only residual doubt among some of the British participants to these discussions, there were emerging insurmountable practical difficulties. Before these became sufficiently obvious to alter Allied plans, Soviet Foreign Commissar Vyacheslav Molotov had visited London and Washington where agreement was reached on a phraseology that could be interpreted as promising an invasion in the West in 1942. The actual text was that "full understanding was reached with regard to the urgent tasks of creating a Second Front in Europe in 1942,"[133] a phraseology obviously not as precise as it sounds on first reading, but it does reflect the hopes in Washington in late May 1942 before the disaster in North Africa.[134] Even before that defeat turned around the situation, the Western Allies were increasingly affected not only by dangers in East Asia which were obviously greater than they had anticipated, but by the catastrophic shipping situation which was being dramatically worsened by the enormous loss of ships to German submarines off the North American coast in the first half of 1942. This subject is examined in more detail in the next chapter, but its effect on Allied strategy in 1942 was to be dramatic: it helped preclude any invasion of Western Europe in 1942, it limited very dramatically any operation in 1942 and 1943 at all (and would thus keep the North African invasion from being mounted on a scale that could have assured a rapid seizure of Tunisia), and it would require that any operation in 1942 temporarily preclude the use of shipping for the dangerous route around northern Norway to the Soviet Arctic ports of Murmansk and Archangel.

It was into this already difficult situation that the great British defeat of late May–early June 1942 burst with shocking impact. By a coincidence, Churchill was himself in Washington for strategy talks when the terrible news of Tobruk's surrender was handed to him.[135] Obviously dramatic steps had to be taken to prevent a collapse of the whole situation in the Middle East. The Americans agreed to strip their new armored division of its Sherman tanks and send them to Egypt; it was the first installment of these that arrived in Egypt during the Alam el Halfa battle that has already been mentioned, and the arrival of the rest was critical to Montgomery's timing of and victory in the great battle of El Alamein in late October, 1942.

But not only armor to replace most of the 8th Army's lost and obsolete tanks with better ones had to be sent. Concerned about the great danger of a complete Axis triumph in the Middle East that would enable the Germans and Japanese to cut the Allied supply route across Iran to Russia and across India to China, the Americans ordered the new bomber force being built up in India under General Lewis Brereton to be shifted to the Egyptian front.[136] This shift in turn had two major implications for the war. In the first place, it put American combat units into the Middle East theater for the first time (the tanks having been shipped without their crews). From now on, an American air force would play its part in the Eastern Mediterranean theater, first contributing to the defense of Egypt and later engaging in such operations as the air raids on the Romanian oil fields. The other side of this transfer was, of course, its effect on the China–Burma–India theater. The promised air reinforcement for Chiang Kai-shek had vanished to another theater, and with it a great part of American influence with Chiang in military affairs, a point of great significance for subsequent United States–Chinese relations in the war.[137] The Americans decided not to send other units to the Middle East, but their confidence in the British—after the earlier disasters—was badly shaken, and they were much less inclined to push their ally in the subsequent talks on strategy for 1942.

Before those talks are discussed, one last repercussion of the summer crisis in Egypt must be mentioned. As agreed upon the year before, the Russians were releasing Polish prisoners of war and civilians deported into Central Asia for the creation of a Polish army under the auspices of the Polish government-in-exile. It had been Sikorski's hope that this army would fight alongside the Red Army on the Eastern Front and eventually reenter Poland from the east (the way de Gaulle anticipated having his troops eventually return with the Western Allies into France). The building up of the Polish army inside the Soviet Union was, however, fraught with endless frictions and difficulties; and the Soviet government, which certainly did not want either a truly independent Polish army in the east or a German army striking at the Soviet Union across the Middle East from the south, decided that the best way to deal with both issues was to send the Poles out in the summer of 1942 to reinforce the British in Egypt. With very mixed feelings, the Poles as well as the British accepted this proposal and the newly forming Polish divisions, accompanied by thousands of civilians, headed for the North African front and would eventually reenter Europe from the south, not the east.[138] By the time the resulting transfers had an impact on operations, new decisions made in London in July were being implemented in Africa.

Talks between the Western Allies took place in London in July, the month after the British defeat in North Africa and even as Auchinleck was halting the Germans at the gateway to Alexandria but was unable to dislodge them. In anticipation of these meetings, both the Americans and the British reviewed their respective positions. All were concerned about the Russians holding on in the face of a new German offensive. The Americans were more determined than ever that a landing in Northwest Europe was essential; they had already decided to shore up the faltering British in the Middle East but they were gravely concerned about any diversion from the concentration on one main front. The fact that it had proved necessary to respond to the great victories of Japan by allocating greater forces to the Pacific made it clear to them, however, that the British would have to carry the main burden of any assault in Northwest Europe that year. And there were those among the Americans, especially Admiral King, who believed that the Pacific War should have greater priority in any case and most assuredly so if nothing were going to be done in Europe in 1942 anyway.[139]

The British, more cautious after the defeat in the desert than earlier, were now certain in their own minds that a cross-Channel assault in force was out of the question that year. Only Mountbatten and some on his Combined Operations staff thought that an attack on the Cherbourg peninsula could be mounted and a beachhead held in that portion of Normandy.[140] Churchill and the three Chiefs of Staff were convinced that this was impossible and that a disaster in the West, quite possibly another disgraceful mass surrender on the model of Singapore and Tobruk, far from helping the Russians would end up by hurting them because of its subsequent relief for the Germans from any threat in the West for a very long time.[141] Furthermore, though on this point the evidence is circumstantial rather than direct, the possibility put forward by Mountbatten of holding a small beachhead looked like a very poor idea even if it were feasible because it would absorb endless resources without in any substantial way bringing about a weakening of the German army in the East. The basic position of the London authorities accordingly was that no offensive against Northwest Europe could or should be launched in 1942.[142]

Churchill argued very strenuously that if a landing on the French–Belgian coast was impossible there should be a landing in north Norway, long a favorite project of his, and periodically examined under the code-name "Jupiter." Such an operation would at least hit at the Germans, would begin unravelling their empire where they had begun to put it together, and ease the difficult sea supply route to the Russian ports of Archangel and Murmansk. The Chief of the Imperial Staff always opposed this concept, arguing time and again with the insistent Churchill and always managing to defeat the idea as too risky, not worth the cost, a strategic dead-end, and unlikely to work in practice because the Germans could always counter from their air bases in southern Norway.[143]

It is by no means quite so obvious in retrospect that Brooke was correct in his view. An invasion of Norway in 1942 would not have had such serious repercussions for any cross-Channel attack in 1943 as operation "Torch" did, and while providing less relief for the Allied shipping problem than Torch, certainly would have given some. The strategic goals of such an operation, which Brooke always claimed did not exist, were evident to Churchill: a safer route to the Soviet Union, a real diversion from the Eastern Front, interruption in winter of the German iron-ore supplies from Sweden, and major implications for the attitude of Sweden and the position of Finland in the war. Certainly the Germans always feared such a move by the Allies, and Hitler as well as the German command in Norway were especially concerned about this possibility. Hitler's insistence that the German battleships and cruiser at Brest be added to the battleship *Tirpitz* and accordingly transferred to Norway, an insistence that led to the famous dash up the Channel of the *Scharnhorst* and *Gneisenau* along with the heavy cruiser *Prinz Eugen* beginning on February 12, 1942, grew out of his worry on this score.[144] For the Germans, this meant a shift from a potential surface naval offensive against shipping in the Atlantic to a defensive posture in Norway; a point obvious to the German navy but not as yet to the British.

To the dismay of the British public, the ships slipped through the Channel under their noses unscathed, but to the at least equally great dismay of the Germans, both battleships thereupon ran onto mines newly laid by the Royal Air Force in the channels cleared by the Germans. The *Scharnhorst* was laid up for months while the *Gneisenau* was bombed beyond further use in the war while undergoing repairs. Other preparations by the Germans, including both getting reassurance from Sweden and making plans to invade her country, all show the German pre-occupation with a possible Allied landing in Norway, which they repeatedly saw as imminent.[145] But on this issue, as on many others, Churchill yielded to the firm and unanimous opposition of his military advisors.

At the conference in London on July 18–22, the conflicting perspectives of the British and Americans had to be reconciled.[146] Since the British made it absolutely clear that they were not about to go forward with operation "Sledgehammer," as the Northwestern Europe project for 1942 was code-named, the Americans had no alternative but to agree to dropping it. Obviously they could not insist on an operation which the British would have to mount and that the latter were certain would lead to a disaster which, after their earlier defeats, they simply could not contemplate. Given the situation at the time, this was very likely a correct assessment of the situation. The question then was what to do next. The Norwegian alternative was clearly out as well, having been earlier rejected in internal British discussions, and not appealing to American military leaders either. Some of the Americans, as already mentioned, wanted to transfer resources to the Pacific. Others did not wish to do this, and on this issue the decision of the American Commander-in-Chief, President Roosevelt, was unmistakably clear.[147]

There had to be action in the war against Germany in 1942 in the President's judgement. If the psychic as well as the material energies of the American people were to be engaged in the European war—as the Japanese on their own had arranged for them to be engaged in the Far East—then it was essential that there be a major operation against the European Axis as early as possible. Waiting for that until 1943 was unacceptable. As for concentrating on the Pacific, that made no long-term sense.[148] A victory in the Pacific lay years off and would hardly affect Germany, while a victory in Europe would have immediate and dramatic repercussions on the war in East Asia. It was, therefore, essential that a major operation be launched in the European theater in 1942, and the obvious possibility was a revival of the project to invade French Northwest Africa, operation "Gymnast," discussed earlier that year and now all the more desirable both because of the great danger in Northeast Africa and the potential contribution to easing the terrible shortage of shipping by clearing North Africa of the Axis.[149] The great dilemma was that either nothing could be done at all in 1942 or "Torch" (the new name for "Gymnast") could be launched at the risk of postponing any invasion of Northwest Europe, now referred to as "Roundup," to 1944.[150] The decision agreed upon was a landing in Northwest Africa later in 1942, to be accompanied by a continued buildup of the American forces in England (operation "Bolero") looking toward a landing in Northwest Europe, hopefully in 1943 ("Roundup"). Here, in "Torch," the Allies had a project that looked difficult but within the realm of the possible to the British and the Americans alike. And the crises on Guadalcanal and in Papua were not allowed to upset the projected operation.[151]

The Russians had to be told of this development, a difficult chore which Churchill planned to undertake in person; and there was a real possibility that with the reinforcements being sent to Egypt, the landing in Northwest Africa could be coordinated with a drive from the east to squeeze the Axis out of Africa entirely and open up Italy to attack from the south.[152] Now all depended on whether Egypt could be held and a counter-stroke launched from there, as well as on the capacity of the British and Americans to prepare and mount their first combined offensive of the war.

The disparate but related parts of the Allied program went forward simultaneously. Churchill went to Moscow on August 12–16 to explain to Stalin the impossibility of a landing in France that year as well as the British–American plan of a landing in Northwest Africa instead.[153] The Soviet leader was, or professed to be, extremely upset at first but had to accept the decisions; having helped the Germans drive the Allies off the European continent in the first place, he was not in a very good position to complain about their difficulty in returning to it. Furthermore, he was impressed and gratified by the recent increase in the British bomber offensive against Germany and the plans to increase this effort substantially. The real difficulties of any major landing on the coast of Western Europe were illuminated in public a few days after Churchill left Moscow when a Canadian division with attached units landed at Dieppe.[a] This major raid had been planned and called off earlier; it was launched on August 19 with disastrous results. The landing force was thrown back with great loss and without any diversion of German troops from elsewhere. The Germans were jubilant, and the Vichy French leaders were so enthusiastic about this victory that Pétain offered to join the Germans in fighting off any future landing attempts.[154] At the same time, however, the operation taught the Allies a number of lessons which would be usefully applied thereafter, including the critically important one of landing on beaches and bringing their own harbors along rather than making a frontal assault on a port.[155] The operation, however bad its later repercussions in Canada, did serve to lift spirits in England and the United States; at least someone was trying.

This was particularly important at that time because the United States was locked into a bitter battle of attrition in the Solomons, while the Russians were desperately trying to hold back the German summer offensive. The preparations for "Torch," obviously, could not be trumpeted in public—though there is evidence that the Soviet ambassador in London foolishly leaked the information to newspapers[156]—and the army in Egypt was not ready to strike back quickly. Churchill wanted a new offensive in September, but Montgomery insisted after Alam el Halfa that his army had to be thoroughly retrained, both to carry out an offensive properly and to integrate the hundreds of new tanks and guns

---

[a] The British commando raid on the French Atlantic port of St. Nazaire in March, 1942, was related to concern about the German battleship *Tirpitz* and is therefore discussed in Chapter 7.

arriving during September. Reluctantly Churchill agreed to an October date, just ahead of the planned landing in Northwest Africa.

On October 23 the 8th Army struck a surprised enemy. The postponement had given the Germans and Italians time to lay out enormous mine-fields, and the British units had a difficult fight. Over a period of twelve days the 8th Army crushed the Axis army facing them, though suffering heavy losses itself. Having rebuilt an effective and self-confident army, Montgomery was able to administer a defeat of such dimensions to the Germans that regardless of Hitler's orders, Rommel, who returned from leave in the midst of battle, frantically tried to extricate the remains of his army. Only a small portion was able to rush back to the Libyan–Egyptian border, could not hold there, and was quickly pushed back toward Tripoli.[157] A more determined pursuit might have destroyed Rommel's forces entirely; but even so, the 8th Army entered Tripoli on January 23, three months after the attack at El Alamein, 1000 miles to the east, had began. The Italians, who pointed to German refusal to follow their insistence on taking Malta before striking into Egypt as the main cause of Axis defeat,[158] had lost the last portion of their African empire, and the Mufti could no longer expect to return to Jerusalem in Rommel's baggage car.[159] At El Alamein, as before Moscow and at Midway, the Allies had won a victory that the Axis could hardly reverse.

The war in the desert had created one popularly regarded hero, Erwin Rommel. A great tactician of armored forces, a hard driving military leader, an enthusiastic admirer of Hitler, he had been given the opportunity to lead in a theater where an individual could stand out. A favorite of the Führer, he had been promoted rapidly, most recently to field marshal, and often disregarded orders and official channels; but his health was no longer the best and he was beginning to have some doubts about Hitler. Perhaps this crushing defeat — which would have been even worse had he obeyed Hitler's order to let his army be destroyed in place — started him on the road to the forced choice between suicide and public trial and hanging, with the same German general who gave him the poison arranging the state funeral to which he was thereupon entitled.

The battle of October 1942 now established another general in the public mind. Montgomery had been Brooke's choice for the 8th Army, and in the ups and downs of his career Brooke would back and shield him. A driving, self-confident professional, "Monty" as he came to be known, seemed a bit mad to many high-ranking officers in the British (to say nothing of the American) army, but he did wonders for the morale of a force that had been badly beaten. His soldiers got more of a sense of him than those in most armies ever get of their commander, and they knew he might lead them to death but never needlessly. He would make his share of mistakes, many of them tied to his inability to work with others of high rank, but he provided a touch of hard professionalism, grim determination, and assertive confidence in carefully worked out plans that Allied armies, and especially the British army, desperately needed.

Long before Montgomery's forces had reached Tripoli, in fact only days after the breakthrough at El Alamein, the Allied landing in North-west Africa had been made successfully. The lengthy political prepara-tions, in which the Americans and British hoped for a peaceful landing received by either a changed Vichy regime or a shift to new elements in North Africa, all failed.[160] The last-minute hopes and predictions of the American Office of Strategic Services (OSS) proved to be completely mistaken.[161] The possible disaster to British and American forces was averted by a combination of factors. The determined bravery of their troops landing in Morocco and Algeria was a key element. The decision of Hitler to occupy the unoccupied part of France convinced the last French soldier that the policy of fighting only the Americans, the British, and other Frenchmen made little sense.[a] The unexpected presence of Admiral Darlan, who had flown to Algiers because of the illness and expected death of his son, would open the way for a political deal to assure a rapid Allied takeover in Morocco and Algeria.[162] Perhaps the most important single factor favoring the success of the highly risky operation was the Allied attainment of complete surprise. The shortage of Allied shipping resulting from the U-Boat successes was thought by the Germans likely to preclude an invasion;[163] the Allies had deliberately excluded de Gaulle from knowing of the projected invasion,[164] and, as the British knew from their reading of German codes, the Germans had no idea of what was coming even as the huge convoys approached the West and North African coasts.[165] In any case, once ashore, there was practically no way for the Axis powers to drive them out.

The problems and implications of the North African campaign which came to concentrate on a race for Tunisia and thereafter on a five-months struggle over that territory are examined in Chapter 8. Whatever the outcome in detail, the Allies had clearly seized the initiative. As Japan had been halted in East Asia and was beginning to be driven back on New Guinea and in the Solomons, so the European Axis powers

---

[a] In October 1942 Pétain was only prevented by the Germans from going to North Africa to whip up enthusiasm for fighting any British–American landing (*ADAP*, E, IV, No. 127); two days before the Allied landing of November 8, there was still discussion in Vichy of the project to reconquer the Free French territories in Africa (ibid., No. 143).

were now on the defensive in the Mediterranean. The hopes of the powers of the Tripartite Pact for joint action had been ended; they were now separately on the defensive.

7

THE WAR AT SEA, 1942–1944, AND THE BLOCKADE

The earliest stages of the fighting on, over, and under the oceans have been integrated into the account of the first years of the war, and the last efforts of the Germans to recover the initiative in the winter of 1944–45 will similarly be included in the account of that portion of the war in Chapter 14. For the war in the Pacific in 1942, the surface naval aspect has been dealt with in the preceding chapter, and the naval battles which accompanied the American advance in the Pacific in 1943–45 form an integral portion of that advance. Special features of the struggle for control of the world's oceans, however, require a separate treatment because they dominated the strategy of both alliances in a manner not all recognized at the time and which is too often ignored in retrospect.

In Europe, the difference between the situation in World War II from that of World War I made control of the seas even more critical for the Allies. In World War I, the Soviets pulled out of the war in the latter portion of the conflict, but by that time Germany had been so weakened by her earlier exertions and losses while the Allies had been so strengthened by the entrance of the United States into the war that it was possible to stop the German onslaught in the West in 1918. This enabled the Western Allies to bring their power to bear directly on Germany and to crush her in the summer and fall of that year. In World War II, on the other hand, the Soviet Union had assisted Germany in driving the Western Allies off the continent in the north, west, and southeast in the first years of war, so that thereafter the Allies faced the fundamental problem of how to bring their power to bear on Germany.

A new front in Europe had to be created from across the sea; it did not already exist. This issue loomed over the diplomacy of the Allies — when could they establish a front on the continent? — even as it created a redoubled vulnerability for Great Britain: how to keep in the war at all unless the seas over which her supplies had to come could be kept open. Control of the sea lanes was, accordingly, crucial for the survival of Britain, for the maintenance of the alliance between Britain, the United States, and the Soviet Union, and for an effective land offensive against Germany from the west. A massive bombing campaign could and did provide a partial substitute for such a land campaign and is discussed in Chapter 10; but if the Allies were to crush Germany, they would have to open a new front or fronts on the continent, land and supply vast forces there, and advance into Germany itself. All this depended on control of the seas.

Some Germans saw this clearly. Although Hitler had initiated a massive naval construction program early in his chancellorship, knowing that big warships could be built only if there were an early start on them, the big blue-water navy was in its infancy when he went to war in 1939. What there was of it could be and was used as effectively as possible, but great reliance was placed on submarines. If the surface ships had been essential for the conquest of Norway and would have been vital for any invasion of Britain, they could only play a subordinate role in the fight to strangle British trade. The submarines played a central role in this effort, and they were simultaneously to make it impossible for the Western Allies to build up and support the huge forces the latter would need to have in England for a major assault on the continent.

The longer the war lasted, the more obvious this point became for the Germans; and as it became increasingly clear to them in late 1941 that the war in the East was not about to end in German victory as quickly as they had anticipated, the issue of keeping Western Europe under German control and preventing the British and Americans from assaulting the continent assumed increasing significance as a major role for the German navy.[1] Furthermore, the success of the navy in sinking Allied ships would not only keep them from supplying Britain and landing on the continent but would also reduce their ability to provide assistance in the form of supplies to the Soviet Union. The focus of German military planning for 1942 and until that time when they finally did attain victory in the East, therefore, had to be on the campaign against Allied shipping. Because of Hitler's assumption of direct command of the army in December 1941 and his pre-occupation with the fighting on the Eastern Front, he did not give the naval struggle the constant attention he paid to operations in the East, but he understood quite early that the way to paralyze his enemies in the West was to destroy the shipping on which the life of Great Britain and any offensive plans of Britain and the United States were necessarily dependent.

Control of sea routes was obviously a key aspect of the fighting in the

Pacific, but here, as we will see, there was a significant difference from the European theater. The Japanese, unlike the Germans, did not really comprehend how important merchant shipping was and how their conquest of Southeast Asia, far from freeing them from dependence on others, in fact made them as vulnerable to blockade by the sinking of merchant ships as Great Britain. The Americans, on the other hand, recognized this early. They soon acted on their comprehension of the obvious fact that Japan's seizing oil wells, tin mines, and rubber plantations did not move the wells, mines, and plantations by one inch; it merely meant that their products had to be moved by ships in war rather than in peacetime.

Of the other major belligerents, the Italians certainly recognized the enormous significance of sea communications. Not only their long coast line and sense of being bottled up in the Mediterranean by the British at its eastern and western entrances kept this issue before their eyes, but the fact that all their fighting in the first year of war was dependent on sea communications reinforced their concern. They had depended on sea transport to Albania to launch their ill-fated attack on Greece; they had been unable to support their garrison in Northeast Africa as it was being crushed by the British in the winter of 1940–41 because they could not send ships there; and, above all, they were entirely aware of the almost complete dependence of their own and Germany's forces in North Africa on sea communications for reinforcements and supplies. Their navy carried the main burden of Axis naval fighting in the Mediterranean; and while they did receive some welcome help in this from the Germans in the form of submarines and planes, they in turn had sent many of their own submarines to assist the German campaign against Allied shipping in the Atlantic.

The Chinese had seen their own sea communications cut off by Japan early in the Sino-Japanese War and were therefore no longer directly involved in the war on the oceans. Once the Burma Road was cut by the Japanese advance in the spring of 1942, supplies had to come in by plane until a campaign in north Burma reopened the possibility of a new road, but all that was far into the future. In the meantime, Chiang Kai-shek had other worries.

The Soviet Union's navy was involved in important operations primarily in the Black Sea and these are taken up subsequently in this chapter, but there is very little evidence on Stalin's recognition then, or Soviet historians' recognition later, of the extent to which Allied strategy was dominated by the problem of shipping. Whether because of the primarily land-locked character of Russia, a concentration on the immediate and terrible danger on the land front, or an unwillingness to accept the fact that her allies were doing the best they could under very difficult circumstances, Stalin appears never to have developed any real understanding of the long and bitter fight for control of the oceanic supply routes. In the pre-war years he had begun to push for the building of a Soviet blue-water navy, and he had utilized the period of alignment with Germany to obtain items useful in such a buildup in exchange for Soviet support of the German war against Allied shipping; but these measures represented a small beginning of naval planning, not a real comprehension of the role of sea power in global war.

The fundamental problem facing the Allies in the war with Germany then was to protect what shipping they had, and to replace, hopefully more than replace, what shipping they lost. Conversely, the challenge for the Germans was to defeat England, paralyze the United States, and divide both from the Soviet Union by destroying Allied shipping at a greater rate than replacement was possible. Important but still subsidiary elements in this struggle were the most efficient use of what shipping there was by careful loading, quick turn-around of ships, and use of the shortest possible routes for the Allies; and interference with short routes and destroying the morale of the crews of merchant ships by heavy sinkings for the Germans. Although the longest part of the struggle involved attacks by and defense against submarines, the Germans also used other weapons, and these can be taken up first.

THE GERMANS VERSUS THE ALLIES AT SEA, 1942–1943

The regular surface ships of the German navy were, by 1942, concentrated in Norwegian waters and the Baltic. In the latter location, they were primarily being used to protect German shipping to and from Finland, Sweden and Norway against Soviet and British interference.[2] Only those warships in Norwegian ports were potentially available for the war against shipping. The largest of them, the battleship *Tirpitz*, worried the Allies most. To make sure that it would not, like the *Bismarck*, try to go raiding into the Atlantic, the British mounted a daring commando attack on the French port of St. Nazaire to put out of commission the one dock on the German-controlled Atlantic coast where this 42,900-ton ship could be repaired. The raid of March 28, 1942, accomplished its objective though it is most unlikely that Hitler would have allowed the *Tirpitz* ever to attempt an Atlantic operation under any circumstances.[3] Because of its size and armament, the *Tirpitz* remained a focus of British attention. Along with the other German warships in Norway it forced the retention of a large surface fleet, including battleships and carriers, in British home waters to protect the convoys to

Russia, and thus precluded the use of these scarce and valuable ships in the Mediterranean, the Indian Ocean, or the Pacific.[4] Repeated attempts were therefore made to destroy the *Tirpitz* by bombs and one-man torpedoes, which failed. On September 21–22, 1943, damage by a British mini-submarine put the ship out of action until March 1944.[5] Hardly repaired, it was damaged again, this time by bombs, on April 3. After being out of service for three months and subjected to a long series of largely unsuccessful air attacks, the ship was finally destroyed in an air raid on November 12, 1944.[6] By that time the battles involving the German surface ships in Norway had affected the war at sea in other dramatic ways.

There was an inner contradiction between the use of the German surface ships against the Arctic convoys to the Soviet Union and their use against any Allied invasion of Norway which, as described in the preceding chapter, the Germans were very concerned about and was the reason for their being stationed in Norway in the first place. The same ships could not interfere with supply convoys — with the attendant risks of engagements and losses — and be available to help fight off any Allied landing attempt.

This confusion of roles contributed to a series of arguments and complications about the ships, several operations against convoys in which the German losses in destroyers off-set the sinkings of Allied ships, and two major British naval victories. The first was a botched German effort to destroy the convoys JW 51A and B at the end of December 1942, which was half beaten off by British escorts and half called off by German command confusion.[7] This defeat, clearly recognized as such by the Germans, led to the dismissal of the Commander-in-Chief of the German navy since 1928, Admiral Raeder, and his replacement by the commander of the submarines, Admiral Dönitz. Furthermore, Hitler simultaneously decided to decommission all the remaining big ships, using the crews for the submarines and small ships and their guns in coastal defense. He was eventually persuaded to reverse this order only by Dönitz himself.

The long-time advocate of concentration on submarines had come to recognize the utility of the big ships for defense against an invasion of Norway if it did come, the training of naval crews, renewed attacks on the convoys to Russia, and, perhaps most important, as a way of forcing the British to maintain major fleet units in home waters instead of presenting them with a gratuitous naval victory, a victory which would provide Britain with relief at home and the prospect of sending the fleet to take part in the war against Japan.[8] In practice, however, the German surface units were unable to do more than restrict the allocation of

British surface ships until in a second major defeat, that of Christmas 1943, the battleship *Scharnhorst* was sunk when sent out by Dönitz in what objective observers must call a useless suicide mission for the ship and the 1900 men who went down with her.[9]

The other main type of surface ship utilized by the Germans in the war against Allied shipping was the auxiliary cruiser. These fast converted merchant ships were designed to fool Allied and neutral ships by sailing alone, in disguise, with false flags and concealed guns, until the last moment when they revealed their true nationality and character. In the first years of the war, they enjoyed considerable success in the South Atlantic, Indian Ocean, and the Pacific, but during 1942 and 1943 they were caught one by one by the Allies. Admiral Raeder himself had been a major promoter of this project, which certainly inflicted substantial losses on the Allies and caused added dispersion of their escort vessels; but in October 1943 the last one was sunk by an American submarine.[10]

The Germans also had a substantial number of very fine E-Boats, as the Allies called them, small but fast torpedo boats utilized for scouting, for escorting German coastal shipping, and for attacks on Allied warships as well as merchant ships in the Channel, the North and Baltic Seas and the Mediterranean. During the course of the war they sank over 225,000 tons of ships. Their most spectacular feat was probably the sinking, on April 28, 1944, of two large LST's (Landing Ships for Tanks) during a major landing exercise, code-named "Tiger," on the south coast of England, in which over 700 American soldiers were killed, an event hushed up by the Allies at the time.[11] At the other extreme in size of warships, the Germans long tried to get their first aircraft carrier ready for use, but this project was eventually abandoned early in 1943.[12]

The German use of long-range airplanes, especially the FW-200, against Allied shipping has already been mentioned. Planes continued to play a role in attacks on shipping from bases in France, but the main contribution of the Luftwaffe was from Norwegian bases in the campaign against the Arctic convoys to Russia. Here, unlike elsewhere, Göring was prepared to devote substantial resources to the struggle for the sea lanes and occasionally with considerable effect. As the other demands on the air force grew, however, the units in Norway were not provided with adequate replacements, so that by 1944 the air attacks on the route to Murmansk became less and less significant. It had been in the Mediterranean that the air force had made its major contribution in 1941–42 to the war at sea; thereafter the pressures of the Eastern Front, the need to defend German-controlled Europe against air attacks, and efforts to strike directly at England again assumed priority.

Two other aspects of the war at sea must be mentioned before the

German submarine campaign is examined. By plane, by small surface ships, and by submarines the Germans, Italians, and Japanese laid mines which contributed a small addition to the losses caused with other means.[13] An additional major source of losses was that of "marine casualty," that is, ships that had worn out, that collided, that ran aground, capsized at sea, or were lost in other kinds of marine accidents. In part because of the constant use of available shipping, the need to move in all kinds of weather and on dangerous routes, less experienced shipyard workers and crews, and similar factors, such losses were quite substantial, usually exceeding those from aircraft, surface ships, and mines combined. The sailors drowned and the ships lost were as much casualties of war as those due to acts of combat—and they too were missing from the rosters of the Allies.

By far the greatest losses inflicted by the Axis and suffered by the Allies were the result of submarine action. The submarines of World War II were not at all the under-water ships of popular imagination. They were so slow when submerged—the most commonly employed German submarine (Type VIIC) could go at 7.5 knots and only for a limited time—that they could be outrun by most ships. Only by staying on the surface—where they could go at 17.7 knots—for a large part of the time was there any prospect of moving in time to designated areas and getting into position to attack. This was, until the last stages of the war, a characteristic shared in basic essentials by the submarines of all belligerents, and it meant that just forcing them to stay under the surface for long periods of time deprived them of most opportunities for attack.

The Germans had decided before the war that the most effective way to use their submarines would be to send them out in groups to try to locate Allied ships, which it was assumed would probably be in convoys, and to attack them at night while on the surface with the members of each group, referred to as wolf-packs by the Allies, summoned by whichever submarine first located the convoy. The German navy had practically no reconnaissance airplanes of its own, the air force refused to provide substantial numbers for the submarine war, and the submarines, unlike some Japanese ones, did not carry small float planes, that could be stowed inside and launched and recovered, to search for possible targets.[a] The only practical approach to the problem of finding Allied ships, therefore, appeared to be a skirmish line of submarines directed from headquarters on land to an area considered most promising, there

---

[a] The Germans did occasionally use a kite from which a lookout, flying some 300 feet in the air, could provide a greatly increased radius of view for the submarine pulling him as it cruised on the surface. See Patrick Beesly, *Very Special Intelligence* (New York: Ballantine, 1977), p. 198.

followed by a call from the first submarine to sight the enemy and a constant series of locator calls thereafter.

Two aspects of this tactic must be noted. It made it possible for Dönitz to utilize the latest intelligence available to him to direct his submarines out in the Atlantic by radio to the most profitable targets, to alter directives as necessary, and to send them to the next position as appropriate; but it also meant a stream of radio signals which could provide material for code-breakers. Whatever the Germans sent, others could hear, even if special devices were utilized to transmit the messages with extreme speed. A second danger was inherent in the wolf-pack's constant sending of location signals so that all could follow and attack the same convoy. The Germans assumed that Allied direction finders on land could locate the general area of the U-Boats, but they would know that from the moment of the initial attack on a convoy anyway. What the Germans did *not* understand was that the Allies were developing and placing on board ships direction finders that could locate the submarines by their radio transmissions from the escorts of the attacked convoy. This equipment, called "Huff-Duff" from the abbreviation HF/DF for High-Frequency Direction Finders, began to be placed on ships in the summer of 1942 and came to play a major role in the eventual victory of the Allies in the war against the submarines. The Germans never caught on to this device and ascribed all Allied ability to locate U-Boats running on the surface to their use of radar. While radar (especially the radar carried by planes) certainly played an important part in the campaign, the convoy escorts more frequently located submarines on the surface by the Huff-Duff device.[14]

When the submarines were submerged, they could not (except at periscope depth) send or receive radio messages and hence could not be located by either land or sea based radio direction finding. Already in World War I the Allies had developed a device, called asdic by the British and sonar by the Americans, which could hear submarine propellers and also send signals through the water bringing back echoes when they bounced off something, sounds and echoes which skilled interpreters could use to locate a submarine at least approximately.[15] Once located under water, the submarine might be damaged or sunk by the explosion of depth charges and later other explosives dropped and fired by the escorts. On the surface, a submarine could be attacked by the guns of warships and those mounted on most merchant ships, or it could be rammed, while airplanes dropped special bombs and could also use machine guns and cannon fire (using a special form of searchlight, called "Leigh" lights after their inventor, in the second half of the war). The submarine used torpedoes and, for smaller ships, often relied on its guns when on the surface. At the beginning of the war, the German torpedoes were defective, but this was largely remedied by 1941. The Americans also had defective torpedoes until well into 1942 and even 1943, but the Japanese had excellent torpedoes from the beginning of the war while the British and Italian ones were generally satisfactory.

Two political aspects of the submarine campaign also have to be reviewed. The Germans had to decide in World War II as in World War I whose ships they would sink and whose they would try to spare. Naturally they tried to avoid sinking those of their allies as well as their own, though occasionally mistakes were made. While hoping to postpone war with the United States until a big navy could be built, Hitler had also restrained the enthusiasm of the German navy for sinking American ships; but as soon as Japan attacked the United States, he ordered all ships of the United States, seven Central American countries and Uruguay to be sunk on sight.[16] Hoping to keep Argentina out of the war, the Germans did try to avoid sinking Argentine ships, and took some steps to smooth out any problems which arose when this did happen anyway.[17] This self-restraint did not, however, apply to others. After several Mexican ships were sunk, she entered the war in May, 1942. Assuming that what defense cooperation existed between the United States and Brazil amounted to effective Brazilian participation, Hitler ordered his submarines to stage systematic attacks on Brazilian ships and drew that country—the largest and most populous in Latin America—into the war on August 22, 1942.[18] This attack on Brazil did for her internal debates what Pearl Harbor had done for the arguments within the United States; a united country was now fully at war.

Another aspect of drawing countries into the war was that of using their territory for bases. For the Germans, the critical country in this regard was certainly Spain. German spies in Spanish towns near Gibraltar regularly observed and took pictures of Allied ships passing through the straits in and out of the Mediterranean.[19] Most useful was the repairing and refueling of German submarines by clandestine operations organized by the navy with the knowledge and support of the Franco regime.[20] These activities took place primarily in 1941 but continued at least until the fall of 1942 when Allied pressure obligated Franco to be more cautious and the Germans to restrict themselves to Spanish coastal waters for travel thereafter.[21]

The converse of German use of Spanish ports was the unsuccessful attempt of the Allies to secure bases in neutral Ireland and their eventual success in obtaining Portuguese agreement to their use of the Azores. After the failure of British attempts in 1940 to persuade the Irish Free State to exchange use of bases for steps leading to reunification (discussed in Chapter 3), the issue rested for a while. The Japanese attack on Pearl Harbor and the German and Italian declarations of war on the United States seemed to open the possibility for a reexamination of the issue. Consideration for Irish–American opinion had operated to restrain the British earlier; now it seemed reasonable to suppose that with the United States in the war and Irish–Americans fighting the Axis, the Irish government might change its policy. Churchill personally once again raised the issue, and the American government also urged Dublin to support the United Nations. But the de Valera government refused to alter its basic policy, though thereafter it was more accommodating in releasing Allied planes and crews which landed in the Free State.[22]

The hope of the Allies that they might be allowed to utilize bases in the Azores was related to one of the most difficult aspects of the struggle against the submarines. Airplanes were useful for patrolling but they were especially helpful in aiding convoys evade attack because the appearance of planes forced the submarines to submerge even if they did not damage or destroy them. The problem was that there were not enough very long-range planes available for this duty, and even those there were could not reach certain portions of the Central Atlantic. Airplanes based on the Azores would have solved this problem before the introduction of small escort carriers assigned to anti-submarine duty became available.[23]

The Portuguese, however, were very vulnerable to German threats of invasion and hence reluctant to take any action until it was obvious that Germany was not in any position to take effective retaliatory measures. In this case, as so often in World War II, the known reluctance of the Allies to deal violently with neutrals, by contrast with German enthusiasm for doing so, worked in Germany's favor. Finally, in August 1943, the Portuguese government thought it was safe to act in accordance with its alliance of 1373 with England and allow the Allies to use the Azores for air and naval forces from October 8, 1943. By that time, the tide in the Battle of the Atlantic as well as the war as a whole had turned clearly in favor of the Allies, but the latter certainly derived considerable if belated help from their new bases.[24]

One other important semi-neutral in the war over the oceans has been referred to repeatedly: Vichy France. Its warships were potentially still important but most remained in port in Toulon and Martinique.[25] Pétain and Darlan publicly declared on December 12, 1941, that these would not be used against the Allies, in order to obtain an American declaration of December 27 that France would keep its territory and place in the world.[26] In private talks with the Germans, however, both Darlan and Laval expressed themselves as vehemently anti-British and pro-German.

Darlan warned the Germans about excessive signalling by their submarines and generally showed himself eager to side with them in December 1941 and January 1942.[27] But as Hitler was absolutely unwilling to make even the slightest concession to the French, the approaches from Vichy did not lead to any basic changes in policy.[28] Laval continued to believe in a German victory in the war and in a Franco-German rapprochement,[a] but the only contribution he and Darlan could make to that objective was to promise to destroy the French cruiser and aircraft carrier in Martinique if the Americans tried to seize these ships for the Free French to use in the Battle of the Atlantic.[29] When the Allies landed in French Northwest Africa in November 1942, the French allowed the Germans to take over their warships in Tunisia;[30] but the attempt of the Germans to seize the French warships at Toulon failed as these sank themselves in the harbor.[b]

By the time the French were scuttling remnants of their navy in Toulon in November 1942, the Battle of the Atlantic was reaching its climax; in fact, that month saw the highest Allied losses of World War II: over 860,000 tons altogether, including over 720,000 sunk by submarines. The most important single measure used by the Allies to protect shipping was the convoy system. Originally developed to cope with the German submarine menace in World War I, it provided some protection to ships by enabling the Allies to allocate whatever escort forces were available to groups of ships scheduled to sail together, necessarily at the speed of the slower boats in each convoy. This had the disadvantage of slowing ships to one of the two speeds generally used, with the slow convoys going at six knots and the fast ones at nine knots, but greatly reduced the loss of ships. Detailed analysis showed that larger convoys lost proportionately fewer ships; and while in 1942 the slow convoys averaged forty-four and the fast twenty-five ships, in 1943 the slow ones averaged fifty and the fast fifty-two ships. By 1944, an intermediate speed had been added and convoys often included eighty to one hundred ships.[31] On the less threatened routes, some ships continued to sail alone, while the very fast liners like the *Queen Mary* and *Queen Elizabeth*

---

[a] The OSS was reading the correspondence between Vichy and its embassy in Washington. On April 30, 1942, it provided President Roosevelt with Laval's report to Ambassador Henry-Haye on his talk with U.S. Ambassador Leahy of 27 April 1942 (*FRUS* 1942, 2: 181–2). The text, handed to Roosevelt in French, includes the following: "My policy is based on a reconciliation with Germany without which I cannot visualize any possibility of peace, neither for Europe nor for France nor for the world. I am certain that Germany will be victorious." FDRL, PSF Box 166, OSS Donovan Reports, # 10.

[b] In July 1943 the chief in Martinique, Admiral Robert, was ordered by Vichy to scuttle the remaining war and merchant ships there, but the crews mutinied and went over to de Gaulle. For German interception of the relevant orders and reports, see OKM, Chef MND III, xB Bericht Nr. 29/43, 21 July 1943, pp. 14–15, NA, RG 457, SRS 548, Vol. 16.

carried their thousands of troops at a speed that made escort impossible and submarine attacks unlikely.[32]

Within range of Allied air bases in Newfoundland, Iceland, Northern Ireland, England, Gibraltar and the Gambia, airplanes could provide additional protection to the convoys; but, as already mentioned, there was a 600-mile wide gap south of Greenland where air support was at first impossible.[33] There was much debate in the British government, especially in 1942, about the allocation of planes to convoy duty since it competed for the larger models with the desire of Bomber Command to utilize all such planes for the bombing offensive against Germany.[34] This issue spilled out into public view occasionally, was a major point of criticism of Churchill's direction of the war at the time, and remains a contentious issue among students of the war.[35] The problem was solved in stages beginning in late 1942 and during 1943. There was the increased assignment of very long range American Liberator B-24s which were in more and more cases equipped with the British-developed Leigh lights that could be used to illuminate U-Boats running on the surface at night. Even more helpful eventually was the building and employment of escort carriers, ships capable of carrying a small but substantial complement of airplanes, which began to be built in 1942 and entered service in the Battle of the Atlantic in 1943.

These small carriers were closing the Central Atlantic gap in air coverage even before the establishment of bases on the Azores and played a critical role in the defeat of the U-Boats in 1943. Barrage balloons occasionally helped keep German planes from low-level and more accurate attacks on shipping, and blimps, small helium-filled airships used for patrol purposes off the coast of North America, provided some assistance; but the main burden of defending the convoys against attack always fell on the escort ships and their crews in endless duty on rough and dangerous seas. For the sailors as for the soldiers, war was a combination in which 99 percent boredom and anxiety alternated with 1 percent terror and exhilaration. But at sea, the likelihood of rescue and survival was generally lower than on land, a truth as ominous for the merchant sailors as for naval personnel.[36]

The northern Atlantic was for most of the war the main battlefield. Early and late in the war the coastal waters around Britain were the site of great activity, and in the first half of 1942 first the coast of North America and then the Caribbean were centers of attention, while periodically some German submarines operated in the South Atlantic, off the Cape of Good Hope and in the Indian Ocean as well as in the Mediterranean; but for the majority of the time most of the action was on the

North Atlantic convoy run. There are several reasons for this. The need to keep Britain supplied and to build up forces and supplies there for any invasion of Europe meant that there was no way for the Allies to abandon that route without losing the war. They could reroute the convoys as far north or south as weather, intelligence, and other factors might indicate, but they had to keep this route open. For the Germans, this area offered both the largest number of targets for their submarines and an approach route substantially shorter than that to any other area, a matter of great importance both as regards fuel consumption by the submarines on the way out and back as well as the length of time taken out of the total operational period for each mission by these two journeys. It was accordingly in this area that both sides concentrated most of their strength. In the early years of the war, both operated with small numbers of ships; in 1942 and 1943 both escorts and submarines became more numerous, until over a hundred submarines confronted literally hundreds of British and American escort ships, with Canada also playing a steadily increasing role.[37]

The most important element in the struggle was always the skill and endurance of the crews on the ships engaged, but intelligence probably played a larger role over a greater period of time in this struggle than elsewhere in the war. If Allied intelligence could discover the present and intended location of submarines, the convoys could be routed around them, and any convoy that was *not* attacked at all represented a small but significant victory: the ships and their crews and cargo survived intact while the by-passed submarines had wasted several of their limited number of days at sea without accomplishing anything.[38] Conversely, if German intelligence could locate a convoy and its assigned route, submarines could be strung out on a patrol line across that route to attack that convoy once the first sighting of the ships had been made.

If air intelligence and its photographic element was potentially useful for the Germans but rarely available, it was increasingly important for the Allies in observing the building of new submarines, their completion, and their trials in the Baltic Sea.[39] As already mentioned, the use by the Allies of locator intelligence, especially Huff-Duff, was of central importance. At times traffic analysis, that is the careful examination of the patterns and frequency of radio traffic (even if it could not be read) provided major clues, for example to the sending out of new groups of submarines or their being given new orders. The most important clues for intelligence, outside of the use of Huff-Duff during convoy battles, was the actual reading of the other side's coded messages. This process was facilitated by the way both sides conducted the major aspects of the battle: from land by radio messages to the convoys and to the submarines. By definition, such direction and redirection from land had the enormous advantage of enabling those in charge to base decisions on the latest information and to act on it swiftly in issuing new directives, while simultaneously providing the other side with enormous quantities of radio traffic for the code-breakers to work on. These issues are discussed in additional detail in Chapter 10, but their relevance to the war at sea calls for comment here. The fact that the Germans were able to break into the British convoy codes and utilize information gleaned in that way to direct their submarines was of enormous help to them in 1941 and 1942 and contributed greatly to their ability to employ submarines effectively. It also reduced the value to the Allies of their breaking into the German codes, to be discussed shortly, because repeatedly the new British orders redirecting the convoys were in turn read by the Germans who then issued new orders to their submarines. It was only when the British eventually broke the new German submarine code in December 1942 that they recognized the vulnerability of their own system and, in June 1943, introduced a new machine code which the Germans apparently never broke.[40]

The ability of the British, developing their code-breaking program on the basis of materials furnished by the Poles, to read at least some of the German enigma code system, enabled them to reroute much of the convoy traffic in 1941 in a manner that greatly reduced sinkings. Combined with increasing American assistance in the North Atlantic and the diversion of German submarines into the Mediterranean, this seemed to give the Allies a distinct edge, especially in the fall of 1941.[41] The balance, however, swung in favor of the Germans early in 1942 from a combination of two factors; the declaration of war on the United States opened American shipping and the American and Caribbean coasts to U-Boat attack, and a new development in the German code system.

The lifting of all restraints on the German submarine campaign in the Western Hemisphere and against American ships—for which the German navy had been pleading for over two years—inaugurated a period of several months in which German submarines sank Allied shipping off the coast of the United States in record numbers. On the one side were experienced U-Boat crews; on the other was a merchant marine not yet in convoy, very poorly protected by the navy, and at night visible to the submarines by the glowing lights of the American coastal area which had not been blacked out. It was fortunate for the Allies that the number of German submarines employed in their operation "Paukenschlag" (Roll of the Drums) was quite small; about a dozen were on station off the North American coast for most of the months from January to May 1942 because of the assignments to other areas, especially the Mediterranean and off the coast of Norway.

In short order, these few submarines, operating independently, sank ships left and right, quite literally in sight of the American coast, as the American navy took an unbelievably long time to wake up to the danger and take appropriate steps. Admiral King for weeks refused to adopt the most obvious lessons which the British had learned at high cost earlier in the war. He had to be prodded by President Roosevelt, General Marshall, Winston Churchill, and an aroused American public. Not until April was a partial convoy system initiated, and over the following months the extension of that system, increased sea and air patrol activity, and the dimming out of the coast pushed the submarines first into the Caribbean—where they sank many of the precious oil tankers—and by July back into the Central Atlantic.[42] By the end of August, the submarines had sunk some 485 ships, a total of almost 2,600,000 tons, off the coast of North and Central America in what must be regarded as the most disastrous defeat ever suffered by American naval power.[43]

The other critical element in the great increase in U-Boat successes during 1942 was the introduction by the Germans of a version of the enigma code machine for submarines, effective from February 1, 1942, which added a fourth wheel to that machine and was not broken into by the Allies until mid-December 1942. For most of the year the British struggled unsuccessfully with the new submarine code, called Triton by the Germans and Shark by the British. This not only kept the British from following the directives to and reports from the U-Boats as had often been possible earlier, but it also concealed from them until the end of 1942 that in the same month as they introduced the new fourth wheel, the Germans also completed their reconstruction of the British Naval Cypher 3, the main code used for and by the Allied convoys in the Atlantic. The result was a steady level of very high sinkings during 1942, culminating in November with losses of 721,700 tons, the worst month of World War II.[44]

Unlike the Poles, who had shared their knowledge of the enigma machine code system with the British in 1939, and the Americans, who had provided them with a machine for reading the Japanese diplomatic "purple" code in January 1941,[45] the British most unwisely did not share their work on German codes with the Americans until months after the United States had been drawn into the war.[46] Given the technological resources of the United States, this contribution to the shipping disaster of 1942 may well have matched that of the tardiness of the American navy in the first half of the year. In the event, it was the capture of important cryptographic material taken from a U-Boat sunk in the Eastern Mediterranean on October 30, 1942, that made it possible to begin breaking the new submarine code machine on December 13, 1942.[47]

In the meantime, the struggle had shifted back to the central North Atlantic with both sides making more efficient use of their respective ships. The Germans had begun in 1941 with the modification of submarines to serve as refuelers for others, and the first of these so-called milch cows, or tanker U-Boats, became available in April 1942. From that time on, these ships played an important role in the Battle of the Atlantic by enabling German submarines, once they had arrived in the central North Atlantic, to extend their stay substantially by refueling at rendezvous with the tankers and sometimes taking aboard additional torpedoes as well.[48] Conversely, after months of debate and preparations, the convoys in June 1942 began to include tankers which refuelled the escort ships, thereby greatly facilitating effective use of these vessels, always in short supply.[49]

In the summer of 1942, the situation in the central North Atlantic was becoming more difficult for the Allies because the number of German submarines at sea was steadily increasing from 22 in January and 16 in May to 86 at the beginning of August and over 100 by October.[50] Dönitz enjoyed the full support of Hitler, who considered the U-Boat war as second in importance only to the new offensive Germany was about to begin on the Eastern Front.[51] It was to assist the Russians that the Allies ran convoys to the north Russian ports of Murmansk and Archangel; and the German navy and air force, on the other hand, fought hard to keep the weapons and supplies from reaching the Soviet Union by the route the latter preferred because it brought them closest to the front.

It was in this connection that the attack on convoy PQ 17, which left for the Soviet Union on June 27, 1942, and was largely destroyed in the following ten days, combined a great victory for the Germans and defeat for the Allies with a major strain on the alliance of the Western Powers with the Soviet Union. The order of Sir Dudley Pound, the First Sea Lord, to the escorts to withdraw and the convoy to scatter was given, against the advice of his intelligence experts, in the mistaken belief that the *Tirpitz* might have sailed to intercept the convoy. In the ensuing slaughter by planes and submarines, 26 out of the 39 ships in the convoy were lost, taking thousands of vehicles and hundreds of tanks and planes—to say nothing of most of the crews—with them; and, as a result, the British government decided that such convoys ought to be suspended until the winter because the demands of "Torch," the planned invasion of Northwest Africa, had to have priority.[52] This caused a major rift in the Alliance as the Soviet government clamored for aid in its time of great peril in the face of the German summer offensive, but the shipping and escorts were simply not available. The other side of this coin, however, was that Torch, once successfully launched, forced the Germans to divert torpedo bombers from northern Norway to the Mediterranean. In the meantime, in September 1942, there had already been resumption of convoys to Russia, now for the first time accompanied by an escort carrier.[53] PQ 18 saw the ratio of loss reversed, with 27 out of 40 arriving safely; and thereafter, following the two months' interruption in convoys to Russia necessitated by Torch, the situation steadily improved.[54] Nevertheless, the shock of what had happened to PQ 17 remained as a warning of what could easily go wrong and what the implications of such set-backs could be.

The fact that Torch coincided with the month of the heaviest Allied shipping losses can be seen as an illustration of how the shipping problem dominated Allied strategy. One of the major reasons for launching this operation in the first place had been the hope of opening the Mediterranean to ships so that the long and wasteful route around the Cape of Good Hope would not be necessary. We have already seen how the demands of Torch forced an interruption in convoys to Russia in July and August and again in September and October. Furthermore, the shortage of shipping imposed restrictions on the scope of Torch that would, as will be discussed in Chapter 8, make it impossible for the Allies to seize Tunisia in the initial stages of that operation. This made it possible for the Germans to hold on in North Africa until May 1943 and hence make an invasion of Northwest Europe impossible before 1944. With shipping losses continuing to exceed new construction, it should come as no surprise that at the January 1943 conference of the Americans and British at Casablanca, top priority should be assigned to the battle against the U-Boats. If this menace could not be conquered, the steady diminution of Allied tonnage would immobilize the Western Allies; even if Britain could be kept supplied, there was nothing a huge American army could do to help defeat Germany if it could not be brought to Europe and supplied there.

At the Casablanca Conference there was a great deal of discussion and disagreement on many issues, but on one there was immediate and general agreement within the American and British delegations and between them.[55] The war at sea had to have the highest priority. "Defeat of U-Boat remains a first charge on the resources of the United Nations" was the opening of the agreed memorandum on the decisions reached at Casablanca.[56] Two decisions were taken to implement this assertion of priority, one affecting the air forces, and one pertaining to the situation at sea.

The decision about the air forces of Britain and the United States was to assign the German submarine construction yards the highest priority as targets for the combined bomber offensive, followed by the aircraft industry, transportation, oil plants and other war industry in that order.[57] The bombing of submarine pens built by the Germans on the French Atlantic coast and of U-Boat building yards in Germany which followed proved to be an expensive failure; expensive in that in January to May 1943 266 airplanes were lost in almost 7000 sorties; a failure in that no bomb ever penetrated one of the U-Boat pens and no appreciable damage was inflicted on the construction yards.[58] Not until 1944–45 could the Allied bombing offensive have an important impact on German submarine construction; in the most critical years of the war, the issue was left to the naval portion of the Allied forces.

The decisions about sea operations concerned the need for continued and accelerated construction of escort vessels, though with the recognition that the "minimum acceptable requirements of escort craft will not be met until about August or September 1943. We ought not to count on the destruction of U-Boats at a rate in excess of the production rate before the end of the year."[59] Since simultaneously the Germans were increasing their construction and commissioning of submarines, the stage was clearly set for the series of great battles which characterized the following months.[60]

In January and February 1943 the convoys were often successfully routed around the lines of waiting submarines; but delays in reading the German warship code settings for the day, German reading of the British convoy code, and the very number of submarines which often led a convoy safely directed around one line of submarines into the search area of another, brought on a number of the most desperate battles in March. In these engagements many Allied ships were sunk, but the convoy escorts were fighting back hard and often successfully. In the next two months, the slugging match turned slowly but effectively in favor of the Allies. Even when the convoy could not be alerted in time, Allied knowledge of which convoys were in danger and which not enabled them to concentrate escort ships and special task forces of escorts organized into "support groups," also called "hunter-killer groups," now including escort carriers, at the danger spots.

The placement of Huff-Duff on all escorts, the increased number of escort vessels, the larger number of very long range planes, and the addition of a "Tracking Room" in Canada to follow and control operations, all helped the embattled convoys. Time and again the U-Boats were driven off with the balance of losses shifting steadily against them: in May the Allies were sinking them at the rate of one per day out of the over 120 out in the Atlantic. Some of the U-Boat aces, who had run up big scores in early 1942, went down at the same time as more and more of the newly commissioned submarines were sunk on their first combat patrol.[61] Signs of reluctance were beginning to be evident in the tactics of some of the submarine commanders, and all the exhortations and complaints of Admiral Dönitz, directing the battles personally and on an hourly basis from headquarters in France, could not reverse the tide which was turning decisively against his ships with a rapidity for which, because of earlier exaggerated claims, he was not prepared. On May 24, 1943, Dönitz acknowledged that the battle had been lost for now, ordered his submarines to move to less dangerous waters further south and looked for new weapons and tactics to return to the northern convoy routes in the future.[62]

Knowing that control of the seas was essential and that the Germans would certainly try again, the Allies did not relax;[63] on the contrary, having earlier determined from their own reading of German signals that their convoy code had been broken, they switched to a new system which helped protect them thereafter.[64] The Germans, on the other hand, answered their own repeated queries about the security of *their* codes in the negative and remained confident that no one could penetrate their machine codes, holding to this view not only during World War II but for decades thereafter.[65] They believed that Allied radar was primarily responsible for the disastrous losses they had suffered and recognized neither the vulnerability of their codes nor the possibility that the escort ships could locate attacking submarines from their radio messages to other wolf-pack ships.

There was still another element in the changing balance of war at sea. The construction of new ship tonnage had exceeded submarine sinkings for the first time in February 1943, the month after the Casablanca Conference. By September or October it was exceeding the losses due to all causes.[66] Thereafter the construction curve continued to rise dramatically even as losses levelled off. Contrary to German expectations, the United States not only built enormous numbers of ships of standardized design more and more quickly; it could man and arm them.[67] By the end of the war, 4900 ships totalling 51.4 million tons had been built for the Maritime Commission;[68] additional ships were built privately. Simultaneously, the continued commissioning of escort vessels and escort carriers made it possible to protect these increasing numbers of merchant ships and to hunt submarines. Opening the Mediterranean in 1943, furthermore, finally enabled the Allies to utilize shipping more effectively. At last it looked as if the shackling of Allied strategy by the shortage of shipping might be ending. But the Germans and their Axis partners did not give up that easily.

From the perspective of the Germans, the war against Allied shipping remained central. They had long stressed this point to the Italians and Japanese.[69] The Italians had deployed a substantial number of submarines into the Atlantic, and during 1942 and the first months of 1943 had sunk over 350,000 tons of Allied shipping there.[70] The collapse of Italian military power with the surrender of Axis forces in Tunisia, however, completely altered this portion of the war at sea. Thereafter the role of the Italian submarines would be increasingly in their use as blockade-breakers by the Germans, an aspect included in the discussion of that topic below. As for the surface ships of the Italian navy, the Germans and even more the Japanese were most anxious that these should not fall into Allied hands as they anticipated Italy's surrender, a surrender which took place in September 1943. In the converse of British anxiety over the French fleet in 1940, the Japanese now hoped that the Germans could capture or sink the Italian fleet. The Germans' hopes and plans for seizing the Italian navy succeeded in part and failed in part; they sank the battleship *Roma* and captured or destroyed more ships than Italy had lost to the Allies in the three preceding years of war, but many of the warships slipped out of the Italian ports. Whether they were used again or not, their absence from the Axis side reduced the pressure on the British navy.[71]

The Japanese submarine fleet had been developed originally as an auxiliary to her surface fleet in the strictest sense, that is, as a means of aiding the fleet in combat against the navies of her enemies, particularly the United States. Before Yamamoto forced Imperial Naval Headquarters to adopt his Pearl Harbor plan in the fall of 1941, the Japanese intended to use their submarines for harrying the American navy, reducing its size by torpedo attacks as it moved across the Pacific, leaving it smaller and damaged enough to be overwhelmed by the Imperial fleet. When this operational plan was scrapped in favor of Yamamoto's concept, there was no reorientation of the submarines' employment doctrine, a reorientation for which there was little time and which was in any case rendered unlikely by the surface fleet orientation of those in the highest command positions of the submarine branch.[72]

The Japanese submarines continued to be used primarily to assist the surface fleet, especially in the long naval campaign in the Solomon

Islands. They had actually been quite successful against shipping in the Indian Ocean in April, 1942, but this was seen as an aberration in the employment of submarines. The Germans repeatedly tried to explain to their ally that the best hope for the Axis was to paralyze their enemies by attacks on shipping, attacks in which the possible increment provided by Japan could be of great significance. To assist them in their project, the Germans offered to provide some of their own submarines as models and eventually gave them two early in 1943. Of these one made it to Japan.[73] But, though some German ideas were copied in Japan, in part because of engineers sent from Germany,[74] the Japanese never were able to act on their newly grasped understanding of the importance of the campaign against Allied merchant ships because of developments in the Pacific War which they had not anticipated.

The combination of American attacks, primarily by submarines, on Japanese shipping with General MacArthur's strategy of by-passing Japanese garrisons in the Southwest Pacific, increasingly forced the Japanese navy into an entirely new pattern of submarine employment. If the Japanese garrisons isolated by American and Australian advances were to remain even minimally effective militarily, they had to be supplied with certain essential items: ammunition, spare parts, and medical supplies. Submarine supply was becoming the only way to deliver these items, and submarine commanders who had once disdained as unheroic a campaign against merchant shipping found themselves engaged in the equally hazardous but even less heroic business of carrying sacks of rice and crates of ammunition to the remnants of Japan's outer garrisons. Simultaneously, the emphasis in the submarine construction program, far from following in the footsteps of German models, was shifted increasingly toward the building of larger supply submarines which would deliver a larger volume of cargo to the isolated units in the Southwest Pacific.[75]

The Japanese were certainly very alarmed by the turn in the Battle of the Atlantic in May 1943, learning about it very quickly from the dramatic change in German announcements of the tonnage sunk by the U-Boats.[76] The Germans explained the role of airborne radar and escort carriers as the main causes of their set-back and informed the Japanese of their plans for new technologies to revive the effectiveness of the U-Boats, thereby unknowingly tipping off the Allies who were reading the Japanese reports.[77] One of the other ways for the Germans to cope with the defeat in the North Atlantic, however, was to shift the submarine campaign into less dangerous areas in which to operate, and in this regard cooperation between Germany and Japan was of special importance.

Since the Japanese did not have submarines to spare for a major campaign against shipping, they provided bases for a small fleet of German submarines sent to Malaya to operate from bases there, primarily at the important port of Penang, against the Allied supply routes across the Indian Ocean. It is no coincidence that the program began in the summer of 1943 with operation "Monsoon," the dispatch of eleven submarines and one supply submarine to Malaya. Five of the submarines actually arrived and others followed. Using the bases provided by the Japanese, these German submarines did have some successes, and more were sent thereafter; but their number was not large enough to make a major contribution in the tonnage war.[78] Their last significant successes in early 1944 were restricted by Allied use of information from broken German enigma codes to destroy their supply ships.[79] In May 1945, the remaining four German and two Italian submarines were taken over by the Japanese when the German naval attaché in Tokyo ordered the local German commander, who wanted to go on fighting, to surrender.[80]

The Allied landing in France in June 1944 led to the capture by the French Maquis and their turning over to the Allies the captain and the May 1943 to June 1944 log of U-188, one of the submarines which had been based in Penang; and this material provided the Allies at the time—as it does historians later—with considerable insight into the situation at that base and in the Indian Ocean.[81] The immediately more obvious result of the invasion was the loss by the Germans of submarine bases on the French Atlantic coast, and their inability to use those which they continued to hold but with hopelessly isolated garrisons. This led the Japanese beginning in September 1944, to urge the Germans to send additional submarines to East Asia; they did send some, but not nearly as many as the Japanese would have liked. Even reference to the sinking of the *Tirpitz* and the resulting release of British warships from European to East Asian waters did not convince Dönitz, who preferred to keep most of his submarines based in Norway and Germany.[82]

In April and May of 1945, as Germany was collapsing, and while Dönitz still hoped for a turn of the tide to be brought about by his new submarine models, the Japanese made a final effort to have the Germans transfer to East Asia large numbers of their submarines. At this time over 350 were in service, and the Japanese appear to have believed that their use in the Pacific War could make a substantial difference there. In spite of repeated and evidently agitated meetings with Dönitz, von Ribbentrop, Keitel and others when he could not get to see Hitler, the head of the Japanese military delegation in Berlin, Vice Admiral Abe Katsuo, was unable to budge the Germans. They explained to their anxious ally that there was not enough oil to send so many on the long journey; only the two or three already scheduled to go would be sent; but when they had recaptured the oil fields near Vienna they would reconsider![83]

The German reaction to their defeat of May 1943 relied on their allies only to a small extent. Other than shifting submarines to less threatened even if less remunerative operational areas, they depended on technical and tactical innovations. For some time the German leadership had considered alternative types of submarines. The most important problems as they saw them were the problems of underwater speed, above surface defense against airplanes, and means for coping with the escorts. In a major conference at Hitler's headquarters on September 28, 1942, the leaders of the navy, then Raeder, Dönitz and Admiral Fuchs, the man in charge of naval construction, had reviewed the U-Boat war. The discussion included the immense advantages of a new type of U-Boat, called the Walter boat after its inventor, which was propelled under water at 20 knots or faster (almost three times the speed of the current U-Boats and faster than most escorts). It was decided to start building a small version of this new type.[84] Dönitz, however, was at this time still confident that his old dependable types could do the job, especially as their numbers were now increasing to the levels he had long demanded.[a] The defeat in May, on which Dönitz, by now Commander-in-Chief of the navy as well as commander of the U-Boats, had to report to Hitler on June 5, led to new decisions.[85]

Dönitz placed much of the blame for the defeat on the lack of air support for the U-Boats, possibly a partially correct explanation, but a deficit which at a time when the demands of the Eastern and Mediterranean fronts and home defense against air raids were steadily increasing was not likely to be remedied.[86] The successes of the Allies were blamed on the radar carried by their airplanes. This was certainly in part correct. The very productive British series of air attacks on U-Boats passing in and out on their way to or from their operational areas across the Bay of Biscay in June and July 1943 reinforced this impression and diverted attention from the Allied successes in code-breaking and the use of Huff-Duff.[87] If this transit had to be made submerged, an intolerable amount of time would be taken up in an unproductive manner. The alternative was to provide the submarines with more anti-aircraft guns

---

[a] Note the memorandum by Admiral Walter Gladisch on a trip to occupied France in October 1942 which reflects his talk with Dönitz on October 15, 1942. It is clear that Dönitz at that time was in no way concerned about the possibility that the Allies might close the air gap in the Atlantic with long-range planes or escort carriers and that he had no comprehension of the possibilities open to the United States. ("Informationsreise Frankreich Oktober 1942," BA/MA, PG 71838.)

so they could fight it out with the planes; this was done but did not solve the problem. What appeared to be needed were new devices to detect and give warning of Allied radar fixes, new torpedoes to cope with the escorts, and, above all, new types of submarines.

The new radar detection devices were never developed; in this field the Germans remained behind the Allies. New acoustic torpedoes which followed the sound of an attacked ship, altering course when necessary, were already under development and began to be used in the fall of 1943. With these, especially the more effective of the two, the "Zaunkönig", called "Gnat" by the British, the U-Boats did attain some successes; but the Allies developed counter-measures rather quickly, and the submariners were often misled as to the effectiveness of this device.[88] The Germans also introduced radio-guided glider bombs, first used, ironically, against the escaping Italian navy in September 1943, and an airborne guided rocket missile; these were highly effective but available only in limited quantities.[89] The main emphasis, as Dönitz explained to the higher commanders of the U-Boat war on June 8, 1943, was on the new types of submarines; the rest of 1943 would be bad, but in 1944, 1945, 1946, and 1947 the situation would become steadily better.[90]

The Germans decided that it would take too long to develop and bring into service the original Walter boat and instead ordered a modified electro-boat version in two sizes, a small one for the Mediterranean, Black Sea, and Baltic (Type XXIII), and a big one for the oceans (Type XXI). Approved by Hitler on July 12, the new construction program called for 140 of the small and 238 of the big boats. In a desperate race against time, the German construction yards, building the new types in sections for later assembly, struggled to get these ships built, beginning in December 1943, even as the Allied bombers attacked the yards and supplies. It was a race which will be examined again in Chapter 14; suffice it to say here that the Allies won. Of Type XXIII, 61 were built, but only five were ready by the end of the war; while of the oceanic Type XXI, 120 were built but only one started on an operational cruise on April 30, 1945.[91]

Like the whole U-Boat program, the effort to construct hundreds of the new submarines dug deeply into the available supply of high-grade steel, desperately needed for making tanks and other weapons. In this regard, the turn in the war in the Atlantic, by leading the Germans to an enormous investment of material and workers into a naval program that never paid off did have an effect on the land battles in Europe in 1944 and 1945. Literally thousands of tanks were not built by the Germans because of their massive allocation of scarce resources to the program for a new form of submarine warfare.[92]

In the meantime, the Allies had to cope with the old types of submarines, of which 250 were under construction in July 1943 when the shift to new types began but the old ones were still being completed.[93] The Allies knew about the German plans for new types as a result of their ability to read the detailed reports on them which the Japanese naval attaché in Berlin sent back to Tokyo. They had every reason to be concerned but would rely on the Japanese to keep them unintentionally informed both of progress and, in their eyes even more encouraging, the delays imposed primarily by bombing on the German program.[94] A major way of striking at the existing type of submarines had been the attacks on them as they crossed the Bay of Biscay. If this was primarily a British operation, the Americans concentrated on exploiting the breaking of German submarine codes to catch the supply submarines when they were on the surface refueling other submarines. Using various techniques to obscure the fact that signal intelligence was the real basis of the strikes, the Americans launched a very successful series of such attacks in the same months of June and July 1943.[95]

With these and other measures, the Germans were held in check, their new torpedoes and anti-aircraft guns warded off, and the tonnage war won by the Allies. Only the underwater breathing apparatus developed by the Germans, called snorkel, and fitted to many of the older submarine models, gave the Germans some relief and the Allies some additional losses and worries,[96] but in the meantime their own construction of merchant ships and escort vessels continued in high gear. The new German offensive of September 1943 to May 1944 was a failure: for sinkings of 411,000 tons in seven months, they lost 119 U-Boats.[97] The submarines fought on, disappointed in the obvious inadequacy of their new weapons, but grimly continuing in fatalism and fear.[98]

It must not be thought, however, that the Allies simply relied on the techniques of anti-submarine warfare that gave them victory in May 1943. Pressed by the desperate shortage of shipping, they too experimented with new devices, some of them on the outlandish side. There had been an early American scheme to construct concrete barges and another to build huge numbers of shallow-draft "sea otters" powered by banks of standard gasoline engines.[99] Beginning in December 1942, the British worked on a device long favored by Churchill called the Habakkuk, a flat-surfaced artificial iceberg, propelled by banks of outboard motors, and designed to serve as floating airfields to close the air gap in the Atlantic, and later to provide air cover for invading Allied expeditionary forces. The inability of the British to provide the necessary resources and the objections of the American navy kept this project from getting very far beyond the drawing boards where it remained after the escort carriers came to be available.[100] Whatever the attraction of the Habakkuk concept, the reality of escort carriers used for escorting convoys, ferrying airplanes and providing air support for actual invasions was too clearly superior.[101]

One of the most engaging of the Allied projects has left its mark on the California tourist industry. The obvious counter to a submarine that could make sustained high speed under water was a cargo plane that touched the surface of the ocean only in port, carrying its cargo through the air and beyond the reach of torpedoes, conventional or acoustic. This was the concept of the huge flying boat, constructed of light wood, powered by multiple engines and capable of either carrying very substantial cargo or ferrying large numbers of soldiers safely across the ocean. The contract for such a plane was issued to the Hughes Aircraft Company and, when the project was first reduced and then dropped, Howard Hughes completed one and flew it. The "Spruce Goose," the largest airplane ever built, was moved in 1992–3 from California to Oregon, a monument to a campaign never fought between submarines designed always to remain below the surface and cargo ships designed always to remain above it. [102]

Two other aspects affecting the war at sea generally must be noted. The participation of Canada has been remarked on repeatedly. The active Canadian role was a product of several factors. The deep involvement of Canada in the war by 1942 and the obvious danger of the submarine campaign—evidenced by numerous sinkings in the St. Lawrence and off the Canadian coast—were the central elements. But there were important contributing factors. President Roosevelt, who always followed the war at sea with special attention, had a greater personal interest in Canada than any American President before (or since).[103] While Churchill was on the contrary extraordinarily insensitive to Canadian susceptibilities, his government recognized the large portion of the Battle of the Atlantic necessarily carried by the Canadians. In this field, Canada really came into its own.

In another area, however, there was no effective participation. While, under the influence of the National Maritime Union, the American merchant marine operated without a color barrier and came to include a very large number of Blacks among the ship crews essential to the war effort, the United States navy was hopelessly unmoving.[104] Even President Roosevelt, the Commander-in-Chief, found that he could hardly budge the navy's insistence that Blacks were to be used only for mess duty.[105] In this regard the ancient prejudices continued to assert themselves unchecked.

THE MEDITERRANEAN

The war on the oceans was, of course, in many ways a unified whole, but some theaters and aspects of it, in addition to the central conflict to control the oceanic supply routes, must be examined at least briefly. Reference has repeatedly been made to the significance of the war in the Mediterranean for both sides. The Axis powers had to supply their forces in North Africa while the Allies hoped to control the Mediterranean to protect their position in the Middle East. The fulcrum, as both sides recognized, was the island of Malta; and the long German–Italian siege of the island, as well as their project of seizing it, grew out of this. The other side of this equation was the need for the British to reinforce the island, and during all of 1942 the battle over such reinforcement raged across the Mediterranean and over the island. Convoys battled their way there from Gibraltar and Alexandria, frequently engaged by the Italian navy, German airplanes and submarines, and often losing many of the ships. Airplanes to defend the island had to be flown in off aircraft carriers approaching close enough for fighter planes to reach it, a task for which the old British carrier *Eagle* was repeatedly used. This was so important a task that the American carrier *Wasp* was, at Churchill's request, twice also used for such missions.[106] The daring of the British navy, the determination of the garrison and inhabitants of Malta, and the miscalculation of the Germans in relying on their air force to contain the island made it possible for the British to hold it through its most difficult days.[107] Thereafter, Malta became an offensive base for the Allies and helped them control the Mediterranean.

An aspect of that control was, of course, the struggle against the Italian navy. While in the end the Allies were victorious in this when much of the Italian fleet surrendered to them in September 1943, it is too often overlooked that the Italians had fought under grave handicaps. The British had broken into some of their codes; and the Germans had foolishly insisted on their ally replacing some of its old-fashioned code systems—which the British could not read—with their own modern and more elegant machine codes—which the British were reading with some regularity![108] The major handicap of the Italian navy, however, was its desperate shortage of fuel oil. With the country itself almost completely dependent on oil imports, inadequate supplies from Romania, followed by the failure of the German 1942 offensive to seize the Soviet oil fields in the Caucasus, meant that only the most limited missions could be run. The fuel shortage dominated Italian naval strategy in 1942–43 and in the end made it impossible for the big ships even to try to interfere with the invasion of Sicily in July 1943.[109]

The one time that massive quantities of fuel were allocated to the Mediterranean theater by the Germans was in the winter of 1942–43, when by ship and plane German and Italian troops and supplies were rushed to Tunisia. This initially successful project certainly had major effects on the course of the war which will be examined in the next chapter. On the one hand it prolonged the North African campaign by four months and hence made an invasion of Western Europe in 1943 impossible; on the other hand it meant that the Axis lost several hundred thousand additional soldiers when the surrender there—the biggest one up to that time in the war—finally came in May of 1943. Practically none of the troops sent out were evacuated, and considerable numbers of Axis ships had been sunk as they attempted to keep the German and Italian units fighting in Tunisia supplied.

THE PACIFIC

The German attempt to defeat Britain and paralyze the United States by sinking as much Allied tonnage as possible had its counterpart in the efforts of Britain and the United States to blockade the Axis powers and to throttle Japan by the destruction of *her* merchant shipping.

The Japanese never took anti-submarine warfare as seriously as the Allies, a fact which served to increase their vulnerability, which was in any case enormous because they could draw on the resources of the great empire they had conquered practically only by sea transport. Similarly, they could supply and reinforce their now far-flung garrisons only by using the sea routes, a point already mentioned in connection with their employment of submarines for this purpose. It is true that they attempted to reduce their vulnerability by drastic measures. The construction of the notorious railway from Thailand to Burma—the railway of "The Bridge on the River Kwai"—which cost the lives of tens of thousands of civilians and prisoners of war, was a part of the effort to create alternative methods of transportation. Similarly, the campaign in China in 1944 discussed in Chapter 11 was designed in large part to open up overland communication by railway across Japanese-controlled China as well as with Southeast Asia.[110] Another way of reducing dependence on shipping was to restore the oil refineries in the Dutch East Indies and then base much of the fleet at Singapore, close to the oil source.[111]

Measures like these, however, only minimally reduced Japan's vulnerability to attacks on her shipping. As a post-war analysis phrased it: "No major power in the world was more dependent upon ocean shipping than Japan."[112] She not only needed ships to carry men and goods to and from her newly won empire, but in the home islands the railway and road networks had not been well developed so that most domestic movement of bulk goods was also carried by ships from port to port. The railway system and its rolling stock were primarily designed for moving people, not cargo, and the road system was designed for local traffic with no major inter-city highways at all. Furthermore, the radical nationalists who had shot their way into power in the country had not the slightest comprehension of the logistical problems of a modern industrial society. They knew how to use swords and guns; but beyond that they were not only ignorant, they tended by background and inclination to look down on anyone who knew anything about subjects which they considered beneath the dignity of the exalted warrior. Masters at fighting enemy soldiers and sacking cities, they were and remained the crudest amateurs in matters of supply.

As Japan moved to expand the war with China into a part of the world war initiated by Germany, she found fewer and fewer foreign ships that could be hired to carry goods for Japan, and this loss of shipping that could be hired as needed was not off-set by the 823,000 tons captured by the Japanese armed forces during the months of conquest in December 1941 to March 1942.[113] This left the country dependent primarily on its six million tons of Japanese ships, and even this inadequate volume was never effectively utilized. It was divided into three separate shipping pools — army, navy, and civilian — which often had ships riding in ballast because the pool to which they were assigned had loads for only one leg of a trip. As if this organizational error were not enough, the Japanese committed a major doctrinal one in addition: they had never paid serious attention to the subject of anti-submarine warfare. There was no convoy system for years; merchant ships had not been armed and only a small portion ever were; and escort vessels were and remained few and far between. If the United States navy took half a year to wake up to reality in the North Atlantic in 1942, the Japanese navy remained somnolent through most of the war. While there was an effort to increase available shipping tonnage by construction, this was never on the scale of the Allied ship-building program, a point which could have been predicted very easily. In the event, Japan added about 3,300,000 tons during the war[114] (as compared with United States construction of over fifty million).

From the beginning of general hostilities in December 1941, the Japanese lost shipping to Allied military activity, and by April, 1942, this had more than balanced out new construction and captures. Unlike the Allies, whose losses exceeded construction until the fall of 1943 but thereafter were consistently below the additions of new ships, the

Japanese were never able to reverse the tide. From April 1942 to the end of the war, the shipping situation for Japan, which was already tight, deteriorated steadily. In the first five months of war, she lost about 375,000 tons; soon thereafter the campaign around the Solomons and New Guinea led to further substantial losses in shipping, primarily to Allied air attacks. In subsequent years, carrier air attacks on ships in port also inflicted heavy damage.

The major impact on Japanese shipping came as a result of Allied submarines, most of them American. In the first year of the Pacific War, the small number of United States submarines employed and the large proportion of defective torpedoes meant that few ships were sunk. In October 1942, submarines for the first time sank over 100,000 tons; in 1943, the monthly *average* was well above that figure, and in 1944 it rose to over 200,000.[a] By the end of the war, submarines had sunk over 4.8 million out of the almost 9 million tons sunk altogether; the other major contributors being land and carrier based airplanes and, especially in the last year of the war, mines laid around the home islands, primarily by the new American very long range bombers, the B-29s.[115]

Two observations about this successful assault on Japanese shipping, primarily by submarines, must be made. First, the highly effective attacks on merchant shipping certainly did not involve neglecting warships. On the contrary, American submarines sank twice as much Japanese naval tonnage as the American surface fleet, and while the totals were far smaller, the same thing was true of British submarines.[116] The largest warship ever sunk by a submarine was the super carrier *Shinano*, one of the three ships of over 60,000 tons built by the navy to outclass all American ships; of the two largest Japanese warships sunk by the British navy in World War II, both heavy cruisers, one was torpedoed by a submarine.[117] And in all their missions, casualties among the submarines were very heavy.

The second point which must be noted is that, unlike the British and Americans, the Japanese were hopelessly slow in recognizing the danger to their supply routes, took forever to start convoys—and did it very poorly—and did not get their first escort carrier into service until July 1944.[118] Of great importance to the Allies, especially to the Americans who carried the major share of the Pacific War on the oceans, was a significant difference in the intelligence war at sea. While at least until the summer of 1943 German ability to break the codes used by the

[a] It is worth pointing out that the Japanese Navy Minister in pre-war conferences in Tokyo had argued that the estimate of annual shipping production of 400,000 tons the first year, 600,000 the second, and 800,000 the third was "too optimistic." The reality was about half that projected. Nobutake Ike (ed.), *Japan's Decision for War* (Stanford, Calif.: Stanford Univ. Press, 1967), p. 189.

convoys gave them a major tool to use against the Allies and somewhat evened the odds in the war over shipping, the Japanese were generally unsuccessful in dealing with Allied naval codes. The Americans, on the other hand, after breaking back into Japanese naval codes in the late summer of 1942, steadily increased their ability to read their radio messages and employed the knowledge gained in this fashion to find their ships.[119]

As they advanced in the Pacific, the United States could also increasingly utilize air reconnaissance either to locate Japanese ships or to provide a plausible alternative explanation for attacks actually based on signal intelligence. Conversely, Japanese radar, direction finding, and air patrols never even remotely matched the skills and resources in these fields which the Allies employed in their war against the U-Boats.

THE BLOCKADE

If the attack on shipping was one way of striking at the economy of the Axis, the blockade imposed by the Allies was another. Having gone to war with all her neighbors except the Soviet Union, Japan was not in a position to draw any benefit from trade with neutral powers; the South American countries which had remained out of the war were too far away for Japan to engage in any substantial trade with them.[a] Germany, on the other hand, bordered on and traded with several neutral countries even after her attack on the Soviet Union:[b] Sweden, Switzerland, Spain, Portugal, Vichy France and Turkey. In these cases, there was an opportunity for Germany to draw directly on their resources and also to try to obtain goods from other neutrals, especially in South America, across them. On the other hand, the Allies were interested both in preventing goods from being sent to Germany across these neutrals and also to keep the neutrals themselves from supplying Germany. It was in opposition to such practices that the Allied blockade operated during the war.[120]

To prevent transshipment of goods, the Allies, with the British generally taking the lead, tried to ration the neutrals so that the Germans could not import goods which were nominally consigned to neutral

---

[a] I have been unable to locate information on Japanese imports from Latin America after December 1941. Several of the South American countries continued to have diplomatic relations with Japan, but it does not appear that the Japanese had much success in obtaining materials from them. The trade between Japan and the Soviet Union in the period December 1941–August 1945 also awaits investigation.

[b] The breach in the blockade created by Soviet assistance to Germany has been discussed in Chapter 2. In February 1943 the British Ministry of Economic Warfare calculated that, with the sole exception of flax and hemp, the Germans had obtained more grain, oil, chrome, tin, rubber, etc. by trade with the Soviet Union than as a result of invasion. PRO, N 1293/75/38, FO 371/36958.

neighbors. A complicated system of controls, operated primarily by the British, served this purpose and worked reasonably well. There was some slippage through the neutrals, but very little, and there was some smuggling of items by individual seamen on neutral ships trying to make substantial profits for themselves.[121] Some materials which the Allies had allowed into Spain and into Vichy France did end up being re-shipped to German-occupied Europe, but the volume was never substantial.[122] The main concern was always the direct shipment of goods from the neutrals to Germany, especially as in some cases the items involved were of great military significance.

As discussed in Chapter 2, the trade between Germany and Sweden was a major focus of concern throughout the war. Germany drew from Sweden a substantial volume of high-grade iron ore and a high proportion of her steel ball bearings. The Germans were continually pressuring the Swedes to deliver more while the Allies were trying to restrict the flow. Three factors influenced the long and tedious struggle over Swedish exports to Germany. The first was the ability and willingness of Germany to pay for what she bought. The Swedes did not wish to allow her to run up debts, in effect borrowing from Sweden to pay for the imports. In 1941, when Germany still seemed to be winning the war and was in a strong position to threaten military action, the Swedes did extend her considerable credits; but, as the tide of war turned, the Germans found it more and more difficult to extort credit. On the contrary, in 1943–44, when they could least afford it, they had to export at last some coal and some war materials to pay for a portion of the imports.[123]

The payments issue already points to the second factor in the picture: the military situation. As long as Germany could effectively threaten Sweden, the latter was more inclined to make concessions to Berlin; as it became more and more obvious that Germany could not afford to take the initiative in beginning hostilities against Sweden and that the Allies were going to win the war—and in the not too distant future—Stockholm was more likely to yield to Allied pressure.[124]

As one follows the difficult negotiations of both sides with Sweden, however, a third facet can be recognized, and that is the general inclination of the Swedish government to assist Germany as much as possible in spite of Allied pressure. In spite of the fact that most of the post-war literature attempts to present Swedish policy in the best possible light, the evidence—even that offered in the most eloquent apologias—shows a consistent and determined effort to slip as much iron ore and steel ball bearings to Germany as possible.[125]

Although a series of agreements between Sweden and Germany

seemed to be more and more restrictive each year, the Swedes did what they could to assist Germany in spite of the appearance of greater restrictions in 1943.[126] The last and most restrictive German–Swedish agreement was signed on January 10, 1944, but even during that winter the Swedes, feeling confident that the Allies—unlike the Germans earlier—would not punish them by invasion, did what they could to circumvent their promises to the Allies by shipping ball-bearings to Germany.[127] In April 1944 they rejected an Allied demand for an end of ball bearing exports at a time when both the Allies and the Germans thought that these were essential for the German war economy.[128] As Allied bombing of German Baltic ports and political pressure on Stockholm increased, the Swedes in August 1944 began to insist that the Germans provide their own ships, refusing to provide Swedish ships any more for war supplies.[129] Later that year, they were still circumventing their own promise to the Allies to cease delivering ball bearings,[130] and only at the end of 1944—when it clearly made very little difference any more—were the Swedes prevailed upon to stop.[131]

The Swedish government was interested in getting and retaining German permission for a minimal level of Swedish seaborne trade with the outside world, but this was as much in German as in Swedish interest. The most plausible explanation for the policy of accommodating Germany in her need for critical materials is to be found in the sympathy of some circles for her in the early part of the war and worry about the advance of the Soviet Union in the latter years of the conflict. Sweden made some important humanitarian gestures during the war, but it insured that it would be one of the very few countries on earth to profit handsomely from it.[132]

Spain was important to Germany as a source of wolfram, needed for the steel-hardening alloy tungsten, iron ore, and mercury and zinc ore. Here also the issue of German payment played an important role. Spain was simply too poor, and its government too nationalistic, to be able or to want to extend credits to Germany. Time and again the Spaniards held up exports to ensure German payment in arms, machines, and other forms of compensation.[133] The Allies, on the other hand, used their economic leverage on Spain with increasing effectiveness to inhibit Spanish exports to Germany, especially wolfram, and also bought as much as they could themselves in a program of preclusive buying.[134]

The Spaniards took advantage of the situation to extort maximum payments from both sides, eventually yielding to Allied pressure in early 1944—after quickly selling as much as possible to the Germans and then letting them smuggle out some more until the Allied advance closed the border in August 1944.[135] The government in Madrid was even more pro-German in its orientation than that in Stockholm. Certainly, if it had not been for Allied pressure, the Germans would have been able to draw more heavily on the Spanish economy; but as it was, they obtained substantial quantities of important goods.[136]

The most critical material for her war effort that Germany needed from Portugal was wolfram, and in this country also pressure from both sides and competitive buying were significant. As in the case of Spain, the Germans obtained a considerable amount but not all they wanted. There were, however, several differences. The Portuguese government, headed by António de Oliveira Salazar, was more sympathetic to the Allies than the Franco regime in Spain. It was, in addition, affected by the decision of Brazil, with which Portugal had special ties dating back to colonial times, to join the United Nations in the war against Germany after a German campaign against Brazilian shipping. On the other hand, Salazar was a man who did not appreciate being pushed around, an issue on which the Americans were generally less inclined to be patient than the British. In this case also the final cutting off came in 1944, ironically a day before the invasion of June 6 made the whole issue theoretical.[137]

The pressures of both sides on Switzerland led to especially complicated negotiations during the war. As explained in Chapter 3, the Germans intended to occupy and partition the country with Italy in the late summer of 1940 but then postponed the disappearance of what they considered an undesirable entity until after victory in the war. Later it would be easy to dispose of Switzerland when its main defense assets, the railway communications through the Gotthard and Simplon tunnels, were no longer of such great importance to Axis military operations. In the meantime, the Germans would provide some coal to keep Swiss industry working—primarily for the Axis. This pattern was shielded against Allied pressure by the economic interest of much of Swiss industry in German orders, and the generally pro-German preferences of the Federal Councillor in charge of foreign affairs, Marcel Edouard Pilet-Golaz. In spite of Allied rationing of imports and repeated pressure attempts, Switzerland's industry worked hard for Germany, substantially increasing its exports, which included arms and ammunition, during 1943 as the bombing of Germany increased her incentive to turn to the safer factories of Switzerland for products.

The occupation of Vichy France in November 1942 gave the Germans an additional means of pressure since their troops now surrounded the country on all sides. By this time, however, the Allies were fed up with Swiss maneuvers and threatened to use, and began to use, their most important weapon. By blacklisting or threatening to blacklist Swiss firms, thereby presenting major segments of the Swiss industrial economy—and their owners and directors—with the prospect of a post-war future in which they were not likely to participate, the Allies waved a stick that the wartime profiteers could understand. By this time, it was obvious to them that the Allies would win the war, and that the exclusion of Swiss firms from a world dominated by the United Nations was certain to end the country's prosperity permanently. Here was a form of pressure that left Switzerland politically independent but imperilled its economic future. The policy of the government now changed, and the new trade agreement of December 19, 1943 met most of the Allied demands. On October 1, 1944, Switzerland embargoed all exports of war materials.[138]

The last of the European neutrals which needs to be discussed is Turkey. Although other products, especially copper, mohair, and skins were a significant element in trade discussions, the most important focus of attention was always chrome. Not only did German war industry need Turkish chrome, the United States also was short of chrome so that Allied purchases were as much for their own use as to preempt the Germans. The Turks had originally stalled off the Germans by allowing the British to purchase chrome in 1942, in effect promising the bulk of 1943 and 1944 production to the Germans. Though formally allied to Great Britain, Turkey was primarily interested in making territorial gains at the expense of Greece and/or Syria if that were possible, and building up her own military power in exchange for whatever she exported to either side.[139] In the background in Ankara was always the fear that either Germany or Russia would win the titanic battle on the Eastern Front and that the winner might then try to dominate Turkey.

Three other factors operated in this situation. One was the great difficulty Germany had in actually delivering the armaments which the Turks insisted on as payment for chrome. If in the end the Germans received substantial quantities of chrome, perhaps some 70,000 tons (compared to over 100,000 in 1939) and not even more, it was due to short-falls in German deliveries rather than to Turkish reluctance or Allied pressure.[140]

Secondly, the Allies were always hoping, especially in 1942 and 1943, that Turkey would come into the war on their side, and they were therefore reluctant to press the Turkish authorities too hard. Churchill's meeting with their President, Prime Minister, and Foreign Minister at Adana at the end of January 1943 appears to have convinced him that they were serious about entering the war, and he remained fooled by the Turks, who had no such intention, for a year.[141] A military mission was sent as well as substantial military equipment to strengthen the Turkish army.

The third factor which assuredly did not assist the Allies was the fact that from October or November 1943 to February 1944 the valet of the British ambassador in Ankara was regularly providing the Germans with copies of secret messages from the ambassador's safe. A serious scholarly examination of the "Cicero" case remains to be written, and the implications for British code security have not as yet been fully investigated — at least in material available to the public. Whatever else may or may not have been compromised, the leak certainly did not make the task of Allied diplomacy in Turkey any easier.[142]

In early 1944, the Allies were tired of Turkish stalling and their continued deliveries of chrome to the Germans. In January they withdrew the military mission and began imposing economic restrictions on Turkey. Patience as well as gullibility had run out in London and Washington. The effects were quick and dramatic. On April 20, 1944, the Turks announced the halting of all chrome deliveries to Germany — and on Hitler's birthday at that — and on August 1 broke diplomatic and economic relations with Berlin. It had become obvious to the authorities in Ankara that the Allies would soon win the war, that the Germans were in no position to do anything to them in the meantime, and that it behoved Turkey to be in the good graces of Britain and the United States when the war was over.[143]

With minimal variations depending on circumstances and conditions, the neutrals tended to follow essentially similar policies in the face of pressures from both sides. They recognized that by their nature the two sides had differing choices, and the neutrals did their best — or worst — to profit from this situation. It was obvious on the basis of their prior record that the Axis powers would as soon crush the neutrals as respect them and that there would be no place for any independent states in a German-dominated Europe. On the other hand, the Allies were clearly inclined to respect the neutrals' right to exist, certainly if they won the war, and probably during the fighting. The one advantage the Allies had, even before their victory appeared certain, was their ability to follow the line being taken by most of the neutrals in negotiations with the Axis by reading the reports of the Japanese diplomats and service attachés stationed there. But this did not greatly help them cope with the basic inclinations of the neutral governments.

In the hope of profiting as much as possible from the needs of others, the neutrals accordingly sold as much as they could at the highest prices possible to the Germans, defying Allied blockade pressures as much as they dared. In the early years of the war this tendency was reinforced by fear of Germany, in the latter years by the hope of insulating their own peoples from the privations which the great struggle imposed on others. But they would make the Allies pay as high a price as possible for defending the freedom of Swedes, Turks, Swiss and others alongside that of their own people.

BLOCKADE-BREAKERS

Anticipating the efforts of the Allies to deprive them of important materials which might be obtained from overseas, the Germans and to a lesser extent the Japanese had looked to ships which slipped through the blockade. Germany needed rubber and vegetable fats from East Asia which were carried across the Soviet Union as long as Germany respected its Non-Aggression Pact with that country, but would have to be brought in some other way once she attacked the Soviet Union; while Japan needed mercury and industrial technology from Europe. As the Germans anticipated that their attack on Russia would close the loophole in the blockade, they made preparations to compensate by other means. The first blockade-breaker had left Japan on December 28, 1940, arriving in France on April 4, 1941.[144] Measures were then instituted on a far larger scale.

A major program of blockade-breakers was organized early in 1941, and during the 1941–42 winter, when the conditions for such trips were best; out of seventeen ships only four were lost. Germany thereby acquired 32,000 tons of rubber plus over 25,000 tires, enough at that stage of Germany's synthetic rubber production to cover her needs for two years.[145] The Allies, who knew of this program but were largely incapable of stopping this first group of ships, made extensive preparations for interfering with the expected resumption of blockade-breaker voyages in the winter of 1942–43.[146] In the face of determined German planning and operations, the Allies did very much better in the second season, sinking most of the ships involved and forcing the Germans to begin building transport submarines to take over by underwater journeys what could no longer be done at reasonable loss rates by surface ships, especially in the Bay of Biscay.[147] The fact remains, however, that four of the blockade-breakers did get through and the 7850 tons of rubber they carried could cover Germany's needs for a full year now that advances in her synthetic rubber industry had further reduced her need for natural rubber.[148]

Both sides made even more elaborate preparations for the 1943–44 winter season; and the Allies were increasingly successful, this time sinking four of the five ships incoming from East Asia and, as a result of this, leading Hitler himself to cancel the planned four outgoing ship journeys. In spite of this apparent Allied victory, which included a British naval victory on December 28, 1943, in which a German destroyer and two torpedo boats were sunk, and an American operation which sank three German blockade-breakers from East Asia in January 1944, the basic fact remains that the *one* ship which had gotten through covered German rubber, tin and wolfram needs for the rest of 1944.[149] The use of surface blockade-breakers had been costly for the Germans and now had to be abandoned, but it had served its purpose.

The high losses in surface ships had led the Germans to consider using transport submarines on occasion in 1942 and 1943. An additional number of originally thirty-six transport U-Boats was ordered in January 1943; and until these could be ready, the Germans took over Italian submarines either already designed for or converted to transport duty.[150]

The interim project with Italian submarines did not work out very well as only two were eventually so employed. Both German submarines headed for or returning from East Asian waters on standard war cruises and some Japanese submarines were, however, used to carry small but significant amounts of cargo. While nothing came of the great plans to carry increasing amounts of rubber, tin and other products with a volume of over 14,000 tons by 1947,[151] some cargo was carried by submarines in the last year of the war. Included were small but significant quantities of rubber and wolfram as well as patents and drawings for new weapons.[152] High-ranking officers and officials also used this means of transport. The trip of Bose to East Asia has been mentioned; Vice Admiral Nomura Naokuni, the Japanese navy representative in Germany, and Rear Admiral Yokoi Tadao, the naval attaché, both also returned to Japan by submarine in 1943.[153]

In the winter of 1944–45, Dönitz decided to send one more series of submarines, eventually scheduled to leave on January 10, 15, and 20 and March 5, 1945, for Japanese waters.[154] Some of these submarines actually left in February and March of 1945.[155] In addition to plans, drawings, and technicians for new weapons such as rockets, jet engines, and the ME-262 airplane—all advanced technologies Germany had developed but Japan lacked—Dönitz was also hoping to send a group of eight line and two engineering officers, who were to be assigned to Japanese battleships, aircraft carriers, cruisers and destroyers to assimilate Japanese experiences for the rebuilt future German navy which Dönitz confidently anticipated.[156] Ironically, while the Japanese agreed in principle to this fantastic project for assigning German officers to ships already on the bottom of the Pacific Ocean, a German actually sent on one of the submarines which left Germany was General Ulrich

Kessler, who was being sent as the new air attaché to replace the one who had been in Tokyo for years; the submarine was surrendered on the Atlantic when the war in Europe ended.[157]

These last-minute gyrations with submarines, whatever they might tell us about Japanese hopes for benefits to draw from a Germany in its death-throes and about German hopes about a huge blue-water navy for some future Fourth Reich, were in part a sign of the desperation for communication between the two powers. The last two years of the war had seen continued agitated discussions of various projects to establish and maintain airplane contact between the Axis partners. All foundered on the inadequacy of available airplanes and Japanese concern about possible Soviet objections to overflights.[158] The interminable discussion of this abortive project at the highest levels does show, however, the importance attached to it by the Germans, Japanese and, until their surrender in 1943, the Italians. Because Japan and the Soviet Union were not at war with each other, there was a courier connection between Germany and Japan across Turkey and the Soviet Union, but all the available evidence suggests that very little was ever transmitted by this route.[159] Basically, what was exchanged by blockade-breaking ships and submarines was what each especially wanted from the other. And what was the balance?

The critical balance is that in spite of the very great effort expended by the Allies in trying to restrict German access to raw materials from neutrals and by blockade-breakers, and the substantial assistance provided to their naval operations against the latter by their breaking of some German and most Japanese codes, the Germans did get what they most needed.[160] By the time that the neutrals were pressured into restricting or ending exports to Germany and the naval and air forces of the Allies had driven the Germans off the surface of the seas into the use of transport submarines, enough critical raw materials had been brought through to Germany to cover her most essential needs. It would certainly have been easier for the Germans to hold out longer had it not been for the blockade, but their armaments industry succumbed to the land and air forces of the Allies, not to shortages imposed by blockade.

On the other hand, it is evident that Japan's inability to cope with the advances of the Americans and, very late in the war of the British, was due to a considerable extent to the successful blockade of Japan. Her war industry, unlike Germany's, was dramatically affected by losses of shipping, and many of the factories bombed by the United States air force in 1945 had already stopped operating because needed raw materials simply could not be brought there. Furthermore, when the Germans late in the war finally decided to assist the Japanese with the production of the new weapons on which they themselves had pinned such great hopes, they found it practically impossible to transfer the needed knowledge and experts to Japan. What knowledge the Japanese did receive came to an industrial economy being paralyzed by the loss of shipping. The fact that Japan could not utilize the added months beyond the collapse of German resistance in early 1945 to bring into effective use the new weapons, which were developed too late for use by the Germans, was surely an important, if little noticed, result of the blockade.

THE SOVIET NAVY

While the battles and difficulties at sea which accompanied the Allied convoys to Murmansk have been mentioned repeatedly in this chapter as well as in Chapter 5, no reference has been made to the Soviet navy and Russian shipping. The role of the Soviet navy was primarily one of supporting land operations. In the north, the units of the fleet there assisted in the defense of Murmansk and played a small role in receiving the convoys from the West. It was precisely because the Soviet Union did not have either the shipping to carry the goods or the warships for escorts that the bulk of the cargo ships and escorts was provided by the British and Americans. Russian ships were regularly included in the convoys and Soviet warships played a role as escorts and in clearing mines laid by the Germans. To reinforce their northern fleet, the Western Powers transferred numerous smaller warships to the Russians, and in 1944, as a compensatory arrangement in connection with the surrender of the Italian navy, turned over a battleship, a cruiser, and a destroyer. All the Russian ships as well as the units of the Red Air Force stationed in the far north played a part in protecting the convoy route.[161]

It was because the Western Allies had to bear the majority of the load on this shortest but most dangerous route to the Soviet Union that it became such a subject of friction. The need to interrupt the convoys in the summer of 1942 and again in the spring of 1943 because of the dangers in the endless summer days, the heavy loss of ships with their cargoes, the competing demands of operation "Torch" in 1942 and the crisis of the war against the U-Boats in 1943, caused enormous trouble. The Russians simply refused to believe that there were real problems, or pretended not to, and repeatedly made life as difficult rather than as easy as possible for those sailors, soldiers, merchantmen, and airmen who were trying to help them at enormous risk to themselves.[162] It was not really until the Moscow Conference of October 1943 that these issues were worked out satisfactorily[163] — not surprisingly at a time when the Russians were winning on the Eastern Front and the Western Powers had finally turned the tide of battle in the North Atlantic.

While about a fifth of the supplies sent by the northern route ended up on the bottom of the ocean, the losses among cargoes sent to the Persian Gulf for shipment to the Soviet Union via Iran were kept at 8 percent.[164] The problems on that route were the enormous distance, the need to build adequate facilities in Iran, and the extra burden placed on the internal Russian transportation system. On this route, of course, the escorts were all British and American as was almost all the shipping as well.

The situation was the reverse on the third major route, that to Vladivostok and other Soviet Pacific ports. The Russians had few merchant ships in the Pacific; the United States, therefore, began transferring ships to the Soviet flag so that they could cross the Pacific from the American Northwest to the Soviet Union without escort, as the Japanese allowed Soviet ships to travel designated routes unmolested. In 1942, relatively few ships were available and the American ports were crowded, but in 1943 vast quantities of food and other supplies were shipped on this route.[165] In terms of volume, this was by far the most important route for deliveries from the Western Allies to the Soviet Union with about half going this way and less than a quarter each by Murmansk and Iran.

This development, not surprisingly, annoyed the Germans. In the very years that the Red Army was tearing the guts out of the German army, a huge volume of supplies was flowing unhindered to the Soviet Union under the noses of their Japanese ally. As the volume of shipments increased in 1943, the level and frequency of German protests to the Japanese increased as well. The latter, however, regardless of their feelings on the subject, believed very strongly that they could not interfere with the shipments or refuse to recognize the transfer of American ships to the Soviet merchant fleet without endangering their own relations with the Soviet Union. The converse of no Japanese interference with American supplies to Russia seemed to them to be no Soviet bases for American planes in the Soviet Far East. Accordingly they regularly turned aside the Germans' demands for action and simultaneously pretended that the volume was really not as great as the Germans correctly suspected and in any case included no war materials.[166]

On the few occasions when the Japanese detained Soviet vessels, the repercussions were immediate. The government of the Soviet Union, with Molotov repeatedly intervening personally, insisted on the release of the ships and let it be understood that any other action by Japan would constitute a violation of the Soviet–Japanese Neutrality Treaty of

1941. As an angry Molotov explained to the Japanese ambassador on July 8, 1943: "We are fighting a war and have to have stuff. We have lost some fine industrial and agricultural land and we must have food, machinery, and raw materials, and we are not going to stand for you Japanese standing in our way of getting them."[167] Ambassador Sato Naotake consistently and insistently urged his government to accede to the Soviet demands and to refrain from ship seizures in the first place. Japan in his view simply could not afford to antagonize the Soviet Union in 1943 and 1944 and was in no position to argue about the legal status of the reflagged American ships. Tokyo gave in reluctantly but comprehensively.[168]

It is in this context also that the obvious alternative to shipping must be mentioned. Many of the airplanes destined for Britain were being flown rather than shipped across the Atlantic; this was one of the first highly important military missions that the United States government entrusted to women pilots in World War II.[169] Why not fly planes to the Soviet Union via Alaska and Siberia? If the Japanese did not interfere with ships once reflagged to Soviet ownership, they would be even less likely to interfere with airplanes once turned over to and then flown by Russian crews. The Japanese lacked not only the political incentive — stopping Russian planes flying from American airports was a bit too close to inviting the flight of American planes from Russian airports — but they also lacked most of the means. Here was a way to move Lend-Lease without use of shipping and without danger from the enemy (though some from the weather).[170]

For a considerable period of time the Soviet government refused to agree to this procedure. We do not know the reason, but it may have been a combination of suspicion of the United States and concern over the Japanese reaction. At the insistence of the Americans, Stalin finally agreed to reconsider in April 1942.[171] In the summer of 1942 this process was begun and, though slow and complicated to begin with, came to be of very great significance.[172] Until the Japanese attack on Pearl Harbor, the Canadians had always forbidden the construction of a highway connecting Alaska to the rest of the continental United States. In the face of the common danger, this obstacle was lifted, and at American expense the road known as the Alaska Highway was begun. Its main function in World War II was to supply the intermediate bases at which the thousands of planes delivered over the ALSIB (Alaska–Siberia) route made their intermediate refueling and service stops. This was surely an unanticipated by-product of World War II shipping shortages.[173]

If the Alaska Highway appears to be a very long way from the Soviet navy and shipping, the connection comes from the smallness of the

Soviet shipping pool which made it necessary for the Allies to use whatever means were at hand to move supplies and weapons to Russia. It was in the Baltic and the Black Sea that the Red navy itself played a significant role. In the Baltic, the Russian navy units based at Kronstadt were of importance in two ways. The possibility of Soviet ships coming out of the Gulf of Finland into the Baltic and interfering with Germany's supply routes to Finland, her trade with Sweden, or her training of submarine crews always agitated the German navy. They therefore felt obliged at all times to lay mine barriers and to keep some fleet units and active submarines in the Baltic as a protection against that contingency. Here the failure of the initial German offensive in 1941 cost the Germans heavily in a way that has not always been recognized: the Baltic did not become a safe German lake as Berlin had confidently expected.

There was, however, a second way in which the Russian navy related to the original halting of the German onrush. At the northern end of the front, the Germans had cut off Leningrad, but they had not been able to clear the whole southern shore of the Gulf of Finland. The Red Army held on to a portion of the south shore: a segment which the Germans called the Oranienbaum Kessel and the Soviets referred to as the Coastal Operations Group. It could obviously survive only by receiving at least minimal reinforcements and supplies from the main defense of Leningrad, and this required the protection of the Soviet navy.

If this latter function of the Red Baltic Fleet was primarily one of army support, the same was true for most of the operations of the Soviet Black Sea Fleet. Its successful evacuation of the Odessa garrison, discussed in Chapter 5, was only one of many operations carried out by what was probably the most effective and efficient portion of Soviet naval forces in World War II. The Black Sea Fleet's role in the Soviet winter counter-offensive in the Crimea has also been mentioned. There the fleet had not only reinforced the garrison but brought in other units, evacuated machinery, and generally organized under Black Sea Fleet Commander Admiral F.S. Oktyabrskiy a defense from which the British defenders of Singapore could have learned some very useful lessons. The amphibious assaults in December 1941 and January 1942 across the Kerch Straits and at Feodosyie succeeded while that at Yevpatoria failed. The German Forces on the Crimea as a result were strained but not, as the Russians had hoped, destroyed. It is, however, a reasonable conclusion that this was due more to the inexperience and confusion of the Red Army commanders in charge of the landing units and the effective if belated German resistance than to any failure of the Black Sea Fleet.[174]

The history of the fleet's actions in the subsequent years of World

War II is, like that just recounted, essentially a part of the fighting on land and will therefore be dealt with in that context. The Soviet leaders had no reason to regret the portion of their resources allocated to the navy; though small and often forgotten by historians, its role was significant at precisely that portion of the Eastern Front where the Germans would make their greatest effort and suffer their greatest defeat at the hands of the Red army in 1942. The naval struggle in the Black Sea was both in kind and in distance far removed from the endless battles in the Atlantic, the Allied blockade of Japan in the Pacific, and the efforts to maintain a blockade of Germany against her resourceful attempts to breach the ring around her; but these were all inter-related portions of a struggle for control of the oceans which cover much of the globe and which claimed so many lives that slid beneath the seas.

8

THE WAR IN EUROPE AND NORTH AFRICA 1942–1943: TO AND FROM STALINGRAD; TO AND FROM TUNIS

As it became increasingly obvious to the Germans in the fall of 1941 that the campaign in the East was not likely to be completed that year, they began to think about 1942 operations. For a while in September, October and November, there were still hopes of seizing both the industrial area around Moscow and the oil fields of the Caucasus by the end of the year. Even before the Red Army defeated the Germans at the southern end of the front and drove them out of Rostov, all German hopes of taking the Caucasus in 1941 had vanished. Similarly, once the euphoria of early October had been offset by the reality of heavy fighting in November, the Germans realized that even if a final push enabled them to seize the immediate Moscow area, there was no prospect of going any further. The dramatic turn in December, when the German spearheads had been first halted and then overwhelmed and pushed back, made it obvious that any 1942 campaign would start a substantial distance away from where the Germans had envisioned as late as early November 1941.

There were additional complications affecting any German offensive plans for 1942. Casualties among the men and horses in the armies fighting the Soviet Union had not been replaced by the trickle of replacements; and while a major effort was made to build up new divisions, provide more men and conscript additional horses, there were simply not enough of either to restore the army to its June 1941 strength. The shortage of horses was doubly serious because the enormous losses of vehicles in the winter made the infantry divisions even more dependent upon horse-drawn transport than before; this alone made a war of movement on more than one segment of the front at a time quite impossible.

The July 1941 shift of industrial production from priority for the army to priority for air force and navy had been replaced in January 1942 by a renewed emphasis on the needs of the army, but this step could not make itself felt in substantial additional production adequate even to make up for the losses of the 1941 campaign until the summer of 1942 at the earliest. The death of the Minister of Munitions, Fritz Todt, in January 1942 was so "convenient" and took place in such an unlikely manner that deliberate sabotage of his plane by a member of Hitler's entourage is likely. In any case, the new man in charge of war production, Albert Speer, quickly proved himself efficient and unscrupulous, both important qualifications in National Socialist Germany. He managed to increase production of war materials, but even so the German army had fewer tanks and the German air force no more planes in June 1942 than in June 1941.[1] Furthermore, the continued drain of the war at sea and in the air with Britain and the United States made it impossible for Germany to concentrate her production on the weapons for the East at the same time as she had to divert forces to other areas of combat.

These factors combined to make two choices clear for Hitler and his advisors. The army could remain on the defensive in the East or it could launch an offensive on *one* sector of the front; the 1941 option of striking in several sectors of the front simultaneously had vanished under the blows of the Red Army and the needs of other theaters. There is no evidence that an essentially defensive stand in the East in 1942 was ever seriously considered. The alternative Mediterranean strategy which the German navy had urged repeatedly had no appeal for Hitler, who saw the Mediterranean as Italy's sphere of expansion while the East was Germany's. If von Brauchitsch ever had a strategic concept before his retirement as Commander-in-Chief of the army in December 1941 it has vanished without a trace. General Halder, the army Chief of Staff who now had to work ever more closely with Hitler, certainly never supported any alternative strategy of his own; on the contrary, his vision was if anything more narrowly land-locked than Hitler's.

The only choice to be made, therefore, was where to strike in the East, and on that subject there was an unusual degree of unanimity. Army Group South had managed to hang on to the most coherent defensive line during the winter fighting, and the weather there would be suitable for German offensive operations earlier than further north. It was therefore assumed, only partly correctly as it turned out, that the preliminary operations considered necessary in the south, the clearing of the Crimea and the destruction of the Izyum pocket, could be finished long before the preliminary operations that would be needed in the center and north could be carried out. A major attack on the southern portion of the front would, therefore, allow more time for a summer offensive.

A second factor which led the Germans to look to the southern segment of the front was the prospect of very significant material and strategic objectives within their reach. The seizure of the oil resources of the Caucasus would have a triple impact on the war. It would relieve the shortage of petroleum products which was hampering the German armored forces, hindering the German navy, and immobilizing the Italian navy even as it made Germany less dangerously vulnerable to the effects of any air attacks on her synthetic oil works and the Romanian oil wells. Secondly, the converse of this was, of course, that of depriving the Soviet Union of a very high proportion of its oil resources. Even if her allies could replace some of this, it would necessarily be at the expense of other weapons and supplies they could have sent instead. Finally, a German force in the Caucasus would be poised for an operation the following year into Iraq and Iran from the north, collapsing the Allied position in the Middle East, turning that region's oil resources from Allied control to the Axis, offering a real opportunity for a meeting with the Japanese and in any case severing the southern supply route of the Western Allies to the Soviet Union. The fact that along the road to such splendid prospects the Germans would seize those portions of the important industrial region of the Donets basin still under Soviet control, as well as the rich agricultural region of the north Caucasus, only made this whole direction more inviting, even mouth-watering.

One other operation appeared to the Germans to be important for 1942, the seizure of Leningrad. The success of the Russians in supplying the city in the winter across the frozen Lake Ladoga and the refusal of the Finns to attack it from the north made it obvious to Hitler that only a major assault could end the siege, create a secure line at that end of the front, and provide a land connection to his Finnish ally. Such an operation, in turn, would provide the base for a new effort to cut the connection between the Soviet Union and the Western Allies via Murmansk. The problem with the Leningrad project, however, was that there were no troops available for it and no adequate air and artillery support even if the troops could be found.

The solution that Hitler and his staff came up with was, to put it mildly, on the bizarre side. He decided, not surprisingly, that this operation could not be launched simultaneously with the main offensive in the south. But since that offensive involved two preliminary operations, the clearing of the Crimea and the elimination of the Izyum pocket, the army engaged in the former would thereafter be sent to seize Leningrad while the forces used for the latter were simply to continue eastward as part of the main offensive operation in the southern sector. What this anticipated in practice was that during the time when Germany's most important 1942 offensive in the East was under way in the south, the divisions of one of its armies would be on the trains, moving behind the long front across all the supply routes of the other armies from the southern to the northern end of the main front.[a]

Two further comments are called for by the German plan for the 1942 offensive. One concerns an internal contradiction; the second its major aim. Although it was assumed that the forces of Army Group South would be adequate for the conquest of the Caucasus, which necessarily included the whole Russian Black Sea coast, even without the German 11th Army in the Crimea which was scheduled to take Leningrad, Hitler did not draw the obvious conclusion from his own confidence, namely that in such an event there would be no need for a preliminary campaign to clear the Crimea. Once the Germans took over the Soviet Black Sea coast, *any* Soviet forces left on the Crimea would be doomed anyway. Rather than risk leaving Soviet units to vegetate on the East and West ends of the Crimea, the Germans decided to attack both in sequence, eventually deciding to clear the eastern end before concluding the siege of Sevastopol at the western end with a massive assault.

The second point which merits noting is the absence of any major emphasis on the city of Stalingrad in the planning for and early stages of a campaign that came to be associated in the eyes of contemporaries and all later observers with the name of that city. There is a curious irony in the fact that the place whose name will always be associated with one of the great battles of World War II was largely ignored by the Germans beforehand and renamed Volgograd by the Soviet Union afterwards.

The situation of the Soviet Union was in some ways very difficult but in others was better than that of the Germans. Casualties in the great offensives of the winter had been heavy, and in the spring were exceptionally numerous. The replacements were in many cases either older or younger; so many of the survivors of the 1941 battles had been squandered in uncoordinated attacks of January, February and March 1942. The total strength of the army appears, nevertheless, to have risen in the first half of 1942 to about five million men, of whom the majority

---

[a] On August 5, 1942, Hitler was to comment that the war in the East would be won if Germany cut the ties to Russia's allies in the north and south and seized the oil wells, while thereafter the war in the West could be won by sending 50 percent of the strength in the East there. Jochmann, *Hitler, Monologe*, pp. 328–29.

were in front-line units facing a German army of about three and a quarter million and some 700,000 of the latter's allies.[2] In spite of the loss of territory with its industrial and mining resources and of the manpower of the occupied territory, the Soviet leadership, partly as a result of getting its evacuated factories back into production, partly by a far more drastic shifting of industrial capacity to war production than the Germans ever accomplished, had increased the production of tanks and guns and maintained the output of planes. In all three categories the Soviet Union was not only turning out more than the Germans but in some fields, especially that of the larger tanks, was making better ones. The Germans were continuing to underestimate Soviet strength and production, while the Soviets were apparently over-estimating the Germans'.[3]

If the Soviet Union endured major defeats in the early stages of the summer offensive it was because of Stalin's misreading of German intentions. Soviet intelligence had accurately discerned that the major offensive would come in the south toward the Caucasus and was likely to be followed by an effort to cut the railway from Murmansk; operations against Moscow and Leningrad were expected to *follow*, not precede the main blow.[4] As mentioned in Chapter 5, the Western Powers were also convinced that Germany would strike for the Caucasus first. Stalin, however, was certain that the main blow would come in the center. His insistence that the Germans would place their emphasis on an offensive to take Moscow may or may not have been reinforced by the German deception operation designed to convey this impression, but in any case it was in front of Moscow that the Red Army concentrated its major forces and its main reserves.[5]

To make matters worse for the Red Army and easier for the Germans, grossly incompetent military leadership brought major disasters on the Russians in May. Marshal Timoshenko launched a badly conceived offensive to seize Kharkov which in a way played into the hands of the Germans who were already planning to eliminate the Izyum bulge further south. Unable to direct the offensive properly, Timoshenko did not break it off quickly enough, and German spearheads thrust into the rear of his advance as well as of the Izyum bulge. The result was one of the great German victories and terrible Russian defeats of the war; about 100,000 Red Army soldiers lost their lives and over 200,000 were made prisoner by the end of May. The Germans had their ready position for the main offensive while the Soviets had lost heavily.[6]

On the Crimea, the Germans had decided to clear the eastern end of the peninsula before making another assault on Sevastopol. At the eastern extremity of the Crimea, the Russian army had substantial superiority in troops and weapons; the terrain gave the Germans little opportunity for maneuver. What evened the odds was the incompetence of the Soviet commanders, Dmitriy T. Kozlov and Lev Z. Mekhlis, and a massive air support operation ordered by Hitler over the objections of the air force staff. In a series of sharp blows, Manstein's 11th Army attacked and destroyed the Crimean Front (Army Group) in the period May 8–20. A jab around its south flank broke the front lines and the Soviet Front commander never regained full control of the situation. Most of the soldiers of the twenty-one Soviet divisions were killed or captured; only a third of the 300,000 Red Army soldiers escaped across the Kerch Strait to the North Caucasus to fight again.[7]

If the very risky operation against the Crimean Front had gone smoothly for the Germans, the following assault on the great fortress of Sevastopol took not eleven days but thirty (a particularly striking contrast to the quick fall of Tobruk on two days of those thirty). The Germans moved up to the siege perimeter a vast array of artillery. Beyond the standard heavy artillery of the German army, they brought in 14 inch howitzers and enormous mortars of 17 and 21 inch diameter. As if that were not enough, a monster $31\frac{1}{2}$ inch railway gun firing a 7-ton shell was hauled in to assist in the destruction of the fortress.[8] The whole operation therefore began under an artillery barrage reminiscent of World War I and included an assault landing across Severnaya Bay, the water inlet north of the city. In a bitter, grinding battle the Germans battered their way through the fortifications, took the city, and seized the peninsula projecting westward south of Sevastopol. By July 5, Manstein could stage a victory parade having taken the great fortress and some 90,000 prisoners. While only a small number from the garrison, including most specialist personnel, had been evacuated by air and submarine, the whole operation cost the Germans very heavy casualties—most likely close to 100,000—and a great deal of time.[9] The Soviet commander Oktyabrskiy was among those evacuated, but his soldiers had made the Germans pay a high price. As the huge siege guns were loaded up for the long trip to the Leningrad front and the surviving soldiers of 11th Army rested a little before also heading north, the big offensive was beginning to roll.

The German plan for the offensive in the south anticipated a series of phases. First an attack toward Voronezh, then a turn southward down the Don river to meet an attack headed east from Belgorod. This in turn would be followed by another attack south down the Don river. The theory was that in this way all Soviet forces west of the Don would be destroyed. The major striking force of the German army would then head south into the Caucasus. Since there were not enough troops to cover the approximately 450 miles of Don frontage which would be left unguarded as the Germans headed south, her allies were to provide the needed units. By the fall of 1942, 24 Romanian, 10 Italian and 10 Hungarian divisions were in the East,[10] the majority of them in three armies on the Don with the Italian 8th Army separating the Hungarian 2nd in the north and the Romanian 3rd in the south, lest they fight each other instead of the Russians.

At the last moment a German officer flying with key documents on the planned offensive crashed in Soviet territory, but Stalin took these maps and papers to be a plant. On June 28, the Germans struck toward Voronezh, crashing through the Soviet defenses, forming a bridgehead across the Don, seizing the city and then heading south. The attack further south also pushed through rapidly and joined the spearhead from the north, but the result was not what the Germans expected. The Russians had not fought as effectively as in prior months and some Soviet units were trapped, but this was no repetition of the 1941 encirclements. The same thing happened with the next blow. The German armor from the north pushed toward Millerovo, a city between the Don and Donets rivers which was also the objective of an attack from the west, but once again the meeting spearheads caught a small, not a huge, haul of prisoners. And when, in a third such massive pincer operation the German units with the exception of the 6th Army (which still headed eastward) converged on Rostov and the lower Don, they found the bulk of the Soviet forces gone and the bridges blown.[a]

The great changes in the 1942, as contrasted with the 1941, operations were several. It was not only that the Red Army leadership had learned a great deal in the hard school of battle and that the Germans had been unable to make up for their losses of the year before. More important was the altered leadership styles of Hitler and Stalin. Both were changing the higher commanders as before, Stalin still more frequently than Hitler, but there was one major divergence. Hitler, who had become accustomed to more and more direct interference into the details of tactical operations in the winter crisis of 1941–42, continued with this procedure. In fact, in order to exert more immediate control over the operation, he moved in mid-July from his field headquarters in East Prussia to a new headquarters near Vinnitsa in the Ukraine, where the officers and secretaries could still smell the lightly buried corpses of the Jews who had been slaughtered after working on its construction.[11]

Stalin, on the other hand, was more willing to listen to his military experts than before, especially on one key point. Shaposhnikov had been replaced (for health reasons that were very real) on June 26, two days

[a] The Germans quickly built new ones and formed a bridgehead on the south bank.

before the start of the German offensive, by General, later Marshal, Vasilevsky as Chief of the General Staff. At his insistence, it would appear, the forces in the southern area were ordered on or about July 6 to make fighting retreats instead of being halted in place to be surrounded and destroyed as had happened in 1941.[a] Although there were some signs of internal trouble in the Red Army and desperate measures were resorted to in order to maintain morale, cohesion, and discipline, the fact remains that units of the army either retreated coherently or at least could be pulled together again. The Germans had conquered a large and in part very rich area by the end of July, but the capture of between 100,000 and 200,000 prisoners in three encirclement battles showed that the great victory which Hitler trumpeted to his officers in Directive 45 of July 23, 1942, was in part illusory. The Soviet Union had indeed been dealt a blow, but the assertion that the goals of the summer offensive had been "reached for the most part" would sound increasingly silly in the following weeks.[12]

This euphoric view of developments was, however, honestly believed at German headquarters, at least by Hitler himself, and on the basis of this belief, new operational orders were issued.[13] These provided for operations conducted simultaneously rather than in sequence. Divisions of the 11th Army as well as the heavy siege artillery, just being freed for new deployment after the capture of Sevastopol, were sent north to take Leningrad instead of being sent eastward into the North Caucasus as contemplated at one point. Even more dramatically, the bulk of the forces of Army Groups A and B, which had originally been assigned to the advance eastwards so that they could prepare for and shield a *subsequent* offensive southward into the Caucasus, were now headed south immediately with only the German 6th Army directed eastwards toward Stalingrad. To put it crudely, of the five German armies available in the south, one was sent to the Leningrad front, one toward Stalingrad, and three (4th Panzer, 1st Panzer and 17th) toward objectives in the Caucasus area. As the latter headed in this direction, they made the great advances to be described shortly, but the 6th Army was left not only practically by itself but for a while without even the minimum of supplies needed to move at all. Hitler's personal role in this eccentric set of

---

[a] The evidence on this issue is reviewed in Ziemke, *Moscow to Stalingrad*, p. 343. It may be, but this is pure speculation, that the initial reaction of Stalin, which was to take the attack toward Voronezh as the first step of what he had anticipated, namely an offensive toward Moscow, made him more amenable to advice when the German spearheads turned south, not north, and it became increasingly obvious that the German offensive was concentrated on an area where the Soviets could give ground, if they had to, more easily than before Moscow.

operations, a role made even more emphatic by his simultaneous insistence on measures to cope with what he considered likely steps by the Western Allies to assist their beleaguered Russian ally, may have set the stage not only for the curious German deployment of forces but for the extraordinary reactions of Hitler subsequently when things began to go very obviously wrong. ·

At first it certainly looked as if all were going swiftly in favor of the Germans and disastrously for the Soviet Union and its allies. By the end of July the three armies headed south and southeast were across the lower 150 miles of the Don and at two places had cut the railway connecting the North Caucasus area with Stalingrad. In the first two weeks of August, German troops, moving through some of the richest agricultural area of the Soviet Union, seized the city of Krasnodar, and occupied the first of the oil field areas—that near Maikop—which were a major goal of the whole 1942 operation.[14] The installations had been wrecked by the Russians, but the Germans expected to fix them while their forces rushed on to the other oil fields, those at Grozny, 200 miles further east and those at Baku, an additional 300 miles away. But they would never reach either of these objectives.[15]

As the Germans raced across the plains of the North Caucasus area and into the foothills of the mountains themselves, they were able to make dramatic advances because the Red Army was still retreating; but in this process the balance began to shift. On the German side, not only were there supply difficulties as the units covered great distances from their bases in the Ukraine, but the spearheads became smaller even as they were increasingly separated by vast distances. By late August, German forces trying to push their way into the Soviet naval base of Novorossysk were 300 miles away from those which had captured Mozdok on the road to Grozny; between those spearheads, others were trying to force the Caucasus passes to seize Tuapse and Sukhumi on the Black Sea. At each of these points steadily smaller and more exhausted German assault units faced the stiffening resistance of a Red Army summoned to desperate exertions by its government.

In the face of the German advance, the Soviet leadership was trying hard to pull together a Red Army which threatened to dissolve into headlong flight. Because so many of the reserves available to the Stavka had been concentrated behind the Central front to defend Moscow, much of the reinforcement went to the defense of Stalingrad and came to play a significant role in slowing the German advance in that direction. Moving units to the two main Soviet commands trying to stem the German onrush further south, the Black Sea Group in the west and the

North Group in the east, both under the Transcaucasus Front, was both difficult and slow. Some reinforcements did get there, partly by rail and partly by sea, but a substantial proportion came from the south, that is, from the border with Turkey.

For some time, the Turkish government had watched developments to the north with a combination of anxiety and greed. There was, or at least seemed to be, the possibility that if the Soviet Union fell apart under German blows, some of the areas with Turkic population might fall to Turkey. There was, however, the alternative possibility that an expanding and aggressive Germany might then be poised on the northern as well as the European border of Turkey and demand the right to drive across the country into Syria and Iraq, both now under British military control. In June of 1942, with the surrender of Tobruk after a two-day siege even while the Germans were blasting their way into Sevastopol, it looked for a moment as if the Germans might show up on Turkey's southern border as well! This situation, however, changed in July and early August as the British held at El Alamein. Whatever else Turkey might or might not do, it was certainly not about to join the Axis. Under these circumstances, the Soviet high command ordered seven divisions and four brigades from the Turkish border north to face the Germans.[16]

THE BRITISH AIR OFFENSIVE

In the terrible emergency, there was for a short time a plan, previously mentioned, to send two British divisions to the Caucasus front; but the British disaster in North Africa made that project impossible. Instead, there was beginning in mid-July a project under the code-name "Velvet" to send a combined British–United States air force to help support the Russian army in the Caucasus. Though at first welcomed by Stalin, it was subsequently rejected by him. As soon as it appeared that the Red Army could hold the Germans, he did not want any British or American forces operating from Soviet bases.[17] Although the Western Allies could not make a landing in Western Europe in 1942 and thereby reduce pressure on the Eastern Front, as Churchill explained to Stalin in August, the very fact that this possibility existed restrained Germany from concentrating all its forces on the Eastern Front. Hitler believed that it was much too risky to denude the West,[18] and even ordered the transfer of one crack division from the East against the contingency of operations in the West or in Norway.[19]

When Churchill was in Moscow in August to explain to Stalin the impossibility of a landing in Western Europe that year at a time when the situation on the southern portion of the Eastern Front was particularly grim, other ways of helping alleviate the terrible pressure on the U.S.S.R. were naturally discussed.[20] Ironically the recent disaster of the convoy PQ 17 and the shipping needs for the forthcoming "Torch" operation in Northwest Africa meant that the convoys to Murmansk were being temporarily suspended. The Torch operation itself, however, would provide relief for the Soviet Union, and after initial doubts Stalin recognized this. A point on which Stalin's views fitted in with the thinking of Churchill as well as the plans, intentions, and capabilities of the British was his insistence on the maintenance and if possible expansion of the British bombing campaign against Germany.[21]

The Royal Air Force had begun bombing Germany in 1940 and had done so on a slowly increasing scale in 1941. It was, however, an effort with much smaller effects than anticipated. Two of the reasons for this either were or soon became evident; the third was not understood until much later in the war. First, there was simply the inadequate number of planes. Throughout 1941 and into 1942, there were never more than 300–400 bombers available and many of them were of the smaller two-engine variety. Only the massive commitment of human and material resources to this effort in the winter of 1941–42 could make a substantial difference as, beginning in 1942, there was a higher proportion of the larger four-engine bombers and a slow increase in the total as new planes more than replaced those lost to the enemy, the weather and accidents. The second reason was that the bomber, forced by antiaircraft fire to fly high above the target and unable to see through the cloud cover, rarely was able to drop a bomb accurately on a small target and even when there were no clouds rarely hit the target. This fact, that bombs generally missed whatever installation or factory they were aimed at, did not become apparent until late in 1941 as it became obvious that the bombing offensive was having little effect on the German war economy. The third reason, not understood until the last months of the war, was that in a well-functioning industrial society, most damage to factories and other installations can be repaired fairly rapidly so that only repeated bombing of the same place can have more than temporary effect.

In early 1942 there had been a real crisis in Britain's consideration of the bombing offensive, and the decisions then made largely set the pattern for the balance of the European war. Here was the one way in which Britain could try to strike at Germany effectively so that the pressures of the Prime Minister's personal inclination,[22] combined with those of practicality in a war then going disastrously badly for the country and the insistence of a Soviet ally who was bearing the brunt of the burden of fighting. As the only visible realistic alternative to abandoning all offensive action against Germany for the foreseeable future, the internal debate was resolved in favor of a new bombing directive of February 14, 1942, which called for aiming points in built up areas, not dockyards and factories. The cities of Germany would be levelled, her air force obliged to defend its home, and German industry incapacitated in the process. A new commander, Arthur Harris, took over Bomber Command on February 22 and assumed, entirely correctly, that this was the program he was supposed to carry out.[23]

The new commander had the support of his government and quickly launched his crews on a new set of operations.[24] At the end of March, a massive raid destroyed large parts of the city of Lübeck; a month later it was the turn of Rostock.[25] The German response was to try to retaliate by attacks on British cities rather than a shift to the defense, a posture then still consonant with the German air force's own preference.[26] There was controversy at the highest levels of the British government over the advantages and prospects of a continued focus on area bombing of German cities, a focus of which Churchill's scientific advisor, Lord Cherwell, was perhaps the most influential advocate.[27] Whatever the doubts, the program went forward. The careful marshalling of all available airplanes, including many from training units, for the 1000 airplane raid on Cologne at the end of May, marked a new stage. The destruction was considerable and the whole concept caught the imagination of a British public at a time of constant defeats.[28] It marked a real break in Hitler's confidence in the Luftwaffe when its first reports proved ridiculous.[29] It has yet to lead observers to question whether the term "success" should be applied, as it so often still is, to Hitler's original building up of a German air force in violation of the 1919 peace treaty and in a world practically without heavy bombers.

In the summer and fall of 1942, there were also suggestions that the bombing offensive might serve not only as an interim form of support for the Soviet Union until a major landing on the continent proved possible but that Great Britain ought so to increase its bomber force that an invasion by a large land army would not be needed. Although for a while Churchill appears to have considered this possibility seriously, especially in June 1942 when the surrender of Tobruk and the whole series of disasters in land fighting in North Africa and Southeast Asia raised questions about Britain's ability to field effective land forces, that concept was pushed aside. A major air offensive would continue against Germany, only temporarily shifted to the Mediterranean in support of

"Torch," but as an aid to a comprehensive effort in which armies would play a major role.[30] In August 1942, 38 percent of Germany's fighters were on the Western Front and 43 percent in the East; by April of 1943, 45 percent were in the West and 27 percent in the East. This was one field in which the Western Allies could provide their hard-pressed ally with some relief even as they themselves struggled, as described in the preceding chapter, to keep the sea lanes open.

Those sea lanes were, of course, essential for any supplies from her allies to reach the Soviet Union, and during 1942 the pace of deliveries did improve, most of the increase coming via the Persian Gulf and the Pacific. Roosevelt in particular tried to get shipments expedited, and as there were difficulties between United States Ambassador William Standley and the Russians, the President had former Ambassador Joseph E. Davies sounded in October 1942 about taking another turn at the embassy. When Davies refused, the President kept Standley there but insisted both on adherence to the unconditional aid policy followed since 1941 and the role of those he trusted to carry it out, especially General Philip R. Faymonville as Lend-Lease Representative to the Soviet Union.[31]

THE EASTERN FRONT: HALTING THE GERMAN ADVANCE IN THE SOUTH

Whatever the diversions to the West and the Mediterranean and whatever direct aid might be sent, the basic problem of stemming the Germans was one for the Red Army. In August and the first weeks of September, that looked frighteningly difficult. German forces were still pushing into the Caucasus; Soviet troops were still retreating. Some of the local people, unhappy with Soviet rule (as most of them had been with the Tsarist rule imposed on them in nineteenth-century conquests), collaborated with the Germans in the foolish hope of receiving better treatment and more independence from Berlin than from Moscow. On July 28, Stalin issued the famous Order No. 227 calling on the soldiers not to take a step back, appealing to their patriotism, and threatening dire punishment for any who retreated.[32] The reinforcements sent did begin to stiffen resistance during September. On the Black Sea coast, in the mountain passes, and before Grozny, the Russian forces were recovering. Fighting more effectively, they were slowing down the German advance. In a few instances, German spearheads still managed to make occasional substantial advances, but by mid-September the situation was clearly changing.

The German reaction to the increasingly difficult fighting they were now facing took two forms. One was of the ordinary type. They tried to speed up the sending of supplies, occasionally air lifting them, and they hoped to move additional troops to the front, including Italian mountain divisions to fight in the Caucasus.[33] The other reaction was rather different. It was a confusion of visionary plans and drastic personnel changes. On September 12 Hitler explained to the commanders of the thrust to the east that they were not only to seize Stalingrad but thereafter to move on to the Caspian Sea, take Astrakhan and carry out all sorts of other projects.[34] While he incorrectly imagined that all was going wonderfully on that eastward thrust (to be reviewed below), Hitler correctly sensed that the Caucasus operation was running into difficulty, and he reacted by a series of drastic personnel changes. Earlier he had sent home the Commander-in-Chief of Army Group B; now he dropped Field Marshal List, the Commander-in-Chief of Army Group A, and for a while took over direction of the Army Group himself on September 10. A few days later he dismissed General Halder, the Chief of the Army General Staff since 1938, and appointed Kurt Zeitzler who had been Chief of Staff of the Army Group in the West. His break with the highest military commanders was such that he ordered stenographic records made of his military conferences thereafter and for a while barely spoke to Keitel and Jodl, intending to replace the latter with General Paulus, the 6th Army commander.[35]

This series of changes should in my judgement be seen as reflecting a real break in Hitler's view of the campaign. If all had been going as well as he thought, and if his revised plan for the offensive with its two simultaneous thrusts was as brilliant as he was certain it had to be, and if the Soviet Union was as exhausted as he believed, and if the Red Army was falling apart and without substantial reserves, as most higher German military leaders asserted, the only possible explanation for the difficulties on the road to Tuapse, Sukhumi and Grozny must be either a bad plan — and he was certainly not about to acknowledge that — or the incompetence of his generals. Change in these was obviously needed and he acted accordingly. But the reality of stiffening Soviet resistance and of exhaustion among the German assault columns was not affected by Hitler's refusal to eat his meals with Keitel and Jodl or by the various personnel changes under way and contemplated. As for reinforcing the German Caucasus offensive with additional divisions, this was impossible, in part because some of the available forces had been sent north for the attack on Leningrad, in part because during August and September the eastward thrust toward Stalingrad was running into trouble of its own and came to have first call on whatever manpower and supplies could be sent.

In July, the Stavka had concentrated on Stalingrad before the Germans had focused their attention on it. Major steps to mobilize additional resources in defense of the city were taken in mid-July, a Stalingrad Front was established, and new forces were sent to it, some of them from reserves originally built up to defend Moscow against the anticipated German attacks there. From the Soviet perspective, Stalingrad was important not only as a major industrial center and as a place where the Germans could halt all shipping on the Volga but as the major connecting point to any operations in the Caucasus. Furthermore, it was far easier to reinforce from the center of the country than the front further south. The original plan was to hold the eastern portion of the great bend of the Don river and the river itself above and below that bend. Above the bend, the Germans were deploying the divisions of their allies to hold the advance line; below it they quickly advanced into the North Caucasus as already described. In the bend itself, the German 6th Army was to advance against the Stalingrad Front.[36]

The diversion of forces and supplies to the advance into the Caucasus had left the 6th Army stranded for ten days without the gasoline needed to move forward. As it resumed its advance in the second half of July, it began to be slowed down not by supply shortages but by stiffening Soviet resistance.[37] The Germans thereupon split their 4th Panzer Army, with the headquarters and three of its corps heading for Stalingrad from the southwest, while one corps was added to the 1st Panzer Army which was going southward. During the first part of August, the 6th Army was able to destroy a large proportion of the Red Army units in the Don bend while 4th Panzer swept up over 50 miles from the southwest. In the last ten days of the month, the northern German attacks broke across the Don, and reached the Volga north of the city of Stalingrad even as the southern pincer reached the city's edge and made contact with the 6th Army. By September 3, the city was besieged from northwest and south with the broad river behind it to the east.[38]

The Russian high command was not about to allow the city to fall without a bitter fight. General (later Marshal) A. I. Eremenko, recovered from wounds suffered earlier in the war, was sent to command the Stalingrad Front; Zhukov was recalled from an assignment on the Central front and sent to direct counter-attacks against the 6th Army on its exposed northern flank between the Don and Volga rivers. In the city itself, another very able commander, General V.I. Chuikov, was put in charge of 62nd Army, the main defending force. A steady stream of reinforcements was sent in during the last days of August and the first days of September so that the Soviet commanders on the spot began to have substantial forces to work with.[39]

Counter-attacks from the north battered the Germans on September 5 and 6 but were held by the Germans who pushed into the city in the following days. As more Soviet troops were sent into the city, the fighting began to be a block-by-block slogging match, moving back and forth in bloody fighting. Heavy losses for both sides characterized the street fighting, but when another major Soviet counter-attack on the 18th and 19th failed to drive back the Germans, the latter were left in control of much of the city. But they did not have all of it, had enormous difficulties in going forward and did not want to go back. The Soviets, on the other hand, were in a difficult situation as well. Their remaining troops in portions of the city were in desperate straits, and the two initial sets of counter-attacks had failed to dislodge the Germans. Both sides had new choices to make.[40]

The Germans could, theoretically, have pulled back to the Don, used their regrouped army to clear out all Soviet bridgeheads across the Don, and simply held there. No serious consideration appears to have been given to this possibility. But if the city were to be taken, additional troops were needed. In the immediate vicinity these could come only from the German units still west of the Don masking the Soviet Don bridgeheads. The decision was taken to do this, replacing the German troops with Romanian divisions previously assigned to the Caucasus campaign. What this meant was that added miles of the northern flank of Army Group B would be assigned to Germany's allies while the German troops of 6th Army battered their way block by block and house by house through the city. It is surely worthy of mention that the tactic frequently utilized by the Germans earlier in the war, the surrounding of a major city by armored spearheads cutting it off, was never contemplated; the forces needed for such an operation simply no longer existed.

There is no evidence that at this time Hitler was willing either to give up one of the major projections on the Eastern Front, like those at Demyansk or Rzhev, to free up reserves which could be sent to nourish or to shield the Stalingrad offensive or to transfer major units from the West on the assumption that after mid-September the weather precluded an invasion across the Channel.[41]

Hitler also deliberately gave up the one other way of rebuilding the strength of the German army divisions which were slowly bleeding away on the Eastern Front. The German air force had tens of thousands of men in excess of its needs and these could have been sent for retraining as infantry replacements. Since Göring was unwilling to give them up to the influence of reactionary army officers, a sentiment Hitler strongly shared, they were organized into "air force field divisions" instead. These units of untrained men led by equally unprepared officers would be the bane of Germany's armed forces in the short period of their existence. Horrendous casualties to no useful military purpose were the result of this grotesque innovation.[42]

The weeks following September 20 were accordingly ones in which the German troops ground forward slowly, in the process focusing public attention inside Germany on the city named for the leader of the Soviet Union. Hitler only added to this fixation by his own repeated references to it in speeches on September 30 and November 8, 1942.[43] This was one city, he assured everyone inside and outside the country publicly, that Germany already held and would never give up. What the German soldiers fighting in the ruins of the city thought of these remarks is not recorded.

Stalin had decided to do everything possible to hold the city or whatever portions of it the Red Army could cling to, but acting with advice from Vasilevsky and Zhukov, he came to see this not merely as a matter of getting reinforcements into the struggle for every house and factory. Beginning on September 12 and continuing thereafter, plans were developed for an operation code-named "Uranus" which looked to a very different form of defense for the city. New armies were to be pulled together for a huge pincer operation that would strike out of the Don bridgeheads in the north and across the steppe in the south to cut off the German forces battering their way forward inside the city. It would be necessary to send minimal, not maximum, reinforcements into the fighting inside Stalingrad so that the Soviet units there might hopefully hold out and in the process keep the German army occupied there. Simultaneously, a carefully coordinated buildup would be organized at the two intended axes of advance with every precaution taken to keep this project concealed from the Germans and to delude them about the strength and direction of the planned operation.[44]

As the exhausted soldiers of both sides grappled with each other in the rubble of the city, the Red Army began to implement its dispositions for "Uranus." With great circumspection, troops and equipment were gathered for the offensive. Unlike the prior counter-attacks into the German 6th Army's northern flank, in which arriving units had been thrown into battle practically from the march and piecemeal, this time massive assault forces were gathered and supplies for them collected, with all such reinforcement held back until the date set for the great counter-offensive. If the center could hold and the Germans could be kept ignorant of the plan, the prospects for success were great.[45]

These prospects were actually increased by four other factors. First, there was the general unwillingness of the Germans at this stage of the war to credit the Soviets with the ability to develop and implement a coherent offensive operation on a major scale and in depth. Secondly, the steps which the Germans themselves had taken to reinforce the push into Stalingrad without providing added German troops left the northern flank of their assault entirely and the southern flank very largely entrusted to Romanian troops, whom the Germans had not provided with the equipment needed to fight off a Soviet attack. Thirdly, the Germans had some information on another Soviet offensive project for the Central front, code-named "Mars," which may well have been intended as an alternative to "Uranus" if the Germans had taken all of Stalingrad, or pulled back there, or if other developments had made "Uranus" impossible.[46] Finally, although it is very difficult to define or to document, there appears to have been a real stiffening of morale in the Soviet Union and in the Red Army after the "no step back" decree of July 28. As the fronts held, the Soviet Union appeared to get a second breath; a new sense that the disasters of the summer could again, as in 1941, be overcome, and that the invader might once more be halted and thrown back appeared in the country. The soldiers fought and died in Stalingrad while the forces for "Uranus" were being assembled. The rest of the Eastern Front, however, had not been quiet all summer and into the fall and must be examined.

THE EASTERN FRONT: NORTHERN AND CENTRAL PORTIONS

At the far northern end of the front, there were no significant land operations after the Soviet spring offensive had been halted. German projects for new attacks had to be scrapped because no new divisions could be sent. On the main front in Finland, there were renewed plans for a German drive on Kandalaksha and a Finnish drive to Belomorsk, both designed to cut the Murmansk railway. Neither of these offensives was ever launched because both depended on the Germans taking Leningrad and thereby relieving Finnish units for the Belomorsk and German reinforcements for the Kandalaksha operation. From the perspective of the Germans, therefore, all land actions in the north depended on the offensive in the Leningrad area, ordered in the basic April directive as a follow up to the main attack in the southern segment of the Eastern Front.[47]

On its own, the German Army Group in the north, after completing the destruction of the Soviet 2nd Shock Army in July discussed in Chapter 5, had developed several similar projects, but of these only one was eventually carried out. The relief route to the Demyansk pocket was so narrow and so frequently under water that in anticipation of a second winter campaign some new steps were clearly necessary. Hitler would not authorize a withdrawal from the pocket, which he saw with some justice as a key part of the German Army Group Center's posture of threatening a renewed offensive against Moscow. The alternative was a local operation to widen the corridor, and in the last days of September and early October, 1942, the Germans were able to carry out such an operation.[48]

The major German effort in the north, however, was to be Operation "Nordlicht" (Northern Lights) against Leningrad. During the summer, the big siege guns that had been used against Sevastopol were moved to the other end of the front, along with some additional heavy artillery. Soon after, five of the divisions which had been in the Crimean campaign followed them north. The argument of the commander of Army Group North, Field Marshal Georg von Kuechler, that the seizure of the Leningrad area and the establishment of a firm land connection to Finland were not the simple operation Hitler imagined them to be, produced not added divisions but the appointment of von Manstein and the air force general who had worked with him, General Wolfram von Richthofen, to run operation "Nordlicht." Having cracked Sevastopol, they were the obvious team to crack Leningrad.[a]

Before this attack could begin, however, the Red Army launched its own offensive. The Volkhov Front under General Meretskov had been preparing an attack of its own designed to break open land communication to Leningrad. Attacking on August 27, before the Germans could start "Nordlicht," the Russian forces broke into the bottleneck which the Germans held east of the city. The fighting was so fierce, and the prospect of the Volkhov Front breaking through to the Leningrad Front so immediate, that one by one the German divisions from the Crimea scheduled for "Nordlicht" had to be thrown into the battle. Dissatisfied with the way the fighting was going, Hitler placed Manstein in charge of it. A German counter-attack cut off the Soviet units which had broken into the bottleneck while a break-out attempt from Leningrad across the Neva river was also beaten off.

The Soviet attempt to relieve the siege had been defeated in a month's fighting by the Germans. By the end of September, the Volkhov Front was back where it had started after suffering close to 50,000 casualties. The Germans, however, had suffered heavy casualties themselves but that was not all. The divisions, equipment and supplies which were supposed to carry out operation "Nordlicht" had been consumed in the defense of the bottleneck. There would be no German offensive against

[a] It should be pointed out that in 1941 Manstein had been a corps commander in the first German offensive toward Leningrad.

Leningrad in 1942 at all, and hence also no attacks further north to cut the railway from Murmansk. All summer the Russians had sent supplies into Leningrad by ship across Lake Ladoga, evacuating civilians on the return trip. In the coming winter, they would again use an ice road across the frozen lake. Manstein received a new assignment elsewhere.[49]

On the central portion of the Eastern Front, both sides had very large forces, and at the end of July, Zhukov's West Front launched a major offensive to collapse the German 9th Army line east and south of Rzhev. For the Red Army, success in this offensive would have meant ending a threatened new offensive toward Moscow; for the Germans, holding on to Rzhev was essential to maintaining any credible threat of a renewed advance on the Soviet capital. All through August and most of September the bitter fighting raged, going first in favor of the Russians and later against them. Zhukov himself was called away by Stalin at the end of August to lead the counter-attacks against the Germans driving into Stalingrad,[50] but the offensive ground on after his departure. When the fighting died down, the Russians had reclaimed an area roughly 15 by 50 miles, but they had been unable to dislodge the Germans from Rzhev or to cut the railway to it.

Casualties on both sides had been very heavy in this fighting as well, but here too a Soviet offensive operation, although not successful in reaching its main objective, had as a significant by-product the spoiling of a planned German offensive. The Germans had hoped to launch a major operation of their own to crush the Soviet forces in the great bulge around Sukhinichi and to clear the main north-south railway at Kirov where the Russian winter offensive had cut it. The Soviet offensive against Rzhev, by absorbing most of the available German reserves, reduced this project to a minimal operation of no strategic significance. If in 1942 the Red Army was not yet able to launch major successful summer offensives of its own, it had certainly found a way to keep the Germans from carrying out even limited offensive operations on two-thirds of the Eastern Front.[51]

By the summer of 1942, the fighting in the East was no longer confined to the front lines daily marked on the maps in Stalin's and Hitler's headquarters and anxiously followed, even if not quite so accurately, by governments and ordinary people around the globe. In the area behind the German front lines, guerillas, generally referred to as partisans, were playing a significant role in organizing resistance to the invader.[52] On the assumption that no enemy forces would be allowed to penetrate the territory of the U.S.S.R., no significant preparations for that contingency had been made before June 1941, but within days of the German invasion, the government called on the population overrun by the Germans to resist. Small partisan groups began to be organized in the late summer and fall of 1941, generally centered around party and police (NKVD) activists, local officials from the administration, Machine-Tractor Stations, or state or collective farms, or army officers who had escaped capture in the encirclement battles. These leaders collected Red Army stragglers, especially from the great battles on the central part of the front, into small bands which in the early months of the war generally hid out in the forests and were more concerned with survival than resistance. As it became increasingly obvious that the overwhelming majority of Russian prisoners of war were going to be shot or allowed to die of starvation and disease, some made successful efforts to escape while being moved or in makeshift holding areas, and these escapees also tended to join the partisans.

As long as the German army was advancing rapidly in 1941, what minimal resistance activities the partisans engaged in was more a nuisance than a threat for the invaders. The woods and marshes which provided shelter for the partisans were being left further and further behind the front; and while they could quite easily pick up discarded infantry weapons on the vast battlefields nearby, the small partisan bands would clearly be no match for the Germans once they had won against the Red Army. But the Germans did not win, and that produced a whole series of changes in the situation. First, it meant that the winter crisis at the front obliged the Germans to send to the front lines as reinforcements many of the rear area security troops whose primary function had been the protection of the German army's lines of communications and the maintenance of order in the rear areas. Although these Security Divisions, as they were called, consisted of low categories of troops commanded by elderly, invalided, or incompetent officers, in the desperate situation the German army faced in the winter of 1941–42 anybody in uniform who could carry a rifle was needed. This obviously relaxed the hold of the Germans on the vast areas they had occupied.

Secondly, the breaks through the German front by the Red Army enabled the latter to open routes of contact to the partisans, routes over which officers and supplies could be brought to them. Furthermore, the slow revival of the Red Air Force and the German need to concentrate its planes on ground support operations at critical points on the front meant that where and as the Soviet Union used small airplanes in single flights to drop or even land officers and critical supplies to the partisans, such flights were most unlikely to be intercepted by the German air force. Soviet inspectors and organizers could be sent in and out. The occupied territories, in other words, had neither a solid wall nor a solid roof.

Perhaps more important than these tactical factors was the overwhelming military–political one that the Soviet system was clearly going to stay, not vanish. The partisans were the local arm of a continuing system, not the remnants of a disappearing regime. They could and did begin conscripting men and women in the villages, they could count on far more support than before, and, above all, they could remind all the Red Army stragglers from the 1941 battles who had made quiet new homes for themselves that their military obligation was still in effect. Only by service in the partisan movement could they expect to redeem themselves in the face of questions about their performance in battle.

In a few months in the winter of 1941–42, the partisan movement grew from a few thousand, scattered in tiny bands, to a substantial force, disparate but significant, enrolling at least a quarter of a million members by the spring of 1942 and growing thereafter by volunteers and conscripts, with these latter categories slowly constituting an ever-increasing proportion of the total as compared with the Red Army stragglers.

It must not be thought that this movement grew evenly in the whole area occupied by the Germans. There were almost none in most of the lands annexed by the Soviet Union under the terms of its agreement with Germany, the northeastern portion of Poland being the sole exception at this time. In the open agricultural area of the central and southern Ukraine there was in effect no place for partisans to hide. While there were small underground movements in some of the cities, and partisans did operate in the mountains and caves of the Crimea, the small bands organized in such open areas, as well as the Northern Caucasus seized by the Germans in the summer of 1942, were generally hunted down by the Germans fairly quickly.[53]

It was in the wooded and swampy areas further north, the northern Ukraine, Belorussia, and the portions of the Russian Soviet Federated Socialist Republic (RSFSR) behind the fronts of the German Army Groups Center and North that the partisan movement flourished. Here they came to control large portions of the rural areas, issuing their own newspapers, punishing any suspected of collaboration with the Germans, collecting intelligence for the Red Army and government or providing a haven for those who did this. They acted generally as the long arm of the Soviet government, reaching back into areas nominally now under German control and reminding the population that the Soviet government was coming back, and probably quite soon. On a continent where, with the exception of Poland and Yugoslavia, most of the conquered peoples were quietly cooperating with the conqueror, those living in the occupied Union of Soviet Socialist Republics were reminded that big brother was watching, not from Moscow or some government in exile, but from a camp just outside the village.

The areas in the central portion of the occupied territories which offered the best terrain for the partisans also furnished a base from which roving partisan bands could be sent into areas which, as experience quickly showed, were not so suitable for guerilla warfare. This meant primarily the central belt of the Ukrainian SSR, an area about which the Soviet government was in any case very much concerned because of its nationalistic tendencies.[54] The dispatch of several partisan bands on what were really showing-the-flag expeditions from the main partisan area into the Ukraine must be understood as a means of reminding the population that Soviet power would be restored there as well as in all the territory temporarily under the control of others.[55] And as will become quickly apparent, the Soviet government could always depend upon the Germans to provide new recruits for the partisan movement.

The military activity of the partisans was quite limited in 1941 and 1942. They attacked small German outposts, made the occupying forces uneasy by occasional raids on villages, and obviously interfered with any effective administration of the occupied area. Their most important military actions from the perspective of the Red Army were their attacks on German communications, especially the railways. They rarely tried to blow up the critical bridges, but repeated cuts in the railway tracks were a serious nuisance for the Germans, who found themselves more and more forced by the lack of adequate security forces to abandon most of the countryside and concentrate on defense and patrolling along the railway lines. Not until 1943 and 1944 were the partisans sufficiently well organized and supplied to conduct systematic strikes against the railways in a manner coordinated with Soviet offensive operations at the front, but the early signs of such dangers were becoming evident in 1942.

The German anti-partisan operations were on the whole both unsuccessful and counter-productive. The exception was operation "Hanover" in the area of Army Group Center described in Chapter 5; in that case the partisans fought alongside the Red Army regulars and were defeated with them. The Soviet casualties in that instance were in fact for the most part actually partisans, and subsequent Soviet efforts to revive the movement there failed.[56] In essentially all other anti-partisan operations, German army, SS and police units swept through previously designated areas, slaughtered thousands of civilians, burnt as many villages as possible, and once in a great while killed a few partisans. The latter for the most part usually escaped or hid out, only to resume activity afterwards, generally supported more than before by the population who had just received a demonstration of German pacification methods.

If the indiscriminate slaughter of civilians provided a major impetus for recruitment into the partisan movement in the main areas of partisan activity in the north and center, another German policy served the same function further south. As will be clear from the review of Germany's occupation policy in the next chapter, in 1942 the Germans instituted a large-scale program of forced labor recruitment in the Ukraine. This was not a matter of requiring the local people to work in their home area, clearing snow, rebuilding roads, or bringing in a harvest for the Germans to confiscate. Instead, they began seizing and deporting people by the tens of thousands to factories in Germany. This program—and the news which trickled back of the wretched treatment accorded such workers—drove thousands into the partisan movement in those areas of the Ukraine where earlier it had been difficult for the partisans to establish themselves. The cycle of violence escalated as the Germans responded to the increase in partisan activity; in the bloody confrontation between the cruelty of the occupier and the determination of the partisans, the Soviet regime increasingly created the basis for the return of the Red Army and Soviet power in territories which the maps showed to be nominally under German control.

THE ALLIED OFFENSIVE IN AFRICA

It was during the period that the Germans were pushing at the gates of the Caucasus and pounding their way into Stalingrad, while the Soviet high command was organizing the forces for operation "Uranus" to entrap and destroy the German and Romanian armies in and near Stalingrad, that the war in Africa changed with significant repercussions for the whole development of the war, including the Eastern Front.[57] At El Alamein the British 8th Army offensive opened in the night of October 23–24, breaking through and driving the Germans fleeing before them by November 4. Four days later, American and British troops landed in operation "Torch" on the Atlantic and Mediterranean coasts of French Northwest Africa. The last stages of the battle in Egypt had in fact been influenced by the knowledge that "Torch" was about to be carried out.[58]

The Northwest Africa landing achieved complete surprise; the Germans and Italians had their attention on the rapidly unravelling situation at the other end of the Mediterranean and thought that the great convoys they were hearing about might be designed either for Malta or a landing on the Libyan coast behind Rommel's retreating army.

The North African landing was a massive undertaking involving huge convoys from Great Britain as well as directly from the United States. In view of the shortage of aircraft carriers—these were the months of the most desperate fighting on and around Guadalcanal—several of the first completed escort carriers, small carriers which were in fact variant versions of merchant ships, quite literally just turned over to the navy, were allocated to the invasion force.[59] While the Soviet Union at the time (and some scholars since) complained about the delays in launching a second front as if American and British men, ships, and planes were resting idle somewhere, the grim reality was one of training cut short to meet deadlines set very optimistically in the hope that all would go smoothly.

The hopes associated with "Torch" for the Allies were, however, only partly realized.[60] It had been anticipated that the French in North Africa would quickly turn from Vichy and join the effort against Germany and Italy, but this proved to be a misassessment.[61] The governors remained loyal to Pétain, who expected them to fight the primarily American landing forces assisted by some British units; the local troop commanders with very few exceptions led their men in resistance to the invaders; and those who sympathized with the cause of the Allies and tried to take over control to swing the area to the Allied side were quickly disarmed and arrested.[62]

The French at first fought at the beaches and landing sites, inflicting considerable casualties, but were pushed back over the next few days by the overwhelming strength, equipment and determination of the landing forces, many of them in action for the first time.[63] The combination of a Soviet front holding in the East and the British victory at El Alamein made it impossible for the Germans to get Spain into the war on their side and thus close off the Mediterranean portion of the landing. Now that the United States and British troops were safely ashore, the great questions were: what next? and how quickly? The question, what next, revolved about the failure to rally the French forces to the Allied side, a situation which threatened to bog down the American forces for months as they conquered the whole huge area and then established a new administration in it.[64] By an extraordinary coincidence, this puzzle was resolved as the result of the fact that Admiral Darlan happened to be in Algiers to see his fatally ill son. Darlan decided to order the French forces to surrender as a result of an agreement with the Commander-in-Chief of the Allied invasion force, General Dwight D. Eisenhower.[65] On Darlan's side, this deal was apparently motivated in part by his recognition that the tide of battle in the war was turning from being in favor of the Axis to the Allies. An opportunist of great sensitivity as to who was winning, the check to the German 1942 summer offensive, which was obvious in November even before the Soviet counter-offensive had been launched, combined with the British victory at El Alamein and the Allied landing in Northwest Africa, showed Darlan which way the wind was blowing.[66] The fact that there was no German or Italian interference with the landing convoys or the landings themselves must have impressed the naval officer. A further factor appears to have been the arrival of General Henri Giraud, an escaped POW, whom the Allies hoped to install in charge of French forces in Northwest Africa, only to discover that he had no influence with anyone. The recognition of Darlan as head of the whole area, Giraud as head of all military forces, and General Juin as head of the army seemed for a moment to calm the situation.

Several aspects of this arrangement did not, however, work out. In the first place, at the most critical point, Tunisia, Darlan could not assert his authority. There the Vichy government found in Admiral Ésteva, the Resident-General, a pliant tool for the policy of continued collaboration with Germany in spite of the fact that German and Italian troops had now occupied hitherto unoccupied France according to Hitler's orders issued on November 10. No resistance had been offered to the Germans; Pétain's message to Roosevelt that the French when attacked would defend themselves applied only to the allies, not the enemies, of France at least until November 19 when it was far too late.[67] The repercussions of the situation in Tunisia on the war would be great.

Secondly, the arrangement with Darlan caused enormous political embarrassment in both Britain and the United States. The idea of a "deal" with so compromised a supporter of the Axis in the most recent past was very much resented, appeared to cast a pall over the cause and consistency of the United Nations, and suggested that similar deals might be made with all sorts of other unsavory figures when expediency appeared to call for it.[68] This uproar appears to have contributed to the timing of the announcement of the "unconditional surrender" policy at Casablanca in January 1943, although not to the adoption of such a policy which long pre-dated its public proclamation.

Finally, the Darlan deal naturally enraged the Free French in general and General de Gaulle in particular and would add further complexities to an already muddled and difficult situation. By a second equally extraordinary coincidence of timing, at least a part of this problem was resolved on December 24 by the assassination of Darlan at the hands of a young monarchist, but enough troubles were left to try the patience of those on the spot and the governments in Washington and London.

The other question, namely how quickly could the Allies move, was the most critical one of all. As early as August it had been evident to the Allied planners that the key to a full success for "Torch" would be the speed with which Tunisia could be seized.[69] The hope was that this could be done still in November 1942, and that such a success would clear North Africa and pave the way for a landing in Western Europe in the late summer of 1943, but a number of factors combined to make this impossible.

The first obstacle to quick success was built into the "Torch" operation itself. There was simply not enough shipping available to the Allies in the fall of 1942 to send to Northwest Africa both the troops and the transportation equipment that the commanders believed necessary. As explained in the preceding chapter, these were the months when the Germans were sinking Allied ships at a terrifying rate. The commanders had opted for troops over vehicles and this resulted in their being short on transport once ashore.[70] The shortage of transport naturally slowed down the movement of troops eastwards from Algiers to Tunis—a distance of well over 500 miles.

A second factor has already been alluded to, the refusal of Admiral Estéva to side with the Allies. He allowed the Germans to land on the Tunisian airfields, and by the time he and other French officers began to think about the possibility of defending the French colonial empire against the Germans and Italians, the Axis forces were far too numerous and well entrenched.[71]

The third element is implicit in the second: the decision of the Germans to fight for Tunis and to make a massive commitment of forces to this theater. While it is correct that from November 7 to 23, 1942, Hitler was away from his regular military headquarters in the East, spending time in Munich for his annual speech to the Party faithful and taking a vacation in Berchtesgaden afterwards, he certainly remained in touch with the situation at the fronts and made a whole series of key decisions.[72] It was at this time that he decided to occupy the unoccupied part of France in violation of the armistice agreement of 1940. He also ordered a rapid and massive buildup of Axis forces in Tunisia, and to include in this buildup large air force contingents from the Eastern Front, including most of the bombers hitherto engaged in the battle against the convoys on the route to Murmansk and a squadron of ninety bombers from support of the German offensive in the Caucasus.[73] In November and December 1942, more than 50,000 German and 18,000 Italian soldiers were rushed into Tunisia, with about another 100,000 German and 10,000 Italians in the subsequent months of the campaign.[74] Vast quantities of equipment were flown or shipped in and hundreds of fighters assigned to this new front.[a]

[a] The sending of troops and supplies by the Axis was very much hampered by friction between the Germans and Italians as well as by the extraordinarily high level of conflict between the

Concerned about a possible collapse of Italy and an attack on Europe from the south, Hitler was now determined to allocate resources to the North African campaign on a scale far greater than ever before in the war. Earlier, when urged by his naval advisors, Hitler had always kept the German commitment in this theater to a minimum; this was Italy's future living space and the fewer German resources were allocated to it the better. But now he saw Germany itself threatened from there, and therefore, at a time of enormous tension on the Eastern Front, he diverted to Tunisia troops and equipment desperately needed there. It must be noted, furthermore, that he thought of the campaign in Tunisia as more than a holding operation. The situation of the Africa Corps had always been difficult as long as supplies could not be sent across the short route from Sicily to the ports of Tunis and Bizerta. Now the Corps could work together with the new army being built up in Tunisia; and, when he discussed the whole situation there with Rommel on March 10, 1943, Hitler was seriously thinking of an operation against Casablanca after what he assumed would be a continued successful holding by Axis forces in Tunisia.[75] In the meantime, on the political side he still deferred in North Africa to Mussolini's preferences,[76] while a new German army headquarters under an experienced general (Hans-Jürgen von Arnim) moved from the Eastern Front was to command the rapidly built up Axis force sent to hold the position in the area.[77]

It had been the original plan of the Allies to cover the route to Bizerta and Tunis quickly with the aid of commandos and parachute troops. These projects had to be scrapped because of concern about the attitude of French troops in the area. The forces, primarily British with some American participation, which raced overland to seize the key harbor of Bône and move into Tunisia, crossed the border into Tunisia by November 16, but it soon became evident that they had lost the race.[78] As the weak Allied spearheads, inadequately covered by air forces without forward bases, ran into the German formation operating out of their bridgehead of Tunis and Bizerta, 20 and 40 miles away respectively, they were checked. In the first fighting, November 16–23, short supply routes and excellent air cover enabled the Germans to hold and push back the first Allied units on the scene. In the race to build up troops and equipment for a new assault, the British, Americans and some French could not pull together sufficient strength to push through the German and Italian forces on November 25–30. A German counterattack in the first days of December followed by more fighting in late

German army, navy and air force—always greater in the Mediterranean theater than elsewhere. For an account which stresses these troubles, see Salewski, *Seekriegsleitung*, 2: 251–68.

December only made the stalemate more obvious as the Allies were obliged to pull back and consolidate their position. They could now build up their strength and move forward the bases for their air cover, but the opportunity of the moment was gone in the face of quickly assembled and growing Axis strength. It would take a two-months pause before a new push could begin.[79]

Some French troops, nominally under General Giraud but actually commanded by General Juin, were participating on the Allied side, but the French forces in Tunisia—obedient to orders from Pétain in German-occupied Vichy—had missed their opportunity. This meant that Pétain had performed his last major service for the Germans: there had to be a major campaign for Tunisia and hence no Allied landing in the West in 1943. All of France could look forward to an additional year of German occupation; if Eisenhower's gamble on Darlan had paid off in terms of a moderately secure base in French Northwest Africa from which to launch a new offensive into Tunisia, the German gamble on Vichy had paid off at least as handsomely; they had kept the Western Allies out of Western Europe for additional months.

This point is especially clear when one sees how the recognition that "Torch" would not include a rapid seizure of Tunisia affected Allied planning for 1943. Into the last days of November, 1942, there was still hope in both London and Washington that an invasion of France would be feasible in the summer of 1943.[80] By December 8, the British Chiefs of Staff had concluded that this idea had to be abandoned and only operations in the Mediterranean would be possible;[81] and by the end of the month, Churchill had been brought to this point of view. As he put it on December 27, "the delay in taking the Tunisian tip in any case throws out all previous calculations."[82] The only concern of the Americans, and especially of General Marshall, was coming to be that the need to clear Tunisia and the follow-up operations in the Mediterranean in 1943 might become so extended as to postpone the cross-Channel attack even beyond 1944.[83]

The campaign for Tunisia thus came to have a role that was in many ways unexpected. Before that campaign is recounted briefly, those ways must be summarized. First, by drawing massive Axis forces into a new theater at a time of crisis on the Eastern Front, it provided important relief to the Soviet Union. The diversion of effort would make it impossible for the Germans to send a substantial army to the relief of Stalingrad—divisions could not be used in Tunisia and the south of Russia at the same time. Simultaneously, German air transport could not be used both to fly troops and supplies to North Africa and to fly supplies into the Stalingrad pocket; the two Allied campaigns greatly assisted each other in this regard.[84]

Second, the American army would receive its real baptism of fire in the war against Germany under circumstances in which set-backs, though unwelcome, were not disastrous. The lessons about training, equipment, and tactics learned in Tunisia would be of great value thereafter, while the testing of the higher commanders would show who could be expected to play a key role in the steadily enlarging American military effort.

Third, the obvious lengthening of the North African campaign required a new look at the strategy the Western Allies might follow. It was accordingly not a coincidence that the next meeting of the Allied leaders took place in North Africa at Casablanca. Stalin at this time did not wish to leave his headquarters even for a few days, so Churchill and Roosevelt met with their respective military leaders but without Soviet participation. Both probably came to feel that they had all the aggravation they needed—and more—in trying to cope with the interminable problems of the French leaders who feuded with each other as enthusiastically as with the British and Americans.

The Casablanca Conference held on January 14–23, 1943, reviewed the situation in all theaters and led to a series of agreements on strategy and priorities. The necessity for giving the highest priority to victory at sea over the U-Boats has been discussed in the preceding chapter. This was one issue on which there was no difference of opinion. It was not so easy to reach agreement on some other questions, but considerable discussions produced it all the same. An invasion of Sicily, near the end of July at the latest, earlier if possible, should follow on the final victory in North Africa as a part of the plan to knock Italy out of the war. An invasion across the Channel in 1943 was, in effect, ruled out in favor of one in 1944; there was as yet no prospect of an adequate number of American divisions in England and the shipping and landing craft for a major landing in France. The preparations for such an operation, however, were to go forward; and at the vehement insistence of the Americans, especially General Marshall, a staff to initiate serious planning for the invasion was set up under Lt. General Frederick E. Morgan soon after.[85] A major bombing offensive was to go forward with the Americans free to try to carry it out in daylight as they insisted was feasible and the British were certain it was not. Limited United States offensive action to keep the Japanese from consolidating their empire was agreed to as was a small British attack in Burma (code-named "Anakim"). Once it was clear that there would be no major northwest France landing in

1943, the Americans were insistent on offensives in the Pacific. Every effort was to be made to increase the delivery of supplies to the Soviet Union, including a resumption of the convoys to Murmansk, and similarly to increase aid to Chiang Kai-shek, including a buildup of the air supply route to Nationalist China.[86]

Even though the professional evaluations the British and American military leaders made of each other were not always flattering—Brooke in particular formed and thereafter maintained uniformly negative opinions of Marshall, Eisenhower and Patton[87]—the actual personal relationships between strong and very different personalities were in fact uncommonly good. It is simply not possible for anyone to spend a great deal of time studying World War II without being impressed by the constant and sincere efforts made by the highest British and American military leaders to work cooperatively with each other even in the face of the most serious differences of opinion on issues of great importance to all.[88]

There was, in addition, agreement on one other point of major significance. In the period preceding the conference, both in London and in Washington the belief had been developing that the war would have to end with the surrender of the enemy powers. In Great Britain, the results of the peace soundings of the winter of 1939–40 had left a residue of very strong doubts about any and all Germans who claimed to be moderates and wanted assurances of some sort as to the future of Germany as a preliminary to overthrowing the Nazi regime. When finally given at least some such assurances, they had proceeded to lead the invasions of a series of neutral countries. By the time of the Casablanca Conference they were also, as the London government knew all too well, involved in the most horrendous persecutions and atrocities. From the perspective of London, the unconditional surrender of Germany was an essential pre-condition for peace.[89] As for Italy, Churchill thought of exempting it in the hope of splitting it away from Germany, but the British Cabinet would not hear of such a policy.[90] As for Japan, the way it had begun and waged war made the same policy an obvious one for her, and the British had every reason to insist on that if only to reassure the Americans that they would stick with them in full force once the war in Europe had been won.

As for the Americans, they had especially bad memories on the question of a surrender from World War I. At that time, the United States Commander-in-Chief in Europe, General Pershing, as well as the domestic Republican opposition, had strongly urged that Germany be required to surrender. It was the Wilson administration—which had included most of the key figures in the Roosevelt administration along with the President himself—that had been involved in paving the way for an armistice instead of a surrender.[91] In domestic American politics, this "weakness" had contributed to the administration's loss of the mid-term elections of 1918; in international affairs, it had facilitated the creation of the German stab-in-the-back legend which pretended that Germany had not been defeated in World War I at all. This time there was to be no confusion after the war as to whether or not the German army had been beaten.[92] The President had stated to the head of the Polish government-in-exile, General Sikorski, on December 2, 1942, that: "We have no intention of concluding this war with any kind of armistice or treaty. Germany must surrender unconditionally."[93] There is every reason to believe that Roosevelt, who had hoped until the last moment to keep the United States out of a general war entirely, had in his own mind no doubt from December 1941 about the need to fight until the Germans and Japanese surrendered.[a]

With both the Western Allies determined on a surrender, the only question to be settled was that of timing and method of a public announcement. The decision on timing was, it would appear, greatly influenced by two factors. The uproar in both England and the United States over the deal with Darlan provided a strong motive for reassuring public opinion in both countries that this was no precedent for similar deals with some prominent Nazi who might offer to shorten the war in exchange for being allowed to continue to run Germany, or any analogous arrangements in the case of Italy or Japan. There was also a foreign or coalition policy reason. Since it was now clear to Churchill and Roosevelt that a major invasion of France could not be launched in 1943, it would be well to reassure the Soviet Union that its allies were indeed in the war to the finish and had no intention—as indeed they did not have—of making any arrangement with an undefeated Germany. If these domestic and international factors explain the timing, the reasons for the method chosen, the oral statement by Franklin D. Roosevelt in opening a press conference rather than inclusion in the official press release, must remain speculative. Having decided to make the policy public at this time, Churchill and Roosevelt may have thought that this was the way to get the greatest amount of publicity for the term; it certainly had that effect.[94]

Whereas on this particular issue the Casablanca formula was to hold for the balance of the war, the strategic plans had to be reviewed once more at the "Trident" Conference in Washington, May 12–25, 1943. If the British were interested in further operations in the Mediterranean,

---

[a] Only the Axis satellites were excluded from this requirement in Roosevelt's view. He tried to have the Hungarians, Romanians, and Bulgarians recall their declarations of war until June 1942.

the Americans were insistent that these be limited so as not to interfere with a cross-Channel invasion in 1944.[95] There was real concern in Washington that the British pre-occupation with Mediterranean operations reflected concern about British imperial interests, holding down casualties, and retroactively validating the Gallipoli operation of World War I. Such a procedure was seen as causing pin pricks rather than real trouble for the Germans and was likely to leave the Soviet Union to make a separate peace with Germany. Then the United States would face a Germany in control of practically all of Europe with Japan still to be defeated thereafter. From the United States perspective, there should be no operations in the Eastern Mediterranean. If the British would not aid China by attacking in Burma, the United States would have to make up for that in the Pacific. If they would not commit themselves to an invasion of Western Europe in 1944, then all bets were off and the United States would concentrate on Japan so that at least one major Axis power could be defeated while the British diddled around in the Mediterranean.[96]

The British approached this conference with great doubts of their own.[97] They were worried about what they saw as excessive American allocation of resources to the Pacific, they were eager to get out of the promise to launch any operation in Burma, and they most wanted to follow up on the recent victory in Tunisia, knocking Italy out of the war after the planned Sicily invasion by landings in Italy, and possibly other Western and Eastern Mediterranean objectives. Since these plans threatened—on the basis of recent experience in North Africa—to create a drain from the buildup in England needed for a 1944 invasion, they could count on determined United States opposition.

In a series of very difficult arguments, the issues were hammered out to an agreement. The Americans received the assurance of an invasion of northwest France in 1944 and limits on Mediterranean operations so that this would be possible. The British obtained American agreement to a possible follow-up operation in the Mediterranean after Sicily, the specifics still to be decided, with the assumption that in this way the victory in Tunisia would be utilized for new operations to tie down German forces and divert them from the Russian front by requiring the Germans to defend Italy (or give it up), and to replace the numerous Italian divisions in the Balkans. There was agreement on the continued bombing offensive against Germany. And, with the British leaders siding with the American air commander in China, General Claire Chennault, the priority in the China–Burma–India theater would go to building up the air supply route to China, the opening of a land route for supplies for the development of a real land army by the Chinese Nationalists being held of lower priority. The American ground commander, General Stilwell, would prove to be correct in his assessment that, without an effective army to defend airfields in China, it made no sense to build up a force of bombers in that country, but the Allies had to learn this lesson the hard way.

Undoubtedly agreement was reached on all these matters in part because some decisions were postponed or left open, and because even as the Allied representatives met in Washington it was becoming evident that they were turning the corner in the North Atlantic. There were signs that the U-Boats were being sunk at a high rate and that American ship-building was finally in high gear. But there was surely another element to ease the tension: the recent great victory in North Africa with its huge bag of Axis prisoners.[98]

Once the Allied onrush toward Tunis and Bizerta had been checked, new plans had had to be made in that theater, not only for the timing of subsequent future operations but for Tunisia itself. The original idea of seizing Tunisia and driving into Libya to catch Rommel's army now had to be reversed. The Allies would have to build up their forces in Tunisia during the two months when rain turned the country's unpaved roads into mud and no offensive was possible. In the interim, the British 8th Army would drive on toward Tunisia, with the Allies now hoping to destroy the new German army in Tunisia as well as that of Rommel. Three possibilities might intervene to prevent a final combined confrontation between the two Allied and the two German–Italian armies within Tunisia.

Montgomery might catch the Africa Corps in its retreat before it reached Tunisia. This did not happen; the 8th Army drove the defeated combined German–Italian force back and kept it from ever again holding a firm front but never caught it. Montgomery proved himself then and later a great professional who would fight and win set frontal battles, when necessary changing his plans and procedures in the midst of battle—and pretending afterwards that he had not done so—but he could not catch opponents. He drove them back enormous or short distances, in North Africa, in Sicily, in Italy, in France, in Belgium, and finally in Germany. He now pushed the German–Italian army out of Libya; Rommel himself in fact preferred to join the other Axis forces in Tunisia and repeatedly advocated such a course when from both Rome and the Führer's headquarters there were still orders to hold a position in Libya.

A second possibility was for the Allies in Tunisia to push to the Mediterranean on the southern extension of the front they were building up. Such an offensive would divide the two German forces from each other and enable the Allies to defeat each in turn; in particular, it would greatly complicate even further the already strained supply situation of the Axis. There was a plan for such an operation, code-named "Satin," to be carried out by the American II Corps; while the British 1st Army and French forces held the Germans in the north. This project had to be cancelled; adequate forces were simply not available for it, and the British 8th Army was following Rommel so slowly that he could readily pull away from it and crush the American spearhead to the sea from the south as von Arnim's army attacked it from the north.

The third possibility was an Axis offensive which used the armored units of *both* armies first against one of the two Allied forces and thereafter against the other. The obvious sequence would be to defeat the Allies in Tunisia first and then the 8th Army as it came through Libya into Tunisia. It was this which the Germans decided to try to do, striking at the southern end of the Allied Tunisian front. This would require the shortest movement for Rommel's units, would strike the Allied forces at the point where they were numerically weakest, and open up the possibility of a drive into the rear of the British 1st Army in northern Tunisia, which frontal attacks in the north could keep from intervening. Success for the Germans depended on getting into Africa enough supplies and soldiers to nourish a real offensive, speed to take advantage of the interval between the arrival of Rommel's army in southern Tunisia and the arrival in force of the British 8th Army, and careful coordination between the two Axis forces.

The last of these conditions was never met at all. The German army in Tunisia was able to push the Allies back into less favorable positions in the early weeks of 1943, in part because they had a temporary numerical superiority over the Allies on the central and southern sections of the front, in part because the French troops on the Allied side were very poorly equipped, and in part because neither the American nor the British units involved were led or fought particularly well.[99] But when it came to changing from local attacks on specific objectives to a general offensive, Axis coordination was hopelessly faulty. Directives from the central German and Italian headquarters were confused, the Germans and Italians were repeatedly at odds with each other, and the two senior German commanders were never in agreement on anything, with Rommel not only arguing for plans that differed from those advocated by von Arnim but from the directives from the German theater commander, Field Marshal Albert Kesselring, as well.[a]

---

[a] It must be pointed out that Kesselring and Rommel were of different minds about almost every strategic issue, not just at this time but during all of 1942 and 1943. They appear to have had such a perpetual series of conflicts that it is difficult to imagine them agreeing on

As for the supplies and reinforcements, the Germans and Italians made really quite enormous efforts to provide these by sea and by air during January and February. In the face of an Allied campaign against their shipping, and the shortage of oil which immobilized most of the Italian navy, they pushed through some tonnage and troops, losing heavily in the process. An airlift involving some two hundred of the standard German transport planes, the three engined JU-52 — and fifteen of the huge six-engine ME-323 — delivered a small but steady stream of supplies and replacements until April when the Allied air force came to be able to inflict prohibitive losses on the German air force.[100]

Everything then depended on speed. The Germans hoped to break rapidly through either the Sbiba or Kasserine Pass into the rear of the British 1st Army by seizing Le Kef. The assault at Sbiba on February 19 was halted by the primarily American forces defending the pass, so that the next day Rommel concentrated on Kasserine Pass where his forces had done better in the first attack. They took the pass on the 20th, defeating the American defenders, and in the following days pushed north and west on the paths leading out of the pass. On both the route north to Thala and that west to Tebessa American and British forces held the Germans on the 21st and 22nd. The Americans had lost heavily, but there was no breakthrough as the Germans had planned. Rather than engage in a continued frontal assault on the stiffening United States and British lines, Rommel now withdrew in order to collect his forces for a thrust at the advance units of the British 8th Army before that army could bring the bulk of its strength to bear in the south.[101]

The American tactical defeat at Kasserine Pass and its two thousand casualties had three repercussions, one immediate, the other two more lasting. The immediate effect was a series of personnel changes. The American corps commander was relieved, as was the British officer heading Allied intelligence. The new American commanders who came to the fore as a result, especially General George Patton and General Omar Bradley, would go on to higher postings and greater fame;[a] the new chief of intelligence, General Kenneth Strong, once British military attaché in Berlin, would hold the same position in Eisenhower's staff in the invasion of France. The two more lasting effects were on the American and British thereafter. The American army learned a great many

anything. And they were much less successful at working things out than British and American commanders.

[a] Patton took over command of II Corps with Bradley as his deputy until the south Tunisian operations were completed. Then Bradley became commanding general of II Corps while Patton was preparing for command of the American army which would take part in the invasion of Sicily.

useful tactical lessons, some applied in battle thereafter and many incorporated into the training of new divisions in the United States and the specifications for American equipment.[102]

The higher commanders of the British army drew an entirely different and fatefully flawed lesson from this event. Both General Montgomery and Field Marshal Alexander, who in February was appointed to command all the ground forces in North Africa now called 18th Army Group, concluded that the Americans were hopelessly trained and led, made poor soldiers, and were unlikely to improve quickly in either performance or leadership.[103] It is difficult to understand why they found it so hard to comprehend that the Americans' taking several months to learn what it had taken their own army and its leaders three years was a good, not a bad, sign for the Allied cause. On the basis of their assessment, they would make a disastrous error in the Sicilian campaign. Thereafter, Alexander, who kept his opinions on this subject quiet until he revised them, would always get along well with the Americans, while Montgomery, who probably never revised his opinion and at times voiced it, never could develop a harmonious relationship with American—or Canadian—commanders.

The withdrawal of the German assault forces from the Kasserine front was designed to enable Rommel to strike quickly at the advance units of the British 8th Army, slowly following him across Libya, before the full weight of that army could be gathered. The German commander had wanted to go all the way back to the narrow line at the Wadi Akarit where only a slender coastal strip offered an invasion route between the Mediterranean and a vast inland lake, but he had been ordered to hold the Mareth Line, an old set of French defenses which the Germans and Italians now rebuilt and reinforced. To strike at Montgomery's advance guard, he gathered his armored units for an assault on the Medenine area. The British knew from intelligence that this attack was coming and defeated it handily on March 16.[104] Between Rommel's attacks at Kasserine and Medenine, the Germans under von Arnim had also launched attacks in the north against the British, making substantial gains but suffering losses they could not afford. The stage was now set for the final steps in the campaign.

The Allies had built up their supplies and had even made a beginning of helping the French sort out their internal quarrels. New airfields had been built so that better air support was available. The plan now was for the British, French and American forces to hit at the Axis lines in north and central Tunisia while 8th Army assaulted from the south. The initial 8th Army attack on the right flank of the Axis position failed to penetrate and had to be withdrawn, but the New Zealanders on the left had pushed rapidly and successfully around the Mareth position by March 22. Montgomery now shifted his axis of attack and reinforced the push inland behind the New Zealanders. The result was that the Axis army defending the Mareth line had to pull back or risk being cut off. Their blocking forces held long enough to enable what was now called the 1st Italian Army under General (later Field Marshal) Giovanni Messe to escape once again.[105] The British assault had been assisted by the American attack to the north, which had drawn one of the German armored divisions away from their front, but the British battered rather than crushed the army in front of them.[106]

Whatever the defects of the operation at the Mareth line, it had so weakened the Axis forces that when the 8th Army attacked the line at the Wadi Akarit on April 6, the defenders crumbled in one day. By April 13, the 8th Army was before Enfidaville, and the Axis forces had been compressed into a small perimeter defense around Tunis and Bizerta. The Allied plan for the final assault had two features worth noting. In the first place, it appeared to Eisenhower and Alexander to make the most sense to have the major offensive, which was to begin on April 19, launched by the British 1st rather than the 8th Army. The latter had had plenty of experience in the desert, the former in the rugged Tunisian terrain. This judgement was certainly confirmed by the event, as Montgomery on several occasions halted the operations of 8th Army, which had been designed to hold the Axis forces facing it, at times which were very bad for the over-all plan. Because of the need to amass a powerful attack force, however, several of 8th Army's most experienced divisions were transferred to 1st Army and took part in its offensive.

The second unusual feature of the Allied plan was the transfer of the bulk of the American II Corps from the southern to the northern end of the front across the whole supply and communication routes of the British 1st Army.[a] To make certain that the American officers and men received the needed further battle experience, the American contingent was to be allocated a section in the offensive instead of being squeezed out as the front contracted. The huge transfer was made successfully, though the lesson that such a procedure was entirely possible appears to have been lost on the participants, as later developments would show.

The Allies, in preparation for the final assault, also took measures by sea and air to prevent an evacuation of the Axis forces, but in this they misjudged Axis intentions. Almost to the last moment, the

---

[a] One American division was already in the north; the other three and all corps troops were moved.

Germans were bringing troops and supplies *into* Tunisia, and no preparations whatever were made for any evacuation. The hope was that the bridgehead could hold and keep the Allies tied down for months; it was assumed that any evacuation preparations would only lower morale.

When the Allies struck in April, the British 1st Army and United States II Corps battled their way forward while 8th Army soon called off its assaults. The 1st Army headed for Tunis, broke the German bridgehead into two portions, and courteously allowed the French units attached to it the honor of clearing the capital. The Americans had learned a great deal, mastered the difficult terrain and the fiercely resisting Germans on their front, and freed Bizerta, also quickly turning it over to French units. Running out of supplies and battered by Allied ground forces and the efficiently managed overwhelming Allied air force,[107] the Axis units fell apart after their initial strong resistance had been broken. Instead of trying to hold out in the Cape Bon area or elsewhere, both German and Italian troops after May 3 surrendered in increasing numbers. The numbers, in fact, increased more rapidly than the Allies had expected. Only about 800 Axis soldiers managed to escape, and in about ten days some 275,000 German and Italian soldiers walked, drove, or rode donkeys into prisoner of war enclosures that repeatedly had to be expanded. It was the largest haul of Axis prisoners in the war to date.

The Western Allies had attained their objective in North Africa but not as quickly as they had hoped. In the process, they had learned some hard lessons in the problems of fighting as Allies with all the difficulties of such an arrangement. They now had some experience in this form of warfare at times of both advances and set-backs, disasters and triumphs, daring strikes and grinding positional warfare. It was experience that would be critical to their future success in the invasion of Sicily, already in the final planning stage, and thereafter. The Americans had begun to learn the realities of fighting experienced and determined soldiers in modern war, a learning process better carried out at a distance from the enemy's main center of resistance than closer to it.

In victory, even the French began to work together, with Giraud and de Gaulle forming the French Committee of National Liberation which the British, United States and Soviet governments then recognized as a de facto government and which pulled together the areas earlier under de Gaulle with those in Northwest Africa. The great issue which underlay the cleavage—whether to overlook or to punish the earlier identification with the Vichy regime of most of Giraud's associates—would continue to divide Frenchmen. But they could begin to work together.

The Axis had lost its hold on parts of North Africa, two armies, and vast quantities of supplies, shipping and airplanes. Its cohesion was strained to the limit as Italian morale was hit by the loss of the last portion of the country's African empire. Time and again Mussolini and other Italian leaders had urged Germany to make peace on the Eastern Front so that all Axis forces could concentrate on fighting Britain and the United States, a subject that is discussed in greater detail elsewhere in this chapter. The Germans had always rejected this concept and were instead planning a new summer offensive in the East in the very days that the Axis forces in North Africa were surrendering by the tens of thousands.

On only one point did the Germans learn something from the disaster. Between October 1942 and June 1943 they lost 1419 transport planes; they now established an air transport command for the first time in the war.[108] The great loss of precious transport planes had been caused by two simultaneous heavy demands on their limited fleet of such aircraft: the need to supply the campaign in Tunisia and the effort to supply the army cut off in Stalingrad.

"URANUS": THE SOVIET STALINGRAD OFFENSIVE

From mid-September to mid-November, while the German army ground its way into Stalingrad, the Soviet high command had worked to build up its forces for the "Uranus" operation designed to cut off the Germans in the area. The internal mechanism of the Red Army was tightened by a dramatic reduction in the power of the commissars and a heavier reliance on the professional officers, symbolized by the decree of October 9, 1942 which at least nominally gave full responsibility to the commanders and Chiefs of Staff.[109] The full mobilization of manpower rebuilt the Red Army to a front line strength of 6.5 million at a time when Germany and its allies could field about 4 million. In spite of the fact that the Germans had overrun additional Soviet territory of great economic importance in terms of both industrial plants and mineral resources, Soviet industry was able to increase production of planes, tanks, and guns. What is perhaps more important than the increase in numbers is that a far higher proportion of the tanks and planes was of the more modern models. In all categories, the Soviet Union by itself was out-producing the Germans.[110]

The Soviet plan for "Uranus" took advantage of the geographic and military advantages on their side and the disadvantages of their enemies, though these disadvantages might have been ameliorated by the Germans if they had exercised some insight and judgement, the former missing from German army intelligence, the latter from both Hitler and his military advisors. The geographic advantage was that the bulge toward Stalingrad practically invited a pincer attack. It was accentuated by the fact that on the northern flank the Red Army had retained bridgeheads across the Don, especially at Serafimovich, and had actually expanded these during the fighting inside Stalingrad. The northern pincer of the offensive, the new Southwest Front of General Vatutin, could therefore begin massing its assault forces across the river even while Red Army engineers built additional bridges for the supplies and reserve units needed to nourish any move into the rear of the Axis troops.

The military advantages of the Soviets were two. The Axis units facing them at the places where the pincers would strike were in both cases mainly Romanian.[a] These had never been provided by the Germans with the equipment necessary for combat on the Eastern Front, and, once actually involved in the fighting using obsolete and inadequate weapons, were never properly supplied.[111] The insistence of the Germans, and this was Hitler's own decision, to drive into the Caucasus at the same time as he pushed the offensive toward Stalingrad made it impossible to keep any substantial number of German units on the flanks of 6th Army and 4th Panzer Army. On the contrary, as the fighting in the city absorbed more and more German divisions, these could be provided only by taking them from the flanks, putting them at the point of the thrust into the city, and increasing the length of front entrusted to Germany's allies.

In the last weeks before the Soviet offensive began, two interacting German errors accentuated the difficulties they would face. The massive diversion of resources to Tunisia has already been mentioned; November 1942 was not the best time for Germany to begin building up a second army in North Africa with all that involved in men, materiel, and transport. Even more important, the careful preparations that the Soviets deliberately shrouded in secrecy completely misled German army intelligence, which for most of the Eastern campaign was great on amassing details but hopelessly mistaken in its strategic assessments.[112] They now

---

[a] The German decision-making process in the winter crisis was complicated by Hitler's absence from his headquarters from November 7 to 23, 1942, first in Munich for his annual speech to the Nazi Party faithful on the anniversary of the 1923 coup attempt, and thereafter at Berchtesgaden on vacation. German communications were therefore especially strained while Rommel was being beaten in North Africa, the Western Allies were landing in Northwest Africa, and the Soviet "Uranus" operation was getting under way.

thought that the main Soviet winter offensive would come on the central portion of the Eastern Front—where the Russians were indeed planning operation "Mars." Not until the last days before the attack did they have even a minimal picture of what might happen, and even then, the persistent underestimation of the Soviet Union would leave them misjudging the situation. Hitler himself repeatedly referred to a possible Soviet offensive across the Don; but the fact that he never insisted on substantial measures to counter this possibility shows that he thought of it neither very seriously nor consistently; it is only in retrospect that his musings on it have assumed any importance.[113] As it was, the Soviet offensive achieved a surprise of dramatic proportions because in the last weeks before its launching the Germans were still giving priority to the push inside the torn city.[114]

The big offensive was postponed for about ten days from its original opening date. On November 19, following a massive artillery barrage, the Southwest Front's infantry opened a path for 5th Tank Army to break through the Romanian 3rd Army. Without either heavy tanks or anti-tank guns adequate to deal with Soviet tanks, the Romanian army disintegrated that day. Some units fought hard, some surrendered, many tried to escape the onrush—but there was no way they could hold up the attacking 5th Tank Army, which had advanced half the 70-mile distance to Kalach on the Don by the end of the day. The Don front of Marshal Konstantin K. Rokossovski assaulted further east, advanced less rapidly, but kept the Germans from moving westwards to support the Romanians. On the following day, while General Andrei I. Eremenko's Stalingrad Front launched its southern pincer through the Romanian units of 4th Romanian Army (assigned to the German 4th Panzer Army), the advance spearheads of 5th Tank Army were closing on Kalach. As German and Romanian remnants and assorted rear area headquarters and installations tried to hold at a few places but mostly to flee the advancing Red Army, the two jaws of the pincers came closer. On the morning of November 22 the spearhead of 5th Tank Army seized the Don bridge at Kalach,[115] and on the following day the two Soviet forces met about ten miles southeast of Kalach. The whole German 6th Army, most of the German divisions in the 4th Panzer Army, and some of what was left of the 3rd and 4th Romanian Armies were surrounded.[116]

The Germans had to make some new decisions quickly, and soon after the Soviet high command also faced new choices. The Germans reacted immediately to the attack on their northern flank by halting the offensive inside Stalingrad and beginning to shift some of the troops near the city westwards, but the big decisions which had to be made in the next two days involved the larger question of whether the 6th Army and the portions of the 4th Panzer north of the breakthrough of Ere-menko's southern pincer should fight their way back in a southwesterly direction through the enveloping Russian armies or try to build up a circular front while a relief force attempted to pry open the encirclement from the outside.[a]

Inside the Stalingrad area, all the highest German commanders thought a breakout was the appropriate step, and on November 22 and 23 began with the preparations for such a move on November 25 and 26. On the outside, the German Army Group commander strongly held the same opinion, and so urged headquarters, where General Zeitzler, Chief of the General Staff of the army, favored such action. The belief of the local air force commander, von Richthofen, that adequate air supply of the isolated army was impossible, reinforced these arguments. Hitler, however, hoped to relieve the encircled army where it was, wanted to avoid the conspicuous humiliation of giving up a city he had just publicly promised to hold, and seems to have believed that the experience of the preceding winter, when Cholm and Demyansk had held out until relieved, could be repeated. Furthermore, he still hoped and expected to win the war, and because for that victory Germany needed to seize the oil resources of the Caucasus and to close off the area by holding the lower Volga from Stalingrad to Astrakhan, it made no sense to him to give up any more territory that had been taken at great cost and would need to be taken again than absolutely necessary. He was encouraged in adopting and holding this attitude by Göring and von Manstein.[117]

The German air force Chief of Staff, General Hans Jeschonnek, had already discussed air supply of Stalingrad with Hitler on the train as they returned to East Prussia from Hitler's vacation in Berchtesgaden. There were now projects for collecting air transports to create a bridge of flights to the isolated garrison, and it seems clear that Göring and his experts saw this very differently. The air force officers, both the transport officers at headquarters and the commanders out in the field, thought that limited tonnage could be flown in for a few days, assuming either a quick breakout or minimum sustenance until a quick relief.[118] Göring, on the other hand, hoped to recoup his own and the air force's position with Hitler by promising a level of deliveries which was quite impossible

---

[a] There were a few German units behind the northern front and more in the south, but in neither case did this make a great deal of difference. The endless debate in Hitler's headquarters about how best to employ these units in the developing battle merely reflects the extent of the Axis defeat. The most dramatic example is the argument about General Heim's 48th Panzer Corps, which has had more pages written about it than it had tanks at the time. See Kehrig, *Stalingrad*, passim. Heim was jailed on Hitler's order for some months and ended up in command of Boulogne!

given German air transport resources—simultaneously being drained by the building up of the bridgehead in Tunisia—the weather conditions in the area, the inadequacy of the infra-structure required for any such air supply effort, especially in the winter, the enormous number of troops to be supplied and equipped and, of course, the obviously to be expected counter-measures of the Red Air Force.[119] Göring assured Hitler that the 6th Army would receive an average of 500 tons daily; 6th Army was promised 300 tons; but even this figure was not reached on one single day.[120]

Field Marshal von Manstein had been summoned by Hitler to take over a newly formed Army Group Don, which included the forces inside Stalingrad and the remnants of 4th Panzer Army southwest of it. Reinforced by a number of new divisions, it was expected to make a relief assault based on Kotelnikovo. The push was to reach the encircled army and thereafter restore the whole situation.[a] If von Manstein could not take Leningrad, at least he could hold Stalingrad. Once arrived on the southern front, von Manstein broke with all the other German army and air force generals and believed that it was possible to hold Stalingrad and relieve the beleaguered forces there by the offensive he was planning; it was his assessment that at least the attempt should be made. Concerned primarily about his reputation as a daring and always successful military commander, both at the time and after the war, he reinforced Hitler's inclination then and faked the relevant portion of his memoirs after the war.[121]

The Germans inside the encirclement were told to make no further withdrawals in the north, east and south. They built up a new front in the west and tried to hold out against the Red Army with hopelessly inadequate supplies, ammunition, and fuel. Outside the Stalingrad pocket the remnants of the 3rd Romanian Army and some German units built up a new front to the west on the Chir river while Manstein gathered the remnants of the German 4th Panzer and 4th Romanian Army to the south. He tried to organize what reinforcements he could get for a counter-attack northeastwards toward the encircled army. He never received all the forces promised—there were far too many other demands on the German army both elsewhere on the Eastern Front and in Tunisia—and by the time he was ready to move, new Soviet operations had altered the situation. By the end of November, even before actually starting the relief operation, Manstein was beginning to see how unrealistic his earlier assessment of the situation had been, especially in regard to air supply;[122] but this made little difference now that firm orders to

[a] Hitler also finally appointed a new commander for Army Group A which he himself had been nominally running since the dismissal of Field Marshal List.

hold had been issued to 6th Army. The most favorable time for initiating a breakout attempt had already passed, and the prospect of the relief offensive which was to be launched in a few days encouraged ridiculously optimistic expectations.

The relief offensive had to be postponed several days as Manstein gathered what units he could. The slowness of the Soviet pursuit after their initial success alone made it possible for the Germans even to start such a move on December 12. The drive included all of two understrength Panzer divisions, joined after much argument by a third, and in ten days pushed approximately half-way across the 80-mile gap separating their starting position from the encircled troops. As it became obvious after seven days that the Red Army was containing this thrust, the only possibility became a breakout attempt toward the stalled relief force. Manstein would not order such an action against Hitler's insistence that Stalingrad be held, and certainly Paulus, the commander inside the pocket, could hardly defy both his immediate military superior and Hitler.[123] No additional opportunities would ever occur because by this time the new Soviet offensive, launched on November 25, was collapsing the Axis front further north; and the problem facing the Germans was not one of rescuing the lost garrison of Stalingrad but instead that of keeping both Army Group Don and Army Group A in the Caucasus from both being cut off themselves by an onrushing Red Army.[124]

The Red Army had caught the German–Romanian forces in the Stalingrad pocket but took some time to exploit the resulting chaos on the Axis front. The Stavka did not realize at first how large a force had been encircled and did not immediately develop appropriate follow-up operations.[a] The plan to destroy the Stalingrad pocket, code-named "Koltso" (Ring), called for an assault eastwards into the German perimeter to the Volga, splitting it into north and south pockets which could then be destroyed in turn. The German relief offensive of December 12 forced the Russians to divert key units destined for "Koltso" to containing Manstein's thrust. In this they entirely succeeded, but Koltso was postponed as a result, eventually until January 10. The four weeks from December 12 to January 10, however, saw a steady weakening of the resistance from the pocket as the German forces were quite literally being starved out.

A vastly larger operation was approved on December 2 under the code-name "Saturn" to drive behind the whole newly formed German front in the Don river bend, behind Manstein's Army Group Don and behind the German Army Group A in the Caucasus by heading for

---

[a] The Soviet original estimate was that 85–90,000 Axis soldiers had been encircled, not three times that number. There is here an interesting reflection on Soviet intelligence.

Rostov. This vast project was modified to "Small Saturn" for two reasons: the Manstein counter-offensive seemed likely to create problems for Saturn as well as Koltso and, in addition, there was what has to be called the failure of still another Soviet offensive called "Mars." This operation, launched on November 25, against Army Group Center, was originally coordinated with the Stalingrad offensive. It had, however, been halted without any major breakthrough by December 10, so that, although heavy fighting between the attacking West and Kalinin Fronts and Army Group Center continued, the Stavka could see that there were good reasons not to repeat the previous winter's over-ambitious offensives.[125]

The "Small Saturn" project called for an envelopment of most of Army Group Don by an attack southwards across the Don through the 8th Italian and 3rd Romanian Army and an offensive westward into the German relief army pushing toward Stalingrad from the southwest. Launched by the Southwest Front on December 16, the Red Army offensive in a few days ripped through the Italian and Romanian armies on the Don, pushed back the German units in the area, and, in the process, not only threatened to collapse the whole Axis front in the south but more immediately to seize the main airfields from which the Stalingrad pocket was being supplied. In the following days, the Germans had to build up a new front west of the Soviet breakthrough, replacing the vanished Italian 8th Army with whatever reinforcements they could locate. Simultaneously, the Soviet attack against the relief force not only halted Manstein's effort but threatened to cut off Army Group A in the Caucasus. As the Red Army pushed forward slowly but successfully, the Germans had to make some quick decisions: whether to try a break-out from Stalingrad or abandon the encircled garrison, and also whether to risk having Army Group A cut off or to pull back the forces there and use them to rebuild the southern front.

One German decision was to abandon the Stalingrad garrison. No break-out was ordered and none was attempted. As the relief force was driven back by the advancing armies of the Stalingrad Front and the German air bases at Tazinskaya and Morozovsk were first threatened and then seized by the armies of Southwest Front, no hope of escape remained for the encircled Germans. When Koltso was mounted by the Don Front under Rokossovski on January 10, an enfeebled German 6th Army was pushed eastwards, losing its main airport at Pitomnik on January 16.[126] In the following weeks, the Red Army battered its way into Stalingrad, splitting the German 6th Army, overrunning the defending forces and eventually ending the fighting on February 2. While the Red Army suffered substantial losses, the German defeat was both total and conspicuous. About 250,000 Germans and tens of thousands of Romanians and Russian auxiliaries had been in the pocket. Some 30,000 wounded were flown out, and the Russians took 91,000 prisoners. About 150,000 German soldiers had been killed or had died of cold, hunger and wounds. Of even greater significance than this loss in dead and captured—which included practically all of the officers—was the public and morale aspect of the Soviet victory and German defeat.

Having himself made Stalingrad the symbol of the 1942 offensive, Hitler had elevated the fight for the city to enormous public attention. The insistence that the German army hold rather than break out only reinforced this aspect of the situation. The crushing defeat administered by the Red Army to the German army at Stalingrad was therefore a major blow to Hitler's prestige—a matter of vast importance in a dictatorship—at the same time as it greatly enhanced the position of Stalin and the Red Army. The public in the Soviet Union was, of course, kept aware of the desperate fight for the city on the Volga, but around the world as well, attention had been drawn to this epic struggle. Few could be found outside the most restricted circle of specialists who had ever heard of Cholm and Demyansk, and even fewer in subsequent years remembered these places and their relief, but everywhere Stalingrad had been in the public eye for months, and the victory of the Red Army there symbolized at the time and thereafter what to most was the great turn of the tide on the Eastern Front.

The dramatic events at Stalingrad hastened the process of change in the relations of the dictator to the military in both the Soviet Union and Germany. This subject has been clouded in both cases by post-war distortions only recently giving way to more objective analysis. In the Soviet Union, the role of the Great Patriotic War, as it is called, in the self-definitions of the society has produced various official theses which change from time to time; in the German Democratic Republic, ideological posturing dominated study of the war; and in the Federal Republic of Germany, the effort to "prove" that all the mistakes were made by Hitler and all the atrocities were committed by the SS obscured the realities of the conflict. It is, however, clear that the great victory reinforced Stalin's willingness to listen to and rely on the professional military, whose growing experience and self-confidence now appeared justified by success. He dominated them but was more inclined to listen to their views.

Hitler's inclination to distrust the military leadership was reinforced by the great defeat. He had always resented his dependence on a professional higher officer corps whom he needed for the wars he expected to fight but whom he hoped to replace at the earliest opportunity with men ideologically more attuned to National Socialism. He had assumed the powers of the Minister of War in February 1938; in December 1941 he had also taken over the position of Commander-in-Chief of the army. He continued to find most of the higher officers complaisant but not sufficiently enthusiastic about National Socialism, and he was more and more inclined to interfere in tactical details. It is by no means certain that his directives were in general any less unrealistic than those recommended by most of the generals; but he now relieved them with greater frequency while pushing up into the higher ranks those whose dedication to extreme National Socialist views made them more congenial to his way of thinking and acting, men like Guderian, Schörner and Model in the army and Dönitz in the navy. Most of the others were kept in line by their self-identification with the German war effort, hopes for promotion and decorations, concern for their soldiers, and a vast secret program of bribery involving practically all at the highest levels of command.[127]

STROKE AND COUNTER-STROKE ON THE EASTERN FRONT, JANUARY–MARCH 1943

Even before the final stage in the grisly drama at Stalingrad had been reached with the surrender of its emaciated garrison and bemedalled generals, the progress of "Small Saturn" had also obliged the Germans to make new decisions about Army Group A, still stalled in front of its objectives in the Caucasus. Having neither seized the Grozny oil fields (to say nothing of those at Baku) nor cleared the Black Sea coast, the German 17th and 1st Panzer Armies risked being cut off if the Red Army reached Rostov. Manstein repeatedly asked for units from 1st Panzer to be transferred to his command so that he could stem the southern thrust of "Small Saturn," but these transfers were made only on a small scale and always too late to make much difference. The basic decision Hitler made was to pull back portions of the 1st Panzer Army into the southern Ukraine to hold open a route of retreat for the supplies and rear area troops of Army Group A, but to have 17th Army hold its front. This decision would make it possible for the Red Army to liberate a large stretch of the area seized by the Germans in 1942, but leave open the possibility of new choices and internal German frictions later.

This new set of decisions was forced on the Germans by a new Soviet offensive, a fact which underlines the extent to which the initiative in the war on the Eastern Front had shifted to the Soviet high command. A major Red Army offensive by the northern section of the Southwest Front crushed the 2nd Hungarian Army and the adjacent portions of the German 2nd Army to the north and 8th Italian Army south of the new large hole torn into the Axis front.[128] The political impact of this disaster on Hungary as well as of the earlier destruction of Romanian and Italian units on those Axis satellites is reviewed later in this chapter; it is the immediate military effect which must be examined first.

The determined and successful Soviet offensive against Army Group B, combined with the Stalingrad Front's assault against Army Group Don, threatened to destroy both German Army groups and simultaneously to cut off the portions of Army Group A still in the Caucasus, though retreating from there, partly under pressure, partly according to plan. The Red Army was not only liberating vast areas and important cities like Kursk and Kharkov, but its spearheads were approaching the Dnepr river near Dnepropetrovsk and Zaporozhye. The Germans had to decide how to cope with the disappearance of still another satellite army from their order of battle, enormous losses of their own men and materiel, and a tactical situation which threatened catastrophe for the whole southern portion of their front. The decisions reached and the arguments over them reveal a great deal about German strategy and aims at this point in the war; similarly, the reaction of the Russians to the German implementation of these decisions sheds significant light on Soviet policy in mid-war.

Hitler decided on three major steps. First, he would authorize more of 1st Panzer Army to pull back across the lower Don to be utilized by Manstein in a series of moves, urged by the latter, to redeem the situation by a counter-offensive. This, however, first required that considerable territory be evacuated rather than fought over so that units could be extricated in good order, reorganized, and assembled in systematic preparation for an offensive into the flank of the Soviet advance. Second, the beginnings of reinforcement of the Eastern Front from the West, already under way as a result of the defeat at Stalingrad, would be both increased and accelerated, a decision now easier to make since the season ruled out any cross-Channel invasion for some months and this was an obvious time for Germany to take advantage of its interior lines of communication. Third, Hitler decided that the other army which had been fighting in the north Caucasus area, the 17th, should pull back but was not to assist in the restabilization of the front in the area north of the Sea of Azov. Instead, it was to establish a defensive perimeter holding the portion of the North Caucasus east of the Crimea with its back to the Sea of Azov, the Kerch Straits and the Black Sea, which was given the designation "Goth's head position" (Gotenkopfstellung), also referred to as the Kuban bridgehead.

Each of these three decisions deserves comment. The last, that of holding a bridgehead in the North Caucasus, is especially important in the light it sheds on the long-term perspectives of the Germans on the Eastern Front in the early months of 1943. While most of Hitler's military advisors appear by this time to have anticipated no more than some sort of stalemate, the Führer still thought of great victories ahead; it is only in this divergence that the arguments over the Kuban bridgehead make sense. The generals wanted 17th Army pulled out, the area east of the Kerch Straits evacuated, and the units freed by this action utilized to assist in the stabilization of the southern portion of the Eastern Front and the defense of the Crimea. Hitler, on the other hand, was still thinking of new great offensives in the East. These would involve the need to seize the Caucasus oil fields, and for such an operation a bridgehead across the Kerch Straits would provide the best possible base.[129]

In the end, the practical implications were of no great moment. Whether 17th Army would have helped the German southern front in the Ukraine more than the release of Red Army units facing it could have helped the Soviet forces fighting there will never be known. Soviet advances on the north shore of the Sea of Azov threatened to cut off the German–Romanian garrison on the Crimea in August 1943; and under these circumstances Hitler, after consulting the Romanian leader Ion Antonescu, gave the order to evacuate the area still held by the German 17th Army. Over a four week period in September-October 1943, the whole army was transferred to the Crimea with relatively little interference from the Soviet Black Sea Fleet. If this ended all theoretical possibilities of a German offensive toward the Caucasus, the real threat had long since passed with the crushing defeat of Germany's 1943 summer offensive on the Eastern Front and the great Soviet advance across the Ukraine.[130]

Hitler's other two decisions had made their impact on the front in the interval between the decision to hold and later to evacuate the Kuban bridgehead. As the Red Army stormed back into the Donets Basin in January–February 1943, driving the Germans back through key industrial areas they had seized the preceding summer, the most critical question was whether Hitler would allow von Manstein the necessary leeway to pull back his scattered units to the old Mius river line, which had been held in the winter of 1941–42, while reorganizing for a counter-offensive against the Red Army advancing on Dnepropetrovsk and Zaporozhye on the Dnepr, over 150 miles further west. On February 6 Hitler agreed to the withdrawal. Perhaps the experience of discovering himself vulnerable to capture by the Red Army when in Zaporozhye for a conference with von Manstein on February 17 and 18 helped persuade the Führer that a slightly different style of leadership might help, and he allowed von Manstein to carry out a project rather different from those of the preceding campaign.[131] For the new operation, several divisions from Western Europe were to be sent East to be added to the heavily armored and manned divisions of the Waffen SS, the armed formations of the SS. Fanatical in spirit, favored over the regular army in delivery of weapons, and not always particularly obedient, these contingents were in the process of becoming a kind of fire-brigade for critical points at the front. Von Manstein would get to use them in Germany's last major tactical success on the Eastern Front in World War II.

The possibility of launching an effective counter-attack was, to a major extent, a result of Red Army inexperience in the exploitation of its own successes. As the initial breakthroughs on the front, north and south of Stalingrad in November 1942 had not been followed up quickly by a determined exploitation, so the repeated ripping open of the Axis front on the upper Don had not led to concerted and carefully coordinated offensives. In the process of advancing, the Red Army had liberated major industrial centers like Kharkov and Voroshilovgrad, but it had not wedged open the front sufficiently to force the German army back to the Dnepr river. Repeatedly the Red Army was on the verge of decisive victories on the Mius, near Slavyansk, and on the road to Dnepropetrovsk, but at the last moment the German defenders barely held. It must also be remembered that in the depth of winter the armies of the Voronezh and Southwest Fronts had moved forward literally hundreds of miles, and were now coming to the end of the offensive strength with which they had started their attacks. The combination of desperation and experience still worked in favor of the German army, but it should have been obvious to the leaders of the latter that this would no longer always be the case.

The German counter-offensive ran from February 19 to March 17, 1943.[132] In a series of swift armored blows from south to north just east of Dnepropetrovsk and in the Donets area, the two panzer armies of Army Group South smashed into the Soviet spearheads. The 4th Panzer Army's assault units, primarily SS divisions, destroyed the advance forces of the Soviet 6th and 1st Guards Armies and pushed northwards, retaking Kharkov and Belgorod before halting and being halted. Further east, the German 1st Panzer Army was able to cut off and destroy much of the Soviet armored force commanded by General Popov, who had misjudged the situation and could rescue only small portions to hold the lower Donets line. When the front settled down as all were immobilized by the spring thaw in late March, only the great westward bulge around Kursk to the north remained of the areas beyond the starting line of the 1942 German summer offensive which the Red Army had freed in the winter offensive; otherwise the two sides were back essentially where they had been a year earlier.

But this was true only in a tactical sense; a great deal had changed, first because of the enormous and conspicuous Soviet victory at Stalingrad, second because of the German rally in February–March, and finally because the basic military position of both combatants on the great front had altered in fundamental ways. The nature and implications of these three changes will form most of the balance of this chapter, but the winter operations on the northern and central segments of the Eastern Front need to be summarized first; in their respective ways, both serve to underline how the situation in the East had changed from the preceding year.

As previously mentioned, German plans for offensives in the north in 1942 had all foundered when Soviet attacks on the ring cutting off Leningrad had forced abandonment of German hopes of seizing that city, but had also failed to break the ring. The Red Army now planned a new attempt, prepared with great care and precision. In a week's bitter fighting from January 12 to 19, the Leningrad and Volkhov Fronts chewed their way through the northern extremity of the German siege lines, clearing a narrow land corridor on the southern shore of Lake Ladoga. The siege had been broken; and while the land bridge to the great city was narrow and still under German artillery fire, its practical and symbolic importance was immense. The practical significance lay in the greatly increased ability of the Soviet Union to move people and supplies in and out of the city in all seasons. The symbolic significance lay in the great boost the victory provided for Soviet morale even as it demonstrated to the Finns that the German cause to which they had so unwisely tied themselves was obviously a losing one, not only in the steppe areas of the Soviet Union many hundreds of miles to the south but on their own doorstep.

The inability of Army Group North to maintain the siege of Leningrad after its earlier warding off of the relief attempts of 1941–42 surely contributed to Hitler's willingness finally to give up the Demyansk salient and to pull out the German divisions stationed there. Here, too, there was symbolic significance. A pincer operation from Army Group North to meet Army Group Center had been assumed to be a necessary preliminary for any renewed offensive toward Moscow. Giving up the northern base for such a pincer movement—and thus in effect writing off that possibility—made it easier for Zeitzler and the Commander-in-Chief of Army Group Center to persuade Hitler to approve operation "Buffalo" (Büffel), the abandonment of the Rzhev salient, the southern base of any such pincer, which had been the scene of such bitter fighting over the preceding year. Carried out during March, 1943, even as the last German units were withdrawing from the Demyansk area, this operation could be seen as strengthening the now shorter German line. In the broader canvas of the war, however, the two withdrawals, however trumpeted as defensive successes and as triumphs of military reason over megalomania, constituted a clear sign that the German tide was ebbing and that all hopes of a renewed offensive toward the Soviet capital had been given up in German headquarters.[133] In a way, the relief of Leningrad brought with it the relief of Moscow.

The more ambitious aims of Soviet winter offensives had been thwarted in early 1943 as in 1942, but there was a major difference. The great victory at Stalingrad had repercussions on the German home front and on her allies in a way that went far beyond those of the preceding winter. Inside Germany, the loss of the 6th Army introduced a somber mood into a country beginning to show signs of weariness at a war that had now lasted three and a half years and whose casualties were steadily rising. The obvious signs that things were not going well in the Mediterranean combined with the impact of bombing to make the war as a whole look far grimmer than ever before.[134] The broader picture of Germany's home front development will be sketched in the next chapter, but it belongs in this context that the major new effort at mobilization of the home front came as a direct result of the defeat at Stalingrad.

The exclusion of Propaganda Minister Joseph Goebbels from immediate responsibility in the new mobilization measures adopted at Hitler's insistence led the ambitious and anxious minister to seize the initiative by staging the spectacle which came to symbolize the whole process: his total war speech of February 18, 1943. Carefully rehearsed, staged before a hand-picked audience, and broadcast and filmed in a closely coordinated propaganda campaign, this action was designed simultaneously to re-elevate Goebbels to a major role in domestic affairs and to reinvigorate flagging morale.[135] Within limits it did both. But while it could harness greater energies to the ongoing conflict, it could not reverse the disastrous defeat suffered at the front or reassure Germany's allies who drew very different lessons from the events on the Eastern Front.

The most immediately hard hit of Germany's allies were those whose armies had been crushed by the Soviet offensives: Romania had lost two whole armies, Hungary and Italy each one. The government of Marshal Antonescu, based as it was on the Romanian army as its main pillar of support at home, was especially hard hit. The string of broken German promises of equipment and support, the disregard of warnings about

Soviet offensive preparations, the unfriendly treatment of retreating Romanian units by German officers and soldiers, and the general German tendency to blame their own military miscalculations and disasters on their allies all combined to produce a real crisis in German–Romanian relations.[136] The Germans made some minimal efforts to improve the situation, while elements inside Romania, including Foreign Minister Mihai Antonescu and the opposition leader Juliu Maniu, began to sound the Western Powers about peace and urged the Italian government to do likewise. The refusal of the Western Powers to do more than listen and call upon Romania to stop fighting against their Soviet ally—where eight Romanian divisions were still at the front—ended the soundings (about which the Germans came to be quite well informed). The stabilization of the southern section of the Eastern Front in March gave the Germans the opportunity to insist on Romania's falling back in line, but the fundamental basis of mutual confidence had disappeared.[137]

The situation with Hungary was essentially similar, although her forces in the East—and hence casualties—were fewer than Romania's. Here too alarm over the great defeat at the front shook the regime and its relations with Germany, which in Budapest as in Bukarest rested heavily precisely on the military officers who saw themselves disappointed and disgraced by what had happened. Here, too, there were recriminations and complaints; here, too, there would be first soundings with the Western Powers about a possible exit from the war.[138] In this case also, the insistence of the Hungarians on *not* making peace with the Soviet Union blocked an exit from the war while the March German counter-offensive provided a basis for a firmer German line toward the reluctant satellite.

If an underlying fear of German actions against themselves came to play an increasing role in Romanian and Hungarian policy, the same element was also coming to be present, if in a somewhat different form, in the Italian reaction to the destruction of the Italian 8th Army. The impact of disaster in the East on the Italian government was to some extent absorbed by the concentration of the authorities in Rome on the turning tide of battle in the Mediterranean which affected Italy even more directly. The British breakthrough at El Alamein followed soon after by the landing of American and British forces in French Northwest Africa pointed to the possible imminent loss of the remainder of Italy's colonial empire and a subsequent direct Allied assault on Italy itself. From the perspective of Rome, the obviously most effective way for the Axis to deal with the growing threat was to make peace with one of their enemies and concentrate all energies on the immediately most dangerous. Mussolini, therefore, began to urge his German ally to do what the Japanese had long been advocating, namely a separate peace with the Soviet Union and the utilization of the released forces for an effective defense against Britain and the United States.

In a lengthy series of soundings, pleadings, and remonstrances, Mussolini, Ciano, and other Italian political, diplomatic and military leaders urged the Germans to work out a compromise peace with Stalin (although simultaneously some of them were also thinking of sounding out Britain and the United States). The conferences between German and Italian leaders at Hitler's headquarters on December 18–20, 1942, and a number of other occasions were used by the Italians to try to broach this subject, but Hitler always rejected the possibility. He made it clear to his Italian ally that he intended first to halt the Soviet offensive and then to go on the offensive himself again in the summer, and that he had no interest in a compromise with the Soviet Union. On the one hand, the enormous Soviet territory he expected to keep under any circumstances—especially the whole Ukraine—were areas the Soviet government would not be willing to give up, and on the other hand, there was no point in his eyes in leaving on Germany's eastern border a strong and undefeated Red Army with the opportunity to recover its strength and build up its armament. Germany did send what forces it could to assist in the defense of Italy—and, as already mentioned, massive reinforcements were sent to build up the new front in Tunisia—but the war in the East would go on, with or without the Italians.[139]

The other important German ally on the Eastern Front was Finland. The impact on the Finnish government and public of the disastrous course of events of the winter of 1942–43 for the Axis can readily be imagined. First there had been the failure of the Germans to launch the planned assault on Leningrad; there had followed the series of defeats at the southern end of the front symbolized by Stalingrad; finally, to cap the avalanche of bad news, came the successful Soviet offensive south of Lake Ladoga in breaking the siege of Leningrad. Not as obvious to the public, but certainly evident to Finland's military leadership, was the transfer of most of the German planes hitherto engaged in the Axis battle against the Arctic convoys from Norwegian bases to the Mediterranean to cope with the Allied landing in Northwest Africa, with the obvious result that the convoys from the West could now be expected to deliver a substantially higher proportion of their cargoes to Murmansk and Archangel. All of these factors produced a renewed interest in a possible accommodation with the Soviet Union by the Finnish government. There were some soundings in the winter of 1942–43 in which the Soviet government, somewhat to the surprise of its British ally, expressed itself as willing to return to the 1941 border. In the face of

German pressure, however, the Finnish government could not or would not muster up the courage to break with Berlin, and thus forfeited its last opportunity to exit from the war without the loss of territory even beyond that ceded to the Soviet Union by the treaty of March 1940.[140]

The most important of Germany's allies, Japan, had been urging Berlin to reach a new agreement with the Soviet Union and concentrate on fighting Britain and the United States for some time.[141] The Axis defeats of the winter of 1942–43 only led Tokyo to conclude that this advice had been correct all along and to redouble its efforts to urge what the Japanese considered reason on their German ally.[142] The latter responded by calling for greater Japanese efforts against the Western Allies in the Pacific; from the perspective of Berlin, it looked as if Germany was bearing the major burden of the war against all of the Allies, and it seemed to its leaders that Japan was surely capable either of attacking the Soviet Union or of greater offensive actions against the British and the Americans. They did not fully understand the extent to which the Japanese war effort was both strained by the fighting in the Southwest Pacific and partially immobilized by the inability of the army and navy to work out a coordinated strategy.[143]

The constant urgings from Tokyo that a German–Soviet peace could and should be made reflected both enormous worry about the future in Tokyo and the total lack of comprehension of German war aims among Japanese leaders. Like the Italians, the Japanese were assured that there was no prospect of peace, that the Germans would halt the Soviet winter offensive, and that a renewed offensive in the summer would inflict even greater blows on a Soviet Union already weakened by great casualties in the 1941 and 1942 fighting. Germany's demands—the Ukraine, the Caucasus, severance from the outside world and demilitarization—were not likely to appeal to Moscow; and Germany, von Ribbentrop assured Ambassador Oshima on December 11, had no interest in saving a tottering Soviet regime.[144] All the predictions from Berlin were met with skeptical comments from Japanese diplomats. As Ambassador Suma Yokichiro in Madrid explained, it "will be the same old story—the beginning of hostilities in the spring, a big push in the summer and a nightmare in the winter; and this time I do not see how she [Germany] could come back again."[145] He only failed to predict that the nightmare would come for the Germans even sooner.

The consolidation of Germany's southern front in the East as a result of the successful Kharkov counter-offensive in March provided Hitler with the opportunity to shake off the doubts created by the Stalingrad disaster. He and a large number of his military advisors simply blamed the great defeat on the failings of their allies—ignoring the central German role in the catastrophic 1942 campaign. Now that things appeared to be going well again the satellite leaders were summoned one by one to appear in headquarters, or at other places Hitler had selected, in order to be lectured on the failings of their soldiers, the great prospects of Germany, and the need to hold together for final victory. In turn King Boris of Bulgaria, Mussolini, and the leaders of Romania and Hungary, Marshal Ion Antonescu and Admiral Horthy, were called on the carpet, with the latter two being instructed to drop their Foreign Ministers, Mihai Antonescu and Miklós Kallay, as appropriate penance for their having authorized contacts with the Allies.

Neither Marshal Antonescu nor Admiral Horthy followed Hitler's bidding in regard to their Foreign Ministers, and all four were reluctant to yield to the insistent and constant pressure of the Germans to turn over the Jewish inhabitants of their respective countries to be slaughtered by the Germans, who were getting impatient about the recalcitrance of their satellites in this regard. It was, however, made clear to all of them that the war against all the Allies would continue in full force and that Germany would tolerate no deviation from the path that led to total victory or total defeat for every member of the Axis.[146]

GERMAN AND ALLIED PLANS FOR 1943–1944

How did the Germans see themselves, and their ever more reluctant allies, continuing the war? Germany placed increasing emphasis on the U-Boat war which, in the spring of 1943, was approaching its climax. In addition, other new weapons were at first thought likely to play a role in the defeat of the British and Americans. At a conference with Speer on June 30, 1942, Hitler had stressed the need to push for German superiority in the field of gas warfare, especially because he believed that the participation of the United States in the war meant that Germany must win by the employment of the new nerve gas, Tabun, since she could not match United States industrial capacity.[147] As stocks of the new gas were beginning to accumulate, however, Hitler was told on May 15, 1943, erroneously as we now know, that Germany did not have a monopoly of the nerve gas which he very much wanted to use against London (no doubt as an additional sign of the love for the British attributed to him by some historians). Before employing the dread weapon, therefore, Germany would have to develop the capacity to defend her own population against such gases — and this she was never able to do.[148] If this was one new weapon the Germans refrained from using for fear of retaliation, others looked more promising.

By 1942, the Germans had made substantial progress with both an unmanned airplane, which came to be called the V-1, and a long-distance rocket, the ancestor of the intercontinental ballistic missile, referred to by the Germans as the A-4 and known subsequently as the V-2. These and other new weapons are discussed in Chapter 10; but two aspects of their development must be mentioned in this context. First, these weapons were beginning to approach a stage of development that seemed to make it realistic to expect their use in the war before much longer.[149] Second, as all were developed with attacks on London in mind, these weapons were expected to exert an enormous influence on the course of the war not only because of their assumed destructiveness but also because of the anticipated morale effect of their use against the population of the British capital. Finally, these two devices were to be joined by a third, a very long-range cannon in which serial explosions along a lengthy barrel were expected to drive a shell all the way to London in a revised edition of the shelling of Paris in World War I.[150] First discussed in January 1943 and ordered in May 1943, this contraption, known as the V-3, was eventually used only in December 1944 and against Luxembourg at that. Its development, however, and the vast resources absorbed by it, as well as by V-1 and V-2, must be seen as a part of German strategy for the future conduct of the war early in 1943.

By one of the great ironies of World War II, it was a conversation on March 22, 1943, between two German generals captured in the fighting in Tunisia which convinced the British, who had bugged their room, that the rumors of secret rocket weapons were based on facts.[151] As the obvious intended victims, the British thereafter made greater efforts to find out about the development and nature of these weapons, efforts which led to the bombing of the experiment station at Peenemünde in the summer of that year.[152] It was this bombing which, together with technical problems, shortages and internal rivalries delayed the introduction of the new devices until well into 1944 when their impact on the war was very much less than the Germans had expected in early 1943 as they looked forward to their employment.[153]

In the more conventional forms of aerial warfare, the Germans in 1943 did begin to pay more attention to defending their cities and industries, where the Allied bombing offensive was making an impact on the public.[154] Although a major shift of resources to the construction of fighter airplanes would not be made until 1944, there were greater allocations and a transfer of air force units from the Eastern Front already in 1943.[155] The reaction which was most important in their own eyes, however, was quite different. In early March 1943, a major new air offensive against Britain was ordered and planned. The hope was that very serious blows would be struck against the British Isles from the air; that these would force the Allies to halt or reduce their own air offensive; that the heavy bombing of London would drive a wedge between the hard-hit British and the as yet immune Americans; and that in this way Germany could reclaim the initiative in the air war. In practice, it all turned out very differently, with a small bombing offensive against England beginning in late January and ending in late May 1944; but for an understanding of German strategy in 1943, it must be noted that the anticipation in Berlin was that here was a major component of the Axis war against the Western Allies.[156]

Against the Soviet Union, the Germans planned a new major offensive. In spite of some skepticism among German officers,[157] Hitler and his top military advisors, Jodl the head of operations in the OKW (high command of the armed forces), and Zeitzler, the Chief of the General Staff of the army, anticipated a major victory for Germany, a victory which would enable her to outlast the shaky alliance of her enemies. Newly strengthened divisions, including hundreds of the new heavy tanks, would smash a major portion of the Red Army in operation "Citadel" (Zitadelle) against the Kursk salient held by the Soviets at the end of the winter's fighting. Tactical withdrawals were to strengthen other sectors of the Eastern Front, and the big offensive would show that German might was and would remain unbroken on the continent even as the submarines kept the Western Allies from returning to it.[158]

There were, however, serious problems with this strategy. The German army would indeed hold together. Fear of defeat, ideological commitment and unit cohesion made up for the loss of confidence after a second terrible winter. An enormous program of systematic bribery of the highest ranking generals and admirals would, Hitler hoped, assure the loyalty of those at the top.[159] For those in the lower ranks, there was in addition to all other incentives the terror of the German system of what passed for military justice; a repressive aspect of the Nazi regime which is only now being examined honestly but whose average of about 5000 executions per year for a wartime total of over 30,000 belongs in any serious examination of German military cohesion into the last bitter days of 1945.[160] But this solidity of the armed forces could not make up for the bravery, inventiveness, strategic planning, and greater armed might of her enemies, who saw the balance of 1943 from very different perspectives.

The Soviet leadership looked toward the future in terms of the most recent and dramatic events on the Eastern Front. On the one hand, the great victory of Stalingrad and the liberation of most of the Caucasus, the Don basin and much of the Donets industrial area, together with the opening of a land corridor to Leningrad, were an enormous boost to morale and self-confidence. The German assault had been halted a second time and on this occasion with a widely recognized and spectacular Soviet victory. On the other hand, the accomplishments had not only exacted an enormous further toll in casualties, they had ended in a very serious set-back at the front. Until more evidence becomes available from the Soviet side, it must be taken as given that the shock of the reverse of March 1943, culminating in the German recapture of Kharkov, the second largest city in the Ukraine, had a major effect on Stalin and his associates. If the Germans could pull themselves together after a second disastrous winter and carry out such a smashing counter-offensive, then the road ahead was certain to be a grim one.

It is from this perspective that one should, I believe, view the soundings for a separate peace with Germany through contacts in Stockholm in the spring and summer of 1943 which are reviewed in Chapter 11. Similarly, the exploration by the Soviet Union government of an alternative government for Germany inherent in the establishment of the National Committee for a Free Germany and the League of German Officers in the summer of 1943 belong in this context. Perhaps there were less horrendously costly ways of ending the war with Germany than fighting centimeter by bloody centimeter all the way to Berlin.

In the absence of a return to Western Europe by British and United States forces for some time as yet, Stalin could contemplate these other alternatives. And if they proved impossible, the news of soundings for a settlement might well induce either greater speed or greater concessions—or both—in the Soviet Union's Western Allies.[a] There would, thus, be pressure on the British and Americans to carry a larger share of the war, but there was every reason to make preparations for the Soviet Union to move forward with its own operations. These preparations took two forms in the spring of 1943, military and political.

On the military side, the Soviet Union systematically strengthened its front, especially the exposed Kursk salient. After considerable internal debate, it was decided that the best procedure for the Red Army was to build up a strong defensive system on the sectors most likely to be attacked by the Germans and then to launch a large summer offensive of its own, using the greater arms production of the Ural area.[161]

---

[a] Surely the celebration of a forthcoming German–Soviet armistice by members of the Soviet embassy in Tokyo on October 23, 1942, was ordered from Moscow and designed to come to the attention of the United States and Britain (as it did). Tokyo Circular 1957 of 26 October 1942, U.S. intercept in NA, RG 457, SRDJ 27500.

The major political plan involved the first and most important neighboring country on the European side of the U.S.S.R.: Poland. Here was the country which the Soviet Union had partitioned with Germany in 1939, whose successor leadership generation the Soviet Union had decimated by the killing of the officers and reserve officers captured in the 1939 campaign, but to whose government-in-exile it had made some concessions in the wake of the German attack in 1941. Now that the tide on the Eastern Front was turning, this last measure could be reversed. Early in 1943 Stalin explained to Polish Communists that a new army and government would have to be established for Poland and that he would soon break relations with the government-in-exile in London.[162] The Soviet government's announcement of January 16, 1943, that all those who were on Soviet territory in November 1939 were Soviet citizens—with its implication that there were now no more Poles in the Soviet Union—meant that Moscow's 1941 promise to the Polish government that interned and deported Poles would be allowed to enter the Polish army had been revoked.[163] By April, the formation of a new Polish army under Soviet auspices, led by General Berling was beginning.[164] The reaction of the government-in-exile to the discovery at Katyn of the graves of those Polish officers from one of the Soviet prison camps provided Stalin with an excuse for breaking relations with the Sikorski government on April 25, 1943.[165] The inability of the Western Powers to provide effective support to the Polish government gave the Soviet Union a clear road to a new system for whatever Poland survived the war,[166] and this road was smoothed further for them by the death of Sikorski in an airplane accident at Gibraltar on July 4.[167] With the leading figure of the government-in-exile gone from the scene, the Soviet Union thereafter disregarded whatever protestations in behalf of an independent Poland came from their Western Allies. If the Red Army had to fight its way across every kilometer into Germany, the intervening area would be under full Soviet control.

As for the Western Allies, they had already committed themselves to fighting for the unconditional surrender of the Axis powers. They had observed the repeated rumors of a German–Soviet separate peace with great concern for some time and continued to be extremely and continually worried about that possibility.[168] These worries were always being reinforced by their interception and reading of Japanese diplomatic telegrams which alluded to the possibility of such an eventuality; and their own inability to launch a massive landing in Western Europe heightened apprehensions. The British government in particular drew from this situation the conclusion that every possible concession should be made to the Soviet Union and, as recounted in Chapter 11, tried hard to persuade the United States of the wisdom of such a policy.[169] Even if the attempt to cooperate in the future with the Soviet Union did not in the end work out, it was in Eden's opinion better at least to try to get along.[170] The British would provide the Soviet Union with whatever intelligence they could glean about German plans for a new offensive from their code-breaking, especially their new success with the German non-Morse secret printer.[171] As for American and British Lend Lease supplies to the Russians, these were steadily being increased, in spite of a row raised by United States Ambassador Standley over the refusal of the Russians to give their allies any credit for them.[172] The negotiations for the Third Supply Protocol in May and June 1943 were made especially difficult by Soviet refusal to help with air protection for the Murmansk route or to exchange information. At Roosevelt's insistence, spurred by fear of a separate Soviet–German peace and knowledge of the postponement of the Second Front, the policy of unconditional aid was continued.[173]

The Western Allies had their eyes focused on the follow-up to Tunisia. They would land in Sicily in the summer of 1943 and were continuing preparations for a landing in Western Europe in May 1944. On the former project, there was a new plan which shifted the United States army from the northwestern section of Sicily to the southeastern, right alongside the British.[a] As for the second project, the big landing in the West, Churchill still had some reservations, as is explained in Chapter 11, but he did want an offensive against Germany as early in 1944 as possible and came back to the invasion of Norway as a possibility.[174] As for the contingency of a German internal collapse, in April 1943 the Western Allies began plans for the rapid occupation of Germany in that unlikely event, plans code-named "Rankin" and later to be important in the context of projects for the occupation and division of the Third Reich.[175] These plans called for the quick landing of United States and British troops on the continent. If Germany did collapse, the Western Allies certainly wanted to be in Central Europe in force as rapidly as possible.

There was, however, little expectation in London or Washington that the war would end either soon or easily. First the U-Boats had to be defeated and then a series of landings on the continent would follow. In the meantime, a massive bombing campaign was continued to soften up Germany, and if any portion of that bombing offensive appeared to be faltering, the timing and other aspects of the raids would have to be

---

[a] Montgomery also wanted the Americans under his own command, but that was turned down. Montgomery to Brooke, 6 May, 1943, Liddell Hart Centre, Alanbrooke Papers, 14/24/13.

shifted—but the objective remained the same.[176] New technical navigation and bomb aiming devices were introduced beginning in March 1943, and increasing numbers of planes were becoming available for ever larger raids on the Ruhr district.[177] The attack on German dams in the Ruhr area on May 16–17, and the planning for the huge July 1943 series of raids on Hamburg, accompanied by the use of a new device to confuse German radar, belong in the context of the escalating bombing campaign.[178]

The difficulty of reaching much of German-controlled Europe from air bases in Britain and North Africa, at a time when the effective range of Allied bombers was only about 600 miles, made the strategic advantage of a landing in Italy and the seizure of the airfields in the Foggia area there appear increasingly important.[179] But here one already moves to strategic planning for operations after the invasion of Sicily. In any case, the summer of 1943 would, as far as the Western Allies were concerned, combine the exploitation of victory in North Africa with the new "Pointblank" bombing offensive.[180] If the three great allies could only hold together, the road ahead was sure to be hard, but the prospects were certainly more encouraging than in the dark days a year earlier.

9

THE HOME FRONT

GERMANY

The early portion of World War II had a curiously bifurcated impact on internal affairs in the Third Reich. On the one hand, the desire of the government to avoid at all costs any repetition of the collapse at home which it believed responsible for the defeat of 1918 made the regime most reluctant to ask for too high a level of sacrifices. While rationing was introduced at the end of August, 1939, every effort was made to keep rations high; and, partly at the expense of looting most of the rest of Europe, German rations were the highest among the European belligerents until the last months of the war.

Similarly, there was no total mobilization of either the population or the material resources of the country. While millions of men served in the armed forces, there was a high level of deferments to work in industry and in the administration, a policy which did not change until early 1942 when the disastrous defeats in the East meant greater priority of the manpower needs of the armed forces over the political preferences of the government. Furthermore, within the realm of German industry, a high level of consumer goods production continued well into the war, so that neither industrial facilities nor raw materials were directed over-whelmingly into war production until 1942.[1]

If Germany did not draw into military service all able-bodied men, the country was even less inclined to mobilize the labor potential of its women. In the first year of war, in fact, the relatively high level of support payments made to dependents of men in the military had the effect of leading many women to withdraw from employment in industry, offices, or shops—they could do better living at home on their allowance. Of those women who were gainfully employed outside the home, farm, or family enterprise, millions were working as maids for middle and upper class households well into the war. Only from 1943 on would this picture begin to change, but until the last stages of the war Germany did not draw its women in to the same extent as Britain and the Soviet Union did; by then the bombing had brought them into the war in a very different way.

In some respects, therefore, what was called the "Phony War" did not dramatically impinge on German life quickly, and the victory over Poland was especially popular in a country where anti-Polish sentiments were very strong. At the same time, there is good evidence that the British and French declarations of war produced a shock in the thinking of many Germans, in part because of memories of World War I, in part because many had come to believe the propaganda of the regime's earlier years that Germany wanted peace, not war, with the Western Powers. The very bad weather conditions of the winter of 1939–40, with the canals freezing so that coal transport lagged, and all sorts of related difficulties, accentuated a feeling of unease in Germany during the first half year of war.[2]

That feeling of unease would have been more widespread had the public known of the massive program for the killing of the elderly, the very sick, people with mental illness, and others, inaugurated in the first weeks of the war but only gradually coming to people's attention. The so-called euthanasia program has been reviewed in Chapter 2; it was an integral portion of waging war as Hitler and his associates saw it. The points to be made in this context are two: first, the regime quickly found that it could count on the enthusiastic, willing, or reluctant support of thousands of doctors, nurses, administrators and other people in a program which cost over one hundred and perhaps two hundred thousand people their lives. Secondly, in this process the regime developed the techniques for selecting categories of people out of a society for killing, carrying out the murders, and disposing of the bodies, while simultaneously acquiring a corps of individuals ready, willing, and experienced at the task of murdering others as a "regular job" on a day after day after day basis. All societies harbor individuals who for any number of reasons kill another person or even act as serial killers who murder repeatedly; people who engage in killing vast numbers of other human beings as a full-time occupation have to be located and trained. Any who found this an uncongenial profession could, as we now know, ask to be transferred or reassigned with no significant risk to themselves, and a few did that.[3] But there was never a shortage of personnel.

During 1940 and the first half of 1941, there was a slow but steady rise in popular unrest over this murder program, culminating in a public denunciation of it by Clemens August Count von Galen, the Bishop of

Münster, in August 1941.[4] Such appeals had an impact inside and outside the country: inside they led Hitler to defer at least part of the euthanasia program until after the war, when the noisy bishop himself could be included. The suggestion that wounded veterans of World War II would be killed by their own government as "useless mouths" — something which had already happened to many disabled World War I veterans — was just too dangerous to have floating around just as the campaign against the Soviet Union was getting under way. Outside Germany, the killing program had become known, and President Roosevelt referred to Galen's sermon as, "a splendid and brave thing."[5]

The summer of 1941, when the "euthanasia" program was somewhat reduced, was a time when the systematic murder of Jews, first in the newly occupied portions of the U.S.S.R. and then in the rest of German-controlled Europe, was initiated. The first mass deportations of Jews from Germany to places in the East where they were murdered began in October 1941. In the following years, the vast majority of those Jews who had not been able to leave pre-war Germany were deported and killed; their emptied homes turned over to others even as the welfare organization distributed their furniture and vast quantities of confiscated clothes — often blood-stained — to the German population. Word soon seeped back of the mass killings in the East; and while the army repeatedly instructed soldiers to stop sending pictures of mass shootings to their folks at home, Goebbels was distributing a letter from a soldier reporting on the mass killings in a propaganda collection of letters from the front.[6] In public, Hitler repeatedly boasted that his promise, that in a new war the Jews of Europe would be exterminated, was now being carried out.[7] There was some unease over all this, and a few brave individuals helped a small number hide and survive, often at great risk to themselves, but most turned aside.

A major concern of the government apparatus from the fall of 1941 on was to obtain the cooperation of the various governments allied with and subordinate to Germany in turning over their Jewish citizens to the Germans for deportation and killing. In this activity, the Germans obtained considerable help from the government of Vichy France,[8] the puppet regimes of Slovakia and Croatia, and, at least for a while, the government of Romania. The Italians were most definite in their refusal to cooperate, sheltering Jews not only in Italy itself but in the portions of France, Yugoslavia, and Greece occupied by the Italian army.[9] To the outrage of the Germans, who saw this as one more sign of Italian incompetence as allies, most Jews in these areas survived until after the Italian surrender of September 1943 opened them to German control and hence to the application of the by then well-established routines of collection, deportation, and murder. Only in the immediate vicinity of Rome was minimal attention paid to possible objections from the Vatican.[10]

As the tide of war turned against the Axis, Romania began to resist German pressure for the turning over of its Jews, while Bulgaria had resisted from the start, and the Danes had helped evacuate their Jewish neighbors to Sweden when the Germans intended to round them up. Until 1944, Hungary had also resisted German demands, including those voiced personally by Hitler and von Ribbentrop, that its well over half a million Jewish citizens be given up. It was again after the occupation of the country by German troops that the process of deportation to the murder factories began. The international uproar occasioned by these events in the summer and fall of 1944 led to a delay which saved the lives of many; it was in this context that the Swedish emissary Raoul Wallenberg played an important role.[11]

From the practical and the propagandistic side, this was one of the major features of life and death in wartime Germany and German-controlled Europe. As a German reporter wrote at the end of a three-week-long trip into the occupied Ukraine in 1943: "We heard entirely clear and explicit announcements about the Jewish question. Among the 16 million inhabitants of the area controlled by the civilian administration in the Ukraine, there used to be 1.1 million Jews. They have all been liquidated... One of the higher officials of the administration explained the executions with the words, 'the Jews are exterminated like roaches'."[12]

This was not only a central objective of the regime but one of which it was inordinately proud. In 1944, even as Germany was everywhere on the defensive, it planned a big international anti-Jewish congress to be held in Cracow in German-occupied Poland to explain and commemorate the wonderful character of such activities.[13] The congress was eventually cancelled, but the mass killing went on. By the last years of the war, there was not only the pressure from the leadership. Thousands involved in the process had acquired a vested interest in it: here was their source of promotion and rewards; and by 1944, to say nothing of 1945, killing defenseless civilians seemed to them vastly preferable to the far more dangerous alternative of serving at the front where those they faced also carried arms.

The killing of the infirm among the Germans and any and all Jews they could get into their hands were not the only components of National Socialist racial policy during the war. There was a somewhat similar program for the mass murder of gypsies, the Roma and Sinti, which

involved the deaths of thousands but is only beginning to be investigated.[14] Furthermore, the government was very worried that Germans
might marry Poles, Hungarians, and others whom Hitler and all in
charge of racial policies considered undesirable.[15] As the government
brought more and more prisoners of war and slave laborers into pre-
1939 Germany, there was endless concern about German women
sleeping with men of Slavic and other backgrounds whom the regime
held to be racially inferior. Illegitimate children were just fine as long as
both parents met the racial criteria of the Nazis, but what was considered
interracial sex was severely punished. The problems posed by the
increasing casualties among the male population as a result of combat
were to be met in the post-war years by a whole series of schemes
discussed during the war. These ranged from Martin Bormann's argument for multiple wives bearing children to one man in what one historian has called the National Socialist principle of crop rotation[16] to a plan
worked out by a high SS official for recruiting for the SS from among
the Germans in North and South America and in Australia.[17] A more
immediate form of population "recruitment" was a large-scale program
of kidnapping of "Germanic-looking" children and the classification as
German of those Poles and Czechs whom the authorities thought plausible candidates for reclassification.

Finally, it was assumed that extensive German settlement in agricultural areas of the U.S.S.R. and Poland would lead to farm families with
large numbers of children who would take the place of those lost in the
fight to seize these territories. As a starter, even during the war the
regime began to allocate estates to its most faithful servants. General
Guderian, for example, between commanding an army on the Eastern
Front and becoming inspector general of armored forces, spent months
travelling around occupied Eastern Europe looking for an estate which
the government could steal for him.[18] The new racial order in Europe
was to have been established in the decades after Germany had won the
war, but a big start was made during hostilities.

Reference has been made to the prisoners of war and other foreign
workers brought into Germany during World War II. This eventually
massive program began with Polish prisoners captured in the campaign
of fall 1939 and came to include over one million French prisoners and
about one million Soviet prisoners of war. The latter, together with
another million who agreed to serve as auxiliaries with the German army,
constituted the survivors of over five million captured Red Army soldiers;
the over three million others having been murdered or allowed to starve
to death. To these must be added approximately four to five million

additional forced laborers, most of them impressed or kidnapped in the
Soviet Union, with smaller contingents from Poland, France, and other
portions of German-occupied Europe. Furthermore, several hundred
thousand Italian workers who had been recruited more or less voluntarily
were joined by additional hundreds of thousands of Italian soldiers captured by the Germans after the Italian surrender of 1943 and converted
into slave laborers soon after.

These seven to eight million forced or enslaved workers came to play
a critical role in the German war economy in several ways.[19] In the first
years of the war, they enabled the regime to refrain from mobilizing
German women for factory work and to replace the men who left farms
for better paying industrial jobs. From 1942 on, the massive increases
in forced labor by the surviving Soviet prisoners of war and enslaved
Russian and Polish civilians made it possible for the German government
to draft very large additional numbers of German men into the armed
services, primarily to replace casualties of the fighting on the Eastern
Front.

Wretchedly housed and fed, constantly harassed and mistreated, brutally punished for real or imaginary offenses, the slave workers were
omni-present in wartime Germany. Every town had its slave labor camps,
every factory its proportion of slave-laborers, ranging from 20 to 80
percent of the work force. The degrees of mistreatment were carefully
calculated on so-called racial lines with the French and other "Western"
workers discriminated against least and those from the Soviet Union
most of all. The greatest concern of the regime was always about sexual
relations between foreign workers and German women, a practice met
by public hangings on the one hand and a national system of brothels
on the other.[20] The slave laborers suffered even more than German
civilians as the Allied bombing offensive destroyed many of their barracks and interrupted the flow of their already miserable food rations.
During the war years, many died of mistreatment, others were killed as
"useless mouths" when unable to work, and the women who constituted
more than half the forced laborers from the East were often subjected
to forced sterilizations and abortions. In the last days of the war thousands were shot on the slightest pretext.[21]

During their years among the Germans, they had played a key role
in the war economy. Simultaneously, their terrible treatment, graded
according to alleged racial categories, accustomed the Germans to the
racialist new order in which all would be expected to live and die in a
German-controlled Europe. In the months before final defeat, most
Germans were concerned primarily with immediate questions of their

own and their families' survival; but in the earlier heady days of anticipated victory, they could already experience the "benefits" of being a "master race" by living on the upper rung of a racial hierarchy as they watched columns of ill-fed and poorly clothed workers in the streets of their cities, and working alongside them in factory and farm. Industrial magnates, at the same time, could reap large profits from underpaying workers who would be replaced by ever more slaves as those who were too weak or old were killed off—and therefore needed no pensions.

The likely future appearance of a German-controlled world was foreshadowed in other ways in wartime Germany. The administrative chaos which had been developing in the years before the war was, if anything, accentuated during the conflict. Once in a great while some superfluous agency was dissolved; von Ribbentrop's private foreign office, for example, was abolished two years after its head had become Foreign Minister of Germany.[22] But for every agency ended, at least ten new ones sprang up, and all struggled for power and jurisdiction with each other. A post-war study which referred to this system as "authoritarian anarchy,"[23] aptly describes the administrative chaos in which rivalry for power was stimulated by ambition and zeal to gain the favor of the Führer—and Hitler himself felt most comfortable. In this mass of rivalries he always had the last word, and, as he saw it, the most ruthless and determined made their way to the top.

This confusion was characteristic not only of the military hierarchy and the civilian administration, it also extended to a project especially dear to Hitler: the transformation of Germany's urban landscape. A whole series of cities was to be completely restructured, not only Berlin but a long list of others. Massive buildings symbolizing the capital of the world were to be erected in Berlin; smaller versions would grace other cities.[24] Work on these projects began during the war; some of the contracts were being worked on for years, and the architectural offices were still busy on their design work in the spring of 1945.[25]

Two aspects of these projects deserve mention because of their significance for the priorities of the regime and its hopes for the future. The priorities were such that all involved in the planning could count on deferments from the draft; like those engaged in murdering Jews and participating in the endless jurisdictional quarrels which characterized the regime, those planning the future of Germany's cities had a strong vested interest in remaining at their current tasks rather than facing the dangers of the front. Secondly, all the plans for cities and towns had one common characteristic: there would be no churches in post-war Germany's urban areas.[26] Here one can see the architectural expression of a goal close to the hearts of the leadership of National Socialist Germany. Whatever temporary accommodations might have to be made in wartime to the objections of the churches to euthanasia, to the removal of crucifixes from the schools, and to the maintenance of a structure of chaplains in the army, once victory had been attained in the war, the existence of the Christian churches in Germany could safely be ended. And if anyone objected, the Gestapo would see to their punishment.[27]

Any number of other things would disappear from a German-controlled Europe, including the independence of most countries on the continent. The economic and political preparations for this were also under way during the war and thus affected German internal affairs as well as those of the occupied countries. There was considerable discussion in some government circles about the "New Order" which Germany would create. In part for propaganda purposes to counter the hopes aroused by the Atlantic Charter and the call for a new world by the United Nations, there were proposals for Germany to give some public presentation of its post-war plans.[28] Until its surrender Italy and, for most of the war, Japan urged Germany to take some steps to reassure the peoples of German-occupied Europe about their future, but all such pleas fell on deaf ears.[29] If there was one thing Hitler did not want, it was promises and commitments which might restrain Germany. At times he gave his immediate associates some hints of what the future of a German-dominated Europe would look like,[30] but beyond the promise that there would be no Jews he would not make any of his intentions public.

All trade would be directed from Germany, and German currency, the Reichsmark, would be the central currency.[31] The economy would be directed by the state with industry strictly controlled and regulated — insofar as it was not actually owned by the government or by the growing empire of the SS.[32]

Under the ambitious leadership of Himmler, the SS was expanding its authority. The SS and police apparatus took over more and more functions from the courts, operated independently in the occupied territories, and built up an industrial empire originally based largely on the concentration camp system.[33] The internal rivalries, which characterized the SS like all other aspects of the Third Reich, should not be allowed to obscure its cohesion in dealings with other segments of society. Its economic role was growing at the expense of private industry and of the economic structure which Albert Speer, with his sharp elbows and the personal support of Hitler, was steadily building up.[34] The military force of the SS, the Waffen SS or armed SS, as it was called, grew steadily in spite of very heavy casualties.[35] Growing rather like a cancer within

Germany's land forces, this army within an army grew ever larger, recruiting not only in Germany itself but from people of real or imagined German ancestry all over Europe.[36] And those officers of the regular army, who were sought out for the higher staff positions in the corps and army headquarters created to command the ever increasing numbers of Waffen SS divisions, were expected to leave whichever Christian Church they belonged to as the price of certain and rapid promotion.[a] The SS, like the cities of Germany and their people, would have no religious inhibitions.

The old rivals of the SS, the brown-shirted SA and the regular Nazi Party organization, came to play significant roles in wartime Germany in two opposite ways. On the one hand, they were utilized to assist in the mobilization of the public. In this process, the party, like the SS, grew more influential in the last year of war. Under the vigorous leadership of Martin Bormann, the central offices of the party gained vastly greater power.[37]

On the other hand, there is good evidence that the party organization became something of a lightning rod for whatever discontent and dissatisfaction existed in the country. Most Germans fell easily into the habit of separating their Führer from the party he led, imagined that all would be well if only he knew about whatever they objected to, and developed an increasingly negative attitude toward the party's officials.[38]

One party formation was not affected by the developing alienation from the Nazi Party in the latter years of the war. The increasing devastation caused by Allied bombing made the population more dependent on the relief agencies of the government, and of these the National Socialist Welfare Organization (NSV) was by far the most important.[b] Bombed out urban families turned to the welfare organization for help, and if they were occasionally disconcerted by the blood and bullet holes which marked some of the clothing distributed to them, they were grateful all the same.

The public supported the German war effort with a high degree of coherence. There was some apprehension in the first winter of war followed by jubilation in 1940 and increasing apprehension about the length of the war in 1941 and thereafter. The propaganda machinery helped sustain public morale in the face of growing troubles and

---

[a] I was personally told by one former German army colonel that this was his reason for declining a request that he transfer.

[b] There is very little substantial literature on the NSV. A factor in this is that most of its records, at least at the national level, appear to be lost. See Herwart Vorländer, "NS-Volkswohlfahrt und Winterhilfswerk des deutschen Volkes," *Vierteljahrshefte für Zeitgeschichte* 34, No. 3 (July 1986), 341–80, and the same author's *Die NSV: Darstellung und Dokumentation einer nationalsozialistischen Organisation* (Boppard: Boldt, 1988).

unease.[39] The dismissals of a series of famous military leaders in the winter of 1941 and the almost simultaneous drive to collect winter clothing and equipment for the troops caused disquiet on the home front, but the Soviet victory at Stalingrad, followed soon after by the surrender in North Africa, had even greater impact in the country.

The bombing at first caused morale to drop, but after a while appears to have caused more apathy than anything else. People concentrated on survival and the most immediate concerns. Anxiety about relatives at the front and the next air raid at home dominated people's thinking to the exclusion of most other topics. There was resentment at what looked to many like an unequal sharing of burdens by the wealthier segment of the population, but the ubiquitous slave laborers were viewed as a normal part of daily life. The mass murders of Jews and others were repeatedly mentioned in public by Hitler himself and by others, but most did not react. Assembled officers applauded Hitler's expressions of satisfaction about the extermination program;[40] the majority of the people shut their eyes and ears.

In the last two years of war, hope for the effects of new weapons provided some solace, but for many Germans strength through fear replaced the "Strength through Joy" recreation and vacation programs of the German Labor Front. Fear of defeat on the Eastern Front and a Russian invasion, fear of the peace which might be imposed on Germany, fear of punishment for past crimes, fear of denunciation to the police for defeatism with its drastic penalties, fear of a future which no one could visualize; these were only some of the characteristics which dominated the thoughts and feelings of many. As a bitter, then current, joke put it: "Better enjoy the war; the peace will be terrible."

There were, however, those who opposed the regime. Already before the war, there were some who had their doubts about the National Socialist system; and although the war not surprisingly brought a cohesiveness to a country with which its citizens identified, there continued to be important elements highly critical of the system. And in many cases their criticism was further stimulated by what they saw and heard of atrocities carried out in the occupied territories as well as at home.[41] Though some became opponents of the regime as it was obviously on the way to defeat, it would be grossly unfair to disregard the fact that many had turned against it in the years of apparent triumph.

The opponents were greatly hindered by two factors. They could see that the vast majority of their fellow citizens supported the government, many of them enthusiastically. This meant, in practice, that only a coup from the inside could topple the government.[42] Isolated acts of public resistance to such policies as the deportation of the sick to killing centers in Germany, or the deportation of Jewish partners of mixed marriages to killing centers in occupied Poland, might slow or even halt such specific actions. There was, however, no massive public opposition to the regime of the sort that toppled the East European Communist governments in 1989, including that in East Germany, once it became clear that the Red Army would not intervene to save Moscow's puppets. The few valiant attempts to arouse the public highlight by their total failure both the bravery of those trying and the futility of that approach. In the 1930s such attempts came from workers, primarily Communists and Socialists; during the war the most famous such attempt was the February 1943 appeal of the "White Rose," a small student group in Munich.[43]

If the mass support of the regime made a coup very difficult, the precautions taken by the regime added to the problems faced by those opposed to it. They came to realize that only by killing Hitler could they disrupt the system, seize power, and explain to the public their reasons for such a step against their own government in the middle of a war. But killing Hitler was not a simple matter; he was increasingly careful, surrounded by loyal and adoring military and civilian guards and associates, very sensitive to the personal loyalty to himself of those he met, and very lucky. He had narrowly escaped Elser's attempt of November 1939, as recounted in Chapter 2. The first time opponents among the military tried to kill him by placing a bomb on his plane in March, 1943, the detonator failed to work.[44]

Several other projects for killing Hitler also failed; that of July 20, 1944, being the most likely to succeed because it had been prepared with some care and included provision for a procedure to take over power in Germany and the occupied territories she still held at that time. By a narrow margin, the bomb itself went off but did not kill Hitler. It is an indication of the overwhelming support Hitler still had that as the orders from the conspirators in Berlin and those from his headquarters in East Prussia landed on the desks of military commanders in German-controlled Europe, all but a brave few sided with him in this, the last "election" of the Third Reich. Most of those in positions of any significance who had been opposed to the regime were uncovered as a result of this attempted coup and killed; some committed suicide lest they reveal too much when tortured; a tiny number survived.

The failure of this attempt underlines the fact that most in the German military hierarchy continued in support of a regime which by July 1944 was obviously not doing very well. Three arguments sometimes advanced to explain this fact ought, in my judgement, to be dismissed. The assertion that most felt bound by their oath of loyalty to Hitler should be seen in the context of prior oaths and subsequent oaths taken and broken by the same individuals, especially those at the highest ranks. They had sworn to uphold the Weimar constitution, and many had sworn to uphold its laws—which included the Versailles Treaty. It was considered desirable, even honorable, to break this oath as often as possible, and anyone who wanted to keep it was despised.[a] After World War II, a substantial number of the military leaders were called on to testify under oath. Anyone who has studied their sworn testimony carefully will have noticed that many took this oath very lightly indeed. If of all the oaths generals and field marshals took, only the one to Hitler is so often cited, that may reveal more about their attitude toward Hitler than toward oaths.

A second explanation sometimes put forward is to the effect that the Allied demand for unconditional surrender inhibited opposition. This is difficult to square with the fact that in the decade from Hitler's becoming Chancellor until the Casablanca Conference the opponents never moved to remove him (except for Elser's bomb of November 1939); all the real efforts to topple the regime came after the call for unconditional surrender. Certainly if the Allies had spelled out in detail their plans for Germany's future, insofar as they could agree on them, that would hardly have provided much new incentive for a revolt in the eyes of those who believed they needed one.

There is finally the argument that the Allies should have encouraged the opposition with assurances about Germany's future. For most of the war, this meant assurances that Germany could keep the territories seized in the 1930s and even some taken during the war; this was never a possibility and reflects more on the nationalistic provincialism of some in the opposition than on the options before the Allies. The constant role of those who were to overthrow the regime in planning and executing the invasion of one neutral after another in the first part of the war and their involvement in the atrocities known to be committed in the occupied territories during the second part made the British and Americans very doubtful.[45] There was always worry about a breakup of the Allied coalition. Above all, there was the belief that if the opponents were really serious, it was *they* who needed to act; thereafter the Allies would see what the situation allowed. Since one of the major war aims of the United Nations was the disarmament of Germany, there was no way that they could give to the periodic emissaries of the opposition assurances which the latter could take to German generals in the hope of getting them to take action. The ones who were willing to act had enough insight and courage to do so without assurances; the others could not

---

[a] The post-World War II discussion of the oath question has barely begun to deal with these matters. See Karl Dietrich Bracher, Wolfgang Sauer and Gerhard Schulz, *Die nationalsozialistische Machtergreifung* (Cologne; Westdeutscher Verlag, 1962), pp. 766–67, 778–79.

be persuaded anyway. Perhaps the fact that most of them were secretly accepting huge bribes from Hitler ought to be recalled in this context.

The failure of the July 20 attempt worked to strengthen the hold of the Nazis on what was left of their empire. Their opponents had come into the open and been crushed. The National Socialist revolution, a process as much as an event, now moved forward more rapidly and more ruthlessly. The SS gained vast additional powers as Himmler consolidated his hold on Germany's various intelligence services and took over the Replacement Army from the military. The Nazi Party increased its power by gaining a major role in the new Volkssturm or people's army, the last great mobilization of manpower. And the population, combining fear and apathy with devotion and hope, continued to support the regime until the last days of the war. Only as Allied troops appeared in Germany itself did substantial numbers turn their backs on the system they had served.

As the last illusions disappeared, relief over the end of bombing and fighting mingled with fear of the Russians and the future, anxiety over food and the fate of loved ones, but above all the daily struggle for survival. As for the National Socialist Party, even before its leaders had fled, committed suicide, or been arrested, it quickly lost the hold it had once held on the faith of millions. On January 27, 1942, Hitler had said that if the German people would not fight, they might as well disappear.[46] But it was not the German people who disappeared. It was the Nazi Party which evaporated from the scene once Hitler was dead about as rapidly as the Fascist Party in Italy had vanished in July 1943.

ITALY

Italy's population generally entered the war with an attitude not unlike that of countries invaded by the Axis. They had not wanted to enter the conflict, might be pleased by the appearance of quick triumph followed by an even quicker end to the war in 1940, but were basically as a people in a position worse than any other. The Poles and Norwegians, the British and French, the Belgians and Dutch, the Greeks and Yugoslavs, the Russians and Americans, to say nothing of the Chinese, would all have greatly preferred not to be drawn into war or attacked at all, but as long as they had been, at least most of them believed they were on the right side and fighting alongside the right allies. For most Italians it was the other way around: they disliked—if they did not hate—the Germans and generally would have been more comfortable fighting alongside their "enemies" if they had to fight at all.

Mussolini and a minute number of others were enthusiastic about attacking France, Greece, and Yugoslavia, but finding anyone in the country who genuinely believed Italy's future would be served by sending thousands of soldiers to fight on the southern part of the Eastern Front against the Soviet Union, or by Italy's declaration of war on the United States, would have been a Herculean task. No analysis of Italy's role and her home front in World War II can overlook the basic fact that, in the eyes of much of the population, the country's entry into the war was a bad idea and that it had picked the wrong side. There remained a residual resentment at the way the Allies had treated Italy at the end of World War I, and there was additional resentment over what looked to some like British blocking of Italian aspirations in the Mediterranean; but these grievances did not translate into a desire for war. Such bizarre episodes as the abortive project to sell the Italian navy to Great Britain in the winter of 1940–41 can be understood only in the context of a society which found itself on the wrong side of a war.[47]

As that war went from a short time of early success for Germany to a string of defeats for Italy, popular attitudes and morale fell. The German rescue operation in early 1941 may have saved the regime at home as it saved the remnants of Italy's empire in North Africa and Albania, but it did nothing for the regime's reputation—quite the reverse. Occupation zones in France, Yugoslavia and Greece, allotted to Italy by the Germans, brought troubles rather than advantages. These troubles were as much or more with the Germans as with the occupied peoples. The Italian zones in all three countries produced endless friction with the Germans over the reluctance of the Italian occupation authorities to hand over the Jews there to be murdered. Most Italian officers simply could not comprehend the German insistence on killing Jews and saw it as merely one more indication of their ally's barbaric inclinations. When the Italian zone in occupied France became a refuge for Jews fleeing from the German occupation of Vichy France in November 1942, the conflict escalated.[48] In occupied Yugoslavia, there was additional controversy with the Germans about the Italian policy of aiding the Cetniks, while in Greece there were disputes about responsibility and remedies for the run-away inflation and misery in that country. In all these areas, the 1943 surrender of Italy followed by German occupation would bring death to the Jews and increased misery to everyone else, but in the preceding years, the symbols of Italy's share in Axis victories, which the occupation zones represented, had provided no glories to off-set the dissatisfaction with war on the Italian home front.

The privations of war thus came to a society that saw little purpose to the sacrifices being imposed on it; the air raids, though small at first, significantly affected morale; and the casualties had a double sting.[a] As if this were not sufficient cause for dissatisfaction, one of Mussolini's favorite devices for running the country, the periodic replacement of incompetent ministers and Fascist Party officials by others who were usually even less qualified, hollowed out the Fascist Party in the very years when it was most needed if the country were to be held together in the war.[49]

The astonishing thing under these circumstances is not that the Italian people failed to live up to the martial standard which Mussolini set for them but that the home front held together as long as it did, and that elements of the armed forces often fought valiantly and effectively.[50] Three essentially simultaneous disasters: the loss of the last portion of Italy's North African empire, acquired by the parliamentarily governed Italy of the pre-Fascist era, the disastrous losses of early 1943 of the Italian forces on the Eastern Front and in Tunisia, and the stepped up bombing of Italy by Allied planes from North African bases, provided the final push. Shortly after the successful Allied landing on Sicily the actions of dissidents among the leaders of the Fascist Party coincided with the plotting of a group of court officials and military men around the King. The July 25, 1943, vote in the Fascist Grand Council precipitated not only the resignation and arrest of Mussolini, but the swift collapse of the Fascist Party and system in Italy. In a few hours, it turned out that whatever earlier gains Fascism might have made among the population, there was practically nothing left of it after three years of war.

The extraordinary incompetence with which the Badoglio government made its exit from the war left Italy, like Caesar's Gaul, divided into three parts. The southern portion was occupied by the Allies who slowly fought their way up the peninsula. The central and northern part was occupied by the Germans who also quickly seized Albania and the Italian islands on the Aegean as well as the Italian occupation zones in France, Yugoslavia and Greece. The third part was the saddest: it constituted hundreds of thousands of Italian soldiers who were carted off by the Germans to forced labor, a fate from which thousands never returned alive.[51]

In the portion of Italy which remained under German control, the latter exercised effective authority. They ran the area as an occupied territory and, now free to act as they wished, did what they could to round up Jews for deportation to murder centers, always their first

---

[a] There were major strikes in the north Italian industrial cities of Turin and Milan in March 1943; nothing of the sort took place in wartime Germany.

priority. In this they were aided by some old Fascists who had long wanted to emulate the Germans in this regard, but they were hindered by other Italians who hid or in other ways protected their fellow citizens.[52]

Murdering Jews, shooting civilians, and deporting captured Italian soldiers to slave labor were not the only German measures certain to alienate the Italian population. During the years of war since late 1940, the planned resettlement of the people who identified with Germany from the South Tyrol to other portions of German-controlled Europe had ground to a halt.[53] Now that the Germans could do whatever they wanted, they took the first steps toward annexing huge portions of northern Italy. Not only the South Tyrol but most of northeast Italy, including the ports of Trieste and Fiume, were designated as "Operational Zones" and placed under complete German control.[54] The new rulers began the process of annexation to Germany in many fields; and since the overwhelming majority of the population was Italian, contributed to ever greater resistance not only there but in the rest of German-controlled Italy.

If Hitler restrained his own inclination for openly annexing parts of Italy, and the even more fervent anti-Italian enthusiasm of some of his associates like Joseph Goebbels, it was because of regard for his old friend Mussolini. The Duce was rescued from Italian captivity by an airborne coup and installed in northern Italy. There he and a group of Fascist fanatics attempted to establish a new Fascist regime under German auspices. They tried hard to raise a new army to fight alongside their Axis partner,[55] and to court public support by a variety of semi-socialist measures.[56]

This shadow system, officially called the Italian Social Republic, and often referred to as the Republic of Saló, may have been a reflection of Mussolini's dreams of earlier years, but it was too obviously a client of the hated Germans; and the Duce himself was no longer the rousing speaker of earlier days. Among squabbling would-be born-again Fascist leaders, Mussolini had a few of those who had voted against him in the Fascist Grand Council—including his son-in-law Count Ciano—shot, but otherwise could rouse himself from a lethargic somnolence only for his mistress. The Germans who held the real power in northern Italy, the military and police commanders, negotiated in 1945 with the Western Allies for a surrender in Italy without informing Mussolini. As the German hold on the area behind the front line collapsed, the partisans there not only seized control of ever greater territory but caught Mussolini and his mistress and shot both of them.

These partisans were a portion of a large resistance movement which blossomed in the part of Italy which remained under German control after the front line stabilized between Rome and Naples in the late fall of 1943. Including both parts of the rural population based in the villages and sometimes protected by the mountains and also the urban resistance drawing especially from the factory workers of northern Italian cities, the resistance as a whole came to constitute a major menace to the Germans and a point of reference for post-war Italy. Here, in the opposition to German occupiers and their Italian stooges there grew up a coalition of a broad range of people from Communists through Catholic political leaders to conservative nationalists who learned to work together and respect each other, at least for a while. These groups cooperated effectively with secret emissaries from the Allies and paved the way first for the latter and eventually for the restoration of Italian self-government. Some of their exploits were exaggerated in the heroic literature of the post-war years, but a major portion of the recovery of Italian self-confidence and revival in the years after 1945 can in fact be attributed to the fact that the extremes of disaster in war were accompanied in their last stage by a second national revival in the resistance.[57]

At least a minimum of cooperation between the various elements of the resistance in the north was made possible not only by their common enmity to the Germans and to Fascism, but also by the temporary restraint which appears to have been urged on Italy's Communist Party by the Soviet Union.[58] This also facilitated their working after a fashion with the government of King Victor Emmanuel and General Pietro Badoglio in the south. There the British and Americans sponsored the reestablishment of the regime which had ignominiously fled from Rome. The most obvious disadvantage under which this government labored in its efforts to reestablish a semblance of Italian sovereignty and self-respect under the shield of Allied military power was that it steadily inherited precisely those portions of the country which had been most ravaged by the fighting as the Allies pushed north. The disruption and suffering caused for Italians by the advance of battle could be and was alleviated somewhat by the relief efforts of the Allied military government.[59] But the greater problem was an internal one. The discredited men around Badoglio and the King were under pressure to open the government to representatives of anti-Fascist parties. In the struggles which followed, the British and Americans increasingly took opposite sides. The British, with Churchill's personal and constant pressure, feared that new elements would bring about an end to the Italian monarchy while the Americans were uninterested in the fate of the monarchy but wanted more liberal elements included in the government.

The difficulties were partially resolved by a promise to hold a plebiscite on the monarchy after Italy was completely liberated—and which produced a majority for ending the monarchy—and by the increasing inclusion of new elements in the government.[60] Even Churchill's firing of the chief British representative, General Mason-Macfarlane, the former governor of Gibraltar, for siding too closely with the wrong Italian party leaders could not halt the drift toward a truly new system in the country after the liberation of Rome in June, 1944.[61]

Liberation not only brought changes in the Italian government, it also changed the situation of the Vatican which had operated under Axis pressure until this point. The Allies had been unhappy about the Pope's silence on German atrocities and his welcoming of a Japanese embassy.[62] Pius XII, who had not been unduly worried by the actions of German occupation forces in Europe, now asked that Black soldiers not be included among the Allied units stationed in Rome.[63] The Allied commanders had other worries. As their troops drove north in 1944 and 1945, the liberated areas came under the control of the restructured Italian government. The resistance formations were disarmed and new political parties came to the fore. The Communist Party came to inherit a large part of the working class and many former Fascists—no European proved as adept at recruiting a mass popular following for communism as Mussolini. On the other hand, as a successor of the "Popular" Party of the pre-Fascist era, the Christian Democrats became the mass party of the center and moderate right. They played a major role in the resistance; and the moderate left new government of the resistance hero Ferruccio Parri which began in June 1945 was succeeded by the first of a long series of Cabinets led by a Christian Democrat in December.[a] As the situation in the war-torn country began to stabilize, the internal and international position of its government very slowly began to regain the status of an independent country which the Fascist regime had sacrificed to German overlordship in the hope of imperial expansion.

THE UNITED KINGDOM

The state which participated in the war longer than any other—from the beginning in September 1939 to the end of August 1945—was Great Britain with its colonies and those Dominions which entered the conflict. It should, under these circumstances, not be surprising that the home front, especially in the United Kingdom, was affected by the war in

[a] This was the first government led by Alcide de Gasperi. The Christian Democrats provided Italy's Prime Ministers until 1981. For a helpful account, see Pietro Scoppola, "Alcide de Gasperi: Sein Weg zur Macht," in Hans Woller (ed.), *Italian und die Grossmächte, 1943–1949* (Munich: Oldenbourg, 1988), pp. 207–40.

innumerable ways. The direct impact of bombing was dramatic in 1940 and 1941; it resumed in the "Baby Blitz" of the early months of 1944; and then began again in June of 1944 with the German V-1 and V-2 weapons which in many ways had a morale effect out of all proportion to their actual destructiveness. This impact on British morale was related to the very length of the conflict and the disappointing reality that early victory had not followed upon the successful defiance of the German onslaught of 1940.

The exhilaration of standing alone in the face of a dictator who had overrun Western Europe after all British efforts to avoid war altogether had failed cemented a temporary political alliance of all political parties, other than the Communists, behind a coalition government led and inspired by Winston Churchill. Subsequent years brought new allies but also, especially in the spring and last month of 1941 and the first half of 1942, a series of setbacks and defeats. Disaster in Greece and on Crete, the total collapse of Britain's position in East Asia followed soon after by stunning defeats in North Africa and accompanied by steady losses at sea—with a humiliating dash of three major German warships the whole length of the English Channel—came closer to upsetting the Churchill government than many realized at the time or since.[a]

As the tide began to turn in ways visible to ordinary Englishmen with the victory at El Alamein and the landing in Northwest Africa, there was a sense of relief; but the very length of the road to victory, coming after long years of sacrifice and defeats, made for a brittle home front. It was in this context that the enormous concern over the impact of the new German weapons launched against English cities in 1944 and 1945 must be seen. The drop in morale affected most and led to serious consideration of the use of poison gas in retaliation.

In the background of all British life was the high level of mobilization. Out of a total work force of about 22 million in 1944–45, 5 million were serving in the armed forces; almost a third of the men from 14 to 64 were in uniform.[64] The military and merchant marine casualties of about 800,000 were very much lower than those of World War I; but their impact was very great all the same, not only because the numbers were still very high indeed, but because the memory of the enormous casualties of the preceding conflict weighed heavily on a country now also suffering over 33,000 civilian deaths from bombing attacks.[65] With most workers not in military service involved in war production of some sort, with tight rationing in effect for years, and with very high levels of

[a] It is instructive that a careful study of the Dieppe fiasco of August 1942 explains the launching of that costly operation largely in terms of the military–political crisis of 1942. Villa, *Unauthorized Action*: chap. 4.

taxation, life became and remained dreary and difficult for most. Obvious to those in the government but not as clear to the public was the fact that even at this extremely high level of manpower, industrial and financial mobilization, the country could carry on the war only because of massive assistance from the United States and large lending by the Dominions and India. Even with British factories producing vast quantities of equipment and munitions, the armies Britain put into the field depended heavily on supplies from others; for example, by 1942 more than half and in 1943 two-thirds of the tanks turned over to the British army came from overseas.[66] While Great Britain, in turn, sent a substantial volume of supplies to the Soviet Union, assisted the building up of the armed forces of the Commonwealth, and provided what was called "reverse Lend-Lease" to the United States, the basic balance was the other way and reversed the old pattern in which during coalition wars Britain had helped finance her allies. Now only the aid of her allies enabled the country to continue in the war.

As the tide of war changed visibly in favor of the Allies, both government and people turned increasingly to consideration of the post-war world. There was the converse of the official domestic political truce. The last general election, that of 1935, receded into an ever more distant past; there would have to be one when the war ended, and that idea by itself pointed both to the future and to the last post-war period. There had then been the hope for a new England, a "land fit for heroes" as the slogan had put it.[67] But those hopes had been disappointed, and the England of the inter-war years had been a place of long-term unemployment, of class strife, of desperation. Statistical analysts could argue with some degree of accuracy that the country eventually had made a better economic recovery from the depression of the 1930s, which had followed the difficult 1920s, than most industrial countries, but many ordinary people did not see it that way. The nation's leaders looked cold and hard to them, and it was this image that hovered over the future.

There was a sense within government circles that plans needed to be made for the country's future, and Churchill himself had a certain sympathy for this. He paid very little attention to domestic affairs during the war—other than pushing for more production of military supplies, ship construction and repairs, and other war-related activities.[a] He did, however, push for some post-war planning beyond schemes for demobilization, and of those made, certainly the most famous was the proposal of William Beveridge for reorganizing the bits and pieces of earlier welfare

---

[a] A look through the volumes of his history of World War II provides an interesting confirmation of this observation.

state legislation into a comprehensive system of social insurance, often referred to as "cradle to grave."[68] Something of a milestone in British history, the report became the subject of much public discussion.

Although Churchill had become the focus of popular attention in the great crisis of 1940 and was increasingly identified with Britain's role as a member of a victorious alliance, it was only in that role that many people saw him. If he was seen as a leader in war, not peace, that was in part his own doing. That was where his own interests were focused, and he could hardly complain if others took him at his word. Thus, in June 1943 he had stipulated that, in addition to his role as Minister of Defence, he would personally deal with important army and air force business whenever the Secretaries of State for War and Air were away.[69] When the coalition government dissolved in the acid of renewed party strife as the end of war in Europe came near, a caretaker government replaced it. The elections which followed produced a landslide for the Labor Party, and Britain would take part in the final stage of World War II and enter the post-war world under a new government.[70] Its leaders had acquired vast experience in the affairs of state in the preceding five years; they would direct Britain's affairs into new channels both at home and in its relations with its colonial empire.

THE BRITISH COMMONWEALTH

In the British Commonwealth and empire, the war brought massive changes. Canada, the largest of the Dominions, played a significant role in the war on land, sea, and in the air. On land, she contributed major troop contingents, primarily in the European theater. At sea, her forces played a key role in the Battle of the Atlantic. In the air, Canada not only built up a substantial air force of her own but provided the training arrangement for thousands of air crew members for the Royal Air Force. In the process, the country changed internally as well. The economy was greatly stimulated by the massive investment in new factories and means of transportation and communication. Although questions were at times raised about the role of United States personnel and institutions in such projects as the construction of the Alaska Highway, the result of it all was that the facilities built were in Canada and under Canadian control when the war was over. Whatever the frictions of wartime, no one in Washington thought of Canada as other than an ally, Roosevelt least of all, and her position vis-à-vis the United States was strengthened, not weakened, by the war.

The relocation of Canadians of Japanese ancestry was handled in a manner even more shameful than the analogous policy in the United States. The most difficult internal problem of the country, that of relations between its English and its French speaking inhabitants, was dealt with by Prime Minister Mackenzie King with extreme care. He could no more avoid some difficulties in this field than his World War I predecessors, but it was clearly a subject very much always on his mind. If Canada did not emerge from the war more united, it certainly did not come out bitterly divided. Perhaps the most important change was a far greater sense of national independence; a self-perception which called for a more independent foreign policy in the future with a more elaborate foreign service of its own. A sentimental tie to England—or France— might remain, but it was only one element of a self-confident independent actor on the world scene.[71]

In both Australia and New Zealand, the war had somewhat similar repercussions. Both felt deserted by the home country in their hour of greatest danger; it may be an exaggeration, but not a completely unjustified one, that a major recent study of Australia's defense position in World War II is entitled "The Great Betrayal."[72] Both looked more to the United States for their defense in the face of any future threat. In the meantime, the war had placed very heavy burdens on the two Dominions. The mobilization of manpower interfered with economic development, especially in Australia; but in other ways, the war also hastened the process of building up home industries while the former trading ties with England were largely in abeyance. Like Canada, Australia in particular would benefit from the disruption that war caused in Europe by receiving the post-war immigration of many thousands uprooted during the great upheaval.[73]

The Union of South Africa, as it was then called, provided important raw materials as well as troops to the Allied cause, but the initial division about entering the war had continuing implications for the Union. The extreme Afrikaaner nationalists sympathized with Nazi Germany and hoped for a compromise peace, if not a German victory. At the same time as soldiers from South Africa helped to defeat the advocates of extreme racism in the fighting, the supporters of similar views grew in strength among the white population in the Union. They would win the election of 1948 and set the country on a new course which imitated that of those whom South African troops had helped defeat in 1945.[74]

In all of Britain's colonial possessions the war stirred nationalist sentiments. The war for the independence of small nations against German and Italian aggression could only invigorate those elements in Britain's African empire which resented foreign rule. This issue has already been discussed in connection with the largest and most important British possession, India. The stabilization there in the fall of 1942 and the defeat of the attempted Japanese invasion of 1944 in no way silenced the continued agitation for change. The force of this agitation was dramatically enhanced by a horrendous famine. Caused by the disruption of trade, shipping shortages, and the extraordinary incompetence of the British administration, the 1943 famine in Bengal cost about 1.5 million lives and in a way destroyed what legitimacy British rule might have had in the eyes of the survivors.

It was in this regard that the contrast between Churchill and the Labor opposition was most dramatic. As Lord Halifax, whose willingness to deal with Gandhi had once aroused Churchill's ire, wrote in July 1940, the Prime Minister's reluctance on according Dominion status to India was "not a matter of argument but instinct, which, in turn, is affected a good deal by his own past on the subject..."[75] The demands for independence from India would be met under Clement Attlee, Churchill's successor, who had once served on the Simon Commission, which developed the new home-rule procedures for India which Churchill had fought all during the 1930s. Partition, accompanied by terribly bloody communal rioting, would divide the Indian sub-continent into separate states, but the turn-of-the-century world in which Churchill in some ways still lived was not coming back.[a]

In Burma, the local collaborators turned against the Japanese in the final stages of the fighting. There, as elsewhere in their newly conquered empire, the Japanese had made some appeal to anti-Western and anti-colonial sentiment; but their own behavior showed the population that they could not expect any real independence under Japanese control. After the colossal defeat Britain had suffered in Southeast Asia in the winter of 1941–42, however, there could be no easy return to the pre-war situation. The prestige of the Europeans had suffered a devastating blow, and, as will be discussed later in this chapter, could not recover.

THE UNITED STATES

The United States was transformed by World War II in ways of which some were recognized at the time but others only came under scrutiny

[a] Lord Louis Mountbatten, who presided over this process as Viceroy, would presumably never have been appointed to that post had he not earlier been in charge of the Southeast Asia Command (SEAC). The man whose appointment the United States had blocked, Air Chief Marshal Sir Sholto Douglas, instead succeeded Montgomery as British military commander in occupied Germany. Without American intervention, their roles might well have been reversed.

decades later. Whatever the confusions attending the beginnings of military and economic mobilization, there was a rapid and drastic economic expansion which quickly absorbed the remaining unemployed workers and unused factories still left idle by the depression. Massive government investments added enormously to the nation's industrial plant. Some existing plant capacity was converted from peacetime functions to war production, but much of the vast industrial system was new. Some of the installations, such as the Maritime Commission's shipyards, the synthetic rubber factories, and the complex of works for the production of atomic materials and weapons, were built directly with government funds. The vast majority were, instead, constructed by private contractors operating for industries which had been awarded huge contracts for the delivery of everything from airplanes to combat boots.

Many of the expanded and new plants were in the old industrial centers of the American East and Middle West, but a substantial number were placed in new locations in California, the Northwest, and parts of the South. Their placement, followed by a massive influx of new workers and their families, dramatically altered not merely the immediately affected cities but the whole economic and demographic pattern of the United States.[76] It was in this context that the growth of aircraft industries in California and Washington, of shipyards in the latter state and on the Gulf Coast, and the new air bases in Arizona and Texas altered the demographic and economic landscape of the United States. An important factor in the selection of Arizona and Texas for training of air crews had been the weather; this also influenced the War Department's decision to place many of the army training camps in the southeast where it was far easier to carry on basic training procedures on a year-round basis. The effort to create and arm huge military forces as speedily as possible changed the country in ways that remained after the new plants and training centers had served their original purpose.

In some ways the war effort also made a beginning in social changes. The political energies of the New Deal had been largely spent by the time the 1938 elections brought conservative victories, and the coalition of conservative Republicans and Southern Democrats controlled the Congress during the war. Public attention was in any case increasingly diverted from domestic to foreign affairs. Nevertheless, some changes in American society did take place, or at least begin, which would greatly alter the country in later years.

In a negative way, the anxiety over the war with Japan led to the forced evacuation of Japanese and Americans of Japanese descent from California and the western portions of Washington, Oregon, and Arizona. Deprived of their rights and their property, these victims of fears aroused by Japanese actions, war hysteria and racial prejudice were herded into camps, called "relocation centers," from which they were not released until late in the war. One unanticipated by-product of this policy was to be a far more even distribution of Japanese–Americans across the United States where, in the post-war years, their educational and professional advances would create one of the great success stories of the American scene.

The impact of war on the nation's Afro-American population was in some ways reminiscent of the World War I experience. Many more moved to the urban areas of the North and Midwest from the rural and small-town South. Some new job opportunities opened up for them, but it took the threat of a mass march on Washington to produce an Executive Order banning discrimination in the employment of Blacks in war industries working on government contracts. More honored in the breach than in reality, such measures hardly altered the pattern of discrimination; but they heralded a new role for the federal government which would become the focus of debate in American society in the last years of the war and has remained so ever since.[77]

The country drew in a limited and segregated way on its Black men and women for the armed forces. Accompanied by endless debate inside and outside the military, this process simultaneously offered some new opportunities for Afro-Americans even as it presented them with many new frustrations.[78] The limitations and restrictions which remained a formal part of the life of Blacks in the American armed forces would not be ended until the Korean War, but the service of hundreds of thousands of soldiers, airmen, and sailors made a far greater impact on American society than had been the case in World War I. A major element in this was a pair of changes which complemented each other. Civil rights organizations were far stronger and political awareness substantially greater in the Black community than earlier. At the same time, there were at least some people in the government who were sympathetic to the struggle of Blacks for their rights, a group of which the President's wife, Eleanor Roosevelt, was the most prominent. This segment of the white community would have its views of the need for American reality to resemble the theoretical promises of the constitution greatly affected by the publication in 1944 of Gunnar Myrdal's widely discussed work, *An American Dilemma*,[79] a searching analysis of the central issue of race in American society. At a time when the country was fighting a racist society in Europe, the persistence of racism at home was all the more incongruous.

The preconceptions of the American public also hindered the full utilization of women in the war effort. Millions were drawn into industrial and other work related to the war, if only by replacing men in the service, but there were real limits on the levels to which they could rise. The image of "Rosie the riveter" fit some who filled critical jobs, but many saw themselves as only temporarily in such capacities.[80] The American military was even slower to accept women. In the face of ever more obvious shortages of men and pressure from patriotic women who wished to serve, the armed forces slowly and reluctantly relented. Under prodding from Chief of Staff Marshall, the army took the lead; and by the end of hostilities, hundreds of thousands of women had volunteered to serve in the army, air force, navy, and marines.[81] Their experience helped to form the basis for subsequent changes in American society.

One of the ways wartime service assisted the later advances of both Blacks and women was their ability, as veterans, to take advantage of the wartime plans for post-war America. These plans were discussed in considerable detail during hostilities and included very important departures in the benefits to be accorded veterans of the armed services. Instead of, or in addition to, the types of benefits which had been a part of prior American wartime mobilization—bonus payments, pensions, medical services—the World War II program included some novel features. A "GI Bill of Rights" emphasized educational benefits, which would enable literally millions of veterans to pursue higher education after the war, and home loan entitlements, which greatly eased the path to house-ownership for millions more. These massive investments by the federal government in those who had served the country in wartime had a major impact on post-war America, and they would provide some new openings for advances by both Blacks and women.[82]

There was also planning for demobilization and reconversion in the domestic economy, but it is probably correct to assert that in President Roosevelt's thinking the most important part of post-war planning was the continuing effort to obtain public support for American participation in a world organization and for a continued active role by the United States in international affairs. Influenced by the disasters which had overtaken the Wilson administration in the 1918 and 1920 elections and which had turned the country in directions that Roosevelt, like increasing numbers of Americans, believed had contributed to the outbreak of another world war, the President was determined to do things differently. Symbolized by the holding of both the preparatory conference and the founding conference of the

United Nations Organization in the United States, these efforts were to be a double success: the organization was formed with United States participation, and the American people would be willing to support a major role for their country in international affairs after the war.[83]

By the time Japan attacked Britain, the Netherlands, and the United States, the country had been at war continuously for almost 4½ years. The conflict with China, which Japan had begun in July, 1937, had already absorbed enormous resources. Whatever could be saved in the periods when a quiet stalemate replaced bursts of heavy fighting had been expended in bouts of border fighting with the Soviet Union in 1938 and 1939, both of which Japan had lost. The country which expanded the war in December 1941 was, therefore, one which had already placed its people and its economy under severe strains. The internal restructuring which Konoe Fumimaro had initiated in the summer of 1940 had in practice made only slight progress; the same bureaucracy which had blunted the efforts at government by political parties thereafter restrained the attempt to establish a mobilizing dictatorship.[84]

The first stages of the Pacific War seemed to make any complete mobilization unnecessary. The enormous and quick victories exhilarated the home front, silenced the doubters, and made the leaders dizzy with success. Nothing seemed impossible; the Japanese were obviously superior to others, especially to Whites; and whatever Japan might want she could get. Extravagant plans were now elaborated for a huge Pacific empire which would include not only the Southeast Asian and South Pacific areas already conquered, but Alaska, the western provinces of Canada, the northwestern United States, and substantial portions of Central and South America.[85]

At home, the set-backs of the summer of 1942 were concealed from the public and even from many in the government. The continued successes in Burma obscured the checks Japan's forces were encountering in New Guinea and the Solomons in the second half of 1942.[86] Although the Tokyo raid of April 1942 had been a shock, it was only the public admission of defeat in the Aleutians in May 1943 that began to show the Japanese people that all was not going well. At home, the regime operated relatively leniently.[87] In the newly conquered empire, however, the story was very different.

Japanese policy in the occupied territories looked in the first place to the elimination of any and all European influence. The Germans were excluded like all others, and only Japan was to draw on the resources and to control the future of the expanded empire.[88] After bitter debate inside the government, a special ministry, the Greater East Asia Ministry, was established to exclude the Foreign Ministry, which was seen as too traditional, from the process of directing an enlarged empire in collaboration with the military.[89] This step itself showed that the periodic announcements from Tokyo that the peoples of Asia were to be liberated and allowed to determine their own fate were a sham and were so intended. If any of the territories nominally declared to be independent were in fact to be so, they could obviously be dealt with by the Foreign Ministry, which existed precisely for the purpose of handling relations with independent states.

As it was, the new ministry in practice had little to do because the military ran the new empire to suit themselves, a subject discussed near the end of this chapter. Aside from sponsoring a great deal of propaganda, the major activity of the Greater East Asia Ministry was to be the holding in early November 1943 of a big conference in Tokyo of key figures from the supposedly independent portions of the empire. With English ironically selected as the only common language of the assembled dignitaries, the nominal Prime Ministers of puppet governments regaled each other with praise for the Japanese and assurances of triumphs to come. As a special guest, the extreme Indian nationalist Subhas Chandra Bose tried out his eloquence, explaining to the presiding General Tojo and the assembled "Allies" of Japan: "If our Allies were to go down, there will be no hope for India to be free for at least 100 years."[90] Less than four years later India was free.

Soon after this meeting in Tokyo, that city and other Japanese cities were beginning to be subjected to American bombing, first from bases in China and then increasingly from bases in the Marianas. These operations are discussed in Chapters 10 and 16; the focus here must be on their effect on the Japanese at home. Unlike the people of China, Poland, Britain, and Germany, which sustained heavy bombing early in the war, this was not the case for the Japanese. The air raids of 1943 and 1944 were small and had a minimal impact on the population as a whole. Far more significant in their effects on the daily lives of Japanese were the lengthening casualty lists from the fronts, the ever greater stringency of rationing and shortages, and the sense of worry about a war that by 1944 had been going on for seven years with no end in sight. But unlike in Germany, Italy and their satellites, there was little resistance to official policy in Japan.[91]

It was the stepping up of the bombing in early 1945 which brought devastation to the cities of Japan. More vulnerable than many European cities because of the heavy reliance on wood supports and rice-paper partitions, huge areas of one city after another burned out in great fire raids. The American capture of bases closer to Japan, first on Iwo Jima and later on Okinawa, facilitated an intensification of the air assault. This assault came to include carrier based American and British planes in ever larger numbers in the spring and summer of 1945; and, to the consternation of the people in coastal cities, this was supplemented by shelling from American and British warships sailing along the coast in broad daylight.[a] The last part of the war in some ways compressed into six months the destruction from the air visited on Germany in three and a half years; and while Japan was not devastated by ground fighting as Germany was in the last half year of the war in Europe, the devastation by fire of her cities was immense. For the people of Japan the war, especially in its final stages, would prove a horrendous ordeal; having sowed the wind, they now reaped a whirlwind.[92] In a way, it was this destruction of the old physical order of the country which prepared the way for the remaking of its political, economic, and social order afterwards. Two and a half million Japanese had died or disappeared, three-fifths of them from the army, and the country had to find room for seven million people repatriated from the former empire.[93] A hard road lay ahead.

CHINA

In China, as in Japan, war had been a fact of life and death since 1937. By December 1941, very large portions of the country were under Japanese occupation, and these included the most important industrial areas, ports, and major urban centers. In the countryside of the area under nominal Japanese control, Communist guerillas drew increasing support from the peasantry. At the front, however, the Communist Party had drawn from the "Hundred Regiments Campaign" of August 1940, which had hurt the Japanese but had seriously damaged the Communist forces, the lesson that a frontal war with Japan was not in the party's interest.[94] In line with earlier views of Mao Tse-tung, they would concentrate hereafter on minor guerilla actions against Japan while preparing for a post-war showdown

[a] When I was in Japan as a soldier in the post-war occupation, foreign residents in Japan during the war told me that it was the appearance of Allied warships visible off the coast in the summer of 1945 that had finally persuaded many of their Japanese neighbors that the war really was lost.

with the Nationalists. As the New 4th Army incident of January 1941 showed, open warfare between Communist and Nationalist Chinese armies was coming to be an accepted feature of the situation.[95]

In unoccupied China, inflation added to the other woes of a torn country. The central government had only the most tenuous hold on the provinces, in which local military leaders starved their own troops, generally avoided fighting the Japanese, and exploited the peasantry. The regime of Chiang Kai-shek was both corrupt and ineffective, expecting the other enemies of Japan, especially the United States, to defeat China's enemy. But both the Japanese hopes and the American fears that China would withdraw from the war were unrealistic. Chiang realized who would most likely win, and he could expect to control the future of China only in alignment with the winners, not the losers, of the war. Even Bose realized that there was no prospect of a switch;[96] instead of choosing to "fight or switch," Chiang preferred to do neither.

The Japanese offensive of 1944 in China, therefore, struck at Nationalist forces which were simply no longer ready to fight.[97] They fled or surrendered, and the Japanese army captured a number of the newly built American air bases. Until the very end of the war, Nationalist control was limited to the interior of China and was tenuous even there. Only a portion of the area lost in 1944 was recovered in the first half of 1945.[98] When Japan surrendered, therefore, Chiang's international position was secure, but his domestic power was fragile.

In the international area, the Nationalist government was one of the victors. Its representatives spoke for a state considered one of the great powers, holding by virtue of that status one of the permanent seats on the Security Council of the new United Nations Organization. Here was surely a dramatic reversal of the situation at the end of World War I when it had been Japan that ranked among the leading Allies—and had been unable to secure a statement on racial equality included in the Covenant of the League of Nations. The last of the so-called "Unequal Treaties," which provided extra-territorial rights for foreigners in China, had been abrogated. A treaty between the Nationalist government and the Soviet Union, worked out in the summer of 1945, promised Chiang's government the full and continued recognition of Moscow.

The domestic picture, however, did not match the international one. As Japanese forces on the mainland surrendered, the Nationalists moved forward; and where they could not move fast enough, the Americans helped them move, sometimes by air-lifting the Chinese troops. But many of the Japanese weapons, especially in the north-eastern part of the country, fell into the hands of Mao's Communist armies, and even in the cities now garrisoned by the Nationalists, there was little enthusiasm for a regime which had been gone for years. As China drifted into open civil war, the regime of Chiang Kai-shek was by no means as secure as it looked, and its huge forces would melt away quickly in the heat of battle.[99] The gamble on saving the fighting strength of the Nationalist armies for the post-war confrontation with the Communists proved a losing one.

THE SOVIET UNION

For the Soviet Union, the ordeal of war was in many ways even worse than for China, whose ordeal was terrible enough. In the occupied areas, discussed later in this chapter, German policies and practices were in general more barbaric than those followed by Japan, whose atrocities were on the whole concentrated in the first period of fighting. Further-more, the very fact that the Red Army drove the Germans out in pro-longed and bitter fighting meant that the destruction in the liberated areas was enormous, with the retreating Germans doing what they could to cart off or destroy whatever they were forced to give up. By contrast, the Japanese surrendered most of the Chinese-occupied areas intact in 1945. The intensity of the fighting on the Eastern Front also implied a total mobilization of the Soviet home front. People and resources were drawn into the conflict on a scale matched by none of the other major belligerents. The enormous casualties reached into every home even as the already low pre-war economy imposed terrible privations.

Three factors operated to hold together the Soviet home front under the hammer blows of war. First, it was immediately and dramatically obvious to increasing numbers of Soviet citizens that, whatever their objections to the policies of their rulers and to the conditions under which they had been living, the policies of the Germans were infinitely worse and the conditions under their rule — for those left alive — were sure to be even more dreadful.[a] And if they were going to be ruled by those they disliked, better their own than those from another country.

A second element was the combination of an effective Communist Party and secret police apparatus which made some concessions during the time of war. The government eased its restrictions on religious

---

[a] The subject of Red Army soldiers' behavior as they entered Germany is a very difficult one. There is considerable anecdotal evidence that the anger of many soldiers was stimulated by the feeling that people who lived as well as the Germans had come to steal what little their own people had.

observances and made other gestures to public preferences even as it had to mobilize all resources for the war and, therefore, impose the most drastic material sacrifices. This process was related to a third factor, that of patriotism, to which the regime effectively and successfully appealed. The war itself was now called not the Second Imperialist War but the Great Patriotic War as the people were summoned to defend their homes.

It is worth noting in this connection that the maintenance of cohesion and the revival of hope and pride can be seen in part as a reaction to the course of the fighting. In World War I, the Russian armies had first defeated the Austrians, then been defeated by the Germans, had then had their front ripped open in 1915, and had thereafter been driven back ever further in a series of see-saw battles. In World War II, on the other hand, the biggest defeats came at the beginning, but thereafter, in spite of a major retreat in the south in 1942 and occasional set-backs — some of them serious — the tide of battle moved steadily the other way. Large portions of the Soviet Union might still be in the hands of the Germans and their allies, but there was hope that they would be freed as the first ones had been in the winter of 1941. Clearly the German army was not invincible; there was hope even if the road to victory might be a long one. In these elements of the situation, and especially the sense of shared dangers and shared accomplishments at the cost of vast sacrifice, one may recognize the experience of World War II as the great consolidating experience of the Soviet Union between the revolutionary upheaval of 1917–22 and the dramatic changes of the 1980s.

As discussed in connection with the review of the fighting in 1941 and 1942, the Russians evacuated many industries from the areas overrun by the Germans, and during the war naturally expanded facilities and production in areas which were considered safe from the invaders, primarily the industrial region in the Urals and in portions of Soviet Central Asia. It was in these expanded and new factories that a long-suffering and very hard working labor force turned out the tanks, guns, planes, ammunition, and other supplies of war which enabled the Red Army to overwhelm the Germans.[100] Standardizing on a series of very fine weapons, especially on heavy tanks, artillery, rocket launchers, and automatic weapons, the Soviet industrial system provided its troops with great volumes of weapons which were often qualitatively superior to those of the Germans as well. Even in the air, where Soviet inferiority had been marked at the beginning of hostilities — in part because of the surprise attack — there was a substantial change as excellent new models were put into service in substantial numbers.

In the process, a country which had barely begun to recover from the ravages of collectivization of agriculture, forced industrialization, and the great purges was burdened by the most drastic further privations. But with these came first hope and then pride. No other country on the continent had been able to stand up to the German army in its hours of great strength. The very price of victory—substantially over twenty million dead, massive destruction, total disruption of the society—came to look in retrospect like special badges of honor. The brutalities of their own regime, including the forced deportations of whole nationality groups suspected of collaborating with the invader, paled by comparison with the horrors imposed by the Germans. The people had seen an alternative to their own system and knew they did not want it. There was hope, which would be cruelly disappointed, that a victorious regime would deal more kindly and leniently with its people, who had suffered and accomplished so much. But for all who survived, the war remained a dominating memory.

AFRICA

The continent of Africa cannot be discussed as if it were a single unit, and its experiences during World War II cannot, except in one important respect, be discussed collectively. The differences must be noted first. The portion of the continent which saw the earliest fighting was also the first to see it end. In the northeastern corner, Ethiopia had been conquered by Italy in 1935–36 and had thereafter been the scene of some guerilla warfare against the Italians and later the base for the Italian conquest of British Somaliland: in the winter of 1940–41 the British armed forces had defeated all the Italian forces, liberated Ethiopia and British Somaliland and occupied Eritrea and Italian Somaliland. There had been considerable destruction from the fighting at a few places, but on the whole the damage was very localized. The Emperor of Ethiopia, Haile Selassie, returned to his capital, long to outlive Mussolini and most of those who had watched him deposed and his land conquered. In Eritrea and Italian Somaliland, a British military administration was established to control the area until the end of the war.[101] Eritrea would be turned over to Ethiopia in spite of considerable local opposition, while Italian Somaliland became independent and absorbed British Somaliland as the country of Somalia. The war years actually brought some economic development to these territories because their importance to the Allied war effort along major oceanic supply routes led to some improvement in port and transportation facilities being made.

What would later become the largest country in Africa, the Anglo-Egyptian Sudan, was only slightly touched by fighting on its eastern border. A major effect of the war there was the development of transportation facilities, especially the airport at Khartoum, the eastern terminus of the Takoradi supply route across Africa to the Middle East theater of war.

The tides of battle which moved back and forth across Egypt and Libya took place for the most part in desert and rocky terrain of little economic value, but there was extreme damage to the towns along the east Libyan coast. The local population in both territories suffered as a result of the dislocations of war, but both also benefited in the long run from large-scale construction of airports and other facilities.

In Egypt, however, there were other developments as well. Egyptian nationalists resented continued British dominance of their country, while both King Farouk and some extreme nationalist officers in the Egyptian army, such as Gamal Abdel Nasser and Anwar Sadat, hoped for a German victory and were in touch with the Germans—never understanding that Axis rule of Egypt was likely to be far more oppressive than British. The officers were arrested and the King was forced to pick a government more willing to cooperate in the war alongside the British.[102] The whole process, however, exacerbated Egyptian antagonism toward the British and left a bitter legacy behind.

In Northwest Africa, only Tunisia suffered serious damage from the fighting in 1942–43. The Vichy regime had kept control before that time and de Gaulle did so thereafter, but the whole concept of rule by France had been called into question by both the population there and President Roosevelt, who ostentatiously met with local dignitaries.[a] In Tunisia, some nationalists sided with the Axis in hopes of a respect for their independence from Berlin and Rome that they had not had from Paris; as so often, neither a wise idea nor a sign of great insight.

In the band of French, British, and Belgian colonial possessions across Africa from the Atlantic to the Indian Ocean, the war meant some recruitment for armies to fight in the war, further development of local industries and transportation facilities, and great difficulties in exporting the products which in peacetime provided much of the earnings of these colonial economies.

The one development which was really general on the continent was the increased nationalist agitation. From whatever level anti-colonialist sentiment had reached before the war, the years 1939–45 saw an escalation. The plans of the Germans for a huge new colonial empire in Africa

---

[a] During the period of Vichy rule, various restrictions had been imposed on the Jews living in French North Africa, and there was considerable trouble over getting these lifted because most of the Vichy officials remained in office for some time after the Allied landing. A good account in Michel Abitol, *The Jews of North Africa during the Second World War*, trans. by Catherine Thanyi Zentelis (Detroit: Wayne State Univ. Press, 1989).

had been thwarted by the Allied victory. The educated elite in each colonial area saw the weakness of the old imperial masters: France, Belgium, and Italy defeated, Britain weak, and Spain and Portugal standing aside. Both the United States and the Soviet Union were strongly opposed to colonialism in their respective views of the world. Italy's colonial territories were certain to have new rulers; and whatever the post-war plans of London and Paris, Brussels, Madrid and Lisbon, there were major changes ahead.[103]

LATIN AMERICA

In Latin America, the years of war brought several significant changes. With the exception of Argentina, the countries of the Western Hemisphere joined the Allies. Their economic ties to Germany had been largely broken by the blockade, and only in the summer of 1940, when it looked briefly as if Germany might win, was there serious consideration of new ties with the Axis in the post-war years. In that brief period, there was serious worry in Washington; as Under Secretary of State Sumner Welles wrote President Roosevelt on June 3, 1940, in words omitted from the published version: "The majority of the American Republics would run helter-skelter to Hitler just as so many of the remaining small neutral nations of Europe are doing today."[104] But except for a few shells from German submarines fired at the Dutch West Indies, and the sinking of their ships off the coast, the Latin American countries were spared the most conspicuous impact of war. There was an ongoing struggle between the intelligence organizations of the Axis and the Allies, but much of this is still shrouded in secrecy and would, in any case, leave no major after effects.[105]

Only Brazil sent troops to the front, in this case to Italy, and those involved with that effort in some instances came to play major roles in post-war Brazilian politics.[106] As for the war years themselves, the possibilities for economic development were largely negated by local ineffectiveness and the incompetence of United States "experts" sent to increase production.[107] The one field in which Brazil and several other Latin American countries made some progress during the war was that of reducing foreign control of the economy. The sale of products needed by the Allied war effort, combined with a reduction in the imports of manufactured goods—almost entirely from Europe—made it possible to reduce the level of foreign ownership of enterprises in Brazil, Argentina, and elsewhere. The pre-war role of both Germany and Britain was lessened, while that of the United States only grew temporarily.

The Germans had hoped to keep the countries of Latin America neutral at first and looked to vastly expanded trade opportunities at the expense of a defeated Britain after the war.[108] There was also some hope that movements based on local Fascist elements, like the Integralists in Brazil and the Peronists in Argentina, combined with pressure from the large German immigrant community in several countries of the region, would open the Western Hemisphere to political as well as economic penetration.[109] Such hopes were not realized.

But there was to be an important legacy of the war all the same. The United States had adopted a "Good Neighbor" policy which included a far less imperious attitude toward Latin America than prior administration had been accustomed to show. This certainly helped in rallying the countries of the hemisphere in the war against the Axis, but it also had another result. The very use of the resources and products of the South American countries in the Allied war effort gave those countries not only a better price for their products during the war but also led them to feel that they had some claim on the gratitude of the victors afterwards. With internal problems of poverty and disease remaining very serious, the nations of Latin America would assert themselves in new ways once the war was over.

THE MIDDLE EAST

Internal developments in the Middle East were directly influenced by the war in several very important ways during the conflict, and in even more dramatic ways thereafter. The collapse of France in 1940 and the fighting of 1941 provided an enormous stimulus to the independence movement in Syria. Whatever the hopes of the French for continued domination of this important area acquired as a mandate carved out of the Ottoman empire at the end of World War I, there was really not the slightest chance of reestablishing rule from Paris. Syrian nationalist aspirations could not be subdued, even by shelling Damascus. The independence of Syria and an enlarged Lebanon was assured by the war. The issue caused much friction between France and Great Britain, especially because the French quite falsely suspected the British of wanting to take over from them, but the fact was that France's time in Syria had run out. The French had actually promised independence; after a double defeat, there could be no road back, even for a France led by Charles de Gaulle.[110]

Turkey was unable to extend its territory at the expense of its neighbors during the war, but it held on to its pre-war gain at Syria's expense. The country's backward economy was somewhat aided by the demand for its products, especially chrome. Both sides had been fooled by the

Turkish government into providing some modern weapons to supplement the army's antiquated and inadequate equipment. The country's small circle of leaders faced the post-war world, and especially the pressure for concessions from the Soviet Union, with a confidence born of what they considered a successful policy of neutrality until they had joined the victors when it no longer mattered.

Iran had been inclined toward Germany before the war and during its initial years. Trade ties and worry about British and Russian imperial expansion had contributed to this orientation. From the summer of 1941 on, the country was occupied by British and Russian forces, but there was an increasing American presence with the building up of the supply route across Iran to the Soviet Union by American transportation corps units. This development had two short-term advantages for the Iranians. In the first place, the country inherited the improved harbor, railway, and highway facilities constructed by the Americans. Secondly, it enabled them to play off the Americans against the Russian and British occupying powers. This would be especially important when, at the end of the war, the Russians were inclined to keep their troops in the country rather than withdraw them as promised.

On the other hand, in Iran as elsewhere in the Middle East, American influence was also resented, especially as it focused increasingly on obtaining a foothold in the exploitation of the region's petroleum resources.[111] Here was a source both of wealth and of foreign interest which enhanced the region's income during the war and thereafter but also brought further threats to the independence of its people.

This was as true of Iraq as of Iran. Once the revolt of 1941 had been suppressed by British troops, the country was ruled by a regime which collaborated with the Allies. The urge to throw off all outside influence, and especially that of the British, remained, however, and would reassert itself not long after the war.

On the Arabian peninsula, the war's most significant impact was in the further strengthening it provided for the role of Ibn Saud and his family in the consolidation of their hold on what was increasingly referred to as the Kingdom of Saudi Arabia. For now, the area deferred to British interest in the war, but the post-war years would be different.

During, as before and after, World War II, most governments in the Middle East had, or pretended to have, a great interest in the developing situation in Palestine. The British had partitioned their mandate along the Jordan river in 1922, calling the east bank "Trans-Jordan" for the obvious, if characteristically colonialist, reason that it was on the other side of the Jordan river from the perspective of London. The client state under King Abdullah was loyal to Great Britain during the war and provided important facilities and transit routes for its military forces. There was, however, no occasion for the massive construction of facilities which took place in Iran and Egypt. Between the Mediterranean and the Jordan river, however, was the other portion of the mandate, now called Palestine, and though a small fraction of the original, it became the focus of the majority of the attention.

Originally held by Britain as a protector for the northern flank of her position astride the Suez Canal, the Palestine mandate performed this function in World War II but only because the British were able to keep the Axis away from the canal by action elsewhere. The German and Italian advance from the western approach via Libya was halted, if with great difficulty, by the British 8th Army in 1941 and 1942 when the threat to the canal was most acute. From the north, the reluctance of Turkey to join Germany and the success of the British, Australians, and the Free French in wresting Syria from Vichy France in the summer of 1941 eliminated German influence there and barred the way. For these developments, the British base in Palestine was an essential prerequisite, but otherwise the area was and after 1942 remained a military backwater. In the political sense, however, it was a center of attention because of the efforts of ever larger numbers of Jews seeking refuge from persecution elsewhere by joining those who had been living in the area for millennia.

From the late nineteenth century on, Jews from Eastern Europe had arrived in Palestine in several waves, adding slowly to the prior Jewish presence. The British had promised to allow further settlement but soon had second thoughts as some local Arabs objected to the influx. The economic development of the area in this period quickly led to an even larger immigration of Arabs from other portions of the Middle East. When Nazi persecution of Jews and the somewhat lesser plundering of German Jews who fled to Palestine as compared with those who went elsewhere increased the immigration of Jews in the 1930s, disturbances in the country led the British first to advocate and then to reject a second partition, this time into Arab and Jewish states. Instead, the British government, fearful of Arab enmity in a looming war with Germany, decided to halt most Jewish immigration in 1939. Ironically this decision came just before the outbreak of World War II provided the German government with a cover to initiate first a program for killing Germans thought unfit to live because of their mental or physical state and then the program to kill all Jews they could get their hands on.

This new development made the Jews more eager than ever to open the gates to those fleeing certain death, some Arabs more determined than ever to keep them out, and others, like the Grand Mufti, interested in collaborating with the Germans so that they could get to Palestine and kill the Jews already there. The British did what they could to restrict both legal and illegal Jewish immigration, but the issue would resurface at the end of the war.[112] The major long-term impact of the war on Palestine was two-fold. The alignment of the Grand Mufti with Hitler, after the former's earlier elimination of rivals for leadership among Palestinian Arabs, meant that with Germany's defeat the Arabs of Palestine were left without any leadership which could obtain respect and attention elsewhere. For the Jews, the enormous slaughter of the Holocaust meant that the major reservoir of potential immigrants from Europe had been decimated and the community of Jews in what came to be Israel would, at least until 1989, therefore, become increasingly one of North African and Middle Eastern origin. As these attained political influence in the country, their prior experience of Arab oppression (as opposed to the European Jews' memory of German, Russian and Polish anti-Semitism), made the community increasingly dubious about concessions to Arab interests.

GERMAN-OCCUPIED EUROPE: NORTH AND WEST

In German-occupied Europe, the occupier began the establishment of a new system of which the outlines only could be developed during the war and which collapsed as the German forces were driven back.[113] In Northern Europe, Denmark and Norway remained under German control from April 1940 until the surrender of May 1945.[a] In the case of Denmark, the German invasion came so quickly that there was no resistance and no opportunity for the government, and especially the King, to flee. Given the acquiescence of the administrative apparatus, it was obviously easiest for the Germans to run the undamaged country by supervising it rather than controlling it directly. There was, in effect, a temporary accommodation between occupier and occupied. As part of this tacit but effective arrangement the Germans did not raise the question of revising the border which had resulted from the World War I peace settlement, much to the dismay of many among the German minority in the area. On the other hand, the Danes not only provided important military bases for the German conduct of the war but furnished vast quantities of food supplies, about one-twelfth of the total annual rations for Germany (including all annexed areas).[114]

As the war—and the occupation—continued, a few Danes became restive, but major changes were forced by the Germans. In October

[a] A small piece of northeast Norway was devastated and then evacuated by the Germans in the winter of 1944–45, but the bulk of the country with essentially all of its population was still in German hands at the end of hostilities. (In fact, the Germans there were still carrying out executions of their own military personnel for some time after the end of hostilities.)

1942 Hitler shifted to a harsher course, instructing his new military representative that Denmark would be annexed to Germany and could not keep her monarchy and her democratic institutions.[115] For a while these intentions were masked, but the antics of Danish Nazis pointed to the future. In August 1943 the Germans proclaimed a military emergency and the Danish government was effectively removed. Ironically this stimulated rather than inhibited resistance, first clearly manifested soon after when the German effort to round up Denmark's Jews foundered as the Danes helped them flee to Sweden. Repression and resistance faced each other for the rest of the war; any hopes the Germans might have had of turning the "Nordic" people of Denmark into loyal Germans had long vanished, while the Danes had abandoned whatever illusions they might once have held about the aims of their powerful neighbor.

The situation in occupied Norway was more confused because there was considerable fighting and a period of negotiations about the possibility of an accommodation between parts of the government and Germany. As these broke down, the picture was further clouded by the appointment of a German Reichs Commissioner, Josef Terboven, who had been—and remained—Gauleiter of the Essen area of the German Rhineland. A long-time member of the Nazi Party, Terboven was going to run Norway the way he saw fit, subject only to Hitler's repeatedly announced intention that Norway would always remain a part of the German empire. In carrying out his policies, Terboven was generally supported by the German army commander in the area, General Nikolaus von Falkenhorst, occasionally obstructed by the representative of the German navy, Admiral Hermann Boehm,[116] and frequently in trouble with Vidkun Quisling, the leader of the Norwegian Nazi Party.

Though willing to help the Germans first conquer Norway and then to recruit Norwegians for the SS,[117] Quisling wanted to run the country as a client state of Germany. The German repressive measures taken in the country were under the cloak of wartime needs—which automatically made him and his followers into traitors in the eyes of Norwegians.[118] Whether inside or outside the government structure established by the Germans in occupied Norway, therefore, he called for a peace treaty, something the Germans always refused as Hitler had no intention of ever letting the country regain a measure of independence. By April 1943 even Quisling had come to recognize that he was merely being used to facilitate annexation by Germany and was embittered over the trend in that direction.[119] If this was the attitude of the man who had once encouraged the Germans to occupy the country, one can easily imagine what the ordinary patriotic Norwegian thought.

Resistance to the Germans grew slowly but steadily and was encouraged rather than halted by the ruthless measures taken to suppress it. A very poor country, Norway could not contribute much to the German war economy; most of its greatest economic asset, its merchant fleet, having escaped to continue in the war. The Germans took what they could, and made the Norwegians suffer great hardships, not the best way of persuading them that as fellow Nordics they shared a community of fate with the Germans.

While Hitler evidently thought of absorbing both Denmark and Norway the way he had incorporated Austria, any such plans depended entirely on a German victory in the war. The people in both countries would have none of it, and everything they saw of the Germans and their minions only reinforced this reluctance. They awaited liberation and return to the type of independent, democratic, political life they had led before the war.

Like Denmark and Norway, Luxembourg was to be incorporated into Germany.[120] Occupied on May 10, 1940, the Grand Duchy was considered a Germanic area. Those held to be non-Germanic, like the Italian workers who had come there for jobs and those considered of Walloon or French background, were deported. Many classified as Germans but not sufficiently enthusiastic about this designation were resettled among German settlers sent to Eastern Europe. The rest, except of course for the tiny number of Jews, were to be governed and treated as Germans.

The Grand Duchess and the ministers had escaped before the Germans could seize them, and formed a government-in-exile. Until the winter of 1944–45, when the Grand Duchy was first liberated and then the scene of bitter fighting during the German Ardennes offensive, the Battle of the Bulge, the people looked forward to a German defeat which could only be brought about by others. There were instances of resistance and of German repression, but Allied victory brought a return to independence. Their wartime experience helped Luxembourgers see the need for a closer association with their northern neighbors in the post-war world. They would remember those who had fought to restore their freedom, and there is a certain propriety in the fact that an American military cemetery in the country includes the grave of General George S. Patton.

If Luxembourgers visit an American cemetery at Hamm, the Dutch go to a British one near Arnhem. The German invasion of 1940 quickly overran the Netherlands, and in spite of the terrible bombing of Rotterdam, most of the country was not devastated in the rapidly moving fighting. For a while it almost looked as if, in spite of the flight of the Queen and the leaders of the government, the people might settle down to a quiet acquiescence, almost glad that the war had passed over them so fast and with such little apparent impact. They were soon awakened by the realities of German policy.[121]

The Germans saw the Dutch as fellow Germanic people, temporarily led astray, and expected to reassimilate them into Germany proper—but at the same time to exploit their economy and possibly also their colonial empire.[122] Hitler wanted to replace the military administration as quickly as possible and did so on May 17, installing as the Reich's commissioner Arthur Seyss-Inquart, who had played a key role in the absorption of Austria into Germany two years earlier and had most recently been assigned to helping Hans Frank exploit and terrorize Poles.[123] He tried to utilize the Dutch administrative apparatus, integrate the country into the German economy, and prepare its people for their future as Germans.

The administration of the country proved more difficult than Seyss anticipated. All sorts of German agencies competed for control with him and each other, and the Dutch Nazis proved a troublesome lot. The most prominent of the latter, Anton Adrian Mussert, wanted to run an enlarged Dutch state as a German client, while the Dutch Nazi most agreeable to a direct fusion with Germany, Meinoud M. Rost van Tonningen, was happy to cooperate with the SS and to help its schemes to settle Dutch farmers in land taken from the Soviet Union. However, he had even fewer supporters in the country than the hugely unpopular and generally incompetent Mussert.[124]

As the country in Europe with the longest record of treating Jews decently, Holland was not the country in which to acquire popularity by deporting its Jewish citizens to be murdered in the death camps in occupied Poland. The first measures to implement this program provoked the first major strike in German-occupied Europe, that of February 1941. In spite of Dutch resistance and some secret sheltering of individual Jews—the case of the German Jewish refugee Anne Frank becoming the most famous—the vast majority of Dutch Jews, over 100,000 out of about 120,000, were killed by the Germans.[125] Although in the Netherlands, as elsewhere in Europe, many local people cooperated in this process and some profited from it, there was more opposition here than anywhere else.

One of the saddest aspects of the German occupation was the impact of its economic exploitation combined with the way the front stabilized in the fall of 1944. The Germans had ruthlessly stripped the country, once a great food exporting nation, of its reserves. When the course of the war left western Holland partly cut off from the rest of German-controlled central Europe, the most desperate food shortage ensued. The winter of 1944–45 was a time of famine in which many died in sight of liberation. At the very end, there were arrangements to bring in food from the Allies; but for many of the Dutch, this came too late. After World War I, many Dutch families had taken in German youngsters so that they could more quickly recover from the undernourishment of the war years. After World War II, the people of Holland for years retained bitter feelings toward a Germany which had repaid charity with death and starvation.

Belgium, like the Netherlands, was headed for inclusion in Germany, but with altered borders. On the one hand, the small pieces of territory transferred to Belgium after World War I as well as the piece ruled jointly with Prussia before that war were added to the adjacent German province.[126] On the other hand, two departments (or administrative districts) of northern France were joined with Belgium. During the war years, Hitler postponed decisions about the final configuration in this case. He placed a moderate general with substantial international experience in charge as military governor while casting about for a long-term solution.

General Alexander von Falkenhausen proceeded to run the least oppressive of all the German occupation administrations. Himself an opponent of Hitler and National Socialism, he tried to assert military rule against the economic and police agencies, to keep the exactions within reason, and to avoid or limit the sorts of horrors inflicted on other occupied peoples. Within the limits of the situation, he had some success in containing the efforts of Göring and Himmler to interfere, kept the people from starving in spite of low rations, and held the murder of Belgium's Jews to some 25,000 out of a total of about 90,000, a terrible toll but still a sign of substantial opposition to the process.[127] No wonder Falkenhausen was placed in a concentration camp, even though his contacts with the group which attempted to kill Hitler were not discovered at the time.

Repeatedly during the war Hitler thought of different Nazi Gauleiters to send to Belgium to take over,[128] but it was not until July 1944, just before the Allies liberated most of the country, that he finally picked Josef Grohé to take over from Falkenhausen. Certainly King Leopold, who had remained in the country, would play no role. The leader of the Flemish Nazis, Staf de Clercq, had few followers, and Léon Degrelle, the Walloon Nazi, could do little better. Even Hitler's backing and Himmler's support could make little out of this self-anointed "French speaking Nordic."[129] The Belgian economy worked effectively for Germany while much of the administrative apparatus remained in place.[130] But there is no evidence that any substantial portion of the population looked on the Germans as anything other than invading barbarians who had come to ravish and loot the country for the second time in thirty years. They had even burned down the Louvain University Library once again as in World War I.[131] On October 10, 1941, the representative of the German Foreign Ministry in Belgium, Werner von Bargen, had written to State Secretary Ernst von Weizsäcker that Germany could get the United States to stay out of the war and England to make peace if she would make a real peace in western and Northern Europe which assured the independence of the states there. The State Secretary could only reply that no one in the National Socialist leadership agreed.[132] German victory would have meant the end of Belgian independence; German defeat brought its restoration.

France was defeated in 1940 under circumstances which gave the Germans an incentive to restrain Italy as well as themselves in order to keep the French government from continuing the war from North Africa and the French fleet and colonies from assisting Great Britain—and hence encouraging that country to keep on fighting. Otherwise, the Germans would do as they saw fit. The armistice of June 1940, which provided for the French government to continue to direct the administration in all of France, was broken before it was signed by the removal of Alsace and Lorraine from its purview and their effective annexation to Germany. Beginning in 1940, hundreds of thousands were deported from the two provinces, which were placed under the government of adjacent German Gaue, Saarland and Baden.[133]

In addition, the Germans treated the two French northern departments placed under the military commander in Belgium as prospective German territory and clearly intended to annex them.[134] Furthermore, a line was drawn separating the area of northeast France curving from the mouth of the Somme river to the Swiss border, which was closed off from the rest of France; those portions of the country together with ports on the Channel and Atlantic coasts were also scheduled to be annexed to Germany. Hitler, however, did not decide on a border during the war.[135] The majority of the remaining country was to be occupied by German troops while the southeastern quarter was left unoccupied for the time being. It was in the little town of Vichy in the unoccupied zone that the new government of France was temporarily located; and since the Germans refused to allow it back to Paris, it remained there until abducted by the Germans in 1944, and came to be known as the Vichy government.

By allowing this puppet regime to operate, the Germans obviated a danger and a problem. The danger was the possibility of continued resistance from French North Africa; the problem was that of staffing an administrative apparatus for an area with over forty million inhabitants. With a tiny supervisory staff, the Germans directly or indirectly controlled an administrative and police apparatus of Frenchmen which functioned for them with a diligence and thoroughness they could never have provided themselves during wartime.

The continuation of the war by Britain worked to strengthen Vichy's negotiating position vis-à-vis the Germans in a way neither the French, nor the Germans, nor the British had anticipated.[136] The campaign in the East had a somewhat similar effect; and the Vichy authorities eventually became more reluctant to make concessions without obtaining concessions from the Germans in turn; but Hitler was determined not to make these under any circumstances.[137] If Pétain dismissed Laval on his own in December 1940, the Germans forced the dismissal of Maxime Weygand as delegate for French North Africa as too anti-German and pro-U.S. a year later.[138] The return of Laval in April 1942 made little difference: neither the Germans nor the French trusted him.[139]

Some of those running the Vichy system believed that in this way they could spare their people a worse fate; some hoped to use the defeat for a reorganization of French society; some genuinely believed in the possibility of reconciliation with the Germans; most were convinced that after the defeat of France, Britain would quickly succumb also. All were in error.

The German government included some individuals who also wanted a real peace with France, and these, not the French collaborators, effected some restraints on German policy and practice. The line set by Hitler, however, was uncompromisingly hostile to France, a country he both hated and despised. Pétain may have thought that France would rise from defeat as Prussia had once risen from defeat at the hands of Napoleon, but Hitler was determined to prevent anything of the sort.

Those who hoped to reorganize French society believed that the Third Republic was responsible for its own defeat and that a new structure, more authoritarian, more efficient, stressing not liberty, equality and brotherhood, but work, family, and fatherland, should rise from the ashes of defeat.[140] With considerable resonance at first among a people stunned and disoriented, this vision of a new France was quickly and hopelessly compromised by the total failure of the hope for reconciliation with Germany. The exactions of the Germans, the steady looting of the country,[141] the exorbitant demands in violation of the armistice terms, the expulsions from Alsace and Lorraine, the rigidities of demarcation borders within France, the retention of French prisoners of war combined with the eventually forced recruitment of labor for work in Germany, and the increasingly terroristic measures employed by the Germans, disillusioned the most devoted believers in any real accommodation with Germany.[a] Finally, the obvious turning of the tide against the Axis showed that the German victory, which most had taken for granted in the summer of 1940, would never come.

Pierre Laval, the symbolic advocate of collaboration, might urge the Germans to make peace with the Soviet Union so that they could concentrate all their forces on the defeat of the British and Americans and thereby remain in control of France, but most Frenchmen increasingly looked forward to liberation by the Western Powers. Ever larger numbers of them turned to resistance against the occupiers, and the vicious eagerness with which the Vichy militia hounded and slaughtered those who opposed the Germans served to discredit the regime they served. The extent to which the Vichy government inaugurated anti-Semitic measures and its police enthusiastically participated in the rounding up of Jews for deportation and murder remained as a blot that time did not erase but instead made more conspicuous.[142]

In November 1942, the Germans occupied the unoccupied zone and allowed the Italians to occupy a portion of it; but, true to the policy of fighting only the friends and not the enemies of the country, the French armistice army allowed to Vichy did not fire a shot against the soldiers of either Axis power.[143] In September 1943, with the Italian surrender, the Germans took over the Italian zone as well; but this end to the old Italian demands on France brought no concessions from the Germans.[144] The complete occupation by the Germans only facilitated both further exactions from the French[145] and the murder of those Jews who lived or had taken refuge first in unoccupied France and later in the Italian zone.

Inside German-occupied France, a small number resisted the authorities, but they were handicapped by the overwhelming support Frenchmen originally gave to Pétain as well as by the surveillance of the Germans. There was, in addition, a reluctance to take actions which might provoke a brutal occupier into massive measures of retaliation against the population when liberation was obviously in the distant future. After the German invasion of the Soviet Union, French Communists who had earlier stood aside or even welcomed the Germans joined the resistance

---

[a] Some French workers were sent to Germany on the basis of one prisoner of war to be released for every three workers, but the Germans soon abandoned this procedure.

and eventually came to form an important part of it. Jews who had little or nothing to lose played a major role, one which post-war accounts of the resistance generally overlooked. Some support was provided by the British Special Operations Executive (SOE), but well into 1942 this was greatly affected by a vast swindle, the so-called Carte network.[146] The rivalry of British military intelligence with SOE produced a calamitous further disaster in which an intelligence agent ended up betraying to the Germans a large portion of the French resistance and numerous other British agents in 1943.[147] In spite of all set-backs, resistance grew, stimulated in part by German measures, the obviously turning tide of the war, and the growing experience of the French themselves and of the British and eventually the Americans in aiding them.

The leader of the Free French organization which continued to fight on the side of the Allies after June 1940, Charles de Gaulle, proved a very difficult man for the Allies to deal with. Field Marshal Brooke commented in his diary: "a most unattractive specimen. We made a horrid mistake when we decided to make use of him!"[148] The language is instructive: Brooke evidently believed that Charles de Gaulle could be used. Whatever might or might not be said about the proud and determined Frenchman, being used by others was not one of them. He made life as difficult as he could and dared for both Churchill and Roosevelt,[149] but he always followed his own star. It took years of war for a steadily increasing number of Frenchmen to rally to him outside or to see him as their leader inside the country, but he proved more capable and determined than his rivals. By the end of 1942 he truly led and symbolized resistance to the Germans. By the end of the war, the leaders of various factions of French collaborators had formed competing "governments-in-exile" on different floors of a castle in southwest Germany, hoping for some last-minute reprieve as their German sponsors and abductors were going down in defeat. De Gaulle headed the French government in Paris.

Throughout occupied Western and Northern Europe, the Germans did what they could to exploit the economy. First it was simply looting, either by confiscation or by nominal payments with money extorted as occupation costs. As the war continued longer than expected, they shifted more and more in two new directions. In the first place, they recruited more and more labor, first voluntarily, then by force. In the second place, they turned increasingly to war production on the spot. This policy, pushed by Albert Speer, harnessed the economies of the occupied countries more effectively and efficiently to the German war effort. It also, in return, provided the workers with exemption from being shipped to forced labor inside Germany. In the process, they could contribute to the maintenance of German rule over them. In every country, German firms tried hard to take over local plants and businesses, preferably at little cost, or to gain the securities which would allow them control. It was a system of exploitation which enormously aided the German war effort; it left behind exhausted workers and run-down industries.

SOUTHEAST EUROPE

From Southeast Europe, the Germans expected to draw important food stuffs, minerals, and other raw materials. They hoped to keep down the standard of living in the area so that it could continue to export to Germany, rather than consume at home, and also provide a source of cheap labor.[150] The area was covered by a net of diplomats and special agents as well as hordes of German industrialists and financiers trying to take over factories, banks, and mines. All feuded with each other; and the complaint of the German Minister to Bulgaria about Franz von Papen, the ambassador to Turkey, that he was getting into everything when he was "ambassador only in Turkey and not in all of the Balkans,"[151] may serve as a sample of endemic competition for influence. In all these countries, Germany ran up huge clearing debts for deliveries provided to Germany but not repaid by the Reich. After Germany had won the war, the countries of Southeast Europe could either write off these debts or buy whatever Germany offered in repayment.[152]

In the old core area of Czechoslovakia, called the Protectorate of Bohemia and Moravia, German rule was indirect but looked to a future in which the Czechs would be partly Germanized, partly expelled or exterminated. In the meantime, they could work for German victory.[153] Not all of them shared the puppet President Emil Hácha's joy at the German victory over France in 1940;[154] some in the country did begin to organize resistance. But this was on a very small scale. The Czech administrators appear to have believed that the Germans needed them — and while the war lasted, the Germans did. That would not have saved them had Germany won the war, and it did not save those, including some high officials, who were in contact with the Czechoslovak government-in-exile; but it did preserve the people from some of the more ruthless measures during the war. The sending of a special team by air from the government-in-exile in London to assassinate Reinhard Heydrich, who had replaced Constantin von Neurath as head of the

German administration, led to savage reprisals but no general resistance.[155] Though restive, the Czechs remained under firm German control to the end of the war.

The Czechoslovak government-in-exile in London had some contacts with the occupied area. It tried to secure the recognition of the Allies for its eventual return to Prague and was successful in this regard. It also wanted the Munich agreement nullified and a return to its pre-Munich borders. Furthermore, though for some time negotiating with Wenzel Jaksch, the leader of the Social Democrats among the Sudeten Germans,[156] they eventually decided to expel the Germans from the country after the war.[157] By the end of the war, the Allies had come to agree to this project. Since the Germans had themselves torn up the agreement under which these 3.5 million people had been transferred to Germany with the land on which they lived, they were now to be transferred without it. Their demand to go "Home into the Reich" was fulfilled in a manner none of them had anticipated.

Slovakia was allowed a temporary respite as a puppet state whose treatment might serve to encourage other governments in Southeast Europe to cooperate with Germany. The special treatment for the Germans living there, however, pointed to a future in which the Slavic element would be expected to vanish.[158] The fact that in the summer of 1939 Hitler for a while thought of sending Arthur Seyss-Inquart there[159] suggests that incorporation into Germany lay in store for this puppet state. During the war, Slovakia could help Germany by its small industrial and agricultural production and some fighting in the East; it might be played off against the occasionally obstreperous Hungarians;[160] but it would be closely watched. The uprising of the Slovak army in 1944 was put down with savage fury. The Jews, like those of Bohemia and Moravia, were for the most part deported and murdered. Until Germany had won its war, Hitler was willing to allow Monsignor Tiso to act as a puppet ruler of a client state. In 1945, that entity would disappear as the Czechoslovak government returned in the wake of the Red Army.

In Hungary, the governments operating under the Regent, Admiral Miklós Horthy, tried to combine participation in the war on a limited basis with independence from Germany. The limits to participation were governed not only by a lack of enthusiasm for fighting Great Britain, the Soviet Union, or the United States.[161] The Hungarians wanted to take back even more of the territory they had lost to Romania after World War I than they had received at the hands of Hitler and Mussolini in 1940; they feared that a greater contribution by Romania to the Axis war effort would prejudice their standing with Berlin when they turned to the war they really wanted to fight, the one with Romania. In view of this set of priorities, they kept as much of their army at home as possible, sent to the Eastern Front only what seemed essential to remain in Germany's good graces, and were enormously upset when those forces were crushed by the Red Army in the fighting of early 1943.[162]

There were additional causes of friction between Budapest and Berlin which grew out of the domestic situation in Hungary. The Germans tried to protect their minority in Hungary and to recruit soldiers from it, both policies which the proud Hungarians resented. On the economic front, German efforts to dominate Hungary's small but significant oil industry aroused resentment. The soundings which the Budapest government began to make in 1943 as the anti-German Miklós Kallay replaced the pro-German László Bárdossy as Prime Minister annoyed the Germans, who tried unsuccessfully to have him dismissed and to influence his Cabinet appointments.[163]

The major source of friction between the Germans and Hungarians, however, was the refusal of the Budapest government to turn over the approximately 800,000 Jews in the country. A whole series of anti-Semitic laws was enacted, but the Regent and Prime Minister balked at murder. Hitler had himself predicted in July 1941 that the Hungarians would be the last to surrender their Jewish population; repeated pressure on the Budapest government and personal bullying by Hitler of the Regent failed in their purpose; and some Jews from other portions of Europe took refuge in Hungary. All this would change only after German troops occupied the country in March 1944. A new government under the former ambassador to Berlin, Döme Sztojay, proved more accommodating. His government assisted in the deportation to their deaths of about half a million Jews, with the rest saved by a combination of international pressure and Horthy's own reluctance, which produced a halt in the deportations in July, 1944.[164]

The SS utilized its own role in murdering Hungarian Jews to obtain a major foothold in the economy of the country, exchanging control of the nation's largest industrial concern, the Manfred Weiss company, for the lives of some of its owners and their families.[165] This dramatic intervention into Hungarian economic life did nothing to endear the Germans to the nationalistic Hungarians. The advancing Red Army made it ever more evident that the Western Allies had been correct in advising their Hungarian contacts that the country should surrender to all the Allies; and Horthy attempted to do so in October 1944. The Germans prevented this by a second coup in the capital and now established a puppet regime under the Hungarian Fascists, the Arrow-Cross movement of Ferenc Szálasi.[166] The change inaugurated further slaughter of Jews but hardly helped the Germans greatly.[a] Administrative chaos was Szálasi's main contribution to Hungary's remaining role in the war on Germany's side. During the winter of 1944–45 the Germans and the few Hungarians still fighting with them were driven out of the country by the Red Army. A new system would be installed in Hungary to last for more than forty years.

Romania was treated with special care by the Germans because of its important oil resources. The fact that production was steadily falling made the Romanian government both unable and unwilling to increase deliveries to the Axis as much as the latter desired—any dramatic increase in exploitation would exhaust the country's most valuable resource all the more quickly. A major concern of the government of Marshal Ion Antonescu was, therefore, to obtain real payment for what was sent and to keep from pumping too much. He was more successful with the latter than the former, and ironically assisted by the efforts of the Americans in 1943 and 1944 to disrupt the oil industry by bombing. Romania was, however, Germany's largest and Italy's only source of natural, as distinct from synthetic, oil from June 1941 on.

Inside the country, the Romanian administration carried on as before. The areas lost to the Soviet Union in 1940 were temporarily recovered, and Romania also administered an additional portion of the Ukraine known as Transnistria. The Germans hoped that such expansion eastward at the expense of the Soviet Union would divert Romanian aspirations from the recovery of the portions of Transylvania lost to Hungary and the northern Dobruja ceded to Bulgaria, also in 1940, but this was a lost cause. The Antonescu government was looking toward the recovery of those areas and anticipated a war with Hungary at the earliest opportunity. In fact, to a large extent the Romanian effort on the Eastern Front was designed to impress the Germans with the merits of Romania's cause.

When the tide turned in the East, the very large commitment of Romanian forces there meant that the disaster was all the greater for the country. As they began to look for a way out of the war, the Romanians, who had hitherto enthusiastically participated in the program to murder the Jews in newly occupied Russian territory, balked at turning over to the Germans the Jews of pre-June 1941 Romania. A last-minute coup in August 1944 came far too late to keep the whole country from being occupied by the Red Army. The government-in-exile created by the Germans under the Iron Guard leader Horia Sima had

[a] It was during this period that Raoul Wallenberg saved many of Budapest's Jews.

no resonance in the country, but the fact that the new government in Bukarest declared war on Germany and participated actively in the fighting on the Allied side led to the restoration of Transylvania to Romania at the end of the war. The new government installed in August 1944 would, however, soon be displaced by a Communist regime; in this regard, Romania shared the fate of both its Hungarian and Bulgarian rivals. In all three, the remnants of the pre-war regime and elites were displaced by new masters.[167]

Bulgaria had joined Germany in the hope of territorial aggrandizement at the expense of its Romanian, Yugoslav, and Greek neighbors and had been rewarded by substantial grants of land from each. What the Germans expected in return had been delivered by Sofia: cooperation in the German campaign of spring 1941 against Greece and Yugoslavia. Thereafter, the major interests of Berlin had been in the position of Bulgaria as a possible spring-board against Turkey, contributions toward their problem of pacifying insurgencies in occupied Yugoslavia, and the turning over of Bulgaria's Jews. On the first two of these the Bulgarians were willing to cooperate, and while the German thrust through Bulgaria and Turkey into the Middle East never materialized, that was due to factors outside Sofia's control. On the third issue, that of the Jews, the results were mixed. The Bulgarians allowed the Germans to have most of the Jews in the occupied portions of Greece and Yugoslavia assigned to her, but refused to sanction the deportation of pre-war Bulgaria's Jews. These were, as a result, saved from being killed, a result due not only to Bulgarian resistance but also to the reluctance of the Germans to push that country too far.

German diffidence in this case—as compared with others—was part of a general policy which recalled that Bulgaria's cracking under the strain of war in 1918 had set off the avalanche of defeat at the end of World War I. Bulgaria, it was believed, could be expected to contribute only so much to the Axis cause. Hitler had some respect for King Boris— the only reigning monarch the Führer evaluated positively—and accepted that ruler's protestations of loyalty and affection at face value.[168] The Germans, therefore, contented themselves with minimal economic deliveries and accepted Bulgaria's refraining from going to war with Russia.

The Bulgarian government, however, added to its seizure of Greek and Yugoslav territory by the fatal step of declaring war on Britain and the United States in December 1941. Once at war with the Western Allies, they would and could not extricate themselves from the self-imposed hostilities in time by an early surrender and switching of sides.

The result was that after the collapse of Romania in August 1944 the Soviet Union declared war on Bulgaria and occupied that country. Under a new Communist-led government Bulgaria re-entered the war on the Allied side, and large forces fought alongside the Red Army in Southeast Europe even as her society was reshaped at home.[169]

In Europe only Poland and the western portions of the U.S.S.R. were more drastically and violently affected by the deaths and destruction of war than Yugoslavia. Upon the German invasion in 1941, large portions in the north were directly annexed to Germany. There the people supposed to be of Germanic ancestry were to be re-Germanized and most of the rest driven out. Some of the expelled Slovenes were settled in Croatia or other parts of occupied Yugoslavia; many perished as a result.[170] Italy annexed large portions of Yugoslav territory both in the north and along the Adriatic coast, while Hungary was awarded a substantial piece of land in the north and Bulgaria in the south. Furthermore, the pre-World War I state of Montenegro was revived, now under Italian control, and Italian-dominated Albania was substantially expanded as well. The rest of the country was divided between a nominally independent state of Croatia and a Serbia under German military administration with a puppet government of its own.

In Croatia, which was supposedly under Italian influence but in practice divided into a German and an Italian zone of occupation, the extreme Croatian nationalists, the Ustasha of Ante Pavelic, were put in charge. A small and violent group of fanatics, they were determined to expel or exterminate all Serbs, Muslims, and Jews in the area under their control. With no discernible administrative skills, the new masters of Croatia quickly plunged the area into bloody chaos, tried to play off the Germans and Italians against each other, and enormously heightened the already bitter feuds between all segments of the population.

In German-occupied Serbia, the major economic aim of the Germans, the exploitation of the Bor copper mines, was attained, but all else quickly sank into an administrative chaos of German civilian, military, and police agencies and plenipotentiaries which rivalled the confusion in Croatia. Led by an unusually fanatic group of military officials of various sorts, and encouraged by the OKW, which complained that far too few prisoners and others were being shot,[171] the German forces stationed in Serbia soon strove to set new records of brutality. Those shot were usually the innocent bystanders,[172] and also Jews who were systematically killed off by the military. It did not take long for the population to realize that, in a situation of indiscriminate slaughter, the resisters had a better chance of survival than the acquiescent.

The result in both Italian and German controlled areas was a steadily escalating growth of resistance to the occupiers. This began in 1941 with former officers and soldiers of the Yugoslav army who had avoided capture and came to be led by General Draja Mihailovic. Known as Cetniks and operating at least nominally under the command of the Yugoslav government-in-exile, these forces recruited increasing numbers of men.[173] Though engaging in some sabotage, the Cetnik movement was essentially designed to rally resistance forces for an uprising against the Germans in connection with and in support of an Allied landing. Until that time, the limited resources available to the resistance and the likelihood of bloody retaliation against the civilian population were adduced as arguments for limiting rather than increasing incidents.

The British began helping Mihailovic with supplies and a liaison mission in September 1941.[174] Their signals intelligence showed that the Germans wanted to crush a movement which, whatever its limitations, did carry out some acts of resistance. The same intelligence, however, also showed that Mihailovic was in touch with the Italians, and that there was in effect a truce between the Italians and the Cetniks and occasionally cooperation between Mihailovic and the Germans, as the Cetniks increasingly concentrated on a civil war with another resistance force, Tito's partisans, in a struggle for control of post-war Yugoslavia.[175] Influenced in part by Communist agents in the British SOE headquarters in Cairo who deliberately distorted information from occupied Yugoslavia, the British in February 1943 began to turn to Tito, and between May and September of that year shifted their support to the partisans, though contacts with Mihailovic remained.[176] What the British did not know was that Tito was trying hard to work out a truce with the Germans.

Like other Communist resistance leaders in Europe, Josip Broz, known as Tito, had waited until the German invasion of the Soviet Union to initiate activity against the occupation. An exceptionally gifted leader, Tito rallied to himself elements from different nationalities in Yugoslavia, not only the Serbs as Mihailovic tended to do, and took action against the occupiers regardless of the retaliation the latter might visit on the civilian population. The atrocities of the Ustasha in Croatia, which at times were too much even for the SS,[177] provided a rich opportunity for recruitment. The partisan forces grew steadily and soon clashed with the Cetniks even as more and more of the population turned to the partisans.

There was thus a brutal civil war in the country simultaneously with fighting against the occupation authorities and endless massacres by the latter. From time to time, the Cetniks tried to arrange a truce with the

Italians—and were often successful in this—while Tito tried hard but failed to work out a truce with the Germans. He was especially interested in such an accommodation because he feared, as the Cetniks hoped for, a landing by the Western Allies. His offer to stand aside so that the Germans could beat off an invasion was discouraged by Moscow and rejected by Hitler.[178]

The Germans learned of the contacts their Italian ally had with Mihailovic, and the Italians, unlike the British, found out about Tito's dealings with the Germans.[179] Needless to say, this hardly improved relations between the Axis partners, but until the Italian surrender of September, 1943, they had to work together as best they could. They watched the Cetniks and partisans fight each other, trying unsuccessfully to crush both themselves, and ravaging the country and its people in an endless orgy of violence.[180] With ever greater supplies from the Western Powers and some aid from the Soviet Union, Tito's forces came to control much of the country.[181] As the Germans retreated in late 1944, the partisans became the heirs of pre-war Yugoslavia. In the last weeks of war and the immediate post-war period, they crushed both the forces of Mihailovic and the remnants of the Croatian army. A devastated and blood-soaked country was under entirely new leadership. But that leadership had established itself by military effort before and during the arrival of the Red Army, not in its wake, and this differentiation from the new regimes in Poland, Hungary, Romania and Bulgaria came to have major repercussions in later years.

Albania had been administered by Italy since early 1939. The southern portion had been temporarily occupied by the Greek army after it repulsed the Italian invasion in the winter of 1940–41. With the defeat of Yugoslavia, large portions of that country, and most especially the Kossovo area with its large Muslim population, were annexed to predominantly Muslim Albania. Little changed under Italian rule, but the collapse of Italy's administration with the surrender of September 1943 opened the way to new developments. The Germans, primarily in hopes of influencing Turkey, tried to create an independent client state but with little success.[182] Both Communist and nationalist insurgents began to harass the German occupation forces and, as these withdrew in late 1944, the former seized control of the country. Their leader, Enver Hoxha, dominated the country until his death in 1986.

The German invasion of Greece in April 1941 led to its defeat and occupation. A part was turned over to Bulgaria—which promptly inaugurated a program of expelling Greeks and settling Bulgarians there[183]—

and a portion of the northwest was annexed to Albania. The bulk of Greece was placed under Italian occupation though the northeast, including the port city of Salonika; most of Crete, several of the Aegean Islands, and a tip of land southeast of Athens came under German occupation. After the Italian surrender, the previously Italian-controlled area, which included Athens, came under German occupation.

A series of collaborationist regimes ran the country for the Italians and Germans while the latter established their usual plethora of agencies to compete with each other for influence. The critical impact on the people of the country came from three aspects of the years of occupation. In the first place, the Axis looting of the country and the disruption of its foreign trade produced a runaway inflation in which the currency was made worthless by the endless printing of money to pay for "occupation costs," money which the Germans used to strip the country like locusts. This in turn was both a cause and a symptom of famine which struck hard, especially in the winter of 1941–42, causing over 200,000 deaths, and which was only minimally alleviated by food imports paid for by the United States and allowed through the blockade by the British.[184]

The second aspect of the occupation period was the German murder of most of the country's Jewish population. The largest number lived in Salonika, and from that German-controlled city over 45,000 were deported to Auschwitz in the first half of 1943. The Jews in the rest of Greece were protected first by the Italians and, after the Italian surrender of September 1943, to a considerable extent by other Greeks so that about half the remaining 12,000 Jews in Greece survived.

The third facet of the war years, and one which would cast its shadow over Greek politics for the balance of the century, was the bitter conflict over resistance to the occupation. King George II and many of the ministers left the country in April, 1941, but they never made any significant effort to organize a resistance movement, either at the time or later in the war. The assumption was that they would sit out the war and return with the British victors at its end. Perhaps the King's identification with the dictatorship of Metaxas made any other course very difficult, but there is no evidence of his ever trying. The effect was that most of what resistance there came to be was organized by the Greek Communist Party, although it never provided more than a small percentage of the organization and membership of the main resistance structure, known by the initials of its Greek name as EAM, or its armed units, known as ELAS. A small separate resistance force under the former republican Colonel Napoleon Zervas, known as EDES, turned monarchist as it became clear that the British would provide arms to a monarchist organization. Both forces opposed the occupation, though ELAS much more effectively, but they also fought each other in the hopes of inheriting control of the country after liberation.[185]

Efforts to unite all resistance forces inside Greece failed, while the Greek politicians and the tiny Greek military units in Egypt during the war squabbled with each other. The evacuation of the German forces in late 1944 was not substantially hindered by the resistance which rather looked to the future. British troops in Athens in December 1944 became involved in the contest for control of the country, with Churchill—who came to the city in person—insisting on a monarchical restoration, at least under a regency. In the immediately ensuing struggle, the royalists won out, rehabilitated most of the collaborators, and began a systematic persecution of the ELAS resistance. The latter had failed in their first bid for power, had shown many Greeks their true colors by the murder of some 4000 hostages,[186] and bided their time for a new round of civil war.

If the internal Greek conflict between parts of the resistance as well as between the largest resistance organization and the government-in-exile set the stage for a civil war which raged in Greece overtly or covertly for decades, the roles of Britain and the Soviet Union in the Greek drama closely followed their division of the Balkans into spheres of interest. The most recent study of the issue shows as clearly as is possible before the opening of Soviet archives that during 1944 and again in early 1945 Moscow used its influence with the Greek Communists to restrain the latter, and hoped to utilize this policy to assure British agreement to the steps the Soviet Union was taking to establish a Communist dictatorship in Romania.[187] For the people of Greece, on whom the war had imposed terrible hardships, the victory of the Allies meant not peace but more swords.

GERMAN-OCCUPIED EUROPE: THE EAST

No country was affected more dramatically by World War II than Poland. In 1939, huge portions of the country were annexed to Germany, and the population in these areas was subjected to a "racial" screening which cost those deemed to be Polish their homes and their possessions. In their eagerness to Germanize their new domains, the Nazi Party leaders in the area combined ruthless expulsions for some with an anomalously "generous" policy of classifying as Germans as many people as they dared.[a] In the rest of German-occupied Poland, German policy aimed

---

[a] Gauleiter Forster of Danzig–West Prussia is reported as explaining on September 1, 1943, that he listed as many Poles as Germans as possible. If Poles are a dirty people, then the clean ones must be Germans. Krogmann Diary, 11 k 11, 1 Sep. 1943, Hamburg, Forschungsstelle für Geschichte des Nationalsozialismus.

at maximum economic exploitation of the material and human resources after the killing of the intellectual, political, and religious leadership. The long-term aim was clearly two-fold: in the coming years, the surviving Poles would work hard at minimal incomes for the Germans, serving as a reservoir of cheap labor. As German settlers became available, they would be driven out or exterminated.[188] The medical experiments in concentration camps aiming at the development of methods of mass sterilization may well have been designed for application to the Poles, among others. By the time any such techniques were available, one large segment of the country's population (about 10 percent) would already have vanished: the Jews.

Though there were local massacres of Jews as well as other measures of persecution in the first two years of German occupation, the mass murder program got under way in the summer of 1941, as the German invasion of the Soviet Union brought the German army and the killing squads attached to it into the part of Poland assigned to the Soviet Union under the 1939 Nazi–Soviet partition agreements. Subsequently, German-occupied Poland became the locale for the construction of special extermination centers, facilities devoted to the systematic killing of Polish Jews and of Jews transported from all over Europe and, when the Germans could reach them as on the island of Rhodes, from outside Europe as well. Over three million Polish Jews were killed, most of them in these installations. A few were aided by their Polish fellow-victims of German occupation, with most of the survivors hounded out of the country by pogroms in post-war Poland. The killing centers themselves, insofar as they remain, and the memorials erected at their sites, will stand for centuries as monuments to what the Germans once called their cultural mission in Eastern Europe. The resistance and defiance of the victims was dramatically symbolized by the final despairing uprising in the Warsaw ghetto in April 1943. Ignored by the Polish population next door, and crushed ruthlessly by the Germans, the first urban revolt in German-occupied Europe became a point of reference for the post-war world.

By the time this grisly drama was enacted, the Germans had added a portion of the eastern Ukraine, allocated to the Soviet Union in 1939, to the territory designated as "General Government" as a residual Polish area though characteristically deprived even of any Polish name. Alone of the occupied countries, Poland produced no collaborationist government. In the face of a harsh and deliberately extreme occupation administration, the population tried to survive and to resist. Hundreds of thousands died of hunger and disease, while hundreds of thousands of others were killed as undesirable intellectuals, hostages, reprisal victims, or whatever other excuses the imagination could conceive. Some 10,000 were killed in mental institutions, hospitals or old people's homes in an extension from Germany to the occupied territories of the program for the systematic killing of those deemed "unfit to live."[189]

These repressive measures, and many more,[190] however, did not bring the Germans the quiet they sought. The Polish underground army had massive support among the population. It drew on its members and supporters for an extensive intelligence network which provided the London government-in-exile and through it the Western Allies highly significant information on subjects ranging from German military moves through the program for the extermination of Jews to key details on secret weapons and even actual parts of them.[191]

The hope of the underground army was to rise against the Germans as they eventually retreated, but in this regard the government-in-exile and the Armya Krajowa leadership made a terrible misjudgement which has not been explained. The plan was to rise in the countryside, so the available weapons were largely hidden there; but in 1944, the uprising was ordered in Warsaw where few preparations for it had been made and equipment was inadequate. The resulting terrible drama, in which the Red Army was halted so that the Germans could crush the Poles, and every possible obstacle was placed in the way of Western efforts to assist the insurgents, is reviewed in Chapter 12. Upon the defeat of the uprising, Hitler ordered Warsaw levelled, a directive carried out with brutal thoroughness.

There was a small Communist underground in German-occupied Poland which grew somewhat as the Red Army approached and built up Polish units, the Berling army, to fight alongside it. The Poland which emerged, battered and terribly depleted, from the conflict would be altered in both regime and borders. A Communist regime was imposed by the Soviet Union and its few Polish supporters. The borders were redrawn to return most of the territory occupied by the Soviet Union under the Nazi–Soviet Pact to it, while in the north Poland acquired the southern portion of what had been called East Prussia as well as Danzig and in the west received the former German territories east of the rivers Oder and Neisse and some land even beyond that line. The country had lost its Ukrainian and Belorussian peoples in the East, its Jewish population had been murdered or was chased out after the war, and the bulk of the Germans in pre-war Poland as well as the large newly acquired former German areas either fled or were driven out.

The Poland which emerged from the war was thus a very different country from that of 1939. It was smaller and had lost enormously in population and wealth; it had acquired land basically more valuable than the territory it had lost; and it was very much more homogeneous than ever before. But it was saddled with a regime and a social system few Poles wanted and had come, at least for the time being, under a new foreign domination which most Poles bitterly resented.

The large remaining European area under German control for much of World War II was the portion of the U.S.S.R. seized in 1941 and 1942 and under German occupation, at least in part, until late 1944 with a minimal bit of western Latvia held until May 1945. As has been explained in Chapter 5, all this territory and more was to be the living space of the Germanic people with vast and steadily expanding German settlements, while a decimated and steadily shrinking indigenous population would be toiling for the new masters until their remnants were either expelled or exterminated.[192] Beyond the role of the area as a place of agricultural settlement, it was to be a source of raw materials for German industry and war production: oil, iron, coal, manganese and other non-ferrous metals. In addition to these known resources, which the Germans expected to exploit much more efficiently than their prior owners had, new crops would be introduced in large areas to make up deficits in the German economy: soybeans to provide vegetable oil and rubber trees to produce the natural rubber of which small quantities were still needed by the synthetic rubber industry.

The Jewish population, which was very numerous in the areas first overrun, was to be killed, and over one and a quarter million were indeed slaughtered, most of them in the first year after June 22, 1941. Some 10,000 mentally ill and elderly people were also murdered in an extension of the so-called euthanasia program into the occupied territory.[193] Communist party officials as well as political officers among the prisoners of war were also to be killed, and enormous numbers became victims of this policy.

The basic assumption always was, and remained until the Germans had been driven out again, that this would all be German territory, at least to the line Archangel–Astrakhan, perhaps to the Urals. Certainly the national aspirations of the non-Russian peoples of the Soviet Union were not to be met. Ironically, those who were most inclined to welcome the initial German invasion because of their hopes of national revival, people in the Baltic States and the Ukraine, lived in regions designed for German settlement and were therefore quickly disabused of their hopes.

The plan to deprive the population of as much food as possible to feed the German army and much of the German population similarly meant that the collective farm system, which allowed the government the first claim on the crop and made the peasant a residual claimant, would be maintained. This source of opposition to the Soviet regime was thus also kept, and the nominal "agrarian reform" instituted early in 1942 made no real change in the system. On the contrary, the Germans were so enthusiastic about the advantages of the collective farm system as a means of getting their hands on the harvest that they forced the last remaining individual farmers, operating in small scattered numbers in the marginal agricultural areas of Belorussia, into collectives. That these measures created both antagonism in the country-side and famine in the cities, especially in the winter, was hardly surprising.

It had been assumed by the Germans that the fighting in the East would be over quickly. The advancing armies would briefly exercise authority over the occupied territory, followed by equally transient Army Group rear area commands, a new creation for this campaign. After the short interval of military government would come the permanent civilian administration under Reich Commissars for huge areas with regional commissars under them, all nominally reporting to a new Ministry for the Occupied Eastern Territories in Berlin headed by the Nazi Party theoretician and supposed expert on the Soviet Union, Alfred Rosenberg. In reality, as the German army was slowed down and then halted, and finally driven back by the Red Army, civilian administration was established in only parts of the occupied U.S.S.R. and about half of the area remained under military administration for the period of German rule.[194]

In general, the military administration was governed somewhat more by practical than ideological considerations and hence proved slightly less harsh. Because a large variety of economic and police agencies operated in both spheres, however, and acted equally ruthlessly in both, this differentiation did not substantially alleviate the situation of the population. Concessions which were made by the military in the Caucasus areas temporarily occupied by the Germans in the second half of 1942 had little significance for the occupied people. They were very much more affected by the forced labor program, established in the same year, under which hundreds of thousands were to all intents and purposes kidnapped and carried off to work in German factories under horrendous conditions.

There was considerable debate within and between the innumerable German agencies which vied with each other for important roles in the occupied U.S.S.R., and some of these involved arguments over policies designed to be more appealing and less repressive to the population under German control; but all these debates, however extensive their paper trail in the archives, produced no significant modification in a ruthlessly exploitive policy.[195] Minimal concessions were temporarily

made in the Baltic States, but as German Foreign Minister von Ribbentrop explained in response to a plea in February 1943 from Finnish
Marshal Mannerheim urging independence for Estonia, Germany was
fighting not for the Estonians but for her own gains.[196] Suggestions
in the same direction from Germany's Japanese ally met with similar
responses; concessions to nationalities within the German-occupied
Soviet territories made no sense to a Hitler determined on the equal
subjugation of all its people.[197] Arguments over this issue, as well as
the related ones of decent treatment for Ukrainians and the possible
recruitment of Russians to fight alongside Germany against the Red
Army under General Vlasov, were put forward in the spring and summer
of 1943 from inside as well as outside the German government, after
the great Soviet victory at Stalingrad might have indicated even to Hitler
that some changes in policy were indicated. He firmly rejected them
all.[198]

The horrendous reprisals taken by the Germans against all real and
imagined resistance, and the massive slaughters of civilians which were
a standard feature of German anti-partisan operations, contributed their
share to the burdens of the people in the occupied territory. As the
Germans retreated before the offensives of the Red Army, deliberate
mass demolitions and the driving off of people and farm animals added
to the destruction of war.

As if all these losses of life, health, and property were not enough,
the Soviet victory did not end the travail of the people overrun by the
Germans. Those deported to forced labor as well as the liberated Soviet
ex-prisoners of war were under suspicion of collaboration with the Germans; they frequently ended up being sent to slave labor camps after
the Allied victory. Even the end of the war did not terminate the horrors
which the German invasion imposed on the Soviet population. A long,
slow and difficult period of reconstruction lay ahead.

COLLABORATION AND RESISTANCE

Throughout occupied Europe, as in the states nominally or actually
independent but under German control, the issues of collaboration or
resistance affected people at the time and influenced perspectives and
controversies afterwards. In most satellites there were different opinions
on the advisability of cooperating with the Axis and the extent to which
that cooperation might forestall German occupation and even worse
treatment of the people. In the areas under more complete German
control, this issue was yet more difficult. Did it help the Germans more

or did it protect the population more to continue in administrative positions in the occupied countries? The Germans clearly lacked the personnel to run the huge areas they dominated, but what would happen if everyone quit? As for resistance activity, how could one risk not only one's life and that of one's family, but also the lives of others likely to be killed in retaliation? These very hard questions were made even more difficult by the general impression in 1940 and 1941 that Germany was likely to win the war and even after 1941 that the Third Reich was unlikely to be completely defeated.

It was in this context that individuals chose to collaborate or to resist or, in a very large number of cases, to do some of both. As the brutality of the Germans became both greater and more obvious and as the appearance of an inevitable German triumph was replaced by first the hope and then the certainty of defeat, more and more turned to resistance. The resisters often assisted the victims of German terror, helped Allied airmen and escaped prisoners of war get back to the Allies, provided intelligence, and, on an ever larger scale, engaged in acts of sabotage and other overt acts of defiance. By such acts they contributed to Allied victory and their own country's liberation, but perhaps their main contribution lay in a different sphere.

The resistance by its existence and its spreading of news through word of mouth, leaflets, and illegal newspapers showed fellow citizens that not all had given up, that there were those with hope and alternatives to collaboration. Furthermore, this reminded those who helped the invaders that they were being watched and might well find themselves called to account for their actions after the war. And there was a still more important long-term contribution made by the resistance. The conquered people of Europe were all liberated primarily by the efforts of others, by the exertions and the sacrifices of the British, the Russians, the Americans, Canadians, New Zealanders and soldiers from additional far away countries. For their own subsequent self-respect and for their later national development, it was of great significance that some Frenchmen and Norwegians, Dutchmen and Belgians, Poles and Yugoslavs, Greeks and people from additional German-controlled areas had made a contribution to the Allied victory which restored a measure of independence to them after dark years of foreign domination. As one of the most talented chroniclers of the resistance concluded: "It gave back to people in the occupied countries the self-respect that they lost in the moment of occupation."[199]

JAPANESE-OCCUPIED AREAS

For the people in the areas of East and Southeast Asia overrun by the Japanese the same thing was true, but in a different way. With the exception of Thailand, all had been under direct or indirect rule by Europeans before 1941. Thailand came to be controlled by Japan and was required to declare war on the Western Allies but kept its formal independence; the war really meant that its economy was developed further, even as there were some strains imposed upon it. For the other territories (except for the Philippines) conquered by Japan, the war meant in the first instance and in the final analysis the destruction of the prestige and status of the former colonial masters. It was they who had been defeated, and defeated completely and quickly, by the Japanese, an Asian people. There might be and temporarily would be a restored control by the European powers—and in the South Pacific, by people of European background from Australia and New Zealand— but the aura of power of the colonial authorities had been shattered permanently.[a] Few situations more precisely fitted the saying that "all the king's horses and all the king's men" could not put the colonial empires together again.

In the interim, the Japanese ran the empire they had won in a manner which did two apparently contradictory things simultaneously. On the one hand, they exploited the area and its people ruthlessly and viciously, showing the population that there could be colonial masters far worse than the Europeans and Americans whose rule they had resented.[200] But this, and the actual destruction of warfare, passed relatively quickly. It was the nominal independence which the Japanese proclaimed in order to obtain more cooperation from the local population and to discourage resistance which appealed to people even as it left them unhappy with their new overlords.[201]

It was in this context that the people in the Japanese occupied areas, unlike those in German-occupied Europe, came to look at the wartime collaborators as patriots rather than traitors. It was easy to forget in places where the Europeans attempted to restore the colonial system of a by-gone era that a Japanese victory, attained with the help of such collaborators, would have meant a worse colonialism than they had experienced before.[202] The Koreans, who had suffered from Japanese colonialism longer than anyone else, would regain their independence

---

[a] The situation in the Philippines was the one important at least partial exception, a point demonstrated by its having the only significant anti-Japanese guerilla movement in Southeast Asia. There these guerillas, not the Japanese-organized groups, would be important in the post-war period.

only to be divided into two contending states by their liberators, while the others who had been under Japanese control for a few bitter but short years looked forward to a new and independent future for themselves, often under the very leaders, like Soekarno in the Dutch East Indies, who had come to prominence as collaborators in wartime.

10

———— • ————

MEANS OF WARFARE: OLD AND NEW

In World War II, the major weapons systems used in World War I and in some instances further developed in the inter-war years dominated all combat well into the war. As a practical matter many countries had kept or bought stocks of World War I weapons, especially those newly made in the last months of that conflict, and used them in the initial fighting. The rifles of the earlier conflict were only slowly replaced by newer models, and the British army in the summer of 1940 was pleased to receive large shipments of American World War I rifles. The general trend in infantry weapons was, however, into a new direction.

Increasingly the belligerents introduced rifles which could fire rounds from a clip or magazine more rapidly—if less accurately—and which thus substituted volume of fire for accuracy, ironically a revival of the way muskets had been used in the seventeenth and eighteenth centuries. The same trend could be seen in the increasing introduction of relatively simply made automatic weapons, which might be called sub-machine guns or assault rifles but which shared the characteristics of rapid automatic or semi-automatic fire, short range, and low accuracy. Designed to be used in infantry combat where a large volume of fire in street fighting, ambushes, and similar situations was called for, these weapons slowly but steadily replaced rifles as a preferred weapon of the infantry. Their very rapid expenditure of ammunition, however, obviously could create supply problems, and most armies relied on rifles for much of their infantry until the end of the war.

All armies in World War II used machine guns and mortars, but the changes made in these were not particularly great. The weight of machine guns was reduced and the caliber and accuracy of mortars increased somewhat, but any World War I veteran would have had no difficulty recognizing the heavy infantry weapons of 1945. Flame-throwers were employed on a large scale, especially by the Americans in the island campaigns of the Pacific War, and some were mounted on tanks; here too new developments were not especially radical.

Cavalry, insofar as it was not changed over to armor, was used on a far lesser scale than in any prior European or Asiatic conflict. The Poles and subsequently the Russians used cavalry fairly extensively, but most armies used horses for transport.[a] In many armies, officers of the infantry, at least in the early stages of the war, rode, but the major use of horses was to pull artillery, pull supply carts of various types, and pull the wagons of medical companies.[1] Millions of horses were thus employed in the German, Russian, Italian, Japanese and other armies, and mules were used by most armies—including the American—as pack animals, especially in mountainous terrain.

If horses still drew many of the guns, the artillery itself changed during the war. In this field as in that of infantry weapons, the beginning of the war saw many armies using World War I artillery pieces. There had, however, been some changes in the inter-war years and these continued, and with increased speed, during the war. The European powers and the United States all moved toward heavier and more rapidly firing guns, large numbers of them mounted on the lower portion of a tank chassis and thus self-propelled and providing greater protection for the gun crews. The major changes in artillery, however, took somewhat different forms.

The Germans developed a superior heavy anti-aircraft gun: the famous "88," a gun named for the millimeter diameter of its barrel but best known for its versatility. It could be utilized as an anti-tank gun and was of deadly effectiveness in that role; modified versions of it were also mounted in tanks. Not nearly as successful was the German tendency toward gigantomania. The investment in huge guns of 14, 17, and 21 inch caliber was most likely wasted as these could be moved only with great difficulty and were rarely used. The epitome of such mis-investment of resources was the "Dora" monster, a $31\frac{1}{2}$ inch railway gun which required the services of 4400 men for loading, firing, transportation and security; it fired all of 48 shells at the siege of Sevastopol in June 1942.[2] The other dead end pursued by the Germans was in regard to distance rather than caliber. In order to shell London from the continent, they developed a gun with a barrel literally over a hundred yards long, in which a sequence of explosions along the way would drive a shell all the way not merely across the Channel but to downtown London. A clear sign of Hitler's special love for the English, the V-3, as this contraption was called, was not ready in time for its intended

---

[a] There was a German SS cavalry regiment, employed in so-called anti-partisan operations in occupied Russia but actually engaged primarily in the slaughtering of civilians.

target; its only use was against Luxembourg in the winter of 1944–45.[3]

The most important innovations in artillery were of a very different kind. One involved a new version of an ancient weapon, the other a revolutionary change in the shell. The first of these was a revival of the use of rockets. The Soviet Union introduced a multiple rocket-launcher, the katyusha, which could be mounted on a truck and fired in salvoes of rockets for relatively short distances but to very great effect. The Germans produced a somewhat similar weapon later in the war, and the Americans constructed such weapons for mounting on landing-craft, to be fired by these in enormous numbers as the craft approached shore in an amphibious assault. Very useful in support of landings on defended coasts, these rocket launchers capitalized on a great advantage of the rocket over traditional artillery—the absence of a recoil. It was this advantage which led the Germans and Americans to introduce handheld small rocket launchers which infantry could use against tanks. The German versions were substantially more effective and efficient than the American bazooka; both pointed in new directions.

The major changes in the shells were of two kinds. One was the shaped charge, an arrangement of the explosive in the head of the shell which made its burst powerful enough to penetrate the increasingly thick armor of tanks. The other was the proximity fuse, a device in the shell which caused it to explode not only if it hit something but if it came close—an obvious advantage, especially in anti-aircraft fire. While the latter development was an innovation of the Western Allies, the shaped charge was used by both sides and affected the development of increasingly heavily armored tanks, a tendency also pushed by competitive pressures.

The armored fighting vehicles, generally referred to as tanks, had been introduced during World War I. Slow, with unreliable engines, and vulnerable to artillery, the tank had been the subject of further experimental development by all major powers in the inter-war years, with the Germans enabled to do so in the 1920s by the Soviet Union. In the 1930s, the Germans had proceeded to continue with this process, eventually concentrating to their later disadvantage on two medium tanks, the Mark III and the Mark IV, both very effective in the early years of the war and used in different models until its end. This was supplemented by a very fine medium tank which had been developed in Czechoslovakia, referred to as the T-38, and built under the German occupation until 1945.[4] It was the experience of the greatly superior Soviet T-34 and KV tanks which shocked the Germans into developing the Mark V, or "Panther," which was to equal it, and the Mark VI, or "Tiger," which was supposed to better the Soviet models.[5]

These new German tanks in their various models were among the most effective built in the war, but they suffered from development problems, were rushed to the front when not yet ready, and could not be built in the numbers Germany needed and wanted because of the diversions caused by bombing and by competing needs. These competing needs included not only submarine construction but a tendency to gigantomania, which was not limited to artillery. There were endless experiments with monster tanks, including a 188 ton "Mouse," which absorbed resources to no conceivable practical purpose.[6]

The French had begun to develop and then to build very good medium and heavy tanks, but the quick collapse of France in 1940— brought about in part by the foolish dispersal of the country's numerous tanks—ended the French role in this field. For reasons which remain unclear, the Germans did not insist on the continued production of the excellent French tanks as they did with the Czechoslovak model.

Mussolini had dreamt of a massive and advanced Italian armored force, but, like many of his military aspirations, this one remained largely in the sphere of dreams.[7] The British had been the great innovators in armored warfare in World War I, British writers on military affairs had emphasized the possible role of armor in the inter-war years, and under the prodding of Secretary of State for War Leslie Hore-Belisha the British army had become the first European army to turn completely to motor from horse transport; but in the field of tank development Britain lagged behind. The steady series of defeats at the hands of the Germans in North Africa was to a considerable extent due to the inferiority of British armor.[8] The models introduced in 1943 and 1944 were a substantial improvement, but in those years British armored units were increasingly equipped with American vehicles, especially the "Sherman" tank.[9]

The "Sherman" came to symbolize the arguments over American armor in World War II.[10] With its reliable engine and substantial armor, it proved distinctly superior to the Mark III and IV but had trouble dealing with the Mark V and VI, generally relying on larger numbers to cope with the more heavily gunned German tanks.[11] Whatever their defects in detail, the American tanks, especially when supported by the excellent American artillery and by the Allied air forces, proved adequate for their task.

There cannot be any doubt that the Soviet Union both developed the most effective tanks and produced and fielded them in huge numbers. The T-34, KV, and Stalin tanks, all improved during the war, proved admirably suited to conditions on the Eastern Front, distinctly superior to the German tanks of 1941 and 1942, and more than able to cope with the new German models of 1943 and 1944.[12] Of probably equal importance on the battlefield was the Soviet development of "tank armies" and their use in the war, first conspicuous in the offensive which encircled the Axis armies in Stalingrad. Although the Germans had introduced large armored formations, eventually named "Panzer Armies," as a practical matter these contained fewer and fewer tanks as the war went on. The Red Army, on the other hand, steadily increased the tanks allocated to their "tank armies" and these came to be the main instruments of the deep penetrations which it was able to make in 1943 and 1944.

Armor played a decidedly smaller role in the Pacific War, in part because the terrain in Burma and the Southwest Pacific was generally not suitable for the employment of armor on any large scale. The Japanese used small and lightly armored tanks;[13] the Americans and British small numbers of their standard models. The modification which the Americans found most useful in the Pacific War was the tank-mounted flame-thrower for dealing with Japanese soldiers and gunners who had dug themselves into caves and other natural obstacles on such islands as Okinawa. The biggest use of armor in East Asia came at the end when Soviet armor, recently transported by train across the U.S.S.R., swept into Manchuria in August 1945.

THE AIR

Far more dramatic changes took place in airplanes. Most air forces still had bi-planes at the beginning of the war, but with the exception of the Russian U-2 (used for liaison and support of partisans throughout the war), these were all phased out. The single-engine single-wing fighter came to characterize all air forces with the initial German and Japanese lead in speed overcome by newer British as well as newer American and Soviet models. The German experiment with two-engine fighters proved a bad mistake; the American ones, on the other hand, turned out to be especially useful in the Pacific with its greater distances. The most important change, discussed in Chapter 11, was the extension of the range, especially of the P-51 "Mustang," to where it could escort bombers great distances. The completely new world of jet-propelled airplanes is discussed later in this chapter.

If fighters became faster, carried heavier armor, came to have self-sealing tanks, and flew further, bombers changed in a different way. The two-engined standard bomber of all air forces continued to be used in varying modifications by all air forces. The major new development was the four-engined bomber, produced in ever larger numbers primarily by the United States and Great Britain. Designed before and in the early stages of World War II, these planes could go further and carry a vastly heavier load of bombs than the two-engine models.[a] They bore the major burden of the strategic bombing offensive, carrying huge loads of high explosive and incendiary bombs to German and Japanese cities, factories, and other installations. The most advanced bombers of the war, the American B-29 and the British "Mosquito" represented opposite lines of development. The B-29 with its huge size, enormous range, and pressurized cabin pointed toward the inter-continental planes of the post-1945 era.[14] The "Mosquito," with its light wood construction, great speed, and very high altitude capability foreshadowed the spy-planes of the Cold War era.

The Axis powers lagged behind in the development of the 4-engine bomber. Misled by their faith in the dive-bomber's ability to hit targets by getting low enough to aim accurately, the Germans moved from the single-engine dive-bomber (JU-87) to a two-engine dive-bomber (JU-88), whose pilots, however, often found diving far too dangerous and tended to fly their planes like any two-engine bomber. To make a four-engined bomber capable of diving, the Germans put two engines onto each of two propellors, a solution which proved more genial in theory than in practice (Heinkel 177). This plane always had problems with its tandem engines, caught fire in the air or on the ground, and was never practical for diving anyway. Unlike the B-29 and the Mosquito, the Heinkel concept turned out to be a dead end.[b]

All air forces continued to use their two-engine bombers, especially to support the ground forces. In this, the Western Allies, after initial difficulties, became especially proficient, using their planes in Europe to attack German military targets with cannons as well as machine guns and with rockets mounted under the wings.[15] In the Pacific the Americans used their two-engine bombers not only in the same way but to skip-bomb Japanese shipping.

The Red Air Force started the war with a large stock of often obsolete or obsolescent planes. Losing huge numbers of planes in the first days of fighting, the Soviet Union soon concentrated production on more modern models and developed planes which were equal to the Germans' in capacity even if the crews often lacked experience. There were,

[a] The project for clearing fog off runways in England, code-named "F.I.D.O.," helped save many returning bombers. There is important relevant material in the Sir Ronald Banks Papers at the Imperial War Museum.

[b] It should be noted that to insure itself against a failure of the B-29, the United States also developed another very long-range bomber, the B-32. Such planes were seen as the intermediate step toward the true inter-continental bomber (B-36) and were ordered, designed, and built initially against the possibility of a German victory in Europe, which would leave the United States with no bases on the other side of the Atlantic, and hence in need of planes which could reach targets in Germany from the continental United States.

however, no great technological breakthroughs. The Soviet Union, like all the belligerents, faced enormous problems in training vast numbers of pilots, navigators, and other aircrew members. It could, however, do this at bases out of reach of enemy planes, something the United States could do in the Western Hemisphere and Great Britain did to a considerable extent through the British Commonwealth air training plan in Canada.[16]

The old standby of the pre-war air enthusiasts, the balloon, played a part in the war in two ways. Primarily, but not only, the Western Allies used balloons very extensively to protect cities, military installations, and convoys from low-level air attack.[17] Here was one area in which women increasingly came to occupy a near-combat role in the West at a time when they were already fighting with arms and in planes in the Soviet military. The other use of balloons, discussed in Chapter 7, was the employment of helium filled — and hence non-inflammable — blimps with crews in anti-submarine patrols, as opposed to the hydrogen-filled captive barrage balloons whose crews were on the ground. The Germans did not repeat their World War I bombing of England with Zeppelins, that is, with dirigibles; but the Japanese unsuccessfully tried to set fire to the forests of western Canada and the United States with incendiary carrying balloons. The 1944 idea of burning down huge portions of the enemy's country — forests, cities, factories and people — in enormous firestorms was Japan's contribution to the conduct of war; it would prove unsuccessful in practice and be repaid the following year by the Americans on a more limited scale but to far greater effect.

NAVAL WARFARE

At sea, there were fewer innovations than on land or in the air. The types of warships developed in the pre-war years, and in fact the ships themselves, dominated in the navies of all belligerents.[18] Aircraft carriers became increasingly important, but except for American adoption of the British concept of the angled flight deck and the introduction of the small escort carrier, these ships became more numerous rather than different. The really new type of ship was the landing ship and landing craft, a variety of ships designed in part by the American marines in the inter-war years, in part by the British Combined Operations Command, and most often built by the Americans, to bring ashore troops, tanks, and other equipment in amphibious operations. By 1945 there were literally thousands of these, essential to all the landings in the Mediterranean and Normandy as well as the many assault landings in the Pacific.

The submarines of World War II were also basically those developed earlier. These ships spent most of their time on the surface, were too slow to overtake ships or convoys when underwater, and had to surface to recharge the batteries which drove them when submerged. The Japanese began the war with the most effective torpedo; those of other powers, especially of Germany and the United States, were defective and only slowly improved. As explained in Chapter 7, the massive effort made by the Germans to by-pass the handicaps of the standard submarines and to employ new types which could stay submerged and move at high speeds failed to produce results in time for their effective employment in the war. The real impact of these new types was their absorption of vast resources and the influence their anticipated effectiveness had on the conduct of German military operations in the Baltic area in 1944 and 1945.

The most significant changes in naval warfare came from the introduction of radar and other electronic devices which are reviewed later in this chapter. The advances of the Allies in these fields gave their navies an enormous advantage over the Italians from 1941 on and over the Germans and the Japanese from 1943 on. The use of these new technologies helped them turn the tide in the Battle of the Atlantic and destroy Axis warships on all oceans from the waters off Norway to the Southwest Pacific.

Acting independently of each other as far as is known, both the Japanese and the Germans had tried to leap-frog the British and Americans for control of the seas by beginning construction in the 1930s on battleships vastly larger than anything being built or even contemplated elsewhere and arming such new ships with 18 inch guns, again larger than any gun in any other navy. The Germans had halted work on their super-battleships in September 1939, had renewed work in the summer of 1940, halted it again later that year, resumed once more in the summer of 1941 only to stop once more and finally in the fall. The deliberate or accidental oversight in the cancelling of the contracts which led to some engines being completed—only to be scrapped—in the summer of 1944 is of interest in showing how seriously the project had been taken in Berlin. The Japanese, on the other hand, completed two 70,000-ton monsters, the *Yamato* and the *Musashi*, while converting a third into a huge aircraft carrier, the *Shinano*. All three were sunk without having had any substantial effect on the war (a fourth one was scrapped quite early during construction). Whatever the theoretical merits of the concept in the context of Japan's *original* war plan, the substitution of the Pearl Harbor concept made the super-battleships of doubtful value. Both Germany and Japan would have derived greater naval power from investing the resources devoted to the monster ships to smaller models.

The United States built somewhat larger battleships in the *Iowa* class, but these were the direct follow-on to the *North Carolina* class. The victory of the Allies at sea was, however, attained by the building of vast numbers of ships rather than any major new types. Naturally there were all sorts of technical improvements, but, except for some of the special ships built for amphibious warfare, the sailors of 1939 would have had no difficulty recognizing the warships of 1945.

ESPIONAGE AND SIGNALS INTELLIGENCE

Another area where the war at first saw little change from prior practice was that of agents and spies. German agents and spies were of considerable effectiveness in France, Holland, and Belgium, but had little success in the United States or the Soviet Union.[19] Those in Great Britain were all captured and shot, jailed, or turned into double-agents controlled by a special organization established for that purpose.[20]

The best known German penetration of Allied diplomacy, the recruitment in the fall of 1943 of the valet of the British ambassador in Turkey, generally known under the code-name "Cicero" given it by the Germans because of the eloquence of the documents he purloined, still awaits a serious—as opposed to sensationalist—investigation. As so often, the highest level information on Allied plans thus obtained by the Germans was either not believed or not particularly useful to them.[21]

British espionage and agent operations in Germany, Italy, and Japan remain shrouded in security restrictions but appear not to have been nearly as extensive as the contemporary imagination—especially of the Germans—supposed. Most successful activities appear to have taken place in German and Japanese-occupied areas where some support from local sympathizers could be expected. Such operations were, however, often disastrous. Sometimes the Germans penetrated the networks established by the British and then lured agents and members of the resistance to their death, simultaneously collecting great quantities of supplies dropped by the British, the most notorious case occurring in the Netherlands in 1942–43.[22] At other times, rivalry between the older intelligence agencies, MI5 and MI6, on the one hand and the new SOE on the other, led to disaster which was then used by the former to discredit the latter.[23] Some valuable information came to the British from German individuals opposed to the government of the Third Reich; the most famous of these, the "Oslo document," listed the major new weapons being developed by the Germans but was for a long time considered too implausible to believe, a fate often accorded to top-level leaks in wartime.[24]

The United States was apparently about as unsuccessful in penetrating Germany as Great Britain was,[25] but did better in occupied Western and Southeast Europe through contacts with underground resistance forces. The OSS at least from March to June 1942 obtained copies of correspondence between Vichy and the French embassy in Washington.[26] There was a massive intelligence research effort in Washington.[27] The United States also gained important insights into developments inside the German government from individuals opposed to the Nazi regime. Some of those associated with the July 20 plot provided such insights; especially important were the German Foreign Ministry materials turned over from October 1943 by Fritz Kolbe.[28]

Polish intelligence, which had made the decisive contribution to the breaking of German machine codes before the war, a subject discussed later in this chapter, continued to supply both Britain and the United States with valuable information not only from German-occupied Poland but from all over Europe and North Africa. The British, for example, received key details about and pieces of German secret weapons, and the Americans were provided German order-of-battle and other significant reports. As American War Department G-2 (Intelligence) commented on two such documents in a long series: "This is an excellent report. . ." and "This type of information is extremely valuable."[29]

There is, in addition, good reason to believe that from time to time the Western Allies received intelligence of importance to them from sympathetic individuals in the military and diplomatic services of several neutrals, Sweden in particular. At times, furthermore, representatives of German satellites unburdened themselves to Allied officials in neutral capitals.[30]

The Italians and the Japanese had espionage networks that were, on the whole, more effective in the pre-war period than during hostilities.[31] Vastly more widespread, and very active during the war, was the Soviet espionage network, or rather, the networks directed separately by the Secret Police and by the Red Army. Much of their activity remains to be illuminated, and much has been distorted by sensational accounts. Some things can, however, be stated with considerable confidence. There was extensive Soviet espionage in Germany, much of it continuing from before the war. A most important Soviet source was either indirectly Rudolf von Scheliha or Gerhard Kegel, of the German embassy in Warsaw; Scheliha was arrested in October 1942.[32] A major Soviet network generally referred to as the "Rote Kapelle" or Red Orchestra had a high-level recruit in the intelligence section of the German air force, Harro Schulze-Boysen, whose arrest in August 1942 further reduced the already low esteem in which air force intelligence was held in Berlin.[33] The literature on the Rote Kapelle is extensive, but it suggests that little was gained from it by the Soviet Union.[34]

The Soviet government clearly received information of much greater importance from the spy ring headed by Richard Sorge in Tokyo, though in this case also truth and fiction have been very much confused.[35] Sorge certainly provided the government in Moscow with a clear picture of Japanese general policy in the years before the Japanese expanded their war against China into the Pacific War in 1941, and he also had considerable access to information originating in the German embassy in Tokyo. Whether his activities and those of his associates compromised Japanese or German codes is not known. A less well-known figure was Ivar Lissner, a key German agent in Manchuria, who collected information on the Soviet Union from there, was accused in 1943 by the Japanese of being a Soviet double-agent, but may well have been so accused merely to enable the Japanese to rid Manchuria of a German who was too well-informed in their eyes.[36]

Soviet espionage in Great Britain also continued, and probably increased, during the war years. This activity, doubtless aided by the British ending work on Soviet codes during wartime, was to attain enormous notoriety in the post-war years. The subject of a vast literature, that espionage has been examined primarily from the perspective of its impact on the Cold War.[37] Beyond demonstrating the tenuous character of the alliance against Germany and the willingness of numerous individuals in Britain to betray their country to the Soviet Union, even when that state was aligned with a Nazi Germany poised to invade the United Kingdom, this espionage activity appears to me to have been significant for two types of information provided Moscow during World War II. In the first place, it would have made certain that the Soviet government knew of British code-breaking successes against Germany; so that the real source of the special information provided them by the British and discussed subsequently in this chapter would have been known, in spite of the attempts at camouflage designed to protect that knowledge for fear of the Germans finding out.[38] Secondly, the extensive information about the British–American effort to develop atomic bombs provided by Klaus Fuchs and others gave the Russians, who were working on such weapons themselves, both a sense of the progress being made by the Western powers and assistance for their own project. Whether, in addition, the Soviet moles in the British government also made it possible for the Russians to read British codes is not known at this time, but, even if given, such information would hardly have been very useful *during* as opposed to *after* the war.

Soviet espionage was similarly active in the United States. Here too such activity was mainly a continuation of pre-war operations. As the United States government learned, espionage was very much directed toward the atomic bomb project but appears to have been less successful, even if as extensive, as in Britain. The American success in reading Japanese codes appears, however, to have remained secret from the Soviet Union; it is difficult to imagine such Soviet leaders as Molotov speaking to Japanese diplomats the way they did had they known that the Americans would read the reports of the Japanese.

Given this background, it should not be surprising that cooperation in intelligence matters, like cooperation in other fields between the Western Powers and the Soviet Union, was on a minimal level.[39] There were some exchanges of information, but most of the traffic was one way: the British and Americans provided material about some of their own technical developments and captured German material to the Russians with little being given in return.[40] At Churchill's repeated insistence, information derived from the breaking of German codes was regularly transmitted to the Soviet government through a specially assigned representative attached to the British embassy, Major Edward Crankshaw.[41] From their own spies in England, especially Kim Philby, the Soviets knew the source of the information provided by Crankshaw; but the British fear that careless use of such information by the Russians or German reading of Soviet codes would compromise the source, which had led them to disguise the latter, was never realized. In spite of repeated requests, however, the Soviet government was rarely prepared to reciprocate by providing products of its own extensive intelligence against the Axis. There is no sign that the massive Russian interrogations of German prisoners of war, capture of German weapons and documents, or other information gathered on the Eastern Front was transmitted on any substantial scale to the other powers fighting Germany.

While there was a very extensive degree of cooperation in both intelligence and technical matters between the Americans and the British, beginning before the United States was drawn into the war, the exchanges between Germany and Japan, though considerable, were clearly less.[42] In most fields, the Germans appear to have been more forthcoming than the Japanese. It should be added that both at times displayed a singular carelessness in their selection of readily penetrated cover names: the Germans by using "Barbarossa" for the invasion of Russia and "Aida" for the offensive toward Suez,[43] the Japanese by using operation MI and operation MO for the attacks on Midway and Port Moresby respectively.

Whatever effects espionage and agents may have had on the war, these were of minor importance compared to those resulting from signals

intelligence. The need for rapid communication with tanks and formations on the ground, planes in the air, headquarters at a distance, ships
at sea, and, in return, the requirement for reports, put a premium on
communication systems. Where possible, these were handled by all belligerents through cables or couriers precisely to preclude the dangers
of interception which always accompany radio messages. Sometimes,
however, there was no way to avoid radio communication: with ships at
sea and planes in the air, to places where cables were not available, and
in the rush of battle when there was often no alternative to radio. One
of the important but rarely noted by-products of strategic bombing in
the last part of World War II in both Europe and the Pacific was that
the destruction of the means of communication, first in Germany and
later in Japan, reached a level where a large volume of messages which
would otherwise have been transmitted by wire, mail, or courier was
instead entrusted to the radio, with the resulting exposure to interception
by the Allies.

Interception by all belligerents involved the establishment of extensive
systems of stations for listening in on, recording, and conveying to central
locations whatever messages could be gathered in by usually large numbers of increasingly well-trained listeners. These listeners, whose organization was referred to as the "Y-Service" by the Western Allies, played
a central role in all radio intelligence efforts.[44] The intercepted messages
could then be utilized for signals intelligence, which consists basically
of three types.[45]

In the first place, the interception of a radio message by two or more
listening posts could, if accurately plotted, provide the location of the
sending station, what is generally referred to as locator intelligence.
Obviously of central importance in the war at sea, it also played a significant role in the locating of headquarters and agents, as well as their
movement. It was the development of a seaborne radio locator system,
HF/DF, nicknamed "Huff-Duff," which was a key contributor to Allied
victory in the Battle of the Atlantic because it enabled the escort ships to
locate and attack, or at least force below the surface, German submarines
signalling while on the surface.

The second form of signals intelligence is traffic analysis. Careful
attention to the pattern of radio traffic, in which trained listeners soon
learned to recognize the hand of each of the enemy operators they were
monitoring, provided very important information on enemy dispositions,
shifts, reorganizations and, as a frequent result, intentions.[46] It should
be noted that neither locator nor traffic analysis required any ability to
decypher whatever messages the enemy had entrusted to the air; what

was needed was an elaborate monitoring system and exceedingly conscientious and able listeners and analysts. Both types of intelligence had existed in World War I but both, like the third form—decypherment—were developed dramatically in World War II.

The third, the breaking of codes, remains the most difficult to analyze in spite of the enormous volume of released documents and literature on the subject, because so much remains closed. Much of the German archival material captured by the Americans and British pertaining to German code-breaking is still classified so that the successes and failures of the Germans are still not well understood. The Soviet Union has released next to nothing on the subject, and there are large gaps in the British and American records due to real or imagined concerns about security. In addition, because so much of the cryptographic record was deliberately destroyed during hostilities to prevent leaks, there will always remain major gaps in the record.

The Germans had several agencies working in the field of code-breaking, and while they had a number of major successes, the very dispersion of effort hampered the Third Reich.[47] The evidence is good that the Germans read a high proportion of French codes and were assisted by this in their rapid conquest of France. German naval intelligence had begun to break several codes used by the British navy, especially the convoy code, and used this effectively in their submarine campaign in the Atlantic. In spite of periodic alterations which caused them temporary difficulties,[48] the Germans were able to read a high proportion of the convoy code messages until the British, finally convinced by the results of their own reading of German naval code messages, realized what had happened and changed to machine cyphers in the summer of 1943.[49] Before this change the German superiority in code-breaking had provided them with an enormous advantage; thereafter the advantage in the crucial battle over the oceanic supply routes shifted to the Allies. When the Americans and British landed at Salerno in September 1943, the German naval signals intelligence organization could only report that the landing had not been recognized beforehand; only radio silence had provided a clue that something was afoot.[50]

Directly, and also on the basis of Italian assistance, the Germans also broke into some American codes, primarily the diplomatic ones.[51] The American machine code systems were apparently not broken into, but in this regard, as well as what the Germans and others may have learned about American codes in connection with the Tyler Kent incident discussed in Chapter 3, there is still a veil of secrecy.

The Germans did have considerable success with lower level Russian codes though less so with the higher level ones. The Soviets apparently protected their most significant communications by the one code system which, if properly used, cannot be broken—the one-time pad, a system where each message is encoded according to a code used only once and only for that message. This was the system also employed extensively by the British and protected their key messages.

The Germans read several codes of their Italian, Bulgarian, Hungarian and Romanian satellites as well as considerable Turkish and Yugoslav traffic. They utilized this information at times to warn their allies lest the British and Americans read them also.[52] Later in the war, the Germans learned from the intercepts about the efforts of Hungary and Romania to negotiate with the Allies about leaving the war and took precautions accordingly.[53] More needs to be learned concerning German code-breaking activities; but in the interim it can probably be stated that apart from tactical benefits on the Western Front in 1940 and the Eastern Front in 1941 and 1942, the Germans benefited primarily from their reading of British naval traffic in the Battle of the Atlantic in 1942 and the first part of 1943, an asset enhanced by considerable American use of the British convoy code.

Italy had long had a large intelligence and cryptographic establishment which succeeded in reading the major Yugoslav and Turkish codes. The former were especially important to them, and the knowledge was used in 1941 for a successful deception operation which probably saved the Italian army in Albania from disaster.[54] The major successes of the Italians, however, were originally based on thefts rather than purely cryptographic methods—but the results were the same. Having acquired important documents from the British embassy in Rome before the war, and other British material early in the conflict, the Italians were able to read a substantial proportion of British diplomatic and naval traffic early in the war.[55]

Probably one of the most important breaks into Allied code security was the result of the theft in August 1941 of the American military attaché code (called Black Code after its binder) from the office of the United States military attaché in Rome. Used by American officers around the globe, the code system provided both the Italians and the Germans, with whom the Italians shared their find, a vast amount of information of the highest value. That value was at its greatest in the Mediterranean and North Africa, where the almost daily detailed reports of Colonel Bonner Fellers, the military attaché in Cairo, involuntarily provided Rommel and the German and Italian naval and air commanders with the most complete information available to any Axis leaders in World War II. The information was utilized very effectively both by

Rommel and by the Axis commanders of the fight against Malta, and contributed in a major way to the Axis victories and Allied disaster in North Africa in the first half of 1942. Only the capture of German documents in North Africa in July, 1942, which gave away the source of German intelligence and led to a code change, closed this hemorrhage of Allied secrets. It is hardly a coincidence that the tide of fortune in that theater of war also changed days later.[56]

The Italians not only read the key codes of pre-war Yugoslavia but during the war broke into the code used by Tito's partisans. This enabled them to confront the Germans with evidence on the negotiations between the latter and Tito.[57] When the Germans, therefore, reproached the Italians about the negotiations of Italy with Mihailovic, Rome had an answer ready to hand. The Western Allies, whose code-breakers read radio messages on the contacts of Mihailovic with the Axis but never matched the Italian feat of reading Tito's messages were left to make their decisions on highly partial evidence.

The Japanese appear to have been the least successful of the major belligerents in the effort to break codes.[58] They had had some success against Chinese codes between the beginning of hostilities in 1937 and the expansion of the war in December 1941, and they appear to have broken some Chinese codes thereafter.[59] They practically gave up, however, on the major American code systems, never broke any of them, concentrated on low-level codes with minimal success, and relied on traffic analysis for most of their communications intelligence on the United States campaign in the Pacific. The Japanese success in penetrating some of the radio traffic of the guerillas in the Philippines proved of little help to them in maintaining control of the islands. Similarly, the substantial accomplishment of breaking into Allied code messages on the northern and central fronts in Burma in May, June, and July 1944, discovered by the Americans from intercepts in October, appears not to have helped the Imperial army in the abortive invasion of India and its great defeat there.[60] What little the Japanese learned about American merchant shipping came to them as a result of the Germans providing them with a codebook captured by one of their raiders; but this information, even on those occasions when it allowed decypherment of messages in a timely fashion, was of little use in Japan's struggle to retain the empire she had conquered so rapidly.[61]

The issue of timeliness was of central importance to all code-breaking in World War II. German reading of the British convoy code and Allied breaking of German and Japanese codes was often not in time for the information to be useful. Such breaks could sometimes still be used to read back into earlier traffic that had been monitored but could not previously be read, and such reading back could be helpful for an understanding of the other side's broader dispositions,[62] but for operational use speed was essential—and frequently not possible. This point must be kept in mind if both the foregoing discussion of Axis and the following review of Allied signals intelligence are to be understood.

One other point frequently overlooked is that even prompt reading of an enemy's code leads only to the decypherment of the messages sent and intercepted; if radio silence is observed or messages are simply not sent on a particular subject, either for security reasons or because the sending agency has itself been kept uninformed, there will be nothing to decypher. It was both radio silence by Japanese ships—which obviated naval locator intelligence—and the deliberate withholding of information about the planned attack on Pearl Harbor from the Japanese Foreign Ministry and representatives to the United States that made the American success in breaking into the Japanese diplomatic code and the United States navy's excellent locator intelligence system incapable of providing warning of the Pearl Harbor attack. There was no reference to it in the codes which had been broken, since those Japanese who used them knew nothing of the plan themselves. Furthermore, there could be no locating by radio intelligence of that portion of the Japanese fleet headed for Hawaii because it sent no signals as it crossed the North Pacific.

The Americans had broken the highest level Japanese diplomatic code in 1940 and, since the Japanese continued to utilize it throughout the Pacific War, maintained their reading of it until 1945. This ability provided the Allies with important information on Japanese policy throughout the war. Furthermore, as repeatedly mentioned in this book, it also gave them significant insight into all manner of other matters because of Japanese diplomats' reporting from the Soviet capital and from Europe on conversations, observations, and developments there.[63] The details which the Allies received from the reading of Japanese diplomatic reports from Europe about new German weapons under development, about the impact of their own bombing effort, and about the political intentions and perceptions of the leaders of the European Axis, were invaluable.[a] These reports were supplemented by those of Japanese military and naval attachés once their codes were similarly broken by the Americans. In this manner, for example, the detailed report of the Japanese Ambassador to Germany on the German defenses against an Allied invasion

---

[a] These reports also provide historians with important conversations between Japanese diplomats and German officials, of which no records survive in the German archives. This is especially true for 1944 and 1945.

was rounded out by a report on a similar inspection trip by a high-ranking Japanese officer.[64]

It should be noted that however complete the American mastery of the Japanese diplomatic and attaché codes, many messages were not intercepted at all because of atmospheric conditions, while others could not be promptly decoded or translated.[65] On the other hand, the Japanese dismissed as improbable or even impossible every hint they received about Allied breaks into their codes; the assumption clearly was that since the Japanese were unable to break into Allied machine cyphers, the inferior Americans and British were certainly incapable of such a feat.[66]

The American partial reading of major Japanese naval codes contributed significantly to the victory at Midway, and the success of the American cryptographers in retrieving access into those codes after an interval in July–August 1942 provided the navy with a great advantage for the rest of the Pacific War. Nowhere was this more evident than in the submarine campaign, in which submarines could be directed to Japanese ships in the vast reaches of the Pacific because the shipping code was being read with great regularity.[67]

The American navy's handling of signals intelligence was unusually effective, in large part because Admiral Chester Nimitz, its Pacific commander, early developed and consistently maintained a very high regard for the excellent naval intelligence officers in his headquarters. From Midway through Kwajalein in the Marshall Islands[68] until the end of the war, he relied heavily and successfully on intelligence from his cryptographers. Such use was always covered by plausible references to other intelligence; thus his approval of the successful attempt to kill Admiral Yamamoto once his route on an inspection trip had been decyphered.[a] Sadly the navy did not make good use of its intercept of a message from the Japanese submarine which in July 1945 torpedoed the heavy cruiser *Indianapolis*; as a result, hundreds of sailors who might have been saved drowned or were killed by sharks.[69]

If the American navy generally made wise use of communications intelligence, the army in the Pacific was less adept at it. This was due primarily, it would appear, to MacArthur's unwillingness to tolerate signals intelligence personnel not under his complete command and his reliance on an intelligence chief, General Charles Willoughby, who had accompanied him from Bataan but whose loyalty was not matched by his ability.[70] Japanese army codes were broken later than the navy's, from

---

[a] Roosevelt and Secretary of the Navy Frank Knox approved Nimitz's decision in the face of the possibility that the breaking of the Japanese naval code might be compromised. Kahn, *Codebreakers*, pp. 595–601; Lewin, *American Magic*, pp. 187–91.

the spring of 1943 and early 1944 (as a result of the capture of Japanese codebooks by the Australians), as compared with the spring of 1942.[71] Thereafter, the use of signals intelligence by MacArthur's headquarters was not as fruitful as the navy's, though the army air force appears to have been more consistent in its use. Certainly in the bitter fighting on Leyte in the Philippines, described in Chapter 16, the neglect of signals intelligence by MacArthur's headquarters was a serious error.[72]

In the final stages of the Pacific War, the intelligence gained by the Americans from reading Japanese codes played a major part.[73] By that time, the heavy bombardment of Japan forced the Japanese to utilize the radio not only for messages to ships at sea but for all manner of other messages of which many might otherwise have been sent by secure routes. The sending out of the super-battleship *Yamato*, for example, was thus revealed to the Americans. Similarly, as reviewed in Chapter 16, the Japanese plan "Damocles" for a suicide airborne landing attempt on the Marianas was precluded, after its details became known, by the last great massed raids in early August, 1945, on the bases from which it was to have been launched. And the atomic bombs would be dropped on Japan when intercepts revealed to the Americans that the Japanese government had considered but rejected the advice of some of its diplomats that she surrender. Rather than save these weapons for the support of the invasion of the home islands, the Americans used them in an effort to get the Japanese government to reconsider its decision to fight on.

Signals intelligence, which played so large a role in the Allied campaigns of the Pacific War, was also of great significance in the war against Germany and Italy. In that theater, the lead was taken by the British who first had their real practice on German and Italian machine cyphers in 1937 during the Spanish civil war.[74] The key steps toward the breaking of the German machine cyphers came from Polish pre-war intelligence, which was assisted by German cypher material sold to French intelligence and provided by the latter to Warsaw.[75] In England (and earlier in France), the rather unproductive effort was thereafter successfully pushed forward, frequently helped by the errors made by German operators—especially in the German air force—in the use of the different enigma machine cyphers.[76]

Very important materials assisting the British in the breaking of German codes were seized from German submarines and weather and supply ships; similarly breaks into Italian codes were facilitated by material taken from Italian submarines and captured in the North African desert war.[77] German diplomatic material provided to the OSS by Hans Bernd Gisevius and Fritz Kolbe, who belonged to the internal opposition to Hitler, was used to further work on codes in the fall of 1943;[78] by that time the British cryptographers had also broken into the German "secret writing machine" (the *Geheimschreiber*), a different encoding system from the enigma.[79] The impact of these cryptographic successes on the war is still being assessed because, as in the earlier American official accounts, all reference to "special intelligence" had been ordered omitted from the published volumes of the British official history.[80]

There can be no doubt that the Allies were greatly assisted by the ability to read at least some Axis codes, beginning in 1940.[81] Repeated reference to the use of information from what was called "ultra" is made throughout this book. By way of summary, the following may help clarify a difficult problem. During the campaign in the West in 1940, as during the German Balkan campaign in the spring of 1941, the British were simply not in a position to take advantage of what they learned.[82] On the other hand, both in the Battle of Britain and in the Battle of the Atlantic, ultra information was of great significance. In the former it aided the proper use of the Royal Air Force, in the latter it helped the steering of convoys around submarines and occasionally in the destruction of the latter. As explained in Chapter 7, the use of ultra played an enormous role in the war at sea until 1945 with ever greater advantage to the Allies from the end of 1942 on.

In the Mediterranean and North Africa, code-breaking was important in the naval war, including the Battle of Matapan on March 28, 1941,[83] the sinking of a high proportion of the Italian supply ships to Libya and later to Tunisia,[84] and also to Montgomery's campaign against Rommel from the fall of 1942 on. At first the Allied landings on Sicily, in Italy, and later in France were affected by the ability of the Axis to use secure land communication systems; but once battle was joined, the Axis used radio extensively and this opened up their messages to interception and decoding. Of the more spectacular examples, one could cite the Allied knowledge of the planned German offensive at Mortain in August, 1944. Considerable reexamination of many details of the operations in Italy and France and the Low Countries will still be needed before a final judgement can be made, but there can be no doubt that time and again ultra information played an important role in the deliberations of Allied commanders.

A further major advantage of ultra for the Western Allies was the information it provided them about the fighting on the Eastern Front. In view of the reluctance of the Soviet Union to share with its allies details about its own or the Germans' operations, the decrypting of German radio traffic was the most important single source the British and Americans had on that portion of the war. This is a subject which still awaits investigation in detail, but ultra at least provided the Western Allies with some idea of what was transpiring on the front where such a large part of the fighting was taking place.

From time to time ultra also provided clues to Axis subterfuges. Thus when in 1942 the Italians decided to conceal gasoline supplies for North Africa on hospital ships, the British learned of this ruse from decyphered messages and sank some of the ships.[85] Similarly, decodes of Japanese radio traffic uncovered their attempt in 1945 to use a hospital ship as a troop transport.[86]

Given the significance of signals intelligence to the Western Allies, it is not surprising that both Churchill and Roosevelt followed it carefully. Churchill had a positive fascination for the subject and constantly insisted on being supplied with it.[87] Roosevelt appears to have paid careful attention to it as well,[88] and was absolutely insistent on maintaining civilian control as well as army and navy involvement.[89]

It must always be remembered, however, that there were constant limitations on the usefulness of signals intelligence. The factor of delay has already been mentioned. The repeated changes in machine settings, the need to provide cover-stories, and the problem of selecting out of the vast quantities of intercepts those of most immediate relevance for decrypting imposed limits on even the most efficient operation at Bletchley Park, the main British center, and Arlington Hall, the American equivalent.[90] On the other hand, a long-term benefit of all the effort was the development of an entirely new computation device—the computer. There was a truly rapid evolution from the Polish Zygalski sheets and cyclometers to the huge British and American computers of 1944–45. Though using tubes where post-war models would utilize chips, the "Colossi" of World War II were indubitably the ancestors of the modern PC.

While all this was in progress, the Germans, like the Japanese, refused to believe that their wonderful machine codes could be broken. Each time they examined the possibility, each time there were hints, they preferred to retain faith in their inventions.[a] Repeated investigations by the navy, which was especially affected by the possibility of its messages to and from the submarines at sea being read, invariably concluded that German communications were secure. At the international conference on signals intelligence held in Germany in the fall of 1978, a number of participants who had played active roles in the events described still found it hard to believe that their machine codes had indeed been read at least in part by the Allies.[91] Those who are directly involved in the

---

[a] In August 1943 the Germans received information from Switzerland that the Allies had broken the German naval enigma but refused to believe it. Chapman, "Signals Intelligence in the Pacific," 146–47.

making of codes and of secure telephone scramblers and related devices are always the last to believe that others—who are by definition not as brilliant as they are—could possibly have found a way to break into their wonderful devices.[92]

A procedure often used in warfare in the past and increasingly tied to signals intelligence in World War II was that of deception, that is, deliberately misleading the enemy about one's intention in order to achieve or at least assist surprise and success at the actual point of attack. Certainly the successful deception operation of the Western Allies, in pursuading the Germans that the major landing was still to come in the Pas de Calais area, depended heavily not only on deceiving the Germans about real Allied strength and intentions but on the ability to monitor the success of this effort by reading German messages to their own headquarters and to the German agents, real and imagined, in England, who were in fact all under British control.[93] Whether or not the simultaneous Soviet success in deceiving the Germans about the planned location of their 1944 summer offensive also included reliance on reading German codes is not known.

Deception efforts in Europe not only accompanied ground operations but were often attempted in air raids, usually to disguise the actual objective of a bombing attack or the direction from which it was coming. These attempts frequently failed, as in the first big American raid on the Ploesti oil fields and refineries on August 1, 1943; at times they succeeded in diverting the defenders, as in the British raid on the German experimental station for missiles and pilotless planes at Peenemünde on August 17, 1943.[94] Perhaps the most serious Allied deception failure in Europe were operations "Starkey" and "Cockade," two hopelessly bungled efforts in 1943 to make the Germans believe that there would be an Allied invasion of Western Europe that year, in the hope of diverting German forces from the Eastern Front.[95] At times, even a successful deception could have reverse implications elsewhere. The total failure of the British attempt to seize islands in the Aegean in the fall of 1943 can be attributed in part to the stupidity of the Italians in the area, in part to the incompetence of the British command, and in part to the refusal of the Americans (for strategic reasons) to support the operation, but a contributing factor was the success of the Allied deception operation "Mincemeat," the ploy with "The Man Who Never Was," in diverting German reinforcements from Sicily to other locations, including the Aegean.[96]

In the Pacific portion of the war, deception was, of course, used at times by both sides. An example of how code-breaking can make a major difference in this regard can be seen in the success of the Americans in making the Japanese believe before the Battle of Midway that several of their carriers were elsewhere,[97] and the failure of the Japanese effort to fool the Americans by a diversionary operation against Alaska and the Aleutians. Whether or not the "Wedlock" operation, an American deception designed to make the Japanese reinforce the Kurile Islands in 1944 when their real target was the Marianas, succeeded is likely to remain contentious.[98]

CHEMICAL AND BIOLOGICAL WARFARE

One of the major weapons innovations of World War I, introduced by the Germans and imitated by the Allies, had been poison gas. The years between the wars had seen both efforts at international agreement to ban poison gas and continued production and experimentation with it. Aside from experimentation carried on in the Soviet Union with the approval of the latter, the Germans simply kept up with other powers in the 1920s and 1930s until major breakthroughs led to the development of nerve gases, beginning in 1936 and their production on an increasing scale during World War II.[99] Tested on prisoners of war and on concentration camp inmates, the nerve gases, Tabun, Sarin, and Somar, also claimed some victims as a result of accidents and errors in the production process but were never employed at the front.

The decision by Hitler not to use the nerve gases, which was made in or about May of 1943, was made on the basis of several considerations. The one which we now know to have been false was the belief that the Allies also had nerve gases.[100] Of great importance was the evident reality of great Allied air strength obviously capable of making good on the repeated public announcements that poison gas would be used in retaliation for any German use of it, either on the Eastern Front or anywhere else.[101] An equally significant restraint on the Germans was their lack of gas masks of any sort for much of the country's civilian population.[102]

The British built up substantial stocks of phosgene and mustard gas, both widely used in World War I. They had been willing to use this weapon in 1940 if the Germans succeeded in establishing a substantial beachhead in an invasion, a point discussed in Chapter 3. In 1944, Churchill would urge the use of gas either against the sites from which the V-1s and V-2s were about to be launched or elsewhere in retaliation for these new forms of indiscriminate bombardment, but contrary advice from his own military Chiefs of Staff and the objections of the Americans prevented any such employment of poison gas.[103]

The requests of the Soviet Union to its allies to threaten retaliation in kind to any German use of poison gas on the Eastern Front were presumably based on a real concern. The Soviet Union had, it would appear, made some preparations of its own in this field but evidently intended to use gas only in retaliation. The opening of Soviet archives may bring new information on the subject, especially since the major German facility for the production of nerve gas, IG Farben's plant at Dyhernfurth, fell into Soviet hands undamaged in 1945.

The United States built up a very large stock of the gases used in World War I for employment in case either the Germans or the Japanese turned to this weapon.[104] Although the possibility of the use of gas in combat was considered in the preliminary discussions of the invasion of Iwo Jima and the Japanese home islands in 1945, such projects were always vetoed by the President or dropped by the military on their own.[105] The shipment of chemical warfare shells to the theaters of war for use if retaliatory employment proved necessary led to the greatest loss of life in a gas accident during the war. A German air force bombing raid on ships in the harbor of Bari in Italy on December 2, 1943, led to the destruction of one ship (among seventeen) which carried 100 tons of mustard gas in bombs; over a thousand Allied personnel and Italian civilians being killed as a result.[106]

Far larger numbers had been killed both accidentally and intentionally by the Japanese, who had built up a large poison gas program beginning in the last months of World War I.[107] They repeatedly used gas for experiments and in the war against China. Perhaps because this employment was almost all carried out before Japan attacked the United States, Britain, and the Netherlands, the Western Powers chose not to retaliate in kind. This subject still awaits further investigation. The employment by the Japanese of a German-invented gas grenade in the Imphal campaign in the summer of 1944 was seen as an isolated, and quite possibly unauthorized, incident.[108] Improper safeguards and processes left hundreds of former workers in the Japanese gas factory at Okunoshima in damaged health.

If a considerable amount of information about chemical warfare projects remains obscure, in part because records are still closed, this is even more the case for biological warfare. Even the World War I attempts by the Germans to spread the cattle and horse disease anthrax in the United States and Canada have been covered by a veil of obfuscation.[109] Some work on biological warfare agents was done in the inter-war years in several countries and continued into the war years.[110]

There was a program during World War II for the development of biological weapons in Great Britain, which had been inaugurated by Neville Chamberlain in response to German threats of secret weapons and was pushed forward with Churchill's full support. With some material assistance from the United States, this project was able to produce a small amount of anthrax (under the code-name N) in 1943 and large amounts in 1944. The whole project was designed for deterrence and, if necessary, retaliation should the Germans resort to biological warfare. No quantities sufficient for use appear to have been made available during the war.[111] There was substantial American research on bacteriological warfare agents, again for any necessary retaliation. Soviet work in this field, whatever it may have been, awaits exploration.

By far the most extensive work in the field of biological warfare appears to have been done by the Japanese.[112] Established already in 1932 in Manchuria, the Japanese center for research and experimentation was employing thousands of workers in a massive installation operating under a 1936 formal Imperial order by the late 1930s. Huge quantities of poisonous bacteria were produced and tried out on human guinea pigs in tests which began in 1932, killed thousands, and were filmed for demonstrations to Japanese army officers. Delivering the biological warfare materials proved a major problem when the Japanese tried them out in their war with China and this use occasionally back-fired.

During the Pacific War, the experimentation was extended to American and British prisoners of war. Allied intelligence came to know about the Japanese program at least in outline from 1942 onward, although the British, unlike the Americans, discounted the evidence that was coming in. For obvious reasons, the Americans were especially concerned about the possible use of the Japanese balloon campaign as a carrier of bacteriological materials. The biological warfare agents were, however, not used against the Western Powers; in August 1945, the Japanese blew up the facilities, murdered the surviving prisoners, and tried hard to cover up the whole episode.[a]

ROCKETS AND MISSILES

A field of weaponry in which the Germans took the lead was that of rocketry and related technologies designed to deliver explosives over great distances if without much accuracy. Though held back during the 1930s and in the early stages of World War II by lack of investment first and low priority later, the theoretical advances made by engineers and enthusiastic amateurs would provide the basis for the prototypes of both the post-war long-range ballistic missiles and cruise missiles.[113] The development of these new types of weapons was aided by the patronage

---

[a] The Soviet Union tried some of those involved after the Red Army overran the ruined facility. The Americans did not try those Japanese who fell into their hands.

of the two Commanders-in-Chief of the pre-war German army, Generals von Fritsch and von Brauchitsch, but held back at first by the low priority assigned them in a war economy of limited resources. The original concept, the development of a liquid-fuel rocket which could be aimed with reasonable accuracy at a distant target, produced technological and design innovations but little in the way of impressive successes. The German anticipation that the war against the Western Powers would be hard but short also kept down resource allocation to weapons not expected to be available in the immediate future.

This constriction changed, though slowly, with two closely related developments. One was the obvious fact that the war was not ending as quickly as Hitler had anticipated, and the other was that a key role in this continuance of the war was obviously played by England which, with its huge capital city of London, offered the largest possible target for any devices which could cover a great distance. It was in this context that Hitler made a series of decisions which either confirmed projects already under way or pushed new ones forward to develop into functioning systems and then to employ, hopefully on a massive scale, four weapons which shared the same basic characteristics.

The four would all be fired or launched at London; they were all at least theoretically capable of covering the distance from German-occupied Europe to the British capital; they did not need to be particularly accurate, given the size of the target city and the aim of striking at British morale; and it was anticipated that all would be fired from fixed launching sites, an assumption which involved additional massive investment of resources, but which in practice turned out to be unnecessary for several of the weapons. The vast allocation of scarce skilled manpower, raw materials, forced labor, and scientific attention to these projects in the years 1942 to 1945 testifies to the importance attached to them by Hitler as well as others in the German hierarchy who urged their development and use. It also demonstrates the real attitude which the German government had toward England at a time when in the imagination of some post-war writers Hitler had only kindly thoughts about the English.

The four systems can most readily be described in the numbered sequence later ascribed to them, V-1 to V-4, although V-2 was actually the earliest one worked on. V-1 was an air force project rushed to completion to compete with the army's rocket, the A-4 which became the V-2. The idea of the V-1 was relatively simple: since the piloted bombers of the Luftwaffe were unable to penetrate the airspace over England effectively, a pilotless small plane powered by a pulse-jet engine would be launched by catapult from a ramp, steered at least minimally by a gyroscope, and land with its explosive contents in London when its fuel had been used up.

The massive effort which the German air force put into this project enabled it to overcome both the army's headstart with rockets and the technical problems caused by hasty development. Although set back by Allied bombing, which is discussed subsequently, the first V-1s were launched at London in the night of June 12–13, 1944, a week after the invasion of Normandy, months after the date originally hoped for – but almost three months before the German army's rocket.

The V-1 carried just under a ton of explosive, flew at a speed of about 375 mph, and caused massive damage primarily by the blast effect of an explosion which, because of the slanting trajectory of the descending missile, was closer to the surface than that of a traditional bomb. This ancestor of the cruise missile could also be launched from an airplane, and of the total of about 22,400 fired, some 1600 were sent on their way in this fashion.[114]

The repeated set-backs caused by technical troubles in development and by Allied air raids had delayed employment of the V-1 until after the Normandy landing. Beginning in mid-June 1944, the pilotless planes were sent to targets in England, primarily London, from German-occupied Europe in volleys and occasionally singly. Well over a third either did not work properly or were shot down, the latter either by fighter planes with higher speed or by anti-aircraft fire using proximity fuses, with both methods increasing their effectiveness over time. As the launching sites were overrun by Allied armies, more and more of the V-1s, eventually more than half of the total, were fired at targets in Belgium, primarily Antwerp. Though causing casualties and property damage and having an effect on the morale of people weary after five years of war, the V-1 was not the war winning weapon the German air force had hoped for. That was certainly also true of the ones with smaller warheads (to obtain longer range) fired at London from Germany in 1945.

The V-2 was a liquid fuel rocket, developed using the ideas of German inventors and the American **Robert H.** Goddard primarily in the 1930s, with the original intention of using it to deliver poison gas. The series began with a unit called A-1; it was the A-4 which came to be the production model. Carrying an explosive warhead of about a ton, the rocket was guided gyroscopically and by fins; its flight could also be minimally corrected by radio. In practice, the rocket had the great disadvantage of a very high rate of defective flights with many being rejected even before use, a fifth to a quarter coming down right after being fired, and over half of those making the full trip coming apart in their descent. The other side of this was first, that there was no way to shoot down a rocket which flew at over two thousand miles an hour; and second, even if it came apart just before impact, the warhead still landed and usually exploded.[115] As the Allied ground forces advanced, the V-2, like the V-1, was increasingly fired at targets in Belgium, with Antwerp, because of its great harbor, again the main target for half the 3200 V-2s launched. Over 15,000 people were killed and more than three times that many wounded.

Since neither the V-1 nor the V-2 could be aimed at targets other than very large cities, the only possible way for them to have had a major effect would have been a truly massive employment, which was far beyond German capabilities. In the case of the old smooth-bore musket in the eighteenth century, huge volleys fired in steady succession by rows of infantry alternately loading and firing had made up for that weapon's well-known lack of accuracy. For a country without the capacity to make up for the deficiencies of the V-1 and V-2, the enormous allocation of resources to these weapons may well have been unwise. As a German scholar has aptly noted, their employment came too soon rather than too late.[116]

The V-3, code-named "Hochdruckpumpe (HDP)" (High pressure pump), was a novel form of artillery in which a shell fired through a barrel about 150 yards long received additional push from explosions as it passed powder charges along the way, thus hopefully acquiring enough velocity to reach London from a firing position being excavated near Calais. The tests and development of this contraption—evidently inspired by the memory of German long-range artillery bombardment of Paris in World War I—were pushed at Hitler's insistence; he clearly preferred it to both the rocket and the cruise missile. The plan to shell London failed completely. It turned out that the shell could not be driven the needed distance. Not a single one of the fifty barrels to be aimed at the British capital had been completed and repaired after Allied bombing when the firing site was overrun. As a substitute, two guns with barrels a mere 50 yards long were aimed at Luxembourg in support of the German Ardennes offensive of December 1944 and fired 183 rounds carrying about twenty pounds of explosive each, a performance out of all proportion to the effort invested.[117]

The fourth weapon designed with the objective of terrorizing London was a four-stage rocket propelled by powder, rather than liquid fuel, code-named "Rheinbote" (Messenger from the Rhine), and developed under army auspices. Initiated before the V-3, this ballistic missile was to carry a warhead of about one hundred pounds a distance of 100 miles, just enough to reach London. Lagging behind the other projects, this multi-stage rocket was almost cancelled in April 1944. Continued work produced a small number; these were also fired in December 1944 and January 1945 at Antwerp, a key port and the goal of the German winter offensive. It turned out that while the city was about 100 miles away, the rocket overshot its aim by about 35 miles, so that not one of the fifty launched hit Antwerp. This was the precursor of the multi-stage solid-fuel ballistic missile of a later age; but its development and production during World War II was another waste of resources which merely serves to underline Hitler's determination to terrorize the British out of the war. A trial firing of the four-stage rocket had landed on a German farm; the explosion damaged the structures, killed all the chickens and a dog and injured two cows.[118]

The enthusiasm for attacks on large cities was not confined to Europe. The pre-war German development of a "New York" bomber, begun in 1937, had not produced a working airplane.[119] During the war, beginning in 1940, the Germans worked on a two-stage rocket version of the A-4, designated the A-9, which was to reach New York from Europe in 35 minutes. A different version was to be launched from a submarine in the Atlantic.[120] Work was also being carried forward on two jet-propelled bombers, the six-engine Junkers 287 and the Junkers 338 which were to operate over the United States from bases in Western Europe.[121] The issue of jet planes is discussed later in this chapter, that the Germans were working on inter-continental types was not clearly understood by the Allies until 1945.

They had, however, learned a considerable amount about the V-1, 2, and 3, before these appeared in combat. The Oslo report had provided some solid indications and had, in particular, called attention to the major German experiment and testing facility at Peenemünde on the Baltic. The British, however, disregarded this warning as they did further information provided them by the same source in August 1941.[122] In subsequent years more and more was learned from prisoner interrogations, air photo reconnaissance, and the interception of Japanese reports, the latter being provided by the Germans with details about V-1 but not V-2.[123] The British effort to piece together the details of what was coming and, drawn from that, what preparations to make, was hindered by the confusion resulting, as is now clear, from the fact that the Germans were working simultaneously on four very different systems; and by the insistence of Lord Cherwell, Churchill's scientific advisor, that the whole project was a bluff.[124] As evidence of German work accumulated, however, the British became convinced that there was a real danger and bombed the Peenemünde station on August 17–18, 1943. This raid, and damage due to other portions of the strategic bombing offensive against aircraft production facilities, set back both the V-1 and the V-2 projects for months and forced dispersal of the projects, some of them going literally underground, a process which entailed further substantial delay.[125]

The interception and decoding of German reports on test flights of the V-1 in late November 1943 gave a clear picture of the characteristics of that weapon, quickly confirmed by photo reconnaissance, and enabled the British to begin the planning of counter-measures.[126] Having been shocked by the unexpected appearance of the excellent German FW-190 fighter plane, the British watched the developing threat of new weapons with some apprehension, an attitude reinforced by the appearance of radio guided rocket missiles and radio controlled bombs in the Mediterranean in August and September, 1943. When first the V-1s and then the V-2s began to land in England, Churchill was sufficiently alarmed to order consideration of the use of poison gas on the Germans in retaliation but was dissuaded by his military advisors and the strong opposition of President Roosevelt.[127] The other measures already mentioned were increasingly effective against the V-1; V-3 and V-4 were never used against England, and there was no direct defense against V-2.

To defend themselves against the new weapons designed to wreck London and British morale, the Allies used two methods, one direct and the other essentially indirect. The direct process was a massive series of air attacks on the launching sites the Germans were building in France. Though damaging to the Germans, these proved futile, primarily because other launching procedures were developed and used without any effective interference. The indirect approach was the impact of the Allied strategic bombing offensive reviewed later in this chapter. It was not only that time and again Allied air raids, and not only the one on Peenemünde, had a drastic impact on German plants involved in the production of V weapons.[128] Even more important was the American success in the air war in early 1944 which pushed aside the German air force, made possible the wrecking of Germany's synthetic oil industry, and thereby made German pilot training for old and new types of planes hopelessly inadequate. This not only reduced the activity of German planes which were supposed to launch many of the V-1s,[129] it also helped win the race for time between the Germans who hoped for additional years of war to perfect their new weapons, and the Allies who wanted a quick and victorious end to hostilities.

The Western Allies were developing new weapons of their own but concentrated most of their industrial and technological capacity on the large-scale production and marginal but steady improvement of the basic weapons systems at hand or developed in the early stages of the war. The Americans worked on a variety of missiles of which the partially guided bomb called "Azon" was the only one extensively used in combat, primarily in the destruction of bridges in Burma.[130] The British were manufacturing ever larger conventional bombs for their strategic bombing offensive. But the basic emphasis of Britain and the United States was, as will be shown presently, on an entirely different type of new weapon. In the field of rocketry, most of their resources went into such tactical uses of rockets as assisting the take-off of planes which were heavily loaded or on carriers, short-range rockets as a form of mass artillery fire to assist amphibious landings, and rocket missiles launched from under the wings of airplanes against tanks, trucks, and other visible targets.

The Soviet Union had long done some experimenting with rocketry, but its main use of rockets in the war was, like that of its Western Allies, in the tactical sphere. The katyusha, a rocket battery fired electrically either from the ground or from a truckbed, proved of real importance on the Eastern Front. Referred to as the "Stalin-Orgel" or Stalin organ by the Germans, its large-scale employment practically through the whole fighting on the Eastern Front made it one of the major effective innovations of the war.

JET AIRPLANES AND RADAR

The development of jet planes has been referred to both in connection with the V-1 which was powered by a pulse-jet, and the German plans for an inter-continental jet plane for bombing the United States. This was a field in which the Germans had begun some work before the war with the world's first pure jet, a Heinkel 178, being flown in August 1939. Other experimental models were developed, but the two which became operational were the Messerschmitt 262 and the Arado 234. The former was a two-engine jet fighter which first flew in July 1943. The dispersion of the German aircraft industry decided on as a response to the Allied strategic bombing offensive delayed the operational deployment of the Me-262 until the late spring of 1944; by that time the American victory over the German air force meant that the jets sent into combat were unable to cope with the vast numbers of Allied planes even if they were not destroyed on the ground. The whole Me-262 program proved largely useless as the fuel supplies were destroyed and the pilots could not be properly trained. There is considerable argument over Hitler's decision to have the Me-262 adapted for bomber employment, but it is not evident that this made much difference at a time when the Germans had irrevocably lost control of the air.[131]

The Arado 234 was a two-jet-engine light bomber, also used for reconnaissance, which came into service in 1944. The forced evacuation of the factory, again due to Allied bombing, delayed any substantial production until the fall of 1944. Employed for reconnaissance flights over England at a time when its high speed of up to 500 mph made it the only plane the Germans could still send on such missions, this model showed what could be done with jet planes some day.[132] Ironically production of the Arado 234 was stopped early in 1945 when only 200 had been delivered. Its production had been delayed by evacuation forced by the bombing of the Western Allies; it was terminated by the Red Army's overrunning the new factory which had been shifted to the supposedly safer eastern area.

The British had begun the development of their own jets in the early war years but had not pushed the program very hard. The earliest operational model, the "Meteor" fighter, was in action a few days after the first German ones, but it played no significant role in the war. Ironically its most useful role was in the shooting down of V-1s.[133]

Certainly one scientific development which affected World War II in a major way was that of radar. The concept of locating and tracking or determining the contours of something by bouncing radio waves off it originated before the war, with scientists in both England and Germany making some advances — the latter probably more than the former. It was, however, the growing fear of German air raids which induced the British to establish a special committee under Sir Henry Tizard to develop and install a radar system consisting of a chain of stations which, using a device developed by Robert Watson-Watt, provided by 1940 a critical factor in the proper employment of Royal Air Force fighters to ward off German assaults. It was this initial success of enormous importance, recognized as such by all in the know, which spurred the British on to further advances in this field. In the following years, they developed increasingly effective radar devices to locate ships as well as planes, a process which showed its utility in the location and sinking of German submarines in the Atlantic and the battleship *Scharnhorst* off the Norwegian coast.[134]

In the air war, the British also developed a series of electronic devices to assist their bombers in finding targets in Germany and in "seeing" through cloud cover at the target areas below. None of these devices proved perfect, but they did enable the strategic bombing offensive at least to find the cities which were supposed to be bombed.[135]

The Germans had an initial advantage on the offensive rather than the defensive side of radio warfare. They used two crossing radio beams to indicate targets to their bomber force over England. It was in the recognition of this system and its effective neutralization by "bending" the beams that R.V. Jones came to play a key role in British electronic warfare and that Churchill came to have a high respect for ultra, the information from German enigma messages, which had made the unravelling of this puzzle possible.[136] In the years 1943–45 the Germans devoted ever greater efforts to a variety of radar systems for locating Allied bombers and steering their fighters, and also for detecting the radar emissions of others. In this process they made a series of major advances but on the whole remained behind the Allies. The Americans increasingly worked out their own radar systems, while the Japanese were not able to catch up with their enemies in the Pacific.

Certainly the role of radar in the war was very great, not only in the Battle of Britain and the air war over Germany but in the war at sea. The electronic advances of the Allies, especially the introduction of Huff/Duff described in Chapter 7, were essential to their victory in the Battle of the Atlantic. Here was also one wartime area of rapid scientific change which would affect not only the nature of future warfare but in addition had major civilian application. The flight of civil aviation and the sailing of ocean-going ships today would be practically inconceivable without the electronic locator devices which were originally developed for military purposes.

NUCLEAR WEAPONS

If radar and related electronic devices provided major boons to post-war travel as well as dramatic changes in the nature of warfare, another scientific development of the war years was to leave a very mixed and dubious legacy: the appearance of atomic weapons. In the first decades of the twentieth century, physicists and chemists had begun to unravel the inside of the atom, once thought to be a stable unit in the construction of matter in the universe, and had discovered instead that it was made up of a variety of electrons, neutrons, and other particles. In the process of radioactivity some of these particles broke apart, and it was discovered that this breaking process could be artificially stimulated by bombarding atoms in devices which were the fore-runners of accelerators and cyclotrons. In 1938, the German chemist Otto Hahn discovered that when uranium was bombarded by neutrons, instead of absorbing them, it split into two different elements each about half the atomic weight of uranium and in the process both creating energy and releasing neutrons which might in turn split other uranium atoms as they were hit, thus potentially creating a chain reaction in which enormous quantities of power would be released in a massive explosion of unprecedented dimensions. If the process were unchecked, it offered the potential of incredible destructiveness; if it were controlled and slowed, it equally promised almost unlimited power which could be used in the form of electricity.

Otto Hahn and another German scientist, the physicist Werner Heisenberg, continued work on this process, trying to determine which material best lent itself to the fission process in a manner that made that process self-sustaining, how much of this material would be needed to make a bomb, and how the process of fission could be slowed down in the manufacturing process to keep it from destroying itself. The answer to the first of these three puzzles had been discovered just before the beginning of World War II by the Danish scientist Niels Bohr; the Germans were never to find the correct answers to the other two. The most suitable material was an isotope, or variant, of uranium 236 known because of its atomic structure as uranium 235. Because there were only minute quantities of U-235 in uranium as found in nature, there was the problem of how to separate it from the rest, a question that made it all the more important to determine how much of this extremely rare material would have to be assembled to make a single explosive device. The Germans miscalculated by a great margin, and the resulting belief that huge quantities would be needed put a damper on all subsequent German efforts to create an atomic bomb.[137] Since the Germans expected to win the war quickly, the idea of a weapon which could only be made ready in several years of arduous effort had little appeal.

This disregard of the potential of atomic weapons was reinforced by two further grave miscalculations. The first of these involved the material needed to slow down the fission process. The Germans correctly recognized that an isotope of water, usually referred to as heavy water, was excellent for this purpose and were happy over their good fortune in capturing the only large factory in the world capable of manufacturing substantial quantities of it when they occupied Norway in April 1940. The "Norsk Hydro" plant became the focus not only of German researchers but also of British and Norwegian saboteurs and bombers. A series of commando raids and air raids in February, July, and November 1943 effectively disrupted the main German source of heavy water at a time when huge American facilities were already being erected.[138] Not only had the German scientists in their fixation on heavy water missed the potential major role of graphite in slowing the fission process, but they had dramatically underrated the ability of the Western Allies.

When the last German chargé and his military attaché in the United States returned to Germany in 1942, they were received by Hitler in late May and treated to a lengthy monolog on the lack of any real war industry in the United States and the absence of engineers and weapons specialists.[139] Such views were not confined to Hitler by any means; they were widely shared among German scientists and intellectuals in general. When in August of 1945 German scientists heard of the dropping of an atomic bomb, they at first refused to believe that the Americans and British could possibly have succeeded where they had failed.

In view of these psychological circumstances as well as the pressing demands of other projects, and the belief that the secret V weapons could be deployed much more promptly, the Germans continued research on the possibility of making atomic weapons but on a small scale. By the summer of 1942 the critical resource allocation decisions had been made; there would be no German atomic bomb.[140] In the summer of 1943 the British were convinced of this, and by the summer of 1944 the Americans had come to the same conclusion, a view reinforced by the special "Alsos" mission, whose task it was to check on German atomic bomb progress.[141]

The British concerns about possible development of atomic weapons had been calmed in the first months of World War II because of scientific advice that many more years of research would be needed before any such weapons became practical.[142] In one of those developments that no one would believe if included in a work of fiction, two scientists who were refugees from Nazi Germany, and who as enemy aliens could not obtain security clearances and hence were only allowed to work on such unimportant matters as atomic physics, Otto Frisch and Rudolf Peierls, in April 1940 worked out how a U-235 bomb could be made out of a tiny fraction of the quantity originally believed necessary. This moved atomic weapons from a far distant future to a prospect a few years off. At Sir Henry Tizard's recommendation, the British government now established the so-called Maud Commission, which urged a British program the following year.[143] For a while British scientists were probably far ahead of all others in the scientific work on nuclear weapons, but their government's refusal to share with the United States when this was suggested to them by the latter in 1941 meant that they soon fell behind the Americans.

Like the British, the Americans had been moved to investigate the possibility of nuclear weapons initially primarily out of fear that the Germans were working on them and were likely to have such a weapon before anyone else, and with dire consequences indeed. Roosevelt had been personally alerted to this possibility; an added urgency came with the Japanese attack and the German and Italian declarations of war in December 1941. A scientific advisor, Vannevar Bush, reported to Roosevelt on March 9, 1942, on the progress to date. He argued that with a major industrial effort a weapon might be completed in 1944 and that a decision on whether to make such a commitment would have to be made soon. After further encouraging news, Roosevelt decided on June 17, 1942, that the United States would go forward with a major atomic program.[144]

As Mark Walker, the major scholar to work on the German atomic bomb project, has wisely pointed out in his discussion of the first official American report on the atomic bomb project, the basic difference between the British and American projects on the one hand and the German on the other, other than the major errors of the German scientists, was their different perception of the war. The Germans expected to win the war quickly and saw nuclear power as a post-war matter, whereas both the Americans and the British saw victory a long way off and hence were interested in the possibility of a weapon in time for use during the conflict.[145] The American project was entrusted to the army which, using at first a headquarters in Manhattan, called the secret project by that name thereafter.[146]

Two issues concerning the development of the atomic bomb in the United States after Roosevelt's decision of June 17, 1942, need a brief discussion. There was first the practical matter of actually going forward with the project. On the major issue of how to acquire sufficient U-235 to make a bomb, the government secretly took what looked like the most reasonable way, namely, it started massive work on all three likely possibilities simultaneously. In addition, the government built a fourth plant to manufacture plutonium, a new type of material correctly believed likely to be usable in atomic bombs. To build the necessarily huge secret laboratories and facilities for all this, vast lands were bought at Oak Ridge, Tennessee, Los Alamos, New Mexico, and Hanford, Washington. Under the direction of General Leslie R. Groves, the massive program went forward in the fall of 1942;[147] the original prediction that the first atomic devices would be ready in 1944 was only half a year off. By late 1944, the American government, or rather the tiny number in it privy to the secret, was assured that enough fissionable material would be available for several bombs in the summer of 1945.

The second issue was that of relations on this subject with America's British and Russian allies. By a coincidence, Churchill was in the United States and talked with Roosevelt about atomic weapons at Hyde Park three days after the President's June 17, 1942, decision. In that conversation—of which no real record survives—the two appear to have agreed to cooperate on atomic matters. That cooperation was, however, limited as the Americans became increasingly skeptical about British security to outsiders and reticence with the Americans. At the end of 1942 Roosevelt approved a policy of limiting the sharing of secrets, a policy Churchill protested at the Casablanca Conference in January 1943, asking Harry Hopkins to resolve this difference.[148]

The Americans relaxed their restrictions somewhat in view of Britain's contribution to the whole enterprise, but even a new agreement arrived at by Churchill and Roosevelt at Quebec on August 19, 1943, did not remove all differences. A coordinating committee in Washington helped, a great deal of information was provided to the British, and the agreement to use in combat any atomic weapons only after consultation was fully adhered to, but some friction remained.[149]

A major aspect of Roosevelt's reticence had been the preference for the United States rather than others to profit from any potential post-war benefits which might be derived from the great investment being made in the nuclear field by the American taxpayer, some two billion dollars by 1945, a sum incomparably greater in those years than later. Of equal if not greater importance, however, were American doubts about British security. These doubts concerned not leaks to the Axis powers but to Soviet espionage which the administration correctly believed was operating in both Great Britain and the United States.[150]

Roosevelt consistently opposed any sharing of nuclear information with the Soviet Union, seeing no prospect of Soviet knowledge of the subject being of use during the war and being vastly more suspicious of and concerned about Soviet intentions after the war than some post-war critics have imagined. While the second group of revisionist historians, those blaming Roosevelt for his alleged anti-Soviet attitude, as opposed to the first ones who criticized his supposed pro-Soviet views, have decried the President's unwillingness to share American atomic secrets with the Soviet Union, the origins of his policy are not hard to find.[151] There was no sign either of Soviet willingness to exchange important secret information about any subject whatever with the Western Allies, nor of any prospect that there would be wartime cooperation in weapons development, atomic or conventional. There were, however, lots of signs that Soviet espionage networks were continuing their activity in the United States, and presumably also in Britain, that these were trying to penetrate work being done in the atomic field, and that all this was likely to be exclusively of post-war application.

In his famous speech to the American Youth Congress in February 1940, denouncing the Soviet invasion of Finland, Roosevelt had described the Soviet Union as "run by a dictatorship as absolute as any other dictatorship in the world."[152] The pro-Soviet audience had booed him, but nothing suggests that Roosevelt ever changed his mind on the subject. He recognized the enormous contribution which the Soviet Union was making in the war against Germany, and with his broad knowledge of the war appreciated this fact more than many Americans then or later; and he very much hoped that wartime cooperation might continue into the post-war era. Like Churchill, however, he saw no reason to take the Soviets into American confidence about a weapons system of potentially great significance in the post-war years, especially since he expected that the United States would dismantle most of the conventional forces it had built up during the war at the conclusion of hostilities as it had done after World War I, and in fact proceeded to do after World War II.

Roosevelt did live to learn that the Germans had dropped out of the race to build atomic weapons, but this in no way caused him to order the vast secret American effort to be relaxed. The available evidence supports the conclusion that he had expected any bombs built in time for use against Germany to be dropped on that country and any not ready in time to be dropped on Japan, in both cases in the hope of bringing a long war to a quick end.

Harry Truman was briefed on both the atomic bomb project and on Soviet espionage efforts at penetration of it as soon as he became President on Roosevelt's death. He adhered to the outlines of his predecessor's policies, becoming, if anything, less willing to share information with America's allies. The accidents of chronology resulted in his presiding over the completion of the first nuclear weapons, [153] so that the decision on their first use had to be made by him. That issue is discussed in Chapter 16; nothing suggests that Roosevelt, had he lived, would have decided differently.

The early stages of the Soviet nuclear program remain shrouded in secrecy, but these may yet become better known as new policies in the former Soviet Union bring new materials to light. Soviet physicists were as well informed on scientific developments in the nuclear field in the pre-war years as any other, but the pressures of the German invasion required that priority be given to the immediate defense needs of the country. A major program was, however, launched in 1942 and continued for the rest of the war. In this endeavor, the Soviets were aided by their espionage efforts in Britain and the United States. A reasonably clear and objective assessment of these matters remains to be written, but it would appear that the major contributions of outsiders were more on the scientific side from British individuals and more on the engineering side from Americans acting as Soviet spies.[154] How these activities, publicly most associated with the names of Klaus Fuchs on the British and Ethel and Julius Rosenberg on the American side, fit into the development of Soviet nuclear weapons in the wartime and post-war era remains to be explained.

The other belligerent apparently most involved in an effort to build nuclear weapons was Japan. While physicists in German-occupied France appear to have continued their essentially theoretical and experimental work during the war, thereby helping prepare the way for the post-war development of nuclear weapons by that country, it was in Japan that several separate attempts were made to turn the discoveries of the 1930s into weapons. Laboratories working for the army and navy were active in this field, but it was outside the practical realm of industrial capacity to devote to the project the resources required for any major production facility.

The handful of people involved in work on a uranium bomb solved some of the theoretical and a few of the laboratory problems. They, therefore, were among the few in Japan who immediately understood what had happened at Hiroshima, but they had thought it impossible for anyone else to have completed the development of nuclear weapons in so short a time.[155] The Japanese would greatly have liked to make nuclear weapons but could not; they simply did not have the resources. The Japanese military attaché in Stockholm prepared a lengthy report on the atomic bomb on December 9, 1944. He was understandably not very accurate on the details of German, British, or American work on it, but few would quarrel with his stress on the bomb as the "most important technical advance in the present war."[156]

STRATEGIC BOMBING

If the atomic bomb was indeed the most important new technical development in World War II, that development was in practice employed within the context of strategic bombing, with that term used as meaning a strike at the enemy's capacity and willingness to continue in the conflict. Nuclear weapons were considered a likely means of support for the landing in Kyushu planned for November 1, 1945; and if Japan had not surrendered after the dropping of the second atomic bomb, the bombs becoming available thereafter would almost certainly have been utilized in such a fashion. But Japan did surrender; the tactical support potential of such weapons was not tested in combat; and no atomic weapons have been used in warfare since 1945.

The actual use of the atomic bombs thus became the last step in a process that was debated in the pre-war years and at times during the war. Should the air forces of belligerents be employed not only in direct support of other military operations or might they fulfill an independent role? There had been theorists in the years after World War I who argued that the new factor introduced into warfare by adding air power to the prior two forms of fighting, that on land and at sea, opened up the possibility of effectively by-passing the fronts of war to strike into the enemy's home territory, a perspective which appeared especially attractive in the wake of the stalemated trench warfare of 1914–18. Bombing, it was argued, might destroy either the *capacity* of the enemy to continue fighting by wrecking the industrial facilities essential for the conduct of war, or the *will* to continue fighting by destroying the morale of the home front, which was equally necessary for the maintenance of a war effort, or to do both simultaneously.

The Germans had attempted to reach such a goal in World War I by bombing English cities, using dirigible airships called zeppelins and also long-range airplanes. The novelty of this approach may well have inspired some of the post-war theorists, but the actual effect of the attempt was not substantial. There was, of course, damage, and there were casualties, especially in London, but the main impact of these operations was to increase hatred of Germany in England for the introduction of this new type of warfare against urban areas far from the front. The raids also inspired the British to build long-range planes of their own capable of reaching Berlin and dropping bombs on that city. The war ended before these new planes could be employed, but the concept which the Germans had introduced into warfare remained.

The inter-war theorists who advocated an independent role for bombers, the Italian Giulio Douhet, the Briton Lord Trenchard, and the American Billy Mitchell, all believed that it would be possible to make direct, major, and independent air attacks upon the enemy which would be likely to force that enemy to make peace. It was assumed that this could be done by long-range bombers striking deep into enemy territory and bombing industrial facilities as well as urban areas. In practice, these theorists had an influence on the development of air power in several ways. It became ever more obvious that airplanes would have to have more than one engine, most likely four, to carry substantial bomb loads the required distance, and that larger numbers of them than originally anticipated would be needed. The discussion also produced widespread public fear of bombing as a likely eventuality in any war which might come. There were, however, several issues which the advocates of the new concept overlooked in all countries and one which was ignored in most. Overlooked everywhere were two inter-related problems of bombing: the plane would have to fly at a great height to avoid being shot down but could not drop its bombs accurately from any substantial height. The idea of the dive-bomber, devised to cope with this difficulty, could not be used for any but the most limited, even if important, targets because such planes could not carry heavy bomb loads. The other problems were those of long-distance navigation and the identification of targets through cloud cover or at night. None of these puzzles was satisfactorily solved by any of the belligerents until the last stages of the war. The issue ignored by most was that of defense against fighter planes, which might be sent up to shoot down the bombers. The Americans eventually did develop a bomber, the B-17, which carried the name of "Flying Fortress" because it was designed to carry such heavy defensive armament that a group flying in close formation could supposedly defend itself against attacking fighter planes. In practice, this approach would not work as well as had been hoped, but it did provide more protection than most World War II bombers could employ.

In actual fighting, Axis bombing beyond immediate ground support quickly became simply the dropping of bombs on cities, maybe hitting industrial targets but more commonly hitting residential areas. Italian bombing of Barcelona in the Spanish civil war, the German destruction of Guernica in that conflict, and Japanese bombing of Chinese cities largely followed this pattern. The German bombing of Polish cities, especially of Warsaw, was in reality at random, whatever the claims sometimes made. The surrender of Warsaw was brought about by doing in practice what in March of 1939 the Germans had threatened to do to Prague—a ruthless and indiscriminate bomb attack on the civilian population.[157] The destruction of central Rotterdam by the German air force in May, 1940, was deliberately intended to accomplish the same purpose. In 1941 the Germans initiated their war with Yugoslavia with a Sunday terror raid on its capital. There is no evidence that the German raids on Paris were ever of a size to make a major impact. French pilots were busy at lunch on June 3, 1940, while some of the attackers were shot down by British fighters,[158] but the main contribution of the German air force to the defeat of France had been in its tactical support operations. Whatever the nature of May and June 1940 air raids on France and England, the invasion of the Low Countries and the air attacks which accompanied those actions led the British government to drop the restrictions earlier placed on their bombers, a point discussed in detail in Chapter 3. The bombing of London, first in daylight and then at night, was met by small raids by British planes on Berlin and other German cities.

Both because they badly miscalculated the nature and productivity of the British, American, and Soviet airplane industry, and because of the drain of fighting on several fronts, the German air force, which had entered the war in 1939 as the strongest on earth, was pushed into the defensive by the Allies.[159] Although the Royal Air Force learned the hard way, perhaps one should say the very hard way, to provide tactical air support for the Allied ground forces fighting in North Africa, the only *offensive* role it could play was to bomb Germany and parts of German-controlled Europe.[160] This was not only the sole way for the British to strike directly at the Germans, it was also the one major way in which Britain and for a long time the United States could directly assist the Soviet Union after Germany attacked that country in June 1941.

As explained in Chapters 3 and 4, the British tried to direct a major portion of their bombing effort at German industry, especially the crucial oil industry. In the process they made a discovery which some realistic exercises would have revealed to them years before: bombers flying at night, to reduce vulnerability to fighters, and at high elevations, to reduce vulnerability to anti-aircraft fire, were unlikely to hit almost any target, even on a clear night, to say nothing of cloudy ones. The choice, fairly obvious by early 1942, was either to abandon most bombing altogether or to make German cities, which were large enough to hit, the targets. In this situation, the London government opted for the latter alternative. They entrusted this project to a newly appointed chief of Bomber Command, Air Chief Marshal Sir Arthur Harris.

An energetic and driving officer, Harris had been in the Air Staff.[161] He knew that there were serious questions about the efficiency of the RAF's Bomber Command operations, and he was determined to change the situation. He knew that in this he had the full, energetic and enthusiastic backing of Churchill. He proceeded to demonstrate the capacity of Bomber Command to locate and destroy urban areas, beginning with the Baltic port of Lübeck. He never made any pretence about his project to "de-house" the Germans; the latter were by this time calling their own raids over England, which were aimed especially at the most famous tourist sites, their "Baedeker raids" after the best known guide books of the time.[162]

The slow but steady escalation in the size of the British bomber force, eventually joined by American flights, brought more and more damage to German cities, in part because the German leadership did not shift its construction priorities to fighter aircraft, still emphasizing the attack in both East and West until the Hamburg raids of July 1943.[163] The shift to emphasis on fighters, and the transfer of additional fighters from the Eastern Front, led to the October 1943 suspension of daylight raids on Germany.[164] By that time, however, the raids themselves had forced the Germans to disperse their aircraft factories, a process that cost them months of production and was, until the oil and transportation raids of 1944, itself the most important blow at German war industry.

The vast attacks on Berlin in the winter of 1943–44 threw the whole issue into relief.[165] Harris was convinced that these area attacks could win the war and received Churchill's support for them, although the Allied "Pointblank" bombing directive had posited the aircraft industry, not urban areas, as the priority target.[166] The attacks on Berlin raised not only the question of whether or not the effort was successful—it most obviously did not cost Germany the war as Harris anticipated— but whether the whole concept of area bombing was correct.

Some British church leaders in public and a few political leaders in private raised the question of the morality of aiming such vast military effort at civilians. Harris wanted the British government to tell the truth, that this was in reality what was being done and why, but the government preferred to prevaricate.[167] It was a distortion which would come back to haunt them (and after the war many surviving fliers) and would be the excuse for not extending to Bomber Command the recognition after the war which had been so generously lavished on it during hostilities.

Even as the bombing went forward, several other aspects became increasingly important. The Germans steadily increased the anti-aircraft batteries on which they depended very heavily for defense. At their maximum in August 1944 there were 39,000 of them, served by over one million men.[168] The Allied commitment of men, materials and other resources was obviously enormous as well. The attempt of the Americans to concentrate on industrial targets did not always work well in 1943, but at other times it did. Thus the August 17, 1943, attack on Regensburg severely damaged the German ME-262 jet plane construction facility.[169] The Soviet Union certainly was greatly encouraged by the bomber offensive; as Stalin explained to the British Ambassador to Moscow on October 21, 1943, he would very much want to take part if the conditions at the front allowed it.[170]

The return of massive bombing in daylight and deep into Germany after the victory of the new Allied long-range fighters over the Luftwaffe in February–March 1944 altered the whole picture. Thereafter the strategic bombers first aided the invasion by destroying German communications, starting with France and Belgium and later moving on to German transportation targets. Both of these efforts were highly successful. The second major truly effective bombing campaign of 1944 was that of the Americans against the German petroleum industry. The problem was that Harris was always against what he called "panacea targets," and refused to shift from area bombing even at a time when the technological deficiencies which had originally led to its adoption had been very substantially ameliorated.

An indication of the way some in the RAF were thinking is the August 2, 1944, planning document "Operation Thunderclap: The Attack on German Civilian Morale," which called for a concentrated effort to destroy central Berlin the way the Germans had in 1940 destroyed the center of Rotterdam. The intent was to destroy morale, force peace, and leave behind in the form of ruins and memory a post-war sense of the "consequences of universal aggression" among the Germans.[171] There can be little doubt that, although the details of this plan were not implemented, the concept was applied, and in many ways applied successfully.

The Allied sense of how the bombing was affecting Germany was very substantially assisted by their deciphering of radio messages. At first this was due to a great extent to their reading of Japanese reports, and on the conversations of Japanese diplomats with German officials about the impact of the bombing campaign.[172] Information from the reading of German coded messages did not become important until later in the war but then turned to a flood.[173] The strategic bombing itself so disrupted the transportation and communications systems first in Germany and then in Japan during the last half year of hostilities that messages which would normally have been sent by cable or wire, by courier or mail, simply had to be sent by radio. This meant that they could be intercepted and often read, and in this fashion strategic bombing as a by-product elicited information on its own effectiveness as well as many other subjects.

The reference to the impact of strategic bombing on Japan in the last months of the war moves the focus to the Pacific theater. There the major role was played by the Americans with a small effort based on China, followed, after the seizure of the Marianas in the summer of 1944, by increasing raids from bases there. In the last months of the war Allied naval air joined in the bombardment of targets in the Japanese home islands.

The major stages in this process, as well as the final portion involving atomic bombs, are discussed in Chapter 16. The point which needs to be made here is that after months of strategic bombing aimed at specific industrial targets, the Americans concluded that at such extreme range and with the violent jet stream over Japan, accuracy was impossible. Knowledge about and understanding of the jet stream over the globe, carefully analyzed by the Japanese in connection with their project of sending balloons to the United States and Canada, was as yet quite rudimentary in American circles; in particular, they had no understanding beforehand of the interaction between the jet stream and the very high altitudes at which the new B-29 bombers were designed to fly. Under these circumstances, the Americans in February–March 1945 in the war against Japan made essentially the same decision the British had made three years earlier in Europe: rather than abandon bombing of distant targets altogether, they shifted to area bombardment of cities, burning them down one by one, beginning with Tokyo.

What did it all mean? On the one hand, the extraordinarily extreme predictions of the advocates of strategic bombing turned out to be erroneous. The massive reports of the United States Strategic Bombing Survey and the British official history of strategic bombing tend, on the whole, to underplay rather than to stress the impact of the strategic bombing offensives in Europe, although the American one assigns greater significance to its role in weakening the Japanese economy.[174] The study of the influence of intelligence on the war from the British perspective stresses, correctly in my opinion, that a major role of the strategic bombing was its aid to the Allies in the race against any renewed turn of the war in Germany's favor with new weapons after 1943, because of the great delays it imposed on their development and production.[175] The morale effects were not those anticipated: the constant bombing eventually produced apathy and dependence, rather than revolt, but it certainly left behind a sense of the impact of war that Germany had not had after 1918. On the other hand, it must also be noted that in the Western countries overrun by the Germans in 1940, seeing the overflight of British bombers headed for Germany showed the people that the war was by no means over and that liberation, however distant, was at least a possibility.

The debate over the role of Air Chief Marshal Sir Arthur Harris is likely to continue.[176] The critical point appears to me to be that the British had no alternative in 1942 but to adopt the procedure that Harris pushed vigorously for the rest of the war, even though by the spring of 1944 other alternatives were available, in part as a result of his efforts. The conclusion of a very careful analysis of the collapse of the German war economy with special emphasis on the truly decisive impact of bombing on the German transportation system is surely correct:

> Looked at from the military perspective, it may be contended that strategic bombing can make a significant contribution to victory in war. But it is not a substitute for a balanced strategy encompassing every component of a nation's military power. It is peculiarly reliant on accurate intelligence, sensibly interpreted. Above all, strategic bombing is not a cheap, easy or quick avenue to

success. It involves a major investment of national resources to build a force powerful enough to be effective. To be successful, strategic bombing requires simultaneous and repeated strikes against a small number of indispensable sectors of the enemy economy after air superiority has been won.[177]

PSYCHOLOGICAL WARFARE

World War II was fought not only with weapons but also with words. In the negative sense, all belligerents imposed some form of censorship both to prevent information of possible help to the enemy from becoming known and to help maintain a solid public opinion on the home front. In the process, the states which already had authoritarian regimes of one sort or another tightened their control of all means of communication; the democracies created new ministries or other institutional structures for that purpose. The measures adopted were, however, aimed not only at a consolidation of the home front and military cohesion by censorship; there was also the positive side, the attempt to provide reasons for the war and confidence in victory by newsreels—then the main visual format for the dissemination of images—by special feature films, and by news releases, posters, radio programs, and other mass media approaches.[178]

In addition, these and other devices were directed at neutrals to induce a favorable attitude toward one side and, even more important, at the enemy to frighten, weaken, divide, or in other ways assist the war effort of one side. German propaganda and psychological warfare had been developed before the war. During hostilities, it came to be distinguished by famous propaganda films like "Sieg im Westen," (Victory in the West), which were especially designed to overawe Europe's neutrals and to show the rest of the world the might of the Third Reich. A massive campaign had been launched in 1940 to try to prevent the reelection of President Roosevelt, and there was even a smaller renewal of this in 1944.[179] In between, the Germans had tried with equally little success to make much of the declarations of war on the United States by Bulgaria, Hungary, Romania, and the puppet states of Croatia and Slovakia.[180]

From time to time, the Germans utilized defectors from the other side to try to score points among their enemies. Thus, in June, 1940, former German Communist leader Ernst Torgler broadcast for them on their French radio program.[181] William Joyce broadcast frequently to England, where the main reaction of the humorously skeptical audience was to refer to him as "Lord Haw-Haw" in reference to his accent.[182] The German efforts to appeal to Red Army soldiers by utilizing defectors, especially in the elaborate "Silberstreif" (Silverlining) operation of 1943, were likewise unsuccessful. Many Red Army men were captured or deserted, but nothing suggests that propaganda played any significant role. In the latter years of the war, German propaganda themes concentrated on the Communist danger and the likely unfaithfulness of the Allied soldiers' wives and sweethearts at home; neither appeal had much impact. The Germans developed a massive organization of special propaganda companies which recorded action at the front for German newsreels and took thousands of pictures which today provide interesting material for historians.

Italian psychological warfare was aimed at undermining Britain's position in the Middle East. Given Italy's own colonial record and imperial ambitions, these efforts were not particularly effective. The string of Italian defeats which began in the fall of 1940 made the discrepancy between Mussolini's ambitions and the country's performance in the war too large and too obvious. The efforts of extreme nationalist agitators like the Mufti of Jerusalem, Rashid Ali al-Gaylani, and Subhas Chandra Bose to play off Rome against Berlin in their attempts to obtain Axis promises of independence, which they could then utilize in propaganda beamed at the Middle East and India, were abortive. The efforts reveal more about the shortsightedness of those who sought the sponsorship of the nation which had destroyed the independence of Ethiopia than about Axis psychological warfare.

The Japanese had in effect written off any prospects for propaganda in China by their atrocious conduct in that country. In the rest of Asia, the line they tried to push was that of "Asia for the Asiatics," an anticolonialist slogan related to the much publicized "Greater East Asia Co-Prosperity Sphere." In some places these slogans at first had some resonance. Many of the colonial peoples of Southeast Asia were not the least bit unhappy to see their European masters defeated, and defeated very quickly at that. While the rapid collapse of British, French, and Dutch colonial rule permanently destroyed the aura of might and strength the Europeans had once held, the people in the newly Japanese conquered areas quickly learned that they had indeed been conquered, not liberated. As it became more and more obvious that the "Co" was for them and all the "Prosperity" for the Japanese, no amount of Japanese propaganda could convince them to tie their future to Tokyo. As for Japanese propaganda toward the Allies, that never amounted to anything. The Australians and New Zealanders positively hated the intruders upon their portion of the globe. The Americans did indeed "Remember Pearl Harbor"; and no broadcasts by "Tokyo Rose," as the Japanese radio propagandist was called, was likely to make American troops forget it.

Great Britain tried early in the war to appeal to the German people over the heads of their government by dropping leaflets which recalled the treaties and promises Germany had broken in bringing on the war. The speculation that the German people might themselves turn against their government proved false. Instead they cheered on their troops to victory in Northern, Western, and Southeast Europe. Thereafter British attention in the field of psychological warfare shifted to the conquered people of the continent. The very continuation of Britain in the war gave them some hope, and this hope was increasingly reinforced by the view and the news of British warplanes flying overhead to bomb Germany (an aspect of early strategic bombing that is often forgotten). Perhaps of even greater importance was the role of the British Broadcasting Corporation (BBC), which acquired and held a reputation for truthful reporting and thereby became the major source of reasonably reliable war news for a continent covered by the blanket of Goebbels's lies. The beam of truth lit the lives of many who lived in the occupied areas and even came to be an important source of information for Germans who defied the ban on listening to foreign broadcasts. The impact of the news programs was in a significant way enhanced by the use of the V for Victory symbol. The people under Nazi rule, often for seemingly endless years, could sustain their morale by the hope of a better future.

The Soviet Union faced what at first looked like a difficult task. Its leaders had been denouncing the Western Powers first as the aggressor in the war and then for continuing to fight Germany when the Soviet Union advocated a negotiated peace with Hitler. Any embarrassment over this situation was quickly eliminated by German policies and actions. It was all too obvious all too quickly that the Germans had invaded the Soviet Union to plunder and to murder, both on the largest possible scale. Whatever the domestic problems which patriotic themes helped to overcome, the difficulties in the foreign psychological warfare field were great. Soviet leaflets addressed to German soldiers were steeped in a Marxist terminology which may have done credit to the orthodoxy of those who wrote them but could only bring derisive smiles to their readers. All the evidence suggests that the appeals of those German officers and soldiers who became members of the National Committee for a Free Germany and the League of German Officers also fell mostly on deaf ears.

The real psychological warfare triumph of the Soviet Union came not from its propaganda but from the hard-won victories of the Red army. The prestige which accrued to the Soviets from their successful defense of the country, the mauling they were obviously giving to the Germans, and the string of spectacular victories which began with Stalingrad was enormous. Here was the power which had stopped the seemingly invincible German army; this was the country which was bravely defending itself and in the process offering a hope of deliverance from the Nazi yoke to those in the occupied territories. Simultaneously, it was the fighting of the Red Army which impressed the public in Britain and the United States and thereby provided a critical cementing factor for the alliance of the Soviet Union with those countries. The prestige of the U.S.S.R. in the world and of Communist Parties in many countries was a product of Soviet deeds at the front rather than words from Moscow.

The United States engaged in extensive broadcasting and movie propaganda, Frank Capra's "Why We Fight" series being perhaps the most famous example of the latter. With footage taken primarily from Axis newsreels, these films, prepared at General Marshall's request, were designed to inform and inspire American soldiers, who often had little background on the developments in Europe and East Asia which had drawn the United States into the war. In the Pacific War, there was practically no opportunity for psychological warfare, given the attitude of Japanese soldiers and the nature of the home front. Only in the last stages of that part of the conflict was there any major effort at the use of leaflets and broadcasts, though to no great effect.

In the European theater, the Americans made a far greater attempt, especially from 1944 on, to persuade German soldiers to surrender rather than fight on in a hopeless cause.[183] The use of an official looking pass for those who gave themselves up proved to be the most effective technique, but it is doubtful that many individual surrenders were induced rather than facilitated by these means.[184] There were "black" radio stations and "News for the troops" and all manner of other devices, but it remains very much an open question whether all these efforts made a great deal of difference.

Once hostilities had started, psychological warfare could serve to reinforce hope for and confidence in victory and to assist in the consolidation of opinion at home in each of the belligerents. In a war that called for enormous sacrifices, that was undoubtedly a matter of the greatest importance. And this was as true of Americans urged to buy War Bonds as of all others. But undermining the will to fight of the enemy proved extraordinarily difficult for every country at war.

MEDICINE

In a war which involved so many new types of weapons, many of them more deadly even than those which had caused such carnage in World War I, there was one field of endeavor in which great advances were made in the saving rather than the destruction of life: Medicine. In the general field of tropical medicine, the invention of new methods of making synthetic quinine assisted in dealing with the terrible problem of malaria. The discovery of sulfa drugs, and of penicillin and additional antibiotics, made it possible for the Allies, especially the British and Americans, to save the lives of thousands of wounded soldiers who would otherwise have succumbed to infections. Here **were new families** of drugs of vast post-war significance.

Closely related in practice, though not in theory, to the life-saving role of antibiotics was the development, application and increasing use of blood transfusions in connection with surgery for battlefield injuries. It was this, together with systems for the more rapid movement of the wounded to advance field hospitals, that increased the survival chances of the wounded. The battlefield—which might be in a town under bombing hundreds of miles from the front as well as at a fox-hole—had lost none of its terror; it had in fact gained some new ones; but the capacity for coping with wounds had greatly improved.[185]

A development of the war which turned out to be a mixed blessing was the discovery of DDT. This powdery chemical proved of enormous value in reducing the incidence of several diseases, especially typhus and malaria, which would otherwise have killed or maimed literally tens of thousands, as had happened in prior wars. There simply cannot be any doubt that during hostilities and in the desperate conditions prevailing in many parts of the world right after the end of hostilities—liberated prisoner of war, internment and concentration camps to mention only some examples—the use of DDT proved a great boon. The indiscriminate use of the new "miracle" dust after the war was to be a cause of great environmental damage, thus showing that it ought to be employed only in the most dire emergencies.

It must also be noted that the war provided the opportunity or the excuse for some of the most awful medical experiments ever carried out on unwilling subjects in German and Japanese camps. Thousands were deliberately wounded, maimed, infected and usually killed during or soon after all manner of horrible procedures ostensibly designed to further the medical or military knowledge of the perpetrators. Though in the German case reported on at professional medical meetings, these activities belong more in the realm of torture than of medicine. At least a few of the "doctors of infamy" were tried after the war; nothing productive came of all their butchery.[186]

It is easy to draw a balance for the war years between the destructive power of weapons and the potential benefits of new technological and medical discoveries. The endless casualty lists are a silent but convincing record of the net impact of these new developments on mankind. On the other hand, for the post-war world, the heritage of radar and jet airplanes as aids to travel, and new drugs, surgical procedures, and other therapies for the protection and maintenance of life have left a positive heritage which has improved and extended the life of millions. But only as long as the new nuclear weapons remain unused.

A related major change which had begun in some ways in World War I but reached its maturity in World War II was the great role of scientists in influencing and even determining government policy. Their role in managerial positions was closely related to this change. The positions of Carl Krauch in Germany, of Lord Cherwell in England, of Arthur Compton and James Conant in the United States, derived from the enormous significance of scientific developments requiring expert knowledge for the successful prosecution of modern war between highly industrialized societies. Any interruption of research, such as the German development stop order of October 10, 1941, could have drastic consequences even if dropped later.[187] The big war produced big science, and that continued into the post-war years.

Another special aspect of the war, reaching back to the first horn sounded in battle, continued into the post-war years as well. Military music had accompanied all wars from ancient to modern times. Except for the large-scale use of recordings and radio transmissions, the nature of military music did not change appreciably during World War II. One incident, however, deserves special mention. In mid-July 1941 the Red Army captured a German regimental band leader. After the war, he reappeared as a band leader in the National People's Army (NVA), the military force of the now vanished German Democratic Republic, conducting the music for its goose-stepping parades. In the 1950s he was sent to Communist China to teach military music in the People's Liberation Army (PLA), the army of the People's Republic of China.[188] One can only hope that the resulting performances sounded as well as Tsingtao beer, the "Chinese beer" sold in this country but made by the pupils of German brewers in the former German colony in China, tastes.

11

———•———

FROM THE SPRING OF 1943 TO SUMMER 1944

AXIS HOPES AND PLANS

As the German leaders looked toward the future in the early spring of 1943, there were both good and bad prospects. The good prospects were of two types. They had stalled off disasters and they were bringing on new weapons. After the great defeat at Stalingrad, they had reversed the tide temporarily with a counter-stroke which offered at least the hope of their being able to launch a new offensive in the East. In North Africa, the outlook was grim for the Axis forces in March—the month of German victory at Kharkov in the East—but at least they had prevented a quick Allied victory which would quite probably have paved the way for a summer or fall 1943 landing in the West. Even if a successful Allied offensive in Tunisia were followed by other such operations in the Mediterranean area, a substantial amount of time had been gained.

Furthermore, new weapons were beginning to come off the assembly lines in large numbers. The production of submarines was at last reaching the levels required to keep about one hundred at sea at any one time. The new Tiger heavy tanks were getting their early troubles fixed; the new Panther medium-heavy tanks were beginning to be delivered; and there was every prospect that, during the course of the year, monthly output of these and other critical weapons—assault guns in particular—would steadily increase. Perhaps of greatest importance was the effect of manpower mobilization. The combination of rationalization in industry and massive employment of prisoners of war and slave laborers was making it possible to provide added manpower to the army, so that by the summer of 1943 the army in the East was at least close to its size two years earlier.[1]

The efforts of the Finns, Hungarians and Romanians to discover an exit from the war had been effectively squelched by the Germans. The submarine war was expected to keep the Western Allies immobilized in 1943; and there was the expectation that during that year the recovery on the southern part of the Eastern Front, combined with the resources freed by the withdrawals from the Demyansk and Rzhev salients would make possible a great attack on at least one section of the Eastern Front. The fighting in that theater would continue to have priority, and it would also continue to be waged with great ferocity.[2] The battering which Germany planned to administer to her enemies in the West at sea and in the East on land would somehow see her through, at least until the alliance of Britain, the Soviet Union and the United States fell apart.[3]

Italian prospects were nowhere near as rosy. Already entirely dependent on Germany, the Mussolini government could only try to convince its powerful ally to make peace in the East—something Hitler refused—and to concentrate more forces in the Mediterranean theater. Some of the latter had been done, but the clear signs of impending defeat in Tunisia opened up the obvious prospect of an assault by the Allies on Italy herself. Morale in the country was poor, especially after the loss of Libya. There had been little enthusiasm for war in June 1940; there was none now. Disaster had followed upon disaster in Greece, East Africa, North Africa, and in the Soviet Union. But there was for a long time no prospect of an overthrow of the regime.[4]

In the Balkans, the Italians greatly worried that they would lose whatever happened: if the Axis lost, all was gone; if it won, the Germans would take over anyway.[5] The scuttling of the French fleet at Toulon in November 1942 had removed the Italian fear of having a French fleet in the Mediterranean larger than their own after the war;[6] but all the German deference to Italian wishes in North Africa and in the Yugoslav–Greek area, on which Hitler always insisted, could not conceal the fact that it was Germany which, if it won the war, would be in effective control.[7] Furthermore, there had been persistent friction between the two European Axis partners on short-falls in German-promised deliveries of coal for Italian industry and oil for the Italian navy, while the Italians also complained about the treatment of the very large number of their workers sent to labor in German industry.[8]

It was in this context that the first peace feelers were extended to the British in December 1942 by agents of the Italian royal family, but they were turned off with the demand that the Italians would have to take action first to remove Mussolini and kick out the Germans themselves, something the British correctly expected they would not do.[9] Other soundings in January 1943 were met by an essentially similar line.[10] Churchill noted on February 13, 1943, that perhaps after the landing in Sicily, then already planned for the summer, it might be possible to get Italy out of the war.[11]

Since Mussolini was entirely unable to persuade Hitler to make an accommodation with Stalin, he could only keep asking for additional German assistance to meet the expected Allied attacks across the Mediterranean. Simultaneously, he made some changes in his own government, in particular dropping Ciano as Foreign Minister, appointing him to be ambassador to the Vatican, while also urging on the Germans a more conciliatory policy toward the conquered peoples of Europe. If the German authorities were enthused by the dismissal of the increasingly anti-German Ciano, they were certainly not about to relax their exploitive policy in the occupied territories. On the contrary, the increasing levy of forced labor was designed to free more German men for the armed forces. There was no room in a New Order for soft policies or even hopeful promises for those whom the Germans considered inferior peoples, a category into which the Italians had every reason to believe their ally had placed them as well.[12] If the British and Americans had their frictions in 1943 with each other and with the Soviet Union, these were mild compared to those between Germany and Italy. In addition, there was no effective coordination of the European Axis partners with Japan.

The Japanese government was, as ever, unable to work out a coherent policy toward China. On the one hand, the Japanese hoped to defeat Chiang Kai-shek but had as yet developed no effective way to do so. Simultaneously, they tried to build up the regime of Wang Ching-wei, but were unwilling to make to him the sorts of substantive concessions which would convert the transparent puppet into an effective alternative to Chiang for self-respecting Chinese. They could persuade Germany and Italy to recognize the Wang government, but neither that action nor the minimal adjustments made in favor of his regime on the old international concessions in China made any real difference. And having Wang declare war formally on Britain and the United States had no practical import either. A key figure within the Wang system, Chon Fo-hai, was continually in touch with Chiang, but that did not produce any change in either of the two ineffective governments.[13] Similarly ineffective was the project for organized volunteer armies to fight alongside the Japanese and recruited among the occupied areas of Southeast Asia; these would become significant in the post-war era, not in wartime.[14]

In the war ahead, the Japanese saw the situation in Europe in somewhat realistic colors and continued to urge the Germans to make peace with the Soviet Union and concentrate on the war against Britain and the United States, especially in the Mediterranean.[15] Tokyo watched anxiously for any sign that their German ally might instead make peace with the Western Powers and leave Japan facing the force and fury of the latter by herself, but on that score they could be as confident as they were disappointed by German insistence on a renewed offensive in the East.[16]

As for their own major war with Britain and the United States, the first concern had to be to keep it limited to those countries. It was essential to keep the Soviet Union from joining the circle of Japan's enemies either by directly entering hostilities against Japan or by allowing the Americans to use air bases in its Far Eastern provinces for air attacks on the Japanese homeland. This meant making whatever concessions might be needed to deal with the current issues on fisheries and other matters in Japanese–Soviet relations;[17] it meant never interfering with United States aid shipments to the Soviet Union across the Pacific—whatever complaints the Germans might make; and it meant doing anything necessary to obtain Soviet reassurances of no aid to the United States when, in early 1943, the American campaign in the Aleutians threatened and eventually destroyed the Japanese position there. It would be a difficult year in Japanese–Soviet relations, because from Tokyo's perspective the Soviet Union's position was likely to become steadily stronger; but there was no alternative to concessions to Moscow now that the war Japan had launched against the United States and Britain had turned into a lengthy conflict in which Japan had already been forced on the defensive.

As for the basic strategy for Japan to follow in this struggle, the review which came after the evacuation of Guadalcanal in February 1943 produced a general strategic concept to which the army and navy tried to adhere for the balance of 1943 and which they modified only in 1944. There was to be for the time being no new offensive either in China or from Burma into India; in both areas the military would hold their current positions (though it was in this regard that there was a change in 1944). In the South Pacific, the Japanese defeat at Buna and Gona made it all the more important to hold on in central New Guinea, just as the defeat on Guadalcanal reemphasized the significance of holding on to the Northern Solomons. The agreed strategy, formalized in a new war plan of March 15, 1943, provided for the defense of the existing perimeter in the south.[18] The American and Australian forces would be made to pay heavily for each advance, however small, until either a major defensive counter-blow by the navy provided a great victory for Japan or the eventual exhaustion of her enemies brought on a new settlement in East Asia.[19] The death on April 18, 1943 of Admiral Yamamoto Isoroku when his plane was intercepted by American airplanes brought no change; his successor, Admiral Koga Mineichi, adhered to the same basic strategy. Japan would fight a defensive war until her enemies decided they had had enough.

PLANS OF THE WESTERN ALLIES

The British and Americans had looked to 1943 from their planning sessions at the Casablanca Conference in January, setting the defeat of the U-Boats as top priority. The air offensive against Germany was to be stepped up, and the Tunisian campaign, which was now expected to last several months, was to be followed by operation "Husky," the invasion of Sicily, which would fully open the Mediterranean, draw German forces from the Eastern Front, and weaken Italy even further. No decision had yet been made on what was to follow on "Husky"; and when the British and American leaders again met in Washington in May 1943 (Trident) the differences were such that no final agreement on a follow-up to "Husky" could be reached. The British and United States air commanders as well as the United States Army Chief-of-Staff, General Marshall, favored reducing Mediterranean operations in order to build up strength in the United Kingdom for the cross-Channel invasion, while the British land and sea commanders, as well as Admiral King, urged continued pressure in the Mediterranean to force Italy out of the war.[20] The decision was made to await a recommendation from the Allied Commander-in-Chief in the Mediterranean, General Eisenhower. By the time that recommendation came in and was approved, the landing on Sicily had already taken place. This operation and other issues in Anglo-United States relations must be reviewed before the new choices of the summer of 1943 can be examined.

Certainly not only strategic issues led to arguments between the Western Allies. The American and British had very different views on economic and colonial policy. All during the war, the United States government was pressuring the British to remove the special imperial preferences which had been adopted during the Depression and which were seen by the Americans, especially Secretary of State Cordell Hull, as interfering with world trade in general and American trade in particular.[21]

The other major field of contention grew out of the American anti-colonialist tradition. Beginning in the winter of 1941–42, the obvious objection of Americans to colonialism caused serious problems for the alliance. This especially focused on the issue of India. In addition, there was President Roosevelt's concern over the impact on domestic support for the war effort if the United States were not seen as pushing for the end of colonialism.[22] The British, on the other hand, and Churchill in particular, were insistent on not becoming involved in discussions about the future of the empire, which was dear to the Prime Minister's heart and most certainly not to be discussed with the Americans of all people. Even in the worst days of the war there had been a reluctance to run risks in this field.[*] Now that the tide appeared to be shifting, the British were even less willing to contemplate alterations in colonial policy to please either nationalists in the empire or the Americans. The suspicion of the Americans that it was British imperial interest which lay behind London's and especially Churchill's insistence on extensive operations in the Mediterranean greatly exacerbated the argument over strategy.

That argument had been papered over in the summer of 1942 with the decision to invade Northwest Africa. It had been dealt with but not resolved at Casablanca; the Germans having won the race for Tunisia in November 1942, it was obvious by January 1943 that an invasion of northern France in the summer of 1943 was practically impossible. But the Americans never developed any great enthusiasm for Mediterranean operations, and whatever was done there always looked to them like a diversion from the main effort.[23] The British, on the other hand, thought that the opportunities in the Mediterranean should be exploited to the full. As will become increasingly obvious, Churchill would time and again display a preference for operations in the Mediterranean in practice over his own belief in principle in the attack across the Channel. The Chief of the Imperial General Staff, Field Marshal Brooke, kept arguing for Mediterranean operations, and especially a landing in Italy, because he believed that it would be more difficult for the Germans to reinforce there than in France, a belief he held sincerely, though it would be disproved by the experience of landings in July and September 1943 and January 1944 — but without ever making any difference in his assessment. Marshall, on the other hand, had objected to the Northwest Africa operation from the start, argued that it would function like a suction pump to draw more resources, and that it was certain to end up interfering with rather than supporting the great invasion, which alone could bring the military power of the Western Allies to bear directly on the Germans. The argument continued for years during the war — and enlivened post-war debates. Ironically, as we shall see, on the one Mediterranean operation that Marshall (like Eisenhower) wanted, the invasion of southern France, it would be the British who would balk. While a series of compromises and agreed strategies was eventually worked out,

---

[*] It is worth noting the concern in London that the Americans, if asked to occupy the Falkland Islands, might hand them over to Argentina. As Brooke noted in his diary on January 2, 1942, "While we argue Japs likely to step in" (Liddell Hart Centre, Alanbrooke Papers).

the arguments left behind an endless trail of nasty comments about Marshall in Brooke's diary.[24]

The most immediate practical issue in the planning of Britain and the United States early in 1943, other than the Battle of the Atlantic, was the forthcoming invasion of Sicily.[25] Because of their inability to relieve pressure on the Soviet Union during the anticipated new German summer offensive by a landing on the Channel coast, the Western Allies were especially eager to launch this operation as early in the year as possible. While the battle in Tunisia was in progress, fixed dates were still argued about, with both Churchill and Roosevelt hopeful that the preliminary estimate of the planners that the landing would have to come in August could be moved forward. Although they pushed for June, the final date was set for early July, an interval of less than two months following the end of the Tunisian campaign.

The initial invasion plan provided for two armies, one British and one American, landing at opposite ends of the island, the British in the southeast and the Americans in the northwest. At the insistence of Montgomery, who was to command the British 8th Army portion of the invasion, this plan was altered to have both armies in the southeast, with the American 7th Army under Patton on the left flank. This change, together with several less spectacular but still significant alterations, was made after considerable and at times heated debate; but Montgomery's insistence that he command the whole operation himself was rejected. The Army Group would be under Alexander, who in turn would be under Eisenhower's Allied theater command. In view of Montgomery's near incapacity for dealing with Americans, this was undoubtedly an essential arrangement, but it only exacerbated his negative attitude toward the American army and would have serious repercussions in and after the campaign.[26]

SICILY AND THE ITALIAN SURRENDER

The planned landing on Sicily would be the first in Europe since the British had been driven out of Greece and Crete in 1941 and it had to be launched not against Vichy French forces as in Northwest Africa but against Italian and German troops on Italian territory. Furthermore, the Allies did not have the benefit of the sort of intelligence which had facilitated the operation in Africa. There, Allied intelligence had excellent sources in the French areas and could decypher a high proportion of the German and Italian radio signals traffic to their forces in North Africa. On Sicily and the Italian mainland, however, the Allies lacked agents in place while the Axis headquarters relied heavily on cable traffic which, unlike radio messages, could not be intercepted and decoded. Only the German air force continued to use radio communication extensively, thereby unwittingly providing the Allies with much useful information.

To confuse the Axis and lead them to disperse their forces, Allied intelligence mounted a major series of deception operations designed to give the impression that landings were planned on Sardinia (as was in fact considered for a while) and in Greece. The most famous of these projects, that of the "Man Who Never Was,"[27] relied on the pro-Axis sympathies of Franco Spain to pass on to the Germans especially forged documents planted on a corpse floated ashore on the Spanish coast.

These schemes did help confuse the Germans about the intended landing and directed some Axis resources elsewhere. The advantage gained was, however, partially cancelled out by horrendous errors made as a result of lack of proper training and coordination between the Allied air and naval commanders, in the handling of the airborne assaults which were to assist both the British and the American landing units move inland rapidly by seizing key positions beyond the beaches. Improperly routed over the badly instructed landing armada, the airborne forces suffered as much from Allied as from Axis fire and therefore could provide only some of the assistance to a rapid advance inland that had been expected of them.[28]

The landings on July 10, 1943 did succeed.[a] The defenders were surprised in spite of the enormous size of the armada carrying the British and American assault divisions.[29] The British forces quickly captured the great port of Syracuse intact, as well as some airfields which would help the Allied air forces in providing close ground support. However, just as the advancing British forces on the eastern coast began to run into coordinated German resistance, Montgomery, whose exuberance ran away with his usual caution, split his forces. Taking over the road north which would have enabled the Americans to move inland, he sent one corps up each of the two flanks of his eastern Sicily landing area. The result was that everything went wrong. The 8th Army coastal thrust—which might have punched through toward Messina and thereby cut off the Axis forces in Sicily entirely—was now too weak and soon stalled in the Catania plain. The 8th Army's inland thrust on the road originally assigned to the Americans moved forward slowly but to no great effect. The Americans had successfully warded off a fierce German

---

[a] Roosevelt personally checked at the Map Room, the White House command center, for any news at 20 minutes after midnight (Log 10 July 1943, FDRL, Map Room Box 195, Log la). On June 6, his scotty Falla had accompanied the President into the Map Room only to be told by Roosevelt that he was not permitted to be there (ibid).

counter-attack at the Gela beaches, in part because of excellent naval gunfire support; they were now shifted toward the northwest, raced for Palermo—which was a spectacular but by then unprofitable prize—and then had to be completely redirected to the east toward Messina.[30]

The upshot of this was that the Allies ground their way forward, captured many Italian soldiers, but pushed the Germans off the island rather than destroying them. In a final souring of the campaign, the Allied air force and navy, in spite of overwhelming superiority, could not prevent the Germans from evacuating the bulk of their forces across the Straits of Messina.[31] The Western Allies had indeed won a local victory; their land forces in particular had fought well and hard, with the British 8th Army (now including a Canadian division) showing successful adjustment from desert warfare to a new kind of terrain, while the American soldiers demonstrated their absorption of the lessons learned in Tunisia. But the higher Allied commanders hardly covered themselves with glory. Eisenhower and Alexander had not controlled their subordinates effectively. Montgomery had miscalculated the situation and lost the great chance at the beginning—greatly antagonizing the Americans in the process—while Patton had disgraced himself, and narrowly avoided dismissal, by the notorious incidents of slapping and cursing some soldiers in two field hospitals.[32] Only General Omar Bradley had distinguished himself as an effective corps commander and moved up to higher command as a result.

If in these ways the aura of success which attended the conquest of Sicily had a side to it that was by no means all positive, in other ways "Husky" did make several major contributions to the war. By far the most important was its impact on the German direction of the war: coming just as the Battle of Kursk had turned critical, the Allied landing in Sicily would, as will be discussed in that context, contribute to the German decision to end all offensive operations on the Eastern Front so that reinforcements of both troops and planes could be sent to Italy and the Balkans. This was critically related to an aspect of "Husky" which became immediately obvious to the Germans: the Italians were simply not prepared and willing to fight Britain and the United States effectively in defense of their homeland. The Germans would have to send additional troops not only into Italy if they expected to hold any portion of it against the Allies but also into those portions of the Balkans garrisoned by Italian troops and hence, it was now obvious, likely to be open to practically unopposed landings.

These German concerns were reinforced by the impact of the Allied advance in Sicily and the bombing of Italian cities on the internal cohesion of Italy. The reports Berlin was getting from Rome were in many ways confusing, but it was obvious that Mussolini's regime, already hard hit by the loss of the African empire, was now even more shaky as Italian home territory was coming under attack. In 1917, the victory of the Central Powers over the Italians at Caporetto had brought about a certain rallying of Italian popular support for the defense of a country clearly in imminent danger of conquest by German and Austrian troops. The picture of civilians in Palermo waving white flags, if not actually cheering American GIs, showed that the attitude of the people this time was very different indeed. Even before Mussolini was toppled from power by his own former friends and associates in the Fascist Grand Council, the Germans were planning to take over control of Italy and Italian-occupied territory in France, Yugoslavia, Greece and Albania.[33]

In the weeks between the collapse of Axis resistance in Tunisia and the landing in Sicily, the Germans had begun moving troops, primarily from their armies in France, into Italy, whether or not the Italian government wanted them. While Mussolini hoped to preserve the appearance of independence at least in his own country, his military leaders realized that the disastrous defeats their army had suffered in North Africa and on the Eastern Front meant that, whatever their preference for holding the reins in their own country, only German troops could make a defense of any portion of Italy effective. This divergence of view naturally made it easier for the Germans to send in to Italy whatever they felt they could spare elsewhere. There was, however, no effective coordination of German and Italian preparations, and the German commanders in the area, especially Field Marshal Kesselring, were excessively optimistic.[34] An air force commander himself, Kesselring had originally been sent to the Mediterranean precisely to gain control of the air over the Central Mediterranean; he now presided over an air contingent which in spite of a steady flow of reinforcements was dwindling under the hammering of Allied air power and could not meet the constant requests of the Italians for more planes and additional anti-aircraft protection.[35] Symbolic for the changing situation in the air war in the Central Mediterranean was the surrender on June 11, 1943, of the island of Pantelleria at the end of heavy air and sea bombardment and before the Allied landing force came ashore.

Right after the Axis collapse in Tunisia, Hitler had ordered the creation of a special staff to prepare measures in case Italy caved in or changed sides.[36] Since Rommel had been recalled from North Africa in part at the insistence of the Italians, he was a logical person to head the preparations, code-named first "Alarich" (and later "Achse" [Axis]), to take over the Italian zones in France and the Balkans, secure the Alpine passes on the French–Italian and German–Italian border, and control as much of Italy itself as possible. German units originally scheduled to invade Spain and Portugal in case of an Allied landing in the Iberian peninsula were now assigned to the new project, while it was incorrectly anticipated that three SS divisions could be removed from the Eastern Front. In practice, the spring 1943 German postponements of the offensive against Kursk and the Allied landing in Sicily altered the details of the German plans—and Rommel himself was briefly transferred to Salonika on July 21—but they had at least begun serious planning to cope with the defection of Italy.[37] The Italians, on the other hand, would botch their intended exit from the war about as dramatically as Mussolini had miscalculated the country's entrance into it.

For some months there had been dissatisfaction in Italy. The loss of empire, the obvious threat of invasion, and the inability of Italy or her German ally to defend Italian cities from Allied air attacks all redoubled the original unpopularity of the alliance with Germany and the war.[38] Furthermore, the Duce, who personified the regime, had lost his magic, his political touch, and, it would appear, his health. The "changing of the guard" of February 1943, Mussolini's way of dealing with the crisis facing his country, simply did not produce the sort of national resurgence which was needed. Three strains of dissatisfaction merged into an upheaval which destroyed the Fascist system. First, there were the doctrinaire and rabid Fascists, led by Roberto Farinacci, who wanted to revive and reinvigorate what they hoped would be an energetic Fascist regime, which would galvanize the masses to fight alongside Germany against the British and Americans.[39] There was a second group led by Dino Grandi, a Fascist also but far less certain than Farinacci that Mussolini was still the man to lead the country. Grandi wanted to reduce Mussolini's authority over the military, which he clearly could not direct effectively. Third and most important, the circle around the court and King Victor Emmanuel III and some of the military leaders, who hoped to replace Mussolini with a regime that could find a way for Italy out of the war.

In a coincidence of timing largely created by the stimulus to all three groups by the obvious inability of German and Italian forces to block the invasion of Italy, these plots came to a head on July 24–26, 1943. At a meeting of the Fascist Grand Council held on July 24–25, the first since October 1939, the opponents of Mussolini carried a motion against him by a vote of 19 to 8. This action made it easy for the King to move up by one day the previously developed plan to dismiss Mussolini, immediately thereafter arrest him, and simultaneously announce the appointment of Marshall Pietro Badoglio as head of a new government. In no time at all, the Fascist Party which had dominated Italian affairs for more than two decades practically evaporated while a new government of bureaucrats attempted to administer the country.[40]

Mussolini appears to have had no real sense of what was actually going on around him.[41] He had completely failed to push Hitler on the critical issues facing Italy when they met at Feltre on July 19; coming during the bloody fighting at Kursk, that meeting had been a particularly poor time for him to urge his idea of a separate peace with the Soviet Union.[42] On July 25, he explained to Japanese ambassador Hidaka Shinrokuro that the only hope for the Axis lay in Germany's giving up the Ukraine, going back to the 1939 border, and taking advantage of the difficulties in the relations between the Soviet Union on the one hand and Britain and the United States on the other—symbolized by the Soviet establishment of the National Committee for a Free Germany— by concentrating all energies on the struggle against the Western Allies.[43] Whatever theoretical sense there may have been in this concept, for which Mussolini wanted Japanese support, it could hardly have any impact on a domestic situation which was collapsing around him. The people remembered the tens of thousands of soldiers the Duce had sent to death and imprisonment on the Eastern Front for his own prestige and no conceivable Italian interest, not his new found insight (naturally kept secret from the public) into the strength of the Red Army.

The new government of Badoglio promised the Germans to continue in the war, though the latter were certain—and correctly so—that it would try to leave.[44] In the ensuing race between Badoglio and his associates and the Germans, the Italians did almost everything as stupidly and slowly as possible. They did not even conceal or guard Mussolini effectively, and in September he was rescued by a German airborne operation and subsequently installed by the Germans as a puppet in northern Italy.[45]

Unwilling either to face the wrath of the Germans or to surrender to the Allies, Badoglio and his military and diplomatic assistants dithered for weeks.[46] In the end Badoglio had to surrender as the Allies had told him from the beginning;[47] but in the meantime the Italians had allowed the Germans to bluff, threaten, and bamboozle them out of important spots in the Italian-occupied territories, the passes through the Alps from France and Germany, and key positions all over north and central Italy as well.[48] As the Allies announced the Italian surrender simultaneously with the landing at Salerno, Italian soldiers began surrendering in great numbers to the Germans. Since they would not fight for their country against the Germans, they would now be hauled off to slave labor camps in Germany, which many did not survive, while the soldiers of other countries fought over and devastated the country they left behind. Even the capital was not properly held by the Italian army, and the planned landing of the United States 82nd Airborne Division to seize Rome was called off at the last moment when the Italians insisted on additional forces.[49]

With Rommel recalled from Salonika on July 26, the Germans had moved quickly to contain the risk of Italian defection and poured troops into Italy. In the last days of July and early August, they had withdrawn crack SS units from the Eastern Front and sent them into central Italy, while their successful evacuation of all units from Sicily enabled them to prepare to defend the northern portion of southern Italy, around Naples. The German garrisons of Corsica and Sardinia were success-fully shipped back to the mainland as the Italians looked on in fear and confusion. As discussed in Chapter 7, a substantial portion of the Italian navy did get away, but even in the home bases of that proud navy, tiny detachments of Germans prevented sabotage, seized key facilities and held some of the warships. If there was anything the new Italian govern-ment could have fouled up that was overlooked, it has yet to come to light.[50]

The Western Allies, who had not settled the details of their Mediter-ranean strategy at the Washington Conference in May, had left it to their theater commander, General Eisenhower, to recommend the next step after "Husky." The division of opinion over a landing on the main-land was resolved in favor of such a project when the Allied air com-manders, who had opposed such a landing, shifted to its support in order to make possible the seizure of the airfields around Foggia on the Adriatic coast of Italy. From there, many of the most important targets of the German and German-controlled aircraft industry could be reached and the fighter defenses forced to divide their effort. The result was that, with the newly won supporters, Eisenhower by July 18, 1943, adopted Brooke's and Churchill's idea of a landing on the Italian main-land and obtained the approval of the Combined Chiefs of Staff for an amphibious assault at Salerno, the northernmost beach within range of fighters from Sicilian bases ("Avalanche"), and a supporting crossing of the Straits of Messina to the Calabrian toe of Italy ("Baytown").[51]

The fall of Mussolini and the soundings of the Badoglio government for an armistice coincided with the early stages of planning for the Salerno and Calabrian landings. Allied diplomats and military leaders hoped that the Italians would coordinate their steps with those of the Allies, pressed Badoglio to get on with the surrender and then, after Badoglio's representative had finally signed, simply landed in Calabria on September 3, and announced the armistice hours before landing at Salerno. Once again, as in Sicily, they would get ashore, but once again there were serious problems because the Germans had been steadily building up forces in the area near Naples. The plan for two landings assumed that the two would assist each other—which they did not—and that the Italians would be helpful—which they were not. Above all, Montgomery was against the whole approach, and the American appointed to command the newly designated 5th Army for the Salerno landing, Mark Clark, was inexperienced. On September 3 the British 8th Army crossed to the Italian mainland and thereafter devoted its efforts to building up supplies, bringing in reinforcements and very little else. Montgomery had become an inspired and inspiring leader, whose soldiers were devoted to him—as he was to them—and he was a folk-hero at home in the United Kingdom where, after years of defeats, he stood out as the one general who seemed able to win victories. Now he missed the opportunity to recover high standing with the Americans by deliberately pausing after his unopposed landing instead of dashing northwards. Alexander would and could not interfere with Montgomery's tactical dispositions; and Brooke, who was the great advocate of both the invasion of Italy and Montgomery as a key figure in it, neither explained to his protégé why the Italian campaign was so important nor sent a rocket to him even while sighing into his diary that the Salerno landing "is doomed."[52] Montgomery never had such a chance again. Newspaper correspondents could drive up the Italian roads toward Naples, but the 8th Army rested on its laurels as their American and British comrades died on the Salerno beaches.[a]

The American 5th Army landing at Salerno started ashore in the early morning of September 9, 1943, a few hours after the Italian surrender had been announced. An American and a British corps landed in Salerno Bay with the British on the left and the Americans on the right. The planned airborne operation against Rome had been cancelled at the last moment. The Germans had anticipated an Allied landing in this general area and mounted a counter-attack after disarming all Italian units in the vicinity. The German 16th Panzer Division was in the immediate area, and other units quickly joined in, while all German forces further south were summoned to the battlefield. In several days of bitter fighting, the Germans drove the British and American forces back some, but their announcement of victory was premature. In the struggle to hold the beachheads, the Allied forces were not only provided heavy air support but very effective naval gunfire and were reinforced by the regiments

---

[a] Nigel Hamilton, Montgomery's adoring biographer, writes: "he now deliberately decided to make Alexander pay for his mistakes. He would not undertake any further operations for the moment, merely sit and watch" (*Monty*, 2: 401). Equally critical, Lamb, *Montgomery*, pp. 32–51.

of the airborne division originally scheduled for the Rome landing. By September 16, the Germans had been held and even pushed back and now began to assume a position across the Italian peninsula designed to hold the Allied forces in the south. The German 10th Army pulled back slowly in the face of the United States 5th Army and the even more slowly arriving forward elements of the British 8th Army.

By October 1 the Americans had taken Naples, where the Germans had wrecked even the museums in fury at their erstwhile ally, while the British had seized the Foggia airfields which had played such a large part in Allied planning. What was to happen next depended on decisions argued about then and still a subject for dispute,[53] but the Western Allies were back on the continent in force for the first time since 1941, and at least some of the divisions they faced had been diverted from the titanic battles in the East where the major land fighting of the war took place during 1943 as in 1942.

THE EASTERN FRONT

The Germans had initially planned to attack on the Eastern Front right after the spring thaws had dried up the terrain sufficiently for their armored forces to move, probably about the middle of April. From their perspective, the sooner the better and especially before the Red Army had recovered from the Kharkov defeat. The original order for the attack, dated March 13, called for von Manstein to strike north into the Kursk bulge while Army Group Center, strengthened as a result of the evacuation of the Rzhev bulge, would strike southwards into that bulge. Army Group North was to follow up with an offensive against Leningrad that would off-set the Soviet success there in January, and seize the city, thereby strengthening Germany's hold on the Baltic and Finland, threatening Sweden and securing the whole northern flank.[54] A major function of the whole operation, code-named "Zitadelle" (Citadel), was to seize the initiative on at least one portion of the Eastern Front and thereby make possible a stabilization of the front as a whole, thus enabling Germany to create a reserve of such substantial proportions that an enemy offensive in the East would be precluded in 1943 and any invasion elsewhere could be crushed.[55]

In the following weeks, other offensive projects were considered but rejected. Not only did discussion over these cause delays, but General (later Field Marshal) Walter Model, the commander of the German 9th Army, which had been made available because of the evacuation of the Rzhev salient and which was to launch the offensive from the north, repeatedly called for postponement until he could build up his forces and, in particular, receive a substantial allocation of the new Panther and Tiger tanks.[56] In the face of the objections of the other German commanders, especially von Manstein and von Kluge, who argued that the longer operation "Citadel" was postponed the more chancy it became as the Russians built up their defenses, Hitler sided with Model, one of his favorites.[57] In the face of increasing doubts among his military advisors, and considerable sentiment for refraining from an offensive altogether, Hitler decided by June 19 to go ahead. He had stated in the April 15 version of the attack order that "the victory of Kursk must have the effect of a lesson to the world."[58] He was quite right in this prediction but not in the way he intended.

The German 9th Army, attacking from the north, and the 4th Panzer Army and the Kempf Army, striking from the south, had been enormously reinforced with replacements and new weapons as well as heavy air support. Some 2700 tanks and assault guns were to provide the push as 1400–1800 German aircraft swarmed overhead. The German forces were keyed up to a major operation even if the objective this time was far less ambitious than in 1941 or 1942; the aim was to seize the initiative and win a great tactical victory, not a knock-out blow.[59]

The Soviet leadership had decided after considerable internal debate that the Red Army would build up defenses on the north and south shoulders of the obviously vulnerable Kursk salient but await a German offensive. A major counter-offensive was, however, planned well ahead of time to strike from the northeast into the bulge around Orel from which the northern German pincer was expected; an offensive in the south would follow the hoped for defeat of Germany's summer attack. As they awaited the expected blow, the Red Army Front commanders received very substantial reinforcements, built up several defensive positions in depth, and trained their units to meet the expected German armored thrusts. Rokossovski's Central Front in the north and Vatutin's Voronezh Front in the south had developed what they had good reason to believe would be strong barriers to any German assault. Both sides had reinforced their armored units to peak strength for what became the greatest tank battle in history.[60]

On July 4 a preliminary and on July 5 the main German offensive began. From the north, the German 9th Army began to blast its way into the Soviet Central Front, while in the south, armored formations cut deeply into the Voronezh Front's defenses. Both sides moved in reinforcements, the Germans to nourish their attacking spearheads, the Russians to assist the defending forces as they were destroyed or obliged to withdraw. The next six days saw a slugging match of unprecedented scale as armor clashes and infantry and artillery fire caused colossal casualties on both sides. The Germans were still advancing, somewhat more rapidly in the south than in the north, but they were entirely unable to accomplish a real breakthrough at either axis of attack in the face of determined and effective Soviet resistance.[61] The delay of months in the offensive had, on balance, probably worked more in favor of the Red Army than the Germans, many of whose long-awaited new Tiger and Panther tanks turned out not to be fully ready for frontline deployment anyway.

By July 12, the northern thrust had been stalled to an extent that Model had been forced into a battle of attrition, a form of combat that obviously tied down whatever reserves German Army Group Center could muster. It was precisely this situation for which the Russians had been waiting. The Red Army's Bryansk Front and West Front now initiated a massive offensive into the northern face of the Orel bulge — in effect into the rear of Model's attacking army — and quickly penetrated the thinly held lines of the 2nd Panzer Army. Not only were the Germans obliged to direct divisions intended for Model's army to meet a threatened collapse of the whole Orel bulge, but to take forces away from the 9th Army itself. The northern pincer of the German offensive had been effectively halted in its tracks and soon faced great dangers of its own.

The southern pincer was still advancing against extremely fierce Soviet resistance and von Manstein wanted to keep going, but Hitler decided on July 13 to call off the "Citadel" offensive. The Orel bulge was in danger, Model's army was in no shape to continue and was instead likely to have to withdraw to its earlier position. There was evidence of another Soviet offensive about to be launched in the Donets Basin. As for the assault forces of the southern pincer that von Manstein wanted to drive forward, Hitler was thinking of pulling some of them out to send to Italy. The landing of the Western Allies on Sicily on July 10 and the obvious collapse of most Italian resistance there meant that German divisions from the Eastern Front would have to be sent to help create an army in Italy and to replace Italian occupation forces in the Balkans. Germany was indeed fighting a multi-front, not a one-front war.[62]

Just as the heavy fighting on the Eastern Front prevented the Germans from devoting much of their resources to the struggle with Britain and the United States, so the need for Germany to leave large forces in the west and south, and to defend her home industries against Allied air attack, relieved the pressure the Third Reich could bring to bear on the Soviet Union.[63] Similarly, as the industrial capacity and material and human resources devoted to the new German tanks designed primarily with the Red Army in mind could not be made available for the construction of submarines to reinforce the Battle of the Atlantic, so the building of hundreds of submarines for the war at sea kept Germany from turning out additional thousands of tanks for the battles in the East.

In the northern segment of the Kursk battle front, Model, with Hitler's agreement, now conducted an elastic defense of the Orel bulge, developing a shortened line behind it, called the "Hagen" position, to which the Red Army had chased him by mid-August. In those four weeks, Orel was liberated and the battered 2nd Panzer and 9th Army pushed back. Their new line was indeed shorter, but the Germans had lost heavily in the initial offensive phase and then in the defense against Rokossovski's attack. The insistence of Hitler that Army Group Center transfer divisions directly to Italy and to Army Group South, to replace divisions sent from the latter to Italy, had made it impossible even to try to hold the Orel bulge. Contrary to post-war apologias by German military memoir writers, Hitler was quite capable of sanctioning retreat when urged by generals he trusted and such action was required by strategic priorities.[a]

By the time this Soviet advance and German retreat were well under way, the Soviet offensive into the Donets basin, planned before "Citadel" and anticipated by Hitler when he called off the offensive on July 13, had begun. On July 17, Southwest and South Fronts attacked the German 1st Panzer Army and the new 6th Army in the Donets area. Although this operation in the remaining two weeks of July did not drive the Germans out of the Donets basin as the Stavka had hoped, it made any renewed German attacks in the south impossible, inflicted heavy casualties, and showed that the initiative had definitively passed to the Red Army in the summer as well as in the winter.

More offensives would be launched by the Soviet Union in August even as the Red Army was liberating Orel, but it is critical to note first that in July 1943 the German army had suffered a shattering defeat. It had thrown its best units and most modern weapons against an exposed Soviet salient and had been beaten back with heavy losses. Certainly Soviet losses were also huge, and the battlefield would be littered for years with burned out German and Soviet tanks, but the signal to the world which Hitler had expected from a victory at Kursk had indeed been given—it was a signal of the triumph of the Red Army over the Wehrmacht in a slugging match of enormous size and ferocity.

---

[a] It should be noted that it was Model who was instrumental first in having "Citadel" delayed and subsequently in obtaining authorization to retreat when the delayed operation failed. Klink (*Operation "Zitadelle"*, p. 271) believes that Model had hoped to have the whole project cancelled.

During August and September, even as the Germans were obliged by the Allied victory over Italy to withdraw units from the Eastern Front to replace Italian ones in that country and in the Balkans, the Red Army pushed forward in new offensive operations, now conducted in the summer and thus altering the pattern which many observers had expected. In August, even as the Red Army cleared the Orel bulge, a massive offensive was launched by the Voronezh and Steppe Fronts against von Manstein's troops still holding parts of the line reached in their July attacks. With the help of very heavy artillery concentrations, the Soviets broke into the German lines, liberated Belgorod and continued to strike both westwards and to the south. By the end of the month, the Germans had been driven out of Kharkov, a victory which redeemed the defeat suffered there by the Red Army in March. This was, however, by no means the end of the Soviet summer offensive; in a way it was only the beginning.

A series of Red Army offensives in the second half of August and during September on practically the whole southern portion of the front drove the Germans out of the Donets basin during September, cleared much of the left bank of the Dnepr, forced the Germans to abandon their old defensive position on the Mius river and obliged Hitler to order the evacuation of the Kuban bridgehead on September 3. By the beginning of October, the Germans had been pushed back on average 150 miles on the whole 650 miles of the southern front, with the Soviet Union thereby reclaiming very important industrial and agricultural areas, the most valuable portion of the country which the Germans had seized. Furthermore, although the retreating Germans were able to escape being encircled, they suffered very heavy casualties and materiel losses, so that when they reached the Dnepr line, even the reinforcements provided by the evacuation of the Kuban could not make up for the weakening caused by the defeats of summer and fall.[64]

The Germans held on to a few bridgeheads east of the Dnepr, one near Zaporozhe which was intended to help protect the manganese mines of Nikopol that she desperately needed for her steel industry, and one on the southernmost portion of the line which covered the land approach to the Crimea. The other side of this equation was, however, far more advantageous for the Red Army and dangerous for the Germans. Not only were the German forces on the new line weakened and exhausted, the Dnepr line itself had in effect been broken even before they could develop and hold it. Facing the possibility of a defense along the Dnepr long before the Germans themselves had decided to retire to it, the Soviet high command had ordered all its units to make every effort to seize crossings on the run, to bounce the river and gain footholds on the other side. In a procedure that was the exact opposite of the one Montgomery would use on the Rhine in 1945, the Red Army set the pattern which the Americans followed, namely to push across a wide river quickly wherever opportunity offered and bravery was sufficient. The gambit worked, and by the time the Battle of the Dnepr River Line began in the first days of October, the Red Army was already across the river at several points, and able to exploit bridgeheads seized the previous month when the Germans were being driven back to the river.

In theory the wide Dnepr river, with a western bank higher for most of its course than a flat eastern bank, would have made an ideal defensive line for the Germans, but there were two great disadvantages. In the first place, the course of the river heading southeast from Kiev and then after a great bend going southwestward to the Black Sea meant that either they would be in an enormous bulge open to the sort of encirclement that had brought on the Stalingrad disaster, or they would have to hold an essentially unprotected ground line south from the bend to the Sea of Azov, thereby shielding the northern approach to the Crimea. In the second place, not only had the Red Army secured several bridgeheads across the river in the September offensive, but the hundreds of miles of the Dnepr line which the Germans did hold had not been prepared for defense in the two years that the Germans had occupied the area. The assumption had always been that Germany would seize and hold vast stretches of territory east of the Dnepr, and by the time the river line became significant as a possible barrier for the Germans to utilize, there was no interval left to establish the needed positions. And the Red Army was determined not to let the Germans have that time. Not only had several of the Fronts pushed bridgeheads across the stream, but the Stavka was building up the armies in several sectors where assaults were to be mounted at a rate which made it possible to attack still in the fall.

The Russians did not repeat the error which the Germans had made in the spring of 1943, when repeated postponements of the summer offensive had afforded the Red Army time to recover from its spring set-back and to construct effective defensive lines. The two Army Groups, South under von Manstein and Army Group A under von Kleist, were not allowed the time either to recuperate or to dig in before the Red Army Fronts, now triumphantly renamed First, Second, Third and Fourth Ukrainian Fronts, attacked.

In the first days of October, Third Ukrainian Front (formerly the

Southwest Front) drove in the Zaporozhe bridgehead in fighting that was very costly for both sides. Soon after, Fourth Ukrainian Front (formerly South Front) attacked the German line running south from Zaporozhe to the Sea of Azov, freed Melitopol, the southern anchor of the German position, and then drove west. By the beginning of November, this thrust had chased the new 6th Army back to the Dnepr and cut off the German and Romanian forces in the Crimea which, in spite of pleas from the 17th Army commander there and from Marshal Antonescu, Hitler would not allow to be evacuated. He feared repercussions on Turkey, as well as air attacks from there on the Romanian oil fields, and hoped that a thrust of German armored forces south from the central Ukraine could reestablish land contact with 17th Army.

These hopes were to prove vain. Even as the Crimea was being cut off, 2nd Ukrainian Front (formerly Steppe Front) launched a smashing attack across the Dnepr between Kremenchug and Dnepropetrovsk, ripping open the front of 1st Panzer Army and threatening the rear of 6th Army. The Germans were able to drive back the most threatening Soviet spearhead, which reached the railway, mining and supply center of Krivoi Rog; but by the end of October the Red Army was deeply into the Dnepr bend area and had removed any possibility of the Germans holding the river line.

Further north, the First Ukrainian Front (formerly Voronezh Front) attacked in the last two weeks of October and the first days of November. After initially holding, the Germans were soon forced back. On November 5–6 the Red Army freed Kiev, the largest Soviet city held by the Germans, and pushed well beyond it. In the subsequent weeks, substantial German armored reinforcements, some of them divisions brought in from the West, cut off Soviet spearheads at Zhitomir; but here too the Dnepr line was gone beyond recall and important territory returned—with much of its population and resources—to Soviet control. By the end of 1943, a very large part of the Ukraine and the whole Northern Caucasus had been cleared of German troops and a substantial combined German–Romanian garrison effectively cut off in the Crimea. And as both sides knew from prior experience, it was the Red Army which launched offensives in the winter. The Soviet winter offensives in the Ukraine and in the north are really a portion of the preparation for the following year's operations and hence discussed in the next chapter; but it is necessary to note that on the central portion of the front, the Soviet victory at Orel by no means ended either the heavy fighting or the summer successes of the Red Army.

On the Central front, the Soviet victory at Orel was followed by a major push which forced the Germans to evacuate Bryansk and Smolensk along with a large portion of the area they had held since the summer of 1941. The German Army Group Center still had more soldiers, proportionally, than those either to the north or the south, although during the fall of 1943 it was obliged to transfer some divisions to von Manstein's Army Group South. The converse of this situation was that, having committed itself to a major series of offensives in the south, the Soviet high command did not have at its disposal the massive reserves which would have been required to drive back the Germans quickly on the Central front. During September 1943, therefore, the Red Army slowly pushed back Field Marshal Kluge's Army Group Center to the "Panther" position, a line about thirty miles east of the upper Dnepr, which the Germans had prepared in the preceding weeks and hoped to hold.

In practice this did not work as well for the Germans as it did in theory. During October, Rokossovski's Belorussian Front (a consolidated and renamed union of the former Bryansk and Central Fronts) drove into the southern flank of Army Group Center. While unable to score a decisive breakthrough, the Belorussian Front pushed the Germans out of Gomel and across the Dnepr. Simultaneously, at the northern flank of Army Group Center, where it joined Army Group North, a Soviet local attack at Nevel crushed one of the newly formed air force field divisions and opened a gap which the Red Army was unable to exploit fully because of commitments elsewhere but which the Germans could not close. During November and December, the Nevel gap was in fact enlarged by the Red Army so that by the end of the year the main northern anchor of Army Group Center, its defensive positions around Vitebsk, remained dangerously exposed, a situation on which the Russians were to capitalize in 1944.[65]

If these obvious signs of continuing military strength by the Soviet Union made it clear that the Red Army could hold and even advance in the summer as well as the winter, the continued strong resistance of the Germans, including their counter-attacks which sometimes succeeded in blunting Soviet advances, also demonstrated that a bitter fight lay ahead if the Red Army was to free all the previously occupied territory and drive on into the heart of Germany. The absence of the forces of the Western Allies from the continent of Europe until September of 1943 — however much the product of the Soviet Union's own earlier policy of helping Germany drive them out of North, West and Southern Europe — made the burden of fighting the bulk of the German army and a large share of its air force a particularly heavy one. This point had been driven home to Stalin most dramatically by the German counter-offensive of March 1943 culminating in the loss of Kharkov.

<h2 style="text-align:center">A SEPARATE PEACE IN THE EAST?</h2>

Until access to Soviet archives enables scholars to see more clearly into these murky episodes, this author will remain convinced that it was the shock of German military revival so soon after the great Soviet victory at Stalingrad which reinforced Stalin's inclinations during 1943 to contemplate the possibility of a separate peace either with Hitler's Germany or with some alternative German government. With the road to Berlin so obviously a difficult one, the temptation to sound possible alternatives was enormous. Surely by now the Germans must realize that their hopes of defeating the Soviet Union were illusory. The German government had had sense enough in 1939 to work out an accommodation with the Soviet Union on terms both sides had found advantageous; the same people were still in charge in Berlin. In the winter of 1940–41 they had refused to reply to the Soviet proposals for Russia to join the Tripartite Pact, but instead had insisted on attacking her; perhaps in the interim they had learned better in the hard school of war. As for the Soviet Union, she had demonstrated conclusively that she could defend herself, but this defense had been immensely costly. A new agreement with Germany would provide a breathing space for reconstruction and recovery, would remove German occupation without either further Red Army casualties or economic destruction, and would leave the Soviet Union dominant in all of Eastern Europe, especially in Poland where a Soviet puppet government would replace the pre-war regime. It may have been known to the Soviet government that there were elements in the German government and military apparatus who wanted an agreement with Moscow, and it was certainly known that Japan was very strongly in favor of a German–Soviet peace.

If a peace on the Eastern Front left Britain and the United States fighting Germany and Japan by themselves, that was not necessarily so sad from Moscow's point of view. Perhaps that would prove to be a more even match than the earlier one Stalin had promoted between Germany and the British–French combination. Whatever happened in such a conflict, victory for one side or a stalemate and accommodation, the combatants were certain to be greatly weakened and the Soviet Union would be secure and in a stronger position than before 1941. And if the prospect of a separate peace on the Eastern Front made the British and American governments more willing to make political concessions to the Soviet Union or to strike earlier against Germany in the West, that would be all to the good even if no such peace actually came about.

The tentative contacts between German and Soviet representatives in 1943, primarily in Sweden and very largely, it seems, through intermediaries, remain shrouded in a fog of controversy and confusion.[66] What is clear is that these contacts were most extensive in the spring and summer of 1943 but continued into the fall, that the Soviet Union informed its Allies about them only months after they had taken place, that the Western Allies found out about them anyway, and that they did not lead to any separate peace. As for their effect on the Western Allies, there can be no doubt that during the period May to September 1943 the British and American governments were very much concerned about the possibility of a separate peace, a concern reinforced by the withdrawal of Soviet ambassadors from London and Washington at the end of June as well as the knowledge gained from the intercepted Japanese telegrams that there was great pressure from Tokyo to bring the two combatants together again.[67]

On the Soviet side, the position appears to have been that Germany must evacuate all the occupied territory, certainly to the 1941 border, possibly later on, after the Soviet victory in July 1943, back to the 1914 border (thus turning over central Poland to the Soviet Union). German Foreign Minister von Ribbentrop appears to have been at least slightly interested in some compromise peace; he saw himself as the architect of the 1939 pact with the Soviet Union and had always given priority to the war against Great Britain. Joseph Goebbels, the Minister of Propaganda, favored negotiations with Stalin and so advised Hitler, almost certainly much more strongly than von Ribbentrop. Hitler, however, was unwilling to have any negotiations with the Soviet Union. Some of the sources make a great deal out of his suspicions about a key intermediary in Stockholm being Jewish, but Hitler's explanations to Goebbels and Oshima go to the core of the issue: he wanted to keep territory, especially the Ukraine, which he was certain Stalin would not give up; and on this point, if no other, his assessment of the Soviet Union was certainly correct.[68] While Stalin might have been willing to negotiate about territory to the west of the 1941 border of the country, he was certainly not about to leave the Germans in occupation of portions of it, least of all the rich agricultural and industrial areas of the Ukraine. The latter would, if necessary, be retaken in battle, and in the fall of 1943 and the winter of 1943–44 that is exactly what the Red Army did.

There was, however, still a third possible path other than a new accommodation with Hitler or a fight to the finish and that was an agreement with some alternative German government willing to abandon Germany's aims of conquest in Eastern Europe in exchange for the Soviet Union's exit from the war. It was obvious by 1943 that the mass working class upheaval which Marxist–Leninist theory had once predicted was clearly not about to occur in Germany. On the contrary, it was all too evident at the front that the workers were, for the most part, fighting hard in the Third Reich's service. There was, however, always the possibility that the German military might break with the regime and return to that cooperation with the Soviet Union which had been so profitable for their rearmament projects in the 1920s. Such a new regime, possibly supported by segments of the German population, could develop good relations with Moscow and provide a junior partner to the Soviet Union in dominating Europe.

The creation in the Soviet Union in the summer of 1943 of the National Committee for a Free Germany (NKFD) and soon after of the League of German Officers (BDO) point in this direction. Recruited from German Communist Party exiles and from German prisoners of war, these organizations were launched with great fanfare. Eventually, as it became obvious that the military were not about to turn on Hitler and the soldiers, with few exceptions, were not about to rise either, these organizations came to serve as propaganda vehicles during the war and as recruitment grounds for the post-war civilian regime and military forces in the Soviet zone of occupation in Germany. But for a while in 1943, their creation was a sign that Stalin was prepared to consider several options in dealing with both his enemy and his allies.[69]

ALLIED INVASION PLANS

Stalin's interest in exploring the possibility of a separate peace with Germany governed either by Hitler or by an alternative regime more sympathetic to and perhaps dependent upon the Soviet Union, was probably stimulated in the summer of 1943 by the information that a large-scale invasion of Western Europe by Britain and the United States would not take place until 1944. And as Soviet intelligence may well have informed him, even that date was not really certain because of continued British interest in pushing Mediterranean operations. At the Trident Conference in May 1943, the Americans, after long and heated debate, finally obtained Britain's agreement on two critical points: a May 1944 target date for the cross-Channel invasion and a commitment that in November 1943 the Allies would begin the transfer of seven battle experienced divisions, four American and three British, from the Mediterranean to the United Kingdom to take part in the great invasion. In the course of the summer, it became clear to the Americans that the British were not holding to this agreement; the latter now called for a halt to the troop transfers and this in turn raised fundamental questions about Britain's willingness to go forward with the cross-Channel invasion in practice, not only in theory.

The constant British emphasis on operations in the central and eastern Mediterranean, repeatedly voiced by Churchill and Brooke, made the American military leaders, Secretary of War Stimson, and President Roosevelt increasingly doubtful about the firmness of Britain's commitment to what was then referred to as "Roundhammer" and came to be known as "Overlord." Stimson himself went to London and in arguments with Churchill and others advocated the United States army's strategy of pushing from the best base with the greatest force at a place where it would have the greatest effect, as against a constantly revived British preference for a peripheral strategy. This in American eyes, would produce a stalemated war in Europe, leave the overwhelming burden of the war against Germany with the Soviet Union, and thus result either in the latter making a separate peace with Germany or, alternately, eventually winning the European war on land by itself and controlling practically all of the continent.[70]

Churchill constantly went back and forth between a firm endorsement in principle of the cross-Channel operation and a concern that the opportunities in the Mediterranean theater be exploited. The forboding sense that a renewed battle in Northwest Europe would involve staggering casualties if the landing failed or if the troops, once ashore, became involved in a lengthy campaign reminiscent of World War I fighting, came back to him time and again. Simultaneously, Field Marshal Brooke, who on other occasions restrained the Prime Minister's impulsive advocacy of all sorts of expeditions and projects, was most reluctant to hold down Mediterranean operations in favor of a future project which he was himself at that time scheduled to command but for which he evidently did not see the prerequisites in place.

It is not, in my judgement, correct to assert that the British opposed a landing in Northwest Europe, but they were simply not yet willing to give it the kind of priority that would be needed if the very obstacles to which they constantly pointed were to be overcome. The fact that both Churchill and Brooke would have reservations *after* the "Quadrant" Conference at Quebec in August, when apparently all had been definitely settled, shows that they did not see the issue the same way as the Americans. The latter believed that unless the energies of the Western Powers were harnessed unreservedly to a firm date, with the operational, shipping, production, and training schedules geared to that date, the project would recede into the indefinite future, and then the United States would either have to carry it out by itself or shift to a Pacific First strategy. It is ironic that Brooke, who so often privately castigated Marshall for being unable to see beyond the end of his nose, neither grasped the American concern with the need to set priorities nor conveyed to Montgomery, his favorite general, just what it was that made the Italian campaign such a highly significant operation. This latter point is important in the face of Montgomery's preference for leaving the Germans in control of the exposed Italian peninsula and concentrating everything for the big blow where it really counted, in the West.[71]

The Americans had three advantages in getting a large part of their strategic concept agreed to in Quebec. First, the recent nasty exchanges between the Western Allies and Stalin on the conduct of the war, the rumors of a German–Soviet separate peace, and the establishment of the National Committee for a Free Germany all suggested that it was essential for Allied unity that the Soviet Union be reassured about the seriousness of purpose in Britain and the United States.[72] Second, President Roosevelt's growing confidence in the advice of General Marshall and the developing strength of the United States helped make him absolutely determined to get a firm and final commitment for a May 1, 1944, "Overlord" at this time, and now with an American rather than a British commander.[a] A third factor was the product of earlier American pressure. At Marshall's insistence, a planning staff for the invasion had been created under General Frederick Morgan and the staff had been at work, preparing an invasion plan. This plan was ready by the time of the Quadrant Conference. It provided for a smaller assault than discussed earlier and actually carried out later (three divisions and two following divisions, plus some airborne units), but it designated the beaches near Caen as the assault site, and called for major supply over the beaches. It stipulated an early effort to seize the port of Cherbourg, set forth the need to have separate sectors in the assault and thereafter for the British and the United States units with the latter on the right flank to facilitate reinforcements, and stressed that it was essential to crush the German fighter planes in the West—all major features of the eventual actual invasion.[73] The submission of the plan as completed at the end of July to the conference immediately and almost automatically made the invasion project a real, practical, actually intended operation of war, not some abstract concept for interminable debate.

---

[a] It was British back-sliding after he had repeatedly received their agreement that led Roosevelt to take an anti-British tack at Teheran. When at Quebec Churchill agreed to an American commander for the invasion, he assumed that the appointment would go to Marshall. At that time Roosevelt appears to have thought so also, but he then believed that the appointment would also include control of the Italian campaign.

The Americans were now advocating implementation of a plan drawn up by an Allied staff headed for the time being by a British general, based on actual Allied combat experience and anticipated available resources, and put forward at a time when the campaign in Sicily was nearing its end, when there were soundings about a surrender from the Italians, and, above all, at a time in the war when the Battle of the Atlantic, though still raging fiercely and likely to provide much hard fighting, was clearly turning in favor of the Allies. In this context, an invasion of Northwest Europe was obviously a realistic proposal, not a pipe-dream.

At the conference in Quebec, the American and British political and military leaders argued out their views of the future of the war with considerable heat, but ended in a substantial measure of agreement.[74] The "overriding priority" which the Americans wanted for "Overlord" was not attained, but the final language made success of "Overlord" the "main object" for 1944. The Americans received the reluctant assent of the British to a reaffirmation of the transfer of seven divisions from the Mediterranean to the United Kingdom for "Overlord." This was a key point, because with forces reduced by such a transfer the Mediterranean theater commander clearly could not be expected to engage in any great array of new operations, however promising in the eyes of the British and however peripheral and diversionary in the eyes of the Americans.

Under these circumstances, it is not surprising that there was agreement that there would be no offensive operations in the Balkans. Guerilla movements in that area would be supplied by air and sea, there might be minor commando raids, and the strategic bombing offensive would attack objectives in Southeast Europe, but there was to be no commitment of ground troops. When, soon after, the British tried to seize the Italian islands in the Aegean and then, as the Italians would not fight the Germans there any more than anywhere else, urged the United States to support operations against Rhodes to assist their own units landed on Cos, Leros and Samos, the Americans absolutely refused. The British suffered disaster in the Aegean in October 1943, losing heavily in ships and planes as well as men. This caused considerable hard feelings between the Western Allies, but the Americans were under no circumstances going to be rushed into major allocations of resources in the Eastern Mediterranean, where they were then in the process of trying to *reduce* American forces and supply commitments.[75]

Agreement was also reached at Quebec on two other issues of importance for the future of the war. For the European theater, the COSSAC staff of General Morgan had produced a plan, code-named "Rankin," for a quick entry into Europe by British and United States forces in case of a sudden German collapse, a contingency examined earlier but now more in need of study because of recent developments in Italy—which might be repeated in Germany—and because of the interest of President Roosevelt in getting troops from the West to Berlin as soon as the Russians reached it from the East, a subject to which he would return later that year.[76] The various alternative versions of the "Rankin" plan attuned to differing contingencies were approved. The other area of major discussion was the war against Japan. The outlines of this issue are reviewed in the examination of the Pacific theater subsequently in this chapter, but in the context of frictions between the United States and Britain resolved at Quebec, a word must be said about the settlement at this time of one of the most difficult controversies ever to arise between the two powers during the war.

The complicated command arrangements in Southeast Asia seemed to both powers to require a supreme commander who could perhaps pull together the disparate Allied forces engaged in the theater, possibly the way Eisenhower was successfully beginning to do in the Mediterranean. The Americans also hoped—perhaps the appropriate term is that they would have turned their prayer wheels if they had had any—that such an appointment would at least and at last reduce the torpor which characterized the British forces in the India–Burma area. The British government, however, came up with the name of Air Chief Marshal Sir Sholto Douglas, the air commander in the Middle East, whom the Americans absolutely refused to accept. Over a two-month period this dispute, the most difficult such controversy of the war, raged. Churchill would not accept any of the alternative British commanders suggested, and Roosevelt, clearly backing Marshall on this, stuck to his objections to Douglas.[77]

At the Quebec Conference, Churchill at last came up with another name: the British Chief of Combined Operations, Lord Louis Mountbatten.[78] Immediately and enthusiastically accepted by the Americans, Mountbatten would go on not only to awaken the sleepy British commands as the Americans had hoped, and enthuse the British soldiers, as Montgomery had done in North Africa, but play a role which perhaps predestined him to become the last Viceroy of India, hardly what Churchill had in mind. But the divisive issue of command was settled; whatever the subsequent endless troubles in the officially designated SEAC, South East Asia Command, Mountbatten had the ability to keep on at least reasonable terms with the perpetually feuding British, American and Chinese commanders on the scene. Marshall was so relieved to have this issue settled that he agreed to the appointment of a personal representative of Churchill to General MacArthur's staff, an opportunity which Churchill made golden by appointing Lt. General Sir Herbert Lumsden, former commander of an armored corps in North Africa, who turned out to have excellent rapport with MacArthur.[79] Here was an ironic but fitting outcome of a quarrel over appointments that at one point had been getting out of hand.

On two further issues relating to the European war there was essentially no difficulty in reaching agreement at Quebec. As a remote contingency if the "Overlord" operation could not be launched, plans should be kept up to date for "Jupiter," the older project, long a favorite of Churchill's, for an Allied landing in Norway. More significant was the sense that the Combined Bomber Offensive against Germany was beginning to hit its stride and could perform a major role in diverting German air power from the Eastern Front, disrupting her production and morale, and preparing the way for the great invasion in 1944. The imminent surrender of Italy opened up the possibility, already mentioned, of seizing airfields from which British and United States airplanes could reach important targets in east Germany and in portions of German-controlled Europe hitherto out of range, and thus forcing a diversion of German air defenses.

THE AIR WAR IN 1943

Even before the Quadrant Conference, the British with United States Air Force help had carried out a series of great air attacks on the city of Hamburg on July 24–27.[80] Enormous damage and heavy casualties (about 40,000 deaths) were inflicted in a succession of raids, which overwhelmed the defenses by sheer numbers, as well as the use of a new device to confuse German radar code-named "Window," the dropping of great quantities of aluminum strips. Vast fires, which produced a massive fire-storm, gutted big portions of Germany's second largest city. This phenomenon, new in modern warfare, created a self-nourishing fire which sucked in people and objects, raised temperatures to levels that caused the asphalt in the streets to burn, and could not be contained or even substantially affected by traditional fire-fighting techniques. The devastation was vast, but with no understanding of German reconstruction efforts, the huge attack on Hamburg would not be repeated on any comparable scale.

After the area raid on Hamburg, the Royal Air Force proceeded to carry out massive attacks on other German cities in September and October 1943, especially Mannheim-Ludwigshafen, Frankfurt am

Main, and Hanover; the raid on Kassel on October 22 created a fire-storm like the one in Hamburg.[81] Believing that heavy bombers acting alone could win the war, Harris now sent his planes on the long and exceedingly dangerous route to Berlin. Here too there was massive damage and great loss of life, but the distance from British bases, more effective German defenses, and difficulty in concentration when attacking a vast built up area attenuated the impact. Without making a judgement on the controversy between those who consider the Battle of Berlin a success or a failure for the Royal Air Force, certain things are clear.[82]

However much the attacks on urban areas diverted from the priority in the "Pointblank" directive for the Combined Bomber Offensive on aircraft factories, they certainly forced a major diversion of German military effort and resources. The August 18, 1943, suicide of the German air force chief of Staff, General Jeschonnek, was only the most obvious sign of the enormous strain and drain imposed by the assault at home simultaneously with the great summer struggle on the Eastern Front.[83] The general disruption of the German economy and the specific raid on the research station at Peenemünde on August 17, 1943, meant that the most dangerous of Germany's new weapons, the ballistic rocket V-2, which was originally to have been fired in masses on London and other cities from November 1, 1943, did not come into action until September 8, 1944, a very significant difference.[84]

Furthermore, the very heavy losses of the Luftwaffe, especially in the fighter forces struggling to defend industry and cities, led to a massive reallocation not only of production resources to fighters and anti-aircraft guns but from the Eastern and Mediterranean fronts to the defense of the skies over Germany. With occasional exceptions, the mass of German air power was concentrated on the home front from the fall of 1943 on.[85] There the increase of aircraft production could not keep up with attrition in the sky, and diversions of resources to the elaborate new weapons hindered rather than helped an air force struggling to cope with streams of Allied bombers. Moreover, the steady increase in anti-aircraft guns with their enormous consumption of ammunition dramatically reduced what was available to the army on the land fronts.[86] The situation had not yet reached the point it did in 1944 when half of Germany's artillery was at home pointing skyward, but the omens were there.

On the other hand, massive increases in German fighter production did make both British night-time and American daylight bomber raids increasingly costly. Larger losses of the four-engine bombers meant heavy casualties among trained crews as the Germans now enjoyed the advantage that the British had held in the Battle of Britain: larger crews in the bombers than in the fighters and a total loss to death or imprisonment of the crew of each bomber shot down, as compared to the possible return to duty of any fighter pilots who bailed out. In the battle over German cities and factories in the fall of 1943 it looked more and more as if the Germans would win out. More especially, the steadily high losses of Bomber Command and such heavy losses by the United States air force as those sustained in the attack on the ball-bearing plants at Schweinfurt on August 17 suggested that the massive fighter production program pushed by Speer and Field Marshal Erhard Milch would triumph over the Combined Bomber Offensive, especially in the absence of long-range fighter escorts.[87]

The Germans were so confident that they were winning in the skies over German-controlled Europe that they again accentuated plans and production projects for bombers, not fighters, in order to strike more heavily at Great Britain.[88] But even before the last big British defeat and German victory in the air during the raid on Nürnberg on March 30, 1944, the Americans had found the answer to the Luftwaffe's challenge in the skies.[89] In the meantime, the British and United States bomber crews fought it out in the skies over Europe in battles in one way similar to those of the German submarines in the Atlantic—steady determination in the face of very low odds on survival. These were lowest for the Americans in the August 1, 1943, raid from North Africa on the Romanian oil fields at Ploesti. As often before and after, considerable damage was inflicted at great cost, but the failure to recognize the need for repeat attacks— and sometimes the inability to mount such attacks because of losses— meant that, within a relatively short time, critical damage to factories could be repaired.[90]

The Royal Air Force and the United States Army Air Force would have to shift their bombing attacks to areas they could reach with fighter escorts until the fighter escorts could be altered to reach the targets that the bombing forces were supposed to reach. In the meantime, the Combined Bombing Offensive had made a major contribution to the Allied war effort by imposing a terrible rate of attrition on the German air force, by forcing its re-allocation from the land fronts in east and south to home defense, by making the Germans disperse their aircraft industry and thereby reducing its output, by inflicting substantial damage on some industries and more cities, and by inspiring the Germans to direct resources to several ingenious but not especially cost-effective devices for retaliating against Britain.

MOSCOW, CAIRO, TEHERAN

The continued Combined Bombing Offensive was the most obvious and immediately implemented of the Quadrant decisions.[91] The invasion of Italy in early September showed that the Western Allies would not be idle after the conquest of Sicily. But the major issue to be worked out remained coordination of the British and American effort with that of the Soviet Union in the war still to be won—and in the years thereafter—now that it looked increasingly as if the Allies could expect to move to the offensive. The Soviet Union had refused to be represented at Casablanca and had been uninterested in participating at the Trident Conference in Washington in May or the Quadrant meeting in Quebec in August; on the contrary Stalin had warded off all British and American attempts to arrange a meeting of the three powers at the highest level and had gone beyond this by withdrawing ambassadors from Washington and London. In the summer of 1943, exchanges between Moscow and the two Western capitals had grown increasingly acerbic. There was now something of a thaw. Until Soviet records on these matters (if they exist) become accessible, it will remain impossible to be certain; but the failure of the Germans to respond to any Soviet overtures, the obvious disinclination of the German generals to overthrow the Hitler regime, and the growing confidence of the Soviet Union in its own military abilities probably contributed as much to this change as the steady increase in Allied aid shipments, the fighting around the Mediterranean and in the skies over Europe and the urgings of the American government. Stalin now agreed to a meeting of the big three to be held later that year and a preparatory meeting with high-ranking British and American officials to prepare the way. Stalin's August 8 statement that a big three meeting was desirable later that year could be recalled as easily as his earlier tentative agreement to meet with Franklin D. Roosevelt in July or August 1943, but the response of Churchill and Roosevelt from Quebec on August 18, agreeing to Stalin's proposal for a preliminary meeting of responsible representatives to prepare the ground for the big meeting later, opened the way for new steps.

The preparations for the preliminary conference included agenda proposals by the three powers, information for the Soviet Union on the decisions about "Overlord" reached at Quebec,[92] and some discussions about the location of the meeting itself. The decision on this last point presumably pleased the Soviet Union: the representatives would meet in Moscow.[93] For twelve days, October 19–30, 1943, British Foreign Secretary Anthony Eden accompanied by General Ismay and others, United States Secretary of State Cordell Hull[a] with a delegation which included the newly designated head of the United States military mission in Moscow, General John Deane, as well as the new Ambassador to the Soviet Union Averell Harriman, met with Molotov, who served as chairman of the conference, a number of Soviet military and diplomatic officials, and, on separate occasions, with Stalin. The Americans especially wanted a Four Power Declaration on wartime cooperation until the surrender of their enemies and on cooperation in the establishment of a post-war international organization. This proposal involved not only Soviet adhesion to the unconditional surrender formula but a major step toward the establishment of the United Nations as well as the inclusion of China as one of the major powers, both points on which Roosevelt and Hull placed great emphasis in their view of the future. The first of these was, with some hesitations, acceptable to both Britain and the Soviet Union while the latter met with strong objections from both. The British and Russians simply refused to accept the American vision of a future for China as one of the world's major powers, and the Russians had the added concern about the reaction of Japan to any Soviet step at that time which could be seen as associating them with Britain and the United States in the Pacific War. This last subject will come up again in several ways, but at the conference, London and Moscow eventually yielded to American insistence and agreed that the Chinese Ambassador in Moscow could be a signer for his government.

If the British and Russians were brought around on this point with great reluctance, the Americans came to agree, perhaps even more reluctantly, to some minimal recognition of the French National Committee of Liberation, as de Gaulle called his provisional government, in the face of Roosevelt's and Hull's objections to him and at Eden's constant insistence (sometimes without support from his Prime Minister). No agreement could be reached on the best way to handle the differences which had developed in Iran in connection with the delivery of supplies across that country to the Soviet Union, but the serious tension between Britain and the Soviet Union over the Arctic convoys was eased a little. On the future treatment of Germany, there was agreement on the need to force a surrender and to disarm and denazify the country. As to its future, there was no agreement on borders, reparation policies,

---

[a] Hull had insisted on going, and this helped precipitate Roosevelt's decision to let Under Secretary of State Sumner Welles go.

or whether the country should be broken up — "dismembered" was the wartime term — or maintained as a smaller unit. As for Italy, that country might work its passage to the side of the Allies by a real contribution in the war, while a council on which the Soviet Union would be represented would advise the Allied military commander in the area. The Soviets wanted a share of the Italian navy and merchant fleet, a point on which the American and British promised agreement which was reached later by the turning over of American and British ships equivalent to what the Soviet Union had requested.

The effort of the Americans to begin serious negotiations on post-war economic relations was met by evasion from the British and Soviet representatives, a most extraordinary form of obtuseness on the part of both powers which would come back to haunt them when, with the end of hostilities in 1945, Lend-Lease ended as provided in the relevant American legislation, legislation which the authorities in both London and Moscow neglected to read.

There was general agreement, reflected in a public pronouncement, that Austria would be separated from Germany again. This was more an effort to stimulate opposition to the Berlin regime in Austria and in German military formations recruited in Austria as well as to show that Germany could not keep its pre-war gains than a recognition of the fact that, while included in Germany, many Austrians had come to realize that they were not Germans after all. It was also announced that war criminals would be tried for the atrocities they committed, with those of local relevance being sent back to the scene of the crimes and those with a broader array of offenses being punished by a joint decision of the Allies, the hope being that this proclamation might discourage at least some Germans from further atrocities as they could see the war turning against the Axis. The three powers also promised to inform each other of peace feelers from the enemy powers, a point of special significance at a time when the satellites of Germany were trying to find a way out of the war without risking the wrath of the Germans, a ridiculous undertaking as the Italian experience might have taught any leader in Helsinki, Budapest, Bukarest or Sofia with eyes and brains.

At the suggestion of the British, who had changed their views on this subject several times, the pre-conference Soviet proposal for a commission to oversee Italy and any other liberated and occupied areas was met by the establishment of the European Advisory Commission (EAC), which was to meet in London (as distinct from the Committee for Italy which began in Algiers), but for which neither Russians nor Americans ever developed great enthusiasm.

The fundamental military divergence between the Allies also appeared to be solved.[94] The American and British military representatives outlined the planned "Overlord" operation for the spring of 1944, the subordination of the Mediterranean campaign to it, and—in practice always the most critical point of all—the planned transfer of seven divisions from the Mediterranean to the United Kingdom. Several aspects of the discussions on this must be mentioned. The Soviet representatives, who were obviously pleased by what they heard, suggested, however, that the Allies try to get Turkey and Sweden to enter the war. These projects would have involved diversions from "Overlord" into the Eastern Mediterranean and Scandinavia, both old favorites of Churchill's and both strongly opposed by the Americans.

Not only were there differences on this issue, but the Soviets were also very cool to the three practical proposals made by the Americans for improving cooperation in the war against Germany: shuttle bombing so that planes from British, Italian or North African bases could land in the Soviet Union and thus carry far heavier bomb loads; exchange of weather information to facilitate the Combined Bomber Offensive; and improved air transport connections between the Soviet Union and the United States and Great Britain. In the face of Soviet reluctance, little came of these three proposals; but the handling of these matters sheds an interesting light on Soviet unwillingness at military coordination.[a] What is in some ways more puzzling is Stalin's apparent willingness, now that the Americans had managed to get the British on record for a shift from the Mediterranean to "Overlord," to waffle on that question himself. When, to the consternation of Eden and the horror of the Americans, Churchill instructed Eden to warn Stalin about the possibility that what Churchill asserted were difficulties in the Italian campaign might well force a postponement in the transfer of divisions from the Mediterranean and hence a postponement of "Overlord," Stalin did not react with anger but instead said kind things about the Italian campaign which would have warmed the hearts of Churchill and Brooke.[95]

The real meaning of these very substantial modifications of prior Soviet positions is not easy to explain. It has been suggested that bringing in Sweden would provide cover toward the United States for a complete Soviet occupation of Finland,[96] and that what Stalin really wanted in regard to Turkey was the halting of British and American arms deliveries to that country once it turned down the request to enter the war, but

---

[a] The alleged reluctance of Britain and France on the issue of close military collaboration had been used by the Soviet Union as an excuse for signing with Germany in 1939. It should be noted that the British believed that the shuttle bombing concept was a poor one in practice because they thought that it would require an excessive allocation of manpower and spare parts to bases in the Soviet Union; see Sinclair to Churchill, 24 October 1943, PRO, PREM 3/11/10 (Churchill agreed with Sinclair's position).

these appear to me somewhat far-fetched speculations.[97] Perhaps these curious aspects of the Moscow discussions merely reflect a far greater confidence of Stalin by late October 1943 in the ability of the Red Army to drive into Central Europe with or without a major land offensive against Germany from the West.[98]

This confidence was also reflected in the handling of questions concerning Eastern Europe. The Soviet Union had been insistent from the time of the German attack in 1941 that its boundaries, including the territory annexed under its earlier agreements with Germany, be recognized. The British had been willing to do that in 1941 but had been restrained by the American government. The British government in preparation for the Moscow Conference had approved Eden's suggestion that they should agree to the Curzon Line, but try to obtain Lwow for Poland, while the Poles would get compensation from Germany. The Baltic States were perceived as lost; the Soviet–Romanian border of 1941 was considered acceptable; and so was the 1941 Soviet–Finnish border. Any Soviet demand for Petsamo was seen as in another category, because it had not been Soviet territory in June 1941, but the British were prepared to agree to this as well.[99]

The Americans had not altered their opposition to boundary commitments during the war, and Hull was not about to become involved in discussions of future governments in Eastern Europe at a time when the British and American governments were engaged in difficult disputes over the new government of Italy. With no prospect of any direct military role by Britain or the United States in Eastern Europe, there was little that either power could do to influence Soviet policy there.[a] The British found themselves obliged to agree to a special treaty between the Czechoslovak government-in-exile and the Soviet Union (described as neighbors on the assumption that the Soviet Union would annex southeast Poland) and could secure no resumption of relations between the Polish government-in-exile and Moscow. Since the fate of Czechoslovakia—which yielded to Soviet territorial demands and otherwise cooperated with the Soviet Union—was to be exactly the same as that of Poland, whose government-in-exile resisted territorial concessions, the bitter debates which later ensued about Poland probably made no substantial difference, but this could hardly be anticipated in 1943.

Enough agreement, however, had been reached on other issues to make for a general sense of satisfaction with the conference. This was

---

[a] The British had been pushing for a federation among the smaller states of East and Southeast Europe, but ran up against a Soviet veto at the Moscow meeting. There is no reason to believe that such a construction would have been created in the absence of Soviet objections.

marked in a special way by Stalin's telling Hull, and Molotov informing Harriman at the end of the meetings, that the Soviet Union would enter the war against Japan after the defeat of Germany. All prior projects for U.S.—Soviet cooperation in case of a Japanese attack on the Soviet Union had foundered on Stalin's opposition.[100] Now Stalin had promised to join in against Japan; discussion of the price and circumstances would come later. For the Western Allies, here was a way of assuring that not only the fighting in Europe but also that in the Pacific would end within a reasonable time.

For the Americans the Four Power Agreement had a special significance. It not only marked a step in their effort to have China recognized as one of the major powers but it promised hope that there would not be a repetition after World War II of what Roosevelt and Hull believed had gone wrong after World War I. The turn of the United States to isolation after 1918, and the repudiation of the peace treaties of 1919 and of the League, were major contributing factors to the subsequent outbreak of a second great war. This was an important aspect of their perception of what had gone wrong in the past as they had themselves experienced it, and they were very conscious of this as they looked ahead. If both Roosevelt and Hull attached much more importance to the anchoring of the United States, and especially of American public opinion, in a new international structure to be created at the end of the war, it was because they saw such a procedure as critical to the avoidance of a repetition of what they in common with many Americans had come to believe had gone wrong earlier.[101]

While in the subsequent preparations for the meeting of the big three some issues were resolved if with difficulty, one major question was fatefully left open. After numerous exchanges, Churchill and even more reluctantly Roosevelt agreed to have the meeting held in Teheran, which was as far as Stalin was willing to go from Soviet territory. Even more complicated was the way found to carry out Roosevelt's desire to meet Chiang Kai-shek. Though increasingly disillusioned by what he heard about the corruption, ineffectiveness and military inefficiency of the Chinese Nationalist government, the President wanted to use a meeting to bolster the sagging morale of the Chinese and to pave the way for a larger role for that nation in the future. Chiang's anti-imperialist views, which had dominated Kuomintang (KMT) policy in the 1920s, were consonant with American preferences; and if Roosevelt felt that his personal relations with Churchill could not stand further comments on the need for India to become self-governing, he could make the same point by public enhancement of a head of state who regularly praised Indian nationalist leaders in and out of British jails. As Roosevelt saw the future,

Britain's imperial role in Asia was nearing its end, even if not as quickly as he expected Japan's to be terminated; and China would assume a major role on the continent, serving at the same time as a counter-weight to excessive Soviet expansionism. That such ideas aroused no enthusiasm in London or Moscow is hardly surprising, and the resulting decision was for Roosevelt to meet Chiang in Cairo on the way to Teheran. Churchill and his advisors would also stop there and hold a preliminary meeting with the Americans, but with an entirely different purpose and with entirely different results.

As the major British book on the Moscow, Cairo, and Teheran Conferences puts it, the main purpose of the Cairo meeting

> was to provide Churchill and the British Chiefs of Staff with the opportunity to persuade the Americans that the date for "Overlord" should not be regarded as governing all other factors to the extent of imposing a rigid straight-jacket on Mediterranean operations. In particular it should not be allowed to dictate an absolutely rigid timetable for the return of troops and landing-craft to the United Kingdom.[102]

Here was the key to a major clash between the British and the Americans. The British had reluctantly agreed to the American urging of a deadline for "Overlord" at the Trident Conference in May. They had then reversed themselves to insist on greater flexibility in favor of Mediterranean operations but had yielded to American pressure and returned to the May 1 target date at the Quadrant Conference in August. In October this project had been set forth to the Russians. Even as that conference was in session, however, there was a lengthy discussion in the British War Cabinet in which the clear sense was that the Italian campaign should have priority over Overlord and that there should be no promise of Overlord in May 1944 in spite of all prior agreements with the Americans.[103] So now the British wanted to open the issues once again.

The Americans had seen signs of this British shift coming and were absolutely determined to reject it. It was their view that at some point in the war Allied strategy simply had to be fixed and adhered to if major plans were ever to be implemented. The Americans had most reluctantly agreed to leave some of the landing-craft scheduled for Overlord in the Mediterranean a little longer, but they would not budge on the troop transfers: the first of the four American divisions, the 1st Infantry Division, embarked from Sicily on October 23, 1943, and was already gone from the Mediterranean by the time of the Cairo Conference; the other three were on the way before the end of the year.[104] In this case an American military move was made deliberately to implement a prior agreement which the British still hoped to reverse.

One way in which the Americans hoped to contain what they correctly perceived as a recurrent British preference for immediate operations in the Mediterranean, regardless of the implications for Overlord, was to propose a single command for both theaters, headed by General Marshall, with separate commanders for the two campaigns under him. He would certainly see to it that Overlord received priority and that operations were conducted in and resources allocated to the Mediterranean in a manner designed to support the great invasion, not postpone it over and over. In the face of vehement British objections to this command set up which would place an American dedicated to Overlord between Churchill (and the British Chiefs of Staff) and the British commanders in the Mediterranean, the Americans were prepared to make a major concession. They would accept a British commander, Field Marshal Sir John Dill, in the position assigned to Marshall in their proposal. The Americans had such confidence in Dill's willingness to adhere to the agreed strategy that they were prepared to place the bulk of American forces in action under his over-all command. But even this was not enough to divert the British from their insistence on revising strategy and keeping the Mediterranean command, in which they wanted to include both the North African and Italian theaters and the Middle East, under a separate structure which they could influence directly.[a]

It was thus clear that the whole issue of strategy for defeating Germany would have to be thrashed out all over again at Cairo, with the British aggravated by what *they* saw as a straight-jacket on operations in the Mediterranean and with the Americans even more aggravated by what they saw as still another effort of the British to wriggle out of prior promises so that they could diddle on indefinitely around the periphery of the continent. What made the argument so difficult was that there was substance to both of these grievances. The British were entirely correct in the belief that opportunities in Italy and in Southeast Europe were being sacrificed to the Americans' insistence on adherence to strategic priorities, though whether they would in the end have been that much happier if their troops had reached the Alps and the Western Powers had occupied Bulgaria while the Red Army liberated Belgium is at least open to question. The Americans, on the other hand, were correct in fearing that any further extension of Mediterranean operations risked almost indefinite postponement of Overlord. Even with eventual reaffirmation of the May target date and the Overlord priority, shortages of assault shipping forced a one-month postponement; two additional

---

[a] The agreement had been that, because an American rather than Brooke was to command the cross-Channel invasion, a British officer would assume Eisenhower's post in the Mediterranean. On the whole command issue, see Sainsbury, *Turning Point,* pp. 159–60; Matloff, *Strategic Planning 1943–1944,* chap. 12; British documents in PRO, PREM 3/101.

months of further delay imposed by diversion of resources to the Mediterranean would almost certainly have pushed Overlord into 1945.[a]

At the Cairo Conference (referred to as Sextant), the Americans and British in sometimes bitter conversations failed to reach agreement on the most important issue. Taking advantage of the more favorable comments on the Italian campaign and the push for Mediterranean operations in relation to Turkey by the Soviets at the Moscow Conference, the British now refused to adhere to the Quebec agreement on strategy and insisted on a decision by Stalin at the forthcoming meeting at Teheran. The British hoped—and the Americans feared—that in a choice between further operations in the Mediterranean at the cost of deferring Overlord and adherence to an early date for Overlord and reduced action in the Mediterranean, Stalin would pick the former. Because of their anger over lost opportunities in the Eastern Mediterranean, symbolized by the arguments over their desire for an attack on the island of Rhodes (operation "Accolade"), the British not only argued their case in Cairo but intended to continue arguing it at Teheran.[105] The result of this approach, which should have been obvious to them at the time but was not (nor to many observers later), was that a very large part of the available time at Teheran was occupied by debates on issues that the British and Americans had thrashed out repeatedly and had apparently settled several times, with the consequence that adequate time was simply not available for other questions.

In addition, the British absolutely refused any idea of an over-all European commander even if the position went to Dill, with Montgomery as Northwest Europe commander. This in turn made it less likely that Marshall would command operations in Europe while Eisenhower went to Washington as Acting Chief of Staff, and instead set the stage for Eisenhower's later appointment for Overlord. The Americans agreed to a general Mediterranean command, including the Eastern Mediterranean, but continued to prefer a landing in southern France to assist Overlord, instead of any operations in the Eastern Mediterranean.

The Americans, furthermore, also accepted minor delays in some

---

[a] That this would also have meant vastly greater damage to British cities, especially London, from the new German weapons was no more apparent in the fall of 1943 than that the schedule implicit in the British proposals would practically certainly have led to the first atomic bombs being dropped on Germany rather than Japan.

It should be noted that Brooke's Diary for 9 November 1943 includes the statement: "First we must go in Italy till we reach the Pisa–Rimini line. This will entail postponing Cross-Channel operation some 2 months" (Liddell Hart Centre, Alanbrooke Papers). Of course additional landing ships would have been built during those months, but the word "some" is instructive. See also Stoler, *Politics of the Second Front*, p. 133.

ship transfers to Northwest Europe so that an additional effort could be made in the interval in Italy; as will be seen, Churchill's success in persuading the Americans to try an amphibious operation in Italy did not produce the great new victory, including the seizure of Rome, which he anticipated. There was, on the other hand, no discussion or agreement on the latest version of the "Rankin" plan. Roosevelt had made clear to his advisors on the trip to North Africa that he wanted the western and eastern occupation zones to meet in Berlin, and for the United States to have the northwestern zone with the North Sea ports rather than the southern zone with access overland across France.[106] These questions would become the subject of long debates later (and after the war as well).

As the Americans had intended, much of the time at Cairo was devoted to the Pacific War and questions involving China. Not only Chiang but Mountbatten and Stilwell were at the meeting.[107] The Americans, with British agreement, promised that the areas Japan had seized from China since 1894 should be returned to her. The British were not then about to return Hong Kong, but it is clear that in their private talks Roosevelt and Chiang were in agreement on the need to end colonial rule in Asia. There would be difficulties in working out a coordination between Soviet ambitions and China's desire to regain all her lost territories, but the existing record of the talks on this point is vague. To help open a land route to China, there would be a land campaign in northern Burma (about which the British were most unenthusiastic), and Roosevelt promised a small amphibious operation against the Andaman Islands in the Indian Ocean ("Buccaneer") to which the British objected even more vehemently. With the Chinese government and military in very poor condition, these steps might help keep them in the war.[108] As the Western Allied leaders left Cairo for Teheran, they had still not agreed on a definite strategy for the defeat of Germany and were by no means in real accord about operations in Southeast Asia either. With Churchill in rather poor health at this point, the setting for Teheran was not at its best.[109]

The insistence of Churchill on repeatedly returning to the charge on extended operations in the Mediterranean and delays in Overlord meant that most of three of the four days at the Teheran Conference was taken up with the arguments over strategy in the European war, although Stalin made his own preference absolutely clear at the very first meeting.[110] Whatever may have caused him to consider further Mediterranean operations earlier, he now insisted that all be subordinated to Overlord in May 1944, with that operation to be accompanied and preferably preceded by a landing on the southern coast of France.[a] A Soviet offensive would be coordinated with the invasion. Stalin's insistence in fact settled the issue, and if it meant that the Soviet Union thereby decided an Anglo-American dispute, one must remember that anyone who asks a question risks receiving an answer. Having put the issue to Stalin in view of their inability to agree, the Western Allies now had his reply.

The British nevertheless kept arguing the point to little purpose except the creation of much aggravation and a common front between the American and Soviet delegations, both with their own suspicions of British intentions: the Americans that the British would always find ways to postpone Overlord, the Russians that the British really did not want to carry it out at all. Though rarely touched on in the meetings, there was in my opinion an issue in the background. The British feared that an invasion attempt might fail, and for them, that would be the end of the road. They had been driven off the continent by the Germans three times in the war; the fourth time would be fatal. The Americans, on the other hand, certainly hoped and expected that the invasion would succeed, but if it did fail, they could and they would try again. The Russians undoubtedly felt that, success or failure, it was about time the Western Powers did their share of the fighting. At Stalin's insistence that the operation would never be launched unless a Commander-in-Chief were appointed for it, the President promised that this would be done within a few days. Since the British had blocked an over-all European command, he decided right after the Teheran Conference to keep Marshall in Washington and appoint Eisenhower.

The obstinacy with which the British argued did lead to slight modifications in the timetable: Overlord would take place during May, not on the first; the landing in southern France would come at the same time as Overlord and possibly even a bit later and with a full two division assault landing; and landing craft would remain in the Mediterranean until mid-January for an amphibious operation in Italy. The Allies also agreed once again to try to persuade Turkey to enter the war, but this was surely considered a futile exercise by both the Americans and Soviets, as indeed it proved to be.[111]

At the first session, Roosevelt had discussed the war in the Pacific at

---

[a] If Stoler's explanation of Stalin's comments at Moscow is correct, namely that the Soviets then hoped for a collapse by Germany in 1943, it would make sense to assume that the German counter-attack west of Kiev just before the Teheran Conference impressed the Soviet leader with the fact that the war was not going to end for some time. Stalin's insistence at the conference on weakening Germany permanently may also have been influenced by the recent set-back to the Red Army at the front.

some length, and Stalin now formally promised him and Churchill to join in after the defeat of Germany. This promise and the desire to increase the operation in southern France would enable the British to insist on the abandonment of the "Buccaneer" operation, a decision reached at the meeting in Cairo afterwards and of great significance in symbolizing a major reduction in the importance of the China–Burma–India theater. China would get back the lands Japan had taken from her, Korea would regain its independence, and the Soviet Union would regain southern Sakhalin and the Kurile Islands. Roosevelt explained that he had raised with a most unenthusiastic Chiang the possibility of the Soviets using the warm-water port of Dairen; Stalin insisted that the Chinese like others had to do their share of the fighting to earn their rewards.

For the future generally, Roosevelt urged an international organization in which the four great powers would have a major role, sketching out what came to be the organization of the United Nations and getting Stalin's agreement. If the great powers could cooperate, it would work; but if they did not, there was trouble ahead. On this as on other occasions, Roosevelt pointed to the early withdrawal of most United States troops from Europe. He did not expect the American public to support long-term stationing of troops overseas, especially with the memory of Bataan so strong, and on this issue he would be proved entirely correct—it took the Korean War to bring a reversal.

With so much time spent on military strategy, there was not much left for political issues. Roosevelt spoke up for Finland (with which the United States was not at war); and Stalin explained that the Soviet Union did not wish to annex it, would insist on the 1941 border but might trade Hangö for Petsamo, would expect the Finns to drive out the Germans during the war and pay reparations in kind afterwards.[112] Both Churchill and Roosevelt agreed to all intents and purposes to the Soviet demand for the 1941 border with Poland with some minor modifications in favor of the Poles where the Curzon Line ran further east. Here the 1939 second partition of the country with Germany paid off for the Russians—the Western Allies could hardly reject a border drawn up by their representatives in 1919 and named for a famous British Foreign Secretary. Roosevelt, however, made it clear that, with the possibility of his having to run for President again if the war were still going on in 1944, he could not afford to make this position public. On the other hand, Poland was to gain extensive territory from Germany between the Oder and its pre-war border in the west, thus acquiring some very valuable agricultural and industrial areas in exchange for the loss of larger but nowhere near as rich a territory. Whether the Polish government-in-exile would agree to this shift westwards, and whether the British and Americans could then persuade Stalin to resume diplomatic relations with that government, remained open but highly doubtful.

As for the Soviet interest in acquiring the northern portion of East Prussia with the port city of Königsberg (with the southern part going to Poland), this was agreeable to the British and Americans, who had been convinced by the incessant German propaganda of the inter-war years that Germans could not live on both sides of Poles and who were therefore certain that East Prussia should never be returned to Germany. The rest of Germany after these amputations in favor of Poland and the Soviet Union would probably be dismembered into several states, but this issue was not resolved. Like so many other matters, this one had to be put off because of lack of both time at the meeting and careful preparations on the question beforehand.[113]

When the British and American leaders met again in Cairo afterwards, the detailed implementation of the Teheran decisions was worked out.[114] It was at this time that the new command arrangements were finalized. Eisenhower was appointed for Overlord,[a] British General (later Field Marshal) Sir Henry Maitland Wilson was put in charge of a consolidated Mediterranean theater, and a new command system for the American component of the strategic bombing offensive combining the long-range bombers in England and the Mediterranean was established. At the insistence of the British and with the reluctant acquiescence of his Chiefs-of-Staff, Roosevelt eventually reversed his promise of "Buccaneer" to Chiang to make possible an enlarged assault lift for Overlord and "Anvil" (the landing in southern France) with a resulting delay in operations in north Burma, a downgrading of the China–Burma–India theater, and greater emphasis on the Pacific approach to attack Japan. The route to the hoped for victory over Germany had been laid out, that for victory over Japan had not yet been finally defined, but both the British and the Soviet Union were expected to join in that campaign.[b]

---

[a] It was clearly understood from the beginning that there would be no intermediate command between Eisenhower and the army groups on the continent as the British at times suggested (with Montgomery in mind). The situation in the Mediterranean, where Alexander commanded the single army group in Italy, was seen as entirely different from that in Overlord with two and eventually three army groups. Note Stimson to Roosevelt, 20 December 1943, Hyde Park, Map Room Box 167, Naval Aide, A 16. This issue had been discussed in the British Cabinet on December 15, see CAB 65/40.

[b] British planning for the reallocation of troops and other resources to the war against Japan after the defeat of Germany began in December 1943, see CAB 119/167, 165; the "Redeployment Program for the War against Japan," 17 November 1944, referred to just

EAST ASIA AND THE PACIFIC, 1943

The Pacific War had reached a stage in early 1943 where new choices certainly had to be made. The campaigns in Papua and on Guadalcanal were now essentially complete, while the stalemate in China continued and the Japanese remained in control of most of Burma. The question was what to do next. For the Japanese, the critical point was to hold what remained of their earlier conquests; and although an outside observer could see that the tide had turned decisively against them in the second half of 1942, this was not fully recognized in Tokyo. There the main concern was to fight hard on the periphery while staving off any entry of the Soviet Union into the circle of Japan's enemies. For most of 1943, that meant a bloody holding operation against her United States and British enemies and an effort at reinsurance with the Soviet Union.

In the South Pacific, the Japanese would try hard to rebuild the strength of their forces on New Guinea, depleted by the Australian–U.S. victory in Papua, in the hope of holding on to the northern portion of the great island, thereby protecting the approaches to their major base at Rabaul.[115] These efforts were thwarted by quick Allied moves, greatly aided by an airlift arranged by Kenney's 5th Air Force, and by a crushing defeat inflicted by the same air force on a major Japanese reinforcement effort in the Battle of the Bismarck Sea at the beginning of February 1943.[116] Recognizing that there was now no hope of major offensive operations by their European allies, the Japanese saw their only hope in efforts to forestall American, Australian and British advances.[117]

It was the erroneous belief that such a defensive victory had been attained which led Admiral Yamamoto to head south to congratulate his winning pilots, only to be intercepted and killed by American air force planes alerted through breaks into the Japanese code.[118] The loss to the Japanese was in some ways more symbolic than substantive; Yamamoto's successor, Admiral Koga Mineichi, followed essentially the same defensive strategy, and he as well as his successors would preside over naval battles in which the navy pursued overly complicated plans that in their own way resembled nothing as much as Yamamoto's divided approach at Midway.

The Japanese not only hoped — and failed — to hold their perimeter in the south; they had decided to hold in the north as well. An effort to reinforce the garrison in the Aleutians failed, and the landing forces

over one million men. Major RAF planning had begun in November 1943 (documents in AIR 20/768).

there faced as best they could an American determination to retake the islands. It could be argued that the United States insistence on retaking Kiska and Attu was almost as unwise as the Japanese insistence on trying to hold on to these indefensible outposts which led nowhere for either side. The Americans had finally ended the interminable squabbles between the army and navy commanders in the theater by the relief of the naval commander. On May 11, 1943, American troops landed on Attu, by-passing and thus effectively isolating Kiska. The supporting fleet included two battleships that Yamamoto imagined he had sunk at Pearl Harbor; his death the preceding month saved him embarrassing questions. In bitter fighting which lasted until May 30, the Japanese force on Attu of about 2500 was destroyed at a cost of over one thousand American lives. The Japanese thereupon decided to evacuate their 5000-man garrison from Kiska, a project they successfully pulled off on July 28 without the knowledge of the Americans, whose big landing force the following month was as astonished as it was relieved to find the Japanese gone.

Only in Burma did the Japanese succeed in holding their own. Incompetent British leadership brought on a new defeat as an attempt was made to drive along the coastal plain to Akyab. Without reinforcements from elsewhere, the Japanese army in Burma drove back the British–Indian 14th Army with heavy losses in men, materiel and morale. This disaster confirmed the belief of British headquarters in Delhi as well as London that Burmese jungles were appropriate only for Japanese to fight in; a curious reversal of the earlier easy assumptions of Japanese inferiority, especially at a time when Australian (as well as American) soldiers were demonstrating the nonsensical nature of such pronouncements in the jungles of New Guinea. The Japanese were equally successful in containing the efforts of the so-called Chindits, a special force organized by Orde Wingate to disrupt Japanese communications in the interior of Burma by the employment of columns of specially trained soldiers supplied by air. The remnants of Wingate's force were chased out, but at least he had shown that, contrary to the belief of many, British and Indian soldiers were not afflicted with some special hereditary incapacity for fighting effectively in Burma. In the meantime, and before this lesson was fully learned, the Japanese drove forward the construction of the railway connecting Thailand and Burma, bringing fame to its "Bridge on the River Kwai" but death to tens of thousands of local people and prisoners of war forced by Japanese guards to labor on it under the most horrendous conditions.[119]

Japanese hopes of successfully defending the perimeter of their empire were heavily dependent on the maintenance of peace with the Soviet Union, and concern over the possibility that the latter might allow American use of air bases in the Soviet Far East was especially high during the fighting in the Aleutians in May of 1943. As the battle for Attu was raging, Tokyo asked for and received renewed assurances from Moscow that the neutrality treaty of 1941 still held and that the Soviet Union would not allow American planes to utilize Soviet bases. While the Americans struggled to get Lend-Lease planes to Alaska for Russian pilots to fly to the Soviet Union, their leaders could read in the intercepted Japanese telegrams the exchange of assurances between Moscow and Tokyo.[120]

The Soviet promise of May 21, 1943, to adhere to the Neutrality Pact did not entirely reassure Tokyo. Though satisfied that American planes could not use Soviet bases, the Japanese government was greatly alarmed by the turn of the European war against Germany and Italy as the collapse in Tunisia and the fall of Mussolini threw the weakness of Japan's European allies into bold relief.[121] A major effort was begun to improve relations with the Soviet Union in which, without informing its allies beforehand, Japan was willing to make substantial concessions in regard to its rights in north Sakhalin and on other issues in current Japanese–Soviet relations in the hope of obtaining a new series of agreements with Moscow.[122] These negotiations dragged on for months inconclusively with the Soviet government steadily but very carefully pushing for practical concessions without committing itself to any new formal agreement on the major political issues.[123] Even Japanese congratulations on the Red Army's recapture of Kharkov from their German ally hardly budged the Soviet Union.[124] The latter could remain confident that the danger of any Japanese interference with the steadily growing stream of American aid across the Pacific—to say nothing of a Japanese invasion of its Far East provinces—was out of the question.

Since the Japanese did not plan to attack the Soviet Union at this time, and the Soviet Union, as their leader told the United States and Britain at the Moscow Conference in October and at Teheran in November, intended to go to war with Japan only *after* the end of the war in Europe, negotiations could proceed.[125] The position of the Russians was steadily improving; that of the Japanese was steadily weakening. As the talks proceeded, the Soviet government secured the termination of the Japanese oil and coal concessions on Sakhalin—originally scheduled for 1970 —by a protocol signed on March 30, 1944.[126] In this agreement, as in the new fisheries agreement signed at the same time,[127] the Japanese made extensive concessions to retain Soviet good-will. If their German ally objected, that was too bad. Having repeatedly but unsuccessfully urged the Germans to make peace with the Soviet Union, the Japanese attempted to maintain peaceful relations with their Soviet neighbor regardless of Berlin's complaints about Soviet troop transfers to the European theater from the Far East and American aid deliveries through East Asian waters.[128] From the perspective of Tokyo, concentration on the fighting with the United States, Great Britain and China was quite enough. During 1944 the Japanese moved twelve infantry divisions from Manchuria to the fronts on which they were fighting in the south.[129] These transfers eventually made it easier for the Red Army to crush the remaining Japanese units; but in the critical situation facing Tokyo, combat in the south had to be nourished even if this meant concessions to Moscow.

While the Japanese hoped to hold on to their earlier conquests, concentrating on a firm perimeter and able so to concentrate because of continued peace with their Soviet neighbor, the British, as has already been hinted, hoped to hold on to their Indian empire but without any major effort to recapture its Burmese portion.[130] From time to time the British staffs in London had to engage Churchill's proclivity for impossible schemes, in this case primarily his repeated urging of a landing on Sumatra (operation "Culverin"), but in general the strategy of London remained defensive. There were several reasons for this preference. The available resources, they believed, should be concentrated on Germany first, and any offensive operations which detracted from that priority would only prolong the war. Once Germany had been defeated, there would be plenty of force available for offensives against Japan, and the British were quite determined to play their part and contribute their share in this endeavor; but the Pacific theater would have to wait.

Furthermore, the British never shared the American belief in the future role of China as a great power, distrusted Chiang with his loudly expressed sympathy for Indian nationalists, and greatly doubted that there was any point to the American concept of opening a land route to China across north Burma. The terrible state of the railway in the Indian province of Assam which supplied both the Allied forces in north Burma and the air bases for the air supply route into China reflected not only the torpor of local British administrators and commanders but also the unwillingness of the leadership in London to put some drive into the situation. One has only to contrast Churchill's constant bullying of subordinates for progress on projects in which he was interested with his passivity in the face of the perpetual troubles of the Assam railway if one is looking for an accurate assessment of London's view of the whole

theater.[a] In view of this attitude, the British let the Americans build up
the air supply route to China as much as they wanted to and themselves
did as little in the theater as they possibly could. As will become apparent, under the prodding of the Americans, the blows of the Japanese,
and the new leadership team, Lord Louis Mountbatten as South East
Asia commander and the very able General William Slim as 14th Army
commander, that turned out to be far more than they had anticipated.

The Americans in looking toward 1943 in the Pacific concentrated
on projects to improve their position for action in subsequent years when
more force would be available.[131] As much Japanese shipping as possible
was to be sunk by Allied submarines and planes, and steps would be
taken to seize bases closer to Japan from which that country itself as
well as its shipping routes could be bombed. The issue of a landing
assault on the Japanese home islands was at this time left open, but the
same operations which brought them within land-based airplane range
would in any case be needed for such an assault. At Roosevelt's insistence and with the full and enthusiastic support of Admiral King as well
as General Marshall, the United States was building the warships and
especially the aircraft carriers for mastery in the Pacific.[132] In September
1942 the first flight tests of the B-29 took place. Planned since 1939,
this very long-range bomber started coming off the production lines in
July 1943 for deployment against Japan, first from China and then from
the Marianas. As a new weapon in warfare, with a 1500–mile range that
was about double that of the standard long-range bombers of the time,
its availability came to play a major role in determining strategy in the
Pacific War.[133]

As the American strategy evolved in 1943, it concentrated first on
plans to seize Rabaul, plans which had to be drastically modified since
the resources to implement them fully were not available.[134] In practice,
MacArthur, disgruntled about Washington's inability—refusal as he saw
it—to provide him with the forces he asked for, ended up by making a
virtue of necessity and developed that strategy of by-passing Japanese
garrisons and strongpoints, including Rabaul, which came to characterize much of the American conduct of the war in the Pacific. The allocation of some resources to MacArthur was matched by some for Nimitz's
Central Pacific command so that a double thrust headed for the Philippines, with plans thereafter left open.[135]

Implementation of the plan for the central Pacific thrust would be

---

[a] Churchill's Personal Minute D 147/3 of 31 July 1943, stating that he did not want the date
1948 mentioned as the hypothetical date for ending the war with Japan, may give some
insight into the timetable being thought about in London. (CAB 120/744).

enormously aided by the fact that the warships ordered under the Two-Ocean Navy Act of July 1940 were coming out of the construction yards into the navy during 1943; in this regard, the hopes of the Americans and the apprehensions of the Japanese connected with that great program proved to be well founded.

It could be argued, and was, that a double thrust, which was designed partly by default to accommodate the army–navy rivalry of MacArthur and Nimitz, should have been replaced by one which gave full emphasis to one of the two regardless of the problems posed by the personalities involved; but there was also much to be said for allocating the steadily growing American forces to two axes of advance, which would assist each other by making it increasingly difficult for the Japanese, with their shrinking resources, to block either one with a concentration which could only be attained by opening an enormous gap for the other one to push through. As long as both American advances were commanded by leaders determined to move forward as rapidly as possible, with neither likely to let any such opportunity slip by unexploited, the double thrust was likely to prove a highly effective way to drive back the Japanese — and so it turned out.

All these plans, however, still included one major project which turned out to be more difficult to implement than all the others: keeping China in the war both for political reasons and to provide a base for air attacks on Japan itself as well as on its key shipping lanes.[136] And the plans for this always revolved around a campaign in north Burma to reopen the land communications across which China might receive the supplies needed to rebuild her armies and provide bases for the attack on Japan.

In China, the Japanese continued to occupy the ports, major cities, and much of the best agricultural area. There was in early 1942 even a possibility that the Kuomintang (KMT) would split, with War Minister Ho Ying-ch'in turning away from Chiang and responding to peace soundings from the Japanese in order to turn against the Chinese Communists right away rather than after the end of the war.[137] The Japanese could never bring themselves to make either Ho or Chiang any substantial offer, but the Chinese armies were in no condition to attempt serious military operations.[138] With Chiang having minimal control directly over his own forces and working sometimes closely, often barely, always suspiciously, and never effectively with the regional armies more under warlord control than his own, there could be no Chinese war strategy except to hold on until others, primarily the Americans, defeated Japan.

Little fighting took place between the Nationalist armies and the Japanese in 1943.[139] What fighting there was came at the end of the year from a Japanese initiative which was produced by changes elsewhere in the Pacific War. The losses of shipping to United States submarines led the Japanese to develop a plan in November 1943 for military operations that would enable them to have a land link for railway traffic from north to south China and occupied French Indo-China. There could then be overland carriage for supplies and troops all the way from Korea to Hanoi and from there a connection to the new Thailand–Burma railway, the whole route without dependence on the vulnerable sea lane.[140] While opening this north–south land route in China, the Japanese would crush Chiang and seize the majority of the airfields being built for the United States air force to use against the home islands of Japan. How had this latter force come to be a serious threat for the Japanese to worry about?

The American commander in the China–Burma–India theater, General Joseph Stilwell, had the full confidence of Roosevelt, Stimson and Marshall.[141] His strategic vision proved to be sound even if his personality—he was not called "Vinegar Joe" for nothing—made him innumerable enemies in high places.[142] He never got along with Chiang, whom he despised, or the British, whom he held in almost equally low esteem. Mountbatten was perhaps the sole exception to Stilwell's poor relations with Allied leaders, and this owed as much to the good sense and forbearance of the former as to the steady and devoted efforts of Field Marshal Dill.[143] Stilwell was, furthermore, in a fundamental difference of opinion with his most important American subordinate, General Claire Chennault, the head of the American air force in China. Unlike Stilwell, Chennault was on good terms with Chiang Kai-shek as well as Madame Chiang, who played a major role in policy making in Chungking.

These personality issues have to be considered in any examination of strategy in the China–Burma–India theater for three reasons. One was that the scarcity of resources allocated to the theater, which was generally at the bottom of the Allied allocation priority list, meant that each project of whatever size always involved acting at the expense of another; there was never enough for one big operation, to say nothing of several. Secondly, this was a theater in which the relations between allies were made most complicated by the simultaneous presence of enormous distances and terrain difficulties and the greatest divergence of political views. Finally, it had become obvious by 1943 that only those Chinese troops directly trained under Stilwell's supervision and inspired by his leadership would at least on occasion fight effectively against the Japanese, something they would, however, only do when Chiang allowed or directed it—and this in turn he was prepared to do only under very limited circumstances. Given the fundamental objection of the policy makers in London to any major operation in Burma, American and Chinese insistence that such an operation to open a land route to China was essential, and the three special complications listed, it is nothing short of a miracle that the Allies were ever able to accomplish anything in this theater.

The basic strategic dilemma was as follows: the low capacity Assam railway, which the British insisted on operating like a minor branch of the Toonerville trolley, could only support a limited air lift of supplies over the rugged mountains to China. The limited air power available could be used either to support land operations in north Burma or expansion of air supply to China. The limited supplies flown by air into China in turn could be utilized to build up the largest possible air force in China or to maintain a smaller air force while building up an effective and properly trained and equipped group of Chinese army divisions. In Stilwell's eyes, the most sensible thing to do was to open a land route to China over which supplies could be moved by truck and eventually also petroleum products by pipeline, while, in China itself, an effective Chinese land force would be needed to defend the air bases, which were certain to become the object of Japanese land attacks as soon as the planes based on them threatened serious danger to the Japanese. General Chennault, on the other hand, had argued that an air offensive from the bases in China could deliver truly damaging blows to the Japanese without a great offensive in north Burma or the diversion of supplies to a rebuilt Chinese army.[144] Chennault had the support of Chiang who was interested in getting the largest possible supplies in by air, was not interested in substantial land operations against the Japanese, saw the centrally controlled air force as a counter to the provincial warlords, and did not believe the British would ever mount a serious offensive anywhere in Burma.

Once the Allies had decided at the second Cairo meeting that they would not launch operation "Buccaneer," only a small land offensive began in northern Burma in November 1943. The Chinese troops Stilwell had trained fought well and alongside small American forces began to push the Japanese back slowly but effectively, eventually enabling a road to be built connecting to the Old Burma Road in the spring of 1945.[145] But long before then, Roosevelt had decided that the only thing to do, in order to keep up Chinese morale, to keep Chiang's government from total collapse, and to give some sign of support in the face of British unwillingness and inability to act, was to side with Chennault on the allocation of the precious cargo carried by air over the "Hump."[146] Stilwell could do whatever was possible with very limited resources — and would eventually be relieved — but the bulk of American supplies was assigned to developing an air offensive based on China against the Japanese home islands and shipping lanes.

As American intelligence had feared, this led to a Japanese land offensive to seize the bases from which Chennault's planes flew.[147] On April 18, 1944, the Japanese opened their "Ichigo" operation, which quickly broke through the weak Chinese armies. On June 18 they began a second phase in fighting around Ch'angsha and then in early August at Hengyang.[148] In the latter stages of the fighting the Japanese army suffered substantial casualties, but the losses of the Chinese were staggering in numbers and nature. At least 300,000 men were lost, but even more significant was the fact that the Chinese Nationalist armies had suffered a blow from which they never recovered.[149] Chiang had no effective control over the provincial armies which were supposed to hold back the Japanese, and he refused to assist those units which fought hard.[a] In the military sense, the "Ichigo" operation meant the loss of many of the major United States air bases in China with only a few still out of Japanese reach. On this point, Stilwell's prediction had proved all too correct. In the political sense, the disastrous defeat of the Nationalist army ended any chance the Kuomintang might have had to rebuild its ties to the people of China.[150]

The collapse of the Chinese Nationalist forces in the summer of 1944 greatly reduced American interest in the China theater; the approach to Japan clearly would not be able to depend on a major base in China.[151] Other approaches and bases would look far more attractive, and this shift helps explain American strategy in the latter part of the Pacific War. Ironically, just as the situation in China was getting dramatically worse, that in Burma was getting equally dramatically better, but only after a crisis caused by a major Japanese offensive into India.

On January 3, 1944, Mountbatten had written to Brooke about the bad effects on morale in his theater of the repeated cancelling of operations after the hopes of the troops had been raised by the prospect of major offensives.[152] The Japanese were about to force the South East Asia Command to fix its internal feuds and fight the real enemy.[153] On January 7, Imperial General Headquarters issued to General Kawabe Mazakazu, the Burma area commander, orders for an offensive into India. His troops were to seize the area around Imphal and the adjacent portions of northeast India.[154] The military aim was to defend control of Burma and simultaneously isolate China by taking a large portion of Manipour and Assam provinces, thus cutting the railway which was essential for the "Hump" air route to China, Stilwell's north Burma

---

[a] There is even an account which argues that Chiang may have withheld support from the units opposing the Japanese in exchange for some deal by which the Japanese puppet governments in China would join him after the Japanese left, in a war against the Communists (Boyle, *China and Japan*, pp. 317–21). The same author also argues, however (pp. 312–13), that in the spring of 1944 the Japanese were seriously considering making peace with the Chinese Communists. These matters await further investigation.

campaign and any British overland thrust into Burma itself. The political aim was to try for a general uprising against British control in India. For this purpose, Subhas Chandra Bose, who had arrived in Tokyo in June 1943, where he had impressed the Japanese leaders including Tojo, rebuilt the collaborationist Indian National Army and for months been urging a big push into India, was attached to the rear of Kawabe's army and allowed to drag his soldiers into the disaster for which they soon headed.[155]

Whatever the political possibilities for a major revolt in India might have been in 1942, they had vanished by 1944. Not only had the Allied military presence in India been strengthened, but the reputation of the Japanese as cruel conquerors who were interested in enslaving, not liberating, the former colonial subjects of European powers had spread widely. Though it was not known in India at the time, the fact that the Japanese reinforcements for the operation had come on the "Death railway," built over ground soaked with the blood of thousands of slave laborers, symbolized the political character of the last great Japanese military offensive in Southeast Asia.

If the political effort was a complete fizzle, the military side created first two major crises for the Allies and then a total rout for the Japanese. They had attacked first near the coast and there cut off the British 14th Army's 7th Indian Division. The latter, however, held on grimly in February and March, nourished from the air by supplies dropped by British air supply flights as well as planes temporarily diverted with American consent from the "Hump." If this threat had been halted decisively by the end of March—and the myth of Japanese invincibility shattered in the process—the situation of the British and Indian troops further north was soon more difficult and even desperate.

On March 12, 1944, the Japanese 15th Army launched its "U-Go" offensive toward Imphal and Kohima with the intention of seizing these towns as a base for a subsequent attack to cut the Assam railway at Dimapur, a mere thirty miles northwest of Kohima. The British and Indian soldiers fought bravely and desperately, allowing themselves to be cut off and surrounded rather than either simply retreating, and continued to fight instead of surrendering when surrounded. Additional troops were flown in and again supplied by air. Mountbatten and the 14th Army commander, General Slim, had changed their soldiers' attitudes; air supply had altered their opportunities for holding on if they were so inclined. With the complicated Allied command structure functioning more effectively than the direct involvement of the British Chiefs of Staff in London and the United States Joint Chief of Staff in Washington might have led one to expect, the necessary transport planes were scraped together from all over to support the 14th Army and the isolated garrisons, enable 14th Army to relieve Kohima and Imphal, and in the process administer a crushing defeat on the Japanese.[156] Although the Chief of the Imperial General Staff in London was terribly worried and, on June 1, saw "disaster staring us in the face,"[157] the adequately supported British troops beat back the invading Japanese in the following weeks. It was the latter who endured disaster because they not only suffered a humiliating defeat in battle but proved incapable of evacuating their starving and beaten army across the mountain ranges into Burma.

Of the over 150,000 Japanese soldiers engaged in the campaign, only a tiny number of sick and exhausted men staggered back to Burma. It had been Japan's costliest defeat on land in the whole war up to that point, and it did wonders for the morale of the 14th British–Indian Army after its ordeal. By mid-July the Japanese had decided that from here on their only hope in the area was propaganda by Bose, not much of a substitute for their lost 15th Army.[158]

Even as the Japanese offensive into India was being blunted and then crushed, Stilwell led a combination of American trained and equipped Chinese divisions and a special American force, modelled on the Chindits and called Merrill's Marauders after their commander, in a series of local attacks which eventuated in the sudden seizure of the key airfield at Myitkyina in mid-May, 1944.[159] In spite of the most bitter fighting, neither side could dislodge the other from positions in the Myitkyina area, but two things were obvious: the Americans and Chinese would clear northern Burma and thus make a new road to China possible, whether the British approved or not; and the simultaneous collapse of Chinese Nationalist resistance to the Japanese "Ichigo" offensive meant that the road would lead to a China which could play little part in the ultimate defeat of Japan.

FIGHTING IN THE PACIFIC, 1943 TO JULY 1944

How that ultimate defeat was to be achieved was certainly not yet obvious in 1943. The twin assaults under primary American army and navy control respectively were being pushed with determination, but they were as yet not nourished by the resources available later and had to contend with fierce resistance at the outer reaches of the empire conquered by Japanese forces earlier. The offensives were pushed, nevertheless, not only because the commanders on the spot were insistent on doing so—the point generally stressed in American accounts—or because this was Admiral King's favorite theater of war—the pet explanation of British authors—but because there were excellent reasons for believing that it was essential to keep the Japanese on the defensive lest they so fortify the islands and build up the air bases on them as to make a deferred assault horrendously costly or even impossible. It would all prove difficult enough as it was. And if a larger share of the fighting was borne by the Americans than one might have expected in an area on the approaches to Australia and New Zealand, this was due not only to the relative sizes of the resources and armed forces of the Allies but also to MacArthur's incapacity for Allied command and the deliberate decision to leave in the Mediterranean theater major Australian and New Zealand units instead of recalling all of them to the South Pacific.[160]

In the Southwest Pacific, there were parallel thrusts in New Guinea and in the Solomons, following up on the earlier victories on both fronts. On New Guinea, American and Australian troops in a series of carefully planned and coordinated moves crushed the main Japanese forces in the Lae and Salamaua area, greatly assisted by a surprise attack of the 5th Air Force which destroyed almost 200 Japanese planes on the ground at Wewak on August 17, 1943, thus both avenging the American losses at Clark Field in December 1941, and depriving the Japanese in central New Guinea of air cover for several weeks in the face of the Allied offensive. A combined U.S.–Australian force, assisted by a parachute assault to capture a nearby area for an airfield, succeeded in taking both Lae and Salamaua in September, 1943, with the surviving Japanese defenders driven into the jungle.

Hardly had the main bases of Japanese power in central New Guinea been taken than the 9th Australian Division landed at Finschhafen at the tip of the Huon peninsula, took the town and harbor after ten days of bitter fighting, and thus anchored an Allied presence on the New Guinea side of the straits separating that great island from New Britain, the long curving island with Rabaul, Japan's major bastion in the Southwest Pacific, at the other end. A follow-on American landing at Saidor further up the New Guinea coast failed to trap the Japanese forces by-passed in this fashion, but did move the Allies another 150 miles toward their later objectives further west.

By the time Finschhafen was secured on October 2, 1943, the other wing of the "Cartwheel" operation to isolate Rabaul, the offensive in the Solomons, had also made major advances. The next main island north of Guadalcanal is New Georgia, and the Americans were alarmed to learn that the Japanese were constructing a big airfield at Munda, an indication of the kind of problem awaiting the Allies if the Japanese were allowed time to harden the perimeter defense of their newly conquered empire. Having seized the Russell Islands between Guadalcanal and New Georgia in February, the Americans now launched a coordinated offensive against New Georgia. The island of Rendova just across a narrow strait from Munda was the scene of a landing on June 30, 1943; three days later the Americans landed on New Georgia itself. The Japanese fought a bitter defensive battle on the island and repeatedly tried to run in reinforcements, primarily on light cruisers and destroyers. Fierce air, sea and land battles raged all during July. In the air, the Americans inflicted heavy losses on the Japanese, in part because the new pilots being sent in were simply not up to the standard of those they replaced. As the Japanese naval air force units were run down, the Americans were increasingly more experienced and their replacements better trained.[161] At sea, the American and New Zealand warships did much better now than in the fighting off Guadalcanal the preceding year, sinking a series of Japanese destroyers loaded with reinforcements for the loss of one destroyer and a light cruiser.[a]

The land fighting was longer and more costly than Admiral Halsey had anticipated; but after reinforcements had been sent in and the American division commander replaced, a series of drives brought the Americans first control of the Munda airfield at the beginning of August and then of the rest of New Georgia by the end of the month. Of the 9000 Japanese soldiers, only a few escaped to other islands in the Solomons; and the Munda airfield, quickly expanded by the Seabees, the special engineer construction units, was quickly converted into an important American air base.[162]

The next island in the Solomons was Kolombangara, even more heavily garrisoned and fortified than New Georgia. Taking a leaf from Admiral Thomas C. Kinkaid's procedure in the Aleutians, where Kiska had been by-passed for an assault on Attu, Halsey now made an almost unopposed landing on Vella Lavella, the large island on the other side of Kolombangara from New Georgia, on August 15. This jump left the Japanese garrison of 10,000 men to sit on their island while the war passed them by after they had failed to dislodge the American 25th Division from Vella Lavella. The Americans, and the Australian and New Zealand contingents fighting alongside them, could now prepare for the attack on the most important island in the northern Solomons, Bougainville, where they would be on the other side of Rabaul from the Australians and Americans at Finschhafen on New Guinea.

The attack on Bougainville had to be prepared with great care. Here was an objective that was obviously menaced by the Allies, had to be defended by the Japanese if Rabaul was not to be outflanked, and simply could not be by-passed if the Americans were to proceed further. The

---

[a] It was in the naval fighting of the New Georgia campaign that John F. Kennedy's "PT 109" was sunk by the Japanese.

Japanese in a series of policy conferences in Tokyo during September agreed on a somewhat modified strategy for the defense of their Pacific empire. They drew a new defensive line—including Bougainville and parts of New Guinea—which they would hold as long as at all possible, with that defense strengthened by extensive reinforcements which were now to be sent to the Southern Pacific. This defensive strategy would be assisted by cooperation with Germany and facilitated by improved relations with the Soviet Union. The time gained by hard defensive fighting was to be used to build more airplanes and ships as well as an inner line of strongpoints for the continuation of the struggle. The following year, 1944, did see Japanese aircraft production reach its World War II peak of 28,180—as well as Germany's of 39,807—but the United States alone produced 100,752, a figure which even understates the discrepancy because of the high proportion of four-engine bombers included in the American production figure.[163]

Long before the new Japanese planes entered service, the Americans had broken into the perimeter at several places. Bougainville was the first. While the Japanese were getting ready to reinforce their 35,000 soldiers on the threatened island with additional troops from New Britain and naval air units from the Combined Fleet, the Allies carried out several diversionary operations to mislead the Japanese and throw them off balance. An American marine unit temporarily landed on Choiseul Island, drawing off Japanese reserves, while the 8th New Zealand Brigade Group landed on the Treasury Islands to make it possible for the Allies to build an advance airstrip for additional coverage of Bougainville. The main assault went into a lightly defended and unlikely portion of Bougainville, Empress Augusta Bay. Attacks by planes and warships on the Japanese air bases at both ends of the island threw off the defenders, who were totally surprised by the 3rd Marine Division's November 1, 1943, landing. The Japanese counter-attack mounted by naval forces already on the way from Rabaul was defeated by the smaller but better handled Task Force 39 of Admiral Aaron Stanton Merrill.

The danger posed to the landing by the dispatch of large Japanese naval reinforcements was averted by Halsey's risking his carriers *Saratoga* and *Princeton* to attack Rabaul. In conjuction with the land-based planes sent by General Kenney from New Guinea, these air attacks destroyed most of the carrier planes the Combined Fleet had sent to Rabaul and damaged six cruisers in the harbor. Perhaps even more important, the raid had the effect of bluffing the Japanese navy out of use of Rabaul because Admiral Koga was simply unwilling to believe that Halsey would have sent in his carriers without massive escorting warships.

These naval air successes left the fighting to the units on Bougainville itself where the 37th Infantry Division quickly joined the 3rd Marines. By the time the Japanese on the island realized that there were going to be no further landings, the Americans had upset all their calculations by building an airfield in the swamps within their Empress Augusta Bay perimeter. The Japanese attack on that perimeter in late November failed, and another attempt by the Japanese navy to bring in reinforcements—the last in the Solomons as it turned out—was beaten off by the United States navy. The fighting on Bougainville continued for months; but without substantial air support and with no prospect of reinforcement, the Japanese soldiers who survived the hard battle on the island became involuntary bystanders in the war.[164]

Rabaul had been isolated and largely neutralized. This was what the Quadrant Conference of August 1943 in Quebec had called for instead of the direct assault MacArthur had insistently urged. By the end of 1943, MacArthur came to embrace a policy of by-passing strong Japanese garrisons, a policy of which he became the loudest advocate and most successful practitioner (and which he later claimed to have invented).[165] A final operation in the process as regards Rabaul was the landing of the 1st Marine Division and army units at Cape Gloucester near the western end of New Britain in late December 1943. Though carefully and effectively carried out, this operation was later considered unnecessary by some.[166] Necessary or not, it helped contain the Japanese forces of over 100,000 men who remained on both New Britain and the nearby island of New Ireland until 1945.[167] "Cartwheel," the operation designed to convert the Japanese base at Rabaul from an effective bastion in defense and a potential basis for new offensives into a wasting liability had been completed.

The extremely large garrisons isolated at Rabaul and elsewhere, furthermore, showed the reverse side of the Japanese strategy of fighting hard to defend the outer perimeter of their empire. Once the perimeter had been pierced, there were after Guadalcanal no large-scale evacuations of the experienced garrisons left behind by Allied thrusts. The Japanese procedure of making the crust hard to crack was costly for them and not merely for the Allies.

One of the major reasons that the Joint Chiefs of Staff had decided against allocating to the Southwest Pacific the resources needed for any direct attack on Rabaul had been their agreement in the summer of 1943, formally settled with the British at the Quadrant Conference, for a push in the Central Pacific. This axis of advance pointed through the Marshall Islands to the Marianas. With forces still limited, the first step to the Marshalls would be into the Gilberts; this operation would provide the experience as well as an important base for the subsequent advance.[168] Unlike the operations in the Southwest Pacific to date, which involved primarily unopposed landings on large islands followed in most cases by bitter fighting in deep jungles for weeks and even months, the whole framework of Central Pacific operations was necessarily different. The islands to be assaulted were in most cases minute or at least very small; because of the enormous distances involved, air cover had to be provided by carriers, not by the nearest land bases; the whole operation would be dependent on a floating supply base, not a land base; the initial landings were generally likely to be extremely difficult in the face of entrenched Japanese resistance; and the fighting that was expected to follow would necessarily be bloody and brief. There was nowhere for the defenders to retreat to: there was no prospect of evacuation, and they could be expected to fight to the end to sell their lives dearly.[169] The Central Pacific thrust would, however, benefit from the simultaneous operations in the Southwest Pacific, which immobilized the Japanese fleet at Truk during the most critical period of the Gilberts operation.[170]

The first of the Central Pacific operations ironically had been made even more difficult by an earlier raid on the Gilberts by Colonel Carlson's raiders in August 1942, which had alerted the Japanese to their weakness there and caused them to reinforce the troops and defenses in the islands, and also by the American lack of recent and accurate navigation charts.[171] The 2nd Marine Division, reconstituted after its ordeal on Guadalcanal, was to land on Tarawa while the 27th Infantry would seize Makin Island. A huge fleet of over 200 ships provided support; with the defeat of the German U-Boats in May 1943 and the completion of warships ordered in 1940 and 1941, it was now possible for the first time to have an adequately supplied large American fleet of carriers, battleships, cruisers, destroyers and other ships provide the basis for a massive amphibious assault hundreds of miles from the nearest base.[172] Furthermore, this operation, code-named "Galvanic," would see the first large-scale use of a new weapon, the "amphtrac," a combined boat and tracked vehicle used as an armored infantry assault carrier that could float or run over ground and coral.[a]

In spite of a heavy bombardment, the Japanese on Tarawa fought effectively on the beaches and inland. In three days of some of the bloodiest fighting of the Pacific War, the marines had first to wade ashore in the face of enemy fire when the uncertain tides left their

[a] It is surely worth noting as a sign of inter-Allied confidence that the Americans provided the British with the full details of their planned operations in the Pacific, including the date of the scheduled landing on Tarawa. See J.S.M. Washington (Dill) to COS, FM D 41 of 20 October 1943, in CAB 120/412.

landing ships stranded or crippled off shore, and then had to fight a
deeply entrenched defending force without adequate artillery support,
which could not be brought in right away for the same reason. By a
combination of bravery and numbers and naval gunnery support, they
overcame and destroyed a force of 4500 Japanese. Of the marines, 1300
were killed and over 2000 wounded.[173] The initial attack on the Tarawa
coral atoll had been on Betio, the main island of under 300 acres with
the airport. The other islands in the atoll were taken quickly after Betio
was secured, while the army division was able to seize lightly defended
Makin. In that part of "Galvanic," the major loss was the torpedoed
escort carrier *Liscome Bay*, in which over 600 crew members lost their
lives.

Although American commanders and the American public were
shocked at the high percentage of casualties in the Tarawa assault, this
was one battle about whose necessity there could be no argument.[174]
The Gilberts were needed for the subsequent attacks on the Marshall
Islands, but much more important were the technical lessons about
equipment, tactics, angle of naval fire, and the needed length and nature
of bombardment learned in this first effort of a type that would have to
be repeated many times. In a way the shock of losses proved salutary;
the deficiencies uncovered really were remedied, and quickly at that.
Nothing shows this more clearly than the next step in the Central Pacific
thrust: the invasion of the Marshall Islands.

The American naval thrust across the Central Pacific had to include
the Marshall Islands as the main intermediate objective on the way to
the Marianas. From the latter, the Americans could strike at the Philippines, the Bonin and Ryukyu islands, or Formosa; but whatever they
might decide once arrived in the Marianas, they could use these islands
as bases for air raids on the Japanese home islands by the new very long
range bombers, the B-29s. Whether the Caroline Islands with their huge
Japanese naval base at Truk could be by-passed or would have to be
assaulted remained open, but there was no question that landings had
to be made in the Marshalls. Nimitz decided in mid-December 1943 to
by-pass the eastern Marshall Islands and, using carrier-air and land-
based-air from Makin and Tarawa, attack and seize first Kwajalein, the
world's largest coral atoll in the center of the island chain — 700 miles
northwest of Makin — and subsequently Eniwetok at the northwestern
end of the chain, another 300 miles closer to Tokyo. The lessons learned
at Tarawa would be applied as a huge American fleet escorted two
infantry and one marine division to islands in the Kwajalein atoll.

The Japanese had seized the Marshall Islands from the Germans in
World War I and had been confirmed as mandate holders for the islands

in 1920. They had therefore had plenty of time to prepare and fortify positions, whatever their treaty commitments to the contrary. As the Americans were launching their attack, the Japanese themselves were planning a counter-attack with their navy, but this project was halted by the American thrust.[175] That operation, code-named "Flintlock," went forward smoothly. Air and naval bombardment helped the new 4th Marine Division to land on January 31, 1944, and crush the Japanese garrison on Roi and Namur at the northern end of the atoll, while the 7th Infantry found the islands of Kwajalein atoll far easier to take than Attu had been. Casualties were heavier for the Japanese and lighter for the Americans than at Tarawa; a great deal had been learned. This portion of the operation had gone so well so quickly that the force commander, Admiral Spruance, agreed to Nimitz's proposal to move up the Eniwetok landing. In three days, portions of the 27th Infantry and a marine regiment took the main islands of Eniwetok atoll, thereby giving the Americans effective control of the whole island group.[176]

But this was not all. To protect the Marshalls operation, a major air assault by Admiral Mitscher's task force was launched against the Japanese base of Truk on February 17. The Imperial navy, it turned out, had already abandoned Truk for the safer Palau islands, but the destruction of planes, ships and installation left a shambles of the "Gibraltar of the Pacific." The combined effect of this successful attack and the seizure of the Marshalls made it possible to by-pass the Caroline Islands entirely; and the large Japanese garrison of Truk, like that of Rabaul, was left to contemplate its shrinking store of supplies.

The disaster of Truk was the last straw for General Tojo; he had the navy Chief of Staff, Admiral Nagumo, sacked and replaced by Navy Minister Shimada while Tojo himself took over as Chief of Staff of the Japanese army.[177] It was apparently Tojo's hope that a greater and more direct personal role in command of operations in the Pacific would enable him to coordinate the army and navy more effectively in resisting the American advance. The effect of his action, however, was negligible in the military sense but made his own position far more vulnerable: the next big Japanese defeat was to cost him all his accumulated jobs.[178]

The broad outlines of American strategy in the Pacific had been agreed upon at the Quadrant Conference at Quebec in August 1943. There it had been formally decided that the Central Pacific thrust would head for the Marianas and that in the Southwest Pacific for the Vogelkop peninsula, the northwest corner of New Guinea. From these positions, an invasion of the Philippines as well as other alternatives would be open.[179] The decision of the second conference in Cairo, to drop "Buccaneer" in favor of a reinforced "Anvil," the invasion of southern

France, had meant down-grading the whole China theater. This appeared feasible in December 1943 because in the interim Chinese military effort had been negligible, the Western Allies had received assurances of Soviet support in the war against Japan after the defeat of Germany, and because of the recent advances in the Pacific theater, in particular the successes in the central and northern Solomons and in New Guinea. It now seemed plausible to look toward the possibility of a victorious end to the war in the Pacific three years hence, that is, in the fall of 1946.[180] Preliminary details were agreed upon in early December by planners of the Combined (U.S.–British) Staffs for operations in 1944 and thereafter.[181]

The original plans for a major air offensive against Japan from bases in China increasingly faded from view with first the logistical problems on the supply route from Burma and then the collapse of Chinese resistance in 1944; the fact that the Marianas were within the 1500 mile range from the Japanese home islands of the new B-29s made the seizure of these islands, therefore, all the more important. Their capture had long loomed as the central feature of a thrust across the Pacific—they were the key island group on the way—but the shift of emphasis from the Asian mainland to the Pacific side of Japan and the availability of a weapon which could reach Japan itself directly from the islands now made them an all the more significant target in the view of the Americans.[182]

From the Japanese perspective, the centrality of the Marianas was equally obvious. Although not well informed about the B-29, the Japanese could see how important the islands were to the control of their routes to Southeast Asia, their hold on the Philippines, and the defense of the home islands themselves. They accordingly built up their garrisons on the islands, of which all but Guam had been in their possession since they had seized them from the Germans in World War I. Even as the authorities in Tokyo prepared to hold on to the Marianas by a combination of new strategies with the fight-to-the-death tactics of earlier engagements, they also inaugurated one more offensive procedure.

Since the fall of 1942, there had been planning for a project to set the forests of the American and Canadian West on fire by balloons carrying incendiary materials and blown across the Pacific by the prevailing winds, especially the jet stream. They would come down in the Western Hemisphere, where they were expected to start more fires than the Americans and Canadians could put out. Here would be a Japanese-created set of fire-storms to devastate the heavily forested western states and provinces of the United States and Canada. In March of 1944 a conference was held to work out the details and production schedules, the whole project being delayed by other demands on the Japanese war economy. From November 7, 1944, to March 1945, some nine thousand balloons were released, of which well over a thousand landed on or exploded over the United States and Canada.[183] They did little damage and caused only a few casualties, in this way no more effective than the earlier occasional shelling of the coast by Japanese submarines; but they do show that the strategy of making the war as costly as possible for Japan's enemies had an offensive as well as a defensive component until the end.

The American double thrust in the Central and Southwest Pacific areas was, however, not likely to be halted by the launching of balloons. The concentration of all Japanese military might would be needed, and Tojo's increased power might have made such concentration possible had he — or anyone else in Tokyo — ever had the needed strategic vision. But it was precisely at the time that the American double thrust moved forward in the spring and summer of 1944 that the Japanese launched their great land offensives in China and into India from Burma, whose course has already been described. Of these operations, that in China succeeded while that into India failed, but both drew resources which were not available to meet the Americans in the Pacific; and in this sense the Americans benefited substantially from the diversion of Japanese resources which was imposed by Japan's view of priorities in the war.

The expectation of the Japanese army and navy was that the Allies would continue their campaign in New Guinea while the American navy would head next from the Marshall Islands into the Palaus. Not only was this latter assumption incorrect and diverted reinforcements from the threatened Marianas to the islands further south, but the basic Japanese naval defense plan proved faulty. The "A-Go" plan as it was called consisted of two main elements. A consolidated fleet of carriers, battleships and smaller warships would hit the Americans from a base between the Dutch East Indies and the Philippines, a location chosen because it made possible direct fueling with oil from Borneo which did not have to be refined before being used (though with bad effects on the engines). The carriers would depend on the greater range of their planes, extended even further by the possibility of landing and refueling on airports in the Marianas or Palaus before returning to the carriers.[184] The second element was a massive allocation of about five hundred land based planes which would harass and weaken the American fleet in concert with the carrier planes. Originally the plan for the destruction of the next major American offensive was aimed at the naval support of MacArthur's forces struggling on Biak, an operation reviewed later in this chapter. But just as the "A-Go" operation was to be mounted against MacArthur under the code-word "Kon," the Japanese learned that the Americans were landing on Saipan in the Marianas. All attention was now focused on that island and the Philippine Sea to the west of it.

On June 15, 1944, two marine divisions landed on Saipan with an army division held in reserve to land there if needed, or to begin the process of taking Tinian and Guam if not. It would be needed. The massive pre-invasion bombardment had damaged the defenses,[185] and air attacks on air bases in the area had almost eliminated air support for the defenders; but the assaulting marines were slowed by an energetic and effective defense by the 30,000 man garrison. Here was an island of some size with mountains and dense jungle, not a small coral atoll, and the marines had to fight their way across it. The 27th Infantry division was sent in to assist them. The Marine Corps commander of the land operation, General Holland M. Smith, fired the 27th Division commander, General Ralph S. Smith, when that division did not perform the way he imagined it should; the best study of the "Smith–Smith" controversy suggests that "Howlin' Mad" Smith was the wrong man to put in charge of what was indeed a most difficult operation.[186] In three weeks of bloody fighting, the Japanese were driven back; after a final and colossal suicide charge in which several thousand of them died, the remaining soldiers and hundreds of civilians who had lived and worked on the island jumped off a cliff to their deaths.

Before this ghastly spectacle had appalled the Americans, who tried to persuade the suicidal Japanese to surrender, the American navy had crushed the "A-Go" operation. Attacks on Japanese air bases had either destroyed the land-based planes or kept them at a distance, but their commander had falsely informed Admiral Ozawa Jisaburo (who commanded the whole operation) that his planes were inflicting great damage on the American fleet. In fact, the United States 5th Fleet had an undamaged seven large and eight escort carriers, protected by a massive screen of battleships, to deal with Ozawa's three large and six smaller carriers. The Japanese carrier pilots were new and inexperienced; they were shot down literally by the hundreds by far more experienced and better controlled American pilots in what came to be called "The Great Marianas Turkey Shoot." Most of those not downed by American planes were brought down by the concentrated anti-aircraft fire of the battleships. In addition, American submarines had sunk several of the Japanese destroyers before the battle was joined and sent to the bottom two of the large carriers; one, the *Shokaku*, had been at the Pearl Harbor raid, the other, the new *Taisho*, blew up when the fumes of the volatile

Borneo oil exploded inside the portion of the ship sealed off after a torpedo hit.

On the afternoon of the following day, Admiral Spruance located what was left of Ozawa's fleet and sent his own planes after it, sinking one carrier and damaging two more, many of the returning American planes having to ditch as they ran out of fuel in the dark. But the Battle of the Philippine Sea, as it came to be known, was a major American victory in which the Japanese navy lost enormously in ships and even more in planes and pilots it could not replace, while United States losses were very low. The Saipan landing was safe, and soon after, first Tinian and then Guam were taken.[187] The victory in the battle, furthermore, made it impossible for the Japanese to cope with MacArthur's advance on New Guinea. Though neither the latter nor the American navy might be willing to recognize it, the double thrust strategy had been dramatically vindicated. The commanders in both areas were more inclined to see opportunities, not only risks and obstacles, and in practice kept the Japanese off balance and incapable of concentrating effectively on halting either.

The American operation saved by the diversion of Japanese attention to the Marianas was that on the island of Biak off the northwest coast of New Guinea. MacArthur's forces had reached this far after a series of bold and dramatic moves. In a gamble which paid off handsomely, the Americans had landed a reconnaissance force in the Admiralty Islands on short notice on February 29, 1944, and, in MacArthur's personal presence, had reinforced the advance party at the moment when the Japanese were still confused. By-passing the bulk of Japanese units in central New Guinea, the Americans had then surprised them by going 600 miles up the coast to Hollandia on April 22, soon making this small community in the Dutch portion of New Guinea into a major base. Because it turned out that the land nearby was not suitable for airfields which could carry the heavy bombers of 5th Air Force, MacArthur quickly threw his forces forward, landing on the little island of Wakde to seize its airfield on May 18 and launching an assault on Biak on May 27, 1944.

While in the Admiralty Islands, at Hollandia, and at Wakde the Americans had surprised the Japanese, on Biak it was the other way around. The airfields which were the objective of the assault were on a narrow coastal plain overlooked by high ground marked by caves. The Japanese commander, who anticipated a landing, withdrew his troops from the beach and entrenched them in the rugged terrain from which they poured fire on the Americans. Sending in reinforcements and replacing the American division commander did not move the fight forward much faster. The Japanese now acted to crush the landing force by reinforcements to deal with the American army; and the world's two largest battleships, the *Yamato* and *Musashi*, to deal with the navy aspect. It was news of American preliminary bombardment of Saipan which led to the cancellation of this project so that Admiral Ozawa could have all the ships needed for the "A-Go" operation, which became the Battle of the Philippine Sea. Under these circumstances, the American troops eventually destroyed the Japanese force on Biak and secured the airfields by June 30.[188]

The purpose of seizing the Biak airfields and those on Wakde had been to provide air support for the last offensive on New Guinea — the seizure of points in the northwest, the area called Vogelkop, the "bird's head," by the Dutch because on a map that is what it looks like. In July 1944, American troops landed first on Noemfoor and then at Sansapor, establishing themselves quickly while the substantial and recently reinforced Japanese garrison in the area, the equivalent of two divisions, faded into the jungle until the 1945 surrender rather than fight it out. Only General Adachi Hatazo's 18th Army of the by-passed Japanese on New Guinea would attempt a major counter-offensive against Aitape, one of the American coastal strongpoints. Beaten off with losses of over ten thousand men, the 18th Army in central, like the Japanese 2nd Army in northwest New Guinea, was left behind by the war. Their containment, and that of the by-passed Japanese garrisons on New Britain and Kavieng, was turned over to the Australians who had provided the majority of MacArthur's ground forces in 1942 and 1943, being now overtaken by the Americans.

The battles in the Pacific theater interacted with the internal political situation in both the United States and Japan. In the United States, the steady stream of publicity about MacArthur, carefully controlled from his headquarters,[a] stimulated both mid-western conservative Republicans opposed to the likely nomination for President of either Thomas Dewey or Wendell Willkie by their party, as well as miscellaneous right-wing kooks and fanatics, to push the general for the nomination. They looked to a deadlock between the two leading contenders for a chance to push MacArthur as a widely and even enthusiastically acceptable alternative, and the general's most reliable biographer believes that some of the time in late 1943 and early 1944 MacArthur was very much interested.[189] The vast majority of Republicans, however, preferred New York Governor

---

[a] The communiqués from the Southwest Pacific Headquarters were notorious not only for their inaccuracy but also for their quite unnecessary slighting of the Australian role in the theater.

Thomas Dewey, whose rout of all opposition in the April 4, 1944, Wisconsin primary effectively ended the miniboom. In the preceding months, MacArthur had had detailed and satisfactory meetings with General Marshall and with Admiral Nimitz, and in Admiral Kinkaid (transferred from Alaska) he had a naval associate with whom he worked well. In spite of his Chief of Staff General Richard K. Sutherland's quite extraordinary talent for antagonizing everyone, MacArthur himself was settling into his role much more successfully and looked forward to the last intermediate operations that would take him back to the Philippines as commander of an American invading force.

The most dramatic political repercussion of the Pacific fighting culminating in the American victory in the Marianas was the resulting crisis in Tokyo. The greater power Tojo had gathered into his own hands now made him the more vulnerable when Japan's armed forces suffered set-backs. The Japanese army's victory over Chiang Kai-shek after seven years of war could not off-set defeats in India, in New Guinea, and on and near the Marianas, the last named an area Japan had held long before the war. The tough-minded general tried hard to hold on to power, but he could not do so. The palace and most leading political and some military figures combined to assure his being dropped from all of his posts; he resigned formally on July 18, 1944.[190] His successor, General Koiso Kuniaki, had been governor of Korea; he did not take over the other portfolios, such as War Minister, that Tojo had held and never attained the commanding position of his predecessor.[191] In July of 1940 he had wanted to lead Japanese troops into the Dutch East Indies,[192] but now, so he claimed at his trial after the war, he feared that the war was lost.[193] The public posture of the new government was, however, one of fighting on to victory. And, for the first time in the war, the Japanese army and navy began to plan jointly for the defense of the Philippines which they correctly saw as the next main American objective.[194]

The Japanese in looking toward defense of their empire also attempted further to improve their relations with the Soviet Union following the signing of the protocols and conventions of March 30, 1944. They hoped to have the duration of the neutrality pact with the Soviet Union extended, preferably well before its expiration, to work out some understanding on China, and to obtain Soviet agreement to a mission of important Japanese personalities to Moscow, a mission behind which there was the hope of bringing about a separate peace between the Soviet Union and Germany.[195] While Molotov listened carefully on April 8, 1944, to Japanese Ambassador Sato's explication of such projects, and discussed the proposals cordially, he always came back to the question of whether there was any German initiative behind Japan's projected commission of notable emissaries.[196] Since there was not, the Soviet Union, which might have been interested in a negotiated peace with Germany at this time—otherwise why ask for details?—always waved off the mission idea. As for a deal with Japan to settle disputes about and in China, Molotov professed no interest at all. The Soviet Union was not about to bind itself by new and far reaching agreements with Japan, and the Japanese had to content themselves with the prior agreement.[197] For the time being they could continue their redeployment of forces from Manchuria to the South Pacific, push the last stage of their offensive in China, and stand on the defensive elsewhere.[198]

ALLIED AND AXIS PLANS FOR VICTORY

The British planning for the Pacific War looking toward its victorious conclusion over a bitterly fighting Japan was to produce little impact on that war but instead the most heated dispute between Churchill and his three Chiefs of Staff of the entire war in March, April and May of 1944.[199] Between Churchill's argument for a major offensive in Southeast Asia and the Chiefs of Staff urging a push alongside MacArthur's advance from New Guinea through the Philippines to Japan, the exigencies of war and timing rather than agreement in London would decide. The Japanese offensive into India led to plans for a major campaign in Burma while the continuation of the war in Europe into 1945 followed by an unanticipated early victory over Japan first precluded and then obviated further major British operations in either theater. A substantial British fleet would assist the Americans in the Pacific offensives of 1945, welcomed there by the Americans, in spite of Admiral King's doubts, at the orders of President Roosevelt.[200]

The President also had had a very direct personal hand in the argument over American strategic planning for the Pacific War. He had, it would appear, played a major personal role in the decision to launch the Doolittle raid on Tokyo and the Guadalcanal operation, but these were not the only strategic choices he influenced. There had been lengthy and at times heated arguments over the most appropriate way to defeat Japan during the whole period from the spring of 1942 to the fall of 1943.[201] The basic decisions had tended increasingly to favor the double thrust in the Pacific, downgrading any approach to Japan from the north and from China because of experience with the weather problems in the former theater and the ineffectiveness of Chinese military effort in the latter. These trends had been reinforced by the successes in the Pacific in the fall of 1943 and early 1944 at a time when Chinese resistance was collapsing. It was increasingly clear that the two thrusts would converge in the central Philippines late in 1944 while the beginning of B-29 bombardment of Japan, first from bases in China and subsequently from the Marianas, was seen as leading either (in cooperation with the blockade of Japan) to the avoidance of an invasion of Japanese home islands altogether or to an effective preparation for such invasion if it proved necessary.

There were two categories of major remaining questions. One was the possible speed of the advance, and that depended on the success of operations in the Pacific and the timing of the defeat of Germany with the resulting release of forces from Europe for redeployment to the Pacific. The other was that of intermediate objectives, especially whether a major American effort should be made to retake the main island of Luzon in the Philippines or to head for Formosa (as Taiwan was then called) instead. On this issue, Roosevelt gave the nod though no final decision to Luzon in his conference with Nimitz and MacArthur in Hawaii on July 26–28, 1944.[202] The decision was finalized when Admiral King was convinced by Nimitz in September that this was the correct course; Formosa would be by-passed and the follow-up to the Philippines would be the Bonin Islands (Iwo Jima) and then the Ryukyus (Okinawa).[203]

Before any of these plans could be implemented, the Americans would have to mount a series of preliminary operations to get into the Philippines at all. A landing on Leyte Island in the central Philippines was originally scheduled for December 20, 1944, with landings on several islands between New Guinea and the Philippines by MacArthur's Southwest Pacific forces, and islands between the Marshalls and the Philippines by Nimitz's Pacific Ocean Area forces, preparing the way. Of the planned landings, several were eventually cancelled, but others were still considered necessary. MacArthur's army units assaulted Morotai on September 15, completely by-passing the large Japanese garrison on Halmahera.[204] If this move cost few casualties, leaving some 25,000 Japanese soldiers stranded on Halmahera while the Americans built airfields to support the invasion of the Philippines on Morotai, the simultaneous attack by marines and soldiers of Nimitz's command on Angaur and Peleliu in the Palau Islands proved terribly difficult and costly. The 81st Division had a difficult six weeks campaign to clear Angaur; the 1st Marine Division had to fight the Japanese on Peleliu until the end of November in a horrendous struggle which, with almost 7000 killed and wounded, cost the highest combat casualty rate of any of the amphibious assaults launched in the Pacific.[205] Admiral Halsey had been doubtful about the Peleliu operation from the start and many have questioned both its concept and its implementation since. It is, however, at least doubtful whether the enormous fleet anchorage at Ulithi in the Palaus, which was seized unopposed by the 81st Division, could have been utilized effectively as a major base by the American navy without a firm United States presence in the islands.

Whatever the merits of the Palaus operation, even while it and the Morotai landings were in the launching stage, highly successful American air raids on the Japanese in the Philippines suggested to Nimitz that the timetable for that operation could be moved forward from December 20 to October 20. The Joint Chiefs of Staff agreed with this change, as did MacArthur's headquarters. The stage was set for an American return to the Philippines. The Japanese had landed there and attacked the United States in December 1941 in order to secure their access to the oil-rich Netherlands East Indies; the American return would both cut them off from their Southeast Asian empire and prepare the way for an assault on the Japanese home islands. The stage for this great operation had been set with the final preliminary assaults on Morotai, Angaur, and Peleliu.

In Europe, the belligerents looked toward a year of the most bitter fighting on all fronts. In the East, the Soviet offensives in the winter of 1943–44 were designed to continue the effort to free all lands occupied by the Germans and their satellites, a process examined in Chapter 12. The Soviet Union had committed itself to launching an offensive in the East to coincide with the invasion of Western Europe, but the exact location of that operation could not be determined until the situation had been clarified by the results of the winter's fighting. The center piece of the Soviet summer offensive in 1944 would be a huge attack to destroy German Army Group Center which had held out so long and still clung to areas from which Moscow could be bombed. It is not known when the planning for what came to be known as operation "Bagration" actually began, but preliminary planning appears to have started early in 1944 with the broad outlines ready by mid-April.[206]

In the interim, there was not only much heavy fighting, but the Soviet government moved on three diplomatic fronts after the conference at Teheran. One of these, the working out of a new set of agreements with Japan signed at the end of March 1944, is reviewed earlier in this chapter. A second is very difficult to analyze in the absence of any evidence from the Soviet side. On January 17, 1944, Pravda printed and Moscow radio broadcast a big entirely fabricated story about separate peace negotiations in Spain between von Ribbentrop and two leading British personalities. The story was, of course, denied in London. The purpose of creating the uproar caused by this fabrication is not easy to understand:

was it designed as a cover or excuse for any Soviet explanation of an agreement with Germany on its part? Was it designed to put pressure on the British to carry out their promise to take part in the "Overlord" operation? We will not know unless material on this episode from the Soviet side becomes available.[207]

Whatever the intentions of Moscow and despite the annoyed reaction of London, the British looked to the Soviet Union not only as a key ally in the war but a power with which they hoped to continue to have good relations in the future. As the War Cabinet's Post-Hostilities Planning Sub-Committee was told on April 12, 1944, the assumption on which it was to operate "should be that it remains the policy of His Majesty's Government to foster and maintain the friendliest possible relations with the U.S.S.R."[208] It was taken for granted in London that the Soviet Union could dominate all of Europe and Asia but was not likely to do so; the only real worry was a possible Soviet threat to Near Eastern oil, while all would in any case have to work together to contain Germany, the power still seen as the most dangerous threat to Britain. The United Kingdom was simply unable to respond favorably to a Soviet request for long-term credit; as Orme Sargent of the Foreign Office minuted on June 1, 1944, "in future we shall have to adapt our diplomacy to the requirements and capacity of a debtor country. In fact the instruments at the disposal of a creditor country, such as loans, credits, foreign investments and subsidies will no longer be at our disposal."[209] British as well as American Lend-Lease shipments to Russia were, however, at a high level at the time, and the Soviet Union for once in the war gave considerable public acknowledgment of it.[210]

Thus Soviet relations with the Western Allies were temporarily eased a little; even the arrangements for shuttle bombing with American planes using Soviet air bases seemed at last to be working with the first raid using them being flown on June 2, 1944. But a successful German air raid on the base at Poltava followed by raids on two other bases led the United States to abandon an effort which had begun with ambitious hopes for Allied cooperation, had been delayed endlessly by the Soviet government and had been carried through in its later stages only as a possible harbinger of future cooperation in the air war against Japan.[211] Military cooperation between the Soviet Union and the Western Allies could only be at arms' length, and, as discussed in Chapter 13, the political relationship was not particularly good in the early months of 1944 either.

The third major Soviet initiative directly related to the conduct of hostilities was the sounding of a possible peace with Finland. Near the end of 1943, the Soviet Ambassador in Sweden, Alexandra Kollontai, presumably on instructions from Stalin following up on the discussion of Finland at Teheran, let it be known that the Soviet Union might deal for a Finnish exit from the war on specified terms rather than unconditional surrender. With the United States urging them on, the Finns decided to investigate this possibility during February and March 1944. The terms offered them provided for a return to the 1940 border, with Hangö exchanged for the Petsamo area, the internment or expulsion of German troops, and reparations payments of six hundred million dollars to be paid in goods over a 5-year period. The Finnish government, pressed hard by the Germans, misled by the temporary ability of the latter to hold onto Estonia, and still not reconciled to the border settlement at the end of the 1939–40 winter war, turned down these terms in April.[212] It was surely a most unwise choice. The Russians now made plans for a major attack which would take Finland out of the war by crushing it as the first step in the 1944 summer offensive.

The planning of the Western Allies for 1944 was, as might be expected, concentrated on the forthcoming invasion of northern France, operation "Overlord". Eisenhower had been appointed as over-all Allied commander, taking over the pre-existing preparatory staff of General Morgan.[213] Montgomery was brought over from Italy to control the land forces in the initial assault and took in hand both changes in the existing plan and the final training of the troops, British, American, and Canadian, destined to take part in the landing. Admiral Sir Bertram Ramsay was appointed to head the Allied naval forces and Air Chief Marshal Sir Trafford Leigh-Mallory was to lead the air forces. With Marshal of the Royal Air Force Sir Arthur Tedder as Eisenhower's deputy, the higher command for Overlord was in place.

The details of planning and preparation are summarized in Chapter 12, but anyone in the United Kingdom could see that vast preparations were in hand for what was obviously an operation of tremendous proportions. The very extent of the preparations gave rise to conflicting reactions. On the one hand it was jokingly suggested that only the barrage balloons kept the British Isles from sinking into the ocean under the weight of weapons and supplies; on the other hand the general discussion could cause apprehension. As General Sir Hastings Ismay, Churchill's military assistant, wrote to Field Marshal Wavell, then in India, on March 7, 1944, with the references to World War I which so heavily affected people's thinking in World War II:

> Feelings at home are very mixed. There are a number of people who go about talking as though all is over but the shouting; on the other hand a lot of people who ought to know better are taking it for granted that OVERLORD is going to be a bloodbath on the scale of the Somme and Passchendaele. Never has

there been an operation so widely advertised. One cannot help recalling Niv-elle's offensive in the watches of the night; however much one tries to put it out of one's mind.[214]

In the meantime, the actual land fighting was of course going forward in Italy, but it was going so slowly [215] that an effort was made, primarily at British insistence, to speed it up by a landing on the Italian coast well beyond the land front on which the Germans had stalled the Allied armies before the Gustav Line. British and American assaults tied down German reserves in anticipation of the landing with the British success-fully crossing the Garigliano river in the east while the Americans were driven back when trying to cross the Rapido river to open a route into the Liri valley in the west. The defeat suffered by the 36th Division—which had done very well at Salerno and would do even better in the later Italian campaign—caused bitter feelings after the war in Texas from which that National Guard division came; but in any case, the Gustav Line, anchored at Monte Cassino, held.[216]

The Allied landing itself at Anzio on January 22, 1944 succeeded, but incompetent leadership by General Mark Clark, the 5th Army com-mander, allowed the opportunity created by the initial surprise to pass unutilized. The Germans sealed off the beachhead and still held on to the Gustav Line across Italy. In the following weeks, they repeatedly tried to drive the Allies into the sea but failed because of a combina-tion of brave fighting and accurate intelligence through code-breaking about German intentions. The lines around the bridgehead and across Italy would be broken only in a new offensive.[217] Before that offensive could move forward, the great abbey at Monte Cassino was blasted to bits at the orders of General Freyberg, the able New Zealand division commander whom Field Marshal Alexander was not about to overrule. The Germans had ammunition under and soldiers and guns around it as the Vatican learned.[218] The operation which freed central Italy and the city of Rome would precede the invasion in France.

The portion of the planning for that invasion which directly affected the Italian campaign in addition to the timing of the major drive in Italy itself was the planned invasion of southern France, then code-named Anvil, which was scheduled to utilize divisions from the Italian front. Having given up all hope of having Turkey enter the war by late January 1944,[219] Churchill was now all the more determined to have Anvil can-celled so that the forces in Italy could continue to fight there. His pres-sure to aid the French resistance and the guerillas in Southeast Europe at this time should be seen in part in connection with his effort to abort Anvil.[220] That campaign belongs to the account of Overlord in Chapter 12, but it should be noted that Brooke was in these months doing what he could to have Field Marshal Wilson, Eisenhower's successor as the Allied commander in the Mediterranean, so write his reports as to assist: "for Heaven's sake get Anvil killed as early as you can," he wrote on March 6, 1944.[221] Wilson, who was more realistic in this regard than Brooke, promised to try but offered little hope.

The other inter-Allied dispute with direct military implications for the Italian campaign was the quarrel over Poland. Because Polish army units played a major role in the Allied campaign in Italy, there was repeated and grave concern that changes in the status of the Polish government-in-exile in London and the new puppet government being created by the Soviet Union would have repercussions on the morale and fighting capability of the Polish divisions which were essential to the 8th Army's effort.[222] The campaign in what Churchill had referred to as the soft underbelly of Europe was not without difficulties.

In one field the Italian campaign was certainly paying dividends in the Allied planning and preparation for Overlord. One of the major object-ives of the invasion of Italy had been the airfields near Foggia so that Allied planes could extend the range of their bombing offensive. (One of the reasons for the repeated attempts to push the Germans back and liberate central Italy up to the Pisa–Rimini Line had been the hope of securing air bases in the region north of Rome to extend the coverage of the combined bombing offensive even further.) The general impact of that offensive on Germany can be seen in the fact that by 1944 half of all German industry was working for the air force [223] which, in addition to tactical support at the fronts, was making desperate efforts to rebuild a bomber force and to defend German-controlled Europe from Allied air raids. The new bomber force project is included in the discussions of German planning for 1944 later in this chapter, but the struggle to defend her cities and industry belongs in this context.

All during the winter of 1943–44, the British continued their attacks on German cities and the Americans their effort to bomb German indus-try. But the losses were high. It was in this context that the success of the Americans in meeting the need for fighter escort of the bombing missions into central Europe was of decisive importance. They had been steadily extending the range of the P-38s and P-47s to the alarm of some Germans.[224] The use of the P-51 "Mustang" fighter, equipped with supplementary fuel tanks which could be dropped, changed the whole situation in the air war, which had looked for a while as if it were going in Germany's favor.

Fighters now accompanied the bombers; and, as the effectiveness of the P-51 became obvious, the bombers were sent deliberately to targets the Germans had to defend, thereby forcing the Luftwaffe into battle.[225]

In January–February 1944 the Americans crushed the defense system which the Germans had laboriously built up; in February alone the German air force lost 1277 frontline planes in battle and an additional 1328 to accidents and other causes, both categories of losses very much a product of inadequate training of crews who were shot down before acquiring substantial experience.[226] The almost total ability of the British and Americans to read the German air force codes helped achieve this spectacular victory as well as revealing the victory's extent to them.[227] Certainly Allied losses were heavy, especially in bombers, but in spite of these, the production and training facilities were increasing the size of the forces the Allies employed, even as the German air force was shrinking in size and dropping in the quality of its surviving crews.[228]

This victory made possible not only the continuation of the bombing offensive itself but the invasion and the two special air operations designed to assist it. One which was long the subject of controversy was the attack on the transportation system, especially in Western Europe. This project was called for to assist the consolidation of a bridgehead in an area where a dense transportation network made it potentially easy for the Germans to bring vastly superior forces to bear, and to bring in reserves more quickly than the Allies could bring in reinforcements. The head of the British Bomber Command was especially vehement in his opposition to using his bombers to support the invasion by transportation and other bombing missions; many in the London government were concerned about the heavy French civilian casualties expected to result from such bombing.[229] The directives to do so were, however, issued by Eisenhower under the authority of the Combined Chiefs of Staff; they were implemented and as it turned out with far greater success (and fewer civilian casualties) than both Harris and the British had anticipated.[230]

The British, however, did continue some area bombing of German cities while their aerial dropping of mines in the North Sea, Baltic, and Danube probably did more serious damage to Germany's powers of resistance.[231] More dramatic in its impact on German industrial and military effort was the great air offensive against the oil industry. Since this closely coincided with the invasion itself, as it began in mid-May, it is reviewed in Chapter 12; in this field also the ability to read German codes quickly provided the Allies with information on the effectiveness of their efforts.[232]

Whatever the dangers and the doubts, there was no way to defeat Germany but by a frontal assault from east and south, from the west and from the air. At one time, air power advocates had asserted that the last named could do it alone. It was obvious, whether he admitted it or not, that Harris's offensive had not done so and could not do so, however great the damage his bombers inflicted. In forwarding on January 27, 1944, to President Roosevelt a report on Germany's war potential by a group of distinguished historians given access to all secret information in American possession, General Arnold, the commanding general of the United States army air forces, expressed himself as concurring in the findings of the committee, which he summarized to the effect that a German surrender would come when the resistance of her ground forces could no longer be maintained because her air defenses were no longer adequate.[233] Bombing could contribute, but no early decision was to be expected; it would all depend on the success of the invasion.

The Germans looked to 1944 with the immediate problem of the Allied bombers preceding the great one of the invasion. The answer to the bombers, in spite of the obvious one of defending fighters, was seen in an air offensive. General Hans-Jürgen Stumpf was finally put in real charge of air defense against Allied air attacks at the beginning of February;[234] there was a long-range plan for putting key industries underground;[235] and a short-term one of dispersing the aircraft industry geographically to reduce its vulnerability;[236] but an offensive was still considered the preferable procedure. A projected strategic air offensive against the Soviet Union was aborted as a result of the situation at the front; the Germans simply could not withdraw bombers from support of ground operations in substantial numbers as the Red Army continued to pound their ground forces, a process which in any case was driving them from the bases needed for long-range bombing operations against the intended targets.[237] Any such projects were further hampered by the continued problems of the long-range bomber, the Heinkel 177, with its four engines driving two propellers, originally so that it could be used as a dive-bomber. Given the tendency of this plane to incinerate its crews, it may have been just as well that the Germans never brought it into large-scale production. What planes of this type and all sorts of other (mostly older) types could be made available were, however, thrown into a last bombing offensive against *England*.

From January to May 1944, a collection of over 500 bombers launched what came to be called the "Baby Blitz" against England. Though involving more planes than any attacks on England since 1941, these raids inflicted little damage and minor casualties while costing over 300 bombers which might have been available to attack the invasion beachheads. The delay in availability of the V weapons—itself in large part as a result of the Allied bombing—and the desire of Hitler to strike at Britain were behind the effort conducted to a large extent with pre-war bomber models and inexperienced crews. This was surely no way to hold off the Western Allies.[238]

The basic German strategy for 1944 was to continue to hold the front in Italy as far south as possible[239] and to hold as well as they could in the East but to concentrate on defeating the expected Allied invasion in the West. The basic assumption was and remained that Germany's best prospect lay in building up the military forces in the West sufficiently to crush the invasion attempt, because this would take advantage of her strong position in the West and the enormous risks of any great amphibious assault (which the Germans themselves had not dared to attempt at the height of their victory in 1940). Such a triumph, because of the losses in men, materiel, and morale inflicted on the Allies, would make it impossible for the latter to launch a second attempt that year, if ever, thereby releasing German forces for a major counter-offensive in the East. This in turn would drive back the exhausted Russians so that they could either be crushed in turn or forced to sue for peace. And while this was in process, the new submarine types would be coming into service to hold off any effort of the Western Allies to mount a new invasion in the West.

At meetings with his own military leaders and with his allies Hitler repeatedly sketched out this strategy in the first months of 1944; and since his actions fitted in with the strategy, it may be accepted that for once he was explaining what he really believed.[240] Urged by the Japanese as before, and now also by his French puppet Pierre Laval, to make a peace with the Soviet Union so that he could concentrate all his forces on the defeat of the British and Americans, Hitler always came back to the strategy just outlined.[241] He was confident that it would succeed, in part because by this time he believed that the mass murder of the Jews and all opposed to the regime had, as he explained to a loudly cheering assemblage of officers on May 26, removed all possibility of problems at home.[242] A Germany not subject to the stab-in-the-back which he imagined responsible for defeat in 1918 could not be beaten this time. He was in fact so confident that early in May 1944 he assured Herbert Backe, the Minister of Agriculture, that Germany would soon retake the richest part of the Ukraine, and that preparations for its control and exploitation should be made promptly.[243]

The real prospects of Germany were much dimmer than Hitler thought. He had in reality not concentrated forces in the West to anywhere near the extent which the danger there called for.[244] And, as the record of his conversation with Japanese Ambassador Oshima Hiroshi on May 27, 1944, reveals, he had been successfully misled by the great deception operations of the Allies. In the East, he had fallen for the

Soviet scheme to make the Germans believe that their summer offensive would be launched in the Lwow area; in the West, he had been equally successfully fooled into believing the Allied army far larger than it really was with plans for several diversionary attacks and then the main landing across the Dover Straits.[245] The German hopes for victory in 1944 would prove to be based on very weak foundations on all fronts.

12

———— • ————

THE ASSAULT ON GERMANY FROM
ALL SIDES

PRELIMINARIES IN THE EAST

In the months after the October 1943 set-backs west of Kiev, the Red Army quickly recovered and launched a new set of offensives. In the south, the winter of 1943–44 was more varied and mild than usual, but the mud caused by the periodic thaws did not hamper the movements of Soviet forces as much as it hindered the Germans. Soviet tanks were equipped with substantially wider treads and were therefore able to move more easily, and, in addition, the Red Army was by this time equipped with thousands of American trucks far more likely to keep going than the German ones. The greatly increased gasoline consumption characteristic of vehicles churning their way through the deep mud imposed a more serious burden on the oil-short Germans than on the Soviets. Furthermore, the Red Army had commandeered far more "panje carts," high wheeled wooden wagons drawn by a single horse, which could often move—and carry equipment and supplies—when all other modes of transport failed. The major factors enabling the Red Army to maintain its offensive pressure, however, were the continued growth in Soviet military production, the greater experience and self-confidence of its military commanders, and the increasing disparity in the size of its forces as compared to the German units facing them.

The Russians were also aided by two aspects of Hitler's control of the German military effort. With an invasion in the West anticipated by the Germans, the basic strategy of the Third Reich, as already described in Chapter 11, looked to a successful defeat of that invasion before troops and equipment could be turned to the East. As codified in Hitler's general directive Number 51 for the conduct of the war of November 3, 1943, this strategy required that for the time being the Eastern Front would have to take care of itself while Germany concentrated her newly mobilized men and manufactured weapons on defending Western Europe against Allied assault.[1] Minor deviations from this policy were required by crises on the Eastern Front in the spring of 1944, but on the whole this policy was adhered to because, as the directive put it: "In the East the size of the [German-controlled] space is such as to allow if worst came to worst even large losses of space without deadly danger to German survival,"[2] while this was not the case in the West.

If this sense of strategic priorities for 1944 meant that Germany would concentrate on building up her forces in the west and south, Hitler was by no means as willing to trade space for time in the East as the quotation might suggest. On the contrary, the economic importance of the Ukraine, both in terms of mineral and industrial resources and as a rich agricultural region, made him especially reluctant to agree to withdrawals urged on him by the commanders on the spot who were often supported by the Chief of the Army General Staff. In rejecting such advice, or following it slowly, Hitler not only acted out of regard for the economic importance of the area but also the fact that shortening the lines freed Russian as well as German units, often meant that heavy equipment and supply dumps could not be evacuated, and was likely to add to the strength of the Red Army, which promptly conscripted any men in the area given up who had escaped being evacuated by the Germans. In their memoirs the German generals, therefore, usually attributed their defeats during the period of retreat to Hitler's insistence on holding ground they believed should have been given up sooner, but the real difference between many of them and Hitler lay elsewhere.

Earlier in 1943 Hitler had agreed to the evacuation of the Demyansk and Rzhev front bulges to gain reserves for operations elsewhere on the Eastern Front, but these other operations had failed in the face of determined and effective Soviet resistance. Later, in September–October 1944, Hitler would agree to two very large withdrawals, one in southwest France and the other in the southern Balkans. Although in some of the other instances when withdrawals were recommended, an excellent case could be made for the earlier retreats urged by the military leaders on the spot, the real difference, it seems to me, lay in quite a different sphere.

Although they would not admit it openly—even to themselves—many of Germany's military leaders were by late 1943, early 1944, becoming convinced that they were losing the war and would be defeated; they preferred that the defeat come about in the least messy way possible. Hitler, on the other hand, still wanted and hoped to win, if not the whole war, at least a major part of it, and saw the need for Germany to hold as much of the occupied territories as possible as a basis for victory or at least an advantageous or partial peace. When given unpleasant advice by those military advisors he trusted, like Admiral Dönitz or General

Model, he was quite prepared to accept it; he sensed—correctly it should be noted—their devotion not only to him personally but to his vision of ultimate German victory. If he distrusted the advice of others, it was because he sensed—equally correctly I believe—a difference not only on tactics but in basic orientation. In the meantime he retained some of them, relieved others, occasionally followed their advice, and continued his program of massively bribing them all regularly in the hope that this would assure their loyalty.

Arguments over appropriate tactics for the Germans in the face of Soviet offensives marked the winter of 1943–44. From the Soviet side, the aim was obvious: a series of hammer blows was designed to force the Germans (together with what satellite troops still fought alongside them) out of the bulk of the Soviet territory they still occupied in the north and south. Most of the economically valuable land still held was in the south and it was here that the Red Army concentrated the bulk of its offensive forces. Beginning in the last week of December and continuing through January, Vatutin's First Ukrainian Front drove the Germans (4th Panzer and 1st Panzer) out of the area west of Kiev where they had earlier won their last tactical victory.[3] In the process the Red Army freed such important cities as Zhitomir, Berdichev and Kirovograd. Furthermore, they cut off and surrounded two corps in an encirclement at Korsun-Shevchenkovsky, a pocket which the Germans referred to by the name of Cherkassy, a nearby city also liberated by the Red Army. Because on this occasion, unlike Stalingrad, the advancing Soviet units were unable to drive back the German front a substantial distance away from their ring, the Germans succeeded in driving a relief column close to the pocket; and again unlike Stalingrad, when that column came close, the encircled units moved to break out. As a result, of some fifty to seventy thousand men in the pocket, possibly as many as a third of those trapped were able to escape but without any of their equipment. However hard the desperate Germans fought, the whole experience showed two things clearly. The initiative was now wholly with the Red Army, and the shock of the Stalingrad experience had made a deep impression on the thinking and the conduct of the German army.[4]

While Manstein's Army Group South was being battered and driven back in the northern Ukraine, Field Marshal Ewald von Kleist's Army Group A was receiving its share of attention farther south, though a few weeks later. Here the Germans still held the major industrial area around Krivoi Rog in the Dnepr bend area and the manganese mines at Nikopol together with a substantial protecting bridgehead south of the great river. A series of massive offensives by the Third and Fourth Ukrainian Fronts drove the Germans out of both areas with heavy casualties in January and

February of 1944; neither the talents of the Army Group commander nor the ruthless fanaticism of General Ferdinand Schörner, one of Hitler's favorites, could contain the well equipped and carefully led Red Army units.[5] As they advanced, the latter did on this sector of the front what they had done at the Dnepr and would do over and over again thereafter: bounce the next river barrier, in this case the Ingulets, on the run, establishing bridgeheads *before* the Germans could establish a firm line on the river banks.[a]

The collapse of German military power in the Dnepr bend area and the loss of the Nikopol bridgehead raised once more the problem of the German and Romanian forces cut off in the Crimea in the fall of 1943 and now more isolated than ever. Marshal Antonescu urged Hitler immediately after the fall of Nikopol on February 8, 1944 (as he had in the preceding October), to evacuate Axis troops from the Crimea now that all hope of regaining contact with them was lost.[6] Only the seven Romanian divisions stationed there could secure the defense of Romania itself from the obviously imminent Soviet invasion. Hitler refused, ostensibly because of concern for repercussions on the policy of Turkey and the danger of air raids against the Romanian oil fields, perhaps in reality more because he still hoped that after a stabilization on the Eastern Front and a defeat of the invasion in the West he could reconquer the Ukraine and thereby reestablish land contact with the Crimea. There was also concern over the Soviet Black Sea fleet regaining the great base at Sevastopol.

When Antonescu visited Hitler's headquarters at the end of February, the Germans were primarily interested in checking whether he was about to leave the war and whether or not to have Romania join Germany in occupying Hungary, which was indeed considering an exit from the conflict far more seriously than Romania.[7] Hitler decided not to have the Romanians participate in his planned action against Hungary because he hoped to keep Hungary fighting on the side of Germany; promising to return to the Romanians the piece of that country which the Axis had awarded to Hungary in 1940 was guaranteed to prevent that. But neither would he agree to an early evacuation of the Crimea. The five German and seven Romanian divisions were to remain there.

A Soviet offensive struck from the north across the Perekop land bridge into the Crimea and from a bridgehead the Russians had earlier secured nearby, while a companion attack came from the east, where they had held a small bridgehead since November 1, 1943, across the Kerch Straits. The two Red Army operations hit the Axis forces on

---

[a] It would be worth investigating why the Red Army regularly did this, the American army usually did it, while the British army almost never did so.

April 8–9, 1944. By mid-May the 120,000 men formally organized as the 17th German Army had been crushed. Only a small proportion was evacuated; there was no long siege as in 1941–42. The Soviet victory and Axis defeat in the Crimea was one of the most complete, if least known, of the war.[8]

A major Soviet victory which had made it foolish for the Germans to try to hold on to the Crimea — and most difficult first to supply and then to evacuate its isolated garrison — had been the massive spring offensive on the southern front. Designed to crush the whole German front from the Prijpet Marshes to the Black Sea, it had freed the important ports of Nikolaev and Odessa from German and Romanian occupation. With Vatutin wounded, Zhukov took over the command of First Ukrainian Front; in a major offensive striking south from the Rovno area, the armored units of First Ukrainian Front staged a Blitzkrieg of their own. In a four-week period of March 1944, they clobbered the German 4th and 1st Panzer Armies, drove to the Carpathian Mountains, and outflanked the various possible German defense lines in the southern Ukraine.

An equally effective if less daring frontal assault by Konev's Second Ukrainian Front demolished most of the German 8th Army while the Third Ukrainian Front of Malinovsky battered the reconstituted 6th Army at the southern end of the front. Although in this process the speedy Soviet advance captured important German supply centers, the Soviet hope of catching the 1st Panzer Army in an encirclement was not realized, in part because of the re-transfer of an SS armored corps from the forces assigned to deal with an invasion in the West. The Red Army's advances in March 1944 were, nevertheless, dramatic. It was obvious that its commanders knew how to maneuver and control vast forces on the move. Prospective German defensive lines to be based on the Bug and Dnestr rivers were bounced in the advance, and the next one, on the Pruth river, outflanked from the north. The Germans and Romanians had been driven out of the main portions of the Ukraine, and the Red Army stood at the entrance to Romania and Hungary.[9]

Neither Romania nor Hungary was in any strong position to defend itself. The Romanian army had, to all intents and purposes, bled to death at Stalingrad and in the Crimea — the collapse of the Romanian forces on the latter battlefield came right after the Soviet offensive, which freed Nikolaev and Odessa, had removed all realistic hope of their relief. The Romanians were, as discussed in Chapter 13, already trying to find a way out of the war; the Germans were in effect giving them every incentive to quit while making it as difficult as possible for them.

As for the Hungarians, their first serious effort to leave the war led the Germans to occupy the country and change its government. The

German leadership had long been suspicious of the Hungarians; they believed that Budapest had not been sufficiently eager to send its best troops to assist the 1942 campaign in the East; and Hitler himself had retained doubts about the steadfastness and loyalty of the Hungarians ever since their government had funked at war in 1938 when he had hoped to enlist them in a joint attack on Czechoslovakia. They were, in his eyes, the least reliable of Germany's allies. It is worth recalling that in July 1941, when at the height of his euphoria over an assumed victory in the East he had discussed the project of murdering all of Europe's Jews, he had predicted that, as the countries of the continent were urged to give up their Jews, the Hungarians would be the last to yield to German pressure.[10] This prediction had proved to be correct.[a] In spite of endless efforts, including heated personal interventions with Hungarian Regent Horthy by Hitler and von Ribbentrop, the government in Budapest had failed the acid test of loyalty to the Third Reich at a time when the vast majority of Jews in German-controlled Europe had already been murdered. If Germany could no longer conquer its enemies, at least it could occupy its allies to keep them from defecting. In the case of Italy, the Germans had struck late but on the whole effectively, aided, as already discussed, by the complete incompetence of the Italians. The Germans now arranged a repeat performance in Hungary under the code-name "Margarethe."

For some time plans and preparations had been made in German headquarters to take over in Hungary, utilizing, as in Italy, troops allegedly on their way through the country to fight Germany's enemies, not its own allies. As the situation on the Eastern Front changed drastically with Zhukov's offensive in March coming closer and closer to the border of Hungary, the urgency for action increased just as the means for the operation decreased. Hitler decided to try to keep the Hungarian army on the German side rather than turning it into a source of slave labor like the Italian one. Horthy was summoned to meet Hitler and browbeaten into accepting a German occupation as well as appointing a new government agreeable to Berlin. By the time he returned to Budapest, German units were in control of much of the country; he was himself surrounded by Nazi soldiers; and the new government he was obliged to install was headed by the former Hungarian Minister in Berlin, Döme Sztojay, a man acceptable to Hitler. Hungarian units were now called on to assist the remnants of German divisions fleeing from

---

[a] Although it is true that neither Bulgaria nor Finland yielded up their Jewish citizens for slaughter, the numbers involved were in both cases so small that the Germans did not think it worth the uproar when initial requests failed. The Wannsee Conference statistical estimates were 48,000 for Bulgaria and 2300 for Finland, but 742,800 for Hungary.

Romania before the advancing Red Army in clearing the passes of the Carpathians. Incidentally, they could thereby imagine themselves to be protecting their country not only from the Soviet Union but also from having to return territory to Romania. The first serious attempt of Hungary to leave the war had been effectively crushed.[11]

The coup in Hungary was not the only step Germany took in the face of its disastrous defeat at the hands of the Red Army in the Ukraine in the early months of 1944. A second step was a new tactic: the designation of essentially arbitrarily selected places as "fortresses," which were to be held to the bitter end by an especially appointed fortress commander who was expected to inspire his troops to hold out until they and he were killed. The intended purpose of this charming innovation was to force the Red Army to devote such large forces to dealing with isolated German garrisons that the advance columns of Soviet tanks would be weakened, bereft of supplies, and eventually halted. The isolated "fortresses" could serve as beacons for German stragglers from units broken up by Soviet offensives and would then be able to hold out all the better until they were eventually relieved—in theory by again advancing German forces, in reality by imprisonment or death.[12]

The third step Hitler took involved the command of the two Army Groups defeated by the Soviet offensive. On March 28, von Manstein and von Kleist were both given high decorations and relieved of their commands. Their successors were the two highest ranking dedicated National Socialists among the Eastern Front commanders, Model for Army Group South and Schörner for Army Group A. Their Army Groups may have shot more German soldiers after rigged courts martial than they had before, but the new commanders would prove just as incapable of halting the Red Army as their predecessors. Changing the names of the Army Groups from South to North Ukraine and from A to South Ukraine pointed to Hitler's hopes and ambitions but also did nothing to enhance German military strength.[13] Ironically, the appointment of the cautious Model would prove of enormous help to the success of the great Soviet deception operation for their 1944 summer offensive because it was *his* Army Group that the pretended Soviet offensive was to strike and which hence drew to itself, with Hitler's enthusiastic support, practically all German reserves.

Simultaneously with the change in the German command on the southern part of the Eastern Front came the confirmation in his position of General Lindemann, who had been acting as commander of Army Group North.[14] In that portion of the front there had also been a major Soviet victory in the winter. The Red Army had built up its forces in the Oranienbaum pocket as well as on other sectors of Army Group

North's front and hoped that a massive offensive could completely free Leningrad and drive the Germans out of the northern Soviet territory they still held. Though the tight siege of Leningrad had been broken earlier, the city was still under constant artillery bombardment and a drastic change at this point would be a signal for all of Scandinavia. The Germans had done some serious contingency planning here, unlike elsewhere on the Eastern Front, and were preparing a defensive line which took advantage of the Narva river and the lakes along the Estonian–Soviet border. Although transfers of German divisions to the endangered southern portions of the front and the withdrawal of the Spanish Blue Division dramatically weakened the German front, the order to withdraw to what was called the "Panther" position was not given.[15] This was due in part to erroneous intelligence of the German 18th Army which led its commander to prefer remaining in place, and in part to the concern in headquarters about the likely repercussions on Finland of a withdrawal on this sector of the front. The result was that the weakened front—which included a number of the air force field divisions—crumbled quickly under the Soviet offensive.

On January 14 the Red Army launched a major attack from the Oranienbaum pocket and south from Leningrad itself, followed soon after by an attack near Novgorod. Here was a far more ambitious project than the prior relief attempts. Neither replacing Army Group Commander Kuechler temporarily with Model and subsequently having Lindemann take over when Model was sent south made much difference. The Germans fought skillfully and fiercely, while the Soviet leadership was not as sure as in the south, but the German army was forced to retreat to the Panther position. The units which arrived there by the end of March had been badly battered in the interim while the Red Army had won another major victory; Leningrad was really and truly freed. Furthermore, although an early spring thaw halted the Red Army as much as the Germans at the Panther line, the Russians had already bounced the Narva river line in their advance and held a small but significant foothold across that river.[16]

It appears likely that the temporary holding of the northern end of the main front at Narva had helped decide the Finns to reject the Soviet terms in April 1944. But the fact remains that at the northern as on the southern ends of the great front in the East the Red Army had driven back the Germans, inflicting heavy losses in men and materiel. At both ends of the main front, the Russians were now essentially back at their pre-1939 borders. There was a major German bulge eastwards only at the center; in the south the Red Army stood at the gates of Hungary and Romania; in the north they could strike at Finland or into the Baltic

States or both. The initiative was with them, and as observers anticipated the summer of 1944 on the Eastern Front, the question now was where the Red Army would strike, not what the Germans might do. The whole initiative had passed to the Soviet Union.

Since March 1944, the Soviet general staff had been working on plans for the summer offensive. If the Finns did not leave the war on their own, they would certainly be driven out of it by a massive attack for which preparations were already under way. The big question was where to strike on the main front? The result of prior failure to drive the Army Group Center out of its Belorussian positions, combined with the great winter successes of the Red Army in the south and north, suggested the possibility of an attack on what was now an eastern bulge; this project simultaneously offered the possibility of deceiving the Germans by making it look as if the attacks were to come in the regions of prior success, especially the northern Ukraine. With Stalin personally canvassing the possibilities and opting for this approach, the stage was beginning to be set for one of World War II's most dramatic battles.

The Soviet plans provided for a massive buildup of forces on the central sector with the old Western Front split into the Second and Third Belorussian Fronts on April 24. This was not a mere name change like the German one of a month earlier. Here was a portion of a carefully calculated buildup in which, however, reinforcements were for the most part fed into existing units and additional units were transferred from the reserve and from other segments of the front in the last weeks before the attack, and under unusually careful provisions for secrecy. At the same time, steps were taken to give the impression of a major offensive against the Army Group North Ukraine with a secondary thrust into the Baltic States. Perhaps most important was the insistence in this offensive plan on concentration on one major objective within reach at one time and on putting all the needed resources into it.

The other side of these preparations was the complete and successful hoodwinking of the Germans. As so often before and later, German army intelligence had lots of accurate minor details while getting the big picture completely wrong. A major Soviet offensive against Army Group North Ukraine was anticipated. All reinforcements and much new equipment was sent to this Army Group, which had the additional advantage of now being under the command of Hitler's favorite, Model. Army Group Center, on the other hand, lost most of its reserve formations to its southern neighbor and had to put all of its strength up front, an arrangement which fitted perfectly into the plans of the Red Army which wanted to crush the Germans facing them in place, not drive them through the forests and swamps of Belorussia. Whatever the signs beginning to come in at the front, both German military headquarters and the Army Group Center commander Field Marshal   Busch himself were certain there would be no major offensive against the Army Group until the day it started; Busch himself was away and would have to fly back to his crumbling command.[17]

The great offensive to destroy Army Group Center and rip open the road to Warsaw was also to be supported by a massive partisan operation in the German rear. The movement had grown substantially in the area still occupied by the Germans with the Belorussian terrain especially suitable for guerillas. The partisans by late 1943 in fact controlled large areas in the rear, drafted men into their ranks, and made it obvious to the rural population that the power of the Soviet state would soon be coming back in full force. In the spring of 1944 the German army launched a series of major anti-partisan operations and inflicted considerable casualties, but by this time there were so many partisans that their military effectiveness from the Soviet point of view was not substantially affected. They were to make thousands of line cuts in the railways in the days and nights just before the Soviet offensive started; their activities helped to paralyze the German transportation system in the critical early days of the Red Army offensive somewhat the way the Allied bombing of the transportation system in France held up the German reaction to the Allied landing in Normandy.

PRELIMINARIES IN THE WEST

In early April, the British and Americans had notified the Soviet Union that the invasion would begin on or about May 31, with the weather determining the exact date. There is no evidence that the precise dates were in any way coordinated; the Soviet Union and the Western Allies both moved at the earliest time that each felt it could, with both having to make some last-minute changes in the timetable. On details in such fields as intelligence between the Soviet Union on the one hand and Britain and the United States on the other, cooperation was very poor.[18] At a time when there were all sorts of political problems between the Allies, only the broad thrust of strategy, not the details of operations, could be coordinated.

The Western Allies had decided to utilize the Italian campaign to help prepare for the invasion in the West in three ways. They would bind German forces in that theater and thus keep them away from both the Eastern Front and the invasion area. Secondly, the liberation of central Italy would provide them with air bases from which the remaining unreachable portions of German-occupied Europe were within the range of their bombers. Finally, experienced divisions from the Italian theater were to provide the needed push for the landing on the south coast of France which would support the invasion of northern France and provide additional port facilities for the Allies once fully ashore.

The campaign in Italy itself proved very arduous, as shown in Chapter 11. While the Germans failed in their repeated efforts to drive the Allied divisions landed at Anzio into the sea,[19] the Allies themselves, in spite of repeated efforts, failed to break the German line across the peninsula. The renewed frontal assault in the period February 15, to March 23, 1944, did not push through to the Liri valley, the route north.[20] Shifting forces from the east coast to the west, the Allies struck again after major preparations on May 11, a date determined with reference both to steps in Italy and the forthcoming invasion in the West. Over a period of several days, the Allied forces battered their way into the German lines, broke through and headed north after joining up with the troops in the Anzio beachhead.[21] As the Allies advanced under General Mark Clark's command, they most unwisely raced for Rome rather than trying to cut off the retreating Germans.[22] On June 4 Rome was liberated (and there is no evidence that the Allies heeded the Pope's plea to refrain from sending Black soldiers into the eternal city); in the following months the British, American, French and Polish troops pushed on, slowly driving the Germans out of central Italy.[23]

In the process of advancing from their positions of May to the end of their offensives in early November, the Allies captured the airfields north of Rome, which had been one of their key objectives. They also released the American and French divisions needed for the invasion of southern France at American insistence and over vehement objections from the British. Whether driving the Germans out of central Italy was worth the cost is at least open to argument; that the alternative to "Anvil," a push into northern Italy and into the Alps toward Austria would have gotten anywhere, is beyond belief. As Stalin had tried to point out to Churchill at Teheran, there were some very high mountains barring that route into Central Europe. Nothing suggests that the armies which had encountered such obstacles in the rugged terrain of Italy, perfectly suited to the needs of the defending Germans, would have found it easy to fight their way up the Alps. The spring offensive in Italy had, however, made it impossible for the Germans to move units from their 10th and 14th Armies out of Italy to meet the dangers looming in France, and in this fashion contributed to the general strain on their military resources as the latter faced the cross-Channel threat.

There the leaders, the soldiers, and the people on both sides looked toward the great invasion which was expected to take place in 1944.

The British and Americans had originally committed themselves to one landing on the Channel coast in May to be accompanied or followed soon after by another on the Mediterranean coast of France. A number of major issues had to be solved to convert these hopes and plans into reality. The staff under General Morgan (COSSAC) had been gathering detailed information and developing plans for months; whatever changes were made later, these provided the basis for all subsequent work. Eisenhower had been made the overall commander with Montgomery to lead the ground forces in the assault,[24] while Admiral Sir Bertram Ramsay headed the naval and Air Chief Marshal Sir Trafford Leigh-Mallory the air contingents. The British Air Chief Marshal Arthur Tedder was made Eisenhower's deputy. Though in the end working together, these individuals often clashed; Montgomery and Leigh-Mallory were evidently very difficult men who had troubles cooperating effectively with high ranking officers of any service or nationality. Fortunately Montgomery's Chief of Staff, General Francis (Freddie) de Guingand, was superb at working with everybody, and Air Chief Marshal Charles Portal, the Chief of the Air Staff, managed to control Leigh-Mallory. He also helped solve one of the most contentious issues, that of the role of the strategic air forces in relation to the invasion. Hoping to win the war on their own and skeptical of the likely success of the invasion, the British Bomber Command and the American 8th and 15th Air Forces preferred to operate independently against targets they considered of strategic importance—industrial cities for Bomber Command and the aircraft industry, later the synthetic oil industry, for the Americans. After endless bickering, the strategic air forces were temporarily subordinated to Eisenhower, especially for the bombing of transportation targets.[25]

The issue of transportation was tied closely to the basic needs of a successful invasion. On the one hand, the Allied landing force had to be large enough and strong enough to seize a substantial beachhead against what was certain to be energetic resistance. This had led to the expansion of the anticipated assault force from three to five divisions supported by three rather than one or two airborne divisions.[a] The greater shipping needs for such an assault and the patent difficulties of the Anzio landing had led to a postponement of the planned invasion from May to June, with dates at the beginning and the middle of the month feasible in view of tides and other technical considerations. But an even larger assault would be launched against an enemy whose forces in the West, over fifty divisions, were certain to be vastly greater than

---

[a] This trend was the reverse of that in German planning for an invasion of England in 1940, which had begun with a 13 division assault but had been reduced to one of nine divisions with two airborne divisions.

those which could be landed in the initial phase of the invasion. Any hopes of success—and it is too often forgotten how many doubted that these were great—rested on keeping down the rate at which the Germans could reinforce the point at which the landing had taken place; and systematic attacks on the transportation system of France were an obvious way to assist with this objective. As already mentioned, the transportation bombing plan was approved and implemented; it proved more effective than its opponents had expected and caused fewer French civilian casualties than an anxious British government had feared. Even while that bombing operation was under way, the American air force began a systematic effort to disrupt Germany's petroleum supplies through massive and repeated attacks on her synthetic oil installations; over time this program would have a major effect on German air operations, pilot training, and mobility in general.

A second key factor in making an invasion feasible by keeping German reinforcements away was, of course, the existence of other fronts at which Germany had to keep substantial forces or deliberately run great risks. Some German divisions were in Italy and some in the Balkans, but in the middle of 1944 about half were on the Eastern Front. The maintenance of Soviet pressure in the East was a prerequisite for any landing in the West in 1944, and the promised Soviet summer offensive was expected to keep the Germans from moving any large units from the Eastern Front to the West once the battle there was joined—as in fact happened.[26] Whatever some of his generals thought and whatever he had himself said, Hitler was simply not prepared to make a major sacrifice of territory deliberately in the East in order to send to the West the massive reinforcements which would have been needed for a successful defense.[27]

The third essential factor in keeping the Germans from concentrating overwhelming forces against the invaders was to deceive them into believing that more than one landing on the Channel coast was planned. The Allies had decided very early that Normandy was the correct place to land; it was more difficult for the Germans to concentrate their troops there, it was within land-based fighter range, it could be reached by over-night shipping runs, and it offered a way of coping with the harbor issue that would also fool the Germans and is reviewed subsequently. But one very important way to protect a beachhead landing there from being overwhelmed was to encourage the Germans to believe that this landing was only the first of two, with the main one yet to come in the Pas de Calais area, the narrowest part of the Channel and the closest to Germany. Any landing at the latter point would not only run into the strongest German defenses but could not possibly be portrayed as a feint to shield the major landing elsewhere. What the Allies therefore had to do and did was to create over time a whole series of notional divisions, corps, armies and one Army Group; with one army, the British 4th, being ostensibly slated to invade Norway, while the fake 1st United States Army Group (FUSAG) would invade France near Calais.[a]

The deception operation ("Bodyguard") was conducted on a very large scale with the direct operational parts under the code-names "Fortitude North" (Norway) and "South" (Calais). The project was carefully worked out, continually monitored, and almost unbelievably successful.[28] In brief outline, it involved the slow buildup of a complex of imaginary headquarters with both radio traffic for the Germans to locate and attempt to analyze and commanders who really existed. Of the latter, Lt. General Patton of FUSAG was by far the best known; and when he was sent to Normandy to command the 3rd Army, he was replaced at FUSAG by the commanding general of the Army Ground Forces, Lt. General Leslie J. McNair. When McNair was killed by an Allied bomb dropped short on July 25, the highest ranking American officer killed in World War II was in turn replaced by Lt. General John L. DeWitt, until then head of the Western Defense Command.[29]

The effectiveness of the deception was reinforced by the fact that every German spy in the United Kingdom had been captured by the British and, if not executed, had been turned around so that a stream of erroneous information was fed to the Germans both before and after the day of the invasion, with special emphasis on the concept that the Normandy landing was a diversion before the main invasion yet to come in the Calais area, thereby keeping units of the German 15th Army there from being sent to reinforce the 7th Army fighting for its life in Normandy. The Allies were able to monitor the effectiveness of the deception and to time the messages from the agents who worked for them but were believed by the Germans to be their own, because of the earlier break into the enigma code systems.[b] Allied ability to decrypt had more than kept up with the German refinements in encrypting, so that at critical times during the "Overlord" operation—when the Germans were especially pressed for time and hence resorted to radio communications—the Allies could determine whether or not the deception was working.

While the pretended project to invade Norway did not look entirely

---

[a] Some of the units were real, not notional, and were then "reassigned" to the actual invasion, being replaced in many cases by imaginary units supposedly newly arrived from across the Atlantic.

[b] The Americans' breaking of Japanese codes also proved most helpful because the Japanese diplomatic and military representatives sent home detailed reports on the German defences in the West which were frequently intercepted and read.

convincing (though no divisions were for a long time removed from there and a special force of German submarines was collected and stationed off the Norwegian coast), the deception worked well because the Germans were prepared to believe it. They readily accepted the existence and location of the extra units in southeast England and were therefore certain that an attack in the Calais area was coming: there were simply too many divisions in England and on the way from the United States to be accounted for. Furthermore, the Germans had an excessively high estimate of the assault shipping available to the Allies, so that the five-division assault in Normandy did not look like the main invasion to them. Finally, the Dieppe experience led the two sides to very different conclusions. The Germans decided that their key task was to defend the ports, which the Allies would obviously need to supply their invasion forces. The emphasis in the massive program of fortifying the coast of France and Belgium was therefore on the ports; this is where the mass of artillery and fortifications was located.[30] The hope was that an Allied effort to seize a major port could be foiled, and that without a port to bring in supplies and reinforcements any beachhead could be destroyed.

The Allies had drawn a rather different conclusion from the Dieppe fiasco. Instead of assaulting a heavily defended port, they would land on beaches, bring their own harbors with them and seize a port *after* consolidating their beachhead. Enormous segments of breakwaters were built of concrete in English ports to be towed across the Channel and sunk in place, together with a large number of old ships, to build two artificial harbors, called "Mulberries," on the French coast, one for the British and Canadian forces, one for the Americans. Floating causeways inside these harbors would facilitate unloading. Once a major lodgement had been secured, the Allied forces would strike out to obtain ports, first Cherbourg and then the Brittany harbors; but for a long time the Mulberries would provide adequate facilities. By the time the Germans began to get an inkling of this extraordinary development, it was far too late to alter their defense arrangements even if they had fully understood the import of the new device.[31] As for the other new supply scheme of the Allies, the pipeline to be laid under the ocean ("Pluto") for pumping gasoline to the beachhead, the Germans did not have even an inkling.[32]

With these misunderstandings and delusions, the Germans expected one or more diversionary attacks, most likely including one in Normandy, followed by the main assault in the Calais area. Even after the Normandy landing, this continued to be the German belief all during June and July; it was only at the end of July that it began to dawn on them that no landing in the Pas de Calais area was planned at all. By that time, it was too late to move reinforcements from there to the invasion front, which was about to be ruptured by the American breakout at its western end.[33]

Both sides faced added problems. On the Allied side, there were those of security, de Gaulle, and broader dedication to the whole project. The strictest rules were developed and rigidly enforced to protect the plans and intentions of the invasion; although causing some hardships and frictions, the security measures proved effective. Even the disaster costing hundreds of lives when German E-Boats ripped into an unescorted landing exercise in Lyme Bay on April 26 did not give the Germans any solid information.[34] What bits of accurate information leaked out were drowned in an ocean of rumors and deliberate misinformation.

There was considerable friction with Charles de Gaulle who, unlike Montgomery, was not blessed with a Chief of Staff capable of working with a variety of British and American leaders. In the preparations for the invasion, the very magnitude of the effort that others had to make to rescue France from German domination made the French leader all the more determined to be as stubborn and difficult as possible, while the enormous risk they were running made the British and Americans especially reluctant to defer to his wishes or to endanger the secrecy of their intentions. Even as de Gaulle successfully consolidated his hold on French North Africa, the relationship with London and Washington remained strained. The Americans, however, were now coming around to a tacit recognition of de Gaulle's effective control of the French resistance which could assist the invasion. In practice Eisenhower was empowered by Roosevelt to deal with de Gaulle's newly established French Committee of National Liberation as the de facto regime; and while this in no way smoothed dealings with it or him, it both facilitated some practical cooperation and greatly helped de Gaulle take over control of the country as it was liberated from the Germans.[35]

The basic commitment of the Allies to the invasion was perhaps more at risk than often realized. Churchill, with nightmares of the Channel running red with blood, a new Dunkirk, and the end of Britain's role in the war as well as his own role as its Prime Minister, had been doubtful for a long time. In April he was still complaining about an operation "forced upon us by the Russians and by the United States Military authorities";[36] it was only at the final review of the invasion plans on May 15, in which Montgomery played a major role, that he described himself as "hardening toward this enterprise."[37] He continued to oppose the planned landing in southern France, as did Brooke and Montgomery, and that project was postponed until August to assure adequate landing ships for Overlord. But for the Americans who saw the need for port facilities to supply the assault into Germany itself as well as the need to feed into France the French divisions being formed in Italy and North Africa, there could be no abandonment of that project. For them, and especially for Roosevelt and Marshall, there was in addition the combined pressure of MacArthur and King for expanding operations in the Pacific and the preference of large segments of the American public for a Pacific First strategy. If in a Presidential election year the United States did not mount a truly major offensive in Europe, the push for deployment elsewhere would become overwhelming. It remains curious that the British, who were so certain that the Europe First strategy was correct, never did appreciate that for the Americans this strategic priority necessarily meant a massive invasion, not puttering around the edges. And if Churchill ever had the forebodings about the Soviet Union which have often been attributed to him, could he really conceive of slogging up the Italian peninsula — to say nothing of climbing over every mountain ridge in the Balkans — while the Red Army liberated Central and Western Europe?

The air force leaders were still doubtful about the whole enterprise but their broader reservations had been silenced. Many of them were not well attuned to cooperating with the ground forces, but they would try. On one aspect opposition remained strong. Fearing enormous casualties to the American airborne landing on the right flank of the invasion, Leigh-Mallory urged first orally and then in writing that this project be dropped. Since it was held essential to the westernmost of the landings — and hence to the whole broad assault scheme — Eisenhower overruled him and kept to the original plan; it is not a coincidence that the famous picture of the Supreme Allied Commander on the night before D-Day shows him with some of the paratroopers about to emplane for their flight across the Channel.[38]

The basic commitment to the operation, with the President and eventually Churchill behind him, was very carefully orchestrated by Eisenhower himself. He had been in charge of the landings in Northwest Africa; his theater command had directed the invasions of Sicily and the mainland of Italy. Now it was his job to repeat the performance, hopefully successfully.[a] There were certainly no doubts or hesitations in Montgomery's thinking once the plan for the invasion had been altered in the way he as well as Eisenhower wanted. Montgomery had put his heart and soul into the enterprise, had exhorted, inspired, and cajoled the troops, had insisted on more training and more supplies, had supported the use of the new kinds of floating tanks and other devices

---

[a] There are hints in the evidence that, given the risks of the entire enterprise, Eisenhower's appointment left open the possibility of Marshall taking over if the invasion failed and a new one had to be mounted. See David Eisenhower, *Eisenhower at War*, p. 44.

developed by the inspired General Sir Percy C.S. Hobart in his 79th Armored Division, and took a certain personal satisfaction out of once again facing his old enemy Rommel, now commanding the German Army Group B, about to be attacked by his own 21st Army Group. He had beaten Rommel once, and he was confident of doing so again.

The full backing of the United States and British governments for "Overlord" was dramatically illustrated by the enormous commitment of men—over a million—along with thousands of ships and planes to the enterprise. If this was clear to any observer of the English countryside then and in pictures now—pictures which suggest truth for the joke that only the barrage balloons kept the island from sinking into the ocean under the weight of stowed weapons and supplies—it is also evident both in retrospect from the then secret evidence and from any comparison with the German side by the command arrangement. All depended on the weather to go ahead and the fortunes of battle if the word were given. For the latter, the Chiefs of Staff of both powers were gathering; if the invasion faltered, they would make whatever decisions needed to be made to retrieve disaster. But the decision to go ahead was Eisenhower's own; he was to consult his weather forecasters and his military subordinates, but he did not have to ask anyone for agreement to give the order for the invasion.

The full authority without the need to check with military or political superiors proved of even greater importance than anyone might have anticipated. The weather forecast for June 5 turned out to be horrendous, with strong winds and dark clouds the preceding night. The invasion had to be postponed. But the weather experts detected a coming short interval of good weather, and on this basis, Eisenhower decided, with his land, air and naval commanders concurring, that the invasion should go ahead rather than wait another two weeks. The Allied domination of the North Atlantic enabled them to detect this slight break in the weather; but the Germans, whose weather stations in Greenland and Canada had been destroyed, whose weather reporting ships had been swept out of the Atlantic, and who could no longer send out long-range airplanes for weather reconnaissance, were ignorant of it. All they saw was the wretched weather which had forced the postponement, and they concluded that there was no prospect of an invasion before the middle of June or early July. Air and sea reconnaissance over and in the Channel were called off, and the coastal radar stations had been knocked out by Allied air attacks. The German commanders were either on leave or at conferences away from their posts—they thought there was plenty of time when in fact thousands of Allied ships were heading for the French coast. German intelligence knew the Allied codes used to alert the

French underground and intercepted these messages, but the skeptics could not believe that the Allies were coming when the weather was so obviously unsuitable. The commitment which empowered Eisenhower to grasp the weather window of opportunity enabled the Allies to gain the enormous advantage of surprise.

The Germans had been working for years on their defenses and were very confident of their ability to crush an invasion attempt. If they could come close to foiling the Allies at Salerno and Anzio, they could certainly succeed where they already had in place large forces, extensive fortifications and the ability to mass very substantial reinforcements. They had, however, significant problems as well. The navy was small and could only send submarines and E-Boats against any invading armada; in the event these proved even less effective than the low expectations of the Germans. The coastal artillery was large in number, and often large in caliber, but much of it was in the Pas de Calais area and around the ports (and the large guns could not, of course, be moved out of their enormous emplacements). The air force had just lost many of its bombers in the "Baby Blitz" and many of its fighters in "Big Week." Again, in the event the Luftwaffe also could do even less than the little expected of it.

Even the army, always Germany's strongest arm, had its difficulties. The long war in the East had drained the military of many of its best officers and men. The forces in the West included a number of fine armored and infantry divisions, but a large proportion of the 58 divisions under the Commander-in-Chief West were second-rate.[39] Furthermore, in the fall of 1943 the Germans had transferred the bulk of the units recruited from Soviet prisoners of war and in the occupied U.S.S.R. to the West, out of fear that with the turning tide in the East, they might not be reliable there. That, however, meant that the majority of German divisions in France had at least one battalion of "Eastern troops" (Osttruppen), soldiers whose enthusiasm for fighting the Western Allies was not likely to be high. There were even stranger oddities in the army. The Indian Legion, recruited from among prisoners captured in North Africa and Italy and nominally a portion of Bose's Indian National Army, was no more likely to succeed in helping hold up an invasion of France than their associates tied to the Japanese army had been in invading India from Burma.[40] It is not likely that Bose's sending Hitler his best wishes for defeating the American and British invaders provided much more than comic relief.[41]

The Germans suffered not only from shortages of troops and equipment but also from an excess of commanders who could neither agree on what to do nor had the authority to do whatever they preferred with the speed required by circumstances. The expectation of invasion had led to the buildup of German headquarters as well as units. Nominally under the Commander-in-Chief West, Field Marshal von Rundstedt, Army Group B, led by Field Marshal Rommel, commanded the 7th and 15th Armies on the Channel coast; Army Group G of General Johannes Blaskowitz with the 1st and 19th Armies was to defend the Biscay and Mediterranean coasts.[42] Directly under the Commander-in-Chief West was a Panzer Group West under General Leo Geyr von Schweppenburg. Rommel and Geyr, however, did not agree on the best way to deal with an invasion. Rommel believed that the landing troops must be crushed quickly and wanted the armored divisions stationed close to the coast; Geyr believed that they ought to be held back in a substantial block to be employed against the beachhead once it was clear where the main landing had occurred. Rundstedt tried to work out a compromise, but the real effect of the squabbling was that the armored divisions were divided, with three assigned to each Army Group but susceptible of being switched to the other, while four were held back as a mobile reserve to be sent to the critical point—but in Panzer Group West at the orders of Hitler and the high command of the armed forces (OKW), *not* the Commander-in-Chief West.[43] When this confusion in command was paired with successful strategic deception by the Allies, which left the Germans mistaken about the location of the main landing for weeks after the Normandy landing, and tactical surprise because of ignorance of the weather, the prospects for the German defenders were far less than they might have been—and the risks for the invaders in the face of overwhelming German numerical superiority in men, guns, and armor in the initial stages of invasion not as great as originally believed.[a]

INVASION IN THE WEST

In the night of June 5–6, while the huge convoys accompanied by six battleships, twenty-three cruisers and eighty destroyers assembled in the Channel for the initial landings, the three airborne divisions were being flown overhead to their drop zones. Dummy parachutists were dropped at several locations to confuse the Germans as the British 6th Airborne Division landed on the eastern flank to secure bridgeheads over the

---

[a] The confused German command structure was even more complicated than presented here. There were also Chiefs of Military Government for France, for Belgium and northern France, and for the Netherlands, assorted SS headquarters, and a host of other special units and commands which had proliferated in the years since 1940 and which no normal person could be expected to understand then or now. Ose, *Entscheidung im Westen*, pp. 60–64, attributes this proliferation to Hitler's distrust of the officer corps; surely some of the staffs were maintained to provide berths for men who preferred the comforts of occupation in the West to the rigors of combat in the East.

Orne canal and river, while the American 82nd and 101st Airborne Divisions were coming down on the western flank to make sure the troops landing at "Utah" beach, the westernmost of the five, could break into the open rather than being contained easily on the coast. The airborne landings were on the whole successful; in spite of substantial casualties, the main objectives were reached on both flanks and without the disaster Leigh-Mallory had anticipated. The British seized a bridgehead east of the Orne river and took key bridges by landing gliders right at them. The American parachutists were somewhat scattered but contributed by that very scattering to the confusion among the Germans. The American soldiers who survived the descent and first hours quickly created points of control inland for the troops which had in the meantime landed on Utah beach.

On the beaches, everything went much better than hoped for on the three British and Canadian sites, Gold, Juno and Sword, and at Utah beach of the American landings. At none of these four could the Allies advance inland on the first day as far as they had hoped, but substantial gains were made with losses below what had been anticipated. The surprised Germans were overwhelmed by the combination of preliminary bombardment from air and sea and the force of the assault. Only at Omaha beach, where the Germans had just moved in an additional first-rate division at the last moment, was there serious trouble for the Americans. As casualties mounted and units at sea could not land, while the soldiers ashore had difficulties pushing off the beaches, the situation looked bad for several hours. By noon, however, brave men with strong naval gunfire support were pushing off the beaches at the same time as the Germans thought they had won and brought in no reinforcements. As at Gela and Salerno, the soldiers held and pushed on; by the end of June 6, the Allies were ashore and beginning a rapid buildup of troops, equipment and supplies.[44]

The key question that day and in the immediately following days was whether the Allies or the Germans could bring additional forces to the fighting more rapidly, and especially whether a coordinated German counter-attack could drive in at least one of the beachheads. Although the Allies fell short of their D-Day objectives and did not succeed in joining their five beachheads into an effective continuous front until June 12, they were steadily if slowly pushing the Germans back. By the time of the great storm of June 19 which destroyed one of the two Mulberry harbors, the Germans had lost their chance of driving the Allies into the sea and were instead obliged to try to contain them—ironically at the very moment that the Americans had already begun their own offensive to cut off the Cherbourg peninsula.

The Allied success in establishing themselves and holding off the German counter-attacks at a time when the Germans had overwhelming superiority in troops, guns, and tanks in the West was due to the combination of several factors. German reaction to the initial landing was slow and hesitant; unwilling to believe that the decisive moment was really at hand in spite of the bad weather, the Germans dithered for hours with the higher military leaders absent from their posts or unwilling to take chances, Hitler literally asleep and not to be woken up, and Jodl determined that the OKW would not allow Rundstedt and Rommel to commit the armored reserve under its control. All this changed by the afternoon of D-Day and thereafter, but by then it was too late. The reinforcements dribbled into the invasion front were never enough, and the Allied air forces as well as the sabotage efforts of the French resistance and Allied special teams slowed down whatever was sent.[45] The German armored divisions, therefore, arrived one at a time and quite slowly, were never able to punch through, and ended up becoming mired in positional warfare because they continued to be needed at the front in the absence of infantry divisions to replace them on the spot. The pressure of the Allies was such as to keep the Germans constantly stretched—especially because the latter continued to believe that the main Allied landing was still to come in the Pas de Calais area. This successful deception kept the bulk of the 15th Army, the largest German army in the West, poised to ward off a landing which never came, while the 7th Army was trying to cope with the concentrated might of the Allies.

Once successfully ashore, the Allies had planned to strike across the Cotentin peninsula to isolate and then capture Cherbourg. This assignment went to the Americans while the British on the left flank, by their location at the edge of good open tank country to the south and east— and hence the threat of rapid exploitation—drew to themselves the majority of the German armored divisions and other reinforcements sent to the front. The attack westward by the American VII Corps began on June 10, gathered speed on the 14th, and had reached the coast on the 18th, thus cutting the peninsula and Cherbourg off from possible reinforcement. The first days of this fighting had been slow and bitter as the Germans held desperately to each hedgerow surrounding each little field, but, as the Americans pushed on, the Germans had not only heavier losses but no replacements. Confused orders, some from Hitler personally, as to whether the defending forces were to retreat north toward Cherbourg or south to retain contact with the rest of the German front, made it easier for the VII Corps, which immediately headed north, feeding newly arrived divisions into the push toward Cherbourg.

The Germans had counted on holding onto the port city for a long time, but the Americans drove north to its defense perimeter in three days, immediately beginning an assault on the fortress. Supported by air attacks and naval as well as ground artillery, the American troops drove into the city during the third week of June. The German commander, General Schlieben, surrendered on June 26; some German soldiers held out in bitter fighting until June 30.

The Allies now had their port, later than they and earlier than the Germans had hoped,[46] but the destruction of its facilities by German demolition experts had been massive. It took almost three weeks to open the port at all and months before it could handle substantial volumes of cargo. Eventually Cherbourg would take more than half of all the cargo landed in France for the American forces,[47] but the delay imposed by the demolitions contributed substantially to the eventual halt in the Allied offensive. Whatever the problems, however, the seizure of Cherbourg meant that the Allies could not be driven into the sea again even if the weather should destroy the remaining Mulberry and make it impossible to land troops and supplies over the beaches. The destruction of one Mulberry right after the capture of Cherbourg in the great Channel storm enormously complicated the supply problem of the Allies, but they were bringing in considerable amounts over the beaches and could look forward to the restoration of Cherbourg's facilities.

While the Americans were cutting off the Cotentin peninsula and taking Cherbourg, the British 2nd Army was battering its way toward Caen, a town which had been included in the anticipated D-Day lodgement. Held up by German armored units, repeated German counterattacks, and the reluctance of Montgomery and his subordinate army commanders to accept heavy casualties, the advance came to an early halt. Montgomery hoped to drive beyond Caen to Falaise in mid-June, but German resistance stalled his drive.[48] On June 18 he ordered new drives for Caen by Lt. General Sir Miles Dempsey's British 2nd Army and for Cherbourg by Bradley's United States 1st Army;[49] the latter succeeded, but the Caen offensive again made minimal progress. Montgomery thereupon decided to build up his forces on the British sector for a big push; as he wrote Brooke on July 14, he had decided on a real "show down on the eastern flanks, and to loose a Corps of three armored divisions in the open country about the Caen—Falaise road." As he put it to his most important backer in the Allied high command: "The possibilities are immense; with seven hundred tanks loosed to the South East of Caen, and armored cars operating far ahead, anything can happen."[50] What did happen was that this big attack on July 18–19, called "Goodwood," was halted with very heavy losses in spite of an immense prior air bombardment and a massive armored assault.[51] This check suffered by the British almost cost Montgomery his position since most of the higher officers at Eisenhower's headquarters, especially the latter's British deputy Tedder, wanted Montgomery relieved, and Eisenhower had had enough of Montgomery's difficult behavior. Montgomery was saved by the backing of Churchill and the American breakthrough on the other flank, which opened up new prospects for the Allies.

In the middle of the Allied front, which included the right flank of the British 2nd Army and all of the American 1st Army, progress had been very slow indeed. The Americans were pushing toward St.Lo in order to secure a good basis for a drive into the open country at the western end of the Normandy front, but they were held up by two factors. The first of these was the bocage, the hedgerow terrain which confined the tanks to narrow roads and the infantry to laborious field-by-field advances under fire from well-concealed German defenders. It might be argued that it would have been better if the British had fought a slowly advancing battle in this terrain while the Americans drove into the open in the perfect tank country at the eastern end of the bridgehead, but the position of the two Allied forces had been determined by transportation factors. The shortage of shipping and the need to bring troops and supplies directly from the United States after the initial landing had led to the decision for the British to take the left and the Americans the right flank in the landing and the subsequent campaign.[a] The result therefore was that the Americans had to slug their way forward in the bocage, a process that only became easier as they welded steel "tusks" onto the front of the tanks so that these "rhinoceroses" could drive right through the hedgerows.

The other factor holding the Americans up was the skillful and determined resistance. Taking advantage of the terrain, German forces, mostly infantry but some armor, fought for every field. By this time they were trying to hold the Americans to the slowest possible advance while launching their heaviest armored attacks against the British. The Americans did not, however, have to assist their ally directly because air attacks kept the Germans from moving their armored divisions quickly enough to the British front to mount a serious threat there at any one time.[52] It was therefore possible for the Americans to concentrate on their own front, and if the Germans made them pay a heavy price in casualties for

---

[a] It was this decision which determined first, that the United States would accept an occupation zone in south Germany, and second, that American units in NATO would be stationed primarily in the southern and British units in the northern portion of the Federal Republic of Germany.

every yard gained, the defenders were also suffering heavy losses which they could not replace as readily as the Americans.[53]

The plans for the big American push were also not disrupted by the introduction of a new weapon by the Germans. Originally scheduled to be launched far earlier, the first salvo of pilotless jet planes, the V-1s, was fired at London on June 12 with the major bombardment beginning three days later. Hitler was most enthusiastic about this project and seriously expected the attacks to lead to an evacuation of London and thus a disruption of the whole Allied effort.[54] The V-1 was supposed to be followed quickly by the V-2, a ballistic missile, but the first of these was not fired until September 8, 1944. Certainly the V-1 caused destruction and casualties, and the renewal of heavy bombing in the fifth year of war had a serious effect on British morale; but many of the pilotless planes were shot down and others crashed or failed on their own. Although the new weapons gave the Allies an added incentive to try to break out of Normandy as quickly as possible in order to overrun the launching sites, they could not interfere seriously with the Allied forces fighting to liberate France. On the other hand, the introduction of the new weapon obviously aimed simply at a big city led Churchill to argue seriously and repeatedly in favor of using poison gas in retaliation. He was restrained by the objections of his military advisors and a veto by the Americans, but the British leader held to his preference even if he could not implement it.[55]

Whatever the effects of the V-weapons, the German reaction to the establishment of a coherent and sustainable Allied bridgehead was a combination of fierce defensive fighting with no effective strategic concept. The fighting slowed down the Allies but could not drive them back. Both in repeated speeches to his generals and to industrial leaders, Hitler tried hard to enthuse those apprehensive about the situation. He looked to new weapons and to fanatical resistance to show the enemy that victory over Germany was impossible; in other words, he was coming to believe that a defensive victory was now Germany's great hope. As for the situation on what now had to be called the Western Front, he had rejected both the suggestion that the first major counter-attack be made against the Americans in favor of one against the British, while rejecting all advice for mobile defense in favor of simply holding all ground.[56] For a short time longer, this approach succeeded in containing British and American advances; but since it wore out the defending troops, including the armored divisions which had to remain in the front line continuously, it also speeded up the rate of German collapse at the front once a major gap had been torn in their lines.

The Allies had originally planned to launch the great offensive in the

American sector code-named "Cobra" at the same time as "Good-wood," but it had had to be postponed repeatedly because bad weather prevented the air forces from providing the needed support. Because the air forces, when they could fly, had not yet fully mastered the techniques of effective cooperation with ground forces, large numbers of bombs were dropped on the American units, causing numerous casualties, but the weight of the heavy bombing fell on the Germans when the operation finally started on July 25.[57] The American troops pushed through the staunch defenders and, in the immediately following days, the German divisions facing the western end of the front began to disintegrate as more American divisions joined those already advancing south. Even as the German front was being ripped open in the west, Montgomery, under pressure from Eisenhower, drove his forces forward in the east; and although these, now reorganized into the 1st Canadian as well as the 2nd British Army, did not make major advances, their determined pressure prevented the Germans from shifting strength to their own threatened left flank. That flank collapsed in the last days of July as the Americans seized Avranches at the base of the Cotentin peninsula and were clearly poised to drive into the open terrain to the south.

Their ability to do so had been assisted by the drawing of most German armor to the British front and its then being held there by a combination of repeated attacks on the part of British and Canadian divisions, as well as Hitler's fixation on concentrating the newly arriving reserves in that sector. The success of the American effort was also greatly aided by the continued effectiveness of the Allied deception operation which, by pretending that another major landing would come in the Pas de Calais area, led the Germans to keep most of their 15th Army away from the fighting front—Normandy. By the time the Germans realized at the end of July that the Normandy landing was the only one and that there would be no other Channel crossing, it was too late for reinforcement from 15th Army to be transferred to the danger points or to relieve the divisions facing the Canadians and British, so that these divisions in turn could move west. Field Marshal Günther von Kluge, who had replaced von Rundstedt early in July,[58] did not get permission to transfer substantial forces until the end of the month—just as the Americans broke through.

Allied control of the air slowed down all German movements, and the earlier attack on the transportation system had reduced its efficiency and its recuperative power. The Germans could not sustain the positional warfare which had characterized the first eight weeks of fighting in the West; and the disaster which the army had suffered in the meantime at the hands of the Red Army meant that massive reinforcement of the

Western at the expense of the Eastern Front was impossible, even if Hitler had been so inclined.

Under these circumstances, the Americans, now reorganized as planned into the 3rd Army under Patton on the right and the 1st Army under General Courtney Hodges on the left with Bradley advanced to 12th Army Group commander, pushed division after division through the gaping hole at the western end of the German front. The 3rd Army's divisions had originally been scheduled to head southwest into Brittany, in order to open up the port of Brest and other harbors for additional American units and supplies to land directly from the United States (as in World War I). Since German resistance in the interior of Brittany was obviously minimal—many of the units originally stationed there having been drawn into the Normandy battle and chewed up in the prior fighting—it was clearly not necessary to commit the whole 3rd Army there. New decisions had to be made and these intersected fatefully with the new decisions now made by the Germans.

With Bradley's and Montgomery's approval, Patton sent only one of his four corps into Brittany. That was more than enough to clear most of the province but not enough for quick seizure of the ports which the German garrisons held stubbornly, Brest falling only on September 19. Two corps were sent racing southeast and south with a fourth held in reserve. With the right flank of American 1st Army also on the move, it looked as if the whole German army in Normandy might be surrounded.

Since about two-thirds of the German front was still holding coherently, Hitler decided on a major counter-attack at Mortain, an operation already being planned by von Kluge who had also replaced Rommel when the latter was wounded. This operation was to strike west and to the sea and cut off the American forces which had pushed through the Avranches gap. When the Germans massed for and launched this counter-attack, they suffered a major defeat to which the tactical air support of the Allied ground forces—now finally functioning effectively—contributed greatly.[59] The Americans were, as we now know, also greatly assisted by the fact that key German messages connected with this attack had been intercepted and decoded. Having shifted the weight of their forces from the British–Canadian front westwards for this operation, the Germans were more vulnerable to encirclement than ever once the Mortain attack had been beaten off by the Americans.[60]

With the Canadian and British forces attacking southward toward Falaise now that some of the German armored divisions previously facing them had been shifted westwards for the Mortain attack, it looked for a moment as if the whole 7th German Army and the Panzer Group West (renamed 5th Panzer Army) might be trapped. The advance units of the American 3rd Army reached north to Argentan as the Canadians pushed toward them, while portions of the American 1st Army had also reached positions south of the German front. Ten days after the Mortain attack had been halted, it looked as if the two German armies were about to be trapped in what came to be known as the Falaise pocket.

The Allies had the possibility of completely destroying most of Army Group B, with the American troops in the south pushing northward to Argentan even as they headed east toward Paris, while the Canadian 1st Army was to close the pincer from the north. In the period August 8–18, the German front was battered, pushed in from the south, pulled back from the west, but not penetrated in the north. Montgomery sent untried Canadian divisions and the Polish armored division instead of more experienced units to close the gap. As a result, the Germans, though losing heavily in equipment and men, were able to extricate a substantial proportion of their soldiers and most of the higher staffs—all of which could be reformed into effective military units with which the Allies would have to cope later. It is also possible that if Bradley had ordered the 3rd Army to drive beyond its designated advance line to Falaise, the pocket could have been sealed off earlier and more effectively; but in the absence of regular meetings between Montgomery and the American commanders (because of Montgomery's unwillingness to have such meetings), such a step would have been difficult to take.

The Allies had indeed won a major land victory in the West, in which their air power had played a highly significant part; they had inflicted well over a quarter of a million casualties on the Germans; and they had wrecked the vast majority of the German divisions in the West. But although they could now race eastward and northward, the Germans, now under the leadership of Field Marshal Model, brought from the East to replace von Kluge, had extricated some 50,000 thousand men, including many experienced officers, from the wreckage of Army Group B.[61]

The immediate situation in France, however, looked spectacularly good for the Allies. The Canadian and British armies raced north, quickly crossing the lower Seine to attack the Channel ports from the rear and also head into Belgium, in the process seizing many of the launching sites for the V-1 and V-2. In the middle, American troops in late August approached Paris, which the Germans intended to defend and even destroy but could not hold in the face of onrushing Allied troops and the beginnings of insurrection in the city. The original plan to by-pass the city was abandoned by Eisenhower, who allowed a French armored division the honor of liberating the capital of France and followed that up by marching two American divisions through the city to make sure everyone understood that the Germans were finished in the area.[62] De Gaulle entered the city to the cheers of the inhabitants; he had greatly wanted to get there quickly to establish himself both against any possible challenge from the Communists and to assert his role against Britain and the United States.[63]

Further south, the landing on the French Mediterranean coast, operation "Anvil," now renamed "Dragoon," had gone ashore successfully on August 15.[64] This landing had been preceded by an exceedingly bitter dispute as the British, with Churchill personally leading the charge, attempted practically until the last moment to have it called off in order to maintain the strength of Allied forces in Italy.[65] In the final days of this debate Churchill even proposed rerouting the operation at the last minute into Brittany. The very absurdity of this proposal probably hardened rather than shook the resolve of the American government, especially Roosevelt and Marshall, to uphold Eisenhower's insistence on going forward as planned.[66]

Once ashore, the United States 7th Army, consisting of one American and one French corps, quickly took the key ports of Marseilles and Toulon and pushed northwards. The threat of the advancing units of United States 7th and 3rd Armies meeting in central France led to the German decision, reluctantly approved by Hitler, to evacuate most of Army Group G from southwest France. Special blocking units were left to hold as many of the ports as long as possible—a subject reviewed in Chapter 14—but the bulk of the German 1st and 19th Army headed northeast. Though harassed by the French resistance, Allied air power, and the advancing American armies, the majority of the soldiers escaped to help build up a new front in the German–French border area and along the Alpine passes into Italy.

Most of France, however, had been liberated by the Allies and Marshal Pétain, Laval, and assorted French collaborators—who in 1940 had found it inadvisable to leave Metropolitan France for French North Africa—now found it expedient or necessary to move back with the retreating Germans, eventually to establish a "government-in-exile" in southwest Germany.[67] At first many of them, with memories of French defeat at the hands of the Germans, seriously expected the German armies to return to the offensive and drive the Allies out of France, and Laval now as earlier wanted the Germans to make peace with the Soviet Union so that they could do so more easily,[68] but the Germans had other worries and different plans.

NEW CHOICES IN THE WEST

The steady series of defeats had been added to the knowledge of enormous crimes and German responsibilities for the outbreak and extension of the war in opening the eyes of opponents of the Hitler regime to the absolute need for an overthrow of the Nazi government, an overthrow that could come only if Hitler—the central figure of that regime—were removed from the scene. Already reviewed in Chapter 9, the internal opposition had made several attempts to kill Hitler and seize power. The bomb attempt of July 20, 1944 had, however, failed narrowly; Hitler survived the explosion. In the choice between opposing orders from Hitler's headquarters in East Prussia and the leaders of the military opposition in Berlin, the overwhelming majority of the military sided with Hitler. In Paris, the military commander was with Hitler's opponents; because the Nazi regime remained firmly in control, however, he and many others were arrested and executed.

The upheaval of July 20 made Hitler even more suspicious of his military leaders, and as he developed a new strategy for the West in the following days, he would not allow the front commanders to have a clear view of his intentions. These he explained to his chief operational advisor, General Jodl, on July 31 in an important conference of which, by a fortunate coincidence, a full stenographic record survives.[69] Hitler hoped to hold the Eastern Front, where the Soviet summer offensive had torn open the central sector, on a new line and wanted to keep the fighting in Italy as far south as possible. In the West, he was now prepared to have a new defensive line reconnoitered and fortified, but the American breakout, which was developing even as the conference took place, would lead to the overrunning of the proposed line before it could be defined. Another portion of his plan for the West would, however, be implemented, and came to have major implications for Allied strategy and the course and duration of the war.

Shocked by the quick fall of Cherbourg to the Allies, Hitler ordered special arrangements for assigning specified units to hold each of the major ports until quite literally the last round of ammunition and the last man. He assumed that these garrisons would not be relieved; their function was to hold the ports and deny them to the Allies as long as possible, thereby keeping the Americans and British from employing, developing, and supplying their human and material resources on the continent. Only the constriction applied by such a procedure could afford the Germans an opportunity to build up new defense lines and first hold and then strike back at the Western Allies with any hope of success.

In accordance with these plans, twelve ports and the Channel Islands continued to be held after they had been cut off. Significant German strength came to be tied up in these holding operations, but while some were crushed in the fall of 1944, several held out until the general surrender of May 1945.[70] Although they could not serve the initial purpose of allowing the German army an opportunity to rebuild a firm front in France, they contributed substantially to the halting of Allied offensive operations in the fall of 1944 and the continuation of the war into 1945.

Whatever the long-term implications of Germany's holding on to as many ports for as long as possible, the sweep of the Allied armies through France liberated most of the country and thereby had two immediate and significant implications for the subsequent course of hostilities. First, the German navy lost the most convenient of the bases on the Atlantic gained in 1940. The isolated garrisons could deny ports to the Allies but they could not support a continued U-Boat war from French Atlantic ports. If the new submarines, with which the Germans still hoped to turn the Battle of the Atlantic in their favor, became operational in substantial numbers in time, they would, therefore, have to go out into the Atlantic and return the long way from German or Norwegian ports.[71] Secondly, the land connection to Spain and across Spain to Portugal was now severed. This meant that, regardless of German efforts, critical raw materials, especially wolfram and chrome, could no longer be imported or smuggled out of the area;[72] the countries of the Iberian peninsula were now effectively cut off from the Third Reich.

As Allied soldiers swept across France and into Belgium, and small parties of German soldiers were still trying to find their way across France back to the main lines being reformed to defend the Third Reich's borders, major issues of command and strategy faced the American and British governments and military. The command issue was in essence quite simple. As the size of the American forces on the continent increased, a new structure was required. The introduction of 3rd Army alongside 1st had led to the creation of 12th Army Group under Bradley; the newly formed 1st Canadian Army alongside the British 2nd Army now constituted Montgomery's 21st Army Group. As of September 1, however, the general supervisory role of Montgomery over all land forces would end as Eisenhower took command of the land battle himself. This was obviously necessary for two reasons, political and personal. The political reason was simple. The American forces were growing while the British were shrinking. A third American army, the 9th, under General William Simpson, was about to be formed at the Army Group border between 21st and 12th Army Group at a time when the American and French forces in the south, organized into 6th Army Group, were being integrated into Eisenhower's command.

Simultaneously with the massive American buildup reflected in these new headquarters, the British army was necessarily shrinking. On August 14 Montgomery had written to Brooke for permission to break up the 59th Division so that other divisions could be kept effective; there were simply not enough replacements available to make up for the casualties being incurred. The request was granted, and even before the liberation of Paris, the 59th became the first British division to disappear from the Allied order of battle.[73]

If the increasing predominance of American soldiers in the Allied armies made an American commander—in this case obviously Eisenhower himself—a political necessity, the personal factor only reinforced it. Montgomery had had great difficulties in working with American military leaders in Sicily and Italy; he had gone out of his way to antagonize Eisenhower in the weeks before the formal change of command on September 1. Instead of participating in regular meetings with Eisenhower and Bradley, he had kept to himself and at times rudely insisted that others should come to him. It is theoretically barely conceivable that Field Marshal Alexander might have been acceptable to the Americans; there was no prospect that Montgomery would be. If there had ever been a possibility, he had himself removed it by his own behavior; and Brooke and British War Minister P.J. Grigg were singularly foolish in encouraging him to hope for a reversal of the decision to implement the new command arrangement. The popular general could be and was promoted to the rank of Field Marshal by the British government, thus recognizing his services in the invasion, but he would have done better to make some effort to cooperate with the American commanders. Since he could not do so with his Canadian and Polish subordinates, that was perhaps asking too much.[74]

There should have been no argument over the command structure, which had been agreed upon before D-Day, but its being agitated by the British, and specially by Montgomery, served to exacerbate the dispute over strategy after the successful breakout. This issue, often phrased in terms of a narrow versus a broad front approach into Germany, had not been worked out in pre-D-Day planning, where the emphasis had been first on getting ashore and, to a far lesser extent, on how to seize a major port and then break out into France during the first ninety days. By late August, the rough target line for those three months had in fact been reached—even if more slowly in the first and more rapidly in the last weeks than originally anticipated. The question now was how to proceed next.

This question was complicated by two factors, supply limitations and the command issue just mentioned. Because the Germans had demolished the harbor of Cherbourg, held onto many of the other ports for a long time, and wrecked the facilities at Brest so effectively that they were never used after the capture of the city, the problem of nourishing any further operations was exceedingly difficult. The further the Allies advanced, the longer the supply route inland; and the later the season, the greater the risks of continuing to bring in supplies over the Normandy beaches. Some supplies were brought forward by air drops, and the Americans organized a special one-way truck delivery procedure called the "Red Ball Express," but these expedients were not a substitute for an effective supply system. That would await the repair of Cherbourg, the capture and opening of Antwerp, and the construction of proper new supply channels in liberated France. Until that stage could be reached, the available supplies could be allocated to either a northern thrust by Britain's 21st Army Group, an eastward thrust by the American 12th Army Group supported by the United States–French 6th Army Group, or provided on a limited scale to both.

It was Montgomery's opinion that if his Army Group were greatly increased by the effective subordination of the American 12th Army Group to it, and provided the full allocation of available logistic support, he could drive northwards across the Rhine into the north German plain, occupy Berlin, and end the war quickly in 1944. Like many in the British command structure in London, Montgomery considered the war practically over and himself the man to end it. The project was impractical for a number of reasons, not the least of them being that it called for crossing the largest river—the Rhine—at its widest and where it had the most branches. Furthermore, it required halting all other offensive operations at a time when Patton was much closer to the Rhine than Montgomery, and assumed that it was safe to send a single spearhead far in advance of the Allied front against a German army which was reforming its units. The only conceivable advantage was the possible earlier seizure of some sites from which V-1s and especially the more dangerous V-2s were being launched against England; but this was offset by the prior experience of the Americans with Montgomery as a commander who had troubles leading the armies of two nations in harmony, to say nothing of the three—British, Canadian, and United States—that this project would require. Eisenhower turned the project down and preferred to move toward the Rhine on a broad front, but, influenced by the need to seize the great harbor at Antwerp and the sites from which the troublesome V-2s were launched, did give considerable support to Montgomery's drive.[75]

Although the American drive south of the Ardennes moved forward rapidly, eventually it literally ran out of gas. The 3rd Army captured some German stocks of gasoline but not enough to keep moving in the face of stiffening resistance. There was, in fact, not enough to go around. The German strategy of holding the ports was making itself felt; and while some might argue that providing all the available supplies to *either* 21st or 12th Army Group could have enabled that one to break through completely and end the war in 1944, it can more easily be argued that the total halt such a strategy would have imposed on the other Army Group would have exposed the one far in advance of the rest of the Allied front to the danger of a major defeat. As it was, with the resources he was given, and the added strength of the Allied airborne army assigned to him, Montgomery made three major errors which assured the halting of further Allied advances for months.

The first two errors were closely related. In early September, British forces racing to liberate Belgium seized Antwerp not only without any serious fighting but before the Germans could dynamite the great unloading cranes or other portions of the extensive harbor facilities. This stroke of enormous good fortune opened up two great opportunities: a quick drive north to cut off the German 15th Army, whose route of retreat was now severed, and a clearing of the Scheldt estuary to open Antwerp for use by the Allies to supply their forces on the continent. Montgomery, who had a few days earlier tried to talk Eisenhower into letting him rush forward with a mass of forty divisions to end the war quickly, now instructed his forces to rest up and thus lost both opportunities. The bulk of the 15th Army escaped — as much of the 7th Army had escaped a month earlier — and the port facilities remained closed until November 27 when a grinding and bloody battle finally made it possible for minesweepers to clear its approaches.

The importance of Antwerp to a successful operation in Western Europe had been stressed in the very earliest plans for an invasion on December 24, 1941, when the invasion project was still code-named "Roundup." The destruction of facilities at Cherbourg and Brest, the latter still in German hands when Antwerp was freed, only accentuated the significance of opening the port. The liberation, primarily by the Canadians, of several smaller Channel ports, could ease the immediate supply problems of 21st Army Group, but any large-scale drive into Germany would be feasible only once Antwerp had been opened. In this instance Eisenhower's efforts to prod Montgomery were undoubtedly warranted, and Montgomery himself in a rare admission conceded that he had made a mistake.[76]

Having obtained Eisenhower's agreement to using the Allied airborne divisions, Montgomery decided on an operation in which two American and one British airborne division were to secure a series of river crossings, with the American 82nd and 101st seizing the southern two and the British 1st Airborne, reinforced by the Polish Parachute Brigade, the northernmost at Arnhem. The British 30th Corps would strike forward to cross and join the seized bridges and thereby establish the Allies in one daring move across the lower Rhine. Though warned by intelligence officers of German armor and other units in the vicinity, Montgomery went ahead with the plan with the approval of Eisenhower. While a similar operation further up the Rhine near Wesel would have required fewer major river crossings, Montgomery appears to have picked the Arnhem route in spite of its greater difficulty because it would have provided a river crossing in an exclusively British sector; if that is a correct assessment, it makes even more serious the planning error, Montgomery's third great mistake, which assigned to the British 1st Airborne Division a drop zone miles away from its bridge. This was designed to avoid excessive casualties in the landing but had the opposite effect. A daring operation cannot be designed to be safe—as the Normandy airborne operations had shown in spite of Leigh-Mallory's doubts.[77]

Launched on September 17, parts of the airborne operation ("Market") and accompanying land drive ("Garden") appeared to go well. The 101st Division took Eindhoven and its bridge, replacing another one blown by the Germans with an engineer-built substitute; and the 82nd after bitter fighting and a river-crossing assault combined with the advancing British armored ground forces to seize the bridge at Nijmegen. The tanks and soldiers pushing up the narrow corridor from Nijmegen loosely made contact with the Polish Parachute Brigade on the south side of the Rhine on September 23, but the 1st British Airborne Division had been dropped too far from the bridge at Arnhem, on the other side of the town, and could not hold the northern exit from the main road bridge across the river. German resistance, hastily organized but based on two SS armored divisions already in the area, forced the British paratroopers away from the river. At the end of ten days of bitter fighting, as the advance of the thrust from the south had ground to a halt, that thin wedge itself under heavy German attack, and the situation inside the Arnhem perimeter hopeless, the survivors of 1st British Airborne either escaped across the river or surrendered. The attempt to "bounce" the great river barrier had failed by a narrow margin in the face of a reviving German resistance, but it had failed nonetheless.[78]

The recovery of German military power, discussed in the next chapter, was obvious not only in the defeat suffered in the operation "Market-Garden" and the bitter fighting endured by the Canadians in their struggle to open the Scheldt in September and October but on the American front in northeast France as well. With Model first in complete command and then limited to Army Group B when von Rundstedt was recalled to take over general command in the West, German reinforcements poured westwards. The staffs of shattered divisions which had escaped from the Falaise pocket and southwest France were put in charge of revived divisions and corps. As Allied supply lines lengthened and became strained, the German ones became shorter. In Lorraine, Patton's 3rd Army ran into heavy fighting which slowed it to a crawl, while further north the American 1st Army battering its way into Germany and Luxembourg found that the old field fortification of the Westwall, as the Germans called it, or the Siegfried Line, as the Allies referred to it, were being rearmed and remanned. By mid-September, the Allied drive had been halted temporarily by a combination of exhaustion, supply difficulties, and renewed German resistance. Months of campaigning still lay ahead.

One obvious tie between the Western and Eastern Fronts had been encountered in Normandy by the British and Americans. As their intelligence had already informed them, the German army in France included large numbers of soldiers recruited from among prisoners of war captured from the Red Army and from people in occupied Soviet territory, and organized into so-called Eastern Battalions incorporated into the regiments of German divisions. Many of these were captured by the Allied armies in Normandy, and, on July 17, 1944, Eden raised the question of what to do with some 1500 or so already in Allied hands. Churchill suggested that Stalin be told about them, and that if he asked for their repatriation the Western Allies would have to agree to send them, though for a while they might be used for agricultural labor. The Cabinet consented to this proposal;[79] and when the subject came up again in early September as more soldiers surrendered, they agreed with Eden that, willing or unwilling, all would be repatriated to the Soviet Union.[80] This issue was to be discussed again at Yalta and lead to considerable controversy after the war, but at the time no one saw any reason to spare those who fought to keep Western Europe under German control. The main concern of the Western Allies was the promised Soviet summer offensive designed to make it impossible for the Germans to shift large reinforcements to the new front in the West.

OFFENSIVES IN THE EAST

As a preliminary to the planned Soviet major offensive, the Leningrad and Karelian Fronts opened an attack against Finland on June 10. The Finns were both surprised and overwhelmed as the Red Army battered in the westernmost section of the Finnish front facing Leningrad. In a few days the Red Army forced the Finns back on the Karelian isthmus, breaking their intermediate defensive position and pushing them back to their last line of defense on the Soviet side of the 1940 border. The Finns appealed for help to the Germans, who sent supplies and weapons withheld earlier when it looked as if Finland might leave the war.[81]

The assistance of the Germans, an evacuation under Soviet pressure of almost all of the eastern Karelian territory occupied by the Finnish army in 1941, the exhaustion of the Red Army offensive, and the transfer of Soviet units from the Leningrad Front to the south enabled the Finns to hold on during July. Their situation was, however, most precarious. They could not replace the casualties suffered. They had promised the Germans, in effect in exchange for the aid received, that they would stay in the war; but there was no real prospect of halting any new major Soviet attack.[82]

As the big Soviet offensives of June and July collapsed first Army Group Center, then threatened to cut off Army Group North, and in August forced Romania to sue for peace on the southern end of the front, the Finnish government realized that there was no choice but to accept whatever terms the Soviet Union offered. The President who had promised the Germans to stay in the war resigned and was replaced by Marshal Mannerheim, who persuaded the Finnish parliament to agree to the demands placed before them and sign an armistice on September 4, 1944. Finland had to go back to the 1940 border, give up the Petsamo area, agree to a lease at Porkkala instead of Hangö, pay substantial reparations, break relations with Germany and intern any German troops left in the country after a two-weeks grace period.[83]

The Germans, who had not been able to send the reinforcements they had promised, were greatly upset but by that time not too surprised. In a badly mishandled operation which had been strongly pushed by Admiral Dönitz, they attempted to seize the key island Suursaari in the Gulf of Finland in order to help keep the Red navy bottled up, but Finland was neither Italy nor Hungary and drove the Germans off.[84] In the north, the German 20th Army began a slow withdrawal, at first trying to hold on to the Petsamo nickel mines but then pulling back into Norway as the need for the nickel turned out to be less than anticipated and the Red Army joined the Finnish in pressuring the German retreat. In the winter, the 20th Army joined the other forces stationed in Norway and except for some units transferred to the main fronts on the continent remained there until the 1945 surrender. In northern Finland and the northernmost province of Norway, they had laid waste everything and burned every building to prevent any pursuit. The general who had replaced their commander Edward Dietl after his death in an airplane crash on June 23, General Lothar Rendulic, proved as efficient in burning buildings and destroying bridges in the far north as the former Austrian officer had been at having Italian officers shot and civilians slaughtered in occupied Yugoslavia the year before. The Red Army, however, had no plans to follow up on the offensive in the far north by working its way along the Norwegian coast and instead pulled back a short distance. The road into central Europe was much shorter further south.[85]

The offensive against Finland began right after D-Day but was clearly *not* to be the major Soviet summer offensive. That was the comprehensively prepared concentric attack designed to rip open the German Eastern Front by destroying its Army Group Center and freeing the Soviet territory still under German occupation on the main route between Warsaw and Moscow. The operation, code-named "Bagration," had been planned with great care and was accompanied by a major deception plan which, like that designed to fool the Germans in the West, succeeded extremely well. German army intelligence fell for every Soviet ploy, and Reinhard Gehlen, the chief of army eastern military intelligence, maintained his record of invariably erroneous predictions.[86] The Commander-in-Chief of the German Army Group about to be annihilated, Field Marshal Ernst Busch, was away from his post; the major reserves of his segment of the front had been transferred to the adjacent Army Group on the south, Field Marshal Model's Army Group North Ukraine, where it was assumed the Red Army would strike. Even the planting of thousands of mines on the railways and roads behind Army Group Center in the largest partisan operation of the war beginning in the night of June 19–20 did not alert the determined sleepers in Army Group Center and higher German headquarters.

Delayed a few days by problems in assembling the needed one and a quarter million troops and massive supplies, the main Soviet summer offensive began on the northern sector, where Marshal Vasilevskiy coordinated the 1st Baltic and the Third Belorussian Fronts in a massive assault on June 22 which broke through the surprised German 3rd Panzer Army right away; the next day it had five divisions surrounded in Vitebsk.[87] That day, the Second and First Belorussian Fronts coordinated by Marshal Zhukov struck toward Orsha, Mogilev, and Bobruisk, quickly breaking open the lines held by the German 4th and 9th Armies. In a series of carefully directed and brilliantly implemented thrusts, the Red Army cut off most of the German 9th Army, drove the defeated German 4th Army back over a single congested and heavily bombed bridge across the Berezina river, and threw the whole rear area of Army Group Center into a panic.

Hitler's appointing Model to take over the latter Army Group in addition to Army Group North Ukraine facilitated the transfer of reserves but did not halt the Red Army's forward momentum. By July 3, the Russians had liberated Minsk; a few German stragglers made it back to new lines Model was desperately trying to put together out of minimal reserves, remnants of Army Group Center which had been pulled back, and rounded up stragglers streaming back terrified and broken. In twelve days, twenty-five divisions with at least 300,000 men had vanished from the German order of battle. The Red Army had shown that conducting Blitzkrieg was no German monopoly and that, in spite of the horrendous losses in the earlier fighting, it had both the means and the ability to drive successfully into a German front that had been held and fortified for many months.

New defensive lines in the center existed mainly in the imagination of Model and Hitler. The Red Army commanders, who could not know of these theoretical halt lines, simply drove on into the open or into the fleeing Germans. A project to push into the advancing Soviet forces from the north—a sort of Eastern Front precursor of the Mortain offensive in the West—never got started because Army Group North lacked the needed Panzer divisions, and the Red Army drove into Lithuania and eastern Poland. Just as the Western Allies had hoped that an active Eastern Front would prevent the Germans from switching troops from the East to drive the invasion back into the sea, so the successful establishment of a bridgehead in Normandy, signaled by the liberation of Cherbourg in the first days of the Soviet summer offensive, made it impossible for the Germans to transfer troops from the West; simultaneously the advance in central Italy after the liberation of Rome prevented them from shifting divisions from the south. By mid-July, the Red Army had advanced more than 200 miles on the Central front and had to pause for bringing up supplies and repairs on the road and railway system. But there would be no respite for the Germans.

Before the extension of the offensive to the north and south can be discussed, something must be said about the symptoms of disintegration which were beginning to appear in the German army during the summer of 1944, both after the Soviet breakthroughs of late June in the East and the American rupture of the Normandy front at the end of July.

There were clear signs of panic in the rear areas on both fronts, with those who had been stationed there in the prior years of occupation rushing back by any means at hand now that the possibility of being engulfed in the fighting suddenly loomed before them. Among the units at the front, most fought very hard at first, and some continued with desperate resistance even after the front had been pierced, but there were now mass surrenders alongside instances of garrisons fighting to the bitter end. On both major fronts, very large numbers of German soldiers surrendered; this was an especially novel development on the Eastern Front. On July 17, the Red Army arranged a mass march of over 57,000 prisoners through the streets of Moscow; the Japanese ambassador reported to his government on the fact that hundreds of thousands of Muscovites watched calmly as the soldiers, robust and full of life, were paraded by them.[88] Unlike the Red Army soldiers captured three years earlier in the same general area, the vast majority of whom had been shot or starved to death by the end of 1941, most of these men would eventually return to Germany—even if later than their comrades captured in France.

Hitler came to attribute the disaster of Army Group Center and the large-scale surrenders on both fronts to treason among the military, especially after the coup attempt of July 20, but the roots of defeat lay elsewhere. The fear of another Stalingrad hung over German soldiers in the East; they had lost heavily in the battles of the preceding years; to the ordinary soldier the prospects looked grimmer and grimmer; to the officers, the sacrifice of their men in holding on to some obscure French or Russian town for a few more days looked ever more dubious as a sound operation of war. While Army Group and army commanders-in-chief might still hope for glory, promotion, and their monthly bribes from Hitler as long as the war lasted, the subordinate division and corps commanders could see less and less sense in fighting on, once cut off. The German military machine still had lots of fight in it, but there were now omens of disaster which could not be obliterated either by enthusiasm and hope on the one hand or fear of the enemy or one's own judicial terror machine on the other. The new army Chief-of-Staff, appointed as a result of the July 20 explosion, General Guderian, could vent his resentment on commanders like von Kluge who had crossed him in prior years, and he could call on all officers to listen to lectures on National Socialist ideology, but beyond that he hardly made a major difference.

The destruction of Army Group Center and the liberation of the still occupied parts of Belorussia had immediate repercussions for the northern segment of the front as the Red Army drove into the open gap between Army Group North and the remnants of Model's forces. As early as July 9 Model proposed to Hitler that efforts to restore contact between the two Army Groups by offensives from both were not feasible and that Army Group North, which might easily be cut off by a Soviet thrust to the Baltic Sea, be pulled back to the river Dvina. In rejecting this concept then and later, Hitler referred to the critical objections of Admiral Dönitz, the Commander-in-Chief of the navy, which needed control of the Baltic to train U-Boat crews,[89] a subject which recurs repeatedly in controlling German strategy in the Baltic area in 1944 and 1945. When the subject was raised again in the following weeks, Hitler also stressed Germany's need for steel from Sweden, nickel from Finland, and oil from Estonian oil shale. But the Red Army was not impressed by all this, continued to roll forward, and drove to the Baltic just west of Riga. In the most desperate fighting, the Germans reopened a corridor along the coast to Army Group North; but because the Soviet offensive had driven the Germans out of their best defensive line from the Gulf of Finland south, utilizing the large Peipus and Pskov lakes, even the fanaticism of the new Army Group commander Schörner, sent in exchange for General Johannes Friessner from the 20th Mountain Army in the far north on July 23, could not hold Estonia forever. At the end of August the front in the north quieted down temporarily as the Red Army regrouped, but there were clearly great dangers ahead for the exposed northern flank which the Soviet Union could exploit when the next offensive was launched.[90]

In mid-July, as the Red Army was advancing on Warsaw on the Central front, the First Belorussian Front of Rokossovski and Konev's First Ukrainian Front smashed into Model's Army Group North Ukraine. By this time, a number of the divisions which Model had amassed earlier had been written off by being sent to reinforce the crumbling front of Army Group Center. The withdrawals Hitler had allowed Model to make before the new Soviet offensive did not provide much relief. In a series of massive attacks, of which the first was moved up to July 13 as Model was pulling back to the new line, the Red Army spearheads, now much more carefully concentrated than earlier, broke the German front and sent the 4th Panzer Army, 17th Army, and 1st Panzer Army—or rather what was left of them—reeling back. In six weeks of battle the First Ukrainian Front, part of it reorganized as the Fourth Ukrainian Front in the meantime (with the staff from the Crimea where it was no longer needed), drove the Germans back to the Carpathian mountains.

In the same period, the First Belorussian Front and the bulk of First Ukrainian Front pushed across several rivers, closed to the Vistula in some places and jumped it to form bridgeheads on the west bank at

Magnuszew, Pulawy, and Baranov. With Galicia now under Soviet control, the Red Army stood practically on the border of Hungary[91] and Slovakia at about the same time as it had reached the German border of East Prussia on the northern flank of the great offensive. The Soviet victory over Army Group South Ukraine included an encirclement of a corps of about 30,000 men of whom only 5000 escaped; the Soviet leadership at the army and the newly reintroduced corps level had learned much about offensive warfare in the age of armor and now applied this effectively to the Germans. The fact that by this time the Red Air Force controlled the skies over most of the front helped; and Soviet artillery could compensate by very heavy firing for the fact that, after their earlier great losses, the Russians now had to be very careful with their infantry in the assault.

In its push into Poland, the Red Army reached two places of special significance in late July. They came to Majdanek, the easternmost and first of the larger death camps established by the Germans. The labor and extermination camp was the only one in the immediate vicinity of a large city, Lublin, and had served for years as a central site for forced labor and mass killing of Jews and of other people primarily from Poland and the Soviet Union. Over 300,000 had been murdered there; it was liberated by the Red Army before the Germans could destroy the crematoria, gas chambers, barracks, and other traces of what would become the major monuments to the penetration of German culture into Eastern Europe. Here pictures could first be taken and circulated around the world of huge piles of shoes, enormous quantities of human hair, and grinding machines for crushing bones into fertilizer.[92]

The nearby city of Lublin, taken by the Red Army on July 23–24, came to be known as the seat of a Soviet sponsored government for Poland, a group generally referred to as the "Lublin Poles" to distinguish them from the government-in-exile in London. This new government had been announced by Moscow on July 22 and was placed in nominal command of the Communist underground and partisan movements organized under Soviet auspices, while the new Polish army under General Berling was under the direct control of the Red Army Fronts to which it was assigned.

The establishment of a Soviet puppet regime had been preceded by months of internal preparations and over a year of dispute, sometimes in public, sometimes quietly, with the Western Allies, who recognized the Polish government-in-exile which had fought the Germans continually since September, 1939. The whole time since the Soviet government had broken relations with the Polish government in the spring of 1943 there had been various efforts, especially by the British, to get relations reestablished, but without success. The nominal stumbling block was the eastern part of Poland, occupied by the Soviet Union under the Nazi–Soviet Pact. Stalin indicated a willingness to accept minor modifications in this border in favor of Poland but expected agreement on it, or on the Curzon Line prepared as a possible border after World War I. Churchill urged the Polish government to accept the new border, especially because Poland was to be enlarged westward and northward at the expense of Germany and because the Red Army was certain to occupy Poland in its advance westwards.[a]

The Polish government-in-exile was itself frequently divided internally, but practically none of its members was prepared to agree to the territorial demands of the Soviet Union. The other Soviet demand, voiced increasingly stridently by Stalin and Molotov, was for a major change in the personnel of the Polish Cabinet; and while the Prime Minister, Stanislaw Mikolajczyk, was willing to make some changes, there were limits to what he would concede. The issues were complicated in 1944 by two further factors. This was an election year in the United States, and President Roosevelt was hesitant to take steps which would alienate the Polish American voters, and hence to be as explicit about the inability of the United States to assist the Polish government in the face of the Soviet advance into Poland as the facts warranted.[b] The other and more important element was the functioning of the Polish underground army, the Armia Krajowa, or AK, inside Poland as the Red Army advanced into the portions of German-occupied Poland where it was active. There were all sorts of problems and frictions, but the major pattern was that the advancing Soviet units utilized the assistance of the AK, especially their local knowledge, until an area was firmly under Red Army control and then arrested and either shot or deported them.

These issues all came to a head in late July 1944 as the Red Army approached Warsaw and soon after crossed the Vistula fifty miles south of the city, and the Germans tried to call up thousands of Polish men in Warsaw for forced labor on the defenses, even as Mikolajczyk flew to Moscow to confer with Stalin. Expecting to overrun the Polish capital quickly, Soviet radio on July 29 called on the public in the city to rise against the Germans as the thunder of artillery could be heard from the nearby front. The British government had made it clear to the Poles

---

[a] The British pressure on the Polish government in 1943–44 is astonishingly similar to that applied to the Czechoslovak government in 1938.

[b] Stalin tried to split the Polish community in the United States by talking in conciliatory terms to two of its prominent members, Professor Oskar Lange (who later represented the new Polish government in the UN), and Father Orlemanski, in June 1944 (see the documents in FDRL, PSF Box 66, File Poland–Orlemanski–Lange [May–June 1944]).

that they could neither fly in the Polish Parachute Brigade nor carry out extensive air operations at enormous distance from British bases and right in front of the Red Army. Given permission to act when ready by Mikolajczyk, the Polish commander in the city on July 31 ordered an uprising for the next day. He and his men could sit it out and be condemned as useless or pro-German—the latter a favorite term of condemnation applied to them by the Soviet government—or take a chance on either winning control of the city at least temporarily or going down to defeat.

The Warsaw commander of the AK, General Tadeusz Bor-Komorowski, decided that it was better to take a chance than to stand aside, and it is clear that the bulk of his associates agreed. What is not so clear is why this reversal from previous AK strategy was made with very little preparation. In prior years, the plan had always been to stage an uprising against the departing Germans in the *rural* areas, and accordingly weapons had been moved by the AK out of Warsaw into the country-side. Now that an uprising was to be staged in the capital, there was a terrible shortage of weapons. When the rising took place as ordered on August 1, the insurgents were unable to seize either the whole city or many key locations, and, as the Germans rallied their forces, the AK was relatively quickly confined to segments of the capital.[93] No one has explained why the Polish underground learned nothing from the uprising in the Warsaw ghetto the year before; for those who have studied the 1944 uprising, as for the civilians in the rest of Warsaw at the time, that event might as well have taken place on another planet.

The next two months saw something like a repeat performance of the 1939 Nazi–Soviet Pact against Poland. The Red Army had slowed down on the approaches to Warsaw; now it halted short of the Vistula—pushing to the river only after the insurgents had been driven away from the opposite bank—and placed its emphasis on expanding bridgeheads over the river south of Warsaw and obtaining bridgeheads across the Narev river to the north.[94] For weeks, the Soviet Union refused either to send aid itself or to facilitate the sending of aid by the British and American air forces. The latter did send some supplies by air drops from Britain and Italy, but these operations were very costly, strongly objected to by the air force commanders, and in any case more effective for morale than supply purposes since a high proportion of the material sent fell into German hands.[95]

The Germans first used police and SS units to slaughter as many Poles and destroy as many buildings as possible. Deploying units primarily interested in killing, raping, and looting, they initially made little headway beyond containing the insurgents. Slowly they added regular units, demolished the city block by block, split the Polish held area, drove the AK from the left bank of the Vistula, and in a steady, murderous advance ground down the defending Polish forces. As the front to the east grew silent, Soviet planes dropped not weapons but leaflets on August 18–19 calling for an end of resistance and berating the Polish government-in-exile.[96] When the Germans were obviously winning, Stalin decided to reduce tension with the Western Allies by indicating he did not object to their helping the Poles—as long as their planes did not land on Soviet airfields—and sent a little help himself. But the strategy had worked; the Germans crushed the AK for him. In early October the remaining AK forces surrendered, and the Germans levelled to the ground most of what was left standing of Warsaw.[97]

The argument that the Germans were blunting the Red Army offensive so that help could not be provided by the Soviet Union will not hold up when nearby offensive operations are examined. Now that the regimes of Poland and the former Soviet Union have publicly admitted Soviet responsibility for the Katyn massacre, the line on the events of 1944 may also change.[98] It is possible that as in the case of Finland in 1939, so in this instance Stalin was initially misled by Communist Party leaders from the area into underrating the strength of the local forces, but this very strength gave him pause. Let the Germans crush them; it would save him the trouble. The advice which Polish Communists gave Mikolajczyk in Moscow—to dissolve his government and the AK—certainly fits in with Stalin's hope of ending Poland's independence. If seizing Warsaw was so hard for the Red Army, surely an uprising in the city would make that task easier, not more difficult. With both the British and American governments pressing him repeatedly, Stalin opted as he had in 1939 for an accommodation, even if tacit and temporary, with Germany if that helped accomplish the final destruction of Polish independence. If the cost was to be great damage to the alliance with his two Western partners, so be it. The priorities in Soviet policy seemed clear to Stalin.

If the spectacular scene of those months was the bloody battle for Warsaw, the quiet one was a permanent change in British and United States attitudes. Neither allowed the issue to cause a break in the wartime coalition against Hitler; with much of the war still ahead, they needed to have the Soviet Union continue in the fight against Germany. But there was a sea change in the attitudes at the top in both countries, and their relationship with the Soviet Union would never be the same afterwards. There was nothing they could do in an area far from their military power and a few miles from the Red Army, but having themselves sent aid to the Soviet Union and to Marshal Tito's partisans, they remembered Stalin's attitude toward an independent Poland.[99] And so did the people of Poland.

When the Warsaw insurgents surrendered on October 2, another uprising in Eastern Europe was also in the process of being brutally crushed by the Germans. Resistance elements in the puppet state of Slovakia had contacts and sympathizers in the Slovak armed forces and were preparing a coup to shift Slovakia to the Allied side, open the door to the Red Army, and begin the return of Czechoslovakia to independent status. The weeks after the First Ukrainian Front reached the border of Czechoslovakia on April 8 were a time of preparation inside the Axis satellite. Pro-Soviet partisans, commanded by Russian officers, carried out a number of attacks on Germans, and this, together with rumors of a coup by the Slovak army, led by Defense Minister Ferdinand Catlos, precipitated a German move to occupy the country on August 29. This in turn provoked the Slovak uprising which quickly came to control large portions of Slovakia.[100] Here there was an opportunity to fly in reinforcements and supplies since the insurgents held airports and substantial areas for drop zones. The Western Allies, though publicly sympathetic and providing a little assistance, had clearly decided not to try for any large-scale supply operation; it seemed pointless to them to try to support another uprising right in front of the Red Army front.[101] Although it had been possible for the Russians to fly in officers for partisan bands, they now sent in few reinforcements and slowly at that. There was an effort, utilizing regular Red Army units and a Czechoslovak army raised and trained in the Soviet Union, to break into Slovakia through the Carpathian mountains at the Dukla Pass. All this was inadequate, however. Mistakes by insurgent leadership on the first days of the rising, German seizure of full control of Hungary in October which opened up the southern flank to them, conflicts among the insurgents between those loyal to the government-in-exile in London and those looking to a Communist Czechoslovakia, and entirely insufficient Soviet aid enabled the Germans to crush the Slovak uprising by the end of October. It had all lasted just as long as the battle in Warsaw and came to the same end. The Germans slaughtered to their hearts' content, though in the rural areas of Slovakia, unlike the urban rubble piles of Warsaw, some guerilla activities continued into the following year.

The Soviet advance on the central portion of the Eastern Front, which had stimulated the risings in Warsaw and Slovakia, had also reversed the geographic situation of the central sector as compared with the north and south. Instead of a German bulge eastwards in the center, there was now a Soviet bulge westwards. This made the German positions both to the south and the north more vulnerable than before; and as the

Soviet offensive on the central sector ran out of steam, the Red Army struck on the flanks. The German forces pushed back into Romania held the front reached at the end of the Soviet spring offensive, but they held a ramshackle line. German units alternated with Romanian armies. The former were steadily weakened during the summer by the transfer of divisions—eventually more than a quarter of the total—to the threatened front further north. The rest were assured by German army intelligence, wrong as usual, that there would be no more Soviet offensive.

The Romanian armies had been greatly reduced by the calamitous defeats of 1943 and early 1944; Romania's best divisions had been lost in the previous battles at Stalingrad and in the Crimea. Furthermore, both the government and the army had lost the will to fight. Although Marshal Antonescu assured the Germans of his loyalty, he had himself authorized peace sounding with the Allies, first in the West and then with the Soviet Union. If the marshal had doubts, most others in the government were certain that Romania should get out of the war as quickly as possible. Only their desire to do so safely—a preposterous hope—had kept them from making peace. The army itself had simply collapsed internally. The officers and men were through with the fighting, and it would take only a forthright push from the Soviet side to reveal in practice that there was to be no effort at resistance.

The Soviet offensive on the Romanian front, following plans largely developed on the spot with only timing determined by the Stavka, began on August 20 with the Second Ukrainian Front under Malinovsky on the right and General Fedor I. Tolbukhin's Third Ukrainian Front on the left. Both had been strengthened by several hundred thousand men conscripted in the recently liberated Ukraine and trained as well as indoctrinated in the preceding months. While the sectors held by the German 8th and 6th Armies resisted, the Romanian 4th and 3rd Armies simply did not fight, and Red Army advance guards quickly pushed through. Soviet armor could drive forward at will, and this meant that the German 6th Army, rebuilt after its disaster at Stalingrad, was once again cut off by the Red Army when its pincers closed around most of it on August 23rd. Its eighteen divisions were destroyed by the Russians as the German 8th Army—or what was left of it—fell back on the Carpathian mountains. In the same days that the Army Group South Ukraine, now commanded by General Friessner who had exchanged places with Schörner earlier, was being destroyed, the Romanian government pulled out of the war.

On August 23 a coup in Bukarest displaced Marshal Antonescu as King Michael and the political leaders tried to arrange peace. An effort by the surprised Germans to salvage their position and their hold on the unoccupied parts of the country, which included an air raid on the Romanian capital, only served to hasten the change of regime and of fronts. Now the Romanians not merely withdrew from the Axis but declared war, on Hungary with great enthusiasm and on Germany with no pleasure but with a sense of taking revenge on an ally who had first exploited, always neglected, and finally turned on them.

In a few days the Red Army rolled through Romania and across the Danube while Romanian units joined with them in the battle toward the northwest. There in the Carpathian passes, the Germans and the Hungarians tried to build up a new front as the Red Army pushed them back in pursuit, and the Romanians now hoped to reclaim the portions of Transylvania they had lost to Hungary in the 1940 territorial settlement. Like Finland at the other end of the front, Romania had switched sides but in far more dramatic circumstances and in a much greater Soviet victory over the German army, which lost more than 380,000 men in about two weeks.[102]

The Red Army occupied practically all of Romania including the Black Sea port of Constanza and the oil fields and refineries of Ploesti, the latter largely wrecked by prior American bombing.[103] The Germans still had in their concentration camps Horia Sima and other Iron Guard members, who had fled or been brought to Germany after their failed coup of January 1941. These now organized a government-in-exile under German auspices since no Romanian military leader, any more than any Finnish one, was willing to rebuild a pro-German regime; instead they fought hard against the Germans. Like the French collaborationists, the Iron Guardists could only conduct feuds with each other and propaganda under German auspices.[104] They were soon joined by still another shadow regime, this one for Bulgaria.

Bulgaria had thought it wise to join Germany in the war, first against Greece and Yugoslavia, then against Britain and the United States. In 1943 and 1944 the Bulgarian government, which had carefully avoided joining the Axis war against the Soviet Union, had carried out some soundings with the Western Allies; but, with a degree of stupidity difficult to credit, had refused to surrender to them when it still had the chance. On the other hand, the Western Allies, of whom the United States in particular had originally tried to persuade the Bulgarians that they could live very happily without a war with America, had not pushed them very effectively.[105] Their effort to pull out of the war now was far too late. On September 5, 1944, the Soviet Union declared war on Bulgaria, on the 8th the Third Ukrainian Front crossed the border, and on the same day Bulgaria declared war on Germany. In a few days, the whole country was occupied by the Red Army, and the Bulgarian army insofar as it did not dissolve began to fight alongside it.[106] A "National Bulgarian Government" under Professor Alexander Zankoff was established in Vienna [107] but would have no influence in the country which the Soviet Union had decided to occupy, place under a Communist dictatorship, and retain in its control.

The collapse of Romania had dramatic repercussions not only for Bulgaria but also for Hungary and the whole German position in Southeast Europe, especially in the Aegean, Greece, Albania and Yugoslavia. In Hungary, the approach of the Red Army to the Carpathians earlier in the year had stimulated both projects to leave the war, and reinforcement of the army. The events in Romania were of special importance in both directions. On the one hand, the Hungarian army now fought more vigorously and effectively than before: the Russian army was at the gates and the Romanian army was fighting alongside it. Especially in the new front being built up in Transylvania, the Hungarian army fought hard, and at first successfully, to halt and even throw back the invaders. The old territorial dispute with Romania provided an added incentive here for the Hungarians as for the Romanians. On the other hand, elements in both the government and in the army, led by the regent, Admiral Horthy, now began sounding the Soviet Union seriously about peace. On September 24, during the fighting in eastern Hungary, Horthy decided to send a delegation to Moscow; he personally wrote a letter to Stalin, now claiming to have been misinformed about the incident in 1941, which had been utilized to have Hungary join Germany in attacking the Soviet Union.[108]

The Hungarian faction hoping for peace planned to pull out of the Axis on October 15, 1944, but botched the operation about as effectively as the Italians had in the preceding year.[109] The Germans seized Horthy and took over the capital. There they instituted a new regime under Ferenc Szálasi, the leader of the Hungarian Arrow Cross movement, a lunatic fringe organization of the right whose chief was seriously thought to be a lunatic himself by many.[110] Much but by no means all of the Hungarian army rallied to the new regime. The Germans were now in direct control of most of Hungary, and with the enthusiastic aid of Szálasi and the Arrow Cross began what they considered their most important task: the deportation to slaughter of Hungary's over half a million Jews. The last refuge for Jews in German-controlled Europe provided the last large contingents of victims until pressure from the Allies and the advance of the Red Army combined to halt the deportations. In the meantime, in late October a German counter-offensive drove back the Second Ukrainian Front temporarily as the Germans tried to protect the agricultural and oil resources of Hungary.[111] By the end of October a coherent front had been put together by what was now being called the German Army Group South, but most of Transylvania had been occupied by Soviet and Romanian troops. The prospects for a continued holding of this front by the Axis were very poor; the Second Ukrainian Front was already in the open Hungarian plain.

The dramatic developments in Budapest led to a long and bitter battle in Hungary which lasted from October 1944 into the last days of World War II, causing enormous devastation and heavy casualties for both sides. The repercussions of the collapse of the German position in Romania on the situation in Greece and related parts of South and Southeast Europe were equally dramatic but less destructive. When the first news of the coup which overthrew Antonescu reached German headquarters on August 23, the Commander-in-Chief in Southeast Europe, Field Marshal Maximilian von Weichs, was at Hitler's headquarters. In the conference held that day, Hitler made several decisions which crucially affected German strategy and general developments in the whole theater of war. For years Hitler had insisted on building up forces and positions in Greece, Crete, and the islands in the Aegean, and in September 1943 the Germans had quickly taken over the portions of Greece occupied by Italy as well as the Italian Dodecanese islands. At one time a basis for possible further advances into the Middle East through Turkey, the German positions in the area had more recently served the purpose of restraining Turkey from entering the war on the Allied side as well as insuring the supply of chrome from that country, simultaneously denying to the Allies air bases from which their planes could more easily attack the Romanian oil fields.

Turkey had already broken diplomatic relations with Germany on August 2.[112] With Romania lost and Bulgaria doubtful, the prior considerations all fell by the wayside; and under the new circumstances Hitler wanted the focus of attention shifted to a defensive posture further north. Southern Greece should be evacuated if attacked, and a key concern must be to make certain that the Bulgarians did not seize the only railway line through Serbia to Greece and turn it over to the Allies. Some garrisons on the islands in the Mediterranean, especially the large one on Crete, would have to be abandoned while others might be evacuated.[113]

It will be noted that here Hitler set the stage for a major withdrawal of German forces in Southeast Europe right after he had agreed to the evacuation of southwest France; clearly he was prepared to go into a defensive position and evacuate substantial areas when this appeared to him to be the appropriate procedure. In this instance, the local commander in fact moved quite slowly in carrying out the evacuations ordered; over a period of weeks German garrisons were evacuated from most of the islands in the Aegean and from southernmost Greece. Only as the danger of a Soviet breakthrough westwards from Bulgaria, cutting the key railway through southern Yugoslavia into Greece, began to develop during October did von Weichs move on the basis of his authorization. In a lengthy and carefully orchestrated withdrawal, German troops evacuated Greece, which they had conquered with such fanfare in 1941, and drew back into Macedonia, establishing a new defensive position in October. On the 10th, the withdrawal started; on the 13th, Athens was evacuated; and at the end of the month German troops pulled out of Salonika. The Germans had deported to their murder factories practically all of the country's Jews; now they themselves left in an almost peaceful evacuation after the liberation of Belgrade and Nish had made the precariousness of their position further south evident. With the forces of the Western Allies fully engaged elsewhere, the latter struck only air blows at the evacuation routes, and the British landing force which began to disembark in the Peleponnesus at the beginning of October made no effort to interfere with the departing Germans. They would soon be in battle with Greek, not German fighters; occupation was soon followed by civil war, but the first of the two ordeals for the Greeks was over.[114] The Soviet Union and Great Britain had already decided that Greece would fall into Britain's sphere of interest while Romania was allocated to the Soviet Union; neither great power was interested in upsetting these arrangements at a time when the war against Germany was still bitter and bloody.

One of the more bitter and bloody of the engagements in that war was taking place at the opposite end of the Eastern Front in the very days of the major changes at the southern part of that front. Army Group North, after land contact had been reestablished with it, still held most of Estonia, much of Latvia, and the western quarter of Lithuania in early September, 1944. Their situation on this portion of the front, like that at the southern end, had however been made extremely tenuous by the Soviet victory in the central sector; and where the Germans had reopened a corridor to their Army Group North just west of Riga, the troops of General Ivan Bagramian's First Baltic Front were less than twenty miles from the Baltic Sea. There were repeated German projects for offensives to widen this corridor by pincer attacks on the three Soviet armies in the bulge toward the sea west of Riga, but these operations were never carried through. The German hopes of regaining the initiative were thwarted by Red Army offensives. On September 17 an offensive by the Leningrad Front broke into the rear of the German Narva Army holding the northernmost end of the front, and this army (named for the city and river it was to defend) and the adjacent 18th Army had to be withdrawn toward Riga. The Third and Second Baltic Fronts pushed against the retreating Germans without breaking through and the First Baltic Front did not or could not reach the sea. The September Soviet offensive, therefore, drove the Germans back, forcing them entirely out of Estonia and out of more of Latvia, but without cutting them off in a major breakthrough of the sort which had taken place in Romania. But that now changed.

Once the German armies had concentrated in the immediate vicinity of Riga, they thought once again of the pincer operation against First Baltic Front; and the Army Group North commander, Field Marshal Schörner, probably looked to Hitler like the ideal leader to drive it through. This time, however, the Red Army redeployed rapidly, effectively, and without German intelligence getting any clear picture of what was afoot. Bagramian shifted his weight from the right to the left flank, and on October 5, before the Germans realized what was happening, launched a major offensive west of Shaulyay to the Baltic. Breaking through the front of 3rd Panzer Army, the Russians reached the Baltic on October 9 both north and south of the port city of Klaipeda (Memel)[115], isolating a German corps in that city and cutting off the two German armies, the 16th and 18th, in western Latvia.

This time the Germans could not reopen a corridor to Army Group North because a major Soviet offensive into East Prussia by the Third Belorussian Front occupied all their attention. The German army recovered sufficiently to contain in mid-October this last major offensive of the Red Army on the northern and central parts of the Eastern Front in 1944; but they simply did not have the strength, especially in armor, to make even an attempt to drive north into the Soviet wedge between East Prussia and the German armies stranded in the Courland area of Latvia.

This set of events merits further examination. On the one hand, the Red Army was clearly coming to the end of its ability to sustain major offensive operations against substantial resistance until there had been time to rebuild communication systems behind the new front line reached in the summer and fall offensives, as well as an opportunity to replace casualties, rest and reform units, and replenish weapons and ammunition. On the other hand, as the fighting approached the old German border, desperate German resistance, shorter German lines of communications, and newly activated German divisions made the going slower and harder for the Allies in both East and West. In the days that the Red Army was trying unsuccessfully to break deeply into East Prussia, the last soldiers of the British 1st Airborne Division had just been rounded up in Arnhem and the American 9th Army was slowly battering its way block by block into the city of Aachen. This was the first major German city to be taken by the Allies, but it was obvious that on all major fronts the time of rapid Allied advances was over and a new stage in the war had been reached.

The other, and related, question was the decision of Hitler to hold on to the Courland portion of Latvia rather than either order Army Group North to break through to the south or evacuate entirely by sea. Some divisions were transferred by sea to strengthen other portions of the Eastern Front, but in spite of the preference of army Chief-of-Staff Heinz Guderian, a large force was left there, fending off a series of Red Army attacks until the final surrender of May, 1945.[116] Why was this piece of Latvia important enough for Hitler to insist it be held at a time when he had just decided to evacuate southwest France as well as all of Greece, Albania and southern Yugoslavia? The possibility of direct communication by sea across the Baltic made it easier to contact, re-supply, or pull out troops from the Courland area than either of the other territories evacuated in the fall of 1944, but this difference facilitated rather than caused the different decisions made about them. To understand that difference, it is necessary to examine German strategy in this period.

In August–September 1944 the German government was once again being urged by its Japanese ally to make peace with the Soviet Union. The hope of the Japanese, as earlier, was that such a peace would make it possible for the Germans to concentrate on fighting the United States and Great Britain. They thought that the prospect of actually obtaining a German–Soviet peace was easier now than earlier as both countries had suffered vast casualties and were back practically where the campaign had started in 1941: the Soviets had regained and the Germans had lost practically everything that the German army had originally overrun. This looked to Tokyo like a good opportunity, especially since in their eyes—opened by frank reporting of Japanese diplomats in Europe—the Germans had suffered very serious defeats on both the Eastern and the Western Fronts.[117]

The efforts of the Japanese to persuade the Germans of the wisdom of such a course did not fall on quite such deaf ears as earlier in the war. It was by now obvious to Hitler and his associates that the invasion in the West had succeeded and that the offensive capabilities of the Red Army in the East remained great. Perhaps it would be wise to get the fighting on one front ended and concentrate on the other. As it was very publicly obvious that the Western Powers were continuing to insist on a German surrender, the possibility of a peace in the East remained.

There is some evidence that in the fall of 1944 Hitler for the first time seriously considered a possibility he had hitherto always dismissed out of hand; it cannot be documented, but there is reason to believe that the fact that the Germans had been driven out of the Ukraine and now had no prospect of retaking it as Hitler had still anticipated earlier in 1944 was a significant factor in his willingness to rethink the question. As long as the Germans had held it, he argued—with Goebbels for example—that Stalin simply could not give up that valuable area; when it was originally lost in the fall of 1943 and the first months of 1944, Hitler was still confident of regaining it by a new offensive after the invasion in the West had been beaten off. Now that the invasion had succeeded and the central and southern sectors of the German Eastern Front had collapsed, there was no visible prospect of reconquering the major goal in the East. Under these circumstances, it would appear, Hitler briefly did think of some accommodation with the Soviet Union.[118]

It is not at all clear whether the Soviet government would have been willing to make peace with Germany in 1944. There appear to have been contacts in Stockholm with adherents of the opposition to Hitler before July 20 as well as with representations of the Nazi regime, and in some instances it is impossible to tell—and was presumably impossible for the Soviets to tell—which group specific individuals represented. But it all made no difference because Hitler came to an entirely different strategy. In combination with the holding of ports in the West to make it more difficult to supply and reinforce the Allied invasion armies, Germany was building up new armies of its own which would strike a major offensive blow at the Western Powers. That offensive was to be two-pronged: a land offensive which eventually became what the Germans called the Ardennes Offensive and the Allies referred to as the Battle of the Bulge. At the same time, a revived U-Boat warfare with the radically new submarines, against which the Allies had no effective defense at all, would sever the transatlantic routes, return the initiative in the war at sea to the Germans, and contribute to a massive victory over the Western Allies who could then neither supply nor reinforce nor evacuate whatever armies they had on the continent. Once that combination of land and sea offensives had succeeded, new blows were to be struck on the Eastern Front by a German army which could then concentrate on that theater. If those blows caused Stalin to try for a settlement with Germany, a new situation would arise for the German government to examine; but in the meantime it was essential that Japan take no steps in Moscow.

While the Japanese reluctantly agreed to this German request, it hardly reassured them about the future; by the last days of September 1944 they began preparations for the fate of their diplomatic personnel in Europe in case of a German collapse.[119] For the Germans, however, this set of decisions had major and immediate implications of a different sort. For the land offensive in the West, they would need the new formations being organized and equipped. For the sea offensive in the West, they would need to train the crews in the new U-Boats—and for *this*, the safety of the training area in the Baltic was essential.

It was the need for keeping the Red Army away from the coast and the Red navy away from the sea in the central Baltic which played the determining role in Hitler's decision to hold on to Courland. He was very much encouraged in this decision by Admiral Dönitz, who expected the new U-Boats to be ready at any moment and who knew that they could not be employed without proper trials of the ships and training of the crews. The whole Courland issue, therefore, revolved about naval strategy against the *West*. The navy worked hard not only to influence Hitler's thinking but also to assist in the holding of portions of the Baltic area.[120]

Eventually, the arguments over the evacuation or retention of the Courland area were to play an important role, first in Hitler's breaking with Guderian as his army Chief-of-Staff and, subsequently, in his appointing Dönitz to be his own successor. In the meantime, the fronts ground to a virtual halt in both East and West as both sides prepared for the final battles. If the German calculations and hopes proved correct, there was a very lengthy conflict still ahead; if they proved wrong and the Allies crushed all resistance, the divisions in Courland—rather like the German division left on the Channel Islands—could be said to have established their own prisoner-of-war camp even as the war was still under way.

13

TENSIONS IN BOTH ALLIANCES

The alliance between the United States and Great Britain, developed in tentative stages even before Japan, Germany, and Italy drew the United States into the war, had from its beginning both built-in tensions and elements making for cooperation. The tensions came in part from their divergent histories and perspectives, in part from their differing situations and strategies. The United States had gained its independence in a long and bitter war with England, a war which had affected the country more deeply than any conflict except for the civil war. The country's national anthem recalls to its citizens an incident from their next war with England, and at later times in the nineteenth century there had been further serious friction about boundaries in the northwest and northeast, about fishery rights and British support of the Confederacy in the civil war, about rivalries in Central and South America, and about projects of some Irish–Americans to seize all or parts of Canada to hold hostage for the freedom of Ireland from British rule.

This last source of friction relates to the role of the Americans of Irish descent, who had become very numerous partly because of developments in Ireland during the middle and second half of the nineteenth century, and who were becoming increasingly influential in American politics in the first half of the twentieth century, especially because of their concentration in a number of large eastern and mid-western cities, where their role was crucial to the Democratic Party coalition which dominated American politics in the 1930s. Although their overt hostility to Britain was diminishing somewhat, it remained a factor in the picture.

Furthermore, Americans generally extended their antipathy for their own former colonial masters to the whole colonial concept. If they had generally very little idea of the extent to which Canada, Australia, New Zealand and what was then called the Union of South Africa were in fact fully in charge of their own internal affairs, they had no doubt that

India and the other colonial possessions of Great Britain were not. Having themselves through Congressional action in 1936 decided to withdraw from the one great deviation from their own anti-colonial tradition, the Philippines, they could see no reason why the British should not do likewise. Whatever the size and nature of other colonial empires held by other powers, any glance at a map—to say nothing of population statistics—showed that in the competition for the greatest empire and hence the worst place in American eyes, Britain indeed had taken the lion's share.

For those concerned about the world trade causes and effects of the Great Depression, and that especially included Secretary of State Cordell Hull and much of the personnel of his State Department, the system of imperial preference instituted by the Ottawa Agreements of 1932 was an abominable restraint on trade and hence an obstacle to both prosperity and future peace. In addition, there was in both government circles and the American public a sense that the British were sharp and unscrupulous dealers, a quality they had most recently demonstrated by defaulting on their debt to the United States from World War I.

The British, on the other hand, resented the American refusal to share in the support of the peace settlement of 1919 as well as the American tariff system which, they believed, had caused many of their difficulties (including their debt default) in the first place. Many of them, especially in the Conservative establishment, objected to American criticism of the British empire in general and of British rule in India in particular. The arrival of large numbers of American troops in England led to many individual cases of friendship and eventually to thousands of marriages, but also produced considerable friction; the Americans, as a popular comment put it, were "over-paid, oversexed, overfed and over here."

There were, in addition to the differences in popular attitudes, divergencies in strategic perception. The Americans constantly argued that the "Germany First" strategy demanded that something really be done against Germany in the European theater, and such favorite projects of Churchill and the British Chiefs of Staff as mounting big operations to seize the Italian islands in the eastern Aegean did not look to them in the least likely to further that aim. On the contrary, the American leaders saw in such projects diversions designed for British imperial purposes more likely, by diverting resources, to delay than to speed up victory. The refusal of the British to provide a reasonable level of support for their own forces in the Indian theater, on the other hand, looked to Washington and its representatives on the spot as a means of holding back on strengthening an anti-colonialist China until Britain could reclaim her colonies after the Americans had defeated Japan.

The British leaders, on the contrary, constantly objected to what they considered excessive American deployment to the Pacific (conveniently forgetting that they had requested it in the first place in order to assure the safety of Australia and New Zealand while much of the force of those Dominions was engaged in the British campaign in North Africa). The British also resented the insistence of the Americans on the priority of the cross-Channel invasion, the willingness of the Americans to sacrifice to that priority opportunities which they believed existed elsewhere, especially in Italy and the eastern Mediterranean, and the failure of the Americans, as they saw it, to see that needs elsewhere precluded for the time being the manpower and resource allocations to the Burma theater, which the British in any case believed unlikely to produce the revived Chinese war effort Americans hoped for.[1]

The other side of this litany of troubles was an array of substantially more significant factors drawing and keeping the two powers together. The American President and the British Prime Minister had established a truly extraordinary personal and working relationship, and if in this the balance whenever they differed shifted increasingly to the more powerful American side, there was obviously on each side an exceedingly high regard for the other and a determination to make the alliance work. This sentiment was very much shared by the higher staffs of both men, so that, whatever differences over policy and strategy developed, the attempts to bridge these were always made in the shared assumption that cooperation was essential for victory. And until his death in November 1944, Field Marshal Dill invariably worked hard, and usually with success, to resolve whatever difficulties arose.[2]

The cooperative attitude at the top had pillars at home and derived strength from implementing organs. At home, Americans admired the steadfastness of the British in their great trial while the British appreciated the help they had received and were continuing to get from the Americans. In practice the cooperation generally worked and in the process generated further cooperation. The various joint boards and committees working under the auspices of the Combined Chiefs of Staff carried out their activities with enormous success. In spite of the inherent difficulties of making combined plans and allocating scarce resources from ammunition to shipping space, it all somehow worked; and in the process large numbers of officers from both countries and all services learned to work together and became accustomed to doing so.[3] Furthermore, there were at least some theater operational commands which were effectively Allied in composition, nature, and functioning.

While MacArthur deliberately kept his headquarters in the Southwest Pacific from being the Allied construction it could (and probably should) have been and Mountbatten, in spite of really trying, simply did not have enough Americans assigned to his Southeast Asia Command to make that a truly Allied one,[a] in the Mediterranean and in Northwest Europe there really did develop a truly integrated form of command structure. As much a tribute to the personal efforts of Eisenhower in this direction, the Allied Forces Headquarters in Algiers and later his Supreme Headquarters Allied Expeditionary Force in London and thereafter on the continent were a new type of organization (which Field Marshal Sir Henry Maitland Wilson continued when he succeeded Eisenhower in the Mediterranean). Quite unlike earlier attempts at liaison or allied command as with Marshal Foch in World War I, these headquarters were of a fundamentally different kind. They developed their own cohesion and atmosphere, friendships and procedures, and they not only contributed immensely to smoothing the otherwise troublesome problems of managing the British–American alliance at the time but prepared the way for the North Atlantic Treaty Organization's (NATO) success in the decades after 1949.

Such structures were especially badly needed in the summer of 1944 and thereafter. The tension which developed over the stalemate, or what looked like stalemate, in Normandy tested the cohesion of Allied command. The troubles between Eisenhower's headquarters, and especially its British members, and Montgomery came close to leading to the latter's relief. Montgomery in turn had the most extraordinary difficulties with his Canadian commanders. As if this were not enough, the disappointing inability of the British, Canadians and Poles under Montgomery's command to close the Falaise gap and completely trap the remnants of the two German armies which had been fighting in Normandy produced more friction.

At almost the same time, the British were still trying to get the landing in southern France cancelled in a bitter dispute with the Americans. The acrimonious nature of this particular argument over strategy[4] was related to British disappointment over the effect of that operation on the Italian front, which they preferred to see supported more heavily, and made all the more bitter by the memory of defeat in the Aegean the preceding fall. Only these factors can explain the complete disregard of logistics by the British: how did they expect the huge armies of the Allies to be supplied without the French Mediterranean ports?

These troublesome military disputes were all resolved or smoothed over, but their sharpness was in part a reflection of other tensions in the

[a] Field Marshal Wavell's command in the winter 1941–42 did not exist long enough.

Anglo-American alliance which had been simmering for some time and which increased in 1944. The most difficult and long-standing of these grew out of the fundamentally divergent views of the two countries on the colonial question.[5] The American public maintained its fundamental opposition to colonialism, a view shared by most military leaders, while a substantial portion of the British public and much of its civilian and military leadership expected a continuation of the British empire in some form. The divergent views could not have been represented more sharply than by the two leaders, Churchill and Roosevelt, themselves. Churchill became positively apoplectic at any mention of decolonization; Roosevelt was even more certain that all colonies of Britain and other colonial powers were and should be headed for the earliest possible independence, after a period of some sort of trusteeship.

The fact that already in 1942 Churchill had threatened to resign rather than make substantial concessions to the movement for Indian independence supported by Roosevelt had made it clear to the latter that this was an issue on which the British leader simply would not budge. The President was on the whole careful not to push this matter too openly thereafter, but there could be no secrecy about his views. The fact that these were shared by his representative in India, William Phillips, a long-time friend of the President, only served to underline the gulf separating London and Washington on this issue.[6]

The fundamental difference over the colonial question was, in a way, closely related to another difference which was much more in the public eye at the time in both Britain and the United States: that over the governments being established or to be re-established in Italy and Greece. In both cases, the sentimental attachment of Churchill to the maintenance of monarchy in Italy and its restoration in Greece ran afoul not only of the antipathy, or at least indifference, of the Americans to the monarchical question but also the general identification in both countries of exceedingly conservative and even collaborationist elements with the monarchy. The reluctance, at least initially, of the Americans to work with such people was matched by Churchill's aversion to anyone in either country whom he suspected of anti-monarchical sentiments. He objected not merely to Communists and those who were willing to work with them but to such respected liberal statesmen as the Italian leader Ivanoe Bonomi.

The American and British attitudes toward the internal evolution of Italian politics were fundamentally different, with Churchill adamant against what he perceived, largely correctly, as an increase in the role of those opposed to the maintenance of the monarchy, even if under King Victor Emmanuel's son Prince Umberto. The Americans were far more ready to accommodate the clear signs in Italian politics pointing in other directions. When the April 1944 agreement of the Allies and Badoglio for the all-party government under Victor Emmanuel to be replaced by one under Umberto after the liberation of Rome was to be implemented in June, the pressure of Italy's parties brought an end to Badoglio's role as Prime Minister. Bonomi, of all people, became the new Prime Minister, to Churchill's outrage and quiet satisfaction in Washington.[7] British–American quarrels over Italy continued thereafter, focusing later that year on Churchill's veto of the appointment of Count Carlo Sforza as Foreign Minister.[8] The steady drift of the Italian government into a moderate liberal direction, which the British government found impossible to halt, made Churchill all the more adamant in his attitude toward developments in Greece.

As the Germans evacuated their troops from Greece, British troops landed there. The major Greek resistance organization, the EAM, was dominated by the Communists, though many of the members and supporters were not aware of this fact.[9] In an increasingly complicated situation, these elements first agreed to a settlement, referred to as the Caserta Agreement, of September 26, 1944, with other elements in the resistance and the British as well as representatives of the Greek government-in-exile, but then reversed themselves and tried to obtain control of Athens. British troops played a major role in putting down this effort; and while the Soviet Union, for reasons to be reviewed later in this chapter, acquiesced in the British suppression of those who looked to the Soviet Union as a model, the American public reacted very negatively to the developments in Greece. An American public statement of December 5, 1944, originally designed to engage the veto of Sforza, also contained a pointed reference to the events in Athens and caused enormous resentment in England but elicited a favorable response from the American public. For weeks something of a publicistic controversy raged and came to be relaxed only by the end of January.[10]

The situation in Greece had exploded into something akin to civil war, with British troops playing a key role in putting down an attempted Communist insurgency in Athens. Whatever the obvious interest in obtaining absolute power on the part of the Communists, those on the British side had in many cases collaborated with rather than fought against the Germans. The voices of dissent in the British Parliament were mild compared to the uproar in the United States; Admiral King had American ships transferred to the Union Jack rather than give the appearance of American support by carrying British troops and supplies to Greece under the Stars and Stripes.[11] A major effort was eventually made to smooth over the troubles, but there was legitimate concern that the two allies would move apart. This was due partly to the greater interest of the American public in such countries as Italy and Greece than Romania and Bulgaria, partly to the perception that British actions were closely connected to her imperial interests which Americans in general deplored, and partly to the impact of the Battle of the Bulge and Montgomery's unfortunate press conference, reviewed in the next chapter.

A further source of friction between the Americans and British was their troubled relationship with de Gaulle. Both found him exceedingly difficult to deal with, in part because the leader of the Free French appears to have thought it important for his own and French self-respect to make things as difficult as he could for the allies on whom he depended. In this he was certainly successful.[12] Because they realized earlier than the Americans that de Gaulle was likely to have behind him the support of the liberated French people, the British made, on the whole, a greater effort to accommodate the difficult French leader. Once they had been concerned to keep him from flying out of England,[13] now they tried hard to work with him and to persuade the Americans of the wisdom of doing the same.[14] Roosevelt remained reluctant, partly because of his concern over the imposition of a military commander on a liberated France in which the last general to try to head the country had been General Boulanger, in part because those closest to him in Washington held an even more negative view of de Gaulle than the President himself. The July 1944 meeting of the two in Washington eased the strain considerably, but de Gaulle's subsequent deliberate flaunting of his newly recognized status hardly helped. Because the British government, in spite of its own endless troubles with the French general, considered itself bound to him and was constantly urging Washington to follow a similar policy, the difficulties of both Britain and the United States with the Free French leader produced tensions in their relationship with each other.

The problem of de Gaulle in Anglo-American relations does not exhaust the catalog of frictions. There was a whole series of economic difficulties. The British realized that they were not only dependent upon American Lend-Lease aid during hostilities but would need assistance both for the interval between the defeat of Germany and the defeat of Japan and during the period immediately thereafter. Having poured their energies and resources into the fight against Germany, and at a level and cost far beyond the resources of their country, Britain's leaders looked to the United States for continued aid until they could once again be self-supporting. It was their hope that the extensive "reverse Lend-Lease" which they were providing to the Americans and the great role they had played in the war would combine with American self-interest in a prosperous post-war Britain to make some assistance program palatable to them.

At the Quebec Conference of September 1944 the Americans had promised a generous treatment of British needs in what was coming to be referred to as Phase II Lend-Lease, the period after the defeat of Germany. The British sent John Maynard Keynes to Washington to work out an agreement on this subject. Keynes, whatever his ability as an economist, was perhaps not the wisest choice, given the attitude of Roosevelt toward him, but that may not have been known to the British.ᵃ Secretary of the Treasury Henry Morgenthau in particular tried to accommodate the British, having himself played a key role at the Quebec meeting; but objections within the United States government and Congress, responsive to doubts among the American public, kept the resulting agreement—if the compromises arrived at can be called that—substantially below what the British had hoped for. And even that would be imperilled by legislative changes in Congress and the early end of the war with Japan.[15]

The difficult discussions of further aid to Britain in the last months of 1944 were complicated by the differences between the American and British delegations at the international civil aviation conference simultaneously taking place in Chicago. At a time when British Airways is the world's largest air carrier and dominates its most important and profitable route, that between New York and London, it may at first be difficult to follow the agitated debate over post-war civil aviation between Americans who wanted open competition and the British who were afraid that American wartime mass production of transport planes, when they themselves were concentrating on fighters and bombers, would drive them out of peacetime passenger traffic altogether. Massive American pressure brought agreement on terms close to what the British strongly objected to, but the pressure itself angered the authorities in London while Washington seethed over what was seen as British intransigence.[16]

Behind the angry dispute over the future of international civil aviation and also in the background of differences about Lend-Lease was always the argument over differing philosophies on international

---

ᵃ In a letter of July 9, 1941, Bernard Baruch had warned Roosevelt not to trust Keynes, referring to very bad experiences at the Paris Peace Conference of 1919. In his reply of July 11, the President, who was generally not inclined to put his thoughts on paper, wrote, "I did not have those Paris Peace conference experiences with the 'gent' but from much more recent contacts, I am inclined wholly to agree." FDRL, PSF Box 117, Bernard Baruch. For British doubts about the American plan to publish the minutes of the Council of Four at Paris, see WM (43) War Cabinet 93(43), 5 July 1943, PRO CAB 65/35.

economic policy. The Roosevelt administration, led on this issue by Cordell Hull, argued in favor of lowering barriers and controls. On this issue, there were two fronts: at home, against the advocates of protective tariffs, especially influential in the Republican Party, and abroad, against the imperial preference agreements embodied in Britain's arrangements with her Dominions and colonies. If in the pre-war years the administration had concentrated its efforts on the passage and implementation of the reciprocal trade agreements act, fighting in the Congress against the domestic opponents of its lower tariff policies, during the war it tried hard to utilize the leverage provided by Lend-Lease to push the British into abandoning their special imperial preferences. The prospect of a terribly difficult recovery from the exertions of war made the London government most reluctant to yield to American pressure on this issue; it would affect relations between the two for years to come.[17]

In the period immediately following the end of the war in Europe, the question of relaxing British restrictions on Jewish immigration into the British mandate of Palestine was to poison Anglo-American relations, but this prospect was not apparent during the period of hostilities. It was the future of Germany and the relationship of the Western Powers with the Soviet Union that gave rise to different opinions in the two capitals and friction between them. On the future of Germany, the differences were worked out in the fall of 1944. After lengthy opposition, Roosevelt was finally converted to the British scheme of occupation zones, which left Berlin deep inside the Soviet sector and allocated the southern rather than the northwestern zone to the United States. The President's mood was not improved by Churchill's change of mind on the zonal question in early 1945, and his successor, Harry Truman, was also unwilling to break the zonal agreement once it had been reached. Both Churchill and Roosevelt at Quebec in September, 1944, agreed to the deindustrialization embodied in the Morgenthau plan and both soon after abandoned it, though not necessarily for the same reasons (an issue reviewed in Chapter 15). The policies of the Western Allies toward Germany would be somewhat different in principle but far more similar in practice than might have been anticipated, a reality which later facilitated the junction of the two zones.

Rather more difficult was the divergence in views concerning relations with the Soviet Union. Here there were on the one hand common Anglo-American perspectives which would produce major frictions between both and the Soviet Union, frictions to be discussed later in this chapter, but there were also significant differences in approach between the two Western Powers.

THE WESTERN POWERS AND THE SOVIET UNION

On some points the British and American governments were in full agreement. Both very much preferred to keep their project to develop the atomic bomb secret from the Russians, though both were aware of Soviet espionage efforts to penetrate the work being done, with the Americans apparently being more aware of it and the British far more deeply penetrated. Both had in prior years made substantial efforts to work with the Russians on military matters and intelligence exchanges; both had been equally rebuffed and were by 1944 about equally disheartened on this score. Both still very much hoped for post-war cooperation with the Soviet Union, though both were becoming somewhat skeptical about the prospects for such cooperation. Where they differed from each other, and hence at times had substantial disagreements, was on how to deal with the Soviet Union in the meantime.

The British Prime Minister and most in his government were concerned that the waning power of Britain in the face of the growing power of the Soviet Union made early agreements with Moscow a necessity. Even if those agreements, and the concessions required to obtain them, were painful—especially for those East Europeans who would find themselves under Soviet control—it was better to get the best terms possible early and try to tie the Soviets down by such agreements than to wait until later when Britain's power had ebbed further and the Russians could do practically what they wanted.[18] This approach explains the course Churchill had tried to adopt in 1941–42 in accepting the essentials of Russia's pre-June 1941 borders, a course from which he had been kept by American objections. As the Red Army beat back the German invaders and headed into Central and Southeast Europe, he wanted to return to it.

Roosevelt's views were based on a different reality and drew quite different conclusions from that reality. The President was opposed to advance commitments about the post-war world not only on general principles, in part because of the believed bad effects of the secret treaties made during World War I, but also due to a view of the realities of power which was entirely different from Churchill's, and for very good reasons. He knew all too well how poorly prepared for war the United States had been in 1939, 1940, and 1941, and how long it was taking to mobilize American military strength. He was equally conscious of the difficulties of projecting the slowly but steadily growing power of the United States across the vast oceans separating her from the European and Pacific enemies in the face of the struggle with German submarines and other sources of ship losses. The obvious implication for a man who believed firmly in the long-term ability of the country to surmount these difficulties and attain victory was that a steady unfolding of American power was certain to improve the position of the United States in Allied councils. Generally averse to making choices before they were absolutely necessary, in regard to the future of Europe Roosevelt believed that he had every incentive to postpone decisions. This was especially true at a time when American forces were not yet deployed on the continent in force; it would continue to be the case for some time thereafter as American strength in France grew.

As it was, American armies were to move far beyond the lines contemplated by Churchill even though there was some reluctance to move east of them in 1945; had the Germans not launched their last great offensive in the West, the Americans would quite likely have pushed yet further. If there was a case to be made for Churchill's belief that a waning power had best make its deals early, then an equally good case can be made for Roosevelt's view that a country growing in strength could benefit from postponing decisions until that power had unfolded to its full potential.

This differentiation in perspective hampered Anglo-American deliberations as they dealt with the Soviet Union and made it very difficult for the two powers to adopt a common line toward Moscow. There was certainly no lack of issues between the London and Washington governments on the one hand and Moscow on the other. These had been there from the beginning of the alliance forced on them by Germany; many came to a head in the summer and fall of 1944.

Undoubtedly the most important of the issues was that of the future of Poland. Neither the British nor the American government was an admirer of the pre-war government in Warsaw, and neither government was especially devoted to the pre-war eastern border of Poland. The point on which there was, however, basic agreement in both governments — as well as the public in the two countries — was a hope and a very strong desire for the future liberated Poland to have its independence. Here was the central and determining problem: given the geographic realities, Poland was most likely to be liberated by the Red Army; could it still be independent?

In the First World War, Serbia had been overrun by the armies of the Central Powers, but at the end of that conflict had emerged larger and independent because of the defeat of those Central Powers at the hand of the Western Allies, Russia having previously been defeated by Germany. Now the situation was going to be different. The Soviet Union was obviously not only not being defeated by Germany, it was making a major contribution to Germany's defeat and the Western Allies had every interest in urging and helping it to do so. How then enable Poland, wedged as it was between Germany and Russia, to retain an independence which Germany had hoped to extinguish along with much of its population and which Stalin appeared unwilling to allow?

The British government, which was closest to the Polish government-in-exile, located in London since the summer of 1940, took the view that the best hope for an independent Poland lay in that government-in-exile making almost any concession to Moscow that the latter might want as a means of assuring its return to a Poland that would in any case be liberated by the Red Army. If they could only get back into the country, the people there would surely rally to them rather than to whatever puppets the Soviet Union might prefer to install. Both before and after the Soviet Union broke off relations with the Polish government-in-exile, the British government, with Churchill playing an active personal role, tried hard to pressure the London Poles into making first territorial concessions and subsequently also some changes in personnel to accommodate Soviet demands.[19]

The Polish leaders in the West were on the whole unwilling to make the extensive territorial concessions asked for, though a few of them were willing to make some changes, especially in view of anticipated gains at Germany's expense. They were, however, not inclined to accept the view that the Soviet Union could be a multi-national unit while Poland could not and were especially reluctant to agree to yield portions of pre-war Poland while the war was on and they were in exile.

It cannot, of course, be known what would have happened had they agreed to Soviet demands. It seems likely, however, that it made no difference and that the British were deluding themselves. There were already the germs of a Polish government and army under strict Soviet control being organized within the Soviet Union. Stalin's policy clearly looked forward to an entirely new regime in Poland; and while he would and did make what he considered concessions to London and Washington to hold down the level of acrimony in the alliance, he appears to have made up his mind very early that none but his own hand-picked Poles would have any real say in Warsaw.[20]

American policy on the Polish question lagged behind that of England but engaged the same basic problem.[21] In part because of domestic political concerns, President Roosevelt was most reluctant to push concessions on the Polish government-in-exile. There was, furthermore, his hope that he could do more for the Poles as American power grew; as late as the Yalta Conference, at a time when the Red Army was in occupation of all of Poland, he still hoped to get a better deal for Poland.[22] This hope would not be realized; geography and the Red Army ruled. But the issue of Polish independence came to the fore dramatically in the summer of 1944, and while it did not sunder the alliance between the Western Powers and the Soviet Union during the war, it turned the possibility of their continued cooperation in the post-war years from a hope to a highly unlikely prospect.

As described in the preceding chapter, the uprising of the Polish underground army in Warsaw which began on August 1, 1944, produced a major crisis in the alliance against Hitler. The Red Army halted its advance and withdrew its spearheads in the outskirts of Warsaw, shifting its emphasis to the creation of bridgeheads across the Narev river north and the Vistula river south of the Polish capital. The Russians, who had called upon the Poles to rise against the Germans, not only stood aside as the Germans crushed the uprising, they refused to allow British and American planes to land on Soviet airfields as they attempted to drop supplies to the insurgents. As a matter of policy, the Soviet Union even refused to allow British planes from Italy to fly over Soviet-occupied Hungary on their long and dangerous journey to the Polish capital.[23] The result of this general policy, as could be expected, was the crushing of the uprising by the Germans, which was followed by the systematic destruction of what was left of the city.

These events, it should be noted, took place very much in the public view. Unlike the relevant exchanges of diplomats and heads of states, most of which did not appear in print until long after the war, the dramatic events of the two months of fighting in the streets of Warsaw reverberated in Britain and the United States. Nothing could have done so much to undercut the admiration for the Red Army and with it sympathy for the Soviet Union as the spectacle of Soviet acquiescence in the defeat of the Poles. Neither Churchill nor Roosevelt could budge Stalin by their messages about the situation; neither believed that the alliance could or should be broken over it; but nothing about that alliance would ever be the same again.

It was not only that friction over the future of Poland, thrust into the limelight by the Warsaw uprising, highlighted the differences between the Western Allies and the Soviet Union. Even with the signs of approaching victory—perhaps because of them—the suspicion and hesitations of the Soviets in their treatment of the British and American military missions continued, and all attempts at more effective coordinations of military activities were frustrated.[24] These difficulties shed an interesting light backwards on the military talks conducted by the British and French with the Soviets in Moscow in the summer of 1939; cooperation on military affairs was most definitely not high on the list of Stalin's priorities. Ironically it was precisely this unwillingness to work out practical arrangements that led to the worst incident in Allied affairs when American planes bombed and strafed a Soviet column believed to be German on November 7, 1944. This tragic event, in which a number of Red Army officers and men were killed, led to the effort to develop a strategic bomb line; but even that attempt never met with Soviet cooperation.[25] These sorts of practical difficulties continued until the end of the war; the problem of what to do about liberated prisoners of war, discussed in the next chapter, being added in the final months.

The future of Poland was, furthermore, not the only liberated area at issue between the Western Powers and the Soviet Union. There were differences over the policy to be followed toward Italy not only between Britain and the United States but also with Russia. While the Western Powers took the lead there—when they could reach agreement—the Soviet Union also insisted on a voice and was eventually accorded one.[26]

The predominance of the Western Powers in Italy has sometimes been cited as a precedent for Soviet control of events in the countries of East and Southeast Europe, but this facile analogy ignores a critical difference. In all the liberated and occupied countries there were Communist Parties. In every area that came under Western control, these parties continued to operate and frequently participated in the government; in Italy, for example, it not only did both of these but remained a major force for decades. The converse was not true in the areas overrun by the Red Army. Precisely because in those states the Communist Parties were minute, the new masters not only put them in charge of the government, army, and police, but quickly pushed out and repressed those movements which represented the bulk of the population (a point which became dramatically obvious in 1989 when the people discovered that their local masters were no longer backed by the Red Army).[a]

As the Red Army in the fall of 1944 occupied first Romania and then Bulgaria and began to push into Hungary and Yugoslavia, the question of whether or not the people there would be able to influence the composition of the new governments came to the fore. The British and Americans discussed this problem at their meeting in September 1944 at Quebec, a conference Roosevelt and Churchill held in part because

---

[a] Yugoslavia was the one exception to this pattern. It had a large Communist Party by 1944 and much of the country was liberated not by the Red Army but by the efforts of the Yugoslavs themselves. These differences had a great influence on Yugoslavia's subsequent history.

Stalin had refused to meet with them. It was at this second Quebec Conference that the Americans originally agreed to the dispatch of British troops to Greece and, in the hope of maintaining Great Britain's power into the post-war years, promised an effort to continue aid beyond the defeat of Germany.[27]

Even before the great offensives of June 1944 in West and East, there had been discussions about the possible switch of Germany's East European satellites to the Allied side. When these had involved the Western Powers, as in the case of Bulgaria which was at war only with them, the Soviets had been kept informed.[28] The converse, however, was not observed: when the Soviet Union began to deal with Romanian diplomats, the Western Powers were not told.[29] Concern over the future of the East European countries had led the British to raise the possibility of a sort of "spheres of influence" agreement with the Russians already early in 1944. In May British Foreign Secretary Anthony Eden and Soviet Ambassador Ivan Maisky had tentatively agreed that Romania would be in the Soviet and Greece in the British sphere, though it was pretended that the arrangement would hold only for wartime.[30]

In the face of American doubts, forcefully expressed by President Roosevelt, Churchill went forward with the concept of an agreement with the Soviet Union which, designed in the Prime Minister's view as a means of restraining the Russians, allocated percentages to the West and the Soviet Union. Proposed by him to Stalin in Moscow in October, the notorious percentage agreement was to have little significance except in two ways.[31] It confirmed Soviet willingness to refrain from interfering in Greece, a policy that it took Greek Communists some time to recognize and accept.[32] The other effect was to show the Soviet leadership that little serious opposition from the West to the imposition of Soviet control was likely; certainly not the message Churchill had intended to give.

The reality was that the Western Powers could do little to interfere in any case. The real question was whether Stalin would pay attention to their protests in order to retain their good will; the events surrounding the Polish uprising of August 1944 showed that he would not. Roosevelt believed that there was little point to constant protests if there were no chance of these being heeded; perhaps in the future the situation would improve, but in the meantime there was in fact little that the Western Powers could do.[33]

This was at the time as true for plans about Germany as its satellites. The British plan for the partition of Germany into occupation zones and the projects for German territory to be turned over to Poland and the Soviet Union are reviewed elsewhere. The major concern of the Western

Powers, that the Soviet Union might sign a separate peace with Germany, was finally fading in 1944. There remained doubts about Soviet plans attached to the National Committee for a Free Germany and the League of German Officers, both organized under Moscow's auspices in 1943; but there came to be no attempt at a counter-organization in the West.[34] If there were to be agreements on the issues concerning the future of Germany, these would have to be worked out in conferences between the three Allied leaders in person, and with Stalin refusing to meet Churchill and Roosevelt, that meant the questions would have to wait until their second (and last) meeting in February 1945.

The relations between the Western Powers and the Soviet Union were further troubled by the friction caused by Soviet espionage in the West, although the extent of this, (referred to in Chapter 10), especially in Britain, was not suspected at the time. There were also arguments about the repatriation demanded by the Russians of any Soviet citizens or agents who attempted to defect to the West.[35] The Soviet government added repeated complaints about Rudolf Hess who was imprisoned in England and should, according to their arguments, have been put on trial immediately. There are signs that Stalin worried alternately about the Western Powers using Hess the way he had tried to use German prisoners in the U.S.S.R. for an alternative government to replace Hitler's and then make peace with it, or their allowing Hess to escape to a neutral country the way Emperor William II had fled to Holland at the end of World War I.[36]

The signs of friction between the Allies were at times very much in the public eye, and the Germans did everything in their power to call attention to them, provide disinformation about them to the Soviets and the Western Powers, and in other ways emphasize the inter-Allied difficulties in the hope of rupturing the alliance they had forged against themselves.[37] They had an obvious interest in splitting the alliance, since, unlike Japan, they were at war with all three. These, of course, realized very clearly that this was precisely what the Germans wanted and for that very reason recognized that, if the Allies expected to win the war, remaining together and overcoming their differences would be essential. By 1944 it was obvious to both sides that the only hope of victory the Axis still had was a split among the Allies, and the very efforts of the Germans to create such a split made the Allied governments more sensitive to the need to work things out. The fact that victory was finally in sight in 1944 thus had a double and contradictory effect on the alliance. On the one hand, the removal of mortal danger made them less inclined to subordinate individual aims to the need for hanging together and hence a greater willingness to disregard the susceptibilities of allies. On the other hand, the imminence of victory and the obvious desperation of the Germans suggested that this was a poor time to allow divergent views of policy and strategy to break up a winning coalition and thereby risk all that had already been attained at huge cost in lives and treasure.

The need to work out differences if at all possible was, it should be noted, perceived even if somewhat differently by the leadership in all three Allied capitals. This is to be seen very clearly in the difficult negotiations which led to the creation of the United Nations Organization, in spite of major differences of opinion which surfaced at the Dumbarton Oaks Conference held in the Washington area from August 21, to October 9, 1944.[38] Already at the Moscow Conference of October 1943 the Allies had agreed that a new international organization should replace the moribund League of Nations, but it was much easier to call for the establishment than to work out the practical details of such a structure. Furthermore, the three major powers approached this question from very different sets of experiences and perspectives.

Only the British had belonged to the League from the beginning and were still formally members in 1944. They looked upon any new structure as an important method for continued American involvement in world affairs, a useful mechanism for resolving at least some disputes, and, hopefully, as a way of smoothing continued cooperation with the Soviet Union, a subject expected to be difficult indeed. There were, however, serious concerns about any new international organizations. On the one hand, the British not only wanted France restored eventually, if not immediately, to a major role and all the Dominions and also India to be represented in such an organization. On the other hand, they were determined, and Churchill was especially insistent on this point, that there be no interference into the affairs of the British colonial structure from the outside. This concern extended both to possible claims on portions of the empire by others, such as China's claim to Hong Kong, and to any prescriptions for the internal development of territories included within the empire.

The Soviet Union had joined the League in 1934 but had been ousted as a result of its attack on Finland in the winter of 1939–40. The denunciations of the League which had preceded its entrance into that organization seemed justified in Moscow's eyes by the subsequent expulsion. While it was clear to Stalin that participation in any new international organization was in theory preferable to staying out, with the obvious risk that such abstention would only facilitate that "ganging-up" on the Soviet Union by others which he always feared, there had to be some protection for the U.S.S.R. in any new structure.

He evidently believed that it was important for the Soviet Union to

play a part in the new organization, and he appears to have been especially interested in the role it could play in preventing any renewed
aggression by a revived Germany. Furthermore, he appears to have had
two major concerns about the whole question. In the first place, he no
more wanted interference of any sort into the internal affairs of his
empire than Churchill wanted in the British one. The result of this was
a general tendency to restrict competence to political matters and to
downplay all others to the extent of having the Soviet Union stay out of
the whole set of new international banking and monetary structures
created at the Bretton Woods Conference reviewed later in this chapter.

His second, and perhaps even more significant interest related to
the organization's internal structure and procedure. He was evidently
concerned that in any voting the U.S.S.R. and the sympathetic regimes
it hoped to establish in Eastern Europe might be hopelessly outnumbered. For this reason, he at first adopted a restrictive attitude
toward membership, only agreeing at Yalta in February 1945 that those
who joined the Allies in war by March 1, 1945, could be invited to the
founding conference. The same worry about what might be called the
optics of voting by all countries appears to have been behind the Soviet
proposal, first made to the horror of the British and American delegations at Dumbarton Oaks on August 28, 1944, that all sixteen Soviet
republics be initial members.[39] This issue, like the preceding one and
the dispute over the veto which is discussed below, was also resolved at
Yalta as described in Chapter 14, but should be seen in the author's
view as a part of Stalin's worries about the way future voting in the new
organization might well look, even if those votes did not mean that
much.[a]

An issue of supreme importance to the Soviet Union, and one on
which Stalin was evidently not prepared to compromise until the last
moment, involved that of unanimity, an issue generally referred to as
that of the veto. While President Roosevelt always favored some form
of the veto, from the beginning of serious discussion of the new organization, the Soviet government was insistent on unanimity on all issues
among the great powers on the executive organ. Their suggestion that
it be called the "Security Council" was accepted by the others at Dumbarton Oaks, and they were willing to accede to proposals that France
and China have permanent seats on the Council; they were also agreeable to a system where majority votes rather than complete unanimity
would be acceptable—provided always that the majority include *all* the

---

[a] It might be noted that had Stalin had his way, the Baltic Republics and the republics of the
Caucasus and Central Asia as well as Moldavia would all have been separately represented
in the UN—as in fact they are becoming on the dissolution of the U.S.S.R.

permanent members. What the Soviet Union said, in effect, was that the other nations, which would be elected on a rotating basis by the body including all members, called the Assembly, could be out-voted by a majority on the Security Council, but no great power, especially the Soviet Union, could be dealt with in this fashion. And that requirement of unanimity was to extend to issues in which it was itself involved.

This insistence, to which the Soviet delegation at Dumbarton Oaks adhered in the face of every objection, was based, it would appear, on two major considerations. One was an element of prestige and one of practical substance. The prestige issue, which at this time may well have been more significant than believed by some, was the definitive recognition of the status of the Soviet Union as a world power. Isolated in pre-war years, clearly making a major contribution and the largest sacrifices in the war to defeat Germany, the U.S.S.R. was to be recognized by all as a state which would properly play a major role on the world stage. This meant that no action should be taken on any subject by the world organization unless the Soviet Union was in accord with it.

The practical issue was, simply put, that the Soviet Union was not going to allow itself to be out-voted on any issue, *especially* including those in which it was itself involved. No urging by either the British or the Americans was going to make Moscow budge on this question, and the Soviet representative in the negotiations, Andrei Gromyko, made it clear that no concessions on it were to be expected. The efforts to show that the public in the United States and Great Britain would not support and might not be willing to join an organization in which a country was to be a judge in a matter in which it was itself involved made no impact on the Soviet delegates, and they were willing to let the conference adjourn without an agreement on the voting question.[40] The final report on the Dumbarton Oaks Conference simply stated that the procedure to be followed on voting in the Security Council was "still under consideration."

The United States had refused to join the League altogether, and those who were in leadership positions in the country in World War II all looked back to that decision as one of the great errors made by America. Their view of that error was redoubled by the fact that it had been a domestic political disaster for them as well; their party, the Democrats, had been crushed in the 1920 election and kept out of power for over a decade. Roosevelt was himself particularly conscious of that turn of the American public. He had been the second man in the Wilson administration's Department of the Navy and he had been the second man on the losing Democratic Party's national ticket in the 1920 election. Furthermore, the one time during the 1930s when Roosevelt had tried as President to obtain the Senate's agreement to have the United States join the World Court, he had suffered a humiliating defeat. With this as background, the careful work of the administration in Washington to get an agreement on a new international organization both with the Allies and at home should be easy to understand.

Cordell Hull was as convinced as Roosevelt that a new international organization would be needed to maintain the peace by settling disputes and bringing collective pressure to bear on any power inclined to take an aggressive path. He worked hard to build up support at home and, with the President's full agreement, tried to avoid what was seen as a grave mistake of the Wilson administration by involving key Republicans in the process of developing and defending the American position. It has become fashionable to denigrate the role of the wartime Secretary of State; this was certainly one field in which he was extremely active and successful. He had obtained Soviet agreement in principle at the Moscow Conference, he had developed a working relationship with key Republican congressional leaders, and he closely monitored the State Department's work on the project.[41]

The stalemate over voting procedure which hampered the Dumbarton Oaks Conference left Roosevelt and Hull, like the British, searching for a solution. In the British government, the belief in the absolute need for what was now being referred to as the United Nations Organization was so strong that the Cabinet, under Churchill's prodding, came to realize that a compromise was desirable but that the Soviet position should be accepted if that proved the only way to get agreement. Though not formulated in quite so explicit a fashion, the American attitude developed along identical lines. It is an interesting indication of the extent to which both governments hoped that, in spite of current and prospective frictions, cooperation with the Soviet Union in the future would be possible, that they were both prepared to jettison their preferred procedure if there were no other way to obtain Soviet participation in the United Nations.

These internal discussions took place between the Dumbarton Oaks and Yalta conferences as both the British and American governments tried to develop compromise proposals which were designed to meet the major Soviet concern, but without crippling the procedures of the United Nations. In one way or another, these new formulae kept a major power which was party to a dispute from stopping discussion of an issue and other procedural matters but retained the unanimity requirement for major actions. It was the hope of President Roosevelt that this would satisfy the Russians and get them to drop the sixteen Soviet republics proposal. The British were agreeable to what they saw as a proposal similar to their own ideas, but Churchill let it be known that, if Stalin insisted, he would be willing to accede to the Soviet position. As the Prime Minister explained to the British Cabinet on November 27, 1944, when a Western bloc was suggested by the Foreign Office: "He was very doubtful himself as to the soundness or practicability of a Western bloc. In his judgement the only real safeguard was agreement between the three Great Powers within the framework of the World Organization. He felt himself that Russia was ready and anxious to work in with us."[42]

When the compromise proposal was discussed at Yalta, Stalin pretended not to have heard of it although it had been submitted to Moscow two months before. In the context of the discussions at Yalta, however, he came to agree to it and also dropped the membership demand for fourteen of the sixteen republics as well. He too clearly thought post-war cooperation within a United Nations Organization was sufficiently in Soviet interests to make at least some concessions to his allies.[43]

On another subject relating to the United Nations the major objections had come from the British. This was the concept of trusteeship, pushed by the Americans and agreeable to the Soviet Union. This proposal was seen at first by the British—and entirely correctly—as yet another American scheme for subverting colonial structures, including their own. The agreement of the Americans to apply this new version of the League's mandate system only to territories taken from the Axis powers removed British objections, if not London's worries. If on this subject it was easier for the Americans and Russians to reach agreement, there was a further one on which, in spite of difficulties, it was the British and Americans who eventually accepted a new set of institutions while the Soviet Union decided to remain outside.

In the first three weeks of July 1944 representatives of most of the United Nations met at Bretton Woods, New Hampshire, to try to develop an international banking and monetary system for the post-war world. It was devoutly hoped that this would preclude the kind of international economic and monetary warfare which had characterized the years before World War II and had in the eyes of many contributed to world economic malaise and the pressure toward war which some had seen in that situation. There is certainly some truth in the view of one scholar that a major objective was "locking the door, or trying to lock it, upon the international trade and fiscal practices of Dr. Schacht."[44] The reference is to the German economic leader of the 1930s who had devised innumerable schemes to defraud foreign investors to assist German trade and rearmament.[45]

For the immediate post-war problems of relief of suffering and devastation, the United Nations Relief and Rehabilitation Administration (UNRRA) had been established at American initiative in 1943 and was already beginning to operate.[46] For the long-term redevelopment of the world economy, however, something far more permanent than such an obviously temporary institution, however important and even vital in the short run, was believed needed. At the Bretton Woods Conference it was decided to establish two permanent institutions, an International Monetary Fund and an International Bank for Reconstruction and Development, the latter usually called the World Bank. While the Monetary Fund was designed to assist international currency transfers and stability, in the process obviating the sorts of competitive devaluations and special currency manipulations which had hampered world trade before the war, the World Bank was expected to provide capital for development and the continued growth of economies UNRRA had helped recover.

If these new institutions, the instruments for which were ratified by numerous nations over the following years, did not always function as effectively as the founders had hoped, this was in large part the result of the war's disruption of the world economy being even greater than anyone had anticipated. They nevertheless contributed enormously to the period of great economic growth which followed the war. Drastically modified in the 1970s because of the greatly altered position of the United States and the dollar in world trade, both the Monetary Fund and even more the World Bank remain major factors in the world economy half a century after their conception. A striking feature of their role is the fact that the very countries of Eastern Europe which were prevented from joining by the Soviet Union after World War II are all or almost all expected to become members by the end of the twentieth century.

Whatever concessions the Western Powers were willing to make to Soviet preferences, and whatever adjustments Stalin was prepared to make to accommodate them in turn, on this question there would be no agreement. Secretary of the Treasury Henry Morgenthau, who had chaired the Bretton Woods Conference, hoped for a while that the Russians could be persuaded to join the new financial institutions; after all, they expected to benefit and did benefit from UNRRA. But there was simply no way in which the Soviet leadership could see its economy linked to that of the rest of the world, and neither the Soviet Union nor the governments it established in Eastern Europe joined the Fund or the Bank. In this field, the gap between the Allies could not be bridged.[47] That divergence was not, however, seen as so serious as to be disruptive of the alliance in a major way as long as agreement could be reached on the establishment of the United Nations Organization (UNO).

The formal meeting to found the UNO was to be held, as agreed at Yalta, in San Francisco in April of 1945. By the time that conference was held, Franklin Roosevelt, its most important sponsor, had died. But he had played a key role in attuning the American public to participating in world affairs, including the UNO. The very fact that this organizing conference was being conducted even as the war in Europe was obviously in its closing stages showed that the alliance of the Western Powers with the Soviet Union, however strained, had held fast to the end.

THE TRIPARTITE PACT POWERS

If the Allies had numerous difficulties in working together, these were minimal when compared to those of the Tripartite Pact powers. There were no institutions comparable to the British–American Combined Chiefs of Staff and the other joint boards and committees. The Tripartite military commissions established between Germany, Italy and Japan in the winter of 1941–42 were good for publicity pictures but practically nothing else.[48] The argument that this was due to geographic factors cannot be sustained in the face of the absence of any real coordination between Germany and Italy in the early years of the war when those two were contiguous—unlike Britain and the United States—and coordination would have been simple to arrange had there been any desire for it. There is no evidence to suggest that either Axis partner had any interest in such coordination; on the contrary, both Hitler and Mussolini far preferred to direct the respective war efforts of their countries entirely independently of each other.[49]

The rapid deterioration of Italy's position in the Axis as her armies were defeated first in Greece, then in East Africa, and finally in North Africa has been recorded. On the one hand, Italy could no longer conduct war independently, as Mussolini had at one time imagined, on the other the Germans were justifiably worried that a total Italian collapse would open up Europe to Allied invasion from the south. Such a situation would require the dispatch of substantial German forces both to whatever new fronts might be created by Allied landings and also as replacement for Italian occupation forces in France and Southeast Europe. Under these circumstances the Germans tried unsuccessfully to prop up the Italian war effort while watching with great suspicion for any signs of defection from the Axis.[50]

The relationship between Germans and Italians was almost always strained. They had fought on opposite sides in World War I; the Italians looked on the Germans as barbarians, and overbearing ones at that, while the Germans considered the Italians inefficient and incompetent. Germany's inability to provide the coal Italy needed in spite of very considerable efforts was matched by the unwillingness of the Germans to treat the vast numbers of Italian workers in Germany decently. This latter problem, a steady irritant in German–Italian relations, would be greatly exacerbated by the deliberately ruthless treatment accorded to the soldiers disarmed by the Germans after the Italian surrender and then deported to slave labor in Germany.[51]

As if these problems were not sufficient, there were, in addition, personal and ideological ones. The personal problem was that some of the highest German officers who dealt with the Italians, notably Field Marshal Erwin Rommel, simply could not abide them, an attitude which was quickly and widely known. The ideological question on which there was a wide difference concerned the proper handling of the Jewish question. Mussolini had introduced a series of anti-Semitic laws in 1938 as a sign of his ideological affinity with the German dictator. These rules, though often enforced on Italy's tiny Jewish community, appear to have been no more popular than the German goosestep, introduced into Italy at the same time and for the same reason under the pompous title of "passo Romano," the Roman step.[52]

The divergence between the Axis partners became ever more pronounced during the war. German initiation of the systematic killing of Jews was no more discussed with the Italian government than any other of their major political, military, or other initiatives, but the Italians were expected to participate fully. On the whole, in spite of Mussolini's willingness to go along, they mostly simply would not do so. In the Italian-occupied portions of France, Yugoslavia and Greece the local commanders, who knew perfectly well what the Germans were doing, refused to turn over the Jews to the Germans to be murdered, and endless arguments over this issue led to no agreement. The Italians were confirmed in their prior belief that the Germans were still barbarians, and the Germans were reinforced in their view of the Italians as indifferent and incompetent allies.

The most significant divergence between Germany and Italy, however, was the one over strategy. As the Allied threat to Italy grew in 1942–43, obvious to all with the British breakthrough at El Alamein in early

November 1942 and the American landing in Northwest Africa a few days later, the Italians began to urge Germany to concentrate its forces on the war against Britain and the United States while working out a compromise peace with the Soviet Union. First put forward to Hitler and other German leaders in December 1942, these proposals always fell on deaf ears, as did the similar Japanese proposals which the Germans had by that time been hearing for over a year. The Germans saw the threat in the Mediterranean, but their response was not what Mussolini wanted.

In early 1941, when there appeared to be all sorts of opportunities for Axis advances in the Mediterranean area, the Germans had committed small forces there, primarily because Hitler saw the area as Italy's living space and hence not worth a major investment of German resources. Now that disaster appeared to threaten Italy, his worry was that the Allies could use Italy as an airbase for attacks on Germany from the south, and might seize the portions of Southeast Europe under Italian control, thereby threatening Germany's access to the mineral resources of that area. Under these circumstances he was prepared to allot a far larger share of his military resources to the Mediterranean theater, a commitment most obvious in the building up of an Axis army in Tunisia. This effort was, however, designed as a protection for Germany's southern flank, not as a support for Italy's ambitions; under no circumstances was he willing to accept the basic reorientation in strategy urged on Germany by both the Italian and the Japanese governments.

Many of the transport aircraft which might have been utilized to fly supplies into the beleaguered German garrison in Stalingrad were instead deployed to Sicily for ferry duties to Tunisia, but Hitler was not about to consider a compromise on the Eastern Front. There was, instead, to be a new German summer offensive on that front. The same difference, if on a smaller scale, affected German–Italian relations in the turmoil that was World War II Yugoslavia. The Italians wanted to arm Mihailovic against the partisans and then crush him later; the Germans preferred to fight both simultaneously.[53]

The collapse of Italian resistance on Sicily in July 1943 followed by that of the whole Fascist system later that month marked a final parting of the ways between Germany and Italy. The extraordinarily clumsy way in which the Italian government left the war merely facilitated Germany's use of considerable Italian territory and resources for a continued war which devastated the country. The puppet state Mussolini organized under German auspices in northern Italy after his rescue from imprisonment could have no influence on German strategy or policy. The most dramatic illustration of this was to be the surrender negotiations which the Germans there carried out behind his back in 1945. They had shot innumerable Italians in various so-called reprisals; they left Mussolini to be shot by his own people.

The relationship between the European Axis powers and Japan was not marked by any closer cooperation than that between Germany and Italy. In the political field, there was very little willingness to work together. Japanese advice to the Germans to allow greater freedom to the subject peoples of Europe, as Japan claimed she was granting in her sphere, fell on deaf ears. Nothing remotely resembling the extensive discussion of post-war plans among the Allies ever took place among the powers of the Tripartite Pact. In November 1942, after a conference of the heads of Japanese diplomatic delegations in Europe, Ambassador Oshima forwarded their recommendations that the Japanese, Germans and Italians must work together as effectively as the Allies were doing.[54] It regularly proved most difficult to iron out minor differences;[55] certainly on the major issues between Germany and Japan nothing changed.

The basic strategy issue remained unsolved in 1943 and 1944. The Germans wanted the Japanese to become offensive again, by which they meant that Japan should move against the British, Americans, or Russians. Certainly Japan was not about to attack the Soviet Union. The Japanese had been badly beaten by the Russians in the 1939 fighting, had no desire whatever for a repetition, feared that the Soviet Union might allow the Americans use of air bases for attacks on the home islands of Japan and, therefore, went to great lengths to keep peace with the Soviet Union. They were most assuredly not going to interfere with the steady stream of American supplies passing by Japan to help the Soviet Union in its fight against Germany. In these years, as earlier, the Japanese were certain that the Germans should make peace with Russia so that Germany could concentrate on fighting Britain and the United States.[56]

As for fighting the British, the Japanese waited until 1944 to launch a major offensive into India from the positions which they had occupied in Burma in early 1942. From the perspective of Berlin, this was too little and too late. Mounted in the summer of 1942 to follow on the earlier Japanese conquest of Malaya and Burma, such an operation might have had a significant impact on the war. In 1944 the Japanese offensive was a strategic irrelevance.

The only other major Japanese offensive was that in China in 1944, and that operation was designed more to prevent American air attacks from Chinese bases and to substitute Japanese land lines of communications for the sea lanes vulnerable to American submarines than part of any broader strategic concept. As for direct engagement of the Americans, the Japanese in 1943 and 1944 were already permanently on the defensive.

The only other possible area of military cooperation was in the war at sea. Time and again the Germans tried to have the Japanese devote greater attention to the war against Allied shipping. Japanese submarines, however, continued to be utilized primarily in fleet support operations and, increasingly, in supplying Japanese garrisons cut off by the advancing American and Australian forces. The Japanese naval leadership never understood the German navy's strategy of trying to do to the Allies what the latter were ever more successful in doing to Japan: cutting the vital oceanic supply routes. The whole field of submarine warfare against shipping as well as the problems of defending against this type of operation was one in which Japanese naval leadership displayed a consistently high level of incompetence unique in the annals of war at sea.

In a long conversation between von Ribbentrop and Oshima on May 19, 1943, the whole situation of the war was reviewed at a time when the balance in the conflict was clearly shifting. The European Axis powers had just lost their last foothold in Africa and the Germans had barely stabilized the situation on the Eastern Front. The Japanese had evacuated their last forces from Guadalcanal and Kiska. They had sent a special mission under General Okamoto Kiyotomi to Germany across the Soviet Union and Turkey in the vain hope of improving cooperation between the two countries; he was present at this meeting.[57]

Their exchange illuminates the divergence in the strategies of Berlin and Tokyo as well as the lack of understanding in each capital of the situation of its partner in the war. Oshima explained why Japan could not attack the Soviet Union and would prefer to mediate a German–Soviet peace. Von Ribbentrop urged a Japanese offensive somewhere, insisted on the necessity for a new attack on the Eastern Front, and denounced the Japanese ambassador to the Soviet Union for his interest in peace between Germany and Russia. Oshima frankly told von Ribbentrop that he doubted Germany could defeat the Soviets and urged the Germans to proclaim the independence of the Baltic States and the Ukraine the way Japan had done in Burma and the Philippines, a proposal the German Foreign Minister rejected out of hand.

It is obvious from this open exchange between two men who had known each other for years, had inaugurated closer relations between their two countries by negotiating the Anti-Comintern Pact behind the backs of their respective foreign offices in 1935–36, and appear to have had a very high personal regard for each other, that there was no real understanding of the other country's true position.[58] The Germans had no comprehension of the weakness of Japan after six years of war and major defeats at the hands of the Americans; the war in East Asia had never drawn their careful attention, and whatever the insights of a few in the German hierarchy, those at the top had no real sense of what was going on in the Pacific. The Japanese, on the other hand, had not recognized the priority of racial dogma and expansionism for their German ally, and as a result never understood German policies. That in the face of such mutual ignorance and incomprehension there would be even less cooperation than between the Allies should not be surprising.

The signs of approaching defeat brought little effective change in the situation. Although the Germans tried to provide some technical assistance to their ally by giving Japan details of at least some of their new weapons, Japan's industrial system was in no condition to take advantage of such knowledge in the little time which remained available. The only real effect of such exchanges was in their unknowingly providing information to the British and Americans who were decyphering them.[59] In economic as in military affairs, in strategy as in politics, the countries of the Tripartite Pact went each its own way to destruction and defeat.

14

THE HALT ON THE EUROPEAN FRONTS

The German armies had suffered catastrophic defeats in the summer of 1944, and these defeats were accompanied by huge losses. It is not possible to give exact figures, but the killed, captured, and missing (most of whom were either dead or prisoners) from the beginning of June to the middle of September were in excess of one million and are likely to have been over one and a half million. These defeats on land in the east, west, and south were accompanied by huge losses of materiel. Vast numbers of tanks and guns were destroyed in the fighting and additional quantities either fell into the hands of Germany's enemies or were destroyed by the Germans themselves, when surrounded or cut off, in order to prevent their capture.

Great losses were by no means confined to the land battle. In the air, the German defenses had been crushed through the intervention of long-range fighters in early 1944 — on top of the steady attrition suffered by the German air force in prior years. This defeat had reduced the once mighty Luftwaffe to the thankless role of trying to get back into the struggle for control of the air with masses of inexperienced and inadequately trained pilots. The American and British air forces dominated the skies over Western, Central and Southern Europe and the Red Air Force had by this time overwhelming superiority in the East. The destruction by the American air force of much of Germany's synthetic oil industry made any revival of the German air effort doubtful: planes were often destroyed on the ground because they lacked fuel.

At sea, the last German surface raiders and larger ships had long since been swept from the oceans or confined to support duties in the Baltic Sea. German submarines had as yet been unable to recover from their 1943 defeat. October 1944 was a month when they managed to sink only one merchant ship of just over 6000 tons on all the world's oceans. Driven out of the Black Sea and Mediterranean, German submarines had also lost their bases on the French Atlantic coast. Simultaneously, the various classes of escorting warships and carriers earlier ordered by the Western Allies were becoming available, manned by ever more experienced crews—as very few were now lost—and able to protect the Allied merchant fleet, which was rapidly growing as construction continued and losses dropped. Even a revived submarine campaign would, therefore, have had to start from a position far more favorable for the Allies and much less hopeful for the Germans than in the fall of 1943, when the Allied construction curve had finally overtaken that of their losses from all causes.

If Germany's military situation in the broader sense looked hopeless, her diplomatic position appeared to be even worse. Her European allies had been knocked out of the war one by one. Italy had left first; and the shadow regime of Mussolini installed on German bayonets in northern Italy was of little more use than the shadow cabinets in exile arranged for Vichy France, Romania, and Bulgaria.[1] Not even a propaganda façade could be erected to replace the Finnish forces which had once fought alongside Germany, while the military forces of the puppet states of Slovakia and Croatia were in revolt or near dissolution. Only in Hungary was a substantial satellite army still fighting alongside the Germans in Europe. In East Asia, the Japanese triumph in China could not offset her crushing defeat in Burma and the steady series of American victories in the Pacific. No substantial assistance could be expected from Germany's only significant ally at a time when that power was bracing itself for what it correctly assumed would be a massive American assault on the Philippines.

The converse of the crumbling of Germany's alliances was the constancy, even increase, in the alliance opposed to her. As shown in the preceding chapter, the alliance of the Western Powers and the Soviet Union was holding together in spite of great tensions. At the point of greatest tension—Poland—the alliance was not only remaining firm, but the immediate military risk related to their friction, the possibility that the Polish divisions in Italy might withdraw from the battle, was being effectively contained. There were now two Polish armies, one under Soviet control and one aligned with Britain and the United States, but both were fighting the Germans; only inside Poland itself were they battling each other.

Furthermore, the Allies were beginning to receive added military power and diplomatic reinforcement from new sources. The slowly rebuilding French army provided a welcome addition on the southern portion of the Western Front and relieved the Allies of rear area security duties there. A small Brazilian expeditionary force was adding its weight to the continuing struggle on the Italian front,[2] where there were also now some Italian soldiers on the Allied side. One by one the remaining neutrals were either openly joining the United Nations or at least reducing their assistance to Germany. Spain and Sweden in particular were no longer providing Germany with the extensive supplies they had once sent her; Turkey had cut off the chrome shipments; and Switzerland, now that Allied soldiers stood on at least one border with her, could afford to take a firmer line. The optics of the war had changed dramatically; the Germans were obviously no longer in a position to retaliate effectively against any neutral who yielded to the pressure of the Allies; and all not under direct German or Japanese control were finding it expedient to get on the best possible terms with those powers which were obviously about to win the war.[3]

This sense of approaching victory, at least in Europe and surely before too long also in the Pacific, also had its effect on the home fronts of the major belligerents. In the United States, there was now a somewhat unrealistic expectation that the war in Europe had been practically won; in Great Britain, there was a degree of war weariness—accentuated by the V-1s and V-2s landing there—and a real hope that the war was about to end at last. The British public paid little attention to the demands the war in East Asia could make on them if fought through to the end; they could not know that the fall of 1944 was the time when detailed planning for the actual transfer of British Commonwealth forces to that theater was begun. In the Soviet Union, the liberation of the last portions of German-occupied territories, a victory dramatically demonstrated by the march of tens of thousands of German POWs through the streets of Moscow in July, gave a promise of better times to come. Reconstruction in the areas freed in 1943 and early 1944 was only beginning; and the degree of privation and sacrifice was still very high; but the signs all pointed to victory. In the early years of World War II, the Germans had sounded victory trumpet fanfares on the radio; now the Russians regularly marked *their* victories with the sound of artillery volleys in Moscow.

The changes at the fronts also had their effects on Germany. The success of the invasion in the West, followed almost immediately by the destruction of Army Group Center and the dramatic advance of the Red Army in the East, aroused great anxiety. Disappointment that the expectation of crushing the Allied landing attempt and of inflicting great damage with the new weapons had not been realized, both symbolized for many by the fall of Cherbourg, had a very depressing effect which was reinforced by the unhindered daylight appearance of hundreds of Allied planes over the Reich.[4]

It was in the early stages of this obviously deteriorating situation that the attempt to kill Hitler and to overthrow his government took place. Some of those involved had been opponents of the regime for years, in some instances from long before the beginning of the war. Some had joined as they saw the horrors accompanying German victories, especially in the East, and others came to participate in view of the unwillingness of the regime to face up to what they saw as the imminence of defeat. The more active members of the opposition realized that in view of the mass support enjoyed by the regime only an insiders' coup had any chance of success; once power had been seized, the mass of the population which had been deluded by propaganda and kept ignorant of critical developments could be informed of the true facts and rallied to a new system. During the war, it was by definition those who had access to weapons and explosives who would have to launch a coup, and there was an increasing recognition of the need to begin by killing the dictator whose orders and whose strand of loyalties held the system together. They had tried for the first time in March of 1943 to kill Hitler by placing a bomb on his airplane, but the fuse did not work properly and the conspirators were left with the ticklish task of recovering the explosive device. Several other attempts failed thereafter; a new element came into the picture with the appointment of Colonel von Stauffenberg to be Chief of Staff of the Replacement Army.

An energetic officer who had been seriously wounded in the Tunisian campaign, von Stauffenberg had become the motor of the conspiracy. The great problem was that there were so few who were both energetic and dedicated that he had to combine his access to Hitler's circle in East Prussia as an opportunity to attempt the assassination with a quick trip to Berlin thereafter to direct the takeover itself, thereby guaranteeing an interval to any surviving supporters of the regime. The planned takeover was to be carried out under the cover of a regularly developed plan for dealing with such emergencies as massive disturbances among the millions of forced laborers in German-controlled Europe by the transfer of full powers to the military districts, a procedure familiar to Germans from having been in effect in World War I.

If the preparations were thus more sensible than some critics have maintained, there were nevertheless problems beyond the anticipated double role of von Stauffenberg himself. In the first place, many of those who might have played a major role had been caught and dismissed and in some cases arrested in the preceding years, and there is considerable evidence that Himmler and his secret police knew at least some details of the planned coup. Secondly, the number of individuals in the governmental and military hierarchy actually or potentially sympathetic to any overthrow of the regime was very small. If one of Germany's most prominent commanders, Field Marshal von Weichs, then Commander-in-Chief in Southeast Europe, noted in his diary on July 22, 1944, that even a successful assassination would not have kept the coup from failing because no one would have followed the orders of the conspirators,[5] one can see how slight the chances of the opposition were. But they were determined to try in order, if nothing else, to demonstrate that there were those in Germany who were so appalled by the misdeeds of the regime that they would risk their lives in the attempt to overthrow it. When the explosion failed to kill Hitler, the overwhelming majority of Germany's military leaders sided with him rather than his opponents. As both sides sent their orders over the teleprinters in Germany's last "election" as a united country until 1990, most generals chose to support the Hitler regime and to reinforce rather than arrest its police.

The triumph of Hitler and his followers in this crisis had a number of critical consequences. It obviously meant in the first instance that his opponents, who had come into the open, were almost all now arrested and killed if they did not commit suicide lest they betray comrades under torture. A wave of arrests, fake trials and summary executions swept through all walks of life, ironically depriving the country of many of precisely those it would most need.[6] Hitler himself now felt reinforced in the belief that destiny had called him to lead the German people, a belief which appears to have been reciprocated by vast masses of Germans who, according to the best evidence, were relieved rather than disappointed by the failure of the attempted coup.[7]

The consolidation of the regime, implicit in these developments, was made explicit by a major further shift of power in Germany to the SS, with Himmler placed in charge of the Replacement Army and other changes accelerating the process of what the historian of the Nazi Party, Dietrich Orlow, has called "partification".[8] If the first great triumph of the National Socialist regime had been the accession to power in January 1933, its last great victory was that over the remnants of domestic opposition in July 1944. Those who now controlled the nation's destiny more completely than ever before were determined to mobilize its resources on the most extreme scale in order to turn the tide in Germany's and their own favor, aware that the fate accorded their opponents quite likely awaited them. Unlike the Japanese ambassador in Berlin, who had a surprisingly clear view of the patriotic and humanitarian motives of the resistance,[9] the Nazi leaders had neither understanding nor mercy. They would fight on all fronts for victory or total disaster.

The Western Allies had a reasonably accurate picture of the situation, partly from their own intelligence services, partly from their reading of the Japanese reports,[10] but we do not know how the Soviet Union at the time saw the event. In any case, the Allies could all see that German resistance on all the fronts continued. For them, too, the war would grind on.

The German push for a more complete mobilization of resources for war had begun before the coup attempt of July 20. The production of war materials had been rationalized under Speer's vigorous management, and the results were showing in large-scale production of the major standardized weapons in the face of Allied bombing—though without the bombing, it would have been higher still. Speer made a general effort to increase the utilization of available resources, in particular of manpower for industry, in July.[11] Simultaneously, Goebbels, who had earlier been excluded from the total war measures, argued strongly for extensive new mobilization steps in the same month and received new powers along with Himmler right after July 20.[12] These steps not only drew additional resources into the German war effort but also met some criticism among the population that the burdens of war were not being equally shared by all.

On this last point the Germans soon had little to complain about. Several hundred thousand additional men were drawn into military service, primarily from industry, and formed into new *Volksgrenadier* (people's grenadier) divisions which were expected to help stabilize the front and then turn to the offensive. A new military defense supplement, a sort of militia for home defense, was also organized under the title of *Volkssturm*.[13] This supplement to the army, whose numerous precursors were subsumed into the general system established by a decree of September 25, 1944, was to include all males from 16 to 60 who could possibly bear arms if any could be supplied. As the Allies approached and entered German territory from both east and west, *Volkssturm* units were expected to provide local support and reinforcement to the regular army and the armed units of the SS. The main concern of many obliged to serve in the *Volkssturm* was, however, not effective fighting but the risk of being shot as a partisan if captured; the German population knew all too well how Germans had treated those they considered partisans in the preceding five years of war.

The extension of military service was not, however, confined to the men who trained in their spare time for the *Volkssturm* while still working in factories and fields. In spite of Hitler's original reluctance, more and more women were drawn not only into war industries but into the armed services as clerks, communications specialists, and in numerous other functions.[14] This was not all. Beginning in 1943, large numbers of teen-age boys had already been enrolled as *Flakhelfer*, or anti-aircraft auxiliaries.[15] Often terrified and sometimes killed or wounded, these youngsters "manned" anti-aircraft guns and search-lights around German cities. Their service contributed substantially to the shooting down of Allied planes; occasionally they found their own homes demolished and their families killed at the end of a night's service. By October 1944, the boys were being joined by girls. Several hundred thousand women were already serving as military auxiliaries in hospitals and communications centers; now some were being trained to fire the anti-aircraft guns.[16]

The Germans were not only mobilizing the last reserves of their own men and women, they were seriously thinking about the surviving Russian prisoners of war in their hands. Many of these had voluntarily or involuntarily been assimilated into the German army as auxiliaries or, as previously mentioned, been organized into battalions attached to German regiments. At Hitler's insistence, and in accord with Nazi ideological preconceptions, no promises as to the future of the conquered portions of Russia were ever made to them—after all, since German settlers were to displace the Slavic inhabitants of Eastern Europe, any promises would come back to haunt the Germans. This attitude meant that those Russian prisoners like General Vlasov, who insisted on some commitments about the future of their country, could not be allowed to operate freely and, in addition, that there could be no effective political warfare against the Red Army.

Now that the last sliver of occupied Soviet territory had been cleared by the Red Army, and Hitler's summer hopes of reconquering the Ukraine after driving the Allies back into the Channel had been dashed, there was some slight relaxation in German attitudes. Perhaps something could still be salvaged, and Heinrich Himmler, always on the lookout for new recruits, overcame his ideological fantasies sufficiently to meet Vlasov and support his movement in a minor way.[17] Nothing much came of this, and Hitler clearly continued to have great reservations;[18] but the willingness to turn for support to those hitherto always held to be *Untermenschen*, sub-humans, shows the extent to which the Third Reich needed and wanted every possible recruit it could get.[19]

If the Germans were drawing their boys and girls into military service and reconsidering their attitude toward those they considered sub-human, it will be easy to understand their ruthless exploitation of what little non-German territory they still occupied. In these months whatever was left to steal was stolen in Czechoslovakia, Norway, Denmark and the portions of the Netherlands and Yugoslavia still under German control. This policy was extended to the remaining nominal allies, Mussolini's north Italian "Social Republic" and what remained of pre-war Hungary. Between expressing hope for victory if there were a break in the alliance of the United States, Britain and the Soviet Union or as a result of the introduction of new weapons, Mussolini regaled Japanese diplomats with a litany of bitter complaints about the endless requisitions of goods and the slaughter of hostages by the Germans, which were wrecking any chance of support for his regime from the people of northern Italy.[20]

In German-occupied Hungary, the Germans, particularly the SS, tightened their hold on the economy. On the one hand they launched a program for the deportation and mass-murder of Hungary's Jews, the last large remaining Jewish community in Central Europe. This process, in turn, provided the opportunity for them not only to seize Jewish property but to blackmail the owners of Hungary's largest industrial complex, the Manfred Weiss firm, into turning over controlling shares to the SS in exchange for their lives. While a tiny number of Jews thus escaped, Germany acquired a stranglehold on the Hungarian economy, rejected all Hungarian protests against such an obvious infringement on their sovereignty, and exploited the economy and what was left of its fighting strength for their own war effort.[21]

Accompanying the effort to draw additional manpower and resources was a redirection of allocations within German war production. As the effort to turn the tide with new weapons went forward, there was also a significant shift in airplane production. In late June 1944 the decision was made to order fighters rather than bombers, a move to the defensive which was accentuated as the attacks on Germany's oil industry made it appear all the more important to counter the Allied air offensive.[22] Ironically this shift would not only fail in its primary purpose, but it also had a direct and negative impact on Germany's defending army on the Eastern Front. There the Germans had relied on their bombing force as a form of artillery; with the number of available bombers steadily falling and few replacements, the situation for them became ever more precarious.

THE EASTERN FRONT

But this change would become obvious only when the Soviets launched their great winter offensive; in the meantime, the German front in the East was temporarily consolidated and holding on. In Hungary, in the face of the offensive of the Red Army, supported by two Romanian armies, the Germans and some Hungarian units had built up a front after Romania switched sides, Bulgaria had been occupied by the Soviets, and the Germans had been forced to evacuate Greece, Albania and southern Yugoslavia. Local German and Hungarian successes blunted the thrusts of Second Ukrainian Front into the Hungarian plain. Simultaneously, the efforts of the Fourth Ukrainian Front to break into Slovakia and through the Carpathians had been slowed practically to a halt. The fact is that the offensive power of the advancing Red Army in the southern segment of the front had been exhausted; the different railway gage in much of the area over which it was advancing added to supply problems; and the Germans, at Hitler's personal insistence, had allocated a disproportionately large part of their armor to this portion of the Eastern Front.

At this time and thereafter, Hitler was especially concerned about protecting the remaining oil fields in southern Hungary, and he appears to have had something of a fixation about Budapest, the Hungarian capital. The puppet government of Arrow Cross leader Ferenc Szálasi was trying to operate under German auspices, collaborating in the murdering of Jews with greater enthusiasm than the much more dangerous task of fighting the Red Army. During October and November, Russian forces pushed forward to the outskirts of Budapest, surrounding it in December, but the Germans had succeeded in their holding operation in three important ways. They had built up a new front in the wake of their disaster in Romania and Bulgaria, they had kept Hungary from changing sides in October somewhat on the Finnish model of September,[23] and they had contributed to the slowing down of the advancing Red Army.

Hungarian formations contributed only a small part of this effort, as Szálasi admitted when he saw Hitler on December 4. He promised to fight on, but urged Hitler to make no compromise with the Anglo-Saxons, crushing them, but doing everything possible "to reach an understanding with the Soviet Union."[24] While Hitler agreed that no compromise was possible with the Western Powers, he was less definite about one with the Soviet Union; he was "willing to reconsider the whole question and adopt some new line of action" but the Red Army had to be driven back first.[a] At the front itself, however, the German effort to relieve Budapest had had no more success than the earlier

---

[a] Hitler also regaled Szálasi with a lengthy account of the past, explaining that the British were responsible for the outbreak of the war, having introduced conscription in 1935/36 (*sic*; in reality in 1939), and that the weakness and defection of Germany's allies had caused the setbacks of the last two years.

attempt of the Red Army to seize the Hungarian capital on the anniversary of the Bolshevik revolution.

On the central portion of the Eastern Front, the Red Army concentrated on building up its bridgeheads across the Vistula and Narev rivers in preparation for future offensives, but the spearheads aimed toward Warsaw had been halted, and the Russians observed the agony of Warsaw from a safe distance. While at Hitler's orders the city was, in effect, razed to the ground, the Red Army in that sector remained quiet; the key concerns for it were the four bridgeheads across the Vistula, several of which were expanded slightly in heavy fighting after earlier German attempts to eliminate them had failed.[25] But, in general, the last three months of 1944 saw the central portion of the Eastern Front from the Baltic Sea to the Carpathians stable, with the Soviets rebuilding the transportation system and destroying the Polish underground army behind their lines and the Germans attempting to create an effective defensive system on their side. Although a Soviet patrol had briefly crossed the pre-war border into East Prussia on August 17, the German defense held until mid-October when the Russians drove onto German territory almost to Gumbinnen, where the front stabilized for several months.[26]

Further north, the portion of western Latvia held by the cut-off German Army Group North was compressed somewhat by Russian attacks; but the Germans refused to evacuate the region, while the Soviets, in a series of local offensives, proved unable to destroy the garrison.[27] The special role of this German-held bridgehead, already referred to in Chapter 12, is examined below in connection with the German hopes for a new form of submarine warfare. In the far north, the German troops withdrawing from the Finnish front were pulled back to the Lyngen position, at first under Soviet pressure, but after the end of October without contact. A buffer zone, devastated by the Germans and soon after controlled by a token police force sent by the Norwegian government-in-exile, separated the German and Soviet forces. The Red Army had other priorities; the Germans could continue to hold most of Norway and looked forward to utilizing its naval bases for that resumption of attacks on Allied shipping which they hoped to carry out with the new submarines.

The basic fact was that the military advance of the Soviet Union had run out of steam as German forces fell back and reformed. The transportation system in the huge area liberated by the Red Army since June had to be restored, replacements had to be provided for the heavy casualties suffered during the summer offensive, and the great losses of equipment had also to be made good. Furthermore, any new offensives required extensive planning, the stockpiling of supplies, especially artillery ammunition, and very extensive regrouping of Soviet forces. This last was a result of geographic factors which created a converse of the problem the Germans had once faced as they headed east. Given the territorial funnel-like opening up of Europe as one moves from Central Europe eastwards, any invader of Russia must deal with the fact that the front—measured from north to south—becomes larger the further east the advance goes. When heading west the opposite is true. The major front in the North European plain between the Carpathians and the Baltic Sea becomes steadily narrower. With the exception of the Soviet units facing the remaining Germans in Courland, the armies which had fought on the northern end of the front from Leningrad through the Baltic States now had to be redeployed. New command arrangements had to be worked out for the final assault on Germany; and if Stalin in the planning for this decided to arrogate to himself the coordination of the central thrust—a role hitherto played by a special Stavka representative—this was a sign as much of the narrower front as of Stalin's personal interest in a direct role in the final assault on Berlin. But during the interval in which the planning and preparations for that offensive were under way, the Eastern Front was uncharacteristically quiet.[28]

There is no clear evidence on the subject, but the Russian four months halt at the Vistula may also have had other motives. The railways behind the advancing Red Army in the Balkans were the same gage as those behind the no longer advancing front in Poland, and therefore required as much work in either reloading railway transport or altering to the wider Russian gage. Perhaps the Soviet leadership believed that it was only appropriate for the Western Allies to do some of the heavy fighting; they had certainly done an enormous amount themselves. It was no secret that Germany was trying desperately hard to create new divisions and to equip them with the newest weapons. It would certainly assist the Red Army's drive into Central Europe if these new units, together with the rebuilt divisions salvaged by the Germans out of their summer defeats, were launched against the armies in the West instead of being fed into the front in the East. As Soviet sources become accessible in the coming years, new light may be shed on this long "quiet on the Eastern Front."

THE WESTERN FRONT

In the West, several factors combined to stall the Allied advance in the very weeks when, as we now know, the Germans were preparing their own offensive. The most important single factor holding back the Allies was the supply situation. As they had advanced rapidly in August, the Allied armies had been unable to seize additional ports. Brest did not fall for months and then turned out to be so badly wrecked that it was not reopened. Other ports continued to be held by German garrisons deliberately left behind with instructions to hold on precisely to prevent use of the port facilities. The great harbor of Marseilles had been wrecked by the Germans almost as much as Cherbourg but soon came to be an essential element in the supply picture.[a] The other major port, and the one which the Allies had counted on as the main base for a drive into Germany, had fallen into their hands intact but could not be used because the Germans controlled its approaches—Antwerp. For months Montgomery would not provide the Canadian army with the logistic and other support it needed to drive the Germans from its approaches; and while the Canadians, eventually assisted by other Allied forces, battered their way forward, all the Allied armies had to be supplied to a large extent from Cherbourg and over the beaches, hundreds of miles from the front.[29]

The supply problem was accentuated by two difficulties inherent in the invasion project but made even worse by the slowness in clearing the ports, especially Antwerp. Since shipping was one of the great bottlenecks, use of the small ports on the Channel coast, the beaches, and the only partially cleared harbor facilities at Cherbourg and later Marseilles tied up ships for inordinate lengths of time. Secondly, the enormous distance from the factories in the United States to the front meant that, in the best of circumstances, it took close to four months for an item ordered in France to reach the battlefield. This long supply route in turn tied up vast quantities en route—usually there were about two thousand tanks in the pipeline from the United States to the front.[30]

The rapid advance in August combined with the repair needs of the French railway system to force a reliance on motorized transport, primarily thousands of large trucks. These were dispatched over designated one-way routes to forward supply centers. The "Red Ball Express" was both the most famous and the most effective of these; when it ceased operating on November 16, the same day that the Normandy beaches finally closed down, it had carried over 400,000 tons of supplies.[31]

Although this system of motorized transport together with the railways and some airlift and barge traffic enabled the Allied forces to maintain

---

[a] The post-war British literature on the controversy over "Anvil"–"Dragoon" has yet to engage fully the fact that as early as September 1944 the southern French ports provided the largest contribution to American supplies for the invading armies. See the revealing table in Ruppenthal, *The European Theater of Operations* 2: 124. The American XV Corps was transferred from 3rd to 7th Army solely so that it could use Marseilles as its base (ibid., p. 17).

their military effectiveness, these measures could not move enough material to the front fast enough to sustain the August rate of advance. The great arguments over a narrow versus a broad front in the West was largely academic—like the dispute over the German advance in the East after late July 1941. Until major ports, especially Antwerp, were operational and the railway system was functioning at a high level of efficiency, there was no prospect of a major advance against the stiffening German resistance on either a broad or a narrow front.[32]

The difficulties with supply affected not only material but manpower. Although Allied casualties had not been as high in the initial assault as had been anticipated, thereafter first the heavy fighting in Normandy and then the combat after the August rush created a massive need for replacements. In the British army, this meant pressure to break up some divisions to provide replacements for others, a process under way by late August in spite of strenuous objections from Churchill, who saw this process, begun in August and continuing during the winter, as leading to a reduced British weight in Allied discussions of strategy.[33] There could certainly be no question of transferring units from the European to the Southeast Asian theater at this time as the Chief of the Imperial General Staff wanted; until victory over Germany had been attained, Great Britain simply had to concentrate its shrinking manpower resources in Europe.[34]

The American manpower situation was also tight though for entirely different reasons. The American army had concentrated on building divisions for combat and had shipped these to Europe as rapidly as possible. Now that these divisions were in combat, providing an adequate stream of replacements was complicated not only by the tight shipping situation but by what most would consider defective replacement policies. Injured men were not systematically returned to their own units when they recovered from their wounds; divisions were kept in combat far too long instead of being periodically rotated for rest and refitting; and the rear area services were over staffed even if necessarily large because of the enormous distance from the American base to the front. Pouring replacements into front units on an undifferentiated basis as these units were kept in constant combat was excessively costly, as the inexperienced replacements themselves became casualties quickly. The whole system worked poorly and served to accentuate rather than remedy the manpower shortages developing at the battle front. A wide variety of expedients was attempted to remedy this situation, from combing out rear area staffs to retraining men as infantry replacements; but these efforts took effect slowly, certainly precluded effective offensive operations in the late fall of 1944, and never quite straightened out a situation which ought to have been anticipated.[35]

The upshot of all this was that the Allied thrust was weakening at the very time that massive German reinforcements built up a new defensive line in the West.[36] As Hitler had explained long before, the defensive depth available in the West was not great; here the Allies could reach Germany's industrial heart. It was, therefore, to this front that most of the new divisions were sent. The American and French armies in the south were able to clear all of Lorraine and, except for a bulge around Colmar, most of Alsace; but American progress in the north was slow around Aachen, held up by German control of dams which could flood their route of advance, while the British made minimal advances in the Venlo area.

The German role in halting the Allied offensive had been the rebuilding of formations, in some cases around cores which had escaped the Falaise battle, in some cases newly organized and equipped by massive manpower mobilization, together with a substitution, in effect, of holding on to the ports as a means of reducing Allied supplies for sinking them with submarines. It was the German hope that new weapons and new formations would now enable them to strike such blows at the Western Powers as to drive them off the continent. There could be no quick renewal of a massive Allied invasion in the West, so that such a German victory could be the prelude to either a compromise peace or a renewed offensive in the East.

Two of the new weapons were already seeing service: the V-1, the pilotless bomber, and the V-2, the ballistic missile. These were now increasingly directed at Antwerp in an effort to destroy the port facilities on which the Allies were correctly believed to depend heavily. But other weapons were already either in service or about to be employed. The Germans had a lead in the design and manufacture of jet airplanes, and it was their hope that the enormous advantage in speed which these planes had over all planes powered by conventional engines would enable them to drive the Allied bombers out of the skies and to regain control of the air over the battlefield. The reality quickly proved otherwise. The new jets did succeed in shooting down some bombers; but they were simply overwhelmed by the great numbers and longer endurance of the American P-51 Mustangs, an outcome also affected by the poor training (because of inadequate fuel) of the German pilots and the greater experience of the American pilots.[37]

There has been extensive discussion in the post-war literature about the delay in production and first introduction of jets by the Germans as a result of Hitler's decision of May 23, 1944, that the only type of plane actually about ready for production, the ME-262, also be equipped to drop bombs. This literature ignores not only the overwhelming numbers of Allied planes after the defeat of German fighter defenses in February–March 1944, but also Allied knowledge of German aircraft innovations—in part as a result of intercepting Japanese reports on them—and as a result the possibility of the Allies pulling forward their own employment of jet aircraft.[38]

If the new jet airplanes were in fact unlikely to produce the results expected of them, the new submarines still remained potentially a major menace to the Allies because there was no way for the convoys to outrun their greater speed or for defending planes and warships to spot them on the surface as they simply remained under water. Even the intermediate step between the old German submarines and the new, the snorkel-equipped older models, caused the Allies substantial losses and great difficulties because it enabled the Germans to return to the waters close to the English coast. The totally new submarines did constitute a realistic German hope, but one that was not realized, primarily because, as discussed later in this chapter, the Allied air offensive so disrupted the German naval construction program that none could be made ready in time. Unlike the factories for jet planes, the facilities where portions of the new submarines were built and assembled could not be placed underground and therefore remained vulnerable to air attacks. But, as explained in Chapter 12, German strategy on the Eastern Front was in the meantime very much influenced by the need to retain control of portions of the Baltic Sea as a trial and training area for the new submarines. The German soldiers in Courland were ordered to hold out until May of 1945 to enable crews to practice on the submarines, which never saw service in the war.

If neither new planes nor new submarines came to play in reality the role prescribed for them in German plans, that left the army, though it should be noted that careful consideration was given in the planning for a new German offensive to the impact of weather on the role of air power. When anticipating the launching of the great offensive in the West which Germany started after numerous postponements on May 10, 1940, one major factor in determining the timing of the attack had been the assurance of several days of *good* weather so that the German air force could use its great strength to support the offensive and hinder all Allied counter blows. Now it was the other way around. All too aware of the enormous superiority of the Allies in the air, the Germans this time planned to attack when they could hope to have several days of *bad* weather, in order to be secure from interference by Allied planes. But the main responsibility for the attack itself was to be carried by the German army and the armed formations of the SS.[39]

THE BATTLE OF THE BULGE

The general concept of the German offensive was first to halt the Allies at the old German border with its pre-war fortifications, now quickly being put back into usable form and provided with men and weapons.[40] The fighting of October, November, and early December forced the Germans to retreat to the Westwall, with the exception of the American push through it to seize Aachen in the north on the one hand and the Germans holding on to the Colmar area on the left bank of the Rhine in the south; otherwise the old fortifications essentially defined the front in early December and provided the basis for a German offensive. The American offensive around Aachen had however drawn into costly battle a number of the German divisions which were supposed to be used in the great attack, and thereby contributed to a postponement in the intended launching from the last days of November to the middle of December.

The plan for a counter-offensive had originated at the end of July, just as the American break-out from Normandy was developing; had been tentatively scheduled by August 19 for November—when the Allied air forces would be hampered by weather; and had been set for the Ardennes area by September 16.[41] Here the Allied front would be split open by a hard and quick blow at the Americans by thirty new and rebuilt German divisions which, in Hitler's view, could make only a minor difference on the Eastern Front. Crossing the river Meuse quickly—Hitler hoped for the second day—and striking for Antwerp, the Germans could cut off and destroy the 1st Canadian, 2nd British, and 9th and 1st American armies; such a blow would change the whole situation in the war. Either the enemy coalition would break or, at the very least, the victory in the West would make possible a massive shift of troops to the East. This latter was not merely a nominal reassurance for General Guderian, the Chief of the General Staff of the army, who objected to the whole idea of employing Germany's last reserves in the West, but Hitler's real intention. He hoped to be done in the West *before* the anticipated Soviet winter offensive could start.

Hitler's view of the Americans as incapable of fighting effectively and of the American home front as likely to crack under a heavy blow at the front reflected his long-held perception of the United States.[42] There is no evidence that Hitler realized or that a single one of his military advisors pointed out to him that, of all the major belligerents, the United

States was the one which up to this point had been *least* damaged by the war and had by far the greatest recuperative powers, so that even a really major defeat was less likely to have a serious impact on its war effort. That what Hitler referred to as a "second Dunkirk" inflicted on the British would, even if accomplished, hardly relieve Germany of major pressure in the West did not occur to any of them either. All debate in the ensuing weeks focused on the details, not the wisdom, of the planned operation.[43]

The commanders in the West, Field Marshals Rundstedt and Model, preferred an offensive with more limited objectives but could never explain why Germany's last reserves should be expended on such an operation. They and their subordinates in great secrecy prepared the detailed plans for the operation outlined by Hitler and Jodl. In the meantime, the divisions for the attack were being rebuilt or organized, moved to the front with careful attention to concealment, the commanders to the division level harangued by Hitler, and the last preparations made.[44] The main thrust was to be made by the 6th SS Panzer Army on the north and 5th Panzer Army on the south with 15th Army providing flank support on the right and 7th Army on the left. When the degree of completion of the preparations and bad weather coincided in mid-December, some 200,000 German soldiers and six hundred tanks supported by about nineteen hundred guns attacked a front held by approximately 80,000 American soldiers, four hundred tanks, and four hundred guns.

The offensive blow of December 16 struck the American front largely by surprise. Overconfidence combined with an absence of clear intelligence signs, though many had indeed expected at least a spoiling attack. When the Germans struck, the American lines held in the north but buckled in the south. The 6th SS Panzer Army ran into solid American defenses on the Elsenborn ridge and at St Vith, the latter quickly reinforced at Eisenhower's orders by the 7th Armored and 82nd Airborne Divisions. In the following days, repeated thrusts by the Germans, with SS armored divisions leading the way, failed to crack the Elsenborn ridge but did succeed in pushing forward some distance and eventually taking St. Vith. This, however, was less than half way to the Meuse river — to say nothing of Antwerp a hundred miles further off—and meant that the intended main thrust of the German offensive had been halted.

Perhaps to make up for their failure to make more than minimal gains, at least one of the SS units, 1st Panzer Division, engaged in an all too frequent SS activity. In what came to be known as the Malmédy Massacre a large number of American prisoners was murdered on December 17; both before and after that date other prisoners and civilians also fell victim to the SS preference for killing the unarmed.[45] News of these atrocities quickly spread among American soldiers, as did stories about a unit of Germans in American uniforms. This formation actually existed, but it was small and proved to be ineffective. It probably caused more confusion by its existence and the resulting suspicion than by its actions; those of its members captured in American uniforms were shot in accordance with standard practice in all armies.[46]

In the southern portion of the offensive front, 5th German Panzer Army broke through relatively quickly, effectively destroying the two American divisions (106th and 28th) in its path. Driving forward rapidly in bad weather, which kept Allied planes out of the air, the Germans headed for Houffalize and Bastogne. They pushed westwards between the towns, took the former but failed to seize the latter as American troops fell back on this key road junction, which was reinforced at the critical moment by the American 101st Airborne Division.

Although the Germans, seeing the failure in the north and some success in the south, put more resources into the southern push, it too began to slow down. They were experiencing shortages of gasoline, not off-set as much as they had counted on by the capture of Allied stocks, increasing American resistance, especially at Bastogne, and counter-attacks against the weak German 7th Army on the southern flank of the bulge driven into the Allied lines. In bitter fighting, the Germans now tried simultaneously to push forward to and perhaps across the Meuse and also to clear the road junction of Bastogne so that they could nourish their own front and their further attack westwards.

Both German efforts failed. The spearheads of 5th Panzer Army reaching for the Meuse were stopped by American armor east of the river, while Bastogne held out, even when surrounded by German forces. These defensive victories were primarily due to the recovery of American forces on the ground, and soon after greatly assisted by clearing weather which enabled the Allied air forces to intervene in the struggle by attacks on German columns, supply routes, and the transportation system in the rear areas. German units in the bulge found themselves exhausting their strength in numbers, equipment, and supplies as routes were choked behind them. The turn of emphasis from a rapid advance to a siege of Bastogne could only favor the Americans. And the siege was soon broken by an American counter-offensive from the south.

In spite of skepticism by some, General Patton quickly broke off the offensive his 3rd Army was developing south of the bulge, swung forces into a new direction, and struck northward toward Bastogne instead of eastward into the Saar area in the forty-eight hours he had promised at a conference at Verdun on December 19. In a few days, his armored units broke through the southern portion of the ring around Bastogne and held against a series of furious German counter-attacks. The hope of utilizing what was now an American salient into the bulge from the south for cutting off the whole German spearhead in the western portion of the bulge was, however, thwarted by skillful German fighting and the developments on the northern flank of the bulge.[47]

There a new command arrangement had been worked out. With Bradley on the southern side of the bulge and often out of touch with 1st and 9th Armies on the northern side, Eisenhower temporarily placed Montgomery in charge of all forces north of the German spearheads.[48] This had the advantage of providing a more coherent command structure on the north flank of the bulge and making British divisions available as a reserve behind the American 1st Army front. It had, however, one short-term and one long-term disadvantage. The short-term problem was that Montgomery applied his slow methodical approach to a counter-stroke which came far too late to prevent the Germans from withdrawing the bulk of their forces. As he explained to Brooke on December 22, he had no confidence in the American 3rd Army attack and expected to "have to deal unaided with both 5th and 6th Panzer Armies."[49] Three days later Montgomery was in a complete panic and called for vast withdrawals in the south, including the evacuation of all of Alsace and Lorraine, as otherwise there could be no offensive in the north in the spring or summer of 1945.[50] These predictions, which were completely erroneous in regard to the Americans, the 3rd Army attack, and the whole course of the fighting, explain his caution when a very different approach might well have been appropriate.[51]

The long-term problem was that, as soon as the situation improved and thus confounded every one of his predictions, Montgomery called a press conference on January 7 in which he made a fool of himself by making it appear as if he had personally retrieved with British forces—of which practically none were engaged—a disaster created by the Americans.[52] By this extraordinarily unwise gesture he ended all hopes he and Brooke still held of permanently attaching substantial American forces to his command. The opportunity provided by the German offensive of pinching off a major assault force as well as of recreating any Allied ground command under Eisenhower had evaporated. The German bulge was squeezed out.

In the last days of 1944, the Germans staged a subsidiary offensive in Alsace, designed to keep the initiative and to take advantage of Allied transfers to meet the offensive further north; but beyond minimal gains and an angry quarrel between Eisenhower and de Gaulle about a possible evacuation of Strasbourg,[53] this operation had no substantial effect.

More important in its implications was a massive German air operation on January 1, 1945. Coordinated mass attacks on Allied airfields were designed to strike a major blow at the Allied air forces but had the opposite effect. Although the thousand German planes involved destroyed about 180 and damaged close to 100 planes, they themselves lost 277 planes; the operation left the German air force weaker than ever and incapable of again mounting any major attack.[54]

What had been the overall impact of the "Battle of the Bulge"? Since the Allied offensive from the west was stalling even before the German attack, the over-all length of hostilities was not extended; in early December Montgomery had estimated a Rhine crossing north of Wesel in the middle of March, 1945 — very shortly before the actual crossing.[55] The casualties on both sides had been heavy: about 80,000 Germans and 70,000 Americans killed, wounded and missing, with a large contingent of the latter, about 8000, having been taken prisoner when two regiments of the 106th Division were forced to surrender.[a] Each side lost about seven hundred tanks and other armored fighting vehicles. This balance, however, obscures the fact that the Germans had used up their last reserves while the Allied forces, if no longer growing, could replace their losses. On November 15, Japanese Ambassador Oshima had recalled to von Ribbentrop that in his judgement Germany would have done better in 1918 not to launch an attack in the West, but von Ribbentrop assured him that Germany would indeed go on the offensive again.[56]

Inside Germany and in the German army, the temporary return to the offensive did have major favorable repercussions on morale, but the failure of the whole project eventually had an even more depressing effect. Here the analogy to 1918, to which Oshima had alluded beforehand, was too close for comfort. The dashing of hopes attached to what was understood to be a last throw of the dice necessarily had a redoubled impact both at the front and at home.

On the Allied side, there were three sets of repercussions. In the American army, there was a fuller recognition that a great deal of hard fighting still lay ahead. After initial confusion and set-backs, the soldiers and the commanders had pulled themselves together; and success at the Elsenborn ridge and at Bastogne had shown that determined and well-led American soldiers could face Germans with tanks better than their own and hold. Between the Americans and the British, the whole episode had caused little but bad blood. The hesitations of Montgomery which had allowed a German army which might very well have been

---

[a] One American soldier, Private Eddie Slovik, was executed for desertion, the first execution for a battlefield offence since 1865 (David Eisenhower, *Eisenhower at War*, p. 586).

completely cut off to withdraw for a *third* time were contrasted with the dash of Patton's shift to the offensive northwards; the press conference incident infuriated the Americans; and the British leaders, especially Brooke and Montgomery, were more certain of American incompetence than ever before.[a]

Perhaps even more fateful than the impact on United States–British relations was the effect on the relative positions of the Western Allies and the Soviet Union in the winter of 1944–45. As the Western Allies had to rebuild their own forces for the final assault on Germany, the commitment of Germany's last reserves to the offensive in the West guaranteed a rapid advance to the Red Army once its winter offensive got started. The German army Chief of Staff, General Guderian, had warned about this beforehand and repeatedly called for ending the Ardennes offensive in order to transfer troops East while that offensive was under way, but to no effect.[57] The position of the Soviet Union in the final stages of the European war could only benefit from the fact that all the new units built up and almost all the new heavy weapons delivered during the halt on the Vistula in the last five months of 1944 had been hurled against the American army in its sternest test of the European war.

By the first days of January 1945, when it was obvious that both German offensives in the West had entirely failed to attain any strategic objective, the other elements in German hopes of reversing the tide of the war had already been dashed as well. The strategy of denying supplies to the Western Allies by holding on to the ports had, in effect, collapsed with the opening of Antwerp to Allied shipping in the last week of November. Shifting the aim of Germany's new weapons, the V-1 and V-2, from London to Antwerp, caused some casualties and damage there but hardly interfered with the effective operation of this key harbor. Already in December over a quarter of American supplies were being unloaded in Antwerp, and in the following months it continued to carry the largest or next to largest share of the load.[58] There might still be some items in short supply, but the hope of stalling the offensive capability of the Western Allies by denying them the harbor facilities they needed had failed in the West; in the Mediterranean it had never had a real chance of success once the British had taken

---

[a] What is one to make of the fact that in his diary Brooke constantly misspells, and in different ways, the name of General William Simpson, the commander of the American 9th Army which he always wanted to have subordinated to Montgomery, although one of his closest assistants, the Director of Military Operations, spelled his name in exactly the same way? On March 3, 1945, it was "Stinson," on March 25 it was "Syrmson;" after the war, around 1955, Brooke referred to him as "Stimson," perhaps confusing the general with the American Secretary of War! (Liddell Hart Centre, Alanbrooke Papers, 3/B/XV, p. 1171).

Syracuse and subsequently the Americans had liberated Naples, with the French and Americans freeing Marseilles and Toulon thereafter.

The other way in which the Germans had expected to halt the danger they faced in Western Europe had been a resumption of the submarine war with new types of U-Boats which were fast enough to overtake the convoys and which could move at high speed under water without the need to surface, either for recharging their batteries or to go at higher speed. Such submarines, employed in substantial numbers, were expected to disrupt the trans-Atlantic supply route, thus leaving the Allied troops on the continent stranded without reinforcements or supplies. The engineering development on the submarine types for this new campaign had been completed: the first boats existed. They met or more than met the expectations of the Germans and the fears of the Allies: the boats were fast and not detectable by radar. But the whole project ended up as an eventually unproductive diversion of German material and manpower resources.

Although the sacrifice of the German army in Courland assured the Germans of control of enough of the Baltic Sea to try out the new submarines and to begin training crews in them, the new submarine campaign never became a reality. The fitting of existing submarines with a snorkel, a device that enabled them to remain submerged while recharging batteries, did make it possible for the Germans to carry on the campaign against Allied shipping on a small scale into the last weeks of the war; but whatever the damage inflicted as a result, there was never any prospect that *this* portion of the German naval effort could possibly catch up with the enormous increase in available Allied shipping produced by the cumulative and ever growing excess of construction over losses since the two lines had crossed in the fall of 1943.[59]

Everything therefore depended on the entirely new electro-boats. Developed during 1942 and 1943, the Germans began building them on a large scale in March, 1944.[60] The first of the new submarines (Type XXI) was delivered in June, 1944; by February 1945, 104 of Type XXI and 49 of Type XXIII had been completed, so that in that month the German submarine force with over four hundred ships reached its largest size in World War II. But not one of the new submarines sank an Allied ship. The whole project suffered from great flaws and fatal defects. The decision to go directly into series production meant that important defects were discovered after many of the submarines had been delivered, so that getting them ready took additional months. Above all, the direct and indirect impact of the Allied bombing campaign pre-cluded any effective renewal of the submarine war by Germany.[61]

The direct effect of the bombing campaign was three-fold. It led to the actual destruction of some submarines or components in harbor or hit factories providing parts. It dramatically reduced the fuel supplies of the German armed forces by attacks on synthetic oil plants and hence the allocations to the factories producing for the navy.[a] Finally it dis-rupted the whole transportation system so that deliveries of steel, coal, and other critical materials steadily fell behind. As if these direct effects of the bombing offensive, which greatly reduced the number of submar-ines that could be produced and delayed the delivery of those actually completed, were not enough, there was the even more dramatic indirect effect.

The new types of submarines had the obvious advantage over their predecessors of being able to remain submerged practically indefinitely, thereby escaping the Allied air and naval defenses which depended heav-ily on radar and radio detection (Huff-Duff) contact with the *surfaced* U-Boats. The other side of this advantage, however, was the even greater dependence of any submerged ship on aerial reconnaissance to locate the convoys. Now that the Germans could no longer read the Allied convoy codes, only long-distance aerial reconnaissance could locate tar-gets for the new submarines, and this was simply not available.

It was not merely the reluctance of Göring to use any portion of his air force in a supporting role for the navy, but actual incapacity in the face of the Allied air offensive. It was this offensive which had forced on the Germans their delayed concentration on building vast numbers of fighters, not costly and complicated four-engined long-distance reconnaissance planes. The key airplane, the JU-290, was produced in minute numbers in 1943 and 1944.[62] Even this minimal program had to be abandoned in the summer of 1944 under the pressure of Allied air power. The loss of the French coastal bases for U-Boat warfare in August 1944 meant that even longer range planes would have been needed for any serious revival of the U-Boat war; and under the hammer blows of the Allied bombers, the Third Reich had not the slightest chance of producing them from the models which existed.

Had the new submarines been available sooner, they would have cruised the North Atlantic under water and blind. If sufficiently numer-ous, or perhaps by luck or mischance, they would have hit upon a needle in a haystack once in a while, but in the absence of aerial reconnaissance the whole massive effort would have been ineffective. Their major role,

---

[a] The new submarines themselves used types of batteries and fuels independent of the navy's oil supply.

then, must be seen in a somewhat different light. The whole construction program represented a massive and useless diversion of labor and materials from other armaments projects but gave the navy, and particularly its chief, Admiral Dönitz, an important role in Hitler's state in that state's last months. Here was a service and a leader who still claimed to have realistic hopes of turning the tide in the war. For his effective presentation of this dubious image, Dönitz would receive his reward.

As already mentioned repeatedly, the Allied bombing of the German oil industry and the transportation system inflicted critical damage on Germany's whole industrial and military system in 1944, and it was in the summer and fall of this year that strategic bombing finally came to play the role earlier assigned to it in the theory, hopes, and claims of air power enthusiasts. Earlier bombing of urban and industrial targets had caused vast destruction, heavy civilian casualties, and some disruption of the Axis economy, but its most significant contributions had been of a very different kind. Bombing had been the one major way in which Britain and the United States had been able to bring their military power to bear on the Third Reich at a time when the earlier support of the Soviet Union had enabled the Germans to drive the Allies off the continent, and had left Russia facing German land forces practically alone. Maintaining that control of western and central Europe with a minimum of interference from the Western Allies had been a main mission of the German submarine campaign; and the resources Germany devoted to that effort until the Allies turned the tide in the Battle of the Atlantic in 1943, and thereafter to the attempt at reviving a new submarine campaign, had been a major diversion of scarce human and material resources from the Eastern Front. The hundreds of old and new types of submarines sent to sea represented thousands of tanks *not* produced for the war in the East.

The other major contribution of the bombing offensive had been the enforced diversion of German resources to the defense of cities and installations, to the defense of the skies. By 1944, over 1.1 million men were employed in firing and controlling 12,000 heavy and 19,000 other anti-aircraft guns.[63] Almost half a million of the crew members were auxiliaries—primarily teenagers and women—who could not have been employed in front-line units; but, on the other hand, not only were enormous quantities of ammunition as well as guns tied up in defense of the Reich against air attacks, but the bulk of the German air force had had to be shifted to this defensive mission. The German air force was absorbing the majority of Germany's military industrial resources, and primarily for defense against British and American bombers.

This basically indirect effect of the bombing on the war effort of

Germany changed in 1944. The primarily American offensive against oil targets launched in May 1944 was to have a fundamentally different effect from all prior bombing operations for several reasons. In the first place, the Americans had earlier succeeded in overwhelming the German fighter defenses by long-range fighter escorts and could now reach the synthetic oil plants deep inside Germany with large numbers of escorted bombers.[64] Furthermore, the advance in Italy enabled them to strike at the Romanian oil fields and refineries at Ploesti not just in an occasional special mission from North Africa but on a regular basis.[65]

Most important to the success of the air offensive against oil, however, was that the Americans did not repeat the British and their own prior mistake of underrating German recuperative powers. Instead of a single big operation, rarely if ever repeated—on the model of Hamburg—the bombers of the 8th Air Force went after the synthetic oil works systematically, repeating the attacks as soon as photo or cryptographic intelligence indicated that repairs had been made.[66] The Germans tried to cope with this development by extraordinary repair efforts and a dramatic increase in fighter plane production. Neither worked: the repairs simply could not keep up, and the fighters, though obviously more easy to build than four engined bombers, simply could not cope. Never built in the numbers Speer pretended,[67] the new fighters were in many instances destroyed on the ground, shot out of the skies by the more experienced and better trained Allied pilots, or left standing around without fuel.[68] Needless to say, the attacks on the synthetic oil plants affected the whole German war effort, not only the air force. The dramatic reduction in fuel production, which varied between 40 and 60 percent of capacity in the fall and winter, had major repercussions on all fronts; the success of the German Ardennes offensive, for example, had been predicated on the assumption that enough petroleum supplies could be captured along the way to Antwerp, as the Germans did not have it themselves.

The other major target to which the Allies paid increasing attention with devastating results for the German war economy was the transportation system. In a localized way, this had been an important part of the preparation for the invasion; the Allies had disrupted the German transportation system in the West just as the Soviet partisans repeatedly concentrated on the German railway network in the occupied U.S.S.R. before major Red Army offensives. Certain, on the basis of this experience and some assessments of air attacks on the transportation system in Italy earlier, that the railway network, including its freight marshalling yards, was potentially a highly rewarding target, some of the British leaders, especially Air Chief Marshal Sir Arthur Tedder, now argued for an offensive against the whole German transportation system, with special emphasis on the railways and canals.[69]

New directives were issued to the Allied strategic air forces in September 1944 to concentrate on oil with transportation as the second target, barely mentioning the area attacks which had become the mainstay of British Bomber Command's operations. In the following months, the head of Bomber Command, Air Chief Marshal Sir Arthur Harris, frequently ignored these directives, successfully defying the Chief of the Air Staff.[70] In spite of the resulting dispersion of Allied bombing effort, the transportation plan worked, drastically reducing German deliveries of coal and other vital materials to factories and stranding parts and finished products at the plants where they were made.

In the fall of 1944 the German railway system, the main artery of the whole economic structure, was being pounded to bits, with industrial production dropping precipitously as a result. Ironically one of the attacks on the railways also dealt the greatest single blow to Germany's highly important water transport system. An American attack on the railway yard at Cologne on October 14, 1944, set off the explosive charges which had been placed by German engineers in the piers of the great new suspension bridge over the Rhine, against the contingency of its being seized by the Allies. Thereupon the whole bridge fell into the river, blocking the Rhine, Germany's most important waterway, to barge traffic.[71] Other attacks, especially by the RAF using the largest bombs of the war, hit the German canal system and blocked it at key points.[72] Here was a way to bring the German war machine to a halt.

Having failed to arrest the Allied air offensive by the mass employment of fighters, the Germans tried other expedients. They had earlier turned to underground facilities for the fabrication of parts for the V-1 and V-2; in early March, 1944, Hitler ordered that all war production be moved into caves, tunnels, and excavated underground spaces; but this was obviously not the sort of thing which could be done quickly.[73] Hitler was most certainly not going to make peace as the fired German air force Chief of Staff, General Werner Kreipe, suggested to Göring on his departure at the beginning of November 1944.[74]

On the contrary, the Germans, like the Japanese, began to give serious consideration to the deliberate use of suicide attacks, though never implementing this tactic on the scale actually employed by the latter. German plans and actions in this regard have never been subjected to a serious and comprehensive scholarly analysis,[75] but they appear to have begun with a June 1944 project, code-named "Carl," for a bombing operation at extreme one-way range of Soviet hydro-electric works on the upper Volga and in the Urals.[76] The German air force planners then shifted to the idea of ramming Allied heavy bombers with single-seater fighters on the assumptions that the trade was worthwhile and that the tactic would shake the morale of the bomber crews; and they exchanged experiences with the Japanese who introduced the kamikaze suicide squadrons into action in the battle for the Philippines in October 1944.[77] Although the German ramming squadron did fly one mission on April 7, 1945, the whole project never played a substantial role in German, as it did in Japanese, planning for defense.[a] There really was no way to put a secure roof over the Third Reich anymore. As there was no reversal of the naval defeat of 1943, there could be no reversal of the air defeat of February–March 1944.

THE SITUATION BY JANUARY 1945

The employment of Germany's last reserves in the failed December offensive in the West and the collapse of Germany's industrial system under the pounding of Allied bombers combined to set up Germany and what remained of its European satellites—Hungary, the puppet states of Slovakia and Croatia together with Mussolini's "Social Republic" in northern Italy—for their final defeat. The counter-attacks of the Western Allies, squeezing out the bulge in the West, and the slow but continued advance of the Red Army in Hungary were harbingers of new major offensives to come: the Soviet winter operation which looked ever more imminent and the resumption of offensives by the Allied forces in the West and also in Italy.

The very fact that the concentric operations of the Allies were continuing showed that the hopes which German leaders had pinned on a disruption of the alliance of their enemies would not be realized. The frictions between the United States and Great Britain, which had originally centered on the debates over the invasion of Western Europe and then on strategy in the Mediterranean, had turned more and more to political issues in the winter of 1944–45, especially in regard to British support of monarchist elements in Italy and Greece. Whatever the significance of these political disagreements, and some of the military

---

[a] A partial parallel was the American project to load up war weary planes with explosives, fly them toward Germany with skeleton crews which would bail out over Allied territory at the last moment, and leave the planes to crash with a big explosion somewhere in the Third Reich. Subsequently the idea of a skeleton crew was replaced by that of mechanical flight control, thus converting the plane into a drone. Roosevelt favored the plan, which Truman eventually dropped in the face of Churchill's adamant opposition. The British leader was concerned about retaliation against London. The American case is put in FDR to Churchill, 29 March 1945, Loewenheim, *Roosevelt and Churchill*, pp. 688–89; Kimball, *Churchill and Roosevelt*, 3: 591–92. The most useful British file, beginning with the receipt of the American proposal of 11 November 1944, is in PRO, AIR 8/838; see also AIR 20/95.

implications which they might have,[78] those at the top in the two countries in general and Roosevelt and Churchill in particular were determined not to allow them to cause any major breach. The death of Sir John Dill, a key figure holding them together, in early November 1944, came at a time when the alliance was firmly set,[79] and when a closer approximation of their respective policies toward de Gaulle reduced one earlier source of friction.

Similarly, the developing difficulties between the British and Yugoslav partisan leader Tito did not lead to any break between them. Churchill was upset about the partisan leader's increasingly close relations with Moscow, but the supply of weapons to him continued. The project for joint British–partisan operations in and later from the area of Zara, the Italian port on the eastern Adriatic, which had been under review since November, 1944, was called off in January, 1945, as it became obvious that from Tito's perspective this was simply another way to acquire equipment and definitely *not* British units. Given the British shortage of troops, with more and more of them being sucked into the contentious situation in Greece, one wonders whether anything substantial would actually have come of the scheme, code-named "Baffle," if it had ever been implemented.[80]

The most critical alliance relationship, however, was that between the Soviet Union and the Western Powers. The possibility that their differences over military operations or, more likely, over the political future of Poland and Southeast Europe, would lead to a breakup of the grand coalition, had been a mainstay of German hopes for the future as it had been a major source of concern for the British and Americans. But if there had been real prospects of such a break earlier in the war, they had vanished by now. The Soviet Union had liberated its own territory, had driven Finland out of the war—on terms which paid some attention to the concerns of her allies—had occupied all of Romania and Bulgaria, was in control of substantial portions of Hungary and Poland, and had begun to move into Czechoslovakia and Yugoslavia. Now that their Western Allies had agreed to a division of Germany which provided for a substantial Soviet zone in the East and the annexation of the northern half of East Prussia to the Soviet Union, what could the Germans possibly offer Moscow, even had they been so inclined?

According to the report the Hungarian Fascist leader Ferenc Szálasi had given to the Japanese ambassador, Hitler had not entirely rejected his advice to reach an understanding with the U.S.S.R., whereas there was no possibility of a compromise with the Western Powers,[81] but all Soviet incentive and interest had vanished by this time. It was obvious to the Soviet political and military leaders that there was still hard fighting ahead, but the possible gains in Europe were substantial; and thereafter portions of the Red Army could be moved to the Far Eastern provinces of the U.S.S.R. to assure further important gains there. Certainly nothing happening in the Pacific War in 1944 argued against such a policy. The Japanese were obviously being beaten by the Americans while the Japanese victory in China was not only off-set by defeat of the attempted invasion of India, but would in addition weaken Chiang Kai-shek's ability to resist whatever demands Moscow might make of him.

The prospect of a series of further bloody campaigns against Japan only enhanced American interest in eventual Soviet intervention in the Pacific War—and hence desire to accommodate her in Europe if possible. The shock received by the Americans in the Battle of the Bulge and the continued slowness of the campaign in Italy served to underline for American leaders the enormous importance of continued pressure by the Red Army to Allied victory in Europe. The dispatch of Air Chief Marshal Tedder to Moscow as Eisenhower's representative in late December 1944 reflected the concern of the Western Powers that the final pushes into Germany be coordinated as carefully as possible; there was as yet no recognition of the effect strategic bombing—after so many earlier disappointments—was at last having on the German industrial system.

As for the British, they were certainly not about to allow their differences with Moscow to produce a breach now. Whatever the arguments about Eastern Europe, it was Western Europe and Greece that mainly concerned them; and in these areas, the cooperation of the Soviet Union appeared to be provided. As for Central and Eastern Europe, there was little hope of the British ever obtaining in reality the occupation zone in northwest Germany, which they had argued for for so long, except in a continuing alliance which assured heavy offensive operations by the Red Army in the East with the aim of occupying the zone allocated, in the British-originated scheme, to the Soviet Union. As for the rest of Central and Eastern Europe, the same attitudes which had once led many in England to accept, reluctantly perhaps, but to accept all the same a German sphere in the region, now argued for a similarly complaisant attitude toward the Soviet Union.[82]

For now the alliance against Hitler's Germany was secure, whatever its internal tensions. The leaders were about to meet again after an interval of a year and a half since Teheran, and they could be expected to find ways to continue the struggle against Germany together. That struggle had now moved very close to the old borders of Germany. In the East, the Red Army had barely crossed into East Prussia, but its bridgeheads over the Vistula in central Poland offered an opportunity for a drive across open and excellent tank country into the industrial center of Silesia and the political center at Berlin. Simultaneously, the Western Allies, who already held a significant piece of German territory, were back on the line before the German Ardennes offensive and, in spite of the slow progress of the American–French offensive in Alsace stood poised to close and cross the Rhine. Germany still controlled most of Norway, all of Denmark, much of Czechoslovakia, and portions of Hungary, Yugoslavia and Italy as well as practically all of pre-1939 Germany. But with the roof falling in and the Allies pounding on the doors, how long could the Germans expect to hold out?

15

THE FINAL ASSAULT ON GERMANY

The Allies early in 1945 hoped to crush Germany that year. It was their expectation that the German army would continue to fight ferociously on the defensive, especially now that it was the German homeland which was being invaded, but there was confidence in victory. The Allied air forces controlled the skies over all the fronts; and although at times the German air force could still muster substantial numbers, the Allies greatly outnumbered them, had better trained and more experienced pilots, and could, when it came to it, replace losses far more easily than the Germans. By this time, furthermore, the air attacks on Germany's synthetic oil plants and the capture of the Romanian oil fields by the Russians had so reduced the supplies available to the German air force that many of its planes simply could not be flown.[a]

Control of the air assured the Allies of full support for their land offensives and the opportunity to attack industrial, transportation, and other targets in the whole area still under German control. What few newly developed jet airplanes the Germans could produce were often destroyed on the ground or simply overwhelmed in the skies. Both the Western Allies and the Soviet Union were producing propeller driven airplanes of improved design in great numbers even as the German air force had, for the most part, concentrated on modified versions of by 1945 obsolescent models of the early war years. In the air, there was obviously a dramatic reversal of the situation from that at the beginning of the war when the Germans had won air superiority first over Poland, then in the Western campaign of 1940 and the Balkan campaign of the spring of 1941, and finally in the first stage of the German attack on Russia. The earlier German insistence on building up a new air force

[a] By the end of 1944 the Germans had also lost two other sources of oil which they had seized earlier in the war and had exploited for several years: the small oil fields in the Boryslav–Drogobycz area of Poland and the Estonian oil shale region.

in the face of their treaty commitments and in a world without great fleets of warplanes no longer looked like the "success" which it had been hailed as by many in the 1930s and is still occasionally referred to in the literature.

The German navy was, as shown in Chapter 14, still hoping to return to the Battle of the Atlantic with new submarines which could go at high speed submerged; but even if these new types, being delivered and tried out in the winter, ever could be put into combat service, they would be blind without aerial reconnaissance — of which there was not the slightest prospect. The submarines in actual service, those of the old types but equipped with a snorkel so that the batteries could be recharged without the need for full surfacing, were now having little success. In all of January, they sank 80,000 tons of shipping in the Atlantic; this and the few remaining months of the war saw a pattern of minimal sinkings but high levels of U-Boats lost, often on a first combat cruise.

The German navy had by this time been effectively driven out of the Mediterranean and the Black Sea, so that the Allies were not only safe in those waters but were beginning to send supplies to the Soviet Union through the Turkish Straits to Soviet Black Sea ports. The first shipments were delivered on this route in January 1945; by March and April, fully a third of the tonnage was being sent this way.[1] Not only were German submarines excluded from the Mediterranean and successfully hunted in the Atlantic, but their operations in the Indian Ocean from Japanese bases were being affected by the deteriorating situation of their Japanese ally. Although the Germans did not have an entirely accurate view of the vast losses which had by then been inflicted on the Japanese navy, they knew enough to realize that the fleet whose accession to the Axis in December 1941 had made them hope for victory at sea was now to a large extent at the bottom of the ocean.[2] Because of the loss of the Philippines, the severing of communications between the Japanese home islands and the conquered areas of Southeast Asia would make it difficult for the Japanese to refuel the German submarines stationed in Malaya, so any new ones sent had better be plentifully fitted out;[3] hardly welcome advice at a time when Germany's synthetic oil industry was being smashed.

The major immediate operational concern of the German navy in the last months of the war was not, however, the ongoing activity of submarines in the Atlantic or the hope of reviving effective submarine warfare with new submarines, but the danger threatening its major training area in the Baltic, which was also the sea over which Germany drew the Swedish iron ore essential to the continuation of the war. Sweden was not willing to join the Allies, as the Germans by this time feared, but it was imperative for Germany to keep the Soviet navy out of as much of the Baltic as possible to protect German trade as well as submarine training. As the German army—in the face of the navy's calling for efforts to seize Leningrad—instead retreated closer to the German border, Dönitz became ever more frantic in his insistence that as much of the Baltic shore as possible be held, a point already repeatedly discussed in connection with the Germans holding on to the Courland area of western Latvia.[4] The converse of the navy's pressure, of course, was the insistence of the army for support of its fighting on land first by naval artillery and, thereafter, in supplying the garrisons in Courland and Memel cut off by the advancing Red Army.[5]

During the winter of 1944, the naval war in the Baltic revolved around the efforts of the Soviet navy to strike into that sea, which the Germans on the whole warded off; and the latter's frantic attempts to supply isolated garrisons, evacuate wounded soldiers and those ordered withdrawn for employment elsewhere, and the evacuation of vast numbers of civilian refugees. In these tasks, the remnant German navy was surprisingly successful. Ironically, it proved to be best in those missions which the founders and leaders of the Imperial and the Nazi navy had pushed aside to pursue world-wide ambitions and offensives; those few who had once argued for a navy attuned to coastal and defensive needs were proved right after all.

But the key question in the last months of war in Europe was not what the German air force and navy could do but whether the German home front would remain solidly behind the army as it fought in the west, east and south. In spite of the enormous casualties of the summer and fall and in spite of the impact of the increasingly heavy Allied bombing offensive, the home front held up. There had been a lift of morale when the first news of gains in the December offensive came through, but that quickly evaporated. There were still hopes for new secret weapons, since the V-1 and V-2 had obviously not turned the tide, but other factors helped to hold the system together.

Certainly a major factor in the cohesion of Nazi Germany was the victory of Hitler and his supporters over the internal resistance on and after July 1944.[6] The success of the secret police in ferreting out opponents as well as the increasing terror at home and in the army appeared to oblige all to go along or at least keep their criticism to themselves. Many Germans were scared of their own government; others were scared of the Allies. The widespread participation in and even wider knowledge of the most awful crimes perpetrated in prior years made for a sense of desperation in the face of possible punishment and retribution. It was assumed that defeat would be followed by the harshest measures and terms for Germany. There was a sad joke circulating in the country: it would be best to enjoy the war while it lasted because the peace would be terrible. Furthermore, in important ways, the massive disruption of the bombing campaign made people more dependent on the social service and support system of the government and thus contributed to a consolidation rather than disruption of public adherence to the existing regime.[7]

There were also strong positive cohesive factors in German society. Many, both among the leadership and in the population, continued to believe in the system. Some enjoyed the benefits of high rank and office, and the regime was especially careful to make sure that the monthly bribes to the highest generals and all field marshals (and their naval equivalents) continued until the end. Many simply could not envisage any alternative and, like numerous soldiers, fought on or held on out of loyalty not to the Nazi state but to their comrades. It should also be recalled that in World War II, unlike World War I, the looting of German-occupied Europe had assured the population the highest rations on the continent until the last portion of the conflict. And there was always the hope that Hitler, who continued to be held in high esteem by most of the public, would find some way to reverse the tide or attain a compromise or hold out until the coalition against Germany split up.[8]

There were some minimal signs of recognition within the German government that peace on whatever terms might be a preferable alternative to fighting to the bitter end; but unlike in Italy, Romania, Finland, Hungary and subsequently Japan, that recognition was never transferred into serious action.[9] When Japanese Ambassador Oshima saw von Ribbentrop and his new State Secretary von Steengracht in early January, he found them less adamant than earlier in response to his usual refrain of urging a German–Soviet peace.[10] Evidently the Foreign Minister, in the interval between the failure of the Ardennes offensive and the beginning of the Soviet winter offensive, had begun to think of some diplomatic initiative and had not been completely prohibited from doing so by Hitler, whose own inclination was toward a settlement with the Soviet Union for a joint war to crush Britain.[11]

In a series of tentative feelers, which von Ribbentrop himself in part cancelled, the German Foreign Minister urged the Western Allies to make peace with Hitler and join Germany in fighting the Soviet Union, lest Germany join the latter in fighting them—while simultaneously either making the opposite suggestion to the Soviet Union or trying to find a way to do so. The details of these soundings made in Sweden, Switzerland, Spain and at the Vatican are not entirely clear; what is clear is that one of those who has written on them is correct in likening them to von Ribbentrop's earlier project, while still a champagne salesman, to peddle German champagne in France, of all places.[12] The very fact that von Ribbentrop in the early months of 1945 could expect any of Germany's enemies to fall for such approaches reveals a great deal about the perceptiveness of the German Foreign Minister.

Now that the foreign ministry could no longer devote most of its efforts to pressuring Axis satellites into yielding up their Jews to be murdered, it was concentrating on dealings with various shadowy governments-in-exile of its own creation for France, Romania, Bulgaria and others along with such old clients as the Grand Mufti of Jerusalem and Rashid Ali Gaylani of Iraq; but all this had no connection with the realities of either the war or the post-war era.[13] More significant were the orders to move nerve gas supplies out of areas about to be overrun by the Allies against the possibility of their use in the last stage of the war. The nerve gas factory at Dyhernfurth in Silesia, nevertheless, fell undamaged into Soviet hands and was taken to the Soviet Union after the war.[14]

SOVIET PLANS

Plans for what to do with and in occupied Germany, as well as the rest of once German-controlled Europe, were already well advanced in all the major Allied countries by the end of 1944; and they had agreed among themselves on some but by no means every one of the major issues which affected all of them. The Soviet leadership may once have believed, as the surviving exiled German Communists in the Soviet Union held, that the German masses, misled and terrorized by their exploiting capitalist masters, would revolt against the Fascist agents of monopoly capitalism as soon as Germany attacked the Soviet Union, but such notions had long since fallen by the wayside. The experience of war on the Eastern Front had shown all too dramatically that the overwhelming majority of German soldiers (as well as officers) fully supported the regime of the Third Reich, and even in the prisoner of war camps the Communists had difficulty finding recruits. Those few they did locate would in subsequent years come to play significant roles in the Soviet zone of occupation in Germany and later in the German Democratic Republic, but their number was and remained small. In the later stages of the fighting in the East, especially in the summer and fall of 1944, German soldiers surrendered in large numbers and at times before they were completely exhausted and without ammunition, and numerous captured generals joined those of the captives of Stalingrad who had called on their fellow officers to end a useless war; but it was as obvious to the devoted German Communists as to the leaders of the Soviet Union that the bulk of the German army would fight to the bitter end and that the home front remained solidly behind it.

Every Soviet effort to find alternative ways out of the war had failed: the existing German government had refused any possibility of a compromise peace when such a peace still seemed to have advantages to the Soviet Union, and there had been neither an uprising from below nor any substantial effort of nationalistic military leaders to displace the regime and make peace. The events of July 20, 1944, only reinforced the impression of a minute and ineffective opposition to the Nazi regime inside Germany. Under these circumstances, Soviet planning for the future of Germany and for the future of the area between the Soviet Union and Germany came to have a basic set of priorities and principles.[15]

As for Germany itself, as much of it as the Red Army could reach, and more if possible, was to be restructured in accordance with a belief that the National Socialist regime was the product of class forces in that society, rather than a result of the beliefs and deeds of individuals. The expropriation of the old ruling elite and the nationalization of banking and industry would automatically end the power of those who had created and led the instruments of aggression. A popular front under the leadership of the German Communist Party would direct affairs in behalf of the Soviet leadership. Since that party was led by men who had emerged from the endless internal divisions of the Party in the years of the Weimar Republic, and subsequently survived the comprehensive purges in their ranks during the years of exile in the Soviet Union, there was not the slightest chance that any independent thought or idea — perhaps one could say any thought or idea whatever — would ever emerge among them.

The very scarcity of opposition to the murderous Nazi regime appeared to reinforce the need for a tight new control, which the Communist Party would exercise through a combination of whatever elements could be rallied, including any ex-Nazis who had seen the light, and which would temporarily make such concessions to other elements as appeared to be needed — including nationalist appeals where appropriate and a deferring of collectivization of agriculture — until firmly and fully in charge. Eventually the restructuring of the German social order would produce a self-conscious and supportive working class which would lead, under Communist direction, a country modelled on the Soviet Union and in the closest possible alignment with it.

The question of whether such a system could be installed in all or only in a part of Germany was obviously open; one would have to see.

But the chances that it would extend to more than any area directly under Red Army occupation, and that it would be cheerfully accepted even in the part held by the Red Army, came to be undermined by two further policies which the Soviet leadership adopted at the same time. In the first place, as an incentive for the soldiers of the Red Army, now that the pre-war territory of the U.S.S.R. had been freed of German occupation, the internal propaganda was concentrated on the theme of vengeance as a replacement for the earlier theme of defending the homeland. In view of the horrendous atrocities inflicted by the Germans on the civilian population in the occupied territories and on prisoners of war, this concept was easy to propagate and fell on ready ears; but the orgy of individual acts of murder and rape which thereafter accompanied the Red Army's advance into Germany served to reinforce rather than ameliorate the already vehement anti-Soviet attitude among the German population.

Many Russian soldiers did not participate in the acts which so terrorized and alienated the Germans, and many officers took steps to restrain the fury of their own men, but the overall effect of the Red Army's advance into Germany would be to make the task of the German Communist Party and its new supporters even more difficult than it was certain to be anyway; they could operate only under the auspices of the Red Army—but their so operating necessarily compromised them in the eyes of the population.

The second policy, about the preparations for which we are not well informed, was one calling for massive reparations to be extracted from the areas overrun by the Red Army and the rest of Germany if at all possible. The vast destruction caused by the Germans in the Soviet Union, both in the fighting and by deliberate measures to wreck as much as possible during the German retreat, left the Soviet government understandably determined to exact whatever goods, machines, and factories it could (as well as the labor of prisoners of war), and equally understandably meant that Moscow preferred for the German rather than the Russian population to pay as large a share as possible of the enormous cost of reconstructing the Soviet economy. In this regard, however, as in that of vengeance, the implications for the German instruments of Soviet policy were likely to be anything but favorable. The new masters who were to be flown in behind the advancing Red Army would inherit a daunting task: how to create a new structure starting from the roof down and covering a population whose earlier anti-Communist and anti-Russian sentiments had been and for years continued to be reinforced by the actions of the very power on whom the new regime depended for support. And these new masters had, as already mentioned, been carefully screened and culled in prior years by processes which guaranteed that only certified blockheads could survive.

For the territory between the Soviet Union and Germany, Stalin's government had a set of policies which combined traditional with radical features. In the first place, the territories which had been acquired under the terms of the Nazi–Soviet Pact of 1939 were in essentially all cases to be kept by Russia. There was a willingness to make some minor modifications in the border with Poland, but the basic assumption always was that the parts of Finland taken in 1940, the three Baltic States, eastern Poland, and the Romanian territories seized in 1940 were to be reincorporated into the Soviet Union. If Stalin had insisted on this in his talks with Eden in December 1941, when the Germans were within striking distance of Moscow, he was certainly not about to allow any changes after a succession of victories. On the contrary, there would be added territorial gains. In the settlement with Finland, he had exchanged a 50-year lease on the base at Porkkala for that at Hangö,[a] but the Finnish port and nickel mines at Petsamo, returned to Finland after the winter war of 1939–40, were now annexed to the Soviet Union. The latter had also obtained the tentative agreement of her allies to the annexation of the northern half of East Prussia (with the southern half going to Poland) and the commitment to support this arrangement at any future peace conference.[b]

In addition to these territorial changes, Stalin wanted two more but obtained only one of them. Having occupied Bulgaria in September 1944, the Soviet Union was in a very much stronger position to put pressure on Turkey, and began a diplomatic campaign to secure bases on the Straits and the cession of the provinces of Kars and Ardahan to the Georgian and Armenian parts of the U.S.S.R..[16] This effort would be thwarted by Turkish refusal, backed in the post-war years by Britain and the United States. In October 1944, the month after the occupation of Bulgaria, however, the Red Army entered the easternmost portion of Czechoslovakia, and here the situation was made very different by the Soviet military presence.

This area, the Carpatho-Ukraine or Ruthenia, had been a portion of Czechoslovakia and was so considered by the Czechoslovak government-in-exile although the region had been annexed to Hungary, partially in 1938 and the remainder in 1939. Once the area was liberated by the

---

[a] The Soviet government gave up this lease in 1955.
[b] It was always assumed that the area of Memel (Klaipeda), which Germany had been obliged to give up in 1919 but had taken back in 1939, would be included in Lithuania.

Red Army, the local commanders, presumably acting on instructions from Moscow, favored local Communist elements, who called for annexation to the Soviet Union now that the incorporation of the Galician part of eastern Poland provided a common border with the Ukrainian SSR. Stalin insisted on the cession of this area by the Czechoslovak government—which could return to Czechoslovakia only in the wake of the Red Army.

Though we have as yet no explicit evidence on the subject, it appears likely that two factors combined to lead Stalin to his demand. In the first place, his sensitivity to the explosive potential of the nationality problems of the Soviet Union, and especially among its largest nationality after the Great Russians, the Ukrainians, probably made him eager to include *within* the U.S.S.R. the one substantial group of Ukrainians left outside the country after the incorporation of the Ukrainians of pre-war Poland, and who might otherwise provide an *outside* focus for Ukrainian nationalist agitation. Secondly, the annexation of the area provided the Soviet Union with a common border with Hungary, which could in the future be more easily cowed by a Red Army now already across the mountain barrier of the Carpathians which runs through the province. Whatever the reason, Stalin did not allow the Czechoslovak government to administer the area; and the latter agreed to the cession, motivated in large part by the fear that if it did not agree, the Soviet Union would go ahead with the annexation anyway and, in addition, incorporate Slovakia, which only the U.S.S.R. outside the Axis had recognized as independent, as a new SSR into the Soviet Union.[17]

If the annexations represent traditional expansionist policy, the Soviet view of the bulk of the territory between the pre-1939 border of the U.S.S.R. and Germany represented a combination of traditional with revolutionary approaches. Although it has been suggested that Stalin at one point seriously considered the possibility of annexing all of Romania as well as the Baltic States to the U.S.S.R., he appears to have decided fairly early *not* to end the formal independence of Finland, Poland, Czechoslovakia, Hungary, Romania and Bulgaria; he did not follow the example of Otto von Bismarck, who had arranged in 1866 for the total incorporation of four states into Prussia at the end of the German civil war in addition to annexing three duchies formerly under the Danish crown. In Stalin's conversations with the United States and Great Britain, most obviously at Teheran, there had always been the assumption that Finland would be independent—just as he assumed that such would *not* be the case with Estonia, Latvia, and Lithuania. Whatever the boundaries or government, however, Soviet discussions with the Western Allies also assumed the existence of a Poland and separate states in Southeast

Europe, and the percentages agreement between Stalin and Churchill was obviously based on such an assumption.

As for the boundaries with each other and third countries, Poland would receive the southern part of East Prussia, the territory of the Free City of Danzig, and all of Germany east of the Oder and western Neisse rivers, but would return the portion of Czechoslovakia it had seized in 1938 to the latter. In addition, it would be allocated the German port city of Stettin (Sczcecin) and some additional territory *west* of the Oder river to compensate it for not getting the northern half of East Prussia with the city of Königsberg (Kaliningrad), originally promised to Poland but now claimed by the Soviet Union.[18] There is no evidence to show whether Stalin thought about any westward expansion of Czechoslovakia, but he agreed to that country's expelling its inhabitants of German background. The British had approved this transfer in early July, 1942; the United States and the Soviet Union in May and June of 1943.[19] As for the long-disputed border between Hungary and Romania, the Soviet government moved back and forth, using the possibility of its support for the claims to Transylvania of one or the other in the hope of drawing each out of the war on the side of Germany and into the front of the Allies. The success of the coup in Romania in August 1944, followed by active Romanian military participation alongside the Red Army, and the failure of the Hungarians to pull off a similar coup in October of that year, settled the matter: Romania would retain its 1919 border with Hungary. This in turn would make it easier to reconcile Romania to its having to leave with Bulgaria the portion of the Dobruja which had been ceded in 1940.

Vastly more important than the territorial changes, which to all intents and purposes reinstated the settlement of 1919 with only the situation of Poland and the Baltic States altered in major ways, were the socio-political transformations on which the Soviet Union insisted. In each country, the old elites were to be dispossessed, if not physically eliminated, and new regimes in which Communists occupied the key positions of power were to nationalize the means of production and establish entirely new structures not yet fully modelled on the Soviet system but on the road to that goal, via what were for a time called "peoples democracies." Since Stalin knew that in all these countries the Communist movements were small and the population (with the possible exception of that in Bulgaria) anti-Russian, he could not think of any way to establish a system congenial to the Soviet Union, other than to make sure that popular attitudes could not express themselves through free parliamentary processes. Thus a radical transformation of each country would go along with a formal preservation of each as a separate state,

leaving open as a result at least the remote possibility of other developments in the future.

The country most directly and spectacularly affected by this process
was Poland. The movement of the Red Army into the eastern part of
pre-war Poland had, to all intents and purposes, settled the boundary
issue there in its broader context. The Soviet and Polish governments
(either the government-in-exile or that installed by the Russians in
Lublin) could discuss modifications of the border as drawn in the
German–Soviet agreements of 1939—and this was indeed done.[a] The
occupation of the area by the Red Army and the agreement of Britain
and the United States to something approximating the Curzon Line as
the basis of the Polish–Soviet border, however, in reality settled the
basic issue.[b] A Poland freed from German control by the Allies could
not reassert its pre-1772 and pre-1939 character as a multi-national
state by force of arms. The Soviet satellite government referred to by
its location for some time as the "Lublin Committee" accepted the new
eastern border; the Polish government-in-exile would not do so,
although some of its members were willing to make modifications in the
pre-war border with the Soviet Union. It has been suggested, and this
appears to have been Churchill's view during the war, that a willingness
to accept the new border with Russia would have made possible a very
different outcome for Poland on the issues of government and internal
institutions; but the fate of the government of Czechoslovakia, which
followed an opposite course and accepted territorial change in favor of
the Soviet Union, suggests otherwise.

In any case both Polish governments had plans for major post-war
territorial revisions vis-à-vis Germany. While both had hopes for the
cession of all of East Prussia, both were willing to accept its division
with the Soviet Union. Both also assumed that the territory of the Free
City of Danzig would be incorporated into a liberated Poland, as that
city had been for centuries before its annexation by Prussia in 1793. As

---

[a] The outcome was a major modification in favor of Poland at the northern end of the border,
leaving the bulk of the Bialystok region to Poland, and smaller alterations at the southern
end, also in favor of Poland, with the Bug river remaining the border in the middle. There is
a very useful map in U.S., Department of State, *Postwar Foreign Policy Preparations*, facing
p. 512. There is a sketch map comparing the Molotov-Ribbentrop line with the 1945 border
in Romain Yakemchouk, *La ligne Curzon et la IIe Guerre Mondiale* (Louvain and Paris:
Editions Nauwelaerts, 1957), p. 117.

[b] The Curzon Line, named after British Foreign Secretary Lord Curzon of Kedleston, had
been drawn up at the Paris Peace Conference of 1919 on the basis of the Austrian census
of 1910, and was supposed to follow approximately the eastern limit of predominantly Polish
as opposed to Belorussian and Ukrainian populations.

for the western border, Sikorski had been urging the government-in-exile to demand a new border along the Oder and western Neisse rivers as the shortest and most easily defensible line.[20] The British government was increasingly favorable to a new border in the west; although there was reluctance in London and Washington, both to thinking of this border change as compensation for Polish territorial losses to the Soviet Union on her eastern border as well as to the massive number of Germans either being included in Poland or being transferred out of these areas, Great Britain and the United States came increasingly to accept both concepts.[21] There would be a great deal of subsequent diplomatic and propagandistic maneuvering about the new German–Polish border, but there was never any likelihood of major change.

On the subject of the new government of Poland, there had been and would continue to be major differences between the Allies, but the Lublin Committee, installed in stages in the territory liberated by the Red Army, intended from the beginning to crush the underground Polish army loyal to the government-in-exile and to establish a "people's democracy" permanently aligned with the Soviet Union in post-war Europe.[22] And there was little anyone could do to stop it—except for the ceaseless hostility of the mass of the population to their new masters.

The plans of the Czechoslovak government-in-exile for the future had two central aims. One was the recognition by the victors that the German destruction of the Munich settlement of 1938 by the occupation of March 1939 ended the earlier borders and thus re-established the pre-Munich boundaries with Germany, Austria, Poland, and Hungary. By 1944, this aim had been attained. So had the second one: as mentioned above, the Czechoslovak government wanted and received the agreement of the major Allies to the expulsion of the country's inhabitants of German descent. The easternmost portion of pre-Munich Czechoslovakia had to be ceded to the Soviet Union, but in the rest, including the territories ceded to Germany, Hungary, and Poland in 1938, the government-in-exile would be installed with the authorization by the Allies to remove the three and a half million Germans.

The prospect of these Germans, added to over nine million from the territories east of the Oder–Neisse line (together with hundreds of thousands more fleeing or expelled from other portions of East and Southeast Europe), being transferred out of their homes into a residual German area opened up the possibility of an entirely new population movement of a size unprecedented in European history. The Germans had rejected the effort made at Versailles in 1919 to adjust boundaries to population, and they had substituted the concept of drawing new lines and then moving or killing the population to fit those lines. This new procedure was now to be applied to them on a massive scale; and in a world the Germans had terrorized, few could muster sympathy.[a]

BRITISH AND U.S. PLANS

The Western Allies also had their plans for Germany and were already ruling a small portion of it in the Aachen area. Both the Americans and the British planned to install military government systems.[23] The policies to be followed were laid down in directives which reflected two basic assumptions. One was that the German people needed to be reoriented toward a democratic order in a lengthy process; the other that this process required not only the end of Naziism and militarism and the removal of industry capable of supporting still a third attempt at military expansion, but some sort of slow political rebuilding from the ground up.

During the mid-years of the war there had been all sorts of schemes for breaking up Germany into small states—the term used at the time was "dismemberment"—and the Soviet Union had also favored such a project, but when the three governments faced the question of how and where to do the dismembering, the concept looked less and less practical. Each of the three Allies slowly abandoned the idea and looked increasingly to a Germany reduced in size and divided into zones of occupation with the zones still constituting parts of a single entity. In their own zones, about the location of which the Americans and British argued at great length, both would expect new democratic institutions to begin at the local level and later grow in scope. Since the Americans and British believed that the Germans had been turned to Naziism by terrible errors and bad leaders, not as a result of the structure of the economy, they saw the future very differently from the Russians. Whatever changes might or might not be made in the German economy—and the Americans were especially keen on applying their ideas of "trust-busting" to Germany—the new Germany would be erected from the bottom up, not from the top down as was contemplated for the Soviet zone. At the beginning, therefore, the British and Americans foresaw a prohibition of political activity rather than the sponsorship of a political party dedicated to one view of the future. As the public became "re-educated" and democratized, new parties and structures would be created on a local and subsequently broader basis.

[a] The fact that in post-war West Germany the political party which represented the refugees and expellees in public selected as its leaders two men, Waldemar Kraft and Theodor Oberländer, who had both played prominent roles in earlier efforts to expel and expropriate non-Germans, effectively undermined whatever resonance German complaints might have had.

On the economic side, several questions dominated discussion within the American and British governments and between them. In the first place, it was obvious that eastern Germany included a major portion of the agricultural land, and that unless the Soviet Union agreed to the continuation of substantial internal transfers of food from the east to the west of occupied Germany, there would be a massive problem of feeding the population of the British and American zones. In case the Soviets declined food shipments westwards, as looked ever more likely and came to be the post-war situation, the population of the western zones would either be allowed to starve or they would be fed either through British and American food shipments—and this in practice would mean American shipments—or they could be allowed to rebuild their economy and earn the cost of importing food. Each of these three possibilities had its own problems: the first—starvation—was incompatible with the values of British and American society and unlikely to be tolerated for any length of time by the people at home, especially as it produced food riots and disease. The second would impose indefinite burdens on the British and American taxpayers and was not likely to receive their long-term support. The third risked the danger of a rebuilt German industrial might which could lead to a renewed bid for European if not world domination and would certainly make even more difficult a post-war recovery of British world trade, an essential pre-condition for a revival of the country drained by years of extraordinary effort in the war.

Ironically, the argument over the first of these alternatives was initially resolved in a Great Britain which insisted on obtaining that portion of Germany in which the economic problem was certain to be the most difficult of all the occupation zones.[24] Some food would simply have to be shipped in. That this would turn out to be an issue of enormous difficulty for the British—and one which would eventually make their policy in occupied Germany practically subservient to American preferences—was due to the division into occupation zones as well as the allocation of zones primarily in accordance with a British proposal. A special committee of the British Cabinet had worked out a division which was marked by two main features, one affecting the division between the Soviet and the western zones of occupation, and the other the location of British and American zones within the western portion. A plan dividing the Soviet and western zones at what came to be the border between East and West Germany was drafted and submitted to the European Advisory Commission, the body established by the three major Allies after the October 1943 Moscow Conference to work out details of cooperation.[25]

This line left Berlin out of the three occupation zones as a separate district for joint occupation but placed that district deep inside the Soviet zone of occupation. At a time when the British government was still gravely concerned about a possible Soviet withdrawal from the war or from active operations on the main front, this proposal gave the Russians a major objective to fight for in Central Europe. It was presented to the European Advisory Commission without prior agreement with the Americans on the doubtless correct assumption that the Americans would object. The Russians promptly accepted the British proposal and thereby left the Americans little choice but eventually to go along.[26] This was in part due to the fact that when these lines were drawn in the spring of 1944 the Red Army was in great strength on the continent whereas the Western Allies had not yet landed on the coast of France. The other reason for American acquiescence was President Roosevelt's order of priorities on the subject of occupation zones.

Roosevelt's own November 1943 map for the occupation of Germany divided the country in such a fashion as to provide a large zone for the Americans in the northwest, and smaller zones for the British in the south and the Russians in the east. The American and Russian zones would meet in Berlin.[27] Earlier, Roosevelt had repeatedly mentioned his interest in having American troops enter Berlin first, but he had not before sketched his ideas in detail. In the discussions at that time, however, he had been most insistent on the United States having the northwest zone with direct access to the Atlantic, not a zone in the south which would be land-locked and dependent on land communications across France. Fearful of post-war disturbances in the latter country, he insisted for a full year that he would not accept a southern zone. Although there is no explicit evidence, he may have been influenced by the memory of the American garrison in the Philippines, so recently cut off and isolated abroad; he was certainly affected by a continuing concern about the internal stability of France.

In the subsequent negotiations, Roosevelt held out far longer on the issue of the northern as opposed to the southern zone but agreed to the border between the eastern and western occupations. The British insisted on the north, citing proximity, their own maritime interest, and the impracticality of having the British and American armies cross over after hostilities, during which they would have moved into Germany with the British on the northern and the American on the southern flank (though experience in Tunisia and later in Germany itself would show these fears largely groundless). There was a further idea behind the British obstinacy. Since the Americans, including Roosevelt, repeatedly said that their troops would not remain in Europe for more than a few, perhaps two, years, it made sense for the French eventually to replace the Americans in the south. Given Roosevelt's concerns about post-war France, this was obviously not an argument to put to him.

The American Chiefs of Staff eventually persuaded Roosevelt to accept the southern zone with the proviso that the United States was to have an enclave in the British zone at Bremen on the coast to assure a means of direct communication across the British zone and the Atlantic without any need to traverse France.[28] Most of the discussion of access and transport was accordingly between the Americans and the British, not with the Russians.

In subsequent years, those problems which had been anticipated turned out to be far easier than expected: France after its liberation settled down much more readily than Roosevelt had feared, the shifting of troops into occupation zones proved much easier than anyone had thought—at the end of hostilities the American XVIII Corps was at Wismar on the Baltic—and the supplying of the American zone across the British proved so smooth that the complicated Bremen arrangement turned out to be unnecessary after all. What remained were two issues which turned out to be vastly more complicated than anyone had thought: transit to Berlin and feeding the vast population of the north-west zone which the British had received but which they had themselves bombed most heavily during the war, and where the question of how the Germans were to be fed was naturally most acute.

The economic future of Germany was of special concern to the Allies. The Soviet Union, after the terrible devastation of war, wanted as large a contribution as possible to its recovery. The British were concerned about the future competition of German exports with her own efforts at economic recuperation from a war into which she had poured her assets and resources. The United States had no desire for a third round with Germany. If there was general agreement that Germany should be stripped of the capacity to make war again, there was much argument over how this could best be done.

In the United States, occupation had traditionally been a military affair under general but remote civilian control. The assumption was that this would be the case with Germany, and in the War Department some preparations were accordingly begun.[29] As these preparations went forward, their generally rather mild implications for occupied Germany alarmed some, especially Secretary of the Treasury Henry Morgenthau. A Hyde Park neighbor and long-time friend of Roosevelt's, Morgenthau was probably the President's closest confidante after Hopkins, and like Hopkins totally devoted to Roosevelt. An administrator of enormous energy and talent, he combined a frugal and conservative fiscal policy with a heart for the disadvantaged. In these regards he was the ideal assistant to the President, sharing his values, tempering Roosevelt's flights of fancy with a dour punctiliousness, while combining the ability to get things done with complete loyalty to the President.[30]

Concerned about the general tone of American military government planning, Morgenthau, with the help of high Treasury Department officials, especially Harry Dexter White, drew up an alternative proposal which came to be known by his name.[31] Turned over to Roosevelt and initially agreed to by him, it provided for removing heavy industry from a Germany of which one substantial portion of the previously most heavily industrialized part would be internationalized, and another ceded to France; but it also provided that most of the major agricultural area east of the Oder-Neisse line would remain German.[a] The not so heavily industrialized area would be divided into a northern and a southern state with the southern one in a customs union with Austria in its old borders. The models which the Treasury officials had in mind were Holland and Denmark, both advanced countries with a high standard of living in pre-1939 Europe, both heavily agricultural, and neither militarily important.[32]

Roosevelt clearly believed that Morgenthau's proposal fitted in with his own view of Germany's future.[33] Its emphasis on dismemberment, its shift from the post-World War I idea of reparations to a transfer of industrial machinery, its assumption that the Germans would have to work hard and build democratic institutions for themselves over a long period of time, and the view that American troops could be withdrawn relatively quickly, all would have appealed to him.[34] Initially, Secretary of State Cordell Hull also agreed with this proposal while Secretary of War Henry Stimson opposed it.

When Stalin would not participate in a three-power meeting in the summer of 1944, Roosevelt and Churchill decided to meet with their advisors at Quebec in September. Hull decided against attending, so Roosevelt invited Morgenthau.[35] Churchill himself dictated the terminology of the Morgenthau plan that Germany be "primarily agricultural and pastoral in its character," which Roosevelt and the Prime Minister then initialled.[36] Both were strongly in favor of the concept at the time, but soon thereafter both modified their views. The two countries moved

---

[a] The post-war critiques of the Morgenthau Plan invariably omit the plan's assumption of Germany's keeping much of the territory later turned over to Poland. Morgenthau assumed that only East Prussia and Upper and Central Silesia would be ceded. See the maps in Henry Morgenthau, *Germany is Our Problem* (New York: Harper, 1945), facing p. 160; and White's map published in David Rees, *Harry Dexter White: A Study in Paradox* (New York: Coward, McCann & Georghegan, 1973), p. 444. The area to be left with Germany was inhabited by at least five million people in 1939; they were, of course, among those who lost their homes in the settlement actually applied. Morgenthau estimated (p. 50) that his plan would require the shifting of just over four million workers from heavy industry to agriculture.

in the direction symbolized by the American directive for occupation policy sent to Eisenhower known as JCS (Joint Chiefs of Staff) 1067, which embodied the generally harsh attitude Roosevelt, Churchill and Morgenthau had favored but without the major emphasis on the elimination of heavy industry.[37] The level of German industry was to be kept low—and many plants dismantled and shipped to Germany's World War II victims—but the country would not be stripped of heavy industry entirely.

Commentators have pointed to the political objections raised against the original Morgenthau plan as a major factor in Roosevelt's and Churchill's change of heart, but this overlooks a major point already alluded to: the increasing likelihood, known to Roosevelt and Churchill, that there would be a massive transfer of agricultural territory from Germany to Poland. However great the advantages of diminishing Germany's war-making capacity, and whatever the blessings to Britain's export trade from the removal of German heavy industry, there was no way to shift millions of Germans from industry into agriculture if one simultaneously took away a huge portion of the country's agricultural land and agreed to the expulsion of the German population living there.[38]

If the British and Americans were developing—and in the case of the Americans in the Aachen area applying—occupation policies as well as territorial plans, the French were as yet excluded from an immediate role. This, however, in no way kept them from making plans.[39] On the territorial side, there were several concepts, all based on the great concern that France had to be protected from any renewed German threat. In the broadest sense, de Gaulle in particular believed passionately that only a recovered great power status for France was both appropriate and safe. It was a subject on which he clashed most directly with his allies, and especially with the United States and the Soviet Union, both of which thought that the defeat of 1940 had in fact ended such a position for France, while the British, though sharing this view for the present, looked more hopefully to a revived France in the future.

By the fall of 1944, however, the success of de Gaulle in establishing himself as de-facto leader of a liberated France, assisted by the American policy of building up a new French army,[40] made the three major Allies increasingly willing to think of France as a power which could play a key role in the future of Europe. If they would not as yet, and for years, take the great power pretensions of de Gaulle as seriously as he wished, there can be no doubt that the signs pointed in a new direction.

From the perspective of Paris, once again the seat of the French government, the key immediate issue was policy toward Germany. There were two concurrent priorities. First, there should be no new German central government, and in the immediate post-war years the French would use the position of importance restored to them by the Allies to block any and all central administrative structures for Germany which those same Allies preferred to establish.

On the more direct and immediate issue of territorial change, the French government had its second main objective. It wanted to detach the left bank of the Rhine from Germany and either incorporate all of it or much of it—most certainly the Saar area—into France. In the 1919 peace negotiations, the French had given up their plan to detach the left bank of the Rhine under pressure from the United States and Great Britain and in exchange for the promise of a defensive alliance against Germany. After making their concession, the French had been cheated out of the promised alliance. They were not about to get trapped into such a bargain again if they could help it. As it turned out, the Russians would not support the larger territorial ambitions and the Americans and British only agreed to the cession of the Saar area. Washington and London would, however, in late 1944 shift their view on the participation of France in the occupation and began to argue for a French zone of occupation, one of the issues that would have to be resolved at the next Allied meeting at Yalta.

When seen as a whole, the plans the Allies were developing for Germany were quite harsh, but given German behavior, hardly surprisingly so. Putting them in front of the Germans instead of simply calling for unconditional surrender was not likely to make ending the war on Allied terms particularly attractive. The Germans could give in or be pounded to bits; unlike all their allies and satellites, they evidently preferred the latter.

WINTER OFFENSIVES IN THE EAST

Even before the new major Soviet offensive in the East began in January, the situation in Hungary was altering slowly but steadily in favor of the Russians. The capital of Budapest had been cut off on December 26 after Hitler refused permission for the German Army to withdraw in time. The huge city was now besieged, but the Red Army halted in the face of German and Hungarian resistance and the exhaustion of its own offensive power on December 28.[41] The Germans planned a major relief offensive, partly for the political reason of breaking the siege and partly as a means of protecting the Hungarian oil fields, which were especially important for the Germans after the loss of the Romanian oil fields and the success of the Allied air attacks on the synthetic oil industry. Here the German army launched its last great offensive of the war. During

January, a series of German attacks drove toward the Hungarian capital, but, as in the case of the attempted relief of Stalingrad two years earlier, failed to break through and reach the isolated garrison.[42]

Ironically it was into this battle that Hitler directed the 6th SS Panzer Army as it was pulled out of the Battle of the Bulge. Instead of sending it or other reinforcements to the central portion of the Eastern Front, where the Red Army was poised to plunge into Germany, Hitler insisted on still another offensive in Hungary. It would in any case come too late to save the crumbling garrison of Budapest, where the remaining German and Hungarian units were crushed in February with only a few hundred men out of over thirty thousand escaping to the German lines.[43]

The main German attack, launched on March 5 primarily to protect the oil fields and the approaches of Vienna—the next obvious Soviet target—proved an enormous and costly fiasco. Although the Second and Third Ukrainian Fronts (fighting north and south of the Budapest area respectively) had to give some ground, they soon crushed the attacking German forces. By the end of the month they had pushed the Germans out of most of the rest of Hungary, though not yet the oil fields, and were poised to strike for Vienna. Hitler's hysterical reproaches could not move even his armed SS anymore; there were signs of demoralization appearing in the German units, signs which may well have reflected the fact that, even as the German soldiers were supposed to push the Red Army out of Hungary, the fronts had moved ever deeper into Germany both from the East and from the West.

The Soviet Union had been building up its forces on the central portion of the Eastern Front during the time when the Germans were using up their reserves of manpower and equipment elsewhere, first in the offensives in the West and thereafter in futile efforts to relieve the siege of Budapest. A third Red Army offensive against the Germans in Courland failed to break that front; but until more is known about Soviet plans and operations in western Latvia from October 1944 to May 1945, we will not be able to determine whether these were intended to drive the Germans into the Baltic Sea or to pin them down there and preclude evacuation until their eventual surrender. The major emphasis of Soviet military planning for their January 1945 offensive was on the Central front looking toward a crushing of the German armies from East Prussia to the Carpathians with a rapid follow-up drive to Berlin which, as Stalin well knew, was inside the occupation zone allocated to the Soviet Union.

The Soviet plan contemplated accomplishing this victory drive to the Elbe river in a first phase of fifteen days, in which the major thrust would be out of the bridgeheads over the Vistula south of Warsaw, and a secondary push out of the bridgeheads over the Narev river north of

Warsaw. The southern offensive by First Belorussian and First Ukrainian Fronts would drive through southern Poland into the key German industrial area of Silesia, while in the north the Second and Third Belorussian Fronts would isolate the German troops in the area around East Prussia by driving to the Baltic Sea behind them and subsequently crushing the cut-off remnants. In both cases, it was assumed that Soviet superiority in manpower, artillery, tanks and mobility would break open the relatively thin crust of German defenders quickly and that mobile Red Army spearheads could then strike deep into the rear of an enemy without substantial reserves. In a second phase of thirty days, which was to follow the first without a pause, the Red Army command would send the southern forces, that is First Belorussian and First Ukrainian Fronts, straight forward through Berlin and to the Elbe river. The assumption was that a drive of about six weeks would end the war in Europe in February or March and release forces for a campaign into Manchuria against Japan.[44]

The first portion of the Soviet plan to end the European war in forty-five days succeeded completely; the second did not. Originally scheduled for about January 15–20,[45] the offensive was moved up a week, in part in response to requests from the Western Allies to relieve pressure, after months of quiet on the main sector of the front in the East had enabled the Germans to concentrate elsewhere. The early attack had the advantage, on the other hand, of surprising many of the German headquarters, which had expected the Red Army to await better weather. The German reserves had largely been sent to Hungary; on the main front practically everything the Germans had was within Red Army artillery range. The great assaults, launched on January 12, 13, and 14 out of the Vistula and Narev bridgeheads, quite literally crushed the German forces before them, shoved aside both the remnants of the German front formations and what few reserves were available behind the German lines, and had broken into the open by January 17. Portions of the German front were surrounded as Red Army armored formations cut in behind them while elsewhere the disorganized remnants of German divisions — preceded by rear area services and administrations — flooded back toward the Reich. As the weather cleared, the Red Air Force held effective control of the skies.

The Soviet victory was of immense proportions, and it caused all the more confusion because the Russians gained in confidence and morale as the Germans, chased over areas hitherto hardly touched by the war and in fact the goal of many evacuated from the West because of bombing there, fled before what looked increasingly like an unstoppable onrush.[46]

The Germans moved some reinforcements from the Western Front eastwards and scraped together others, but the main effort to shore up the collapsing front was of a different sort. Hitler sent two of his experts at holding fast by having lots of Germans shot, Schörner and Rendulic, to take over critical sectors and then Himmler to head up a new, largely fictional, Army Group named "Vistula." None of this substantially slowed down the Red Army; by the end of January Soviet forces had drawn to the Baltic just east of Danzig (Gdansk) and cut off the remnants of the German 3rd Panzer and 4th Armies, were on and across the Oder river in the center of the front, and had captured almost all of Silesia east of that stream. Practically all of pre-war Poland had been liberated from Germany and was now under Soviet control, a large portion of the Silesian industrial and mining area had fallen to Konev's First Ukrainian Front practically intact, and hundreds of thousands of German civilians were now crowding the roads as refugees. Here and there surrounded islands of resistance held out—the city of Breslau (Wroclaw) until May—but it was obvious that these were all certain to fall.[a] The area through which the Red Army had moved included Auschwitz (Oswiecim) with its branch camps, its vast factories and its murder centers. The Germans had not had time to cart off seven tons of women's hair.

It can, however, be argued that the determination—or desperation—with which the German garrisons fought at the northern and southern flanks of the front, combined with last minute reinforcements on the Oder, contributed to the halting of the Soviet offensive during February. Zhukov's bulge to the Oder river east of Berlin included some bridgeheads across that river but was not wide enough to provide a basis for the second phase of the planned Soviet offensive; and most of February, as the winter weather allowed, was a time when the Red Army pushed forward in East Prussia, Pomerania, and northern Silesia on the flanks of the line reached at the end of January.[47] A small German counter-offensive at Stargard on February 16 appears to have shaken the self-confidence of the Soviet high command; and, as a result, the decision was made that the second phase of the great offensive into central Germany would require a full preparation. Occupying Berlin and the assigned zone in Germany would not be easy or quick for the Russians, but this also meant that it would be even more bloody and devastating for the Germans.[48] In between the

[a] From the isolated coastal areas about two million military and civilians were evacuated. On Breslau, see Karol Jonca, "The Destruction of 'Breslau': The Final Struggle of the Germans in Wroclaw in 1945," *Polish Western Affairs* 2, No. 2 (1961), 304–33.

two now separated phases of the Soviet offensive there occurred the previously planned Allied conference at Yalta in the Crimea.

There had been lengthy exchanges about a possible new meeting of the leaders of the Allies, and Stalin had once again refused to travel any great distance, a point of particular difficulty for Roosevelt who had an election to face in November 1944 and whose health showed signs of exhaustion from overwork.[49] The decision to meet at Yalta meant a long trip for him as well as Churchill; the Chiefs of Staff of the Western Allies arranged to meet beforehand at Malta. At this meeting, the final offensives of the Western armies into Germany were worked out. The British still had visions of a single thrust in the north commanded by Montgomery, but there was no prospect of American agreement. The possibility of replacing Tedder as Eisenhower's deputy with Field Marshal Alexander was also canvassed before and after this meeting; but once it became clear that he would not assume a full ground forces command position, the British themselves dropped the idea.[50] The basic strategy agreed to with considerable British misgivings provided for a series of offensives, beginning in the north, to destroy German forces on the left bank of the Rhine, then a major crossing of that river and an offensive to surround the Ruhr industrial area, to be followed by advances to the Baltic in the north, toward the Russians in the center, and into Bavaria in the south.

There was also considerable discussion of the shipping problem, once again difficult because of the need for both relief shipments to liberated portions of Europe and the plan to redeploy troops from the European theater of war to the Pacific for the final assault on Japan. There was still some concern about the possible appearance of the new types of German submarines, but these were likely to create problems only if the war against Germany were prolonged. To speed up the process of defeating Germany, both the Americans and Canadians insisted on, and the English Chiefs of Staff reluctantly agreed to, the transfer of five divisions, three of them Canadian, from the Mediterranean to the main front in the West.

As for the Pacific War, agreement was reached on the landings on Iwo Jima and Okinawa and the eventual invasion of the home islands of Japan. With the expectation that the war in Europe would end between July and the end of that year, it was calculated that another year and a half would be needed to crush Japan. Victory, the Combined Chiefs of Staff informed Churchill and Roosevelt, would hopefully come in 1947.

At Yalta, the Allied leaders met from February 4 to 11, 1945, in a series of sessions which have gained more fame—or notoriety—than perhaps they deserve. Most of the major diplomatic choices were prefigured at the Teheran Conference, and the most contentious political issue between the Soviet Union and the Western Allies—the fate of Poland and Southeast Europe—had been effectively settled between Teheran and Yalta by the occupation—or liberation—of practically the whole of that area by the Red Army in the interim. By the time of the meeting at Yalta, the "Lublin Committee" was installed in Warsaw, and already the Czechoslovak government-in-exile had followed Soviet wishes by recognizing it, not the London government-in-exile, as the legal regime of its northern neighbor.

If one major factor overshadowing the Yalta deliberations was the control which the Soviet Union in fact already exercised over almost all of Eastern and Southeastern Europe, the converse was the British control of Greece, and American and British predominance in Italy, France, and most of the Low Countries. The Americans and British found that they would get very little in the way of concessions on the government of Poland, and the concessions which they did obtain were quickly repudiated soon after the meeting: the expansion of the Lublin regime by representatives of the London government-in-exile and others from within Poland was quickly and effectively sabotaged, while the free elections, which Stalin promised could be held as early as a month off, were not held until 1989, forty-four years later. Since the Soviet Union had not interfered in the fighting between the British and the Greek Communists when the latter had attempted to seize power, Stalin may have felt entitled to repress all opposition in the area controlled by his army, though agreeing to the American proposal of a declaration assuring all liberated and occupied territories the freedom to choose their own government. The Soviet Union wanted "friendly" regimes in East and Southeast Europe, and there was no way that governments which Stalin considered friendly were likely to emerge from free elections.[51]

On the other hand, the Western Powers had become increasingly committed to a major role for France in post-war Europe. With very great reluctance Stalin agreed to an occupation zone for the French in Germany but insisted absolutely and successfully that this zone (and a corresponding sector of Berlin) be carved out of the zones (and sectors) allocated to the United States and Great Britain. The Soviet Union was not about to give up any portions of the territory assigned to it; Stalin may well have thought of France as simply a satellite of the Western Powers. Furthermore, it was only after Roosevelt changed his mind on the subject of assigning France a place on the Allied Control Council for Germany that Stalin also agreed to this.

The British insistence on American and thereafter Soviet acquiescence in a full role for France was presumably related to the repetition by Roosevelt of his Teheran pronouncement that large numbers of American troops would not remain in Europe for more than two years after the defeat of Germany. Not only would many be needed for the war against Japan, but it was thought unlikely that the American public would agree to any long-term stationing of American units in Germany. Always conscious of the disruption of President Wilson's hopes and plans at the end of World War I, Roosevelt had been cautious both about commitments for the future and building up domestic support for those he did make. At least in the anticipations of the British and possibly also his own, the French could eventually take over the American zone in southern Germany which Roosevelt had just agreed to accept, and which would certainly be adjacent to any French zone.[52]

Getting the American public to accept the compromises the Western Powers had made on Poland was going to be difficult. Both the British and Americans agreed to an eastern border for Poland based on the Curzon Line—as they had previously indicated they would at Teheran— but Roosevelt did try very hard, though unsuccessfully, to salvage the primarily Polish city of Lwow as well as the nearby oil fields for Poland.[53]

The resolution of the difficult chore of selling this in the United States, or at least blunting opposition to it, was tied closely to the issue of the planned new international organization. On this topic, Roosevelt was understandably eager to avoid the failure of the Wilson administration, a failure in which he had been deeply and personally involved and which he like many others saw as having contributed so greatly to the outbreak of a second world war. He was determined at the Yalta Conference to have the critical remaining issue left open at the Dumbarton Oaks Conference, that of the voting procedure in the Security Council, resolved. He had taken to Yalta the new Secretary of State, Edward Stettinius, as he had not taken Hull, recently retired because of illness, to Teheran; and Stettinius carefully explained the United States compromise proposal at the meeting when Stalin claimed not to have studied it beforehand. Although on this point the Soviet leader, to the enormous relief of the American delegation, agreed to accept the proposal to the effect that the great power veto would not apply to procedural matters, he insisted on another concession which Roosevelt was most reluctant to approve.

Earlier the Soviets had asked for sixteen seats (and votes) in the Assembly of the United Nations, one for each of the constituent Soviet Socialist Republics in the U.S.S.R.. The Americans had objected, but the British, who wanted a place for India as well as for each of the self-governing Dominions, were not so sure. Now Stalin insisted on two extra votes, one each for the Ukrainian and the Belorussian SSRs;[a] the British agreed to the demand;[54] and the Americans reluctantly went along. Roosevelt, who remembered the domestic American opposition to what the public had seen as multiple British votes in the League of Nations with one for each of the Dominions, both insisted on keeping this concession secret and British and Soviet support for two extra votes for the United States in the Assembly if that should prove desirable. When the whole deal leaked out soon after, there was a temporary uproar, but this tempest in a teapot was quickly calmed by two other measures, one taken at Yalta, one soon after.

At the Yalta Conference, it was agreed that those countries which declared war on Germany by March 1 should be invited to the April 25 founding conference for which France would be one of the inviting powers, and also that this conference was to be held in the United States, a point on which the Americans were particularly insistent. If the American public was to be permanently weaned from its isolationist proclivities, the best way to engage their attention for a new world security organization was to organize it in the United States, San Francisco being chosen as the location. And Roosevelt, unlike Wilson, would include key leaders of the Republican Party in the United States delegation. With Senator Arthur Vandenberg, the key spokesman on international affairs of the opposition in the Senate, appointed to the delegation, Roosevelt effectively co-opted the most likely opponent of the Yalta agreements.[55]

The future of Germany was certainly a major topic of discussion. The agreement on occupation zones, previously worked out in the European Advisory Commission, was approved with the addition of a French zone. An Allied Control Council, meeting in Berlin, would set policy, but other than the negative aims of de-nazification and de-militarization, there was little agreement on what to do. The Soviet Union and the Western Powers interpreted "democratization" very differently as already described. Since the line between the eastern and western zones had been agreed upon, the extent of territorial cession to Poland would, in effect, be left to the Soviets, and the line of the Oder and western

[a] Why Stalin thought this issue so important remains to be investigated.

Neisse would come to be the new border, in spite of doubts by both the British and the Americans and the formal reference to final determination at a peace conference. Once the German inhabitants had fled or been expelled, there was not likely to be any more change.

With Poland firmly under Soviet control, and both Poland itself and the Soviet occupation zone pushed far westwards, Russia could feel safe from any future German invasion. As for that country itself, the issue of dismemberment came up once more. There was again theoretical agreement that this would be a good idea, with the Soviets especially insistent, but the German Communists in Moscow were already working on the assumption of a single German state, while the Soviet government reversed itself and came out for keeping a unified Germany soon after Yalta.[56]

This shift might have been related to the Soviet view on the reparations issue on which it did not receive the results Stalin wanted at Yalta; later he may have believed that keeping the French from annexing large portions of the industrialized parts of western Germany would more likely make facilities there available for transfer to the Soviet Union. In any case, the Russians argued at Yalta that a reparations sum of twenty billion dollars should be set with half going to them and the balance to the other countries at war with Germany. The Americans and British both read their experience with reparations in the years after World War I as showing that a fixed sum was a poor idea, the British because their zone of occupation would be in need of endless subsidies after its industry had been removed, the Americans because of their belief that American loans had paid for German reparations and might end up doing so again. No agreement was reached, and the issue was left for the Allied Foreign Ministers to resolve, but there was a general sense that massive amounts of industrial equipment would be removed from Germany to help those who had suffered from the Third Reich's policy of aggression.[57]

Before any plans for the future could be implemented, Germany and Japan would have to be defeated. The way to crush Germany appeared to be rather obvious: concentric attacks on the Reich. There was some exchange of military information, but there was in practice no more direct and detailed coordination of operations between the Soviet Union and the Western Allies now than earlier, and the minimal attempts — such as arrangements for American planes to use airfields in Hungary — quickly evaporated in the face of Soviet refusal to implement the promises made. More important were the discussions of the participation of the Soviet Union in the war against Japan.

Since Stalin had originally promised to join the war in East Asia for a suitable price after the defeat of Germany, several major changes had taken place in that war. The Americans and Australians had made major advances in the Southwest and the Central Pacific theaters and the British had defeated the Japanese in Burma, but the fighting had been exceedingly bloody and bitter; at the Malta Conference, the Combined Chiefs of Staff had posited another year and a half of fighting after victory over Germany. Nationalist China, the main land base for the assault on Japanese forces on the mainland of Asia as well as air attacks on the Japanese home islands on which the Americans had counted at the time of Stalin's promise at Teheran, had in the interim collapsed militarily in the face of Japan's great "Ichigo" offensive. Although the air supply of China over the Hump continued, and the first convoy of trucks over the Ledo Road had reached the Chinese border on January 28, just before the Yalta Conference, it was obvious that no major offensive against Japan could be based on the crumbling remnants of Chiang Kai-shek's China.

These alterations in the Pacific War appeared to make the final attack on Japan on the one hand more feasible and on the other hand more dependent on Soviet entrance into the war. With this background, American and British willingness to agree to the Soviet Union regaining its losses from the Russo-Japanese War of 1904–5 looked reasonable enough. There were, however, additional Soviet demands, such as the Kurile Islands, and a recognition of the Soviet satellite status of Mongolia, without the participation of Chinese representatives. Roosevelt had hinted at some of the demands to Chiang at the Cairo Conference; he now undertook to obtain Chiang's agreement to them. In exchange, he obtained not only Stalin's promise to join the war against Japan two to three months after the end of hostilities in Europe, but two concessions highly important for the Chinese government. Stalin agreed to help the Chinese Nationalists and he recognized that, once cleared of Japanese troops by the Red Army, Manchuria would be returned to Chinese sovereignty. In view of the situation in China at the time, these were major concessions indeed; and had the Nationalists won the Chinese civil war, would no doubt have brought Stalin reproaches from Chinese Communists as vehement as those which Roosevelt's and Churchill's agreement to the Yalta terms were later to bring on the American President.[58] No one yet knew whether the atomic bomb would work, nor, if it did work, what its impact on Japanese resistance might be. In the meantime, the Americans and British had secured a major ally for the war against Japan; the Americans to support the invasion of the Japanese home islands, the British to divert Japanese land forces from the planned campaign in Malaya scheduled to follow on that in Burma.

Two secondary topics were also dealt with at the conference. The effort to bring some representatives of the Yugoslav government-in-exile into the new regime being established by Tito proved as unsuccessful as that to create a coalition government for Poland. An agreement with more dramatic repercussions was that designed to assure the return to Britain and the United States of their many soldiers who had been captured by the Germans and kept in prisoner of war camps overrun by the Red Army. There had been endless difficulties in this regard.[59] In return for assurances on their prompt repatriation, the Western Powers committed themselves to returning to the Soviet Union all Soviet citizens—prisoners of war, forced laborers, or those who had agreed to serve in or with the German army. There were two bad aspects of this arrangement.[60] The Soviet Union made endless difficulties about the return of United States and British prisoners, especially because their desire for the crushing of all opposition in Poland made the Russians unwilling to allow into the camps in Poland any western representatives who might observe developments in that country. The resulting clashes with American diplomats, especially Ambassador Harriman and chief of the military mission General Deane, contributed greatly to their negative attitudes toward the Soviet Union and thus to the development of the Cold War.[61]

The other result was the forced repatriation of many who feared for their lives. The British had taken the lead in returning such men already in August 1944; they extended the program to pre-1939 Soviet émigrés and to those from the areas annexed by the Soviet Union from 1939 on. On both of these issues the United States followed a different policy, refusing to repatriate émigrés against their will and allowing those who lived outside the pre-war Soviet Union to decline repatriation.[62] Even so, tens of thousands were forcibly returned by both countries. Until well after the war, there was little sympathy for those who had fought to help Germany keep Europe in subjection, whatever their motives had been; the episode brought grief and suffering to many and no credit to anyone.

Of more immediate concern to both Britain and the United States was the impact of the Yalta agreements on the Polish corps fighting in Italy and the division in Montgomery's forces on the Western Front. Would these men, who were very much still needed by the Allies, continue to participate as valiantly as in the past in a cause that must have looked already irretrievably lost to most of them? In anxious talks and soundings between the two parties, it became clear that until victory over Germany the Polish soldiers would indeed continue to fight alongside the Western Allies.[63] As for those Poles who fought the Germans inside

Poland, if they did not speedily join the forces of the new Polish Communists regime, they could expect to follow the representatives of the Polish anti-German underground who were arrested by the Soviets at the end of March 1945 when they agreed to appear for negotiations in response to a Soviet invitation.[64]

In subsequent years, the Yalta Conference came to be denounced as a sell-out to the Soviet Union, especially in the United States where, in the first great wave of revisionist writing on war time relations between the Allies, American leaders were accused of giving away everything to the Russians. Later, when a new group of revisionists asserted that those same leaders had in fact been plotting against the Soviet Union during the same period when earlier critics thought they were plotting *with* her, the emphasis came to be on the concessions made by the Soviet Union. Perhaps it would be more reasonable to take a view which sees the three Allies as trying hard for an accommodation of divergent ideologies and interests, with the great problem being that some of the agreements reached were not afterwards carried out, so that the high water mark of cooperation was followed by new crises rather than more steps toward continued working together.

Certainly at the time American public opinion was highly favorable to the Soviet Union, in spite of earlier frictions, and continued to be so for some time.[65] Churchill, who had tried unsuccessfully to arrange a prior meeting with the Americans to coordinate negotiating strategy, was absolutely euphoric at the end of the conference and reported to the British Cabinet in glowing terms on Soviet desire to work with Britain and the United States, and on Stalin's willingness to make concessions to that end.[66] The great reversal came soon after: the February 27, 1945, coup in Bukarest, organized by Soviet Deputy Foreign Minister Vyshinskii, which installed a Communist regime there, the refusal to hold free elections in Poland but instead, on March 27, the arrest of the leaders of the Polish underground when they were supposed to meet Marshal Zhukov, quickly ended the euphoria in London.[67] The American reaction took slightly longer, and would be accelerated by Stalin's extraordinary reaction to the negotiations for a surrender of German troops in Italy, but it came basically over the same issues: the divergence over any degree of real independence for the liberated peoples of eastern and Southeast Europe.

On the other hand, more of the neutrals, after Yalta, decided to join in the war in order to obtain admission to the United Nations Organization, a step for which the conference had set a deadline. Turkey had broken diplomatic relations with Japan at American insistence on January 5 and at about the same time had opened the Straits to Allied shipping;

on February 25 the country declared war on Germany and Japan.[68] Those countries of Latin America which had remained neutral, in some cases at American urging, in the case of Argentina very much against United States preference, now hastened to join in. Sweden cut back on its deliveries to Germany, feeling increasingly secure from German retaliation.[69] As if the isolation of the Axis were not sufficiently advanced, the savagery of Japanese soldiers on the rampage in Manila, where they burned down the Spanish consulate after butchering the officials and refugees in it, led Spain to renounce its representation of Japanese interests with the Allies and to break relations with Japan on April 12.[70] The Germans, like the Japanese, would have to stand alone on the funeral pyre they had insisted on building for themselves, while others rushed to join the Allies as quickly as they could and the Allies would let them.

OFFENSIVES IN THE WEST

But in the meantime, the war ground on. Just as the Red Army's offensive was coming to a halt on the Oder, and the Germans were getting ready for still another counter-attack in Hungary, the Allies in the West, having eliminated the bulge caused by the German December offensive, were getting ready to attack again. As a preliminary, Eisenhower insisted on the clearing of the Colmar bulge west of the Rhine by the French and American troops of General Devers's 6th Army Group. Here, as elsewhere, the Germans would expend their defensive effort on the left bank of the Rhine and then have little strength remaining to defend the line of the river itself. In bitter fighting, the Allies drove to the upper Rhine by February 9.[71] The plan was to follow up on this by a series of operations, starting in the north with a British–Canadian attack southeastward toward Wesel, code-named "Veritable," which would meet an American offensive northeastward called "Grenade." These operations would close the lower Rhine and prepare the way for the great follow-up: a major assault crossing of the Rhine under Montgomery's command into the German plain north of the industrial area of the Ruhr. Following on Veritable-Grenade, Bradley's forces would strike to the Rhine and Mosel rivers farther south (operation "Lumberjack") and, if all went well, could then strike southeast across the Mosel into the rear of German forces in the Westwall along the old Franco-German border from Luxembourg to the Rhine (operation "Undertone"). The possibility of early crossings of the Rhine in these operations was left open, but it was assumed that subsidiary cross-Rhine operations would eventually be launched south of the Ruhr to envelop that region, and in the direction beyond Frankfurt. Montgomery's 21st Army Group was being reinforced by three Canadian and two British divisions from Italy, and the Americans sent the last available division from the United States. Over 400,000 British and Canadian, 1.5 million American, and more than 100,000 French soldiers were poised for the assault on Germany.

The Canadian 1st Army launched "Veritable" on February 8 and drove forward slowly against bitter German resistance.[72] Flooding due to snow melt and the opening of floodgates by the Germans combined with the determined German defenders to slow both the Canadian advance and the American 9th Army attack launched subsequently in operation "Grenade" to meet them. On March 3 the Canadian and American spearheads met, and in the following days what was left of the German defenders withdrew across the Rhine, blowing up the Rhine bridges as they retreated. Although the fighting had been bitter, there were signs that some German units were becoming demoralized: over 50,000 prisoners fell into Allied hands. Montgomery now began enormous preparations for a crossing of the Rhine barrier, but even as he was engaged in this vast endeavor, the Americans further south were busy cutting through the German defenses west of the Rhine and crossing that river on the run.

On February 23 General Hodges's 1st Army attacked southeastwards and pushed toward Cologne. They rapidly drove into the outskirts of the great city and headed south into the rear of German troops still on the German–Belgian border. As they reached the heights overlooking the railway bridge at Remagen on March 7, the 9th Armored Division advance guards saw the bridge still standing and rushed it while the Germans desperately tried to blow it up. Ironically, the October 1944 explosion caused by an American air raid, which had dropped the suspension bridge into the Rhine, had led the Germans to rewire the explosives on the other bridges lest a similar accident befall them; and the greater difficulty of blowing up the re-wired bridge now kept them from destroying the Remagen bridge in the rush of the American advance. With the approval of Bradley and Eisenhower, Hodges quickly pushed American forces across the river, built up a perimeter on the other side against desperate German efforts, and had other bridges in place by the time German artillery and bombs caused the structure, weakened by the original demolition effort, to collapse. The last barrier into Germany from the west had been broken.[a]

---

[a] Knowledge of the bridge seizure first reached 1st Army headquarters from a decyphered *German* message; Adolph G. Rosengarten, Jr., "With Ultra from Omaha Beach to Weimar, Germany—A Personal View," *Military Affairs* 42, No. 3 (1978), p. 131; see also London report "Sunset 860" of 8 March 1945, SRS 1869, Part VI, p. 121, NA, RG 457. Montgomery learned of the bridge capture on the same day and immediately informed Brooke (Tac Hq 21st Army Group to War Office M. 1020 of 7 March 1945, Liddell Hart Centre, Alanbrooke

By this time, Patton's 3rd Army had driven the Germans back to the Mosel on 1st Army's right flank and, in the fashion Patton knew best, now drove across the Mosel into the rear of the German forces facing an attack by the American 7th Army of 6th Army Group. When the German commander in the West, von Rundstedt, wanted to withdraw these units across the Rhine, Hitler replaced him with Field Marshal Albert Kesselring, who had been so successful in stalling the Allies in Italy. This made no difference to the American 3rd Army, which cut the German Army Group G into shreds, captured huge numbers of prisoners, reached the Rhine near Oppenheim on March 21 and late on the following day crossed the river. Before the great assault in the north, not only had the Americans put troops on the east bank of the Rhine at two places, but the French 1st Army had crossed a barrier of its own: on March 19 they had planted the Tricolor on German soil.[73]

The Allied operations had been assisted both by the massive deployment of tactical air support and by continued heavy attacks on German oil, transportation, and industrial targets. At the Yalta Conference, the Russians had asked for major attacks by the air forces of the Western Allies on cities behind the Eastern Front. This request coincided with British plans for massive bombing raids to disrupt German defenses in the East, to aid the next Soviet offensive. As a result, February and March of 1945 saw very large attacks on such German cities as Berlin and Dresden, with massive fires and destruction in the former and a firestorm in the latter.[74] By the end of March, Churchill, who had been a strong advocate of area bombing, began to change his views on this subject,[75] but by then enormous destruction had been caused by the fleets of British and American bombers which were now at their most numerous and, with their fighter escorts, simply overwhelmed any remaining defenders.

In the meantime, Montgomery's preparations for the Rhine crossing (operation "Plunder"), which he had ordered to begin in October 1944, when the failure to seize the last bridge in the Arnhem operation had become obvious, were nearing completion.[76] Montgomery had forbidden General Simpson, the commander of the American 9th Army which was temporarily assigned to his command, to attempt a surprise assault across the Rhine early in March; after the failure of the daring attempt at Arnhem, the Field Marshal had become extraordinarily cautious. Having underestimated German resistance to "Veritable" and "Grenade," he appears not to have realized that the Germans had used up the bulk of their defensive resources in the West *before* the Allies reached the Rhine;

Papers, 14/7/16), but there is no reference to the event, or to Patton's Rhine crossing, in Brooke's Diary.

since early February the Allies had captured almost 300,000 men and had inflicted another 60,000 casualties.[77] Furthermore, as the date set for the crossing approached—and Montgomery was still thinking of possible postponements if the weather were not right—most of what few Germans reserves were left had been sent south to contain the American divisions that had been across the Rhine for two weeks at Remagen. But with enormous artillery preparatory fire, great naval support, a huge aerial bombardment, and a two-division airborne drop, the great operation went forward as planned on March 23–24 with both Churchill and Brooke (as well as Eisenhower) watching in person.

The assault succeeded quickly and, except for the heavy casualties suffered by the British and American airborne divisions,[78] fairly easily. German resistance was spotty: heavy at a few points but almost non-existent at others. Pontoon bridges were built quickly, and within days the British 2nd and the American 9th Armies were across the river in great strength. As Montgomery put it in his March 28 order for 21 Army Group, the enemy was effectively finished: "there are no fresh and complete divisions in rear and all the enemy will be able to do is to block roads and approaches from schools, bath units, pigeon lofts, and so on."[79] Although 21st Army Group headed northeast at a fast clip, there were two problems which affected Montgomery's advance, and they were in important ways related to each other and his own personal qualities. One concerned command and strategy, the other the actual progress of his own armies.

If Eisenhower had ever meant to leave the American 9th Army under Montgomery's command, the Rhine crossing at Remagen and the contrast between the rapid moves of Hodges and Patton and the deliberation of "Plunder" combined with resentment among Americans over the British Field Marshal's press conference at the time of the Ardennes fighting to convince him not to do so. He decided, and so informed the British, that as soon as the American 9th and 1st Armies met on the far side of the Ruhr, enclosing that industrial area and the German Army Group B trapped there, 9th Army would revert to Bradley's 12th Army Group. Montgomery, like Brooke, thought this a terrible mistake, though it is hard to see how they could have been so surprised. They, and Churchill, were at least as startled, and considerably angrier, to learn that Eisenhower had also decided with the approval of Washington to direct the main thrust eastwards toward Saxony, thus by-passing any opportunity to get to Berlin before the Russians.

Since Eisenhower knew by this time that the Allies had agreed on a zonal division of Germany which placed Berlin deep inside the Soviet zone—a plan developed by the British in the first place—he wanted to take advantage of the rapid successes of the American armies which had crossed the Rhine in force earlier and were now joined by the American 7th and French 1st Armies further south. With little faith in Montgomery's ability to exploit a breakthrough rapidly and drive to Berlin as the Field Marshal confidently expected,[80] Eisenhower preferred to concentrate on crushing the remaining German forces in the West, letting the Russians pay the price in blood for the zone assigned to them, and having the British get as quickly as possible to the north German ports and the Baltic to seal off Denmark.[81]

The British leaders were livid but could not budge Eisenhower; the extraordinary delays in Montgomery's subsequent advance would appear to justify the Supreme Commander's doubts. In spite of repeated urgings from Churchill as well as Eisenhower, Montgomery found ever new reasons for not advancing rapidly, eventually came to think of crossing the Elbe south of Hamburg in a huge operation similar to a crossing of the Rhine, and asked for and received additional American divisions to reach the Baltic and enter Wismar just ahead of the Russians.[82] It may be that his dawdling in this instance was merely a repetition of his sulking at the southern end of Italy in September 1943 because of his dissatisfaction with the role assigned to him in that operation, and that he would have operated very differently had he been left in control of the American 9th Army, but that is pure speculation. The record of his control of that army when he did have it was all to the contrary; he had not allowed them to "bounce" the Rhine and there is nothing to indicate that he had any intention of "bouncing" the Elbe.

In accordance with earlier plans, the Canadian 1st Army on the northern flank drove into northern Holland and the adjacent portion of Germany, in the process cutting off a German garrison in western Holland, where they were left alone militarily because of their threat to flood the whole area. The Dutch population was already starving, and a whole variety of efforts was undertaken to arrange for them to be fed. Since this involved contacts with Germans who had no intention of surrendering, a Soviet representative was involved in the talks. The suffering in the cut-off area was reduced somewhat, but only the final surrender of the German forces in May ended the appalling ordeal of the Dutch.

To the south and east of the Canadians, the 2nd British Army headed for Bremen and Hamburg. As already mentioned, this advance did not go as rapidly as both Churchill and Eisenhower wanted. Churchill wrote on April 3: "When the cease-fire sounds in Germany, I hope Field Marshal Montgomery will be shaking hands with the Russians as far as possible East of the Elbe. Our zone is marked out and after salutations, which may be marked, we shall retire to its limits."[83] Kicked and pushed from above, Montgomery's army took the important port city of Bremen, drew up to the Elbe river and then crossed it, dashing to the city of Lübeck while American divisions moved toward the Baltic on the right flank of the advance. Hamburg surrendered on May 3, but by then the war in Europe had already reached its concluding stage.

The American 9th Army, in addition to providing the northern pincer to cut off the Ruhr, also advanced across the Weser toward the Elbe, now in 12th instead of 21st Army Group. Those of its forces assigned to the containment and then the splitting and destruction of the Ruhr pocket combined with that portion of 1st Army assigned to the task from the south in one of the great encirclements of history. Over 300,000 German prisoners were taken during April as Field Marshal Model, their commander, committed suicide.[84]

Even before the Ruhr had been surrounded, Hitler had issued strict orders that all industrial, transportation and other facilities inside Germany should be destroyed lest they fall into Allied hands. Such orders had automatically accompanied all other retreats forced on the Germans, and in most cases German commanders had carried them out ruthlessly to the greatest extent possible, with no thought to the future survival of people who had already suffered enormously. In a few instances there had been reluctance to leave only ruins—Florence and Paris being examples—but in general, the speed of some German retreats rather than humanitarian inhibitions had caused some facilities, structures, and supplies to fall into Allied hands undestroyed. That attitude started to change once the fighting moved *inside* Germany. Speer began to sabotage the sabotage orders, and many German commanders filed rather than implemented the orders to destroy everything that might support life in territory occupied by the Allies.

As Allied forces advanced rapidly, they even encountered cases where the local German population tried to discourage the military from defending a particular community in order to keep it from being destroyed. Soldiers, for obvious reasons, do not want to die, but they particularly do not want to be the last person killed in a war. A common pattern, therefore, was that when an American unit came to a seriously defended island of resistance, it would simply draw back slightly, call for the artillery and air force to pound it to bits, and then move through. Many Germans, now losing confidence in the possibility of victory or even stalemate, preferred to spare their communities the fate which the war Germany began had brought to so many other towns. The white— or more likely grey—sheets of surrender appeared more and more frequently even as in some locations fierce resistance still flared up. In addition, vast numbers of German refugees from the East, fleeing before the Soviet advance, poured westwards; and increasing numbers of German soldiers found ways to absent themselves from units fighting on the Eastern Front in hopes of substituting American for Russian prisoner of war camps.

This was only a portion of what the 9th Army and to its south the 1st Army ran into on the Elbe river and in the Harz mountains of central Germany. Of the first two bridgeheads quickly thrown across the Elbe near Magdeburg by Simpson's 9th Army, one was driven back by the Germans even as other American divisions battled fanatical German resistance in the Harz mountains.[85] What had happened was that miscellaneous units, put together by the Germans at Hitler's orders into the new 12th Army under General Walther Wenck, were forming up for a counter-offensive westwards to open up a corridor to Model's Army Group B, of which remnants were still fighting in the Ruhr pocket. In the Führer's imagination, this bold move with an army made up of fanatical youngsters and battle-wise veterans would split the whole American front open in the middle. What it really did was to slow the Americans down for a few days and convince them that it was silly to try to drive for Berlin in the face of real resistance at a time when the Russians, who were just breaking open the German defenses on the Oder, were far closer. By the time Hitler turned most of Wenck's recoiling army around to head east instead of west and to halt the Russians rather than the Americans, the offensive power of that German force had already been spent.

Eisenhower ordered 1st Army with 3rd Army on its right flank into Saxony deep into what had been agreed upon as the Soviet zone of occupation, both to close down the industrial production of arms there and to engage the German forces which could otherwise interfere with the big push into southern Germany. He had notified the Russians of his intention to do so, much to the annoyance of the British government and Chiefs of Staff but with full support from Washington.

The big issue on this portion of the front was the land equivalent of the earlier debates over the air force aspect of coordination with the Soviet Union in practical day-to-day operations to preclude, or at least minimize, possible mistakes. As the forces of the Allies rushed toward each other in Central Europe, there was the great danger of incidents and clashes. A whole series of efforts was made by the Western Allies in order to try to cope with this, but the Russians were most reluctant to cooperate.[86] The Red Army, like the Red Air Force, would give out practically no information so that operations could be coordinated, and in the end the arrangement generally applied was notification by the British and Americans of their intentions, followed by implementation if the Russians did not make a fuss. Eisenhower for good geographic reasons picked the Mulde as the most likely tributary of the Elbe at which to stop; patrols across this smaller stream met advance formations of the Red Army at Torgau on April 25, the same day on which Berlin was completely surrounded by the Red Army and the United Nations Conference opened in San Francisco.

To the south of 1st Army, the 3rd Army, which had crossed the Rhine near Oppenheim, first headed east and then northeast into Thuringia, then southeast into Bavaria and Czechoslovakia. Its rapid advance was designed to preclude a new development of resistance in the south. There was some concern that in the mountains of south Germany and adjacent parts of Austria the Germans would try to hold out in an Alpine redoubt. Although intelligence reports on this project varied, the extent to which the Germans held on fanatically in Italy and even tried to launch new offensives in Hungary in the last months of the war suggested that there could be more nasty surprises awaiting the Allies in the mountains.[87]

The American 7th Army on Patton's right flank also turned southeast after crossing the Rhine and battered its way into Nürnberg, the old site of Nazi Party rallies, on April 20, Hitler's birthday, in the face of last-ditch resistance. While Patton's army continued into Austria in order to meet the Red Army there, Patch's 7th headed south with the aim of meeting Allied forces striking north in Italy. In Munich a local uprising on April 28, one of the very few in those months, tried to topple Nazi control of the city but was suppressed; soon after, on April 30, the Americans came in and then headed for the Brenner Pass to join advance units of the American 5th Army near the Austrian–Italian border on May 4.

These shifts in direction from heading east to heading southeast had implications for inter-Allied relations in the final campaign. On the eastern flank of the advance, the halt line vis-à-vis the Red Army which was pushing into Czechoslovakia from the east had to be worked out. This was done in a series of contacts between Eisenhower's headquarters and the Red Army General Staff and left the interior of Bohemia, with its capital of Prague — already in the hands of insurgents — to the Red Army. It has been suggested that this was a silent quid pro quo for Soviet restraint to facilitate Western liberation of Denmark.[88] On the right flank, the turn cut off the route of the French 1st Army and headed it south into the southeast corner of Germany and the mountainous western end of Austria. This process led to friction with de Gaulle, who insisted on his forces holding the German city of Stuttgart until the borders of the French zone of occupation were settled, a maneuver which further soured his relations with the Americans, which had hardly been improved by his refusal to meet with President Roosevelt on the latter's return from the Yalta conference shortly before.

The meeting of the American 7th and 5th Armies at the Brenner Pass in the Alps marked an extraordinary conclusion of the long campaign in Italy. There a sustained air campaign against the transportation system through the Alps had so reduced the ammunition and fuel supplies of the German Army Group C that its two armies, though fighting fiercely against the Allied forces trying to break into the Po valley, were in a very difficult situation. Any breakthrough anywhere in the front was sure to lead to a disaster, and under these circumstances a few German leaders began to try for a negotiated surrender of the Army Group by establishing contact with the OSS in Switzerland in March, 1945.[89] The SS chief in Italy, Karl Wolff, and a few German military were involved in this effort; the military appear to have been primarily interested in a quick and less bloody end of the fighting while Wolff and other SS officers were primarily concerned about immunity for themselves from prosecution for war crimes. The military, partly because of changes in command, partly because of opposition to what many considered "too early" a surrender, lest a new stab-in-the-back legend blame them for Germany's defeat,[90] delayed actually surrendering until April 29, effective on May 2; as for the hopes of SS leaders, President Roosevelt had denied the December 1944 request of the OSS's Chief Donovan for authority to grant immunity to individual Germans.[91]

The final Allied offensive on the Italian front began on April 9, broke into the valley of the Po river in mid-April and across that river on April 23. It led the German commander in Italy, General von Vietinghoff (who had replaced the great Hitler admirer Kesselring when the latter was sent to the Western Front) to move the surrender negotiations forward a bit. Even while Vietinghoff was trying to end hostilities in Italy by a local surrender, Mussolini attempted to escape to Switzerland but was caught and shot, along with his mistress, by partisans on April 28. The surrender speeded the end by a few days and had the effect of facilitating an early junction of the Allied armies fighting in Italy with the 7th Army at the Brenner as well as the forward rush of British troops on the Adriatic coast to Trieste simultaneously with the arrival of Tito's partisans.[92] The main impact of the surrender negotiations however, was to be on relations between the Allies.

Once the Western Allies informed the Russians of the contacts, the latter became increasingly annoyed. While they had never before involved western officers in their surrender negotiations with German forces, the Soviets were increasingly violent in their objections to the continuation of shadowy soundings in which they were not invited to participate. Stalin sent Churchill and Roosevelt an increasingly nasty series of messages which made ever worse impressions on the recipients. Perhaps in the hope of influencing the President during a time when the agreements reached at Yalta were breaking down over the refusal of Moscow to implement its promises on Poland and the coup in Romania, Stalin now let it be known that Molotov would not go to San Francisco after all.[93] This rather rude step was later reversed; but the evidence is clear that in what turned out to be the last days of his life, Roosevelt was increasingly annoyed with Soviet actions.

Stalin's actions in this situation are not easy to understand.[94] Perhaps he was concerned that a German surrender on other fronts would leave him at a disadvantage.[95] The Western Allies regularly waved away all German offers of wider surrenders unless made unconditionally and to all three major Allies;[96] perhaps because he himself was hoping for some last-minute deal on his front that would assist his purposes, he assumed that Britain and the United States would do likewise. Perhaps he felt that heavy fighting, rather than surrenders, elsewhere would assist the Red Army's campaign for Berlin by drawing off German forces or at least keeping them busy. Certainly the final campaign for the German capital was not easy. It had been delayed much longer than the earlier Soviet planning for the winter offensive had contemplated, and it had been this delay which both worried Eisenhower and had appeared to dangle the prize of Berlin in front of the American 9th Army.

BATTLE FOR BERLIN

During the latter part of February and all of March 1945 Soviet military effort was concentrated on clearing the flanks of the forthcoming assault on the Nazi capital while building up forces and supplies for that assault. In battles of tremendous ferocity, the Red Army first failed and then succeeded in destroying most of the German forces in Pomerania and driving back the remnants across the Oder. The two German armies which had been cut off in East Prussia were split into several pockets and, except for those evacuated by sea and a tiny enclave still held until May, also destroyed. Relying heavily on their artillery, the divisions of the Third Belorussian Front pounded their way into Königsberg—now Kaliningrad—and quite literally smashed the bulk of the remains of the old northern wing of the German Eastern Front to pieces. The German general who finally surrendered what was left of Königsberg was condemned to death in absentia and his family arrested, but such actions no more held up the Red Army than the ever increasing German practice of hanging soldiers in public with signs attached to them calling attention to the fate of traitors to the Third Reich. The Germans on the Eastern Front fought with the bravery born of desperation to save their own lives and what they believed was the future of their families and homes, and for this flying execution squads were quite unnecessary. Once the front situation had collapsed and there appeared to be a way out, the equally desperate effort to escape by heading west or surrendering in place could not be held up by summary executions either. As Field Marshal Montgomery explained to Admiral Friedeburg on May 3, when the latter wanted to have German armies surrender to the Western Allies but not to the Russians, "The Germans should have thought of some of these things before they began the war, particularly before attacking the Russians."[97]

One by one the isolated garrisons surrendered; tiny numbers escaped or broke through; the forces in Courland and two of the remnants of the East Prussian forces held out until May of 1945. It could easily be argued that the men trapped in these places were much more likely to survive their post-war stays in Soviet prisoner of war camps than they would have survived a return to battle on the main Eastern Front had they been evacuated earlier. But neither Hitler who wanted them to hold in place nor Guderian who wanted them evacuated was concerned about their survival; they merely had different views on how best to prolong the war. Hitler hoped to turn the tide or split the alliance against himself while Guderian hoped to hold a front in the East. Both were hopelessly unrealistic.

Further south, the Red Army cleared more of Silesia and surrounded Breslau, which held out until May. In Bohemia, the Fourth Ukrainian Front had enormous difficulty pushing back the German Army Group Center which was being substantially reinforced, partly because the Germans had believed that the major spring offensive of the Red Army would come here, partly because its commander, Field Marshal Schörner, was a great favorite of Hitler. In Hungary, the last great German offensive of the war collapsed in the face of the resistance and drive of the Second and Third Ukrainian Fronts, which cleared the Germans out of Hungary and southern Slovakia.[98] While beyond Bratislava (Pressburg) the Red Army headed for Vienna, at the southern end of the front they took the Hungarian oil fields on April 2 even as Tito's army was pushing back the Germans in Yugoslavia, where they faced the possibility of being taken in the rear by the British advancing in Italy. The day before the capture of the Hungarian oil fields, Stalin had set the date for the great offensive on Berlin.[99]

On April 1, Stalin informed Eisenhower that Berlin was of little importance and that the Red Army would attack it in late May; both lies since this was to be the main object of Soviet offensive operations which on that day he ordered launched on April 16 at the latest. What purpose these deceptions were to accomplish remains unclear, but in the same message Stalin agreed to further advances of Western troops into the zone allocated to the Soviet Union as well as to Eisenhower's plan to drive into Austria to meet the Red Army there. As for the big drive on Berlin, Stalin had earlier stated his preference for Zhukov to take that city; he now gave final orders for the offensive to be conducted by three Fronts, the Second Belorussian (Rokossovski), the First Belorussian (Zhukov), and the First Ukrainian (Konev).

There was to be a prior attack by Fourth Ukrainian Front further south which, combined with a pretended offensive on the left flank of First Ukrainian, was to fool the Germans into thinking that the next big attack would come in that area. This effort was to be completely successful. Just as on the Western Front the Germans in March were tricked into thinking Patton's 3rd Army would move through the Remagen bridgehead eastward—thereby helping open the way for his drive across the Mosel southeastward—so in April Hitler and the German high command were fooled into sending most of what few reserves they had to the southern end of the front in Germany, and leaving the key central sector, about to be struck by a massive offensive, with almost no reserves at all.

In the north, Rokossovski's Second Belorussian Front had had the most difficult preliminary re-shuffling and faced the worst terrain: an assault crossing over a river divided into branches in an area of flooded ground traversed by dykes easily shelled by the defenders. His Army Group, therefore, was scheduled to attack several days after the other two; in the event, they struck on April 20 with only the northernmost of the three assault crossings successful. Rokossovski quickly shifted emphasis to that sector and then drove into Mecklenburg. Directly east of Berlin was Zhukov's First Belorussian Front, which already had bridgeheads across the Oder and was to move out of them in three thrusts: to strike north of the German capital and eventually surround it, to head directly toward it, and to head southwest, thus cutting off the defending German 9th Army from the north.

Konev's First Ukrainian Front, while pretending to attack on its left flank, was in fact to launch assault crossings of the Neisse river into the German 4th Panzer Army, head northwest to join in cutting off 9th Army, as well as reaching further west both to meet the Americans and to surround Berlin from the south. The drive to meet the Americans would split the whole German military mechanism apart and make it far

more difficult for them to maintain resistance centers in the north and
south; in this regard Soviet planning essentially coincided with Eisenhower's. Hitler recognized the same possibility—as a danger rather than
an opportunity of course—and even before the launching of the Soviet
offensive began preparations for that contingency, designating Admiral
Dönitz as commander of the northern and Field Marshal Kesselring for
the southern remnants of the armed forces. He had picked two extremely
loyal adherents of his regime whom he correctly believed fully prepared
to sacrifice the lives of any and all Germans in support of the Nazi state.

In the first two weeks of April, while the Third Ukrainian Front
was driving deep into Austria, taking Vienna by April 3, the massive
preparations for the main offensive went forward, greatly aided like previous such prepared offensives by the thousands of trucks which the
United States had delivered under Lend-Lease. With some two and a
half million soldiers in place, the offensive opened on April 16. Stalin
had told his commanders he wanted it completed in twelve to fifteen
days, and at enormous cost in casualties they delivered essentially what
he had ordered.

Although Zhukov's 1st Belorussian Front started out with bridgeheads
across the Oder, its first attacks, launched at night with searchlights
supposed to blind the Germans, barely drove the defenders back frontally. For three days the assaulting formations piled up against the defenses. Driven forward by Zhukov at Stalin's insistence, the attackers
ground forward. As artillery wore down the defenders, Red Army units
broke into and through the front of Army Group Vistula toward and
north of Berlin. There were very heavy casualties on both sides, and
numerous Soviet tanks were destroyed, many by hand-held anti-tank
rockets carried by Hitler Youth members; but the overwhelming power
of the offensive slowly drove all before it.

Further south, Konev's forces made their assault crossings of the
Neisse river with great success on the heels of a tremendous artillery
barrage. In short order several divisions of the 4th Panzer Army simply
disintegrated, and, before the Germans quite realized what was happening, Konev's spearheads were cutting in behind the 9th Army. Within
five days, it was clear that the Eastern Front had been ripped open; the
only remaining question was whether the Germans would try to fight on
or give up.

In a summary of the situation and predictions for the future, General
Marshall had reported to Roosevelt on April 2 that the war would end
as the pockets of resistance collapsed one by one, the key question being
the location of Hitler. The Germans would fight hard at that point,
but there would be little guerilla warfare. The southern redoubt would

function as a center of resistance only if Hitler went there in person, but there would be no overthrow of the Nazi regime from the inside. The misery in occupied Germany was vast, but there was no political interest. The area occupied by the Western Allies was experiencing great hunger because it was a food deficit area, and would continue to do so as no food shipments from east Germany could be expected, while the population was rapidly growing as a result of a vast movement of refugees westward.[100]

Although in early April the Nazi leaders still professed to be confident,[101] Marshall's predictions proved to be correct. The last minute concerns of the German leaders hardly engaged the real dilemmas facing them: they were worried about evacuating their supplies of poison gas lest the Allies utilize their finding of stocks as a pretext for using gas against the Germans; they puzzled over Japanese requests for orders to the German naval forces in the Far East to continue operating with the Japanese if their European base were lost; they rejoiced over the death of President Roosevelt as a sign that all would be well for Germany.[102] There is no evidence that anyone in Berlin had even the slightest interest in or knowledge about the new American President; there was instead an increasing tendency to move non-existent forces around and to engage in the most bizarre historical reminiscences.[103]

At this time, the Western Allies were driving toward the Baltic and into Austria, the Red Army was pushing into the suburbs of Berlin even as it moved to surround the city entirely, while on the German side a fissure was finally beginning to open up. Hitler and a number of key political and military aides were intent on continuing the fighting in preposterous hopes of stabilizing a new front. The orders Hitler himself gave to reorient Wenck's 12th Army from heading west to heading east as well as his fantastic hope that a new organization, an "army" headed by the SS General Felix Steiner and consisting mostly of imaginary formations, would drive south from Mecklenburg and cut off Zhukov's advancing spearheads, must be seen in this light; so should the support Goebbels and Bormann from the political, Keitel and Jodl from the military side gave to such projects.

Increasing numbers among the German military leaders, however, had by this time a rather different perspective. They recognized that the war was lost and that there was no prospect of stabilizing the front once more. With Russian shells falling in the capital, Red Army and American troops about to meet in central Germany, while other American armies from north and south could be expected to join hands at the Brenner Pass, the only point of continued fighting as they saw it was to gain time for civilians fleeing from the east to the west, and possibly to enable a large proportion of their soldiers to be captured by the Western Allies rather than the Red Army.[a] Unlike Field Marshal Schörner, who deserted his men to try to evade capture as a civilian—the sort of step he had regularly penalized with shooting or hanging when attempted by others—most of them remained with their troops and took their chances.

Those chances looked so slight by mid-April 1945 that some of the Nazi leaders wanted to try their hand at ending the war either for themselves or for the country. Many simply fled and tried to vanish; of these, some were caught by the German political or military police and summarily shot. A few attempted negotiated surrenders not of a front sector, like Wolff in Italy, but on a wider scale. The SS chief Himmler, of all people, imagined himself in such a role and made contact with the Swedish Count Folke Bernadotte, while at one point Göring thought of arranging an end to the war. All these soundings were met by the demand for unconditional surrender to all the Allies, and rumors about them which leaked out only served to enrage Hitler.

The advancing Russians were breaking into Berlin from north, east and south even as the spearheads of Zhukov's and Konev's Fronts met west of the city on April 25, the same day Konev's troops came in contact with the Americans. The German capital was completely surrounded and at a time when the main defense force, the 9th Army, had itself been surrounded in a separate encirclement by the Red Army. Hitler's frantic efforts to have the capital relieved had no substantial effect on operations. In hammer blows from all sides, Red Army units battered their way into the city, suffering substantial casualties but moving forward nevertheless. Hitler had decided to stay in the capital and commit suicide there if the relief schemes did not work.

What elements of the German armies near Berlin could escape not unreasonably tried to get away from the scene of horrendous disaster, not toward it, and inside the underground shelter Hitler and his entourage alternated between dreams of last-minute redemption and despair. The last garrison commander, General Helmuth Weidling, had been appointed to the post by Hitler right after he was supposed to have been shot for not handling his corps command the way Hitler wanted. He told Hitler that the last ammunition would run out on April 30. Since Hitler had by then implemented the earlier plan to have Dönitz and Kesselring direct the war in the northern and southern segments of remaining territory, he now had only his personal situation to tend to,

[a] It seems to me that General Gotthard Heinrici, the Commander in Chief of Army Group Vistula, belongs in this category, and that his firing from that post by Field Marshal Keitel reflects quite accurately the distinction between the two types of leaders suggested in the text. See Ziemke, *Stalingrad to Berlin*, pp. 484–87. Note also Gellermann, *Armee Wenck*, chapter 5.

having also sent away many of those still at headquarters until the last moment.

The process of enveloping and penetrating the city had taken only a few days longer than Stalin had originally specified. As the leading American authority on the Eastern Front has put it: "The fighting in Berlin lasted as long as it did because a great metropolis, bombed out though it may be and no matter how amateurishly fortified, cannot quickly be taken even against a lame defense, particularly not by troops who know the war is over and intend to see their homes again."[104] As the fighting neared the immediate vicinity of the bunker which was used as Hitler's headquarters, the Führer married his mistress Eva Braun and dictated his political and private testaments on April 29. In the former he defended his policies, made nasty comments about his generals whom he blamed for the defeat,[a] and called on any surviving Germans to continue his racial policies of slaughtering Jews. He appointed Dönitz as his successor.[105] The following day, he and his new wife committed suicide. The bodies were located by the Russians soon after—there had not been enough gasoline for the complete destruction Hitler had ordered in his private testament—but for years the Soviet government pretended in public that Hitler might still be alive.[106] The rest of the world was soon reassured on that point.[107] Only the head of the Irish Free State, Eamon de Valera, thought the occasion called for a condolence visit to the German Legation in Dublin, a gesture he had not considered appropriate when Roosevelt died.[108] Few others shared his sadness.[109]

The Berlin garrison—or rather what was left of it—was surrendered to the Red Army soon after the attempts of the last acting German army Chief of Staff, General Hans Krebs, to work out a broader surrender had failed.[110] The battle for Berlin was over; according to one careful study, it had cost half a million people their lives or their health by the most conservative estimates.[111] Even as the last of the defenders were marched off into captivity, Soviet patrols searched for fugitive Nazi leaders, while a group of German Communists led by Walter Ulbricht was flown in from Soviet exile to establish a new government in occupied Germany.

North and south of Berlin some fighting continued in the following days. The announcement that Hitler was dead finally convinced the commanders in Italy to surrender their units. In Bohemia, a final Soviet offensive drove into the remaining German Army Group in that area,

---

[a] Since so many of them survived, German generals took their revenge on Hitler by blaming *him* in their memoirs for all the battles they lost, while claiming for themselves the credit for whatever victories their forces had attained.

which had to surrender as part of the general capitulation. There the units organized by the former Red Army General Vlasov, recruited from among Soviet prisoners of war to fight alongside the Germans against the Soviet regime, became involved in the last struggles for Prague and fell into the hands of the Russians or were turned over to them by the Americans. Those who did not commit suicide were shot or sent to labor camps.[112] The Czechoslovak government-in-exile of Benes was returned to Prague, but under circumstances which hardly promised a bright future.

THE END OF THE WAR IN EUROPE

In the north Admiral Dönitz had taken control of both what remnants of a government could be put together and the German armed forces which still controlled western Holland, all of Norway and Denmark, a substantial portion of north and small pieces of south Germany as well as portions of Austria, Czechoslovakia and Yugoslavia. The pieces of Italy were about to be surrendered. The admiral had been a dedicated adherent of Hitler and believed practically until the last minute that the tide could yet turn in Germany's favor. His dedication to National Socialist ideas and his close identification with Hitler's strategy in the last stages of the war[113] made him a logical, not a surprising, choice by Hitler as his successor. And that in his own strange way Hitler had assessed Dönitz accurately can be seen in the insistence of the latter when in jail as a war criminal as late as January 1953 that he was still Germany's legal chief of state; only a system in which all parties including the National Socialists were allowed to participate could legally choose a successor![114]

When he took over the immediate heritage of Hitler at the beginning of May 1945, however, Dönitz realized that the war was lost.[115] He hoped to end it in such a fashion as to rescue as many as possible of the soldiers of the Eastern Front from becoming prisoners of war of the Russians and to enable as many as possible of the civilians to flee west as well. As the Russians had refused the offer by General Krebs of a local surrender, so the Western Allies refused to allow Dönitz to surrender only to them but insisted that he surrender the armed forces to all three Allies.[116] The Army Group in Italy and subsequently that in northwest Germany as well as the force in Holland could surrender in military capitulations similar to those of earlier surrenders on the Eastern Front. At the northern end of that front, the 3rd Panzer and 21st Armies surrendered to the Americans as they were squeezed between the advancing Second Belorussian Front and 21st Army Group, and some of the

German soldiers in the central sector also entered American POW cages. But the vast majority of those who had fought on the Eastern Front, over one and a quarter million, became Russian prisoners with the general surrender.[117]

That surrender was signed in two installments, once in Reims on May 7 and again in Berlin on May 9.[118] These complications show up clearly both the common aims and the divergent perspectives of the Western Allies and the Soviet Union. All were agreed that this time the German military leaders must sign an unconditional surrender; there could be no pretence as after World War I that the army had not really been defeated, and there would be no civilians to blame afterwards for agreeing to give up. Furthermore, there was agreement that the Dönitz government would be utilized to assure an orderly and swift surrender. All were interested in getting the various isolated German garrisons from the French Atlantic ports to the Baltic as well as German submarines at sea to surrender rather than attempt last-ditch stands.[119] But once that had been accomplished, those associated with the Dönitz government, if not already arrested, would be locked up (with some of them later tried as war criminals) on May 23, after Eisenhower had checked with London, Washington and Moscow. Dönitz himself and the remnants of his government and headquarters were all arrested by the British army, which controlled the area around Flensburg where it had been located.[120] As Montgomery had written to Brooke on May 6, he would use a few Germans to help get most of the enemy into the POW cages and in the end put those Germans used in this process into the cages as well.[121]

In Austria the Soviet Union had already begun to implement the concept agreed upon by the Allies at the Moscow Conference, that the country would be revived as an independent state, by establishing a new government under the elderly Socialist Karl Renner, with the assumption that Austria would also be temporarily divided into four occupation zones and a four-power controlled capital in Vienna; their sponsorship of the Ulbricht group precluded a similar situation for Germany. The Austrians would eventually regain their unity and independence within ten years; the Germans, on the other hand, had no central institutions of their own once the Dönitz government had been arrested. With no civilian government in existence, the four Allied supreme commanders on June 5 in Berlin proclaimed the end of the German government and assumed all sovereign power for their governments to be exercised through the Allied Control Council. The Third Reich had come to an end and with it the German state founded by Otto von Bismarck less than three-quarters of a century earlier. Since the Germans had begun the war with an attack on Poland, which they often referred to as a "state for a season," it was perhaps appropriate that their own disappeared for decades from the map of Europe after less than one-tenth of the time from Poland's becoming a kingdom in 1025 until its disappearance in the partition of 1795.

One of the three major Allied war leaders would not live to see its European end; another was thrown out of office soon after. President Roosevelt had won reelection to a fourth term in 1944, but the pressures of campaigning on top of the enormous pressures of the war had strained his health. Instead of some real opportunity for relaxation, there had been not only the continued drain of the war—with the Battle of the Bulge in December—but also the long trip to Yalta, which proved most exhausting.[122] It was when reporting to the Congress after Yalta that Roosevelt for the first and only time made public reference to his physical handicap in explaining why he was sitting rather than standing during his speech. There followed the collapse of Allied unity over Poland and Stalin's insulting messages about the surrender negotiations with German forces in Italy as well as the terrible fighting and heavy casualties on Iwo Jima. No wonder Oliver Lyttelton, who saw Roosevelt on March 29 as a member of the British delegation to the San Francisco Conference for the founding of the United Nations, telegraphed Churchill that he "was greatly shocked by his appearance."[123]

In the first days of April, not only the current disputes with Stalin were on the President's mind, but also the old one over the deal with Darlan. As we know that Roosevelt could still laugh uproariously over a very heavy maid's hope that she might be reincarnated as a canary,[124] he may have thought it amusing to recall being attacked for cooperating with a Fascist while currently under assault for working with Stalin. In any case, he authorized William Langer to have access to White House materials for his study of American policy toward Vichy on April 6.[125] Always hopeful of a brighter future, Roosevelt wanted to steer the country to a peaceful world in which it would play a more constructive role than it had after World War I. He hoped that it would participate in an international organization to which one by one the former colonies of the age of imperialism would be admitted as independent states; and he very much wanted the Philippines to be among the very first.[126] On April 12, even while resting at Warm Springs he died.

President Roosevelt had guided the United States through the travails of the great depression and had given his people hope in desperate times. He had tried, but without success, to keep the country out of war by assisting others to defeat Germany and to stall off Japan. Driven into the war by the Tripartite Pact powers, he had set the basic priorities and aims in the great conflict: the defeat of Germany first, an engagement of American troops against the Germans in 1942, the double thrust toward Japan in the Pacific, the direct thrust at Germany across the Channel, and the development of atomic weapons. He had selected the key figures in the American military and civilian war effort, and he had set the goal as the surrender of the country's enemies. During hostilities, he had worked hard to prepare the American public for a new role in the post-war world, a world in which he hoped that a new international organization, the United Nations, would provide a framework for continued cooperation among those he considered the four great powers. And whatever the frictions and the troubles, he had striven to keep them working and fighting together during the ordeal of war. Now others would be called on to lead, but at least victory was in sight.

The new American President, Harry S. Truman, had been a follower of Roosevelt's who had come to public attention through his chairmanship of a Senate committee checking war plants for waste and fraud. Himself a veteran of front-line fighting in World War I, he was not likely to make immediate or major changes in the war policies of his predecessor, though he had not been briefed on them in any systematic way before suddenly assuming the presidency. But he was a quick learner, very conscientious in his work, and with the self-confidence needed to make decisions.[127]

Ironically one of the most important issues Truman would be called upon to decide early in his administration was one on which Roosevelt had most reluctantly accepted a British proposal but on which Prime Minister Churchill had now changed his mind half a year after finally obtaining American agreement to his earlier position: the occupation zones in Germany. Roosevelt's first preference had been to draw no lines at all until the Allies arrived in Germany; his general inclination to deferring choices reinforced by the knowledge that American power was steadily increasing and that a better deal could be made once American troops were in Europe, rather than in the training camps of the American South. When pushed into drawing lines, he had drawn a map which had an American zone in the northwest running to Berlin. It then turned out that the British government had drawn a map with the Americans in the southwest and Berlin deep inside the Soviet zone and obtained quick Soviet agreement to it. As the third preference, Roosevelt had grudgingly accepted this proposal, subject to special access rights and a port enclave (Bremen and Bremerhaven) in the British zone for the Americans. In the course of the fighting of the spring of 1945, American troops had advanced far beyond the zonal borders of the British map in central Germany and also a smaller distance beyond the line as part of 21st Army Group in the north. Now Churchill wanted the Western Allies, in effect, to hold on to the territory occupied by their armies—Roosevelt's original first preference—until the Soviet Union made concessions on a number of current matters in dispute.[128]

On this issue, Churchill not only broke with his own earlier views and the inclinations of Field Marshal Brooke[129] but ran into the strongest opposition from the Americans. The earlier commitments to the Soviet Union were clear and in writing and were tied to the entrance of Western troops into Berlin, Vienna, and parts of Austria occupied by the Red Army.[130] The idea of running the risk of war with the Soviet Union was "unthinkable" to the British Chiefs of Staff;[131] they thought the chances of success "quite impossible;"[132] nothing indicates that the American Chiefs thought otherwise. Truman decided against Churchill's preference that the prior agreement would be adhered to; American forces withdrew from the two-fifths of the Soviet zone they had occupied—though after moving out German scientists, records, and other materials—and the zonal and sector issues for Germany and Austria, for Berlin and Vienna, were resolved by June 29 with implementing moves scheduled for July 1–4, 1945.

The entrance of troops of the Western Allies into their sectors of Berlin paved the way for a final meeting of the victorious allies in Potsdam. It was during this meeting that the results of the British election, which removed Churchill as Prime Minister and installed Clement Attlee, the leader of the Labor Party and former Deputy Prime Minister, as head of the British government and delegation, became known. The coalition government which had directed British affairs since May 1940 was ended on May 23, the same day as the arrest of Dönitz and his associates.[133] Churchill then headed a Conservative Party caretaker government until the election, held on July 5, but with the results not announced until July 26 so that the ballots of soldiers could be sent in and counted. Those results showed a decisive victory for Labor, primarily because a majority of the people wanted a new government in the post-war world. It had been ten years since the last election in the United Kingdom, and people had bad memories of the Conservative governments of the years after World War I. A Cabinet led by Attlee would direct Great Britain's effort in what was expected to be at least another year of war.

Churchill had led Britain to victory in Europe from a time of terrifying peril to the largest wartime surrender ever of German soldiers to Montgomery's 21st Army Group. In the last months of his years as Prime Minister and Minister of Defense, he had become increasingly alarmed over the implications in Eastern Europe of Stalin's insistence on absolute Soviet control of Poland, as well as other signs of deterioration in the grand alliance which had seemed to have been restored at Yalta. He had tried to retrieve at the last moment some of the concessions to the Soviet Union he had himself wanted made earlier from a sense of Britain's waning power, in the belief that it made more sense to delimit Soviet expansion by concessions early rather than late. He was greatly perturbed to see that it was now too late—but given the geographic and military realities, it was in any case certain that the Western Allies would move into Europe from the west while the Red Army would come from the east. Nevertheless Churchill still hoped that he could effect some changes in the situation. He also very much wanted to lead Britain to a share of the victory over Japan, which looked much more imminent as a result of the successful atomic bomb test in the interval between the voting and the counting and announcement of the results.

Whatever his differences with the Labor Party on domestic policy, on the subject of nationalization of industry as well as the field of social insurance, he had a huge difference with them on a subject close to his heart: the empire. All during the war, he had fought off pressures and even hints from the Americans on the issue of independence for India and steps toward independence for other colonial possessions. He had literally exploded on the Americans at the least reference to the subject, most recently in a violent outburst at Stettinius during the Yalta Conference. As a result, the Americans had restrained themselves somewhat, though Roosevelt could not refrain from occasionally twitting the Prime Minister.

A major concern of Churchill's in connection with the war against Japan was his firm belief that British power had to be restored in Burma, Malaya, the British portions of Borneo and Hong Kong. He also strongly favored the full return of the former French and Dutch possessions in Southeast Asia to their previous colonial masters, in opposition to American preference for moving them toward independence. It is true that in Syria and Lebanon Great Britain followed a different line in the spring of 1945 in the face of vehement French opposition, but in this case there were earlier firm promises of independence which the French had made, the British had guaranteed, and the local population absolutely insisted upon. After the small share of the fighting which the French had done in Europe, Churchill was not about to help them in a major campaign to subdue the people of Syria and Lebanon.[134]

With the exception of an area where there were earlier promises of independence, the old order was to be restored, and the Prime Minister, who kept up with the latest techniques of radar and code-breaking, still lived in the late nineteenth century whenever the colonial question was discussed. And he knew all too well that on this issue Labor held views of a very different sort: Attlee himself had been on the Simon Commission on the development of self-governing institutions for India, over which Churchill had broken with the Conservative Party and gone into the political wilderness for a decade. And now Attlee was to be Prime Minister. It was a double blow, but as a firm believer in free parliamentary government, Churchill immediately resigned and advised King George VI to have Attlee form a new government. Churchill had in fact taken Attlee along to the Potsdam Conference against that contingency, and after a brief break, when the conference resumed, the new Prime Minister represented Great Britain.

Before the Potsdam Conference, to which Churchill had given the code-name "Terminal," could meet, there were other matters left over from the hostilities which had ended in early May. The most anxious question secretly examined by the Allies was the discovery that the Germans had developed a series of new types of nerve gases, Tabun, Sarin, and Soman, of which they had had no inkling and for which they knew of no antidotes. The question was whether the Germans had passed on this weapon to the Japanese; when they learned that they had not, the British and Americans—and presumably also the Russians—decided to keep the information secret so that such gases could be used in retaliation against the Japanese should the latter decide to start the use of poison gas themselves.[135] It was a long time since the British government had decided to use gas if the Germans were successful in establishing a beachhead on the British coast.

In public, there was a major inter-Allied dispute over the question of Lend-Lease. The Lend-Lease Act and the appropriations for American deliveries under it provided that it was to continue only for the duration of the war. The Americans and British had worked out an agreement for the period following the end of hostilities in Europe, what was referred to as "Second Stage" aid, during the Quebec Conference of October 1944. But the renewal of Lend-Lease in the spring of 1945, at a time when the administration's relations with Congress were at their worst since 1933, had made emphatically clear that no money could be used after the war ended. There was endless bickering over the delivery of items ordered and in the pipeline but not delivered until after the end of the fighting.

What the Congress clearly wanted to avoid was post-war aid programs for relief and reconstruction under the cover of Lend-Lease; any such programs would have to come under special and separate legislation.[136] The head of the Foreign Economic Administration, Leo T. Crowley, was in favor of a strict interpretation of the law as it affected all of America's allies. President Truman had himself cast the tie-breaking vote against even more restrictive language on April 10 when still Vice-President; in signing the bill extending Lend-Lease on April 17 as the first law of his administration he was thus naturally very conscious of the tenuous status of the whole Lend-Lease program. It should, therefore, not have surprised any of America's allies that victory in Europe was quickly followed by dramatic reductions in aid, but both the British and the Russians who equally ignored the text of the relevant American legislation professed to be surprised and even shocked. While the cut-off in supplies not needed for the war against Japan was handled especially poorly in regard to the Soviet Union, the reality remains that American shipments to the Soviets reached their highest level of the war in May 1945.[137] The stream of supplies, however, was hardly consistent with a deterioration of American–Soviet relations at a time when Soviet actions in Poland lent weight to those in the American government, such as the ambassador to the Soviet Union Averell Harriman, and the head of the American military mission there, General John R. Deane, urging a tougher line on the new American President.

Both the Americans and the British felt that they had treated the Soviet Union most generously in providing aid while the Russians believed that, since they had done the bulk of the fighting, they were entitled to all they received and more.[138] In this area, as in so many others, it had been a common enemy and a common danger which had held the alliance together and provided an incentive for settling outstanding differences; the defeat of that enemy dissolved the incentive.

In a smaller but equally dramatic way, the confrontation over the Italian–Yugoslav border also demonstrated the dissolving alliance. The race for Trieste, which has already been mentioned, was only the most conspicuous element in a very dangerous situation where British troops (backed by the United States),[139] faced Tito's army, which they had largely armed earlier in the war. In a series of tense confrontations, the danger of new hostilities was narrowly averted. The "Morgan Line," named after the British commander on the spot, divided British and Yugoslav forces until a peace treaty with Italy settled the border, with Yugoslavia receiving much, but not all, of the territory Tito claimed. The city of Trieste remained the key to the dispute. Its hinterland was heavily Slovene in population, but the city itself had a majority of Italians. Whatever the economics of the situation, a division which ended up by allotting the hinterland to Yugoslavia and the city to Italy may have been the fairest way to cut the baby.

If there were great differences among the Allies, there was one subject on which there was increasing agreement. During the fighting, reports on Nazi atrocities had led the Allies to announce that those responsible would be held to account. Repeatedly grisly news stories of new outrages had rebuilt interest in this subject, but nothing so placed the horrors committed by the Third Reich in front of the public in the Western allied nations as clearly as the arrival of their troops at concentration and labor camps in 1945. The Red Army had overrun some of the great murder factories earlier, and pictures had been printed in the United States and Great Britain; but somehow these places seemed far away, even if the numbers murdered in them were vastly greater than in the camps in western and central Germany. No one had to convince the Russians of the awful nature of the Nazi regime; now the American and the British peoples received a lesson on the reality of what they had been fighting against that was far more dramatic than the worst reports they had heard or read.

On April 12, 1945, near the town of Gotha in Thuringia, Eisenhower, Bradley and Patton toured Ohrdruf. They saw the gallows, the dead and the still dying, while Signal Corps photographers took pictures which would stun the American public.[140] German civilians as well as GIs were instructed to see this camp or others like it; there were literally hundreds of these. In the following days, American and British troops liberated other far larger and later more famous — or notorious — camps: Buchenwald, and Dachau, Bergen-Belsen and Nordhausen, Mauthausen and, and, and. The whole impact was undoubtedly enormous. In an age when newsreels and magazines like *Life* provided the main visual impressions of events, the pictures of the camps brought reality to the home front the way nothing else had. It was known to some at the time and to more later that these camps were in fact but the tiny tip of a vast iceberg; that there were places where perhaps as many people had been murdered in one day as in the Ohrdruf camp as long as it existed, but the impressions had been made. Here was something quite different from the specific massacres — such as that of American prisoners of war near Malmédy or of British commandos after their capture. Here were the most tangible signs of a general horror in a form the ordinary person could only try to grasp.

These developments provided a major basis of public support and further impetus for American policy which looked to trials for war criminals after the end of hostilities. The experience with allowing the Germans to conduct such trials after World War I had been very bad;[141] there was now no German government. There was no inclination to turn the issue over to neutrals like Spain and Argentina — by definition the countries which had refused to join the war against Germany — and there was no indication that any of them was the least bit interested in doing so.[142] The Allies would have to do it themselves. The initiative was taken by the Americans who, following the terms of the 1943 Moscow "Declaration on German Atrocities in Occupied Europe," wanted criminals involved in a single area returned for trial there, and an international tribunal for those whose offenses were of a broader geographical nature. Roosevelt had taken a basic summary of the United States position to Yalta, and Truman appointed Supreme Court Justice Robert H. Jackson to represent the United States in preparing for such international trials. On the basis of a trip to Europe and plans discussed at the San Francisco Conference, Jackson represented the United States at a special conference held in London from June 26 to August 8, 1945.[143]

On this subject, the Soviet Union was, in general, closer to the American position than the British government.[144] The latter from at least 1943 and into 1945 preferred declaring the top Nazis to be outlaws and summarily shooting them; and they most certainly opposed any Allied tribunal, a position the Cabinet confirmed as late as April 12, 1945.[145] The Americans, with their fundamental objection to the bill of attainder concept, an objection growing out of eighteenth-century experience and anchored in the United States Constitution (Article I, Section 9,2, and Section 10, 1), were adamant on this subject; and by early May 1945, the British were coming around.[146] At the London Conference, agreement was reached on the establishment of an international tribunal and the procedures it would follow. Here was the charter for the Nürnberg trial; and the jail of those sentenced there would become, along with the air control system for Berlin, the last remnant of four-power cooperation in World War II.

The most obvious and striking aspect of the situation in Europe, however, was the general misery. There was destruction and hunger everywhere. Millions had been uprooted from their homes; many could not or believed they could not go back. The new term "Displaced Person" or DP was added to the vocabulary, and the immediate post-hostilities situation such as the expulsions from the German territories administered by Poland and the Soviet Union and from Czechoslovakia added to the numbers. Soon anti-Semitic riots in Poland convinced those Jews who had survived and attempted to return home that this would be impossible for them, so they too streamed into the DP camps in the western zones of occupation.[147] The United National Relief and Rehabilitation Administration (UNRRA) under Herbert Lehmann had been set up at Roosevelt's initiative to cope with these problems; it worked hard at the enormous task, but there was enough misery to daunt even as dedicated a humanitarian as the former governor of New York.

These issues in the aftermath of war were all greatly complicated by the shortage of food which, in turn, was in part caused by a shortage of shipping. The end of hostilities meant that much shipping was needed for returning troops home; however, many of them were not going home but toward new battles. The pressing need for shipping was only one reflection of the fact that the war in the Pacific overshadowed the war in Europe in 1945; whether it was the need for ships to redeploy troops or the diplomatic discussions among the Allies, the war in East Asia was a determining factor in everything.

The last stages of the war in East Asia, reviewed in the following chapter, were getting more difficult even as the European War was winding down. The alternation in developments of the first half of the year underlines the pattern. January was the month of the Soviet breakthrough from central Poland into Germany; February was the month of the bitter battle for Iwo Jima; March saw the seizure of the Remagen bridge and other crossings of the Rhine; April, May, and June were the months of the bloodiest fighting of the Pacific War on the island of Okinawa. The Americans were planning to remove the bulk of their forces from Europe quickly, some to be discharged but many for redirection to the Pacific. "Redeployment" was the key word. On May 1, even before the end of hostilities in Europe, the headquarters of the American 1st Army was withdrawn for redeployment; on August 1 it was reactivated in Manila to participate in the 1946 landing in Tokyo Bay. The concern of Eisenhower as well as Roosevelt and Truman over troubles with the Soviet Union in the spring of 1945 cannot be understood without reference to their awareness of the terrible price being paid in the war against Japan, and the anticipation of worse to come when American forces landed in the home islands later that year.

Certainly the Japanese had no plans to quit, and Allied intercepts of Japanese telegrams made this as obvious as the terrible fighting on and around Okinawa. The Japanese Minister in Switzerland, Kase Shunichi, passed on the advice of German officials who urged Japan *not* to follow Germany's example but to end the war quickly.[148] But Tokyo made it as clear as it could that the war would continue. The Japanese would try to take over German warships in East Asia; they would not allow a German government-in-exile to be established; but they would fight on without Germany and avoid recriminations over her violation of the treaty of December 1941 not to make a separate peace.[149] As the Allied leaders headed for Potsdam, they looked not only to the problems of a settlement for Europe but a continuing war in East Asia.

The Potsdam Conference of July 17 to August 2 was the longest of the Allied wartime conferences.[150] The French did not participate as both the Soviet and American governments saw no reason to invite them. The weakness of France was a key factor; in Soviet eyes this was a minor Western satellite whose presence would have called for admission of a Soviet satellite, perhaps Poland, which in turn would have caused problems for Britain and the United States. The Americans had no enthusiasm for the French either. Much attention has been paid to Truman's rough treatment of Soviet Foreign Commissar Molotov when the latter was in Washington on April 23, 1945, without reference to the fact that the new President was an outspoken man who did not pull his punches with anyone, foreign or American, who in his judgement had broken his promises. On May 18 and 21 Truman read the riot act to French Foreign Minister Georges Bidault over the refusal of French forces in Germany to obey orders—a reference to the difficulties over Stuttgart and in northern Italy a short time earlier.[151]

While France, therefore, was excluded from the Potsdam Conference, many of the agreements reached on the German question would subsequently founder on French opposition. The French government did not feel bound by decisions in which it had not participated, and French vetoes quickly blocked the implementation of those portions of the Potsdam agreements which called for the administrative and economic unity of Germany. The question of Germany, however, was but one of two dominating the conference; the other was the continued war with Japan.

Certainly President Truman went to Potsdam determined both because of the advice of American military leaders and his own inclination to obtain an early entrance of the Soviet Union into the war in the Pacific. He had approved the invasion of Kyushu for November 1 in June and was aware of the large anticipated cost in casualties. Stalin had previously promised to enter the war against Japan, but for Truman, as for Roosevelt, the critical issue was one of timing. All sorts of countries had rushed to declare war on Germany when they would no longer be called on to participate actively. The Soviet Union might well do the same thing in East Asia, and what the Americans as well as the British wanted was a timely entrance of Russia which would tie down the Japanese forces in Manchuria and north China. At a time when the high casualty list of Okinawa was on everyone's mind in Washington, this was Truman's key concern.

It is in this context that his great pleasure on learning from Stalin at their first meeting on July 17 that the Soviet Union would enter the Pacific War on August 15 must be understood.[152] As he wrote Mrs. Truman on the following day: "I've gotten what I came for—Stalin goes to war August 15 . . . I'll say that we'll end the war a year sooner now, and think of the kids who won't be killed! That is the important thing."[153] The other major issue, that of Germany, occupied much of the discussion thereafter, but the leaders knew that they would return to the Pacific War at the end of the conference.

The fate of Germany was, naturally enough, the subject of lengthy discussion at Potsdam. President Roosevelt had predicted with considerable accuracy the basic nature of the problems which the Allies faced. He had expressed dislike for "making detailed plans for a country which we do not yet occupy"[154] and had repeatedly based this reluctance on the inability to predict "what we and the Allies find when we get into Germany."[155] It had turned out that the Allies found a Germany without government or administration, but with massive destruction, misery, and dislocation. As for what they could do about it, another prediction of Roosevelt's proved to be correct: "In regard to the Soviet government . . . we have to remember that in their occupied territory they will do more or less what they wish. We cannot afford to get into a position of merely recording protests on our part unless there is some chance of some of the protests being heeded."[156]

There were three practical issues about Germany facing the Potsdam Conference. One was the establishment of a government machinery, the second was that of borders, and the third reparations. On the first, agreement was reached on an administration which would be directed and controlled by an Allied Control Council, with each zonal commander able to act on his own if no agreement or policy were reached in the ACC. Since the French vetoed the establishment of a common central German administrative apparatus and the four ACC representatives rarely agreed on policy, this really ended up meaning that each zone would go its own way. Dismemberment had been rejected in theory but was put into effect in practice. Certainly the new government the Soviet Union had begun establishing in its zone would not be accepted in the other zones, and the Soviet edict of June 10 authorizing political parties only reinforced the trend toward differing development in the zones.

The border and reparations issues were partially related. Soviet insistence on having the future border between Poland and Germany on the western rather than the eastern Neisse and actually turning that area, along with the rest of eastern Germany (except for northern East Prussia) over to Polish administration had a double impact on the reparations issue. It meant that Germany would have substantially less agricultural land at the same time as there would be more mouths to feed in the western zones—because of the settlement of refugees expelled from areas turned over to Poland. The British and the Americans were still a little reluctant to agree to such enormous territorial and population transfers, and they argued that there was no way to reconcile such a procedure with reparations from the over-burdened western zones.

The Soviet Union wanted Poland pushed to the western Neisse but also wanted massive reparations; at Potsdam Stalin repeated the demand, for half of a total of twenty billion dollars, which he had voiced at Yalta. The British, who had the zone with the greatest food deficit, insisted on food deliveries from the eastern zone so that the German workers could be fed; the Americans were sure, on the basis of their reading of the post-World War I experience, that they themselves would end up paying for the reparations as they paid to keep the Germans in all three western zones from starving.

The Soviet Union, nevertheless, insisted on heavy reparations, very reasonably arguing that the terrible destruction wrought by the German invasion of their territory should be repaid as much as possible by German labor, German machinery, and German goods; the United States, on the other hand, was reluctant to endorse forced labor and could not see how goods for reparations could be produced by a wrecked economy and hungry people. A compromise, suggested by the new United States Secretary of State James Byrnes, was eventually agreed upon. The Western Allies agreed to Soviet action in transferring the territory east of the Oder and western Neisse to Polish administration while reserving final border settlement to the peace conference. Since they also agreed to the removal, supposedly under humane conditions, of the German population from this area, they had in reality accepted the new border as permanent in fact if not in law: no one was likely to reopen the border issue for any but the most minimal corrections once the German population had been replaced by new Polish settlement.

In return, it was agreed by all that the Soviet Union would satisfy its reparations needs primarily out of *its* zone of occupation and would receive a portion of the industrial facilities from the other zones ruled to be not needed for Germany's peacetime economy. Part of this would be transferred to the Soviets without any payment—thus fulfilling the Russian demand for 50 percent of all German reparations—while part would be exchanged for food and coal from the Russian zone, so that less of the food deficit in the western zones would have to be made up by the Western Powers.[a] In practice, the reparations agreements soon

---

[a] William H. MacNeill in *America, Britain, and Russia*, p. 625 n 1, has pointed out that Soviet insistence on deliveries from the western zones contributed to the American abandonment of support for internationalization of the Ruhr. It should be noted that Truman had accepted the resignation of Morgenthau rather than take him along to Potsdam. The Potsdam agreements meant abandoning both Morgenthau's ideas on the Ruhr and his intention of leaving much more of eastern Germany to the future Germany. The resignation of Morgenthau is linked by Alan P. Dobson, *U.S. Wartime Aid to Britain* (New York: St. Martin's, 1986), p.222, to the decision on the following day to allow no Lend-Lease aid to Britain except for

led to further disputes and eventually a breakdown, but the compromise deal did give the Soviet Union recognition for the border it wanted for Poland and western acceptance of its exactions from its zone of occupation plus some from the western zones. In exchange, the Western Powers had accepted a border change they could not alter anyway and had made theoretical economic concessions the practical scope of which they could themselves control.

Other issues were at least partly worked out at Potsdam. There was to be a Council of Foreign Ministers to start meeting to prepare the peace treaties, with the first session scheduled for London in September. On the most important of these treaties after the one with Germany, that with Italy, preliminary agreements were not reached; but the Soviet Union did agree to put the treaty with Italy at the head of the agenda and to support Italy's admission to the United Nations, in spite of very clear signs that the British and Americans were not prepared to agree to the Soviet Union's receiving a share of the Italian colonial empire. Stalin had pushed for this, as well as for a role in Tangier, but it is not clear at this time whether this was a serious plan and hope or a negotiating ploy for exchange on other issues.[157]

On Poland, there was also at least minimal progress. Truman had earlier succeeded in obtaining from Stalin a small concession on the new government by the admission of Mikolajczyk and some others to it. These changes appear to have been the result of Harry Hopkins's mission to Moscow from May 26 to June 6 at Truman's request, and to represent a willingness of Stalin to make at least changes in appearances now that the Red Army was in full control of the country and the Lublin Committee had been firmly established in Warsaw.[158] By the time of the Potsdam meeting both the British and American governments were reluctantly moving toward an acceptance of the new Polish government, and they agreed to let it take over former Polish assets abroad. They were, however, not prepared to agree to the requested forced repatriation of the Polish soldiers who had fought alongside them against the Germans. It was one thing to repatriate against their will those who had fought on the German side; it was quite another to do so with your own comrades in arms. Once again free elections for Poland were promised for the immediate future—but not then held. The division of the remnants of Germany's merchant and naval shipping was worked out. The first international trial of German war criminals was set. A number of

---

fighting Japan, in violation of the Quebec phase II agreement. There is a helpful review of the workings of the reparations settlement, including the original terms and the experience in the first years after the war, in Inter-Allied Reparation Agency, *Report of the Secretary General for the Year 1949* (Brussels: Inter-Allied Reparation Agency, 1950).

other issues was postponed by referral to the new Council of Foreign Ministers or simply left unresolved. On one final great question there was agreement: the warning to Japan.

On the way to Potsdam, Truman learned of the successful testing of an atomic bomb in New Mexico. He now obtained Churchill's agreement to tell Stalin about it.[159] The contemporary record does not indicate, but we know today, that Stalin not only knew of the American and British work on the A-bomb from his espionage network—and that the Soviet Union itself was hard at work on producing one—but that Truman had been briefed on Soviet atomic espionage when first informed about the A-bomb after his swearing in as President. What he therefore knew would be really news for Stalin was the report on the success of the test.

Truman was hopeful that the bomb would end the war with Japan quickly.[160] Although he doubted that the Japanese would respond to any appeal for a prompt surrender, Truman was greatly concerned about the casualties and destruction the new weapon would cause and therefore wanted "a warning statement advising the Japanese to surrender and save lives."[161] This concern led to the Potsdam Declaration which called on Japan to surrender, a call which they dismissed, as discussed in Chapter 16. But the Potsdam Conference also provided an opportunity for a coordination of war plans for the final assault on Japan if that should still prove necessary. British forces would participate in the 1946 landing on the main island of Honshu, and the Russians would attack the Japanese army in Manchuria. One way or another, Japan was to follow Germany in defeat. If the call for surrender from the center of an occupied Germany did not get them to see the light, other steps would.

As the Allied leaders left Potsdam for their respective countries, they could look back on a terrible struggle which had finally ended in complete victory over Hitler's Germany and its European allies. But the very completeness of that victory left them both in full control of a devastated continent and face to face with each other in its center. They could look back with satisfaction on a great task accomplished— a point symbolized by exchanges of decorations and the holding of parades—but they also had to look forward to the difficult problems of reconstruction and the challenge of finding ways to live alongside one another without still another great conflict. Both of these assignments would occupy them for years.

16

THE WAR IN THE PACIFIC: FROM LEYTE TO THE *MISSOURI*

LEYTE

Allied plans for the defeat of Japan were developed in the summer and fall of 1944. The success in the Marianas and northern New Guinea opened the possibility for new strikes at the Japanese empire. It was not yet settled among the American planners whether an attack on Luzon, the largest and most important island in the northern Philippines, was preferable to a landing on Formosa (Taiwan) as the basis for the direct attack on Japan itself, but agreement had been reached on an invasion of Leyte in the central Philippines as an essential prerequisite for either of the two alternatives. From Leyte, with its great anchorage facilities and its assumed potential for air bases, subsequent assaults could be mounted over the intervening space to either Luzon or Formosa.

The Formosa project, especially dear to Admiral King, however, fell victim to three developments in the fall of 1944. The collapse of the Chinese Nationalists made the idea of a base off the China coast for the coordination of operations from there in the great assault on Japan an unrealistic project. The continuation of the war in Europe into 1945 precluded the early transfer to East Asia of the troops and shipping needed for the Formosa operation. The logistic needs of a Formosa landing, especially past a Japanese-controlled Luzon, were beyond the anticipated resources of the Central Pacific theater, so that Admiral Nimitz increasingly favored a Luzon over a Formosa operation as a follow-up to Leyte. Even while the Leyte plans were being developed, therefore, the central Philippines landing increasingly took on the character of a prelude to a landing on Luzon as a step to an assault further north—toward Japan itself—and with less and less direct connection to the war on the Chinese mainland.

There were three further repercussions to this change. In the first place, there came to be increasing concern in Allied headquarters about the possibility of a continuing campaign against the large Japanese forces in China even after a defeat of Japan in its home islands. The huge area held by the Japanese armed forces in China, together with their control of some industry there, seemed to open up the possibility of an extended further war to reduce those units.[1] The question of trying to make the Japanese surrender *all* of their forces simultaneously, on the mainland of Asia as well as in the cut-off islands of the southwest Pacific, assumed increasing importance in Allied thinking. In view of their experience with the way the Japanese held on to the bitter end, the prospect of further years of fighting in all sorts of places on the continent and the islands raised very serious questions indeed, questions which included concern about the willingness of the American—to say nothing of the British—public to support bloody "cleaning-up operations" for years on end.

Secondly, the steady deterioration of the situation in China might well lend credence to the British disdain for the Chinese Nationalists and China's role as a great power, but it also made any British operation in Southeast Asia far more a separate endeavor to recapture their colonial empire than a portion of the general campaign against Japan. In the third place, the centrality of the Philippines to the final defeat of Japan in the eyes of Washington as well as the view of General MacArthur, who had always seen this as the supreme test of his own and his country's war effort—and he never could distinguish between the two—would assure solid support from Washington for practically anything he wanted to do in the Philippines campaign.

That campaign, it was decided, could begin even earlier than the December 20, 1944, date originally set for it. When a massive attack by American naval air on September 11 into the Philippines area destroyed large numbers of planes and ships, leaving little effective resistance at that moment, Admiral Halsey called on Nimitz to scrap the Palau Islands operation and strike for Leyte right away. Nimitz and his staff thought it too late to drop the Peleliu attack but agreed to an earlier drive for Leyte and offered the XXIV Corps, ready for another operation which would now be cancelled, to join MacArthur's forces if he too were willing to move early. The Joint Chiefs of Staff, in Quebec for the Octagon Conference, asked for and received the concurrence of MacArthur,[a] and moved up the date of the Leyte invasion to October 20. If the war against Japan could be speeded up, so much the better.

At Octagon, plans were also approved for a British fleet to participate

---

[a] MacArthur was actually not at his headquarters but on a warship keeping radio silence as it took part in covering the landing on Morotai (the Southwest Pacific parallel to the Palaus operation), and his Chief of Staff answered for him. It was too late to call off the landings on Morotai, Peleliu, and Angaur, and, as a result of the last two, the navy was able to make extensive use of Ulithi's superb harbor in the eastern Carolines.

in the Pacific as the ships became available from Europe. King had his doubts, but the President ruled that the British would take part.[2] The latter were also developing plans for their participation in the main attacks on Japan in other ways. A project for British very long range bombers, refueled en route to Japan from bases to be captured or built on Luzon and Okinawa, had originated in late 1943; it received the code-name "Tiger force" and the cooperation of General Arnold.[3] Churchill originally did not want British troops serving under General MacArthur but instead preferred to concentrate on regaining the British possessions in Southeast Asia, especially Singapore.[4] It was, however, intended that Commonwealth forces would be redeployed after victory in Europe, and the plans for the participation of British, Canadian, Australian, New Zealand, and South African units in the final assault on Japan were developed in the summer and fall of 1944.[5] There was certainly no inclination in London to stop short of the unconditional surrender of Japan.[6]

The Americans now went forward with the plans for a landing on Leyte. The 6th Army under General Walter Krueger, MacArthur's main ground force, was to land on the island's east coast, drive inland, and make possible the building of new and expansion of old airfields to provide land-based air support for the invasion of Luzon, now moved forward to December. This was to be the first time a whole American army with two corps would go into action in the Pacific at one time.[a] The former responsibilities of 6th Army in New Guinea fell to the newly designated 8th Army under General Robert Eichelberger. Air support for the landing would be provided primarily by carrier based planes; both Admiral Kinkaid's 7th Fleet, long attached to MacArthur's command, and Admiral Halsey's 3rd Fleet from Nimitz's Central Pacific theater would support and shield the great invasion, in which eventually over a quarter of a million men were landed on the island.[7] Thereafter an invasion of Luzon would be possible and from there, in turn, amphibious landings could be launched against the Bonin and Ryukyu Islands and then the home islands of Japan itself.

The Japanese were certainly not about to let the Americans return to the Philippines without a major effort to throw them back into the sea. Just as the conquest of the islands had looked to Tokyo in 1940 and 1941 as an essential prerequisite for both the occupation of Southeast Asia and the effective control of that area afterwards, the whole structure

---

[a] The Australians had been invited to participate but refused to send a division; they wanted to take part but only if a whole corps under an Australian corps commander could be sent and thought that this might be the case elsewhere in the Philippines (see the Lumsden–Blamey talk of 9 August 1944 reported by the former to Ismay in PRO, CAB 127/33).

of communications between the Japanese home islands and the oil, tin, and rubber of the territories Japan conquered in the winter of 1941–42 depended on continued Japanese domination of the Philippines. Whatever the forms of sham independence Tokyo might temporarily allow collaborating elements in both areas, there was never any doubt that complete control of all military affairs and the major economic resources would be retained by Japan.

The Japanese army and navy leadership was for once in the war united on defensive planning. They were desperately trying to mobilize additional resources for war, in a manner not unlike the German exertions of the same year. The Japanese, in fact, hoped to draw on German technological advances for their own use, especially to exploit the German lead in design, testing, and production of jet fighters. Throughout 1944 and into 1945, they attempted to obtain the latest German advances. The slowness of the Germans in providing detailed information and the poor handling of what they did send negated all these efforts; the only real result was the unwitting one of providing the Allies with a great deal of intelligence on the progress of German and Japanese jet airplane development, because the reports on them were transmitted in code systems that the Americans were reading.[8]

Not only were the Japanese, to all intents and purposes, unable to profit from the latest weapons developments by Germany—exchanges of information about suicide airplanes hardly qualify—they had to anticipate in 1944 the real possibility that in the near future their German ally would follow Italy into defeat, with or without surrender. Japanese diplomats in Europe were cautioning the government in Tokyo not to count either on long continued German resistance or on a split in the Allied coalition.[9] There might be minimal advantages for Japan from the Axis disasters in Europe: the withdrawal of Finland from the war could open a new route to Sweden across the U.S.S.R.,[10] and the Mufti of Jerusalem, fresh from recruiting soldiers for the Germans from among the Muslims of Southeast Europe, now wanted to do the same favor for the Japanese in Southeast Asia and India [11]—perhaps following Bose to East Asia before a German collapse—but all such trifles could not obscure the main danger.

That danger was the redeployment of American and British forces from Europe to East Asia after the defeat of Germany, with the real possibility that the Soviet Union might join them in a concentric attack which, in its fundamentals, if not in its details, would be similar to the concentric assault on German-controlled Europe in the summer of 1944. The most important hope of Tokyo was that of keeping the Soviet Union neutral. Beginning in August 1944, the Japanese government attempted diplomatic steps to encourage the Soviet Union to adhere to the 1941 Neutrality Pact. Japanese Foreign Minister Shigemitsu Mamoru appears to have thought of the possibility of some new Japanese–Soviet agreement which might lead to their jointly developing a program for a general settlement of the whole war, a project which assumed that the Moscow government was prepared to abandon its allies, relieve Germany of its Eastern Front, and thereby in effect force the Western Allies into making peace through a revived Tripartite Pact, with the Soviet Union taking the place of Italy.[12] Once upon a time, in the winter of 1940–41, Stalin had been seriously interested in such an arrangement; but as the Japanese ambassador in Moscow, Sato Naotake, repeatedly told his government, there was not the slightest chance of such a project now. Why should the Soviet Union leave a winning alliance for a losing one and give up the enormous advantages of victory for the minimal advantages Japan offered?[13] Tokyo kept trying for months but simply could not get anywhere with its scheme. Whether or not massive Japanese concessions to the Soviet Union could at this time have turned things around remains an open question, but there was no inclination in Tokyo in *1944* to make the sorts of offers put forward in *1945*, when any interest Stalin might conceivably once have had was long gone.[14]

Even their military victory in China could not be turned to political advantage by the Japanese at this stage of the war. A wild scheme to make peace with Chiang on terms agreed by the Supreme War Council on September 5, 1944, hedging as usual on the withdrawal of Japanese troops from China, insisting on holding on to Manchuria, but promising to turn over Hong Kong and perhaps French Indo-China, never received a reply.[15] As for the alternative, the puppet government of Wang Ching-wei, established under Japanese control in occupied China, that had already lost its real significance by this time. The death of Wang on November 10, 1944, after months in a Japanese hospital, put a formal end to what had always been a dubious project.[16] As if all this were not enough, the Japanese again had to worry about a break with Portugal over the Japanese occupation of Portuguese Timor, a break which would have closed one of the few remaining Japanese windows on European developments. Minor concessions were made to Lisbon, but Japan made no concession on the critical issue: the evacuation of Japanese troops from the Portuguese portion of Timor. Tension continued.[17]

None of these problems affected basic Japanese strategy. The armed forces of the country were prepared to fight fiercely for every one of the islands and territories under Japanese control in the hope of so raising their enemies' cost in lives and treasure that at some point the latter would prefer a negotiated end to hostilities. If, in the process, major defeats could be inflicted on the Americans or the British—as the Japanese had hoped to do in 1944, first in the invasion of India and then in the "A-Go" operation against the Americans in the Marianas or New Guinea—that was, of course, all to the good. But no one in Tokyo expected that the Americans or the British could be discouraged from further operations by a single such event. It would be the cumulative effect of the fighting, win or lose, which was expected to wear them down. And the fighting would become more ghastly as the Allies came closer to the center of Japanese strength, the home islands. The fighting on Saipan and Biak and at Kohima had shown what the terrible battle for Peleliu confirmed: whatever the defects of Japanese naval and army leadership, whatever the superiority of the resources which the Allies could bring to bear, the soldiers and sailors of Japan would fight to the death in loyalty to the Emperor and in obedience to officers who died with them. And they would exact a fearful price.

In the summer of 1944, as a reaction to the defeats Japan had suffered, the Japanese leadership began the organization of suicide formations on a large scale.[18] At a time when Japanese pilots received inadequate training and flew what had become inferior planes against better trained and more experienced American pilots in superior airplanes, and when the massing of anti-aircraft fire from large concentrations of Allied warships made possible the throwing up of a huge volume of fire, battle sorties by Japanese planes were ever more likely to end in their being shot down. Not only that, they were most likely to be shot down without having either brought down any American planes or damaged any Allied warships.

There are as yet no western language studies of Japanese army and naval aviation which plot construction, front-line strength and losses as comprehensively as Williamson Murray has prepared for the German air force, but the outlines are clear.[19] The Japanese built 20,000 planes in 1943 and an additional 26,000 in 1944, but the losses in training, ferrying, accidents, and combat were so large that total front-line strength barely grew in numbers. From a force flown in 1941 by some of the world's most skilled and experienced pilots, the Japanese army and navy air forces—always operating quite separately—had come to be by 1944 a force of dedicated men with little training or experience who in a high proportion of cases went down in their first combat.

It was in this context that it increasingly made more sense to many Japanese air force leaders to do with intent and to a useful purpose what was already being done unintentionally and to little effect. Planes would be fueled for a one-way mission and aimed at Allied ships, the assumption being that the explosion would damage or sink the ship hit. There was no reason to believe that many more planes would be lost this way than any other, but it was assumed that in this fashion there would at least be something to show for the sacrifice. This tactic also had some other advantages: less modern planes could be used, the pilots did not need a great deal of training, and the morale of the Allied fleets hit by mass suicide attacks might well suffer. Named kamikaze, or divine wind, for the wind which had once dispersed an invading armada in the thirteenth century, this form of suicide attack was first put into action by the Japanese in the struggle for the Philippines in October, 1944, and on an increasing scale thereafter, with over 5000 held back to meet the invasion of the home islands.

By the end of the Okinawa campaign there had been 2,550 kamikaze missions of which 475 had secured hits or damaging near misses.[20] Whatever one may think of the concept, it was under the circumstances certainly not an unreasonable or preposterous effort to match Japan's resources to her goals. The one major miscalculation made by those who developed and oversaw what became a very large enterprise was that they appear never to have thought through the most obvious practical side of the project. Instead of carrying the largest possible explosive cargo—a 1000-pound bomb or more—the kamikaze planes were generally loaded with a 500-pound bomb, so that the ones which actually hit an American or British ship inflicted nothing like the damage which might have been wrought at no greater cost in Japanese pilots and planes.

As for the specific plans to defend the Philippines, which the Japanese correctly assumed would be invaded by American forces at some time in 1944 or 1945, there appears to have been a minor miscalculation on timing: the Japanese naval headquarters believed that no invasion would be attempted before the American Presidential election in November because of the repercussions of any reverse on Roosevelt's chances for reelection.[21] In reality, of course, the original post-election date was advanced to a pre-election date for reasons unrelated to partisan politics, an interesting reflection on continued Japanese misassessment of the American people.

The major Japanese plan was called "Sho-go", or "Victory" operation with four numbered variants to deal with an American assault on the Philippines, Formosa, the Kuriles or the home islands. The Philippines—Sho-1—seemed the most likely contingency. The land defense of the islands' quarter million men garrison was to be coordinated by Field Marshal Terauchi Hisaichi. Reinforcements were being sent to the islands; land based planes lost to earlier American attacks were being replaced; and General Yamashita Tomoyuki, who had been shelved as a possible rival of Tojo after the conquest of Singapore, was sent in to take control of the 14th Army, the major land force. After their earlier experiences with American landings, the Japanese had decided to assume that the landing itself could not be blocked. Instead of fighting at the water's edge, they would station their main forces a short distance inland, hold there while the navy and naval and ground air decoyed off or destroyed the American fleet which covered the landing, and then drive the unsuppliable and unreinforceable Americans into the sea. It was a strategy which involved risking practically every remaining Japanese warship, and it almost worked.

The American plan provided for a substitution of sea-borne for land-based air support in the initial phase of the operation; for the first time MacArthur was sending his soldiers into an area where they would be dependent on the navy beyond the initial landing. Because of the wretched terrain intelligence, which was the more inexcusable since Leyte had been under American control for decades and there was fairly constant communication with guerillas on the island, MacArthur's Southwest Pacific headquarters erroneously assumed that large airfields could readily be built on the central Leyte plain. The idea was that in short order the 6th Army could seize that plain and thereafter be supported by General Kenney's land based planes until Leyte was cleared. Thereafter, it was assumed equally erroneously, the big new air bases on Leyte would provide the basis for air support of the Luzon landings. Had MacArthur and his staff had a reasonably accurate idea of what the island they planned to retake from the Japanese was actually like, they would presumably have picked a different target in the central Philippines for a major landing.

The preliminary air attacks launched from Halsey's 3rd Fleet on air bases on Formosa led the Japanese to make two great errors of their own. In the first place, they temporarily believed that the Americans were planning to attack Formosa, not the Philippines, and reacted by throwing a high proportion of their navy planes at Halsey's ships. In a series of air battles on October 11–14, the Japanese lost over five hundred planes to fewer than one hundred American planes. This action, of course, very much depleted Japanese air strength for dealing with the subsequent American operation in immediate support of the Leyte landing. Compounding this misallocation of scarce resources was a complete misunderstanding and misrepresentation of what had happened. Unwilling or unable to comprehend that Japan's naval air force had suffered one of its greatest defeats of the war, the commander informed

Imperial headquarters that eleven American aircraft carriers, two battleships and one cruiser had been sunk while an additional eight carriers,
two battleships, one cruiser and thirteen other ships had been damaged—when in reality one carrier and one cruiser had been damaged.
There was much celebration in Tokyo and the Emperor announced a
special holiday in honor of this great victory.[22]

In fact, Halsey's approximately one thousand carrier planes had eliminated a large portion of the Japanese naval aviation available for the
defense of the Philippines; as the intact United States 3rd Fleet headed
back from the Formosa area to provide close coverage of the Leyte
landing, the whole Japanese defense plan had been gravely weakened.
Whether the Japanese naval high command would have risked practically
the whole navy had the full extent of the Japanese defeat and American
victory been understood in Tokyo will never be known. Perhaps they
would have gone ahead anyway. As it was, by the time the Japanese
naval commanders on the spot realized that the planes on which they
had counted had been shot down a week earlier, but the American fleet
and its complement of naval aviation was essentially intact, it was too
late to change plans. When the Japanese learned on October 17 that an
American landing force was obviously headed for Leyte, not Formosa,
plan "Sho-1" was ordered into effect as the only possible option.

The Japanese navy plan provided that a group of four aircraft carriers
and two carrier-battleships plus escorts under Admiral Ozawa Jisaburo
would head southward from home waters with only 108 planes to serve
as a decoy for Halsey's fleet. The Japanese hoped that this would divert
the 3rd Fleet from close protection of the Leyte landing force, making
it vulnerable, once the troops were ashore, to their main battle fleet,
which would destroy the unprotected American transports and supply
ships off the beaches once the few smaller warships guarding them had
been sunk. The main Japanese fleet, however, was not in one body; as
in the plan for Midway, the naval leadership had made its dispositions
as complicated as possible. In addition to the decoy fleet, no fewer
than four groupings were to act as two strike forces, of which one was
supplemented by still a fifth coming from Singapore.[23] While the
Japanese were assembling and sending out the components of their great
operation, the Americans were already landing on Leyte, and many of
the transports would in any case be gone by the time the Japanese
arrived. Without substantial air support, the Japanese were sending seven
battleships, four carriers, two hybrid battleship-carriers, and twenty
cruisers against the American 3rd and 7th fleets with twelve battleships,
thirty-two carriers and twenty-three cruisers, assisted by well over 1200

planes. The Americans, in addition, had a force of submarines out scouting and ready to strike. Ironically, while the Japanese navy had for decades stressed the role of submarines as one of attacking the enemy fleet to reduce its size so that it could be overwhelmed in surface battle, it was American submarines which played this role in World War II's greatest naval battle.

As the American warships provided cover and Japanese striking forces gathered for battle, the American 6th Army was approaching Leyte in several hundred transports. A bombardment group of old battleships under Admiral Oldendorf pounded beach defenses, engineers cleared obstacles, and the first assault units of four divisions went ashore on a 10-mile front in the morning of October 20, 1944. There was little resistance in the beachhead area, and the American soldiers quickly pushed about two miles inland.[24] The landing operation was on a scale resembling the June invasion in Normandy; involving smaller forces but having come over a very much greater distance, it encountered far less *initial* resistance. Two events of the first day were of major significance, one political, the other military. General MacArthur had personally accompanied the invasion force, went ashore in a scene widely reported with a famous photograph, and spoke by radio from the beachhead to the people of the Philippines, telling them that he had indeed returned and calling on them to rally to him. The Philippine Commonwealth flag flew alongside the Stars and Stripes as he was speaking, and on October 23 the civilian government of the Philippines was formally reinstated at Tacloban, the island capital, under President Sergio Osmeña, who had replaced Manuel Quezon after the latter's death. Whatever one may say about MacArthur's grandstanding or the problems faced by the civil government of the Commonwealth, there could be no doubt that MacArthur really did intend for the islands to continue on their road to independence, and he had every reason for believing that on this critical issue he fully and accurately represented the views of President Roosevelt.

The military event which was to have even greater significance than anyone immediately anticipated was the quick capture of the Tacloban airfield by a swing northward from the invasion beaches. With personal attention from General Kenney, this rather primitive and narrow field was built up quickly so that land-based airplanes could replace those from the escort carriers of Admiral Kinkaid when the carriers would have to leave for refitting and refueling. As the fighting on Leyte developed into a long and bitter slugging match, the Tacloban field, in spite of its narrowness and small size—it was located on a small sand spit—became an essential part of the American effort.[25] For a moment, however, the fate of the whole invasion hung in the balance as the Japanese navy implemented its plan for defeating the Americans.

The Japanese naval contingents under Admiral Kurita Takeo and Admiral Nishimura Shogi left Brunei anchorage in northwest Borneo on October 22. Kurita was to take his ships through the San Bernadino Strait north of Samar Island (to the north of Leyte), while Nishimura was to go south of Leyte through the Surigao Strait ahead of still a further naval force, with all meeting in Leyte Gulf on the east side of the island, where the Americans had landed and where the Japanese hoped to destroy them. Kurita's force was sighted by American submarines which radioed the approach of the Japanese and sank two while damaging a third of the heavy cruisers, one of the submarines being lost. One of the cruisers sunk had been Kurita's flagship; being dumped into the water and forced to transfer to the super-battleship *Yamato* cannot have helped his disposition in the battle about to heat up.

Kurita's force now became the target of a series of attacks by carrier planes of Task Force 38, the main carrier and fast battleship component of Halsey's fleet under Admiral Marc Mitscher. They attacked on October 24 after losing the aircraft carrier *Princeton* to a bombing attack the day before. A long series of torpedo and bomb hits first crippled and then sank the *Musashi*, the world's largest battleship; other ships were damaged, including the battleships *Yamato* and *Nagato*. Without air cover from either land or carrier based planes, Kurita decided to turn back from the Sibuyan Sea westward lest all his ships be sunk before even reaching the San Bernadino Strait. But even as the Japanese warships turned away, the American attacks were slackening. The decoy maneuver had drawn off Halsey's main force, and Kurita turned his surviving ships around once again to head for the San Bernadino Strait and Leyte Gulf. Although neither observed nor hindered by the Americans, he could no longer expect to meet Nishimura's ships coming north through Surigao Strait. The southern arm of the Japanese pincer was destroyed that night.

Nishimura's force had also been sighted shortly after Kurita's and was subjected to some air attacks as it headed for the Surigao Strait. Admiral Kinkaid ordered the bombardment group of Admiral Oldendorf to block the Strait, which he did by deploying the six old battleships across the exit from the Strait, placing his eight cruisers in front of them, and having the destroyers and PT boats on station to attack the approaching Japanese in front of the larger ships.

In what would be history's last great surface contest, the Japanese attack force was utterly defeated. The PT boats did little beyond disorienting the Japanese, but the destroyer attacks badly damaged several of their warships. Oldendorf had successfully performed the dream maneuver of all navies, he had crossed the "T". As the Japanese battleships and cruisers approached his own line, they were met by withering broadsides. The battleship *Fuso* had already been split in two by the torpedoes of American destroyers; the battleship *Yamashiro* and the cruiser *Mogami* were sunk, the latter after running into the heavy cruiser *Nachi*, which was the flagship of the Japanese follow-up naval squadron under Admiral Shima Kiyohide. The latter had sense enough to make off, but Nishimura was dead and most of his force sunk or damaged. Of Oldendorf's six battleships, two had been "sunk" and three badly damaged in the attack on Pearl Harbor.[a]

In the meantime, Halsey's scout planes had discovered Admiral Ozawa's decoy force of carriers. Believing them to be the most important portion of the Japanese fleet and assuming that Kurita's main attack force had been driven back after its heavy losses, Halsey now raced north as the Japanese had hoped. The carrier planes attacked Ozawa's force on the 24th and soon scored hits on the four Japanese carriers which were sunk one after the other. Ozawa's signals, however, did not reach or make clear to Kurita that the main American naval force was attacking him, and therefore was not protecting the Leyte landing. This was one of the most fateful failures in communications during the war. The sacrifice of the large carrier *Zuikaku*, last survivor of the carriers of the Pearl Harbor attack, and of the smaller carriers *Chiyoda*, *Zuiho*, and *Chitose* was to prove useless. The two carrier-battleships and most of the other escorts of Ozawa's force were, however, saved from destruction because Halsey had to order his fast battleships to turn around and head back for Leyte Gulf, where Kurita's fleet was threatening the American landing force now defended only by the light carriers and escorts of Kinkaid's 7th fleet; Oldendorf's heavy ships being by now short of fuel and ammunition.

The calls for assistance from Leyte had led Admiral Nimitz to make one of his few interventions in tactical decisions; whatever Halsey might think and say—and quite profanely at that—Nimitz knew that first priority had to go to the Leyte landing force and its naval protection. The navy had let down a landing force in the Pacific badly when it left the marines stranded on Guadalcanal in August, 1942; there was to be no repetition. In the event the fast battleship force under Admiral Willis Lee arrived too late to take part in the naval battle off Leyte, as Halsey

[a] The *West Virginia* and *California* had been "sunk" by settling in the mud; the *Tennessee*, *Maryland*, and *Pennsylvania* had been hit. Only the *Mississippi* had not been damaged in the Pearl Harbor raid, having been transferred to the Atlantic from Hawaii in the summer of 1941.

had anticipated; but if Kurita had handled his ships with determination, there would have been plenty of action for Lee's battleships.

What had happened in the interim and had caused the anguished queries about the location of Halsey's main fleet was the decision of Kurita to turn around and head for the San Bernadino Strait once more after reforming his fleet. He was, therefore, approaching the Strait unobserved while Halsey was off chasing the decoy fleet commanded by Ozawa. The result was that Kurita's battleships and cruisers now ran into the small escort carriers of Kinkaid's 7th Fleet rather than the big fleet carriers and fast battleships of Halsey.

The escort carriers were small converts from merchant ship designs which were supposed to ferry planes, escort convoys against submarines, and, as in the North African landing of November 1942 and on other occasions like this one, provide temporary air cover for landing operations. Never built, armored or armed for major fleet action, the six escort carriers and six destroyers commanded by Admiral Cliften A. F. Sprague were on October 25 the only protection of the unloading transports and supply ships for 6th Army against Kurita's four battleships, eight cruisers, and accompanying destroyers.[26]

Kurita and Sprague each made a decision as their forces collided, and these decisions, it turned out, very largely determined the outcome of the wild encounter battle which ensued. Kurita was and remained fooled by faulty intelligence, hopelessly inaccurate ship identification, the total lack of Japanese air reconnaissance, and complete failure of radio communication with Admiral Ozawa. He believed that he was facing the fleet carriers which in reality were hundreds of miles away chasing Ozawa's decoy fleet. Kurita never realized that what he was up against was a small group of vulnerable escort carriers supported by a handful of destroyers. Throughout the battle, Kurita acted on this erroneous assumption, never recognized that the decoy concept had worked, and handled his ships as if engaged in battle with a major enemy fleet.

Sprague, who knew all too accurately what he was up against, called for reinforcement but decided that, in these circumstances, attack was the best defense. He hurled his force against the approaching Japanese fleet, ordering the destroyers to charge with torpedo attacks and the escort carriers to launch and relaunch their planes in air attacks with bombs, torpedoes, and anything else they could find to drop on the Japanese warships. In a way this tactic served to reinforce Kurita's confused assessment: with his ships constantly swerving to avoid torpedoes and dodge bombs, the admiral neither reconsidered his view of the situation nor kept a close rein on his own warships. Ironically, in some instances the thin armor of the escort carriers helped them: armor piercing shells occasionally went clear through both sides of the ships without exploding.

In the wild melée, which went on for about two hours, three of the Japanese cruisers were severely damaged while Kurita's flagship, the *Yamato*, turned to avoid torpedoes and thereby kept the admiral from effective control of his ships. One of the American escort carriers, the *Gambier Bay*, was sunk as were several of the destroyers which had charged the larger and more numerous Japanese warships with incredible bravery, but the continuing bombing damaged two more of Kurita's cruisers which the Japanese had to scuttle. Confused by the bombing and the daring torpedo attacks from American destroyer escorts, Kurita decided to turn away a second time and leave the area to reorganize his forces. He had no idea that the decoy ships of Ozawa were even then being attacked by the carrier planes he imagined himself to be facing.

While Kurita reorganized his scattered naval force, Sprague's ships were the objective of the first major coordinated kamikaze attack. The escort carrier *St. Lo* was sunk and two others were damaged, but, as Kurita returned to the charge, he failed to take advantage of the situation. Confused by reports of still another carrier force approaching and by renewed air attacks, Kurita finally turned away from Leyte and retired through San Bernadino Strait. A few planes from Halsey's returning carriers chased after him but scored no hits. The greatest naval battle in history was over, and the landing force was safe.

The Japanese navy, which had remained a major asset after its earlier losses and defeats, could never recover from the loss of three battleships, four carriers, and six cruisers, losses which, together with substantial damage to other ships, left her with an ill-matched assortment of survivors. Now there was not only the already very difficult problem of training naval aircraft fliers to replace hundreds lost in battle; there were only three carriers left and one ship being converted so that the role of carrier based naval aviation had practically come to an end. Whatever chance Japan's surface fleet had ever had of slowing down the American advance was gone. It too would turn to suicide missions as a last resort. In the meantime, the defense of the Philippines against the Americans was primarily up to the Japanese army and the kamikaze. As the Americans soon discovered on Leyte, that was quite a significant barrier on the way to Tokyo.

The critical decision in the land fighting for Leyte was made in late October by Field Marshal Terauchi when, against Yamashita's advice, he ordered massive reinforcement of the Leyte garrison. As Japanese troops were moved into the island, the original force there grew in size instead of shrinking as had been the case in every prior island campaign. This meant on the one hand that the struggle for the island was much bitterer, harder, and longer than the Americans had ever imagined; on the other hand, it meant that the Japanese had used up a far higher proportion of their forces than they had originally intended and were therefore unable to defend the remaining Philippine islands as effectively as would otherwise have been likely.

The growing strength of the Japanese intersected with increasing problems for the Americans. Not only was Japanese resistance on the island growing rather than waning, the air situation deteriorated badly. The escort carriers had to be refitted after the battering they had taken. As for the buildup of land bases for airplanes, it soon turned out that there had been a terrible intelligence failure. The central Leyte area which 6th Army had begun to clear as it drove inland proved quite unsuitable for airfield construction. The steel mats sank in the swampy ground, and the resulting inadequate air support meant that the steadily reinforced Japanese air attacks by the 2500 planes of the Japanese 4th Air Army often dominated the sky over Leyte. Continued Japanese air raids hampered the progress of airfield construction and operations in general. Naval air support from the fleet carriers proved necessary for the Americans, but even so a slogging match ensued in which the Americans gained ground slowly and at high cost.

During November 1944 the Americans fought the steadily reinforced Japanese army on Leyte in bloody positional warfare resembling the trench fighting on the Western Front in World War I and the early fighting in Normandy. The American units were also reinforced and continued to be supported by both naval air and increasing land-based air. The latter became the target of a spectacular Japanese suicide operation in which planes crash landed on the airstrips around Tacloban and paratroopers landed nearby. This was a major effort to seize the airstrips as Japanese ground forces counter-attacked toward them.[27] In bitter fighting from November 27 to December 12, the Americans succeeded in defeating this effort. By that time, an additional major American landing near Ormoc on the west coast of Leyte on December 7 had created a critical situation for the Japanese on the island.

The American Xth Corps had pushed north up the Leyte valley around the central Leyte mountains and threatened the Ormoc valley from the north even as the new American landing drove into it from the south. Ormoc itself was freed on December 10, thus depriving the Japanese of a port they had used to send in reinforcements. On December 21 American spearheads from north and south met in the middle of Ormoc valley. The remaining Japanese had been divided into several separate groups, which fought on until April 1945 against units of the American 8th Army, which by then had taken over from 6th Army, which was scheduled to land on Luzon.

The fighting had been heavier and longer than the Americans had anticipated. As usual, MacArthur's announcement at the end of December that the fighting was over was premature by months. United States casualties had been heavy, over 15,000. The Japanese losses had been even higher, including well over 50,000 dead.[28] At the time MacArthur was declaring the operation over, Yamashita informed the Japanese commander of the 35th Army on Leyte, General Suzuki Sosaka, that no further reinforcements could be sent; he and his forces were on their own. They had already set back the scheduled attack on Luzon by about a month but had been unable to hold on to key positions on Leyte.[a]

The seizure of Leyte, or most of it, provided the American armed forces with a position from which Japanese communications with their southern empire, already shredded by American submarines, were effectively blocked. The campaign had led to the greatest naval battle in history and had consumed a large proportion of the land and air forces at Japan's disposal for holding on to the Philippines.

One major objective of the Leyte operation was not achieved because it turned out to be unattainable. The island was not appropriate for large-scale airfield development as the Southwest Pacific theater planners had hoped. The major bases for the air support needed for the Luzon landing, therefore, had to be built elsewhere. The ideal location for this as well as other purposes in the last stages of the Pacific War proved to be the island of Mindoro, about 250 miles northwest of Leyte and within a short distance of Luzon itself. Originally scheduled for December 5 but postponed because of the Leyte battle, a landing on Mindoro on December 15 quickly led to control of the airfields there, and these were soon expanded. Kamikazes killed hundreds on the escorting naval ships but could not halt the invasion. Even as the airfields were developed, their importance and the essential character of land-based planes for the Luzon invasion were underlined by the impact of a terrible typhoon which struck the 3rd Fleet with massive force on December 18, 1944. Three destroyers capsized and sank; hundreds of planes were destroyed or damaged.[29] Neither the typhoon nor a Japanese navy-supported counter-attack to sink the shipping at San Jose, Mindoro's main port, interfered substantially with the major American project on the island: the construction of airdrome facilities from which targets

---

[a] Suzuki was able to evacuate a portion of the Leyte garrison to other islands to continue fighting there.

on Luzon could be attacked and from which a major landing on that island could be protected and supported.[30]

The bitter fighting on Leyte had delayed the Americans and forced postponements of the whole Pacific timetable; the Mindoro, Luzon, Iwo Jima and Okinawa landings all had to be set back in time—and the struggle on Leyte itself continued as all those operations were underway. On the other hand, the Japanese decision to risk at Leyte their main fleet and a large proportion of their air force as well as a substantial part of the ground forces available for the defense of the Philippines meant that thereafter they could continue to contest every step on the road to Tokyo, but never again with a coordinated land–air–sea strategy. Even as General Yamashita pondered the losses his command had suffered and prepared to meet an American landing on Luzon with what was left, the American plans for that landing were completed with a new target date on December 30, subsequently postponed to January 9, 1945.[31] The new year would not open auspiciously for the Japanese empire.

CHINA AND BURMA

While the Americans and Japanese fought on, near and over Leyte, the war in Southeast Asia was continuing at an accelerated pace. The Japanese chain of victories in China was impinging on that campaign but not decisively. The deteriorating situation in China gave rise to the final clash between Chiang Kai-shek and Stilwell, as a result of which the latter was recalled. His successor, General Albert Wedemeyer developed, at least for a while, a better relationship with Chiang, but this had little effect on major operations. The beginning of long-range bombing by B-29s from Chinese bases, operation "Matterhorn," was inefficient in terms of cost effectiveness—every bit of fuel and every bomb had to be flown in over the Hump for small raids from bases ever more distant from their targets. Wedemeyer himself recommended the transfer of the 20th Bombardment Force with its B-29s to the Marianas; and the United States Joint Chiefs of Staff, who commanded this unit directly, eventually followed his advice.[32]

Since the plans of Wedemeyer for a really effective Nationalist Army to drive to the coast also remained just that, plans, the original hopes for basing a major portion of the assault against Japan itself on the Chinese mainland receded permanently from the view of Washington planners and President Roosevelt.[33] The major concern about China in Washington shifted almost completely to the political one of attempting to bring the Chinese Nationalists and Communists together in some form of coalition, a project which proved as elusive as a mainland base for the final offensive against Japan.[34]

Ironically the military concern in late 1944 and early 1945 was that of maintaining Chiang's control of Chungking, his capital, and Kunming, the Chinese base of the Hump airlift. The Japanese seemed likely to push their own land offensives to a conquest of these key cities; and to meet this threat Chiang withdrew from Burma the only Chinese army divisions which were trained, equipped and above all willing to fight rather than loot and retreat—the new Chinese divisions which Stilwell had whipped into shape and led into battle. This diversion retarded but did not abort the Allied, primarily British, offensive in Burma, without having much effect on operations in China where the Japanese had earlier themselves decided not to strike for either Chungking or Kunming. The inability of the Japanese leadership to devise a coherent strategy for their war against China and then stick to it remained characteristic of that theater from 1937 to 1945.

In the spring and summer months of 1944 the Allies had pushed the Japanese out of key positions in northern Burma, especially the air, road, and rail center of Myitkyina, after very heavy and costly fighting. The operations there as well as the subsequent push into central and southern Burma were not helped by endless feuding within the British command structure as well as between the British and Americans, but the key point was that the British army after the Imphal–Kohima campaign was a changed force. Under increasingly aggressive leadership it now believed it could win, instead of being almost certain it would lose, and proceeded to move forward under the leadership of Mountbatten, Slim and, newly arrived from Italy, General Sir Oliver Leese.[35]

Driving southward in an effort to free all of Burma from the Japanese if at all possible, the British–Indian 14th Army decided on a flanking movement which, with great daring, would cross the Irrawaddy river below Mandalay and cut off the portions of the Japanese 15th Army holding that city and central Burma. In one of the most extraordinary river assault crossings of World War II, this effort succeeded in spite of some confusion and heavy Japanese resistance in February 1945.[36]

The prospects for the Burma campaign had been immeasurably improved not only by the attitudinal change but by the success, at last, of the third British attempt to seize the port of Akyab on the Arakan coast. An amphibious operation had seized the port in January 1945, and provided a basis from which an assault toward Rangoon could be launched once the offensive from the north had eliminated the main Japanese force in central Burma.

Slim's pincer movement against Mandalay succeeded as the troops which had crossed the Irrawaddy south of the city pushed toward those which had crossed the great river north of the capital a month earlier. With British and Indian units already pursuing the Japanese further south, Mandalay itself was retaken on March 20. Substantial portions of the Japanese 15th and 33rd Armies still remained, but the British were determined to push on before the monsoon rains began in late April or early May. They had over 300 miles to go, but vastly increased air support offered at least a hope of success for the attempt.

In one of the more spectacular demonstrations of what a daring and driving army could do when provided with a full complement of air transport, the British divisions were, in effect, leap-frogged south from Mandalay toward Rangoon in the face of crumbling Japanese resistance. An amphibious force supported from Akyab landed near Rangoon at the beginning of May. The monsoon had started but could not halt the determined British. Rangoon was freed on May 3.[37]

The dramatic last stages of the war in Europe largely overshadowed the Allied victory in Burma, but this did not make it any the less complete. The flag which had once flown over the city had been taken as a souvenir by the Japanese unit which seized it, carried by them to the Aleutian campaign where it was recaptured by the Americans. At the Quebec Conference of 1943 Marshall had given it to Brooke; now it was run up in Rangoon once more.[38] Plans for new operations toward Singapore were already being made at Mountbatten's Southeast Asia Command.

LUZON, THE SOUTHERN PHILIPPINES, AND BORNEO

The fight for central Burma coincided in time with the American invasion of Luzon. The new empire which Japan had conquered in the winter of 1941–42 was being assaulted simultaneously from both sides and Japanese forces in these widely separated campaigns proved no more able to coordinate their efforts than the Allies had three years earlier. Field Marshal Terauchi could not provide substantial reinforcement to either of his embattled garrisons any more than Field Marshal Wavell in his earlier role as Allied theater commander. If in this regard there were similarities, there were also great differences. The forces engaged on both sides in both battles were substantially larger than those of the earlier struggles.[39] The Japanese army in Burma in 1944–45, unlike the British one in 1942, remained in small battered clumps of survivors in the country; they did not move out for an eventual return. The Japanese army in Luzon, on the other hand, did not make MacArthur's big mistake of trying to hold an untenable perimeter only to be driven into a siege without adequate preparations to hold out as the focus of retreat; instead Yamashita followed a far shrewder strategy and kept some of his forces fighting on Luzon until the surrender of September 1945.

The invasion plan as finally approved by MacArthur called for the major landing at the southern end of Lingayen Gulf with later subsidiary landings just north of Bataan and southwest of Manila. Though the obvious place to attack — and defend — the Lingayen Gulf itself afforded a sheltered bay for the huge conglomeration of ships, a set of very good beaches for the landing, and an open plain toward Manila, 130 miles to the south, for the employment of armor on the main axis of the advance. Staging from bases on the northern shore of New Guinea and in the Solomon Islands as well as Leyte, the invading forces, which would grow to over a quarter of a million men, were supported by a huge array of naval power. As in the case of the Leyte landing, Admiral Kinkaid commanded the amphibious assault while Admiral Halsey's 3rd Fleet and General Whitehead's 5th Air Force provided the support needed for General Krueger's 6th Army.[a] The two corps of 6th Army successfully landed on January 8, 1945.

The kamikazes had caused very serious casualties among the escorts, sinking one escort carrier and damaging many other ships; among the hundreds of dead was General Lumsden, the British liaison officer attached to MacArthur's headquarters, whose place would be taken by General St. Clair Gairdner.[40] The ordeal of the warships also led to the destruction of most of the Japanese planes committed to the Luzon defense. That defense could not include the ambitious naval operation which the Japanese had launched against the Leyte invasion. With so much of the Japanese navy sunk or disabled in that great battle, Yamashita had to rely on his ground forces, weakened by earlier transfers to reinforce the army on Leyte. But he had over 280,000 army and navy soldiers left[b] and believed that he had a real opportunity to defeat the landing or at least deny use of the air and sea bases of Luzon to the Americans for a very long time. He would certainly keep them occupied in bloody battle for months.

Yamashita divided his force into three groups. The largest, the Shobu Group, was assigned to northern Luzon; it would help the others crush the invasion or, alternatively, retreat to the northern part of the island and hold out there. A second force, the Kembu Group, was to block the route across the plain from Lingayen Gulf to Manila, while a third,

---

[a] Whitehead had succeeded Kenney after the latter's promotion to command the Far Eastern Air Force, which also included the 13th Air Force, in June 1944.

[b] General Willoughby, MacArthur's intelligence chief, had estimated 152,000.

the Shimbu Group, would defend the capital itself as well as southern Luzon.

The 6th Army, once ashore, pushed south and east from the bridge-head gained the first day. The push inland was too fast for Yamashita to mount an effective counter-attack, which might have contained the Americans for some time the way the Germans had initially contained the Normandy invasion. As more American troops came ashore, they shouldered the Shobu Group aside and headed south. Fighting was very bitter with heavy casualties on both sides, but MacArthur was deter-mined to push forward and prodded his ground commanders. A hard drive into the mountains on the left flank of the advance pushed back the Japanese, destroyed their most dangerous counter-attack, and effectively eliminated the 2nd Tank Division, the main Japanese armored force on Luzon. Shobu Group was pushed into the northern mountains by the middle of February but it had prepositioned substantial supplies for a long fight there.[41]

Krueger, pushed by MacArthur, now sent XIV Corps south to seize the key airfields collectively referred to as Clark Field and defended by the Kembu Group. In a week's hard fighting, the fields were retaken and, with their paved runways, could provide excellent bases for the American air force. Several of Krueger's divisions now raced for Manila with the 1st Cavalry Division breaking into the city's suburbs on Febru-ary 3. In the meantime, the American 8th Army's 11th Airborne Division had landed by sea and parachute southwest of Manila and was also pushing toward the city.

Clearing Manila of the Japanese was to prove far more difficult and costly than the spectacular rush into its northern portion and horrend-ously different from the victory parade MacArthur had hoped for. Yama-shita's original plan to pull all forces out of the city was altered dramatic-ally. His deliberate destruction of the harbor facilities produced an enormous fire which engulfed a very large part of northern and western Manila; American troops found themselves fighting the raging fires and not only the Japanese. The latter, under the command of Admiral Iwaba-chi Sanji, decided to hold the southern portion of the city below the Pasig river (which bisects the city as it flows into Manila Bay). Neither Yamashita nor Iwabachi would or could control the Japanese naval gar-rison and army men who, quite aside from fighting the Americans, pro-ceeded to butcher and rape Filipinos and all others they could get their hands on in a massacre reminiscent—if on a smaller scale—of the notorious rape of Nanking.

For a month the approximately 20,000 Japanese in the city fought the Americans, who had to batter their way forward block by block and house by house. Both the heavy modern reinforced concrete buildings designed to withstand earthquakes and the ancient solid stone walls of the old core-city fortress Intramuros ("between the walls") provided extraordinarily good protection for the defenders and difficulties for the assaulting Americans. MacArthur refused to allow air support so that the Americans relied on artillery; whether this saved civilian lives as MacArthur intended is doubtful. At the end of the fighting over 12,000 American soldiers and over 16,000 Japanese soldiers had died in the street fighting. The Japanese massacres and the battle had cost over 100,000 Filipinos their lives and left Manila the most damaged Allied capital after Warsaw.

By the time fighting flickered out in the streets of Manila, the Americans had cleared Bataan and most of the shore of Manila Bay. The island of Corregidor had been bombarded and bombed since January 22, and a combined parachute and amphibious assault was launched on February 16. Although the Japanese garrison was more than five times as large as estimated and therefore outnumbered the air and seaborne assailants, it was caught by surprise. After the Americans had established footholds on the island, they repulsed a series of uncoordinated banzai charges with heavy losses. In the night of February 21–22 a tremendous explosion of ammunition and other explosives in the underground fortifications—set off either by accident or as a mass suicide—killed about 2000 of the garrison. Two more underground explosions killed most of the remaining Japanese in the following days, and by March 1 the fighting was over. On the following day, one day before the conclusion of the struggle for Manila, MacArthur saw the American flag raised again on the old flag pole of Corregidor.

With the capital and its immediate surroundings cleared, the government of the Commonwealth of the Philippines was returned to a city which Americans and Filipinos began to clean up as best they could. It was in these days that MacArthur began to implement two decisions which he appears to have made earlier and which would have major long-term effects, one on the internal affairs of the Philippines, the other on the further conduct of military operations in the war.

MacArthur had long been a friend of Manuel Roxas, and the latter was one of the very few who knew of the huge sum of money Quezon had given MacArthur early in 1942. Roxas had remained in the Philippines and had become a leading figure in the collaborator government of José P. Laurel. While Laurel was flown out of Luzon by the Japanese, Roxas and others remained. MacArthur claimed that his old friend had in reality been a source for American intelligence and had aided the resistance to Japanese occupation, but evidence to this effect has yet to surface. By openly favoring Roxas and many of his associates in the months following the liberation of Manila, MacArthur not only assured the election of Roxas to the presidency of the country but effectively spiked any serious confrontation with the issue of collaboration. The Commonwealth did not regain its independence with as much of a new start as the liberated countries of Western Europe, which had enough trouble dealing with the issue of collaboration without having one of the most prominent ones heading their government.[42]

MacArthur's other decision concerned the next stage in the liberation of the Philippines. It had been assumed in the discussions of the Joint Chiefs of Staff that the campaign for Leyte and subsequent landing on Mindoro were preparatory steps needed for the Luzon landing and that the latter would be the last major campaign in the islands. To secure the airports, cities, and harbors of Luzon for the subsequent strike toward the Japanese home islands, the whole, or at least the main ports, of Luzon would have to be freed, but there was no intention to project operations southward into the central and southern Philippines—a direction opposite to that in which further operations were to be aimed. General MacArthur, however, had other ideas on this subject and instead proceeded to direct General Eichelberger's 8th Army, only marginally involved in the Luzon operation, to stage a series of amphibious attacks into the islands south of Luzon.

Although retroactively authorized from Washington, the over fifty landing operations in which 8th Army assaulted and liberated most of the central and southern Philippines were essentially MacArthur's own project. They provided very significant experience in amphibious operations for those units of 8th Army which were expected to participate in the invasion of the Japanese home islands; and they opened up a large additional series of ports and bases for the staging of American divisions expected from Europe after the end of hostilities there, even as they liberated millions of Filipinos from Japanese rule. The campaign was successful; and no one in Washington appears to have objected; but it had very serious implications for the effort of the 6th Army to complete operations on Luzon.[a]

With some of its divisions and most of its reserves diverted from the Luzon campaign to 8th Army operations further south, the American 6th Army found itself battering the large remaining forces of General Yamashita left on the island. In a long, difficult and costly campaign, most of Luzon was indeed cleared, but in the process the American divisions involved repeatedly faced Japanese forces of equal or superior

---

[a] James, *The Years of MacArthur*, p. 738, suggests that the locally initiated operations in the Philippines influenced MacArthur in his defiance of Washington during the Korean War.

numbers in well-entrenched positions. With massive assistance from Filipino guerillas, Yamashita's army was steadily battered down. At the time of surrender in September, Yamashita had some 50,000 men left in his command, and several of the 6th Army divisions which had been engaged in the hard fighting needed a great deal of rebuilding.[43]

If any who doubt the need for and wisdom of the campaign in the central and southern Philippines are likely to have the best of the argument, the other new series of landings MacArthur carried out, this time with the prior rather than the retroactive consent of the Joint Chiefs, needs to be seen in a different context. The landings in the Dutch East Indies, primarily on Borneo, grew out of discussions between the Americans and Australians and were, although it is difficult to prove, also influenced by concern that Japanese forces in the East Indies, drawing on the resources there, might well continue fighting an active war long after their home islands had been occupied.

The Australian army had replaced American divisions containing the by-passed Japanese forces in the Southwest Pacific. The Japanese 18th Army on New Guinea, 17th on Bougainville, and 8th Area Army on New Britain still headquartered at Rabaul, presented no major threat; but the question of dealing with their approximately 160,000 to 200,000 soldiers remained. Though short of supplies, especially ammunition and medicine, these were still formidable numbers, and the key Australian military figure, General Thomas Blamey, ordered aggressive operations against the 17th and 18th Armies by the Australians facing them. Only on New Britain, where the Japanese 8th Area Army greatly outnumbered the Australian 5th Division, was a policy of containment rather than constant attacks followed. Whether these operations, and the casualties incurred in them, were wise is likely to remain a source of arguments.[44]

Even more arguments greeted MacArthur's plans, code-named "Oboe I-VI," for a series of invasions of the islands of Borneo and Java in the Dutch East Indies and of British Borneo as well. Though reluctantly approved by Washington and Canberra, one of these landings, that at Balikpapan on the east coast of Borneo, was originally the subject of a serious controversy between MacArthur and the Australian government.[a] In part observed personally by MacArthur, the first "Oboe" operations went forward successfully in June and July, 1945. The landing of two Australian divisions on Java was fortunately aborted by the Japanese

---

[a] The controversy concerned the employment of the Australian 7th Division, which, it was feared, would suffer excessive casualties. MacArthur was allowed to go ahead and called in a sixteen-day massive pre-invasion bombardment; the operation proved a tactical success. The key exchange is summarized in James, *The Years of MacArthur*, pp. 752–54.

surrender before this most dubious project against greatly superior Japanese forces could be implemented.[45]

BOMBING THE HOME ISLANDS AND IWO JIMA

The bombing of the Japanese home islands from the Marianas—one of the main purposes of the American landings there in June 1944—had begun in the fall.[46] The B-29 bomber had been especially designed for long-range attacks on Japan, and bases were being built on Saipan, Guam and Tinian to accommodate the big bombers as they became available from the factories, and when those previously assigned to Chinese airports were transferred to the Marianas in early 1945. But the first stages of the B-29 campaign did not go as well as hoped. The plane represented a major departure from earlier designs not only in being the first bomber with a pressurized cabin but in a large number of other ways. Not surprisingly, the plane had all sorts of teething troubles which took time to fix. The enormous distance, increased by the need to try to avoid Japanese fighters from the Bonin Islands, made navigation errors more likely. The tremendous strength of the jet stream and other causes of turbulence caused almost impossible aiming problems at high altitudes over Japan.[47]

The early raids from the Marianas—the first against Tokyo was flown on November 24, 1944—showed the Japanese people far more dramatically than the prior small air raids based on China that the American air force could now reach the home islands; but the weather and winds interfered with bombing from the high altitudes at which the B-29s flew. They were out of range of Japanese anti-aircraft fire and beyond the altitude most fighters could reach, but the distance and weather took their toll, while most of the bombs dropped from 30,000 feet and even higher missed the aircraft factories and other targets at which they were aimed.[48] There was considerable damage, but as the Emperor was told at a meeting with senior statesmen on February 26, 1945, this was not at all as bad as what Germany had had to endure.[49]

Two American steps altered the situation in the air war against Japan dramatically. The landing on Iwo Jima on February 19 followed by the subsequent conquest of the island and expansion of the Japanese airports on it shortened the distance to be flown from the Marianas, because there was no need to depart from the direct route on account of Japanese fighters based on Iwo. The island provided an intermediate base on which B-29s could land, and allowed the stationing of fighters to escort the bombers to Japan.[50] This latter became important because of a second measure adopted in March: flying low—and thus subject to fighter attack—in order to carry masses of incendiaries to burn Japanese industry out instead of flying high to destroy factories with explosive bombs. The two operations proved dramatic indeed.

The Americans had long looked toward a landing on Iwo Jima as the best place in the Bonins for an intermediate base for the air, sea and land attack on Japan. The Japanese could readily see the identical geographic realities.[51] They had evacuated the small civilian population and developed a complicated series of defenses, most of them underground, to fight any American landing force. It was assumed by the Japanese commander, General Kuribayashi Tadamichi, that the Americans could get ashore, but that, once on land, the Japanese would inflict enormous casualties on the assaulting Americans while the kamikaze would take their toll of the escorting and supporting fleet. If the Japanese could not defeat the invaders, they would die themselves after inflicting the greatest number of casualties possible by utilizing the underground defenses they had built, instead of the practice followed by other garrisons of losing vast numbers in futile banzai charges which disconcerted the Americans but led to a quick death for the Japanese.

The Americans knew in general that the Japanese planned a very hard defense of the island, but they could not know all the details. The prospect of extremely heavy casualties in the conquest of the island was daunting enough to lead to a recommendation to President Roosevelt that poison gas be used on the island: there were no civilians there; and the United States was not legally bound by the treaty banning the use of poison gas. The President, however, was totally opposed to its use except as a retaliatory measure, and he rejected the proposal made to him.[a]

The obvious alternative to the use of gas was an extremely heavy bombardment. Here there was a serious deficiency in American coordination of the operations in the Pacific. The continued use of many of the battleships in the Philippines and a major series of carrier plane assaults on the home islands of Japan reduced the naval bombardment substantially below that called for by General Holland Smith, who commanded the three marine divisions (3rd, 4th and 5th) assigned to the assault.[52] With the landing already postponed a month because of the heavy fighting in the Philippines and the need for naval air to support operations still under way in those islands, there was a reluctance to

[a] There is an account in Harris and Paxman, *A Higher Form of Killing*, p. 135. It is not clear whether Roosevelt's chief military advisors really did wish to use gas in this operation or—knowing as they did Roosevelt's strong opposition to gas warfare—used this means to alert him to the very high casualties expected from the Iwo operation. See on this point also the somewhat different account in John Ellis van Courtland Moon, "Chemical Warfare: A Forgotten Lesson," *Bulletin of the Atomic Scientists* 45, No. 6 (July–Aug. 1989), 40–43.

postpone any other action. Neither the weeks of bombing from the air nor the three days of naval gunfire provided instead of the requested ten days were to prove sufficient. The bombing was largely ineffective, and the naval bombardment was too short to deal with the vast number of targets, though many of these simply could not be reached by naval gunfire. And given the small size of the island—some 5 miles by 2.5 miles—there was little opportunity for naval gunfire to support the marines once they were ashore, as had assisted the landing forces in Normandy.[53] The situation of the Americans would have been worse still had not a premature reaction of some Japanese gunners to the ships carrying the pre-invasion obstacle demolition teams on February 17, the second day of the American naval bombardment, revealed the location of some hitherto hidden Japanese gun emplacements.

On February 19 the marines landed and immediately ran into terrific opposition. Some units were literally pinned down on the beaches, while others began to make their way inland slowly. The loose ashes of the island—which had only appeared above sea level due to volcanic action half a century before—made progress difficult and defense relatively simple. A shallow beachhead was obtained on the first day, and in the following days the marines fought their way forward slowly and at great cost. By February 24, they had reached the crest of volcanic Mt. Suribachi, planting a flag which encouraged the marines struggling for control of the airfields and inspiring through a famous news picture the monument to the marines in Arlington today.

The seizure of Mt. Suribachi gave the Americans control of the southern end of the island and good observation on major portions of the rest, but the fight went on. In the bitterest of fighting, the marines slowly inched forward, first splitting the defenders and then destroying the remaining pockets of resistance. Of the Japanese garrison of slightly over 20,000, only 200 were taken alive; the rest were killed, with General Kuribayashi one of the last on March 24. The battle cost 6000 deaths and 25,000 wounded marines, the first and last time that American casualties exceeded Japanese deaths in the Pacific offensive.

The terrible price of victory pointed to ever higher casualties as the Americans approached the home islands. The great distance from Tokyo had held down the kamikaze attacks on the escorting ships which, during the weeks they were needed, would otherwise have been very vulnerable—a point the Japanese took into their calculations for the Okinawa campaign and which the United States navy would have done well to factor into its plans for Iwo Jima: a longer pre-invasion bombardment would have reduced, not lengthened, the time of naval exposure to attack by Japanese submarines and planes. But the island had been won, and even before the last Japanese had been killed in the underground bunkers, the first American bombers were using the airfields on the island, which had been repaired and extended by the Seabees, the American navy's construction experts.[54] In addition, the American planes flying from the Marianas to attack Japan no longer had to skirt the Bonin Islands or worry about fighters from there.

The island base was useful not only as an emergency landing strip for the B-29s—by the end of the war, about 2,400 had made such landings—but it also helped with the organization of the elaborate air–sea rescue system being established to rescue crews from crashed or ditched bombers on the long routes to and from the targets in Japan.[55] This was of special importance both to save large numbers of highly trained crew members and also because the Japanese had earlier publicly announced their killing of captured American air crews who had bailed out over Japan, and who now ordered that B-29 crew members who crashed at sea were also to be killed as a matter of policy, a policy known to the Americans who had intercepted and decoded it.[56]

The B-29 bombing effort from the Marianas had originally been something of a disappointment. From October 1944 into early 1945 a series of raids had produced some effects, especially on the Japanese aircraft industry against which it was primarily aimed, but not anywhere near the results hoped for and at considerable loss to fighters, anti-aircraft fire, and—most of all—weather, accidents, and other operational problems. General Arnold, the head of the army air force, replaced General Haywood S. Hansell, the commander of the 21st Bomber Command, with General Curtis LeMay who had been heading the 20th Bomber Command in China. In United States Air Force headquarters there had been considerable discussion of using the B-29 not for daylight high altitude precision bombing but for incendiary attacks at night. The idea was that the vulnerable Japanese cities with their wood and paper structures densely clustered around decentralized industrial facilities might simply be burned out by massive loads of incendiary bombs.[57] A few experimental fire raids had been mounted, primarily against Hankow by 20th Bomber Command and against Tokyo by the 21st.

With Arnold's support, LeMay now changed the tactics in the field. The target areas of Japan had almost invariably been covered by clouds in daytime and had to be bombed by radar, a system which with the technology of the time and the tremendous strength of the jet stream and winds over Japan almost guaranteed misses. At night the clouds were thinner, Japanese anti-aircraft fire was nowhere near as strong and accurate as that over Germany, the Japanese had very few night fighters, and low-flying planes could carry far heavier loads of incendiaries.[a] In addition, LeMay decided to take a chance by removing the ammunition in the planes to increase bomb loads. The invasion of Okinawa was only three weeks off; the change in tactics would inaugurate a new bombing offensive preparatory to the next great landing operation.

On the night of March 9–10, 1945, LeMay sent 334 B-29s over Tokyo. Flying low, unarmed, and without having to stay in tight formations against fighter attacks, the big bombers showered a huge load of incendiaries on the Shitamachi section of Tokyo. The Japanese were caught by surprise, and their preparations to deal with large-scale fires were in any case hopelessly inadequate. For over three hours, the procession of B-29s lumbered over Tokyo, turning the great mixed area of homes and industry into a raging inferno. Between 80,000 and 100,000 died in the flames, which consumed some 16 square miles of Tokyo's built up area in the raid which probably caused the largest number of casualties of World War II. Dozens of large factories and hundreds of feeder-workshops had been destroyed. A new stage of the air war against Japan had begun.

On March 18, more than a week after the great fire raid on Tokyo, Emperor Hirohito himself inspected the tremendous damage.[58] The 21st had by that time applied an essentially similar technique to Nagoya, Osaka, and Kobe. In several of these cities, modern buildings of stone and reinforced concrete held up somewhat better than the Tokyo tinderbox, but in each of them enormous areas were devastated, with industrial facilities, docks and shipyards being destroyed on a large scale along with vast residential districts. The well-informed German naval attaché reported to his government (and unknowingly to American intelligence) that these raids had been "amazingly effective,"[59] and that the additional air attacks which followed were more damaging than had been expected and were crippling Japanese industry.[60]

With relatively little debate, the American air force embraced in the last stages of the Pacific War the concept of area attacks which it had so long opposed in Europe, where it had for years been advocated and practiced by the Royal Air Force. In the face of a series of ever bloodier battles at the front, there were few if any qualms about launching a rain of death on Japan's cities, which now experienced what the Japanese air force had first visited on China and which the Japanese balloon operation had been designed to do on an even larger scale to Canada and the

---

[a] In all discussion of World War II planes one must always remember that the conventional propeller engine is less efficient, and hence consumes more fuel and wears out more quickly, the higher the plane flies; the exact opposite of the jet powered plane.

United States. With another big raid on Nagoya, the B-29s had made their contribution to the preparations for the Okinawa landing.[61]

PLANS FOR THE DEFEAT – AND DEFENSE – OF JAPAN

The invasion of Okinawa had become the last in the series of operations preliminary to the assault on the Japanese home islands themselves. Planning for those supreme efforts, for which Okinawa was to provide a major base, was well under way in early 1945. The central concept in American planning for the defeat of Japan was the invasion of the home islands in two stages, first a landing on the southern island of Kyushu, "Olympic," scheduled for September 1, 1945, to be followed by an even larger landing on the main island of Honshu, "Coronet," which was to take place on December 1. Both tentative landing dates had to be postponed because of fierce Japanese resistance, "Olympic" to November 1, 1945, and "Coronet" to March 1, 1946. There was some discussion in Washington about the possibility of avoiding such landings, and the enormous casualties they were certain to cost, by strangling Japan through blockade, encirclement and bombardment from the sea and air, but the weight of opinion among the Chiefs of Staff was in favor of the landings. It was agreed that British naval forces would participate in these operations, and the anticipation of this increase in available warships was an argument Admiral King and James Forrestal, who had become Secretary of the Navy after the death of Knox, used to counter the proposal that vast additional warships had to be built to replace the heavy losses expected in this Pacific version of "Overlord."[62]

The actual operation "Olympic" was to be carried out by the American 6th Army, staged primarily from the Philippines and Okinawa, and including both army and marine divisions. Two very small islands off the west coast of Kyushu would be seized as emergency bases a few days before two corps of army and one of marine divisions would land on the southern shore of Kyushu, primarily around Kagoshima Bay. The intent was to take only enough of Kyushu to provide naval and logistic bases and to make possible land-based air support for "Coronet," the supreme operation of the war in the Pacific.

"Coronet," unlike "Olympic," could not be mounted with the forces already in the Pacific theater of war; the more than twenty-five divisions needed were simply not available. From the Pacific would come the American 8th Army and the new 10th Army organized for the Okinawa operation and expected to be reorganized and refilled with replacements in time for the big landing south and east of Tokyo.[63] The third American army destined for "Coronet" was, however, fighting in Europe as these plans were being made. The American 1st Army, which had landed in Normandy on D-Day, was destined for the Pacific; on May 1, 1945, it was pulled out of the line in the last stage of the battle against Germany, and its headquarters was reactivated in Manila on August 1.

Both Olympic and Coronet were to be preceded by very lengthy air and sea bombardment, while Coronet would also involve the participation of a corps of three to five divisions from the British Commonwealth as well as a French corps. In addition, it was assumed that the contingent from the Royal Navy already attached to the American fleet in the Pacific would grow, and that British long-range bombers based in the Philippines would play a part in the bombing of Japan's home islands before and during the great land battle that was expected.[64]

The discussion for United States–British cooperation in the final assault on Japan did not always go smoothly—any more than it had in the planning for the Normandy invasion—but was close and trusting all the same. Thus the outline of the plan for Olympic, with the target landing date of November 1 was sent to the British on June 12, 1945, a few days *before* President Truman formally approved the operation.[65] The whole problem of redeploying one and a half million Americans and almost half a million British soldiers and airmen from Europe to the East Asian and Southeast Asian theaters of war was likely to be immense, but it could be, and surely would have been mastered.[66] The gist of a report of early April on the unwillingness of the Japanese to accept unconditional surrender from the Swedish Minister in Tokyo, which was passed on to the British, elicited the Foreign Office comment on May 9: "the Japanese will have to have a much harder knock than they have yet had."[67] In this endeavor, the British were no less determined to share than the Americans.[68]

The projected invasions of Japan were clearly not going to be substantially aided by Chinese Nationalist troops and were, therefore, thought to require a massive engagement of Japanese forces in Manchuria by a Red Army attack, somewhat similar to the way the Normandy invasion pre-supposed the tying down of much of the German army by the Russians on the Eastern Front. There had been earlier discussions of this question in the American staffs and between the Americans and the Russians; now the commander designated for the Allied invasion, General MacArthur, repeatedly stressed to Washington the essential character of a major Red Army operation in Manchuria.[69]

Because the invasion of Japan was expected to be horrendously costly, there was concern that the Japanese army on the mainland of Asia might well continue fighting there for a long time, even after the occupation of the home islands, and because it was assumed that the Soviet Union would move to attain its objectives in East Asia after the end of the European war in any case, it only made sense to have them join in the fighting while it was still difficult rather than wait until the struggle was over. The time tables worked out at Yalta and Potsdam, and the shipments of American supplies for the Red Army to use in its campaign against Japan, were keyed to Soviet participation at a date well *before* the Olympic landing. The intent was to make Japanese reinforcement of the home islands from Manchuria, North China, and Korea impossible during the fighting in Japan.

The Soviet Union had every intention of going forward with the agreed upon attacks in Manchuria. Detailed planning began in March 1945. Some shifts of headquarters to the Soviet Far East began that month, but the major redeployment took place in May, June, and July, as the fighting in Europe ended. Two Front (Army Group) and four army headquarters headed east on the Transsiberian railway, with special attention to sending experienced commanders and units for a role in the expansion of the Red Army in the Far East from forty to eighty divisions.[70]

The Soviet plan for a major offensive looked to a huge pincer operation from the eastern and western sides of Manchuria and beginning any time after July 25, 1945.[71] Long before that date, the endless Soviet trains heading eastward across the Soviet Union were observed with anxiety by the Japanese—whose reports were deciphered, presumably with relief, by the Western Allies—and by the representatives of neutral powers in the country.[72] The Soviet government clearly looked toward major operations on the ground and was also preparing for the possibility of Japanese air attacks when hostilities began, and even cooperated minimally, and at a very much lower level than originally promised, with the Americans.[73] As Japan's sun was sinking rather than rising, the Indian nationalist leader Bose, who had once staked his hopes on a German and Japanese victory in the war, tried to hitch his wagon to the rising Soviet star,[74] but died in an airplane crash on the way to Moscow. Once preferring Japanese and German colonial policies to those of Britain, he had discovered too late the advantages of Soviet imperialism.

The Japanese were expecting an Allied invasion attempt and were doing what they could to prepare for it. The major political measure was the converse of the arrangements the United States and Great Britain had made for the entrance of Russia in the Pacific War. In a long and agitated series of exchanges and negotiations, the government in Tokyo tried to assure the continued neutrality of the Soviet Union. The government hoped for this in the face of both the doubts of its own ambassador in Moscow, Sato Naotake, and its own unwillingness in the winter of 1944–45 to make such substantial offers of concessions to the Soviet Union as might conceivably have raised doubts in Stalin's mind. As the April deadline for denunciation of the 1941 Neutrality Pact approached, the Foreign Ministry in Tokyo was still hopeful, but a formal Soviet note of April 5, 1945, declared that the Neutrality Pact would be allowed to expire rather than be renewed.[75]

In the months after the Soviet Union had denounced the Neutrality Pact, the Japanese government wanted to reopen negotiations for some new treaty, but their own ambassador was doubtful and the Soviet government was not encouraging. The Soviets were helpful in the repatriation of Japanese diplomats from the positions of Europe being occupied by the Allies in the spring of 1945 — but they may well have been thinking of the fate of their own diplomats in Japanese-controlled areas once they had attacked Japan. It was far too late for hints of extensive Japanese concessions to move Moscow.[76] Whatever the civilian authorities in Tokyo believed or hoped, the Japanese Army General Staff was fairly certain by late January 1945 that the Soviet Union would enter the Pacific War against Japan but made little serious preparation in time to meet a contingency which had been on their mind for a decade.[77]

Although far less important to the Japanese than their relations with the Soviet Union, the question of Portugal's possessions in East Asia — parts of Timor in the East Indies and Macao on the south China coast — also worried the Japanese. Especially after the break with Spain due to Japanese atrocities in Manila, and Turkey's break of relations with Japan under Allied pressure, Tokyo wanted to preserve one of its few remaining listening posts in Europe.[78] From its shrinking diplomatic corps in Europe, the Japanese hoped to receive information on Allied plans, troop redeployments, and other political and military details. It may all have been bad news, but the Japanese military leaders certainly wanted it anyway.[79]

The only field of political activity on which the Japanese could record any advance in 1945 was, as in the case of Germany the preceding year, in its dealings with a satellite government. As the Germans had become worried about the loyalty of Hungary and had occupied that country in March 1944, so the Japanese became concerned about the situation in French Indo-China and proceeded to occupy all of it in March 1945. Worried that with the liberation of France the local French colonial authorities might transfer their loyalties from a Vichy regime, now evacuated to Germany, to the de Gaulle government, now installed in Paris, the Japanese broke the agreements they had made with Vichy in 1940 and 1941 and effected a coup on March 9, 1945.[80] They extended their control over the whole of the area in a quick move which, like their earlier steps in the French colony, was not resisted.

The replacement of the French colonial administration by Japanese military rule and a tentative beginning of a new local self-government was to pave the way for further dramatic changes later. When Japan surrendered in August, the way was open for Ho Chi Minh and the Viet Minh to stage a coup and take over. If the French were to reestablish themselves, it would have to be not against the Japanese but against a local coalition of Communists and nationalists.

The Japanese military leaders had a rather realistic picture of what was ahead, and it was this picture which had contributed to their decision to take over direct control of French Indo-China. In late January they expected that by the middle of 1945 the Americans, after heavy bombing of the home islands, would land on them, while the British were expected to stage a landing in Malaya. They expected continued resistance from both Chinese Nationalists and Communists and described the peoples of the occupied "Greater East Asia Co-Prosperity Sphere" as all uncooperative. The Soviet Union would enter the Pacific War in the second half of the year, a time by which the Japanese Army General Staff expected Germany to have been defeated. In the face of all these developments, Japan would fight on.[81]

A supplementary appreciation similarly sent to Japanese military attachés in Europe on March 8 discussed the plans to meet the expected invasion of the home islands after the serious impact of the intervening defeats on Luzon and Iwo Jima. The Japanese war effort would now have to be reoriented to take account of the loss of access to the empire won in Southeast Asia earlier in the war. Shipping losses were described as Japan's "severest difficulty," and the biggest air raids were—quite correctly—assumed to be still ahead. The Japanese would do their best to fight off the anticipated invasion.[82]

How did the Japanese expect to fight and to what purpose? In Southeast Asia, they moved in the direction of concentrating their forces at key points, withdrawing troops from outlying regions and islands, and using a variety of means including hospital ships to facilitate these troop movements.[83] They especially hoped to hold on to Singapore, and they proclaimed the independence of the Dutch East Indies though retaining effective control. As for the home islands, a new command structure was established in early April. The 1st Army and an attached air command would direct the defense of northern Honshu and Hokkaido from a headquarters under Field Marshal Sugiyama Hajime in Tokyo; the 2nd Army under Field Marshal Hata Shunroku would defend western

Honshu and the islands of Kyushu and Shikoku from headquarters in Hiroshima.[84]

Some of the Japanese military plans were offensive in nature. The balloons, sent aloft with incendiaries attached to burn out American and Canadian forests as they landed in North America after being carried across the Pacific by the prevailing winds, have already been mentioned. As these began to land in the United States and as the Americans learned at least some details of Japanese experiments with biological warfare agents, there was initially great concern in the American government.[85] These worries quickly ended as the balloons failed to start the great fires they were supposed to bring and it turned out that they were not carrying disease germs.

On a more dangerous note, the Japanese began in December 1944 with the training of a special outfit, the Yamaoka Parachute Brigade, of about 300 men who were to be landed on the California coast near Santa Barbara and were expected to shoot their way to the Douglas and Lockheed aircraft factories in the Los Angeles area to destroy these before being killed.[86] In May of 1945, this project for a submarine-carried operation in California was altered to an airborne assault on the Marianas. A massive attack involving some 2000 men carried on several hundred planes was to be mounted against the B-29 bases in the Marianas with the objective of destroying the planes and facilities there in an operation somewhat similar to, but far larger than, the one aimed at Tacloban airfield in the Leyte campaign. Codenamed "Damocles," this project became known to American intelligence because the destruction of Japanese land communications by bombing obliged the Japanese to send messages by radio and these were intercepted and read.[a] Just before the operation was to be launched, Admiral Halsey with the 3rd Fleet was ordered north for a special attack operation on August 4, 1945, in which almost 400 Japanese planes were destroyed or damaged.[87] The Americans did not want to risk having a Japanese suicide squad seize the atomic bombs being assembled on Tinian.

The projects for assaults first on Los Angeles aircraft factories and subsequently on American air bases in the Marianas involved a suicide formation. It was only one of a very large number of suicide projects which the Japanese military developed from the fall of 1944 until the end of the war. The special air attack tactics, generally referred to as kamikaze, have already been mentioned. Though not much employed in the defense of Iwo Jima, they were to play a major role in the Okinawa

---

[a] The California coast landing project did not become known until after World War II. When it was being planned, bombing had not yet so disrupted Japanese communications, and hence all relevant orders went by secure land channels.

campaign; but the largest number—over 5000 airplanes—was being held back and readied for the American invasion of the home islands.[88] In addition, two other types of suicide weapons were being designed and built especially for the last-ditch defense of Japan, the oka (or ohka) guided bomb and the kaiten suicide assault torpedo.[89]

Accepted by the naval staff already in February 1944, the kaiten was a modification of the very powerful Japanese naval torpedo generally referred to as the "long-lance." Stretched out, the torpedo was fitted with a tiny conning tower and held one man who was to steer the torpedo into the target. Originally brought to the scene of action by submarines especially fitted to carry two to six attached to the outside of the hull, the kaiten were later to be used from land against invaders. Never very effective in their first configuration, they might indeed have proved a most dangerous weapon against ships off-loading landing craft near an invasion beach.

The ohka was a steered mini-plane carried to the vicinity of a target by a two-engined bomber, released in the air, and aimed by its own pilot, who activated rocket engines which gave the ohka such speed in the last moments of flight that it could in practice not be shot down. The problem with this device—after the first fifty had gone down with the carrier *Shinano*—was that the airplanes which carried the ohka were generally so slow and had to come so close to Allied ships to release their ohkas that most were shot down on the way by the experienced American and British pilots.

The major reliance was, however, on the suicide airplanes which were to have such an impact on the Okinawa battle and which were expected to play an even greater role when the Allies tried to land on the home islands of Japan. In any consideration of their pilots—as well as those for the kaiten and ohka—one must remember that this was no sudden decision immediately implemented; but that in most cases weeks and even months intervened between the voluntary or coerced decision to participate in such an operation and the final action, with the latter not infrequently preceded by missions recalled or aborted because of weather conditions or changed orders. Those who were to die had to steel themselves more than once. There were no signs of a break in morale in either navy or army—about half of the suicide candidates came from each—and as yet no willingness to surrender at the top.

Why were the Japanese still fighting and to what end? The series of defeats in February and March followed by the American landing on Okinawa and the Soviet denunciation of the Neutrality Pact led to the fall of Prime Minister Koiso Kuniaki. His successor, Admiral Suzuki Kantaro, was a man whose heroic role in the Russo-Japanese War of

1904–5 made him immune to charges of cowardice if he steered the country toward peace; and this may well have been a contributing factor to his selection. But Japan was not ready to end the war; Suzuki expected it to last several more years.[90]

The Tokyo government was being urged by some of its diplomats in Europe to end the war by whatever means it could and as soon as possible. The example of Germany in April and May of 1945 was, in the eyes of some, hardly one that Japan should emulate.[91] The response of Tokyo, however, was that war would continue after Germany's surrender. The treaties with Germany, which the latter had broken by giving up, were null and void, but Japan would fight on.[92] Some rumors of peace negotiations via Stockholm and Switzerland, with the American OSS chief Dulles involved in the latter, were cut off by the Japanese government.[93] The key point was that, whatever the interest in peace, the idea of surrender was as yet unacceptable.[94] Even such a strong advocate of ending the war as Marquis Kido, the Lord Privy Seal, drew up peace terms on June 8, at a time when he expected an early collapse of the last Japanese resistance on Okinawa, which assumed that there would be no occupation of Japan and which were predicated on a procedure involving detailed negotiations, not a surrender.[95]

If in private there was as yet no disposition to surrender, in public the process of mobilization for defense against invasion continued apace. The kamikaze were the heroes of the hour, and on June 12 the Diet passed legislation requiring all males 15–60 and all females 17–40 years old to join the Peoples' Volunteer Fighting Corps. Simultaneously, an equivalent of martial law was declared as the nation prepared to ward off the anticipated assault.[96] By mid-June, both the Japanese and the Americans had obtained at great cost a small preview of what it would all be like in the bloodiest campaign of the Pacific War; the fight for Okinawa.[97]

OKINAWA

The Japanese expected an American invasion of Okinawa, which with its large airfields within easy range of the home islands and its excellent harbor was an obvious target for an operation preliminary to the assault on Japan itself. The 32nd Army under General Ushijima Mitsuru had over 100,000 men to defend the island. His strategic concept, coordinated with that of army and navy headquarters, was simple. There would be no attempt to defend the beaches of the long, narrow island or its relatively flat central and northern portions. Instead, three defensive lines had been established and were being developed in the mountainous southern portion of the island which had been under Japanese control since 1895. Once the Americans were stalled in front of these lines — in which the Japanese would be practically immune to naval gunfire — the expenditure of supplies and ammunition needed for any attack on them would make the Americans wholly dependent on their great ship-borne supply system. This was to be decimated by massive suicide attacks from several hundred kaiten and even larger numbers of kami-kaze planes flown from Kyushu. Weakened by loss of supplies and deprived of full air support by destruction of their aircraft carriers, the American landing force would succumb to a counter-attack from the Japanese garrison which had husbanded its strength in the south of the island.

The Americans expected a bitter fight and were prepared for some of it, but once again intelligence substantially underestimated the strength of the Japanese army to be fought.[a] A new army, the 10th, under General Simon B. Buckner, the former commander in Alaska, was organized to control the army and marine divisions assigned to the operation. Wide-ranging preliminary air operations against bases in Kyushu were provided, and a prior landing on the Kerama Islands off the southwest coast of Okinawa was to provide a base for repairing naval ships damaged in the operation and long-range artillery support for the fighting on the island itself. This operation, successfully carried out on March 26–27, turned out to be even more important than anticipated. On Kerama Retto the Americans found and seized about 300 suicide boats designed for use against the landing craft in combination with the kamikazes from the air — a welcome and easy victory but one which pointed to dangers ahead.[98]

A tremendous naval bombardment was to precede a four-division landing on the western beaches of central Okinawa, selected for their general suitability and closeness to two of the airfields on the island. Supported by a vast naval array and backed up by further marine and army divisions in reserve, the landing force was to seize the airfields and cut the island in two. The marine divisions would head north and the army divisions head south. It was hoped that after a hard battle in the beachhead area, the over 150,000-man attacking force could defeat the Japanese garrison, estimated at less than half this strength, in a fairly short time.

An enormous armada of American and British warships preceded the

---

[a] A study of the under-estimation of Japanese garrisons in the Pacific in spite of substantial breaks into Japanese codes and extensive aerial reconnaissance might shed some interesting light on American perceptions of the war and MacArthur's leadership style. Drea's book, *MacArthur's Ultra*, is only a beginning.

invasion, launching sweeping raids over southern Japan in late March 1945. Numerous Japanese planes were destroyed in the process, but others survived, having been carefully dispersed and concealed. Japanese attacks on the Allied task forces included large numbers of kamikaze, which put three American carriers out of action, and ohka bombs which proved useless when the planes carrying them were shot down. The kamikaze proved much more effective against American carriers with their thin decks than the British carriers with their heavy steel decks. The latter carried fewer planes but proved much more resistant to the planes which crashed themselves onto their superstructure. The B-29s of the 21st Bomber Command in the Marianas also flew support missions instead of urban air raids. For days preceding the landing itself, the landing area was bombarded in a manner that would have been most effective had it been applied to Iwo Jima. Then, on L-Day, April 1, 1945, operation "Iceberg" began as a fleet of over one thousand ships stood off the invasion beaches.

The initial landings proved both easier and simpler than anticipated. There was practically no resistance, and the two big airfields in central Okinawa were captured on L-Day. The island was quickly cut in two, and the marines turned north while the army divisions headed south. The former had little opposition as they cleared the whole of northern Okinawa by April 13; only small Japanese units had to be destroyed. The push south quickly ran into trouble.

From their initially seized portions of central Okinawa, the XXIV Corps quickly came up against the Machinato line, Ushijima's first defensive position anchored on the west coast town of Machinato and taking advantage of the rugged ridges crossing the island to its east coast. In three weeks of bitter and costly fighting, the army divisions, soon reinforced by an additional division, battered their way forward. By April 25, Ushijima decided to abandon the Machinato line and draw back to his most heavily defended position, the Shuri line, across the island in the mountain ridges covering the capital of Naha on the west coast and the old fortifications of Shuri in the center.[99]

The 10th Army battered its way into the outlying portions of the Shuri Line in the last days of April and early May. Ushijima, who may have thought the Americans more weakened by the fighting than they really were, launched a major counter-offensive on May 4 which was repulsed with heavy casualties and deprived him of reserves. It also forced him to reveal many of the hitherto concealed artillery positions. In the following weeks, the Americans went back to the offensive, fighting against a determined enemy and relying on superior fire-power and large-scale use of flame throwers to crush one position after another.

While this battle was raging, another one was taking place on and over the seas around Okinawa. In periodic waves, hundreds of Japanese planes attacked Allied naval ships in conventional or more often kamikaze attacks. In this fighting, in which almost two thousand planes hurled themselves at their targets, the American navy suffered its heaviest casualties of the war and lost a number of ships. The morale effect of these attacks was also considerable, but there were critical shortcomings on the Japanese side. The planes tended to concentrate on the destroyers and destroyer escorts which were out on picket duty to warn of approaching planes. Often kamikazes continued attacking such ships obviously already disabled instead of heading for the larger units these pickets were protecting. The Allies did what they could to cope with what most American naval leaders considered Japan's most effective weapon of the war. Air strikes were flown against the bases of the kamikaze from land bases and carriers; a complicated picket system of warships and submarines was established; evasion tactics for ships under attack were developed; but the most important and effective defenses were always the same. Carrier planes tried to shoot down as many of the attacking planes as they could; the crews on the ships stood to their guns, putting up tremendous volumes of fire which destroyed many of the kamikazes; and the crews, especially the damage control parties, tried their best to cope with the terrible damage often caused by the planes which exploded on and in the ships.

The Allies not only coped with the kamikazes, though with heavy losses, but they also succeeded in beating off the one Japanese surface naval attempt to interfere with the Okinawa landing with practically no casualties. The Japanese super-battleship *Yamato*, her damage from the battle near Leyte of the preceding October repaired, was sent out on April 8, escorted by a light cruiser and several destroyers. Sighted on the next day, the *Yamato* was attacked by waves of carrier-based planes, which sent torpedoes into the huge ship and dropped bombs on it. The *Yamato*, the escorting cruiser, and three of the destroyers were sunk with over 3000 men. There is some argument over whether this was intended as a deliberate suicide mission; but without air support the sortie was certain to have that result and, unlike the kamikaze, to no effect.[100]

On Okinawa itself, the defeat of the Japanese counter-offensive was followed by a renewed American attack. Concentrating on the eastern flank of the Shuri Line, the Americans pounded forward in driving rain. On May 21, Ushijima decided to abandon what his troops still held of the line and pulled back into the mountainous southwest corner of the island. There the remnants of the Japanese 32nd Army were destroyed in the following four weeks of bitter fighting. The American casualties included General Buckner, killed on June 18; Ushijima committed suicide four days later. Over 100,000 Japanese soldiers had died on the island as had tens of thousands of Okinawa civilians. American casualties numbered 75,000, an indication of what could be expected. After the temporary designation of a Marine Corps general, General Stilwell was appointed to take Buckner's place in command of 10th Army, but it was expected to take a long time to rebuild the divisions which had conquered the island. The Japanese had shown here as on Iwo Jima that the closer the Allies came to Japan the harder the fighting. The reaction to victory on Okinawa in Washington and to defeat in Tokyo was astonishingly similar: grim determination.

ENDING THE WAR

The basic question in June of 1945, during the final days of the three months' battle for Okinawa, was whether to go forward with "Olympic," the Kyushu invasion, as planned, or to try first some other operations preliminary to an invasion in the Tokyo Bay area of Honshu, or, alternatively, to try to starve the Japanese out without any further invasions at all. General MacArthur, who was consulted by Marshall, was clear and emphatic in his response: the Kyushu landing was the wisest choice; all other operations were sure to run up the casualties to no great advantage, and the longer Olympic was postponed, the harder and costlier it would become. It would benefit greatly from a Soviet invasion of Manchuria, but in any case, Olympic was the only reasonable next step.[101] The navy leadership, both Nimitz and King, had come to the same conclusion, and the air force commanders were also of this opinion.

President Truman was clearly disturbed by the casualties incurred in the Okinawa campaign and wanted a careful review of the alternatives before giving the green light for Olympic and Coronet, operations which were expected to involve even more desperate fighting with an even higher cost in lives. On June 18 he held a conference at the White House with the Joint Chiefs of Staff (General Eaker representing General Arnold) and the Secretaries of War and the Navy.[102] The President's advisors were unanimously in favor of Olympic in spite of the anticipated cost in lives, though the possibility that the dropping of newly available atomic bombs (reviewed below) might end the war before that invasion had to be launched was mentioned. It was agreed by all that Olympic was needed as the next step, whether or not Coronet would follow. If the Japanese surrendered after an initial defeat in the home islands, well and good. If they did not, the possession of southern Kyushu would provide the essential base for *either* strangling the main island of Honshu or for landing on it if that were to be decided on. Olympic would be launched and the preparations for Coronet were to go forward. The President would try to get whatever assistance the United States could obtain from Russia in the war, but the Americans would go ahead. "He had hoped that there was a possibility of preventing an Okinawa from one end of Japan to the other. He was clear on the situation now and was quite sure that the Joint Chiefs of Staff should proceed with the Kyushu operation."[a]

On July 10, Admiral Halsey began with the preliminary operations for Olympic.[103] In the Philippines and elsewhere, the American armed forces began massive preparations for the landing operation, even as the Japanese, who expected such an assault at essentially the very places the Americans had in mind, made their own elaborate preparations to meet it. A most interesting post-war analysis of the planned invasion by a British team which looked at records and interviewed officers from both sides points to an enormous battle, greatly affected by a huge Japanese commitment of suicide planes and torpedoes.[104]

While these preparations for Olympic were going forward, another major Allied offensive was being planned for Southeast Asia. As the campaign in Burma was ending in the largest Allied victory over the Japanese army in World War II, the British looked toward the reconquest of Singapore. A new British army, the 12th, was formed to direct the final clearing of Burma, while the 14th, fresh from its success in the Burma campaign, was to be the main land force for operation "Zipper," the series of actions designed to retake Singapore and open the Molucca Straits to Allied shipping.[105]

The preparations for "Zipper" were to be influenced by two new factors. Thought eventually scheduled for September 9, 1945, the size and possible success of the operation was very much affected by the decision of London after victory in Europe to release soldiers with long service overseas (three years four months). This meant stripping the forces in Mountbatten's command and led to one of the few British World War II revivals of the bitter arguments between military and civilian leaders which had been such a prominent feature of World War I.[106] The problem was resolved but left plenty of hard feelings. There was certainly no doubt in anyone's mind that Zipper had to go forward.[107]

The second factor affecting Zipper was that Mountbatten could not

---

[a] *FRUS, Potsdam*, 1: 909. On June 21, Field Marshal Brooke noted in his diary after meeting with General Clayton Bissell, the U.S. army's chief of intelligence: "He is very interesting about Japan and evidently considers that the required results can only be obtained by invasion, and that encirclement is unlikely to achieve our object" (Liddell Hart Centre, Alanbrooke Papers).

have all the carrier air support he wanted because carriers were needed in the Pacific, and he could not expect to keep all his resources after Zipper because of the British commitment to a major role in Coronet. The assumption was that Zipper would take place while Olympic was under way. Thereafter all other operations, follow-up actions in Southeast Asia as well as operations elsewhere, were to be subordinated to the anticipated enormous needs of Coronet.

Even as the preparations for Olympic and the planning for Zipper and for Coronet went forward, other developments were under way which ended the war before any of these landing operations had to be carried out. These developments, intersecting in time and in part influencing each other, were the plans for dropping atomic bombs on Japan, internal debates about ending the war in the Japanese government, and the Soviet entrance into the war. The decisions about the first of these issues would be greatly influenced by American partial knowledge about the discussions within the Japanese government from decoded Japanese diplomatic correspondence.

The atomic bomb project had originally been designed in what was believed to be a race with Germany to build weapons of tremendous power. It was assumed that if the Germans made such weapons they would certainly use them; and it was the fear that German scientific and engineering genius would first accomplish this goal that had inspired, perhaps driven would be a more accurate term, the effort in Britain and the United States to try to get ahead of the Germans. In that effort, there was a built-in assumption that, when ready, such bombs would be used against Germany. Two other decisions were also arrived at in the course of the combined American-British atomic bomb project. It was agreed that the weapon would be utilized in the war only by agreement between the two powers, and it was also decided that, while the need for raw materials required for bomb production involved Canada and the Belgian Congo, the two governments cooperating in the main project would not share their knowledge with others, and in particular not with the Soviet Union.

Both decisions reflected an awareness of the possibility that the new weapon could either greatly affect the post-war international situation or at least off-set the major reduction in their armed forces which both Washington and London expected to make after World War II as they had after World War I.[108] The American and British leaders may also have been influenced by their knowledge of Soviet espionage activities directed at the atomic facilities, a knowledge which was quite fragmentary at the time but substantial all the same. Furthermore, although neither London nor Washington appears to have been aware of the massive

Soviet atomic bomb project under way at least since 1942, it most certainly was known that the Soviet Union had steadfastly refused to share with its allies any information on its own weapons research projects and had been most reticent about exchanging even routine intelligence.

By 1943 the British and by late 1944 the American governments had reached the conclusion that Germany had dropped out of the atomic bomb race. By the last months of 1944 however, it had become reasonably certain that the first of the two types of bombs being built, one based on uranium, the other based on plutonium, would be ready in the late spring or summer of 1945, when the enormous special facilities for refining and making the materials needed for bombs were expected to have produced a sufficient quantity for a few of the new weapons.[109] Although it was correctly assumed that by then the European war would be nearing its end so that there would be no point to dropping the bombs on Germany, the prospect of reducing the war against Japan below the expected year-and-a-half after the defeat of Germany looked very inviting, especially in the shadow of growing casualty lists from the Pacific War.

Roosevelt had always opposed the use of gas or biological warfare except in retaliation. On the other hand, he had evidently assumed that the atomic weapons, when available, would be employed as essentially very much larger explosives.[110] It is clear that Truman, when briefed on the bomb project after his accession, was brought into the same assumption; and although his papers show some questioning of this assumption, they invariably also show him coming back to it.[111] If the new devices worked, and most but by no means all informed about the project believed they would, and if they were even remotely as destructive as anticipated, and on this point also there were divergent estimates, then their use might shock the Japanese into surrender, ownership of them enhance the general diplomatic position of the United States, and knowledge of their potential discourage any and all nations from ever again resorting to war.

It was the first of these which was by far the most important issue at the time. This was so not only because of the experience of Okinawa and the anticipation of a terrible battle on the home islands of Japan, but because of the coincidence in timing between the availability of the first atomic bombs, the interval between the Okinawa battle and "Olympic," and also because of American knowledge of the internal debate over surrender in Tokyo. It was assumed in Washington, surely correctly, that once the Olympic landing had begun, the Japanese would fight to defend at least the home island of Kyushu with determination and to great effect. The estimates of American intelligence, that Japan had about ten thousand planes—about half of them kamikazes—and two million soldiers in the home islands, were for once essentially accurate.[112] But before these forces engaged the American invasion, even while the American naval, air, and land preparations for it were under way, the Japanese were reviewing their options—and the Americans knew about it.[113]

In the Japanese government, several key leaders were seriously trying to think of ways to end the war.[114] For the most part, as already mentioned, they could not, or would not, think of a surrender, but there were those who hoped that Japan could obtain the cooperation of the Soviet government in arranging peace on terms which did not require a surrender or involve the occupation of the home islands by foreign troops. It is not clear why these Japanese imagined that the Soviet Union, which had given notice of the termination of the Neutrality Pact, had been defeated by Japan in the Russo-Japanese War of 1904–5, had hopes of revising the peace made at the end of that war, and had been successful in beating off Japanese border attacks in 1938 and 1939 should have been expected by the peace advocates in Tokyo to have any interest in aiding Japan to maintain portions of her power in East Asia, as well as to break openly with her American and British allies in the hour of victory in Europe. There is, however, plenty of evidence that it was in line with this concept that the Japanese tried to enlist the Soviet government in June and July of 1945.[115]

The leaders in Moscow had no interest in such approaches, and passed on some of them to their allies. These approaches, however, had the important effect of alerting the Americans and British to the internal deliberations of the Japanese, because they were intercepting and decoding the radio instructions from the Tokyo government to the Japanese embassy in Moscow and the reports of the ambassador there back to his government. Furthermore, in addition to reporting the negative reaction of the Soviet government, Ambassador Sato also sent his own views to Tokyo. He called the Japanese approaches to Moscow ridiculous and futile and recommended that Japan instead accept the Allied call for unconditional surrender,[116] a suggestion independently sent to Tokyo by several other Japanese diplomats in Europe.[117]

The Americans not only read these calls for surrender but also the responses from Tokyo. The repeated assertions from Tokyo that this unsolicited advice had been rejected, and that the Japanese government would not accept the concept of unconditional surrender even if the institution of the imperial house were preserved,[118] told the Americans two very important things.

In the first place, these exchanges showed that the subject of surrender was actually under discussion in Tokyo, an entirely new feature of the situation. Secondly, they demonstrated that so far the advocates of continuing the war were winning out over those who were prepared to surrender, but they might not always be able to do so. Perhaps the blows of atomic bombs and of Soviet entrance into the war could swing the balance to the faction which urged surrender.

Sato's repeated advocacy of a new meeting of the Japanese Governing Council in the presence of the Emperor, in response to Tokyo's assertion of unanimity, including the Emperor, in opposition to surrender, only accentuated these two points and stressed the significance of still another issue: the role of the Emperor in any surrender.[119] A personal intervention of the Emperor would be needed to control the advocates of continued fighting in Tokyo and to assure obedience to any orders to surrender by the huge Japanese forces still in the field on and off the mainland of Asia as well as in the home islands.[120]

There was, under these circumstances, agitated discussion in the highest levels of the United States government of two closely related issues. First, should the call for unconditional surrender be accompanied by some assurance to Japan about the retention of the imperial system; and, second, should there be some public call for Japan to surrender now rather than face total destruction and defeat later, possibly including a reference to the new weapon. There was no agreement on the issue of the Emperor, though increasingly there was a sense that a new Japan could keep a constitutional monarchy if the people so chose, and in the meantime the Emperor under Allied control could effectively end hostilities in the home islands and throughout the areas still controlled by Japanese forces. President Truman had issued a call for Japan's surrender combined with some reassurances on May 8;[121] there had been no response, but he was leaning toward a new public statement. However, he wanted to postpone that until the atomic bomb test scheduled for mid-July showed that the weapon was almost certainly going to work and until the call for Japan's surrender could be issued from Potsdam — the old center of Prussian power, now the meeting place of the Allies who had triumphed over Germany. Perhaps the Japanese would draw the obvious conclusion from Germany's fate.[122]

In the days that Truman and other American leaders prepared to go to the Potsdam conference, the materials for two atomic bombs were sent to Tinian in the Marianas, and the test site in New Mexico was prepared. While the Americans were operating on the assumption that the atomic bombs would be used to try to shock Japan into surrender, the final order had been deferred for a decision by the President.[123] Even before the American decision, the British government had formally given its approval for the new weapon's use.[124] Two weeks later, on July 15, the test of the first atomic bomb in the New Mexico desert showed that the weapon was even more terrible than anticipated.[125] Now was the time, in the President's opinion, both to notify Stalin of the successful test and to issue a warning to the Japanese. The former step was a simple one; since Truman knew of Soviet atomic espionage and assumed that they were working on a bomb themselves, this would only confirm the fact that weapons could now be produced. Stalin merely expressed the hope that the weapon would soon be used on the Japanese. As for the warning to the Japanese to surrender before they were destroyed, that could now be issued in the knowledge that, if they refused, the new weapon could and would be used.

While the military planners at Potsdam therefore agreed on future operations against Japan, with Stalin even agreeing to the establishment of American weather stations in the Soviet Far East,[126] the highest commanders present at the conference knew or were now informed that there was a possibility that Japan would surrender before Olympic and Zipper, scheduled for November and December of that year, had to be launched.[127]

The Potsdam Declaration combined a call for unconditional surrender with extensive assurances about Japan's future. Designed to appeal to the peace faction in the Japanese government, the document was based on the prior drafts discussed in Washington and assuring a future for a peaceful Japan which could eventually pick its own government. The imperial system was not mentioned, but the implication of its possible retention was clearly there, and the document was so read in Tokyo.

In the internal debates in the Japanese government, the advocates of acceptance did not as yet include the Prime Minister, so that the official pronouncement rejected the Potsdam Declaration. That declaration had been joined in by the Chinese Nationalists who were involved in negotiations with the Soviet Union about the concessions Russia wanted before entering the Pacific War and supporting Chiang Kai-shek.[128] The Japanese therefore knew that they faced the combined views and power of the United States, British, and Chinese governments at a time when these were in conference with the Soviet Union. The Japanese government was also being urged to accept the Potsdam terms through their contacts in Switzerland with the American Office of Strategic Services;[129] but they were unwilling to accept the Potsdam terms and so announced in public.

The Americans waited a few days to see whether there were second thoughts in Tokyo;[130] the President then gave the orders to go ahead with the atomic bombs. Both bombs then available were to be dropped a few days apart on a schedule determined by weather conditions and with the intent of fooling the Japanese into thinking that the United States had an indefinite supply which could be unloaded on the home islands. The reality was quite different. There was only one more near to being ready, and others would follow quite slowly,[131] but the hope was that the shock of seeing done with one bomb what up to that time had required hundreds of planes dropping thousands of bombs (in raids on Germany since 1943 and on Japan since March 1945) might tilt the balance within the Japanese government to the advocates of surrender.[132]

The first of the bombs was dropped on Hiroshima on August 6, causing enormous damage in the center of the city, killing fifty to eighty thousand people and wounding an equal number. An official announcement from Washington explained what had happened; now it was expected that the Japanese would understand what was meant by the total destruction promised them if they did not surrender.[133] The internal debates in the Japanese government continued. The Emperor had on June 26 called on the government to find a way to end the war, but the opponents of surrender both urged delay until the latest approach to the Soviet Union had been answered and also held to their original position on the basic issue. If the strategy of awaiting the American invasion was sound, if the expectation of inflicting very heavy casualties on the invader was realized, and this in turn offered a hope of a negotiated settlement, then the question of whether tens of thousands died in "conventional" air raids or as a result of the new weapon made little difference. The Minister of War and the Army and Navy Chiefs of Staff still wished to continue the struggle.

The Japanese received their answer from the Soviet Union on August 8: it was a declaration of war followed immediately by an attack in very great force on the Japanese army in Manchuria.[134] This was a significant double blow to the Japanese. Their military intelligence had misled them as to the timing of a likely Soviet attack; it was assumed that there was much more time available to prepare for this invasion.[135] On the political and diplomatic side, the blow was in some ways even more serious. In spite of all signs to the contrary, there had still been hopes in Tokyo that the Soviet Union would remain neutral and either act as an intermediary in negotiations for peace terms with the Western Powers or, if assured of sufficient concessions by Japan, might even join Japan. In spite of all the warnings from the ambassador in Moscow, such illusions still flourished in Japanese government circles in the summer of 1945; the Soviet declaration of war, therefore, came as an all the more effective psychological blow. Before any detailed news on the advance of the Red Army in Manchuria could reach Tokyo, word was received of the second atomic bomb's dropping on Nagasaki.

Originally destined for another target, the Nagasaki bomb was actually more powerful than the one dropped on Hiroshima, but primarily because of local terrain features caused less destruction and fewer casualties than the earlier one. It is, however, doubtful whether such details were known in Tokyo at the time or would have made any difference. The key point was that the atomic bombs were falling, that one plane with one bomb could now accomplish the effect of hundreds of planes dropping thousands of bombs at a time when the Americans were known to the Japanese to have enormous numbers of planes. At an Imperial Council held in the night of August 9–10, the equal division of the Council, three for surrender against three for continued war, was broken by the Emperor personally. For the first time since a prior Emperor had intervened in 1895 (to obtain the yielding of the Japanese government to an ultimatum from European powers to change the peace terms a victorious Japan had then imposed on a defeated China), the Emperor took a personal role when the government was divided rather than simply giving his sanction when presented with a previously agreed upon policy; he ordered the Japanese government to accept the Potsdam terms.[136]

The Japanese surrender offer which followed included a reservation on the status of the imperial system. Two critical issues now remained to be resolved if the war were to end promptly: first, the Japanese government had to remain in power in the face of those in the Japanese military who objected to ending the war, and, second, the Allies in general and the Americans in particular had to decide how to handle the question of the retention of the Emperor.

One side of this puzzle was whether the victims of Japanese aggression would agree to the retention of the imperial system.[137] The subject had been debated at length within the American government. Secretary of War Stimson and Under-Secretary of State Joseph Grew, who had served as ambassador to Japan, urged a concession on this issue. The new Secretary of State, James Byrnes, and Assistant Secretary Dean Acheson as well as most of the more liberal members of the administration were opposed. Public opinion in the United States was in general also opposed, as were the articulate organizations of the American left who, perhaps mindful of the deal with Darlan in November 1942, wanted no concessions to the old order in Japan and urged the dropping of additional atomic bombs instead. The imperial system had produced war before and might well do so again.

President Truman, who appears to have leaned in the direction of allowing retention, approved a compromise response which implicitly accepted the imperial system by referring to the Emperor's authority being "subject to the Supreme Commander of the Allied Powers,"[138] with the Japanese people promised that they could establish their own form of government. Truman also ordered a suspension in the dropping of atomic bombs but had the conventional bombing continued to pressure the Japanese into acceptance.

The Americans obtained the reluctant agreement of the Soviet Union and China to this answer while agreeing to a very sensible British proposal that the Emperor be required to instruct *others* to sign the surrender rather than sign it himself. Now came the question of whether the Tokyo government could accept this wording and remain in power.

The opponents of surrender claimed that the provision that the people of Japan would be free to decide on their future form of government was incompatible with Japan's basic system. Once again the Emperor had to intervene personally in an evenly divided Council and insist on acceptance of these terms. He would make a broadcast to the people of Japan explaining the necessity of ending the war.

Inside Japan, the opponents of the course ordered by the Emperor made a major effort to reverse the decision to accept the Potsdam declaration. Military figures in key positions in the capital tried to kill their opponents, seize and destroy the recording with the Emperor's broadcast to the people of Japan, and take over power with the intention of continuing in the war. A full scholarly examination of this last in a long series of military coups in modern Japan is not available in any Western language, but what is known appears to show that the coup failed primarily because the Minister of War, General Anami Korechika, refused to support the plotters.[139] Himself an advocate of continued fighting, Anami was, on the other hand, not prepared to defy the orders of the Emperor repeatedly and personally expressed in his presence. He committed suicide in this dilemma, and the plotters failed in their attempt to overthrow the government. It was a close call, and in a way shows that the earlier fears of the peace advocates within the government, that any open move to end the war could lead to a coup which would prolong rather than shorten the conflict, was warranted. But the Emperor, who had assured himself of backing from the imperial family, was able to assert his will against those who still refused to contemplate surrender.

There were now two further issues remaining: the formalities of surrender as a prelude to the occupation of the home islands of Japan, and the surrender of the vast Japanese garrisons remaining on the mainland of Asia and on islands scattered over the South Pacific and off the coast of Southeast Asia. Over a period of a month, both of these matters were resolved. In spite of tense moments, the surrender process moved forward without major problems. With imperial princes sent out from Tokyo, the Japanese commanders in the various garrisons were persuaded to lay down their arms. A series of local surrenders made prisoners of war of the 5,400,000 men remaining in the Japanese army and an added 1,800,000 in the navy.[140] Certainly Allied soldiers everywhere were ecstatic at the prospect of not having to kill every one of these soldiers with great losses to themselves as had once looked all too likely.[141] Furthermore, the surrender obviated Japanese plans to slaughter Allied prisoners of war as fighting approached the camps where they were held, a project for which considerable preparations had evidently been made, to the horror of prisoners who had already suffered enormously.[142]

The famous surrender ceremony on the battleship *Missouri* on September 2 came in the midst of a series of dramatic activities. Although August 15 had been the official date of victory, the fighting in Manchuria continued until August 21, and the last major Japanese army units in the Pacific theater were not disarmed until October 24.[143] By that time, American troops which had begun landing in Japan itself on August 21 were in occupation of the whole country.[a] In spite of fears to the contrary, the occupation proceeded peacefully. Prime Minister Suzuki had been replaced by an Imperial prince; and in this instance once again, imperial authority had been invoked to assure a quick and effective transition from a policy of fight to the last breath to one of peaceful accommodation to a new system.[144] Japan had been battered by bombing and isolated from what remained of her empire by submarines and mines destroying most of her shipping, but it had not been fought over inch by inch; and the vast majority of her soldiers and sailors would survive to come home and share in the rebuilding of a damaged but not devastated country.

The existing government structure would be simultaneously kept and remade, its personnel utilized and purged. The Americans arrived not to conquer but to reform. They planned to transform Japanese society, and in many ways they succeeded so well that the Japanese came to maintain many of the changes then made long after the American occupation had ended.[145] Whatever the subsequent taboos in Japan about that country's role in bringing on and conducting the Pacific War, in Japan after World War II, unlike Germany after

---

[a] Subsequently the western portion of the island of Honshu and the island of Shikoku were assigned to the British Commonwealth Occupation Force (BCOF).

World War I, no one ever came to doubt that the country had indeed been defeated—and without what President Truman had called "an Okinawa from one end of Japan to the other."[146]

CONCLUSIONS

━━━━━━ • ━━━━━━

THE COST AND IMPACT OF WAR

When the war in the Pacific ended with the Japanese surrender, the fighting in Europe had been over for more than four months. In both areas, peace was accompanied by turmoil. In East Asia, the stages of Japanese forces surrendering in widely scattered areas from Burma to New Guinea, from Luzon to Java, were a lengthy and complicated process, and one followed soon after by new troubles between local nationalist groups and returning colonial powers. Only in Japan itself, ironically, was there a real peace at a time when China was about to dissolve in renewed—or continued—civil war. But everywhere there was at least a sense of hope that, with the end of the fighting, things would somehow be better.

The world looked back on years of fighting which had caused enormous casualties and vast destruction. The Soviet Union had suffered the largest number of deaths. Earlier estimates of 20 million, which were occasionally derided as too high, now turn out to have been too low. New research growing out of the more open atmosphere in recent years has been pointing to figures closer to, and possibly in excess of, 25 million deaths. Of these, at most one-third were military, thus demonstrating in this case what was true for the war as a whole: the civilian casualties exceeded the military. Chinese casualties are much more difficult to estimate than those of the Soviet Union, but 15 million dead is a reasonable approximation. In Poland, close to 6 million lost their lives, while Yugoslavia suffered between 1.5 and 2 million deaths. About 400,000 United Kingdom soldiers and civilians lost their lives; about 300,000 from the United States. Germany lost over 4 million and Japan over 2 million lives in the war.[1] The total for the globe as a whole probably reached 60 million, a figure which includes the six million murdered because they were Jewish.

At the war's end, the movement of people caused by the great upheaval did not come to a halt. Millions had been displaced as refugees or deportees, and many of them found it difficult or impossible to go home.[2] In some instances political conditions in their prior home areas had so changed as to make return inadvisable. In other cases, the people who did try to go home found themselves so unwelcome on return that they had to flee once again. One of the more dramatic instances of this was the fate of surviving Jewish Poles who, on attempting to return, were chased back out, sometimes to the accompaniment of pogroms. British Foreign Secretary Anthony Eden's hope that Jews could stay—or go back to where they had been—proved illusory.[3] That, in turn, would add to the major difficulties of adjustment in the Middle East.

Another movement of people had begun in the last stages of the war and continued on an even larger scale after the cessation of hostilities. In Europe, many Germans had fled in view of the growing signs of defeat on the Eastern Front, especially in the winter of 1944–45. The insistence of the Germans on fighting until the last moment—unlike all of their allies—combined with irresponsible and incompetent evacuation procedures by the Nazi Party to condemn tens of thousands to their deaths.[4] Prior Allied agreement to the expulsion of the Sudeten Germans from Czechoslovakia and subsequent agreement to similar expulsions from East Prussia, Danzig, and the other former eastern German territories turned over to Poland added millions more. It is impossible to sort out reasonably accurately the numbers of those who had fled by May 1945 from those who were subsequently expelled, but the total was well over ten million and thus constitutes the largest single migration of people in a short period of which we know. This uprooting was accompanied by great suffering to which little attention was paid elsewhere, partly because the whole process of moving people to fit boundaries— as opposed to the 1919 effort to adjust boundaries to people—had been inaugurated by the Germans themselves, partly because in post-war Germany the expellees and refugees picked as their spokespersons individuals who had themselves been enthusiastic advocates of or participants in the expelling of others from *their* homes.

The process of moving large numbers of people in the last days of the war and the immediately following period was not limited to Germans. Millions of Poles had to move from the eastern portions of their pre-1939 country, which had been assigned to the Soviet Union, and found new homes in the lands taken over from Germany. There were other such movements, though on a smaller scale, elsewhere in Europe. By a supreme irony, those who had been selected by the Germans in January 1937 as the first people to be subjected to this sort of treatment, the German-speaking minority in the South Tyrol,[5] would for the most part escape that fate, remain in Italy, and eventually have their rights protected somewhat by an agreement between the Italian and Austrian governments. The mass transfers were, moreover, not limited to Europe. Approximately seven million Japanese were repatriated from the former Japanese empire to the home islands, while tens of thousands of Koreans, many of whom had been forced laborers, were returned to Korea. Other upheavals would follow on the mainland of Asia.

There was something of a converse in the repatriation of prisoners of war. Those American and British prisoners held by Germany and Japan who had survived the war were returned home promptly except for some freed by the Russians, who made difficulties about repatriation. The very large numbers of French prisoners as well as the disarmed former Italian soldiers, who had been employed as forced laborers in the German economy, also went back. There were serious problems about the Soviet soldiers who had enlisted in the German military, willingly or under pressure. At least for a while, the Western Allies forcibly repatriated those they had captured or who tried to get into their prisoner of war camps upon the German surrender; even more than the Red Army men who had survived in German prisoner of war camps, they were subjected to dire punishment on their return.

German soldiers fell into Allied hands in enormous numbers, especially in the last weeks of the war and with the surrender of May 1945. They were released over a period of ten years. The Americans moved rather promptly with those they kept in their own custody but turned over many to the French and British, who included many of them among those they held as laborers for a while; hundreds of thousands were kept in the Soviet Union for years to assist in the reconstruction of that country's economy. The Western Powers released the few Japanese prisoners they had captured during hostilities and the vast numbers who surrendered at the end of the fighting fairly quickly, while the Soviet Union moved more slowly in repatriating the numerous Japanese soldiers who fell into its hands as a result of the campaign in Manchuria in August, 1945.[6]

Although not always successful, an effort was made to hold back Axis prisoners who were suspected of war crimes so that, along with civilian suspects, they could be tried. The subject has only recently begun to draw serious attention, but there had clearly been a distinctive break in the military traditions of both Germany and Japan. Armies which had conducted themselves on the whole rather honorably before, the Germans in World War I, the Japanese in that war and in the prior Russo-Japanese War of 1904-5, acted fundamentally differently in World War II. Nothing like the systematic bayonetting of prisoners of war, for example, as practiced by the Japanese in Malaya and elsewhere, had characterized the conduct of that army in prior wars; large-scale participation in the massacre of civilians, which came to be a hallmark of German army activities in World War II had harbingers but no real precedents in World War I.[7]

The experience of the Allies in connection with the handling of war crimes after World War I had been discouraging, to put it mildly. One of the many concessions made to the Germans in modifications of the 1919 peace treaty had been to allow them to conduct their own trials. The result had been a fiasco; this time the Allies would, at least initially, conduct the trials themselves; and it would be years before the Germans began to prosecute mass murderers and other offenders themselves.[8] Some trials were also conducted of Japanese accused of war crimes by the Allies; unlike the Germans, the Japanese post-occupation government has preferred to hold no trials but instead to pretend that no crimes were committed.[9] Some individuals escaped trial by suicide; some were sheltered by one or another of the victors for political, intelligence, or other reasons; some managed to disappear; and some escaped to neutral countries, which in many cases refused to extradite them, often benefiting from help by individuals associated with the Vatican, where such fugitives from justice sometimes found more sympathy than those fleeing the Nazi murderers earlier.[10]

The destruction caused by the war had been tremendous. It was worst in Eastern and Southeast Europe; in addition, bombing had affected numerous cities in Western Europe, Germany and Japan. There had been extensive damage in China, especially in the early years of fighting there; there had been great destruction in the Philippines, and much of Manila had been wrecked in the fighting for that city. Innumerable other cities, towns and villages in both the European and Pacific theaters had been dramatically and directly damaged during hostilities. Millions of tons of shipping had been sunk; factories destroyed or damaged; bridges and dams deliberately blown up by one side or the other.

All participants had poured enormous financial resources into the conflict. In the case of Germany, a very substantial portion of the cost of war had been exacted from conquered territory by looting, direct exactions of various sorts, and the imposition of forced loans from her satellites in the form of trade clearing debts.[11] Both Italy and Japan had used up their financial resources. The Soviet economy had been drained by that state's great exertions, while Great Britain had fought a war far beyond her means and was left with huge debts to the members of the Commonwealth and to India. The United States had poured vast sums into her own and her allies' war efforts, but emerged from the war with her economy strengthened rather than weakened as a result. The big question that would face her people afterwards was whether they would rise to the challenge of assisting others in rebuilding their economies. The new institutions that would make that feasible had been established or soon would be; the open question was whether and how they would work.

The costs in human life and suffering, in destruction and economic dislocation, had been of absolutely unprecedented magnitude. If the question is asked, was victory worth such tremendous exertions and the price paid for their success, one is obliged to consider the consequences of Axis victory. Whatever the more limited imperial objectives of Italy, Japan had intended to create an enormous exploitive empire in East, Southeast, and South Asia, reaching into the Western Hemisphere and, as the Korean model showed, disastrous for the lives and welfare of the oppressed.

By far the most far-reaching objectives, however, had been sought by Germany. World-wide in scope, the Germans looked first to a complete demographic reordering of the Eurasian land mass in which tens of millions would be slaughtered, sterilized, or deliberately left to die of starvation. The reach of this new dark age was confidently expected by its advocates to extend to the exploitation of vast portions of the African continent, the Middle East, and the Western Hemisphere. The view held by some extreme nationalists in the European colonial empires that a victory of Germany, Italy and Japan over Great Britain, the Soviet Union and the United States would, thereafter, facilitate the attainment of independence against the new masters of the globe is too ridiculous to be worthy of serious discussion. Those powers had already demonstrated *their* way of controlling conquered territories, and not one of the colonies would have been liberated but for the triumph of the Allies.

At the beginning of the century, the German Emperor William II had held up the Huns to his nation as the people they should emulate.[12] The German governor general in World War II occupied Poland proudly proclaimed the intent of naming his province after the Vandals instead. A new dark age was to descend on the earth, wrecking the existing features of civilization the way the barbarian invasions had once snuffed out whatever advances had been made in the ancient Mediterranean world. Only this time the destruction was to be more complete and the instruments of continued repression were certain to be more sophisticated. If the costs of victory were immense, those of an alternative outcome would have been even more horrendous. And not only for the losers in the war; as the great theologian Dietrich Bonhoeffer and some other German opponents of Hitler recognized at the time, even for the peoples of the Axis, defeat would be better than a world dominated by evil.

The most basic challenge which the events of the war years placed before all inside and outside Germany was an unprecedented aspect of that evil: the deliberate attempts to eliminate physically from the face of the earth whole populations, whose members were to be killed regardless of age, sex, or conduct but instead solely as a punishment for having been born. Applied on a huge scale to the Jews of Europe and in a substantial way to its Gypsies, such a procedure was almost unprecedented, the World War I massacres of Armenians being perhaps the clearest precursor. For Germany, this meant essentially that the two religions which had arrived there simultaneously during the period of Roman rule, Judaism and Christianity, were removed simultaneously by the Germans themselves, to be replaced first by the worship of Moloch, the idol of blood, and thereafter by Mammon, the idol of gold. Whether that former area of cultural vigor could recover a spiritual foundation would surely be one of the critical issues for its post-war history, in many ways far more significant than the problem of rebuilding its bombed cities.

For the rest of the world, which had watched this process with a mixture of horror and indifference, the challenge to established values and beliefs was different but in some ways equally threatening. It is hardly surprising that, in the face of that threat to the concept of what human beings were capable of doing, some should take refuge in the assertion that the terrible need not be confronted because it had never happened. In the face of mountains of documents and pictures, such escapism neither brought back to life a single one of the victims nor assisted the mass of astounded and puzzled onlookers with the difficult problem of comprehending the dangerous capacities of human beings with the highest levels of education and training and a total absence of moral sensibility.

The purely economic losses of the victors were expected to be made up, at least in part, by reparations from the defeated. Although there was far less noise about this issue in the post-war era this time than after World War I, the reality was that Germany paid far more than earlier. The Russians extracted huge reparations from the portion of Germany they occupied and received some reparations from the western zones as well. The Federal Republic of Germany, created out of the three western zones of occupation in 1949, though much smaller and more seriously damaged by the war than the Germany of 1919, paid far more in reparations than in the inter-war years, the key difference being that of a government with the political will to follow a new policy, a will embodied in its leader Konrad Adenauer.[13] The result was that instead of impoverishing herself, first by run-away inflation, later by horrendous deflation, in order to prove that Germany could not pay, this time she became wealthier than ever as she returned constructively to the world economy.

This dramatic change in Germany was, perhaps, due not only to her new leadership but also to another major difference between the impact of the two great wars on the country. World War I had been fought almost entirely outside Germany; though hard on that country as well, it had damaged the enemies of Germany far more than herself. This time the war had come home: first in the bombing which her own foolish defiance of the earlier peace treaty had provoked and then in the form of invading armies, which Germany had also brought on herself. The experience of World War II was not only terrible for others; this time the conflict had indeed left its mark inside the country. There is more than symbolic significance in the decision of several German cities to keep at least one large ruined building as a conspicuous reminder of the devastation of war.

The extraordinarily inept way in which Italy first entered and then left the conflict had led to a destructive campaign almost the whole length of the Italian peninsula as well as the loss of her whole colonial empire, substantial territory to Yugoslavia, and hundreds of thousands of casualties. The country was beginning to work its way back toward a new status already in the last years of the war, and with some outside help toward a new role in Europe. In the decades when Italian governments had attempted to play the role of a major power, Italy had never had the resources to sustain such a posture. It was only after the disaster of World War II—by contrast with the victory of World War I—that the Italian economy eventually became modernized, and under new leadership there emerged a significant middle-size power. The memory of the resistance to Fascism, especially to Mussolini's "Social Republic" in the north, provided something of a unifying myth, especially as it grew out of all proportion to the real accomplishments of that resistance. The development of functioning democratic institutions proved a more difficult task, but one that was assisted rather than hindered by Italy's having lost a colonial empire which had always been a drain on the country's slender resources.

France had been defeated in 1940 but had been liberated by her allies. The effort of Charles de Gaulle to assert his own authority in France upon liberation had been successful, but his insistence on retaining the great power status to which he devoutly believed France entitled would lead his successors into a series of disastrous colonial wars from which he, once again, would have to extricate the country. At the insistence primarily of the British government, France was accorded a major role in the formation of the United Nations Organization and in the control of occupied Germany and Austria; the French would repay these favors by vetoing Britain's joining the European Economic Community.

For decades, France, like many of the West European countries which had been temporarily occupied by the Germans, was wracked by the problem posed by the collaboration of many Frenchmen with the occupiers. In the years immediately after liberation, the purges were in some cases very severe and at times arbitrary.[14] There followed a period of years in which all seemed to be forgotten and forgiven; eventually there would be a revival of questions and recriminations. Pierre Laval, Vidkun Quisling, and numerous others had been executed, but questions about the behavior of many remained open.

Although the realities were concealed from the view of many contemporaries, the impact of war was especially great on Britain. Its power declining in the pre-war years, Britain had maintained herself in the long war partially as a result of assistance from the United States. Furthermore, the members of the Commonwealth had provided massive support and credits to the mother country in addition to their own direct military contributions. The ties of empire had been loosened further, and in spite of Churchill's own preference for the maintenance of Britain's imperial role, especially in India, the very success he had had in leading the country through the great ordeal contributed to the sapping of its strength. It had been in part his recognition of this process which had led him to advocate a policy of extensive concessions to the Soviet Union, in order at least to set specific limits to Soviet expansion before Britain had been weakened even more, but the extent to which he tried to portray himself in his memoir-history of the war as the advocate of a policy opposite to the one he had followed in practice shows how difficult that recognition had been for him. Under a new government, the United Kingdom would become a more just society at home even as it shed many of the remaining imperial trappings; finding a new place for itself in a changed world was to prove a lengthier and more difficult task.

The terrible winter of 1944-45 in the Netherlands left a heritage of redoubled bitterness toward the Germans, but there as in Luxembourg the return of the government-in-exile brought with it a slow and difficult but effective recovery. That recovery would be aided by the United States, as was true for Belgium, a country rent by the question of what to do about the monarch who had remained behind—and who had to abdicate—as well as by the friction between its Flemish and Walloon population. The fact that when Germany surrendered her armies were still in occupation of Denmark and Norway meant that with the exception of the extreme northeastern portion of Norway, which the retreating German army had devastated in the winter of 1944-45, those two countries had suffered relatively little physical damage in the war. The Red Army had turned over the liberated northeasternmost portion to the Norwegian government-in-exile right away; it took until 1946 for the Soviets to return the island of Bornholm to the Danes. Both Scandinavian countries had been ruthlessly exploited by the Germans, but a continuity of democratic regimes assisted a return to normal life.

Finland had tried to leave the war in September 1944 but soon found itself fighting its erstwhile German ally. Once the German forces had retreated from the northern portion of the country—devastating it as they left—Finland faced the problems of reconstruction and the requirement of paying reparations to the Soviet Union from a country weakened by the exertions of war, territorial losses, primarily in the north, going beyond those of March 1940, and the continuing suspicion of her large and victorious neighbor. A Soviet lease on the Porkkala area was substituted for the one on Hangö required by the March 1940 treaty; the Soviet Union voluntarily giving up this lease in 1955. But the country did retain its independence.

With the possibility of Soviet archives finally opening up, it may be easier to determine the reasoning which led Stalin to allow the Finns to retain their domestic institutions as long as they could be depended upon to pursue no foreign policy hostile to the U.S.S.R.. It would appear that a combination of concern for the maintenance of the alliance with the Western Powers and a recognition of the fierce determination of the Finns to maintain their freedom led him to decide that a neutral and at least outwardly friendly Finland was preferable to a restive province whose retention was also costly for Soviet relations with the West.

No country, except for the defeated, was changed more drastically as a result of the war than Poland. The armies of Germany and the Soviet Union had moved across it several times, leaving enormous destruction in their wake. In addition, the Germans had systematically destroyed the city of Warsaw and had done what they could to wreck the nation's economy. The human losses included the overwhelming majority of the country's Jewish population, and hundreds of thousands of civilians killed during the fighting and as a prelude to the systematic extermination of the Poles scheduled for the period after a German victory. Additional millions had been deported by both the Germans and the Soviets. Furthermore, with the country's boundaries practically completely different after 1945 from what they had been in 1939, there were additional population shifts, difficult at first even if leading to a more nationally uniform population on a somewhat richer territory when it was all over. As if these massive changes were not enough, the end of the war saw the imposition of a Soviet-style dictatorship on the state.

Poland had been anything but a democracy before the German invasion of 1939, but the system imposed in 1945 and the immediately following years had essentially no roots in the country at all. Consolidated by a combination of internal warfare against the remnants of the underground army, the Armia Krajowa, with Stalinist terror, the new structure involved a complete reordering of Polish society on a model practically no segment of the population favored. When the free elections promised at Yalta were finally held more than forty years later, the whole edifice — or what by then was left of it — was swept away, leaving the Polish people to pick up where they had left off in 1939, changed in many ways by the war, but with the additional burdens left behind by decades of brutality and mismanagement.

The three Baltic States of Estonia, Latvia, and Lithuania had lost their independence during and as a result of the war but, unlike the smaller countries of Western Europe, did not regain it at the end. The insistence of the United States on a refusal to recognize their annexation to the U.S.S.R. still stood, and in reluctant deference to Roosevelt's preference the British maintained a similar position formally, but the reality of life in the three states was very different. They were reabsorbed as Soviet Socialist Republics into the U.S.S.R., with a persistent, if by no means entirely successful, effort being made to model them completely on the system installed in the other SSRs. As a part of the earlier territorial reorganization arranged by Hitler and Stalin, Lithuania received the long-disputed area of Vilna from Poland, and in subsequent decades this city and its surrounding territory would, for the first time, become solidly Lithuanian in population. On the other hand, deliberate settlement of Great Russians in the Baltic States would create new nationality problems. In 1990 these three countries finally resumed their real, as opposed to nominal, independence, picking up where they had left off half a century earlier. The fact that Lithuania now separated the northern portion of former German East Prussia, since 1945 included in the Soviet Federated Socialist Republic, from the rest of Russia's territory would mean that an additional complication was certain to face

Lithuania as it dealt with a Russian state emerging from the collapsing U.S.S.R.

That country, by far the largest in Europe and in the world, was transformed by the experience of the war. Its casualties had been by far the highest of all belligerents, and the physical damage to its cities, industries, and transportation system was immense. In addition to the damage in the areas directly affected by hostilities, enormous dislocations in the economy, the running down of industrial plant and the imposition of tremendous hardships on the population had had a major impact on the huge portions of the state never reached by the invader. The country had received substantial assistance from its allies, and this had been especially important in sustaining the civilian population, but the stand- ard of living at the end of the war was grim indeed. Reconstruction would be an immense charge on the economy, and the foreign policy of the Stalin government insured that there would be no outside aid beyond the initial relief support of the United Nations Relief and Rehabilitation Administration. It is not surprising that under these circumstances the Soviet government did what it could to extract economic benefits from its domination of Eastern Europe and its control of a zone of occupation in Germany, but it would be a long, hard pull all the same.

The new boundary agreement worked out with, or perhaps one should say imposed on, the puppet Communist regime of post-war Poland expanded Soviet territory at the expense of pre-war Poland. The eastern portion of that country was annexed as was the northern part of former East Prussia and the easternmost part of Czechoslovakia. In the north, parts of Finland additional to those annexed under the peace treaty of March 1940 were included in the Soviet Union, the most important of these being the Petsamo area, a shift which deprived Finland of an outlet to the Arctic Ocean while giving the nickel mines — and a border with Norway — to the U.S.S.R. Romania, on the other hand, was not required to cede territory additional to that which the Soviet Union had seized in the summer of 1940, perhaps because the Romanians had changed sides in August 1944.

But these territorial accretions, and the domination over the countries of East and Southeast Europe, were not the most significant parts of the new status of the Soviet Union. Instead, it was a double effect of the war on the internal and international situation of the country. Inside the U.S.S.R., the war, called the Great Patriotic War, was the major consolidating experience. Decades later the whole structure of the system would fall apart, but in the period immediately after the war, the ordeal the country had gone through and the victory it had attained gave a sense of pride and cohesion which had not been there since 1917 and took a long time to erode. That pride, engendered by a major role in the defeat of Germany, a role magnified by Soviet propaganda to the practical exclusion of all others, surrounded the regime with an appearance of legitimacy it had not had before and never regained.

In international affairs, the result of the war was that the very country which the Germans had expected to obliterate from the face of the earth—with most of its citizens—instead became and was recognized as one of the dominating powers of the globe, its territory expanded, its influence enhanced, its status unchallenged. Instead of being crushed, the Soviet Union had played a major role in crushing Germany, had advanced into Central and Southeast Europe, and was a founding member of the new United Nations Organization with that status symbol of a great power: a permanent seat on the Security Council. Instead of derision, the Soviet Union inspired respect and even fear. No greater reversal from 1917 or 1939 could be imagined. The day would come when some might question whether getting so many millions of one's citizens killed was truly a sign of genius; but for the time being, Stalin, the only 1939 leader of a major country other than Chiang Kai-shek remaining in power in 1945, looked like the biggest winner from the war.

Czechoslovakia had not been as badly damaged during the war as most other portions of Eastern and Southeast Europe, though there had been substantial fighting in the Slovak portion. Because Czechoslovakia had been taken over by the Germans without war and its Czech population's transfer or annihilation postponed by the Germans until after their victory, the western portion of the country had suffered the usual economic exactions, and the Jewish population had, for the most part, been killed as in other areas under German control; but the basic economic structure of the country had not been affected. The easternmost part of the pre-Munich country was annexed by the Soviet Union, and the puppet state of Slovakia had vanished, leaving its leaders to be tried and in many cases executed after the end of the war. The territory turned over to Germany under the Munich agreement was returned to Czechoslovakia, but the German inhabitants were now expelled in a process which deprived all of their property and many of their lives. For a short time it looked as if the country might provide that bridge between East and West that many of its leaders hoped it could be, but early in 1948 this prospect was crushed in a Communist coup. Forty years of darkness lay ahead.

Hungary, Romania and Bulgaria were all under the control of the Red Army at the end of the war. Though having by no means suffered equal damages and casualties during hostilities, each would encounter the same immediate fate: a process of total social and political reorientation as all three became Soviet satellites. Hungary lost all the territories she had acquired as a partner of Germany; in addition, a small piece of land (the Bratislava bridgehead) was turned over to Czechoslovakia. Romania regained what had been lost in 1940 to Hungary but not what the country had been obliged to cede to the Soviet Union and to Bulgaria. The last named was the only state defeated in the war which actually increased its territory, being allowed to retain the southern Dobruja obtained from Romania in 1940 (and which Bulgaria had lost after World War I). All also had to pay some reparations, but these were to be paid in goods.[15]

Yugoslavia had suffered a civil war as well as occupation and a long struggle with the various occupiers. Terribly ravaged and exploited, the country hardly made up for the enormous suffering by acquiring substantial territory from Italy. The liberation of the country was, however, largely the result of its own resistance forces so that the Soviet Union could not control Yugoslavia as it did its northern and eastern neighbors. Tito imposed a Communist dictatorship on the country but soon broke with Moscow. The Communist insurgents came to control Albania when the nationalist insurgents waited too long to resist the Axis occupiers. Fearful of domination and possibly even absorption by Yugoslavia, they turned toward the Soviet Union for defense against a Yugoslavia which in one of its provinces contained a majority of people who were really Albanians, rather than Serbs (who controlled it). For decades, that new dictatorship was to attempt a remolding of Albania even as it insisted on an independent status in international affairs.

Greece had been spared the devastation of fighting in 1944 when the German troops pulled out, but the years of occupation had drained the country. Greece received the Dodecanese Islands in the Aegean from Italy, certainly a welcome addition, but peace with Italy did not bring peace at home. The civil war which had taken place inside the country already under Axis occupation would continue in various forms thereafter; the Greek agony was to last for years.

The African continent was affected dramatically by the war even though only relatively small portions of it had seen much fighting. The end of Italy's colonial empire pointed the way to new developments. Ethiopia regained its independence and received the former Italian colony of Eritrea, an acquisition that was to prove a very mixed blessing indeed. Italian Somaliland, soon expanded by British Somaliland, became an independent country, as did Libya.[16] These changes point toward a most significant effect of the war. The imperial ties which had bound most of Africa to European states had begun to be loosened as a result of World War I; World War II practically broke them. The defeat of France in 1940 had destroyed that country's prestige and nothing de Gaulle did in what was then French Equatorial Africa or subsequently in Algiers could erase the reality of prior French defeat. Since neither the Americans nor the British who had played the key role in freeing French Northwest Africa from Axis influence had any interest in taking over those areas for themselves, the key issue involved the restoration of French rule. In the short term this was possible, but in the long run it proved quite impossible. The immediate post-war revolt in Madagascar was crushed, but the war which began soon after in Algeria destroyed the French Fourth Republic without restoring French domination. New forms of association with France might be found; the French colonial empire in Africa was gone.

The impetus to decolonization was different for British than for French Africa, but the impetus was there all the same. The Egyptians chafed under the continued presence of British troops: with the Axis defeated, against whom were they to defend the Suez Canal? The majority of the Whites who ruled the Union of South Africa voted in 1948 for those who had opposed entrance into the war; they preferred to wage an internal war of sorts against the Black and Colored majority of the population. In any case, they would not look to London for guidance. The various British-controlled areas on the continent between Cairo and the Cape of Good Hope all moved toward independence in the immediate post-war years, the Gold Coast, renamed Ghana, being the first to attain that status fully in 1957. Substantial European settlements in Kenya and Southern Rhodesia complicated but could not halt the process which was, in any case, enormously facilitated by a changed perception of the imperial idea in the erstwhile colonial power itself.

Decolonization in Asia was both retarded and speeded up by the war. In Syria and Lebanon, the promise of independence made by both the British and the Free French at the beginning of the fighting there in June 1941 precluded any possible return to French rule. Whatever de Gaulle might imagine, there was no road back to the mandate system in the face of powerful nationalist movements, especially in Syria. In Iraq, the alignment of the al-Gaylani government with the Axis had provoked a temporary reassertion of direct British influence; but with the end of the war, that country would resume its troubled path to independence. The situation of Iran was in some ways similar even if different in detail. The British and Soviet occupation of 1941 had lost its rationale in 1945 very much the way Britain's role in Iraq now had no justification, and the British indeed withdrew. The Soviet Union at first was disinclined to honor its promise to do likewise, and it took massive outside pressure, primarily from the United States, to induce a withdrawal of the Soviet military from the northern part of the country. The opening of archives in Moscow may bring new light on this issue. In any case, the war years eventually left Iran with a massively improved internal transportation system as a result of the development of the supply route across the country for allied aid to Russia; it also left a new relationship with the United States that was to prove troublesome.

In the hope of restraining Arab hostility at a time of danger from Italy and Germany, the British government had dramatically restricted Jewish immigration into Palestine just before Germany's initiation of its mass murder campaign made that British mandate almost the only possible refuge for the prospective victims. Earlier, the British had divided the Palestine mandate into two separate units at the Jordan river and had entirely excluded Jews from about three-fourths of the area; now the remaining portion was also about to be closed to further immigrants if they were Jewish (Arab immigration being permitted at all times). The war was to have a whole series of complicated and inter-acting effects on this situation.

The Arab nationalist movement grew in strength during the war every-where, furthered by the obvious weakening of the British and French. The leader of the Arab nationalists in Palestine, however, had aligned himself with the Axis and had thereby discredited himself and left the local Arab population without a credible local spokesman. On the other hand, the full revelation of the extent of the slaughter of European Jews at the end of the war made at least some portions of world opinion more sympathetic to the plight of the survivors of the Holocaust, at the same time as those survivors were increasingly desperate to find a home in Palestine. Once the British government had decided to abandon its role in India, the whole rationale for maintaining British control of the northern approach to the Suez Canal lifeline to India—a key element in the original interest of London in the mandate for Palestine—had evaporated. Under these circumstances, the strife flaring up again inside the mandate looked to the British more trouble than holding the mandate was worth. They therefore left, and the United Nations decided to partition the area into two states, an Arab one and a Jewish one, with international status for Jerusalem.

While the representatives of the Jewish population were willing to accept this U.N. decision, the Arab countries were not and attacked both the newly proclaimed Jewish state and the international area of Jerusalem, anticipating a quick capture of both. That effort failed in the face of a successful Jewish defense which held the areas allotted to the new state by partition, portions of the land originally destined for the

Arab state, and a sliver of the Jerusalem area, most of the latter remaining under Arab control. A series of armistice agreements ended hostilities temporarily but did not lead to peace. The reason why these matters need to be recalled in connection with World War II is that the new Jewish state, called Israel, was so drastically affected by aspects of the war as were the surrounding newly independent Arab states.

The decision of many extreme Arab nationalists to side with Germany in the war undoubtedly influenced the U.N.'s approval of a Jewish state substantially larger than the minute one envisaged by the pre-war British Royal Commission, the Peel Commission. Some unit of that type was clearly going to emerge once the crisis which had led to its postponement had passed; in that sense the postponement has to be seen as similar to the delay in the independence of Iraq, Egypt, and Iran, but it would have been one far different from what actually came to develop.

The obvious desperation of the Jewish survivors of the Holocaust, and the pogroms in Poland which made the return home of those from that country impossible, rendered some new solution essential, and brought a substantial influx of Jewish immigrants the moment independence facilitated their entry into a state one of whose declared objectives was to be a haven for any Jew who wished to enter. In the long run, on the other hand, the enormous scale of the slaughter of Jews in Eastern Europe meant that the main reservoir from which prior Jewish immigrants had come was only a small fraction of what it had once been. Before long, Jewish refugees from the newly independent Arab countries in North Africa and the Middle East would therefore come to outnumber those from Europe. These and related issues would trouble the area for years.

In India, also, the war had both a retarding and an accelerating effect on decolonization. Without the war, Churchill would certainly not have become Prime Minister of the United Kingdom. His steadfast opposition to increased home rule for India in the 1930s had isolated him from all parties in England at the same time as it made Sir Samuel Hoare, who had pushed the Government of India Act of 1935 through the House of Commons over Churchill's last ditch resistance, the obvious next Viceroy. Hoare would presumably have played in the early or mid-1940s the role that Lord Louis Mountbatten performed a few years later.

That the war simultaneously retarded and speeded up the process of India's gaining independence can be seen when the retarding effect of Churchill's imperial vision is contrasted with the collapse of British power and prestige as a result of the exertions of war and the defeat at the hands of Japan in the early stages of fighting in Southeast Asia. The association of Mountbatten with the recovery of British military prestige in the region, because of his position as head of the South East Asia Command during the defeat of the Japanese invasion of India and the liberation of Burma, made him a logical choice for the post-war Labor government in London to charge him with the responsibility for arranging the independence of India.[17] The new British Prime Minister, Clement Attlee, had been Labor's representative on the British Statutory Commission, whose recommendations had once aroused Churchill's wrath. There was no turning back to the vanished days at the turn of the century where Churchill's imagination still lived.

The war had contributed to a horrendous famine in Bengal but had in general assisted the economic development of India. Vast numbers had served in the British Indian Army; many had acquired experience in new factories; the port facilities had been vastly improved. Tensions between the divergent religious communities in the sub-continent had, unfortunately, also risen and made the emergence of a single state impossible. Those opponents of Gandhi, like Subhas Chandra Bose, who had long argued that violence was an appropriate tool if used for the right ends by sincere people, merely contributed to the deadly rash of communal violence which accompanied the partition of India and would repeatedly stain the area's history thereafter. This would be true for all four, eventually five, states which emerged out of the British empire in southern Asia: India, Pakistan, Burma, Ceylon (Sri Lanka), and eventually Bangladesh.

Similar processes applied to Southeast Asia. The Philippines were the most obvious example of the mixture of delay and speeding up in decolonization as a result of the war. The United States had decided to leave before the war; independence was to come in 1944 and the last American bases were to be given up in 1946. The Japanese invasion delayed the former and concern over Soviet power in the Pacific delayed the latter deadline. But there was never any doubt that the islands would be independent. The destruction of war, the fighting of so many Filipinos alongside American forces, and the new defense agreements meant that independence would be accompanied by vastly greater American financial aid to the new state than could otherwise have been anticipated.

In the British and Dutch possessions of Southeast Asia the tides of nationalism had been accentuated by the war at the same time as the prestige of the colonial powers Britain and the Netherlands had been shattered. It took several years for the various areas on the continent and in the islands to secure their independence, but the process was irreversible, and in the case of the former Netherlands East Indies vigorously pushed by the United States. That country, with President Roosevelt's personally urging such a policy, had originally objected to a return of the French to their former control of French Indo-China. The American secret service in the field, the OSS, had worked with and assisted the Vietnamese nationalists under Ho Chi-minh as these fought the Japanese. The planning for the final operation of the Pacific War, the invasion of the Japanese home island of Honshu in the spring of 1946, was accordingly deliberately designed to include those two French divisions which de Gaulle's government had originally hoped to send to Indo-China. But in the face of its assessment of the situation in post-war Europe, the United States changed its policy from opposition to support of the reestablishment of the French colonial position; a reversal that was to have immense consequences.

The most dramatic decolonization took place in the colonial empire Japan had accumulated. The attempt to expand that empire by new seizures beginning in 1931 had failed. Not only were the remaining conquests of the 1930s and 1940s (including Thailand) freed of the Japanese presence, but the portions of the empire acquired earlier were now stripped from Japan as the Allies had promised at the Cairo Conference. Formosa was to be returned to China, and Korea was to regain its independence though after an intermediate period of American and Russian military occupation. When that occupation ended, two states emerged but certainly neither of them would again be ruled from Tokyo. Japan also lost the islands in the Pacific acquired from Germany after World War I, with these passing through American trusteeship into independence or commonwealth status, and the southern half of the island of Sakhalin and the Kurile Islands, which had been taken from Russia at the end of the Russo-Japanese War. When they occupied the Kuriles, the Soviets also seized some small islands off the shore of Hokkaido which had been Japanese for centuries; whatever might have been the military advantages derived from this step, the political repercussions were to plague Russo-Japanese relations for decades.

Under the terms of a preliminary agreement reached at Yalta and a subsequent treaty between the Chinese Nationalist government and Moscow, the special facilities Japan had held at and near Port Arthur in Manchuria went to the Soviet Union, not China; but after some years were retroceded to China anyway. The area which had been the focus of international dispute in East Asia since the end of the nineteenth century, Manchuria, was returned to Chinese control where it was to remain. Ironically, the decade and a half of Japanese occupation had brought a demographic revolution in this huge territory: for the first time the massive influx of Chinese workers into the factories and farms of the region had made it predominantly Chinese rather than Manchu in population. The industrial facilities in Manchuria were stripped and carried off by the Russians, who claimed them as Japanese property; the population, except for the Japanese immigrants, remained.[18]

The surrender of the Japanese at a time when their troops were still in occupation of vast stretches of China, including many of its most important cities, led to a race between the Chinese Nationalists and Communists to claim both the territory and the surrendered Japanese weapons. Although very greatly assisted by the United States in this process, the Nationalists proceeded very quickly to throw away their advantage. Their confiscation of economic assets in the liberated areas and establishment of an exchange rate from the occupation to their own currency which wiped out savings turned the business interests in these areas against them.[19] The failure in the latter years of the war to engage in serious fighting against the Japanese left the Nationalist armies demoralized when now—after the war was supposed to be over—they were required to fight once again. Within a short time, mainland China came under the control of the Communists who would rule it for decades in, first, uneasy alliance with the Soviet Union, and then in equally uneasy enmity to that power. Chiang was left with Formosa (Taiwan), the area restored to China fifty years after its loss to Japan. One of the more preposterous excuses advanced by Japanese expansionists for their course of action had been that of extirpating the danger of Communism from East Asia; they had instead played a major role in destroying the Chinese Nationalists and turning the world's most populous country to Communist rule.

Japan itself, stripped of its colonial empire and with its major cities largely destroyed, was in a desperate condition. The whole country was occupied by Allied troops, most of it by American soldiers, the western portion of Honshu and the island of Shikoku by the British Commonwealth Occupation Force. There were, however, mitigating factors which contributed to the country's recovery. Unlike Germany and Italy, the home islands of Japan had not been fought over mile by mile; the surrender induced by the atomic bombs and Soviet entrance into the war meant that the process of destruction had not included ground fighting with its attendant destruction of small towns and facilities, to say nothing of the accompanying casualties. Similarly, the surrender at a time when the military still had over seven million men in uniform meant that these men would almost all return home rather than fight to the death, either in the far-flung territories where they had been holding out or in the home islands as had been their practice in the preceding years. The country to which they were repatriated was in dire straits, and many of them were now happy to secure menial jobs with the occupation forces in order to make a living—I recall sharing my lunch with some of them.

But they had survived along with the energies and skills they brought back with them.

Of additional significance was the fact that Japan, unlike Germany, was not divided into occupation zones which were sealed off from each other. The central administration continued to operate under supposedly Allied but in reality American supervision; and a restructuring of the society by extensive land reform, the development of free labor unions, the extension of political rights to women, and the establishment of a parliamentary democracy far more broadly based than the one Japan had tried in the 1920s, provided the basis for a relatively quick and massive recovery. That recovery was undoubtedly aided by the economic stimulus provided by the Korean War from 1950-53, but it had already started well before then. Japan was on the political and economic road to recovery; only the unwillingness to deal honestly with the darker elements in its own past continued—and continues—to hold it back.

The United States had been propelled into the war by countries intent on fighting against the power which had made the most elaborate efforts to remove itself from the power plays of the international scene. The war saw the United States change in its attitude toward the world in two closely inter-related ways. On the one hand the dramatic way in which the country was drawn in, the attack on Pearl Harbor, showed the American people in a way nothing else could have that their preference for stopping the world and getting off was simply not a feasible policy line. "Don't shoot until you see the whites of their eyes" may well have been sound advice at a time of limited home industry and resources as well as inaccurate weapons; it made no sense in an era of long-distance planes. Concern over any possible new surprise attack, very much like Soviet concern about any new surprise invasion, dominated thinking about defense policy in post-war America, but perhaps more important was the general recognition by much of the population that an involvement in international affairs was an essential part of any sensible policy. Possible dangers had to be met by policies designed to engage them at a distance, preferably preventing them from becoming dangerous in the first place.

This broad turn in public sentiment was both directed and assisted by a conscious effort on the part of the administration to avoid what were believed to have been errors made in 1918-20 and to anchor the new international policy of the country firmly in both political parties and in the population at large. It was no coincidence that the Roosevelt administration insisted that the preparatory conference for the United Nations Organization, the organizing meeting for it, and its headquarters once it was established, should all be located in the United States.

Although President Roosevelt lived only to see the first one of these three events, he was clearly trying to get the American people to think of the United Nations as something essential to them, not just to others, and to accustom them to a new role in the world. The details of that role were left to his successors, and they were to find the American people even more willing to follow new concepts than Roosevelt himself had thought likely.

If the most conspicuous effect of the war on the United States was its impact on the nation's position in international affairs, there were also major internal changes. The slow economic recovery from the great depression was very much speeded up by the rearmament and later the war programs of the country. The placing of numerous training facilities and new factories in the south and the west played a major role in rearranging the internal economic and demographic picture of the country. The role of Alaska and Hawaii during hostilities contributed to their subsequent admission as states into the union. New opportunities for women and for Blacks contributed substantially to the development of the later movements for equal rights and opportunities in American society. The 1946 election saw the Republicans regaining control of the Congress after years of Democratic control; but there is surely significance in the fact that while the Republican candidate for President in the wartime 1944 election had promised to replace the female Secretary of Labor with a man, the next Republican President appointed as the first woman to serve in a Republican Cabinet the former head of the Women's Army Corps (WAC).[20] As usual, Blacks had to stand at the end of the line, but in that regard, too, the first efforts at legal procedures to establish fair employment practices during and right after the war pointed in new directions.

Those few countries which had remained neutral throughout the conflict were not, thereby, exempt from the changes of the times. Nowhere was this more obvious than in the process of decolonization. Spain and Portugal held on to their colonial possessions for years, but the dissolution of the Italian, Japanese, British, French, Dutch, Belgian and United States colonial empires was not without effect on those of the two Iberian states. Portuguese Timor had been occupied by the Japanese during conflict; it was seized by the Indonesian state which emerged from the Dutch colonial empire very much the way the Portuguese colony of Goa was seized by newly independent India. In both cases, the local population was by no means happy with its new masters. In the far larger colonial empires of Spain and Portugal in Africa, the tides of independence could not be halted at the borders which the Europeans had arbitrarily imposed on that continent.

The economies of all the neutrals had been very substantially affected by the war as well, and this, and their eventually being drawn into the United Nations Organization, was to make them parts of the world scene from which they had tried so hard to remain aloof.

The military developments of the war left their own special heritage. Enormous quantities of unexploded bombs and shells, like those left over from the battles of the previous world war, killed and maimed people for decades, while some areas had to be kept closed off because of the enormous danger of such explosives. To this danger was now added the effect of radiation from the two atomic bombs and from the various tests and processes associated with their prior and subsequent development. This new type of weapon posed an extraordinary challenge; although the United States made only tiny numbers of them for years and others were barely beginning to do so, here was a truly revolutionary development in warfare.[21]

Even if the development of science and technology in this field eventually led to weapons which were as much more destructive than the ones used in 1945 as those were compared to the largest conventional bombs of that time, for the vast majority of people the bomb dropped on Hiroshima became the symbol and the standard of measurement for a new era of potentially total destruction. The arms race of the post-war years was dominated not only by this innovation of the war but by its combination with the other most radical departure from the weapons systems of previous wars: the ballistic missile. This weapon, introduced in the form of the A-4 or V-2 by the Germans, pointed the way to the long-range and eventually inter-continental ballistic missile with a nuclear warhead. The possibility of the use of such weapons reinforced the sense of danger to all on the one hand, and the necessity for extreme caution by the major powers on the other.

Other technological developments of the war had equally significant, even if not quite so dramatic, implications for the post-war world. The advance of radar technology had peacetime as well as military applications; without it the growth of international mass transport by scheduled airplanes would be almost inconceivable. The jet airplane, which would have been built anyway but surely considerably later, altered not only the nature of any future war in the air but also the civilian air travel system which benefited from radar. The first computers in the world had been built to assist in the code-breaking activities of the Allies; their successors became ever smaller and simultaneously more powerful and were increasingly utilized for an endless array of civilian purposes. New drugs and medical procedures were applied to peacetime as they had been used in wartime applications.

A host of other advances in weapons, discussed in Chapter 10, had contributed to making this the most deadly war ever, and continued development of at least some of them would reinforce their potential impact on any conflict thereafter. In addition, new operational doctrines reshaped the nature of war. The armored thrust on land, first applied by the Germans successfully in the West in May 1940, came to be characteristic of first the Red Army and later the forces of the Western Allies. At sea, also, operational doctrine changed. In part because of the Pearl Harbor attack, the United States navy found itself forced to rely far more heavily than anticipated on aircraft carriers. This was to prove a blessing in extraordinarily effective disguise; the American navy hereafter led the world in the large-scale and effective employment of aircraft carriers, sometimes in great numbers, with the traditional mainstay of all navies, the ship-of-the-line, by this time the battleship, relegated effectively to a subordinate role. When this development is combined with the appearance at the end of the war of the very first true submarines, that is ships which actually remained under water instead of merely being capable of submerging briefly, the basic contours of naval warfare had clearly changed.

Whatever the nature of changes in weapons, the war had certainly not altered the fundamental fact that it was human beings, soldiers and their leaders, who made war. It had been especially difficult for the British and Americans to turn their young men into effective soldiers. The repudiation of war as an enterprise, which had reached major dimensions in both countries, made it extremely hard to remake civilians into warriors capable of coping with the rigors of modern war, and fighting the soldiers of countries which had for decades glorified the profession of arms instead of deprecating it.

The two democracies had operated under two additional handicaps in this endeavor. In the first place, both had to create large citizen armies under officers who were for the most part essentially civilians rather than professional soldiers themselves, and who had to fight armies which had acquired prior experience on the battlefield. Secondly, both had to employ a far higher proportion of their available manpower for skilled positions in the navy, in large air forces, and in the logistical structure required by the need to fight campaigns at enormous distances from home. Such manpower allocations made it far more difficult to develop battle-worthy infantry than it was for the Germans or the Japanese. In spite of these obstacles, the Western Allies were successful, assisted by the massive use of fire-power to support their infantry. As the fighting in North Africa and Italy, Burma and Northern Europe showed, after a difficult start, British and British Indian armies could fight effectively;

from Guadalcanal to Sicily, from Bastogne to Okinawa, the Americans demonstrated the same thing. And as the Germans had found out in the first days of fighting in the East, the Russian soldier could do so too. If the Chinese were ineffective in the last stages of the war, this was due primarily to wretched leadership; they had shown on many earlier occasions that they could be turned into highly effective fighting men.

The human element was critical not only in the ranks but in leadership positions. The type of warfare which characterized World War II called for a kind of military leadership which combined the traditional military virtues of decisiveness, courage, an eye for terrain, a sense of the capabilities of one's own and the enemy's forces, and a fair portion of luck with some new qualities which were apparently harder to come by. It was essential for those in command to develop an appreciation for and understanding of the best way to combine different types of weapons: infantry and armor, artillery and airpower. The Germans had some generals who came to be rather good at this, and the Red Army by 1942 had a substantial number who came to be superb at it, especially the combining of high quality armor and massed artillery with an infantry that could not be kept to a very high standard because of earlier huge losses.

The Japanese made up with determination what their leadership frequently lacked in skill; it was only in the final stages of the war that they began to realize that suicide charges by officers wielding sabres and men carrying bayonets were not nearly as effective as a carefully drawn out holding operation from cover. With few exceptions, their handling of combined arms operations did not measure up to the standards of other armies, and their naval commanders, however technically skilled and brave, all too often succumbed to Yamamoto's penchant for extremely complicated plans which were then at times abandoned prematurely. Perhaps more than any other belligerent, they had been hampered by an almost total failure of coordination between army and navy; all armed forces had inter-service rivalries to spare, but the Japanese carried the practice to extraordinary length. They also appear to have been handicapped by the periodic deliberate misleading of higher headquarters by fabricated reports of victories; there is, for example, no known parallel to the imaginary destruction of Admiral Halsey's naval force in the Formosa air battle of 1944 with the resulting complete misleading of Japanese headquarters.[22]

Although a good case can be made for the British military leaders having been extraordinarily slow learners, they did learn. In the latter stages of the war, British forces were increasingly commanded by men of great ability and effectiveness. The same thing proved true of the Americans, who fortunately learned very much more quickly. Like all armed forces, the American ones had to relieve generals and admirals on occasion, and such actions generally led to considerable recriminations afterwards, but this was hardly a new development in war. What was new was that the war called for still further qualities in the highest levels of command, qualities that proved scarce.

In a global war of great complexity, personal relationships at the top were of even greater importance than usual; and, in addition, at least a few of the highest commanders had to acquire the ability to work with allies and to understand global relationships.

In all the forces, able commanders developed, if they did not already have, the skills needed to inspire and work with others.[23] Some, like German Field Marshal von Kesselring, were particularly abrasive; some like Field Marshal Montgomery, General Patton, and General MacArthur, were essentially egomaniacs; some had more pleasant qualities matched with firmness that made them especially good leaders: Admiral Nimitz, Generals Eisenhower, Bradley, Krueger, and Eichelberger; some inspired respect by the obvious force of their personalities and intellect: Field Marshal Brooke and General Slim, to mention two examples. What was most obviously lacking among both German and Japanese leaders were the two other qualities which the war called for: an ability to work with allies and a broad, global perspective.

With very few exceptions, German generals were simply not capable of working with the leaders of the countries allied with them. Feeling certain of their own superiority and the inferiority of all others, they showed these attitudes and thus made real cooperation practically impossible. The Japanese military leaders were, if anything, even more supercilious in their treatment of the military units recruited by them in the occupied areas of South and Southeast Asia. Furthermore, with very few exceptions, neither German nor Japanese leaders in either the military or naval sphere had much of a sense of the global inter-relationships of a global conflict. The admirals were, on the whole, less blinkered than the generals, but no individuals with broader vision could be found in either country's leadership. What capabilities in either of these fields might have existed among the higher commanders of the Red Army and the Red Navy were so inhibited by the restraints imposed by Stalin on all in the country, and by the fact that the Soviet Union alone among major belligerents fought on only one front at a time, that it is impossible to tell. It was therefore among British and American commanders that one must look for these qualities.

Some of the higher commanders of the Western Allies were quite incapable of working effectively with Allied military leaders and staffs; Montgomery on the British and MacArthur on the American side are striking examples of this. But there were many who developed if they did not already have quite considerable abilities in this regard. Field Marshal Alexander, General Ismay and Air Marshal Tedder, and Admirals Ramsay and Mountbatten among the British, and Generals Eisenhower, Bedell Smith, Arnold, and Devers among the Americans obviously had this quality. These were practically invariably personal characteristics, though they were at times, especially after the war, alleged to be related to national rivalries. But Montgomery was no more British than Tedder, and Patton was no more American than Smith. Personal qualities and characteristics still counted in the most mechanized of wars.

Roosevelt and Churchill both had a sense of the war as a global one. The "Europe First" strategy which they adopted, and to which they held, certainly made good sense. And Roosevelt, as Eric Larrabee has pointed out, was particularly thoughtful and successful in picking the right men for the top posts.[24] At least some of their higher military leaders also attained a truly global perception of the war. Field Marshal Brooke had a measure of this, and in spite of his endless criticism of Eisenhower, eventually entrusted some favorable comments on him to his diary.[25] Even more than Eisenhower, Marshall and Arnold had a global view of the war. It is surely worth noting that Arnold would entitle his memoirs *Global Mission*,[26] and that Marshall subsequently saw his name attached to the plan for Europe's economic recovery.

This points to one of the most important if rarely discussed effects of the war. Whatever the destruction and the dangers, whatever the new challenges and problems, constructive individuals with a combination of insight and enterprise were entirely capable of coping with them. The enormous damage left behind by the years of conflict looked at first beyond the capacity of humans to repair, but in the years after 1945, the European continent, most affected by the damage, emerged into the most prosperous era in its history. The new weapons suggested the possibility of eliminating life from the planet, but the decades after the war became the longest period of European peace since the introduction of the modern state system half a millennium earlier. The massive migrations of wretched refugees, "displaced persons" as they were officially called, came to contribute their energies and their talents toward the flowering of those countries in which they found refuge; as so often before in history—if rarely on such a huge scale—it turned out that the most important possession of human beings was what they carried between their ears, and that could not be taken from them as long as they remained alive.

The years of seemingly endless warfare had shown all too clearly the capabilities of individuals for harming one another, for devising new methods of destruction, and for harnessing the power of society and nature for military purposes. But humans could also learn from prior mistakes and utilize their talents for reconstruction and for the creation of international mechanisms to preserve the peace. The establishment of cooperative arrangements for the rebuilding of a shattered Europe was limited to the continent's western portion by the creation of a new Soviet empire in the very years that the old empires of the Western European states were being broken up, but there was no guarantee that the new Soviet and the old Russian empire would not eventually reach the same end, even if by a different path.

Already in the anti-German resistance movements during the years of occupation, there had been considerable informal discussion of the possibility of new arrangements in the future which would deemphasize the nation state and create in all or parts of Europe some type of structure which might embrace them all and eliminate or at least greatly attenuate conflict between them. In the years after 1945, the impetus toward European unification would continue, even if periodically interrupted. Greater success was attained earlier in the economic and then in the military sphere with political unity lagging far behind; but the impetus itself remained.

The vast dimensions of World War II certainly demonstrated the capacity of human beings for destroying each other and themselves, but in a way they also provide a clue to the enormous potential for organizing constructive programs and policies to which the energies of humanity might be harnessed. The new weapons of mass destruction not only brought the threat of unlimited disaster but inspired extreme caution. They could not preclude the possibility of miscalculation, but they certainly created an enormous incentive for avoiding catastrophe. It had become all too obvious that another world war would be the last. A combination of care and luck, inventiveness and insight might enable humanity to harness its capacities for constructive purposes. The great conflagration stood as a warning for all.

BIBLIOGRAPHIC ESSAY

No attempt will be made here either to list all the works cited in the text or to provide a detailed bibliography of World War II. All books and articles referred to in the footnotes and endnotes have been provided with full citations at their first mention in the endnotes; the purpose of this essay is to suggest to the interested reader a highly selective list of books and articles, including some utilized but not cited in this book, which appear to me to be of special note. The personal element in this selection is unavoidable. The existing literature is so vast, and is in my judgement of such greatly varied quality, that it makes more sense to offer suggestions and evaluations based on extensive acquaintance instead of trying to be exhaustive—something a printout from a computerized catalog can do far better. This essay begins with a section on bibliographies, for the benefit of those who wish to start with a broader set of references, and it contains many works which include bibliographies themselves, bibliographies which are in many cases very extensive indeed. Although the emphasis here will be on books and articles in English, there are subjects on which the most important literature is in other languages, primarily German, French, and Italian, so that some of these are included.

Just as it seems to me to make little sense to append a complete list of the works used in this book's preparation, so I do not believe the reader will be aided by a list of archival folders consulted. Whenever a document from an archive is cited in the text, the reference provided has deliberately been made sufficiently specific to enable anyone either desirous of checking my interpretation or wishing to pursue further research to locate the original. At the end of this essay, therefore, there is a short discussion of major archives which have proved helpful, together with an even shorter list of works which describe archives and provide information on their status and organization. That has also appeared to be the appropriate place to comment on archival materials either still closed or only now being opened up and which may offer new perspectives on the war as they are made accessible and used.

The best place to begin any search is Janet Ziegler, *World War II: Works in English, 1945–65* (Stanford, Calif.: Hoover Institution Press, 1971). Arthur L. Funk has prepared sequels to this book, the first covering the years 1965–75 issued by the World War II Studies Association (formerly the American Committee on the History of the Second World War), and the second, entitled *The Second World War: A Select*

Bibliography of Books in English Since 1975, published in 1985 by Regina Books of Claremont, California. Current bibliographic coverage is in the "Newsletter" of the World War II Studies Association. For more extensive listings, including items in languages other than English, the *Jahresbibliographie* issued annually by the Bibliothek für Zeitgeschichte (Library for Contemporary History) in Stuttgart and the *Bibliographie* of the *Vierteljahrshefte für Zeitgeschichte* are most helpful. The main French journal in the field, the *Revue d'histoire de la deuxième guerre mondiale*, has changed not only its title but its coverage and emphasis.

There are specialized bibliographies on aspects of the war and on specific theaters. Myron J. Smith has prepared a considerable number of very good ones; there is also a fine one by John J. Sbrega, *The War against Japan: A Bibliography* (New York: Garland, 1989). On the Holocaust, see Jacob Robinson and Philip Friedman, *Guide to Jewish History under Nazi Impact* (New York: YIVO, 1960), and Jacob Robinson and Mrs. Philip Friedman, *The Holocaust and After: Sources and Literature in English* (Jerusalem: Israel Universities Press, 1973). On war crimes and trials, Norman E. Tutorow, *War Crimes, War Criminals, and War Crimes Trials: An Annotated Bibliography and Source Book* (New York: Greenwood Press, 1986), is most comprehensive. For the diplomatic origins of the Cold War, Joseph L. Black, *Origins, Evolution, and Nature of the Cold War: An Annotated Bibliographic Guide* (Santa Barbara, Calif.: ABC-Clio, 1986), is a good place to start. Additional bibliographies of a specialized kind are listed by Ziegler and Funk.

For single-volume histories of the war, Martha Byrd's *A World in Flames: A History of World War II* (New York: Atheneum, 1970, reprinted by Univ. of Alabama Press) for the military side is complemented on the diplomatic side by John L. Snell, *Illusion and Necessity: The Diplomacy of Global War 1939–1945* (Boston: Houghton Mifflin, 1963). There is a good German one-volume account in Lothar Gruchmann, *Der Zweite Weltkrieg: Kriegführung und Politik* (Munich: Deutscher Taschenbuch Verlag, 1967). The best collection of maps remains that in volume 2 of Vincent J. Esposito (ed.), *The West Point Atlas of American Wars* (New York: Praeger, 1959), which, in spite of the apparent limitation in its title, covers all fronts and sides of World War II. An excellent general survey of the European aspect of the war is in Gordon Wright, *The Ordeal of Total War, 1939–1945* (New York: Harper & Row, 1968); there is nothing like it for the war in East Asia. F. C. Jones, *Japan's New Order in East Asia: Its Rise and Fall, 1937–1945* (London: Oxford Univ. Press, 1954), and Ienaga Saburo, *The Pacific War, 1931–1945* (New York: Pantheon Books, 1978), are helpful. John Costello, *The Pacific War* (New York: Quill, 1982), and Ronald H. Spector, *Eagle against the Sun: The American War with Japan* (New York: Free Press, 1985), cover the conflict in the Pacific; Christopher Thorne, *Allies of a Kind: The United States, Britain, and the War against Japan, 1941–1945* (New York: Oxford Univ. Press, 1978), emphasizes the diplomatic and political side at the expense of the conduct of operations and with vast emphasis on the tensions between the two Western Powers.

Alan S. Milward, *War, Economy and Society, 1939–1945* (Berkeley, Calif.: Univ. of Calif. Press, 1977) reviews the social and economic aspects of the war as a whole; Mark Harrison, "Resource Mobilization for World War II: The U.S.A., U.K., U.S.S.R., and Germany, 1938–1945," *Economic History Review*, 2d series, 41 (1988), 171–92, is an excellent introduction to its subject. John F. Kreis, *Air Warfare and*

Air Base Defense, 1914–1973 (Washington: GPO, 1988), is even more comprehensive than its title. Of the books of pictures and documents, Hans-Adolf Jacobsen and Hans Dollinger, *Der Zweite Weltkrieg in Bildern und Dokumenten*, 3 vols. (Wiesbaden: Löwit, 1963), remains the best.

There are several large collections of published documents on the war. The official American series, *Foreign Relations of the United States*, has appeared for all the war years; the volumes on the wartime conferences are especially significant. The Eisenhower papers have been issued in a very well edited set, Alfred D. Chandler, Jr. (ed.), *The Papers of Dwight David Eisenhower: The War Years*, 5 vols. (Baltimore: Johns Hopkins Press, 1970); those of General Marshall, Larry I. Bland (ed.), *The Papers of George Catlett Marshall*, are still being published (Baltimore: Johns Hopkins Press). *Pearl Harbor Attack: Hearings before the Joint Committee on the Investigation of the Pearl Harbor Attack* was originally published in 39 parts as a Congressional document in 1946; like the Nürnberg trial set, it has been reprinted with an introduction of mine by AMS Press.

The British publication of diplomatic documents stops in 1939 and only picks up again with 1945. For the war years, there are the published *Telegrams and Memoranda of the War Cabinet* issued by the Public Record Office, the *Weekly Political Intelligence Summaries* of the Foreign Office, published by Kraus International, and the documents appended to Churchill's memoirs, Winston S. Churchill, *The Second World War*, 6 vols. (Boston: Houghton Mifflin, 1948–53).

Extensive documentation from German and Japanese archives is in the sets on the great international post-war trials: *Trial of the Major War Criminals before the International Military Tribunal* (Nürnberg) and *Proceedings of the International Military Tribunal for the Far East* (Tokyo). There is extensive coverage of German diplomacy, especially for the first years of the war, in the originally Allied, subsequently joint, and eventually German publication of documents primarily from the German Foreign Ministry archives. The English language edition, *Documents on German Foreign Policy, 1918–1945*, goes up only to December 1941; the German edition, *Akten zur deutschen auswärtigen Politik 1918–1945*, covers the rest of the war and is the version cited in this book.

On the German side, there are also the published diaries of Franz Halder, the Chief of Staff of the army from 1938 to 1942, edited by Hans-Adolf Jacobsen, *Generaloberst Halder, Kriegstagebuch*, 3 vols. (Stuttgart: Kohlhammer, 1962–64), and several translations into English, as well as of the high command of the armed forces, the *Kriegstagebuch des Oberkommandos der Wehrmacht, 1940–1945*, 4 vols. in 7 parts and 2 supplements (Frankfurt/M: Bernard & Graefe, 1961–65); and the surviving portions of the texts of Hitler's situation conferences edited by Helmut Heiber, *Hitlers Lagebesprechungen: Die Protokollfragmente seiner militärischen Konferenzen 1942–1945* (Stuttgart: Deutsche Verlags-Anstalt, 1962), of which portions have been published in English by Felix Gilbert, *Hitler Directs His War* (New York: Oxford Univ. Press, 1950). The war diary of the high command of the German navy, the Kriegstagebuch der Seekriegsleitung, Teil A, is currently being published (Herford: Mittler, 1988–), but the volumes are cited in this book from the originals. There is a useful collection of Hitler's speeches in Max Domarus (ed.), *Hitler: Reden und Proklamationen, 1932–1945*, 2 vols. (Neustadt a.d. Aisch: Verlagsdruckerei Schmidt, 1962) of which an English translation is to appear shortly.

A collection of translated intercepts of Japanese diplomatic documents from 1941 was issued in 1977 by the U.S. Department of Defense: *The "Magic" Background of Pearl Harbor*, 5 vols. in 8 parts, but there is no such publication for the period from December 1941 to the end of the war (see the discussion below for the U.S. National Archives). The Italian government has published a large collection of its diplomatic documents from September 1939 to July 1943, and the Portuguese collection also covers the war years; though of great interest, these are not likely to be used by many. The major publication of French documents is that pertaining to the armistice negotiations with the Germans: *La Délégation française auprès de la Commission allemande d'armistice: Recueil de Documents*. The large and excellent edition of Hungarian documents for the war years is fortunately provided with German language summaries of each document: *Diplomáciai iratok külpolitikájáhaz 1939–1945*. The two major series of documents from and relating to the Vatican are described very well in Victor Conzemius, "Le Saint-Siège et la deuxième guerre mondiale: deux éditions de sources," *Revue d'histoire de la deuxième guerre mondiale*, No. 128 (1982), 71–94.

One of the very best, but unfortunately least used, forms of coverage of the war is the large number of official histories. Written in many cases by highly trained scholars with early and almost unlimited access to the archives, these are frequently of extremely high quality. The opportunity their authors had to consult individuals who had held key positions no doubt at times led to the smoothing over of criticisms, but it also helped illuminate issues and events which might otherwise have remained obscure. This is particularly true of the British and American series.

The British official history is divided into several series: *Grand Strategy, The Mediterranean and Middle East, The War Against Japan, Victory in the West, The War at Sea, The Strategic Air Offensive, Civil Affairs and Military Government*, individual volumes on the campaigns in Norway, in the West in 1940, and on the defense of the United Kingdom; there is a series covering the civilian side including such important topics as the blockade, supplies from North America, and the food, manpower, and financial situation; and a medical series as well. Of special interest is a 5–volume set on *British Foreign Policy in the Second World War* by Sir Llewellyn Woodward. Extraordinarily useful in spite of some limitations is the recently completed series of Francis H. Hinsley, *British Intelligence in the Second World War*, 5 vols. in 6 parts (New York: Cambridge Univ. Press, 1979–90). Early volumes of the British official history were not provided with footnotes to the records—a fraud on libraries and scholars if there ever was one because they must now purchase reprint volumes which include the notes!

The American series are separated by service. The distinguished historian Samuel Eliot Morison wrote in large part and coordinated the balance of the 15–volume *History of United States Naval Operations in World War II* (Boston: Little, Brown, 1947–62). This most important—and most readable—set includes extensive coverage of Marine Corps operations, but these are also covered by a preliminary set, of which some volumes are cited in the body of this book, and a more detailed one: *History of U.S. Marine Corps Operations in World War II*. The best introduction, however, remains Jeter A. Iseley and Philip A. Crowl, *The U.S. Marines and Amphibious War: Its Theory and Practice in the Pacific* (Princeton, N.J.: Princeton Univ. Press, 1951). The American air force had its 7– volume official history prepared under the supervision of Wesley F. Craven and James L. Cate, *The Army Air Forces in*

World War II (Chicago: Univ. of Chicago Press, 1948–58; reprinted by the Office of Air Force History in 1983). The numerous reports of the United States Strategic Bombing Survey added enormous quantities of information on both the European and Pacific theaters, and some of them are cited in the text. These reports are also a mine of statistical and descriptive material on the economies of Germany and Japan.

The American army's *U.S. Army in World War II* set is made up of several series. That on *The War Department* includes essential works on planning, logistics, and the relationship with America's allies. There are series on each of the theaters as well as on each of the services; in addition, there are special studies on such subjects as women and Blacks in the army and rearming the French. The volumes, written with great care by very capable historians, are based not only on access to American archives but systematic even if preliminary work in German and Japanese records, and were provided with citations to the documents and bibliographic essays which are of enormous value to anyone wishing to pursue a specific topic further. Many of these books are cited in the text; the more I have worked with them myself, the more favorably I have been impressed by their quality.

The Soviet Union has published two sets of official history, and its successors are in the process of issuing a third. The problems of utilizing this material are best described in the works of Erickson and Ziemke, listed below, and it should be noted that the first two are available in German translation. Only the earlier of the Soviet sets has been translated into English and is available on film from Scholarly Resources; the volumes as a group are primarily of interest to the specialist. The sets published by the Canadian, Indian, Australian, New Zealand, and South African governments are helpful on specific campaigns, while those of Italy, China, Holland, Norway, and some others are not likely to be of interest or easy access to American and British readers. There is a most helpful introduction to the whole subject, with details on each program, in the important volume edited by Robin Higham, *Official Histories: Essays and Bibliographies from around the World* (Manhattan, Kans.: Kansas State Univ. Library, 1970).

The most significant recent development in this field has been the appearance of the first volumes of the series *Das Deutsche Reich und der Zweite Weltkrieg* being prepared by the Military History Research Office of the German Federal Republic. Five volumes and the first part of a sixth have appeared to date, and the rest may be expected during the next few years. These massive works have been written with great care and are based not only on available German records of the war but considerable utilization of the literature of the last half century; they are also being published in English translation by Oxford University Press under the title *Germany and the Second World War*.

On Germany's role in the war, by far the best work in English is Norman Rich's two volumes on *Hitler's War Aims* (New York: Norton, 1973–74). An especially careful analysis in German is Andreas Hillgruber, *Hitler Strategie: Politik und Kriegführung, 1940–1941* (Frankfurt/M: Bernard & Graefe, 1965 and later eds.). Briefer yet more comprehensive, but unfortunately not translated, is Jochen Thies's book on Hitler's objectives, *Architekt der Weltherrschaft: Die "Endziele" Hitlers* (Düsseldorf: Droste, 1976). Important source publications include the Goebbels diaries edited by Elke Fröhlich, *Die Tagebücher von Joseph Goebbels, Sämtliche Fragmente*, of which the part for 1924–41 has been published in four volumes and an index (Munich: Saur, 1987), and the rest is yet to appear; the conferences of Hitler with Armaments Minister Speer edited by Willi A. Boelcke, *Deutschlands Rüstung im Zweiten Weltkrieg: Hitlers Konferenzen mit Albert Speer 1942–1945* (Frankfurt/M: Athenaion, 1969), and the same editor's *Kriegspropaganda 1939–1941: Ministerkonferenzen im Reichspropagandaministerium* (Stuttgart: Deutsche Verlags-Anstalt, 1966); and the conferences of Hitler with his naval chief edited by Gerhard Wagner, *Lagevorträge des Oberbefehlshabers der Kriegsmarine vor Hitler 1939–1945* (Munich: Lehmanns, 1972), of which there are several English language editions, none of them entirely satisfactory. Also of major importance for an understanding of the German navy are the three volumes of Michael Salewski, *Die deutsche Seekriegsleitung, 1935–1945* (Frankfurt/M: Bernard & Graefe, 1970–75); Eberhard Rössler, *The U-Boat: The Evolution and Technical History of German Submarines*, trans. by Harold Erenberg (Annapolis, Md.: Naval Institute Press, 1981); and Günter Hessler, *The U-Boat War in the Atlantic, 1939–1945*, 3 vols. (London: HMSO, 1989 [but written right after the war]).

On the German air force, the best books are Williamson Murray, *Luftwaffe* (Baltimore: Nautical & Aviation Publishing Co. of America, 1985), and Horst Boog, *Die deutsche Luftwaffenführung 1935–1945: Führungsprobleme, Spitzengliederung, Generalstabsausbildung* (Stuttgart: Deutsche Verlags-Anstalt, 1982). The German army is dealt with in this essay in terms of the various campaigns; on the armed units of the SS the most recent comprehensive treatment is Bernd Wegner's *Hitlers politische Soldaten: Die Waffen-SS, 1933–1945* (Paderborn: Schöningh, 1982), recently translated as *The Waffen SS: Ideology, Organization and Function* (New York: Blackwell, 1990). Providing more insight into the German military than the endless and generally unreliable memoirs of German generals who claim credit for any battles won, blame Hitler for all battles lost, and display an astonishing degree of ignorance, actual or pretended, of much of what they were doing, is the very revealing study of Nazi terror within the military's own ranks: Manfred Messerschmidt and Fritz Wüllner, *Die Wehrmachtjustiz im Dritten Reich: Zerstörung einer Legende* (Baden-Baden: Nomos, 1987). Very important for Germany's gas warfare preparations is Rolf-Dieter Müller, "Die deutschen Gaskriegsvorbereitungen 1919–1945: Mit Giftgas zur Weltmacht?" *MGM* 21, No. 1 (1980), 25–54. On German propaganda and home front attitudes, excellent works are Robert E. Herzstein, *The War that Hitler Won: Goebbels and the Nazi Media Campaign* (New York: Paragon House, 1987), and Marlis Steinert, *Hitler's War and the Germans*, ed. and trans. by Thomas E.J. de Witt (Athens, Ohio: Ohio Univ. Press, 1977).

The ideological side of Germany's conduct of the war, other than the Holocaust and special aspects of the Eastern Front (both covered subsequently), are handled very well in Helmut Krausnick and Hans-Heinrich Wilhelm, *Die Truppe des Weltanschauungskrieges: Die Einsatzgruppen der Sicherheitspolizei und des SD, 1938–1942* (Stuttgart: Deutsche Verlags-Anstalt, 1981), and Ernst Klee, *"Euthanasie" im NS-Staat: Die "Vernichtung unwertes Lebens"* (Frankfurt/M: S. Fischer, 1983). A most thoughtful discussion of the role of the German Foreign Ministry is by Hans-Jürgen Döscher, *Das Auswärtige Amt im Dritten Reich: Diplomatie im Schatten der "Endlösung"* (Berlin: Siedler, 1987). The other side is well represented by David H. Kitterman, "Those Who Said 'No!': Germans Who Refused to Execute Civilians during World War II," *German Studies Review* 11 (1988), 241–54; but the most comprehensive treatment of this subject is Peter Hoffmann, *The History of the German Resistance 1933–1945* (London: Macdonald & Jane's, 1977).

Helpful for an understanding of the German economy during the war are Edward L. Homze, *Foreign Labor in Nazi Germany* (Princeton, N.J.: Princeton Univ. Press, 1967); Ulrich Herbert, *Fremdarbeiter: Politik und Praxis des "Ausländer-Einsatzes" in der Kriegswirtschaft des Dritten Reiches* (Berlin: Dietz, 1985); Ludolf Herbst, *Der Totale Krieg und die Ordnung der Wirtschaft* (Stuttgart: Deutsche Verlags-Anstalt, 1982); and Alfred C. Mierzejewski's superb study, *The Collapse of the German War Economy, 1944–1945: Allied Air Power and the German National Railway* (Chapel Hill, N.C.: Univ. of North Carolina Press, 1988).

The best introduction to the literature and issues of the Holocaust is Michael R. Marrus, *The Holocaust in History* (Hanover: N.H.: Univ. Press of New England, 1987). Excellent treatments of most major aspects and controversies may be found in the published papers of three sets of conferences: Henry Friedlander and Sybil Milton (eds.), *The Holocaust: Ideology, Bureaucracy, and Genocide* (Millwood, N.J.: Kraus, 1980); Peter Hayes (ed.), *Lessons and Legacies: The Meaning of the Holocaust in a Changing World* (Evanston, Ill.: Northwestern Univ. Press, 1991); and Jürgen Rohwer and Eberhard Jäckel (eds.), *Der Mord an den Juden im Zweiten Weltkrieg: Entschlussbildung und Verwirklichung* (Stuttgart: Deutsche Verlags-Anstalt, 1985). The very fine work of Raul Hilberg, *The Destruction of the European Jews* (Chicago: Quadrangle, 1961), has been revised, but one of the revisions is an abbreviated students' edition and the other one has been spread over three volumes, making it impossibly expensive. Very important are Richard Breitman, *The Architect of Genocide: Himmler and the Final Solution* (New York: Knopf, 1991), and the books and articles of Christopher Browning cited in the text. A disturbing but significant book is Ernst Klee et al.(eds.), *"Schöne Zeiten": Judenmord aus der Sicht der Täter und Gaffer* (Frankfurt/M: Fischer, 1988), now translated by Hugh R. Trevor-Roper as *"The Good Old Days": The Holocaust as Seen by Its Perpetrators and Bystanders* (New York: Free Press, 1991).

Many of the books dealing with German-occupied Europe are listed in the two volumes of Rich listed above. Two very significant works which must be added to his bibliography on Poland are Gerhard Eisenblätter, "Grundlinien der Politik des Reiches gegenüber dem Generalgouvernement 1939–1945" (Frankfurt/M, Phil. diss, 1969), and Czeslaw Madajzyk, *Die Okkupationspolitik des deutschen Imperialismus in Polen 1939–1945* (Berlin-East: Akademie Verlag, 1987), a revised version of the same author's 1970 book with extensive material from Polish as well as German archives.

On Britain in the war, the justly famous memoir-history of Winston Churchill has already been mentioned, though it is also necessary to recall that its composition was affected not only by Churchill's desire for self-justification but also by what he saw as the needs of partisan politics and possible future office holding at the time. The authorized biography by Martin Gilbert, volumes 6–8 (London: Heinemann; Boston: Houghton Mifflin, 1983–88), contains much supplementary material. All of Churchill's wartime speeches, including those in secret sessions of Parliament, may be found in Robert Rhodes James (ed.), *Winston S. Churchill: His Complete Speeches, 1897–1963* (New York: Bowker, 1974), vols. 6–7. Tuvia Ben-Moshe's article, "Winston Churchill and the 'Second Front': A Reappraisal," *JMH* 62 (1990), 503–38, is a fine discussion of a major controversy. Of great importance is David Dilks's edition of *The Diaries of Sir Alexander Cadogan, O.M., 1938–1945* (New York: Putnam's, 1972), which provides the insider's view of the permanent head of Britain's Foreign Office. The diaries of Field Marshal Lord Alanbrooke, Chief of the Imperial General Staff for most of the war, have been edited with extensive commentary by Sir Arthur Bryant as *The Turn of the Tide, and Triumph in the West* (Garden City, N.Y.: Doubleday, 1957–59). The text has, however, been seriously tampered with, and until a reliable edition is published, one must consult the original at the Liddell Hart Centre in London (see below). I must record my strong belief that one of the outstanding soldiers of this century and one of the architects of Allied victory has been badly served by an adoring editor's ill-advised "prettifying" of the record which has the long-term effect of calling attention to the very wrinkles and misjudgements concealed in that process. David Fraser's solid biography, *Alanbrooke* (New York: Atheneum, 1982), unfortunately follows too closely in Bryant's footsteps to make up for this.

The three volumes of Nigel Hamilton's authorized biography *Monty* contain very extensive extracts from the papers of Britain's best known general; General Lord Ismay's *The Memoirs of General Lord Ismay* (New York: Viking, 1960) may serve as an example of a large number of such works, in this case from the very center of the direction of war. The controversies of the British strategic bombing offensive may be approached through Max Hastings, *Bomber Command* (London: Pan Books, 1981); Norman Longmore, *The Bombers: The RAF Offensive against Germany 1939–1945* (London: Hutchinson, 1983); John Terraine, *A Time for Courage: The Royal Air Force in World War II* (New York: Macmillan, 1985); the spirited defense in the authorized biography, Dudley Saward, *"Bomber" Harris: The Story of Marshal of the Royal Air Force Sir Arthur Harris* (Garden City, N.Y.: Doubleday, 1985); and the 4–volume set in the official British history. Much insight into the workings of the British government and its direction of the war may be found in Brian L. Villa, *Unauthorized Action: Mountbatten and the Dieppe Raid* (Toronto: Oxford Univ. Press, 1989); the relations of London with various resistance forces are surveyed in David Stafford, *Britain and European Resistance: A Survey of the Special Operations Executive* (Toronto: Univ. of Toronto Press, 1980).

France and the German victory in the West are covered by Brian Bond, *France and Belgium, 1939–1940* (London: Davis-Poynter, 1975), and the key works of Hans-Adolf Jacobsen, *Fall Gelb: Der Kampf um den deutschen Operationsplan zur Westoffensive 1940* (Wiesbaden: Steiner, 1956), *Dokumente zur Vorgeschichte des Westfeldzuges 1939–1940* and *Dokumente zum Westfeldzug 1940* (Göttingen: Musterschmidt, 1956). Jeffrey A. Gunsberg, *Divided and Conquered: The French High Command and the Defeat of the West, 1940* (Westport, Conn.: Greenwood Press, 1979), tries to defend French strategy; Don W. Alexander, "Repercussions of the Breda Variant," *French Historical Studies* 8 (1974), 459–88, demolishes it rather effectively. Bertram M. Gordon, *Collaborationism in France during the Second World War* (Ithaca, N.Y.: Cornell Univ. Press, 1980); Robert O. Paxton, *Vichy France: Old Guard and New Order, 1940–1944* (New York: Columbia Univ. Press, 1972, 1982); and Eberhard Jäckel, *Frankreich in Hitlers Europa* (Stuttgart: Deutsche Verlags-Anstalt, 1966), seem to me to be the best introductions to the still troubled subject of occupation and collaboration. Eleanor M. Gates, *End of the Affair: The Collapse of the Anglo-French Alliance, 1939–*

1940 (Berkeley, Calif.: Univ. of California Press, 1981), offers a reasoned defense of French policy in 1940; R.T. Thomas provides an introduction to a complicated subject in *Britain and Vichy: The Dilemma of Anglo-French Relations 1940–42* (New York: St. Martin's, 1979).

There is now a series of outstandingly helpful biographies of French leaders: Marc Ferro, *Pétain* (Paris: Fayard, 1987); Hervé Coutau-Bégarie and Claude Huan, *Darlan* (Paris: Fayard, 1989); and Bernard Pujo, *Juin: Maréchal de France* (Paris: Albin Michel, 1988). On Charles de Gaulle, his own memoirs in their various editions (an English language one, *The War Memoirs* [New York: Viking, 1955]), seem to me still the best introduction.

The military operations in Scandinavia are well introduced by Earl F. Ziemke, *The German Northern Theater of Operations, 1940–1945* (Washington: GPO, 1960). The political side is covered in Hans-Dietrich Loock, *Quisling, Rosenberg und Terboven: Zur Vorgeschichte und Geschichte der nationalsozialistischen Revolution in Norwegen* (Stuttgart: Deutsche Verlags-Anstalt, 1970). A major work on German–Finnish relations is Gerd R. Ueberschär, *Hitler und Finnland 1939–1941: Die deutsch-finnischen Beziehungen während des Hitler–Stalin Paktes* (Wiesbaden: Steiner, 1978).

On Italy's role in the war and relations with its Axis partners by far the most helpful book is MacGregor Knox, *Mussolini Unleashed 1939–1941: Politics and Strategy in Fascist Italy's Last War* (Cambridge: Cambridge Univ. Press, 1982). The materials of Mussolini's Foreign Minister in Hugh Gibson (ed.), *The Ciano Diaries 1939–1943* (Garden City, N.Y.: Doubleday, 1946), and Malcolm Muggeridge (ed.), *Ciano's Diplomatic Papers* (London: Odhams, 1948), are both of great importance and make for fascinating reading; the challenges once made to the authenticity and contemporaneity of the diary have been largely refuted. Important for its discussion of key sources is A. Repagi, "Le Procès Graziani," *Revue d'histoire de la deuxième guerre mondiale*, No. 9 (Jan. 1953), 30–37. Two most interesting articles by James J. Sadkovich present a rather favorable view of Italy's military effort and attempt to correct distortions due to excessive reliance on materials from the German side: "Understanding Defeat: Reappraising Italy's Role in World War II," *JCH* 24 (1989), 27–61, and "Of Myths and Men: Rommel and the Italians in North Africa, 1940–1942," *International History Review* 13 (1991), 284–313.

Frederick W. Deakin, *The Brutal Friendship: Mussolini, Hitler, and the Fall of Italian Fascism* (New York: Harper & Row, 1962); Conrad F. Latour, *Südtirol und die Achse Berlin-Rom 1938–1945* (Stuttgart: Deutsche Verlags-Anstalt, 1962); and two major studies by Gerhard Schreiber, *Revisionismus und Weltmachtstreben: Marineführung und deutsch-italienische Beziehungen 1919–1945* (Stuttgart: Deutsche Verlags-Anstalt, 1978) and *Die italienischen Militärinternierten im deutschen Machtbereich 1943–1945* (Munich: Oldenbourg, 1990) are the most important works on Italy's relations with Germany. The country's dispute with the Germans over the enthusiasm of the latter for killing Jews is covered by Jonathan Steinberg, *All or Nothing: The Axis and the Holocaust 1941–1943* (London: Routledge, 1990), while Italy's exit from the war is covered by Josef Schröder, *Italiens Kriegsaustritt 1943* (Göttingen: Musterschmidt, 1969).

The fighting in the Italian peninsula remains covered best in the British and American official histories; there is a most helpful survey in Dominick Graham and Shelford Bidwell, *Tug of War: The Battle for Italy, 1943–1945* (New York: St. Martin's, 1986); and there is an especially fine description of the fighting as seen from the perspective of the New Zealand division in Geoffrey Cox, *The Race for Trieste* (London: Kimber, 1977). A good introduction to the Vatican's role may be found in Owen Chadwick, *Britain and the Vatican during the Second World War* (Cambridge: Cambridge Univ. Press, 1986).

On Spain's role in the war, Charles B. Burdick, *Germany's Military Strategy and Spain in World War II* (Syracuse: Univ. of Syracuse Press, 1968); Donald S. Detwiler, *Hitler, Franco und Gibraltar: Die Frage des spanischen Eintritts in den Zweiten Weltkrieg* (Wiesbaden: Steiner, 1962); Denis Smyth, *Diplomacy and Strategy of Survival: British Policy and Franco's Spain, 1940–1941* (Cambridge: Cambridge Univ. Press, 1986); and David W. Pike, "Franco and the Axis Stigma," *JCH* 17 (1982), 369–407, are particularly good. Important for its use of Spanish and Italian archives is Javier Tusell, *Franco y Mussolini: La política española durante la segunda guerre mundiale* (Barcelona: Planeta, 1985). Very new and different perspectives, drawn from German and Spanish archives, are in the 1991 North Carolina PhD dissertation of Norman J.W. Goda, "Germany and Northwest Africa in the Second World War: Politics and Strategy of Global Hegemony."

The fighting in the Mediterranean is excellently covered by the British and American official histories; in addition, there is an important book by Michael Howard, *The Mediterranean Strategy in the Second World War* (London: Weidenfeld & Nicolson, 1968). Essential for the central role of the question of Malta is Mariano Gabriele, *Operazione C 3: Malta* (Rome: Ufficio Storico Marina Militare, 1965), in the Italian official history; significant for an understanding of the role of signals intelligence is Alberto Santoni, *Ultra siegt im Mittelmeer* (Koblenz: Bernard & Graefe, 1985). Arthur L. Funk, *The Politics of Torch: The Allied Landings and the Algiers Putsch 1942* (Lawrence, Kans.: Univ. Press of Kansas, 1974), remains helpful; David Killingray and Richard Rathbone (eds.), *Africa and the Second World War* (New York: St. Martin's, 1986), provides a good introduction to the changes on the continent during the war; Douglas A. Farnie, *East and West of Suez: The Suez Canal in History, 1854–1956* (Oxford: Clarendon Press, 1969), is a most important book on a frequently ignored subject; and A.B. Gaunson, *The Anglo-French Collision in Lebanon and Syria, 1940–45* (London: Macmillan, 1986), supplements the official accounts of the fighting in Syria as well as covering the subsequent political problems.

It is astonishing that the fighting in Poland has not received the attention one might have expected. The second volume of the official German work deals with it, and there is a very extensive literature in Polish, but the best English language accounts remain Robert M. Kennedy's study for the U.S. army, *The German Campaign in Poland (1939)* (Washington: GPO, 1956), and Nicholas Bethell, *The War Hitler Won: The Fall of Poland, September 1939* (New York: Holt, Rinehart, & Winston, 1972).

Southeast Europe has been the subject of a vast literature. Broader issues are treated in Martin van Creveld, *Hitler's Strategy 1940–1941: The Balkan Clue* (London: Cambridge Univ. Press, 1973); Phyllis Auty and Richard Clogg (eds.), *British Policy towards Wartime Resistance in Yugoslavia and Greece* (London: Macmillan, 1975); Elizabeth Barker, *British Policy in Southeast Europe in the Second World War* (London: Macmillan, 1976); George Ránki, "Hitlers Verhandlungen mit osteuropäischen Staatsmännern, 1939–1944," in Klaus Hildebrand and Reiner Pommerin (eds.), *Deutsche Frage und europäisches Gleichgewicht: Festschrift für Andreas Hillgruber* (Cologne: Böhlau, 1985), pp. 195–228; and Jürgen Förster, *Stalingrad: Risse im Bündnis 1942/43* (Freiburg: Rombach, 1975).

In terms of individual countries, Hungary is still introduced most effectively by the two volumes of Carlile A. Macartney, *October Fifteenth: A History of Modern Hungary 1929–1945* (Edinburgh: Univ. Press, 1956). Important other works include the studies collected by Nandor F. Dreisziger for the special volume *Hungary and the Second World War* issued as *Hungarian Studies Review* 10, Nos. 1–2 (1983), and Margit Szöllösi-Janze, *Die Pfeilkreuzlerbewegung in Ungarn: Historischer Kontext, Entwicklung und Herrschaft* (Munich: Oldenbourg, 1989). On Romania, Andreas Hillgruber, *Hitler, König Carol, und Marschall Antonescu: Die deutsch-rumänischen Beziehungen 1938–1944* (Wiesbaden: Steiner, 1954) remains important in spite of its deficiencies. Philip Marguerat, *Le IIIe Reich et le pétrole roumain, 1938–1940* (Geneva: A.W. Sijthoff, 1977); Jürgen Förster, "Rumäniens Weg in die deutsche Abhängigkeit: Zur Rolle der deutschen Militärmission 1940/41," *MGM* 25 (1979), 44–77; and Armin Heinen, *Die Legion "Erzengel Michael" in Rumänien: Soziale Bewegung und politische Organisation* (Munich: Oldenbourg, 1986), represent more recent scholarship. On Bulgaria, the most helpful books are Marshall Lee Miller, *Bulgaria during the Second World War* (Stanford, Calif.: Stanford Univ. Press, 1975), and Hans-Joachim Hoppe, *Bulgarien—Hitlers eigenwilliger Verbündete* (Stuttgart: Deutsche Verlags-Anstalt, 1979). On Greece, there is a chronological account of the fighting in Robin Higham, *Diary of a Disaster: British Aid to Greece 1940–1941* (Lexington, Ky.: Univ. Press of Kentucky, 1986). There is a general survey in John L. Hondros, *Occupation and Resistance: The Greek Agony, 1941–44* (New York: Pella, 1983). A thoughtful introduction to a difficult subject is Peter J. Stavrakis, *Moscow and Greek Communism, 1944–1949* (Ithaca, N.Y.: Cornell Univ. Press, 1989). By far the best book on Turkey is Zehra Önder, *Die türkische Aussenpolitik im Zweiten Weltkrieg* (Munich: Oldenbourg, 1976).

Of the many books on Yugoslavia during the war, Walter A. Roberts, *Tito, Mihailovic, and the Allies, 1941–1945* (New Brunswick, N.J.: Rutgers Univ. Press, 1973); Ladislaus Hory and Martin Broszat, *Der kroatische Ustascha-Staat 1941–1945* (Stuttgart: Deutsche Verlags-Anstalt, 1964); and Hans Knoll, *Jugoslawien in Strategie und Politik der Alliierten 1940–1943* (Munich: Oldenbourg, 1986) are particularly helpful. The most comprehensive account of the diplomatic issues early in the war may be found in Alfredo Breccia, *Jugoslavia 1939–1941: Diplomazia della Neutralità* (Milan: Giuffrè, 1978). For a sense of the fighting and the growth of Tito's partisan movement, Milovan Djilas, *Wartime* (New York: Harcourt Brace Jovanovich, 1977), is most revealing. Very important is the publication of the memoirs and papers of the German military representative to the puppet state of Croatia, Peter Broucek (ed.), *Ein General im Zwielicht: Die Erinnerungen Edmund Glaise von Horstenaus,* Vol. 3: *Deutscher Bevollmächtigter General in Kroatien und Zeuge des Untergangs des "Tausendjährigen Reiches"* (Cologne and Vienna: Böhlau, 1979–88). For Albania, see Reginald Hibbert, *Albania's National Liberation Struggle: The Bitter Victory* (London: Pinter, 1991).

The war on the Eastern Front made up the majority of the fighting but, certainly in Western languages, has not been the subject of the majority of the literature. On its origins, Andreas Hillgruber's recapitulation, "Noch einmal: Hitlers Wendung gegen die Sowjetunion 1940," *Geschichte in Wissenschaft und Unterricht* 33 (1982),

214–26; Robert Cecil, *Hitler's Decision to Invade Russia 1941* (London: Davis-Poynter, 1975); and Gerhard L. Weinberg, *Germany and the Soviet Union, 1939–1941* (Leyden: Brill, 1954, 1972) will be found helpful. The best general surveys of the fighting are the two books of Earl F. Ziemke, *Moscow to Stalingrad: Decision in the East* (Washington: GPO, 1987), and *Stalingrad to Berlin: The German Defeat in the East* (Washington: GPO, 1968); and the two of John Erickson, *The Road to Stalingrad* (New York: Harper & Row, 1975), and *The Road to Berlin* (Boulder, Colo.: Westview Press, 1983). Peter Gosztony, *Hitlers Fremde Heere: Das Schicksal der nichtdeutschen Armeen im Ostfeldzug* (Düsseldorf: Econ, 1976), surveys the fate of the armies of Germany's satellites in the campaign.

Important accounts of specific parts of the fighting are Jacob W. Kipp, *Barbarossa, Soviet Covering Forces and the Initial Period of War; Military History and the Airland Battle* (Fort Leavenworth, Kans.: Soviet Army Studies Office, 1987); Klaus Reinhardt, *Die Wende vor Moskau: Das Scheitern der Strategie Hitlers im Winter 1941/42* (Stuttgart: Deutsche Verlags-Anstalt, 1972) which is to appear in English translation; Manfred Kehrig, *Stalingrad: Analyse und Dokumentation einer Schlacht* (Stuttgart: Deutsche Verlags-Anstalt, 1974); Geoffrey Jukes, *Hitler's Stalingrad Decisions* (Berkeley, Calif.: Univ. of California Press, 1985); Ernst Klink, *Das Gesetz des Handelns: Die Operation "Zitadelle" 1943* (Stuttgart: Deutsche Verlags-Anstalt, 1966); Christopher Duffy, *Red Storm on the Reich: The Soviet March on Germany, 1945* (New York: Atheneum,1991); and Tony Le Tissier, *The Battle for Berlin 1945* (New York: St. Martin's, 1988). German strategy in the last year of the war is seen in a new light in Howard Davis Grier, "Hitler's Baltic Strategy," a 1991 North Carolina PhD dissertation.

There is an excellent selection of portions of Soviet memoirs in translation in Seweryn Bialer (ed.), *Stalin and His Generals* (London: Souvenir Press, 1970). The dominating role of logistics, which in 1941 precluded any of the brilliant strategies devised for the Germans afterwards, is illuminated by the highly significant book of Klaus A.F. Schüler, *Logistik im Russlandfeldzug: Die Rolle der Eisenbahn bei Planung, Vorbereitung und Durchführung des deutschen Angriffs auf die Sowjetunion bis zur Krise vor Moskau im Winter 1941/42* (Frankfurt/M: Lang, 1987). On the role of partisans and anti-partisan warfare, the most significant work remains John A. Armstrong (ed.), *Soviet Partisans in World War II* (Madison: Univ. of Wisconsin Press, 1964). The best account of the Vlasov movement is Catherine Andreyev, *Vlasov and the Russian Liberation Movement: Soviet Reality and Emigré Theories* (Cambridge: Cambridge Univ. Press, 1987). For the Soviet home front, there is useful information in Mark Harrison, *Soviet Planning in Peace and War, 1938–1945* (Cambridge: Cambridge Univ. Press, 1985), and John Barber and Mark Harrison, *The Soviet Home Front, 1941–1945: A Social and Economic History of the U.S.S.R. in World War II* (New York: Longman, 1991).

The role of Stalin in the conduct of operations and the control of the Soviet war effort at home remains one of the most difficult topics to examine; it was so loaded politically that it came to be a function of the current official line—with little relationship to the realities of the war years. The biography of Dmitri Volkogonov, *Stalin: Triumph and Tragedy*, ed. and trans. by Harold Shukman (New York: Grove & Weidenfeld, 1991) is the first major effort to penetrate the veil of distortions. There is no doubt more to come.

Soviet foreign policy during the war is likely to be greatly redrawn on the basis of new material just beginning to become available. Of the existing literature, Alexander Fischer, *Sowjetische Deutschlandpolitik im Zweiten Weltkrieg 1941–1945* (Stuttgart: Deutsche Verlags-Anstalt, 1975); Jan T. Gross, *Revolution from Abroad: The Soviet Conquest of Poland's Western Ukraine and Western Belorussia* (Princeton, N.J.: Princeton Univ. Press, 1988); Vojtech Mastny, *Russia's Road to the Cold War: Diplomacy, Warfare, and the Politics of Communism, 1941–1945* (New York: Columbia Univ. Press, 1979); and Anna M. Cienciala, "The Activities of Polish Communists as a Source for Stalin's Policy Towards Poland in the Second World War," *International History Review* 7 (1985), 129–45, are particularly noteworthy.

On the German occupation, mistreatment of prisoners of war, and the transformation of the German army which made its large-scale participation in the most horrendous crimes possible, see Alexander Dallin, *German Rule in Russia 1941–1945: A Study in Occupation Policies* (London: Macmillan, 1957); Theo Schulte, *The German Army and Nazi Policies in Occupied Russia* (Oxford: Berg, 1989); Christian Streit, *Keine Kameraden: Die Wehrmacht und die sowjetischen Kriegsgefangenen 1941–1945* (Stuttgart: Deutsche Verlags-Anstalt, 1978); and two books by Omer Bartov, *The Eastern Front, 1941–45: German Troops and the Barbarization of Warfare* (New York: St. Martin's, 1985) and *Hitler's Army: Soldiers, Nazis, and War in the Third Reich* (New York: Oxford Univ. Press, 1991). The last of these is in my opinion overdrawn, but it deserves attention.

The central figure in the American war effort and home front was undoubtedly Franklin D. Roosevelt. A superb introduction to his role is William R. Emerson, "F.D.R. (1941–1945)," in Ernest R. May (ed.), *The Ultimate Decision: The President as Commander in Chief* (New York: George Braziller, 1960), pp. 135–77. A fine biography is James M. Burns, *Roosevelt: The Soldier of Freedom 1940–1945* (New York: Harcourt Brace Jovanovich, 1970). Important papers from his files are in Elliott Roosevelt (ed.), *F.D.R.: His Personal Letters, 1928–1945*, 2 vols. (New York: Duell, Sloan & Pearce, 1950). The correspondence between Roosevelt and Churchill has been published in two editions, Francis L. Loewenheim et al. (eds.), *Roosevelt and Churchill: Their Secret Wartime Correspondence* (New York: E.P. Dutton, 1975), and Warren F. Kimball, *Churchill and Roosevelt: The Complete Correspondence*, 3 vols. (Princeton, N.J.: Princeton Univ. Press, 1984). Robert E. Sherwood, *Roosevelt and Hopkins: An Intimate History* (New York: Harper, 1948), remains essential to any understanding of the period.

American strategy in general as well as the country's foreign policy during the war were subjected to two schools of revisionist writings; the first designed to show that the leadership of the United States was a combination of stupidity and short-sightedness with treasonous "softness" toward the Soviet Union, the second arguing the precise opposite, namely that the same leaders were scheming to confront, weaken, and in other ways act to the detriment of the Soviet Union and thereby brought on the Cold War. Most of the writings of these schools illuminate currents of thought in the United States at the time they were written rather than the events they are supposed to describe. I have found very few of them useful in the writing of this book.

Not substantially affected by these problems are Waldo Heinrichs, *Threshold of War: Franklin D. Roosevelt and American Entry into World War II* (New York: Oxford

Univ. Press, 1988); Kent Roberts Greenfield, *American Strategy in World War II: A Reconsideration* (Baltimore: Johns Hopkins Univ. Press, 1963); Robert Dallek, *Franklin D. Roosevelt and American Foreign Policy, 1932–1945* (New York: Oxford Univ. Press, 1979); Gaddis Smith, *American Diplomacy during the Second World War 1941–1945* (New York: John Wiley, 1965); John L. Gaddis, *The United States and the Origins of the Cold War, 1941–1947* (New York: Columbia Univ. Press, 1972); Richard W. Steele, *The First Offensive, 1942: Roosevelt, Marshall, and the Making of American Strategy* (Bloomington, Ind.: Indiana Univ. Press, 1973); Mark Stoler, *The Politics of the Second Front: American Military Planning and Diplomacy in Coalition Warfare, 1941–1943* (Westport, Conn: Greenwood Press, 1977); and Warren F. Kimball, *Swords or Plowshares? The Morgenthau Plan for Defeated Germany, 1942–1946* (Philadelphia: Lippincott, 1976).

The whole range of issues in the conduct of war by the United States can probably be followed best in the second and third volumes of Forrest C. Pogue's outstanding biography, *George C. Marshall, Ordeal and Hope, 1939–1942*, and *Organizer of Victory, 1943–1945* (New York: Viking Press, 1965, 1973). On the home front, John M. Blum, *V Was for Victory: Politics and American Culture during World War II* (New York: Harcourt Brace Jovanovich, 1976) is particularly good. The extensive literature on the internment of Japanese–Americans is now supplemented by Stephen Fox, *The Unknown Internment: An Oral History of the Relocation of Italian-Americans during World War II* (Boston: Twayne, 1990). Of the innumerable books dealing with operations by American forces in all parts of the world, the official histories remain most helpful. Only where the cryptographic material had to be withheld when those works were published but can now be integrated into a new narrative is the more recent literature an essential supplement; a good example is William T. Y'Blood, *Hunter-Killer: U.S. Escort Carriers in the Battle of the Atlantic* (Annapolis, Md.: Naval Institute Press, 1983). To the literature already mentioned and the official histories, the following need to be included for the fighting in the West from D-Day to the end of the war: Hermann Jung, *Die Ardennen-Offensive 1944/45: Ein Beispiel für die Kriegführung Hitlers* (Göttingen: Musterschmidt, 1971); John Keegan, *Six Armies in Normandy* (New York: Viking, 1982); Richard Lamb, *Montgomery in Europe, 1943–1945: Success or Failure?* (London: Buchan & Enright, 1983); Dieter Ose, *Entscheidung im Westen, 1944: Der Oberbefehlshaber West und die Abwehr der alliierten Invasion* (Stuttgart: Deutsche Verlags-Anstalt, 1982); and Russell F. Weigley, *Eisenhower's Lieutenants: The Campaign of France and Germany, 1944–1945* (Bloomington, Ind.: Indiana Univ. Press, 1981).

On the relationship of the United States to its British ally, there is a substantial literature. Especially good are Alex Danchev, *Very Special Relationship: Field Marshal Sir John Dill and the Anglo-American Alliance 1941–44* (London: Brassey's, 1986); David Reynolds, *Lord Lothian and Anglo-American Relations, 1939–1940, Transactions of the American Philosophical Society* 73, Part 2 (1983); Axel Gietz, *Die neue Alte Welt: Roosevelt, Churchill und die europäische Nachkriegsordnung* (Munich: Fink, 1986); Robert M. Hathaway, *Ambiguous Partnership: Britain and America, 1944–1947* (New York: Columbia Univ. Press, 1981); and Lothar Kettenacker, "'Unconditional Surrender' als Grundlage der angelsächsischen Nachkriegsplanung," in Wolfgang Michalka (ed.), *Der Zweite Weltkrieg: Analysen, Grundzüge, Forschungsbilanz* (Munich: Piper, 1989), pp. 174–88.

The American relationship with France is treated extensively in the book by Gietz listed in the preceding paragraph. There is a useful recent work, Raoul Aglion, *Roosevelt and De Gaulle: Allies in Conflict, A Personal Memoir* (New York: Free Press, 1988).

The alliance of the Western Powers with the Soviet Union is dealt with by an extensive body of works of which the pioneering study, William H. MacNeill, *America, Britain, and Russia: Their Co-operation and Conflict, 1941–1946* (1953 ed. reprinted, New York: Johnson Reprint, 1970), remains extremely useful. The most helpful memoir remains James R. Deane, *The Strange Alliance: The Story of Our Efforts at Wartime Co-operation with Russia* (New York: Viking, 1946). Important scholarly works are Mark Elliott, *Pawns of Yalta: Soviet Refugees and America's Role in Their Repatriation* (Urbana, Ill.: Univ. of Illinois Press, 1982); George C. Herring, Jr., *Aid to Russia 1941–1946: Strategy, Diplomacy, and the Origins of the Cold War* (New York: Columbia Univ. Press, 1973); Richard C. Lukas, *Eagles East: The American Air Force and the Soviet Union, 1941–1945* (Tallahassee, Fla.: Florida State Univ. Press, 1970); John D. Langer, "The Harriman–Beaverbrook Mission and the Debate over Unconditional Aid for the Soviet Union, 1941," in Walter Laqueur (ed.), *The Second World War* (London: Sage, 1982), pp. 300–19; Joan Beaumont, *Comrades in Arms: British Aid to Russia, 1941–1945* (London: Davis-Poynter, 1980) and her article, "A Question of Diplomacy: British Military Mission in the U.S.S.R. 1941–1945," *Journal of the Royal United Services Institute for Defence Studies* 118 (1973), 74–81; Steven M. Miner, *Between Churchill and Stalin: The Soviet Union, Great Britain, and the Origins of the Grand Alliance* (Chapel Hill, N.C.: Univ. of North Carolina Press, 1988); Lothar Kettenacker, "The Anglo-Soviet Alliance and the Problem of Germany, 1941–1945," *JCH* 17 (1982), 435–58; Jan Karski, *The Great Powers and Poland, 1919–1945* (Lanham, Md.: University Press of America, 1985); and Sarah M. Terry, *Poland's Place in Europe: General Sikorski and the Origin of the Oder-Neisse Line, 1939–1943* (Princeton, N.J.: Princeton Univ. Press, 1983).

The role of the members of the British Commonwealth is generally neglected in books on World War II; their contributions and forces often subsumed under the term "British" with little attention to geographic origin. It is thus all too often overlooked that at the last and decisive Battle of El Alamein, the majority of the "British" troops were not from the United Kingdom. The Commonwealth members Canada, Australia, New Zealand, the Union of South Africa, and India have all issued their own official histories, and these are of great importance. The key figure in the Canadian program was Charles P. Stacey who also wrote a kind of summary: *Six Years of War: The Army in Canada, Britain and the Pacific* (Ottawa: Queen's Printer, 1955), and two very interesting books which supplement the official history, *Arms, Men and Governments: The War Policies of Canada 1939–1945* (Ottawa: Queen's Printer, 1970), and *Canada and the Age of Conflict*, Vol. 2: *1921–1948, The Mackenzie King Era* (Toronto: Univ. of Toronto Press, 1981). Summaries of Australia's role are the excellent work of Gavin Long, *The Six Years' War: A Concise History of Australia in the 1939–1945 War* (Canberra: Australian War Memorial and Australian Government Publishing Service, 1973), and John Robertson, *Australia at War* (Melbourne: William Heinemann, 1981). Supplementing the official history are John Robertson and John McCarthy (eds.), *Australian War Strategy, 1939–1945: A Documentary History* (St. Lucia: Univ. of Queensland Press, 1985), and David M. Horner,

High Command: Australia and Allied Strategy, 1939–1945 (Canberra: Australian War Memorial; Boston: Allen & Unwin, 1982).

The developments inside Japan and in its foreign policy which led to its decision to expand the war already being waged against China into one with Britain, the Netherlands, and the United States as well have provided the subject for some excellent books. The central figures in the Japanese leadership are the subjects of important biographies. On the man who led Japan into the war with China and to the edge of war with the Western Powers, see Yoshitake Oka, *Konoe Fumimaro: A Political Biography*, trans. by Shumpei Okamoto and Patricia Murray (Tokyo: Univ. of Tokyo Press, 1983). The general who led Japan from the fall of 1941 to the summer of 1944 is covered by Robert J.C. Butow, *Tojo and the Coming of the War* (Stanford, Calif.: Stanford Univ. Press, 1961), and Alvin D. Coox, *Tojo* (New York: Ballantine, 1975). A study which examines his role in the management of Japan's strategy and war effort in some detail would be most welcome.

Helpful for an understanding of the internal development of Japan as well as its moves toward aggression are Michael A. Barnhart, *Japan Prepares for Total War: The Search for Economic Security, 1919–1941* (Ithaca, N.Y.: Cornell Univ. Press, 1987); Gordon M. Berger, *Parties out of Power in Japan, 1931–1941* (Princeton, N.J.: Princeton Univ. Press, 1977); Richard Storry, *The Double Patriots: A Study of Japanese Nationalism* (Boston: Houghton Mifflin, 1957); Stephen E. Pelz, *Race to Pearl Harbor* (Cambridge, Mass.: Harvard Univ. Press, 1974); Gerhard Krebs, *Japans Deutschlandpolitik 1935–1941*, 2 vols. (Hamburg: MOAG, 1984); and two collections of important pieces edited by James W. Morley: *The China Quagmire: Japan's Expansion on the Asian Continent 1933–1941*, and *The Fateful Choice: Japan's Advance into Southeast Asia 1939–1941* (New York: Columbia Univ. Press, 1983 and 1980).

The immediate antecedents of the Pearl Harbor attack are illuminated by Nobutaka Ike (ed.), *Japan's Decision for War: Records of the 1941 Policy Conferences* (Stanford, Calif.: Stanford Univ. Press, 1967); Robert J.C. Butow, *The John Doe Associates: Backdoor Diplomacy for Peace, 1941* (Stanford, Calif.: Stanford Univ. Press, 1974); Dorothy Borg and Shumpei Okamoto, *Pearl Harbor as History: Japanese–American Relations, 1931–1941* (New York: Columbia Univ. Press, 1973); and two books by Gordon Prange, *At Dawn We Slept: The Untold Story of Pearl Harbor*, and *Pearl Harbor: The Verdict of History* (New York: McGraw-Hill, 1981 and 1986). In spite of the passage of time, Herbert Feis, *The Road to Pearl Harbor* (Princeton, N.J.: Princeton Univ. Press, 1950), remains one of the best books on the subject.

On Japan's armed forces in the war, there is Hayashi Saburo, *KOGUN: The Japanese Army in the Pacific War* (Quantico, Va.: Marine Corps Association, 1959); Paul S. Dull, *A Battle History of the Imperial Japanese Navy (1941–1945)* (Annapolis, Md.: Naval Institute Press, 1978); and Alvin D. Coox, "The Rise and Fall of the Imperial Japanese Air Forces," *Aerospace Historian* 27, No. 2 (June 1980), 74–86. The Japanese home front is covered by Thomas R.H. Havens, *Valley of Darkness: The Japanese People and World War II* (New York: Norton, 1978), and Ben-Ami Shillony, *Politics and Culture in Wartime Japan* (Oxford: Clarendon Press, 1981). The best account of the ending of the war remains Robert J.C. Butow, *Japan's Decision to Surrender* (Stanford, Calif.: Stanford Univ. Press, 1954), though a new edition using the declassified American and Japanese documents now available would be most welcome.

On Japan's relations with Germany, a most important source, which is also very revealing about Japan itself, is John W.M. Chapman (ed.), *The Price of Admiralty: The War Diary of the German Naval Attaché in Japan, 1939–1943*, 3 vols. to date (Lewes, Sussex: Univ. of Sussex Printing Unit, 1982–84). Also useful are Bernd Martin, *Deutschland und Japan im Zweiten Weltkrieg* (Göttingen: Musterschmidt, 1969), and Johanna M. Meskill, *Hitler and Japan: The Hollow Alliance* (New York: Atherton, 1966). On other aspects of Japanese foreign policy during the war, George A. Lensen, *The Strange Neutrality: Soviet–Japanese Relations During the Second World War 1941–1945* (Tallahassee, Fla.: Diplomatic Press, 1972), and Joyce C. Lebra, *Japanese-Trained Armies in Southeast Asia: Independence and Volunteer Forces in World War II* (New York: Columbia Univ. Press, 1977) are of interest.

The long war between Japan and China awaits its English-language historian. Dick Wilson, *When Tigers Fight: The Story of the Sino-Japanese War, 1937–1945* (New York: Penguin, 1983); F.F. Liu, *A Military History of Modern China, 1924–1949* (Princeton, N.J.: Princeton Univ. Press, 1956); and Hsi-sheng Ch'i, *Nationalist China at War: Military Defeats and Political Collapse, 1937–45* (Ann Arbor, Mich.: Univ. of Michigan Press, 1982) are the best surveys currently available. John H. Boyle, *China and Japan at War 1937–1945: The Politics of Collaboration* (Stanford, Calif.: Stanford Univ. Press, 1972); Gerald R. Bunker, *The Peace Conspiracy: Wang Ching-wei and the China War 1937–1941* (Cambridge, Mass.: Harvard Univ. Press, 1972); and John W. Garver, *Chinese-Soviet Relations, 1937–1945: The Diplomacy of Chinese Nationalism* (New York: Oxford Univ. Press, 1988), provide excellent coverage of significant subjects. There is much of interest in the *Symposium on the History of the Republic of China*, vol. 4: *War and Resistance against Japan* (Taipei: China Cultural Service, 1981).

For the Pacific War, by far the best introduction is Louis Morton's volume *The War in the Pacific, Strategy and Command: The First Two Years* (Washington: GPO, 1962) in the U.S. Army's official history. A major resource is the now published manuscript of Grace P. Hayes, *The History of the Joint Chiefs of Staff in World War II: The War against Japan* (Annapolis, Md.: Naval Institute Press, 1982). There are two extremely good volumes covering the first seven months of the Pacific War by H.P. Willmott, *Empires in the Balance: Japanese and Allied Strategies to April 1942*, and *The Barrier and the Javelin: Japanese and Allied Pacific Strategies, February to June 1942* (Annapolis, Md.: Naval Institute Press, 1982 and 1983). A different perspective is provided by John Dower, *War Without Mercy: Race and Power in the Pacific War* (New York: Pantheon, 1986).

Of special interest on Japanese naval leadership is the translation of large portions of the diary of a key figure in the Imperial Japanese navy, Ugaki Matome, *Fading Victory: The Diary of Admiral Matome Ugaki* (Pittsburgh: Univ. of Pittsburgh Press, 1991). The best works on Douglas MacArthur are D. Clayton James, *The Years of MacArthur*, Vol. 2: 1941–1945 (Boston: Houghton Mifflin, 1975), and Carol M. Petillo, *Douglas MacArthur: The Philippine Years* (Bloomington, Ind.: Indiana Univ. Press, 1981). There are useful tactical details, even if a lot of political nonsense, in Ohmae Toshikazu, "Die strategischen Konzeptionen der japanischen Marine im Zweiten Weltkrieg," *Marine-Rundschau* 53 (1956), 179–203. On submarines, the best introductions are Carl Boyd, "The Japanese Submarine Force and the Legacy of Strategic and Operational Doctrine Developed between the World Wars," in

Larry Addington et al. (eds.), *Selected Papers from The Citadel Conference on War and Diplomacy 1978* (Charleston, S.C.: The Citadel Development Foundation, 1979), and Wilfred J. Holmes, *Undersea Victory: The Influence of Submarine Operations on the War in the Pacific* (Garden City, N.Y.: Doubleday, 1966).

On specific engagements in the Pacific, it is still wise to start with the official histories. In addition, Brian Garfield, *The Thousand-Mile War: World War II in Alaska and the Aleutians* (Garden City, N.Y.: Doubleday, 1969), provides an excellent survey of that campaign; John J. Stephan, *Hawaii under the Rising Sun: Japan's Plan for Conquest after Pearl Harbor* (Honolulu: Univ. of Hawaii Press, 1984), is essential reading on the early part of the Pacific War; Bert Webber, *Silent Siege: Japanese Attacks against North America in World War II* (Fairfield, Wash.: Ye Galleon Press, 1983), provides the most comprehensive coverage of the Japanese effort to burn down the western portions of the United States and Canada; and three of the critical battles are brilliantly handled in the books of Harry A. Gailey: *Bougainville, 1943–1945: The Forgotten Campaign* (Lexington, Ky.: Univ. Press of Kentucky, 1991), *Howlin' Mad versus the Army: Conflict in Command, Saipan 1944* (Novato, Calif.: Presidio Press, 1986), and *Peleliu, 1944* (Annapolis, Md.: Nautical and Aviation Publishing Co. of America, 1983).

On the war in South and Southeast Asia, once again the official histories are most useful. On India in the war, there are Milan Hauner, *India in Axis Strategy: Germany, Japan and Indian Nationalists in World War II* (Stuttgart: Klett-Cotta, 1981), and Johannes H. Voigt, *Indien im Zweiten Weltkrieg* (Stuttgart: Deutsche Verlags-Anstalt, 1978). Of the vast literature on the campaign in Malaya and the fall of Singapore, I have found Louis Allen, *Singapore 1941–1942* (London: Davis-Poynter, 1977), most helpful; certainly his *Burma: The Longest War 1941–1945* (London: Dent, 1984) is the most comprehensive and thoughtful account of that campaign. The theater is also covered by the official American army histories of Charles Romanus and Riley Sutherland; focusing on the central American figure is the very readable book by Barbara Tuchman, *Stilwell and the American Experience in China 1911–1945* (New York: Bantam, 1972, and other eds.). The final land campaign in Asia is most effectively handled by David M. Glantz, *August Storm: The Soviet 1945 Strategic Offensive in Manchuria* (Fort Leavenworth, Kansas: Combat Studies Institute, 1983).

As records pertaining to intelligence operations and weaponry have been declassified in recent years, there has been a substantial literature of a serious type slowly, but far too slowly, replacing the fanciful inventions of earlier publications. On intelligence activities, see Christopher Andrew and David Dilks (eds.), The *Missing Dimension: Governments and Intelligence Communities in the Twentieth Century* (London: Macmillan, 1984); Horst Boog, "German Air Intelligence in the Second World War," *Intelligence and National Security* 5 (1990), 350–424; John W.M. Chapman, "German Signals Intelligence and the Pacific War," *Proceedings of the British Association for Japanese Studies (History and International Relations)* 4 (1979), 131–49; Aileen Clayton, *The Enemy is Listening* (London: Hutchinson, 1980), a marvellous memoir of a "Y" service officer; Michael L. Handel (ed.), *Strategic and Operational Deception in the Second World War* (London: Frank Cass, 1987); Walter T. Hitchcock (ed.), *The Intelligence Revolution: A Historical Perspective* (Washington: GPO, 1991); Wilfred J. Holmes, *Double-Edged Secrets: U.S. Naval Intelligence Operations in the Pacific during World War II* (Annapolis, Md.: Naval Institute Press, 1979); Reginald V. Jones, *Most*

Secret War: British Scientific Intelligence, 1939–1945 (London: Hamish Hamilton, 1978); three books by David Kahn: *The Codebreakers: The Story of Secret Writing* (New York: Macmillan, 1967), *Hitler's Spies: German Military Intelligence in World War II* (New York: Macmillan, 1978), and *Seizing the Enigma: The Race to Break the German U-Boat Codes, 1939–1943* (Boston: Houghton Mifflin, 1991); two books by Ronald Lewin, *Ultra Goes to War* (New York: McGraw-Hill, 1978), and *The American Magic: Codes, Cyphers and the Defeat of Japan* (New York: Farrar Straus Giroux, 1982); Wladyslaw Kozaczuk, *Enigma: How the German Machine Cypher Was Broken, and How it Was Read by the Allies in World War II*, ed. and trans. by Christopher Kasparek (Frederick, Md.: University Publications of America, 1984); Richard Langhorne (ed.), *Diplomacy and Intelligence during the Second World War* (Cambridge: Cambridge Univ. Press, 1985); Jürgen Rohwer and Eberhard Jäckel (eds.), *Die Funkaufklärung und ihre Rolle im 2. Weltkrieg* (Stuttgart: Motorbuch, 1979); and Nigel West [pseud. of Rupert Allason?], *The SIGINT Secrets: The Signals Intelligence War, 1900 to Today: Including the Persecution of Gordon Welchman* (New York: Morrow, 1988).

For sabotage and similar activities, the best introduction is Michael R.D. Foot, *SOE: An Outline History of the Special Operations Executive, 1940–1946* (London: BBC Publications, 1984). On weapons systems, Fritz Hahn, *Waffen und Geheimwaffen des deutschen Heeres 1933–1945*, 2 vols. (Koblenz: Bernard & Graefe, 1986–87); Dieter Hölsken, "Die V-Waffen: Entwicklung und Einsatzgrundsätze," *MGM* 38, No. 2 (1985), 95–122; and Alfred Price, *Instruments of Darkness: The History of Electronic Warfare* (London: Macdonald & Jane's, 1977), are particularly helpful. Many aspects of the air war are dealt with by experts on them in Horst Boog (ed.), *The Conduct of the Air War in the Second World War: An International Comparison* (New York: Berg, 1992).

On atomic weapons, the best works remain two official histories: Richard G. Hewlett and Oscar E. Anderson, *A History of the United States Atomic Energy Commission, Vol. 1: The New World 1939–1946* (Philadelphia: Univ. of Pennsylvania Press, 1962), and Vincent C. Jones, *Manhattan: The Army and the Atomic Bomb* (Washington, GPO, 1985). There is much scientific information along with political polemics in Richard Rhodes, *The Making of the Atomic Bomb* (New York: Simon & Schuster, 1986). The British side is summarized in an originally secret book by John Ehrman, *The Atomic Bomb: An Account of British Policy in the Second World War* (London: Cabinet Office, July 1953).

The listings and suggestions which have been provided are necessarily incomplete; not only have most memoirs been omitted but so have whole bodies of publications like unit histories. There are also many topics not covered at all. The notes in the back of this book will provide additional references for those subjects covered in the text, and the bibliographical aids mentioned at the beginning of this essay will offer assistance in the location of further publications.

The volume of archives surviving from World War II is enormous. A general introduction to the subject is in James O'Neill and Robert W. Krauskopf (eds.), *World War II: An Account of Its Documents* (Washington: Howard Univ. Press, 1976). On the various categories of captured records, a fine place to start is Robert Wolfe (ed.), *Captured German and Related Records* (Athens, Ohio: Ohio Univ. Press, 1974).

For the main depository of British records, see *The Second World War: A Guide to Documents in the Public Record Office* (London: HMSO, 1972).

On German records still in the United States, see Gerhard L. Weinberg, *Guide to Captured German Documents* (Montgomery, Ala.: 1952), and "Supplement to the Guide to Captured German Documents" (Washington: National Archives, 1959); those returned to Germany are covered by the inventories (*Findbücher*) of the German Federal Archives in Koblenz. The microfilms made before their return are described in Howard M. Ehrmann, *A Catalogue of the Files and Microfilms of the German Foreign Ministry Archives 1867–1920* (Washington: American Historical Association, 1959); George O. Kent, *A Catalog of the Files and Microfilms of the German Foreign Ministry 1920–1945*, 4 vols. (Stanford, Calif.: Hoover Institution Press, 1962–72); and the series "Guides to German Records Microfilmed at Alexandria, Va." issued by the U.S. National Archives since 1958. For a helpful introduction to the fate of Italian archives in the war, see Howard M. Smyth, *Secrets of the Fascist Era* (Carbondale, Ill.: Southern Illinois Univ. Press, 1975); there is also a 3-volume series of "Guides" to captured Italian records microfilmed in the United States which has been issued by the National Archives.

The major collection of Japanese World War II records accessible to those who do not read Japanese is in the National Archives in Washington. There are several series of intercepted Japanese diplomatic, military attaché, naval attaché, army and navy, as well as related German messages—with some of them running to tens and even hundreds of thousands, which are included in the Record Group 457 of the National Security Agency, the inheritor of the American wartime decoding records. These materials are of immense importance because they reflect not only affairs internal to the Japanese diplomatic and military services but because they report on the countries where Japanese diplomats were stationed. Furthermore, for the Japanese as for the German records, the destruction of war has in many cases left the translated intercepts the *only* surviving copies of documents of which no German or Japanese originals exist.

Other major collections in the U.S. National Archives which have been canvassed for this book are the records of the War Department's G-2 (Intelligence) Section and the vast assemblage of materials gathered for the post-war trials of war criminals. In the difficult choice of which of the many huge archival collections to work through personally, I decided to emphasize the Franklin D. Roosevelt Presidential Library at Hyde Park. There is a vast amount of material on all aspects of the war which, if studied patiently, reveals a good deal about the way in which the President ran the American war effort. There are good finding aids at the library which also contains the papers of Henry Morgenthau and numerous other high officials of the Roosevelt administration. Items from Hyde Park are cited as from the Roosevelt files unless otherwise noted, and they are referred to by the filing system in use at the library.

The major depository in England is the Public Record Office (PRO) at Kew. There the prospective reader will find the major collections of the papers of the Cabinet, Prime Minister, Foreign Office, the three service departments, some important personal papers, and a great deal more, all covered by "class lists" from which one selects the files needed and then calls them up via an unusually polite computer. The bulk of British wartime records has been opened, but there are annoying exceptions, a subject commented on at the end of this essay. Those documents cited in this book are referred to by the designation used at the PRO, including the class and file number—which locates the file in which the original is to be found—and in the case of Foreign Office documents the archive designation originally applied to the item in the Foreign Office.

The other archives which have been consulted for this book are the Liddell Hart Centre for Military Archives at King's College of the University of London and the Imperial War Museum Library. The former is an institution which has been collecting the papers of individuals who played a significant role in World War II; the most important papers are those of Lord Alanbrooke, the Chief of the Imperial General Staff for most of the war, and of General Lord Ismay, Churchill's key military assistant during the war and his most important aide in writing the 6–volume memoir-history afterwards. Both of these collections are very well organized and serviced by a helpful staff; they are cited here by the designations used at the Centre. The library of the Imperial War Museum also holds substantial collections of private papers of which several have been utilized and are cited here. Churchill College of Cambridge University has an even larger archive of papers of World War II figures.

If American and British records are at least to some extent centralized in a national depository, German records held in Germany were originally divided between the two states and are only now being reunited in a process likely to be lengthy and complicated. Furthermore, the German Federal Republic, as a part of its original perception of itself as a temporary entity with a temporary capital, decided deliberately not to create a new national archive in Bonn but instead divided its records and placed the main depository in Koblenz. There, after decades of using rented quarters, the Federal Archive had built for it a large permanent structure—a few years before the division of Germany was ended. The *Bundesarchiv* as it is called issues guides to its holdings, is on the whole extremely well organized, and, an unheard of innovation in Europe, is even open in the evening. Records cited from there, primarily from the Reichs Chancellery, the Ministry of Finance, and collections of directives and reports to news agencies, are referred to by the reference system in use at the archive.

The Federal Archive in Koblenz did not, however, obtain immediate custody of all the returned records. The records of the German Foreign Ministry were allotted to an internally controlled archive of the Ministry itself. These records, therefore, are located in Bonn, and they have unfortunately not always been handled with regard for Germany's treaty commitment to make them fully available to scholars. This revival of the "scrap of paper" attitude toward international agreements has in recent years been replaced by a far more cooperative one. Documents from the German Foreign Ministry archive are cited here under the rubric AA, followed by the name of the collection as commonly abbreviated, the title of the folder series, and the volume number (if there is one), followed by the frame number if the document was microfilmed at one time and such a frame number was stamped on it. It should be noted that the Bonn archive also hold the records of former German missions abroad, and these, where cited, are listed with the name of the embassy or legation; the same procedure has been followed with the collections of private papers held.

The German military records are in the custody of what is now a branch of the Federal Archives located in Freiburg (but alas perhaps to be moved to Potsdam).

This is an extremely well organized and serviced archive with a most important collection of German naval records, a major collection of army records, and fragments of air force records—a descending order which reflects the extent to which the papers of the three services survive. There are finding aids available in Freiburg and a helpful staff. The archive in Freiburg has made a systematic effort to collect the papers of German military figures, and many of these will be found referred to in the notes. All references to the Freiburg collection are prefaced by BA/MA, for its German name *Bundesarchiv-Militärarchiv*, followed by the collection and folder numbers, with folio numbers where there is pagination. If it seems strange at times to see references to naval records for information apparently having little to do with the German navy, the peculiarities of the survival of archives mentioned above must be kept in mind.

The Institute for Contemporary History (Institut für Zeitgeschichte) in Munich and the Research Center for the History of National Socialism in Hamburg (Forschungsstelle für die Geschichte des Nationalsozialismus in Hamburg) both combine important library holdings with collections of papers. In Munich there are not only deposited papers but also extensive depositions and post-war correspondence about the war period. These are all referred to by citation systems utilized at the two institutions. Scholars will find the reference staffs most helpful. In Munich as in Bonn, Koblenz, and Freiburg, the archivists will assist researchers who need permission to use those personal papers deposited under restrictions; they cannot, of course, guarantee permission, which is, however, usually granted.

Although, like all who work on World War II, I have found it impossible to work in all the available records—otherwise no book on the war would ever be finished—it does appear to me that some comment is in order about records which are still closed to all research. Two points are central to this issue. In the first place, it becomes increasingly ridiculous to assert that records which are half a century old have anything to do with any country's security today. It is certainly conceivable that there are technical details of weapons systems which ought still to be kept closed—and which scholars generally have no interest in anyway—and there are undoubtedly some records pertaining to private matters, such as medical and court martial records, which need to be kept closed for the obvious protection of privacy (but in some cases could surely be made accessible under protective rules requiring the omission of names). For the rest of the documentation, however, "national security" sounds quite hollow.

The second general consideration is that of the physical quality of the paper. The records of the war, insofar as they have not been microfilmed, are literally disappearing as the original paper deteriorates. In all countries, the quality of paper was deliberately made worse during the war in order to conserve resources needed elsewhere in stressed and stretched wartime economies; the result of this is that the wood acetate paper of the war period is disintegrating rapidly. If it is not microfilmed, it will literally vanish. If it is not made accessible to scholars very soon, it will have deteriorated beyond use before anyone can see it, with the effect that countries that keep such material closed will cut themselves off from an important part of their own past.[a]

[a] For a more extended discussion of this issue, see Gerhard L. Weinberg, "The End of Ranke's History?" *Syracuse Scholar* 9, No. 1 (1988), 51–59.

Specific examples of records now closed which should certainly be made available are numerous. The huge collection of Allied intercepts of German diplomatic traffic, referred to as the "Floradora" material, ought to have been released a long time ago. As in the case of the already declassified "ultra" and "magic" intercepts of German and Japanese messages, many of these documents are likely to be the only surviving copies of the original texts, so they are important for that reason as well as what they can tell us about Allied knowledge of German activities. It is similarly ridiculous that documents at Hyde Park are returned by the agencies to which they are referred for declassification with the answer that they still cannot be opened.

Some years ago, as chair of a committee of the Conference Group for Central European History of the American Historical Association, I was successful in having the Inter-Agency Classification Review Committee direct the National Security Agency to declassify substantial quantities of German documents pertaining to German code-breaking activities before and during World War II. Those records have transformed our understanding of major aspects of the Battle of the Atlantic, to mention just one example. The bulk of the German records pertaining to cryptography, however, remain closed under joint British–American control. Since these records, by definition, are now at least almost half a century old, their continued classification serves only to discredit the whole concept of "national security."

The same thing is true for much of the British withholding of documents. Now that the Duke and Duchess of Windsor are both deceased, they are only made to look even sillier and more dangerous than they were by the continued closure of whole files, and individual items from other files, to protect them. The same thing is true for the bulk of intelligence records still closed from the 1930s as well as the war years; surely there is no need to cover events now from scrutiny either by a long-since defeated Axis or a vanished Soviet Union. Against what and whom are the secrets of World War II being protected now?

There has been a steady trend toward more open records in Germany and Italy and toward more closed records in Japan. Just as the one is encouraging, the other is discouraging and can only arouse, and should only arouse, concern. The major issue in the area of archives opening is, however, in the former German Democratic Republic, the states of the former Soviet block, and in the former Soviet Union. The East German archives are now under the control of the German Federal Archive, and although there is undoubtedly going to be a messy period of transition, one can expect that eventually the more liberal and sensible practices of the post-war German archivists will prevail. One of the many reasons why it was fortunate, not unfortunate, that the East German state collapsed as swiftly as it did was that a longer period of transition would undoubtedly have led to a vastly greater "disappearance" of records, of which there appears to have been a good deal anyway. In the former satellite states, some of which had begun to be more liberal in their access policies even before the collapse of the old regime, the major problem is likely to be a lack of resources, not a lack of will. There, as in the former Soviet Union, the problem of deteriorating paper and the need for microfilming is likely to make the need for open access especially acute: if steps are not taken soon, it may be simply too late. The archives of the former satellites and the former Soviet Union contain not only enormous quantities of their own records, records which have in the past not been made accessible to scholars, but also extensive collections of papers captured during and at the end of World War II. Here too time is of the essence.

The very volume of archives from World War II, both those available and those either still closed or inaccessible until quite recently, guarantees that there will be new perspectives and interpretations. There will be no lack of issues to probe and prior interpretations to review. World War II will justifiably continue to excite the interest of both historians and the public.

NOTES

I: FROM ONE WAR TO ANOTHER

1 See Gerhard L. Weinberg, "The Defeat of Germany in 1918 and the European Balance of Power," *Central European History* 2 (1969), 250–51.

2 A convenient summary in Fritz Fischer, *Germany's Aims in the First World War* (New York: Norton, 1967).

3 For a summary of the relevant treaties, including the role of Japan, see *FRUS, The Paris Peace Conference 1919*, 13 (Washington: GPO, 1947), pp. 237–41; on Japan's activities in practice, see the examples cited in Gerhard L. Weinberg, *The Foreign Policy of Hitler's Germany: Diplomatic Revolution in Europe, 1933–36* (Chicago: Univ. of Chicago Press, 1970) (hereafter cited as *Foreign Policy 1933–36*), p. 85 n. 138.

4 Denis Mack Smith, *Mussolini's Roman Empire* (New York: Viking, 1976); MacGregor Knox, *Mussolini Unleashed 1939–1941: Politics and Strategy in Fascist Italy's Last War* (Cambridge: Cambridge Univ. Press, 1982), chap. 1.

5 Some of the recent literature, e.g. Robert J. Young, *In Command of France: French Foreign Policy and Military Planning 1933–1940* (Cambridge, Mass.: Harvard Univ. Press, 1978), and Jeffery A. Gunsburg, *Divided and Conquered: The French High Command and the Defeat of the West, 1940* (Westport, Conn.: Greenwood Press, 1979), takes a more charitable view of French leaders. The evidence adduced is interesting, but I am not convinced.

6 See Stephen A. Schuker, *The End of French Predominance in Europe: The Financial Crisis of 1924 and the Adoption of the Dawes Plan* (Chapel Hill, N.C.: Univ. of North Carolina Press, 1976).

7 Weinberg, *Foreign Policy 1933–36*, chap. 1, provides a brief summary with evidence from the pre-1933 period.

8 Rudolf Hess to Walter Hewel, March 30, 1927, published in Gerhard L. Weinberg (ed.), "National Socialist Organization and Foreign Policy Aims in 1927," *JMH* 36 (1964), 428–33.

9 Werner Jochmann (ed.), *Im Kampf um die Macht: Hitlers Rede vor dem Hamburger Nationalklub von 1919* (Frankfurt/M: Europäische Verlagsanstalt, 1960), p. 103.

10 The classic work on the subject remains Karl D. Bracher, Wolfgang Saur and Gerhard Schulz, *Die Nationalsozialistische Machtergreifung* (Cologne: Westdeutscher Verlag, 1952). Recent scholarship is summarized in the lectures sponsored by the Berlin Historical Commission, Wolfgang Treue and Jürgen Schmädeke (eds.), *Deutschland 1933: Machtzerfall der Demokratie und Nationalsozialistische "Machtergreifung"* (Berlin: Colloquium, 1984).

11 This author's argument in *Foreign Policy 1933–36* that the coup in Austria in July 1934 was authorized from Berlin is now conclusively supported by evidence on Hitler's prior

knowledge of the date and plans of the conspirators; see the excerpts from the memoirs of General Wilhelm Adam published in Wolfgang Benz (ed.), *Miscellanea: Festschrift für Helmut Krausnick* (Stuttgart: Deutsche Verlags-Anstalt, 1980), pp. 47–48.

12 The best treatment of the subject is Christopher Thorne, *The Limits of Foreign Policy: The West, the League and the Far Eastern Crisis of 1931–1933* (New York: G.P. Putnam's Sons, 1973).

13 See John McVickar Haight, Jr., *American Aid to France, 1938–1940* (New York: Atheneum, 1970).

14 Gerhard L. Weinberg, *The Foreign Policy of Hitler's Germany: Starting World War II, 1937–1939* (Chicago: Univ. of Chicago Press, 1980) (hereafter cited as *Foreign Policy 1937–39*), p. 578 n 178, and p. 608.

15 See document No. 333 of June 19, 1939, in Ministry of Foreign Affairs of the U.S.S.R., *Soviet Peace Efforts on the Eve of World War II (September 1938 – August 1939): Documents and Records*, 2 vols. (Moscow: Novosti, 1973): cf. Weinberg, *Foreign Policy 1937–39*, pp. 604–5.

16 Sidney Aster, *1939: The Making of the Second World War* (London: Deutsch, 1973), p. 317; see also Jacob B. Hoptner, *Yugoslavia in Crisis, 1934–1941* (New York: Columbia Univ. Press, 1962), p. 125 n 41; Gordon Brook-Shepherd, *The Storm Petrels: The Flight of the First Soviet Defectors* (New York: Ballantine, 1982), pp. 155–61.

17 On earlier efforts by Stalin to arrange an agreement with Germany, see Weinberg, *Foreign Policy 1933–36*, pp. 82, 220–23, 310–12; *Foreign Policy 1937–39*, pp. 214–15.

18 Cripps to Halifax, 16 July 1940, PRO, FO 371/24846, f. 10, N 6526/30/38. Internally the Soviet government expressed itself more directly. An instruction of the Soviet Commissariat for Foreign Affairs to the Ambassador in Tokyo of July 1, 1940, contains the sentence: "The conclusion of our agreement with Germany was dictated by the need for a war in Europe." Full text in James W. Morley (ed.), *The Fateful Choice: Japan's Advance into Southeast Asia* (New York: Columbia Univ. Press, 1980), pp. 311–12.

19 The text of the secret protocol has been published repeatedly; see *ADAP*, D, 7, No. 229. After years of pretence to the contrary, the accuracy of this text has now been acknowledged by the Soviet government.

20 Weinberg, *Foreign Policy 1937–39*, p. 456.

21 Ibid., chaps. 3 and 4: the evidence is summarized in Gerhard L. Weinberg, "Hitler and England, 1933–1945: Pretence and Reality," *German Studies Review* 8 (1985), 299–309.

22 The evidence is cited in Weinberg, *Foreign Policy 1937–39*, pp. 462–63.

23 Ibid., chap. 12.

24 The evidence on Hitler's speech of November 10, 1938, to several hundred German journalists on this subject is summarized in ibid., pp. 515–16.

25 The early history of the JU-88 can best be followed in Edward L. Homze, *Arming the Luftwaffe: The Reich Air Ministry and the German Aircraft Industry, 1919–39* (Lincoln, Neb.: Univ. of Nebraska Press, 1976). It is now clear that German air force intelligence was much too optimistic in its May 1939 assessment of German and British air strengths and that the famous demonstration of new models for Hitler at Rechlin in July 1939 was deliberately misleading and designed by the German air force to try to reduce the priority accorded to the navy. See Horst Boog, *Die deutsche Luftwaffenführung 1935–1945: Führungsprobleme — Spitzengliederung — Generalstabsausbildung* (Stuttgart: Deutsche Verlags-Anstalt, 1982), pp. 91–92.

26 Some of the extensive evidence is cited in Weinberg, *Foreign Policy 1937–39*, p. 432 n 231; p. 663 n 10.

27 Ibid., pp. 306–7, 389–90.

28 Ibid., pp. 484–86. According to the memoirs of Juozas Urbsys, the last pre-war Lithuanian Foreign Minister, published in 1988, the Lithuanian and Soviet governments had arrived at a gentlemen's agreement to inform each other about their respective moves in

international affairs; see Klaus Hildebrand et al. (eds.), *1939: An der Schwelle zum Weltkrieg* (Berlin: de Gruyter, 1990), p. 337.

29 Weinberg, *Foreign Policy 1937–39*, pp. 494–97.

30 Gerhard L. Weinberg (ed.), "Die geheimen Abkommen zum Antikominternpakt," *VjZ* 2 (1954), 193–201.

31 The author has dealt with this issue in "National Style in Diplomacy: Germany," in Erich Angermann and Marie-Luise Frings (eds.), *Oceans Apart? Comparing Germany and the United States* (Stuttgart: Klett-Cotta, 1981), p. 150.

32 Weinberg, *Foreign Policy 1937–39*, pp. 558–62.

33 A summary of the talk, with citations to the evidence, in ibid., pp. 610–12. The context makes it obvious that the *Schweinehund* Hitler had in mind was Neville Chamberlain. It has recently become known that a report on this talk was apparently being shown around in German army circles; the German general attached to the puppet government of Croatia mentions reading the text in his diary for August 1942. See Peter Broucek (ed.), *Ein General im Zwielicht*, 3 vols. (Vienna: Böhlau, 1988), 3: 135.

34 Weinberg, *Foreign Policy 1937–39*, pp. 610–12 and 643 n 80.

35 Ibid., chap. 14.

36 Ibid., pp. 428–29, esp. n 219.

37 On this, see Norman H. Gibbs, *Grand Strategy*, (London: HMSO, 1976), 1, chap. 13.

38 Weinberg, *Foreign Policy 1937–39*, p. 643 n 78. Hitler had not the slightest idea of the critical role Canada could and would play in any new war and paid no attention to this warning.

39 Aster, *1939*, pp. 314–19. The American documents reflecting this leak were published in *FRUS*, 1939, Vol. 1 (Washington: GPO, 1956). The two sides of the story may be found in the relevant memoirs: Charles E. Bohlen, *Witness to History, 1929–1969* (New York: Norton, 1973), chap. 5; and Hans von Herwarth, *Zwischen Hitler und Stalin: Erlebte Zeitgeschichte, 1931–1945* (Frankfurt/M: Propyläen, 1982), pp. 175ff.

40 See Weinberg, *Foreign Policy 1937–39*, p. 638.

41 Franz Halder, *Kriegstagebuch*, ed. by Hans-Adolf Jacobsen, Vol. 1 (Stuttgart: Kohlhammer, 1962), August 30, 1939.

42 Weinberg, *Foreign Policy 1937–39*, pp. 644–45.

43 The entry in the diary of German State Secretary Ernst von Weizsäcker concludes for the day with: "So now we again face war. R.[ibbentrop] goes home beaming." (Damit stehen wir von Neuem vor dem Krieg. R. geht strahlend nach Hause.) Leonidas Hill (ed.), *Die Weizsäcker-Papiere, 1933–1950* (Frankfurt/M: Propyläen, 1974), p. 162.

44 For the text of Hitler's speech, see Max Domarus (ed.), *Hitler: Reden und Proklamationen, 1932–1945* (Neustadt a.d. Aisch: Verlagsdruckerei Schmidt, 1962), 2: 1311–18.

45 A study of "Hitlers Osterlass vom 1. Februar 1939" by Andrzej Brozak is in Joachim Hütter et al. (eds.), *Tradition und Neubeginn: Internationale Forschungen zur Deutschen Geschichte im 20. Jahrhundert* (Cologne: Heymann, 1975), pp. 367–76.

46 *ADAP*, D, 7, No. 433.

47 Sven Hedin, *Ohne Auftrag in Berlin* (Tübingen: Internationaler Universitäts-Verlag, 1950), pp. 51–56. The contemporary German record of this conversation contains the same sentiment phrased "Czechoslovakia could not be discussed." *ADAP*, D, 8, No. 263.

48 Birger Dahlerus, *Der letzte Versuch* (Munich: Nymphenburger Verlagsgesellschaft, 1948), pp. 125–26. For British Foreign Office comments on the planned and then realized publication of this book, see PRO, C 13562/11874/9, FO 371/39178; C 1640/45/18, FO 371/46784; C 6002/45/18, FO 371/46787.

49 *Documents on British Foreign Policy 1919–1939*, Series 3, Vol. 7, No. 604.

2: FROM THE GERMAN AND SOVIET INVASIONS OF POLAND TO THE GERMAN ATTACK IN THE WEST

1 On the Polish campaign, see *DRuZW*, 2: 79ff; Nicholas Bethell, *The War Hitler Won: The Fall of Poland, September, 1939* (New York: Holt, Rinehart & Winston, 1972).

2 Bertil Stjernfelt and Klaus-Richard Böhme, *Westerplatte 1939* (Freiburg: Rombach, 1979); Herbert Schindler, *Mosty und Dirschau 1939*, 2d ed (Freiburg, Romback 1979). The bridge was not repaired until the end of August 1940; see Forster to Hitler, 30 Aug. 1940, BA, NS 10/18, f. 40.

3 Many have overlooked the hope of some in the Polish government that war might be averted altogether and their attuning of policy in both diplomatic and military spheres to this possibility. The desperate military situation could only reinforce such a tendency. The other side of this equation was that the postponement of the German invasion from the planned date of August 26 to September 1 was that additional German divisions were ready on the later date *(DRuZW*, 2: 87–88).

4 A striking example, in which State Secretary in the German Foreign Ministry Ernst von Weizsäcker endorsed in August 1939 a repetition toward Poland of the tactic Hitler had ordered followed in the preceding year toward Czechoslovakia: that of always raising the demands so that agreement could not be reached, is published as *ADAP*, D, 7, No. 119.

5 The account in Francis H. Hinsley, *British Intelligence in the Second World War*, 5 vols. (New York: Cambridge Univ. Press, 1979–90), 1: 488–93, needs to be supplemented by Wladyslaw Kosaczuk, *Enigma* (Frederick, Md.: UPA, 1984), pp. 58–60, 292–318, and David Kahn, *Seizing the Enigma*, pp. 78–81 (the German who had sold key documents to the French was shot in July 1943, Kahn, p. 115).

6 See n 1, above. The Poles were not psychologically prepared for war, least of all for German policies in occupied territory, see Karl Dietrich Bracher et al. (eds.), *Deutschland zwischen Krieg und Frieden* (Düsseldorf: Droste, 1990), pp. 54–62. On the air war in Poland, see John F. Kreis, *Air Warfare and Air Base Defense, 1914–1973* (Washington: GPO, 1988), pp. 54–62.

7 See the map in *DRuZW*, 2: 116.

8 Weinberg, *Foreign Policy, 1937–39*, p. 536 n 4. Worth noting is Hitler's comparison of Slovakia's role with that of Hungary and "another state" (presumably Lithuania) in a conversation with the Slovak Minister to Germany on Oct. 21, 1939 *(ADAP*, D, 8, No. 286).

9 Weinberg, *Foreign Policy, 1937–39*, pp. 477, 497.

10 On the policy of Hungary, see *Hung. Docs.*, 4, Nos. 329, 331, 332, 334, 341, 353, 354, 372, 377, 379, 381, 388, 392; *ADAP*, D, 8, Nos. 9, 45, 48, 51, 67, 95; Gyula Juhász, *Hungarian Foreign Policy 1919–1945* (Budapest: Akademiai Kiado, 1979), pp. 163–64; Hildebrand et al., *1939*: pp. 163–64. The Hungarians were encouraged in their reserved attitude by Italy *(Hung. Docs.*, 4, Nos. 338, 363, 377–79, 385).

11 Weinberg, *Foreign Policy, 1937–39*, p. 486; *ADAP*, D, 8, Nos. 36, 41, 57, 58, 65, 76, 84, 121, 164; von Nostiz, "Pol I M 4552g.II," 8 Sept. 1939, AA, St.S., "Litauen," Bd. 11, fr. 193119. The Germans had begun their effort to draw Lithuania into the war already on August 29; see Weizsäcker to Kovno citissime of 29 Aug. 1939, AA, Büro RAM., "Litauen," fr. 117606.

12 Note Jörg K. Hoensch's piece in Gottfried Niedhart (ed.), *Der Westen und die Sowjetunion* (Paderborn: Schöningh, 1983), pp. 135–52.

13 The subject is discussed in both volumes of Weinberg, *Foreign Policy*, and Jiri Hochman, *The Soviet Union and the Failure of Collective Security, 1934–1938* (Ithaca, N.Y.: Cornell Univ. Press, 1984).

14 *ADAP*, D, 7, No. 567; 8, Nos. 2, 5, 34, 35, 37, 39, 46, 59, 70.

15 Robert M. Kennedy, *The German Campaign in Poland (1939)* (Washington: GPO, 1956), p. 124.

16 John Erickson, *The Road to Stalingrad* (New York: Harper & Row, 1975), p. 14. A full study of the Soviet invasion of Poland in 1939 would be most useful.

17 See James W. Morley (ed.), *Deterrent Diplomacy: Japan, Germany and the U.S.S.R. 1935– 1940* (New York: Columbia Univ. Press, 1976), pp. 123, 173. The whole incident is reviewed in detail in Alvin D. Coox, *Nomonhan: Japan against Russia, 1939*, 2 vols. (Stanford, Calif.: Stanford Univ. Press, 1985).

18 Morley, *Deterrent Diplomacy*, pp. 123, 169–70.

19 Ibid., pp. 174–75.

20 Bethell, *War Hitler Won*, p. 306, overlooks the fact that Soviet ambassadors do not return to the Soviet Union on their own initiative but under instruction.

21 On this point, see the extensive suspicion about German adherence to the August 23 line first summarized in Gerhard L. Weinberg, *Germany and the Soviet Union, 1939–1941* (Leyden: Brill, 1954), pp. 54–56, and further substantiated by additional evidence since (*ADAP*, D, 8, Nos. 90, 101, 103).

22 *ADAP*, D, 8, Nos. 78, 80, 94.

23 Jan T. Gross, *Revolution from Abroad: The Soviet Conquest of Poland's Western Ukraine and Western Belorussia* (Princeton, N.J.: Princeton Univ. Press, 1988). There is a fine collection of essays in Keith Sword (ed.), *The Soviet Takeover of the Polish Eastern Provinces, 1939– 41* (New York: St. Martin's, 1991).

24 On the technical problems involving German troops moving into the part of Poland that was to go to the Soviet Union and Soviet troops entering the Vilna area at a time when Lithuania, increased by that territory, was still scheduled to be in the German sphere, see Weinberg, *Germany and the Soviet Union*, pp. 54–58; *ADAP*, D, 8, Nos. 114, 123. For similar problems in the naval sphere, see Norbert von Baumbach, "Die Angelegenheit des 20. Längengrades Ost 25.–30. Oktober 1939," 9 March 1945, BA/MA, M1676, PG 31874a; *ADAP*, D, 8, Nos. 305, 309, 313.

25 A good account of these events in *DRuZW*, 2: 129–33. On the German air force terror raids against Warsaw and Modlin to force surrender, see Samuel W. Mitcham, *Men of the Luftwaffe* (Novato, Calif.: Presidio Press, 1988), pp. 72–73.

26 *DRuZW*, 2: 133.

27 The view expressed in ibid., that these casualties had major repercussions in subsequent years, is one this author cannot share. The losses have to be set against the experience gained by the overwhelming majority of German officers and soldiers who survived the campaign and went into subsequent battles with higher morale, greater cohesion, and more knowledgeable in the ways of war.

28 Weinberg, *Germany and the Soviet Union*, p. 63. The quote is from Stalin's reply to von Ribbentrop's congratulations on his 60th birthday. The full text was published in *Pravda* on December 25, 1939, alongside exchanges with such dignitaries as Father Tiso, the President of the Nazi puppet state of Slovakia, and Otto Kuusinen, "Head of the National Government of Finland," the leader of the puppet government Stalin intended to install in Helsinki.

29 These preparations are reviewed in Chapter 4, below.

30 The new boundaries went far beyond the old everywhere except for a 50–mile segment of southeast East Prussia, and at this point additional Polish territory (the district of Bialystok) was later added to East Prussia. There are maps of the partition of Poland in many books; one of the few which shows the 1914 border for comparison is that in the back of the fine book by Martin Broszat, *Nationalsozialistische Polenpolitik, 1939–1945* (Stuttgart: Deutsche Verlags-Anstalt, 1961).

31 It appears that the concept of population transfer was first raised with the Italians by Hermann Göring when he visited Rome in January 1937 (Weinberg, *Foreign Policy 1937–*

39, pp. 270–71). No evidence of prior discussion of the issue between Hitler and Göring has come to light. The exchange of population between Greece and Turkey in the 1920s belongs in this writer's opinion in the context of the post-World War I settlement of nationality issues.

It should be added that the population shuffling planned by the Germans was not completed during the years of German occupation. What is remarkable is not that some of the terrible changes intended in 990 years of rule by the Third Reich were left unfinished, but rather how far they were carried in the first five. See Richard C. Lukas, *Forgotten Holocaust: The Poles under German Occupation, 1939–1944* (Lexington, Ky.: Univ. Press of Kentucky, 1986).

32 Bernhard Stasiewski, "Die Kirchenpolitik der Nationalsozialisten im Warthegau," *VjZ* 7 (1959), 46–74.

33 Alexander Dallin, *German Rule in Russia, 1941–1945* (London: Macmillan, 1957), p. 90.

34 On Hitler's reference to the massacres of the Armenians being forgotten, see the recent discussion in Richard Breitman, *The Architect of Genocide: Himmler and the Final Solution* (New York: Knopf, 1991), p. 258 n 47.

There is a good summary of German policy in Poland in Norman Rich, *Hitler's War Aims,* 2 *The Establishment of the New Order* (New York: Norton, 1974), chap. 4; see also Waclaw Dlugoborski's piece in Karl Dietrich Bracher et al. (eds.), *Nationalsozialistische Diktatur* (Düsseldorf: Droste, 1983), pp. 572–90; Gerhard Eisenblätter, "Grundlinien der Politik des Reiches gegenüber dem Generalgouvernment 1939–1945" (Frankfurt/M. Phil. diss., 1969); Czeslaw Madajczyk, *Die Okkupationspolitik des deutschen Imperialismus in Polen 1939–1945* (Berlin-East: Akademie, 1987). The entry in the diary of the commander of the German northern Army Group, von Bock, of September 22 1939, that Hitler wanted to get rid of the population of Warsaw, points to his subsequent plans for the eradication of Moscow and Leningrad (cf. Eisenblätter, p. 117 n 6).

On mass murders in the early months of the occupation, see also Christian Jansen and Arno Weckbecher, *Der "Volksdeutsche Selbstschutz" in Polen 1939–40* (Munich: Oldenbourg, 1992).

35 For the text of Frank's speech of December 16, 1941, see Werner Präg and Wolfgang Jacobmeyer (eds.), *Das Diensttagebuch des deutschen Generalgouverneurs in Polen 1939–1945* (Stuttgart: Deutsche Verlags-Anstalt, 1975), p. 459 (henceforth cited as *Frank Diary*; there is something like a translation of the relevant passages in Rich, *Hitler's War Aims,* 2: 89.

36 *ADAP*, D, 8, No. 104.

37 Ibid, No. 131.

38 This whole issue remains to be explored in detail; there is a preliminary analysis in Weinberg, *Germany and the Soviet Union*, pp. 56, 57, 60, 70; see also *ADAP*, D, 8, Nos. 109, 115.

39 I am not aware of any study of this question. German military plans contained provisions for an occupation of Lithuania whether or not that state resisted, and in the immediate office of Foreign Minister von Ribbentrop a draft convention for German military control of Lithuania was prepared (*ADAP*, D, 8, No. 113). The Lithuanian Foreign Minister was summoned to Danzig to surrender his country to the Third Reich (ibid., No. 121; note by von Sonnleithner, 4 Sept. 1939, AA, St.S., "Der Krieg," Bd. 3, fr. 35641–42). The trading of Lithuania to the Soviet Union by Germany meant that instead he had to go to Moscow.

40 *ADAP*, D, 8, No. 152.

41 Robert Koehl, *RKFDV: German Resettlement and Population Policy 1939–1945* (Cambridge, Mass.: Harvard Univ. Press, 1957), remains the best introduction to the subject in English.

42 The September 28 agreements have been published in *ADAP*, D, 8, Nos. 157–63. To this should be added: Ingeborg Fleischhauer (ed.), "Der deutsch-sowjetische Grenz- und

Feundschaftsvertrag vom 28, September 1939: Die deutschen Aufzeichnungen über die Verhandlungen zwischen Stalin, Molotov und Ribbentrop in Moskau," *VjZ* 39 (1991), 447–70.

43 It is often overlooked that the Soviet government initially moved at both the northern and the southern portions of its European border and only postponed moves at the southern end when the negotiations with Finland ran into difficulties and then broke down.

44 The Soviet Union promised to deliver an additional quantity of petroleum products equivalent to the annual production of the Polish oil fields and to facilitate the transport of Romanian oil to Germany across the Soviet-occupied part of Poland. This latter point was especially important for the Germans not only because the railway in question was single-tracked but because the Russians under the agreement kept it at the old gage, rather than converting to the wider Russian gage with a resulting double transfer of cargo. On this issue see *ADAP*, D, 8, No. 386. Statistics of the German Ministry of Transport show a steady rise in the quantities shipped over this route (BA, R 43 II/332a, f. 119).

45 On the economic negotiations, see Weinberg, *Germany and the Soviet Union*, pp. 65–75; *ADAP*, D, 8, passim; *DRuZW*, 4: 103; St.S., No. 688 of 6 Sept. 1939, AA, St.S., "Russland," Bd. 1, fr. 111578; Notiz für Büro RAM, 10 Sept. 1939, AA, St.S., "Der Krieg 1939," Bd. 3, fr. 35794–95; Russland-Ausschuss der Deutschen Wirtschaft, Bericht, 3 Oct. 1939, BA, R 43 II/1489a, f. 163–66; KTB Skl A, 4, 7 Dec. 1939, BA/MA, RM 7/7, f. 45–46; KTB Skl A, 5, 10 Jan. 1940, BA/MA, RM 7/8, f. 62–63; Ritter (Moscow) tel. 9 of 3 Jan. 1940, AA, St.S., "Russland," Bd. 2, fr. 111933, and memorandum by Ritter (Berlin) of 10 Jan. 1940, fr. 111943–45. For a recent Soviet assessment, see Michail Semijarga's statement in Hildebrand et al., *1939*, p. 298.

46 On the transit issue, see Weinberg, *Germany and the Soviet Union*, pp. 65–75; *ADAP*, D 8, No. 320. On transit shipments of rubber and tin from East Asia, see Berlin tel. to Tokyo, zu W VII 74 of 12 Jan. 1940; Berlin tel. to Tokyo, zu W 543/40g II of 7 Feb. 1940; Tokyo tels. No. 108 of 10 Feb. 1940 and No. 124 of 15 Feb. 1940, all in AA, HaPol, Clodius, "Japan," Bd. 3. On early development of the transit trade in soybeans (critical for Germany's need for vegetable fats for human and animal consumption), see the Reichschancellory, "Vermerk, betreffend Deutschlands Versorgung mit Sojabohnen," 13 Feb. 1940, BA, R 43 II/1422. There are detailed statistics on the transit trade and its importance for Germany in BA, R 2/17315. The German press was prohibited from mentioning the transit trade, see Reichspropagandaamt Berlin, "Geheim! Presse-Rundschreiben Nr. II/9/40," 9 Jan. 1940, BA, Nadler, ZSg. 115/19, f. 23.

47 Weinberg, *Germany and the Soviet Union*, pp. 75–85; *ADAP*, D, 8, Nos. 195, 248, 257; Moscow tel. 273 of 5 Sept. 1939, AA, St.S. "Der Krieg 1939," Bd. 3, fr. 35657; KTB Skl A 1, 11 and 25 Sept. 1939, BA/MA, RM 7/4, f. 59,162; KTB Skl A 2, 7, 11, 17, 23, 25, 30 Oct. 1939, BA/MA, RM 7/5, f. 68, 94–95, 135–37, 191–92, 203, 247–48. The British learned about the provision of naval facilities by the Soviet Union to Germany in north Russia by April 8, 1941, at the latest and were greatly worried about this; see N 4087/283/38, PRO, FO 371/24852. The war diary of the German navy for January 1940 also contains extensive material on Soviet assistance for the transfer of an auxiliary cruiser to the Pacific by the northern sea route (BA/MA, RM 7/8, passim).

Obviously Soviet assistance to Germany also enabled the latter to divert naval forces from the Baltic to the Atlantic to prey on Allied shipping; a point the German navy had recognized as soon as the Nazi–Soviet Pact was signed (KTB Skl A 1, 23 Aug. 1939, BA/MA, RM 7/4, f. 8).

The Soviet government also had meteorological information provided for the German air force, but the details of this remain to be investigated.

48 Cripps to Halifax, 18 Sept. 1939, N 4571/57/38, PRO, FO 371/23678. The British government hoped to keep Moscow as far apart from the Germans as possible (Salisbury

to Halifax, 28 Oct. 1939, Halifax to Salisbury, 31 Oct. 1939, PRO, FO 800/325, f. 129–33, 147–49); but Stalin at this time was obviously interested primarily in accommodating Berlin.

49 See Hochman, *Soviet Union and Collective Security*, chap. 5.

50 Donald C. Watt, "Stalin's First Bid for Sea Power 1933–1941," *Naval Institute Proceedings*, 90 (June 1964), 88–96; Malcolm Muir, Jr., "American Warship Construction for Stalin's Navy Prior to World War II: A Study in Paralysis of Policy," *Diplomatic History*, 5 (1981), 337–51; see also Weinberg, *Foreign Policy, 1937–39*, pp. 416–17.

51 On the discussion of this issue in the high command of the German navy (Skl), the high command of the German armed forces (OKW) and with Hitler, which shows Hitler reversing himself to approve important sales to the Russians in view of the significance of Soviet aid to Germany, see the documents of 30 and 31 Oct. 1939 in BA/MA, RM 7/198, f. 287–91. The fact that the German naval construction program had been carried out in violation of the Anglo-German Naval Agreement of 1935 from the beginning was now coming back to haunt them when the Russians asked for the drawing for major warships constructed or laid down supposedly under its terms.

52 On the *Lützow*, see Weinberg, *Germany and the Soviet Union*, pp. 76–78. British intelligence had learned of its being towed to the Soviet Union by 1 June 1940 (N 5854/360/98, PRO, FO 371/24853).

53 Weinberg, *Foreign Policy, 1937–39*, pp. 649–52.

54 Robert Fisk, *In Time of War: Ireland, Ulster and the Price of Neutrality 1939–45* (London: Deutsch, 1983), pp. 150–53.

55 Ibid., pp. 91, 94–96. See also *ADAP*, D, 8, No. 216.

56 Gibbs, *Grand Strategy*, 1: 668.

57 War Cabinet 6³⁹, PRO, CAB 65/1, f. 41.

58 *Documents diplomatiques français, 1932–1939*, 2d series, Vol. 1, No. 334.

59 See Robert A. Doughty, *The Seeds of Disaster: The Development of French Army Doctrine 1919–1939* (Hamden, Conn.: Archon, 1985).

60 Waclaw Jedrzejewicz (ed.), *Diplomat in Paris, 1936–1939: Memoirs of Juliusz Lukasiewicz* (New York: Columbia Univ. Press, 1970), p. 217. It is indicative of the apologetic approach of Gunsberg, *Divided and Conquered* p. 80, that this commitment is mentioned with no reference to its fundamentally mendacious character. Only French memoirs are cited as sources (ibid., p. 85 n 58).

61 Ibid., p. 89.

62 Bethell, *War Hitler Won* p.161.

63 See the minutes of the first meeting of the Supreme War Council on September 12, 1939, in François Bédarida (ed.), *La Stratégie secrète de la drôle de guerre* (Paris: Editions du CNRS, 1979), pp. 93–94.

64 The French also kept the British from mining the Rhine river (operation "Royal Marine") for fear of reprisals. See on this PRO, FO 800/312, f. 28–29. The project was a favorite of First Lord of the Admiralty Winston Churchill and is discussed at length in his *The Gathering Storm* (Boston: Houghton Mifflin, 1948), pp. 508ff.

65 Max Hastings, *Bomber Command* (London: Pan Books, 1981), pp. 13–39. British concentration on bombing no more meant that the bombs actually exploded than that German planning for submarine warfare meant their torpedoes worked. When the British attacked the pocket battleship *Scheer* on September 4, 1939, four bombs hit but none exploded (ibid., p. 16). The Germans eventually solved the problem with their torpedoes, but the British never really solved the bomb problem: of the bombs dropped by the RAF on German oil targets in the last year of the war, almost a fifth failed to explode (ibid., p. 403).

66 On the leaflet campaign, see Charles Webster and Noble Frankland, *The Strategic Air*

Offensive against Germany 1939–1945, 4 vols. (London: HMSO, 1961), 1: 105–6, 134–35.

67 KTB Skl A, 1, 5 and 6 Sept. 1939, BA/MA, RM 7/4, f. 41, 43.

68 *ADAP*, D, 8, No. 4.

69 BA/MA, PG 33626 passim. (There is a detailed account of the fate of the crew of *Graf Spee* in Ronald C. Newton, *The "Nazi Menace" in Argentina, 1937–1947* [Stanford: Stanford Univ. Press, 1992], chap. 15.) Similarly the Russians helped the crews of German ships stranded in Iran by the outbreak of war to return home across the Soviet Union (E 506/48/38, PRO, FO 371/24571). The route via Japan and the Soviet Union was also utilized for those stranded in the United States (Japanese Consul General New York to Tokyo, No. 2 of 4 Jan. 1940, NA, RG 457, SRDJ 002742).

70 *DRuZW*, 2: 170–74; *ADAP*, D, 8, Nos. 460–63, 467; Longmann (Montevideo) No. 177 of 14 Dec. 1939, copy in BA/MA, RM 6/71, f. 137.

71 Michael Salewski, *Die deutsche Seekriegsleitung, 1935–1945*, 3 vols. (Frankfurt/M: Bernard & Graefe, 1975), 1:141ff; *DRuZW*, 2: 164ff. The arguments over the dismissal, first of Admiral Hermann Boehm and later of Admiral Wilhelm Marschall cannot be reviewed here. Whatever the merits of the cases, the incidents certainly reflect confusion at the top of the German navy. There are some interesting comments on this in Rolf Johannesson, *Offizier in kritischer Zeit* (Herford: Mittler, 1989).

72 On the torpedo problem, see Salewski, *Seekriegsleitung*, 1: 188ff. When the United States was drawn into the war more than two years later, the same thing happened with American torpedoes.

73 Jürgen Rohwer and Eberhard Jäckel (eds.), *Die Funkaufklärung und ihre Rolle im 2. Weltkrieg* (Stuttgart: Motorbuch, 1979), p. 128; *DRuZW*, 2: 168.

74 KTB Skl *A*, 5, 23 Jan. 1940, BA/MA, *RM* 7/8, f. 184. The Germans did not understand that the British were also greatly improving their radio location devices and eventually installed them on the convoy escorts, thus enabling the latter to locate and attack U-Boats during convoy battles. The subject is reviewed in Chapter 10, below. Note Rohwer and Jäckel, *Funkaufklärung*, pp. 126, 131–32; Jürgen Rohwer, *Geleitzugschlachten im März 1943* (Stuttgart: Motorbuch, 1975), pp. 29–32, 63–66, picture facing p. 289, 310–14.

75 David Dilks, "The Twilight War and the Fall of France: Chamberlain and Churchill in 1940," *Transactions of the Royal Historical Society*, series 5, 28 (1978), pp. 70–71. A file of documents on the project, code-named "Catherine," is in PRO, ADM 205/4.

76 KTB Skl A 1, 5 Aug. 1939, BA/MA, RM 7/4, f. 6.

77 As is now clear, the *Altmark* was armed and so was part of the crew; see the material in BA/MA, *PG* 33627, esp. f. 35, 283–84. See also Hans-Dietrich Loock, *Quisling, Rosenberg und Terboven: Zur Vorgeschichte und Geschichte der nationalsozialistischen Revolution in Norwegen* (Stuttgart: Deutsche Verlags-Anstalt, 1970), pp. 245–49; "Bestellungen aus der Pressekonferenz vom 19 Februar 1940," BA, Brammer, ZSg. 101/15, f. 85. The Germans became a bit more sensitive about transporting prisoners of war across neutral countries thereafter; see Hans-Jürgen Lutzhöft, *Deutsche Militärpolitik und schwedische Neutralität 1939–1942* (Neumünster: Wachholtz, 1981), pp. 154–55; *ADAP*, D, 13, No. 181.

78 See E.F. Gueritz, "Nelson's Blood: Attitudes and Actions of the Royal Navy," *JCH*, 16 (1981), 487–99.

79 There is a two-volume official history by William N. Medlicott, *The Economic Blockade* (London: HMSO, 1952–59), but the subject has not attracted much scholarly attention since the opening of the archives. Williamson Murray argues in "The Strategy of the 'Phony War': A Re-evaluation," *Military Affairs* 45, No. 1 (1981), 13–14, that the blockade had major effects on the German economy in the first months of the war, but this overlooks the fact that the blockade was seen as a means of weakening

Germany not for a few months but during the years that Britain and France built up their forces.

80 On this question, see Alan S. Milward, "Could Sweden have Stopped the Second World War?" *Scandinavian Economic History Review* 15 (1967), 127–38; Jörg-Johannes Jäger, "Sweden's Iron Ore Exports to Germany," ibid., pp. 139–47.

81 On these problems, see the minutes published by Bédarida, *Stratégie secrète*; Llewellyn Woodward, *British Foreign Policy in the Second World War*, 5 vols. (London: HMSO, 1970–76), 1: chaps. 2–4; Hans-Joachim Lorbeer, *Westmächte gegen die Sowjetunion 1939–1941* (Freiburg: Rombach, 1975).

82 Weinberg, *Foreign Policy 1937–39*, pp. 563–67.

83 Knox, *Mussolini Unleashed*, pp. 44–46.

84 Important for Ciano's visit, in addition to *ADAP*, D, 8, No. 176: Malcolm Muggeridge (ed.), *Ciano's Diplomatic Papers* (London: Odhams, 1948), pp. 309–16; and Hugh Gibson (ed.), *The Ciano Diaries 1939–1943* (Garden City, N.Y.: Doubleday, 1946), 1 and 2 Oct. 1939, is the report of the Soviet chargé in Rome, Leon Helfand, to United States Ambassador William Phillips on his conversation with Ciano in Phillips's diary for 10 Oct. 1939 (Harvard, Houghton Library). (These two publications are henceforth cited as Ciano, *Diplomatic Papers* and Ciano, *Diary*, respectively.) Ciano liked Helfand and later helped him defect; such personal relationships and attitudes greatly influenced Ciano's conduct of official business. On Italian prodding for a peace with Poland, see also *ADAP*, D, 8, No. 38.

85 This interpretation is also shared by Knox, *DRuZW*, 3, and the older study of Ferdinand Siebert, *Italiens Weg in den Zweiten Weltkrieg* (Frankfurt/M: Athenäum, 1962).

86 This was true in spite of British and French efforts to help themselves and split the Axis by trying to obtain deliveries of military supplies from Italy; see the reports of the German naval attaché in Rome of 21 and 24 Jan. 1940, BA/MA, Case 17/3, PG 645170; *ADAP*, D, 8, Nos. 593, 599. On the blockade and Italy, see Knox, *Mussolini Unleashed*, pp. 70–75.

87 Knox, pp. 59–61; Conrad F. Latour, *Südtirol und die Achse Berlin-Rom 1938–1945* (Stuttgart: Deutsche Verlags-Anstalt, 1962), chap. 4. On the issue of publicity, see Reichspropagandaamt Berlin, "Presse-Rundschreiben Nr. II/13/40," 11 Jan. 1940, BA, Nadler, ZSg. 115/19, f. 26.

88 Knox, pp. 63, 66.

89 See the books cited in n 85, above.

90 Knox, pp. 63–65;, *ADAP*, D, 8, No. 205.

91 Weinberg, *Germany and the Soviet Union*, pp. 91–96.

92 The analysis of Spanish attitudes on this question in Donald S. Detwiler, *Hitler, Franco und Gibraltar* (Wiesbaden: Steiner, 1962), pp. 13–14, is persuasive.

93 Weinberg, *Foreign Policy 1937–39*, pp. 160–63, 503.

94 See *ADAP*, D, 8, No. 173.

95 Detwiler, *Hitler, Franco*, pp. 17–18.

96 Elke Fröhlich (ed.), *Die Tagebücher von Joseph Goebbels*, Part 1 (4 vols. plus index) (Munich: Saur, 1987), 22 and 27 Jan. 1939. (Henceforth cited as Fröhlich, *Goebbels Tagebücher*.)

97 KTB Skl, gKdos. "Organisation und Aufgaben der Etappen (Erfahrungen der Spannungszeit, Ölnachschub)," Jan. 1939, BA/MA, RM 6/58.

98 A good source is the file of the German embassy in Madrid, "Seekrieg und seine Auswirkungen auf Spanien," two vols., in AA. For information on a secret fund available to the Germans inside Spain for use in these activities, see Weinberg, *Foreign Policy 1937–39*, pp. 151–52.

99 Charles B. Burdick, " 'Moro': The Resupply of German Submarines in Spain, 1939–1942," *CEH* 3 (1970), 256–84; *ADAP*, D, 8, Nos. 284, 604, 616; KTB Skl A, 3, 4 Nov.

1939, BA/MA, RM 7/5, f. 17–18, and 19 Jan. 1940, RM 7/8, f. 153; AA, Botschaft Madrid, "Seekrieg," passim.

100 Klaus Wittmann, *Schwedens Wirtschaftsbeziehungen zum Dritten Reich 1933–1945* (Munich: Oldenbourg, 1978), pp. 241–43.

101 See n 80, above.

102 The Swedes were so enthusiastic about trade with Germany that their trade agreement with the Third Reich of December 22, 1939, violated the one they had signed with England on December 7. See Wittmann, *Schwedens Wirtschaftsbeziehungen*, pp.160–72; Lutzhöft, *Deutsche Militärpolitik*, p.68.

103 Lutzhöft, pp. 32–34.

104 Wittmann, p. 396, appropriately stresses these points. See also KTB Skl A, 17, 2 Jan. 1941, BA/MA, RM 7/20, f. 23–24. An apologia for Swedish policy, based mainly on the Swedish Foreign Ministry archives, may be found in William M. Carlgren, *Swedish Foreign Policy during the Second World War*, trans. Arthur Spencer (New York: St. Martin's, 1977).

105 Norman Rich, who is generally very cautious in his assessment of Hitler's long-term aims, concludes (*Hitler's War Aims*, 2: 401) that the Austrian model would probably have served for Sweden.

106 Note *ADAP*, D, 8, Nos. 165, 297, 298, 304.

107 Sweden also supplied steel ball-bearings and some other important materials, but iron ore was the key element.

108 Weinberg, *Foreign Policy 1937–39*, pp. 242, 591.

109 On Turkey at this time, see Lothar Krecker, *Deutschland und die Türkei im Zweiten Weltkrieg* (Frankfurt/M: Klostermann, 1964); Zehra Önder, *Die türkische Aussenpolitik im Zweiten Weltkrieg* (Munich: Oldenbourg, 1976).

110 Hoptner, *Yugoslavia in Crisis*, pp. 167–72, remains the best English language account but is now superseded by chapt. 4 of Alfredo Breccia, *Jugoslavia 1939–1941: Diplomazia della Neutralita* (Rome: Giuffrè, 1978), which is based on extensive work in the Italian and Yugoslav archives in addition to British, U.S., and German documents. See also Elizabeth Barker, *British Policy in South-East Europe in the Second World War* (London: Macmillan, 1976), pp. 13–19.

111 When discussing the problem of the Polish government leaders who had fled to Romania with the Japanese Minister on September 22, 1939, Romanian Foreign Minister Grigore Gafencu predicted a war between Germany and the Soviet Union in the future (Oshima to Tokyo No. 1058 of 24 Sept. 1939, NA, RG 457, SRDJ 001825–28).

112 The account in Andreas Hillgruber, *Hitler, König Carol und Marschall Antonescu* (Wiesbaden: Steiner, 1954), pp. 8off, must now be modified in light of Philippe Marguerat, *Le IIIe Reich et le pétrole roumain, 1938–1940* (Leyden: Sijthoff, 1977), chap. 5. See also the documents in PRO, AIR 19/12.

113 Weinberg, *Foreign Policy, 1937–39*, pp. 174–76; Gerhard Krebs, *Japans Deutschlandpolitik 1935–1941*, 2 vols. (Hamburg: MOAG, 1984), 1: 117–47; John P. Fox, *Germany and the Far Eastern Crisis 1931–1938* (Oxford: Clarendon Press, 1982), chap. 9.

114 On this, see Hsi-sheng Ch'i, *Nationalist China at War 1937–45* (Ann Arbor, Mich.: Univ. of Michigan Press, 1982), pp. 118–21.

115 Chiang himself appears to have thought on occasion of German mediation in the war with Japan. The Germans, however, were not interested in trying once more, at least not until after Japan had moved southward and committed herself against Britain, because otherwise a Sino-Japanese settlement could easily pave the way for a settlement between Japan and the Western Powers. See *ADAP*, D, 8, Nos. 32, 201, 217.

116 John H. Boyle, *China and Japan at War 1937–1945: The Politics of Collaboration* (Stanford, Calif.: Stanford Univ. Press, 1972), deals with only aspects of the broader problem.

117 I am not aware of any recent study of this route and its utilization. There are descriptions of the route in Owen Lattimore, "China's Turkestan–Siberia Supply Road," *Pacific Affairs*

13 (1940), 393–412; Aitchen K. Wu, *China and the Soviet Union* (New York: John Day, 1950), pp. 259–60. There is a little information in Andrew D.W. Forbes, *Warlords and Muslims in Chinese Central Asia: A Political History of Republican Sinkiang, 1911–1949* (Cambridge: Cambridge Univ. Press, 1986), p. 146; John W. Garver, *Chinese–Soviet Relations, 1937–1945: The Diplomacy of Chinese Nationalism* (New York: Oxford Univ. Press, 1988), pp. 39, 107–8; Allen S. Whiting (ed.), *General Sheng Shih-ts'ai, Sinkiang: Pawn or Patriot?* (E. Lansing, Mich.: Michigan State Univ. Press, 1958), pp. 49, 61–62. In spite of its title, the 1981 New York University PhD dissertation of Arthur C. Hasiotis, Jr., "A Study of Soviet Political, Economic and Military Involvement in Sinkiang from 1928 to 1949," does not discuss the Soviet supply route.

118 James W. Morley, (ed.), *The Fateful Choice: Japan's Advance into Southeast Asia, 1939–1941* (New York: Columbia Univ. Press, 1980), pp. 32–41.

119 On Wang Ching-wei, see Gerald E. Bunker, *The Peace Conspiracy: Wang Ching-wei and the China War* (Cambridge, Mass.: Harvard Univ. Press, 1972). The defection of two key aides of Wang, who released documents on his negotiations with the Japanese on January 21, 1940, which showed him as subservient to extreme Japanese demands, effectively discredited Wang. See Boyle, *China and Japan at War*, pp. 278–80, 293–337.

120 The fullest account is Coox, *Nomonhan*.

121 Morley, *Deterrent Diplomacy*, pp. 174–76.

122 *ADAP*, D, 8, No. 93. The new Japanese ambassador, Kurusu Saburo, who temporarily replaced the extremely pro-German Oshima Hiroshi, did not make himself popular in Berlin by urging that Germany not attack in the West, but attain her aims in Europe by peaceful means and then mediate the war in East Asia; all this on the basis of the assumption that Germany could not defeat Britain because of American power (ibid., No. 590). Anyone this clear-sighted was certain to be ignored in the Third Reich.

123 On German efforts in this direction, see Morley, *Fateful Choice*, pp. 20–22; Morley, *Deterrent Diplomacy*, pp. 197–98; *ADAP*, D, 8, Nos. 11, 29, 75, 77, 79, 140, 549.

124 *ADAP*, D, 8, Nos. 40, 132, 292, 448.

125 Stephen E. Pelz, *Race to Pearl Harbor* (Cambridge, Mass.: Harvard Univ. Press, 1974).

126 Dorothy Borg and Shumpei Okamoto (eds.), *Pearl Harbor as History* (New York: Columbia Univ. Press, 1973), pp. 242–43. There is an excellent account of the whole project in Malcolm Muir, Jr., "Rearming in a Vacuum: United States Naval Construction and the Japanese Capital Ship Threat, 1936–1945," *Journal of Military History* 54, No. 4 (1990), 473–85.

127 Note the material in Morley, *Fateful Choice*, pp. 241–43.

128 Krebs, *Japans Deutschlandpolitik*, 1: 337–78.

129 Borg and Okamoto, *Pearl Harbor*, p. 43.

130 Michael Schaller, *The U.S. Crusade in China, 1938–1945* (New York: Columbia Univ. Press, 1979), pp. 25–29, 32–33.

131 Morley, *Deterrent Diplomacy*, pp. 192–93, 195; Borg and Okamoto, *Pearl Harbor*, pp. 144–46. Eugen Ott, the German ambassador to Japan, predicted the likelihood of failure in Japan's negotiations with Britain and the U.S. and success in the negotiations with Russia as early as Oct. 16, 1939 (*ADAP*, D, 8, No. 264).

132 Note the 2–4 year estimate in Berlin to Hsinking No. 178 of 15 Sept. 1939, NA, RG 457, SRDJ 1708.

133 Japanese Ambassador to Poland from Bukarest to Tokyo No. 84 of 24 Sept. 1939, ibid., SRDJ 1818–20.

134 See Berlin to Tokyo No. 220 of 11 Oct. 1939, ibid., SRDJ 1957–58; Ott (Tokyo) to Berlin No. 303 of 4 Apr. 1940, AA, HaPol, Clodius, "Japan," Bd. 3. German complaints about Japan in *ADAP*, D, 8, No. 421; Emil Helfferich, *1932–1946 Tatsachen, Ein Beitrag zur Wahrheitsfindung* (Jever, Oldenbourg: C.L. Mettcker, 1968), chap. 7.

135 John W.M. Chapman (ed.), *The Price of Admiralty: The War Diary of the German Naval*

Attaché in Japan, 1939–1943, Vol. 1 (Lewes, Sussex: Univ. of Sussex Printing Unit, 1982), passim; *ADAP*, D, 8, No. 646;9, No. 50; Ott (Tokyo) to Berlin No. 204 of 8 Mar. 1940, AA, St.S., "Japan," Bd. 2, fr. 398404–5; AA, HaPol, Clodius, "Japan," Bd. 3, passim.

136 Morley, *Fateful Choice*, pp. 23–24; Krebs, *Japans Deutschlandpolitik*, 1: 368–69.

137 On the period of the Yonai government (Jan.–July 1940), see Krebs, 1: 379–437.

138 Donald Smythe, *Pershing, General of the Armies* (Bloomington, Ind.: Indiana Univ. Press, 1986), chaps. 5–26, provides a good picture of the American role.

139 The author has placed this issue in a broader perspective in Jürgen Rohwer and Eberhard Jäckel (eds.), *Kriegswende Dezember 1941* (Koblenz: Bernard & Graefe, 1984), pp. 73–74.

140 This is the burden of Robert A. Divine's *Second Chance: The Triumph of Internationalism in America during World War II* (New York: Atheneum, 1967).

141 These issues are discussed in William L. Langer and S. Everett Gleason, *The World Crisis and American Foreign Policy*, 2 vols. (New York: Harper, 1952–53); Robert A. Divine, *The Reluctant Belligerent*, 2d ed (New York: Wiley, 1979); Wayne S. Cole, *Roosevelt and the Isolationists, 1932–45* (Lincoln, Neb.: Univ. of Nebraska Press, 1983); Robert Dallek, *Franklin D. Roosevelt and American Foreign Policy, 1932–1945* (New York: Oxford Univ. Press, 1979).

142 Haight, *American Aid to France*.

143 There is a good study of Bullitt by Beatrice Farnsworth, *William C. Bullitt and the Soviet Union* (Bloomington: Indiana Univ. Press, 1967), and his brother prepared an edition of his correspondence, Orville H. Bullitt (ed.), *For the President, Personal and Secret* (Boston: Houghton Mifflin, 1972). (Henceforth cited as *Bullitt Papers*.) There is no scholarly study of Strauss, the first American ambassador to Paris in twenty years who spoke French. A friendly account is Reginald W. Kauffman, *Jesse Isidor Strauss* (New York: private print, 1973). Neither Bullitt nor Strauss is included among those covered in the fine collection of Kenneth P. Jones, *U.S. Diplomats in Europe, 1919–1941*, repr. ed. (Santa Barbara, Calif.: ABC-Clio, 1983).

144 Langer and Gleason, *World Crisis*, 1: 222; Dallek, *Roosevelt and Foreign Policy*, p. 201.

145 For an account of this struggle which is very strongly biased in favor of the isolationists, see Cole, *Roosevelt and the Isolationists*.

146 Elliott Roosevelt (ed.), *F.D.R.: His Personal Letters 1928–1945*, 2 vols. (New York: Duell, Sloan & Pearce, 1950), 2: 934. (Henceforth cited as *FDR Letters*.)

147 The final vote in the Senate was 55 to 24; in the House of Representatives, 243 to 172. In both houses, the vote was mainly along partisan lines.

148 *ADAP*, D, 8, 22, 54, 56, 85, 88, 129, 220, 301.

149 Gerhard Wagner (ed.), *Lagevorträge des Oberbefehlshabers der Kriegsmarine vor Hitler 1939–1945* (Munich: Lehmanns, 1972), p. 27.

150 It should be noted that Roosevelt's own experience as second man in the Navy Department had sensitized him to the problem of shipping which would become so crucial. See the memorandum by D.J. Callahan for Roosevelt of 11 Dec. 1939, FDRL, PSF Great Britain, Kennedy, Box 53.

151 Gerhard L. Weinberg, *World in the Balance* (Hanover, N.H.: Univ. Press of New England, 1981), pp. 53–74. On the pre-war development of German–American relations, see Weinberg, *Foreign Policy, 1933–36*, chap. 6, and *1937–39*, pp. 249–55.

152 Jochen Thies, *Architekt der Weltherrschaft: Die "Endziele" Hitlers* (Düsseldorf: Droste, 1976), chap. 3.

153 Friedrich von Boetticher, "Soldat am Rande der Politik," BA/MA, N 323/56, p.209.

154 Gerhard L. Weinberg (ed.), *Hitlers Zweites Buch* (Stuttgart: Deutsche Verlags-Anstalt, 1961), pp. 138ff.

155 Borg and Okamoto, *Pearl Harbor*, pp. 176–77.

156 See *FDR Letters*, p. 920.

157 The preceding *USS North Carolina* was to have been completed in the 1920s but was

scrapped in 1923 under the terms of the Washington Naval Treaty. Here is one of the many examples of the extent to which German propaganda about the failure of the victors of World War I to disarm was unrelated to the truth. There is some irony in the fact that the scrapped *North Carolina* was to have been essentially the size of the *Bismarck;* the one subsequently built was smaller. A short account in John R. Corbett, *Ships by the Name of North Carolina* (Wilmington, N.C.: Corbett, 1961).

158 A good summary in Dallek, *Roosevelt and Foreign Policy*, pp. 172ff.

159 A comprehensive study of the work of the British and French purchasing missions in the United States would be most helpful.

160 Summary in Dallek, pp. 205–6.

161 The personal feuds within the leadership of the State Department have sometimes obscured the extent to which the best-known rivalry, that between Hull and Welles, masked common perceptions on many policy issues.

162 A brief summary of the pre-war situation in Weinberg, *Foreign Policy, 1937–39*, pp. 255–60. It should be noted that one of the most spectacular pieces of evidence on German interference in Latin America, the so-called Patagonia Document – demonstrating German territorial interest in the southern part of Argentina – which was denounced as a forgery after its publication by an Argentine parliamentary investigating committee, now turns out to have been authentic (*ADAP*, C, 6, No. 137). For an earlier account, see Alton Frye, *Nazi Germany and the American Hemisphere 1933–1941* (New Haven, Conn.: Yale Univ. Press, 1967), pp. 122–23. Reiner Pommerin, *Das Dritte Reich und Lateinamerika, 1939–1942* (Düsseldorf: Droste, 1977), pp. 65–67, accepted the allegation that the document was a fabrication.

163 This whole subject has been studied in great detail, and emphasized far beyond its real significance, by Hans-Jürgen Schröder. A summary of his views may be found in his piece in Manfred Funke (ed.), *Hitler, Deutschland und die Mächte* (Düsseldorf: Droste, 1977), pp. 339–64.

164 *FRUS*, 1939, 1: 424; *FDR Letters*, 2:938–39; *Wiener Library Bulletin* 18 (1964), 32.

165 On William R. Davis, see Dallek, *Roosevelt and Foreign Policy*, p. 207; Beatrice Bishop Berle and Travis B. Jacobs (eds.), *Navigating the Rapids 1918–1971: From the Papers of Adolf A. Berle* (New York: Harcourt Brace Jovanovich, 1973), p. 265; *ADAP*, DP, 8, No. 242 n 13; Moffat to Leland Harrison (Bern), 14 Nov. 1939, Harvard, Houghton Library, Moffat Papers, Vol. 15. It was in this connection that Roosevelt tried to think of ways to get a mission to the Vatican (*FDR Letters*, 2: 930–32), which was eventually entrusted to Myron Taylor in December 1939.

166 See C 17219, 17220/13005/18 of 24 Oct. 1939 in PRO, FO 371/23099. On James D. Mooney, see also C 17285, C 17419 in ibid.; War Cabinet 61(39) of 26 Oct. 1939, PRO, CAB 65/3, f. 154–55; Kirk to Moffat, 19 Apr. 1940, Moffat Papers, Vol. 18; Dallek, *Roosevelt and Foreign Policy*, p. 216; *ADAP*, D, 8, No. 656; FDR to Mooney, 25 Mar. 1940, FDRL, PSF Safe File, Cont. 4, Germany, and FDR to Mooney, 2 Apr. 1940, FDRL, PSF Cont. 79, Navy Dept. Jan.-Apr. 1940.

167 Presidential Diary, 3 Oct. 1939, FDRL, Morgenthau Papers, Diary, Vol. 2, p. 317; cf. *ADAP*, D, 8, No. 291. For some British minutes on Kennedy's defeatist and anti-British views, see A 605, 1317, 1384, 1723, 1848, and 1945/605/45, 18 Jan.-22 Aug. 1940, in PRO, FO 371/14251. For a balanced and fairly sympathetic account of Kennedy's term as ambassador, see Jane K. Veith's chapter in Jones, *US Diplomats*, pp. 165–82.

168 On the mission of Welles, see Stanley E. Hilton, "The Welles Mission to Europe, February–March 1940: Illusion or Realism?" *Journal of American History* 58 (1971), 93–120; Dallek, *Roosevelt and Foreign Policy*, pp. 216–18. The whole peace question is covered here and elsewhere in this book in detail and on the basis of archival research because the main monograph on the subject, Bernd Martin, *Friedensinitiativen und Machtpolitik im Zweiten Weltkrieg* (Düusseldorf: Droste, 1974), is not reliable (see, e.g., J. W. Brügel,

"Dahlerns als Zwischenträger nach Kriegsausbruch," *Historische Zeitschrift* 228 [1979], 70–79; D. Albrecht, "Zur Friedensdiplomatie des Vatikans 1939–41: Eine Auseinandersetzung mit Bernd Martin," in *Politik und Konfession: Festschrift für Konrad Repgen* [Berlin: Duncker & Humblot, 1983], pp. 447–64). Unfortunately one of the best recent accounts, that in chap. 6 of Marion Thielenhaus, *Zwischen Anpassung und Widerstand: Deutsche Diplomaten 1938–1941* (Paderborn: Schöningh, 1984), depends on Martin at many points.

169 *ADAP*, D, 8, pp. 177–80.
170 On the Göring–Dahlerus soundings, see ibid., No. 138; Brügel, "Dahlerus", pp. 70–97; Helmut Krausnick and Harold C. Deutsch (eds.), *Helmuth Groscurth: Tagebücher eines Abwehroffiziers 1938–1940* (Stuttgart: Deutsche Verlags-Anstalt, 1970), p. 385. (Henceforth cited as *Groscurth Tagebuch.*) British documents in C 13916/15/18, PRO, FO 371/22983; C 18882–83/15/18, FO 371/22986; C 15620/13005/18, FO 371/23097, C 15875 and 16448/13005/18, FO 371/23098; C 16662, 16731, 16840 and 17015/13005/18, FO 371/23099; C 20525/13005/18, FO 371/230100; FO 800/317, f. 60–62, 70, 75, 77–78, 121–24, 141; Cabinet meetings of 2, 6, 10, 12, 15, and 16 Oct. 1939, in PRO, CAB 65/3, f. 88–91, 102–3, 114, 119, 133–34, 138–39. On Göring's soundings via Max von Hohenlohe, see *ADAP*, D, 8, No. 645; C 17016/13005/18, PRO, FO 371/23099. On a sounding via the Swedish Baron Borde, see C 1187/89/18, FO 371/24405. On Baldwin Raper, see C 3537/89/18, FO 371/24406, C 4917 and 5506/89/18, FO 371/24407.
171 Hans-Adolf Jacobsen, *Fall Gelb: Der Kampf um den deutschen Operationsplan zur Westoffensive 1940* (Wiesbaden: Steiner, 1956); Hans-Adolf Jacobsen (ed.), *Dokumente zur Vorgeschichte des Westfeldzuges 1939–1940* (Göttingen: Musterschmidt, 1956).
172 There were also probes launched by other Germans such as the one of Franz von Papen, then German ambassador in Turkey, who put forward ideas characteristically too silly to be taken seriously; see Papen tel. 367 of 3 Oct. 1939, AA, St.S., "Friedensbemühungen," fr. 471603; C 15221, 15356, 15435, 15442/13005/18, PRO, FO 371/23097; C 15944–45, 15972/13005/18, FO 371/23098; C 16892/13005/18, FO 371/23099; War Cabinet 34³⁹ of 2 Oct. 1939, CAB 55/3, f. 77–81, 83–84; FO 800/317, f. 238–41; Mackensen to Weizsäcker, 18 Jan. 1940, AA, Nachlass Mackensen, Bd. 4, fr. 64913–22.
173 A preliminary account in Weinberg, *Germany and the Soviet Union*, pp. 64–65; see also Johann W. Brügel (ed.), *Stalin und Hitler: Pakt gegen Europa* (Vienna: Europaverlag, 1973), Nos. 136ff. A scholarly account of the whole campaign remains to be written. The Germans reprinted Molotov's October 31 speech on the subject and dropped it over France, see Luther notes of 9 and 10 Nov. 1939, in AA, St.S., "Der Krieg 1939," Bd. 6.
174 Knox, *Mussolini Unleashed*, pp. 49–52; Thielenhaus, *Zwischen Anpassung und Widerstand*, pp. 196–202; *ADAP*, D, 8, Nos. 73, 97, 127, 180; Lorraine No. 1000, secret, of 4 Oct. 1939, C 15721/15/18, PRO, FO 371/22984. The Italian effort was pushed with special determination by Bernardo Attolico, the Italian ambassador in Berlin, whom the Germans soon after had recalled.
175 *Hung. Docs.*, 4, Nos. 380, 386; Budapest tel. 326 of 15 Sept. and Ribbentrop's answer No. 364 of 18 Sept. 1939, AA, St.S., "Der Krieg 1939," Bd. 4, fr. 223955–56.
176 Thielenhaus, *Zwischen Anpassung und Widerstand*, pp. 191–96.
177 Ibid., pp. 185–91; C 20492/13669/62, PRO, FO 371/22947 (Halifax–Berggrav meeting of 15 Dec. 1939); PRO, FO 800/322, f. 214–21 (Halifax–Berggrav meeting of 27 Jan. 1940 with Chamberlain's comment: "This doesn't get us any further"); *ADAP*, D, 8, No. 550; Frederick A. Sterling (U.S. Minister Stockholm) to Moffat, 16 Jan. 1940 (with a report on Berggrav's Dec. trip to England), Moffat Papers, Vol. 18 (Houghton Library, Harvard); Weizsäcker note, St.S. No. 249, 21 Mar. 1940, AA, St.S., "Aufzeichnungen btr. nicht-Diplomatenbesuche," Bd. 2, fr. 36560–62.

178 See *ADAP*, D, 8, Nos. 25, 87; *Hung, Docs.*, 4, No. 386; PRO, FO 800/317, f. 179–82.

179 War Cabinet 9(39) of 9 Sept. 1939, PRO, CAB 65/1, f. 59. After the soundings were to all intents and purposes over, Neville Chamberlain on February 2, 1940, wrote to Lord Brocket, a long-time advocate of concessions to Germany, that he would not accept peace at any price. "I did not want this war and did my best to keep out of it. Having been forced into it, I am not prepared undefeated to accept terms which would give away just what we are fighting to preserve." He wrote that he had no desire to cut up Germany into little bits but they must "get rid of the gangsters." PRO, PREM 1/443, f. 3–5.

180 Weinberg, *Foreign Policy, 1937–39*, pp. 618–19.

181 In addition to the other British documents cited in this section, see Sargent Memorandum of 11 Sept. 1939 (C 15050/13005/18, PRO, FO 371/23097); Halifax to Earl of Lytton, 11 Nov. 1939 (FO 800/317, f. 196–99); and Halifax to Lord Lothian, 21 Nov. 1939 (FO 800/311, f. 374–81). The last two documents summarize the situation as seen from London particularly effectively and also reflect British concern that any French insistence on the dismemberment of Germany would harden German resistance. There is a review of the Cabinet discussions in Christopher Hill, *Cabinet Discussions on Foreign Policy: The British Experience, October 1938–June 1941* (Cambridge: Cambridge Univ. Press, 1991), chap. 5. See also Lothar Kettenacker, *Krieg zur Friedenssicherung: Die Deutschlandplanung der Britischen Regierung während des Zweiten Weltkrieges* (Göttingen: Vandenhoeck & Ruprecht, 1989), pp. 40–51.

182 Memorandum by Kirkpatrick, 1 Oct. 1939, C 15649/13005/18, PRO, FO 371/23098. A 31 October memorandum by Strang, which particularly impressed Cadogan, noted that Poland had regained its independence when *both* Germany and Russia collapsed but that the Soviet Union now would be strong when Germany was defeated. He asserted that this would be less dangerous for Western Europe than for Germany to maintain herself, and that whatever happened in Eastern Europe after Germany's defeat would probably not be within the control of the Western Powers (C 17105/13669/62, FO 371/22946).

183 See esp. Bullitt to Roosevelt, 16 Sept. 1939, Bullitt, *For the President*, pp. 374–75.

184 See the documents about the Dahlerus soundings cited in n 170, above.

185 On this point, see Halifax to Osborne, 17 Feb. 1940, PRO, FO 800/318.

186 See Foreign Office comments of May 7, 1939 in C 6612/7/62, PRO, FO 371/24362.

187 Note Christie to Vansittart, circulated with Halifax's approval, 15 Sept. 1939, C 14293/15/18, PRO, FO 371/22983; Halifax minute of 4 Dec. 1939, C 19589/13005/18, FO 371/23100.

188 S. Payne Best, *The Venlo Incident* (London: Hutchinson, 1950). Thielenhaus (*Zwischen Anpassung und Widerstand*, p. 167) imagines that the kidnapping took place in Germany. On the British background, see Hinsley, *British Intelligence*, 1: 56–57n; Christopher M. Andrew, *Her Majesty's Secret Service* (New York: Viking, 1986), pp. 433–39; Chapman Pincher, *Too Secret Too Long* (New York: St. Martin's, 1984), chap. 45; Nigel West, *The SIGINT Secrets* (New York: Morrow, 1988), pp. 142–43.

189 PRO, FO 800/317, f. 27.

190 War Cabinet 40(1939) and 42(39), PRO, CAB 65/1, f. 222, 230.

191 For the drafting of the speech, see PRO, PREM 1/395; for Churchill's reference, see his letter to R.R. Stokes, M.P. of 23 July 1940, PREM 4/100/2.

192 See the formal statement of British war aims of Dec. 15, 1939, in C 20438/13669/62, PRO, FO 371/22947. In view of this position, it should not be surprising that the London government did not welcome the Welles mission, tried to dissuade Roosevelt from sending him, and correctly suspected that it reflected the President's doubts about the strength of Britain and France. See the documents filed under C 1839ff/285/18 in FO 371/24417–18; J. A. Bayer, "British Policy towards the Russo-Finnish Winter War 1939–

1940," *Canadian Journal of History* 16, No. 1 (1981), 50. The basic British objection to Welles's mission was that while he thought of a possible peace *with* the Hitler government, the British made it clear that not only did Poland and Czechoslovakia – and if they so voted, the Austrians – have to be freed, but that the German government itself had to be shown to its own people to be a failure; see Cabinet 67(40) of 13 Mar. 1940, C 3949/89/18, FO 371/24046, and the Halifax memorandum of the same date in FO 800/326, f. 73–78. To avoid antagonizing Roosevelt, Halifax sent him a message through Arthur Murray to tell him how much he and Chamberlain liked Welles personally and had tried to be perfectly frank with him (Murray to FDR, 5 Apr. 1940, FDRL, PSF Box 53, Great Britain). Documents on the mission that were not printed as well as sections omitted from the published ones in FRUS, 1940, Vol. 1, are in FDRL, PSF Safe File, Box 9, Welles Reports 1940.

193 On Hitler's views, see his comments of Sept. 26 in *ADAP*, D, 8, No. 138; his comments to the pro-German Swedish explorer Sven Hedin on Oct. 16 in ibid., No. 263, and in Hedin, *Ohne Auftrag*, pp. 51–56; Fröhlich, *Goebbels Tagebücher*, 24 Oct. 1939.

194 Fröhlich, *Goebbels Tagebücher*, 14 Oct. 1939. Goebbels directed that the word "peace" was absolutely not to appear in the German press; Willi A. Boelcke (ed.), *Kriegspropaganda 1939–1941* (Stuttgart: Deutsche Verlags-Anstalt, 1966), p. 300. See also the entries in Goebbels's diary for 24 Oct., 7 and 9 Nov., 12 and 19 Dec. 1939.

195 Harold C. Deutsch, *The Conspiracy against Hitler in the Twilight War* (Minneapolis: Univ. of Minnesota Press, 1958).

196 On the contacts of the military, see, in addition to the books of Thielenhaus and Deutsch, Owen Chadwick, *Britain and the Vatican during the Second World War* (Cambridge: Cambridge Univ. Press, 1986), pp. 86–99; Peter Hoffmann, "Peace through Coup d'État: The Foreign Contacts of the German Resistance," *CEH*, 19 (Mar. 1986), 18–21; Kettenacker, *Krieg zur Friedenssicherung*, pp. 51–67; Weizsäcker to Mackensen, 14 June and 18 Oct. 1940, Mackensen to Weizsäcker 28 July 1940, AA, Nachlass Mackensen, Handakten Bd. 4, fr. 65571–72, 65586; documents in the PRO, FO 800/317–18, 321; C 19745/3005/18, FO 371/23100; C 770, 1137, 2522, 3044/89/18, FO 371/24405; C 2339/6/18, FO 371/24387; C 4743/5/18, FO 371/24380; War Cabinet 12(39) of 11 Sept. 1939 and 16(40) of 17 Jan. 1940, *CAB* 65/1, f. 71–72, 65/5, f. 67 and 65/11, f. 158–59.

Carl Goerdeler was also in touch with the British at this time; see C 15792, 16893/15/18, FO 371/22985; C 2524/89/18, FO 371/24405; C 3245/89/18, FO 371/24406; C 1189, 1865/6/18, FO 371/24387. Related documents and comments are in C 15720/53/18, FO 371/23010; C 2577/89/18, FO 371/24405; C 297/6/18, FO 371/24386; C 3439/6/18, FO 371/24389; a summary in C 4216/324/18, FO 371/26542.

It is worth noting that many of these contacts involved, or records about them were submitted to, Sir Robert Vansittart, who was incensed by the nationalistic tones of those who claimed to be about to overthrow Hitler; his conclusions are in his memorandum of 14 Mar. 1940, "The Nature of the Beast" (C 4229/6/18, FO 371/24389).

197 On the contacts established by the intermediary J. Lonsdale Bryans, see the documents from the papers of Lord Halifax in PRO, FO 800/326. One of the items on Bryans is closed until 2016 and presumably involves some checking into his background. On March 17, 1940, Lord Brocket, Bryans's main sponsor in England, wrote to Cadogan about Bryans's request for money to pay his debts and overdrafts; Cadogan commented "enlightening." See also Thielenhaus, *Zwischen Anpassung und Widerstand*, pp. 181–82. Bryans tried to establish contact with the Foreign Office again repeatedly in 1943 but was always turned away, see C 7963/155/18, FO 371/34449; C 10397/155/18, FO 371/34451; C 11893/188/18, FO 371/34451; C 13306/188/18, FO 371/34452.

198 Lothar Gruchmann (ed.), *Autobiographie eines Attentäters: Aussage zum Sprengstoffanschlag*

im Bürgerbräukeller München am 8. November 1939 (Stuttgart: Deutsche Verlags-Anstalt, 1970); Anton Hoch, "Das Attentat auf Hitler im Münchener Bürgerbräukeller 1939," *VjZ* 17 (1969), 383–413. A photocopy of the order "to liquidate" Elser is in Best, *Venlo*, between pp. 208 and 209.

199 Text of the speech in Domarus (ed.), *Hitler*, 2:1047–67. Whenever Hitler subsequently referred in his public speeches to this open announcement of his intention of killing Europe's Jews, he would shift the date of the January 30 speech to September 1 to bring the whole murder program into the context of the war.

200 The literature on this subject was for many years quite sparse; the subject was not popular in post-war Germany. There has been a substantial outpouring in recent years; Norbert Frei (ed.), *Medizin und Gesundheitspolitik in der NS-Zeit* (Munich: Oldenbourg, 1991), summarizes the current state of research and contains an excellent selective bibliography. The best recent monographs are Ernst Klee, *"Euthanasie" im NS-Staat* (Frankfurt/M: S. Fischer, 1983); and Hans-Walter Schmuhl, *Rassenhygiene, Nationalsozialismus, Euthanasie: Von der Verhütung zur Vernichtung "LebensunwertenLebens" 1890–1945* (Göttingen: Vandenhoeck and Ruprecht, 1987). By March 1941 the Germans knew of British, American and Vatican knowledge of the program (*ADAP*, D, 12, No. 199). On January 31, 1941, Goebbels noted in his diary that 80,000 had been killed, 60,000 remained to be killed, and the head of Hitler's chancellery, Philipp Bouhler, was the right man for the job (Fröhlich, *Goebbels Tagebücher*, 4: 485). He wanted British propaganda carefully watched lest it spread the news that the Germans intended to kill their own wounded (something they were already doing with World War I invalids); Boelcke, *Kriegspropaganda*, pp. 710–11.

201 A brief survey of public reaction in Marlis Steinert, *Hitler's War and the Germans* (Athens, Ohio: Ohio Univ. Press, 1977), pp. 79–83; also Frei, *Medizin*, pp. 235–51.

202 Some of the details in Broszat, *Polenpolitik*, pp. 28–31.

203 Fröhlich, *Goebbels Tagebücher*, 14 Oct. 1939.

204 Hitler was especially annoyed about the complaints of General Johannes Blaskowitz, the military commander in occupied Poland, about excesses against the local population. Hans Frank eventually succeeded in having Blaskowitz removed in May 1940 (Broszat, p. 76).

205 A good summary in Rich, *Hitler's War Aims*, 2: 32–42.

206 Note that from September 1, 1939 to May 10, 1940 the number of Czech tanks in German armored divisions increased from 274 to 391 (*DRuZW*, 2: 268). Of the two types included, the models 35 and 38, the latter was still being built and used into 1945 (Friedrich M. von Senger und Etterlin, *German Tanks of World War II* [New York: Galahad Books, 1969], pp. 29–30).

207 Rich, 2: 58–61.

208 Seppo Myllyniemi, *Die baltische Krise 1938–1941* (Stuttgart: Deutsche Verlags-Anstalt, 1979), pp. 57–81.

209 It is clear from the evidence that the Soviets provided the Lithuanian government with the precise border agreed to by Stalin and von Ribbentrop; see von Weizsäcker's comment in *ADAP*, D, 8, No. 200.

210 There is no satisfactory account of this whole question. A useful introduction in Boris J. Kaslas, "The Lithuanian Strip in Soviet–German Secret Diplomacy, 1939–1941," *Journal of Baltic Studies* 4, No. 3 (1973), 211–25. When the German Foreign Minister informed his subordinates that the Baltic States and Finland had been signed over to the Soviet sphere of influence, he did *not* refer to the piece of Lithuania reserved for Germany (*ADAP*, D, 8, No. 213).

211 See Hochman, *Soviet Union and Collective Security*, pp. 61–64, for one of the few accounts which notes the difference in Soviet handling of this issue from all other Russian territorial losses after World War I.

212 Hillgruber, *Hitler, König Carol*, pp. 59–63.

213 On Soviet–Bulgarian relations at this time, see Hans-Joachim Hoppe, *Bulgarien – Hitlers eigenwilliger Verbündete* (Stuttgart: Deutsche Verlags-Anstalt, 1979), pp. 70–71; Önder, *Türkische Aussenpolitik*, p. 75.

214 On this point, see Weinberg, *Germany and the Soviet Union*, pp. 46, 101; *ADAP*, D, 10, No. 10. On December 12, 1939, U.S. ambassador to Italy William Phillips recorded in his diary the report given him by Fred Walcott on a long interview the latter had just had with von Ribbentrop. According to von Ribbentrop, Germany had agreed to what the Soviet Union had been refused by England: "A free hand in the Baltic and a free hand in the Balkan States." Harvard, Houghton Library, Phillips Diary, p. 3590.

215 Accounts in Gerd R. Ueberschär, *Hitler und Finnland 1939–1941* (Wiesbaden: Steiner, 1978), pp. 42–45, 49–51; E. Schulin (ed.), *Studien zur europäischen Geschichte: Gedenkschrift Martin Göhring* (Wiesbaden: Steiner, 1968), pp. 338–52.

216 There is an extensive bibliography in Ueberschär. See also Weinberg, *Germany and the Soviet Union*, pp. 85–91.

217 The map in Ueberschär, p. 326, provides a good picture of the negotiating positions about southern Finland. The map in H. Peter Krosby, *Finland, Germany and the Soviet Union, 1940–1941: The Petsamo Dispute* (Madison: Univ. of Wisconsin Press, 1968), facing p. 78, shows the post-Russo-Finnish War border with the whole Rybachi peninsula (called Fischer–Halbinsel by the Germans) included in the U.S.S.R. The Soviets, who already held the eastern portion, had asked for all of it in October; the Finns eventually offered them the northwestern portion but wanted to hold on to the southwestern part.

218 See Ueberschär, p. 123, n 404; Arvo Tuominen, *The Bells of the Kremlin* (Hanover, N.H.: Univ. Press of New England, 1983), pp. 315–17; J. J. Fol, "A propos des conversations finno-soviétiques qui ont précédé la 'guerre d'hiver,'" *Revue d'histoire de la deuxième guerre mondiale*, No. 77 (Jan. 1977), 25–40.

219 English text in Vyacheslav M. Molotov, *Report to the Supreme Soviet, 31 October 1939* (New York: Workers Library, 1939).

220 The major literature on the war is largely in agreement on this point; some further insight into the likely role of Kuusinen (who was close to Stalin as a key official in both the Soviet government and the Comintern) in misleading Stalin can be obtained from the memoirs of Kuusinen's wife, Aino Kuusinen, *The Rings of Destiny: Inside Soviet Russia from Lenin to Brezhnev* (New York: Morrow, 1974), pp. 230–32. After his puppet government was abandoned, Kuusinen became head of the Karelo-Finnish SSR, which included most of the territory seized from Finland in 1940, and continued to hold other high Communist Party and state offices until his death from natural causes in 1964.

221 On the war, see Seweryn Bialer (ed.), *Stalin and His Generals* (London: Souvenir Press, 1970), pp. 130–37; Ueberschär, *Hitler und Finnland*, pp. 130–34; John Erickson, *The Soviet High Command* (London: Macmillan, 1962), pp. 541–52; D. W. Spring, "The Soviet Decision for War against Finland, 30 November 1939," *Soviet Studies* 38 (Apr. 1986), 207–26. A survey of the operations in Tomas Ries, *Cold Will: The Defence of Finland* (London: Brassey's 1988), chap. 4.

222 Weinberg, *Germany and the Soviet Union*, pp. 87–89. Some additional material on the Soviet request, German agreement, and eventual Soviet declination of German naval assistance for the Soviet blockade of Finland is now available. Perhaps the Soviets were merely testing German attitudes and dropped the request when Berlin passed the test. See *ADAP*, D, 8, Nos. 433, 437; Note by Federer and Foreign Ministry to Moscow No. 1036 of 10 Dec. 1939, AA, St.S., "Russland," Bd. 2, fr. 111858–59; KTB Skl A, 4, 12 Dec. 1939, BA/MA, RM 7/7, f. 87.

223 Enrica Costa Bora, *Helsinki–Ginevra, Dicembre 1939–Marzo 1940: La guerra d'inverno e la società delle nazioni* (Milan: Giuffrè, 1987). It should be noted that the British government,

though in the end voting for expulsion, had tried to restrain League action to keep the focus on Germany and avoid war with the Soviet Union (Bayer, "British Policy", pp. 36–37).

224 For a report from the British embassy in Paris of 22 Nov. 1939 about the French Communist Party's propaganda against the war and samples of its documents and leaflets, see C 19065/90/17, PRO, FO 371/22914. Other examples may be found in Angelo Rossi (pseud. of Angelo Tasca), *Les Communistes français pendant la drôle de guerre* (Paris: Iles d'or, 1951); Angelo Rossi (ed.), *Les Cahiers du Bolshevism pendant la campagne 1939–1940* (Paris: Dominique Wapler, 1951).

225 Bayer, "British Policy", pp. 34–35. On French concern over British reluctance to take steps leading to open war with the Soviet Union, see C 4723/9/17, PRO, FO 371/24298.

226 Some of the literature, e.g. Juho K. Paasikivi, *Meine Moskauer Mission 1939–1941* (Hamburg: Holsten, 1966), p. 163, stresses that the change in the Soviet negotiating position with the dropping of the Kuusinen government and a willingness to deal with the real government of Finland came at the end of January *before* the great Soviet offensive of February 1940, but this seems to me to ignore the obvious fact that the massive troop movements and accumulation of ammunition and other supplies had had to be ordered at the very least two weeks before the date of the first big attack on February 1. The military success of the Soviet offensive, once launched, may have contributed to some further increase in Soviet territorial demands, or to a harder line in the Moscow peace talks; but that is another, and less significant matter. The negotiations with the Finns via Sweden, by-passing Kuusinen, actually began on January 10 (Ueberschär, *Hitler und Finnland*, pp. 142–50), so the main decisions were made in Moscow around the turn of the year and presumably at the same time. The Soviets had intimated to the Germans that they might drop Kuusinen as early as January 8 (*ADAP*, D, 8, Nos. 513, 521).

227 Note Molotov's comments on March 5, 1940, in *ADAP*, D, 8, No. 664.

228 Soviet willingness to settle for an agreement rather than occupy the whole country now that they had clearly won very greatly puzzled Hitler at the time. Note the comments of his air force adjutant, Nicolaus von Below, "Aufzeichnungen aus dem Winter 1948/1949: Zwischen Aufstieg und Absturz, Hitler und die Luftwaffe," p. 142, Institut für Zeitgeschichte, Irving excerpts, p. 49.

229 See Travis Beale Jacobs, *America and the Winter War, 1939–1940* (New York: Garland, 1982). Note, especially FDR to Welles, 22 Dec. 1939, *FDR Letters*, 2: 974, asking Welles to hint to the Soviet Ambassador at the possibility of a break in relations, a point of great importance in view of Roosevelt's having opened them in the first place.

230 Ueberschär's explanation (*Hitler und Finnland*, p. 157), that this was done out of consideration for England, seems entirely unconvincing to me.

231 Rumors that Polish prisoners in the officers' camps were being moved were being pursued by the International Red Cross as early as March 14 (*ADAP*, D, 8, No. 676).

232 The best account currently available, but likely to be superseded when recent Soviet revelations are taken into account, is Janusz K. Zawodny, *Death in the Forest: The Story of the Katyn Forest Massacre* (Notre Dame, Ind.: Univ. of Notre Dame Press, 1962). An initial new account from the Russian side is Dmitri Volkogonov, *Stalin: Triumph and Tragedy*, ed. and trans. by Harold Shukman (New York: Grove & Weidenfeld, 1991), p. 360. The official Russian government statement is printed in the *New York Times* for Oct. 15, 1992. Zawodny notes (chap. 8) that 448 officers were kept out and began training for a new pro-Soviet Polish army in the summer of 1940; this became a core of the Berling army. The Katyn site was discovered for what it was in 1943, only a few months before the Germans evacuated it in the face of the Red Army's summer offensive; a second site of such mass graves appears to have been located in 1991. The officers at Katyn were shot with German bullets sold

to the Russians in the 1920s and 1930s; Elke Fröhlich, "Katyn im neuen Licht?" *Geschichte in Wissenschaft und Unterricht* 37 (1986), 234–35.

233 *ADAP*, D, 8, No. 657 n 2.

234 Weinberg, *Foreign Policy, 1937–39*, pp. 371, 382.

235 Ibid., pp. 579–81.

236 See "B Wi 9332/gKdos III, Besprechung bei Generalfeldmarschall Göring am 19.5.39," 19 May 1939, BA/MA, RM 7/257, f. 3–5. On the dive-bomber concept and its problems, especially the JU-88's loss of distance and speed capability sacrificed for a rarely utilized diving capacity, see Boog, *Luftwaffenführung*, pp. 183–90.

237 Homze, *Arming the Luftwaffe*, p. 231; Chef des Stabes AHA, "Tagebuch V," 6 and 7 Sept. 1939, Imperial War Museum, MI 14/981; Reichert to Poensgen, 6 Sept. 1939, BA, R 13/692.

238 Rolf-Dieter Müller, "Die deutschen Gaskriegsvorbereitungen 1919–1945," *MGM* 27, No. 1 (1980), 40–41.

239 Below, "Aufzeichnungen," p. 128 (Irving's excerpts, p. 44).

240 *Kriegstagebuch des OKW*, 4 vols. (Frankfurt/M: Bernard & Graefe, 1961–65), 1: 951; Hans-Adolf Jacobsen (ed.), *Generaloberst Halder, Kriegstagebuch*, 3 vols. (Stuttgart: Kohlhammer, 1962–64), 27 and 28 Sept. 1939. (Henceforth cited as *KTB Halder.*)

241 On this, see also *DRuZW*, 2: 245–46. Note Jacobsen, *Vorgeschichte*, p. 29.

242 See also the detailed letter of the Minister of Finance, Schwerin von Krosigk, of Nov. 6, 1939, to Göring arguing against an offensive in the West (BA, R 2/24243).

243 *DRuZW*, 2: 241–44; Deutsch, *Conspiracy*.

244 Weinberg, *Foreign Policy, 1937–39*, pp. 384–85.

245 Klaus-Jürgen Müller, *Das Heer und Hitler, 1933–1940* (Stuttgart: Deutsche Verlags-Anstalt, 1969), pp. 675–76.

246 Ibid., pp. 459–67.

247 See *KTB OKW*, 1: 951–52.

248 The memorandum is printed in *Trial of the Major War Criminals before the International Military Tribunal*, 42 vols. (Nürnberg, 1947–49), 26: 466–86, and Jacobsen, *Vorgeschichte*, pp. 4–21. On the conference of Nov. 23 there is a whole series of reports, see *ADAP*, D, 8, No. 384; *Grosscurth Tagebuch*, p. 414; von Reichenau notes in BA/MA, N 372/22 and 29; von Waldau notes in BA/MA, Tagebuch von Waldau. A good summary in *DRuZW*, 2: 249. Hitler's comment that the German army had been built up for employment in war has numerous pre-war antecedents; see the von Rintelen "Vermerk," probably of April or May 1939, in BA/MA, N 433.

249 Ciano, *Diary*, 26 Dec, 1939, 2 Jan. 1940.

250 The U.S. also received such warnings, especially in November (Moffat Diary, 10–12 Nov. 1939, Moffat Papers, Vol. 43), and this was the basis of FDR's offer of refuge in the U.S. to the Belgian and Dutch royal families on Nov. 11, 1939 (*FDR Letters*, 2: 953; cf. ibid., p. 971).

251 At one point Hitler thought it possible that Holland might be occupied peacefully (the way Denmark and Romania would be), while he always assumed that Belgium would fight (Jodl Diary, 1 Feb. 1940, *TMWC*, 28: 397–98; Hans-Adolf Jacobsen, "War die deutsche Westoffensive 1940 eine Präventivmassnahme?" *Wehrwissenschaftliche Rundschau* 7 [1957], 288–89 n 62). The use of Dutch uniforms by German troops was a feature of German plans for the seizure of Holland at least from Nov. 1939 on (see "Besprechung beim Führer am 20. November 1939, Abw.II Nr. 32/39 Chefs." Imperial War Museum, AL 1933).

252 Inside the German government during the war, Raeder always called attention to his own role in pushing the invasion of Norway; after the war, he invariably blamed it on the British. There is a discussion of this issue by Patrick Salmon in Richard Langhorne (ed.), *Diplomacy and Intelligence during the Second World War* (Cambridge: Cambridge Univ.

Press, 1985), pp. 258–59. See also Loock, *Quisling, Rosenberg*, pp. 207 n 1, 271 n 1, n 5.

253 Carl-Axel Gemzell, *Raeder, Hitler und Skandinavien* (Lund: Gleerup, 1965).

254 A survey of the background in *DRuZW*, 2: 190–96.

255 *ADAP*, D, 8, No. 188; KTB Skl A, 6, 5 Oct. 1939, BA/MA, RM 7/5 f. 52–54; Dönitz memorandum "Stützpunkte in Norwegen," 9 Oct. 1939, *TMWC*, 34: 159–61; Raeder note of 10 Apr. 1944 on Boehm's report in which Raeder refers to a letter from Admiral Carls and a discussion with him before the meeting with Hitler on Oct. 10, 1939, in BA/MA, Boehm Nachlass. It should be noted that all of these materials, as well as the Hitler–Raeder meeting of Oct. 10, date long before any German concern about an Allied action in Norway.

256 Text in Wagner, *Lagevorträge*, pp. 26–28. This edition is good for text and technical terms; the commentary is generally apologetic and often unreliable.

257 DRuZW, 2: 197–98; Loock, *Quisling, Rosenberg*, pp. 217–24, 230–34.

258 DRuZW, 2: 200; Rich, *Hitler's War Aims*, 2: 140. Commenting on Denmark and Norway to Goebbels on April 8, 1940, Hitler said that "we will never give up the two countries" (die beiden Länder geben wir nie wieder heraus) (Fröhlich, *Goebbels Tagebücher*, 4:102).

259 Some recent efforts to rehabilitate Quisling are not likely to be successful. A good account in Oddvar K. Hoidal, *Quisling: A Study in Treason* (Oslo: Norwegian Univ. Press, 1989), chaps. 9–10. Loock's book remains very useful. As the German landing date approached, Quisling wanted to meet a German officer in Copenhagen so that he could provide details on the Norwegian army and indicate places which ought to be seized (Bürkner memorandum of 29 Mar. 1940, BA/MA, RM 6/72, f. 57–58). He met Lt.Col. Hans Pieckenbrock of OKW intelligence on April 4 (Hermann Boehm, *Norwegen zwischen England und Deutschland* [Lippoldsberg: Klosterberg, 1956], p. 63, claims this meeting was requested by the Germans).

260 Earl F. Ziemke, *The German Northern Theater of Operations 1940–1945* (Washington: GPO, 1959), p. 46.

261 On the *Jan Wellem* and its use of the Soviet-provided naval base near Murmansk, see the documents in BA/MA, Case 20/3, PG 48804; KTB Skl A 8, 2, 5, 9, 13 Apr. 1940, RM 7/11, f. 17, 37–38, 73–75, 123; RM 7/111, f. 117, 123; Walther Hubatsch, *Die deutsche Besetzung von Dänemark und Norwegen 1940* (Göttingen: Musterschmidt, 1952), p. 111 (this book is useful only for operational details).

262 These fairy tales then had to be protected in later years. Note the warning of State Secretary von Weizsäcker that an article on the military operations could not be published without revealing that the claim of having merely responded to British mining of Norwegian waters was false (von Weizsäcker to Schumburg, 9 Jan. 1941, AA, St.S., "Aufzeichnungen über interne Angelegenheiten," Bd. 2, JPD 1333; see also Loock, *Quisling, Rosenberg*, pp. 259–60). Raeder had been especially insistent that the Germans invade Norway after it became certain that the British were not going to do so (ibid., pp. 256–57).

263 KTB Skl, "Notiz für das Kriegstagebuch 1.4.40 über den Vortrag der Befehlshaber, Führer und Kommandeure über das Unternehmen 'Weserübung'," BA/MA, M 1689, PG 33955; cf. KTB Skl A 7, 5 Mar. 1950, RM 7/10, f. 114.

264 Text in *ADAP*, D, 8, No. 644.

265 Churchill to Halifax, 14 Mar. 1940, PRO, FO 800/328, f. 424–26; Halifax answered that the location was bad for the exercise of British power (ibid., f. 428–29).

266 Henry Denham, *Inside the Nazi Ring: A Naval Attaché in Sweden 1940–1945* (London: John Murray, 1984), p. 4; on the British intelligence failure, see Kahn, *Seizing Enigma*, p. 121.

267 Ziemke, *Northern Theater*, pp. 39, 60.

268 Ibid., map p. 50.

269 Ibid., pp. 51–52; see also Loock, pp. 281–83, 287–330.

270 The views expressed in the text are, in general, shared by Ziemke, Salewski, and Bernd Stegemann, the author of the relevant section of the German official history.

271 Hans-Adolf Jacobsen and Jürgen Rohwer, "Planungen und Operationen der deutschen Kriegsmarine im Zusammenhang mit dem Fall 'Gelb'," *Marine-Rundschau* 57, No. 2 (1960), p. 75; *DRuZW*, 2: 221–25. A document of 30 April 1940 appended to the British Cabinet minutes shows that the real change in Germany's naval position as a result of the Norwegian operation was fully understood there (PRO, *CAB* 65/6, f. 302).

272 *The Times*, 5 Apr. 1940.

273 Some details, generally understated to make the best possible case for Sweden, in Lutz-h öft, *Deutsche Militärpolitik*, pp. 81–82; Wittmann, *Schwedens Wirtschaftsbeziehungen*, pp. 182–85, 187–95.

274 Note the Goebbels diary for 21 April 1940 where there is discussion of Norway as a "super-Singapore" against England (Fröhlich, *Goebbels Tagebücher*, 4: 121–23, also 9 July 1940, 4: 234).

275 On Greenland, Iceland, and the Faeroe Islands, see FRUS, 1940, 2: 343ff; *ADAP*, D, 9, No. 235; Donald F. Bittner, *The Lion and the White Falcon: Britain and Iceland in the World War II Era* (Hamden: Conn.: Archon, 1983); Stetson Conn and Byron Fairchild, *The Framework of Hemisphere Defense* (Washington: GPO, 1960), pp.45–56.

3: THE WORLD TURNED UPSIDE DOWN

1 Jacobsen, *Vorgeschichte*.

2 See the Memorandum of 21 Oct. 1940 on a conversation with the former Dutch Counsellor of Legation in Berlin, in NA, RG 165 (War Dept. G-2), Entry 77, Box 1428, File 6910 – Holland and Belgium; Moffat Diary, 7 May 1940, Moffat Papers, Vol. 44.

3 Chamberlain to Churchill, 16 Sept. 1939, quoted in Dilks, "Twilight War," p. 67.

4 Gunsburg (*Divided and Conquered*) claims that the French learned from the Polish campaign, but see Patrick Facon and Arnaud Teyssier, "Les leçons de la campagne de Pologne vues par l'état-major aérien français," *Revue historique des armées* 161 (1985), 103–8. The best account of French strategy and its defects is Don W. Alexander, "Repercussions of the Breda Variant," *French Historical Studies* 8, No. 3 (1974), 459–88. On the French air force, see A.D. Harvey, "The French Armée de l'Air in May-June 1940: A Failure in Conception," *JCH* 25 (1990), 447–65.

5 The evolution of these plans can be followed in Gunsburg, chaps. 6 and 7, and Alexander, "Breda Variant". On British–Belgian and French–Belgian staff contacts, see C 46, 1585/460/4, PRO, FO 371/30787.

6 See War Cabinet 47[39] of 14 Oct. 1939, PRO, CAB 65/3, f. 123–27, War Cabinet 119[40] of 10 May 1940, CAB 65/7, f. 58. On the German losses in airplanes during their overwhelming of the Dutch, see Kreis, *AirBase Defense*, pp. 66–69. On German terror bombing, see the material in Olaf Groehler's contribution to Horst Boog (ed.), *The Conduct of the Air War in the Second World War: An International Comparison* (New York: Berg, 1992), pp. 282–83.

7 Anton Hoch, "Der Luftangriff auf Freiburg am 10. Mai 1940," *VjZ* 4 (1956), 115–44. The German fakery about this attack figured prominently in the 1943 publication designed to prove "Britain's Sole Guilt for the Bombing War against the Civilian Population." Germany, Auswärtiges Amt, *Weissbuch Nr. 8: Dokumente über die Alleinschuld Englands am Bombenkrieg gegen die Zivilbevölkerung* (Berlin: Deutscher Verlag, 1943).

8 Though not always reliable, a useful introduction is Hermann Götzel's edition of the memoirs of the key German airborne commander, *Generaloberst Kurt Student und seine Fallschirmjäger* (Friedberg: Podzun-Pallas, 1980). On the Louvain library, see Wolfgang

Schivelbuch, *Die Bibliothek von Löwen: Eine Episode aus der Zeit der Weltkriege* (Munich: Hanser, 1988).

9 See War Cabinet 121(40) of 14 May 1940, PRO, CAB 65/7.

10 As in the case of Warsaw, the Germans insisted on unconditional surrender. See *KTB Halder*, 1: 322; KTB Skl A 9, 27 May 1940, BA/MA, RM 7/12. For the American intercept of the report on this by the Japanese ambassador in Paris, see Paris to Washington for Tokyo No. 434 of 28 May 1940, NA, RG 457, SRDJ 4519. A thoughtful account in Jan Vanwelkenhuyzen, *1940, Quand les chemins se séparent: Aux sources de las question royale* (Paris: Duculot, 1988).

11 The British Minister in Paris, Sir Ronald Campbell, commented on May 27 in a letter to Lord Halifax: "The rot evidently started at the top" (PRO, FO 800/312, f. 72).

12 There is a balanced account in Brian Bond, "Leslie Hore-Belisha at the War Office," in Ian F.W. Beckett and John Gooch (eds.), *Politicians and Defence: Studies in the Formulation of British Defence Policy 1846–1970* (Manchester: Manchester Univ. Press, 1981), pp. 110–31, which, however, omits reference to Hore-Belisha's making the British army the only one in Europe which went into World War II no longer using horse transport. See also A.J. Trythall, "The Downfall of Leslie Hore-Belisha," *JCH* 16 (1981), 391–412.

13 Phipps to Halifax, 23 Mar. 1940, PRO, FO 800/312, f. 21–23.

14 On Reynaud's firing of Alexis Leger, a key figure in the French Ministry of Foreign Affairs, under her influence, see Erika Ostroyski, *Under the Sign of Ambiguity: Saint John Perse/Alexis Leger* (New York: New York Univ. Press), pp. 144–46. See also Marc Ferro, *Pétain* (Paris: Fayard, 1987), pp. 63–64.

15 Note Martin Gilbert, *Winston S. Churchill*, Vol. 6: *Finest Hour 1939–1941* (Boston: Houghton Mifflin, 1983), p. 385.

16 War Cabinet 121(40) of 14 May 1940, PRO, CAB 65/7.

17 Gilbert, *Churchill* chap. 21.

18 Hans Meier-Welcker, "Der Entschluss zum Anhalten der deutschen Panzertruppen in Flandern 1940," *VjZ* 2 (1954), 274–90. Hitler's air force adjutant emphasized the importance attached to keeping the French from stabilizing a new front (Below, "Aufzeichnungen," p. 152 [Irving's excerpts, p. 52]). See also Hans-Adolf Jacobsen, *Dunkirchen* (Neckargemund: Scharnhorst, 1958).

19 The order to destroy the French and British forces in Flanders was also issued on May 24 (*ADAP*, D, 9, No. 427).

20 Very useful on this is the diary of the head of the German air force Operations Staff, "Tagebuch Gen. von Waldau, Chef Luftwaffenführungsstab," p. 14, in Munich, Institut für Zeitgeschichte.

21 *ADAP*, D, 9, No. 357.

22 See Williamson Murray, *Luftwaffe* (Baltimore: Nautical & Aviation Publ. Co., 1985), p. 42.

23 David Fraser, *Alanbrooke* (New York: Atheneum, 1982), pp. 160–65; P. M. H. Bell, *A Certain Eventuality: Britain and the Fall of France* (Farnborough: Saxon House, 1974), pp. 21–29. Documents pertaining to the possible holding of a portion of Brittany are in PRO, WO 106/1713.

24 The German record is in *ADAP*, D, 9, No. 1; the Italian in Ciano, *Diplomatic Papers*, pp. 361–65. See also Ciano, *Diary*, 8 Feb. 1940; *KTB Halder*, 12 Feb. 1940.

25 See his comments to Goebbels on March 20 in the latter's diary.

26 Weinberg, *Germany and the Soviet Union*, pp. 91–95 (related documents have since been published in *ADAP*, D, 8 and 9).

27 See *ADAP*, D, 9, Nos. 40, 92, 138, 164.

28 Mackensen to the Foreign Ministry, 30 Apr. 1940, AA, Botschaft Rom (Quir.) Geheim 43/2, fr. E 086906–8.

29 In addition to the numerous documents on these appeals published in the various

document collections, see Loraine to Halifax, 7 June 1940, C 7179/5/18, PRO, FO 371/24383. After the Germans seized the Italian archives in 1943, they checked carefully for any signs of disloyalty by Mussolini but found none, see Hencke's report for von Ribbentrop, "Pol XI 9677g," 20 Nov. 1943, AA, St.S., "Italien," Bd. 18, fr. 71169–73.

30 MacGregor Knox, "The Sources of Italy's Defeat in 1940: Bluff or Institutional Incompetence," in Carole Fink et al. (eds.), *German Nationalism and the European Response, 1890–1945* (Norman, Okl.: Univ. of Oklahoma Press, 1985), pp. 247–66.

31 Note the report of the Japanese embassy in Rome No. 455 to Tokyo of 29 May 1940 on a May 15 speech by Mussolini, NA, RG 457, SRDJ 4565; *ADAP*, D, 9, Nos. 350, 356, 357, 360, 371, 387, 408. Interesting are the comments of the representative of the German navy to the Italian navy, Admiral Weichold, in BA/MA, N 316/1, f. 5, 20, 28–29, 39–40. Weichold points out that the Italians had prepared in Libya to fight the French, not the British, and that prestige attacks by Italian planes sent to Belgium to fly against England could not affect the situation in the Mediterranean. See also Weichold's comments in his 23 Dec 1953 letter to Bürkner in the Bürkner Papers, N 565/11.

32 Roosevelt's speech of June 10, 1940 is in *The Public Papers and Addresses of Franklin D. Roosevelt*, Samuel I. Rosenman (ed.), Vol. 3 (New York: Macmillan, 1941), pp. 259–64. On the refusal of King Victor Emanuel III to block the declaration of war, see Denis Mack Smith, *Italy and its Monarchy* (New Haven, Conn.: Yale Univ. Press, 1989), pp. 287–92.

33 *ADAP*, D, 9, No. 129.

34 See AA, Deutsche Botschaft Madrid, "Seekrieg und seine Auswirkungen auf Spanien," 2 vols.; *ADAP*, D, 9, Nos. 169, 330; Reichsfinanzministerium, "Sparpeseten in Spanien," BA, R 2/24–26.

35 Léon Papeloux, *L'Amiral Canaris entre Franco et Hitler* (Tornai: Castermann, 1977), pp. 82–84; *ADAP*, D, 9, No. 380.

36 Detwiler, *Hitler, Franco*, pp. 18–19.

37 These promises were made during a trip to Germany by Spanish Air Minister General Juan Vigón Suerodíaz; see the summary in ibid., pp. 22–25. The view that Franco was very much in earnest about wanting to join the war on Germany's side if only his major conditions could be met is shared by Denis Smyth, *Diplomacy and Strategy of Survival: British Policy and Franco's Spain, 1940–1941* (Cambridge: Cambridge Univ. Press, 1986), pp. 31–36; and is very strongly supported by the new evidence in Norman Goda, "Germany and Northwest Africa in the Second World War: Politics and Strategy of Global Hegemony," Ph diss., Univ. of North Carolina, Chapel Hill, 1991.

38 In June and July of 1940 the defenses of Gibraltar were (like those of Singapore) all on the sea side; there were no modern land defenses at all, and the fortress would have fallen in days. See Imperial War Museum, Mason Macfarlane Papers, MM 30.

39 See Hoare's letters to Halifax of 3, 7, and 11 June 1940, PRO, FO 800/323, f. 89–90, 95–97, 101–4.

40 *ADAP*, D, 9, Nos. 32, 70, 75, 85, 109, 175, 229, 238, 300, 332. See also *DRuZW*, 4: 110–11; Reichswirtschaftsministerium, "Niederschrift über die Sitzung des Interministeriellen Ausschusses für die deutsch-sowjetischen Wirtschaftsbeziehungen vom 7. Juni 1940," BA, R 2/17315. The Soviet government was willing to cooperate with the Germans in some wild schemes in Afghanistan (*ADAP*, D, 8, Nos. 369, 445, 449, 468, 470), but was not as yet ready to have Stalin or Molotov visit Berlin (ibid., 9, Nos. 20, 28).

41 Ueberschär, *Hitler und Finnland*, pp. 155–59; KTB Skl A, 10, 10 June 1940, BA/MA, RM 7/13, f. 104.

42 *ADAP*, D, 9, Nos. 73, 94.

43 Ibid., No. 226.

44 See the June 22, 1940, summary of a cable of June 14, 1940, from the People's Commissariat for Foreign Affairs to the Soviet ambassadors in Japan and China prepared

by the Japanese Consulate-General in Harbin which had obtained access to the document there, in Morley, *Fateful Choice*, pp. 310–11 n 65.

45 Mario Toscano, *Designs in Diplomacy* (Baltimore: Johns Hopkins Press, 1970), pp. 124ff. *ADAP*, D, 9, Nos. 286, 303, 308, 332, 353, 382, 388, 392, 454.

46 Marguerat, *Pétrole Roumain*, chap. 5.

47 See Hillgruber, *Hitler, König Carol*, pp. 63–69.

48 See the report of 14 Dec. 1939, PRO, FO 800/322, f. 134; Halifax to Reginald Hoare, 19 Jan. 1940, ibid., f. 135–44.

49 *ADAP*, D, 8, No. 514; *KTB Halder*, 3 July 1940.

50 Hillgruber, *Hitler, König Carol*, pp. 70ff. Fabricius report G 164 of 14 Sept. 1940 enclosing a copy of the report of the Romanian Minister in Moscow to the Romanian Foreign Minister of 9 Sept. 1940, AA, U.St.S., "Südosten," Bd. 3, fr. 177007–14. The Germans in Bessarabia and the Bukovina were also evacuated.

51 Hoppe, *Bulgarien*, chap. 9. For current problems in German–Bulgarian economic relations, see "*RK* 2904B," 9 Feb. 1940, BA, R 43 II/1428b, f. 20–22.

52 Hoppe, chaps. 4, 10, 11, is useful though somewhat exaggerating the caution.

53 *ADAP*, D, 9, No. 478. It is too often forgotten that into the fall of 1940 Germany held to Hitler's earlier view of Italy's having a predominant role in the area south of Austria and did not change this position until the Italian disaster in Greece. For the understanding of this point, and the changing picture after the Italian defeats in Greece and Africa, by the Japanese ambassador in Berlin, see Kurusu's tel. 119 of 14 Feb. 1941, NA, RG 457, SRDJ 98201.

54 The views of Molotov, presumably reflecting Stalin's, are clearest in the reports of the Italian ambassador Augusto Rosso, translated in Toscano, *Designs in Diplomacy*, pp. 151–62. See also *ADAP*, D, 10, Nos. 21, 130, 165, 286.

55 The Germans had first tried to worsen Soviet–Turkish relations by publishing documents seized in France and showing Turkish knowledge of the preliminary planning for Allied attacks on Soviet oil fields; and also to compromise the Turkish Foreign Minister. They succeeded in scaring the Turks from honoring their treaty with the Allies and into signing an economic agreement, but could not get further with Ankara at the time. See Krecker, *Deutschland und die Türkei*, pp. 85–95; Frank G. Weber, *The Evasive Neutral: Germany, Britain and the Quest for a Turkish Alliance in the Second World War* (Columbia, M O : Univ. of Missouri Press, 1979), pp. 50–61; Selim Deringil, *Turkish Foreign Policy during the Second World War* (Cambridge: Cambridge Univ. Press, 1989), p. 95; Günter Kahle, "Die Publikation des deutschen Weissbuches Nr. 6: Zur Reaktion in London, Moskau, Ankara und Teheran," in *Vom Staat des ancien régime zum modernen Parteienstaat: Festschrift für Theodor Schieder zu seinem 70. Geburtstag* (Munich: Oldenbourg, 1978), pp. 451–66.

56 Ueberschär, *Hitler und Finnland*, pp. 188–91.

57 Ibid., pp. 188, 197–99; Krosby, *Petsamo Dispute*, chap. 2.

58 Ueberschär, pp. 191–92.

59 A useful summary in Bell, *Britain and the Fall of France*, pp. 55–58.

60 Compare Hastings, *Bomber Command*, pp. 101–2, and *ADAP*, D, 9, No. 421.

61 The Germans were quite accurately informed about the situation inside the French government; relevant documents in *ADAP*, D, 9.

62 Most useful on the Vichy regime are Ferro, *Pétain*; Eberhard Jäckel, *Frankreich in Hitlers Europa* (Stuttgart: Deutsche Verlags-Anstalt, 1966); Robert O. Paxton, *Vichy France* (New York: Columbia Univ. Press, 1972, 1982).

63 See Bédarida, *Stratégie Secrète*, pp. 42–49; Léon Noël, "Le project d'union franco-britannique de juin 1940," *Revue d'histoire de la deuxième guerre mondiale* 21 (Jan. 1956), 22–37; Gilbert, 6: 558–61; C 5162, 5614, 5818, 6307/9/17, PRO, FO 371/24299, C 6566, 6942/9/17, FO 371/24300.

64 See War Cabinet 169[40] of 16 June 1940, PRO, CAB 65/7; Noël, p. 52.

65 *DRuZW*, 2: 28.

66 See Boelcke, *Kriegspropaganda*, p. 399.

67 See esp. *ADAP*, D, 9, No. 479, with its emphasis on the British need for destroyers.

68 Ibid., No. 525.

69 On the armistice, see Jäckel, *Frankreich*, chap. 1; Hermann Böhme, *Der deutsch-französische Waffenstillstand im Zweiten Weltkrieg* (Stuttgart: Deutsche Verlags-Anstalt, 1966); Marine Attaché Rom, "Tätigkeitsbericht Nr. 26 der Italienischen Waffenstillstandskommission," 17 Feb. 1942, BA/MA, Case 580, PG 33654.

70 F.-A. Babtiste, "Le régime de Vichy à la Martinique (juin 1940 a juin 1943)," *Revue d'histoire de la deuxième guerre mondiale*, No. 111 (July 1978), 1–14; Pierre Pluchon, *Histoire des Antilles et de la Guyane* (Toulouse: Edouard Privat, 1982), pp. 431–33. Vichy instructed Admiral Robert to fight the British, Americans, or Free French if they invaded, to send the ships there to West Africa or to scuttle them, destroy the American planes on the aircraft carrier *Béarn* and send the gold out as well. See the intercepted Vichy order of 25 Oct. 1940 in OKM, Skl, 3. Abt. "B-Bericht 43/40," 1 Nov. 1940, Anlage 10, NA, RG 457, SRS 548/5.

71 Eleanor M. Gates, *End of the Affair: The Collapse of the Anglo-French Alliance, 1939–1940* (Berkeley: Univ. of California Press, 1981), p. 567 n 5; Thomas J. Knight, "Belgium Leaves the War, 1940," *JMH*, 41 (1969), 62–63; Boelcke, *Kriegspropaganda*, pp. 405–6; *ADAP*, D, 10, No. 222 n 5; Koecher (Bern) No. 516 of 24 June 1940 and the note on it by von Weizsäcker of 25 June 1940, AA, U.St.S., "Krieg Westen," Bd. 2; Memoirs of General von Falkenhausen covering June–July 1940, BA/MA, N 246/46, f. 188; KTB Skl A, 11, 3 July 1940, BA/MA, RM 7/14, f. 145. On British knowledge of secret Belgian soundings, see War Cabinet 171(40) of 18 June 1940, PRO, CAB 65/7.

72 *ADAP*, D, 10, No. 138; other relevant documents are in AA, Gesandtschaft Lissabon, "Deutsch-polnischer Krieg," Bd. 5.

73 Some details in Broszat, *Polenpolitik*, pp. 17–18; Boelcke, *Kriegspropaganda*, pp. 283, 284; Fröhlich, *Goebbels Tagebücher*, 9, 13, 21, 23 Feb. 1940; *Frank Diary*, pp. 170, 450–51; Weizsäcker to Major von Harbou, 25 Jan. 1940, AA, St.S., "Schriftwechsel von A-K," Bd. 4, fr. 470584–92.

74 Relevant documents are in AA, Gesandtschaft Lissabon, "Deutsch-polnischer Krieg," Bd. 5, 7. See also Sarah M. Terry, *Poland's Place in Europe: General Sikorski and the Origin of the Oder-Neisse Line, 1939–1943* (Princeton, N.J.: Princeton Univ. Press, 1983), p. 50 n 9; R 7493/3700/22, PRO, FO 371/38240.

75 It is worth noting how far reticence about the Duke of Windsor still goes; there is no reference to him in Bell, *Britain and the Fall of France*. On the British effort to suppress German documents pertaining to the Duke, see Paul R. Sweet, "Der Versuch amtlicher Einflussnahme auf die Edition der 'Documents on German Foreign Policy, 1933–1941', Ein Fall aus den fünfziger Jahren," *VjZ*, 39 (1991), 265–303.

76 The text of WP(40) No. 168, also COS(40) No. 390, is in PRO, CAB 65/7. See also the book by Bell, which derives its title from this document, esp. chap. 3; Gilbert, *Churchill*, 6: 357.

77 A table of the daily landings in England is printed in Winston S. Churchill, *The Second World War*, 6 vols. (Boston: Houghton Mifflin, 1948–53), 2: 102. Key documents are the Confidential Annex of WM(40) 139th Conclusion, 28 May 1940, Minute 1, in PRO, CAB 65/13, WM(40) 140th Conclusions, 26 May 1940, ibid., Cabinet Paper W.P.(40) 170 of 26 May 1940, R 6309/58/22, FO 371/24946; Chamberlain diary, 26 May 1940, quoted in Dilks, p. 82; WM(40) 142 War Cabinet Conclusion Confidential Annex, 27 May 1940, CAB 65/13, and 145th Conclusion Confidential Annex, 28 May 1940 in ibid; Halifax to Sergent, 12 Oct. 1942, R 7017/3700/22, FO 371/33240. See also Lord Halifax, *Fulness of Days* (New York: Dodd, Mead, 1957), pp. 226–27; Hill, *Cabinet Decisions*, chap. 6. There is a rather confusing discussion of the Cabinet meetings in

Jonathan Knight, "Churchill and the Approach to Mussolini and Hitler in May 1940: A Note," *British Journal of International Studies* 3 (1977), 92–96. Gilbert, *Churchill*, 6: 418–21, adds some detail but is not, in my judgement, entirely accurate. Bell, *Britain and the Fall of France*, pp. 38–48, summarizes the discussion and correctly relates it to the proposed approach to Mussolini. His conclusion on p. 48 is, however, contradicted on p. 50. Bell's chap. 6 summarizes popular support for the policy adopted. See also Kettenacker, *Krieg zur Friedenssicherung*, pp. 68–77.

78 See the files C 7074/5/18, PRO, FO 371/24383, and C 6828/5/18, FO 371/24382 on the period 16 May-26 June 1940 and Hankey's minute of 18 June 1940 on what had been done since May 27 in FO 800/312. Cf. Bell, pp. 48–52.

79 See also War Cabinet 6(39) of 6 Sept. 1939, PRO, CAB 65/1, f. 40.

80 A full report in Alfred Draper, *Operation Fish: The Race to Save Europe's Wealth 1939–1945* (London: Cassell, 1979). Draper was able to utilize the collected materials of Leland Stowe, whose article, "The Secret Voyage of Britain's Treasure," *Reader's Digest* 34 (Nov. 1955), 17–26, first provided an account of this episode. Draper's book also discusses the evacuation of the Yugoslav, Norwegian, and Dutch gold. Through the cooperation of U.S. Secretary of the Treasury Henry Morgenthau the Papal gold was moved to the United States in late May, 1940 (Chadwick, *Britain and the Vatican*, pp. 117–18).

81 See Dilks, "Twilight War," pp. 82–84; Gilbert, *Churchill*, 6: 332, 425–26, 474; Halifax to Samuel Hoare, 11 June 1940, PRO, FO 800/323, f. 98–100. In December 1940 Lloyd George also declined an offer of the embassy in Washington (Gilbert, 6: 442–43, 946, 953). For a sympathetic account of Lloyd George's ideas in 1940, see Paul Addison, "Lloyd George and a Compromise Peace in the Second World War," in A.J.P. Taylor (ed.), *Lloyd George – Twelve Essays* (New York: Atheneum, 1971), pp. 361–84.

82 See, e.g., *ADAP*, D, 8, Nos. 580, 621, 648. Examples of the sort of information to which the Duke had access as a result of trips of inspection and attendance at conferences with French army leaders in the period Oct. 1939–Feb. 1940 may be found in PRO, WO/106.

83 See Samuel Hoare to Halifax, 26 June 1940, PRO, FO 800/323, f. 115–18. Already on 19 June extricating the Duke – then still in France – had been mentioned in the Cabinet; see WM(40) War Cabinet 172(40), CAB 65/7. Many of the relevant documents in the papers of Lord Halifax (FO 800/326, f. 185–215) are closed until 2016, that is, for 75 years!

84 *ADAP*, D, 10, No. 9.

85 Note Franklin Mott Gunther (US Minister to Romania) to Sumner Welles, 26 June 1940, FDRL, PSF Box 90, State, June-Dec. 1940. Cf. Boelcke, *Kreigspropaganda*, p. 242; Fröhlich, *Goebbels Tagebücher*, 17 July 1940, 4: 242.

86 See Weinberg, *Foreign Policy, 1933–36*, p. 281. Hitler had given Lloyd George an interview in 1936; each had favorably impressed the other. Note Hitler's comments to Mussolini on 2 June 1941 in *ADAP*, D, 12, No. 584, p. 786.

87 This part of the tempest in the Windsor teapot is best followed in the files A 3532, 3580, 4271/434/45, PRO, FO 371/24249, f. 146–248. Churchill got the Duke to accept the appointment on July 4 and informed Roosevelt on July 9. Like the other available papers, these show the Duke in a rather shabby light, worried about his medals, his valet, etc., etc. – everything except his country in its desperate situation.

88 Gilbert, *Churchill*, 6: 613–14, 698–709, 984.

89 The account in Peter Allen, *The Crown and the Swastika: Hitler, Hess and the Duke of Windsor* (London: Hale, 1983), chaps. 11–13, is useful but contains some dubious details and assertions. The documents published in *ADAP*, D, 10, supplement chap. 11 in Walter Schellenberg, *Hitler's Secret Service* (New York: Pyramid Books, 1958). See also Stohrer (Madrid) tel. of 28 July 1940, marked "Führer vorgelegt," in BA, NS 10/18, f. 89; John Costello, *Ten Days to Destiny* (New York: William Morrow, 1991), chap. 14.

90 This is especially obvious from any reading of the Cabinet meetings of 12 and 16 June 1940 in PRO, CAB 65/19. See also the documents in AIR 20/296.

91 A useful summary in Bell, *Britain and the Fall of France*, chap. 7; added details in Gilbert, *Churchill*, 6; Ferro, *Pétain*, pp. 57–61; Hervé Coutau-Bégarie and Claude Huan, *Darlan* (Paris: Fayard, 1989), chap. 10. Very critical of Churchill's decision, Richard Lamb, *Churchill as War Leader – Right or Wrong?* (London: Bloomsbury, 1991), chap. 6. The British then had to consider the possibility of a French declaration of war, but Vichy limited itself to an air attack on Gibraltar (cf. PRO, CAB 104/211).

92 The full text is in Robert Rhodes James (ed.), *Winston S. Churchill: His Complete Speeches, 1897–1963* (New York: Bowker, 1974), 6: 6247–50 (the quotation is from p. 6250).

93 See Robert Harris and Jeremy Paxman, *A Higher Form of Killing: The Secret Story of Chemical and Biological Warfare* (New York: Hill & Wang, 1982), pp. 101–15. There is a brief discussion in Peter Fleming, *Operation Sea Lion* (New York: Simon & Schuster, 1957), pp 293–94; see also Gilbert, *Churchill*, 6: 434, 617–18, 762. The account in Günther W. Gellermann, *Der Krieg der nicht stattfand* (Koblenz: Bernard & Graefe, 1986), pp. 140–42, is very poor; the book has been demolished in a review by Rudibert Kunz in *MGM*, 44, No. 2 (1988), 201–5. The volume in the British official history, Basil Collier, *The Defence of the United Kingdom* (London: HMSO, 1957), contains no reference to the intended use of gas.

94 See the notes by General Hans Reinhardt on his role in the preparations for the invasion in BA/MA, N 245/7, f.26. Reinhardt's ideas and activities are described in Walter Ansel, *Hitler Confronts England* (Durham, N.C.: Duke Univ. Press, 1960), but there is no reference to gas in the book.

95 On the intended employment of horses in the assault, see *KTB Halder*, 26 July 1940; Fleming, pp. 249–50 (with an appropriate cartoon); Karl Klee, *Das Unternehmen "Seelöwe"* (Göttingen: Musterschmidt, 1958), p. 87. Horses were being put on barges to accustom them to their anticipated use. At the other extreme of technology, the Germans were experimenting with submersible tanks; see Paul W. Zieb, *Logistische Probleme der Marine* (Neckargemünd: Scharnhorst, 1961), pp. 96–99.

96 John P. Duggan, *Neutral Ireland and the Third Reich* (Totowa, N.J.: Barnes & Noble, 1985), pp. 136–37. Although not always reliable and confused chronologically, this book does contain some interesting details.

97 Although Fisk (*In Time of War*) describes such attitudes, he never recognizes the impact of the antics of those who were eager to welcome the Germans (e.g. pp. 373–77), combined with the massive IRA thefts of weapons, on the British government of the time.

98 On the pro-Nazi sympathies of General Hugo MacNeill, see Duggan, *Neutral Ireland*, chap. 8. A more balanced account, though still strongly biased in favor of the Irish and against the British perspective, is that of Fisk.

99 Fisk, pp. 201–7, 214–16.

100 The various German contacts with the IRA as well as with the official Irish government are discussed by Fisk, Duggan, and Carol J. Carter, *The Shamrock and the Swastika: German Espionage in Ireland in World War 2* (Palo Alto, Calif.: Pacific Books, 1977), but still await a definitive treatment. Particularly important are the as yet unclarified plots of the IRA with Edmund Veesenmayer, von Ribbentrop's subversion expert, for the overthrow of the de Valera government and the extent of de Valera's knowledge of these machinations.

Aspects of the British offers of June 1940 and Dec. 1941 to negotiate an end to partition in exchange for Irish participation in the war also remain unclear. The accounts in Fisk, pp. 158ff, and Duggan, pp. 173–74, are a beginning. De Valera used these offers in his negotiations with the Germans (*ADAP*, D, 9, No. 506); see also Gilbert, *Churchill*, 6: 433.

101 Important examples of such aid were the relatively rapid release of Allied airmen who landed in the Free State and allowing Allied planes from the base at Lough Foyle to fly

to their patrol stations in the Atlantic across Irish territory, the "Donegal Corridor," rather than detouring around Malin Head and thereby using up flying time that could have been spent on patrol.

102 See War Cabinet 170(40) of 17 June 1940, PRO, CAB 65/7.

103 Note Churchill's 7 July 1940 minute for Lindemann calling for weekly reports on the status of each of England's thirty divisions and the progress of arming the Home Guard at least with rifles, in PRO, PREM 3/54/11.

104 There is a general survey of the "auxiliary units" in David Lampe, *The Last Ditch* (New York: G.P. Putnam's, 1968); a report by one of those involved, in Fleming, *Sea Lion*, pp. 268–73; a discussion of the broader context, in Gerhard Schulz (ed.), "Zur englischen Planung des Partisanenkrieges am Vorabend des Zweiten Weltkrieges," *VjZ*, 30, No. 2 (1982), 329–30. The official history by Basil Collier, *Defence*, refers to the subject briefly, pp. 130, 297.

105 Most of those interned were themselves refugees from the Nazis and were later released.

106 *ADAP*, D, 9, No. 394; cf. Halifax to Hoare, 19 June 1940, and Hoare to Halifax, 26 June 1940, PRO, FO 800/323. Sir Samuel Hoare had been sent to Madrid to work on keeping Spain out of the conflict (Woodward, *British Foreign Policy*, 1: 435–37; Smyth, *British Policy and Franco's Spain*, pp. 26–29); Churchill, who had fought Hoare tooth and nail over the plan to allow steps toward Dominion status for India, was not about to appoint him to the position of Viceroy (where Hoare would surely have done a far better job than Linlithgow).

For contingency planning to seize the Cape Verde and Azore Islands if either Spain or Portugal or both came into the war or were obviously about to do so, see Smyth, pp. 66–67; CAB 104/210, WO 106/2947–48.

107 The account in Collier, *Defence*, should be supplemented by Murray, *Luftwaffe*, pp. 43–65; *DRuZW*, 2: 375–408.

108 Murray's assertion that it was the whole RAF and not merely Fighter Command which the Germans saw as their opponent (p. 47) seems to me entirely correct and also helpful in explaining the German battle program. For very serious errors in estimates and predictions by German air force intelligence, see Boog, *Luftwaffenführung*, pp. 95–100, 105–8.

109 Boog, p. 104; Dr. Kausch, "Streng vertraulicher Informationsbericht," BA, Brammer ZSg. 101/36, f. 219–25. Goebbels at first believed all the German reports of success; only on Oct. 4 does there appear in his diary (4: 350) a sense that things were not going perfectly according to plan. The Germans employed the approach they had used on Warsaw, Rotterdam, London and other British cities again in 1941 with their attack on Belgrade to accompany the invasion of Yugoslavia.

110 The article on this by Harvey B. Tess, "Churchill, the First Berlin Raids, and the Blitz: A New Interpretation," *MGM*, No. 2, (1982) pp. 65–78, is entirely unconvincing.

111 See Fleming, *Sea Lion*, pp. 276–78; *DRuZW*, 2: 386–87.

112 The victor in the Battle of Britain, Sir Hugh Dowding, was rewarded by prompt retirement; an extraordinary action which Churchill, though critical of it, did not reverse (on this, see now Reginald V. Jones *Reflections on Intelligence* [London: Heineman, 1989], pp. 288–89). See also Weinberg, *World in the Balance*, p. 17 n 28; documents in PRO, PREM 4/68/9.

113 Murray again makes an important point: the night attacks in the winter also produced a very high German accident rate (*Luftwaffe*, p. 59).

114 Gilbert, *Churchill*, 6: 580–84, 609–13, 655, 687–88. The term "ultra" for readings of German enigma machine ciphers did not come into use until later. The beam system was called "Knickebein" by the Germans. The assertion that measures were not taken against the Nov. 14, 1940, raid on Coventry to avoid compromising ultra has been shown to be entirely false (ibid., 912–16; Hinsley, *British Intelligence*, 6: Appendix 9).

115 See David Stafford, *Britain and European Resistance: A Survey of the Special Operations*

Executive, with Documents (Toronto: Univ. of Toronto Press, 1980), and his articles, esp. "Britain Looks at Europe 1940: Some Origins of the SOE," *Canadian Journal of History* 10, No. 2 (Aug. 1975) 231–48, and "The Detonator Concept: British Strategy, SOE and European Resistance after the Fall of France," *JCH* 10 (1975) 185–217, on the assumptions and hopes underlying the establishment of SOE.

116 Robert H. Keyserlingk, "Die deutsche Komponente in Churchills Strategie der nationalen Erhebungen 1940–1942: Der Fall Otto Strasser," *VjZ* 31 (Oct. 1983), 614–45.

117 See Churchill to Mackenzie King, 5 June 1940 (clearly meant for President Roosevelt) in David Reynolds, *Lord Lothian and Anglo-American Relations, 1939–1940* (Transactions of the American Philosophical Society, Vol. 73, Part 2, 1983), p. 20.

118 On Cripps, see Gabriel Gorodetsky, *Stafford Cripps' Mission to Moscow, 1940–42* (Cambridge: Cambridge Univ. Press, 1984), p. 61; on O'Malley (Budapest), see his No. 298 of 18 July 1940, C 7729/5/18, PRO, FO 371/24384.

119 All the evidence now points in this direction; see C 7324, 7377, 7542, 7578/89/18, PRO, FO 371/24407; C 7825, 7828/5/18, FO 371/24384; C 8015/89/18, FO 371/24408. On the approach via Malcolm Lovell to Lord Lothian, see War Cabinet 201⁴⁰ of 22 July 1940 and 209⁴⁰ of 24 July 1940, CAB 65/8; Reynolds, *Lord Lothian*, pp. 22–23; Chadwick, *Britain and the Vatican*, pp. 137–39; *ADAP*, D, 10, No. 188; Ansel, *Hitler Confronts England*, pp. 153–57; Kelly (Bern) to London No. 365 of 8 July 1940, in CAB 65/8. The supposed statement by Under-Secretary of State for Foreign Affairs R.A.B. Butler to Swedish Minister in London, Björn Prytz, on a possible peace turns out to have no basis in reality; see Thomas Munch-Petersen, " 'Common Sense not Bravado': The Butler-Prytz Interview of 17 June 1940," *Scandia* 52, No. 1 (1986) 73–114; N 6894, 6968, 7788/865/42, FO 371/43509; *The Times*, 11 Sept. 1965 and *Düsseldorfer Nachrichten*, 10 Sept. 1965; relevant documents in FO 800/322f. 272–74, 277–82; C 8837, 8974, 9092, 9598, 13302/89/18, FO 371/24408; the Halifax–Lothian exchange of Sept. 1940 communicated to Roosevelt, in FDRL, PSF Box 4, Safe, File Great Britain. Costello, *Ten Days*, Appendix 10, is not convincing; generally reasonable is the account in Kettenacker, *Krieg zur Friedenssicherung*, pp. 77–83.

120 Halifax, *Fulness of Days*, p. 229, gives his own view of the circumstances of the speech.

121 Text in Domarus, *Hitler*, 2: 1540–59.

122 On July 23 Churchill explained to a Member of Parliament that there was no need to go into detail in the government's answer to Hitler since the government had formulated and publicly announced its policy in October 1939 (Churchill to R.R. Stokes, PRO, PREM 4/100/2). He replied similarly to the King of Sweden on August 3 (PREM 4/100/3). See also *ADAP*, D, 10, Nos. 65, 220, 236; Record of interview with Dr. Albert Plesman, Institut für Zeitgeschichte, ZS 115; Hewel to Max von Hohenlohe, 30 June 1940, AA, Handakten Hewel, "Deutschland E-H," fr. 371067–70.

123 WM(40) War Cabinet 181(40) of 25 June 1940, PRO, CAB 65/7. Churchill's first message to Roosevelt as Prime Minister called attention to the forthcoming exhaustion of Britain's ability to pay.

124 *ADAP*, D, 8, Nos. 655, 659; Hugh Wilson to FDR, 7 Mar. 1940, FDR to Wilson, 15 Mar. 1940, FDRL, PSF Box 90, State, Jan.-Mar.1940.

125 *ADAP*, D, 9, Nos. 141, 163; Weinberg, *World in the Balance*, pp. 53–74.

126 Compare *ADAP*, D, 9, No. 127, p. 153, with Bureau of Demobilization, Civilian Production Administration, *Industrial Mobilization for War: History of the War Production Board and Predecessor Agencies*, Vol. 1 (Washington: GPO, 1947), 1: 542. Similarly, see the reaction to Siebel to Udet of 7 Oct. 1940, *DRuZW*, 5: 527–28, 573–74.

127 See Morgenthau Presidential Diary, 24 Jan. 1940, FDRL, Morgenthau Papers, 2: 420, 28 June 1940, 3: 598–99; cf. Cole, *Roosevelt and Isolationists*, pp. 388–89; Lothian to Halifax, 28 Dec. 1939, A 384/39/45, PRO, FO 371/24233.

128 *FDR Letters*, 2: 1045–48; Samuel Rosenman, (who prepared a draft of a speech for

FDR declining the nomination), FDRL, Oral History Transcript, pp. 150–51; Rosenman, *Working with Roosevelt* (New York: Harper, 1952).

129 Thomas F. Troy, *Donovan and the CIA: A History of the Establishment of the Central Intelligence Agency* (Frederick, Md.: University Publications of America, 1981), pp. 29–31; Donald R. McCoy, *Landon of Kansas* (Lincoln, Neb.: Univ. of Nebraska Press, 1966), pp. 215–19, 431–38; Forrest C. Pogue, *George C. Marshall*, 3 vols. (New York: Viking Press, 1963–73), 2: 39–42. See also the Japanese report, in Washington to Tokyo No. 934 of 22 June 1940, NA, RG 457, SRDJ 4876–79. The retiring Secretary of the Navy (who was about to run for Governor of New Jersey) urged Roosevelt to appoint Rear Admiral Ernest J. King as Commander-in-Chief of the U.S. fleet in order to shake the navy out of its peacetime psychology (Edison to Roosevelt, 24 June 1940, FDRL, PSF Box 82, Navy, Charles Edison).

130 On German spies in the United States, see David Kahn, *Hitler's Spies* (New York: Macmillan, 1978).

131 Some documents on these efforts have been published in *ADAP*, D, 8–11, note esp. 10, No. 112. See also Boelcke, *Kriegspropaganda*, p. 307; Schoenfeld to Moffat, 20 and 24 Jan. 1940, Moffat Papers, Vol. 18; "Besondere Bestellung für die Redaktion," 29 Mar. 1940, BA, Brammer, ZSg. 101/15, f. 158; KTB Skl A, 10, 3 June 1940, BA/MA, RM 7/13, f. 19–20. Cf. Muto (San Francisco) to Tokyo No. 109 of 28 June 1941, NA, RG 457, SRDJ 34172–74.

132 For a perceptive analysis of the domestic American repercussions of the fall of France, see J. Henriette Louis, "Réactions américaines a la défaite française de 1940," *Revue d'histoire de la deuxième guerre mondiale*, No. 119 (July 1980), 1–16.

133 There is an excellent examination of this in Michaela Hönicke, "Franklin D. Roosevelt's View of Germany before 1933: Formative Experiences of a Future President," MA thesis, Univ. of North Carolina, Chapel Hill, 1989.

134 On this concern, see Dallek, *Roosevelt and Foreign Policy*, pp. 233–35.

135 *FDR Letters*, 2:1016; Stanley E. Hilton, *Hitler's Secret War in South America, 1939–1945: German Military Espionage and Allied Counterespionage in Brazil* (Baton Rouge, La.: Louisiana State Univ. Press, 1981), p. 190; Conn and Fairchild, *Framework*, passim, esp. pp. 32–34, 47–48. On contingency planning against the possibility of the surrender of the British fleet, see the 22 May 1940 memorandum from the files of the Chief of Naval Operations in NA, RG 38, Box 245, Records of the CNO, Headquarters Cominch 1942–Secret (I am indebted to Prof. Michael Gannon for reference to this document).

136 Pogue, *Marshall*, 2: 18.

137 Dallek, *Roosevelt and Foreign Policy*, pp. 221–22.

138 Pogue, *Marshall*, 2: 28–32. See also Richard G. Davis, "Carl A. Spaatz and the Development of the Royal Air Force – U.S. Army Air Corps Relationship, 1939–1940," *Journal of Military History* 54 (1990), 453–72.

139 Borg and Okamoto, *Pearl Harbor*, p. 218.

140 Ibid., p. 43; *FDR Letters*, 2: 969; Dallek, pp. 236–37; *ADAP*, D, 8, No. 573.

141 Cole, *Roosevelt and Isolationists*, p. 354; Robert J.C. Butow, *Tojo and the Coming of the War* (Stanford, Calif.: Stanford Univ. Press, 1961), p. 191; Herbert Feis, *The Road to Pearl Harbor* (Princeton, N.J.: Princeton Univ. Press, 1950), pp. 88–94; Michael A. Barnhart, *Japan Prepares for Total War: The Search for Economic Security, 1919–1941* (Ithaca, N.Y.: Cornell Univ. Press, 1987), pp. 184ff; Jonathan G. Utley, "Upstairs, Downstairs at Foggy Bottom: Oil Exports and Japan, 1940–41," *Prologue* 8, No. 1 (1976), 17–28.

142 Note the comment of the American naval commander in East Asia to the Chief of Naval Operations on holding down expenditures in the Philippines: "Anno 1946 is not far away." Hart to Stark, 12 Apr. 1940, FDRL, PSF Box 79, Navy Dept. Jan.-Aug. 1940. On Hart's appointment, see James Leutze, *A Different Kind of Victory: A Biography of Admiral Thomas C. Hart* (Annapolis, Md.: Naval Institute Press, 1981), chap. 6.

143 War Cabinet 38[39] of 6 Oct. 1939, PRO, CAB 65/3,f. 92ff; Halifax to Churchill, 19 Jan. 1940, A 434/434/45, PRO, FO 371/24248. A large selection of the Roosevelt–Churchill correspondence was first published by Francis L. Loewenheim et al. (eds.), *Roosevelt and Churchill: Their Secret Wartime Correspondence* (New York: E.P. Dutton, 1975); a fuller one has been edited in 3 vols. by Warren F. Kimball, *Churchill and Roosevelt: The Complete Correspondence* (Princeton N.J.: Princeton Univ. Press, 1984).

144 The collection of these reports is in FDRL, PSF Great Britain, Boxes 50–52, 47, 48. After Mar. 3, 1942, they were sent to the Secretariat of the Combined Chiefs of Staff rather than to the White House. A few of the reports from July and Dec. 1941 were published in *Pearl Harbor Attack: Hearings before the Joint Committee on the Investigation of the Pearl Harbor Attack*, 39 parts (Washington: GPO, 1946), 20: 4545–48.

145 The Tyler Kent Papers are at Yale University as HM-120; the trial transcript included in these papers makes it clear that the Germans received information obtained through him, though other evidence indicates that the spy ring was an Italian one which appears to have been penetrated by the Soviets. See on these issues E.H. Cookridge (pseud. of Edward Spiro), *The Third Man* (New York: G.P. Putnam's, 1968), pp. 94–98; Reynolds, *Lord Lothian*, p. 17; Gilbert, *Churchill*, 6:485–86; Kahn, *Hitler's Spies*, p. 96 and notes p. 564; David Kahn, *The Codebreakers*, (New York: Macmillan, 1967), pp. 494–95; *Pearl Harbor Attack*, 11: 5523–30; Warren F. Kimball, *The Most Unsordid Act: Lend-Lease, 1939– 1941* (Baltimore: Johns Hopkins Press, 1969), pp. 40–41; James Leutze, "The Secret of the Churchill–Roosevelt Correspondence: September 1939–May 1940," *JCH 10* (1975), 465–91; *ADAP*, D, 9, No. 305; Costello, *Ten Days*, chaps. 5–6, Appendix 5; WM(40) 133 War Cabinet Conclusions, Minute 9, Confidential Annex, PRO, CAB 65/13; Wiley to Moore, 9 Nov. 1934, FDRL, Bullitt Papers; Thomsen (Washington) tel. 4003 of 17 Nov. 1941, AA, St.S., "U.S.A.," Bd. 10, fr. 44616–18; Schulenburg report "A 509/41," of 12 Feb. 1941 and note by Luther for Ribbentrop of 26 Feb. 1941, AA, Inland IIg, "Berichte über Amerika," Bd. 2, fr. K 204628–30. Cole *(Roosevelt and Isolationists)* never mentions the Kent episode and thus fails to see its influence on Roosevelt (see p. 460).

146 The article by David G. Haglund, "George C. Marshall and the Question of Military Aid to England, May–June 1940," *JCH 15* (1980), 745–60, rather overemphasizes the reluctance in Washington but is a useful corrective to earlier accounts.

147 Pogue, *Marshall*, 2: 50–52; Gilbert, *Churchill*, 6: 427, 462, 513–15, 676.

148 See the note by Eden, then Secretary of State for War, to Churchill of 13 July 1940 stating that American rifles being unloaded from a convoy were issued directly to troops (PRO, PREM 3/54/11).

149 See his handwritten addition to the secret daily military report for 3 June 1940: "You will notice the steady loss of destroyers. The damaged ones are also piling up in our repair yards." FDRL, PSF Great Britain, Box 50.

150 See his letters of 9 Jan. and 1 June 1940, *FDR Letters*, 2: 986, 1036.

151 Very good on this is Reynolds, *Lord Lothian*, pp. 25–29. British pressure could be counter-productive: warnings about the possibility of a successor government in London yielding the British fleet to the Germans endangered the destroyer deal, while emphasis on the Atlantic risked creating pressure to move the American fleet from the Pacific (ibid., pp. 21–22).

152 Bittner, *Britain and Iceland*, p. 119; Fred E. Pollock, "Roosevelt, the Ogdensburg Agreement, and the British Fleet: All Done with Mirrors," *Diplomatic History* 5 (1981), 203–19.

153 Reynolds, *Lord Lothian*, pp. 24–25; Conn and Fairchild, *Framework*, pp. 51–61; *FDR Letters*, 2: 1050–51; Dallek, pp. 243–47. A popular account in Philip Goodhart, *Fifty Ships that Saved the World: The Foundation of the Anglo-American Alliance* (Garden City, N.J.: Doubleday, 1965).

154 Note the 17 June 1940 memorandum of Alexander Kirk in FDRL, PSF Germany, 1940–41.

155 See Deborah W. Ray, "The Takoradi Route: Roosevelt's Prewar Venture beyond the Western Hemisphere," *Journal of American History*, 62, No. 2 (1975), 340–58, which concentrates on 1941 but shows the connection to earlier developments. See also the documents in PRO, WO 106/2878, which show the early development of the route, the need to build up defenses on it against a possible attack by Vichy France and the problems associated with the use of German JU-52 transports bought by the Belgians before the war.

156 Vincent C. Jones, *Manhattan: The Army and the Atomic Bomb* (Washington: GPO, 1985), pp. 13–15, 21–25, 65.

157 See Fritz T. Epstein, "National Socialism and French Colonialism," *Journal of Central European Affairs* 3 (1943), 52–64; Bell, *Britain and the Fall of France* pp. 199–201; Charles de Gaulle, *The War Memoirs*, vol. 1 (in 2 parts) (New York: Viking, 1955), 1: 112, 116–18. The large island of New Caledonia in the Southwest Pacific turned to de Gaulle in September 1940 under British and Australian pressure: Gavin Long, *The Six Years War: A Concise History of Australia in the 1939–1945 War* (Canberra: Australian War Memorial and Australian Government Publishing Service, 1973), p. 38.

158 Bell, pp. 225–27. Arthur Marder, *Operation "Menace:" The Dakar Expedition and the Dudley North Affair* (London: Oxford Univ. Press, 1976), is the most comprehensive account. Elmar Krautkrämer, *Frankreichs Kriegswende* (Bern: Peter Lang, 1989), provides an account (pp. 44–47) but is so biased against de Gaulle (usually referred to as "the rebel') as to be misleading.

159 See esp. *ADAP*, D, 11, No. 33. There is to the best of my knowledge no comprehensive study of the various projects to reclaim the area for Pétain.

160 Churchill's broadcast of 1 Oct. 1939 is in James, *Churchill Speeches*, 6: 6161. Note that early in July 1940 the British preferred Soviet to German control of the Petsamo nickel mines, Günter Kahle, "Die Publikation des deutschen Weissbuches Nr. 6: Zur Reaktion in London, Moskau, Ankara und Teheran," p. 456 n 17.

161 The account of the Cripps mission by Gorodetsky is not adequate. There is a useful survey in H. Hanak, "Sir Stafford Cripps as British Ambassador in Moscow, May 1940 to June 1941," *English Historical Review* 94, No. 370 (Jan. 1979), 48–70. Very helpful is Steven M. Miner, *Between Churchill and Stalin: The Soviet Union, Great Britain and the Origins of the Grand Alliance* (Chapel Hill, N.C.: Univ. of North Carolina Press, 1988). I have used the reports in the PRO: Cripps's tels. 399–404, 408, 409 of 1 and 2 July 1940, in N 5937/30/38, FO 371/24844; Kahle, "Die Publikation des deutschen Weissbuches Nr. 6," pp. 453–54; Cripps's report of 16 July 1940, N 6526/30/38, FO 371/24845; WP⁴⁰ 254, "Comment on the Recent Conversation between His Majesty's Ambassador at Moscow and M. Stalin," PRO, CAB 66/9; the Italian intercept of a report of July 6 by the Greek Minister in Moscow on a conversation with Cripps as passed to the Germans, Mackensen (Rome) tel. 1354 of 15 July 1940, AA, St.S., "Russland," Bd. 3, fr. 112315–16, and the full text of the decoded Greek telegram forwarded with Mackensen's report 361 of 16 July in Botschaft Rom (Quir.), Bd. 43/4, fr. 481432–36.

162 *DRuZW*, 4: 58.

163 *ADAP*, D, 10, No. 164.

164 On the journey and activities of the *Komet*, code-named "Schiff 45," see Weinberg, *Germany and the Soviet Union*, pp. 83–84; "Lagebesprechung beim Chef der Seekriegsleitung," 26 June 1940, KTB Skl A 10, BA/MA, RM 7/13, f. 271; KTB Skl A 12, 1 Aug. and 12 Aug. 1940, RM 7/15, f. 7 and 264; German Naval Attaché Moscow report of 9 Sept. 1940, RM 7/92, f. 588–93; KTB Skl A 13, 12 Sept. 1940, RM 7/16, f. 160–61; Jürgen Rohwer and Gerhard Hümmelchen, *Chronik des Seekrieges 1939–45* (Oldenburg: Stalling, 1968), pp. 58, 88, 89, 93, 156, 158, 187, 194.

165 "Vortrag Marineattaché Moskau, Kapitän z.S. Baumbach, bei Chef 1/Skl," 12 Sept. 1940, KTB Skl A 13, BA/MA, RM 7/16, f. 156; *ADAP*, D, 10, No. 206. Given the limited cargo space available, the Soviet Union was willing to carry such critical raw materials as tin, rubber, molybdenum and wolfram from East Asia to Germany but preferred to transport other items only if really essential for war industry. See Ian D. Mac-Donald, "Diplomacy, Trade and War: The British Naval Blockade and the German Search for Raw Materials in the Far East, 1939–1941," MA thesis, Univ. of North Carolina, Chapel Hill, 1987.

166 *ADAP*, D, 10, No. 162; Schulenburg (Moscow) tels. 1398 of 13 July 1940 and 1502 of 29 July 1940, AA, St.S., "Litauen," fr. 193334 and 193351.

167 *ADAP*, D, 10, Nos. 77, 84, 141, 182, 214, 217, 223, 242.

168 There is an excellent account in Toscano, *Designs in Diplomacy*, chap. 3. See also Schulenburg (Moscow) tel. 1497 of 29 July 1940, AA, St.S., "Russland," Bd. 2, fr. 112342, and Tippelskich (Moscow) tel. 1046 of 30 Apr. 1941, St.S., "Russland," Bd. 4, fr. 113383.

169 It should be noted that Soviet relations with the U.S. remained very cool at this time, a fact known to the Germans (*ADAP*, D, 10, No. 59).

170 See People's Commissariat for Foreign Affairs to the Soviet embassy in Tokyo, 1 July 1940, in Morley, *Fateful Choice*, pp. 311–12.

171 On Soviet–Japanese relations, see the project for a partition of China between Japan and the Soviet Union put forward by the Soviet ambassador to Japan on June 28, 1940 (ibid., p. 311) which extraordinarily resembles a plan set forth by Shiratori Toshio on July 19, 1939. Cf. ibid., pp. 41–44.

172 David Dilks (ed.), *The Diaries of Sir Alexander Cadogan, O.M. 1938–1945* (New York: G. P. Putnam's, 1972), p. 331.

173 A summary with documents in Brügel, *Stalin und Hitler*.

174 Summary in Woodward, *British Foreign Policy*, 1: 473–74. The full text, which was sent to Churchill, is in N 6029/283/38, PRO, FO 371/24852.

175 Ch'i, *Nationalist China*, pp. 56–60, 89–92, 128–30.

176 *ADAP*, D, 9, Nos. 29, 233, 327, 414, 491; Joachim Peck (ed.), *Kolonialismus ohne Kolonien: Der deutsche Imperialismus und China 1937* (Berlin East: Akademie Verlag, 1961), No. 134; Gordon M. Berger, *Parties out of Power in Japan, 1931–1941* (Princeton, N.J.: Princeton Univ. Press, 1977), pp. 241–42, 254, 258–59.

177 See Ott (Tokyo) tels. 355 of 17 Apr. 1940 and 367 of 20 Apr. 1940, AA, St.S., "Japan," Bd. 2, fr. 136289–90 and 136291; documents in AA, HaPol, Clodius, "Japan," Bd. 3; the diary of the German naval attaché in Tokyo edited by Chapman, *Price of Admiralty*, passim; and the thesis by MacDonald cited in n 165, above.

178 Morley, *Fateful Choice*, p. 157.

179 Ibid., p. 243.

180 Boyle, *China and Japan at War*, pp. 274–75.

181 Morley, *Fateful Choice*, pp. 243–44; *ADAP*, D, 9, No. 123.

182 *ADAP*, D, 9, Nos. 234, 261, 262, 273, 280, 302, 502; Morley, *Fateful Choice*, p. 244; Arita (Tokyo), to Washington No. 968, to the Hague No. 149 of 11 May 1940, NA, RG 457, SRDJ 4196; Arita (Tokyo) to Washington No. 230 of 15 May 1940, SRDJ 4282; Tokyo to Batavia No. 209, to Berlin No. 280 of 16 May 1940, SRDJ 4714. On Japan's insignificant production of shale and synthetic oil, see Barnhart, *Japan Prepares*, pp. 29, 146–47.

183 Morley, *Fateful Choice*, pp. 38–41.

184 Ibid., pp. 245–46.

185 Gordon W. Prange, *At Dawn We Slept: The Untold Story of Pearl Harbor* (New York: McGraw-Hill, 1981), p. 14, which places this in March or April.

186 Morley, *Deterrent Diplomacy*, pp. 206–7. For German recognition of this shift and the immediate desire of the German navy to take advantage of it to obtain assistance for its

operations in the Indian and Pacific Oceans, see KTB Skl A 10, 1 June 1940, BA/MA, RM 7/13, f. 2.

187 The Japanese army as well as the navy now wanted to move south; see Barnhart, *Japan Prepares*, pp. 158–59. On the French giving in, see Morley, *Fateful Choice*, pp. 158–60, 162–88, 254–55, 301–2. The Germans watched this process with care: they wanted the Japanese to commit themselves by occupying French Indo-China but saw no reason to assist the Yonai government's shaky domestic position by pressuring Vichy in their behalf; *ADAP*, D, 9, Nos. 484, 511, 514; D, 10, No. 6. The original agreement had been signed by Georges Catroux as governor but he was replaced (and joined de Gaulle) by Vichy with Jean Decoux who agreed to the Japanese occupation.

188 On the British answer to Japanese demands, see the War Cabinet meetings 172 of 19 and 173 of 20 June 1940 in PRO, CAB 65/7, and 194 of 5 and 199 of 10 July 1940 in CAB 65/8; Arita (Tokyo) to Washington No. 313, to London No. 513 of 29 June 1940, NA, RG 457, SRDJ 5007–8.

189 Morley, *Deterrent Diplomacy*, pp. 208–14; Morley, *Fateful Choice*, pp. 247–49, 249–53; Butow, *Tojo*, pp. 139–41; Yamaji (Vienna) to Tokyo No. 121 of 26 June 1940, NA, RG 457, SRDJ 4994–98 and No. 140 of 24 July 1940, SRDJ 5470–73, Inoue (Budapest) to Washington and Tokyo No. 122 of 6 July 1940, SRDJ 5142–50; *ADAP*, D, 10, No. 147.

190 Note Yamamoto's sensing of this timetable for Japan as noted in the diary of the German naval attaché on Sept 13. 1940, Chapman, *Price of Admiralty*, 1: 264.

191 Morley, *Fateful Choice*, pp. 140–41, 254.

192 Kido Koichi, *The Diary of Marquis Kido, 1931–45: Selected Translations into English* (Frederick, Md.: University Publications of America, 1984), pp. 244ff (esp. the entry for July 11, 1940). (Henceforth cited as *Kido Diary*).

193 See Berger, *Parties out of Power*, pp. 268–69.

194 The best account in English remains James B. Crowley, *Japan's Quest for Autonomy: National Security and Foreign Policy, 1930–1938* (Princeton, N.J.: Princeton Univ. Press, 1964), pp. 358–75. See also the account in Barnhart, *Japan Prepares*, chaps. 4 and 5.

195 Berger, *Parties out of Power*, pp . 254–70; *ADAP*, D, 10, No. 241.

196 On these debates and their conclusion, see Krebs, *Japans Deutschlandpolitik* 1: 438–40; Berger, pp. 269–70; Butow, *Tojo*, pp. 140–53; Morley, *Deterrent Diplomacy*, pp. 216–21; Morley, *Fateful Choice*, pp. 44–45, 264–65; Boyle, *China and Japan*, p. 300. On the domestic aspect of the new policy, see esp. Berger, pp. 272–92.

197 Borg and Okamoto, *Pearl Harbor*, p. 251; Morley, *Fateful Choice*, p. 266.

198 The quotation is from Matsuoka's draft of a Tripartite Pact policy; the full text is in Morley, *Deterrent Diplomacy*, pp. 283–88; discussion of it in ibid., p. 221, and Morley, *Fateful Choice*, pp. 47–49, 265–66.

199 Borg and Okamoto, pp. 99–101; documents in F 3634/677/23, PRO, FO 371/24741.

200 *ADAP*, D, 10, No. 273; Morley, *Deterrent Diplomacy*, pp. 223–28.

201 Ian Kershaw, *The 'Hitler Myth': Image and Reality in the Third Reich* (New York: Oxford Univ. Press, 1987), pp. 154–60.

202 Note *ADAP*, D, 9, No. 397.

203 See the comments by Goebbels on June 16, 1940, that France must be crushed absolutely and not allowed to recover as Germany had after 1918. Britain would be made into an enlarged Holland (Boelcke, *Kriegspropaganda*, p. 392).

204 This is also the interpretation in the books of Paxton and Jäckel (see Bibliographic Essay, p. 928).

205 On the invasion plans and preparations, see the works of Lampe, Ansel, Fleming, Wheatley, Klee, and the detailed notes by General Reinhardt in BA/MA, N 245/7. There is a facsimile reprint of the German occupation handbook in *German Occupied Great Britain: The Official Secret Documents, Ordinances of the Military Authorities* (Scutt: Foord,

1971); the German arrest list with over 2800 names has been reprinted, *The Black Book (Sonderfahndungsliste G.B.)* (London: Imperial War Museum, 1989).

206 *ADAP*, D, 10, Nos. 73, 129; Douglas A. Farnie, *East and West of Suez: The Suez Canal in History, 1854–1956* (Oxford: Clarendon Press, 1969), p. 621.

207 Knox, *Mussolini Unleashed*, pp. 146–48.

208 The best recent account in ibid., pp. 150ff. Knox is correct in stressing Mussolini's concern about an early peace between Germany and England in which Italian aspirations would be disregarded by the Germans and the role this concern played in his futile efforts to get his generals and admirals moving. A rather different view is presented in James J. Sadkovich, "Understanding Defeat: Reappraising Italy's Role in World War II," *JCH* 24, No. 1 (Jan. 1989), 27–61. More balanced, Brian R. Sullivan, "The Italian Armed Forces 1918–1940," in Allan R. Millett and Williamson Murray (eds.), *Military Effectiveness*, Vol. 2, *The Interwar Period* (Boston: Allen & Unwin, 1988), pp. 169–217.

209 Weinberg, *World in the Balance*, pp. 96–136; Klaus Hildebrand, *Vom Reich zum Weltreich: Hitler, NSDAP und koloniale Frage 1919–1945* (Munich: Wilhelm Fink, 1969). For a perspective from the former German Democratic Republic (where the major German colonial records were located), see Helmuth Stoecker (ed.), *German Imperialism in Africa* (London: C. Hurst, 1986), chap. 12. See also Lammers to Schwerin von Krosigk, "RM Nr. 4992/39," of 20 Nov. 1939, BA, R 2/4509, and the references to Hitler's meeting with Ritter von Epp on 7, 8, and 19 July 1940 for a total of 9.5 hours, in BA, Nachlass Epp 20/3.

210 Hitler's views were set forth by him to the chief of the high command of the armed forces (OKW), Wilhelm Keitel, the prospective Minister for the Colonies, Ritter von Epp, and the OKW representative on colonial matters, Colonel Werner von Geldern-Crispendorf, in conferences on July 13, 1940; see the account of the last named in BA/MA, N 185/4, f. 1191–97; cf. Weinberg, *World in the Balance*, p. 114, and Hildebrand, pp. 666–67. By July 19 the Italians knew the dimensions of the planned German colonial empire, see *ADAP*, D, 10, No. 193.

211 On German negotiations with the nationalist opposition in the Union of South Africa, see *ADAP*, D, 8, Nos. 577, 629; 9, No. 25. Both Hertzog and Malan were at this time urging an immediate peace with Germany; see Kenneth Ingham, *Jan Christian Smuts, The Conscience of a South African* (New York: St. Martin's, 1986), p. 210. German plans for the recovery of German Southwest Africa assumed the exclusion of Walfishbay; see "Verwaltungsorganisation Deutsch Südwestafrika," 18 Jan 1940, BA, R 2/4985a.

212 Proof coins are in BA, R 2/30737.

213 Interesting clues to Hitler's thinking on this point are in his comments to Abetz, the new Foreign Ministry representative in France, on 3 Aug. 1940 (*ADAP*, D, 10, No. 345).

214 Recent accounts of the Madagascar plan are in Breitman, *Architect of Genocide*, passim, and Hans-Jürgen Döscher, *Das Auswärtige Amt im Dritten Reich: Diplomatie im Schatten der "Endlösung"* (Berlin: Siedler, 1987), pp. 215–20. See also Christopher R. Browning, *The Final Solution and the German Foreign Office: A Study of Amt D III of Abteilung Deutschland 1940–43* (New York: Holmes & Meier, 1978), pp. 35–43; Boelcke, *Kriegspropaganda*, pp. 510–11; Fröhlich, *Goebbels Tagebücher*, 26 July 1940, 4: 253.

215 A summary in Eberhard Jäckel, *Hitlers Herrschaft: Vollzug einer Weltanschauung* (Stuttgart: Deutsche Verlags-Anstalt, 1986), pp. 89–99.

216 Note Hillgruber's summary in Jürgen Rohwer and Eberhard Jäckel (eds.), *Der Mord an den Juden im Zweiten Weltkrieg: Entschlussbildung and Verwirklichung* (Stuttgart: Deutsche Verlags-Anstalt, 1985), pp. 218–20.

217 See also the Goebbels conference of July 9, 1940, Boelcke, *Kriegspropaganda*, p. 421.

218 For suggestions that Germany annex a portion of Hungary that the latter had acquired in the 1919 peace settlement, see the material on "Der Anschluss Ödenburgs an das Reich, zu 40/41 geh.Reichssache," in AA, Pol XII.

219 The editor of von Leeb's papers, Georg Meyer, *Generalfeldmarschall Ritter von Leeb: Tagebuchaufzeichnungen und Lagebeurteilungen aus zwei Weltkriegen* (Stuttgart: Deutsche Verlags-Anstalt, 1976), p. 58, claims that this was merely routine staff work, but the entries in von Leeb's diary for 28 June, 1 July, 10 July and 1 Oct. 1940, as well as other evidence, contradict Meyer's apologia. (Publication henceforth cited as *Leeb KTB*.)

220 There is an important file of German documents on the invasion plans from the records of the German headquarters for the planned invasion, von Leeb's Army Group C, in the Imperial War Museum in London, MI14/570/2, Box E 356. A useful survey in Hans Rudolf Kurz, *Operationsplanung Schweiz: Die Rolle der Schweizer Armee in zwei Weltkriegen* (Thun: Otto, 1974), pp. 36ff. Documents which the Germans had captured in France were to be used to justify the invasion when the time for it came, Georg Kreis, *Auf den Spuren von La Charité: Die schweizerische Armeeführung im Spannungsfeld des deutsch-französischen Gegensatzes 1936–1941* (Basel: Helbing & Lichtenhahn, 1976), pp. 7–10, 207; *ADAP*, D, 11, Nos. 11. 138, 301. On the Italian role in this project, see also Knox, *Mussolini Unleashed*, pp. 138, 140.

221 The Swiss had been greatly alarmed by the German invasions of various neutrals and their victory over France which left them isolated. Their willingness to defend themselves, however, especially by blowing up the key railways tunnels, protected them only as long as other powers kept Germany occupied. Liechtenstein would have followed in Switzerland's wake into oblivion; a survey of the whole subject of German–Liechtenstein relations in Joseph Walk, "Liechtenstein 1933–1945: Nationalsozialismus im Mikrokosmos," in Ursula Büttner (ed.), *Das Unrechtsregime*, 2 vols. (Hamburg: Christians, 1986), 2: 376–425.

222 Werner Jochmann (ed.), *Adolf Hitler: Monologe im Führerhauptquartier, 1941–1944* (Hamburg: Albrecht Knaus, 1980), 26 Aug. 1942, p. 366. See also Hitler's comment to Mussolini on 2 June 1941, *ADAP*, D, 12, No. 584, p. 792.

223 Rich, *Hitler's War Aims*, 2: 401–2; Jürg Fink, *Die Schweiz aus der Sicht des Dritten Reiches 1933–1945* (Zurich: Schulthess, 1985), pp. 91–92, also stresses Switzerland as a place for the exchange of gold.

224 Sweden allowed hundreds of German "medical" personnel to go across Sweden to Narvik and permitted submarine crews and the officers and men of the German destroyers sunk at Narvik to return to Germany across Sweden; not one was interned. See *ADAP*, D, 9, Nos. 108, 153, 154, 171, 179, 183, 259, 268, 348; KTB Skl A 8, 26 Apr. 1940, BA/MA, RM 7/11, f. 287; KTB Skl A 10, 30 June 1940, RM 7/13, f. 311.

225 *ADAP*, D, 9, Nos. 306, 351, 386.

226 Lutzhöft, *Deutsche Militärpolitik*, pp. 75ff.

227 Ibid., pp. 81–108. A survey of the transport and related services Sweden had provided to the German war effort in the period July 1940–1 Nov. 1941 was handed to the German military attaché by the Swedes and is summarized in KTB Skl A 28, 14 Dec. 1941, RM 7/31, f. 215–16.

228 Wittmann, *Schwedens Wirtschaftsbeziehungen*, pp. 204–7, 235–40.

229 See ibid., pp. 221–28; *ADAP*, D, 9, No. 510.

230 Ley to Ribbentrop, 10 June 1940, NA, RG 238, PS-1223.

231 *ADAP*, D, 10, Nos. 200, 243.

232 Ibid., No. 17.

233 Wagner, *Lagevorträge*, pp. 108–9; Salewski, *Deutsche Seekriegsleitung*. 1: 237–38; Andreas Hillgruber, "Noch einmal: Hitlers Wendung gegen die Sowjetunion 1940," *Geschichte in Wissenschaft und Unterricht* 33 (1982), p. 218; Weinberg, *World in the Balance*, p. 113 n 47. Information on the future German navy provided by Raeder to the Japanese on 21 Apr. 1941 is in Japanese naval attaché Berlin to Tokyo "N" Serial 12, No. 1905 of 23 Apr. 1941, NA, RG 457, SRNA 38–39.

Before World War I there had been some detailed planning for an invasion of the

United States in Germany; it is summarized in Holger Herwig, *The Politics of Frustration: The United States in German Naval Planning, 1889–1941* (Boston: Little, Brown, 1976), pp. 42–54, 57–66. The absence of similar planning activity before and during World War II – no one this time debated whether to give priority to landing on Cape Cod or on Long Island – has misled some historians into thinking war with the United States was no part of Hitler's intentions. The real difference was in the status of German naval construction – on which Hitler was very well informed – not in intent.

234 *DRuZW*, 2: 345; Sadkovich, "Understanding Defeat," p. 49; KTB Skl A 11, 24 July 1940, BA/MA, RM 7/14, f. 282–83; documents on Italian-German cooperation in the submarine war in the Atlantic in PRO, ADM 223/3.

235 On the Trondheim project, see Thies, *Architekt der Weltherrschaft*, p. 131; Wagner, *Lagevorträge*, pp. 108, 263; Salewski, *Deutsche Seekriegsleitung*, 1: 193–94; Alfred Speer, *Erinnerungen* (Berlin: Propyläen, 1969), p. 196; Admiral Werner Fuchs, "Geschichtliche Entwicklung des Baues einer Grosswerft in Drontheim," BA/MA, RM 7/98, f. 85; Admiral Boehm's adjutant to Raeder, 1 July 1940, BA/MA, Nachlass Boehm, N 172/3. The naval facilities were to accommodate 55,000 families of navy crews and workers, make possible the construction of one battleship annually, and the simultaneous repair of 2 battleships, 6 cruisers, and 24 submarines. See the Raeder material on the Trondheim project in RM 6/74, f. 238, 239, 243. Hitler explained part of the scheme to Mussolini on 4 Oct. 1940 (*ADAP*, D, 11, No. 149).

236 Speer, *Erinnerungen*, p. 196; Winston G. Ramsay, *The War in the Channel Islands* (London: Battle of Britain Prints, 1981); Charles Cruikshank, *The German Occupation of the Channel Islands* (London: Oxford Univ. Press, 1979); Note for the CIGS, "Operations against the Channel Islands 1940–1945," May 1947, PRO, WO 106/3017.

237 German naval leaders also advocated additional bases all over the globe, but there is no clear evidence that these projects ever became the basis of official policy.

238 The German plans for these bases are most thoroughly explored in Goda, "Germany and Northwest Africa."

239 For signs that Franco seriously intended to go to war, see *ADAP*, D, 10, Nos. 3, 88. Goda demonstrates Franco's clear preference for war if his conditions – which he himself believed reasonable – were met. On Spain's bad economic situation, see Smyth, *British Policy and Franco's Spain*, pp. 77–83.

240 *ADAP*, D, 9, No. 488; 10, No. 16.

241 Most recently, *DRuZW*, 2:34.

242 Weinberg, *World in the Balance*, pp. 120–23; Goda, "Germany and Northwest Africa"; Smyth, *British Policy and Franco's Spain*, pp. 84–93, 98.

243 Thies, *Architekt der Weltherrschaft*, pp. 138ff.

244 Nicolaus von Below, *Als Hitlers Adjutant 1937–1945* (Mainz: Hase & Koehler, 1980), p. 217.

245 Note Hitler's comments to Goebbels recorded in the latter's diary on 14 Nov. and 29 Dec. 1939 and 13 Jan. 1940. Translations of the first two of these may be found in the generally unreliable English edition of Fred Taylor, *The Goebbels Diaries 1939–1941* (New York: Penguin Books, 1984), pp. 48, 77. A devastating analysis of this edition is in the *Bulletin of the German Historical Institute, London*, Autumn 1983, pp. 16–19. It should be noted that in his 29 Dec. comments Hitler repeated his view about the fortunate (for Germany) removal of the capable Germanic elite by the bolsheviks.

246 A useful summary of the evidence in Hillgruber, "Noch einmal," pp. 218–19.

247 See Hitler's comments to Raeder on July 21, 1941, in Wagner, *Lagevorträge*, pp. 120–21; a somewhat more detailed account of the same conference is in BA/MA, RM 7/14, f. 236–39. The argument of Hartmut Schustereit, *Vabanque: Hitlers Angriff auf die Sowjetunion 1941 als Versuch, durch den Sieg im Osten den Westen zu Bezwingen* (Herford: Mittler, 1988), is not convincing in this regard.

248 31 July 1940, from the Halder Diary, *ADAP*, D, 10, No. 73.

249 This summarizes the position of Weinberg, *Germany and the Soviet Union*; Hillgruber, "Noch einmal"; and *DRuZW*, 4. On Hitler's views on fighting in winter, see *ADAP*, D, 8, No. 591. As late as July 28, 1940, it was assumed in the high command of the German navy that the attack was scheduled for the fall of 1940; see "Betrachtungen über Russland," 28 July 1940, BA/MA, RM 6/66, f. 36–42. Jodl explained at an internal meeting in OKW on July 29 that the attack was to take place in 1941.

250 *DRuZW*, 4: 114–16; Andreas Hillgruber, "Das Russland-Bild der führenden deutschen Militärs vor Beginn des Angriffs auf die Sowjetunion," in Alexander Fischer et al. (eds.), *Russland–Deutschland–Amerika* (Wiesbaden: Steiner, 1978), pp. 296–310.

251 Dr. med. Erwin Giesing, "Bericht über meine Behandlung bei Hitler," Institut für Zeitgeschichte, pp. 85–86. See also KTB Skl A 10, 18 June 1940, BA/MA, RM 7/13, f. 186.

252 The economic considerations mentioned in *DRuZW*, 4: 111–13, appear to me to have been more important in a later stage of the preparations.

253 Its Chief of Staff, General Marcks, prepared one of the first of the plans for an attack on the Soviet Union. See *DRuZW*, 4: 216–19, 226–27; Ingo Lachnit and Friedhelm Klein (eds.), "Der 'Operationsentwurf Ost' des Generalmajors Marcks vom 5. August 1940," *Wehrforschung*, No. 4(1972), pp. 114–23.

254 The draft of this order had been reviewed in the high command of the armed forces on 2 Aug. 1940, see KTB OKW, 1: 5. The date shows the close connection with the internal discussions of 29–31 July.

255 *DRuZW* 4: 708.

256 Rolf-Dieter Müller, "Die deutschen Gaskriegsvorbereitungen," pp. 42–43.

257 This point is repeatedly and correctly stressed in *DRuZW*, 4: 168–89, and elsewhere.

258 OKW, Abt. L, Keitel, "349/40 gKdos. Chefs." of 14 June 1940 in BA/MA, Case 422, PG 32019.

259 Hillgruber, "Noch einmal," pp. 219–20.

260 Ueberschär, *Hitler und Finnland*, pp. 170–79.

261 The earlier discussions, especially of July 21, also assumed the involvement of Finland on Germany's side, but it is not absolutely certain that this reflects Hitler's (as contrasted with Halder's) views.

262 Weinberg, *Germany and the Soviet Union*, pp. 126–26; Ueberschär, pp. 202–17 (but without any comprehension of the tie to the 31 July decision).

263 See *ADAP*, D, 10, No. 171; Mackensen (Rome) tel. No. 1356 of 15 July 1940, AA, St.S., "Der Krieg 1939," Bd. 8, fr. 232269–71. In explaining the German guarantee of Romania to Goebbels, Hitler took the opposite view, that is, that Germany absolutely needed the oil (Fröhlich, *Goebbels Tagebücher*, 4 Sept. 1940, 4: 307).

264 *ADAP*, D, 9, No. 545; 10, No. 119. Hungary and the Soviet Union had resumed diplomatic relations in the fall of 1939.

265 Ibid., 10, No. 73; *I Documenti diplomatici italiani*, 9th series, Vol. 5, No. 161. The reference was to information in documents seized by the Germans in France.

266 KTB Halder, 13 July 1940.

267 *ADAP*, D, 10, Nos. 63, 75, 81, 105, 146, 393.

268 On the negotiations leading to the award, see Juhász, *Hungarian Foreign Policy*, pp. 172–75; Hillgruber, *Hitler, König Carol*, pp. 89ff; Nandor F. Dreisziger, "The Hungarian General Staff and Diplomacy," *Canadian–American Review of Hungarian Studies* 7, No. 1 (1980), 11–14.

269 It was a great convenience for the Germans that Romanian King Carol had originally invited a German military mission (*ADAP*, D, 10, Nos. 80, 161), but at first Hitler had held back (ibid., No. 196).

270 Weinberg, *Germany and the Soviet Union*, p. 134; Gerhard L. Weinberg, "Der Deutsche

Entschluss zum Angriff auf die Sowjetunion," *VjZ* 1 (1953), 318, 2 (1954) 254; *ADAP*, D, 11, Nos. 236, 376.

271 Knox, *Mussolini Unleashed*, pp. 141–42.

272 *DRuZW*, Vol. 3, is one of the few books which clearly recognizes the importance of this framework for all German actions in the period Sept. 1940 to May 1941.

4: THE EXPANDING CONFLICT

1 Thus Hitler's letter to Mussolini of 5 Dec. 1940 asserting that the German divisions to be used in Spain were needed back in April at the latest because they were required for the war against England (*ADAP*, D, 11, No. 452) has to be read as really referring to the attack on the Soviet Union about which Hitler had not yet informed his Italian ally. On June 21, 1941, Hitler told Goebbels that he had been working on the preparations since July 1940 (Fröhlich, *Goebbels Tagebücher*, 4: 710).

2 The planning is surveyed in *DRuZW*, 4: 119–326; the directive of 18 Dec. 1940 is in *ADAP*, D, 11, No. 532. See also Schustereit, *Vabanque*.

3 David Thomas, "Foreign Armies East and German Military Intelligence in Russia 1941–45," *JCH* 22 (1987), 261–302.

4 *DRuZW*, 4: 188–89; *KTB OKW*, 1: 72; Boog, *Luftwaffenführung*, pp. 85 n 413, 109–10. In the spring of 1941, the Soviets began to complain about the systematic overflights (*ADAP*, D, 12, No. 381).

5 Ueberschär, *Hitler und Finnland*, pp. 162–65.

6 Domarus, *Hitler*, 1: 642.

7 This has been demonstrated particularly carefully in Christian Streit, *Keine Kameraden: Die Wehrmacht und die sowjetischen Kriegsgefangenen 1941–1945* (Stuttgart: Deutsche Verlags-Anstalt, 1978). A good example of the careful obscuring of the import of criminal orders at the time they were given is the entry on a situation conference in the high command of the German navy on 20 Mar. 1941 in KTB Skl A 19, BA/MA, RM 7/22, f. 280.

8 Especially important is the section by Jürgen Förster in *DRuZW*, 4, and the book by Helmut Krausnick and Hans-Heinrich Wilhelm, *Die Truppe des Weltanschauungskrieges: Die Einsatzgruppen der Sicherheitspolizei und des SD, 1938–1942* (Stuttgart: Deutsche Verlags-Anstalt, 1981). The intention to wage the war in the East in an exceptionally brutal fashion was known to the German general in Croatia by May 5, 1941; see Peter Broucek (ed.), *Ein General im Zwielicht*, 3: 108.

9 See the entry for 5 June 1941 in the von Bock diary, BA/MA, N 22/1, f. 21.

10 An important survey in Rohwer and Jäckel, *Der Mord*; a recent analysis in Breitman, *Architect of Genocide*.

11 Krausnick and Wilhelm, *Truppe des Weltanschauungskrieges*, Part I, chaps. 1 and 2.

12 Ibid., chap. 3; also Streit, *Keine Kameraden*, chap. 3.

13 This is made particularly clear by Andreas Hillgruber in "Die 'Endlösung' und das deutsche Ostimperium als Kernstück des rassenideologischen Programms des Nationalsozialismus," reprinted in his collection, *Deutsche Grossmacht- und Weltpolitik im 19. und 20. Jahrhundert* (Düsseldorf: Droste, 1977), pp. 252–75.

14 A preliminary survey in Weinberg, *Germany and the Soviet Union*, p. 122; more details in Salewski, *Seekriegsleitung* 1. See also KTB Skl A 16, 29 Dec. 1940, BA/MA, RM 7/19, f. 232–40. Jodl's 3 Dec. 1940 memorandum placing the offensive against England at the top of the priority list, with the defense against England second and the attack on the Soviet Union third, reflects his assessment of the relative *difficulty* of these operations, not their *desirability*; see *DRuZW*, 4: 177–78.

15 *DRuZW*, 4: 283–84.

16 Schwerin von Krosigk to Göring, 19 April 1941, BA, R 2/24243.

17 See esp. *VjZ* 23 (1975), 333–40; see also Oron J. Hale Interrogation of Köstring, 30–31 Aug. 1945, U.S. Army Center for Military History files.

18 *ADAP*, D, 12, No. 423; Hewel Diary, 28 Apr. 1941, Institut für Zeitgeschichte.

19 *ADAP*, D, 12, No. 419.

20 See the diary of Hamburg's Lord Mayor Carl Vincent Krogmann for 26 May 1941, in Hamburg, Forschungsstelle für die Geschichte des Nationalsozialismus in Hamburg, 11 k 9.

21 Weinberg, *Germany and the Soviet Union*, pp. 118–19; in more detail, *DRuZW*, 4: 168–89, 259–72, 5/1: 488ff, 786ff, 833ff.

22 Best survey in *DRuZW*, 4: 277–86, 299–317; a good analysis and useful statistics in Murray, *Luftwaffe*, pp. 59, 83–84.

23 Note the quotation from the Goebbels diary in *DRuZW*, 4: 317. See also Hinsley, *British Intelligence*, 2: 193.

24 *DRuZW*, 4: 98–161.

25 See *ADAP*, D, 11, No. 651 n 6; numerous documents in AA, St.S., "Japan," Bd. 2 and 3.

26 Ueberschär, *Hitler und Finnland*, pp. 210–13; *DRuZW*, 4: 876.

27 Ueberschär, pp. 221–25; Weizsäcker to Ribbentrop, "St.S. No. 812," of 2 Nov. 1940 enclosing a memorandum by Blücher of 1 Nov. 1940, AA, St.S., "Aufzeichnungen über interne Angelegenheiten," Bd. 2, fr. 235330–32.

28 *KTB Halder*, 16 Dec. 1940 (also *ADAP*, D, 11, No. 54); Weinberg, *Germany and the Soviet Union*, pp. 149–50; *ADAP*, D, 11, p. 1024.

29 This was especially obvious in the German attitude toward the Finnish–Soviet negotiations about the nickel concession at Petsamo, see Krosby, *Petsamo Dispute*.

30 *DRuZW*, 4: map 24; Hewel Diary, 15 May 1941, Institut für Zeitgeschichte. The Finns provided the Germans with a list of demands to be made of Russia if there were a negotiated settlement but were informed that there would be a military, not a diplomatic solution (*ADAP*, D, 12, No. 592).

31 Lutzhöft, *Deutsche Militärpolitik*, pp. 109–21, 160–63; *DRuZW*, 4: 41. For Swedish insistence on a form of neutrality, see Helsinki No. 321 of 10 May 1941, AA, Gesandtschaft Helsinki, "Berichte 251–550," fr. H 067181. Had Sweden been willing to join in fully, Hitler was prepared to take the Aland Islands from Finland and give them to Sweden (*KTB OKW*, 1: 229; *DRuZW*, 4: 408).

32 The conflict in Romanian internal affairs in January 1941, discussed below, led to the abandonment of initial plans for a major offensive into the Ukraine from Romania; see Jürgen Förster, "Rumäniens Weg in die deutsche Abhängigkeit," *MGM* 25 (1979), 67.

33 Beauftragte für den Vierjahresplan, "Ergebnisse der Vierjahresplan-Arbeit, ein Kurzbericht nach dem Stande vom Frühjahr 1942," BA, R 261/18, f. 33.

34 *KTB OKW*, 1:227; Fröhlich, *Goebbels Tagebücher*, 26 Nov. 1940, 4:41; György Ránki, "Hitlers Verhandlungen mit osteuropäischen Staatsmännern, 1939–1944," in Klaus Hildebrand and Reiner Pommerin (eds.), *Deutsche Frage und europäisches Gleichgewicht*, (Cologne: Böhlau, 1985), pp. 195–228. See also Weizsäcker to Heydrich, 30 Mar. 1941, AA, St.S., "Politischer Schriftwechsel," Bd. 6, fr. 331594.

35 See, e.g., *ADAP*, D, 11, Nos. 381, 389, 12, No. 614. Antonescu also lectured Mussolini (Fabricius tel. 2131 of 18 Nov. 1940, AA, U.St.S., "Südosten," Bd. 4, fr. 177247–48; Ciano, *Diary*, 14 Nov. 1940).

36 *ADAP*, D, 11, Nos. 17, 19, 21, 652, 691, 696, 699, 700, 705, 706, 709, 715, 12, No. 94; Hillgruber, *Hitler, König Carol*, pp. 119ff; Welles to FDR with enclosure, 1 Feb. 1941, FDRL, PSF Box 96, State, Welles, Jan.-May 1941; Förster, "Rumäniens Weg," pp. 63–66; Clodius to Ribbentrop, 18 Nov. 1940, AA, U.St.S., "Südosten," Bd. 4, fr. 177251–57; Armin Heinen, *Die Legion "Erzengel Michael" und Rumänien* (Munich: Oldenbourg, 1986), pp. 242–53; General Hansen's account in Institut für Zeitgeschichte, ZS 1130;

and notes by a German correspondent in Bucharest, in BA, Brammer, ZSg 101/38, f. 131–67. Carol had abdicated in favor of his son Michael on Sept. 5, 1940.

37 See *ADAP*, D 12, Nos. 387, 398. Nothing was spelled out to Antonescu before the attack on the Soviet Union, but as in the case of Finland, restoration of the territory recently lost to the Soviet Union plus a bonus on the other side of the old border was anticipated.

38 Useful surveys of Turkish policy are Önder, *Türkische Aussenpolitik*; Krecker, Diringil, *Turkish Foreign Policy*; and, in spite of some serious defects, Weber, *Evasive Neutral*. See also Weizsäcker's memorandum, "St.S., Nr. 109," 12 Feb. 1941, AA, St.S., "Türkei," Bd. 2, fr. 172600–1.

39 The best account remains Toscano, *Designs in Diplomacy*, chap. 3. Some additional documents are in AA, St.S., "Italien," Bd. 4.

40 Miklós Szinai and László Szücs (eds.), "Horthy's Secret Correspondence with Hitler," *New Hungarian Quarterly* 4 (1963), 189–90; *ADAP*, D, 12, Nos. 431, 631.

41 *ADAP*, D, 12, No. 511; ibid., p. 769; Oshima to Tokyo from Rome, 14 May 1941, NA, RG 457, SRDJ 11693–94.

42 Köstring to Tippelskirch, 19 Sept. 1940, BA/MA, N 123; Hermann Teske, *General Ernst Köstring* (Frankfurt/M: Mittler, 1966), p. 272; *ADAP*, D, 11, No. 113.

43 *ADAP*, D, 11, Nos. 1, 7, 13, 24.

44 On the journey of the *Komet*, code-named "Schiff 45," see above, Chap. 3 n 164. In Aug. 1940 the navy gave up its base on the Murmansk coast since all of Norway was by then under German control.

45 German naval attaché Moscow KTB, 11 Jan. 1941, BA/MA, PG 48803, fr. 38; KTB Skl A 21, 21 May 1941, RM 7/24; Memorandum by Baumbach, 27 Jan. 1941, Case 20/3, PG 48807. The ship returned to Germany in November 1941 and was sunk with all hands in October 1942.

46 Teske, *Köstring*, p. 271; *ADAP*, D, 11, Nos. 111, 128, 275; KTB Skl A 13, 20 Sept. 1940, BA/MA, RM 7/16, f. 269; Moscow tel. 2613 of 30 Nov. 1940, AA, St.S., "Russland," Bd. 3, fr. 112691.

47 *ADAP*, D, 11, Nos. 277, 539; Moscow tel. 2225 of 20 Oct. 1940, AA, St.S., "Russland," Bd. 3, fr. 112607.

48 Ettel (Teheran) to Hewel, 16 Nov. 1940, AA, Handakten Hewel, "Deutschland E-H," fr. 371017–19; Ronald Lewin, *The American Magic: Codes, Ciphers and the Defeat of Japan* (New York: Farrar Straus Giroux, 1982), p. 206.

49 Milan Hauner, *India in Axis Strategy* (Stuttgart: Klett-Cotta, 1981), pp. 239–44; Weizsäcker to Kabul, No. 31 of 2 Feb. 1941, AA, St.S., "England," Bd. 4, fr. 108640, and Schulenburg No. 278 of 10 Feb., ibid., fr. 108650.

50 Kaslas, "Lithuanian Strip"; *ADAP*, D, 8, No. 376 n 5; official Soviet note of 12 Aug. 1940, in AA, Botschaft Moskau, "Pol. Beziehungen Sowjetunion–Deutschland," Bd. 3, fr. 35776–78. It should be noted that in the fall of 1939 the Germans had asked for minor changes in the September border in Poland. The Soviets had offered some alterations; but when the Germans did not accept or answer promptly, Moscow withdrew the offer and insisted that with one minimal exception the originally agreed border be kept. The Soviets clearly wanted to avoid the uncertainties and disturbances of repeated redrawing of the lines.

51 Memorandum of Rintelen, 19 Sept. 1940, AA, St.S., "Russland," Bd. 3, fr. 112524–25; Schulenburg tel. 1734 of 23 Aug. 1940, St.S., "Litauen," fr. 193360, and St.S. No. 717 of 20 Sept. 1940, ibid., fr. 193361. The area contained about 1100 square miles with a population of 180,000 including eight to nine thousand Germans; see Botschaft Moskau, "Litauischer Grenzstreifen," fr. 204147–52. There is a good map in the German edition of *ADAP*, D 11, Annex V; the map in the English language edition does not distinguish the former Lithuanian territory from the former Polish territory around Suvalki and thus gives an erroneous impression.

52 *ADAP*, D, 11, Nos. 109, 176, 211; see also Richthofen tel. "Pol V 3372," 30 Oct. 1940, AA, Botschaft Ankara, "Geheime Erlasse," Bd. 12, fr. E 028345.

53 *ADAP*, D, 11, Nos. 309, 317–19. The German draft was provided to the Japanese ambassador in Berlin, whose report No. 1440 to Tokyo of 11 Nov. 1940 was intercepted and read by the U.S., see NA, RG 457, SRDJ 7794–95.

54 Directive 18 is in *ADAP*, D, 11, No. 323. The original draft of this directive had gone out on Nov. 7; see *KTB Halder*, 7 Nov. 1940; Heinz Holldack, *Was wirklich geschah* (Munich: Nymphenburger Verlagsgesellschaft, 1949), p. 424.

55 The British had intended to send Cripps only for the special negotiations; Sir Maurice Peterson was to have been ambassador (note by Halifax, 25 May 1940, N 5660/40/38, PRO, FO 371/24847).

56 Heinrich Bartel, *Frankreich und die Sowjetunion 1938–1940* (Stuttgart: Steiner, 1986), pp. 314ff.

57 See Butler–Halifax talk of 13 Sept. 1939, C 13856/15/18, PRO FO 371/22833; War Cabinets 67, 112, 116(39) of 1 Nov., 12 Dec. and 15 Dec. 1939, CAB 65/2, f. 24, 266, 290; War Cabinet 66(41) of 12 Mar. 1940, CAB 65/6, f. 62–63.

58 Word of a possible British–Soviet deal without Polish participation had so worried the Polish government-in-exile that its leader, General Sikorski, tried for a rapprochement with the Soviet Union himself. The Soviets were not interested and Sikorski was almost dropped (Terry, *Poland's Place in Europe*, pp. 51–55; C 14/14/62, PRO, FO 371/26419).

59 Cripps reports 591 of 8 Aug. 1940, N 6105/40/98, PRO, FO 371/24847, and 715 of 31 Aug. 1940, N 6458/283/38, FO 371/24852; Cripps to Halifax, 10 Oct. 1940, FO 800/322, f. 353–60.

60 Accounts in Woodward, *British Foreign Policy*, 1: 467–96; Medlicott, *Economic Blockade*, 1: 312–17, 633–48; Miner, *Between Churchill and Stalin*, pp. 74ff. See also Dalton to Halifax, 30 Oct. 1940, PRO, FO 800/322, f. 361–63; Foreign Office comments on Cripps No. 976 of 10 Nov. 1940, N 7163/283/38, FO 371/24852; Halifax to Cripps, 27 Nov. 1940, FO 800/322, f. 365–70; Cripps Nos. 1077–78 of 8 Dec. 1940, N 7387/40/38. For German information on these negotiations and their failure, see Weizsäcker to Schulenburg, "Pol VII 75gRs." 13 Feb. 1941, AA, St.S., "Türkei," Bd. 2, fr. 172597.

61 See Cripps No. 980, N 7164/283/38, PRO, FO 371/24852.

62 Weinberg, *Germany and the Soviet Union*, pp. 141–44; Köstring to Tippelskirch, 14 Nov. 1940, BA/MA, N 123; Skl memorandum, 16 Nov. 1940, RM 6/73, f. The German propaganda directives on the visit were apparently removed from the German records by the East Germans or the Soviets; see Boelcke, *Kriegspropaganda*, pp. 194, 565.

63 While urging the Soviet Union to take over Iran, the Germans were reassuring the Iranian Minister in Berlin that there was nothing to worry about (St.S., No. 838 of 18 Nov. 1940, AA, Büro RAM, "Iran," fr. 45242).

64 *ADAP*, D, 11, No. 404.

65 Ibid., No. 403. The similarity to Soviet calls for treaties of mutual assistance with the Baltic States in Sept.-Oct. 1939 is striking.

66 Ibid., Nos. 409, 412, 425, 437.

67 *ADAP*, D, 11, No. 568; Ministry of Finance Memorandum of 16 Jan. 1941, BA, R 2/17315; Russland–Ausschuss der Deutschen Wirtschaft, "Orientierung der Firmen über das deutsch-russische Wirtschaftsabkommen vom 10. Januar 1941," 17 Jan. 1941, R 2/17282; "Wirtschaftliche Pressekonferenz vom 11. Januar 1941," and " . . . vom 14. Januar 1941," ZSg. 115/3.

68 *ADAP*, D, 11, No. 669.

69 Ibid., 12, No. 140. This document records a Soviet instruction explaining acquiescence in Germany's Balkan push as consistent with the Soviet Union's most important goal: the destruction of the British empire.

70 Note the report on a conversation with the Soviet assistant military attaché in Germany

on 11 Apr. 1941, NA, RG 165, Entry 77, Box 1417, File 6900 Germany, weekly reports.

71 Ueberschär, *Hitler und Finnland*, pp. 263–65; Moscow tel. 1280 of 1 June 1941, AA, St.S., "Russland," Bd. 5, fr. 113467.

72 *ADAP*, D, 12, No. 351; KTB, Marineattaché Moskau, Mar.-Apr. 1941, BA/MA, Case 20/3, PG 48803.

73 Details in Weinberg, *Germany and the Soviet Union*, pp. 161–62.

74 Ibid.; see also *ADAP*, D, 12, Nos. 280, 380, 521; KTB Skl A 19, 12 Apr. 1941, BA/MA, RM 7/23. The Soviets also offered new economic negotiations to Italy (Moscow tel. 1046 of 30 Apr. 1941, AA, St.S., "Russland," Bd. 4, fr. 113383).

75 *DRuZW*, 4: 290.

76 *ADAP*, D, 12, Nos. 333, 468, 505, 628; Schulenburg (Moscow) to Grosskopf, 29 May 1941, AA, Inland IIg, "Volkstumsfragen gRs," fr. H 297725–27.

77 On this famous speech, of which a reliable text may soon be made available, see *ADAP*, D, 12, No. 593; Hinsley, *British Intelligence*, 1: 466; Erickson, *Road to Stalingrad*, p. 82; Ribbentrop to Mackensen, 19 Dec. 1942, AA, Botschaft Rom (Quir.), Geheim 58/1, "Kriegführung Sowjetrusslands," Bd. 1, E 260213–35.

78 Note the comment of the Soviet ambassador in Sweden that her government expected until the last moment that there would be an opportunity for negotiations, in Wied (Stockholm) No. 731 of 24 June 1941, AA, St.S., "Russland," Bd. 5, fr. 113602.

79 *KTB Halder* 23 June 1941, 3: 8–9; *Leeb KTB*, 22 June 1941, pp. 275–77. British Ambassador Cripps had returned to London in disgust over Soviet appeasement of Germany. He explained to the British Cabinet that the Soviet leadership was willing to make major concessions to Germany. He expected the Soviet Union to hold out no more than three or four weeks in a war but thought they might hang on in Siberia if they could extricate some of their troops; WM(41) War Cabinet 60 of 16 June 1941, Confidential Annex, PRO, *CAB* 65/22; compare the account in Gorodetsky, *Stafford Cripps*, pp. 170–72.

80 Köstring to Matzky, 21 May 1941, BA/MA, N 123. A detailed study, showing Stalin vetoing projects to interfere with the German buildup in the spring of 1941 by a preventive Red Army offensive, in Timothy P. Mulligan, "'Stalin's Surprise' and German Preventive War: Synonymous or Separate?," paper at the Conference on "Barbarossa" at the University of Waterloo, May 1991.

81 Barton Whaley, *Codeword Barbarossa* (Cambridge, Mass.: MIT Press, 1973). On the American warnings, based on information provided to the U.S. by Dr. Erwin Respondek, see Waldo Heinrichs, *Threshold of War: Franklin D. Roosevelt and American Entry into World War II* (New York: Oxford Univ. Press, 1988), pp. 21–23, n 11 on pp. 224–25, pp. 88–89; John V. Dippel, *Two against Hitler: Stealing the Nazis' Best-Kept Secrets* (New York: Praeger, 1992), chaps. 4–5.

82 Hewel Diary, 13 and 20 June 1941, Institut für Zeitgeschichte.

83 KTB Skl A 22, 13 June 1941, BA/MA, RM 7/25, f. 135.

84 *KTB OKW*, 14 June 1941, 1: 415; *KTB Halder*, 14 June 1941, 2: 455; Tagebuch von Waldau, 14 June 1941, Institut für Zeitgeschichte.

85 Hillgruber, *Hitlers Strategie*, pp. 504–8.

86 Hewel Diary, 18–19 June 1941, Institut für Zeitgeschichte; *ADAP*, D, 12, Nos. 654, 655, 662.

87 See *KTB OKW*, 7 Dec. 1940, 1: 227.

88 See Hitler–Hewel meeting of June 8, 1941, Hewel Diary, Institut für Zeitgeschichte; draft of directive 32, *ADAP*, D, 12, No. 617, also Walther Hubatsch (ed.), *Hitlers Weisungen für die Kriegführung 1939–1945* (Frankfurt/M: Bernard & Graefe, 1962), pp. 129–35; Karl Klee, "Der Entwurf zur Führer-Weisung Nr. 32 vom 11. Juni 1941," *Wehrwissenschaftliche Rundschau* 3 (1956), 127–41 (with silly assertions in the introduction but some important

technical details); "Lagebesprechung beim Chef der Seekriegsleitung," 23 June 1941, KTB Skl A 22, BA/MA, RM 7/25, f. 283–84.

89 *DRuZW*, 4: 182.

90 The best account remains Jäckel, *Frankreich in Hitlers Europa*, chaps. 3–9.

91 See above, pp. 133–34.

92 Halifax to Hoare, 30 July 1940, PRO, FO 800/323, f. 134–40; Hoare memorandum of 23 Sep. 1940, ibid., f. 183–87; Halifax to Hoare, 29 Sep. 1940, ibid., f. 201–2.

93 *ADAP*, D, 10, Nos. 346, 369, 373.

94 Good accounts in Detwiler, *Hitler, Franco*, and Goda, "Germany and Northwest Africa." See also Weizsäcker's memorandum No. 644 of 9 Aug. 1940, in AA, Botschaft Rom (Quir.), geheim, Bd. 43/5; Huene memorandum of 1 Oct. 1940, Gesandtschaft Lissabon, "Deutsch–polnischer Krieg," Bd. 5.

95 Ciano, *Diary*, 1 Oct. 1940, p. 297; Smyth, *British Policy and Franco's Spain*, pp. 84–93, 98; Hoare No. 816 of 3 Oct. 1940, C 10595/113/41, PRO, FO 371/24517; Mr. Garran's minute of Z 11696/11696/41, FO 371/49663.

96 Hoare memorandum of 18 Oct. 1940, PRO, FO 800/323, f. 217–19; Hoare No. 506 (Saving) of 22 Oct. 1940, C 11369/113/41, FO 371/24517.

97 See David W. Pike, "Franco and the Axis Stigma," *JCH* 17 (1982), 377–39; Smyth, *Diplomacy and Strategy of Survival*, pp. 93–94, 99–105.

98 Charles B. Burdick, *Germany's Military Strategy and Spain in World War II* (Syracuse: Syracuse Univ. Press, 1968), chaps. 1–4.

99 Hinsley, *British Intelligence*, 1: 256; Smyth, *British Policy and Franco's Spain*, pp. 160–63, 169; Hoare No. 816 of 3 Oct. 1940, C 10595/113/41, PRO, FO 371/24517; Hoare No. 383 (Saving) of 15 Oct. 1940, C 11145/113/41, ibid. The Japanese also learned of Franco's refusal when Serrano Suñer returned from his Berlin visit; Takata (Madrid) to Tokyo, No. 185 of 3 Oct. 1940, NA, RG 457, SRDJ 7082.

100 *ADAP*, D, 11, No. 268, 13, Nos. 122, 391, 403. Documents on support for German warships and the repatriation of crews from German ships by Spain are in AA, Botschaft Madrid, "Seekrieg," Bd. 1.

101 Detwiler, *Hitler, Franco*, chaps. 4–7; Hillgruber, *Hitlers Strategie*, pp. 178ff, 316ff; Papeleux, *L'Amiral Canaris*, pp. 150–59.

102 The report of Sir Samuel Hoare of 22 Oct. 1940 on a conversation with Franco may be taken as accurately reflecting the latter's views; C 11492/113/41, PRO, FO 371/24517.

103 See Hoare's report No. 1234 of 13 Dec. 1940 on recent Spanish Army Council meetings, C 13404/113/41, ibid.

104 *ADAP*, D, 11, Nos. 490, 506, 428, 434; KTB Skl A 15, 21 Nov. 1940, BA/MA, RM 7/18, f. 376.

105 Burdick, *Germany's Military Strategy and Spain*, chap. 5; KTB Skl A 21, 5 May 1941, BA/MA, RM 7/24, f. 53.

106 A summary of the Italian preparations and the German veto in Knox, *Mussolini Unleashed*, pp. 165–77. See also KTB Skl A 12, 28 Aug. 1940, BA/MA, RM 7/15, f. 328; German naval attaché Rome to Admiral Bürkner, 24 Aug. 1940, BA/MA, Case 17/3, PG 45171, f. 82–85.

107 Ciano, *Diary*, 8 Oct. 1940, p. 299. Von Ribbentrop had at least hinted at this ten days earlier, but the Germans had then deliberately kept their actual movements quiet (Knox, *Mussolini Unleashed*, pp. 190, 205–7).

108 Mussolini as quoted in Ciano, *Diary*, 12 Oct. 1940, p. 300. The concept of equilibrium in Southeast Europe was very important to Mussolini; the prior example was his action in Albania in April 1939 after the German occupation of the remainder of Czechoslovakia in March. The refutation by Knox (*Mussolini Unleashed*, p. 346 n 84) of the doubts expressed by Hillgruber and van Creveld (see Bibliography, p. 930) about this quotation appears to me to be sound. On the other hand, I cannot agree with the view of Knox (p.

209) that the Italian attack on Greece was certain to come at some point. Maybe so – but hardly after the Italian disasters in Africa later in 1940. There is a fascinating translation of the minutes of a meeting on Oct. 15, 1940, in Mussolini's office in Appendix A of ZM 3420/1176/82, PRO, FO 371/49933. It shows general enthusiasm for the invasion.

109 A summary of the September negotiations in Knox, pp. 155–56.

110 Ibid., pp. 191–93. Knox also argues (pp. 196–98) that Ciano wanted to move on Greece in order to have something in hand if the war ended in a compromise peace, but note the report of the Japanese ambassador in Rome on a conversation with Ciano on Sept. 24, in which Amau concludes that Ciano expected a long war (NA, RG 457, SRDJ 6917–18).

111 Knox, pp. 209–30. Ciano also told the Japanese of the attack on the evening of the 27th (Amau [Rome] to Tokyo No. 1120 of 27 Oct. 1940, NA, RG 457, SRDJ 7479).

112 Clemm von Hohenberg, "Kurzer Überblick über den italienisch–griechischen Krieg 1940/1941 und seiner Vorgeschichte," BA/MA, N 449/4, f. 2.

113 Ibid., passim (a survey by the former German military attaché in Athens); other accounts in Knox, pp. 231–60; *DRuZW*, 3: 394–414.

114 Reconnaissance planes supplied by the U.S. and flown from Malta had helped scout the harbor (Gilbert, *Churchill*, 6: 901). There is some evidence that this attack contributed to Japanese Admiral Yamamoto Isoroku's fixation on a carrier-launched torpedo attack as the way to strike at the U.S. fleet in Pearl Harbor. It led the U.S. Chief of Naval Operations, Admiral Stark, to warn Hawaii to put in torpedo nets, but the U.S. fleet commander, Admiral Richardson (subsequently replaced by Kimmel), turned the idea down (Prange, *At Dawn* pp. 40, 43, 45–46).

115 The Italians were also always worried about possible German concessions to the French which might allow the latter to build up their military strength in Tunisia on Libya's western border (Marineattaché Rom Bericht "3101/40 Gkds.," 15 Sept. 1940, BA/MA, Case 17/3, PG 45171).

116 I.S.O. Playfair, *The Mediterranean and Middle East* (London: HMSO, 1954), 1: 190–204, 241–56.

117 Knox, *Mussolini Unleashed*, pp. 253–56; Playfair, chaps. 14, 15, 19; Gavin Long, *Six Years War*, pp. 54–58; *DRuZW*, 3: 591–98. There is a very interesting file of Italian 10th Army documents of the period May-Dec. 1940 captured by the British at Bardia, in PRO, WO 106/2129.

118 The campaign may be followed in Playfair, chaps. 21–23. The last Italian forces surrendered on May 16, 1941.

119 Ibid., pp. 326–32.

120 On Ciano's role, see the memorandum of the German embassy Rome, 4 Dec. 1940, AA, Botschaft Rom (Quir.) Geheim 44/3, fr. 481754–63.

121 Knox, *Mussolini Unleashed*, pp. 269–70; *ADAP*, D, 11, No. 731.

122 Full text in James, *Churchill Speeches*, 6: 6322–25.

123 Knox, pp. 260–72, surveys the internal situation in the critical winter months. See also Horikiri (Rome) to Tokyo No. 1221 of 14 Dec. 1940, NA, RG 457, SRDJ 8480. There appears to have been some consideration of defection in the Italian navy beginning in November, 1940, but the evidence is fragmentary; see Denham, *Inside the Nazi Ring*, pp. 133–38; Alberto Santoni, *Ultra siegt im Mittelmeer* (Koblenz: Bernard & Graefe, 1985), pp. 74–77; docs. in R 8939/60/22, PRO, FO 371/24952; R 530, 1004, 1314, 2070, 2489, 3017, 7013/218/22, FO 371/29940, and PREM 242/11A, f. 463–64.

124 See the observation of the Japanese ambassador in Berlin in his tel. No. 119 of 14 Feb. 1941, NA, RG 457, SRDJ 9820.

125 KTB Skl A 13, 9 Sep. 1940, BA/MA, RM 7/16, f. 255–56.

126 Note von Bock Diary, 11 Nov. 1940, BA/MA, N 22/7, f. l; *ADAP*, D, 11, No. 353. The Germans were also sensitive about Greece as a result of memories of the collapse of

Bulgaria when Allied troops pushed up from the Salonika front in World War I.

127 Wagner, *Lagevorträge*, pp. 301–4; KTB Skl A 26, 28 Oct. 1941, BA/MA, RM 7/29, f. 474–80.

128 Knox, *Mussolini Unleashed*, p. 272.

129 Playfair, *Mediterranean*, 1: 315–28; *DRuZW*, 3: 599, 606–7; Murray, *Luftwaffe*, p. 76. Fliegerkorps X had more experience in attacks on shipping than most German air force units. See also von Waldau Diary, 3 Dec. 1940, Institut für Zeitgeschichte.

130 Farnie, *East and West of Suez*, pp. 623ff.

131 Knox, pp. 279–81.

132 Ibid., pp. 279–82; Playfair, 1: 366–68; *DRuZW*, 3: 599–605.

133 *ADAP*, D, 11, Nos. 320, 324, 334, 417. The Yugoslav leaders of the time never grasped that once almost completely surrounded by German-controlled territory their own independence would be over.

134 An excellent account in Breccia, *Jugoslavia, 1939–1941*, pp. 331–569.

135 On Greek reluctance to allow any British measure likely to be read as menacing Germany, see Robin Higham, *Diary of a Disaster: British Aid to Greece 1940–1941* (Lexington, Ky.: Univ. Press of Kentucky, 1986), p. 51; John L. Hondros, *Occupation and Resistance: The Greek Agony, 1941–44* (New York: Pella, 1983), pp. 48–51. My interpretation of the peace soundings and their rejection by Hitler differs from that of Knox primarily on the basis of the material in the papers of Clemm von Hohenberg, BA/MA, N 449/4, f. 16–21. See also Ehrengard Schramm-von Thadden, *Griechenland und die Grossmächte im Zweiten Weltkrieg* (Wiesbaden: Steiner, 1955), pp. 217–21; FRUS, 1940, 3: 572; *ADAP*, D, 11, No. 584, 12, Nos. 143, 155, 170, 179, 180, 189. Of interest is the summary of a conference in the high command of the German navy on March 19, 1941: "The Führer has confirmed that even if there is a peaceful solution of the Greek question the whole country is to be occupied" (KTB Skl A 19, BA/MA, RM 7/22, f. 265). The Germans, who were able to read some relevant Greek telegrams, knew that their official pretext for action, namely that there were British troops in Greece, was false (Greek Foreign Ministry to Greek Legation Berlin, 14 Mar. 1941, AA, Botschafter Ritter, "Verschiedenes, Aufzeichnungen, Telegramme," fr. E 220961–62).

136 Note the 5 June 1940 memorandum in R 6476/58/22, PRO, FO 371/24948.

137 An excellent account in Higham, *Diary of a Disaster*, pp. 26–27, 34.

138 Sir Francis de Guingand, *Operation Victory* (London: Hodder & Stoughton, 1947), pp. 85–86.

139 Higham, pp. 74–75.

140 Ibid., pp. 88–89; Playfair, *Mediterranean*, 1: chap. 20; *DRuZW*, 3: 433–35; Sir John Kennedy, *The Business of War* (London: Hutchinson, 1957), pp. 81–87; David Carlton, *Anthony Eden* (London: Allen Lane, 1981), pp. 170–79; Ismay notes in Liddell Hart Centre, Ismay Papers, II/3/57/2.

141 Knox, *Mussolini Unleashed*, p. 283; Hinsley, *British Intelligence*, 1: 404–6; Higham, *Diary of a Disaster*, p. 193; *DRuZW*, 3: 608–11.

142 Hoppe, *Bulgarien*, chap. 12; Marshall Lee Miller, *Bulgaria during the Second World War* (Stanford, Calif.: Stanford Univ. Press, 1975), pp. 41–51. See also Hans Bauer, *Hitler's Pilot* (London: Muller, 1958), p. 119.

143 Thomas F. Troy, *Donovan and the CIA* (Frederick, Md.: University Publications of America, 1981), p. 39; FRUS, 1941, 1: 282; *ADAP*, D, 11, Nos. 685, 713; British records in PRO, AIR 8/368.

144 On the futile British efforts, see Carlton, *Eden*, pp. 179–80; Woodward, *British Foreign Policy*, 1, chap. 16.

145 Numerous documents on this are in AA, St.S., "Türkei," Bd. 2–3; also *ADAP*, D, 12, No. 303; E, 1, No. 250. The map in *DRuZW*, 3, facing p. 492, shows the piece of

Greece adjacent to Turkey as all under German control without reference to the special concession to Turkey.

146 Note Roosevelt to Hull, 20 Feb. 1941, *FDR Letters*, 2: 1126–27.

147 The Germans had learned by Feb. 13 that the Soviet Union would not support Turkey or work with Great Britain but rather watch Germany's moves into the Balkans from the sidelines (Weizsäcker to embassies in Moscow and Ankara, 13 Feb. 1941, AA, St.S., "Türkei," Bd. 2, fr. 172597–99).

148 Hitler refused the suggestion of the German Minister in Belgrade that the secret protocols to Yugoslavia's adhesion to the Tripartite Pact be shown to the leaders of that country's opposition (Interrogation of Kurt von Kamphoevner by Oron J. Hale, 14 Aug. 1945, U.S. Army Center for Military History).

149 *DRuZW*, 3: 449–54.

150 The German shift from support of Vladko Macek's autonomist movement to the Ustasha can be followed in a report by Walter Malletke of Apr. 1941 in BA, R 43 II/1458, f. 11–17.

151 *DRuZW*, 3: 454–84, covers the fighting in both Yugoslavia and Greece.

152 *ADAP*, D, 12, Nos. 224, 226.

153 Ibid., No. 215.

154 Relevant documents have been published by the Hungarians in *Hung. Docs.*, Vol. 4. The Hungarians imagined that they would get an outlet to the Adriatic but soon learned otherwise (*ADAP*, D, 12, No. 282). Before committing suicide, Teleki wrote a last letter to Gabor Apor, a prominent Hungarian diplomat then serving as Minister to the Vatican, recounting the crisis and his views. A copy of the text is in Donovan to Roosevelt, 30 Mar. 1945, FDRL, PSF 171, OSS March 16–31, 1945.

155 *ADAP*, D, 12, No. 216.

156 See the summary of Hitler's views, prepared c. 2 Apr. 1941, in AA, Handakten Ritter, "Verschiedenes geheim I & II," fr. 280709.

157 *ADAP*, D, 12, Nos. 465, 478.

158 An early sample may be found in a report of 7 May 1941, Item 8 of the Canaris/Lahousen file, Imperial War Museum, AL 1933.

159 Higham's book, *Diary of a Disaster*, is one of the few which stress this aspect. See Farnie, *East and West of Suez*, pp. 624–25; Playfair, *Mediterranean*, 1: 326–28. For continued German mining of the canal in July, Aug. and Sep. 1941, see the reports in PRO, CAB 160/864.

160 *ADAP*, D, 12, Nos. 350, 427, 446, 13, No. 49.

161 See Brooke Diary, 23 Oct. 1941, 31 Mar. 1942 (both omitted from the published version), Liddell Hart Centre. An additional problem for the British was the relationship with the Australian government which did not appreciate – and with a one-vote margin in its Parliament could not abide – the repeated failures of British military leadership, at least in *Australian* eyes; see John Robertson, *Australia at War* (Melbourne: Heinemann, 1981), pp. 47–48.

162 On this issue, see Chadwick, *Britain and the Vatican*, chap. 10.

163 Hewel Diary, 19 May 1941, Institut für Zeitgeschichte.

164 Ibid., 29 May 1941.

165 Daniel Silverfarb, *Britain's Informal Empire in the Middle East: A Case Study of Iraq, 1929–1941* (New York: Oxford Univ. Press, 1986), pp. 123–40; Richard A. Stewart, *Sunrise at Abadan: The British and Soviet Invasion of Iran, 1941* (New York: Praeger, 1988), chap. 3; *DRuZW*, 3: 448–555; an earlier account in Lukasz Hirszowicz, *The Third Reich and the Arab East* (London: Routledge & Kegan Paul, 1966), chaps. 7–8.

166 See Önder, *Türkische Aussenpolitik*, pp. 110–17, for German pressure on Turkey. The bait offered was now Bulgarian territory.

167 Burkhart Mueller-Hillebrand et al., "Germany and Her Allies in World War II,"

USAREUR (United States Army, Europe), Historical Division, P-108, pp. 260ff (copies in National Archives and reprinted in Donald S. Detwiler et al. [eds.], *World War II German Military Studies*, vol. 20, New York: Garland, 1979); Stewart, *Sunrise at Abadan*, pp. 40–41; Great Britain, Air Historical Branch, "The Middle East Campaign, Vol. IX: The Campaign in Syria June 1941," Royal Air Force Narrative (First Draft), pp. 7–9; A.B. Gaunson, *The Anglo-French Collision in Lebanon and Syria 1940–45* (London: Macmillan, 1986), pp. 33–34.

168 Jäckel, *Frankreich*, pp. 162ff; Elmar Krautkrämer, "General Giraud und Admiral Darlan in der Vorgeschichte der alliierten Landung in Nordafrika," *VjZ* 30 (1982), 212–13; Coutau-Bégarie and Huan, *Darlan*, chap. 14; Werner-Otto von Hentig, *Mein Leben: Eine Dienstreise* (Göttingen: Vandenhoeck & Ruprecht, 1962), pp. 342–45; Fridolin von Senger und Etterlin, "Report on his Activity as German Representative at the Italian Armistice Commission," 1942, BA/MA, N 64/9, f. 26–30; Hewel Diary, 18 May 1941, Institut für Zeitgeschichte.

169 *ADAP*, D, 10, No. 370; 12, No. 12.

170 Some of the communications from Rashid Ali to Berlin were handled by the Japanese legation in Baghdad (Ettel [Teheran] tel. 357 of 9 May 1941, AA, Botschafter Ritter, "Verschiedenes geheim I & II," fr. 280845–48).

171 *ADAP*, D, 12, No. 590, 13, Nos. 180, 183, and docs. in E, 1.

172 Various German government, Nazi Party, and military agencies were involved in plots and controversies in and about Afghanistan. The main effect was to provide draft deferments for German bureaucrats engaged in these endless disputes and subventions for some Afghan exiles. See *DRuZW*, 3: 145–48; Inge Kircheisen and Johannes Glasneck, *Türkei und Afghanistan – Brennpunkte der Orientpolitik im Zweiten Weltkrieg* (Berlin-East: Deutscher Verlag der Wissenschaften, 1968); Pilger (Kabul) to Weizsäcker No. 121 of 7 Apr. 1941, AA, St.S., "Italien," Bd. 4, fr. B 001686.

173 Walter Ansel, *Hitler and the Middle Sea* (Durham, N.C.: Duke Univ. Press, 1972), chaps. 11–13, 15–23; *DRuZW*, 3: 485–511.

174 *DRuZW*, 3: 612.

175 The bridge was blown up, but the landing had shown once again the possibilities of airborne forces.

176 The author first demonstrated this point in some detail in *Germany and the Soviet Union*, pp. 163, 180–82.

177 An unconvincing summary in *DRuZW*, 3: 508.

178 R. T. Thomas, *Britain and Vichy* (New York: St. Martin's, 1979), pp. 106–7. It was in May 1941 that the British made plans to evacuate Palestine if necessary. The troops and the *non-Jewish* British civilians were to be evacuated; Jews as well as Arabs were to be left to the Germans (Ronald W. Zweig, "British Plans for the Evacuation of Palestine in 1941–1942," *Studies in Zionism* 8 [Autumn 1983], 291–96).

179 On the campaign in Syria, see *DRuZW*, 3: 561–67; Long, pp. 87–97; Hirszowicz, *The Third Reich*, chap. 9. The report on the fighting of the 1st Australian Corps in Syria observed: "The Vichy French, in this campaign, displayed fighting qualities in defence that make it difficult to understand the ease with which they were defeated in their own country." John Robertson and John McCarthy (eds.), *Australian War Strategy, 1939–1945: A Documentary History* (St. Lucia: Univ. of Queensland Press), doc. 93, p. 120.

180 Note *ADAP*, D, 12, Nos. 83, 103. The Turks had asked the Germans to be allowed to take northern Syria in the last stages of the fighting there (Önder, *Türkische Aussenpolitik*, pp. 120–21).

181 Joseph Schechtman, *The Mufti and the Führer: The Rise and Fall of Haj Amin el-Husseini* (New York: Thomas Yoseloff, 1965); Klaus Gensicke, *Der Mufti von Jerusalem, Amin el-Husseini, und die Nationalsozialisten* (Frankfurt/M: Lang, 1988).

182 At this time, however, the Japanese had a low opinion of Bose, see Konoe to Berlin to Matsuoka, No. 267 of 27 Mar. 1941, NA, RG 457, SRDJ 10708.

183 On "Crusader," see *DRuZW*, 3: 658–81; James J. Sadkovich, "Of Myths and Men: Rommel and the Italians in North Africa, 1940–1942," *International History Review* 13 (1991), pp. 298–301; John Gordon IV, "Operation Crusader: Preview of the Non-linear Battlefield," *Military Review* 71 (1991), 48–61.

184 These were "Stuart" tanks. The superiority of the British in armor had to await the arrival of "Sherman" tanks in large quantities in the late summer of 1942.

185 On the superiority of German armor and anti-tank guns note Hinsley, *British Intelligence*, 2: 297–99, 304ff.

186 Ibid., Appendix 14.

187 Hitler Directive 38 of 2 Dec. 1941, in *ADAP*, D, 13, No. 535, and Hubatsch, *Hitlers Weisungen*, pp. 169–70. See also R. J. Overy, *The Air War 1939–1945* (New York: Stein & Day, 1981), p. 66; Hinsley, *British Intelligence*, 2: 291, 322–25.

188 The assertion in *DRuZW*, 3: 681, that this diversion practically halted the U-Boat war in the Atlantic is exaggerated, but there was a very substantial effect. See Salewski, *Seekriegsleitung*, 1: 472–85; Hinsley, *British Intelligence*, 2: 326–28.

189 Note KTB Skl A 12, 14 Aug. 1940, BA/MA, RM 7/15, f. 163, and A 13, 7 Sept. 1940, RM 7/16, f. 80. The British were confident that there would be no invasion in 1940 by Oct. 31 (Gilbert, *Churchill* 6: 879–81).

190 Hastings, *Bomber Command*, p. 110; Webster and Frankland, *Strategic Air Offensive, 1*: 163

191 Note the Churchill minute of 20 Oct. 1940 in Churchill, *Second World War* 2: 603–4, and Hastings, pp. 125, 126, 136–37, 140–42.

192 Webster and Frankland, 1: 155–66; Hastings, pp. 116–17.

193 On British concentration on the air force and navy as the implements of victory, see Kennedy, *Business of War*, pp. 96–97. On the shift to the bombing of cities as it became clear in the summer of 1941 that specific targets could not be hit, see Dudley Saward, *"Bomber" Harris* (Garden City, N.J.: Doubleday, 1985), pp. 108–11; Hastings, pp. 127–47. There is a helpful discussion of Harris in the review articles, "'Bomber' Harris in Perspective," *Journal of the United Service for Defence Studies*, 130, No. 2 (1985), 62–70. On Lord Cherwell's role, see esp. PRO, PREM 3/119/10.

194 A good survey in Salewski, *Seekriegsleitung*, 1: 425–49. On the combat experience of the "Condor," see Kenneth Poolman, *Focke-Wulf Condor: Scourge of the Atlantic* (London: Macdonald & Jane's, 1978).

195 Note, e.g., the acrimonious meeting of Göring and Dönitz recorded in "Unterredung B.d.U. mit Reichsmarschall am 7.2.41," BA/MA, RM 6/74, f. 43–45.

196 There is a massive literature on the *Bismarck* episode. Good accounts in Salewski, *Seekriegsleitung*, 1: 392–98; *DRuZW*, 6: 370–83; Donald F. Steury, "Naval Intelligence, the Atlantic Campaign and the Sinking of the Bismarck: A Study in the Integration of Intelligence and the Conduct of Naval Warfare," *JCH* 22 (1987), 209–34. The *Prinz Eugen* escaped but had to return to port on account of engine trouble.

197 Hinsley, *British Intelligence*, 2: 165.

198 Salewski, 1: 449–70; Hinsley, *British Intelligence*, 2: 179–88; *DRuZW*, 6: 384–88. To make sure that the Germans could not resume such operations, the British on March 17, 1942, staged a special raid against the drydock at St. Nazaire on the French coast, the only one large enough to repair the *Tirpitz*, Germany's newest battleship (Hinsley, 2: 192).

199 This meant that the British limited shipments to Ireland; they were reluctant to risk more lives and ships than necessary to assist the Free State which refused to assist them.

200 Churchill's regular minutes to the First Sea Lord, pushing the naval war in all details, from 1941 to 45, are in PRO, ADM 205/10, 13, 14, 27, 35, 43.

201 Hinsley, *British Intelligence* 2: 165ff; Jürgen Rohwer, "'Special Intelligence' und die

Geleitzugsteuerung im Herbst 1941," *Marine-Rundschau* 75, No. 11 (Nov. 1978), 711–19. The German navy was invariably confident on reexamination that its coding system was so wonderful that no one could break into it, or that if there were breaks these were so minimal as to be insignificant. See diary of the Seekriegsleitung, 19 Mar. 1941, BA/MA, RM 7/22, f. 263; 20 Sep. 1941, RM 7/28, f. 323; 21 Oct. 1941, RM 7/29, f. 354; 30 Oct. 1941, RM 7/29, f. 517; 10 Nov. 1941, RM 7/30, f. 191; 18 Nov. 1941, RM 7/30, f. 330–31.

202 Medlicott, *Economic Blockade*, 1: 648–59, 669–71; Halifax to FDR, 11 Feb. 1941, FDR to Halifax, 19 Feb. 1941, FDRL, PSF Box 52, Great Britain, Halifax; FDR to Hull, 3 Mar. 1941, *FDR Letters*, 2: 1130–31.

203 Stafford, *Britain and European Resistance*, pp. 59–69. The British thought until quite late that the German buildup in the East was to pressure the Soviet Union rather than to invade (Hinsley, *British Intelligence*, 1: 470–71).

204 See the documents in PRO, PREM 261/1, and Liddell Hart Centre, Alanbrooke Papers, 14/58.

205 One of the intermediaries involved in the contacts between the British and the German opposition to Hitler in the winter of 1939–40, Lonsdale Bryans, now turned out to be, in Under Secretary of State Alexander Cadogan's phrase of 11 Feb. 1941, "an idiot – and something of a crook" (C 1143/14/62, PRO, FO 371/26419; see also C 1072/324/18, FO 371/26542).

206 C 610, 1426, 1705/324/18, PRO, FO 371/26542. See also C 1301/18/18, FO 371/26508; C 2505, 5695, 6735/324/18, FO 371/26542. The references back to the December 1939 soundings show the impact of the failure of the German opposition to act at that time.

207 Ribbentrop to Stockholm No. 84 of 21 Feb. 1941, AA, St.S., "England," Bd. 4, fr. 108666; Werner Dankwort, "Infernalische Reise," f. 76, Dankwort Papers.

208 The text is in C 7642/324/18, PRO, FO 371/26543. Churchill brought this to the Cabinet's attention and approval on 7 July, WM(41) War Cabinet 66(41), *CAB* 65/19. Cf. C 7759/324/18, FO 371/26543.

209 C 9472, 10855/324/18, PRO, FO 371/26543.

210 M 8881 in ibid. Lothar Kettenacker claims in "Die alliierte Kontrolle Deutschlands als Exempel britischer Herrschaftsausübung," in Ludolf Herbst (ed.), *Westdeutschland 1945–1955: Unterwerfung, Kontrolle, Integration* (Munich: Oldenbourg, 1986), p. 55 n 16, that Churchill may have been open to dealing with a government installed by a military coup that displaced Hitler in November 1941. The major point, of course, always was whether someone in Germany would actually *do* something other than always carry out Hitler's orders; the opponents had had their chance in the winter of 1939–40. See also Kettenacker, "The Anglo-Soviet Alliance and the Problem of Germany, 1941–1945," *JCH* 17 (1982) 444.

211 On the Hess affair, see my *Germany and the Soviet Union*, pp. 122–24, where the then available evidence was first analyzed. See also Gilbert, *Churchill*, 6: 1087–88; Bauer, *Hitler's Pilot*, pp. 124–26; Fröhlich, *Goebbels Tagebücher*, 4: 638–47, 653–64; additional documents in *ADAP*, D, 11 and 12; PRO, PREM 3/219. 1–7; C 12104/18/18, FO 371/26513; PRO, AIR 19/564; 22 June 1941 memorandum in FDRL, PSF Box 96, State, Welles, June-Dec. 1941.

Speculation about the Hess mission continues in view of the still partially closed British records. Professor Richard Breitman has found a document from the fall of 1941 asserting that Hess did mention the forthcoming German invasion of the Soviet Union; it remains to be seen whether this was in fact the case. On this, see Costello, *Ten Days*, chap. 17.

212 Note Lothian to Halifax, 29 Aug. 1940, PRO, FO 800/324, f. 290.

213 Weizsäcker to Ribbentrop, "St.S. No. 250," 12 Apr. 1941, AA, St.S., "Aufzeichnungen über interne Angelegenheiten," Bd. 2. The navy's view was due not only to its interest

in sinking ships but also to a recognition that the American deliveries would increase to substantial proportions (KTB Skl A 27, 13 Aug. 1941, BA/MA, RM 7/27, f. 210).

214 "Was sind schon die USA," Plesman statement, Institut für Zeitgeschichte, ZS 115, p. 4. See also Boog, *Luftwaffenführung*, pp. 118–21.

215 *ADAP*, D, 11, No. 633. A German correspondent who heard a briefing on Jan. 19, 1941, in which American aid to Britain was belittled commented that this sounded very much like what had been said in 1917 and early 1918 (BA, Brammer, ZSg. 101/38, f. 91–93).

216 *ADAP*, D, 11, Nos. 307, 313, 12, No. 608; *KTB OKW*, 1: 253–58; Salewski, *Seekriegsleitung*, 1: 406–15; Hewel Diary, 22 May 1941, Institut für Zeitgeschichte; von Waldau Diary, 9 Jan. 1941, Institut für Zeitgeschichte.

217 KTB Skl A 19, 22 Mar. 1941, BA/MA, RM 7/22, f. 309; now cited in *DRuZW*, 6: 283 n 34.

218 Skl IIIa "17233/gKdos," 31 July 1941, BA/MA, RM 6/83, f. 49–50.

219 Salewski, *Seekriegsleitung*, 2: 514.

220 *FDR Letters*, 2: 1057.

221 Ibid., pp. 1093–95 (FDR to F.B. Sayre, 31 Dec. 1940).

222 Robert J.C. Butow, "The FDR Tapes," *American Heritage* 33 (Feb.-Mar. 1982), 16–17.

223 *FRUS*, 1942, 2: 833–42; cf. ibid, 1: 916.

224 Peter Herde, "Pearl Harbur aus unbekannter revisionistischer Sicht: Neue Materialien über den nachrichtendienstlichen Hintergrund des japanischen Angriffs vom 7. Dezember 1941," *Historisches Jahrbuch der Görres Gesellschaft* 104/1 (1984), pp. 83–85; James Bamford, *The Puzzle Palace: A Report on America's Most Secret Agency* (New York: Penguin Books, 1983), pp. 394–97.

225 William F. Friedman, "SRH 125," NA, RG 457, pp. 35–37; Kahn, *Seizing Enigma*, pp. 235–36.

226 Abraham Sinkov and Leo Rosen, "Report of Technical Mission to England," 11 Apr. 1941, in NA, RG 457, SRH 145, pp. 2–4.

227 Jürgen Rohwer, "Die USA und die Schlacht im Atlantik," in Rohwer and Jäckel (eds.), *Kriegswende*, pp. 97, 99, 101.

228 This interpretation differs somewhat from that in ibid., pp. 89–101. See also Waldo Heinrichs, *Threshold of War: Franklin D. Roosevelt and American Entry into World War II* (New York: Oxford Univ. Press, 1988), pp. 166–68.

229 As late as Sep. 17, 1940, Lindbergh was trying to persuade American officers that Britain would be beaten in a few weeks (see Thomsen [Washington] No. 1987 of 18 Sep. 1940, AA, St.S., "England," Bd. 3, fr. B 002749–50).

230 Butow, "FDR Tapes," p. 12.

231 Reynolds, *Lord Lothian* pp. 39ff; British Cabinet Minutes for 20 Feb. 1941, WM(41) War Cabinet 19(41), PRO, CAB 65/17.

232 A good summary in Kimball, *Most Unsordid Act*.

233 The idea of shipping gold from South Africa to the U.S. on the cruiser USS *Louisville*, which so annoyed Churchill, had originally been suggested by the British representative in the negotiations. See ibid., p. 149; Alan P. Dobson, *U.S. Wartime Aid to Britain* (New York, St. Martin's, 1986), pp. 26–28.

234 The British records are filled with negative comments about Kennedy. Roosevelt, who believed he needed his political support, replaced him after the Nov. 1940 election. Note Douglas Fairbanks to FDR, 19 Nov. 1940, FDRL, PSF Box 53, Great Britain, Kennedy. Useful for background are Michael R. Beschloss, *Kennedy and Roosevelt* (New York: Norton, 1980), and Ralph F. de Bedts, *Ambassador Joseph Kennedy 1938–1940* (New York: Peter Lang, 1985).

235 See Murray to FDR, 25 Dec. 1940, FDRL, PSF Box 53, Great Britain, Arthur Murray 1940–44; Earl of Birkenhead, *Halifax: The Life of Lord Halifax* (Boston: Houghton Mifflin, 1966), pp. 467ff. A full study remains to be written.

236 Gilbert, *Churchill* chap. 51 is the most recent account.

237 Theodore A. Wilson, *The First Summit: Roosevelt and Churchill at Placentia Bay 1941* (Boston: Houghton Mifflin, 1969); Pogue, *Marshall*, 2: 142–45. This was when Marshall and Dill first met, becoming friends right away.

238 Kirk to Welles, 15 Dec. 1940, and Phillips to FDR, 21 Jan. 1941, FDRL, PSF Box 57, Italy 1941; Welles to FDR, PSF Box 96, State, Welles, Jan.-May 1941; NA, RG 457, SRH 281, pp. 83, 84, 86–130; KTB Skl A 20, 4 Apr. 1941, BA/MA, RM 7/23, f. 43.

239 Although the German embassy in Washington generally denied the allegations, sometimes in good faith, the fact is that many consular officials were working for one or another of the rival German intelligence organizations. Note Thomsen tel. 2226 of 15 Oct. 1940, AA, St.S., "USA," Bd. 3, fr. 22994–95.

240 *FDR Letters*, 2: 1079–80; *ADAP*, D, 11, No. 394.

241 Ray, "The Takoradi Route," pp. 342, 347–56.

242 *FRUS*, 1941, 2: 35–72; *ADAP*, D, 12, Nos. 308, 309, 314, 315, 318, 327, 329; *FDR Letters*, 2: 1142–43. See also the section omitted from FDR to Hull, 20 Feb. 1941, ibid., p. 1127, in FDRL, PSF Box 93, Cordell Hull, 1941–42.

243 A good account in James Leutze, *Bargaining for Supremacy: Anglo-American Naval Relations, 1937–1941* (Chapel Hill, N.C.: Univ. of North Carolina Press, 1977). On the key role of Chief of Naval Operations Admiral Harold Stark in this, see B. Mitchell Simpson, *Admiral Harold R. Stark: Architect of Victory, 1939–1945* (Columbia, S.C.: Univ. of South Carolina Press., 1989), chaps. 3–4.

244 Borg and Okamoto, *Pearl Harbor*, pp. 220–22.

245 See Admiral Ingersoll memorandum for Captain Callaghan, 21 Feb. 1941, in FDRL, PSF Box 82, Navy, Daniel J. Callaghan; *FDR Letters*, 2: 1137. The Germans were incensed by this practice which mirrored their own use of Swedish ship-building facilities (Wittmann, *Schwedens Wirtschaftsbeziehungen*, pp. 252–57).

246 Prange, *At Dawn*, pp. 122–24, 130–34, 139–40; Danckwerts for the Combined Chiefs of Staff in Halifax (Washington) No. 1883, 29 Apr. 1941, A 3153/384/45, PRO, FO 371/26220.

247 Pogue, *Marshall*, 2: 130–31.

248 Bittner, *Britain and Iceland*, pp. 124–34; Heinrichs, *Threshold*, pp. 85–88, 110–11. It may well be that the cruise of the *Bismarck* and the fate of Crete influenced the President. The marine brigade first sent to Iceland had been scheduled for the Azores if Germany invaded Portugal.

249 Note Stimson to FDR, 8 July 1941, FDRL, PSF Box 9, Safe File War Department.

250 Sherman Miles memorandum for the Chief of Staff, "Battle of the Atlantic," 5 May 1941, NA, RG 165, entry 77, Box 1419, A6: British Estimate of German Intentions towards NE Africa and Spain winter 1941–1942.

251 Sherman Miles memorandum for the Chief of Staff, "Estimate of the Russo-German Situation," 19 June 1941, ibid. When the Russians had kept insisting that the Germans show them their tanks bigger than the Mark IV and had refused to believe that there were none, the Germans had failed to draw the obvious conclusion, namely that the Red Army had larger ones itself. They would find out about the T-34 and KV tanks of the Red Army on meeting them in battle (see also Earl Ziemke, *Moscow to Stalingrad* [Washington: GPO, 1987], p. 11).

252 John D. Langer, "The 'Red General': Philip R. Faymonville and the Soviet Union, 1917–52," *Prologue* 8 (1976), 214–19; James S. Herndon and Joseph D. Baylen, "Col. Philip R. Faymonville and the Red Army, 1939–43," *Slavic Review* 34 (1975), 483–505; Thomas A. Julian, "Philip Ries Faymonville and the Soviet Union," paper read at the SHAFR Conference, 9–11 June 1988. When F. was recalled in 1943 over differences with the American embassy staff, he was replaced by General Sidney Spalding who had recommended F. in the first place (Langer, p. 220).

253 Cole, *Roosevelt and Isolationists*, p. 433; *FDR Letters*, 2: 1204–5; George C. Herring, *Aid to Russia 1941–1946* (New York: Columbia Univ. Press, 1973), chap. 1; FDR memorandum for Myron C. Taylor, 1 Sept. 1941, FDRL, PSF Italy.

254 On the worries, see *FDR Letters*, 2: 1179; on the lack of contact, note that Roosevelt saw the Soviet ambassador on July 10, 1941, for the first time since the summer of 1939 (Dallek, *Roosevelt and Foreign Policy*, p. 279).

255 Joan Beaumont, *Comrades in Arms: British Aid to Russia, 1941–1945* (London: Davis-Poynter, 1980), pp. 36–42.

256 Morgenthau Presidential Diary, 4 Aug. 1941, Vol. 4, pp. 951–53, FDRL; FDR to Wayne Coy, 2 Aug. 1941, PSF Box 68, Russia 1941.

257 Heinrichs, *Threshold*, pp. 104–5, 136–41. The famous map FDR spoke of in October 1941 showing German plans for the Western Hemisphere now turns out to have been put out by Nazis in Argentina, obtained by the British, doctored up by them in Canada and then passed on by them to the Americans. See John F. Bratzel and Leslie B. Rout, Jr., "FDR and the 'Secret Map'," *Wilson Quarterly* 9 (1985), 167–73; Donovan to Roosevelt, No. 350, 26 Mar. 1942, FDRL, PSF Box 165, OSS Donovan Reports # 8.

258 Note Beaumont, *Comrades in Arms*, pp. 46–49.

259 Pogue, *Marshall*, 2: 145–54.

260 Ibid., p. 79.

261 Jones, *Manhattan*, pp. 30–32. Soon after, the President got the navy to convert light cruisers under construction into carriers, another project that worked out in practice (*FDR Letters*, 2: 1226).

262 Dallek, *Roosevelt and Foreign Policy*, p. 270; Schaller, *U.S. Crusade in China*, pp. 36–38.

263 Schaller, pp. 47–51.

264 *FDR Letters*, 2: 1233–34.

265 Borg and Okamoto, *Pearl Harbor*, p. 46.

266 *FDR Letters*, 2: 1077.

267 Borg and Okamoto, pp. 450–51.

268 An excellent account in Robert J.C. Butow, *The John Doe Associates: Backdoor Diplomacy for Peace, 1941* (Stanford, Calif.: Stanford Univ. Press, 1974). It would seem that State Department official Stanley Hornbeck saw through Drought's action (p. 140), but the project still went forward. See also Barnhart, *Japan Prepares*, pp. 204–7, 219–24.

269 Borg and Okamoto, pp. 149–64; Hilary Conroy, in Richard D. Burns and Edward M. Bennett (eds.), *Diplomats in Crisis: United States–Chinese–Japanese Relations, 1919–1941* (Santa Barbara, Calif.: ABC-Clio, 1974), pp. 307–9, argues that Nomura deliberately withheld information to help the negotiations along.

270 Note Pogue, *Marshall*, 2: 186ff.

271 FDR to Welles, 19 Feb. 1941, FDRL, PSF Box 96, Welles State Jan.-May 1941. Cf. *FDR Letters*, 2: 1126; Butow, *John Doe Associates*, p. 391.

272 Butow, *John Doe Associates*, chap. 4.

273 Washington to Tokyo No. 98 of 7 May 1941, NA, RG 457, SRA 18359–60 (translated in Aug. 1945).

274 Morley, *Fateful Choice*, pp. 255–62; Barnhart, chaps. 1–2.

275 See Horinouchi No. 1347 of 22 Aug. 1940, NA, RG 457, SRDJ 6935, The conclusion of the conference in Washington was that joining Germany and Italy meant war with Britain and the United States and that thereby Japan would be "drawn into a useless war of exhaustion and this will in the end prove disadvantageous to us."

276 The relevant documents in F 3782, 3992, 4009, 4071, 4489/43/10 in PRO, FO 371/24668–70, make it clear that this was a British decision made without American encouragement or promises because Britain's situation in Europe looked better and because the concession which had been made to Japan had strengthened the extremists rather than the moderates in Tokyo. The argument in Frederick W. Marks, III, "The

Origins of FDR's Promise to Support Britain Militarily in the Far East – A New Look," *Pacific Historical Review* 53 (1984), 447–62, does not stand up.

277 Nigel J. Brailey, *Thailand and the Fall of Singapore: A Frustrated Asian Revolution* (Boulder: Westview Press, 1986), pp. 91–94; Morley, *Fateful Choice*, pp. 209–34, 283–85. As Matsuoka explained to the Germans, Tokyo wanted "Thai's lost territory restored . . . so that we could better get at British territory" (No. 865 to Berlin, 5 Dec. 1940, NA, RG 457, SRDJ 58329).

278 Berger, *Parties out of Power*, pp. 290–318; Butow, *Tojo*, pp. 158–59.

279 See Konoe's note on Preliminary Liaison Conference on Tripartite Pact, 14 Sept. 1940, in Morley, *Deterrent Diplomacy* pp. 238–39. See also Morley, *Fateful Choice*, p. 276; Butow, *Tojo*, pp. 161–68.

280 Johanna M. Meskill, *Hitler and Japan: The Hollow Alliance* (New York: Atherton, 1966), pp. 17–22; *ADAP*, D, 11, Nos. 119–21. On earlier German interest in these former colonial territories, see Weizsäcker memorandum, "St.S. Nr. 952," 6 Dec. 1939, and Bielfeld memorandum of 15 Dec. 1939, AA, St.S., "Japan," Bd. 1; Marinekommandoamt, "2330/39 gKdos." of 14 Oct. 1939, BA/MA, Case 561, PG 33624.

The other side to this peculiar relationship is that one day after the signing of the Tripartite Pact Lammers had great difficulty getting Hitler's permission for a German to marry a person of mixed German–Japanese parentage; something permitted in this instance only because it had been allowed before and a change would cause problems. But there would be no repetitions. See Lammers's memorandum "zu Rk.J.Rot 5.10/B," 21 Sep. 1940, BA, R 43 II/722, f. 58–59.

281 Morley, *Deterrent Diplomacy*, pp. 242, 245–49; Morley, *Fateful Choice*, pp. 49–50, 276; Butow, *Tojo*, pp. 168–77; Borg and Okamoto, *Pearl Harbor*, p. 618 n 38; conference text in Nobutaka Ike (ed.), *Japan's Decision for War: Records of the 1941 Policy Conferences* (Stanford, Calif.: Stanford Univ. Press, 1967), pp. 4–13.

282 Morley, *Fateful Choice*, pp. 275–76; Butow, *Tojo*, pp. 177–83.

283 Netherlands Foreign Office to Sir Nevile Bland, 27 Sep. 1940, F 4368/2739/61, PRO, FO 371/24717. On the mission of Kobayashi Ichizu, see Morley, *Fateful Choice*, pp. 143–46; Isigawa (Batavia) to Tokyo No. 1131 of 11 Dec. 1940, NA, RG 457, SRDJ 8412–14. See also Batavia No. 68 of 12 Oct. 1940, SRDJ 7217–19, No. 84 of 19 Oct. 1940, SRDJ 7308–9, and Batavia No. 272 of 7 Apr. 1941, SRDJ 10969–71. A subsequent mission to the Netherlands East Indies under Yoshizawa Kenkichi had no more success (Morley, *Fateful Choice*, pp. 146–53; Ike, *Japan's Decision for War*, pp. 36–39, 43–45, 49).

284 Morley, *Fateful Choice*, pp. 188–200, 203–8; Butow, *Tojo*, pp. 192–93.

285 *ADAP*, D, 11, Nos. 257, 299, 311, 315; Boyle, *China and Japan*, pp. 301–4. Relevant Japanese diplomatic messages intercepted by the Americans are in NA, RG 457, SRDJ 7738–39, 7888–89, 7893–94, 8054, 8127–28, 8198–99, 8298–300 (also in SRH 018), 8328, 8374, 8566–67.

286 Morley, *Fateful Choice*, pp. 272–73, 285–86.

287 Ibid., pp. 45–70; Butow, *Tojo*, pp. 205–6; Japanese intercepts in NA, RG 457, SRDJ 7693–96, 8003, 8021, 8132–36, 8251, 8252, 8260, 8782–86. The Japanese, of course, kept a wary eye on the Soviet Union; when they learned of the murder of the Soviet defector Walter Krivitsky in Washington, they wanted to learn whether he had been killed by the same person who had killed Leon Trotsky (Matsuoka to New York No. 17 of 12 Feb. 1941, SRDJ 9878).

288 Morley, *Fateful Choice*, pp. 75–81; Dallek, *Roosevelt and Foreign Policy*, pp. 273ff; Butow, *Tojo*, p. 207. Matsuoka did not take the full record of his talks with Stalin and Molotov back to Tokyo with him, so the Japanese government had to ask its embassy in Moscow for that record in 1945! See Tokyo to Moscow No. 281 of 17 Feb. 1945, NA, RG 457, SRDJ 91558.

289 Tatekawa No. 1530 of 6 Dec. 1940, NA, RG 457, SRDJ 8345–46. At that time Matsuoka

had not wanted to hurry, see his No. 871 to Berlin of 11 Dec. 1940, SRDJ 8415–16. Simultaneously the Soviets were sending more supplies to Chiang in hopes of keeping the Japanese busy in China (Garver, *Chinese–Soviet Relations*, pp. 107–8).

290 *ADAP*, D, 12, No. 361.

291 Ibid., 11, No. 341, 12, No. 190; numerous documents in AA, St.S., "Japan," Bd. 2; Shanghai to Tokyo No. 512 of 2 Apr. 1941 and Tokyo to Shanghai No. 263 of 5 Apr. 1941, NA, RG 457, SRDJ 10808 and 10956; KTB Skl A 21, 23 May 1941, BA/MA, RM 7/24, f. 339–40. The Japanese had helped a little in the outfitting of German raiders, see the file W 39 in PRO, FO 371/28814.

292 Butow, *Tojo*, pp. 205–6; Morley, *Fateful Choice*, pp. 72–74; Wagner, *Lagevorträge*, p. 184; *ADAP*, D, 12, Nos. 78, 81, 100, 218, 222, 230, 233; German naval attaché Tokyo, "Nr. 174/41, Japans Beteiligung am europäischen Krieg," 13 Mar. 1941, and Skl to Ritter, "25142/41g.Kdos," 19 Nov. 1941, BA/MA, RM 7/253; KTB Skl A 19, 17 Apr. 1941, RM 7/23, f. 236–37; KTB Skl A 21, 13 May 1941, RM 7/24, f. 170–71 and 31 May, f. 458–59; KTB Skl A 22, 25 Oct. 1941, RM 7/29, f. 426–27; Oshima to Tokyo No. 308 of 26 Mar. 1941, NA, RG 457, SRDJ 10684–85; John W.M. Chapman, "Forty Years On – The Imperial Japanese Navy, The European War and the Tripartite Pact," *Proceedings of the British Association for Japanese Studies* 5, Part 1 (1980), p. 219 n 46. It must be noted that for Matsuoka's talks in Berlin there are only German reports. M. decided to report in person and apparently did so orally; see message cited in U.S. Pacific Strategic Intelligence Section, "The Problem of the Prolongation of the Soviet–Japanese Pact," 12 Feb. 1945, NA, RG 457, SRH 069, p. 2. The only report of Matsuoka from Berlin is his one paragraph No. 369 of 5 Apr. 1941, SRDJ 10828.

293 See Chapman, *Price of Admiralty*, 2: 336–37, on this action of 12 Dec. 1940. The document in question had been seized by a German auxiliary cruiser from the *Automedon* (ibid., pp. 582–83); *DRuZW*, 6: 148–49. Earlier the British naval attaché in Tokyo in a private letter of 10 Oct. 1940 to the director of naval intelligence had suggested that in case of war Britain should send an aircraft carrier with planes carrying incendiaries to burn down Japanese cities (F 5308/193/61, PRO, FO 371/24711).

294 KTB Skl A 19, 10 Apr. 1941, BA/MA, RM 7/23, f. 127–28, 22 Apr. 1941, f. 317; "Unterredung mit Admiral Nomura am 6.8.1941," RM 7/94, f. 407–12; Skl "26519/41 gKdos," 20 Nov. 1941, RM 7/206, f. 440–47.

295 Krebs, *Japan's Deutschlandpolitik*, 1: 284. Ribbentrop was speaking on 16 June 1939 to Shiratori in the presence of Attolico and Ciano.

296 Wenneker to Schniewind, 22 Nov. 1940, Chapman, *Price of Admiralty*, pp. 511–13; cf. ibid., pp. 514–21; KTB Skl A 19, 3 Mar. 1941, BA/MA, RM 7/22, f. 38–39; German naval attaché Tokyo, "75/41 gKdos. Der Eintritt Japans in den europäischen Krieg, Möglichkeiten und Auswirkungen," 3 Feb. 1941, RM 7/253, f. 25–35; Meskill, *Hitler and Japan*, pp. 26–29.

297 *ADAP*, D, 12, No. 266.

298 Oshima to Tokyo, 14 Aug. 1941, NA, RG 457, SRDJ 14100. Oshima reports a German back from Hitler's field headquarters as quoting Hitler that if there were a clash between Japan and the U.S. Germany would "at once open war against the United States." Similarly, the report on the Ribbentrop–Oshima conversation of 28 Nov. 1941, *Pearl Harbor Attack*, 12: 202 (a British intercept and translation of the same document in Part 35, p. 677). See also the comments of Friedrich Gauss, head of the legal division of the German Foreign Ministry, on Dec. 1, 1941 which obviously reflect the general understanding of German policy at the Ministry in Berlin (U.S. Department of Defense, *The "Magic" Background of Pearl Harbor*, 5 vols. [Washington: GPO, 1977], 4, No. 831).

299 Ike, *Japan's Decision for War*, pp. 17–19, 20–24, 26, 28–36; Butow, *John Doe Associates*, pp. 172–73, 178, 182–84; *Kido Diary*, 19 Apr. 1941, p. 272; *ADAP*, D, 12, Nos. 454–56, 480, 483–84, 487–89, 496, 507, 517–18, 537; Hewel Diary, 8 and 10 May 1941,

Institut für Zeitgeschichte; Rintelen to Mackensen No. 1058 of 9 May 1941 and Mackensen's reply No. 10862 of 10 May, AA, Botschaft Rom (Quir.), Geheim 46/2, fr. 482072 and 482074–77.

300 *KTB OKW*, 1: 328–29; *ADAP*, D, 12, Nos. 125, 418; KTB Skl A 18, 11 and 22 Feb. 1941, BA/MA, RM 7/21, f. 133–34, 295–96; A 19, 10 Mar. 1940, RM 7/22, f. 138; A 20, 17 Apr. 1941, RM 7/23, f. 236–37; German naval attaché Rome, "Pro-Memoria," 3 Jan. 1941, Case 19/1, PG 45197.

301 Morley, *Fateful Choice*, pp. 89–94; *Kido Diary*, 18 Apr. 1941, pp. 271–72, 6 and 20 June 1941, pp. 279, 283; Hinsley, *British Intelligence*, 1: 478.

302 Summarized in Hillgruber, "Japan und der Fall Barbarossa," in *Deutsche Grossmacht und Weltpolitik*, pp. 225–28.

303 Ibid., pp. 230–33, and appended documents; Morley, *Fateful Choice*, pp. 98–101; *ADAP*, D, 13, No. 241 and Appendices 2 and 4; KTB Skl A 22, 13 June 1941, BA/MA, RM 7/25, f. 133–34; KTB Skl A 26, 28 Oct. 1941, RM 7/29, f. 477–78.

304 See, e.g., Sato (Hanoi) to Tokyo, 21 and 23 Nov. 1940, NA, RG 457, SRDJ 7998–8001 and 8090–91.

305 Butow, *Tojo*, pp. 196–97. Cf. Butow, *John Doe Associates*, pp. 124–25.

306 Text in Ike, *Japan's Decision for War*, pp. 34–43. A speech Matsuoka gave in public a few days later was so strange that the Home Minister banned the distribution of copies. See Burns and Bennett, *Diplomats in Crisis*, p. 291; Butow, *John Doe Associates*, pp. 399–400; Krebs, *Japans Deutschlandpolitik*, pp. 442–51.

307 Ike, pp. 51–56; Butow, *Tojo*, pp. 210–11; Morley, *Fateful Choice*, pp. 234–35; Heinrichs, *Threshold*, pp. 118–27; cf. *ADAP*, D, 12, No. 611.

308 Morley, *Fateful Choice*, pp. 82, 94–104, 236; Butow, *Tojo*, pp. 212–21, 228–33; *Kido Diary*, 22–23 June 1941, pp. 284–86; Ike, *Japan's Decision for War*, pp. 55–90; *ADAP*, D, 13, Nos. 14, 33, 35–36, 53, 63–65, 72, 88–89, 105, 117.
This decision may be in the background of Japan's finally and rather reluctantly giving in to German pressure to end diplomatic relations with the Polish government-in-exile in the fall of 1941. See Weizsäcker to Lammers, "Völkerrechtliche Bedeutung des Zerfalls des Polnischen Staates," 15 May 1940, NA, RG 238, PS-646; Ott reports to Berlin of 6 and 16 Aug. 1941, IMTFE, IPS 4064 and 4053; Privy Council Meeting of 1 Oct. 1941, IPS 1196; Robert Craigie, *Behind the Japanese Mask* (London: Hutchinson, 1946), p. 126; Heydrich to Ribbentrop, 7 Aug. 1941, AA, Inland IIg, "Berichte und Meldungen zur Lage in und über Japan 1940–1944," fr. 280088–100.

309 Kurusu (Berlin) to Tokyo No. 119 of 14 Feb. 1941, NA, RG 457, SRDJ 9817–21.

310 The quotation is from Hilary Conroy, "Nomura Kichisaburo: The Diplomacy of Drama and Desperation," in Burns and Bennett, *Diplomats in Crisis*, p. 311.

311 Ike, *Japans Decision for War*, pp. 76–77.

312 *Kido Diary*, 7 Aug. 1941; Butow, *Tojo*, pp. 236–38.

313 Borg and Okamoto, *Pearl Harbor*, pp. 253–54. The Japanese military attaché in Washington was equally cautious; see his report 159 of 9 Aug. 1941, NA, RG 457, SRA 17353–55.

314 Ike, pp. 93–110; Butow, *John Doe Associates*, pp. 224–25; Morley, *Fateful Choice*, pp. 236–38.

315 Tokyo to Japanese naval attaché Washington, 15 July 1941, NA, RG 457, SRNA 99.

316 Ruth R. Harris, "The 'Magic' Leak of 1941 and Japanese–American Relations," *Pacific Historical Review* 50 (1981), 90. See also *FDR Letters*, 2: 1173–74.

317 Butow, *John Doe Associates*, pp. 228–38, 249; Prange, *At Dawn*, pp. 167–9; *Kido Diary*, 31 July 1941, pp. 296–97.

318 Note Matsuoka to Washington No. 495 of 28 Sep. 1940, NA, RG 457, SRDJ 7043.

319 Utley, "Foggy Bottom," pp. 23–28; Borg and Okamoto, *Pearl Harbor*, pp. 48–49; Heinrichs, *Threshold*, pp. 133–36, 141–42, 177–78, 246–47 n 68; Morgenthau Presidential

Diary, 18 July 1941, FDRL, Vol. 4, f. 946–48; Barnhart, *Japan Prepares*, pp. 225–42.

320 Roosevelt to Hopkins (in London), 26 July 1941, FDRL, PSF Box 152, Hopkins; *FDR Letters*, 2: 1189–90; Butow, *John Doe Associates*, pp. 249–56.

321 Borg and Okamoto, *Pearl Harbor*, pp. 165–88; Pogue, *Marshall*, 2: 201–3.

322 On this project, which was aborted as it became clear that the Japanese were not about to abandon their move south, see Butow, *John Doe Associates*, chap. 19; Butow, *Tojo*, pp. 242–46; Ike, *Japan's Decision for War*, pp. 124–29; Heinrichs, *Threshold*, pp. 185ff; *Kido Diary*, 5 Aug. 1941, pp. 298–99.

323 The Soviets blew up a huge Japanese fuel and ammunition dump at Tatutzuchuan in eastern Manchuria. See John Erickson, "Reflections on Securing the Soviet Far Eastern Frontier: 1932–1945," *Interplay* 3 (1969), 57.

324 Morley, *Fateful Choice*, pp. 106–13; Ike, pp. 112–18; Uchiba Diary, 8 Aug. 1941, quoted in Prange, *At Dawn*, p. 177; Butow, *Tojo*, p. 246; Meskill, *Hitler and Japan*, pp. 284–85.

325 KTB Skl A 25, 27 Sep. 1941, BA/MA, RM 7/28, f. 455–56; KTB Skl A 26, 4 Oct. 1941, RM 7/29, f. 66; Admiral Groos, "Unterredung mit Vizeadmiral Nomura am 6.8.1941," RM 7/94, f. 407–12; Nomura (Washington) to Tokyo No. 894 of 3 Oct. 1941, *Pearl Harbor Attack*, 12: 52, and Tokyo to Berlin No. 969 of 21 Nov. 1941, ibid., p. 165; Ott to Berlin No 1974 of 4 Oct. 1941, in Meskill, p. 296, and also pp. 301–2, 304; David J. Dallin, *Soviet Russia's Foreign Policy 1939–1942* (New Haven, Conn.: Yale Univ. Press, 1942), pp. 350–51.

326 The original pledge was made by Moscow on Aug. 13, 1941, and the Japanese asked for a repetition at the time of the American landing on Attu in the Aleutians; see Sato (Kuibyshev) to Tokyo No. 556 of 17 May 1943, NA, RG 457, SRDJ 36685–86; George A. Lensen, *The Strange Neutrality: Soviet–Japanese Relations During the Second World War 1941–1945* (Tallahassee, Fla.: Diplomatic Press, 1972), pp. 35–37.

327 Ike, *Japan's Decision for War*, pp. 129–63; Butow, *Tojo*, pp. 246–59; Prange, *At Dawn*, pp. 208–12; *Kido Diary*, 6 Sep. 1941, p. 304. Until he had obtained the decision for war, Konoe refused to see American Ambassador Grew (unlike Roosevelt who repeatedly met Nomura). Now he invited Grew to dinner (Butow, *John Doe Associates*, p. 428 n 268).

328 Ike, pp. 179–84; Butow, *Tojo*, pp. 262–85.

329 Ike, pp. 184–239; Butow, *Tojo*, pp. 314–27; *Kido Diary*, 4 Nov. 1941, p. 317. The reluctance to reopen a question once settled in the endless talks in Tokyo – regardless of what had been settled and how – is very much emphasized in Krebs, *Japans Deutschlandpolitik*.

330 Ike, pp. 239–49; Butow, *Tojo*, pp. 327–30; Japanese Foreign Ministry Circular 2319 to Hong Kong of 14 Nov. 1941, NA, RG 457, SRDJ 104736–37.

331 Butow, *Tojo*, pp. 399–401; Butow, *John Doe Associates*, pp. 197–98; Barnhart, *Japan Prepares*, pp. 260–61; Ike, pp. 249–53. It should be noted that the relevant reports from and instructions to the Japanese embassy in Washington were being read by the Americans so that the Japanese insistence on war was understood there.

332 Ike, pp. 253–60; Butow, *John Doe Associates*, pp. 301–2; Butow, *Tojo*, pp. 334–35, 344–48; German naval attaché Rome "1884/41, Politische Lage Japan/Vereinigten Staaten," 3 Dec. 1941, BA/MA, Case 17/3, PG 45172; Masao Maruyama, *Thought and Behavior in Modern Japanese Politics*, Ivan Morris ed. (London: Oxford Univ. Press, 1963), pp. 88–89. The Emperor had his doubts to the end, but the government was unanimous (see Ike, pp. 262–83; Butow, *Tojo*, pp. 337–43, 358–63). The navy wanted to start war without any warning but the Emperor and others wanted one, so there was supposed to be a 20–minute interval between the final note – which contained neither a declaration of war nor an announcement of a break of relations – and the attack. It all meant nothing. The delay in the delivery of the final appeal of President Roosevelt to Emperor Hirohito was a matter of routine and not aimed at this particular document (Butow, *Tojo*, pp. 371–97).

333 Morley, *Fateful Choice*, pp. 277–82.

334 Prange, *At Dawn*, p. 81.

335 Morley, *Fateful Choice*, p. 260.

336 Ibid., pp. 292–95; Butow, *Tojo*, p.204 n 43; Takushiro Hattori, "Japans Operationsplan für den Beginn des Pazifischen Krieges," *Wehrwissenschaftliche Rundschau* 7 (1957), 257.

337 Richard Storry, *The Double Patriots: A Study of Japanese Nationalism* (Boston: Houghton Mifflin, 1957), p. 285 n 3. On the army war games of early October, see Hattori, p. 261; see also Japanese military attaché Bangkok to Japanese General Staff, No. 289 of 18 Oct. 1941, NA, RG 457, SRA 17313–14.

338 Morley, *Fateful Choice*, p. 274. The reference is to October 1940. Yamamoto had turned to an anti-U.S. stance in September 1940 because of the American naval construction program (Chapman, *Price of Admiralty*, p. 264).

339 Prange, *At Dawn*, p. 14.

340 Ibid., p. 15.

341 Ibid., pp. 16–17, 21, chap. 3.

342 Ibid., pp. 285, 296–99, 301–2; Toshikazu Ohmae, "Die strategischen Konzeptionen der japanischen marine im Zweiten Weltkrieg," *Marine-Rundschau* 53 (1956) 188. Because of the intervening international date line, Dec. 7 in the U.S. was Dec. 8 in Tokyo.

343 Prange, p. 261.

344 Ibid., p. 35.

345 Ibid., p. 229. Cf. ibid., pp. 133–34; Hattori, "Japans Operationsplan," p. 261.

346 Prange, p. 323.

347 One of the scholars who shares this perspective is Raymond G. O'Connor, *War, Diplomacy and History* (Washington: Univ. Press of America, 1979), pp. 45, 75. See also H.P. Willmott, *Empires in the Balance: Japanese and Allied Pacific Strategies to April 1942* (Annapolis, Md.: Naval Institute Press, 1982), pp. 134–41.

348 John J. Stephan, *Hawaii under the Rising Sun: Japan's Plans for Conquest after Pearl Harbor* (Honolulu: Univ. of Hawaii Press, 1984), chap. 5.

349 Quoted in Borg and Okamoto, *Pearl Harbor*, p. 259. In the published version of the diary, Chihaya Masataka (trans.), *Fading Victory: The Diary of Admiral Matome Ugaki 1941–1945* (Pittsburgh: Univ. of Pittsburgh Press, 1991), this entry is summarized on pp. 40–41.

350 Borg and Okamoto, pp. 252–58.

351 Cole, *Roosevelt and Isolationists*, p. 479; *ADAP*, D, 13, No. 541; Reichspropagandaamt Berlin, "Presse-Rundschreiben Nr. II/132/41," 9 Dec. 1941, BA, Nadler, ZSg. 115/20, f. 114; OKW, WFSt., Abt. L (Warlimont), "Überblick über die Bedeutung des Kriegseintritts der U.S.A. und Japan," 14 Dec. 1941, BA/MA, RM 7/258, f. 133–64, also f. 119–20; James C. Gaston, *Planning the American Air War: Four Men and Nine Days in 1941* (Washington: National Defense Univ. Press, 1983), pp. 96–100. I have not been able to locate any reference to Japanese reactions to this most dramatic leak from the U.S. government in World War II.

352 See Butow, *Tojo*, p. 336.

353 Pogue, *Marshall*, 2: 221–22.

354 Hull to FDR, 17 June 1942, FDRL, PSF Box 13, Confidential File, State Department 1941–42. The collection was published in two volumes in 1943: *FRUS, Japan, 1931–1941*.

355 There is an excellent account of the issues in Gordon Prange, *Pearl Harbor: The Verdict of History* (New York: McGraw Hill, 1986). This should now be supplemented by George H. Lobell, "Secretary of the Navy Frank Knox and Chief of Naval Operations Admiral Harold R. Stark," in William B. Cogar (ed.), *New Interpretations in Naval History* (Annapolis, Md.: Naval Institute Press, 1989), pp. 247–62, and David Kahn, "Pearl Harbor and the Inadequacy of Cryptanalysis," *Cryptologia* 25, No. 4 (Oct. 1991), 273–94 (see n 56 on the nonsense about Churchill knowing ahead of time).

356 Comments on Admiral Dankwerts for the Combined Chiefs of Staff in Halifax to London No. 1697 of 17 Apr. 1941, A 4782/384/45, PRO, FO 371/26220.

357 On the salvage of most ships "sunk" at Pearl Harbor, see Homer N. Wallin, *Pearl Harbor: Why, How, Fleet Salvage and Final Appraisal* (Washington: GPO, 1968).

358 On Japanese interest in cooperating with Italian intelligence, see Rome to Tokyo No. 419 of 26 Nov. 1941, NA, RG 457, SRA 3062.

359 Rome to Tokyo No. 985 of 3 Dec. 1941, *Pearl Harbor Attack*, 12: 228–29.

360 *ADAP*, D, 13, No. 527, cf. No. 543. An important study based on extensive work in the Italian (as well as United States) archives is Peter Herde, *Italien, Deutschland und der Weg in den Krieg im Pazifik* (Wiesbaden: Steiner, 1983).

361 A detailed account in Weinberg, *World in the Balance*, pp. 75–95. On May 8, 1941 Hitler had told Goebbels that the United States could not produce as much war material as Germany since the latter had all of Europe to draw on (Fröhlich, *Goebbels Tagebücher*, 4: 631).

362 KTB Skl A 28, 9 Dec. 1941, BA/MA, RM 7/31, f. 135–36; Oshima No 1437 of 8 Dec. 1941, *Pearl Harbor Attack*, 12; 253. Countries included were Uruguay, Panama, Costa Rica, Nicaragua, Honduras, Haiti, El Salvador, and the Dominican Republic.

363 Speech in Domarus, *Hitler*, 2: 1794–1811.

364 *ADAP*, D, 13, No. 572.

365 The idea had originated with the Japanese, see Weizsäcker to Ribbentrop, 7 Nov. 1941, AA, St.S., "USA," Bd. 9, fr. 422316; Ike, *Japan's Decision for War*, pp. 260–62. As early as Nov. 21, 1941, von Ribbentrop had assured the Japanese that Germany would not make a separate peace with the United States in any war, however it started (*ADAP*, D, 13, No. 487). The treaties themselves were signed after Pearl Harbor.

366 *FDR Letters*, 2: 1257, 1282; *FRUS*, 1942, 2: 833–42, cf. ibid., 1: 916; Miller, *Bulgaria*, pp. 68–70.

5: THE EASTERN FRONT AND A CHANGING WAR

1 Von Hardesty, *Red Phoenix: The Rise of Soviet Air Power, 1941–1945* (Washington: Smithsonian Institution Press, 1982), pp. 11–15; *DRuZW*, 4: 652–56. Horst Boog, the author of the latter piece, points out that the mass destruction of Soviet planes on the ground meant that many of the crew members survived to take part in the rebuilding of the Red air force. The German air force expected that the whole campaign in the East would last two months so that the Luftwaffe could then concentrate on England (Goebbels' Diary of 29 Sept. 1942, cited in *DRuZW*, 4: 317). The effort of Bryan I. Fugate, *Operation Barbarossa: Strategy and Tactics on the Eastern Front, 1941* (Novato, Calif.: Presidio Press, 1984), to put a new interpretation on the early fighting is effectively refuted in Barry D. Watts and Williamson Murray, "Inventing History: Soviet Military Genius Revealed," *Air University Review* 36, No. 3 (Mar/Apr 1985), 102–12.

2 *KTB Halder*, 3: 38.

3 Halder to Louise von Benda [Jodl], 3 July 1941, provided to Anton Hoch at the Institut für Zeitgeschichte by Louise Jodl. I am grateful to Professor Harold Deutsch for sending me a copy. There is a quotation from this letter in Louise Jodl's memoirs, *Jenseits des Endes: Leben und Sterben des Generalobersten Alfred Jodl* (Vienna: Fritz Moldau, 1976), p. 55.

4 *DRuZW*, 4: 269–70.

5 Ibid., p. 317.

6 Though very early Hitler learned that the Soviets had a heavy tank the Germans could not match, see his letter to Mussolini of June 30, 1941 (*ADAP*, D, 13 No. 50). That did not keep him from ordering on July 13 that no new tanks were to be sent to the Eastern Front; they were to be retained in Germany for the equipment of new formations destined for the follow-up campaign into the Middle East (*DRuZW*, 4: 975).

7 Jochmann, *Hitler Monologe*, 5/6 July 1941, p. 39, 27 July, p. 48; *DRuZW*, 4: 990–91, 994–95; Streit, *Keine Kameraden*, chaps. 6 and 7.

8 *ADAP*, D, 13, No. 114; *DRuZW*, 4: 856, 1007.

9 See *ADAP*, D, 13, Nos. 3–6, 18, 37, 39, 223; AA, St.S. "Litauen," fr. 1933369–94, 96–401.

10 Czeslaw Madajczyk (ed.), "Generalplan Ost," in *Polish Western Affairs* 3, No. 2 (1962), 391–442, contains many bibliographic references.

11 *ADAP*, D, 13, No. 149. Not only Germans but others, for example Dutch, were to be settled.

12 *ADAP*, D, 13, Appendix III. One page of the record of the Hitler–Kvaternik meeting of July 22, 1941, appears to be lost because of an error made by the German wartime microfilm operator; perhaps it will yet turn up if another copy of the record survived.

13 The text was first published in *IMT*, 26: 266–67. For a careful review of the basic source, see Ronald Headland, *Messages of Murder: A Study of the Reports of the Einsatzgruppen of the Security Police and the Security Service, 1941–1943*. (Rutherford, N. J.: Fairleigh Dickinson Univ. Press, 1991).

14 Mathias Beer, "Die Entwicklung der Gaswagen beim Mord an den Juden," *VjZ* 35 (1987), 403–17. The initiative came from an inspection of the mass shootings by Himmler; the new device derived its techniques and personnel largely from the Euthanasia program. Rosenberg informed a large audience (the Reichsarbeitskammer) on Nov. 18, 1942, that the killing of all Jews was to be applied to all of Europe (BA, ZSg Nadler, 115/4, f. 99).

15 Wilhelm Deist (ed.), *The German Military in the Age of Total War* (Dover, N.H.: Berg, 1985), p. 297; Seekriegsleitung, "1385/41 Gkdos Chefs. Absichten für die Weiterführung des Krieges nach Beendigung des Ostfeldzuges," 8 Aug. 1941, BA/MA, RM 7/234, f. 106–9; *DRuZW*, 5/1: 567–69.

16 Boog, *Luftwaffenführung*, pp. 112–14.

17 KTB Skl A 23, 17 July 1941, BA/MA, RM 7/26, f. 255; Canaris/Lahousen file, 20 July 1941, Imperial War Museum, AL 1933, item 11; Skl, "Lagebeurteilung 29.7.41," BA/MA, III M 502/4, f. 9–22; *KTB Halder*, 11 Aug. 1941, 3: 170.

18 Warlimont's memorandum of 6 Aug., sent to the navy on 15 Aug., "441339/41 g.K.Ch. Kurzer strategischer Überblick über die Fortführung des Krieges nach dem Ostfeldzug," is a key document (BA/MA, RM 7/258, f. 4–15); see also OKW L, "441465/41 g.K.Ch. Die strategische Lage im Spätsommer 1941 als Grundlage für die weiteren politischen und militärischen Absichten," 27 Aug. 1941 (ibid., f. 19–26). The change also meant that the German navy had to postpone any thought of using the northern seaway around north Russia to the Pacific and Japan (KTB Skl A 24, 18 Aug. 1941, RM 7/27, f. 290).

19 The author has covered the partisan movement in this area in a study, much of it reprinted in John A. Armstrong (ed.), *Soviet Partisans in World War II* (Madison: Univ. of Wisconsin Press, 1964), pp. 389–457. There is a good account of the fighting around Yelnya in Timothy A. Wray, *Standing Fast: German Defensive Doctrine on the Russian Front during World War II, Pre-War to March 1943* (Fort Leavenworth, Kansas: Combat Studies Institute, 1986), pp. 39–47. See also the interesting discussion in Andreas Hillgruber, *Die Zerstörung Europas: Beiträge zur Weltkriegsepoche 1914 bis 1945* (Frankfurt/M: Propyläen, 1988), pp. 296–312, and Samuel J. Lewis, *Forgotten Legions: German Army Infantry Policy, 1918–1945* (New York: Praeger, 1985), pp. 136–44. Very important, Klaus A. F. Schüler's study discussed in the next note, pp. 351–53, 358–62, 380–81; Walther Lammers (ed.), *Fahrtberichte aus der Zeit des deutsch-sowjetischen Krieges 1941* (Boppard: Boldt, 1988), pp. 11–12, 24–25.

20 This point is made absolutely clear by a very fine study of the problems of logistics which rendered any further German major offensive on the central portion of the front impossible and in other ways doomed the German armies to delay and frustration; see Klaus A.F. Schüler, *Logistik im Russlandfeldzug: Die Rolle der Eisenbahn bei Planung,*

Vorbereitung und Durchführung des deutschen Angriffs auf die Sowjetunuion bis zur Krise vor Moskau im Winter 1941/42 (Frankfurt/M: Lang, 1987). See also Martin van Creveld, *Supplying War: Logistics from Wallenstein to Patton* (Cambridge: Cambridge Univ. Press, 1977), chap. 5.

21 A useful summary in Alan F. Wilt, "Hitler's Late Summer Pause in 1941," *Military Affairs* 45 (1981), 187–91. The documents on Hitler's views are published in *KTB OKW*, 1: 1061–81. See also *DRuZW*, 4: 118; von Bock Diary, 13 July 1941, BA/MA, N 22/9, f. 23–24. In the papers of Field Marshal von Weichs in BA/MA there are interesting letters by von Sodenstern of Feb. 9 and Apr. 15, 1951 which point out how very much wiser the Kiev operation was than any attack toward Moscow, which could not be reached in 1941 anyway, and stating that von Rundstedt had been of the same opinion (N 19/13, f. 131–34). *DRuZW*, 4: 651, comes to essentially the same conclusion. Schüler's book, cited in n 20, shows that any operation on the Central front could not have been launched before late Sept., early Oct. in any case.

22 *DRuZW*, 4: 710.

23 The order was repeated on Oct. 7 when the possibility of Leningrad or Moscow actually falling seemed imminent (*ADAP*, D, 13, No. 388). The intention of making the two cities disappear from the earth had been communicated to the German press as early as Aug. 20, 1941; see Kausch, "Vertrauliche Bestellungen," 20 Aug. 1941, BA, Brammer, ZSg. 101/21, f. 162, cf. ibid., f. 232. The earliest reference of Hitler to the concept appears to be the one mentioned in *KTB Halder* on July 8, 1941.

24 Note *DRuZW*, 4: 1013; Schüler, *Logistik in Russlandfeldzug*, pp. 328–31. A useful sidelight in Sergei Varshasky and Boris Rest, *The Ordeal of the Hermitage: The Siege of Leningrad, 1941–1944* (St. Petersburg: Aurora Art, 1985).

25 See *ADAP*, D, 13, Nos. 248, 262.

26 On the British and American pressure on Finland at Soviet request, and on German contrary pressure, see Prime Minister personal minutes 704/1 of 5 July 1941, 725/1 of 10 July, and 731/1 of 16 July to Eden, PRO, PREM 3/170/4; Eden to Cripps No 227 (N 5096/78/G) of 4 Sep. 1941, PREM 3/170/1; Churchill to Mannerheim, 28 Nov. 1941, PREM 3/170/1; *ADAP*, D, 13, 85, 160, 264, 301, 331, 353, 436, 461, 477, 533, 540; Woermann note, "U.St.S. Pol Nr. 741," 4 Aug. 1941, AA, St.S., "England," Bd. 4, fr. 108867; *DRuZW*, 4: 819–20, 850, 854–55; *FDR Letters*, 2: 1207–8; FRUS, 1941, 1: 81–108; Heydrich to Ribbentrop, 27 Oct. 1941, forwarding intercepted information on the conversations of the Finnish Minister in Washington, AA, Inland IIg, "Berichte über Amerika," Bd. 4, fr. E 024612–17; U.S. military attaché Berlin, "Conversation with the Finnish Military Attaché," 10 Sep. 1941, in NA, RG 165, Entry 77, Box 1417, File 6900, Report 18,629 of 15 Sep. 1941, pp. 1–3.

A helpful account in R. Michael Berry, *American Foreign Policy and the Finnish Exception* (Helsinki: Societas Historica Finlandiae, 1987), pp. 121–46, 192–206.

27 Note Helsinki to Tokyo No. 388 of 18 Dec. 1941, NA, RG 457, SRDJ 17978.

28 Schüler, *Logistik in Russlandfeldzug*, pp. 410–13; Boog, *Luftwaffenführung*, p. 116; *ADAP*, D, 13, Nos. 424, 433; "Bestellungen aus der Pressekonferenz vom 9. Oktober 1941," BA, Brammer, ZSg. 101/22, f. 27; "Vertrauliche Informationen Nr. 264/41–266/41," 8–10 Oct. 1941, BA, Oberheitmann, ZSg 109/26, f. 26–37 (for more realistic assessments by 25 Oct., see ZSg 101/22, f. 76, ZSg 109/26, f. 85).

At this time the Germans who assumed that Moscow would be taken passed out the new jobs. Thus Siegfried Kasche, the Minister to the puppet state of Croatia, was to head the Moscow area (AA, Gesandtschaft Sofia, "Persönliche Aufzeichnungen des Gesandten Beckerle," 4 Oct. 1941, Bd. l, f. 69); while one of the city officials of Hamburg, Senator von Allwörden, was happily looking forward to running the economy of the Moscow area all the way across the Urals (Hamburg Forschungsstelle, Krogmann Diary, 1941, 11 k 9, 27 Nov. and 4 Dec. 1941).

29 Erickson, _Road to Stalingrad_, p. 29. On the plans for evacuating the different commissariats, see John A. Armstrong, "The Relocation of the Soviet Commissariats in World War II," in Karl-Heinz Manegold (ed.), _Wissenschaft, Wirtschaft und Technik: Studien zur Geschichte_ (Munich: Bruckmann, 1972), pp. 92–97; a critical piece for understanding the self-perception of Soviet leadership in the face of the possible fall of Moscow.

30 See _ADAP_, D, 13, No. 265; _DRuZW_, 4: 585.

31 See _DRuZW_, 4: 585–92; Earl Ziemke, "Franz Halder at Orsha: The German General Staff Seeks a Consensus," _Military Affairs_ 39 (1975) 173–76; Schüler, _Logistik in Russlandfeldzug_, pp. 468–75; Heinrich Bücheler, _Hoepner: Ein deutsches Soldatenschicksal des 20. Jahrhunderts_ (Herford: Mittler, 1980), pp. 156–57.

32 Two analyses of German army intelligence blunders illustrate the point with numerous examples: Hans-Heinrich Wilhelm, "Die Prognosen der Abteilung Fremde Heere Ost 1942–1945," in _Zwei Legenden aus dem Dritten Reich_ (Stuttgart: Deutsche Verlags-Anstalt, 1974), pp. 7–75; David Thomas, "Foreign Armies East and German Military Intelligence in Russia, 1941–45," _JCH_ 22 (1987), 261–301.

33 The German strength assessment of the Red Army as of Dec. 1, 1941 asserted that it had no substantial reserve units left (_KTB OKW_, 1: 1075–76); on Dec. 4, 1941, German army intelligence concluded that the Red Army was for the time being incapable of launching a major offensive (_DRuZW_, 4: 600).

34 The whole issue of Germany's allies on the Eastern Front has been little studied. A comprehensive work is Peter Gosztony, _Hitlers Fremde Heere: Das Schicksal der nichtdeutschen Armeen im Ostfeldzug_ (Düsseldorf: Econ, 1976). Concentrating on the later period of the war and excluding Finland is Jürgen Förster, _Risse im Bündnis_ (Freiburg: Rombach, 1975). Both books list literature on the individual armies in their bibliographies.

35 An especially useful source on this issue is in the frank comments of former German General Erik Hansen, "Antworten in erweiterter Berichtform auf eine Anfrage des Instituts für Zeitgeschichte-München," 21 Jan. 1956, IfZ, ZS 1130, f. 13–18.

36 See Erickson, _Road to Stalingrad_, pp. 210–11.

37 The area was formally turned over to Romania on Aug. 19, 1941. Although published in 1957, Alexander Dallin's "Odessa 1941–1944: A Case Study of Soviet Territory under Foreign Rule," Rand Memorandum 1875, U.S. Air Force Project Rand Research Memorandum, Astia Document No. AD 123552, is still the most comprehensive work on the subject. There is a survey of the Holocaust in this area in Julius S. Fisher, _Transnistria: The Forgotten Cemetery_ (Cranbury, N.J.: Thomas Yoseleff, 1969).

38 Killinger to Ribbentrop, No. 2882 of 9 Sep. 1941, AA, St.S., "Türkei," Bd. 4, fr. 173230–32.

39 _ADAP_, D, 13, No. 58.

40 Gosztony, _Hitlers Fremde Heere_, pp. 84–85.

41 Ibid., pp. 86–87.

42 For balanced accounts, see ibid., pp. 116–23; Nandor F. Dreisziger, "The Hungarian General Staff and Diplomacy, 1939–1941," _Canadian–American Review of Hungarian Studies_ 7 (1980), 16–21; Juhász, _Hungarian Foreign Policy_ pp. 188–90; and the articles by Dreisziger and Thomas Sakmyster in the special volume on "Hungary and the Second World War," _Hungarian Studies Review_, 10 (1983).

43 Gosztony, pp. 153–62.

44 Canaris/Lahousen file, 2 Sep. 1941, Imperial War Museum, AL 1933, item 15; Juhász, _Hungarian Foreign Policy_, pp. 199–200.

45 Dreisziger, "Hungarian General Staff", p. 23 (see n. 42).

46 Weizsäcker memorandum "St.S. No. 816," 12 Dec. 1941, AA, St.S., "Aufzeichnungen über nicht-Diplomatenbesuche," Bd. 2, fr. 36806–7; Juhász, p. 201; _ADAP_, D, 13: 381–82, E, 2, No. 291.

47 Gosztony, _Hitlers Fremde Heere_, pp. 94–95, 127–30, 173–77.

48 See *Ciano Diary*, 21 and 22 June 1941, pp. 368–69; *ADAP*, D, 13, No. 62. A general review in J. Calvitt Clarke III, "Italy and Barbarossa, June 22 1941," paper given at the American Association for the Advancement of Slavic Studies, Nov. 1991.

49 The account in *Ciano Diary*, 5 July 1941, p. 373, should be supplemented by that in Plessen to AA, "Betr.: Äusserungen des Duce über die Lage," 11 July 1941, AA, Botschaft Rom (Quir.), "Geheim Bd. 45/1a," fr. 481923–24. At the same meeting Mussolini expressed the hope that following the Russian collapse, it would be possible to attack into Egypt via Turkey and Syria. He assumed that the U.S. would enter the war which he expected to be a long one. He did not explain why in view of this expectation he was so eager to send troops to the Eastern Front.

50 Gosztony, *Hitlers Fremde Heere*, pp. 124–27, 162–73.

51 Note the coincidence in time of the beginning of Croatia's involvement on the Eastern Front and the massive terror and expulsion measures of the summer of 1941 within Croatia; Ladislaus Hory and Martin Broszat, *Der kroatische Ustascha-Staat, 1941–1945* (Stuttgart: Deutsche Verlags-Anstalt, 1964), p. 99.

52 *ADAP*, D, 13, No. 46; Gosztony, pp. 131–35, 177–80.

53 Gosztony, pp. 135–37; cf. *ADAP*, D, 13, Nos. 45, 78. An account of the French military collaborators is in Bertram M. Gordon, *Collaborationism in France during the Second World War* (Ithaca, N.Y.: Cornell Univ. Press, 1980), chap. 9.

54 A good account in Gerald R. Kleinfeld and Lewis A. Tambs, *Hitler's Spanish Legion: The Blue Division in Russia* (Carbondale, Ill.: Southern Illinois Univ. Press, 1979). See also Smyth, *British Policy and Franco's Spain*, pp. 229–30; Klaus-Jörg Ruhl, *Spanien im Zweiten Weltkrieg: Franco, die Falange und das "Dritte Reich"* (Hamburg: Hoffman & Campe, 1975), pp. 27–31. On the anthem incident, see *ADAP*, D, 13, No 70 n 2.

55 The heavy losses incurred by the division, and German inability to provide relief for it, put a real strain on German–Spanish relations in the winter of 1941–42 (*ADAP*, E, 1, Nos. 109, 205, 268; 2, No. 62).

56 On the German attempt to obtain Turkish entry into the war with offers of territory at the expense of French Syria, see Önder, *Türkische Aussenpolitik*, pp. 127ff. Greek islands were also dangled in front of Turkish eyes but never in sufficient quantities to move the Ankara government. All the Germans could get was a new non-aggression pact (AA, St.S., "Türkei," Bd. 3, passim).

57 Waley, *Codeword Barbarossa*; note also the references to Stalin's rejection of warnings, cited in Chalmers Johnson, *An Instance of Treason: Ozaki Hotsumi and the Sorge Spy Ring*, expanded edition (Stanford, Calif.: Stanford Univ. Press, 1990), p. 290 n 16.

58 Erickson, *Road to Stalingrad*, chaps. 1 and 2; Jacob W. Kipp, "Barbarossa, Soviet Covering Forces and the Initial Period of War: Military History and Airland Battle" (Fort Leavenworth, Kans.: Soviet Armies Studies Office, 1987); Volkogonov, *Stalin*, chaps. 41–43.

59 Erickson, chap. 3, esp. pp. 132–35.

60 Ibid., p. 225.

61 A preliminary discussion of the evacuation of people (c. 16.5 million including refugees) and of industrial facilities, in Mark Harrison, *Soviet Planning in Peace and War, 1938–1945* (Cambridge: Cambridge Univ. Press, 1985), pp. 63–79.

62 Gordon A. Prange, *Target Tokyo: The Story of the Sorge Spy Ring* (New York: McGraw Hill, 1984); Johnson, *Instance of Treason*.

63 Text in James, *Churchill Speeches*, 6: 6428–31. See also John Colville, *The Fringes of Power: 10 Downing Street Diaries 1939–1955* (New York: Norton, 1985), 21–22 June 1941, pp. 403–6; Gilbert, *Churchill*, 6: chap. 58.

64 See the account of his talk with Soviet Ambassador Maisky in London on June 19, 1941, N 3099/3/38, PRO, FO 371/29466.

65 War Cabinet 59(41) of 12 June 1941, and related documents, in N 3500/3014/38, PRO,

FO 371/29561; War Cabinet 61(41) of 19 June and 62(41) of 23 June 1941, CAB 65/18. RAF documents on plans beginning on 19 June 1941 are in AIR 8/928 and AIR 20/25.

66 Kettenacker, "Alliance," *JCH* 17 (1982), 436–37. Obviously, though, a Soviet victory would reduce Britain's role; see Leeper memorandum of 7 July 1941, N 3718/78/38, PRO, FO 371/29486.

67 Note the letter to the People's Commissar for Foreign Affairs dated 24 June handed to MacFarlane on 25 June 1941, PRO, WO 216/124.

68 Ibid. See also MacFarlane's letter of 1 Aug. 1941 in ibid, and Cadogan's and Eden's comments on the underestimation by the British military in London, in N 77/30/38, PRO, FO 371/32904.

69 Brooke to MacFarlane, 27 Oct. 1941, PRO, WO 216/124.

70 Whitney to Donovan No. 5392 of 12 Nov. 1941, FDRL, PSF, COI Donovan File 1–41.

71 Beaumont, *Comrades in Arms* pp. 32–34; Gilbert, *Churchill*, 6: chap. 61.

72 See the documents in PRO, AIR 8/564, 840, 937, 939; AIR 20/1398; WO 106/5729.

73 Brian Schofield, *The Russian Convoys* (London: Pan, 1984), first published in 1964, remains an excellent account. See now also Simpson, *Admiral Stark*, pp. 143–45.

74 The best account of the supply route is still T. H. Vail Motter, The *Persian Corridor and Aid to Russia* in the U.S. Army in World War II series (Washington: GPO, 1952). As Beaumont, *Comrades in Arms* pp. 82–85, points out, very little use could be made of the route in the first months of the war in the East. A detailed account of the occupation of Iran is in Stewart, *Sunrise at Abadan*, chaps. 4–10.

75 Gilbert, *Churchill*, 6: chaps. 63–64.

76 Murray, *Luftwaffe*, p. 83. On the transfer of Kesselring, see also Schüler, *Logistik im Russlandfeldzug*, p. 475 n 101.

77 Woodward, *British Foreign Policy*, 2: 5–14.

78 The best account currently available is Terry, *Poland's Place in Europe*, pp. 56–65. See also Detlef Brandes, *Grossbritannien und seine osteuropäischen Alliierten 1939–1943* (Munich: Oldenbourg, 1988), pp. 155–61.

79 See Terry, *Poland's Place in Europe*, p. 61 n 40, p. 64 n 47.

80 Ciechanowski to Donovan, 27 Sep. 1941, FDRL, PSF Box 141, Coordinator of Information. See also Richard C. Lucas, *The Strange Allies: The United States and Poland, 1941–1945* (Knoxville: Univ. of Tennessee Press, 1978), pp. 7–14.

81 A basic account remains Raymond Dawson, *The Decision to Aid Russia, 1941: Foreign Policy and Domestic Politics* (Chapel Hill, N.C.: Univ. of North Carolina Press, 1959). More recent accounts are John L. Gaddis, *The United States and the Origins of the Cold War, 1941–1947* (New York: Columbia Univ. Press, 1972), pp. 34–41; Herring, *Aid to Russia*, chap. 1. On Roosevelt's belief from the beginning that the Russians would hold out, see Owen Lattimore and Fujiko Isono, *China Memoirs: Chiang Kai-shek and the War against Japan* (Tokyo: Univ. of Tokyo Press, 1990), pp. 82–83.

82 Memorandum of Hopkins, 25 Nov. 1941, FDRL, PSF Safe File, Cont. 7, Russia. Similar comments by Roosevelt can be found on a 17 Feb. 1942 U.S. Maritime Commission document in PSF Safe File, Cont. 1, ABCD Folder; a 21 Feb. 1942 letter to the Maritime Commission in Lend-Lease PSF Safe File, Cont. 5, Marshall; and Roosevelt's comments to Morgenthau on 11 Mar. 1942 in Morgenthau Presidential Diary, 5: 1075.

83 *ADAP*, D, 13, Nos. 225, 239, E, 1, No. 12; Japanese military attaché Washington to the Vice Chief of the Japanese General Staff in Tokyo No. 179 of 4 Sep. 1941, NA, RG 457, SRA 15810–11.

84 The President's worry about a Japanese attack on the Soviet Union is documented in Roosevelt to Admiral Stark and General Marshall, 4 Mar. 1942, FDRL, PSF Safe File, Box 5, Marshall. On China's retention of Sinkiang, see Garver, *Chinese–Soviet Relations*, chap. 6; Garver also argues (chap. 8) that it was the German–Soviet War which enabled Mao Tse-tung to emancipate the Chinese Communist Party from Moscow.

85 On the Hopkins trip, see George McJimsey, *Harry Hopkins: Ally of the Poor and Defender of Democracy* (Cambridge, Mass.: Harvard Univ. Press, 1987), chap. 12; Erickson, *Road to Stalingrad*, p. 181; John D. Langer, "The Harriman–Beaverbrook Mission and the Debate over Unconditional Aid," in Walter Laqueur (ed.) *The Second World War* (London: Sage, 1982), pp. 300–19.

86 See esp. Beaumont, *Comrades in Arms*, pp. 45–46, 52–66; McJimsey, *Harry Hopkins*, pp. 189–92; Herring, *Aid to Russia*, chap. 2; Hans Knoll, *Jugoslawien in Strategie und Politik der Alliierten 1940–1943* (Munich: Oldenbourg, 1986), pp. 477–88. The article by Langer cited in n 85, above, also stresses the hope of Churchill and Roosevelt for better post-war relations; it is the best summary of the issue on the basis of solid research.

87 Note *ADAP*, E, 1, No. 4.

88 See, e.g., Oshima's reports 377 and 378 on his meeting with Ribbentrop on 17 Mar. 1942, NA, RG 457, SRDJ 20696–98.

89 Ingeborg Fleischhauer, *Die Chance des Sonderfriedens: Deutsch-sowjetische Geheimgespräche 1941–1945* (Berlin: Siedler, 1986). This book is especially useful for its examination of Swedish, American and German records.

90 Beaumont, *Comrades in Arms*, pp. 50–52; Woodward, *British Foreign Policy*, 2: chap. 20; Gilbert, *Churchill*, 6: chap. 62.

91 Hinsley, *British Intelligence*, 2: 58ff; Gilbert, 6: 1209.

92 It would appear that some of the British intelligence gathered from decrypts was passed to the Russians through a special mission in Moscow while some was fed into an espionage network in Switzerland that was nominally working for the Soviet Union.

93 Beaumont, *Comrades in Arms*, pp. 69–71; Heinrichs, *Threshold*, pp. 105–8; Kettenacker, "Alliance," pp. 439–42; Woodward, 2: chaps. 20, 26; Erickson, pp. 293–96; Axel Gietz, *Die neue Alte Welt: Roosevelt, Churchill und die europäische Nachkriegsordnung* (Munich: Fink, 1986), pp. 184–88; Ross, *Foreign Office and Kremlin*, chap. 3.

94 Woodward, 2: 220–21.

95 Note Halifax to Churchill, 11 Jan. 1942, warning that in view of the possibility of a good offer from Hitler to Stalin, Britain could not simply say "No" (PRO, PREM 4/29/9). See also Graham Ross, "Foreign Office Attitudes to the Soviet Union 1941–1945," *JCH* 16 (1981), 523. The key documents are Eden's memorandum "Policy toward Russia," of 8 Feb. 1942, WP⁴² 69 in PRO, CAB 66/21, and his memorandum of 24 Feb. 1942, WP⁴² 96, CAB 66/22.

96 Mason-MacFarlane to Brooke, 22 Dec. 1941 and 8 Jan. 1942, PRO, WO 216/24; Ross, *Foreign Office and Kremlin*, p. 524; Beaumont, *Comrades in Arms*, pp. 100ff; Kettenacker, "Alliance", pp. 442–44; N 7471/3/38, PRO, FO 371/29655. According to a paper by Gabriel Gorodetsky given at the American Association for the Advancement of Slavic Studies in 1991, the Soviet Union attached great importance to the project for a landing at Petsamo.

   At one point in the difficult talks, Churchill evidently thought of going to Moscow himself; see Brooke diary, 5 Mar. 1942, Liddell Hart Centre.

   Hugh Phillips in "Mission to America: Maksim Litvinov in the United States, 1941–1943," *Diplomatic History* 12 (1988), 261–75, claims on the basis of published Soviet documents that at a meeting on Mar. 12, 1942, Roosevelt agreed to the Soviet 1941 border. The assertion is contradicted, not supported, by other evidence and subsequent events.

97 Hinsley, *British Intelligence*, 2: 116–17.

98 Note that of the German air force losses from June 22, 1941 to the end of the year, three-quarters were in the East (*DRuZW*, 4: 699–700). On land the ratio was even higher; only at sea were German losses greater in the West than in the East.

99 See esp. Churchill's growling message to Cripps of Oct. 28, 1941, in Gilbert, *Churchill*,

6: 1227–28, which includes the portions changed in the final text in Woodward, *British Foreign Policy*, 2: 44–45.

100 Louis Morton, *The War in the Pacific, Strategy and Command: The First Two Years* (Washington: GPO, 1962), pp. 156–57; Beaumont, *Comrades in Arms*, chap. 4.

101 The U.S. War Department G-2 appreciation of the situation of 5 Dec. 1941 noted that the Germans appeared to be in considerable trouble in the East but attributed no offensive capability to the Soviet Union (Sherman Miles Memorandum for the Chief of Staff, NA, RG 165, Entry 77, Box 1419).

102 Erickson, *Road to Stalingrad*, pp. 267ff.; Klaus Reinhardt, *Die Wende vor Moskau: Das Scheitern der Strategie Hitlers im Winter 1941/42* (Stuttgart: Deutsche Verlags-Anstalt, 1972 (an excellent study showing that the Germans had been effectively defeated before the winter battles); Schüler, *Logistik im Russlandfeldzug*, pp. 401ff; Ziemke, *Moscow to Stalingrad*, chaps. 4–5. For Soviet perspectives, see Alexander M. Samsonov, *Pages from the History of the AntiFascist War* (Moscow: U.S.S.R. Academy of Sciences, 1978)), pp. 6–55; Michael Parrish (ed.), *Battle for Moscow: The 1942 Soviet General Staff Study* (Washington: Pergamon-Brassey, 1987).

103 *DRuZW*, 4: 620–21; Bücheler, *Hoepner*, pp. 167–72; Walter Chales de Beaulieu, *Generaloberst Erich Hoepner: Militärisches Portrait eines Panzerführers* (Neckargemünd: Vowinckel, 1969), pp. 246–53. On the appalled reaction of another general to the use of scarce trains to ship Jews to be murdered rather than supplies and reinforcements to the front, see Hans Rothfels (ed.), "Ausgewählte Briefe von Generalmajor Helmuth Stieff," *VjZ* 2 (1954), 302–3 (letter of 19 Nov. 1941); cf. Schüler, *Logistik im Russlandfeldzug*, pp. 472–73.

104 The text of Hitler's speech at this last meeting of the Reichstag is in Domarus, *Hitler* 2: 1865–77. The relevant documents on the end of any rule of law in Germany are in BA, R 43 II/958, f. 38–129. For the place of the Hoepner incident in a broader context, see Gerhard L. Weinberg, "The Nazi Revolution: A War against Human Rights," in Moses Rischin and Raphael Asher (eds.), *The Jewish Legacy and the German Conscience* (Berkeley, Calif.: Judah L. Magnes Museum, 1991), pp. 287–96. An interesting British reaction is in the Cabinet Memorandum "Hitler's Speech of April 28, 1942," 30 Apr. 1942, WP(42) 182, PRO, CAB 66/24.

105 The original plan appears to have been to replace Halder by Jodl and the latter by Manstein when the last named had completed the conquest of the Crimea, see the diary of the Chef des Stabes AHA, 19 Dec. 1941, Imperial War Museum, M 114/981/2, f. 2.

106 "Meldungen aus dem Reich (Nr. 248) vom 5. Januar 1942," in Heinz Boberach (ed.), *Meldungen aus dem Reich* (Herrsching: Pawlak, 1984), 9: 3120–22.

107 Note the comment by Konrad Weygold, "Die Nachfolge des Ob.d.H.," Feb. 1956, BA/MA, Nachlass Förste, N 328/53. De Beaulieu, *Erich Hoepner*, pp. 220–42, argues strongly the other way. All plans to reduce Hitler's responsibilities now that he had taken on the daily direction of the army were rejected by him on Jan. 16, 1942; see BA, R 43 II 1958, f. 8–31.

108 Erickson, *Road to Stalingrad*, pp. 277–92, chap. 8; *DRuZW*, 4: 600–50; Ziemke, *Moscow to Stalingrad*, pp. 134–42.

109 Note the lengthy report of 25 Feb. 1942 by the British chargé in Kuibyshev on the recapture of the town of Mozhaisk on 20 Jan. 1942 (N 1585/30/38, PRO, FO 371/32906).

110 An excellent survey in Catherine Andreyev, *Vlasov and the Russian Liberation Movement: Soviet Reality and Emigré Theories* (Cambridge: Cambridge Univ. Press, 1987).

111 On the Cholm and Demyansk air supply operations and their cost to the Germans, see Murray, *Luftwaffe*, pp. 116–17.

112 Ziemke, *Moscow to Stalingrad*, pp. 143–55, 186–98, 254–60.

113 Ibid., pp. 161–85, 249–52.

114 Ibid., pp. 240–49. Much of the author's study of the war and the partisans in this area, Gerhard L. Weinberg, *The Partisan Movement in the Yelnya–Dorogobuzh Area of Smolensk Oblast* (Maxwell AFB, Ala.: HRRI, 1954), has been reprinted in Armstrong, *Partisans*, pp. 385–457.

115 On the Izyum offensive, see Ziemke, *Moscow to Stalingrad*, pp. 156–61; for the destruction of the pocket, see pp. 269–82.

116 Ibid., chap. 6. The naval aspect is examined in Chapter 7, below.

117 There is an excellent account of this, perhaps the most successful German deception operation of World War II, in Earl F. Ziemke, "Operation Kreml: Deception, Strategy, and the Fortunes of War," *Parameters, Journal of the U.S. Army War College* 9, No. 1 (1979), 72–83. The Soviet General Staff study, *Battle for Stalingrad* (Louis C. Rotundo, ed.) (Washington: Pergamon-Brassey, 1989), chap. 2, prepared in 1943, still held to the mistaken belief in Moscow as the primary target.

118 Erickson, *Road to Stalingrad*, pp. 335–42. The British thought that the Russians, like themselves and the Americans, also expected an attack in the south (Hinsley, *British Intelligence*, 2: 96–98).

119 Earl F. Ziemke, *The German Northern Theater of Operations, 1940–1945* (Washington: GPO, 1960), pp. 223–28; Ziemke, *Moscow to Stalingrad*, pp. 226–33.

120 Erickson, *Road to Stalingrad*, pp. 344–47; Ziemke, *Moscow to Stalingrad*, pp. 269–82.

121 *DRuZW*, 4: 698–99.

122 Ibid., pp. 710–11. Some useful information on Udet is in Armand van Ishoven, *The Fall of an Eagle: The Life of Fighter Ace Ernst Udet*, Chaz Bowjer, trans. (London: Kimber, 1979).

123 *DRuZW*, 4: 1023, 5, 1: 629, 1000.

124 Diary of the Chief of Staff, Befehlshaber des Ersatzheeres, 20 Mar. 1942, Imperial War Museum, MI 14/981/3.

125 See *DRuZW*, 4: 1085. See also Hitler's order of Aug. 20, 1941, to push forward with the development of the V-2 which would obviously not be ready for some time (Dieter Hölsken, "Die V-Waffen: Entwicklung und Einsatzgrundsätze," *MGM* 38, No. 2 (1985), 95–122).

126 "Notizen über den Vortrag des Chefs H. Rüst und B d E beim Führer ... am 23.12.1941," 28 Dec. 1941, Imperial War Museum, MI 14/981/2.

127 ADAP, E, 1, Nos. 51, 106.

128 Boog, *Luftwaffenführung*, p. 65. For British knowledge of the shift, see Hinsley, *British Intelligence*, 2: 149ff.

129 Jochmann, *Hitler Monologe*, 26/27 Feb. 1942, p. 300.

130 *DRuZW*, 4: 702–3. On the Luftwaffe's declining effectiveness on the Eastern Front, see Murray, *Luftwaffe*, pp. 91–103, 115–17.

131 ADAP, E, 1, Nos. 14, 54, 71, 91, 92, 98, 130; *KTB Halder*, 3: 361 (20 Dec. 1941); Rintelen and Mackensen to Ribbentrop No. 3140 of 2 Dec. 1941, AA, St.S., "Italien," Bd. 7, fr. 331841–42. Some German troops were, in addition, withdrawn from the Balkans and replaced by Italian and Bulgarian units (Gosztony, *Hitlers Fremde Heere*, pp. 195–207; Jürgen Förster, *Stalingrad* [Freiburg: Rombach, 1975], pp. 13–23).

132 *ADAP*, E, 2, No. 7. For early examples of armed formations of Russian soldiers fighting alongside the Germans, see Weinberg, *Yelnya-Dorogobuzh*, pp. 103–9 (reprinted in Armstrong, *Partisans*, pp. 440–43); Alexander Dallin, "The Kaminsky Brigade, 1941–1944" (Harvard Univ. Project on the Soviet Social System, 1952), pp. 1–26. Hitler did approve of a unit of Crimean Tatars (*ADAP*, E, 2, No. 132).

133 Hitler–Oshima meeting of Dec. 13, 1941: German record in *ADAP*, E, 1, No. 12, Japanese record in Oshima No. 1471, NA, RG 457, SRDJ 17775–76; Hitler–Ribbentrop–Oshima meetings of Jan. 2–3, 1942: German record in *ADAP*, E, 1, Nos. 84, 87, Puttkamer, "Niederschrift über Äusserungen des Führers vom 4.1.42," BA/MA, RM

6/75, f. 225–26, Japanese record in Oshima No. 17, SRDJ 18661–64; Oshima–Ribbentrop meeting of Mar. 17, 1942: German record in *ADAP*, E, 2, No. 48, Japanese report in Oshima Nos. 377–78, SRDJ 20696–98. For Oshima's perceptive report on the Eastern Front of 18 Jan. 1942, see his No. 80 in SRDJ 19000–5.

134 On American anticipation of a German attack toward Stalingrad and the Caucasus, see FDR to Combined Chiefs of Staff, 24 Feb. 1942, FDRL, PSF Box 80, Navy 1942; U.S. military attaché Moscow Report 2036, "Analysis of the German Failure in 1941 and An Estimate on Future Events," 10 Mar. 1942, NA, RG 165, Entry 77, Box 1418, 6900–Germany.

135 The best account is in Streit, *Keine Kameraden*, chaps. 6–7. Streit has summarized and updated this account in Gerd R. Ueberschär and Wolfram Wette (eds.), *"Unternehmen Barbarossa" Der deutsche Überfall auf die Sowjetunion 1941* (Paderborn: Schöningh, 1984), pp. 197–218. The German general in Croatia had a fairly clear understanding of the mass murder of POWs and Jews by Aug. 27, 1941 (Broucek, *Ein General im Zwielicht*, 3: 127).

136 Note Fröhlich, *Goebbels Tagebücher*, 20 June 1941, 4: 705.

137 The details may be followed in Breitman, *Architect of Genocide*, chaps. 7–9.

138 Jochmann, *Hitler Monologe*, p. 99, also 25 Oct. 1941, p. 106; Krogmann Diary, 21 Oct. 1941, Hamburg Forschungsstelle, 11 k 9.

139 The record of this notorious conference has been published repeatedly; the surviving one of the thirty original copies is the one from the German Foreign Ministry, *ADAP*, E, 1, No. 150; see also Döscher, *Auswärtige Amt im Dritten Reich*, pp. 221–37. Those who still believe in Hitler's desire for good relations with England have not considered the implications of the inclusion of that country's Jews in the murder program.

140 Note that at a meeting of representatives of the press on Nov. 15, 1941, it was explained that the term "Sonderbehandlung" (special treatment) meant shooting or liquidating ("Bestellungen aus der Pressekonferenz vom 15. November mittags," BA, Brammer, ZSg 101/22, f. 141). Any who failed to understand were personally briefed by Rosenberg who spoke to the press on Nov. 19 to explain that six million Jews in Russia and all of Europe were to be killed (Dr. Kausch, "Streng vertraulicher Informationsbericht," ZSg. 101/41, f. 347–51).

141 Döscher, *Auswärtige Amt im Dritten Reich*, pp. 246–48.

142 Ibid., pp. 238ff. For contemporary German reactions, see Ernst Klee et al. (eds.), *"Schöne Zeiten": Judenmord aus der Sicht der Täter und Gaffer* (Frankfurt/M: Fischer, 1988).

143 *ADAP*, E, 1, No. 227, No. 104 n 4.

144 Ibid., D, 13, No. 516.

145 See Christopher R. Browning, "Wehrmacht Reprisal Policy and the Mass Murder of Jews in Serbia," *MGM* 1/83 (1983), 31–47. This piece has been reprinted in Browning's *Fateful Months: Essays on the Emergence of the Final Solution* (rev. ed., New York: Holmes & Meier, 1991), chap. 2.

146 Quotations from the directives of Reichenau, Manstein, and Hoth are in Streit, *Keine Kameraden*, pp. 115–17. The quotation in the text is from Reichenau's. See also Krausnick and Wilhelm, *Truppe des Weltanschauungskrieges*, pp. 258–61; Jehuda W. Wallach, "Feldmarschall Erich von Manstein und die Judenausrottung in Russland," *Jahrbuch des Instituts für Deutsche Geschichte* (Tel Aviv), 4 (1975), 457–72; Omer Bartov, *Hitler's Army: Soldiers, Nazis and War in the Third Reich* (New York: Oxford Univ. Press, 1991), chap. 3.

147 The main works on the subject are Walter Laqueur, *The Terrible Secret* (New York: Penguin Books, 1981); and Walter Laqueur and Richard Breitman, *Breaking the Silence* (New York: Simon & Schuster, 1986).

148 Hinsley, *British Intelligence*, 2: 671, 673. Since there are no file references for these statements, the records themselves are scheduled to be kept secret permanently (ibid., p. x).

149 On the Vatican and the killing of Jews at this time, see Chadwick, *Britain and the Vatican*, chap. 9.

150 Donald Hendrick and Grattan Puxon, *The Destiny of Europe's Gypsies* (New York: Basic Books, 1972), chap. 7; Joachim S. Hohmann, *Zigeuner und Zigeunerwissenschaft: Ein Beitrag zur Grundlagenforschung und Dokumentation des Völkermordes im "Dritten Reich"* (Marburg/Lahn: Guttardin & Hoppe, 1980).

151 An analysis of the systematic killing of the inmates of mental institutions and old folks' homes in the Eastern occupied areas remains to be written. The topic is touched on in Krausnick and Wilhelm, *Truppe des Weltanschauungskrieges*. A good introduction in Angelika Ebbinghaus and Gerd Preissler (eds.), "Die Ermordung psychisch kranker Menschen in der Sowjetunion, Dokumentation," in Götz Aly et al., *Aussonderung und Tod: Die klinische Hinrichtung der Unbrauchbaren* (Berlin: Rotbuch Verlag, 1987).

152 The relevant section of Alexander Dallin's fine study, *German Rule in Russia*, pp. 310–19, is appropriately entitled: "The Geopolitics of Starvation."

153 On these issues, see Michael Kater, *Doctors under Hitler* (Chapel Hill, N.C.: Univ. of North Carolina Press, 1990). The experiments with new techniques were included in the pioneering work, Alexander Mitscherlich and Fred Mielke, *Das Diktat der Menschenverachtung* (Heidelberg: Lambert Schneider, 1947), pp. 149–62.

154 This is not contradicted by the fact that some individuals argued for the sterilization instead of the murder of all Jews; see the July 8, 1941 entry in *Leeb KTB*, p. 288.

155 A detailed account in Dallin, *German Rule in Russia*, chap. 14.

156 Relevant documents are in BA, Reichskommissar für die Festigung deutschen Volkstums, and in Reichskanzlei, R 43 II, 985, 985a–c, 986, 1092, 1092a–b, 1087a, 1565, 1620–22. Some of the generals used their money to purchase land inside pre-war Germany. The appearance of my piece, "Zur Dotation Hitlers an Generalfeldmarschall Ritter von Leeb," *MGM* No. 2, (1979) pp. 97–99, led the German magazine *Stern* to publish a summary of the bribery program by Peter Meroth, "Vorschuss auf den Endsieg," 12 June 1980, pp. 86–92. There is a brief reference in Helmut Heiber (ed.), *Hitlers Lagebesprechungen: Protokollfragmente seiner militärischen Konferenzen 1942–1945* (Stuttgart: Deutsche Verlags-Anstalt, 1962), p. 618 n 4.

157 Maurice Matloff and Edwin M. Snell, *Strategic Planning for Coalition Warfare 1941–1942* (Washington: GPO, 1953), pp. 98–111; J. M. A. Gwyer, *Grand Strategy*, Vol. 3, Pt. 1 (London: HMSO, 1964), chaps. 14–15; Gilbert, *Churchill*, 7: chaps. 1–2; Mark A. Stoler, *The Politics of the Second Front* (Westport, Conn.: Greenwood Press, 1977), pp. 22–26; Knoll, *Jugoslawien in Strategie*, pp. 245–50; Krautkrämer, "Vorgeschichte," p. 225; Dallek, *Roosevelt and Foreign Policy*, pp. 321–22; Pogue, *Marshall*, 2: chap. 12.

158 An excellent account in Alexander Danchev, *Very Special Relationship: Field Marshal Sir John Dill and the Anglo-American Alliance 1941–44* (London: Brassey's, 1986), pp. 10–25.

159 Forrest C. Pogue, *George C. Marshall, 3: Organizer of Victory, 1943–1945* (New York: Viking Press, 1973), pp. 481–83.

160 See JIC[42] 377 (o) Final, War Cabinet, Joint Intelligence Sub-Committee, "Communications between the Far East and German Europe," 3 Oct. 1942, p. 5, PRO, PREM 3/74/3.

161 Berlin to Tokyo No. 1765 of 9 Oct. 1941, AA, St.S., "Japan," Bd. 5, fr. 60685–86; BA/MA, PG 48808.

162 *ADAP*, D, 13, No. 216; Theo Michaux, "Rohstoffe aus Ostasien: Die Fahrten der Blockadebrecher," *Wehrwissenschaftliche Rundschau* 5 (1955), 487–94; "Blockade Running between Europe and the Far East by Submarine," SRH 019, NA, RG 457; U.S. War Dept., G-2, "'Magic'–Far East Summary No. 256," 1 Dec. 1944, SRS 256, NA, RG 457.

163 *ADAP*, E, 1, Nos. 251, 270; KTB Skl A 30, 17 and 22 Feb. 1942, BA/MA, RM 7/33, f. 443, 511; Skl Chefs., 21 Mar. 1942, RM 7/253, f. 226–29; Oshima's reports 377 and

378, 17 Mar. 1942, NA, RG 457, SRDJ 20696–98; Salewski, *Deutsche Seekriegslaitung*, 2: 72ff.

164 Oshima No. 1508 of 23 Dec. 1941, NA, RG 457, SRDJ 18113.

165 Jochmann, *Hitler Monologe*, 17/18 Sep. 1941, p. 64. The statement of Hitler on 27 Nov. 1941 to Danish Foreign Minister Erik Scavenius that, if the German people were ever no longer sufficiently strong and willing to make sacrifices to shed their own blood for its existence, it would deserve to be crushed and to vanish (which is sometimes cited as a first recognition of coming defeat), is in fact nothing of the sort. The context is one of dealing with the fighting by others on the Eastern Front; the Czechs being the people just mentioned. The Germans, Hitler argued, would and should do their own fighting (*ADAP*, D, 13, No. 510).

166 Ribbentrop to Papen No. 1429 of 26 Sep. 1941, AA, St.S., "Türkei," Bd. 4, fr. 173278–80; cf. Ribbentrop to Schwerin-Krosigk, 30 Aug. 1941, BA, R 2/24243. No technical conclusions were, however, drawn from these prospects of a war lasting many years (note *DRuZW*, 4: 710).

6: HALTING THE JAPANESE ADVANCE, HALTING THE GERMAN ADVANCE

1 After almost 40 years, the best account remains Louis Morton, *The Fall of the Philippines* (Washington: GPO, 1953) in the U.S. Army in World War II series. I had the benefit of discussing the problems of writing that work in the absence of much important evidence with its late author. See also Paul S. Dull, *A Battle History of the Imperial Japanese Navy (1941–1945)* (Annapolis, Md.: Naval Institute Press, 1978), chap. 2.

2 A good account in James Leutze, *A Different Kind of Victory: A Biography of Admiral Thomas C. Hart* (Annapolis, Md.: Naval Institute Press, 1981), chap. 9.

3 Carol M. Petillo, "Douglas MacArthur and Manuel Quezon: A Note on an Imperial Bond," *Pacific Historical Review* 48 (1979), 107–17.

4 The best account of this terrible episode is Stanley L. Falk, *Bataan: The March of Death*, originally published in 1977 (New York: Jove Books, 1983). There is also a good discussion of the fighting in Willmott, *Empires*, chap. 13.

5 S. Woodburn Kirby, *The War against Japan*, Vol. 1 (London: HMSO, 1971 [1953]), chaps. 8–9.

6 Dull, *Imperial Japanese Navy*, chap. 3; Willmott, *Empires*, pp. 161–72; Kreis, *Air Base Defense*, pp. 94–111, 133–35; Louis Allen, *Singapore 1941–1942* (London: Davis-Poynter, 1977).

7 Arthur J. Marder, *Old Friends, New Enemies: The Royal Navy and the Imperial Japanese Navy* (Oxford: Clarendon, 1981), pp. 213–31, on the origins of "Force Z" and Vol. 3 on its fate.

8 Willmott, pp. 178ff; Long, *Six Years' War*, pp. 124ff.

9 Note Willmott, pp. 186–90.

10 Ibid., chaps. 8, 11.

11 It should be noted that for the first two days the Japanese landed only infantry on Singapore island; the greatly feared tanks came thereafter. See the British study of March 1945, "The Japanese Attack on Singapore Island – February 1942," pp. 3–4, PRO, WO106/2623.

12 For a report countering the allegation that it was the Indian troops who let everybody down, see PRO, WO 106/2590. On individual escapes from the disaster, see Joseph Kennedy, *When Singapore Fell: Evacuation and Escapes, 1941–42* (New York: St. Martin's, 1989).

13 Wavell to Brooke, 17 Feb. 1942, PRO, WO 106/2609A; this is the letter quoted in Kirby,

War Against Japan, p. 468. See also Wavell to Brooke No. 1200 of 8 Apr. 1942, Liddell Hart Centre, Alanbrooke Papers, 14/60.

14 See PRO, WO 106/2609A, 2812.

15 Relevant documents are in PRO, WO 106/3317.

16 See, e.g., *ADAP*, E, 1, No. 225; Tokyo No. 124 to Berlin of 15 Feb. 1942, NA, RG 457, SRDJ 19854; Oshima's No. 241 of 18 Feb. 1942, SRDJ 19876; KTB Skl A 28, 21 Dec. 1941, BA/MA, RM 7/31, f. 322. See also Woodward, *British Foreign Policy*, 4: 42–45. It should be noted that only on Timor did Allied (Australian) forces continue with guerilla warfare for a year before being evacuated.

17 Note Roosevelt's concern in *FDR Letters*, 2: 1281.

18 Leutze, *Different Kind of Victory*, chap. 10; Dull, *Imperial Japanese Navy*, chap. 4; John Costello, *The Pacific War* (New York: Quill, 1982), pp. 204–10; Marder et al., *Old Friends, New Enemies*, Vol. 2, *The Pacific War, 1942–1945* (Oxford: Clarendon, 1990), chaps. 2–3.

19 Willmott, *Empires*, chap. 12.

20 A good account of the campaign in ibid., chap. 4.

21 See Peggy Warner, *The Coffin Boats: Japanese Midget Submarine Operations in the Second World War* (London: Leo Cooper, 1986), chap. 9.

22 Charles F. Romanus and Riley Sunderland, *Stilwell's Mission to China* (Washington: GPO, 1953), pp. 63–74. See also Barbara Tuchman, *Stilwell and the American Experience in China, 1911–1945* (New York: Bantam, 1972), pp. 308–14; Pogue, *Marshall*, 2: 355–61.

23 For Java, see Joyce C. Lebra, *Japanese-Trained Armies in Southeast Asia: Independence and Volunteer Forces in World War II* (New York: Columbia Univ. Press, 1977), 78–83; for Sumatra, see ibid., pp. 126–27, 156–57; cf. Willmott, *Empires*, pp. 363–65.

24 See Nigel J. Brailey, *Thailand and the Fall of Singapore: A Frustrated Asian Revolution* (Boulder, Col.: Westview Press, 1986).

25 See Japanese Consul General New York to Tokyo No. 507 of 22 Nov. 1941, NA, RG 457, SRDJ 23540; U Saw's message of 31 Dec. 1941 is in Oshima to Tokyo No. 32 of 7 Jan. 1942, SRDJ 18768–73; see also Oshima No. 31 of 8 Jan. 1942, SRDJ 19511–12, 19523–34; Oshima No. 33 of 8 Jan. 1942, SRDJ 19533–34; Tokyo to Oshima No. 30 of 19 Jan. 1942, SRDJ 19016–17; and the documents filed under F 1740/662/61 in PRO, FO 371/31776. On the Burmese Independence Army formed and then dissolved by the Japanese, see Lebra, *Japanese-Trained Armies*, pp. 64–65.

26 An excellent account is still Yale Candee Maxon, *Control of Japanese Foreign Policy: A Study of Civil–Military Relations 1930–1945* (Berkeley: Univ. of California Press, 1957).

27 For material on the leisurely British plans for a scorched earth policy in Fiji, see the documents in PRO, WO 106/2605.

28 See Willmott, *Empires*, chap. 15; H.P. Willmott, *The Barrier and the Javelin: Japanese and Allied Pacific Strategies, February to June 1942* (Annapolis, Md.: Naval Institute Press, 1983), chaps. 1–2; Stephan, *Hawaii under the Rising Sun*, chaps. 6–7.

29 On these issues, see Johannes H. Voigt, *Indien im Zweiten Weltkrieg* (Stuttgart: Deutsche Verlags-Anstalt, 1978), and Milan Hauner, *India in Axis Strategy* (Stuttgart: Klett-Cotta, 1981).

30 See the piece on the years 1936–40 in C.H. Philips and Mary D. Wainright (eds.), *The Partition of India: Policies and Perspectives 1935–1947* (London: Allen & Unwin, 1970), pp. 79–94. Interesting in spite of the absence of documentation is the book on Lord Linlithgow based on his papers amd written by his son, John Glendevon, *The Viceroy at Bay* (London: Collins, 1970). Very helpful is Robin J. Moore, *Churchill, Cripps, and India, 1939–1945* (Oxford: Oxford Univ. Press, 1979). Kenton J. Clymer, "Franklin D. Roosevelt, Louis Johnson, India and Anticolonialism: Another Look," *Pacific Historical Review* 57 (1988), 261–84, shows that the American government backed off from pushing

for concessions to the Indian nationalist movement only when Churchill threatened to resign.

31 It is worth noting the views of the generally rather pro-Japanese Sir Robert Craigie, "India and the 'Co-Prosperity' Sphere," 14 Oct. 1942, F 7103/845/23, PRO, FO 371/31833. See also Lebra, *Japanese-Trained Armies*, pp. 23–25; Tokyo to Rome No. 349 of 31 Dec. 1941, NA, RG 457, SRDJ 18418–19.

32 In addition to Voigt and Hauner, cited in n. 29 above, see Leonard A. Gordon, *Brothers against the Raj: A Biography of Indian Nationalists Sarat and Subhas Chandra Bose* (London: Columbia Univ. Press, 1990), pp. 456–60, 486, 524; Oshima No. 243 of 19 Feb. 1942, NA, RG 457, SRDJ 19915–16; Oshima No. 17 of 4 Jan. 1942, SRDJ 18661–64; Rome to Tokyo Nos. 813 and 814 of 16 Dec. 1941, SRDJ 17796–98; Rome No. 833 of 20 Dec. 1941, SRDJ 17989–90; Rome No. 840 of 26 Dec. 1941, SRDJ 18227; Berlin to Tokyo No. 1492 of 19 Dec. 1941, SRDJ 18306; Tokyo to Berlin No. 158 of 27 Feb. 1942, SRDJ 20171; Japanese military attaché Berlin No. 3469 of 29 Jan. 1942, SRA 17360–62; Japanese military attaché Rome No. 585 of 12 Feb. 1942, SRA 16216; U.S. National Archives, *Guides to Microfilmed Records of the German Navy*, No. 2, p. 60.

On Bose in early 1942, see German press directives of 28 Feb., 11 and 27 Mar. 1942, BA, Brammer ZSg. 101/23, f. 88, 107, 134; Oshima No. 574 of 3 May 1942, SRDJ 22299–300; Japanese military attaché Rome No. 453 of 4 May 1942, SRA 16982; Rome No. 352 of 21 May 1942, SRDJ 22866; Oshima No. 715 of 4 June 1942, SRDJ 23353; Oshima No. 845 of 4 July 1942, SRDJ 24456–59; *ADAP*, E, 3, No. 198.

When Bose saw von Ribbentrop in October 1942, he expressed a wish for German help in training the Indian police; here was evidently a subject on which he thought the Germans had something to teach his people (*ADAP*, E, 4, No. 50). Bose left Germany on 9 Feb. 1943 on U-180 and reached Tokyo on 21 May; Martin Brice, *Axis Blockade Runners of World War II* (Annapolis, Md.: Naval Institute Press, 1981), p. 130; "Vertrauliche Informationen Nr. 148 (1. Ergänzung)," 18 June 1943, BA, Oberheitmann ZSg. 109/43, f. 30–32. The Allies followed his travels by reading the relevant Japanese telegrams; these may be found in NA, RG 457, SRDJ 30414, 30444, 31314, 35584, 35682, 36621.

33 Francis G. Hutchins, *India's Revolution: Gandhi and the Quit India Movement* (Cambridge, Mass.: Harvard Univ. Press, 1973), stresses the long-term political and psychological impact of the upheaval.

34 Note Auchinleck to Brooke, 3 May 1942, pointing out that six of his fourteen divisions in the Middle East were from India (Liddell Hart Centre, Alanbrooke Papers, 6/D/4 (e), Item M).

35 On the sortie into the Indian Ocean, see Willmott, *Empires*, pp. 441–46; Dull, *Imperial Japanese Navy*, chap. 7; Marder, *Old Friends, New Enemies*, 2: chaps. 4–6; "Notes on the Military Situation in Ceylon," 17 Mar. 1942, Pownall Diary, March 1942–Sep. 1943, Liddell Hart Centre.

36 Oshima's Nos. 377–378 of 17 Mar. 1942, NA, RG 457, SRDJ 20696–98; KTB Skl A 28, 22 Dec. 1941, BA/MA, RM/31, f. 242; Wenneker and Ott No. 487 of 19 Feb. 1942, Ott No. 500 of 20 Feb. 1942, and Berlin reply No. 579 of 27 Feb. 1942, AA, St.S., "Japan," Bd. 6, fr. 39694–96, 39726–28; *ADAP*, E, 2, Nos. 48 (the Japanese report on this was passed by the U.S. to Britain with Roosevelt's request that it be shown to Churchill; Hinsley, *British Intelligence*, 2: 85n), 178, 195.

37 See Brooke Diary, 10 Dec. 1941, Liddell Hart Centre; De Gaulle to Churchill, 16 Dec. 1941, PRO, PREM 3/265/1 and other documents in this file.

38 Brooke Diary, 18 Dec. 1941, Liddell Hart Centre; Churchill minute on Eden to Churchill, PM 42/46 of 5 Mar. 1942, and Personal Minute D.68/2, 30 Mar. 1942, PRO, PREM 3/265/1. Eventually the area was turned over to de Gaulle; see the documents in FO 371/31898, 31900.

39 Churchill to Smuts, 18 Feb. 1942, Z 1480/23/17, PRO, FO 371/31897; Churchill to Smuts No 488 of 24 Mar. 1942, PRO, PREM 3/265/2; Balfour to Sinclair, 24 and 28 Feb. 1942, PRO, AIR 20/2828. On the internal situation in South Africa, see the documents in PRO, WO 106/4932. On U.S. pressure to move, see Dill to COS, JSM 66 of 24 Feb. 1942, PRO, PREM 3/265/2; Samuel E. Morison, *History of United States Naval Operations in World War II*, 15 vols. (Boston: Little Brown, 1947–62), 1: 167–68.

40 Brooke Diary, 12, 13, 18 Mar. 1942, Liddell Hart Centre; Admiralty to Foreign Office No. 1641 of 19 Mar. 1942, PRO, PREM 3/265/2; Thomas, *Britain and Vichy*, pp. 184–85; Simpson, *Admiral Stark*, p. 150; Stephen W. Roskill, *The War at Sea, 1939–1945*, 3 vols in 4 parts (London: HMSO, 1954–61), 2: 185–92; Marder, *Old Friends, New Enemies*, 2: 155–61; documents in PRO, AIR 20/4498, WO 174/1–2. Cf. *ADAP*, E, 4, No. 113.

41 Robert O. Paxton, *Vichy France: Old Guard and New Order, 1940–1944* (New York: Columbia Univ. Press, 1982), p. 313 n 43; see also COS to all British C-in-C's in Africa, OZ 138 of 4 May 1942, Alanbrooke Papers, 6/D/4(e), Item K, Liddell Hart Centre.

42 Peggy Warner, *Coffin Boats*, pp. 146–49; Wilfred J. Holmes, *Undersea Victory*, (Garden City, N.Y.: Doubleday, 1966), p.131.

43 Stephan, *Hawaii under the Rising Sun*, pp. 92–94.

44 The full text of the Dec. 1941 memorandum is printed in Storry, *Double Patriots*, pp. 317–19.

45 Stephan, pp. 103–5.

46 Holmes, *Undersea Victory*, p. 96. In June other submarines shelled the Oregon coast and Vancouver island.

47 On the Japanese deliberations, see Stephan, *Hawaii under the Rising Sun*, pp. 106–13; Toshikazu Ohmae, "Die strategischen Konzeptionen der japanischen Marine im Zweiten Weltkrieg," *Marine-Rundschau* 53 (1956), p. 194; Willmott, *Empires*, chap. 15; Willmott, *Barrier*, chaps. 1–2. The text of the official policy adopted at the Liaison Conference of 13 Mar. 1942, is in Morton, *Strategy*, pp. 611–13.

48 Ibid., p. 143.

49 Alfred D. Chandler, et al. (eds.), *The Papers of Dwight D. Eisenhower: The War Years*, 5 vols. (Baltimore: Johns Hopkins Press, 1970), 1: No. 1.

50 Matloff and Snell, *Strategic Planning, 1941–1942* pp. 148–50; Morton, *Strategy*, pp. 208–10.

51 *ADAP*, E, 2, No. 72. Vichy enthusiasm for the Japanese remains to be investigated.

52 Morton, *Strategy*, p. 203.

53 A useful survey in Mark Clayton, "The North Australian Air War, 1942–44," *Journal of the Australian War Memorial* 8 (1986), 33–45.

54 Roosevelt to Admiral Land and enclosure, 21 Feb. 1942, FDRL, PSF Box 5, Marshall.

55 Dallek, *Roosevelt and Foreign Policy*, pp. 336–37.

56 Willmott, *Barrier*, pp. 56–63.

57 See also Hopkins to Roosevelt, 14 Mar. 1942, FDRL, PSF Box 152, Hopkins.

58 On the internment in the Soviet Union and Japanese concern about this issue, see Tokyo to Kuibyshev No. 267 of 1 May 1942, NA, RG 457, SRDJ 26975; Tokyo circular No. 775 to Harbin and Hsinking, 2 May 1942, SRDJ 22644–46.

59 On the Doolittle raid and its impact, see Willmott, *Empires*, pp. 447–50; Butow, *Tojo*, pp. 516–17; Stephan, *Hawaii under the Rising Sun*, pp. 113–17; Morton, *Strategy*, p. 217; Toshikazu Ohmae, "Strategische Konzeptionen," p. 195; Alvin D. Coox, "The Rise and Fall of the Imperial Japanese Air Forces," *Aerospace Historian*, (June 1980), p. 83; Donald M. Goldstein and Katherine V. Dillon (eds.), *Fading Victory: The Diary of Admiral Matome Ugaki, 1941–1945*, trans. by Masataka Chihaya (Pittsburgh: Univ of Pittsburgh Press, 1991) (henceforth cited as *Ugaki Diary*), 18–21 Apr. 1942, pp. 111–15. See also the assessment of a shrewd German observer, Dr. Hans Kolb of the German Foreign Ministry, "Aufzeichnung über japanische Kriegsausweitung," 28 Apr. 1942, AA, St.S.,

"Diplomatische Aufzeichnungen Betr. Japan, Apr. 42–Apr. 43," fr. J 000146–48.

60　For a very useful account, see NA, RG 457, SRH–230. The Japanese were also afflicted by over-confidence in their code security: the April attack on Ceylon was called Operation C, that on Port Moresby, Operation MO, that on the Aleutians, Operation AL, that on Midway, Operation MI. The U.S. Office of Chief of Naval Operations, "Secret Supplement Summary of Japanese Naval Activities" of 27 May 1942 noted that the Japanese 14th Air Group not only planned to be based on Midway but wanted its mail forwarded there! (NA, RG 457, SRNS–44).

61　See esp. Costello, *Pacific War*, chap. 14. There is an ironic aspect to the suggestion of the German navy that the way to help the Japanese assure long-term code security was to send them German enigma machines, OKM, Skl B, Chef MND, "1557/42gKdos., Deutsch-japanische Schlüsselmittel," 2 Apr. 1942, BA/MA, RM 7/253, f. 265–67.

62　The subject is reviewed in Kahn, *Codebreakers*, chap. 17; Lewin, *American Magic*, chap. 4.

63　Merrill Bartlett and Robert W. Love, "Anglo-American Naval Diplomacy and the British Pacific Fleet, 1942–1945," *American Neptune* 42 (1982), 205–7; Willmott, *Barrier*, pp. 331–35; Costello, *Pacific War*, pp. 373–74. Marshall still hoped for one or two British carriers in June, see Pogue, *Marshall*, 2: 379.

64　On the Coral Sea battle, see Willmott, *Barrier*, chaps. 6–8, with clear text and maps. Cf. *Ugaki Diary*, 7–9 May 1942, pp. 121–25.

65　KTB Skl A 33, 9, 12, 27 May 1942, BA/MA, RM 7/36, f. 181–82, 242–43, 521; *ADAP*, E, 2, Nos. 195, 212. The Germans naturally thought that the victory they believed Japan had won would enable the latter to drive the British out of Madagascar where they had just landed, but by June 11 the Germans had figured out what had actually happened (KTB Skl A 34, RM 7/37, f. 218).

66　The carrier was sunk by an American submarine in June 1944.

67　The fullest account of these matters is in Willmott, *Barrier*, chap. 3.

68　On the Alaska–Aleutian fighting, see Brian Garfield, *The Thousand-Mile War: World War II in Alaska and the Aleutians* (Garden City, N.Y.: Doubleday, 1969). No theater of war had worse weather or more fierce inter-service clashes. Note Roosevelt's concern about defense preparations there in his memorandum for Captain McRae of 20 Jan. 1942, FDRL, PSF Safe File, Cont. 1, Alaska.

69　An excellent account in Willmott, *Barrier*, chaps. 6–16. See also Costello, *Pacific War*, chaps. 15–16; Dull, *Imperial Japanese Navy*, chaps. 9–11; *Ugaki Diary*, 18 May–15 June 1942, pp. 127–64; Toshikazu Ohmae, "Strategische Konzeptionen," pp. 195–96; Carl Boyd, "American Naval Intelligence of Japanese Submarine Operations Early in the Pacific War," *Journal of Military History* 53 (1989), 169–89. Ugaki wrote in his diary (5 June, p. 152): "Don't let another day like this come to us during the course of the war!"

70　The table in Willmott, *Barrier*, p. 522, does not include the U.S. commissionings of 1945. Of course, the U.S. navy was also engaged in the Atlantic, but then it turned over an additional 37 carriers to the British (see Ernest J. King, *U.S. Navy at War 1941–1945: Official Reports to the Secretary of the Navy* [Washington: GPO, 1946], pp. 253–57).

71　Note *Kido Diary*, 8 June 1942, pp. 335–36. This would be June 7 at Midway.

72　See Skl KTB A 34, 29 June 1942, BA/MA, RM 7/37, f. 548–49; Wenneker No. 110 of 10 June 1942, NA, RG 457, SRGL 101; Skl to Tokyo No. 32 of 15 June 1942, SRGL 19; Kretschmer and Ott No. 1768 of 11 June 1942, AA, St.S. "Japan," Bd. 7, fr. E 362179; Salewski, *Seekriegsleitung*, 2: 104. The Germans refused the sale. Unfortunately we have no indication of what the American cryptographers thought of the idea of hauling an uncompleted German aircraft carrier from European waters to the Pacific.

73　Morton, *Strategy*, pp. 284–85.

74　Stephan, *Hawaii under the Rising Sun*, p. 120.

75　On May 10, 1942, a German raider seized an Australian ship with a document among the mail it was carrying that showed some Allied decyphering of Japanese naval messages, and this information was passed on to the Japanese at the end of August 1942; John W.M. Chapman, "German Signals Intelligence and the Pacific War," *Proceedings of the British Association for Japanese Studies (History and International Relations)* 4 (1979), 140–41. See also ibid., p. 144; KTB Skl A 36, 17, 31 Aug. 1942, BA/MA, RM 7/39, f. 326–27, 622; A 37, 3 Sep. 1942, RM 7/40, f. 40.

76 The chapter on this in Lewin, *American Magic*, is entitled: "The Stab in the Back."

77 The only warships hit by the land-based bombers were the two heavy cruisers which had collided.

78 Willmott, *Barrier*, p. 521.

79 Morton, *Strategy*, pp. 289–94.

80 Pogue, *Marshall*, 2: 325–26.

81 Morton, *Strategy*, pp. 284–85.

82 Ibid., pp. 316–17.

83 Excellent accounts in the American army's official history, Samuel Milner, *Victory in Papua* (Washington: GPO, 1957), and the Australian official history, Dudley McCarthy, *Southwest Pacific Area – First Year: Kokoda to Wau* (Canberra: Australian War Memorial, 1957). See also D. Clayton James, *The Years of MacArthur*, Vol. 2: *1941–1945* (Boston: Houghton Mifflin, 1975) chaps. 4–6; Long, *Six Years' War*, pp. 197ff. Important for details on the campaign and especially the role of the American general sacked by MacArthur as well as the division involved, Leslie Anders, *Gentle Knight: The Life and Times of Major General Edwin Forrest Harding* (Kent, Ohio: Kent State Univ. Press, 1985). On the public relations aspect of this and other campaigns in the Southwest Pacific, see Michael Schaller, *Douglas MacArthur: The Far Eastern General* (New York: Oxford Univ. Press, 1989), pp. 71–73.

84 Morton, *Strategy*, pp. 336–37, 340.

85 McCarthy, *Southwest Pacific Area*, pp. 121–22, 155–88; Long, *Six Years' War*, pp. 210–14; Edward J. Drea, *MacArthur's Ultra: Codebreaking and the War against Japan, 1942–1945* (Lawrence, Kans.: Univ. Press of Kansas, 1992), pp. 44–48.

86 Morton, *Strategy*, pp. 306–7.

87 John Miller, Jr., *Guadalcanal: The First Offensive* (Washington: GPO, 1949), and Morison, *US Naval Operations*, vol. 5: *The Struggle for Guadalcanal*, remain most helpful. See also Dull, *Imperial Japanese Navy*, pp. 180–260; Kreis, *Air Base Defense*, pp. 220–34; Toshikazu Ohmae, "Strategische Konzeptionen," pp. 196–98; *Ugaki Diary*, 7 Aug.-31 Dec.1942, pp. 177–319 passim. Eric Larrabee, *Commander in Chief: Franklin Delano Roosevelt, His Lieutenants, and Their War* (New York: Harper & Row, 1987), pp. 256ff, stresses the personal involvement of Roosevelt in the launching of the operation and its support.

88 Morton, *Strategy*, pp. 352–56.

89 Ibid., p. 340.

90 Ibid., pp. 364–67.

91 See *FDR Letters*, 2: 1355, 1356, 1371–72; Dill to Brooke, 19 Oct. 1942, Liddell Hart Centre, Alanbrooke Papers, 14/38; Dill No. 442 of 27 Oct. 1942, PRO, AIR 20/7472.

92 For some time the Japanese fooled themselves as well as their German ally about the battle; eventually the Germans discovered at least a part of the truth. See KTB Skl A 36, 15 Aug. 1942, BA/MA, RM 7/39, f. 299–300; A 37, 2 and 6 Sep. 1942, RM 7/40, f. 47, 128; A 38, 11 and 17 Oct. 1942, RM 7/41, f. 212, 356; A 39, 13, 22, 25 Nov. 1942, RM 7/42, f. 353, 601, 675; cf. OKM, Skl, 3.Abt. 7 Dec. 1942, RM 7/253, f. 481–95.

93 The Japanese decision to evacuate was formalized on Jan. 4, 1943, text in Morton, *Strategy*, pp. 624–26.

94 *ADAP*, E, 1, No. 276; 2, No. 168; 4, Nos. 76, 121; Tokyo Nos. 622 and 624 of 3 Mar. 1942, BA, R 9/573; Kolb, "Aufzeichnung über die Behandlung des deutschen Vermögens

durch Japan," 28 Apr. 1942, AA, St.S., "Diplomatische Aufzeichnungen Betr. Japan Apr. 42 -Apr. 43," fr. J 000149–54; Tokyo to Shanghai No. 520 of 15 Apr. 1942, NA, RG 457, SRDJ 21811; Bangkok to Tokyo No. 1096 of 4 June 1942, SRDJ 23452–54; Tokyo to Berlin No. 471 of 13 June 1942, SRDJ 23817; Madrid to Tokyo No. 1025 of 23 Sep. 1942, SRDJ 26649–51; Jochmann, *Hitler Monologe*, pp. 269–70.

95 *ADAP*, E, 3, Nos. 251, 254, 316; Togo to Oshima No. 351 of 1 May 1942, NA, RG 457, SRDJ 22637; Berlin to Tokyo No. 1130 of 23 Sep. and No. 1133 of 24 Sep. 1942, SRDJ 26976–77, 26647–48; Tokyo to Berlin No. 769 of 15 Oct. 1942, SRDJ 27198; Meskill, *Hitler and Japan*, chap. 4; Bernd Martin, *Deutschland und Japan in Zweiten Weltkrieg* (Göttingen: Musterschmidt, 1969), chap. 6.

96 They also discussed at great length how they could use the Mufti for propaganda to the Muslims of the Near East and India (Berlin No. 1491 of 19 Dec. 1941, NA, RG 457, SRDJ 17994; Tokyo to Rome No. 344 of 27 Dec. 1941, SRDJ 18273; *ADAP*, E, 2, No. 87).

97 On these negotiations, only a small sampling of the documents can be listed here; the main contribution the project appears to have made to the Axis war effort was the time of Allied cryptographers taken up by the interminable exchanges. See *ADAP*, E, 3, Nos. 68, 92, 113, 208, 4, No. 50; NA, RG 457, SRDJ 22020–23, 23901–2, 24232, 26915– 16, 27037–38, 27377–78, 27778–79,29025; Ribbentrop to Göring, 1 Sep. 1942, AA, Handakten Ritter, "Japan," Bd. 4–5, fr. 310188–89; Meskill, *Hitler and Japan*, pp. 412– 13.

98 On the Italian plane, see Tokyo to Rome No. 179 of 3 June 1942, NA, RG 457, SRDJ 23552; Tokyo to Japanese military attaché Rome No. 308 of 2 Aug. 1942, SRA 02375– 77. Information on the trip provided by an Italian air force officer who flew on it is in U.S. Navy, CNO, Intelligence Division, Intelligence Report 210–44 of 21 Mar. 1944, NA, RG 165, Box 2413, File 9900–Japan.

99 Compare Hitler's attitude in Apr. 1942 (*ADAP*, E, 2, No. 182) with that in July (ibid., 3, No. 76). On Japanese sensitivity about Soviet reaction to any overflight, see ibid., No. 35; Tokyo to Berlin No. 441 of 3 June 1942, No. 974 of 3 June 1942, No. 472 of 15 June 1942, NA, RG 457, SRDJ 23414–15, 26463–64, 23931–32; Berlin to Tokyo No. 734 of 8 June 1942, SRDJ 23486–87. The formal Japanese "No" to the suggestion that they attack is in Tokyo to Berlin No. 588 of 27 July 1942, SRDJ 25150–59; see also SRDJ 21937–40, 21956–58, 21975–79, 24223–25, 27052; SRGL 368–70; SRA 16218–19.

100 Note Donovan's reports to Roosevelt No. 153 of 15 Jan. 1942 and 164 of 16 Jan. 1942, FDRL, PSF Box 164, OSS Donovan Reports, Folder 4.

101 See KTB Skl A 33, 10 May 1942, BA/MA, RM 7/36, f. 184–85.

102 Seekriegsleitung, "Besprechung mit Admiral Nomura am 4.2.1943," 5 Feb. 1943, BA/MA, RM 7/254, f. 35–39, ". . . am 18.2.2943," 22 Feb. 1943, ibid., f. 45–53; ". . . am 27.3.42," RM 7/253, f. 230–31; ". . . am 8.4.1942," ibid., f. 279–82; " . . . am 13.5.42," ibid., f. 312–20; KTB Skl A 36, 16 Aug. 1942, RM 7/39, f. 304–5; Oshima to Tokyo No. 309 of 28 Feb. 1942, NA, RG 457, SRDJ 20178–79, Tokyo to Berlin No. 655 of 26 Aug. 1942, SRDJ 32229–30; *ADAP*, E, 3, Nos. 142, 295; Meskill, *Hitler and Japan*, pp. 64–67. German army Chief of Staff General Halder was more cautious and did not expect the German army to operate south of the Caucasus until 1943 (Salewski, *Deutsche Seekriegsleitung*, 2: 94–95).

103 Oshima to Tokyo No. 820 of 26 June 1942, NA, RG 457, SRDJ 24192; *ADAP*, E 3, No. 39; KTB Skl A 34, 27 June 1942, BA/MA, RM 7/37, f. 497, A 38, 5 July 1942, RM 7/38, f. 94–95; Seekriegsleitung, "Niederschrift über Besprechung mit jap.Verb.Stab am 22.6.1942 beim Chef der Seekriegsleitung," 27 June 1942, RM 6/76, f. 164–70; ". . . am 7.9.1942," RM 7/253, f. 399–410.

104 KTB Skl A 37, 4 Sep. 1942, BA/MA, RM 7/37, f. 552; Skl, "Vermerk," 25 Oct. 1942, RM 7/253, f. 433–35; *ADAP*, E, 3, No. 76.

105 Holmes, *Undersea Victory*, p. 162; KTB Skl A 37, 4 Sep. 1942, BA/MA, RM 7/40, f. 79, A 39, 6 Nov. 1942, RM 7/42, f. 102; A 40, 4 Dec 1942, RM 7/43, f. 94–95; OKW, Gruppe Ausland, "Niederschrift über die Besprechung am 16.10.42 im Führerhauptquartier," 17 Oct. 1942, RM 7/253, f. 424–29; Seekriegsleitung, "Niederschrift über die Besprechung mit Vizeadmiral Nomura bei C/Skl am 5.11.1942," 9 Nov. 1942, ibid., f. 438–42; Seekriegsleitung, "Vermerk," 24 Nov. 1942, ibid., f. 470; Nomura's letter of 3 Dec. 1942, ibid., f. 471–72; OKW, Gruppe Ausland, "Niederschrift über die Besprechung am 4.12.1942 Führerhauptquartier mit Japanern," 7 Dec. 1942, ibid., f. 499–503; documents on a meeting with Nomura on 18 Dec. 1942, ibid., f. 528–33; Oshima to Tokyo No. 1433(?) of 12 Dec. 1942, NA, RG 457, SRDJ 28960–61; Jürgen Förster, "Strategische Überlegungen des Wehrmachtführungsstabes für das Jahr 1943," *MGM* (1973), 100 n 21, 107 n 60. See also OKM, 1 Skl IOp, "2625/42 gKdos.Chefs. Einsatz der japanischen Ubootswaffe," 6 Dec. 1942, RM 7/253, f. 475–79.

106 Motter, *Persian Corridor*, pp. 482–83.

107 Oshima to Tokyo No. 1121 of 22 Sep. 1942 and No. 1128 of 23 Sep. 1942, NA, RG 457, SRDJ 26634–35, 26661–62, 26818–19.

The German naval attaché in Tokyo, Admiral Wenneker, who saw this clearly and so reported in December 1942, was reprimanded for his pessimism but also defended by some in the navy for accurately reporting the facts and reflecting the new situation as seen by the Japanese themselves: the war in the Pacific had changed with Midway and the Solomons campaign and there was no prospect of a Japanese move into the Indian Ocean. See KTB Skl, A 40, 18 Dec. 1942, BA/MA, RM 7/43, f. 354–56, and 28 Dec. 1942, ibid., f. 521; Ob.d.M., "Verschl.Tel. aus Tokio: Lagebeurteilumg zu Jahresende," 17 Dec. 1942, RM 7/253, f. 512–13; Chef OWK WFSt Op Nr. 552243/42 gKdos.Chefs., 24 Dec. 1942, ibid., f. 514; see also Amt Ausl/ABW, Ag Ausland Nr. 00 478/42 gKdos of 22 Dec. 1942, ibid., f. 528; *ADAP*, E, IV, No. 20.

108 German military attaché Rome, "Zur seestrategischen Lage der italienischen Flotte," 31 Dec. 1942, BA/MA, PG 45172, Case 17/3; KTB Skl A 32, 8 Apr. 1942, RM 7/35, f. 123–25; Gerhard Schreiber, *Revisionismus und Weltmachtstreben: Marineführung und deutsch-italienische Beziehungen 1919–1944* (Stuttgart: Deutsche Verlags-Anstalt, 1978), pp. 331ff.

109 Note Hitler's serious interest in shifting the supplying of North Africa to submarines (*ADAP*, E, 1, No. 181).

110 See the summary in *KTB OKW*, 1942, 1: 1001–103; Salewski, *Deutsche Seekriegsleitung*, 2: 60–72. For Hitler's suggestion that Malta be taken *after* the British had been defeated in North Africa in the face of Cavallero's objections, see Schmundt's memorandum in *MGM*, 1972, No. 1, p. 120.

111 A recent account in John W. Gordon, *The Other Desert War: British Special Forces in North Africa, 1940–1943* (New York: Greenwood Press, 1987), pp. 100–3, which also explains how the British got onto this source and turned it.

112 Hinsley, *British Intelligence*, 2: 356–63, Appendices 14, 16; *DRuZW*, 6: 570–647; Sadkov-ich, "Rommel and the Italians," pp. 302–5.

113 A view from British intelligence in Hinsley, 2: 368ff. Auchinleck was planning to hold Tobruk and at the Egyptian border as late as June 16 (CS 1270 to Churchill, PRO, WO 106/2238A). An inquiry into the disaster was conducted by General Wilson, see WO 106/2234–36, 2238A. Of the captured soldiers, 49 percent were from the United Kingdom, 42 percent from South Africa, 9 percent from India. For Churchill's concern about

the disaster, see PRO, PREM 3/54/10. There had already been discussion of the reintroduction of the death penalty for desertion or cowardice (abolished in 1930), but this was not done; see, e.g., Grigg to Churchill, 5 June 1942, PRO, WO 259/75.

114 *KTB OKW*, 1942, 1: 104–7; Mariano Gabriele, *Operazione C₃: Malta* (Rome: Ufficio Storico Marina Militare, 1965), pp. 268–86.

115 *ADAP*, E, 3, Nos. 42, 43, 49, 56, 59, 60, 66, 129, 299, 4, No. 101; German embassy Rome documents of July–Aug. 1942 in AA, Botschaft Rom (Quir.) "Geheim, 59/5," fr. E 261726ff. For British capture of the relevant German–Italian document of 28 Aug. 1942, see British Minister of State No. 63 of 24 Nov. 1942, J 4867/1145/16, PRO, FO 371/31586. The Italians were very suspicious of German intentions, but Hitler certainly intended to leave them in charge. It is astonishing that the Axis assurances are still taken at face value in *DRuZW*, 6: 652.

116 KTB Skl A 35, 1 July 1942, BA/MA, RM 7/38, f. 3–4.

117 *Rommel Papers*, pp. 243–56, 520; Hinsley, *British Intelligence*, 2: 392–407; Donald G. Brownlow, *Checkmate at Ruweisat: Auchinleck's Finest Hour* (North Quincy, Mass.: Christopher Pub. House, 1977); McNarney to Roosevelt, FDRL, PSF Safe File, Marshall, Cont. 5; Farnie, *East and West of Suez*, p. 628; Brooke to Auchinleck, 17 July 1942, Liddell Hart Centre, Auchinleck Papers, 6/D/4(f) item D.

118 An account in Nigel Hamilton, *Monty: The Making of a General 1887–1942* (Toronto: Fleet Books, 1982), Part 4, chap. 17, Part 5, chaps 1–3. Omitted from the published version of the Brooke Diary for Aug. 17, 1942 is the sentence: "The more I look back on our decision to get rid of Auchinleck the more convinced I am that we were correct" (Liddell Hart Centre, Alanbrooke Papers). Numerous other high-ranking officers from GHQ Cairo and HQ 8th Army and its corps were also relieved.

119 Zweig, "British Plans for the Evacuation of Palestine," pp. 296–99; Daniel Silverfarb, "Britain, the United States, and the Security of the Saudi Arabian Oilfields in 1942," *Historical Journal* 26 (1983), 721–25; Santoni, *Ultra*, p. 264 n 89; WM(42) War Cabinet 85(42) of 3 July 1942, PRO, CAB 65/27. The remaining British warships at Alexandria were withdrawn. There was concern about the French warships immobilized there. The latter were of special interest to the Japanese; note Mitani (Vichy) to Tokyo No. 309 of 16 July 1942, NA, RG 457, SRDJ 24839.

120 In spite of its generally very laudatory tone, the authorized biography by Nigel Hamilton is especially good on this. See also Grigg to Churchill, 11 Sep. 1942, PRO, PREM 3/54/11.

121 Hinsley, *British Intelligence*, 2: 418ff; Dill correspondence file 52 in PRO, CAB 106/323.

122 Hamilton, *Monty*, pp. 637–711. See also *ADAP*, E, 3, No. 153; Hinsley, 2: 408–16.

123 Stoler, *Politics of the Second Front*, chap. 2; Fraser, *Alanbrooke*, chap. 11; Richard W. Steele, *The First Offensive, 1942* (Bloomington, Ind.: Indiana Univ. Press, 1973), chaps. 1–3; Butler, *Grand Strategy*, 3, Part 2, chaps. 24, 27.

124 See Chapter 7, below.

125 JP(41) 1028 of War Cabinet Joint Planning Staff, "Operation 'Roundup'," 24 Dec. 1941, PRO, WO 106/4126, and the following documents in this file and in WO 106/4127, 4191.

126 See Pogue, *Marshall*, 2: 305–6, for Roosevelt's 25 Mar. 1942 approval of this approach.

127 Note Roosevelt to Marshall, 17 Mar. 1942, *Bullitt Papers*, pp. 548–50; Kirk to Welles No. 608 of 17 Apr. 1942, FDRL, PSF Box 96, State, Welles 1942, and other documents in this file, esp. No. 1366 of 2 Aug. 1942.

128 See Stimson to Roosevelt, 20 July 1942, FDRL, Map Room 167, Naval Aide, A 16–3 Middle East.

129 Note the comments of Sir Michael Howard on "Scholarship on World War II: Present and Future," *Journal of Military History* 55 (1991), 378–80.

130 Pogue, *Marshall*, 2: 336; Marshall memorandum for Roosevelt, "American Forces in the

Middle East," 23 June 1942, FDRL, Map Room 167, Naval Aide, A 16–3 Middle East; Maxwell to War Dept. 10 July 1942, ibid.

131 Note Brooke Diary, 6, 10, 28 Mar. 1942, Liddell Hart Centre; Eden to Churchill, PM 42/52 of 23 Mar. 1942, PRO, CAB 120/410 and PREM 3/135/1; Combined Commanders 3rd Meeting, 23 May 1942, P 129/314, CAB 106/1027. The emerging British argument was not over a landing but about its *location*, with Brooke arguing for the Calais or Boulogne area because it could be covered by land-based planes while Admiral Mountbatten, the Chief of Combined Operations, argued for the Cherbourg area. See esp. Brooke Diary, 28 Mar. 1942. The editor of Brooke's diary, Sir Arthur Bryant, was determined to prove Brooke a consistent opponent of what both men by the post-war years considered the foolish American advocacy of a 1942 landing and left out of the printed version all sections of the original diary which point to Brooke's rather different views in March 1942.

132 On the visit of Marshall and Hopkins to England in April, 1942, see *FDR Letters*, 2: 1303–5; Pogue, *Marshall*, 2: 308–20; McJimsey, *Harry Hopkins*, pp. 242–49; Steele, *The First Offensive*, chaps. 4, 6; Stoler, *Politics of the Second Front*, chap 3; Dill to Brooke, 23(?) Apr. 1942, Liddell Hart Centre, Alanbrooke Papers, 14/38. Note also Sikorski's memorandum of 13 Apr. 1942, forwarded to Roosevelt, in FDRL, PSF Safe File, Cont. 5, Marshall.

133 *FRUS*, 1942, 3: 587.

134 On Molotov's visit, see Stoler, chap. 3, though I do not entirely agree with the interpretation.

135 Ibid., chap. 4; Pogue, *Marshall*, 2: 332–33.

136 Marshall memorandum for Roosevelt, "Prospective Movement of Planes to the Middle East," 26 June 1942 (corrected to 25 June), FDRL, Map Room 167, Naval Aide A 16–3 Middle East; Lewis L. Brereton, *Diaries: The War in the Pacific, Middle East and Europe* (New York: Morrow, 1946, henceforth *Brereton Diary*), pp. 130–31, 145–49.

137 Pogue, *Marshall*, 2: 365.

138 See Clark Kerr (Moscow) No. 51 of 30 June 1942, C 6553/19/55, PRO, FO 371/31084. Terry (*Poland's Place in Europe*, pp. 225–44) argues convincingly that the British had always wanted the Polish forces for the Middle East and that General Wladyslaw Anders, the Polish Commander-in-Chief in Russia, worked toward the same end against Sikorski's preference and orders.

139 Matloff and Snell, *Strategic Planning, 1941–1942*, pp. 217–19; Pogue, *Marshall*, 2: 327ff; *FDR Letters*, 2: 1329–30; Robert E. Sherwood, *Roosevelt and Hopkins* (New York: Harper, 1948), pp. 602ff; Roosevelt-Marshall exchanges of 1–6 May 1942, and 19 June–15 July 1942, FDRL, PSF Safe File, Box 5, Marshall; Winant to Roosevelt, 3 June 1942, PSF Box 9, Winant.

140 Note Mountbatten to Roosevelt, 15 June 1942, FDRL, Map Room 164, Naval Aide's File, which evidently reinforced American opinion that gaining a foothold in Normandy was feasible.

141 An excellent case for the fear of another mass surrender as a key factor in British policy is made in Joseph L. Strange, "The British Rejection of Sledgehammer, An Alternative Motive," *Military Affairs* 46, No. 1 (Feb. 1982), 6–14.

142 There is a good outline history of "Sledgehammer" in PRO, WO 106/4289; another summary is in WO 106/4175. See also Hinsley, *British Intelligence*, 2: 464; Strange; Churchill memorandum WP[42] 311 of 21 July 1942, CAB 66/26.

143 See Brooke's comments in his diary of 27 May 1942 in Liddell Hart Centre, Alanbrooke Papers, 3/A/IV, p. 403; Brooke Diary of 5 June 1942, 25 Sep. 1942; PRO, AIR 8/938; British Joint Planning Staff memorandum of 17 July 1942, CAB 119/56; Butler, *Grand Strategy*, Vol. 3, Part 2, pp. 646–50.

144 Puttkamer, "Niederschrift über Äusserungen des Führers vom 4.1.42," BA/MA, RM

6/75, f. 225–27; Salewski, *Deutsche Seekriegsleitung*, 2: 3–31, 39–40; Wolfgang Wilhelmus, "Vorbereitungen der faschistischen Wehrmacht zur Besetzung Schwedens," *Zeitschrift für Geschichtswissenschaft* 23 (1975), 1034–35; Raeder to Boehm, 19 Feb. 1942, and Boehm to Raeder, 5 Oct. 1942, Boehm Nachlass, BA/MA, N 172/4; Ziemke, *Northern Theater*, pp. 216–19; Beesly, *Very Special Intelligence*, pp. 122–28; *ADAP*, E, 1, No. 181. The report of the British board of inquiry into this episode is in PRO, AIR 20/3356.

145 Carlgren, *Swedish Foreign Policy*, p. 127; Ziemke, *Northern Theater*, p. 215; Wilhelmus, pp. 1036–37; Förster, "Strategische Überlegungen," p. 104 and n 42; Woermann to Helsinki No. 297 of 26 Feb. 1942, AA, Gesandtschaft Helsinki, "Drahtberichte," fr. H 069326; Berg to Lammers, 14 Mar. 1942, BA, R 43 II/1494, f. 74–75.

146 Pogue, *Marshall*, 2: 342–48; Steele, *The First Offensive*, chaps. 7–8; WM(42) 94th Conclusions, Confidential Annex, 22 July 1942, PRO, CAB 120/82; Alex Danchev, "A Special Relationship: Field Marshal Sir John Dill and General George C. Marshall," *Journal, Royal United Service for Defence Studies* 130, No. 2 (1985), 59.

147 Sherwood, *Roosevelt and Hopkins*, pp. 610–11; Roosevelt to Hopkins, Marshall and King, London [23 July 1942?], FDRL, PSF Box 4, Hopkins; Roosevelt memorandum of 29 July 1942, ibid., Box 5, Marshall; Roosevelt memorandum of 6 May 1942, ibid., Box 106, War Department, Marshall. Note that this appears to have been the first time in the war that Roosevelt checked with the Map Room to see whether any message from London had come in, 24 July 1942, Map Room Box 195, Chart Room Logs and Standing Orders, 1, p. 92.

148 Morton, *Strategy*, pp. 308–11.

149 Marshall to Roosevelt, 30 July 1942, FDRL, PSF Safe File, Cont. 1, Marshall.

150 See the documents in PRO, CAB 119/56; but see Roosevelt to King, 24 Aug. 1942, FDRL, PSF Cont. 5, King, which suggests that Roosevelt believed after the decision for "Torch" that "Roundup" would be possible in the fall of 1943. There is evidence, cited in Chapter 8, that Churchill thought so also.

151 Morton, *Strategy*, pp. 333ff; Matloff and Snell, *Strategic Planning, 1941–1942*, chap. 14; Richard M. Leighton and Robert W. Coakley, *Global Logistics and Strategy, 1940–1943* (Washington: GPO, 1955), chap. 17.

152 Churchill to Auchinleck OZ 829 of 27 July 1942, Liddell Hart Centre, Alanbrooke Papers, 6/D/4(f) item F.

153 Stoler, *Politics of the Second Front*, pp. 60–62; Gilbert, *Churchill*, 7: chap. 11.

154 *ADAP*, E, 3, Nos. 205, 217. Hitler's comments of 26 Aug. 1942 are in Jochmann, *Hitler Monologe*, p.368.

155 Butler, *Grand Strategy*, Vol. 3, Part 2, pp. 638–42; Hinsley *British Intelligence*, 2, Appendix 13; Roskill, *War at Sea*, 2: 239–42; John Keegan, *Six Armies in Normandy* (New York: Viking, 1982), pp. 120–25; Daniel J. Webb, "The Dieppe Raid – An Act of Diplomacy," *Military Review* 60, No. 5 (1980), 30–37; Hamilton, *Monty*, pp. 548–57; Ronald Atkin, *Dieppe 1942: The Jubilee Disaster* (London: Macmillan, 1980). The material on the Dieppe raid collected after the war by Ismay in helping Churchill write his memoirs shows that Churchill had very strongly pushed the project and that the Germans had no prior knowledge (Liddell Hart Centre, Ismay Papers, II/3/260). A very detailed analysis in Brian Loring Villa, *Unauthorized Action: Mountbatten and the Dieppe Raid* (Toronto: Oxford Univ. Press, 1989), is summarized in his article, "Mountbatten, the British Chiefs of Staff, and Approval of the Dieppe Raid," *Journal of Military History* 54 (1990), 201–26, with commentary by Philip Ziegler and a rejoinder by Villa.

156 Grigg to Churchill, 19 Oct. 1942, PRO, WO 259/75.

157 Hamilton, *Monty*, Part 5, chaps. 12–20; Hinsley, *British Intelligence*, 2: 425–35; *DRuZW*, 6: 725ff (which shows that it rained on the Germans as well as the British when the former escaped the slow follow-up of the latter); Neurath to Weizsäcker, 5 Oct. 1942, AA, St.S., "Schriftwechsel mit Beamten," Bd. 7, fr. 70443–45.

158 See Löwisch, "Kurze Inhaltsangabe des Vortrages Marineattaché Rom beim Herrn Ob.d.M. am 13. Oktober 1942," BA/MA, RM 7/233, f. 431–32.

159 On problems in German–Italian–Arab relations in the fall of 1942, see *ADAP*, E, 3, No. 250; items 34 and 35 in the Canaris/Lahousen file, Imperial War Museum, AL 1933.

160 It had been these hopes which had earlier affected United States policy toward the Free French; note *FDR Letters*, 2: 1268–69, 1315–16; Arthur L. Funk, *The Politics of Torch* (Lawrence, Kans.: Univ. Press of Kansas, 1974), chaps. 1–8; Krautkrämer, "Vorgeschichte," pp. 244–45.

161 David A. Walker, "OSS and Operation Torch," *JCH* 22 (1987), 667–79.

162 Krautkrämer, "Vorgeschichte," pp. 250–51.

163 Ibid., pp. 247.

164 Ibid., pp. 230–31.

165 Hinsley, *British Intelligence*, 2: 476–82. The first German knowledge of the landing was the broadcast from Algiers radio that the landing was under way; see OKM, Skl, Chef MND III, "X.B. Bericht Nr. 45/42," 12 Nov. 1942, in NA, RG 457, SRS 548, Vol. 13. On the German dilemmas in coping with any Allied landing, see Kontrollinspektion Afrika, "Studie über die französischen Abwehr-Möglichkeiten und -Aussichten bei einem Anglo-Amerikanischen Angriff auf Franz.-Marokko," 28 May 1942, BA/MA, PG 33651, Case 579, f. 191–93. The Germans had reassured the anxious Japanese that no landing was likely on Sep. 7 and again on Nov. 5, 1942, see RM 7/253, f. 399–410, 438–43.

7: THE WAR AT SEA AND THE BLOCKADE

1 Förster, "Strategische Überlegungen."

2 There is a good account in Salewski, *Seekriegsleitung*, 1: 354ff., 2: 21ff.

3 Ibid., 2: 33–35; Roskill, *War at Sea*, 2: 168–73.

4 Studies of this issue are David Woodward, *The Tirpitz* (London: Kimber, 1953, and other editions); Ludovic Kennedy and Henry Coverlay, *Menace: The Life and Death of the Tirpitz* (London: Sidgwick & Jackson, 1979). See also Villa, *Unauthorised Action*, pp. 111–13.

5 Hinsley, *British Intelligence*, 3/1: 258–62.

6 Ibid., pp. 271–78, Appendix 13. On Soviet cooperation in one of these raids, see N 5858/5858/38, PRO, FO 371/34442.

7 Salewski, *Seekriegsleitung*, 2: 196–201; Roskill, *War at Sea*, 2: 291–99; important revisions of earlier accounts in *DRuZW*, 6: 418–24; see also Dudley Pope, *"73 North" The Battle of the Barents Sea* (Annapolis, Md.: Naval Institute Press, 1989).

8 The crisis is reviewed in Michael Salewski, "Von Raeder zu Dönitz: Der Wechsel im Oberbefehl der Kriegsmarine 1943," MGM, 1973, No. 2, pp. 101–46; see also his *Seekriegsleitung*, 2: 202–38. Hitler's violent reaction to the events off the Norwegian coast was surely in part related to his hope that a signal German victory there might off-set the gloom associated with the simultaneous defeat at Stalingrad. Raeder, who always wanted to appear to be in the right about everything, had the war diary of the navy altered to support his own interpretation of events (Salewski, "Raeder zu Dönitz," p. 116). On Japanese interest in the Germans *not* decommissioning their big ships, see ONI London, "X 4646" of 19 Nov. 1943, NA, RG 38, Chief of Naval Operations, ONI Attaché Reports 1940–46, u-1-i #7510-E.

9 Salewski, *Seekriegsleitung*, 2: 333–45; Hinsley, *British Intelligence*, 3/1, pp. 269–71 and Appendix 14; OKM, Skl, Chef MND III, "XB-Bericht Nr. 52/43," 30 Dec. 1943, NA, RG 457, SRS 548, Vol. 16, pp. 6–8, 12, Anlage 4.

10 Salewski, 2: 351; Hinsley, 2: 538–40; Roskill, *War at Sea* 2: 177–82, 257, 265–69, 405, 411–12; Patrick Beesly, *Very Special Intelligence* (New York Ballantine, 1977), pp. 228–31; *DRuZW*, 6: 388–94. On difficulties between the Germans and Japanese about a German auxiliary cruiser in the Indian Ocean, see Skl, "Stichwortartige

Zusammenstellung der Verhandlungen mit der japanischen Admiralität über das Operationsgebiet für den deutschen HSK im Indischen Ozean und im südlichen Pazifik," 25 Oct. 1942, BA/MA, RM 7/253, f. 433–35.

11 See Hinsley, *British Intelligence*, 3/1: 123–25; 3/2:, 56. A good brief survey in Paul Beaver, *E-Boats and Coastal Craft: A Selection of Pictures from the Bundesarchiv Koblenz* (Cambridge: Stevens, 1980). The Slapton Sands disaster is discussed in connection with the Normandy invasion in Chap. 12; an account in Edwin P. Hoyt, *The Invasion before Normandy: The Secret Battle of Slapton Sands* (New York: Stein & Day, 1985).

12 Salewski, *Seekriegsleitung*, 2: 123–25; Donovan to Roosevelt, 3 Oct. 1941, FDRL, PSF Safe File, Germany, Box 4; British Admiralty to Opnav, Personal for CNO, 1645A/16, NCR 148, 17 Jan. 1943, NA, RG 457, SRMN 35, p. 12; "Besprechungsnotiz 109/42," Göring conference of 29 June 1942, Imperial War Museum, Milch Papers, Vol. 62, p. 5234.

13 Morison, *US Naval Operations*, 1: 411–12, 10: 184–88, 374.

14 Ibid., 1: 226–28; Rohwer, *Geleitzugschlachten*, pp. 29–32, 64–66, 310–14.

15 Morison, 1: 212–19.

16 The written confirmation of the oral order of Dec. 8 is in the diary of the Seekriegsleitung for 9 Dec. 1941, BA/MA, RM 7/31, f. 135–36. Hitler was especially down on Uruguay because of its role in the loss of the *Graf Spee*. The Central American countries were Costa Rica, the Dominican Republic, El Salvador, Haiti, Honduras, Nicaragua, and Panama; of these the last named was of special importance because so many ships were operating under Panamanian registry.

17 See *ADAP*, D, 9, Nos. 365, 412, 519; Buenos Aires to Tokyo No. 561 of 25 June 1942, NA, RG 457, SRDJ 24182–83.

18 Frank D. McCann, Jr., *The Brazilian–American Alliance, 1937–1945* (Princeton: Princeton Univ. Press, 1973), pp. 275–90; Roskill, *War at Sea*, 2: 203; Morison, *US Naval Operations*, 1: chap. 15. Badly wrong on this, *DRuZW*, 6: 350.

19 See, e.g., the picture in Rohwer, *Geleitzugschlachten*, facing p. 289. A good account in Hinsley, 2: Appendix 15. See also document 377–PS, NA, RG 238.

20 Salewski, *Seekriegsleitung*, 2: 350.

21 A full account of Spanish support of German naval operations in World War II may yet be written now that Spanish archives are becoming accessible; the subject has been ignored by German historians who have preferred to discourse upon the alleged violations of neutrality by those fighting their submarines rather than by those aiding them. The best account currently is Charles B. Burdick, "'Moro': The Resupply of German Submarines in Spain, 1939–1942," *Central European History* 3 (1970), 256–84. The scene in the movie "Das Boot" makes the stop in Spain rather more public than the facts warrant. See also KTB Skl A 34, 12 June 1942, BA/MA, RM 7/37, f. 222. The Germans continued to maintain a radio monitoring station in Sevilla, being notified by the Spanish navy ahead of time when it was about to be raided (KTB Skl A 53, 15 Jan. 1944, RM 7/56, f. 260). See also Robert Cecil, "C's War," *Intelligence and National Security* 1 (1986), 181; Hinsley, *British Intelligence*, 2: 172, 719–21; Skl, "Abwehr feindlicher Angriffe in spanischen Hoheitsgewässern," 21 June 1944, BA/MA, PG 33751, Case 643.

22 Fisk, *In Time of War*. pp. 278–84; Brooke Diary, 8 Dec. 1941, Liddell Hart Centre, Alanbrooke Papers; *ADAP*, E, 1, No. 24. Though extremely pro-de Valera, T. Ryle Dwyer, *Strained Relations: Ireland at Peace and the U.S.A. at War, 1941–1945* (Totowa, N.J.: Barnes & Noble, 1988), and Ronan Fanning, "The Politics of Irish Neutrality During World War II," *Les Etats neutres europeens et la seconde guerre mondiale, Colloque international* (Neuchâtel: Editions de la Baconnière, 1985), pp. 125–33, contain additional details.

23 See the map in Roskill, *War at Sea*, 2, facing p. 205.

24 The crisis of spring 1943 in the Battle of the Atlantic on the one hand, and the Allied

victory in North Africa on the other, made that time a good one to raise the issue with Lisbon; see Woodward, *British Foreign Policy*, 4: 48–57. Churchill had wanted to move earlier and to use force, but the Cabinet refused to go along. See also "Vertraulicher Informationsbericht von Herrn Seligo, Lissabon, vom 15.10.1943," 23 Oct. 1943, BA, ZSg 115/7, f. 109–11; *FDR Letters*, 2: 1466–67. On Japanese concern that this could be used as a precedent for the Soviet Union allowing the use of bases by the United States, see the exchanges between the Japanese embassy in Berlin and Tokyo of 13–14 Oct. 1943, in NA, RG 457, SRDJ 44270, 44332–34, 44380, 44385–86, 44390, 44395–98, 44400.

25 Note de Gaulle's comment on their getting steadily older unused in Harold Nicolson, *The War Years 1939–1945*, Vol. 2 (New York: Atheneum, 1967): 139.

26 Krautkrämer, "Vorgeschichte," pp. 220–21.

27 Ibid., pp. 219–20, 222–23; Paxton, *Vichy*, pp. 387–90; *ADAP*, E, 1, No. 182; documents on Darlan's dealings with the German navy in Dec. 1941–Jan. 1942, in BA/MA, RM 6/75, f. 250–63 and M 1697/71826 a-f.

28 Jochmann, *Hitler Monologe*, 31 Jan. 1942, p. 245.

29 *ADAP*, E, 2, Nos. 196, 200, and related documents in AA, St.S., "USA," Bd. 11.

30 Rudolf Rahn memorandum of 19 Aug. 1943, AA, Nachlass Renthe-Fink, Paket 5, Bd. 1, fr. D 514473. See also Tagebuch Koller, 21 Nov. 1942, Institut für Zeitgeschichte.

31 Rohwer and Jäckel, *Funkaufklärung*, pp. 160–61.

32 Roskill, *War at Sea*, 2: 211; Morison, *US Naval Operations*, 1: 329. The only German submarine attack was a miss with three torpedoes fired at the *Queen Mary*, carrying 12,000 mostly American soldiers, in April 1944 (Hinsley, 3/1: 238 and note).

33 Maps in Rohwer and Jäckel, *Funkaufklärung*, p. 163; Roskill, 2, map 40.

34 Roskill, 2, chap. 3.

35 See Stephen W. Roskill, *Hankey: Man of Secrets*, 3 vols. (New York: St. Martin's, 1970–74), 3: 546–47, 559–61. Note WP.(42) 302, also COS(42) 204(0) Final, "Provision of Aircraft for the War at Sea," 18 July 1942, PRO, PREM 3/119/7; Roosevelt to Marshall and King, 18 Mar. 1943, FDRL, Map Room Box 164, Naval Aide's File.

36 Morison, *US Naval Operations*, 1: 250–51, and 10: 187, 190, 194, 223–24, is very skeptical about the usefulness of blimps. See also Alfred Price, *Aircraft versus Submarines: The Evolution of the Anti-Submarine Aircraft 1912–1972* (London: Kimber, 1973), pp. 146–47. On U.S. blimps turned over to the British, see documents in PRO, AIR 20/1311. On the crews of merchant ships, see Tony Lane, *The Merchant Seamen's War* (Manchester: Manchester Univ. Press, 1990), which is quite useful but overemphasizes the author's "discovery" that these men were people.

37 A good introduction in John A. Swettenham, *Canada's Atlantic War* (Toronto; Sarasota, Fla.: Samuel Stevens, 1979).

38 This point is well made in Rohwer, *Geleitzugschlachten*, p. 64. Of course, occasionally an evading route brought a convoy into the view of a different group of submarines.

39 See Beesly, *Very Special Intelligence*, p. 115.

40 Ibid., pp. 166–67; Hinsley, *British Intelligence*, 2: 554, 637; Kahn, *Seizing Enigma*, pp. 211–13, 262–63, 263–64. The word "apparently" is used because much of the material on German code-breaking in World War II remains closed to research.

41 On this, see Rohwer and Jäckel, *Funkaufklärung*, pp. 171–73; Jürgen Rohwer, "'Special Intelligence' und die Geleitzugsteuerung im Herbst 1941," *Marine-Rundschau*, 75 (1978), 711–19; Rohwer and Jäckel, *Kriegswende*, pp. 97–99; Kahn, *Seizing Enigma*, chap. 13.

42 On this episode, see Morison, *US Naval Operations*, 1: chap. 6; Hinsley, *British Intelligence*, 2: 228–29; Roskill, *War at Sea*, 2: 93–106; Rohwer and Jäckel, *Funkaufklärung*, p. 158. A major study of the whole disaster is Michael Gannon, *Operation Drumbeat: The Dramatic True Story of Germany's First U-Boat Attack along the American Coast in World War II* (New

York: Harper & Row, 1990). A major result of the American navy's great defeat was the building of pipelines to carry petroleum products from the fields and ports of the American southwest and south to the northeast; the most important of these, "Big Inch," was constructed in just under a year, Aug. 1942 to July 1943; see James A. Clark and Michael T. Halbouty, *The Last Boom* (New York: Random House, 1972), pp. 266–71. In the Caribbean, German submarines also shelled the refineries and oil storage facilities in the Dutch West Indies (Morison, 1: 145; Combined Intelligence Committee, "Scale of Attack on Bermuda, The West Indies and the Guianas," 22 June 1942, NA, RG 165, Entry 77, Box 1417, File 6900, Germany–General). On the Canadian aspect of this German submarine operation, see W.A.B. Douglas, *Creation of a National Air Force; The Official History of the Royal Canadian Air Force*, Vol. 2 (Toronto: Univ. of Toronto Press. 1986), pp. 486–92.

43 The statistics, which cannot be regarded as absolutely precise, are based on the table in Morison, 1: 413–14.

44 See Hinsley, *British Intelligence*, 2: 179, 229–30, 233, 548–49, 551; Kahn, *Seizing Enigma*, p. 210, chaps. 17–18.

45 Kahn, *Codebreakers*, p. 23.

46 On this issue, see Hinsley, 2: Appendix 19, esp. p. 748.

47 Ibid., pp. 749–51.

48 Ibid., pp. 229, 683; Morison, *US Naval Operations*, 1: 129, 312–13; Kahn, *Seizing Enigma*, chap. 22. The German navy had first practiced refueling at sea during operations connected with the Spanish civil war; see Paul Zieb, *Logistische Probleme der Kriegsmarine* (Neckargemünd: Vowinckel, 1961), pp. 83–85.

49 Roskill, *War at Sea*, 2: 107.

50 Hinsley, 2: 232.

51 Hitler's comments to Field Marshal von Bock, the Commander-in-Chief of the armies scheduled to participate, on June 1, 1942, in the von Bock Diary, BA/MA, N 22/13, f. 88–89. Hitler at that point believed that submarines had sunk 900,000 tons in May; the correct figure was just under 600,000 with another 100,000 lost due to other causes (Hinsley, 2: 485). See also KTB Skl A 29, 18 Jan. 1942, RM 7/32, f. 300–2.

52 On the PQ 17 disaster and its impact on relations between the Western Allies and the Soviet Union, see Hinsley, 2: 213–23; Salewski, *Seekriegsleitung*, 2: 48–50; Roskill, *War at Sea*, 2: 134–45; Beesly, *Very Special Intelligence*, pp. 129–46; Ziemke, *Moscow to Stalingrad*, pp. 428–30; Morison, *US Naval Operations*, 1: 179–92; Beaumont, *Comrades in Arms*, pp. 108–10, 128–31; Villa, *Unauthorized Action*, pp. 114–17; DRuZW, 6: 413–17. German intelligence on the course of the battle can be found in OKM, Skl Chef MND III, "Bericht Nr. 27/42," 9 July 1942, NA, RG 457, SRS 548, Vol. 11.

53 Hinsley, 2: 227.

54 Schofield, *Russian Convoys*, chap. 8; Morison, 1: 360–65.

55 The best account in Michael Howard, *Grand Strategy*, Vol. 4, chap. 13.

56 The text is in ibid., pp. 21–22. See also Saward, *"Bomber" Harris*, pp. 186–87.

57 The full text of the "Pointblank" directive is in Howard, *Grand Strategy*, pp. 623–24. See also Wesley F. Craven and James L. Cate, *The Army Air Forces in World War II* (Chicago: Univ. of Chicago Press, 1948–58), 2: 305–6.

58 Roskill, *War at Sea*, 2: 351–53; Hinsley, *British Intelligence*, 2: 563, 753–56.

59 Howard, p. 625.

60 The U.S. navy's perception of the course of the war against the U-Boats from 1 Sep. 1942 to 1 May 1945 can be followed in the bi-weekly COMINCH "Biweekly U-Boat Trends," reports Nos. 1–65 in NA, RG 457, SRMN 030.

61 On this issue, see the JIC(43) Final, War Cabinet Joint Intelligence Sub-Committee, "Axis Strength 1943," 11 Feb. 1943, p. 6, PRO, CAB 119/55, which is now entirely confirmed by the record.

62 On the Battle of the Atlantic in the spring of 1943 and the turn in May, see Rohwer, *Geleitzugschlachten*; Beesly, *Very Special Intelligence*, chap. 11; Hinsley, *British Intelligence*, 2: 547–72; Morison, *US Naval Operations*, 1, chap. 14; Rohwer and Jäckel, *Funkaufklärung*, pp. 164–66, 177–90; Salewski, *Seekriegsleitung*, 2: 293–308. There is an excellent National Archives "Guide to the Microfilmed Records of the German Navy, 1850–1945," No. 2: "Resources Relating to U-Boat Warfare, 1939–1945" (Washington: NARA, 1985). Note that at the height of the battle, Roosevelt was in the Map Room asking about the situation, FDRL, Map Room Box 195, Log 1a, 10 and 13 May 1943. On the latter occasion, Churchill, Leahy and Hopkins were there as well.

63 See Churchill's Personal Minute M 363/3 to Secretary of State for War, 27 May 1943: "Now that shipping is the stranglehold upon all military operations, it should be a matter of loyalty to the nation to economize by every possible means." PRO, WO 259/77.

64 Hinsley, 2: 554–55; Rohwer and Jäckel, *Funkaufklärung*, pp. 191–92.

65 Rohwer and Jäckel, pp. 128–30, 145; Kahn, *Seizing Enigma*, pp. 202–3, 205–7, 213, 260–62; *DRuZW*, 6: 356–58. Note the earlier German self-congratulation in KTB Skl A 34, 18 Jan. 1942, BA/MA, RM 7/37, f. 332. For a critique of Dönitz's reluctance to face facts collected by his own intelligence service, see Weichold to Rohwer, 10 June 1959, Nachlass Weichold, BA/MA, N 316/101. Salewski (2: 301) notes Dönitz's pre-occupation with Tunisia at this time.

66 See the table in Rohwer and Jäckel, *Funkaufklärung*, p. 165.

67 Morison, *US Naval Operations*, 1: 290–96; Canada's role in Douglas, *Creation of a National Air Force*, chap. 16.

68 U.S. War Production Board, *Industrial Mobilization for War; History of the War Production Board and Predecessor Agencies, 1940–1945* (Washington: GPO, 1947), p. 962.

69 Note Rome to Tokyo Nos. 132 and 143 of 28 Feb. 1943, NA, RG 457, SRDJ 32092–93, 32542–44; *ADAP*, E, 5, Nos. 148, 158.

70 See Hans-Adolf Jacobsen and Hans Dollinger (eds.), *Der Zweite Weltkrieg in Bildern und Dokumenten*, 3 vols. (Wiesbaden: Löwit, 1963), 2: 192; Sadkovich, "Understanding Defeat," p. 49.

71 Salewski, *Seekriegsleitung*, 2: 376–80; Santoni, *Ultra siegt im Mittelmeer*, 234–40; Josef Schröder, *Italiens Kriegsaustritt 1943* (Göttingen: Musterschmidt, 1969), pp. 274–80, 302–13. On Japan's interest, see *Kido Diary*, 9 Sep. 1943, p. 366; Tokyo to Oshima Nos. 690, 698, and 773 of 9 Sep. and 1 Oct. 1943, NA, RG 457, SRDJ 42854, 43225, 43735; Oshima's reports Nos. 1054, 1070, 1111 of 9, 11, and 18 Sep. 1943, SRDJ 42858, 42935, 43290; Japanese naval attaché Stockholm No. 296 of 10 Sep. 1943, SRA 2988; Tokyo to Vatican for Hidaka No. 159 of 1 Dec. 1943, SRDJ 51140–41.

72 This point is well made and documented in Carl Boyd, "The Japanese Submarine Force and the Legacy of Strategic and Operational Doctrine Developed between the World Wars," in Larry Addington et al. (eds.), *Selected Papers from the Citadel Conference on War and Diplomacy 1978* (Charleston, S.C.: The Citadel Development Foundation, 1979), pp. 27–40, which is also heavily drawn upon in the following account.

73 See Oshima Nos. 104 and 107 of 24 Jan. 1943, NA, RG 457, SRDJ 31266–67, 31342–43 (no German record of this Hitler–Oshima conversation has been found); *ADAP*, E, 5, No. 150, 6, No. 53; Seekriegsleitung to OKW/WFSt, "556/43 g.K.Chefs.," 22 Feb. 1943, BA/MA, RM 7/254, f. 45–47; Skl, "Indopazifischer Raum (Vortrag vor Ob.d.M. am 2. März 1943)," ibid., f 62–70; KTB Skl A 42, 8 Feb. 1943, RM 7/45, f. 126; Theo Michaux, "Rohstoffe aus Ostasien: Die Fahrten der Blockadebrecher," *Wehrwissenschaftliche Rundschau* 5 (1955), 497–98; St.S., No. 82 of 5 Feb. 1943, AA, St.S., "Japan," Bd. 11, fr. 17135–36. On the sinking of one of the two submarines turned over to Japan (RO 501, ex U-1224) on 13 May 1944 during her trip to Japan see William T. Y'Blood, *Hunter-Killer: U.S. Escort Carriers in the Battle of the Atlantic* (Annapolis, Md.: Naval Institute Press, 1983), pp. 215–16.

74 U.S. War Dept., G-2, "Magic Far Eastern Summary, Naval Section, No. 304, 1 Jan. 1945, NA, RG 457, SRS 287.

75 See Boyd, "Japanese Submarine Force," pp. 31–32; USSBS, *The War against Japanese Transportation, 1941–1945* (Washington: GPO, 1947), p. 63.

76 KTB Skl A 45, 23 May 1943, BA/MA, RM 7/48, f. 399; Skl, "Niederschrift über die Besprechung mit Vizeadmiral Abe beim Chef des Stabes der Seekriegsleitung am 25. Mai 1700 Uhr," 31 May 1943, RM 7/254, f. 127–31; Tokyo to Berlin No. 476 of 5 July 1943, NA, RG 457, SRDJ 39872; Oshima to Tokyo No. 731 of 6 July 1943, SRDJ 39930–33.

77 Oshima's report No. 1138 of 24 Sep. 1943 on a conversation with Dönitz on 22 Sep., NA, RG 457, SRDJ 43444–46; Hinsley, *British Intelligence*, 3/l: 220–22.

78 Michaux, "Rohstoffe aus Ostasien," pp. 503–6; NA, RG 457, RG 232; Tokyo to Berlin Skl No. 67 of 1 June 1943, SRGL 720; Hinsley, 3–1: 218; Beesly, *Very Special Intelligence*, pp. 197–99; Morison, *US Naval Operations*, 10: 303–4; Marder, *Old Friends, New Enemies*, 2: 206–15, 250ff. A preliminary survey in Allison W. Saville, "German Submarines in the Far East," *U.S. Naval Institute Proceedings* 87, No. 8 (Aug. 1961), 80–92. The book by Hans Joachim Brennecke, *Haie im Paradies: Der deutsche U-Boot-Krieg in Asiens Gewässern, 1943–45* (2d ed., Herford: Kochler, 1967), is in fictional form, but the documents in it contain some interesting details.

79 Hinsley, 3/1: 229–31.

80 Pacific Strategic Intelligence Section, "Japanese Reaction to German Defeat," 21 May 1945, NA, RG 457, SRH-075, pp. 5–7; U.S. War Dept., G-2, "Magic Far Eastern Summary," No. 432, Naval Section, 9 May 1945, SRS 412.

81 See NA, RG 457, SRGL 1188–89; Chief of Naval Operations, ONI Attaché Reports 1940–46, F-6-e # 24309-H, NA, RG 38; National Archives, "Records Relating to U-Boat Warfare 1939–45," p. 62. On the revival of the French navy for participation in the Battle of the Atlantic and other operations on the side of the Allies, see Marcel Vigneras, *Rearming the French* (Washington: GPO, 1957), chap. 22.

82 On this question, see the intercepts of relevant Japanese messages of 7 Sep.–21 Dec. 1944, in NA, RG 457, SRNA 2350–51, 2602–4, 3553–4, 3597–98; "Magic" Far Eastern Summaries No. 195 of 1 Oct. 1944 and No. 279 of 24 Dec. 1944.

83 This episode can be followed in the intercepted Japanese and German telegrams of 15 Feb.–16 May 1945, NA, RG 457, SRNA 4135–37, 4216–17, 4653–56, 4737–42, 4751–52, 4755–57, 4760–62, 4778, 4796–97, 4807–8, 4840, 4907; SRDJ 98570; SRGL 2843, 2847.

84 Wagner, *Lagevorträge*, pp. 420–25; Heinrich Waas, "Eine Besprechung über den U-Boot-Krieg bei Hitler in der Reichskanzlei im Herbst 1942 und ihre Bedeutung für den Kriegsverlauf," *Geschichte in Wissenschaft und Unterricht* 38 (1987), 684–95.

85 The June 5 conference is in Wagner, pp. 507–11. Dönitz had prepared Hitler for the bad news on May 14 when he had argued for the invasion of Spain (which Hitler rejected as no longer feasible) as a means of recovering the initiative in both the U-Boat and North African campaigns (ibid., pp. 504–5).

86 Salewski, *Seekriegsleitung*, 3: 357–63. The minimal efforts of the Luftwaffe are covered in ibid., 2: 498–500. Although Dönitz did not mention it, the loss of weather ships and stations by the German navy surely also played a major role (Kahn, *Seizing Enigma*, chaps. 12, 14).

87 On the campaign in the Bay of Biscay, see Morison, *US Naval Operations*, 10: 89–92; Hinsley, *British Intelligence*, 3/1: 214–17.

88 On the acoustic torpedo, see Hinsley, 3/1: 222–23. There was much debate about sharing this secret with the Japanese. It was eventually decided in favor of giving it to them; relevant documents in NA, RG 457, SRGL 1032, 1098, SRA 11190; War Dept. G-2, "Magic" Far Eastern Summary No. 183 of 19 Sep. 1944, No 337, Naval Section, No.

347 of 2 Mar. 1945; of 3 Feb. 1945; KTB Skl A 53, 15 Jan. 1944, BA/MA, RM 7/56, f. 261. Another part of the German fall 1943 offensive was the establishment of a small automatic weather broadcasting station in Canada, see Alec Douglas, "The Nazi Weather Station in Labrador," *Canadian Geographia* 101 (Dec. 1981/Jan. 1982), 42–47.

89 On the FX 1400 glide-bomb and the HS 293 rocket, see Wagner, *Lagevorträge*, p. 511; Hinsley, 3/1: 47, 337–42.

90 "Ansprache an Oberbefehlshaber 8.6.43," BA/MA, RM 7/97, f. 518–21.

91 Waas; "Eine Besprechung über den U-Boot-Krieg"; Hinsley, 3/1: 239, 244–45, Appendix 11; Salewski, *Seekriegsleitung*, 2: 503–28. Note that on May 1, 1945, the COMINCH warned that the new Type XXI submarines could appear in the North Atlantic in May; see NA, RG 457, SRMN 30, p. 118. See also Douglas, *Creation of a National Air Force*, pp. 600ff.

92 Waas, p. 692, estimates a steel equivalent of thirty tanks per U-Boat. By this reckoning, the 170 Type XXI boats ordered "cost" the Germans 5100 tanks.

93 Hinsley, 3/1: 239–40.

94 Ibid., pp. 46–51, Appendix 11; Op-20-G, "Technical Intelligence from Allied C[ommunications] I[intelligence]," Vol. 4 of "Battle of the Atlantic", NA, RG 457, SRH-025, pp. 1467–69; Japanese naval attaché Berlin No. N Serial 233 of 26 May and N Serial 235 of 28 May 1944, SRNA 1450–54. Allied intelligence profited particularly from the report on a 29 Aug. 1944 inspection of a Type XXI submarine in Danzig; Japanese naval attaché Berlin Nos. 420 of 12 Sep. and 423 of 13 Sep. 1944, SRNA 2414–17, 2420–22; cf. Beesly, *Very Special Intelligence*, p. 254.

95 Hinsley, 3/1: 312–14.

96 Note Beesly, pp. 246–47; Morison, *US Naval Operations*, 10: 317–19, 327. In the summer of 1944 Hitler also abandoned his 1942 project of having submarines refuel airplanes so that they could bomb New York; see KTB Skl A 35, 16 July 1942, BA/MA, RM 7/38, f. 310–11; "Persönliches Kriegstagebuch des Generals der Flieger [Werner] Kreipe als Chef des Generalstabes der Luftwaffe für die Zeit vom 22,7,-2.11.1944," entry for 21 Aug. 1944, Center for Military History, P-069.

97 Jacobsen and Dollinger, *Zweite Weltkrieg*, 3: 154; Salewski, *Seekriegsleitung*, 2: 501–3, 506; Morison, 10: chaps. 9–12.

98 See the interesting report on morale as of Dec. 1943 written by a U-Boat commander of Austrian background captured that month; CNO, Op-16-z, Spot Item No. 286, in FDRL, Map Room, Box 167, Naval Aide, Germany; and the comments in Gottfried Hoch, "Zur Problematik der Menschenführung im Kriege, Eine Untersuchung zur Einsatzbereitschaft der deutschen U-Boot-Besatzungen ab 1943," in Vito Housselle et al. (eds.), *Die Deutsche Marine* (Herford: Mittler, 1983), p. 199.

99 Morison, 1: 290–91, derides these projects. More dramatic and successful was the capture on May 31, 1944, of U-505 with its code books and machines (Kahn, *Codebreakers*, pp. 504–6); it is now on display at the Chicago Museum of Science and Industry.

100 On this project, see the summary in Bernard Fergusson, *The Watery Maze: The Story of Combined Operations* (New York: Holt, Rinehart & Winston, 1961), pp. 145–46, 287, 289, 298–99; documents in PRO, CAB 120/840, AIR 20/4546, PREM 3/216/2-6; FDRL, Map Room Box 162, Naval Aide, Habbakuk [the misspelling used at the time]; Arthur Bryant, *The Turn of the Tide* (Garden City, N.Y.: Doubleday, 1957), pp. 569–70, 583–84.

101 Very useful is by Y'Blood, *Hunter-Killer*.

102 John J. McDonald, *Howard Hughes and the Spruce Goose* (Blue Ridge Summit, Penn.: Tab Books, 1981); Charles Barton, *Howard Hughes and his Flying Boat* (Fallbrook, Calif.: Aero Publishers, 1982).

103 Charles P. Stacey, *Canada and the Age of Conflict, Vol. 2: 1921–1948, The Mackenzie King Era* (Toronto: Univ. of Toronto Press, 1981), pp. 230–31, 325.

104 Morison, *US Naval Operations*, 1: 198.

105 Roosevelt to Secretary of the Navy, 9 Feb. 1942 and 22 Feb. 1943, FDRL, PSF Box 11, CF Navy 1940–42, and CF Navy 1943. A tiny number of Black seamen was commissioned in March 1945, there is a summary in the obituary of one of them in *New York Times*, 11 Jan. 1992.

106 Morison, 1, chap. 8; Roskill, *War at Sea*, 2: 61–62, 75.

107 Charles A. Jellison, *Besieged: The World War II Ordeal of Malta, 1940–1942* (Hanover, N.H.: Univ. Press of New England, 1984); Kreis, *Air Base Defense*, pp. 113–35. When in April 1942 the London government saw, or thought it saw, signs that the governor of the island, Lt.Gen. Sir William Dobbie, might be thinking of surrendering or in any case was buckling under the pressure, Field Marshal Gort was sent instead. Whatever Gort's deficiencies as head of the BEF in 1940, no one ever had any doubts about his steadfastness as a fortress commander, and he was clearly no longer needed at Gibraltar (Jellison, pp. 212–14; Bryant, *Turn of the Tide*, pp. 305–6).

108 Santoni, *Ultra siegt im Mittelmeer*, passim.

109 Hinsley, *British Intelligence*, 3/1: 87; *ADAP*, E, 4, Nos. 80, 85; "Stand der Heizöllage der deutschen und italienischen Kriegsmarine Anfang April 1942," BA/MA, RM 6/76, f. 78–81; German naval attaché Rome, "Italienische Urteile zu Admiralstabsbesprechungen in Garmisch," 23 Jan. 1942, BA/MA, PG 45923, Case 19/3.

110 This is made particularly clear by the map in Ch'i, *Nationalist China*, p. 75.

111 Note JP(44) 54 (Final), War Cabinet Joint Planning Staff, "Appreciation on Move of Japanese fleet," 24 Feb. 1944, PRO, AIR 8/1277.

112 USSBS, *Transportation*, p. 1.

113 Ibid., p. 2.

114 Ibid., p. 54.

115 The most useful table is that in ibid., p. 47. It should be noted that some of the sinkings were caused by British and Dutch submarines, Australian, British, and Russian planes, and, of course, by marine casualties.

116 Joint Army–Navy Assessment Committee, *Japanese Naval and Merchant Shipping Losses during World War II by All Causes* (Washington: GPO, 1947), pp. vii-viii.

117 On the sinking of the *Shinano* on Nov. 29, 1944, see Captain Joseph F. Enright with James F. Ryan, *Shinano! The Sinking of Japan's Supership* (New York: St. Martin's, 1987); on the sinking of the *Ashigara* on June 8, 1945, see Alistair Mars, *British Submarines at War, 1939–1945* (Annapolis, Md.: Naval Institute Press, 1971), pp. 227–29.

118 See Boyd, "Japanese Submarine Force," p. 33.

119 Kahn, *Codebreakers*, pp. 579–85 on the Japanese, 586–94 on the Americans. As Drea repeatedly shows in *MacArthur's Ultra*, the breaking of the code used for transport shipping aided the Allies enormously.

120 There is no history of American blockade measures, and hence Volume 2 of the British official history, William N. Medlicott *The Economic Blockade*, serves, in effect, as the only general account for both countries.

121 Ibid., pp. 165–69, 435–45.

122 Ibid., pp. 433–35, 669–72.

123 Wittmann, *Schwedens Wirtschaftsbeziehungen*, pp. 263–73, 278–79.

124 Note the 1943 documents of the German navy detailing its thoughts on the disadvantages of a war with Sweden, in BA/MA, RM 7/162, f. 120–32.

125 A semi-official apologia is Wilhelm M. Carlgren, *Swedish Foreign Policy during the Second World War*, trans. by Arthur Spencer (New York: St. Martin's, 1977). The study of Sweden's economic relations with Germany by Klaus Wittmann has a very strong pro-Swedish and anti-Allied bias, but the material presented in it fully supports my interpretation.

126 Wittmann, pp. 361–69; Oshima's No. 940 of 16 Aug. 1943, NA, RG 457, SRDJ 42045–46.

127 Wittmann, pp. 354–60.

128 Ibid., pp. 372–73 (Wittmann himself, however, does not share this view).

129 Ibid., pp. 380–81.

130 Ibid., p. 377.

131 Ibid., pp. 384–90.

132 Statistics on Swedish exports to Germany are in ibid., pp. 243, 248, 359; Medlicott, *Economic Blockade*, 2: 665–66.

133 *ADAP*, E, 2, Nos. 245, 278; 3, No. 11; Klaus-Jörg Ruhl, *Spanien im Zweiten Weltkrieg: Franco, die Falange und das "Dritte Reich"* (Hamburg: Hoffmann & Campe, 1975), pp. 157–65; Memorandum by Weizsäcker, "St.S. Nr. 199," 26 Mar. 1943, AA, St.S., "Aufzeichnungen über Diplomatenbesuche," Bd. 13, fr. 290549–51.

134 Although dated in some ways, Herbert Feis, *The Spanish Story: Franco and the Nations at War* (New York: Knopf, 1948), remains important; see esp. chaps. 24–26.

135 Ruhl, *Spanien*, pp. 233–42; Oshima's No. 427 of 7 May 1944, NA, RG 457, SRDJ 57894–95; Donovan to Roosevelt, 24 July 1944, FDRL, PSF Box 168, OSS Reports 15–29 July 1944.

136 Some statistics in Medlicott, *Economic Blockade*, 2: 667. Chaps. 10 and 19 recount the negotiations and activities in detail. Most of the smuggling from Latin America appears to have been done via Spanish ships as well.

137 Ibid., chaps. 11 and 20. The statistics on p. 668 also refer to the transit shipment of sisal (for making rope) from the Portuguese colonial empire. There is extensive documentation on the German concern about wolfram imports in the German diplomatic documents, and material on German worry that Japan's occupation of Portuguese Timor and the refusal to allow the Portuguese administration there to function would lead the Lisbon government to cut off wolfram supplies. Examples of intercepted Japanese documents in NA, RG 457, SRDJ 26652–54, 47636–37, 47762–63, 47917–18. See also OKM, "Niederschrift über die Besprechung zwischen dem kaiserlichen japanischen Vizeadmiral Abe und dem Chef des Stabes der Seekriegsleitung Vizeadmiral Meisel am 21.12.1943," 24 Dec. 1943, BA/MA, RM 7/254, f. 208–10; KTB Skl A 53, 19 Jan. 1944, RM 7/56, f. 332–33.

138 The issues can be followed in Medlicott, *Economic Blockade*, 2: chaps. 7 and 17. As for the other neutrals, numerous documents are published in the relevant volumes of *ADAP* and *FRUS*.

139 See Önder, *Türkische Aussenpolitik*, pp. 190–91, on the negative British reaction to the Turkish effort to acquire Aleppo from the French mandate of Syria. Deringil (*Turkish Foreign Policy*), maintains a discreet silence on the subject of Turkish territorial aspirations.

140 On the Turkish ore delivery agreement of Oct. 9, 1941, see Önder, pp. 130–31, 154–55.

141 The British minutes are published in ibid., pp. 274–96; a full account of Churchill's visit in Gilbert, *Churchill*, 7: 316–25.

142 Hinsley, *British Intelligence*, 3/2: 43n, takes a very charitable view. Kahn (*Codebreakers*, pp. 451–52) correctly notes that the most important British cables were sent using one-time pads so that matching a code text with a clear text would provide no clues for any other message – the great advantage of the one-time pad. What is not clear is whether other codes were compromised. The "Cicero" affair is reviewed in Chapter 10.

143 A full account in Medlicott, *Economic Blockade*, 2: chaps. 8 and 18; some statistics on p. 666. See also Önder, *Türkische Aussenpolitik*, pp. 212, 227–28, 232–37.

144 Michaux, "Rohstoffe aus Ostasien," p. 486.

145 Salewski, *Seekriegsleitung*, 2: 349; Hinsley, *British Intelligence*, 2: 190–91; Beesly, *Very Special Intelligence*, p. 231; Medlicott, 2: 170–72; NA, RG 457, SRDJ 114015–180, passim; Earl of Selborne (Minister of Economic Warfare) to First Lord of the Admiralty, 18 Mar. 1942ff, PRO, AIR 19/343.

146 Salewski, 2: 350–55; Roskill, *War at Sea*, 2: 182–84; Medlicott, 2: 446–48; documents in PRO, AIR 8/1746 and PREM 3/74/3; Admiralty to COMINCH, 25 June 1942, NA, RG 457, SRMN 35, pp. 1–2; Oshima to Tokyo No. 822 of 27 June 1942, SRDJ 2444–45, Tokyo to Berlin No. 717 of 26 Sept. and No. 744 of 9 Oct. 1942, SRDJ 26694, 27012–15.

147 Salewski, 2: 352–54; Hinsley, 2: 540–47; *ADAP*, E, 5, No. 258; Michaux, pp. 494–97; Beesly, pp. 231–32; Roskill, *War at Sea*, 2: 273–76; Oshima to Tokyo Nos. 103, 105, 106 of 23 Jan. 1943, NA, RG 457, SRDJ 30741–43, and No. 194 of 13 Feb. 1943, SRDJ 31543–44; Japanese military attaché Berlin to Tokyo No. 439 of 29 July 1943, SRA 03655–56.

148 Salewski, 2: 355–57; Beesly, pp. 232–33; Medlicott, *Economic Blockade*, 2: 448–52; Morison, *US Naval Operations*, 10: 226–28; Lewin, *American Magic*, chap. 9; Hinsley, 3/1: 247–52; Roskill, 2: 408–11; Wagner, *Lagevorträge*, p. 570; Michaux, pp. 499–503; intercepts of Japanese documents in NA, RG 457, SRDJ 43045, 43765, 45497–99, 45622; SRA 01238, 01278; SRNA 603–6.

149 Salewski, 2: 357–59; KTB Skl A 53, 6 Jan. 1944, BA/MA, RM 7/56, f. 87–88. This does not mean, of course, that vast quantities were not lost; see the reference to the 200 lb bale of cured rubber floating ashore at the special American HF/DF station set up on Jan Mayen Island to locate German weather reporting stations on Greenland; "U.S. Naval Supplementary Radio Station on Jan Mayen Island, November 1943–December 1945," NA, RG 457, SRH 299, p. 12.

150 Salewski, 2: 353–55; Michaux, p. 498; Martin Brice, *Axis Blockade Runners of World War II* (Annapolis, Md.: Naval Institute Press, 1981), pp. 129–34; Berlin to Tokyo No. 38 of 15 Apr. 1943 and No. 152 of 25 May 1943, NA, RG 457, SRDJ 39059, 37063; OKW, HKW (Gross) report for Keitel, 5 June 1943, BA/MA, RM 7/224.

151 Salewski, 2: 359.

152 Intercepted Japanese documents on this are in NA, RG 457, SRDJ 50472–74A, 56497–98, 68946–47, 83729–30, 93871; "Magic" Far East Summaries 152, 156, 224, 273, SRA 12782. German naval attaché Tokyo to Berlin No. E 2470 of 5 Oct. 1944, with its detailed shipping list provides an excellent example of the sort of cargo sent; it is in SRGL 1598 (see also SRGL 1571). Additional information in SRNA 603–6, SMMN 33, pp. 4290–92.

153 *Kido Diary*, pp. 364, 375; U.S. Army Center for Military History, Shuster file, interrogation of Bohle by Oron J. Hale, 26–27 July 1945.

154 Japanese naval attaché Berlin to Tokyo No. 848 of 30 Dec. 1944, and No. 131 of 4 Apr. 1945, NA, RG 457, SRNA 3697–98, 4593–94; "Magic" Far East Summary No. 156, 23 Aug. 1943, NA, RG 457, SRS 156.

155 Chief Inspector in Germany to Tokyo Nos. 165 and 176 of 15 Apr. 1945, NA, RG 457, SRNA 4707–10, 4692–96; "Magic" Far East Summaries Nos. 347, 354, 403.

156 Dönitz's very interesting project, which awaits a serious study, can be traced in the American intercepts of German and Japanese messages about it from 25 Nov. 1944–19 Mar. 1945. The German messages are in NA, RG 457, SRGL 1794–96, 1982, 1996, 2194, 2221–23, 2288–89, 2472, 2494; the Japanese messages are in ibid., SRNA 3520–23, 3742, 3743–44, 3799–800, 4423–24. The Germans also wanted plans and details of the guns and ammunition used on the Japanese surface ships, including their 16-inch guns (see the Japanese naval attaché message of 29 Jan. 1945 quoted in "Magic" Far East Summary No. 337, 3 Feb. 1945, p. 3).

157 The replaced German air attaché Colonel Wolfgang von Gronau was to return to Germany by submarine thereafter. When Kessler was captured in May, the two Japanese officers on the submarine committed suicide. Japanese documents on this, intercepted by the Americans, are in NA, RG 457, SRNA 3607–8, 4871–72, 4875, 4908–10, SRDJ 88665. A German message of 14 Apr. 1945, is in SRH 075, p. 3. See also COMINCH

to CINCPAC and Commander 7th fleet No. 162034 of 16 May 1945 in SRMN 33, p. 4450; Morison, *US Naval Operations*, 10: 360.

158 Japanese documents on this for the period Jan. 1943–Apr. 1945, intercepted by the Americans, may be found in NA, RG 457, SRDJ 31342–44, 32785, 33942, 34350, 36954, 37957, 38946–49, 40323–24, 66833, 85409–11, 87373–74; SRNA 2086–87, 2458–59, 2812–13, 3792–95, 3796, 4667–71; SRA 00235–36, 15627, "Magic" Summary Japanese Army Supplement, No. 77 (SRS 77), "Magic" Far East Summary No. 201 (SRS 201). German documents are in *ADAP*, E, 5, No. 180 and in AA, St.S., "Japan," Bd. 11. There is evidence that a Japanese airplane attempted to fly to Europe from Singapore in May 1943 and disappeared along the way (Tokyo to Berlin No. 272 of 16 May 1943, SRDJ 38950–51; Japanese military attaché Berlin to Madrid No. 351 of 9 July 1943, SRA 01169).

159 For British and American concerns about this issue, see W 1137, 3033/1137/804, PRO, FO 371/42507; War Dept., G-2 Estimate of the Enemy Situation, Japanese empire and Manchuria, 12 Apr. 1944, NA, RG 165, Entry 77, Box 2364, File 6000–Japan. The Western Powers were concerned primarily about the possible sending of blueprints; the Soviets refused to cooperate unless clear evidence of the improper use of the diplomatic pouch could be presented – and that, of course, was inside the pouches.

160 Note Salewski, *Seekriegsleitung*, 2: 359; Roskill, *War at Sea*, 2: 482–84.

161 Some information in Nikolai Alexeevich Piterskii (ed.), *Die Sowjet-Flotte im Zweiten Weltkrieg*, trans. by Erich F. Pruck, ed. by Jürgen Rohwer (Munich: Stalling, 1966), esp. chap. 3. See also Friedrich Ruge, *The Soviets as Naval Opponents, 1941–1945* (Annapolis, Md.: Naval Institute Press, 1979); Jürg Meister, *Soviet Warships of the Second World War* (New York: Arco, 1977).

162 See Beaumont, *Comrades in Arms*, pp. 116–25, 131–37, 140–42, 161–63.

163 Ibid., pp. 164–65.

164 Morison, *US Naval Operations*, 1: 159.

165 Herring, *Aid to Russia*, pp. 72–73, 97, 115–16; detailed statistics in Motter, *Persian Corridor*, pp. 481–83.

166 *ADAP*, E, 5, Nos. 104 and n 3, 356; 6, No. 68; Tokyo to Berlin No. 1744 of 4 June and No. 1873 of 17 June 1944, AA, St.S., "Japan," Bd. 12; "Magic" Far East Summary No. 267, 12 Dec. 1944, NA, RGS, SRS 267; German naval attaché Tokyo to Berlin No. 178 of 21 Nov. 1944, SRGL 1905; and Japanese intercepts in SRDJ 34675–76, 37898–900, 39622–23, 39801, 65346–51.

167 Sato quoting Molotov in his tel. No. 57 of 10 July 1943, NA, RG 457, SRDJ 40394. When a Soviet ship was sunk by a submarine in the summer of 1944, the Japanese insisted to the Russians that it had been done by an American submarine (on the basis of "signals" intelligence). The issue was quickly smoothed over while the Americans checked to make sure that the Japanese knowledge came from locator, not code-breaking, intelligence (Tokyo to Moscow No. 868 of 11 July 1944, SRDJ 64401–2; Moscow to Tokyo No. 1480 of 21 July 1944, SRDJ 65425–29).

168 The Americans were following this argument by reading the exchanges between Tokyo and the Japanese embassy in Kuibyshev and later Moscow. These documents, from 26 May to 13 Aug. 1943 (and a last item from 24 July 1944), are in NA, RG 457, SRDJ 38480, 36987, 37115–16, 37136, 37726–32, 37733–34, 37739–40, 38060, 38095–113, 38170–71, 38182–84, 38455–57, 38364–68, 38458, 38526, 38572, 38610–12, 38630–31, 38756–63, 40265–66, 40325–27, 41274–75, 41276–80, 42081–82, 65643–46.

169 Sally van Wegener Keil, *Those Wonderful Women in Their Flying Machines* (New York: Rawson, Wade, 1979).

170 Memorandum for Roosevelt, early May 1942, FDRL, PSF Box 68, Russia 1942–43.

171 *FRUS*, 1942, 2: 702.

172 Lukas, *Eagles East*, pp. 166–67; Herring, *Aid to Russia*, pp. 70, 72; C. P. Stacey, *Arms*,

Men and Governments: The War Policies of Canada, 1939–1945 (Ottawa: Queen's Printer, 1970), pp. 379–82. The papers of General Follett Bradley, the key American figure in this, are in the U.S. Air Force Academy Library as M.S. 1.

173 On the Alaska Highway and its role, Stacey, *Canada and the Age of Conflict*, pp. 155, 361–62; Stacey, *Arms, Men and Governments*, pp. 348, 382–83; Joseph Bykofsky and Harold Larson, *The Transportation Corps: Operations Overseas* (Washington: GPO, 1957), pp. 57–64; Phillys Lee Brebner, *The Alaska Highway: A Personal and Historical Account of the Building of the Alaska Highway* (Erin, Ont.: Boston Mills Press, 1985). There is a 2–volume official account by the U.S. Army Service Forces, *The Alaska Highway* (Washington, 1945), which has been filmed by the Library of Congress (No. 51360).

174 Ziemke, *Moscow to Stalingrad*, chap. 6; Erickson, *Road to Stalingrad*, pp. 289–91, 329–30.

8: THE WAR IN EUROPE AND NORTH AFRICA

1 Ziemke, *Moscow to Stalingrad*, pp. 283–86, 327–28.

2 Ibid., pp. 301, 303; *KTB Halder*, 3: 436, 5 May 1942. After the war Halder pretended that he had opposed the 1942 offensive; there was in fact no opposition from him or anyone else in German headquarters (*DRuZW*, 6: 774).

3 Ziemke, *Moscow to Stalingrad*, chap. 14; *DRuZW*, 6: 788ff.

4 The relevant segments of the Soviet appreciation are translated in Ziemke, *Moscow to Stalingrad*, pp. 302–3.

5 Ibid., pp. 307–8, 328–30.

6 Ibid., pp. 269–82; Erickson, *Road to Stalingrad*, pp. 344–47; *DRuZW*, 6: 852–64.

7 Erickson, *Road to Stalingrad*, pp. 347–50; Ziemke, *Moscow to Stalingrad*, pp. 261–69; David M. Glantz, *Soviet Military Deception in the Second World War* (London: Cass 1989), pp. 182–88; *DRuZW*, 6: 841–45. The Germans captured over 150,000 prisoners.

8 A good account of the monster gun in Charles B. Burdick, "DORA: The Germans' Biggest Gun," *Military Review* 11 (1961), 72–75.

9 Ziemke, *Moscow to Stalingrad*, pp. 309–21; Erickson, *Road to Stalingrad*, pp. 350–52; *DRuZW*, 6: 845–52; Alfred Philippi and Ferdinand Heim, *Der Feldzug gegen Sowjetrussland 1941 bis 1945* (Stuttgart: Kohlhammer, 1962). p. 124, refer to 24,000 German casualties. The Soviet official work, *Istoriya Vtoroi Mirovoi Voyny* (12 vols. Moscow: Voyennoye Izdateltsvo, 1973–82), 5: 137, says about 150,000.

10 Philippi and Heim, p. 129; *DRuZW*, 6: 816ff.

11 See the account by Colonel von Geldern-Crispendorf in his papers in BA/MA, N 185/1, f. 785. Ziemke (p. 351) gives July 14; Hillgruber (*KTB OKW*, 2, Part 1: 58) July 16 as the date of Hitler's move. The most recent account of Hitler's dismissal of Field Marshal von Bock is in *DRuZW*, 6: 876–75; it shows Halder and the whole high command of the army as in agreement with Hitler.

12 The text of the 23 July 1942 directive is in Hubatsch, *Hitlers Weisungen*, pp. 196–200. The directive for the main operation itself, No. 41 of 5 April 1942, is in ibid., pp. 183–88. There are good accounts of the fighting in Ziemke, *Moscow to Stalingrad*, pp. 321–57; Erickson, *Road to Stalingrad*, pp. 353–63; *DRuZW*, 6: 868ff (with special stress on the hopelessly inadequate logistical preparations and maintenance for the German 6th Army).

13 The detailed orders are in Directive 45 cited in the preceding footnote (see also *KTB OKW*, 2, Part 1: 60–62). Hitler's July 10 decision that the conquered Caucasus area would be under the Ministry for the Occupied Eastern Territories rather than falling under the jurisdiction of the German Foreign Ministry (*ADAP*, E, 3, No. 83) may fit into this context. See also Andreas Hillgruber, "'Nordlicht'–Die deutschen Pläne zur Eroberung Leningrads in Jahre 1942," in Andreas Hillgruber (ed.), *Deutsche Grossmachtund Weltpolitik im 19. und 20. Jahrhundert* (Düsseldorf: Droste, 1977), p. 295–316.

14 Note the anxious memorandum of American intelligence on the dangers for all the Allies of the German advance into the Caucasus, War Dept., Military Intelligence Service, "Military Potentialities in the Caucasus," 17 Sep. 1942, NA, RG 165, Entry 77, Box 3484, File U.S.S.R. 6910.

15 Ziemke, *Moscow to Stalingrad*, chap. 18; Erickson, *Road to Stalingrad*, pp. 376–81.

16 Önder, *Türkische Aussenpolitik*, pp. 142–57; *ADAP*, E, 2, No. 33, 3, No. 284; Ankara to Tarabaya No. 92 of 27 July 1941 and Rohde to Papen, 28 July 1942, AA, Botschaft Ankara, "Geheime Erlasse, Berichte," Bd. 17, fr. 488605–6; German embassy Turkey, "Die aussenpolitische Stellung der Türkei," 1 Sep. 1942, ibid., Bd. 18, fr. 488676–83; Ziemke, *Moscow to Stalingrad*, p. 370.

17 On Project Velvet, see the documents in PRO, AIR 8/ 1055–58, AIR 19/557, AIR 20/2483–84, 3878–80, CAB 120/291; FDRL, Map Room Box 170, A 16, Air Warfare U.S.S.R.. Accounts in Lukas, *Eagles East*, chap. 10; Beaumont, *Comrades in Arms*, pp. 125–26.

18 Geoffrey Jukes, *Hitler's Stalingrad Decisions* (Berkeley, Calif.: Univ. of California Press, 1985), pp. 38–40.

19 The unit was the Grossdeutschland division which, however, ended up being sent to the central part of the Eastern Front (Ziemke, *Stalingrad to Berlin*, pp. 357–58, 364–65, 375, 405–7).

20 The most recent account in Gilbert. *Churchill*, 7: chap. 11. Information obtained on this by the Japanese is in Kuibyshev to Tokyo No. 843 of 4 Sep. 1942, NA, RG 457, SRDJ 26655.

21 Roger Beaumont, "The Bomber Offensive as a Second Front," *JCH* 22 (1987), 10–12.

22 Note, for example, Churchill's personal pushing of the fog dispersal system FIDO, starting in October 1941, to save planes and to make more frequent raids possible (documents in PRO, AIR 8/781).

23 On these issues, see Webster and Frankland, *Strategic Air Offensive*, 1: chaps. 5–6; Hastings, *Bomber Command*, pp. 156–64. On the speech of Sir Stafford Cripps of Feb. 25, 1942, which was interpreted by some as a sign of loss of confidence in the bomber offensive, see also Saward, *"Bomber" Harris* pp. 116–17, and the documents in PRO, AIR 8/619.

24 The British were also finding out more about the German defenses; the commando raid on St. Bruneval to seize a German "Würzburg" radar took place on Feb. 27–28, 1942 (see Hinsley, *British Intelligence*, 2: 248–49). The successful air raid on the Renault works was on Mar. 9, 1942 (Hastings, pp. 172–73).

25 Saward, *"Bomber" Harris*, pp. 118–26, 132–33; Hastings, pp. 173–77.

26 Boog, *Luftwaffenführung*, p. 133.

27 Hastings, pp. 149–54; Saward, pp. 149–50; Roger Beaumont, "Bomber Offensive," pp. 7–9. An account sympathetic to Lord Cherwell is in the authorized biography: Earl of Birkenhead, *The Professor and the Prime Minister* (Boston: Houghton Mifflin, 1962), pp. 258–67.

28 Saward, pp. 138–46; Hastings, pp. 177–80; Webster and Frankland, 1: chap. 7.

29 Boog, *Luftwaffenführung*, p. 524. The first Japanese report was also ridiculously inaccurate by contrast with later reports on the bombing of Germany which were generally very frank (Berlin to Tokyo No. 710 of 3 June 1942, NA, RG 457, SRDJ 23755).

30 See Saward, pp. 160–81; Portal to Brooke, 28 Sep. 1942, PRO, AIR 8/878; Brooke Diary 22 and 23 Oct. 1942, Alanbrooke Papers, Liddell Hart Centre.

31 Herring, *Aid to Russia*, pp. 74–75, 84–85; John D. Langer, "The 'Red General': Philip R. Faymonville and the Soviet Union, 1917–52," *Prologue* 8 (1976), 219.

32 Much of the text is quoted in Ziemke, *Moscow to Stalingrad*, pp. 361–62. See also Erickson, *Road to Stalingrad*, pp. 370–71; *DRuZW*, 6: 928–30; Welles to Roosevelt, 12 Aug. 1942, reporting very alarming comments by Ambassador Litvinov which had been repeated to

him by the Mexican ambassador to the U.S. (FDRL, PSF Box 68, Russia 1942–43).

33 *ADAP*, E, 3, Nos. 153, 181.

34 Maximilian von Weichs, "Erinnerungen über die Sommer-Offensive 1942 im Ostfeldzug," BA/MA, Nachlass Weichs, N 19/17, f. 18; Kurt Zeitzler, comments on a paper by Gotthard Heinrici on Stalingrad, "Unternehmen Fischreiher, Hitlers weitfliegende Pläne," 10 Dec. 1953, BA/MA, Nachlass Zeitzler, N 63/15, f. 11–12; *KTB OKW*, 1942, 1: 66.

35 See *DRuZW*, 6: 951ff; Ziemke, *Moscow to Stalingrad*, pp. 276–78, 449–50; Förster, "Strategische Überlegungen," p. 96 and n 9, 10; Paulus Papers, BA/MA, N 372/10, f. 85; Zeitzler, "2 Jahre Chef des Gen.St.d.H. im 2. Weltkrieg" [circa 1953], N 63/18, f. 43, and his statement of 19 May 1946 in N/63/1, f. 39–40; Heiber (ed.), *Hitlers Lagebesprechungen*, pp. 11–12, 14–16. The stenographers were provided by the Reichstag, the German parliament, which had met for the last time in April of that year.

36 Ziemke, *Moscow to Stalingrad*, pp. 352–54.

37 Ibid., pp. 357–58.

38 Ibid., pp. 382–91; *DRuZW*, 6: 962ff.

39 Erickson, *Road to Stalingrad*, pp. 363–70. A detailed account in Louis C. Rotundo (ed.), *Battle for Stalingrad: The 1943 Soviet General Staff Study* (Washington: Pergamon-Brassey, 1989).

40 Ziemke, *Moscow to Stalingrad*, pp. 391–95; Erickson, *Road to Stalingrad*, pp. 383–86.

41 Note Zeitzler's post-war comments in his Nachlass, BA/MA, N 63/15, f. 10–11. The latter type of transfer would provide the basis for the German counter-offensive at Kharkov in Feb.-Mar. 1943.

42 A serious study of the air force field divisions remains to be written. See Egon Denzel, *Die Luftwaffenfelddivisionen, 1942–1945, sowie die Sonderverbände der Luftwaffe im Kriege, 1939–1945*, 3d ed. (Neckargemünd: Vowinckel, 1976); Werner Stang, "Zur Geschichte der Luftwaffenfelddivisionen der faschistischen Wehrmacht," *Zeitschrift für Militärgeschichte* 8 (1969), 196–207.

43 Text in Domarus, *Hitler*, 2: 1916, 1937–38. On the details of the fighting inside Stalingrad, see Erickson, *Road to Stalingrad*, pp. 391–93, 402–22, 431–45. A major contribution of Bernd Wegner's account in *DRuZW*, 6, appears to me to be his demonstration of the fact that even if the German 6th Army had taken Stalingrad, its supply situation was so deperate that there was no way for it to hold on through the winter. It should be noted that because of the extended street fighting, most of the army's horses were pulled out in October so that neither adequate supply nor rapid withdrawal or breakout would have been possible thereafter (R.L. Di Nardo, *Mechanized Juggernaut or Military Anachronism: Horses and the German Army of World War II* [New York: Greenwood, 1991], p. 60).

44 Glantz, *Soviet Military Deception*, pp. 108–19.

45 Ziemke, *Moscow to Stalingrad*, pp. 440–45; Erickson, *Road to Stalingrad*, pp. 374–76, 388–93, 422–31, 445–53.

46 On "Mars," see Ziemke, *Moscow to Stalingrad*, pp. 445–47; *DRuZW*, 6: 999 n 164. This is a subject on which the new openness in the former Soviet Union may shed more light.

47 On June 4, 1942, Hitler made a brief visit to Finland for Mannerheim's 75th birthday. Bernd Wegner (ed.), "Hitlers Besuch in Finnland: Das geheime Tonprotokoll seiner Unterredung mit Mannerheim am 4. Juni 1942," *VjZ* 41 (1993), 117–37; Michael Berry, *American Foreign Policy and the Finnish Exception: Ideological Preferences and Wartime Relations* (Helsinki: SHS, 1987), pp. 218–19. According to the Japanese Minister in Lisbon, the Finnish chargé there told him on Sep. 2, 1942 (presumably on the basis of a report from the Finnish Foreign Ministry), that Hitler had told Mannerheim that the war would last two more years. Germany and Finland would confer after the fall of Leningrad (Lisbon

[Chiba] to Helsinki, 4 Sep. 1942, copy of No. 686 to Tokyo, NA, RG 457, SRDJ 26032). A very important study of operation "Nordlicht" is that of Andreas Hillgruber.

48 Ziemke, *Moscow to Stalingrad*, pp. 421–22; *DRuZW*, 6: 902–3.

49 Glantz, *Soviet Military Deception*, pp. 96–98; Ziemke, *Moscow to Stalingrad*, pp. 408–23; *DRuZW*, 6: 903–6.

50 Erickson, *Road to Stalingrad*, p. 383.

51 Ibid., pp. 381–82; Ziemke, *Moscow to Stalingrad*, pp. 398–408; Glantz, pp. 88–95; *DRuZW*, 6: 906–10.

52 On this subject, the most useful English language introduction remains Armstrong, which combines a general survey with the reprinted texts of portions of many of the partisan warfare studies of the War Documentation Project, all now declassified. There is an excellent summary in Ziemke, *Moscow to Stalingrad*, chap. 10.

53 This is the main burden of the studies of early partisan bands in the Ukraine and the north Caucasus by John Armstrong and Alexander Dallin respectively.

54 John A. Armstrong, *Ukrainian Nationalism, 1939–1945* (New York: Columbia Univ. Press, 1955).

55 The most famous of these partisan bands, those of Aleksei F. Fyodorov, Sidor A. Kovpak, Alexander Saburov, and M. I. Naumov, all operated in 1942–43 in essentially this fashion and did have some success in organizing local partisans in the northern Ukraine (Armstrong, *Partisans*, pp. 113–16).

56 See the excerpts from Gerhard L. Weinberg, "The Partisan Movement in the Yelnya-Dorogobuzh Area of Smolensk Oblast," in ibid., pp. 444–57.

57 Note that by Sep. 7, 1942 the British had realized that the main German effort was at Stalingrad (Hinsley, *British Intelligence*, 2: 103–6).

58 George F. Howe, *Northwest Africa: Seizing the Initiative in the West* (Washington: GPO, 1957); Richard W. Steele, *The First Offensive* (Bloomington, Ind.: Indiana Univ. Press, 1973). See also Santoni, *Ultra*, pp. 182–88.

59 Y'Blood, *Hunter-Killer*, pp. 13–26.

60 Note the report of the Japanese Minister to Vichy to Tokyo No. 454 of 12 Nov. 1942, NA, RG 457, SRDJ 28229–31. The landing did, however, put an end to Vichy interference with the flights of British planes from Gibraltar to West Africa for the Takoradi route (see documents in PRO, AIR 8/691). On Churchill's interest in the building up and subsequent running down of that route see AIR 8/483. There is a general history of the route prepared by the Air Historical Branch in AIR 41/32.

61 This misassessment is especially striking since the Americans, as the OSS reports to President Roosevelt show, were reading the diplomatic telegrams of the Vichy French embassy in Washington, and the British had obtained the code of the Vichy French naval attaché there (H. Montgomery Hyde, *Cynthia* [New York: Dell, 1966], chap. 8).

62 The most comprehensive account is Funk, *The Politics of Torch*. See also Howard, *Grand Strategy*, 4: chaps. 7–9; Howe, *Northwest Africa*, chaps. 3–4; David A. Walker, "OSS and Operation Torch," *JCH* 22 (1987), 667–79. On Darlan's role and fate, see now Coutau-Bégarie and Huan, *Darlan*, chaps. 19–21.

63 There is a most interesting account of the fighting in Morocco evidently written in Nov. or Dec. 1942 by a high French staff officer at General Nogues's headquarters, in PRO, WO 106/2703. The intent there was obviously to fight, with a readiness to quit when clearly beaten by the Americans. See also Robert O. Paxton, *Parades and Politics at Vichy: The French Officer Corps under Marshal Pétain* (Princeton, N.J.: Princeton Univ. Press, 1966), pp. 344–58; Howe, chaps. 5–14.

64 Note Roosevelt's comments to Morgenthau, 17 Nov. 1942, FDRL, Morgenthau Presidential Diary, 5: 1193–94.

65 Paxton, *Parades and Politics*, pp. 358–61; Krautkrämer, "Vorgeschichte," p. 212; Raeder's answers to Assmann's question of 28 Aug. 1944, "Möglichkeiten eines Ausgleichs mit

Frankreich," BA/MA, PG 71826; Assmann memorandum, "Die Rolle des Admirals Darlan" [1944?], BA/MA, III M 502/1; Assmann to Raeder, 28 Nov. 1944, BA/MA, III M 502/7; Krogmann Diary, 10 Dec. 1942, Hamburg, Forschungsstelle, 11 k 10.

66 Note the Japanese reaction, Tokyo to Vichy Circular No. 2054 of 11 Nov. 1942, NA, RG 457, SRDJ 27877. For a German appreciation of Darlan's switch, see "Die Rolle des Admiral Darlan," n.d., probably 1944, BA/MA, III M 502/1.

67 On the situation in Tunisia, see Paxton, *Parades and Politics*, pp. 363–71; on the unoccupied part of metropolitan France and the determination not to resist the Germans, ibid., pp. 371–90. The French army which had finally reversed its humiliation in the Dreyfus case by removing its Jewish commissioned and non-commissioned officers (ibid., pp. 176–77) surrendered to the Germans without a shot.

68 Howard, *Grand Strategy*: 174–79. This uproar also led to the writing of William L. Langer's book, *Our Vichy Gamble* (New York: Knopf, 1947), with U.S. Government support; see the relevant documents in FDRL, PSF Box 82, Navy: Wilson Brown.

69 Hinsley, 2: *British Intelligence*, 464–66.

70 John D. Millett, *The Army Service Forces: The Organization and Role of the Army Service Forces* (Washington: GPO, 1954), pp. 61, 63.

71 See the letter of General Kenneth Anderson to Brooke, 16 Nov. 1942, Liddell Hart Centre, Alanbrooke Papers, 14/50.

72 On this issue I cannot agree with Jukes, *Hitler's Stalingrad Decisions*, pp. 97, 103. Since Hitler made decisions on several important issues in those days, his failure to make such decisions concerning the situation in the Stalingrad area seems to me to be due more to his unwillingness to make those particular decisions than to his location at the time.

73 Hinsley, 2: *British Intelligence*, 486–91. Salewski, *Seekriegsleitung*, 2: 251, understates Hitler's initial reaction to the importance of Tunisia.

74 See Howe, *Northwest Africa*, Appendix B, p. 683; Santoni, *Ultra*, chaps. 6–7; Kreis, *Air Base Defense*, pp. 169–73, for details. On British recognition of the Axis success in supplying Tunisia in Jan.-Feb. 1943, see Hinsley, 2: 573–77.

75 *Rommel Papers*, p. 419. See also Admiral Wagner's comments on Jan. 13, 1943, quoted in Salewski, 2: 229–30.

76 This point is clear from the internal German debate about whether or not to send the Mufti to Tunisia as the latter very much wanted; *ADAP*, E, 4, Nos. 181, 225, 267, 294, 320, 5, No. 7; Canaris "Vortragsnotiz," 9 Dec. 1942 and Lahousen, "Aktenvermerk," 11 Dec. 1942, Imperial War Museum, AL 1933, Canaris/Lahousen file, items 39 and 40; Weizsäcker to Ribbentrop, 12 Dec. 1942, AA, St.S., "Aufzeichnungen über interne Angelegenheiten," Bd. 2, fr. 472313–14; Berlin to Rome, No. 76 of 7 Jan. 1943, AA, St.S., "Italien," Bd. 12, fr. 123787.

77 Note Jodl's views of Nov. 29, 1942, on strategy for 1943 in Förster, "Strategische Überlegungen," pp. 95–96. The recollections of General von Arnim, suddenly called on Dec. 3, 1942, from the defense of Rzhev to take over as commanding general of 5th Panzer Army, are in his memoirs, BA/MA, N 61/4, f. 1–4.

78 Hinsley, *British Intelligence*, 2: 493–98.

79 Howe, *North west Africa*, chaps. 15–17; Hinsley, 2: 504.

80 See Churchill's Minute COS(42) 421(o) of 29 Nov. 1942 arguing that "July 1943 should be fixed as the target date" (PRO, AIR 8/878); his note as Minister of Defence COS(42) 429(o) of 3 Dec. 1942 calling for a landing in July or Aug. 1943 (ibid.); and his comments to the War Cabinet on 30 Nov. 1942 in WM(42) War Cabinet 162 (CAB 65/28). The redrafting of Churchill's message to Roosevelt forwarding his 24 and 27. Nov. exchange with Stalin also shows the early hopes for a 1943 landing on the assumption that Tunisia would be taken by the end of Dec. 1942 and Libya by the end of Jan. 1943 with a landing in northern France in Aug. or Sep. 1943 (CAB 120/411). Cf. Bryant, *Turn of the Tide*, pp. 428–37. Similarly, the drafts of Roosevelt's message to Prime Minister Curtin of

Australia on the return of the 9th Australian Division from the Middle East were changed to assume a final defeat of Rommel to "early in the year" instead of "the first of the year" between Nov. 23 and Dec. 2, 1942; FDRL, Map Room Files Box 12, Miscellaneous Presidential Messages 1942. But see the documents in PRO, AIR 20/2471.

81 Formalized in a document JP(42) 1005 (Revise) (Final) of 10 Jan. 1943, PRO, CAB 119/55.

82 PM personal minute D 228/2, PRO, CAB 120/411. It should be noted that Montgomery thought a cross-Channel invasion in 1943 would be easier than a Mediterranean invasion other than Sicily (Montgomery to Brooke, 12 Dec. 1942, Liddell Hart Centre, Alanbrooke Papers, 14/61).

83 See Dallek, *Roosevelt and Foreign Policy*, pp. 369–70. See also Roosevelt to Leahy, 7 Dec. 1942, FDRL, Map Room Box 167, Naval Aide, Warfare Northwest Africa.

84 On this point, see Hinsley, 2: 109–10.

85 This was the staff which came to be known by its initials as COSSAC. That the impetus to serious planning came from the *American* side and led to the creation of this staff and to its really getting to work is clear from the key files of the British DMO (Director of Military Operations), 22 Jan. 1943 – 3 July 1944, PRO, WO 106/4147–48; cf. WO 106/4243. It must, however, be noted that it was Brooke who on Mar. 11, 1943, asked General Sir Percy C. S. Hobart to take on the job of developing the floating tanks and other devices which would play such an important part in the invasion (Brooke Diary, 11 Mar. and 1 Apr. 1943, comment in 3/A/VIII, p. 656, Liddell Hart Centre, Alanbrooke Papers).

86 On the Casablanca Conference, see Howard, *Grand Strategy*, 4: chaps. 13–14; Morton, *Strategy*, pp. 376–86, 439–41. An appreciation by the Combined Intelligence Committee on "German Strategy in 1943" of 26 Jan. 1943 is in NA, RG 165, Entry 77, Box 1418, File 6900–Germany.

87 There are, in addition to the numerous negative views of American generals in the published volumes of Brooke's diary, many others which may be found in the diary and Brooke's later notes; see entries for 16 and 19 Jan. 1943, notes 3/A/VIII, pp. 601, 609, Liddell Hart Centre, Alanbrooke Papers.

88 See the letter of Lt.Col. Howkins of the Office of the War Cabinet to Major Davidson in the British Secretariat of the Combined Chiefs of Staff in Washington, 23 Jan. 1943, PRO, CAB 119/59.

89 Note Lothar Kettenacker, "Die alliierte Kontrolle Deutschlands als Exempel britischer Herrschaftsausübung," in Ludolf Herbst (ed.), *Westdeutschland 1945–1955* (Munich: Oldenbourg, 1986), p. 56, and *Krieg zur Friedenssicherung*, pp. 186ff.

90 Howard, *Grand Strategy*, 4: 283. At the Trident Conference in May 1943, this attitude toward Italy was upheld again by Roosevelt and Churchill (ibid., pp. 456–57).

91 Harry R. Rudin, *Armistice 1918* (New Haven, Conn.: Yale Univ. Press, 1944) remains an excellent account. Raymond G. O'Connor, *Diplomacy for Victory: F.D.R. and Unconditional Surrender* (New York: Norton, 1971), pp. 4–5, suggests that Roosevelt, then Acting Secretary of the Navy, leaned toward a surrender demand in 1918. The best recent account is Lothar Kettenacker, "'Unconditional Surrender' als Grundlage der angelsächsischen Nachkriegsplanung," in Wolfgang Michalka (ed.), *Der Zweite Weltkrieg: Analysen, Grundzüge, Forschungsbilanz* (Munich: Piper, 1989), pp. 174–88.

92 Note the draft by Robert Sherrod, dated 17 May 1944, giving the background of the unconditional surrender policy, in C 6775/236/62, PRO, FO 371/39024. As minutes by Churchill in the same file show, he then thought it unwise to deviate from the formula when the Allies were planning to shift millions of Germans out of extensive territories to be turned over to Poland.

93 Sikorski's account is quoted in Terry, *Poland's Place in Europe*, p. 302. A minimally different translation is in Wlodzimierz T. Kowalski, "The Western Powers and the Polish–

German Frontier during the Second World War (1943–45)," *Polish Western Affairs* 6, No. 1 (1965), p. 91, but is there erroneously dated to Jan. 3, 1943. In any case, the choice of words obviously reflects World War I experience.

94 See O'Connor, *Diplomacy for Victory*, pp. 50–53. A careful examination of National Socialist propaganda has shown that, in spite of post-war assertions to the contrary, the Unconditional Surrender formula had little resonance there; see Günter Moltmann, "Nationalklischees und Demagogie: Die deutsche Amerikapropaganda im Zweiten Weltkrieg," in Ursula Büttner (ed.), *Das Unrechtsregime: Internationale Forschung über den Nationalsozialismus* (Hamburg: Christians, 1986), 1: 223.

95 Note that in Mar. 1943 the British had, on reconsideration, once again rejected a cross-Channel operation as a replacement for the invasion of Sicily (Hinsley, 3/1: 3–4).

96 Mark A. Stoler, "The American Perception of British Mediterranean Strategy, 1941–1945," in Craig L. Symonds (ed.), *New Aspects of Naval History* (Annapolis, Md.: Naval Institute Press, 1981), pp. 332–33; Morton, *Strategy*, pp. 454–59; Maurice Matloff, *Strategic Planning for Coalition Warfare, 1943–1944* (Washington: GPO, 1959), pp. 123–24 (full text in JCS for the President, "Recommended line of action at coming conference," 8 May 1943, FDRL, Map Room Box 164, Naval Aide File).

97 Brooke's diary entry for 10 May 1943 as quoted in *Turn of the Tide*, p. 500, is very much toned down from the original entry at the Liddell Hart Centre.

98 On Trident, see Howard, *Grand Strategy*, 4, chaps. 22–23; Stoler, *Politics*, chap. 7.

99 Howe, *Northwest Africa*, chaps. 20–22.

100 Ibid., pp. 366–67.

101 On the Kasserine Pass battle, see Howe, chaps. 23–24; Martin Blumenson, "Kasserine Pass, 30 January – 22 Feb. 1943," in Charles E. Heller (ed.), *America's First Battles, 1776–1965* (Lawrence, Kans.: Univ. Press of Kansas, 1986), pp. 226–45, 394–97. On the disputed issue of intelligence before the battle, see Hinsley, *British Intelligence*, 2: 577–86; E. E. Mockler-Ferryman's privately printed memoirs in the Imperial War Museum, p. 323, barely touches on the subject.

102 A summary in Howe, pp. 479–81, 671–73.

103 See Alexander's long, most secret, private and confidential letter to Brooke of 3 Apr. 1943, in Liddell Hart Centre, Alanbrooke Papers, 14/63. Montgomery's views are both cited and reflected in Hamilton's *Monty, Master of the Battlefield, 1942–44*.

104 Hinsley, 2: 593–95; Hamilton, *Monty, Master*, pp. 152–70.

105 Hinsley, 2: 600–5.

106 Sir Francis de Guingand, *Operation Victory* (London: Hodder & Stoughton, 1947), pp. 248–49; Howe, chaps. 26–28; Hamilton, *Monty, Master*, pp. 182–207; Martin Blumenson, *Patton: The Man behind the Legend, 1885–1945* (New York: Berkley Books, 1987), p. 184. Because Patton was not satisfied with the handling of the 1st U.S. Armored Division in this operation, he replaced General Orlando Ward with General Ernest Harmon as division commander.

107 See David R. Mortensen, *A Pattern for Joint Operations: World War II Close Air Support, North Africa* (Washington: GPO, 1987). By this time, Allied control of the sea around Tunisia was also almost total; only about 800 Axis soldiers escaped across the Mediterranean (Santoni, *Ultra siegt im Mittelmeer*, p. 229).

108 Boog, *Luftwaffenführung*, pp. 25–26.

109 Ziemke, *Moscow to Stalingrad*, pp. 437–40.

110 A summary in ibid., pp. 440–41; more detail in Harrison, *Soviet Planning in Peace and War*, chap. 3.

111 Jürgen Förster, *Stalingrad: Risse im Bündnis, 1942/43* (Freiburg: Rombach, 1975), pp. 25–29; *ADAP*, E, 2, No. 231, 3, No. 85.

112 Wilhelm, "Die Prognosen der Abteilung Fremde Heere Ost 1942–1945," pp. 47–48. The erroneous summary of German army intelligence for the Eastern Front (OKH/FHO)

of 12 Nov. 1942 is printed in *KTB OKW*, 1942, 2: 1306–7. For another, quite idiotic, assessment by Reinhard Gehlen, that agency's chief, see ibid., p. 1283. Cf. Ziemke, *Moscow to Stalingrad*, pp. 454–56.

113 Hitler's references are summarized in Ziemke, *Moscow to Stalingrad*, p. 456, and discussed in *DRuZW*, 6: 1014.

114 Ziemke, *Moscow to Stalingrad*, pp. 458–68.

115 Erickson, *Road to Stalingrad*, p. 469.

116 Ibid., pp. 453–72; Ziemke, *Moscow to Stalingrad*, pp. 468–77.

117 The most complete examination of these matters in Manfred Kehrig, *Stalingrad: Analyse und Dokumentation einer Schlacht* (Stuttgart: Deutsche Verlags-Anstalt, 1974), pp. 195–234; additional details in Johannes Fischer, "Über den Entschluss zur Luftversorgung Stalingrad," MGM 6 (1969), 7–67; more recently, *DRuZW*, 6: 1024ff.

118 See Boog, *Luftwaffenführung*, p. 22 n 23 and p. 24.

119 Note Kehrig, *Stalingrad*, pp. 286–98.

120 The best statistics in ibid., p. 670. The table in Hans-Detlef Herhudt von Rohden, *Die Luftwaffe ringt um Stalingrad* (Wiesbaden: Limes, 1950), p. 100, gives a daily average of 96.16 tons. Ziemke, *Moscow to Stalingrad*, p. 497, reads the evidence as showing that on one day, Dec. 2, 1942, the 300 ton figure was reached.

121 A few samples of Manstein's distortions are noted in Kehrig, pp. 224, 390f, 395, 396; see also Ernst Alexander Paulus (son of the field marshal) to General Arthur Schmidt, 11 Nov. 1957, Nachlass Paulus, BA/MA, N 372/43, f. 131. Because of the sensitivity of the Stalingrad question in post-war Germany, Manstein worked as hard to distort the record on this matter as on his massive involvement in the murder of Jews.

122 See Kehrig, *Stalingrad*, p. 279.

123 For Hitler's own view at this time there is the surviving, but damaged, record of the situation conference of Dec. 12, 1942 in Heiber, *Hitlers Lagebesprechungen*, pp. 71–119.

124 On the relief operation, see Ziemke, *Moscow to Stalingrad*, pp. 478–83; Kehrig, pp. 307ff. On Soviet countering of the relief effort, see Glantz, *Soviet Military Deception*, pp. 124–29.

125 Ziemke, *Moscow to Stalingrad*, pp. 485–86; Erickson, *Road to Stalingrad*, pp. 449–50; Glantz, pp. 120–24.

126 On "Koltso," see Ziemke, *Moscow to Stalingrad*, pp. 492–502.

127 For personnel management, see Manfred Messerschmidt, *Die Wehrmacht im NS-Staat: Zeit der Indoktrination* (Hamburg: Decker, 1969); Dermot Bradley and Richard Schulze-Kossens (eds.), *Tätigkeitsbericht des Chefs des Heerespersonalamtes General der Infanterie Rudolf Schmundt* (Osnabrück: Biblio-Verlag, 1984). The bribery system understandably does not figure prominently in the endless memoir literature of the recipients and has attracted little scholarly attention. For an introductory journalistic survey, see Peter Meroth, "Vorschuss auf den Endsieg," *Stern*, 12 June 1980, pp. 86–92; for detailed examination of a single case, see Gerhard L. Weinberg, "Zur Dotation an Generalfeldmarschall Ritter von Leeb," *MGM*, No. 2 (1979), pp. 97–99. The more general issues for both the Soviet Union and Germany are discussed in Ziemke, *Moscow to Stalingrad*, pp. 506–10; Erickson, *Road to Stalingrad*, pp. 461–62.

128 On the disastrous defeat of 2d Hungarian Army, see Glantz, pp. 131–41; German military attaché Budapest (Pappenheim) to Berlin, "Unterredung mit ungar. Genstb.Chef über Versagen ungar. 2.Armee," 1 Mar. 1943, AA, Handakten Ritter, "Verschiedenes I, II," fr. 280665–70.

129 See Zeitzler's comments in his papers, BA/MA, N 63/12, f. 69–71.

130 An account of the evacuation and its background in Friedrich Forstmeier, *Die Räumung des Kuban-Brückenkopfes im Herbst 1943* (Darmstadt: Wehr & Wissen, 1964).

131 Earl F. Ziemke, *Stalingrad to Berlin: The German Defeat in the East* (Washington: GPO, 1968), pp. 85–94.

132 Ibid., pp. 90–97; John Erickson, *The Road to Berlin* (Boulder, Colo.: Westview Press, 1983), pp. 48–55; Glantz, *Soviet Military Deception*, pp. 141–46. The account in Eberhard Schwarz, *Die Stabilisierung der Ostfront nach Stalingrad: Mansteins Gegenschlag zwischen Donez und Dnjepr im Frühjahr 1943* (Göttingen: Muster-schmidt, 1985), though marred by adulation for Manstein, is very useful on military details because it is based on Manstein's papers, now in the BA/MA.

133 Ziemke, *Stalingrad to Berlin*, pp. 110–17; Erickson, *Road to Berlin*, pp. 59–62.

134 Note Hugh R. Trevor-Roper (ed.), *The Bormann Letters* (London: Weidenfeld & Nicolson, 1954), p. 6; Steinert, *Hitler's War* pp. 184–215.

135 Peter Longerich (ed.), "Joseph Goebbels und der Totale Krieg: Eine unbekannte Denkschrift des Propagandaministers vom 18. Juli 1944," *VjZ* 35 (1987), 294–5 and 302 n 44. L. believes much of the effect of Goebbels's push was lost as a result of the March victory at Kharkov (ibid., p. 296).

136 The best account in Förster, *Stalingrad*, pp. 46ff.

137 Ribbentrop to Killinger No. 737 of 11 Mar. 1843, AA, St.S., "Italien," Bd. 12, fr. 124028–29; Mackensen to Ribbentrop, No. 1916 of 23 Apr. 1943, AA, Botschaft Rom (Quir.), Geheim, Bd. 56/2, fr. E 258342–44; *ADAP*, E, 5, No. 332.

138 Förster, *Stalingrad*, pp. 54ff. For German information on Hungary's peace soundings, see the Forschungsamt summary of intercepts of 30 Sep. 1943 in AA, St.S., "Ungarn," Bd. 10, fr. 106683–87; also Woermann to Budapest No. 547 of 15 Mar. 1943, AA, St.S., "Ungarn," Bd. 9, fr. 106077–78.

139 On Italian efforts to urge a separate Axis–Soviet peace, see Förster, *Stalingrad*, pp. 54–57; Josef Schröder, *Bestrebungen zur Eliminierung der Ostfront 1941–1943* (Göttingen: Musterschmidt, 1985), pp. 18–25; Meskill, pp. 415–16; *Ciano Diary*, 28 Dec. 1941, 6 and 16 Dec. 1942; Memorandum from the German embassy Rome, "1443/42geh.," 2 Sep. 1942, AA, Botschaft Rom (Quir.), "Italienische Kriegführung," Bd. 1, fr. E 257436–39; *ADAP*, E, 4, Nos. 146, 303, 6, No. 95; Rintelen to Warlimont, 26 Feb. 1950, Rintelen Papers, BA/MA, N 433; Mackensen to Ribbentrop No. 665 of 11 Feb. 1943, AA, St.S., "Russland," Bd. 10, fr. 33573–75; Ribbentrop to Mackensen No. 720 of 15 May 1943, AA, St.S., "Türkei," Bd. 8, fr. 41379–80; Zeitzler to Heinrici, 14 Jan. 1954, BA/MA, N 63/15, f. 50–51. Japanese telegrams concerning the unsuccessful Italian effort which were intercepted by the Americans are in NA, RG 457, SRDJ 32092–93, 32542–44, 34186–88, 34330–32, 34383–85, 39609, and SRA 02613–14.

140 On the possibility of a Soviet–Finnish peace in the winter of 1942–43, see *ADAP*, E, 4, Nos. 116, 263; Memorandum by Weizsäcker, 11 Nov. 1942, AA, St.S., "Russland," Bd. 9, fr. 33442–43, also St.S. No. 713 of 7 Dec. 1942, fr. 33494; Memorandum by Weizsäcker, St.S. No. 155, 10 Mar. 1943, AA, St.S., "Aufzeichnungen über Diplomatenbesuche," Bd. 13, fr. 289947–48, also St.S. No. 204, 1 Apr. 1943, fr. 289957–60, and St.S. No. 278, 3 June 1943, fr. 289970–78; Blücher tel. No. 422 of 24 Feb. 1943, AA, Gesandtschaft Helsinki, "Drahtberichte 400–960, 1943," fr. H 062660; Maisky to Churchill, 29 Mar. 1943, PRO, PREM 3/170/2 and other documents in this file; Ingeborg Fleischhauer, *Die Chance des Sonderfriedens: Deutsch-sowjetische Geheimgespräche 1941–1945* (Berlin: Siedler, 1986), p. 104; Oshima to Tokyo No. 434 of 17 Apr. 1943, NA, RG 457, SRDJ 34401, Helsinki to Tokyo No. 120 of 7 June 1943 and No. 200 of 26 May 1943, SRDJ 38356 and 38391.

141 On earlier Japanese interest in a German–Soviet separate peace, see Meskill, *Hitler and Japan*, pp. 409 n 3, 414; *ADAP*, E, 2, Nos. 4, 19, 48, 72, 78, 3, Nos. 255, 295; Memorandum by Weizsäcker, St.S. No. 671 of 14 Nov. 1942, AA, St.S., "Japan," Bd. 10, fr. 17060–61; Japanese documents intercepted by the Americans in NA, RG 457, SRDJ 21456–61, 21747, 25705–6, 28403, 28744. After the Germans seized the files of the Italian Foreign Ministry in September 1943, they prepared an analysis of Italian–

Japanese joint efforts to urge a compromise peace on the Eastern Front, "Pol.XI 2221gRs.," 21 Oct. 1943, AA, St.S., "Italien," Bd. 18, fr. 70822–25.

142 *ADAP*, E, 4, No. 275, 5, Nos. 145 n 8, 188, 272 n 6, 318, 6, Nos. 12, 15, 16, 41; Memorandum by Weizsäcker, St.S. No. 701 of 27 Nov. 1942, AA, St.S., "Japan," Bd. 10, fr. 297776–77; Ribbentrop to Stahmer No. 1256 of 20 May 1943, St.S., "Japan," Bd. 12, fr. 398593–94, and 847 of 25 May 1943, fr. 17248–52; Schröder, *Bestrebungen*, pp. 8–18; Oshima's telegrams 10 of 23 Feb., 303 of 16 Mar., 305 of 17 Mar. 1943, NA, RG 457, SRDJ 32015–16, 32936, 32940, and Tokyo to Berlin No. 312 of 6 May 1943, SRDJ 35741–43; a series of reports by the Dienststelle Ribbentrop prepared for Hitler by Likus, Dec. 1942 – June 1944, stresses Japanese interest as expressed by members of Oshima's staff (NA, T-120, Serial 146a, Roll 161, fr. 129238–488). Fleischhauer, *Sonderfrieden*, pp. 105ff, takes Weizsäcker's and Ribbentrop's interest as serious; I have been unable to find any evidence for this interpretation.

143 It should be noted that the Japanese similarly overestimated German capabilities when they suggested in April 1943 that Germany reverse the tide in the Mediterranean by taking Gibraltar; see Seekriegsleitung to OKW, 17 Apr. 1943, BA/MA, RM 7/254, f. 101–5; OKW, "Niederschrift über die Besprechung mit japanischen Offizieren im F.H.Qu. am 18.4.1943," 27 Apr. 1943, RM 7/254, f. 108–14. German intelligence concluded in July 1943 that a Japanese attack on the Soviet Union would be of no real help to Germany (ibid., f. 158–60; but see also NA, RG 457, SRDJ 41746–48).

144 Oshima No. 1433 of 12 Dec. 1942, NA, RG 457, SRDJ 28955–56 (*ADAP*, E, 4, No. 275). Oshima concluded that since the German situation on the Eastern Front was very bad and there was no prospect of a compromise peace, Japan should attack the Soviet Union, concentrate on sinking Allied shipping, and exchange detailed plans with the Germans (see his No. 116 of 26 June 1943, SRDJ 30560–62).

145 Madrid No. 224 of 3 Mar. 1943, NA, RG 457, SRDJ 32477. On Dec. 21, 1942 Ambassador Sato in Kuibyshev had sent home a very clear survey of the real situation on the Eastern Front concluding that Germany had no chance of either succeeding or obtaining a compromise there, see his No. 1211 of 21 Dec. 1942, SRDJ 29486–88; cf. his No. 182 of 20 Feb. 1943, SRDJ 32088–91. The conclusion of Tokyo was that there would be a new German offensive, "but one thing is certain – she [Germany] cannot defeat Russia" (Tokyo circular No. 24, 10 Jan. 1943, SRDJ 30163–66). This appears to have been the view of the Japanese Foreign Ministry, not of Prime Minister Tojo who was much more optimistic (*Kido Diary*, 12, 15 Feb. 1943, pp. 351–52). For Japanese criticism of the German 1943 plan to attack in the East, see Tokyo to Berlin No. 291 of 28 Apr. 1943, SRDJ 34892–98; Oshima's assessment is in his No. 518 of 9 May 1943, SRDJ 35084–88.

146 Förster, *Stalingrad*, pp. 121–30, has a good summary.

147 Rolf-Dieter Müller, "Die deutschen Gaskriegsvorbereitungen 1919–1945," *MGM* 27, No. 1 (1980), p. 44.

148 Ibid., pp. 44–45.

149 The first accurate launch of an A-4 over 120 miles took place on 3 Oct. 1942 (Hinsley, *British Intelligence*, 3/1: 357ff).

150 See Olaf Groehler, "Die 'Hochdruckpumpe' (V-3)–Entwicklung und Misere einer 'Wunderwaffe'," *Militärgeschichte* 5, No. 16 (1977), 738–44. (This weapon is the model for the "Supergun" developed for Iraq by a Canadian arms technician in the 1980s.)

151 Hinsley, 3/1: 362–63.

152 Ibid., pp. 370ff. On the question of these weapons, Churchill's favorite scientific advisor, Lord Cherwell, turned out to be completely wrong (see ibid., pp. 373–74, 386, 397, 398, 400–1, 410–11).

153 Brooke Diary, 29 June 1943, Liddell Hart Centre, Alanbrooke Papers.

154 Note the censorship analysis of letters to German prisoners of war held by the British in

the Middle East in Headquarters, U.S. Army Forces in the Middle East, "Brief Digest of British M.E.F. Military Censorship Fortnightly Summary of Prisoner of War Correspondence Covering Examination Period May 5th – May 18th, 1943," 27 May 1943, NA, RG 165, Entry 77, Box 2209, File 5970–Italy I.

155 Hinsley, 2: 521–23; Boog, *Luftwaffenführung*, p. 141. On the basis of captured German documents, the Western Allies had a summary of the German air force program for 1943 by July 6, 1943 (ibid., Box 1482, File 9910–General Western Front).

156 See the British Air Intelligence report of 1 Mar. 1944, "The G.A.F. and the London Raids," in ibid.; Boog, *Luftwaffenführung*, p. 134; Jeschonnek comments of 1 May 1943 quoted in BA/MA, RM 7/260, f. 173–79. There is a summary of the "Baby Blitz" of 1944, which resulted in heavy German aircraft losses, in Murray, *Luftwaffe*, pp. 237–38, but the account does not set this operation in its strategic context as a product of decisions made in March *1943*.

157 Note Förster, "Strategische Überlegungen," pp. 95 n 2, 97.

158 See Scheidt Papers, Institut für Zeitgeschichte, B 2, S 266, pp. 272, 299–300; Kempf, "Stellungnahme zu den 'Betrachtungen Zitadelle'," 22 Apr. 1958, Nachlass Zeitzler, BA/MA, N 63/12, f. 33–38; Junge to Dönitz, 15 May 1943, BA/MA, RM 7/260, f. 194–96.

159 See n 127, above. Important documents are in BA, R 43 II, 985b, 985c, 986, 1987a, 1092b.

160 An initial study in Manfred Messerschmidt and Fritz Wüllner, *Die Wehrmachtjustiz im Dritten Reich: Zerstörung einer Legende* (Baden-Baden: Nomos, 1987). An analysis of the death sentence statistics is in chap. 5. The statistics have been challenged but not convincingly.

161 Glantz, *Soviet Military Deception*, pp. 148–54; Volkogonov, *Stalin*, chap. 47. Note the comments of Morishima in *Kido Diary*, 3 Mar. 1943, pp. 352–53.

162 Anna M. Cienciala, "The Activities of Polish Communists as a Source for Stalin's Policy Towards Poland in the Second World War," *International History Review* 7 (1985), 133–34.

163 Terry, *Poland's Place in Europe*, pp. 335–36; Joanna K. M. Hanson, *The Civilian Population and the Warsaw Uprising of 1944* (Cambridge: Cambridge Univ. Press, 1982),

164 Cienciala, p. 136.

165 Terry, pp. 337–38. For the British and U.S. governments getting full information on the correct background of Katyn, see O'Malley to Eden No. 51 of 24 May 1943, C 6160/258/55, Foreign Office Print, sent by Churchill to Roosevelt 13 Aug. 1943 and initialled by the latter, FDRL, PSF Box 53, Great Britain, Churchill 40–43 (published in Kimball, *Churchill and Roosevelt*, 2: 389–419).

166 See Stafford, *Britain and European Resistance*, pp. 133–36

167 On the death of Sikorski, see esp. PRO, AIR 8/779, which points to troubles in the controls as decisive. Sabotage of these by a Soviet agent cannot, in my judgement, be ruled out. See also Brooke Diary for 5 and 15 July 1943 as well as earlier entries, all very favorable to Sikorski (Liddell Hart Centre). The comments of General Mason Macfarlane, then British commander at Gibraltar, are in his 18 July 1945 notes at the Imperial War Museum, MM 30.

168 Hinsley, *British Intelligence*, 2: 615; Brooke Diary, 9 Dec. 1942, Bryant, *Turn of the Tide*, p. 531; documents 31 July 1942 – 28 Apr. 1943 in War Dept., G-2, File, NA, RG 165, Entry 77, Box 3481, File 6900–Peace, on possible German–Soviet separate peace.

169 Kettenacker, "Alliance," pp. 446–47.

170 Ibid., pp. 447–50. Eden was here advocating precisely the policy Chamberlain had adopted toward Hitler's Germany. He had General Sir P. Le Q. Martel recalled as head of the British military mission to Moscow for taking too hard a line with the Russians. See the

latter's "Notes on Important and Unknown Features in 1943 on the Russian Front," PRO, CAB 106/323.

171 See Hinsley, 2: 624 and Appendix 22; 3/1: 191. The Western Allies generally received very little intelligence from the Russians in return; see ibid., 2: 618–20.

172 Richard C. Lukas, *Eagles East* (Tallahassee, Flo.: Florida State Univ. Press, 1970), pp. 171–72; Herring, *Aid to Russia*, pp. 88–97.

173 Lukas, pp. 173–74; Beaumont, *Comrades in Arms*, pp. 142–47; Herring, pp. 97ff.

174 See Prime Minister's Personal Minute D 134/3 of 19 July 1943, PRO, AIR 8/1077.

175 There is a very useful file of key documents on the "Rankin" plan, 26 Apr. – 15 Dec. 1943, in PRO, WO 106/4245.

176 See W.P.(42) 580, "Air Policy: Note by the Prime Minister and Minister of Defence," Dec. 1942, PRO, CAB 120/10.

177 Saward, *"Bomber" Harris*, pp. 93–95; Webster and Frankland, *Strategic Air Offensive*, 2: chap. 10, 4: Annex 1. For Churchill's pressure to keep up the volume of bombs dropped, see his Personal Minute 387/3 to the Chief of the Air Staff (Portal) of 16 June 1943, in PRO, CAB 120/292.

178 On the dam raid, see Saward, pp. 197–200; Paul Brickhill, The *Dam Busters* (New York: Ballantine, 1955). On the use of "window" (strips of aluminum foil) in connection with the Hamburg raid, see Hinsley, 2: 518–19; Brooke Diary, 23 June 1943 (Liddell Hart Centre). On the Hamburg raid in general, see Boog, *Luftwaffenführung*, pp. 135–36; Saward, pp. 208–11; Hastings, *Bomber Command*, 241–46; a detailed Japanese naval attaché report is in NA, RG 457, SRNA 508–11.

179 See the documents in PRO, AIR 8/1146.

180 Saward, pp. 207–8.

9: THE HOME FRONT

1 This is a major theme of *DRuZW*, 5/1. See also Alan S. Milward, *War, Economy and Society 1939–1945* (Berkeley, Calif.: Univ. of Calif. Press, 1977), pp. 220–21; Ludolf Herbst, *Der Totale Krieg und die Ordnung der Wirtschaft: Die Kriegswirtschaft im Spannungsfeld von Politik, Ideologie und Propaganda 1939–1945* (Stuttgart: Deutsche Verlags-Anstalt, 1982). There is a very helpful comparison in Mark Harrison, "Resource Mobilization for World War II: The U.S.A, U.K., U.S.S.R., and Germany, 1938–1945," *Economic History Review* 2d ser., 41 (1988), 171–92.

2 The best account remains Steinert, *Hitler's War*.

3 The post-war argument that the murderers had no choice but to carry out their grisly orders or suffer the direst penalties themselves was effectively demolished by prosecutors in the Federal Republic of Germany. See David H. Kitterman, "Those Who Said 'No!': Germans Who Refused to Execute Civilians during World War II," *German Studies Review* 11 (1988), 241–54; Jehuda L. Wallach, "Befehlsnotstand: A Matter of Fact or Subterfuge," in Haim Shamir (ed.), *France and Germany in an Age of Crisis, 1900–1960: Studies in Memory of Charles Bloch* (Leiden: Brill, 1990), pp. 162–68. An especially dramatic example of a battalion commander inviting any of his men who did not wish to participate in mass slaughter of Jews to step aside is described by Christopher R. Browning, "One Day in Jozefow: Initiation to Mass Murder," in Peter Hayes, ed., *Lessons and Legacies: The Meaning of the Holocaust in a Changing World* (Evanston, Ill.: Northwestern Univ. Press, 1991), pp. 200–1; added detail in the same author's *Ordinary Men: Reserve Police Battalion 101 and the Final Solution in Poland* (New York: Harper Collins, 1992).

4 See Ludwig Volk (ed.), "Clemens August Graf von Galen: Schweigen oder Bekennen? Zum Gewissensentscheid des Bischofs von Münster im Sommer 1941," *Stimmen der Zeit* 194 (1976), 219–24. Complete documentation in Peter Löffler (ed.), *Bischof Clemens*

August Graf von Galen: Akten, Briefe und Predigeen 1933–46, Vol. 2, *1939–1946* (Mainz: Mathias-Grünwald, 1988).

5 *FDR Letters*, 2: 1220. The text of Galen's denunciation of Gestapo terror is in FDRL, PSF Box 70, Vatican, Myron C. Taylor 1941.

6 Wolfgang Diewerge (ed.), *Feldpostbriefe aus dem Osten: Deutsche Soldaten sehen die Sowjetunion* (Berlin: Limpert, 1941), p. 38.

7 Hans-Heinrich Wilhelm, "Wie geheim war die 'Endlösung'?" *Miscellanea: Festschrift für Helmut Krausnick*, ed. Wolfgang Benz (Stuttgart: Deutsche Verlags-Anstalt, 1980), pp. 131–48. Both in his public speeches and their officially published texts, Hitler's numerous references to his prediction of Jan. 30, 1939, that in any future war the Jews of Europe would be exterminated, now being implemented, was post-dated to Sept. 1, 1939, presumably to reinforce the concept of its being connected with the war (just as his October 1939 order for the "euthanasia" program was pre-dated to Sept. 1, 1939).

8 Michael R. Marrus and Robert O. Paxton, *Vichy France and the Jews* (New York: Basic Books, 1981).

9 There is now a careful examination of this matter in Jonathan Steinberg, *All or Nothing: The Axis and the Holocaust, 1941–1943* (London: Routledge, 1990).

10 Owen Chadwick, "Weizsäcker, the Vatican and the Jews of Rome," *Journal of Ecclesiastical History* 28 (1977), 179–99. The original idea appears to have been to murder the Jews of Rome in northern Italy, see Moellhausen (Rome) to Ribbentrop No. 192 of 6 Oct. 1943, AA, St.S., "Italien," Bd. 17, fr. 123580.

11 Randolph L. Braham, *The Politics of Genocide: The Holocaust in Hungary*, 2 vols. (New York: Columbia Univ. Press, 1981). Wallenberg's activities were financed by the U.S. government. Note Donovan to Roosevelt, 17 Oct. 1944, FDRL, PSF Box 169, OSS Reports Oct. 1944.

12 "Auszug aus einem Bericht von einer dreiwöchigen Fahrt in die Ukraine," 28 June 1943, BA, Nadler, ZSg. 115/6, f. 154. The statistics, of course, refer not to the Ukraine as a whole but to the portions administered by the Reichskommissariat Ukraine.

13 An account in Max Weinreich, *Hitler's Professors* (New York: Yiddish Scientific Institute–YIVO, 1946), pp. 219–35. Japanese Ambassador Oshima was most hesitant about accepting his invitation, see his tel. No. 614 to Tokyo of 22 June 1944, NA, RG 457, SRDJ 62675–76. He was concerned that the racial policies proclaimed at the congress would conflict with those of Japan. One wonders what he would have thought of the special brothel planned for the attendees – with Polish and Ukrainian women excluded as racially inappropriate!

14 The systematic terrorization and killing of gypsies is surveyed in Sybil Milton, "Nazi Policies toward Roma and Sinti, 1939–1045," *Journal of the Gypsy Lore Society*, Feb. 1992.

15 See "Rk 7723B, Betrifft: Eheschliessungen Deutscher mit Polen und Tschechen," 16 June 1940, BA, R 43 II/1502a, f. 14.

16 Trevor-Roper (ed.), *Bormann Letters*, p. xx. See also Oron J. Hale (ed.), "Adolf Hitler and the Postwar German Birthrate," *Journal of Central European Affairs* 17 (1957), 166–73.

17 Bernd Wegner (ed.), "Auf dem Wege zur pangermanischen Armee: Dokumente zur Entstehung des III. ('pangermanisches') SS-Panzerkorps," *MGM* (1980/2), p. 102.

18 Guderian did not think the huge estate finally offered to him was adequate: see Weinberg, "Zur Dotation Hitlers an Generalfeldmarschall Ritter von Leeb," p. 99 n 20.

19 The best English-language study remains Edward L. Homze, *Foreign Labor in Nazi Germany* (Princeton, N.J.: Princeton Univ. Press, 1967); the most comprehensive recent survey is Ulrich Herbert, *Fremdarbeiter: Politik und Praxis des "Ausländer-Einsatzes" in der Kriegswirtschaft des Dritten Reiches* (Berlin: Dietz, 1985) (now available in an English translation). There was considerable publication in the former German Democratic Republic; some of it is discussed in Herbert's introductory chapter. Because of the

involvement of millions of Germans with the slave labor program, it has been something of a taboo in post-war German work. A good general summary in Milward, *War, Economy and Society*, pp. 221–28.

20 Herbert, *Fremdarbeiter*, pp. 127–28.

21 Ibid., pp. 336–40.

22 Note Hess to Rosenberg, 30 Jan. 1940, NG-1078, cited in Paul Seabury, *The Wilhelmstrasse* (Berkeley, Calif.: Univ. of California Press, 1954), p. 181 n 40.

23 Walter Petwaidic, *Die autoritäre Anarchie* (Hamburg: Hoffmann & Campe, 1946). Note also Dieter Rebentisch, *Führerstaat und Verwaltung im Zweiten Weltkrieg* (Stuttgart: Steiner, 1981).

24 The best introduction is Jost Dülffer, Jochen Thies and Josef Henke, *Hitlers Städte: Baupolitik im Dritten Reich* (Cologne: Böhlau, 1978).

25 Ibid., p. 17.

26 Ibid., p. 20.

27 Very important is Bernhard Stasiewski, "Die Kirchenpolitik der Nationalsozialisten im Warthegau 1939–1945," *VjZ* 7 (1959), 46–74. On the actual functioning of the Gestapo, see Robert Gellately, *Gestapo and German Society: Enforcing Racial Policy, 1933–1945* (Oxford: Clarendon, 1990).

28 A good source on internal German discussion of schemes for the post-war world is AA, Nachlass Renthe-Fink, Paket 5, Bd. 1–3.

29 On Italian, Japanese and Romanian urgings, see Berlin to Tokyo No. 80 of 19 Jan. 1943, NA, RG 457, SRDJ 30619–20; Madrid to Tokyo No. 458 of 13 May 1943, SRDJ 35839–41; Memorandum by Bismarck with a 15 Mar. 1943 covering note by Mackensen marked "cessat," AA, Botschaft Rom (Quir.), Geheim, Bd. 51/2, fr. E 257522–24.

30 The various editions of Hitler's table-talk are full of material on this topic. See also Stuckart to Weizsäcker, 19 Oct. 1942, AA, St.S., "Politischer Schriftwechsel," Bd. 9, fr. 304013–15.

31 Note Wittmann, *Schwedens Wirtschaftsbeziehungen*, pp. 228–35. There was rivalry between various agencies as to which one was to direct the European economy but no argument over the intention of running it all from Berlin.

32 Important on the broader issues: Rainer Zitelmann, *Hitler: Selbstverständnis eines Revolutionärs* (Hamburg: Berg, 1987). On the Austrian economy, see Norbert Schausberger, "Sieben Jahre deutsche Kriegswirtschaft in Österreich," *Jahrbuch 1986*, Dokumentationsarchiv des Österreichischen Widerstandes (Vienna: Österreichischer Bundesverlag, 1986), pp. 10–60. There is an excellent review of the literature on Austria in Evan B. Bukey, "Nazi Rule in Austria," *Austrian History Yearbook* 23 (1992), 202–33.

33 Still useful is the first serious exploration of this question, Enno Georg, *Die wirtschaftlichen Unternehmungen der SS* (Stuttgart: Deutsche Verlags-Anstalt, 1965).

34 An excellent discussion of Speer and the literature on him is in Alfred C. Mierzejewski, "When did Albert Speer Give Up?" *Historical Journal* 31 (1988), 391–97.

35 Bernd Wegner, *Hitlers politische Soldaten: Die Waffen-SS 1933–1945* (Paderborn: Schöningh, 1982); English ed.: *The Waffen SS: Ideology, Organization and Function*, trans. by Ronald Webster (Oxford: Blackwell, 1990).

36 See the forthcoming book of Valdis O. Lumans, *Himmler's Auxiliaries* (Chapel Hill, N.C.: Univ. of North Carolina Press).

37 Dietrich Orlow, *The History of the Nazi Party: 1933–1945* (Pittsburgh: Univ. of Pittsburgh Press, 1973), chap. 7.

38 On this issue see Steinert, *Hitler's War*, ; Ian Kershaw, *The 'Hitler Myth' Image and Reality in the Third Reich* (New York: Oxford Univ. Press, 1989), chaps. 6–8; and the series of *Meldungen aus dem Reich* edited by Heinz Boberach. On Bavaria, see Martin Broszat et al. (eds.), *Bayern in der NS-Zeit*, 1 (Munich: Oldenbourg, 1977), pp. 571ff. A very graphic account from the personal side in Mathilde Wolff-Mönckeberg, *From the Other Side, To*

my Children: From Germany 1940–1945, trans. and ed. by Ruth Evans (London: Peter Owen, 1979), which consists of letters written in wartime Hamburg.

39 Robert E. Herzstein, *The War that Hitler Won: Goebbels and the Nazi Media Campaign* (New York: Paragon Books, 1987), chaps. 11–12; USSBS, *The Effects of Strategic Bombing on German Morale*, 2 vols. (Washington: GPO, 1946–47). For an excellent study of a specific area, see Gordon J. Horwitz, *In the Shadow of Death: Living Outside Mauthausen* (New York: Free Press, 1990). A useful summary in Christoph Klessmann (ed.), *Nicht nur Hitlers Krieg: Der Zweite Weltkrieg und die Deutschen* (Düsseldorf: Droste, 1989), chaps. 2–4.

40 A particularly dramatic example is cited in Wilhelm, "Wie geheim war die 'Endlösung'?" pp. 134–36.

41 The best short introduction is Peter Hoffmann, *German Resistance to Hitler* (Cambridge, Mass.: Harvard Univ. Press, 1988). New and important are Horst Mühleisen, "Hellmuth Stieff und der deutsche Widerstand," *VjZ* 39 (1991), 339–77; Elizabeth Chowaniec, *Der "Fall Dohnanyi" 1943–1945* (Munich: Oldenbourg, 1991).

42 The American OSS saw the situation the same way; see OSS Report A-29084, "Resistance Forces within Germany," 1 June 1944, NA, RG 165, Entry 77, Box 1418, File 6900–Germany.

43 On the circulation of a translation of a White Rose leaflet to the British government by Sir Stafford Cripps, see PRO, CAB 118/74.

44 On this attempt, see Heinz W. Doepgen, *Georg von Boeselager* (Herford: Mittler, 1986), pp. 71–72. An exceptionally well-informed member of the German resistance told the American embassy in Madrid of the March bomb fiasco in December; see enclosure 2 to Despatch 1741 of 14 Dec. 1943, NA, RG 165, Entry 77, Box 1418, File 6700–Germany, Military Operations Nov. 1943. See also enclosure 1 with its accurate report on the situation in Germany.

45 Some material on these contacts may be found in FDRL, PSF Safe File, Hohenlohe; PSF Box 6, Safe File OSS; PSF Box 96, Sumner Welles, June-Dec. 1940; Welles to Roosevelt, 13 Nov. 1940, PSF Germany; Lochner to Currie, 19 June 1942, OF-198a; Welles to Roosevelt, 18 May 1942, PSF State; Donovan to Roosevelt, 29 July 1944, PSF Box 168, OSS Reports July 1944; in the PRO, C 10645/5/18, FO 371/24385; N 4956/48/18, C 4799/4799/18, C 5428/48/18, FO/30912; C 4548/155/18, FO 371/34448. The subject is now reviewed in detail in Klemens von Klemperer, *German Resistance to Hitler: The Search for Allies Abroad, 1938–1945* (Oxford: Clarendon Press, 1992).

46 Jochmann, *Hitler Monologe*, p. 239.

47 On this project, see Santoni, *Ultra*, pp. 74–77, and Chapter 4.

48 For summaries, see Yehuda Bauer, *A History of the Holocaust* (New York: Franklin Watts, 1982), pp. 236–37; Manfred Funke, *Starker oder Schwacher Diktator?* (Düsseldorf: Droste, 1989), pp. 172–74. More details in Steinberg, *All or Nothing*; Liliana Picciotto Fargion (ed.), "Italian Citizens in Nazi-Occupied Europe: Documents from the Files of the German Foreign Office 1941–1943," *Simon Wiesenthal Center Annual* 7 (1990), 93–144.

49 Note Edward R. Tannenbaum, *The Fascist Experience: Italian Society and Culture, 1922–1945* (New York: Basic Books, 1972), p. 308.

50 In a somewhat exaggerated fashion, this is the burden of the two articles by Sadkovich, "Understanding Defeat," and "Rommel and the Italians."

51 See Tannenbaum's comments on p. 313. An excellent comprehensive treatment in Gerhard Schreiber, *Die italienischen Militärinternierten im deutschen Machtbereich 1943–1945* (Munich: Oldenbourg, 1990).

52 Tannenbaum, pp. 316–17; Harry Fornari, *Mussolini's Gadfly: Roberto Farinacci* (Nashville: Vanderbilt Univ. Press, 1971), pp. 188–89.

53 Latour, *Südtirol und die Achse*, chaps. 5–7.

54 Ibid., chap. 8: Arnold J. Toynbee, *Hitler's Europe* (London: Oxford Univ. Press, 1954), pp. 96–97. Note the budget for the operational zone "Adriatisches Küstenland" (Adriatic Coastal Area) for the first quarter of 1945 in BA, R 2/11407.

55 Note the report on this issue by the Japanese military attaché in Italy, No. 103 of 25 Apr. 1944, NA, RG 457, SRA 9054–56; see also Memorandum by Gottfriedsen, 18 Sep. 1943, AA, St.S., "Japan," Bd. 13, fr. 17375–78.

56 Tannenbaum, *Fascist Experience*, pp. 313–16; Alan Cassels, *Fascism* (New York: Crowell, 1975), pp. 315–18. Of interest is the apologia of Fascist Italy's last ambassador to Germany, Filippo Anfuso. Originally published in 1949 in French as *Du palais de Venise au lac de Garde*, it has appeared in two editions in Italian, *Roma–Berlino–Salò* and *Da Palazzo Venezia al lago di Garda*; there is an abbreviated German edition, *Rom–Berlin im diplomatischen Spiegel* (Essen: Pohl, 1951).

57 Cassels, pp. 318–19; Charles F. Delzell, *Mussolini's Enemies* (Princeton, N.J.: Princeton Univ. Press, 1961); Maria de Blasio Wilhelm, *The Other Italy: Italian Resistance in World War II* (New York: Norton, 1988). Massimo De Leonardis, *La Gran Bretagne e la resistenza partiziana in Italia, 1943–1945* (Naples: Scientifiche Italiane, 1988) is important.

58 Note the U.S. military intelligence reports on "Russian Policy in Italy," 25 Apr. 1944 and 18 May 1944, in NA, RG 165, Entry 77, Box 2179, File 3850–3900–Italy.

59 Military government in Italy has not attracted as much attention as its counterpart in Germany. See David W. Ellwood, *Italy 1943–1945* (New York: Holmes & Meier, 1985), and *L'alleato nemico: la politica dell'occupazione anglo-americana in Italia 1943–1946* (Milan: Feltrinelli, 1977); Robert M. Hill, *In the Wake of War: Memoirs of an Alabama Military Government Officer in World War II Italy* (University, Ala.: Univ. of Alabama Press, 1982); and the volume in the British official history, Charles R. S. Harris, *Allied Military Administration of Italy 1943–1945* (London: HMSO, 1957).

60 On the purge of Fascists, there is an excellent summary in Hans Woller, "Die Anfänge der politischen Säuberung in Italien, 1943–1945: Eine Analyse des Office of Strategic Services," *VjZ* 38 (1990), 141–90. For the establishment of the Italian government in the area under Allied control, see Edgar R. Rosen, *Königreich des Südens: Italien 1943/44* (Göttingen: Erich Goltze, 1988).

61 Churchill to Wilson T 00241215Z of 24 Feb. 1944, Liddell Hart Centre, Alanbrooke Papers, 14/44. Mason-Macfarlane's own views are very well presented in his "Draft Notes on Chapter 18 of Badoglio's 'Italy in the Second World War'." He is certain that Roosevelt was correct in insisting on a new government under Bonomi after the liberation of Rome. He also reinforces the view that Stalin left the British and Americans to work things out in Italy as they thought best (Imperial War Museum, Mason-Macfarlane Papers, 20).

62 Rome (Quir.) to Tokyo No. 63 of 22 Jan. 1942, NA, RG 457, SRDJ 19127; Rome (Vat.) to Tokyo No. 15 of 27 May 1942, SRDJ 23097–98; Tokyo to Vichy No. 157, SRDJ 23462. In 1942, American policy toward the Pope was very courteous, in part because of U.S. relations with Latin America; see Welles to Roosevelt, 8 July 1942, FDRL, PSF Welles. Note also the section of Welles's 18 Mar. 1940 comment on Pius XII omitted from *FRUS*, 1940, 1: 108, in FDRL, PSF Box 9, Safe File, Welles Reports 1940.

63 Chadwick, *Britain and the Vatican*, p. 290.

64 There is a very fine series of British official histories of the home front called the United Kingdom Civil Series, edited by W. K. Hancock. It includes a *Statistical Digest of the War* prepared by the Central Statistical Office (London and Nendeln: HMSO and Kraus Reprint, 1975). The statistics in the text here are from the table on p. 8.

65 Ibid., pp. 13, 37.

66 Ibid., p. 149. On the sending of British children out of the country, see Michael Fethney, *The Absurd and the Brave* (Lewes: Book Guild, 1990). On British women in the military, compare D. Collett Wadge (ed.), *Women in Uniform* (London: Dampson Low, 1946), for

a view from above, with Mary Lee Settle, *All the Brave Promises: Memories of Aircraft Woman 2nd Class 2146391* (London: Heinemann, 1966), with its view from below.

67 Paul B. Johnson, *Land Fit for Heroes: The Planning of British Reconstruction, 1916–1919* (Chicago: Univ. of Chicago Press, 1968).

68 *Social Insurance and Allied Services, Report by Sir William Beveridge* (New York: Macmillan, 1942). See also Milward, *War, Economy and Society*, p. 340; Gordon Wright, *The Ordeal of Total War, 1939–1945* (New York: Harper & Row, 1968), p. 246.

69 Prime Minister's Personal Minute D 95/3, 13 June 1943, PRO, CAB 120/1.

70 On the 1945 election, see Gary McCulloch, "Labour, the Left, and the British General Election of 1945," *Journal of British Studies* 24 (1985), 465–89; Kenneth O. Morgan, *Labour in Power, 1945–1951* (New York: Oxford Univ. Press, 1984); Henry Pelling, *The Labour Governments, 1945–1951* (New York: St. Martin's, 1984). The background is dealt with in Kevin Jeffries, *The Churchill Coalition and Wartime Politics, 1940–1945* (Manchester: Manchester Univ. Press, 1991), chaps. 2–8. Churchill's role in the election campaign is described in the last volume of Martin Gilbert's biography.

71 Most useful are two of the books of C.P. Stacey, *Arms, Men and Governments*, and *Six Years of War* (Ottawa: Queen's Printer, 1955). On women in the Canadian navy, see Rosamond Greer, *The Girls of the King's Navy* (Victoria, B.C., Canada: Sono Nis Press, 1983).

72 David Day, *The Great Betrayal: Britain, Australia and the Onset of the Pacific War, 1939–42* (New York: Norton, 1989). For the new relationships developing out of the war situation, see Roger John Bell, *Unequal Allies: Australian–American Relations and the Pacific War* (Carlton, Victoria: Melbourne Univ. Press, 1977).

73 Long, *Six Years War*, chap. 16, summarizes the impact on Australia.

74 A very helpful account in Patrick J. Furlong, *Between Crown and Swastika: The Impact of the Radical Right on the Afrikaner Nationalist Movement in the Fascist Era* (Hanover, N.H.: Univ. Press of New England, 1991).

75 Halifax to Amery, 15 July 1940, PRO, FO 800/318, f. 151. Cf. ibid., 24 July 1940, f. 159. On the famine in Bengal, see Paul R. Greenough, *Prosperity and Misery in Modern Bengal: The Famine of 1943–44* (New York: Oxford Univ. Press, 1982); Milward, *War, Economy and Society*, pp. 280–81.

76 These issues are reviewed in two books by Gerald D. Nash, *The American West Transformed: The Impact of the Second World War*, and *World War II and the West: Reshaping the Economy* (Lincoln, Neb.: Univ. Of Nebraska Press, 1990), and Roger Lotchin, *Fortress California, 1910–1961* (New York: Oxford Univ. Press, 1992). On changes in the South, see the thoughtful analysis in Pete Daniel, "Going among Strangers: Southern Reactions to World War II," *Journal of American History* 77 (1990), 886–911.

77 A summary stressing the lack of change is Harvey Sitkoff, "American Blacks in World War II: Rethinking the Militancy-Watershed Hypothesis," in James Titus (ed.), *The Home Front and War in the Twentieth Century: The American Experience in Comparative Perspective* (USAFA Tenth Military History Symposium, 1982) (Washington: GPO, 1984), pp. 147–55 and following comment and discussion. On Eleanor Roosevelt's role, see Joan Hoff-Wilson and Marjorie Lightman (eds.), *Without Precedent: The Life and Career of Eleanor Roosevelt* (Bloomington, Ind.: Indiana Univ Press, 1984), pp. 88–107. A corrective for the view that only Japanese–Americans were affected by the panic in the American West in 1942 and for primarily racial reasons, can be found in Stephen Fox, *The Unknown Internment: An Oral History of the Relocation of Italian-Americans during World War II* (Boston: Twayne, 1990). The whole issue of restrictions on all "enemy aliens" in World War II America awaits research.

78 An especially good introduction to this process through one person's eyes is the memoir of a Black woman officer, Charity Adams Early, *One Woman's Army: A Black Officer Remembers the WAC* (College Station, Tex.: Texas A & M Press, 1989). On Marshall's

role, see Pogue, *Marshall*, 3: 96–99. On the army air force's handling of African-Americans, the Foreword in Craven and Cate, *Army Air Forces*, 6: xxxi, is especially interesting.

79 Gunnar Myrdal, *An American Dilemma*, 2 vols. (New York: Harper, 1944).

80 Maureen Honey, *Creating Rosie the Riveter: Class, Gender and Propaganda in World War II* (Amherst, Mass.: Univ. of Massachusetts Press, 1985). For general surveys of the American home front, see John M. Blum, *V Was for Victory: Politics and American Culture during World War II* (New York: Harcourt Brace Jovanovich, 1976); Richard Polenberg, *War and Society: The United States 1941–1945* (Philadelphia: Lippincott, 1972).

81 On Marshall's major role, see Pogue, 3: 103–14. The best general work on women's role in the army remains Mattie Treadwell, *The Women's Army Corps* (Washington: GPO, 1954), in the official U.S. Army in World War II series. The army air force's history by Craven and Cate places the discussion of women in Vol. 6 entitled, of all things, *Men and Planes* (Chicago: Univ. of Chicago Press, 1955, reprint, Washington: GPO, 1983), pp. 678–90. See Adela R. Scharr, *Sisters in the Sky*, 2 vols. (New York: Patrice, 1986–88). There is an important collection of materials on the women air service pilots in the papers of Lt. Col. Yvononde C. Pateman, U.S. Air Force Academy Library, MS 31.

82 Theodore R. Mosch, *The G.I. Bill: A Breakthrough in Educational and Social Policy in the United States* (Hicksville, N.Y.: Exposition Press, 1975); Davis R.B. Ross, *Preparing for Ulysses: Politics and Veterans during World War II* (New York: Columbia Univ. Press, 1969).

83 A fascinating way to follow the administration's efforts is to see them through the eyes of Isaiah Berlin's weekly political reports from the British embassy in Washington published as *Washington Despatches 1941–1945* (Chicago: Univ. of Chicago Press, 1981), ed. Herbert G. Nichols.

84 Ben-Ami Shillony, *Politics and Culture in Wartime Japan* (Oxford: Clarenden Press, 1981), p. 36.

85 See the text of the "Land Disposal Plan in the Greater East Asia Co-Prosperity Sphere," Dec. 1941, of the Research Section in the Japanese War Ministry, IMTFE Exhibit 1334, published in Storry, *Double Patriots*, pp. 317–19. Cf. an alternative plan of 14 Dec. 1941 from the Japanese Foreign Ministry, IMTFE Exhibit 1333A, discussed in Francis Clifford Jones, *Japan's New Order in East Asia: Its Rise and Fall, 1937–1945* (London: Oxford Univ. Press, 1954), pp. 332–33.

86 On the failure to adjust the economy even after the set-backs of 1942, see Bernd Martin, "Japans Kriegswirtschaft 1941–1945," in Friedrich Forstmeier and Hans-Erich Volkmann (eds.), *Kriegswirtschaft und Rüstung 1939–1945* (Düsseldorf: Droste, 1977), pp. 266–67.

87 Note the statistics on political prisoners and on executions in Japan during the war in Shillony, *Wartime Japan*, pp. 12–13, 34–35, 79. In the years 1941–45 a total of 79 persons were executed in Japan; inside Germany, that many were being executed every *week*. Even the elections held on Apr. 30, 1942, were relatively free, with official candidates receiving two-thirds of the votes and independents one-third (ibid., pp. 21–27; there is a study of this election by Edward J. Drea). The chapter entitled "The War at Home: Democracy Destroyed," in Ienaga Saburo, *The Pacific War, 1931–1945* (New York: Pantheon Books, 1978) concentrates on the period 1937–41.

88 See Stahmer (Tokyo) to Berlin No. 1139 of 8 Apr. 1943, AA, St.S., "Japan," Bd. 12, fr. 298548–53; cf. *ADAP*, E, 5, No. 231. On plans for Japanese control of post-war China, see Tokyo circular No. 755 of 28 Apr. 1942, NA, RG 457, SRDJ 22764–65; Tokyo to Berlin No. 504 of 15 May 1942, SRDJ 24102–4.

89 The struggle over the creation of the Greater East Asia Ministry is summarized in Jones, *Japan's New Order*, pp. 334–35. Foreign Minister Togo was forced out in the process (*Kido Diary*, 1 Sep. 1942, pp. 339–40). The Foreign Ministry retaliated by refusing to

turn over files to the new ministry in Tokyo, see Tokyo to Peking No. 226 (Circular 1688) of 11 Sep. 1942, NA, RG 457, SRDJ 26368.

90 The speeches delivered at the meeting were published in *The Japan Year Book 1943–44*, issued by the Foreign Affairs Association of Japan (Tokyo: The Japan Times, 1943) and reprinted by the U.S. Interdepartmental Committee for the Acquisition of Foreign Publications (Washington: GPO, 1945), pp. 1049–76 (the quotation from Bose is on p. 1075). On the conference, see also Shillony, *Wartime Japan*, pp. 141–51; Lebra, *Japanese-Trained Armies*, p. 12; Jones, p. 368.

91 This is the import of Ienaga, *Pacific War*, chap. 10.

92 An interesting account in Thomas R. H. Havers, *Valley of Darkness: The Japanese People and World War II* (New York: Norton, 1978).

93 Butow, *Tojo*, p. 443.

94 Ch'i, *Nationalist China*, p. 118.

95 Ibid., p. 121; Schaller, *U.S. Crusade in China*, pp. 42–43.

96 See Tokyo to Nanking No. 303 of 13 Dec. 1943, NA, RG 457, SRDJ 47198–99.

97 The Japanese had repeatedly considered making a major offensive earlier and then dropped the idea; one wonders what would have happened had they tried (Ch'i, pp. 69–70).

98 For a summary of the last months of fighting, see Dick Wilson, *When Tigers Fight: The Story of the Sino-Japanese War, 1937–1945* (New York: Penguin, 1983), pp. 243–45. On the whole subject, see also James C. Hsiung and Steven I. Levine (eds.), *China's Bitter Victory: The War with Japan 1937–1945* (New York: M. E. Sharpe, 1992).

99 For a study of the comparative evolution of Chinese Nationalist and Communist military forces during the latter years of war, see Ch'i, pp. 122–31.

100 The official Soviet account is Nikolai Alekseevich Voznesenskii, *The Economy of the U.S.S.R. during World War II* (Washington: Public Affairs Press, 1948, translated from a 1947 original). Good recent surveys in Klaus Segbers, *Die Sowjetunion im Zweiten Weltkrieg: Die Mobilisierung der Verwaltung, Wirtschaft und Gesellschaft im "Grossen Vaterländischen Krieg" 1941–1943* (Munich: Oldenbourg, 1987); Arthur Marwick (ed.), *Total War and Social Change* (New York: St. Martin's, 1988), chap. 4; John Barber and Mark Harrison, *The Soviet Home Front, 1941–1945: A Social and Economic History of the U.S.S.R. in World War II* (London: Longman, 1991).

101 Lord Rennell of Rodd, *British Military Administration of Occupied Territories in Africa during the Years 1941–1946* (London: HMSO, 1948); chap. 10 of this book covers Madagascar.

102 On Egypt, see John H. Turner, "Caught in the Middle: Egypt's Wartime Relations with Britain and the Axis Powers, 1939–1942," MA thesis, Univ. of North Carolina, 1987; internal changes in Africa are summarized in David Killingray and Richard Rathbone (eds.), *Africa in the Second World War* (New York: St. Martin's, 1986).

103 William Roger Louis, *Imperialism at Bay: The United States and the Decolonization of the British empire, 1941–1945* (Oxford: Clarendon Press, 1977), is a fine study of British and American plans and controversies.

104 FDRL, PSF Box 96, Sumner Welles June–December 1940. Cf. *FRUS*, 1940, 5: 1157.

105 Stanley E. Hilton's, *Hitler's Secret War in South America: German Military Espionage and Allied Counterespionage in Brazil* (New York: Ballantine, 1982) concentrates, as the sub-title indicates, on Brazil. German support of an attempted revolution in Bolivia in August 1944 was uncovered by interception of German clandestine radio traffic (NA, RG 457, SRH 062, p. 7). See also Blasier Cole, "The United States, Germany and the Bolivian Revolution (1941–46)," *Hispanic American Historical Review* 52, No. 1, Feb. 1972.

106 A useful account in Frank D. McCann, Jr., *The Brazilian–American Alliance, 1937–1945* (Princeton, N.J.: Princeton Univ. Press, 1973), chaps. 12, 14.

107 Ibid., chap. 13, presents a sorry picture of Brazil's economy during the war.

108 See *ADAP*, D, 9, No. 470, 10, Nos. 41, 80, 92, 145.

109 Alton R. Frye, *Nazi Germany and the American Hemisphere 1933–1941* (New Haven, Conn.: Yale Univ. Press, 1967); Ronald C. Newton, *The "Nazi Menace" in Argentina, 1931–1947* (Stanford, Calif.: Stanford Univ. Press, 1992).

110 A good summary in Philip Shukryi (Philip Khoury), *Syria and the French Mandate: The Politics of Arab Nationalism, 1920–1945* (Princeton, N.J.: Princeton Univ. Press, 1986), chap. 23. See also A.B. Gannon, *The Anglo-French Collision in Lebanon and Syria, 1940–1945* (London: Macmillan, 1986); Aviel Roshwald, *Estranged Bedfellows: Britain and France in the Middle East during World War II* (New York: Oxford Univ. Press, 1990).

111 On the developing U.S. interest in Middle East oil, see Aaaron D. Miller, *Search for Security: Saudi Arabian Oil and American Foreign Policy, 1939–1949* (Chapel Hill, N.C.: Univ. of North Carolina Press, 1980), chaps. 2–5; David S. Painter, *Oil and the American Century: The Political Economy of U.S. Foreign Oil Policy 1941–1954* (Baltimore: Johns Hopkins Univ. Press, 1986), chaps. 1–3; Michael B. Stoff, *Oil, War, and American Security* (New Haven, Conn.: Yale Univ. Press, 1980).

112 See Bernard Wasserstein, *Britain and the Jews of Europe, 1939–1945* (New York: Oxford Univ. Press, 1979). For a British wartime partition plan slightly different from the earlier one see WP(43) 563, 20 Dec. 1943, PRO, CAB 66/144, f. 102–11. The British War Office was especially negative about a Jewish unit in the British army in spite of Churchill's insistence; see PRO, WO 259/52, 79.

113 The best account remains Rich, *Hitler's War Aims*.

114 *ADAP*, E, 3, No. 148. The Danes also sold the German navy eight torpedo boats (KTB Skl A 17, 25 Jan. 1941, BA/MA, RM 7/20, f. 340–41).

115 *ADAP*, E, 4, Nos. 6, 104, 108.

116 This can be followed in the papers of Boehm in the BA/MA, N 172/1, 4, 6, 7.

117 Note *DRuZW*, 4: 877.

118 See the Quisling-Boehm talk of 23 Jan. 1942 in BA/MA, N 172/4. The best account is Hoidal, *Quisling*, chaps. 11–16.

119 *ADAP*, E, 5, No. 310.

120 Rich, *Hitler's War Aims*, 2: 162–69; *DRuZW*, 5/1: 58; Willard A. Fletcher, *"Plan und Wirklichkeit:* German Military Government in Luxemburg, 1940," in George O. Kent (ed.), *Historians and Archivists* (Fairfax Va.: George Mason Univ. Press, 1991), pp. 145–72; Paul Dostert, *Luxembourg zwischen Selbstbehauptung und nationaler Selbstaufgabe: Die deutsche Besatzungspolitik und die Volksdeutsche Bewegung 1940–45* (Luxembourg: Imprimerie Saint Paul, 1985). A major study of Luxembourg in World War II will be published by Willard A. Fletcher.

121 Note Werner Pfeiffer's report of 18 May 1943, in BA, ZSg. 115/6, f. 101–5.

122 Rich, *Hitler's War Aims*, 2: 141–63; Gerhard Hirschfeld, *Nazi Rule and Dutch Collaboration: The Netherlands under German Occupation, 1940–1945* (Oxford: Berg, 1988). There is a multi-volume official Dutch history summarized in English, Louis De Jong, *The Netherlands and Nazi Germany* (Cambridge, Mass.: Harvard Univ. Press, 1990).

123 Konrad Kwiet, "Vorbereitung und Auflösung der deutschen Militärverwaltung in den Niederlanden," *MGM* 5 (1969), pp. 129, 149–51.

124 There is an important publication of Rost van Tonningen's papers in E. Fraenkel-Verkade, *Correspondentie van Meinoud Marinus Rost van Tonningen* (s'-Gravenhagen: Nijhoff, 1967). On plans for Dutch settlements in German-controlled Russia, see Dallin, *German Rule in Russia*, p. 285 (Rost van Tonningen was a key figure in these projects).

125 Hilberg, *Destruction of the European Jews*, 2: 570–97.

126 Arnold H. Price, "The Belgian–German Frontier during World War II," *Maryland Historian*, 1 (1970), 145–53.

127 Hilberg, 2: 599–608.

128 According to the diary of the mayor of Hamburg, Hitler planned to send the Gauleiter of that city, Karl Kaufmann (Krogmann Diary, 6 June 1940, Hamburg Institute, 11 k 8). Some of the Austrian Gauleiter were considered for the position in early 1942 (Rich, *Hitler's War Aims*, 2: 179).

129 The Nazis had originally pushed away Degrelle (see Boelcke, *Kriegspropaganda*, p. 597) but changed their minds as the military situation deteriorated. See German Foreign Ministry to von Bargen, No. 184 of 15 Feb. 1943, in AA, Inland IIg, "Namen D," fr. D 441614; *ADAP*, E, 5, No. 51 n 5. For some candid comments by Degrelle, anticipating an almost endless war and a union of Belgium with Germany, see *ADAP*, E, 5, No. 51.

130 A good summary in Rich, 2: chap. 7.

131 Wolfgang Schivelbuch, *Die Bibliothek von Löwen: Eine Episode aus der Zeit der Weltkriege* (Munich: Hanser, 1988).

132 Bargen to Weizsäcker, 10 Oct. 1941, AA, St.S., "Briefwechsel mit Beamten," Bd. 6, fr. 122709–19, Weizsäcker to Bargen, 16 Oct. 1941, fr. 122708.

133 A good survey of German policy in occupied France in Rich, 2: chap. 8; more details in Jäckel, *Frankreich*; for another perspective, see Marwick (ed.), *Total War*, chap. 6. On the situation in annexed Alsace, see Johnpeter Horst Grill, *The Nazi Movement in Baden, 1920–1945* (Chapel Hill, N.C.: Univ. of North Carolina Press, 1983), chap. 12.

134 As early as July 31, 1940, coal deliveries from these departments were to be considered German coal (*ADAP*, D, 10, No. 267).

135 Note the comments by Hitler reported by Engel to the Commander-in-Chief of the Army, 25 Dec. 1940, Imperial War Museum, AL 2828, Box E 284.

136 Note the meeting of Churchill and Halifax concerning relations with France on 31 Oct. 1940, C 11713/9/17, PRO, FO 371/24303.

137 KTB Skl A 22, 19 July 1941, BA/MA, RM 7/26, f. 284–85; Puttkamer to Raeder, 11 Aug. 1941, RM 6/81, f. 60–61; Fridolin von Senger und Etterlin, Bericht, 1942, BA/MA, N 64/9, f. 33.

138 Krautkrämer, "Vorgeschichte," pp. 214–17; Krautkrämer, *Frankreichs Kriegswende*, pp. 56–57.

139 See Mitani (Vichy) to Tokyo No. 62 of 12 Feb. 1943, NA, RG 457, SRDJ 31528–30.

140 A good introduction in Paxton, *Vichy France*.

141 Hitler even planned to strip the Louvre, see Boelcke, *Kriegspropaganda*, p. 550.

142 See Marrus and Paxton, *Vichy France and the Jews*; Ferro, *Pétain*, pp. 238–47, 414–19. On Pétain's attitude toward the resistance, see Ferro, pp. 566–67. On broader issues, see John F. Sweets, *Choices in Vichy France: The French under Nazi Occupation* (New York: Oxford Univ. Press, 1986) which concentrates on the Clermont–Ferrand area. On the way these issues came to be viewed – and the views changed – see Henry Rousso, *The Vichy Syndrome: History and Memory in France since 1944*, trans. Arthur Goldhammer (Cambridge, Mass.: Harvard Univ. Press, 1991).

143 Paxton, *Parades and Politics*, pp. 372ff. Large numbers of officers of the French armistice army in France subsequently escaped to join the French army in North Africa fighting alongside the Allies (ibid., pp. 398–99).

144 See "Streng vertraulicher Informationsbericht," 15 Oct. 1943, BA, ZSg. 115/7, f. 99.

145 Note *ADAP*, E, 3, No. 275.

146 Stafford, *Britain and European Resistance*, pp. 92–93.

147 Robert Marshall, *All the King's Men: The Truth behind SOE's Greatest Wartime Disaster* (London: Collins, 1988).

148 Brooke Diary, 15 Dec. 1941, Liddell Hart Centre, Alanbrooke Papers.

149 A good introduction in Raoul Aglion, *Roosevelt and De Gaulle: Allies in Conflict, A Personal Memoir* (New York: Free Press, 1988). This book stresses the significance of the influence of anti-de Gaulle sentiments among prominent Frenchmen in the United States, especially Alexis Leger, on Roosevelt's attitude. See also Gietz, *Die neue Alte Welt* pp. 141–77.

150 Beauftragte für den Vierjahresplan, "Zur Frage der künftigen Wirtschaftspolitik gegenüber Südosteuropa," 15 Jan. 1941, BA, R 2/10382.

151 Adolf Heinz Beckerle, "Tagebuch, 2. September 1941," AA, Deutsche Gesandtschaft Sofia, Persönliche Aufzeichnungen des Gesandten Beckerle, Bd. 1, f. 43.

152 Note Der Reichsminister der Finanzen, "F 7003–891, Garantien für Nachkriegsgeschäfte," 3 Mar. 1944, BA, R 2/30936.

153 Rich, *Hitler's War Aims*, 2: 27–55; Detlef Brandes, *Die Tschechen unter deutschem Protektorat* (Munich: Oldenbourg, 1969); Vojtech Mastny, *The Czechs under Nazi Rule: The Failure of National Resistance* (New York: Columbia Univ. Press, 1971). We can now look forward to new work on this important subject.

154 See Hácha to Hitler, 7 or 8 June 1940, BA, Adjutantur des Führers, NS 10/19, f. 73–77.

155 Callum MacDonald, *The Killing of SS-Obergruppenführer Reinhard Heydrich* (New York: Free Press, 1989).

156 See C 10778/6/18, PRO, FO 371/24392 and C 4795/18/18, FO 371/26510, to correct Jaksch's memoirs, *Europas Weg nach Potsdam* (Stuttgart: Deutsche Verlags-Anstalt, 1958).

157 Radomír Luza, *The Transfer of the Sudeten Germans: A Study of Czech-German Relations, 1933–1962* (New York: New York Univ. Press, 1964); Detlef Brandes, *Grossbritannien und seine osteuropäischen Alliierten* (Munich: Oldenbourg, 1988).

158 Rich, *Hitler's War Aims*, 2: 55–67.

159 Lammers memorandum, "Rk 17178A," 16 June 1939, BA, R 43 II/1416, f. 16–17.

160 See Memorandum by Woermann, "Zu Pol. IV 1559," 28 May 1942, AA, St.S., "Dipl. Aufzeichnungen, April-Juni 1942," fr. J 000491–92.

161 On the regrets of many Hungarians about the declaration of war on the United States, see the letter of Robert T. Pell, the last U.S. Minister, to Roosevelt, 10 Feb. 1942, in FDRL, PSF Box 96, State, Welles, 1942. Pell predicted that the Germans would wreck all of Europe as they went down.

162 A summary in Rich, *Hitler's War Aims*, 2: 241–51.

163 *ADAP*, E, 3, No. 183; Schmidt (Presse), "Notiz für Herrn St.S.," 9 Mar. 1942, AA, St.S., "Ungarn," Bd. 6, fr. 104672; Weizsäcker to Stuckart, 19 Mar. 1942, AA, St.S., "Politischer Schriftwechsel," Bd. 8, fr. 470730–31.

164 Braham, *Politics of Genocide*; Randolph L. Braham (ed.), *The Destruction of Hungarian Jewry: A Documentary Account*, 2 vols. (New York: Pro Arte, 1963).

165 *ADAP*, E, 8, Nos. 40, 48. There are numerous related documents in the file AA, Inland IIg, "Judenfrage in Ungarn, Angelegenheit Manfred Weiss, 1944."

166 A fine survey in Margit Szöllösi-Janze, *Die Pfeilkreuzlerbewegung in Ungarn: Historischer Kontext, Entwicklung und Herrschaft* (Munich: Oldenbourg, 1989).

167 On Romania, see Rich, *Hitler's War Aims*, 2: 251–58; I. C. Butnaru, *The Silent Holocaust: Romania and its Jews*, (Westport, Conn.: Greenwood 1992); Hillgruber, *Hitler, König Carol*, which also covers the Horia Sima government-in-exile (pp. 226–28). On the latter, see also Heinen, *Die Legion "Erzengel Michael"*, pp. 459–63.

168 The Germans also provided financial support to his father, the ex-king Ferdinand, because the latter advised Boris in a pro-German sense (Weizsäcker to Ribbentrop, 21 Jan. 1942, AA, St.S., "Aufzeichnungen über interne Angelegenheiten," Bd. 2, fr. 472298).

169 On Bulgaria in the war, see Rich, 2: 258–63; Hoppe, *Bulgarien*, pp. 128ff. On the fate of Bulgaria's Jews, see Frederick B. Charny, *The Bulgarian Jews and the Final Solution 1940–1944* (Pittsburgh: Pittsburgh Univ. Press, 1972); Marshall Lee Miller, *Bulgarian Jewry during the Second World War* (Stanford, Calif.: Stanford Univ. Press, 1975).

170 The German Minister to the puppet state of Croatia pointed out that the expulsions made even the Italians look good (Kasche, "Abschliessender Bericht über die Umsiedlung," 20 Nov. 1941, AA, Inland IIg, "Fremde Volksgruppen," fr. H 296639–49).

171 The OKW order of 8 Dec. 1942 is quoted in Christopher R. Browning, "Harald Turner

und die Militärverwaltung in Serbien 1941–1942," Dieter Rebentisch and Karl Treppe (eds.), *Verwaltung contra Menschenführung im Staat Hitlers* (Göttingen: Vandenhoeck & Ruprecht, 1986), p. 366. See also Christopher R. Browning, *Fateful Months: Essays on the Emergence of the Final Solution*, rev. ed. (New York: Holmes & Meier, 1991), chap. 2.

172 Note *ADAP*, D, 13, No. 432.

173 A good account in Matteo J. Milazzo, *The Chetnik Movement and the Yugoslav Resistance* (Baltimore: Johns Hopkins Press, 1975). There is additional detail, and a balanced set of judgements, in Lucien Karchmar, *Draja Mihailovic and the Rise of the Cetnik Movement, 1941–1942*, 2 vols. (New York: Garland, 1987).

174 Stafford, *Britain and European Resistance*, pp. 73–74.

175 The shift in British policy can be followed in Hinsley, *British Intelligence*, 3/1: chap. 33.

176 Ibid., pp. 151–56; Hugh DeSantis, "In Search of Yugoslavia: Anglo-American Policy and Policy-making 1943–45," *JCH* 16 (1981), 544–47; Lamb, *Churchill as War Leader*, chap. 19.

177 See *ADAP*, E, 1, No. 277; cf. Kasche to Weizsäcker, 12 Oct. 1942, AA, St.S., "Schriftwechsel mit Beamten," Bd. 7, fr. 122283–85; Broucek (ed.), *Glaise Horstenau*, 3: 292–93, 302–3, 371–72.

178 On the approaches of Tito to Hitler, see the introduction by Peter Broucek to his edition of the Glaise Horstenau papers, 3: 33ff, 145 n 1, 220–21. Broucek's whole introduction is an excellent survey of wartime events in Croatia. See also Milovan Djilas, *Conversations with Stalin* (New York: Harcourt, 1962), pp. 9–10, 33; Milovan Djilas, *Wartime* (New York: Harcourt Brace, 1977), pp. 198–99, 229–45; *ADAP*, E, 5, No. 262; 7, No. 105; 8, No. 240; and AA, Gesandtschaft Zagreb, "geheime Reichssachen" files for 1943–44. According to a post-war account by a member of the historical staff in Hitler's headquarters, Dr. Claus Grimm, Hitler rejected Tito's offers with the comment: "mit Rebellen verhandle ich nicht" (I don't negotiate with rebels) (BA/MA, MSg-1/705, f. 123–24). Tito does appear to have been able to work out a temporary truce with the Hungarians in late 1943.

179 *ADAP*, E, 3, No. 310; Weizsäcker to Kasche, 9 Apr. 1942, AA, St.S., "Schriftwechsel mit Beamten," Bd. 7, fr. 122266–67; Mackensen to Berlin No. 2451 of 25 May 1943, AA, St.S., "Italien," Bd. 13, fr. 124411.

180 *ADAP*, E, 7, No. 156. The German military and diplomatic archives are literally filled with records on the subject; a systematic analysis and account remains to be written.

181 For a very thoughtful 1 Mar. 1944 report on Mihailovic by an American officer (Capt. W.R. Mansfield USMCR) at his headquarters, 18 Aug. 1943 – 15 Feb. 1944, see FDRL, PSF Box 167 OSS. There are important related documents in PSF Box 167 OSS, Donovan, and Box 168, OSS Reports Apr. – July 1944.

182 Rich, *Hitler's War Aims*, 2: 299–302; Christoph Stamm, "Zur deutschen Besetzung Albaniens 1943–1944," *MGM*, No. 2, (1981) pp. 99–120; Reginald Hibbert, *Albania's National Liberation Struggle: The Bitter Victory* (London: Pinter, 1991).

183 This was an early German violation of the armistice and surrender terms; see the Greek memorandum of June 1941 in the papers of Clemm von Hohenberg, BA/MA, N 449/2, f. 5–20.

184 On the allowing of food through the blockade, see Medlicott, *Economic Blockade*, 2: 263ff. A short survey of German policy and practice in Hagen Fleischer, "Das Beispiel Griechenland," in Norbert Frei and Hermann Kling (eds.), *Der nationalsozialistische Krieg* (Frankfurt: Campus, 1990), 205–19; a general review in Hondros, *Occupation and Resistance*, pp. 61–76. On German insistence that all the problems were Italy's concern see *ADAP*, E, 4, No. 64; Ribbentrop to Rome No. 1274 of 10 Oct. 1942, AA, St.S., "Italien," Bd. 10, fr. 125121–124.

185 A good account, rather favorable to ELAS, in Hondros, chaps. 4–6. See also Thanasis

D. Sfikas, "The People at the Top Can Do Those Things Which Others Can't Do: Winston Churchill and the Greeks, 1940–45," *JCH* 26 (1991), 307–32.

186 See Hondros, p. 250.

187 Peter J. Stavrakis, *Moscow and Greek Communism, 1944–1949* (Ithaca, N.Y.: Cornell Univ. Press, 1989).

188 Lukas, *Forgotten Holocaust*: See also Czeslaw Madajczyk, "Besteht ein Synchronismus zwischen dem 'Generalplan Ost' und der Endlösung der Judenfrage," in Michalka (ed.), *Der Zweite Weltkrieg*, pp. 844–57.

189 Schmuhl, *Rassenhygiene, Nationalsozialismus, Euthanasie*, pp. 240–47.

190 An extraordinary record is in the diary of the German governor, Hans Frank. A complete film is available at the National Archives as T-992; a large selection has been edited by Präg and Jacobmeyer, *Das Diensttagebuch des deutschen Generalgouverneurs in Polen*, here cited as *Frank Diary*.

191 A helpful summary in Michael A. Peszke, "The Polish Government's Aid to and Liaison with its Secret Army in Occupied Poland, 1939–1945," *Military Affairs* 52 (1988), 197–202.

192 The best account remains Dallin, *German Rule in Russia*. A summary with some other material in Rich, *Hitler's War Aims*, 2: chap. 11.

193 Schmuhl, pp. 240–47.

194 This point is overlooked in much of the literature which deals with the German occupation, as if the civilian-administered areas were the whole and not just a portion (and of the pre-1939 U.S.S.R. the smaller portion) of the occupied territory. An example of this error is Harvey Fireside, *Icon and Swastika: The Russian Orthodox Church under Nazi and Soviet Control* (Cambridge, Mass.: Harvard Univ. Press, 1971). A far more realistic perception of the situation underlies Theo J. Schulte's *The German Army and Nazi Policies in Occupied Russia* (Oxford: Berg, 1989).

195 A good recent analysis in Timothy P. Mulligan, *The Politics of Illusion and Empire: German Occupation Policy in the Soviet Union, 1942–1943* (New York: Prager, 1988).

196 *ADAP*, E, 5, No. 149.

197 See Tokyo to Oshima No. 250 of 16 Apr. 1943, and Oshima to Tokyo No. 444 of 19 Apr. 1943, NA, RG 457, SRDJ 34430–34.

198 Hans-Erich Volkmann, "Das Vlasov-Unternehmen zwischen Ideologie und Pragmatismus," *MGM* 2 pp. 125–29, (1972), and the documents cited there.

199 M.R.D. Foot, *Resistance: European Resistance to Nazism, 1940–1945* (New York: McGraw-Hill, 1977), p. 319.

200 They certainly disregarded Franco's plea to take account of Spanish culture in the Philippines (Suma [Madrid] to Tokyo No. 9 of 4 Jan. 1942, NA, RG 457, SRDJ 18649). A survey in Ienaga, *Pacific War*, chap. 8, is entitled "The Greater East Asia Co-Prosperity Sphere: Liberation or Exploitation?" and shows why the latter is the correct description.

201 An example is the situation in Burma, surveyed in Pacific Strategic Intelligence Section, "Japanese–Burmese Relations," 9 May 1945, NA, RG 457, SRH-074.

202 Note the analysis in Peter Herde, "José P. Laurel: Konservativer Katholizismus und japanische Sozialphilosophie als philippinische Variante der 'Neuen Ordnung' in der 'Grossostasiatischen Wohlstandsphäre' (1942–1945)," in Sabine Weiss (ed.), *Historische Blickpunkte: Festschrift für Johann Rainer* (Innsbruck: Amoe, 1988), p. 269.

10: MEANS OF WARFARE: OLD AND NEW

1 One of the best semi-fictional books on World War II, Kurt Emmrich (pseud. Peter Bamm), *The Invisible Flag* (New York: Day, 1956, and other eds.), records the adventures of a German medical company on the Eastern Front which generally relied on horse transport. A general survey in Di Nardo, *Mechanized Juggernaut*.

2 Fritz Hahn, *Waffen und Geheimwaffen des deutschen Heeres 1933–1945* 2 vols. (Koblenz: Bernard & Graefe, 1986–87), 1: 191–94. For other German monster guns, see ibid., 2: 107–9. Dora's use at Sevastopol is reviewed in Chapter 8.

3 An account in Groehler, "Die 'Hochdruckpumpe',"pp. 738–44. The installation in France from which London was to be bombarded by this weapon was wrecked by Allied bombers on July 6, 1944.

4 Von Senger und Etterlin, *German Tanks of World War II*, pp. 29–31. Such tanks were still used by the Germans in the final defense of Berlin.

5 Hahn, 2: 45–47.

6 See ibid., pp. 89–91. The various monster tanks would, if built, have been untransportable by train and too heavy for practically all the bridges then in place or being built by German engineers.

7 An excellent account in John J. Sweet, *Iron Arm: The Mechanization of Mussolini's Army, 1920–1940* (Westport, Conn.: Greenwood, 1980).

8 This is repeatedly stressed by Hinsley, *British Intelligence*. See the study by David Fletcher, *The Great Tank Scandal: British Armor in the Second World War*, of which Part 1 (London: HMSO, 1989) has appeared.

9 See the *Statistical Digest of the War* in the British official series, p. 148.

10 Charles H. Bailey, *Faint Praise: American Tanks and Tank Destroyers during World War II* (Hamden, Conn.: Archon, 1983). Also useful, R.P. Hunnicutt, *Sherman: History of the American Medium Tank* (San Rafael, Calif.: Presidio Press, 1978).

11 Note the favorable comments in Keegan, *Six Armies in Normandy*, pp. 197–98.

12 John Milsom, *Russian Tanks, 1900–1970* (London: Arms and Armor, 1970).

13 See Donald B. McKean, *Japanese Tanks, Tactics and Antitank Weapons* (Wickenburg, Ariz.: Normount Technical Publications, 1973).

14 The closest German plane in general use was a military version of a civilian plane, the FW 200 "Condor." On German projects for long-range bombers, see Horst Boog, "'Baedeker-Angriffe' und Fernstflugzeugprojekte 1942: Die strategische Ohnmacht der Luftwaffe," *Militärgeschichtliches Beiheft zur Wehrwissenschaftlichen Rundschau* 5, No. 4 (1990), 2–9; Richard J. Overy, "From 'Uralbomber' to 'Amerikabomber': the Luftwaffe and Strategic Bombing," *Journal of Strategic Studies* 1 (1978), 125–33.

15 There is excellent material on the British problems in developing sound air–army cooperation in PRO, PREM 3/119/8.

16 See William A.B. Douglas, *Creation of a National Air Force: The Official History of the Royal Canadian Air Force* (Toronto: Univ. of Toronto Press, 1986), 2: 293.

17 See Great Britain, Air Ministry, Air Historical Branch, "Balloon Defences, 1914–1945: The Development and Employment of Balloon Barrages with Particular Reference to the Work of Balloon Command, Royal Air Force," Royal Air Force Monograph (First Draft), London [1945?], PRO, AIR 41/1.

18 It can be argued that the 18.1 inch gun carrying Japanese super-battleships *Yamato* and *Musashi*, discussed below, constituted a new type. Had there been a fleet action, as the Japanese originally intended, instead of Yamamoto's Pearl Harbor scheme, this would probably have been demonstrated with disastrous results for the Americans. See Malcolm Muir, Jr., "Rearming in a Vacuum: United States Naval Intelligence and the Japanese Capital Ship Threat, 1936–1945," *Journal of Military History* 54 (1990), 473–85.

19 A useful survey in Kahn, *Hitler's Spies*. On German agents in Latin America, see Hilton, *Hitler's Secret War*. A systematic German wartime operation destroyed records of agent operations in the United States as well as in parts of Latin America; note German Minister in Santiago to Berlin No. 926 of 2 Aug. 1942, AA, St.S., "U.S.A.," Bd. 11, fr. 39204–5.

20 The 1945 account of John C. Masterman, *The Double-Cross System in the War of 1939 to 1945* (New Haven, Conn.: Yale Univ. Press, 1972), was prepared for publication

before the release of information about the Allied breaking into German enigma machine codes. It must, therefore, be read with the understanding that the "secret sources" repeatedly mentioned were derived from code-breaking. There are very substantial additional details in Hinsley, *British Intelligence*, 4 and 5. The process of turning German agents continued with those left behind in the areas liberated in the West in 1944; see Nigel West, *The Circus:* MI5 Operations 1945–1972 (New York: Stein & Day, 1984), pp. 24–25.

21 Elyesa Bazna (with Hans Nogly), *I was Cicero* (New York: Harper & Row, 1962). A puzzle which awaits resolution is whether the British found out, or could have found out, about this leak from reading reports from the German embassy in Ankara, which sent them by radio and not always with the highest security classification (including references to Cicero). Relevant documents are in AA, St.S., "Türkei," Bd. 9, including a 17 Nov. 1943 item which refers to Cicero documents and carries only a "geheim" classification (fr. 41768–70). For material from the Cicero documents in the diary of Alfred Jodl for September 1944 see the transcript in the Imperial War Museum, AL 930/4–3, f. 38. The continued British–American secrecy concerning the "Floradora" documents, the fruit of the breaking of German diplomatic codes, makes any even reasonably accurate assessment of questions like the one raised by the Cicero affair impossible. Hinsley, 4: 213–15, downplays the whole matter.

22 West, *SIGINT*, pp. 241–42; Hinsley, 4: Appendix 14.

23 This was best, or worst, illustrated in France; see Robert Marshall, *All the King's Men.* The similarity between the rivalries of intelligence agencies in Germany, Britain and the U.S. in World War II simply cries out for a comparative analysis.

24 On the Oslo document, see Andrew, *HM Secret Service*, p. 433; Hinsley, *British Intelligence*, 1: Appendix 5 and numerous references in this and other volumes. Reginald V. Jones, *Reflections on Intelligence* (London: Heinemann, 1989), pp. 319–27, identifies the author as Hans Ferdinand Mayer (I am indebted to Richard Breitman for calling this work to my attention).

25 See Joseph E. Persico, *Piercing the Reich: The Penetration of Nazi Germany by American Secret Agents During World War II* (New York: Viking, 1978).

26 Note those submitted by Donovan to Roosevelt (in French) in FDRL, PSF Box 165, OSS Donovan Reports 7–13; and Donovan to Roosevelt, Memorandum No. 566, 29 May 1942, Box 166, OSS Donovan #12.

27 Barry M. Katz, *Foreign Intelligence: Research and Analysis in the Office of Strategic Services, 1942–1945* (Cambridge, Mass.: Harvard Univ. Press, 1989).

28 The activities of Kolbe, code-named George Wood, and whose material is referred to in documents as "Boston" (Kappa) material, await scholarly investigation. See also Foot, *Resistance*, pp. 218–19; Klemens von Klemperer, *German Resistance against Hitler: The Struggle for Allies Abroad*, 1938–1945 (Oxford: Clarendon Press, 1992), pp. 321–23; Donovan to Roosevelt, 15 Apr. 1944, FDRL, Map Room Box 163, Naval Aide Intelligence A-8-2.

29 The huge file is in NA, RG 165, Entry 77, Box 1431, File: Polish O/B Intelligence. Recent changes in Poland may open the way for a review of Polish intelligence, combining information from both inside and outside the country.

30 Note the comments by the Finnish chargé in Lisbon reported by the U.S. naval attaché there on 31 July 1943, NA, RG 165, Entry 77, Box 1311, File 6000–Germany. For an example of information provided by the Hungarian Minister to the British Minister in Stockholm in Feb. 1944, see C 2946/1343/12, PRO, FO 371/38941. There were also minimal low-level German–British contacts which both sides tried to use for intelligence purposes; see Bern to Berlin No. 1164 of 14 Apr. 1944, AA, St.S., "Ungarn," Bd. 11, fr. 110140–42.

31 On Japanese intelligence, see Walter T. Hitchcock (ed.), *The Intelligence Revolution: A Historical Perspective* (Washington: GPO, 1991), section 3.

32 Ulrich Sahm, *Rudolf von Scheliha 1897–1942: Ein deutscher Diplomat gegen Hitler* (Munich: Beck, 1990).

33 Boog, *Luftwaffenführung*, p. 81.

34 Heinz Höhne, *Codeword: "Direktor": The Story of the Red Orchestra*, trans. by Richard Barry (New York: Coward, McCann & Georghegan, 1971), pp. 148–49, 165–67, 191, 202; and *The Rote Kapelle: The CIA's History of Soviet Intelligence and Espionage Networks in Western Europe, 1936–1945* (Washington: University Publications of America, 1979), are among the more useful. It is quite possible that the main source of "Lucy" (Rudolf Roessler) was the Swiss general staff, which used him to pass information to the Soviet Union. See also Richard Aldrich, "Soviet Intelligence, British Security and the End of the Red Orchestra: The Fate of Alexander Rado," *Intelligence and National Security* 6 (1991), 196–217.

35 The most reliable books are Prange, *Target Tokyo* and Johnson, *An Instance of Treason*. In the *Kido Diary* (p. 333) Sorge is referred to as Zolge.

36 The Lissner story awaits serious study. See *ADAP*, E, 2, Nos. 83, 94; Shigemitsu to Berlin No. 426 of 15 June 1943, NA, RG 457, SRDJ 38584; Stahmer to Berlin No. 1757 of 5 June 1943, AA, St.S., "Japan," Bd. 12, fr. E 489973–74; and documents in the file AA, Inland IIg, "Namen Le-Li," fr. 437798, 437802, 437864–67.

37 Useful works include Chapman Pincher, *Too Secret Too Long* (New York: St. Martin's, 1984); John Costello, *Mask of Treachery* (New York: Morrow, 1989); Hitchcock (ed.), *The Intelligence Revolution*, pp. 251ff.

38 West, SIGINT, pp. 232–33.

39 On exchanges about low-level German Air Force codes, see documents in PRO, AIR 20/2766. See also J. Dane Hartgrove (ed.), *The OSS–NKVD Relationship, 1943–1945* (New York: Garland, 1989).

40 See documents in PRO, AIR 20/2075; Donovan to Roosevelt, 22 Feb. 1944, FDRL, Map Room, Naval Aide Intelligence A-8-2.

41 Crankshaw left for Russia on Sep. 19, 1941 (PRO, WO 165/38). On Churchill's insistence, see Rohwer and Jäckel, *Funkaufklärung*, pp. 391, 393–94.

42 Most interesting is the British ADI (Science) Air Scientific Intelligence Report No. 131, "Air Technical Liaison between Germany and Japan," of 16 Oct. 1944. A very fine analysis in John W. M. Chapman, "Signals Intelligence Collaboration among the Tripartite Pact States on the Eve of Pearl Harbor," *Japan Forum* 3, No. 2 (Oct. 1991), 231–56.

43 Salewski, 2: *Seekriegsleitung*, 95–96.

44 An especially good account of such operations may be found in the memoirs of a distinguished British woman Y-service officer, Aileen Clayton, *The Enemy is Listening* (London: Hutchinson, 1980). A file of RAF Wireless Intelligence Service "Periodical Summary" reports for Oct. 1939 – May 1941 in PRO, AIR 20/335, provides some insight into the Y-system.

45 The best introduction remains Kahn, *Codebreakers*, supplemented by the same author's collection, *Kahn on Codes: Secrets of the New Cryptology* (New York: Macmillan, 1983) and his *Seizing the Enigma*. Most helpful, but unfortunately not translated, are the materials collected in Rohwer and Jäckel, *Funkaufklärung*.

46 A number of examples from the Allied side of the war in the Pacific are in Lewin, *American Magic* index p. 329. For examples of Japanese use of traffic analysis, see *Ugaki Diary*, pp. 322, 324.

47 Much information is summarized in Rohwer and Jäckel, *Funkaufklärung*. The point about dispersion of effort is also made in Horst Boog, "German Air Intelligence in the Second World War," *Intelligence and National Security* 5 (1990), 350–424. See also Doran Arazi,

"Die deutsche Funkaufklärung im Zweiten Weltkrieg," in Michalka (ed.), *Der Zweite Weltkrieg*, pp. 501–12; John W.M. Chapman, "Signals Intelligence in the Pacific," pp. 131–49.

48 Note OKM Skl Chef MNDB, "XB Bericht Nr. 2/42," 16 Jan. 1942, f. 3, NA, RG 457, SRS 548/12; Nigel West, *SIGINT*, pp. 163, 190–91.

49 The question is discussed at length in Beesly, *Very Special Intelligence*, and Rohwer and Jäckel, *Funkaufklärung*. The changeover is reflected in OKM Skl Chef MNDIII, "XB-Bericht Nr. 24/43," 17 July 1943, f. 5, NA, RG 457, SRS 548/15.

50 OKM Skl Chef MNDIII, "XB-Bericht Nr. 37/43," 16 Sep. 1943, NA, RG 457, SRS 548/16.

51 Santoni, *Ultra siegt im Mittelmeer*, pp. 64–65; Rohwer and Jäckel, *Funkaufklärung*, p. 107; Steengracht, "St.S. Nr. 277," 3 June 1943, AA, St.S., "Aufzeichnungen über nicht-Diplomatenbesuche," Bd. 2, fr. 371875–77.

52 Woermann Memorandum, "U.St.S.Pol. Nr. 600grRs.," 28 Sep. 1942, AA, St.S., "Italien," Bd. 10, fr. 125074–75; Woermann Memorandum "U.St.S.Pol. Nr.64 g Rs," 26 Jan. 1943, ibid., Bd. 12, fr. 123858–59.

53 "Zusammenstellung der F[orschungs]A[mt]-Meldungen über ungarische Bemühungen um ein Abrücken vom Bündnis mit dem Reich (15.6.-30.9.43)," 30 Sep. 1943, AA, St.S., "Ungarn," Bd. 10, fr. 106683–87; related documents are in the same file, fr. 106688–93, and Bd. 11, fr. 109770–82.

54 Kahn, *Codebreakers*, pp. 469–70.

55 Santoni, *Ultra siegt im Mittelmeer*, pp. 6off.

56 Ibid., pp. 64–65; Hinsley, *British Intelligence*, 5: 65; Kahn, *Codebreakers*, pp. 472–77; Gordon Welchman, *The Hut Six Story: Breaking the Enigma Codes* (New York: McGraw-Hill, 1982), pp. 234–35. Examples of Fellers's signals deciphered by the Germans are in Hans-Otto Behrendt, *Rommel's Intelligence in the Desert Campaign, 1941–1943* (London: William Kimber, 1985), Appendix II.

57 Mackensen to Berlin No. 2451 of 25 May 1943, AA, St.S., "Italien," Bd. 13, fr. 124411. See also the discussion of this in Chapter 9, above.

58 A survey in Kahn, *Codebreakers*, pp. 579–85; see also Chapman, "Signals Intelligence in the Pacific."

59 Thus the Americans learned from an intercept of a Japanese telegram of 9 Mar. 1944 of the Japanese reading a report by the Chinese ambassador in London on his meeting with Eden on March 3 (Tokyo Circular 938 of 9 Mar. 1944, trans. 13 Mar., NA, RG 457, SRA 07510).

60 See the extensively "sanitized" page 2 of the "Magic" Far East Summary No. 224 of 30 Oct. 1944, NA, RG 457, SRS 224.

61 Kahn, *Codebreakers*, p. 582.

62 Lewin, *American Magic*, p. 245.

63 In addition to the numerous specific documents from the SRDJ, SRA and other series cited in notes throughout this book, there are several articles by Professor Carl Boyd, who is preparing a book on the subject of Allied knowledge about Europe from intercepted Japanese reports.

64 See Oshima to Tokyo No. 1349 of 10 Nov. 1943, NA, RG 457, SRDJ 45465–69; and Colonel Ito's inspection report quoted in U.S., Army Security Agency, "Examples of Intelligence Obtained from Cryptanalysis," 1 Aug. 1946, SRH-066, f. 5–6.

65 See, e.g., the footnotes on SRDJ 33800 (a document of 26 Mar. 1943), SRDJ 33941 (31 July 1942), and SRDJ 34050 (18 Jan. 1943). In addition, the documents intercepted often needed interpretation; see Leahy to Roosevelt, 23 Jan. 1944, FDRL, Map Room Box 163, Naval Aide Intelligence A-8-2.

66 Note Japanese military attaché Lisbon to military attaché Rome No. 360 of 1 July 1943, NA, RG 457, SRH 01629; Japanese military attaché Budapest to military attaché

Stockholm, 25 June 1944, SRA 07047–48 (sanitized); and the material about the OSS theft of Japanese code materials from their embassy in Lisbon cited in SRH-066, f. 7, and SRH 113.

67 Very helpful are the two books by Holmes, *Undersea Victory*, and *Double-Edged Secrets* (Annapolis, Md.: Naval Institute Press, 1979); a good survey in Lewin, *American Magic*, chap. 10.

68 Lewin, *American Magic*, pp. 195–96.

69 Kahn, *Codebreakers*, pp. 609–10; Morison, *US Naval Operations*, 14: 319–30. Many of those who survived the week-long ordeal, one of whom I had an opportunity to interview, were never the same afterwards.

70 Numerous examples of Willoughby's underestimation of Japanese strength are included in the text. There is no evidence that MacArthur ever called him to account. The fairest summary may be in Lewin's assessment, *American Magic*, pp. 147–49, 180–81.

71 Ibid., pp. 196–97. See also Alexander S. Cochran, "MacArthur, Ultra et la guerre en Pacifique, 1942–1944," *Revue d'historie de la deuxième guerre mondiale*, No. 133 (Jan. 1984), 17–27. The Australian discovery of abandoned and not destroyed Japanese code materials is recounted in Drea, *MacArthur's Ultra*, pp. 92–93, 226.

72 Some details in Lewin, *American Magic*, pp. 268ff. A detailed scholarly study of the fighting on Leyte utilizing the now available materials would be a major contribution to our understanding of the Pacific War.

73 It also uncovered such issues as last-minute German–Japanese cooperation in landing agents in India (Magic Far Eastern Summary No. 401, 25 Apr. 1945, and No. 407, 1 May 1945, NA, RG 457, SRS 401, 407).

74 West, *SIGINT*, p. 127.

75 Jean Stengers, "Enigma, the French, the Poles and the British, 1931–1940," in Christopher Andrew and David Dilks (eds.), *The Missing Dimension: Governments and Intelligence Communities in the Twentieth Century* (London: Macmillan, 1984), pp. 126–37, 267–73; Kozaczuk, *Enigma*; Hinsley, *British Intelligence*, 3/2: Appendix 30; Kahn, *Seizing Enigma*, chaps. 3–9.

76 The best account of this process currently available is Gordon Welchman, *The Hut Six Story*.

77 On the seizure of German enigma materials, see Beesly, *Very Special Intelligence*; Kahn, *Seizing Enigma*; Hinsley, 3/2: 955. The capture of Italian materials is referred to in Santoni, *Ultra*, pp. 66–71, 101–2.

78 Andrew Boyle, *The Climate of Treason: Five Who Spied for Russia* (London: Hutchins, 1979), pp. 239–44. For examples of American reading of German diplomatic traffic, see NA, RG 457, SRH-066, f. 8–9. It was such a break in Oct. 1943 which led to the arrest of a key German agent in Argentina, Osmar Hellmuth (SRH-066, f. 8; Hinsley, 4: 203; Newton, *The "Nazi Menace" in Argentina*, chap. 16). See also von Klemperer, *German Resistance*, pp. 321–23.

79 West, *SIGINT*, pp. 225–28; Lewin, *Ultra Goes to War*, pp. 131–32. Unlike the enigma with three or four rotors, the Geheimschreiber had ten and sent its code text directly by radio without a human transmitter. The details of how the Allies managed to break into this system remain closed.

80 David A.T. Stafford, "'Ultra' and the British Official Histories: A Documentary Note," *Military Affairs* 42, No. 1 (1978), 29–31.

81 Accounts by Hinsley, Kahn, Rohwer and Jäckel, Lewin, and Bennett supersede the early book by F.W. Winterbotham, *The Ultra Secret* (New York: Harper & Row, 1974).

82 Note the example of Crete, Santoni, *Ultra siegt im Mittelmeer*, pp. 246–47.

83 Ibid., pp. 85–99.

84 Ibid., pp. 255–56.

85 Ibid., p. 172.

86 NA, RG 457, SRH-066, f. 4–5.

87 Note Christopher Andrew's comments in Hitchcock (ed.), *The Intelligence Revolution*, pp. 113ff.

88 For an example of an ultra supplement at Hyde Park see FDRL, Map Room Box 127, MR 450(4) Enemy Raiders (a 10 Dec. 1942 document declassified at my request on 7 Oct. 1975). For American practice in general, see NA, RG 457, RHH-107. Very helpful, David Kahn, "Roosevelt, MAGIC, and ULTRA," in Kent (ed.), *Historians and Archivists*, pp. 115–44.

89 Note Roosevelt to Knox, copies to Stimson, Leahy, FCC Chairman Fly, 7 Sep. 1943, NA, RG 457, SRMN-7.

90 A good summary of the problem in Santoni, *Ultra*, pp. 252–53.

91 This is the conference recorded in Rohwer and Jäckel, *Funkaufklärung*. The author discussed the point with several of the German participants. See also Kahn, *Seizing Enigma*, pp. 202–3, 205–7, 213, 260–62.

92 This point is repeatedly and effectively made by Welchman. The whole question of the extent to which the Soviets broke German machine cyphers in World War II, captured some of the machines, and used their knowledge remains open. For some discussion of the subject, see the exchange between Geoff Jukes and Ralph Erskine in *Intelligence and National Security* 4 (1989), 374–84, 503–11.

93 A survey in Thomas L. Cubbage II's piece in Michael L. Handel (ed.), *Strategic and Operational Deception in the Second World War* (London: Frank Cass, 1987), pp. 327–46. See also Hinsley, *British Intelligence*, 5: chap. 6.

94 Welchman, *The Hut Six Story*, pp. 240–41.

95 See John P. Campbell's piece in Handel (ed.), pp. 92–113; Hinsley, 5: 76ff. For the serious effects of this disaster on the SOE and on French resistance networks, see Marshall, *All the King's Men*.

96 Hinsley, 3/1: 119–21, 5: 89–92. I do not find Klaus-Jürgen Müller's argument on this (Handel, pp. 307ff) convincing. At the key point (p. 324 n 36), he relies on the notoriously unreliable David Irving for his evidence.

97 Katherine L. Herbig in Handel, pp. 263–64.

98 Ibid., pp. 265–78.

99 The best account in Rolf-Dieter Müller, "Die deutschen Gaskriegvorbereitungen 1919–1945: Mit Giftgas zur Weltmacht?" *MGM* 27, No. 1 (1980), 25–54. See also Hahn, *Waffen und Geheimwaffen*, 1: 227–30; Harris and Paxman, *A Higher Form of Killing*, chap. 3. The account in Gellermann, *Der Krieg der nicht stattfand*, is not reliable and has been effectively challenged in the review by Rudibert Kunz (*MGM*, 44, No. 2 [1988], 201–5).

100 Rolf-Dieter Müller, "Gaskriegsvorbereitungen", pp. 44–45; Harris and Paxman, *A Higher Form of Killing*, p. 64. On British ignorance, see Hinsley, 2: 119–21.

101 Such warnings had been issued in May 1942 and April 1943; see documents in PRO, AIR 8/449. An implementing plan for that contingency of 9 July 1943 is in AIR 20/27; further documents are in AIR 20/6112. Note the report that Hungarian Regent Horthy had urged the use of gas on the Eastern Front (Dörnberg memorandum of 20 Apr. 1942, AA, St.S., "Ungarn," Bd. 6, fr. 104879–94).

102 Hahn, *Waffen und Geheimwaffen*, 1: 235.

103 The formal consideration of gas use began with War Cabinet 8(44) of 18 June 1944 (PRO, CAB 65/41). See also Jones, *Reflections*, pp. 251–55.

104 The statistics in Harris and Paxman, pp. 155ff, overstate the size of the American stockpile, because the authors fail to take into account that all smoke bombs and shells were included in the figures, since these too came under the jurisdiction of the Chemical Corps. See Brooks E. Kleber and Dale Birdsall, *The Chemical Warfare Service: Chemicals in Combat* (Washington: GPO, 1966).

105 Harris and Paxman, p. 117; John Ellis van Courtland Moon, "Chemical Warfare: A

Forgotten Lesson," *Bulletin of the Atomic Scientists* 45, No. 6 (1989), 40–43, and "Project SPHINX: The Question of the Use of Gas in the Planned Invasion of Japan," *Journal of Strategic Studies* 12 (1989), 303–23.

106 Glenn B. Infield, *Disaster at Bari* (New York: Macmillan 1971, Ace Book, 1973).

107 A preliminary account in Yuki Tanaka, "Poison Gas: The Story Japan Would Like to Forget," *Bulletin of the Atomic Scientists* 44, No. 8 (1988), 10–19. See also Ienaga, *Pacific War*, pp. 187, 239.

108 Louis Allen, *Burma: The Longest War 1941–1945* (London: Dent, 1984), pp. 301–2. Note the reference to the discontinuing of "hand thrown self-exploding bottles" in an intercepted Japanese circular of 15 July 1944, Warren F. Kimball (ed.), *Churchill and Roosevelt*, 3: 256.

109 Professor Reinhard R. Doerries has been trying to penetrate this veil. See his *Imperial Challenge: Ambassador Count Bernstorff and German-American Relations, 1908–1917* (Chapel Hill, N.C.: Univ. of North Carolina Press, 1989), p. 189.

110 See Stockholm, International Peace Research Institute, *The Problems of Chemical and Biological Warfare*, vol. 1, *The Rise of CB Weapons* (New York: Humanities Press, 1971).

111 Harris and Paxman, *A Higher Form of Killing*, chap. 4; Jones, *Reflections*, pp.251–55. Barton J. Bernstein, "Churchill's Secret Biological Weapons," *Bulletin of the Atomic Scientists* 43 (1987), 46–50, uses important British materials but is marred by his vehement bias against Churchill. More reliable, Julian Lewis, *Changing Direction: British Military Planning for Post-War Strategic Defence, 1942–1947* (London: Sherwood Press, 1988), pp. 211–14, Appendix 8.

112 A pioneering work on the subject is Peter Williams and David Wallace, *Unit 731: Japan's Secret Biological Warfare in World War II* (New York: Free Press, 1989). It does, however, contain much speculation set forth as facts.

113 An excellent survey of the projects in Hölsken, "Die V-Waffen", pp. 95–122. See also Hahn, *Waffen und Geheimwaffen*, 2: 162ff.

114 Hölsken, p. 116.

115 On British efforts to deceive the Germans as to the impact of V-2s, see Masterman, *The Double-Cross System*, p. 181.

116 Hölsken, p. 117; *DRuZW*, 5/1: 597; Murray, *Luftwaffe*, p. 181.

117 Hölsken, p. 114; Groehler, "Hochdruckpumpe"; Hahn, *Waffen und Geheimwaffen*, 2: 155–62; Hinsley, 3/1: 405 and n t, 413, 435–36, 439, map facing p. 593, 594–95.

118 The report is quoted in Hölsken, p. 114. Much additional material in Heinz D. Hölsken, *Die V. Waffen: Enstehung–Propaganda–Kriegseinsatz* (Stuttgart: Deutsche-Verlag-Anstalt, 1984).

119 A preliminary account in Thies, *Architect der Weltherrschaft*, pp. 136–48.

120 Hahn, *Waffen und Geheimwaffen*, 2: 168–72.

121 Hinsley, 3/1: 51 n t, 335, 347; 3/2: 594–95.

122 Arnold Kramish, *The Griffin* (Boston: Houghton Mifflin, 1986), pp. 99–102 (the identification of the source may need to be changed).

123 Berlin to Tokyo (Vice Minister of War) No. 146 of 9 Feb. 1944, NA, RG 457, SRA 06766–72; see also Madrid to Tokyo No. 577 of 15 Jan. 1945, SRA 15571.

124 Rohwer and Jäckel, *Funkaufklärung*, p. 366; Hinsley, *British Intelligence*, 3/1: chaps. 40–42.

125 Hinsley, 3/1: 382–87. The dispersal to Poland led to important Polish intelligence reports for the British; see ibid., pp. 437–38, 441–42.

126 Ibid., pp. 402–3. The British later acquired large portions of a V-2 which had landed in Sweden. For an Aug. 1944 offer by the latter to provide complete and reliable information on V-2, 3, and 4 in exchange for British plans to return to Norway, see N 4807/865/42, PRO, FO 371/43509.

127 Note Hinsley, 3/1: 339 and n, 415 and n, 448–49.

128 Several examples are mentioned in Hölsken, *Die V-Waffen*, p. 101.

129 Ibid., p. 112. See also Hinsley, 3/1: 46–50. The German target date for use of the V-2 had been Nov. 1, 1943. Bombing was primarily responsible for the delay until Sep. 8, 1944; see Collier, *Defence*, p. 339; Hinsley, 3/1: 375.

130 Jacob Neufeld, *The Development of Ballistic Missiles in the United States Air Force, 1945–1960* (Washington: GPO, 1990), p. 11. Other projects are described in chaps. 1 and 2 of this book.

131 Eugene Emme, *Hitler's Blitzbomber* (Maxwell Air Force Base, Alabama: Air University Documentary Research Study, 1951), takes one side; the best survey of the issue, J. Richard Smith and Eddie J. Creek, *Jet Planes of the Third Reich* (Boylston, Mass.: Monogram Aviation Publications, 1982), pp. 101, 356, argues that Hitler's decision was the correct one. So does the most recent examination, Alfred Price, *The Last Year of the Luftwaffe: May 1944 to May 1945* (London: Arms and Armour Press, 1991). See also Hinsley, 3/1: 332ff; 3/2: 595ff; Werner Girbig, *. . . mit Kurs auf Leuna: Die Luftoffensive gegen die Treibstoffindustrie und der deutsche Abwehreinsatz 1944–1945* (Stuttgart: Motorbuch, 1980), p. 148; Olaf Groehler, *Kampf um die Luftherrschaft* (Berlin–East: Militärverlag der DDR, 1988), pp. 156–68.

132 Smith and Creek, *Jet Planes*, chap. 17; Hinsley, *British Intelligence*, 3/1: 333; 3/2: 598.

133 Smith and Creek, pp. 123–24; Hinsley, 3/1: 336n. The first reference to jets in Brooke's diary is dated 17 Feb. 1944: "Had intended to visit the display of new jet aircraft but weather was too bad" (Liddell Hart Centre, Alanbrooke Papers).

134 A good survey in Alfred Price, *Instruments of Darkness: The History of Electronic Warfare* (London: Macdonald and Jane's, 1977).

135 On these devices, "Gee," "Oboe," and "H2S," see Webster and Frankland, *Strategic Air Offensive*, 4: Annex 1. There is also a most interesting report, prepared in Oct. 1945, Royal Air Force, Headquarters Bomber Command, Signals Branch, "War in the Ether, Europe 1939–1944, Radio Countermeasures in Bomber Command: An Historical Note," in PRO, AIR 20/1492.

136 Reginald V. Jones, *Most Secret War: British Scientific Intelligence, 1939–1945* (London: Hamish Hamilton, 1978). Very helpful, his piece in Rohwer and Jäckel, *Funkaufklärung*, pp. 228–54.

137 The best account is Mark Walker, *German National Socialism and the Quest for Nuclear Power, 1939–1949* (Cambridge, Mass.: Harvard Univ. Press, 1989). A good summary in his "Legenden um die deutsche Atombombe," *VjZ* 38 (1990), 45–74, which also discusses the relevant literature, especially the post-war lies of German scientists who worked on the project.

138 For the raids on Norsk Hydro, see Cruikshank, *SOE in Scandinavia*, pp. 198–202; Kramish, pp. 167–73; M.R.D. Foot, *SOE: An Outline History of the Special Operations Executive, 1940–1946* (London: BBC Publications, 1984), p. 211, Walker, pp. 185–88. According to Kramish, *The Griffin*, pp. 83–89, much of the supply on hand in April 1940 had been saved at the last minute and sent to France and subsequently to England.

139 Memoirs of Boetticher, BA/MA, N 323/56, f. 232–33, 235–36.

140 Kramish, pp. 126–32; Tagebuch Chef des Stabes AHA, 12 Jan. 1942, Imperial War Museum, MI 14/981/2. The whole process is described in detail in Walker's book.

141 See Hinsley, 3/2, Appendix 29; Samuel Goudsmit, *ALSOS* (New York: Schuman, 1947).

142 See the comment of the Minister for the Coordination of Defence at the War Cabinet meeting of 7 Oct. 1939 (War Cab. 40[39], PRO, CAB 65/3, f. 110–11); and of Professor Lindemann (Lord Cherwell) on 9 Oct. 1939 (PRO, ADM 205/4).

143 Hinsley, 2: 122–28. See also John Ehrman, *The Atomic Bomb: An Account of British Policy in the Second World War* (London: Cabinet Office, July 1953), a secret print based on British sources and now declassified; and Margaret Gowing, *Britain and Atomic Energy, 1939–1945* (New York: St. Martin's, 1964).

144 Jones, *Manhattan*, pp. 37–44. On the American program, see also Richard G. Hewlett and Oscar E. Anderson, *A History of the United States Atomic Energy Commission, Vol. 1: The New World, 1939–1946*, (Philadelphia: Univ. of Pennsylvania Press, 1962); and Richard Rhodes, *The Making of the Atomic Bomb* (New York: Simon & Schuster, 1986), a work which combines much scientific information with political polemics.

145 Walker, *Quest for Nuclear Power*, chap. 20.

146 Jones, pp. 43–44. The British used the code-name "Tube Alloys."

147 See Jones, pp. 74ff; Leslie R. Groves, *Now It Can Be Told: The Story of the Manhattan Project* (New York: Harper, 1962).

148 Jones, pp. 228–35.

149 See the summary in Robert M. Hathaway, *Ambiguous Partnership: Britain and America, 1944–1947* (New York: Columbia Univ. Press, 1981), pp. 212–15; Dallek, *Roosevelt and Foreign Policy*, pp. 416–17.

150 Note the material in FDRL, PSF Box 104, War Department 1943. Cf. Jones, pp. 228–32.

151 The most forceful statements of the second view are Martin J. Sherwin, *A World Destroyed: The Atomic Bomb and the Grand Alliance* (New York: Knopf, 1975), and Barton J. Bernstein, "Roosevelt, Truman and the Atomic Bomb, 1941–1945: A Reinterpretation," *Political Science Quarterly* 90 (1975), 23–69.

152 Samuel I. Rosenman (ed.), *The Public Papers and Addresses of Franklin D. Roosevelt*, 13 vols. (New York: Harper, 1950), 9: 93. See also Loewenheim et al. (eds.), *Roosevelt and Churchill*, pp. 57–58.

153 David A. Rosenberg, "U.S. Nuclear Stockpile, 1945 to 1950," *Bulletin of the Atomic Scientists* 38 (1982), 25–30, provides the most accurate information currently available.

154 One of the few serious works in a most difficult field is Robert C. Williams, *Klaus Fuchs, Atom Spy* (Cambridge, Mass.: Harvard Univ. Press, 1987), which also has a fine bibliography. See Professor David Holloway's forthcoming book, *Stalin and the Bomb*, to be published by Yale Univ. Press, on the Soviet nuclear program, for which he has been able to utilize newly released information and which he has discussed with me.

155 There is an account of the Japanese project in Pacific Research Society, *The Day Man Lost: Hiroshima, 6 August 1945* (Tokyo, Palo Alto, Calif.: Kodansha International, 1972), pp. 1–64. This is poor on other matters, as is J.W. Dower, "Science, Society, and the Japanese Atomic-Bomb Project during World War II," *Bulletin of Concerned Asian Scholars* 10, No. 2 (1978), 41–54. Note the Japanese request for radioactive materials from the Germans intercepted by the U.S. (Tokyo to Berlin No. 057 of 24 Aug. 1943, NA, RG 457, SRA 02321). See also Shillony, *Wartime Japan*, p. 202 n 13.

156 Stockholm to Tokyo No. 232 of 9 Dec. 1944, NA, RG 457, SRA 14628–32.

157 Samuel W. Mitcham, *Men of the Luftwaffe* (Novato, Calif.: Presidio Press, 1988), pp. 72–73.

158 See PRO, AIR 20/2759.

159 Note the Luftwaffe report of 29 July 1941 cited in *DRuZW*, 4: 706–7, as an example of miscalculation.

160 A key figure in the development of British tactical air support is described in Vincent Orange, *Coningham: A Biography of Air Marshal Sir Arthur Coningham* (London: Methuen, 1990). On the pressures on the British government to do something in early 1942, see Villa, *Unauthorized Action*, chap. 4.

161 See, e.g., his 13 Mar. 1941 memorandum on the absolute need for air superiority before landing troops, in PRO, AIR 20/2759.

162 Note Charles Whiting, *The Three-Star Blitz: The Baedeker Raids and the Start of Total War 1942–1943* (London: Cooper, 1987). I do not find the discussion of these matters in *DRuZW*, 6, convincing.

163 Boog, *Luftwaffenführung*, pp. 135–36.

164 Hinsley, *British Intelligence*, 2: 521–23.

165 See Martin Middlebrook, *The Berlin Raids: RAF Bomber Command Winter 1943/44* (London: Viking, 1988).

166 Hastings, *Bomber Command*, pp. 306ff; Saward, *"Bomber" Harris*, pp. 158–60.

167 Hastings, pp. 201–5.

168 Boog, *Luftwaffenführung*, pp. 204–14.

169 Smith and Creek, *Jet Planes*, p. 66.

170 Clark Kerr to London No. 53 of 22 Oct. 1943, PRO, PREM 3/11/10.

171 PRO, AIR 20/3357, p. 4.

172 See the papers beginning in late August 1944 in PRO, AIR 19/818; cf. Alfred C. Mierzejewski, *The Collapse of the German War Economy, 1944–1945: Allied Air Power and the German National Railway* (Chapel Hill, N.C.: Univ of North Carolina Press, 1988), pp. 70–71.

173 Mierzejewski, p. 167, explains how much of this information was ignored.

174 The reports of the USSBS were published by the GPO; the British survey was not published, but a four volume study by Webster and Frankland appeared in the official United Kingdom history of World War II instead. There is a helpful discussion of the two projects in Volume 4, Annex V, of the latter.

175 Hinsley, *British Intelligence*, 3/1: 46–51.

176 The appearance of Dudley Saward's biography, *"Bomber" Harris* produced very important information and provoked a most interesting series of reviews in the *Journal of the Royal United Service Institute for Defence Studies* 130, No. 2 (1985), 62–70.

177 Mierzejewski, p. 186.

178 A survey of all belligerents and fronts in Anthony Rhodes, *Propaganda, The Art of Persuasion: World War II* (New York: Chelsea House, 1976). For additional insights, stressing the racial angle, see John Dower, *War Without Mercy: Race and Power in the Pacific War* (New York: Pantheon, 1986).

179 The extensive German intervention into the 1940 American election awaits its historian. For 1944, see "Vermerk Gesandter Megerle, Führerhauptquartier: Amerika-Aktion," 7 Feb. 1944, and Megerle to Legation Zagreb, No. 128 of 30 Jan. 1944, AA, Gesandtschaft Zagreb, "Geheime Reichssachen," Bd. 1/44 – 50/44.

180 "Vertrauliche Informationen Nr. 328/41" and "Nr. 329/41" of 14 and 15 Dec. 1941, BA, Oberheitmann, ZSg. 109/28, f. 41–43, 45.

181 Boelcke, *Kriegspropaganda*, pp. 375–81.

182 On German radio propaganda, see Herzstein, *The War that Hitler Won*. Though dated, Ernst Kris and Hans Speier, *German Radio Propaganda* (London: Oxford Univ. Press, 1944), is still useful.

183 A helpful introduction in Daniel Lerner, *Sykewar: Psychological Warfare against Germany, D-Day to VE-Day* (New York: Stewart, 1949).

184 The pass is pictured in Anthony Rhodes, *Propaganda*, p. 147.

185 Both the American and the British official histories include extensive series dealing with the medical aspect. For a brief history of the "British Medical History of the Second World War," see Sir Arthur S. MacNulty's account in Robin Higham (ed.), *Official Histories: Essays and Bibliographies from around the World* (Manhattan, Kans.: Kansas State Univ. Library, 1970), pp. 515–17. For the American navy see the piece by Quirtin M. Sanger, ibid., pp. 536–42; there is a preliminary report on the army's extensive series by John Boyd Coates in ibid., pp. 595–602. The Canadian official medical history was edited by W.R. Fensby (Ottawa: Queen's Printer, 1953–56); Bishen L. Raina edited the Indian one (Delhi, 1961–62); Thomas D.M. Stout the New Zealand volumes (Wellington, 1954–58); Allan S. Walker the Australian ones (Canberra, 1952–61). The U.S. army also published an interesting volume on *The U.S. Army Veterinary Service in World War II* by Everett B. Miller (Washington: GPO, 1961).

186 The title is that of an early book on the subject by Alexander Mitscherlich and Fred Mielke (New York: Schumann, 1949). The best recent survey of the German activities is included in Michael Kater, *The Nazi Doctors* (Chapel Hill, N.C.: Univ. of North Carolina Press, 1989). I am not aware of any similar survey of Japanese experimentation.

187 See *DRuZW*, 4: 708.

188 Lammers, *Fahrtberichte*, p. 88 n 97.

11: FROM THE SPRING OF 1943 TO SUMMER 1944

1 On the tanks, see von Senger und Etterlin, *German Tanks of World War II*, pp. 59–74.

2 On Mar. 10, 1943 Hitler, after a talk with Goebbels, decided that postcards from German prisoners of war in the U.S.S.R. were not to be delivered to the addressees (AA, St.S., "Russland," Bd. 10, fr. 33600).

3 Note "Vertraulicher Bericht von Herrn Seligo-Lissabon," 17 Mar. 1943, BA, ZSg. 115/6, f. 45–101; Ankara to Tokyo No. 94 of 11 Mar. 1943, NA, RG 457, SRDJ 32483–85.

4 See the U.S. Military Intelligence reports on morale in Italy in 1942–43, in NA, RG 165, Entry 77, Box 2209, File 5970–Italy-I; a Japanese report in Rome to Madrid No. 756 of 7 Dec. 1942, NA, RG 456, SRDJ 28932–34; and the German naval attaché's report of 19 Mar. 1943 in BA/MA, RM 7/233, f. 528–33, with the military attaché's comments in ibid., f. 527 and 534.

5 Note General Roatta's comments reported in a U.S. Naval Intelligence report of 7 Apr. 1944, NA, RG 165, Entry 77, Box 1197, File 3850–Germany.

6 Von Senger und Etterlin, "Bericht der deutschen Delegation bei der italienisch-französischen Waffenstillstandskommission Turin," 22 June 1942, BA/MA, N 64/9.

7 Rintelen to Weizsäcker, 13 Sep. 1942, AA, St.S., "Italien," Bd. 10, fr. 125016–17; Mackensen memorandum of 13 Nov. 1942, AA, Nachlass Mackensen, Bd. 6, fr. 65367–68; KTB Skl A 39, 15 Nov. 1942, BA/MA, RM 7/42, f. 382; Rome to Tokyo, no number read, 7 June 1943, NA, RG 457, SRDJ 29861–62.

8 These frictions have yet to be carefully investigated; they are touched on in Frederick W. Deakin, *The Brutal Friendship: Mussolini, Hitler, and the Fall of Italian Fascism* (New York: Harper & Row, 1962), and Schröder, *Italiens Kriegsaustritt*. Numerous documents have been published in the German and Italian editions of diplomatic documents; there is much more in the archives.

9 William S. Linsenmayer, "Italian Peace Feelers before the Fall of Mussolini," *JCH* 16 (1981), 653–54; Hinsley, *British Intelligence*, 3/1: 70, 102 n; Woodward, *British Foreign Policy*, 2: 461–64.

10 Chadwick, *Britain and the Vatican*, pp. 250–52, 257–58; WP(43) 27, Eden memorandum "Proposal Received from Certain Anti-Fascist Elements in Italy," 14 Jan. 1943, and Cabinet WM(43) 18 Jan. 1943, 9th Confidential Annex, both in PRO, PREM 3/242/9; Denis Mack Smith, *Italy and Its Monarchy* (New Haven, Conn.: Yale Univ. Press, 1989), p. 298.

11 PM Minute 58/3, in PRO, PREM 3/242/9. Churchill added: "I am not going to take the responsibility of carrying on this war a day longer than is necessary to achieve full victory."

12 See Schröder, *Italiens Kriegsnaustritt*, chap. 2. The projects for a mild New Order were primarily identified with Giuseppe Bastianini, who as Under Secretary ran the Italian Foreign Ministry after Ciano's dismissal.

13 Boyle, *China and Japan*, pp. 308–10, 323–26; Burns and Bennett, *Diplomats in Crisis*, pp. 171–93; Tokyo to Tientsin Circular 109, NA, RG 457, SRDJ 28399–402. On the unsuccessful effort to have Finland recognize Wang's government, see Helsinki to Tokyo No. 64 of 9 Mar. 1943, SRDJ 33324. On continued German interest in possible Japanese-

Chinese negotiations, see Steengracht, "Inland II B 115gR," of 1 Aug. 1942, AA, Inland IIg, "Berichte zur Lage in und über Ostasien 1941–1944," fr. 267318.

14 See Lebra, *Japanese-Trained Armies*, pp. 10–11.

15 Hesse to Ribbentrop, 5 Nov. 1942, AA, St.S., "Politischer Schriftwechsel," Bd. 9, fr. 303944–50; Sakamoto (Bern) to Tokyo, Special No. 6, 3 Mar. 1943, NA, RG 457, SRDJ 32276.

16 For examples of Japanese worry, see NA, RG 457, SRA 01401–2, 01815–16, 02781–87 (all Feb. – Mar.1943).

17 Sato (Kuibyshev) to Tokyo No. 189 of 22 Feb. 1943, ibid., SRDJ 31948–49, No. 214 of 26 Feb. 1943, SRDJ 32129–35, and No. 283 of 19 Mar. 1943, SRDJ 32961–63.

18 Most of the text is printed in Morton, *Strategy*, pp. 636–40.

19 See the U.S. Naval Intelligence report of 10 Mar. 1943, NA, RG 165, Entry 77, Box 2360, File 5900 National Defense General–Japan; *ADAP*, E, 5, No. 218; Ohmae, "Strategischen Konzeptionen," pp. 198–99.

20 The issues are summarized in Alexander S. Cochran, Jr., "The Avalanche/Baytown Decision: British Ascendancy or Allied Consensus?" paper delivered at the Southern Historical Association meeting in 1983.

21 The most recent treatment is in Warren F. Kimball, *The Juggler: Franklin Roosevelt as Wartime Statesman* (Princeton, N.J.: Princeton Univ. Press, 1991), chap. 3.

22 Ibid, chap. 7; Louis, *Imperialism at Bay*: Dallek, *Roosevelt and Foreign Policy*, pp. 324ff.

23 Note Dill to Nye, 30 Mar. 1943, Liddell Hart Centre, Alanbrooke Papers, 14/38.

24 See, e.g., the reference in the Brooke Diary for 24 July 1943: "He [Marshall] cannot see beyond the tip of his nose and is maddening." Or the full text of the relevant portion of his entry for 12 Aug. 1943 in connection with the Quebec Conference: "I only wish to heaven that I could go on escaping into the country instead of having to face up to a conference with our American friends who have no strategic outlook, cannot see beyond the end of their noses, and imagine that this war can be run by a series of legal contracts based on false concepts of what may prevail six months ahead! I am tired of arguing with them." Liddell Hart Centre, Alanbrooke Papers. Fraser (*Alanbrook*, pp. 360–61) implies that Brooke's black mood was related to his disappointment over the decision, communicated to him rather insensitively by Churchill, that the command of the cross-Channel invasion would be assigned to an American, not to Brooke himself. I do not agree with this interpretation; Brooke was surely disappointed, but he was always the model of the "good soldier" in the best sense of the term.

25 See Carlo d'Este, *Bitter Victory: The Battle for Sicily, July–August 1943* (London: Collins, 1988).

26 There is a very strongly pro-Montgomery account of these disputes in Hamilton, *Monty*, 2: 241–68. There are helpful accounts in the American army and navy official histories. Thoughtful and critical of Montgomery is Richard Lamb, *Montgomery in Europe 1943–1945: Success or Failure?* (London: Buchan & Enright, 1983), pp. 21–31. See also Blumenson, *Patton*, pp. 186–95; Schröder, *Italiens Kriegsaustritt*, pp. 158–76, 258–66. On April 9, Brooke commented on the difficulties with "Husky" planning owing "to Montgomery's egotistical outlook"; on May 28 he wrote, "Alexander too is somewhat disappointing and only realizes half the situation." Liddell Hart Centre, Alanbrooke Papers.

27 Ewen Montague, *The Man Who Never Was* (Philadelphia: Lippincott, 1954). For Axis evaluation and acceptance of the fake, see Schröder, *Italiens Kriegsaustritt*, pp. 112–14; Papeleux, *L'admiral Canaris*, 178–81, 184–87; Hinsley, *British Intelligence*, 3/1: 119–21; KTB Skl 45, 7 May 1943, BA/MA, RM 7/48, f. 125ff. See also the discussion of this deception operation in Chapter 10, above.

28 For an account based on interviews and published materials, see William B. Breuer, *Drop Zone Sicily: Allied Airborne Strike July 1943* (Novato, Calif.: Presidio Press, 1983).

29 Bad weather hurt the airborne operation but persuaded the defenders that there could be no landing at that time. See A.A. Nofi, "Sicily: The Race for Messina 10 July – 17 August 1943," *Strategy and Tactics* 89 (1981), 9.
30 Blumenson, *Patton*, pp. 198–207.
31 See Hinsley, *British Intelligence*, 3/1: 95–99.
32 Blumenson, *Patton*, pp. 209–16, provides an excellent, fair, and brief summary of the whole affair. The relevant documents are in the published Patton and Eisenhower papers: Martin Blumenson (ed.), *The Patton Papers 1940–1945* (Boston: Houghton Mifflin, 1974), pp. 326–42; Chandler et al. (eds.), *Eisenhower Papers*, Nos. 1190, 1396, 1397, 1401, 1414, 1416, 1418, 1423. (Henceforth cited as *Eisenhower Papers.*) See also David Eisenhower, *Eisenhower at War, 1943–1945* (New York: Random House, 1986), pp. 36–38.
33 On German troops in Aug. – Sep. 1943 replacing Italians in the Balkans, see Hinsley, 3/1: 11–13, 29.
34 Schröder, *Italiens Kriegsaustritt*, pp. 116–31.
35 Ibid., pp. 138–56.
36 Already on 1 Apr. 1943 Berlin had ordered its Rome embassy to send home older sensitive files as a precaution (Berlin to Rome No. 1354, AA, St.S., "Italien," Bd. 13, fr. 124146–48); on 10 May 1943 Tokyo ordered its embassy in Rome to be ready to destroy codes and cypher machines (Tokyo to Rome No. 394, NA, RG 457, SRDJ 36812).
37 The best analysis of "Alarich" remains Schröder, *Italiens Kriegsaustritt*, pp. 176–95.
38 See Hidaka (Rome) to Tokyo No. 309 of 31 May 1943, NA, RG 457, SRDJ 37492–96.
39 Harry Fornari, *Mussolini's Gadfly: Roberto Farinacci* (Nashville: Vanderbilt Univ. Press, 1971). Most interesting is the report of the Japanese ambassador Hidaka Shirokuro of 23 Aug. 1943, No. 624, NA, RG 457, SRDJ 42310–14.
40 Rome to Tokyo No. 243 of 30 July 1943, NA, RG 457, SRA 02409–16. See also Smith, *Italy and its Monarchy*, pp. 300–6.
41 Note that on July 18 Mussolini had neither approved nor forbidden Bastianini's plan to sound the Allies about peace (Linsenmeyer, "Italian Peace Feelers," pp. 151–52).
42 *ADAP*, E, 6, No. 159; Deakin, *Brutal Friendship*, 4, chap.3; Dino Alfieri, *Deux dictateurs face à face. Rome–Berlin 1939–1943* (Geneva: Les éditions du cheval oilé, 1948), pp. 311–28.
43 Hidaka to Tokyo No. 488 of 25 July 1943, NA, RG 457, SRDJ 40965–74; see also Hidaka No. 602 of 18 Aug. 1843, SRDJ 41818. The Japanese Foreign Minister passed on the gist of Hidaka's report to the German ambassador in Tokyo who responded, as instructed, that Germany sought victory, not peace (*ADAP*, E 6, No. 191).
44 Note the belief of Enno von Rintelen, the German military representative in Italy, that Badoglio thought the war lost when he took over, preferred to make peace jointly with Germany, but went his own way when this was clearly impossible (Rintelen to Egon Heymann, 13 May 1948, Rintelen Papers, BA/MA, N 433).
45 Schröder, *Italiens Kriegsaustritt*, pp. 252–58, 320–25.
46 For an astonishing illustration, see Adrian Carton de Wiart, *Happy Odyssey* (London: Jonathan Cape, 1950), chap. 17.
47 Linsenmeyer, "Italian Peace Feelers," pp. 656–57.
48 The Germans discovered that the excavations for explosives to block the Brenner Pass were all empty; the Italians had alarmed the Germans by their preparations but had never gotten around to making these effective (see the transcript of the Rommel Tagebuch for 31 July 1943 in the Institut für Zeitgeschichte, AL 1708/1).
49 See the account in Richard Lamb, *The Ghosts of Peace 1935–1945* (Wilton, England: Richard Russell, 1987), chap. 8.
50 In spite of its silly comments about the Allies, Schröder's account, pp. 196ff, remains the best; cf. Smith, *Italy and its Monarchy*, pp. 306–23.
51 Alexander S. Cochran's account cited in n 20, above, covers the issue.

52 Brooke Diary, 13 Sep. 1943, Liddell Hart Centre, Alanbrooke Papers. He added negative comments on both Eisenhower and Alexander: "neither will ever have sufficient vision to be big soldiers."

53 By Oct. 2, 1943 the Allies had learned from ultra that the Germans were planning to hold a front south of Rome but believed themselves not in a position to mount an offensive to drive the Allies off the continent because of Russian pressure in the East (Hinsley, *British Intelligence*, 3/1: 173–75).

54 The full text of the order is in *KTB OKW*, 1943, 2: 1420–22; it is discussed in Ziemke, *Stalingrad to Berlin*, pp. 124–26. The revised order of 15 Apr. is in *KTB OKW*, 1943, 2: 1425–28. A fine account of the operation in Ernst Klink, *Das Gesetz des Handelns: Die Operation "Zitadelle" 1943* (Stuttgart: Deutsche Verlags-Anstalt, 1966).

55 Note Klink, p. 48.

56 On the new position of Guderian as Inspector General of Armored Forces on Feb. 28, 1943, see ibid., pp. 41–46.

57 Ibid., pp. 110–16 (Guderian sided with Model, pp. 140–43).

58 "Der Sieg von Kursk muss für die Welt wie ein Fanal wirken" (*KTB OKW*, 1943, 2: 1425).

59 See Ziemke, *Stalingrad to Berlin*, pp. 128–33; Erickson, *Road to Berlin*, p. 97. For Hitler's speech to the Army Group and army commanders on July 1, 1943, see Klink, *Operation "Zitadelle"*, pp. 197–98. Very helpful, Timothy Mulligan, "Spies, Cyphers and 'Zitadelle'": Intelligence and the Battle of Kursk," *JCH* 22 (1987), 235–60.

60 Soviet preparations are covered in detail by Erickson and in more summary form by Ziemke. See also Glantz, *Soviet Military Deception*, pp. 154–63. On the Eastern Front from Leningrad south about three million Germans and 350,000 Hungarians and Romanians with 2000 tanks faced close to six million Soviet soldiers with over 8000 tanks (figures in Ziemke, p. 144).

61 An excellent account in Charles W. Sydnor, Jr., *Soldiers of Destruction: The SS Death's Head Division, 1933–1945* (Princeton, N.J.: Princeton Univ. Press, 1977), pp. 281–90.

62 Ibid., pp. 291ff recounts the subsequent operations of the SS divisions which were sent to Italy; in the event, two of the three remained on the Eastern Front and only one was actually transferred to Italy.

63 Hitler's comments to the Japanese ambassador on Oct. 3, 1943, exaggerated the situation but are nevertheless of interest; see Oshima's 1186 of 4 Oct. 1943, NA, RG 457, SRDJ 43965–69 (no German record of this conversation has been found, *ADAP*, E, 7, No. 15 n 5).

64 Ziemke, *Stalingrad to Berlin*, chap. 8; Erickson, *Road to Berlin*, pp. 121ff; Glantz, *Soviet Military Deception*, pp. 165–79, 182–86, 216–21.

65 Ziemke, *Stalingrad to Berlin*, chaps. 9–10; Glantz, pp. 186–216, 243–49, 258–78.

66 Very useful is Ingeborg Fleischhauer, *Die Chance des Sonderfriedens*. She has worked in German, British, and U.S. archives, was able to obtain access to Swedish materials, and interviewed some of the key participants. Her use of intercepted Japanese telegrams is, however, based on the Magic Summaries, not the full collection of intercepts. Her interpretation differs from the one presented here in down-playing Soviet interest in the contacts. Schröder, *Bestrebungen*, surveys the 1942–43 contacts (pp. 25–32), but is very brief and uses none of the Japanese material. For additional information see Diether Krywalski (ed.), "Zwei Niederschriften Ribbentrop's über die Persönlichkeit Hitlers und die letzten Tage in Berlin," *Geschichte in Wissenschaft und Unterricht* 18 (1967), 739; Meskill, *Hitler and Japan*, pp. 414, 423; Harold Nicolson (ed.), *The War Years, 1939–1945* (New York: Atheneum, 1967), pp. 277, 345; Bryant (ed.), *Turn of the Tide*, pp. 531, 535; Stockholm to Tokyo No. 156 of 9 June 1943, NA, RG 457, SRA 02022–23; Tokyo to Berlin No. 757 of 14 Oct. 1942, SRDJ 27253, and No. 29 of 12 Jan. 1943, SRDJ 30140; Oshima to Tokyo Nos. 549 of 21 May, 858 of 4

Aug., 1142 of 25 Sep. and 1185 of 4 Oct. 1943, SRDJ 37447–52, 41430–31, 43486–91 and 43769–74; Bukarest to Tokyo No. 37 of 20 Mar. 1943, SRDJ 33451; Bürkner to Wagner, 28 Dec. 1950, and Bürkner to Lutz, 14 July 1953, BA/MA, Nachlass Bürkner, N 565/5 and 9; Karl Werner Dankwort, "Infernalische Reise," a post-war memoir in AA, Dankwort Nachlass; Scheidt Papers in Institut für Zeitgeschichte, B 2, f. 267; Ribbentrop to Stahmer No. 847 of 25 May 1943, AA, St.S., "Japan," Bd. 12, fr. 17248–52; U.S. War Department G-2 documents in NA, RG 165, Entry 77, Box 3481 File 6900–Peace. Some British documents in Admiralty to Foreign Office, 16 Aug. 1943, C 6896/155/18, PRO, FO 371/34449; War Cabinet 129^{43} of 20 Sep. 1943, CAB 65/35; Dill to Brooke, 16 and 22 Oct. 1943, Liddell Hart Centre, Alanbrooke Papers, 14/38.

On German knowledge of Italian–Japanese cooperation in urging a separate peace with the Soviet Union as well as greater concessions in occupied areas gathered from Italian documents seized after the German occupation of Rome, see Memorandum of Hencke, "Pl XI 2221gRs," 21 Oct. 1943, AA, St.S., "Italien," Bd. 18, fr. 70822X-25X.

67 Note Dallek, *Roosevelt and Foreign Policy*, pp. 413–17; Memorandum by Colonel Harvey H. Smith, "Possible Developments on the Soviet–German Front," 20 Sep. 1943, NA, RG 165, Entry 77, Box 1419 File 6900 Peace. See the conversation Kawahara–Hencke of 7 Sep. 1943 in which the former argued that Germany and Japan should take advantage of the split among the Allies the way Germany had done in the summer of 1939, when the Soviet Union had faced the choice between making sacrifices for the West and making an agreement with Germany and had settled for the latter (*ADAP*, E, 6, No. 288). Earlier the Japanese had speculated that the Russians might simply stop when they reached their old border and let their allies carry the rest of the fight (precisely the possibility which greatly worried the British); see Tokyo to Berlin No. 98 of 13 Feb. 1943, NA, RG 457, SRDJ 31415–16.

68 See Goebbels' diary for 8 May, 10 Sept. and 23 Sep. 1943 (currently available in the Lochner edition but soon to be published by Fröhlich in the complete German edition); Oshima to Tokyo No. 858 of 4 Aug. 1943, NA, RG 457, SRDJ 41430–37. On Nov. 17, 1943, Hitler told Rosenberg to keep his most effective administrators of the evacuated territories in the East in reserve for a possible redeployment (Memorandum by Albrecht of Bormann's staff, BA, R 43 II/684, f. 4).

69 OSS, "Memorandum for the Planning Group," 29 July 1943, FDRL, Map Room Box 78, File MR 210(3), National Committee for Free Germany; John C. Wiley to Roosevelt, 11 Aug. 1943, FDRL, PSF Box 167, OSS Donovan, 1941, 1943; Sato (Kuibyshev) to Tokyo No. 906 of 12 Aug. 1943, NA, RG 457, SRDJ 42041–42; Tokyo Circular No. 74 of 12 Aug. 1943, NA, RG 457, SRA 02707–8; Clark Kerr to London No. 53 of 22 Oct. 1943, PRO, PREM 3/11/10; Fleischhauer, *Sonderfrieden*, p. 172; Bodo Scheurig, *Freies Deutschland: Das Nationalkomitee und der Bund deutscher Offiziere in der Sowjetunion 1943–1945* (Cologne: Kiepenhauer & Witsch, 1984); James Donald Carnes, *General zwischen Hitler und Stalin: Das Schicksal des Walter v. Seydlitz*, trans. Friedrich Forstmeier (Düsseldorf: Droste, 1980). Kai P. Schoenhals, *The Free Germany Movement: A Case of Patriotism or Treason?* (New York: Greenwood Press, 1989), is interesting but marred by a complete lack of appreciation of the situation in Soviet prisoner of war camps and in post-war Soviet-occupied Germany.

70 Maurice Matloff, *Strategic Planning for Coalition Warfare, 1943–44*, (Washington: GPO, 1959), chaps. 5, 6, 8; Stoler, *Politics of the Second Front*, chaps. 6–7. Stimson's memoranda are in FDRL, Map Room, Box 164, Naval Aide's File. Before the conference, Churchill had sent Roosevelt the British diplomatic report showing that the Soviets were almost certainly responsible for Katyn. The text is published in Kimball (ed.), *Churchill and Roosevelt*, 2: 389–99; Roosevelt initialled and dated the covering letter, an unusual action on his part.

71 Hamilton (*Monty*, 2: 71–73, 253, 422ff) presents the evidence on this but without ever drawing any conclusion from it.

72 See Dallek, *Roosevelt and Foreign Policy*, pp. 413–17.

73 A fine summary in Matloff, *Strategic Planning 1943–44*, pp. 168–73. Criticism of Morgan and his plans overlooks the key point: if you never began work on a plan, you were never likely to get an invasion started. For an account which stresses the key role of COSSAC in really getting Overlord moving forward, see Kent Roberts Greenfield, *American Strategy in World War II: A Reconsideration* (Baltimore: Johns Hopkins Univ. Press, 1963), p. 42.

74 Stoler, *Politics of the Second Front*, chap. 8.

75 On the British disaster and German victory in the Aegean in 1943, see Matloff, *Strategic Planning 1943–44*, pp. 253–59; Stoler, pp. 124–28, 131; Lamb, *Churchill as War Leader*, chap. 18. On this occasion, Brooke, partly out of concern about the likely American reaction, tried hard but unsuccessfully to restrain Churchill. The most recent detailed account, Jeffrey Holland, *The Aegean Mission: Allied Operations in the Dodecanese* (New York: Greenwood Press, 1988), is very critical of Churchill's role.

76 Matloff, *Strategic Planning 1943–44*, pp. 225–27.

77 Danchev, *Very Special Relationship*, pp. 108–10, cites the relevant evidence (much of which is in PRO, PREM 3/53/3). The objection appears to have been based on the belief, possibly erroneous, that Douglas was anti-American. In any case, the endless prolongation of the argument by Churchill was surely unwise; Dill helped straighten it out.

78 Brooke, who had wanted Douglas, "still considered that he [Mountbatten] lacked balance for such a job" (Diary, 15 Aug. 1943, Liddell Hart Centre, Alanbrooke Papers). Montgomery, on the other hand, thought the appointment a good one (Montgomery to Brooke, 3 Sep. 1943, ibid., folder 14/24).

79 On the Lumsden appointment, see Matloff, *Strategic Planning 1943–44*, p. 238. Lumsden's report on his first meeting with MacArthur together with a letter to Brooke of 22 Nov. 1943 is in PRO, WO 216/96. He was killed when a kamikaze struck the battleship *New Mexico* on 6 Jan. 1945. MacArthur had become good friends with Lumsden (see James, *The Years of MacArthur*, p. 619); the latter was replaced by General St. Clair Gairdner who also developed an excellent relationship with MacArthur. Simultaneously with the Lumsden appointment, General Carton de Wiart was appointed to represent Churchill with Chiang Kai-shek (an interesting parallel!); see his memoirs, *Happy Odyssey* (London: Cape, 1950), chaps. 18–19.

80 Hastings, *Bomber Command*, pp. 241–46; Saward, *"Bomber" Harris*, pp. 208–11; Murray, *Luftwaffe*, pp. 162–64; Gordon Musgrove, *Operation Gomorrah: The Hamburg Firestorm Raids* (New York: Jane's, 1981); Martin Middlebrook, *The Battle of Hamburg: Allied Bomber Forces against a German City in 1943* (New York: Scribner's, 1981); Norman Longmate, *The Bombers: The RAF against Germany, 1939–1945* (London: Hutchinson, 1983), chap. 19; Hans Brunswig, *Feuersturm über Hamburg* (Stuttgart: Motorbuch Verlag, 1978).

81 Summary in Murray, *Luftwaffe*, p. 199. Silly in its political and historical portions but useful for its documents, Werner Dettman, *Die Zerstörung Kassels im Oktober 1943: Eine Dokumentation* (Kassel: Hesse, 1983).

82 For the argument that the attacks on Berlin were a mistake and a failure, see Hastings, *Bomber Command*, pp. 306ff; Murray, *Luftwaffe*, pp. 199–206; Longmate, chap. 20 (now reinforced by Hinsley, *British Intelligence*, 3/1: 301–3). For a carefully reasoned defense of the attacks, see Saward, *"Bomber" Harris*, pp. 219–25. See also the "Streng vertraulicher Informationsbericht über Berlin, Die Lage nach den drei Grossangriffen," 3 Dec. 1943, BA, ZSg. 115/7; Gordon Musgrove, *Pathfinder Force: A History of 8 Group* (London: Macdonald and Jane's, 1976). For a German account, very dubious in parts, see Werner Girbig, *Im Anflug auf die Reichshauptstadt* (Stuttgart: Motorbuch Verlag, 1970), pp. 59–141.

83 See Boog, *Luftwaffenführung*, p. 260; Murray, *Luftwaffe*, pp. 174–77.

84 Collier, *Defence*, p. 339; Hinsley, 3/1: 375; Murray, *Luftwaffe*, p. 173; Saward, pp. 211–12.

85 Murray, *Luftwaffe*, pp. 176–77, 214. With less experienced pilots and fewer training flight hours, the accident rate also rose. From 1941 through 1944 between 40 and 45 percent of German air force total losses were due to *non*-combat causes.

86 Ibid., pp. 178–82, 215–18.

87 On Schweinfurt, see Thomas M. Coffey, *Decision over Schweinfurt: The U.S. 8th Air Force Battle for Daylight Bombing* (New York: McKay, 1977); Friedhelm Golücke, *Schweinfurt und der strategische Luftkrieg 1943: der Angriff der U.S. Air Force vom 14. Oktober 1943 gegen die Schweinfurter Kugellagerindustrie* (Paderborn: Schöningh, 1988); Martin Middlebrook, *The Schweinfurt–Regensburg Mission* (New York: Scribner, 1983). See also Hinsley, *British Intelligence*, 3/1: 293–96, 308–16; Murray, *Luftwaffe*, pp. 164–68.

88 Boog, *Luftwaffenführung*, p. 145.

89 On Nürnberg, see Murray, *Luftwaffe*, pp. 206–9; Hastings, *Bomber Command*, pp. 318–19; Hinsley, 3/1: Appendix 21; Martin Middlebrook, *The Nürnberg Raid, 30–31 March 1944* (London: A. Lane, 1980); Geoff Taylor, *The Nürnberg Massacre* (Richmond, Victoria: Hutchinson of Australia, 1979).

90 On Ploesti, see Murray, *Luftwaffe*, p. 169; Leon Wolff, *Low Level Mission* (New York: Arno Press, 1972 [1957]). There is a very useful chart of U.S. 8th Air Force heavy bomber crews and planes and losses in Murray, p. 170; his analysis of British bomber losses is in ibid., pp. 210–11.

91 The text of the final approved plan for the defeat of the Axis of Aug. 24, 1943, is in Morton, *Strategy*, pp. 650–53.

92 The British files on the issue of what to pass on to Moscow about the Overlord plans, PRO, WO 106/4161–62, include much discussion of the Soviet refusal to reciprocate with information about their own military plans. The record for the fall of 1943 also reflects the remaining tentativeness in the British commitment to Overlord.

93 The best record at present is Keith Sainsbury, *The Turning Point: Roosevelt, Stalin, Churchill and Chiang Kai-shek, 1943, The Moscow, Cairo and Teheran Conferences* (Oxford: Oxford Univ. Press, 1985), chaps. 1–4. My account does not always follow Sainsbury's interpretation. See also Stoler, *Politics of the Second Front*, pp. 128–32. The question of Austria is discussed in the work of Robert H. Kayserlingk, *Austria in World War II: An Anglo-American Dilemma* (Kingston and Montreal: McGill–Queen's Univ. Press, 1988).

94 Note Lisbon to Tokyo No. 568 of 24 Oct. 1943, NA, RG 457, SRA 08127–28.

95 Stoler, *Politics of the Second Front*, pp. 130–32; Matloff, *Strategic Planning 1943–44*, p. 302; Sainsbury, pp. 63, 96. The key document is Churchill to Eden, 20 Oct. 1943, T 1677/3, PRO, CAB 120/412. This action of Churchill must be seen in connection with his order of the preceding day for a secret study of operations in the Mediterranean if the British commitments to the U.S. on Overlord could be modified (Hinsley, *British Intelligence*, 3/1: 15).

96 On Finland at the Moscow Conference, see Bernd Martin, "Deutsch-sowjetische Sondierungen über einen separaten Friedensschluss im Zweiten Weltkrieg," in Inge Auerbach et al. (eds.), *Felder und Vorfelder russischer Geschichte* (Freiburg: Rombach, 1985), pp. 310–13.

97 Sainsbury, *Turning Point*, pp. 33, 66.

98 Stoler, p. 134, speculates that perhaps the great Red Army successes that fall may have led Stalin to think that a push in the Mediterranean at that time might bring on a German collapse in 1943.

99 See Eden's memorandum, WP(43) 438, "Western Frontier of the U.S.S.R.," 5 Oct. 1943, PRO, CAB 66/41.

100 Morton, *Strategy*, pp. 528–29; U.S.S.R. Ministry of Foreign Affairs, *Correspondence between the Chairman of the Council of Ministers of the U.S.S.R. and the Presidents of the U.S.A. and*

the Prime Ministers of Great Britain during the Great Patriotic War, 2 vols. (Moscow: Foreign Languages Publishing House, 1957), 2: Nos. 64ff.

101 This view, and the steps taken to implement it, are described in the title of Divine's very fine book: *Second Chance: The Triumph of Internationalism in America During World War II.* See pp. 149–55 for Hull's role in connection with this issue at the Moscow Conference and the unprecedented invitation to him to report to the U.S. Senate on his return.

102 Sainsbury, *Turning Point*, p. 136; cf. ibid., pp. 125–26. In a personal minute of 6 Nov. 1943 Churchill had raised the question whether it would be possible to increase the number of British divisions for Overlord so that the British could carry greater weight in the discussion "and might well enable us to secure any necessary retardation of 'D' Day" (PRO, WO 259/77).

103 See WM(43) War Cabinet 147th Conclusions, Confidential Annex, 27 Oct. 1943, and Churchill's tele. No. 142 to Eden [in Moscow] of 26 Oct. 1943, PRO, CAB 65/40.

104 Matloff, *Strategic Planning 1943–44*, p. 268. The 1st Infantry Division was officially assigned to the ETO on Nov. 1, and to 1st Army's VII Corps on Nov. 6; it actually arrived in England on Nov 8. See Society of the First Division [U.S.Army], *Danger Forward: The Story of the First Division in World War II* (Washington, 1947; reprint Nashville: Battery Press, 1980), pp. 419, 421.

105 Brooke's diary entry for 1 Nov. 1943 (Liddell Hart Centre, Alanbrooke Papers) is more vehement than that in Bryant, *Triumph in the West*, pp. 2: 37–38.

> We are to discuss plans for another Combined Chiefs of Staff meeting, and the stink of the last one is not yet out of my nostrils! My God! how I hate those meetings and how weary I am of them! I now unfortunately know the limitations of Marshall's brain and the impossibility of ever making him realize any strategical situation or its requirements.
>
> In strategy I doubt if he can ever even see the end of his nose.
>
> When I look at the Mediterranean I realize only too well how far I have failed in my task during the last 2 years! If only I had had sufficient force of character to swing those American Chiefs of Staff and make them see daylight, how different the war might be.
>
> We should have been in a position to force the Dardanelles by the capture of Crete and Rhodes, we should have the whole Balkans ablaze by now, and the war might have been finished in 1943!!
>
> Instead, to satisfy American short sightedness we have been led into agreeing to the withdrawal of forces from the Mediterranean for a nebulous 2nd front, and have emasculated our offensive strategy!! It is heartbreaking.

In his post-war comments, Brooke connects this outburst with a bad cold, not having recovered from the strain of the Quebec Conference, and being not far from having a nervous breakdown. That may all be true, but I would be inclined to note the coincidence in timing with the American transfer of troops and the use of the term "nebulous" for Overlord, then scheduled for a date six months later.

106 Roosevelt's map is reproduced in Matloff, *Strategic Planning 1943–44*, facing p. 341; see also Earl F. Ziemke, *The U.S. Army in the Occupation of Germany 1944–1946* (Washington: GPO, 1975), pp. 120–21.

107 Roosevelt's letter to Mountbatten of 8 Nov. 1943 (*FDR Letters*, 2: 1468) is especially important as it gives a good picture of Roosevelt's views on China and Southeast Asia as he explained them to a person he thought of as a friend and whom he was happy to see in the SEAC position.

108 Dallek, *Roosevelt and Foreign Policy*, pp. 426–29.

109 On the first Cairo Conference, see Sainsbury, *Turning Point*, chap. 7; Stoler, *Politics of the Second Front*, pp. 135–43; Matloff, *Strategic Planning 1943–44*, pp. 334–56.

110 Recent accounts of the Teheran meeting in Sainsbury, chap. 8; Stoler, chap. 10; Keith Eubank, *Summit at Teheran* (New York: Morrow, 1985). On this, as on so much else, there is unfortunately little new in Eden's authorized biography, Robert Rhodes James, *Anthony Eden* (London: Weidenfeld & Nicolson, 1986), pp. 279–80.

111 By Dec. 9, 1943, the Germans and Japanese knew that Turkey had refused to enter the war and that the Turks believed Stalin had promised Roosevelt to enter the Pacific War after the end of the European War (Kurihara [Ankara] to Tokyo No. 453 of 9 Dec. 1943, NA, RG 457, SRDJ 46871–72).

112 Martin, "Deutsch-sowjetische Sondierungen," pp. 314–18; Berry, *American Foreign Policy*, pp. 360–63.

113 Note Eden's report to the British Cabinet on 13 Dec. 1943, PRO, CAB 65/36, 40.

114 Sainsbury, *Turning Point*, chap. 9; Matloff, *Strategic Planning 1943–44*, pp. 369–87. See also Hinsley, *British Intelligence*, 3/1: 16–17, for the original British ideas for Mediterranean operations.

115 Note Seekriegsleitung, "Niederschrift über die Besprechung mit V.Adm. Nomura beim Chef des Stabes der Seekriegsleitung am 18.2.1943," BA/MA, RM 7/254, f. 48–53; KTB Skl A 42, 21 Feb. 1943, RM 7/45, f. 359–60.

116 Costello, *Pacific War*, pp. 390–91; Kenney, *General Kenney Reports*, chap. 7; Drea, *MacArthur's Ultra*, pp. 68–72.

117 Note Japanese military attaché Rome to Tokyo No. 095 of 3 Apr. 1943, NA, RG 457, SRA 01107–8; German naval attaché Tokyo to Berlin No. 14, Chefsache, of 14 May 1943, BA/MA, RM 7/254, f. 124–26. Although deception attempts were made to induce the Japanese to believe that an attack might come from the north (see Chapter 10), no such projects were ever developed beyond initial planning; for a recent look at this, see Galen R. Perras, "Eyes on the Northern Route to Japan: Plans for Canadian Participation in an Invasion of the Kurile Islands- A Study in Coalition Warfare and Civil-Military Relationships," *War & Society* 8, No. 1 (May 1990), 100–17.

118 Morton, *Strategy*, pp. 413–15. Important additional details in *Ugaki Diary*, 18–25 Apr. 1943, 18 Apr. 1944, pp. 330–31, 350–60 (Ugaki was Yamamoto's Chief of Staff and survived the shooting down of the plane in which he was being ferried). The latest details from the American side in Richard H. Kohn, "A Note on the Yamamoto Aerial Victory Credit Controversy," *Air Power History* 39, No. 2 (Spring 1992), 42–52. It is indicative of the peculiarities in German–Japanese cooperation that the Germans had to ask for details of Yamamoto's career after his death in order to award the famous admiral a posthumous medal! Berlin, OKM 1334g to German naval attaché Tokyo of 2 June 1943, NA, RG 457, SRGL 670.

119 16,000 out of 46,000 prisoners of war and 60,000 out of 150,000 Asian forced laborers died (Butow, *Tojo*, p. 511). A good recent account in Peter N. Davies, *The Man Behind the Bridge: Colonel Toosey and the River Kwai* (London: Athlone, 1991).

120 Tokyo (Shigemitsu) to Kuibyshev (Sato) Nos. 420,446, 421 (sic) of 16, 22, 25 May 1943, NA, RG 457, SRDJ 36162, 36555, 37167–68; Kuibyshev to Tokyo Nos. 556, 558, 587, 593 of 17, 21, 21, 23 May 1943, SRDJ 36685–87, 36987–70 (sic), 36971, 36961–62; Tokyo Circular No. 418 of 24 May 1943, SRDJ 37368. In April 1944 the Japanese were alarmed to hear of an American flyer who had been in the Doolittle raid of April 1942, had landed near Vladivostok in the Soviet Far East, and was now flying from England on air raids against Germany. See Shigemitsu to Sato No. 418 of 24 Apr. 1944, and Sato to Shigemitsu No. 846 of 26 Apr. 1944, SRDJ 56581, 56665 (note that both of these documents were decyphered immediately).

121 Tokyo Circular No. 535 of 26 June 1943, NA, RG 457, SRDJ 39661–62; Japanese military attaché Rome to Tokyo No. 214 of 13 July 1943, SRA 03191–95; Madrid to Tokyo No. 775 of 26 July 1943, SRDJ 41026; Japanese military attaché Helsinki to Tokyo

No. 280 of 28 July 1943, SRA 03127–29; Berlin to Tokyo No. 897 of 4 Aug. 1943, SRDJ 41346–68; *Kido Diary*, 26 July 1943, p. 363.

122 Tokyo to Kuibyshev No. 460 of 26 May and No. 547 of 28 Jun 1943, NA, RG 457, SRDJ 37387–88, 39597; Tokyo to Moscow No. 21 of 1 July 1943, SRDJ 40067.

123 Moscow to Tokyo No. 46 of 4 July 1943, NA, RG 457, SRDJ 40170–73; Tokyo to Moscow No. 704 of 12 Aug. 1943, SRDJ 42226.

124 Moscow to Tokyo No. 961 of 24 Aug. 1943, NA, RG 457, SRDJ 42339, 47656.

125 Molotov and Sato reassured each other after the Moscow Conference; see Sato's No. 1375 of 11 Nov. 1943, NA, RG 457, SRDJ 46829–32.

126 The account Lensen, *The Strange Neutrality* chap. 4, can now be supplemented by the intercepted Japanese diplomatic documents of Jan.-Mar. 1944, in NA, RG 457, SRDJ 49897–98, 49566–90, 49616–17, 49726–38, 50128–35, 49809–13, 50693–94, 50229–30, 52070–71, 51808, 51815–16, 51851–52, 52074–77, 54708–9, 56402–3. The text of the concession liquidation treaty is in Lensen, pp. 279–81; an American analysis is in the Weekly G-2 Estimate of 3 Apr. 1944, NA, RG 165, Entry 77, Box 2364, File 6000-Japan, Wkly G-2 Estimates – 1944.

127 Lensen, chap. 5; text of the fisheries agreement in ibid., pp. 281–87. See also Kolb's "Aufzeichnung über das Verhältnis Japan-Sowjetunion," 9 Sep. 1943, AA, St.S., "Japan," Bd. 13, fr. E 541912–17; Sato to Tokyo Nos. 689 and 696 of 1 Apr. 1944, NA, RG 457, SRDJ 55031–34, 56975–76.

128 *ADAP*, E, 6, Nos. 15, 36, 41, 68, 364; 7, Nos. 44, 65, 104; Tokyo to Berlin Nos. 841 and 842 of 21 Oct. 1943, NA, RG 457, SRDJ 44625–26, 44623–24. The Japanese were always alert for any signs of a German separate peace with the West, see Tokyo Circular No. 752 of 10 Nov. 1943, SRA 05836. German propaganda continued to praise all Japanese victories, including the imaginary ones, see, e.g., "Tagesparolen des Reichspressechefs," 6 Nov. 1943, BA, Nadler, ZSg. 115/9.

129 Edward J. Drea, "Missing Intentions: Japanese Intelligence and the Soviet Invasion of Manchuria, 1945," *Military Affairs* 48, No. 2 (1984), p. 67.

130 Note Brooke's Diary for 30 Sep. 1942, Liddell Hart Centre, Alanbrooke Papers.

131 The U.S. Joint Chiefs of Staff memorandum of 22 Jan. 1943 on "Conduct of the War in the Pacific Theater in 1943" is printed in Morton, *Strategy*, pp. 627–29.

132 See Roosevelt to King and Marshall, 24 Aug. 1942, FDRL, PSF Box 5, King.

133 See Stanley L. Falk, "General Kenney, the Indirect Approach, and the B-29s," *Aerospace Historian* 28, No. 3 (Sep. 1981), pp. 147–55. The history of the B-29 is summarized in Craven and Cate, *Army Air Force*, 6: 208–10. See also Steve Birdsall, *Saga of the Superfortress: The Dramatic Story of the B-29 and the Twentieth Air Force* (Garden City, N.Y.: Doubleday, 1980); Curtis LeMay and Bill Yenne, *Superfortress: The Story of the B-29 and American Air Power in World War II* (New York: McGraw-Hill, 1988).

134 A good account of the Pacific strategy conference in Morton, *Strategy*, pp. 394–97.

135 Ibid., pp. 447ff. The Joint Chiefs of Staff and Combined Chiefs of Staff plan for the defeat of Japan of May 19, 1943, is in ibid., pp. 644–48.

136 Ibid., p. 136.

137 Boyle, *China and Japan*, pp. 310–11.

138 A summary in Ch'i, *Nationalist China*, pp. 63–67.

139 Ibid., pp. 98–106.

140 Ibid., pp. 72–74.

141 Note Stimson to Roosevelt, 3 May 1943, FDRL, PSF Box 14, CF War Jan 43–Aug 43.

142 Field Marshal Brooke belonged to the circle of Stilwell's critics; see his diary for 14 May 1943, Liddell Hart Centre, Alanbrooke Papers. A good general account in Tuchman, *Stilwell*.

143 See Mountbatten to Brooke, "SC 4/198C," 3 Feb. 1944, Liddell Hart Centre,

Alanbrooke Papers, 14/49; Dill's file of correspondence "30/15A" on a great ruckus of Feb.-Mar. 1944 in PRO, CAB 106/329.

144 See Chennault to Roosevelt, 26 Jan. 1944, FDRL, PSF Box 1, Army Air Force. On Chennault's career and views, see Martha Byrd, *Chennault: Giving Wings to the Tiger* (Tuscaloosa, Ala.: Univ. of Alabama Press, 1987).

145 Ch'i, *Nationalist China*, pp. 80–81; Tuchman, pp. 466ff.

146 The best account remains William H. Tunner, *Over the Hump* (New York: Duell, Sloan & Pearce, 1964; Washington: GPO, 1985). See also Bliss K. Thorne, *The Hump: The Great Military Airlift of World War II* (Philadelphia: Lippincott, 1965).

147 Note the memorandum by the chief of the Far Eastern Division of War Department G-2 of 13 Feb. 1944, "Japanese Reaction to V[ery]L[ong]R[ange] Operations from Chengtu Area," in NA, RG 165, Entry 77, Box 2366, F.file 6010–20–Japan.

148 Ch'i, *Nationalist China*, pp. 74–77.

149 Ibid., p. 80.

150 Ibid., pp. 238–39; Boyle, *China and Japan*, chaps. 14–16.

151 Ch'i, pp. 106–11.

152 Letter in Liddell Hart Centre, Alanbrooke Papers, 14/49.

153 An excellent source on these squabbles is Mountbatten's correspondence in PRO, CAB 127/24, 25. In commenting on the feuds between Mountbatten and Admiral Somerville, the commander of the British fleet in the area, Marder (*Old Friends, New Enemies*, 2: 321) wrote: "Not having the Japanese to fight, the Admirals fought one another."

154 See Lebra, *Japanese-Trained Armies*, pp. 23, 31. An excellent account of the background of this offensive in Allen, chap. 3.

155 Lebra, pp. 28ff; Leonard A. Gordon, *Brothers against the Raj*, pp. 467ff, 495ff. None of those who have written on Bose's Indian national army has investigated whether, while they were trained by the Japanese army, they were permitted to share in the "comfort" provided by the thousands of kidnapped Korean young women held as sex slaves by the Imperial Japanese army at its camps. This might have provided them with some insight into the nature of Japanese, as opposed to British, colonial rule, as well as what might be in store for their sisters and daughters.

156 The complicated transport plane arrangements can be followed in Ehrman, *Grand Strategy*, 5: 408–15. What the author does not point out is that the prior American reluctance and the 1944 American willingness to assist can be understood in terms of justified suspicions earlier that the British were not going to do any serious fighting in the theater anyway, and a swift change in U.S. attitude when it became obvious that the British had changed: they were clearly fighting it out this time around. Mountbatten and Slim had done for the British–Indian 14th Army in 1943–44 what Alexander and Montgomery had done for the British 8th Army in 1942. The Imphal–Kohima battle itself is well described in Allen, *Burma*, chap. 4. See also Raymond Callahan, *Burma, 1942–1945* (London: Davis-Poynter, 1978), chap. 4; Sir Geoffrey C. Evans and Antony Brett-James, *Imphal: A Battle on Lofty Heights* (London: Macmillan, 1964).

157 Brooke Diary, Liddell Hart Centre, Alanbrooke Papers. The entry continues with scathing comments about Mountbatten, General Pownall (his Chief of Staff), and General Giffard, the 11th Army Group commander.

158 Japanese Army General Staff Tokyo to military attaché Berlin No. 949 of 15 July 1944, NA, RG 457, SRA 14260–61.

159 On the Myitkyina campaign and Merrill's Marauders, see the still useful book, Charles Ogburn, Jr., *The Marauders* (New York: Harper, 1956); also Tuchman, *Stilwell*, pp. 564ff.

160 Note Roosevelt to the Prime Minister of New Zealand in *FDR Letters*, 2: 1428.

161 Elmer B. Potter, *Bull Halsey* (Annapolis, Md.: Naval Institute Press, 1985), p. 221.

162 Kreis, *Air Base Defense*, pp. 234–36.

163 The Japanese discussion of strategy is reviewed in Morton, *Strategy*, pp. 543–50, 655–

60; Louis Morton, "Japanese Policy and Strategy in Mid-War," *U.S. Naval Institute Proceedings* 85, No. 2 (Feb. 1959), 52–64. The statistics on aircraft production are from Coox, "The Rise and Fall," p. 81.

164 On the Bougainville campaign, see Costello, *Pacific War*, pp. 422–27; James, *The Years of MacArthur*, pp. 339–41; a full account of the invasion and fighting in Harry A. Gailey, *Bougainville, 1943–1945: The Forgotten Campaign* (Lexington, Ky.: Univ. Press of Kentucky, 1991), chaps. 4–9.

165 See James, pp. 332–35.

166 Ibid., pp. 341–46.

167 Costello, *Pacific War*, pp. 446–47.

168 Morton, *Strategy*, pp. 460–72.

169 An early study, Jeter A. Iseley and Philip A. Crowl, *The U.S. Marines and Amphibious War: Its Theory and its Practice in the Pacific* (Princeton, N.J.: Princeton Univ. Press, 1951) remains the best introduction to the subject in this author's opinion.

170 Morton, *Strategy*, pp. 571, 575.

171 Ibid., pp. 444–47. In the subsequent operation against the Marshall Islands the Americans captured secret Japanese charts which proved enormously helpful.

172 The report of a British naval observer on the carrier *Essex* during "Galvanic" stresses how essential the huge number of fleet and escort carriers (over 20) turned out to be (PRO, WO 106/3402).

173 An excellent account in Iseley and Crowl, *The U.S. Marines*, chap. 6. Captain James R. Stockman, USMC, *The Battle of Tarawa* (Washington: GPO, 1947), remains useful. See also Costello, chap. 25; the "official" account by Henry I. Shaw, Jr. et al. *History of U.S. Marine Corps Operations in World War II*, Vol. 3: Central Pacific Drive (Washington: GPO, 1966), Part 2. Morison, *US Naval Operations*, 7: Part 2, covers the whole operation in detail.

174 The British ambassador to the U.S., Lord Halifax, repeatedly suggested that the island be given to the U.S. as a war memorial, but objections from the United Kingdom, Australia and New Zealand prevented the offer from being made (File AN 355 in PRO, FO 371/44623).

175 Morton, *Strategy*, pp. 590–91.

176 Good accounts in Iseley and Crowl, chap. 7; Costello, pp. 448–52; Shaw et al., *US Marine Corps*, part 3; Morison, *US Naval Operations*, 7: part 3.

177 Butow, *Tojo*, pp. 427–28.

178 Note the report from the German embassy in Tokyo of Mar. 1944 with a clear understanding of the implications for Japan of the loss of the Marshalls (once a German colony) and of the failure of the Japanese to realize the extent to which their earlier victories derived from Germany's having drawn Allied forces into fighting elsewhere. The report recognized Japan's need for good relations with the Soviet Union and shows comprehension of the nature of the American double thrust strategy (Hencke to OKW and others, 31 Mar. 1944, AA, Handakten Etzdorf, "Ferner Osten," fr. 313280–83).

179 Morton, *Strategy*, pp. 517–20.

180 Ibid., pp. 592–601.

181 Ibid., pp. 668–74.

182 Ibid., pp. 602–5; see also Falk, "General Kenney," p. 153.

183 Yasushi Hidagi, "Attack against the U.S. Heartland," *Aerospace Historian* 27, No. 2 (June 1981), 87–93; NA, RG 457, SRMA-6; Douglas, *Creation of a National Air Force*, pp. 425–26; quite detailed, Bert Webber, *Silent Siege: Japanese Attacks against North America in World War II* (Fairfield, Wash.: Ye Galleon Press, 1983).

184 Ohmae, "Strategischen Konzeptionen," pp. 200–1; *Ugaki Diary*, 25 May – 14 June 1944, pp. 376–99.

185 Included among the battleships were three of those "sunk" at Pearl Harbor. By a curious

coincidence, the man who had been in charge of the Pearl Harbor raid, Admiral Nagumo Chuichi, had in the meantime been relegated to the tiny naval command of Saipan (and committed suicide at the end of the Saipan fighting).

186 Harry A. Gailey, *Howlin' Mad Versus the Army: Conflict in Command, Saipan 1944* (Novato, Calif.: Presidio Press, 1986).

187 On the Marianas, see Iseley and Crowl, *The U.S. Marines*, chap. 8; Morison, *US Naval Operations*, 8: part 3; Costello, *Pacific War*, pp. 475–86; Dull, *Imperial Japanese Navy*, pp. 302–11; Shaw et al., *US Marine Corps*, 3: parts 4–6; *Ugaki Diary*, 14 June – 24 June 1944, pp. 398–425. Useful studies of the way in which increasing size went hand-in-hand with decreasing effectiveness in the Japanese naval air force as well as the Japanese army air force are in the "Magic Far Eastern Summary" No. 112 of 10 July 1944 (NA, RG 457, SRS 112). For German navy perceptions, see KTB Skl A 58, 20 June 1944, BA/MA, RM 7/61, f. 610–11. Comment on Japanese concern that the Allies had been able to mount the Saipan operation at the same time as the invasion of Normandy is in ibid., A 59, 9 July 1944, RM 7/62, f. 220–21.

188 On the Biak operation, Robert Ross Smith, *The Approach to the Philippines* (Washington: GPO, 1953), chaps. 12–16, in the U.S. Army official history remains a fine account. Smith estimates American casualties from battle and disease at just under 10,000 (p. 392). See now also Drea, *MacArthur's Ultra*, pp. 135–41.

189 James, *The Years of MacArthur*, chap. 10. When James wrote, the information of MacArthur's enormous gratuity from President Quezon had not become public. One wonders what a leak would have done to his candidacy had he been nominated. Those who speculate on MacArthur's relationship with President Roosevelt have not as yet engaged the implications of Roosevelt's and Interior Secretary Harold L. Ickes's knowledge of this transaction (and the fact that MacArthur, of course, knew that they had been asked for their approval).

190 Butow, *Tojo*, pp. 432–33; Shillony, *Wartime Japan*, pp. 60–64; *Kido Diary*, 13 July 1944ff, pp. 387ff; Marder, *Old Friends, New Enemies*, 2: 388–98.

191 Robert J.C. Butow, *Japan's Decision to Surrender* (Stanford, Calif.: Stanford Univ. Press, 1954), pp. 30–37.

192 Morley, *Fateful Choice*, pp. 140–41.

193 See Butow, *Japan's Decision*, p. 37.

194 Ohmae, "Strategischen Konzeptionen," p. 201; Shillony, *Wartime Japan*, pp. 69–70.

195 Shigemitsu (Tokyo) to Sato (Moscow) No. 352 of 2 Apr. 1944, NA, RG 457, SRDJ 54704–5.

196 See Sato's telegrams No. 747 of 8 Apr., 754 of 10 Apr., and 773–74 of 12 Apr. 1944, NA, RG 457, SRDJ 55688–97, 55622–29, 55630–31.

197 For further details on these negotiations, see the intercepted Japanese telegrams of 5 Apr. – 4 Aug. 1944, in NA, RG 457, SRDJ 56013–14, 59589–90, 61093–103, 62953–54, 63331–36, 63495–503, 64338–39, 66199–203, 66907, and the analysis in SRH-069. On the possibly related trip of Soviet ambassador to Tokyo, to Moscow, see Shigemitsu to Sato No. 699 of 17 June 1944, SRDJ 62144–48; Stoller (Shanghai) to Berlin No. 524 of 22 June 1944, AA, Handakten Ritter, "Japan," Bd. 4–5, fr. 363345–46; Donovan to Roosevelt, 6 July 1944, FDRL, PSF Box 168, OSS Reports Apr. – July 1944.

198 Note the analysis of this Japanese strategy in the Allied Pacific Order of Battle Conference of 3–19 July 1944 in NA, RG 457, SRH-097. The one point missed by those in attendance was that the utilization of the Marianas for the bombing of Japan was something that the Japanese did not fully understand at this stage of the war. There is no evidence that they considered simply giving up on defending the home islands as too vulnerable and fighting on with their army in mainland China in hopes of a compromise peace as suggested in a G-2 appreciation of 13 May 1944 (NA, RG 165, Entry 77, Box 2265, File 6000 Army-General). The possibility of such extended fighting on the mainland and by other garrisons

after a successful Allied campaign had conquered the home islands, however, played an important role in Allied thinking until the final Japanese surrender.

199 A useful summary in Fraser, *Alanbrooke*, pp. 410–21; the relevant papers of Field Marshal Brooke are now available in the Liddell Hart Centre, Alanbrooke Papers, 14/20–23. See also *Old Friends, New Enemies*, Marder, 2: chap. 12, part 1.

200 A major substantive argument against British naval participation had been the different pattern in British and U.S. naval operations in the war. The British had always relied on fixed bases. The American fleet in the Pacific was to a large extent based on a fleet-train, a floating group of tankers, supply ships, hospital ships, etc. In this context, a British contingent might simply reduce the number of American warships that could be maintained.

201 Summary in Morton, *Strategy*, pp. 592–605; details in Grace P. Hayes, *The History of the Joint Chiefs of Staff in World War II: The War against Japan* (Annapolis, Md.: Naval Institute Press, 1982), chaps. 21–25.

202 Hayes, pp. 610–11; James, *The Years of MacArthur*, pp. 526–36; Costello, *Pacific War*, 492–93; M. Hamlin Cannon, *Leyte: The Return to the Philippines* (Washington: GPO, 1954), pp. 5–6. See also the report on the Lumsden–MacArthur meeting of 1 Aug. 1944 in Liddell Hart Centre, Alanbrooke Papers, 19/54.

203 Hayes, p. 623; James, pp. 533, 536–37.

204 James, pp. 486–89.

205 Ibid., pp. 491–92; Costello, *Pacific War*, pp. 493–98. An excellent account in Harry A. Gailey, *Peleliu, 1944* (Annapolis, Md.: Nautical and Aviation Publishing Co., 1983); the fighting man's perspective is impressively presented in Eugene B. Sledge, *With The Old Breed at Peleliu and Okinawa* (New York: Oxford Univ. Press, 1990 [1981]), chaps. 3–6. A good case can be made for the view that the 1st Marine Division was not a large enough force for Peleliu, that the 81st Division should not have been committed to the Angaur operation until Peleliu had been secured, and that the marines were simply too stubbornly proud to ask for army help when they needed it.

206 Glantz, *Soviet Military Deception*, p. 251.

207 On this incident, see Eden's memorandum, WP⁴⁴ 150, "Information from the Soviet Union," PRO, CAB 66/47; Federal Communications Commission, Foreign Broadcast Intelligence Service, "Special Release: 'Pravda' Report on British-German 'Secret' Peace Negotiations, Together with Early Radio Reaction," 18 Jan. 1944, NA, RG 165, Entry 77, Box 1417, File 6600–Germany, Military Operations; Fleischhauer, *Sonderfrienden*, pp. 225–26.

208 PRO, CAB 119/128.

209 N 2996/302/38, quoted in Beaumont, *Comrades in Arms*, p. 179. Sargent was referring to the standard British practice in prior wars.

210 Ibid., pp. 170, 173–75.

211 Lukas, *Eagles East*, Kreis, pp. 204–12; *Air Base Defense*, pp. 192–201; Stockholm to Tokyo No. 326 of 10 June 1944, NA, RG 457, SRDJ 61959–60.

212 Erickson, *Road to Berlin*, p. 205; Ziemke, *Northern Theater*, pp. 273–75; Berry, *American Foreign Policy*, pp. 386–98. For reports of Japanese diplomats in Berlin, Stockholm, and Helsinki, intercepted by the Americans, see military attaché Helsinki to Tokyo Nos. 40 of 16 Feb., 42 of 18 Feb., 58 of 28 Feb., 60 of 1 Mar., 65 of 3 Mar., 76 of 13 Mar. 1944, NA, RG 457, SRA 7582–83, 7015–18, 7335–37, 7759, 7437, 7633–36; military attaché Stockholm to Tokyo Nos. 521 of 19 Feb., 526 of 23 Feb., 562 of 21 Mar. 1944, SRA 7321–27, 7639–42, 7969–71; embassy Berlin to Tokyo Nos. 185 of 28 Feb., 414 of 3 May 1944, SRDJ 51823, 57740–42; Legation Stockholm to Tokyo No. 153 of 10 Mar. 1944, SRDJ 53930; Legation Helsinki to Tokyo No. 46 of 11 Mar. 1944, SRDJ 53930. German documents have been published in *ADAP*, E, 7 and 8.

213 In Eisenhower's case as in others, Brooke had a vehemently negative opinion at the time

which Bryant for the most part suppressed in the published version. Compare, e.g., the entry for 24 Jan. 1944 in Bryant with that in the original diary, Liddell Hart Centre, Alanbrooke Papers.

214 Liddell Hart Centre, Ismay Papers IV/Con/2/4. The Somme and Passchendaele references involve bitter battles of 1916 and 1917 on the Western Front; Nivelle's offensive was a much heralded French operation in 1917 whose failure led to the great mutinies in the French army.

215 See de Guingand, *Operation Victory*, pp. 332–34.

216 A fair account in Martin Blumenson, *Bloody River: The Real Tragedy of the Rapido* (Boston: Houghton Mifflin, 1970).

217 On Anzio, see the comments by Harold Deutsch in Rohwer and Jäckel, *Funkaufklärung*, pp. 313–14; Hinsley, *British Intelligence*, 3/1: 184–87, 190–91, 196–97. A balanced account in William L. Allen, *Anzio: Edge of Disaster* (New York: E.P. Dutton, 1978). An extraordinarily vivid account of the fighting is in William Woodruff, *Vessel of Sadness* (London: Chatto & Windus, 1970).

218 Chadwick, *Britain and the Vatican*, pp. 278–84.

219 Önder, *Türkische Aussenpolitik*, pp. 223–24.

220 See Arthur L. Funk, "Churchill, Eisenhower, and the French Resistance," *Military Affairs* 45, No. 1 (1981), 29–33.

221 Brooke to Wilson tel. 74890 of 6 Mar. 1944, Liddell Hart Centre, Alanbrooke Papers, 14/44. Related documents, including Wilson's answer of 8 Mar., are in the same file.

222 See the extensive documentation for the period May 1944 – July 1945 in PRO, WO 106/3973.

223 Roger Beaumont, "Bomber Offensive," p. 15.

224 Murray, *Luftwaffe*, pp. 216–22.

225 On the P-51, see Robert W. Gruenhagen, *Mustang: The Story of the P-51 Fighter*, revd. ed. (New York: Arco, 1980), esp. pp. 87ff; Jeffrey Ethell, *Mustang: A Documentary History of the P-51* (London: Jane's, 1981).

226 See Boog, *Luftwaffenführung*, pp. 28–31.

227 Hinsley, *British Intelligence*, 3/1: 317–22.

228 An account which focuses on the German and American aspects, largely omitting the British, in Murray, *Luftwaffe*, pp. 223–32.

229 Saward, *"Bomber" Harris*, pp. 246–48.

230 Ibid., pp. 248–52. A detailed discussion of the decision in Walt W. Rostow, *Pre-Invasion Bombing Strategy: General Eisenhower's Decision of March 25, 1944* (Austin: Univ. Press of Texas, 1981). On the debate in the British Cabinet, see WM(44) War Cabinet 61(44) Conclusions, Confidential Annex, 2 May 1944, PRO, CAB 65/46.

231 Note Hinsley, 3/1: 41–42.

232 Williamson Murray, "Ultra: Some Thoughts on its Impact on the Second World War," *Air University Review* 35, No. 5 (1984), 59.

233 Arnold to Roosevelt, 27 Jan. 1944, and enclosure, FDRL, Map Room Box 164, Naval Aide's File, Axis War Potential.

234 Boog, *Luftwaffenführung*, pp. 130–33.

235 "Punkte aus der Besprechung beim Führer am 5. März 1944" (Milch, Bodenschatz, Below), Imperial War Museum, Milch Papers, Vol. 64: 6506.

236 Murray, *Luftwaffe*, pp. 240–41.

237 Ibid., pp. 232–33; Boog, *Luftwaffenführung*, pp. 200–2.

238 On this operation, see Murray, *Luftwaffe*, pp. 237–38; Hinsley, *British Intelligence*, 3/1: chap. 38; Gerald Kirwin, "Waiting for Retaliation – A Study of Nazi Propaganda Behaviour and Civilian Morale," *JCH* 16 (1981), 575–77; War Department G-2, "The

G.A.F. and the London Raids," 9 Mar. 1944, NA, RG 165, Entry 77, Box 1482, File 9910–General Western Front. On the German air force conferences under Göring's leadership on May 23–25, 1944, see Imperial War Museum, Milch Papers, Vol. 64: 6826–96; Boog, *Luftwaffenführung*, p. 145.

239 Japanese military representative in German-controlled Italy to the Vice Chief of the Imperial General Staff, No. 33 of 18 Dec. 1943, NA, RG 457, SRA 06577–81.

240 Oshima's Berlin to Tokyo Nos. 81–82 of 24 Jan. 1944, NA, RG 457, SRDJ 49910–20, 49886–93 (German record in *ADAP*, E, 7, No. 179); F.C. Jones, *Japan's New Order*, p. 419; *Rommel Papers*, pp. 465–66; Oshima's report on his meeting with Dönitz, No. 440 of 10 May 1944, NA, RG 457, SRDJ 58167–69; Weichs–Papen meeting of 9 May 1944, BA/MA, Nachlass Weichs, N 19/3, F 151.

241 For Japanese urgings, see the preceding note. The Japanese ambassador in Moscow, it should be noted, anticipated that the Allies would succeed in getting ashore and saw no signs of a German–Soviet peace; see Sato's No. 995 of 20 May 1944, NA, RG 457, SRDJ 59053–55. On Laval, see the reports of Mitani, the Japanese representative in Vichy, Nos. 45 of 16 Feb., 207 of 19 June, and 208 of 19 June 1944, SRDJ 51113–16, 62400, 62237. That such supposedly anti-Communist collaborators with the Germans as the Hungarian Szálasi and the French Laval favored peace with the Soviet Union so that Germany could concentrate her strength on fighting the Western Powers is an aspect of World War II which awaits its historian. Goebbels, who had urged peace with the Soviet Union on Hitler in 1943, did so again in the spring of 1944 (Rudolf Semmler, *Goebbels – The Man Next to Hitler* [London: Westhouse, 1947], pp. 119–22, 127–28).

242 The text and commentary on it in Hans-Heinrich Wilhelm (ed.), "Hitlers Ansprache vor Generalen und Offiziere am 26. Mai 1944," *MGM* 20 (1976), 123–70, esp. pp. 134–35.

243 Backe to Rosenberg M 2130/44 of 8 May 1944, Library of Congress, Manuscript Division, Container 834. On Nov. 17, 1943, Rosenberg had been told by Hitler not to let the best of the occupation administration officials be drafted so that they would be available for redeployment (Albrecht memorandum, BA, R 43 II/684, f. 4).

244 See Heinz Magenheimer, "Das Gesetz des Schwergewichts: Zur strategischen Lage Deutschlands im Frühjahr 1944," *Wehrwissenschaftliche Rundschau* 31 (1981), 18–25.

245 Earlier Hitler had been sure that the invasion would come in Normandy, ibid., p. 24. On Hitler's views in May, see the German record in *ADAP*, E, 7, No. 41; the Japanese record is in Oshima's No. 511 of 28 May, 1944, NA, RG 457, SRDJ 59971–79.

12: THE ASSAULT ON GERMANY FROM ALL SIDES

1 Text in Hubatsch, *Hitler's Weisungen*, pp. 233–38.

2 "Im Osten lässt die Grösse des Raumes äussersten Falles einen Bodenverlust auch grösseren Ausmasses zu, ohne den deutschen Lebensnerv tödlich zu treffen."

3 For an interesting report on the Eastern Front by a group of American officers, led by the commanding general of the Persian Gulf Command, who were permitted a tour on 3–16 Jan. 1944, see U.S. military attaché Moscow, "Trip to Kiev Front, 3–16 Jan. 1944," 24 Jan. 1944, NA, RG 165, Entry 77, Box 1431, File 6910–Germany (Russia) Jan. 1944. For a joint British–U.S. estimate of Red Army casualties as of February 1944, see Annex I to the U.S. Army ETO Intelligence Committee Minutes of 14 Mar. 1944, in ibid., Box 1417, File 6900–Germany-General.

4 Ziemke, *Stalingrad to Berlin*, pp. 218–38; Erickson, *Road to Berlin*, pp. 163–67, 176–79; Trevor N. Dupuy, *Great Battles on the Eastern Front: The Soviet–German War, 1941–1945* (Indianapolis: Bobbs-Merrill, 1982), pp. 129–38; Glantz, *Soviet Military Deception*, pp. 306–22. It was at this battle that the National Committee for a Free Germany made its major – but unsuccessful – effort to induce a surrender (see refs. in Friedrich Freiherr

Hiller von Gaertringen [ed.], *Die Hassell-Tagebücher: Ulrich von Hassell, Aufzeichnungen vom Andern Deutschland* [Berlin: Siedler, 1988], p. 608 n 13). The stabilization of the northern sector of German Army Group South's front after the Soviet liberation of Rovno is covered by Ziemke, pp. 244–47; Glantz, pp. 322–26.

5 Erickson, *Road to Berlin*, pp. 165–67, 179–80.

6 Notes of General Hansen in Institut für Zeitgeschichte, Zg. 1130, f. 18ff; Ziemke, *Stalingrad to Berlin*, p. 244.

7 Hillgruber, *Hitler, König Carol*, pp. 180–81; *ADAP*, E, 7, Nos. 236–38.

8 Ziemke, *Stalingrad to Berlin*, pp. 291–95; Erickson, *Road to Berlin*, pp. 193–95; Gosztony, *Hitlers Fremde Heere*, pp. 282–84; Dupuy, *Great Battles*, pp. 139–49. The role of the German navy is covered by Salewski, *Seekriegsleitung*, 2: 383–400, in a manner very critical of Dönitz's encouraging the policy of holding on to the peninsula.

9 Ziemke, *Stalingrad to Berlin*, pp. 272–85; Erickson, *Road to Berlin*, pp. 180–87; Glantz, *Soviet Military Deception*, pp. 326–48.

10 See the report on the Hitler–Kvaternik conversation of 22 July 1941 in *ADAP*, D, 13, Appendix III.

11 On this episode, see Ziemke, *Stalingrad to Berlin*, pp. 287–88; Carlile A. Macartney, *October Fifteenth: A History of Modern Hungary 1929–1945*, 2 vols. (Edinburgh: Edinburgh Univ. Press, 1956), 2: 221ff; Mario D. Fenyo, *Hitler, Horthy, and Hungary: German–Hungarian Relations, 1941–1944* (New Haven, Conn.: Yale Univ. Press, 1972), chap. 9; György Ranki, *Unternehmen Margarethe: Die deutsche Besetzung Ungarns*, trans. by E. and M. Pogány (Vienna: Böhlau, 1984); Gustav Hennyey, *Ungarns Schicksal zwischen Ost und West: Lebenserinnerungen* (Mainz: Hase & Koehler, 1976), pp. 55–65, 161, 166–67; *KTB OKW*, 1944/45, 1: 179–246; extensive material in BA/MA, Nachlass Weichs, N19/3; Jodl Diary transcript, 28 Mar. 1944, Imperial War Museum; numerous documents in AA, St.S., "Ungarn," Bd. 11. The original German candidate for heading the new government had been Béla Imrédy. It should be noted that initially the Germans planned a similar operation code-named "Margarethe II" for Romania.

12 The first directive on this general concept, Führer Order No. 11 of 8 Mar. 1944, is in Hubatsch, *Hitlers Weisungen*, pp. 243–49; a brief discussion in Ziemke, *Stalingrad to Berlin*, p. 277. The discussion of Hitler's concept of the *Wellenbrecher*, the "wave breaker," in *KTB OKW* 1944/45, 1: 53–54, confuses the holding of isolated points with the holding of ports in the West which had entirely different purposes and is discussed in this and the following chapters.

13 Ziemke, *Stalingrad to Berlin*, p. 286.

14 The inter-relation between the defeats at the front and the name and personnel changes is shown clearly in the entry for 31 Mar. 1944 in Dermot Bradley and Richard Schulze-Kossens (eds.), *Tätigkeitsbericht des Chefs des Heerespersonalamtes General der Infanterie Rudolf Schmundt, 1.10.1942 – 29.10.1944* (Osnabrück: Biblio, 1984).

15 On Soviet anticipation of a possible German pull-back, see Erickson, *Road to Berlin*, p. 169.

16 Ibid., pp. 167–76; Ziemke, *Stalingrad to Berlin*, pp. 248–66; Glantz, *Soviet Military Deception*, pp. 297–306, 308–9.

17 On Soviet planning and deception operations, see Glantz, pp. 348–79; Erickson, *Road to Berlin*, pp. 189–204, 207–15; Ziemke, *Stalingrad to Berlin*, pp. 313–19; Magenheimer, "Das Gesetz des Schwergewichts," pp. 22–23. Charles G. FitzGerald, "Operation Bagration," *Military Review* 44, No. 5 (1964), 59–72, summarizes the then available literature.

18 JIC[44] 81 (O) Final, "No. 30 Mission [to the Soviet Union]: Report by the Joint Intelligence Sub-Committee," 8 Mar. 1944, PRO, CAB 119/128, and other documents in this file. On Soviet cooperation in the deception operation, see Hinsley, *British Intelligence*, 5: 111–12.

19 Note the title of William L. Allen, *Anzio: Edge of Disaster*.

20 On Mar. 24, 1944, Wilson wrote Brooke that he would soon replace Clark with Patch as commander of the 5th Army (Liddell Hart Centre, Alanbrooke Papers, 14/10/1). On

Patch, whose record on the whole appears superior to Clark's, see William K. Wyant, *Sandy Patch: A Biography of Lt. Gen. Alexander M. Patch* (New York: Praeger, 1991). He was to command the 7th Army.

21 Note the report by the Japanese military attaché Rome, No. 134 of 29 May 1944, NA, RG 457, SRA 11356–62.

22 See Hinsley, *British Intelligence*, 3/1: 206–7 note *.

23 Much too slowly for Brooke; see his comments on the diary entry for 7 June 1944 in Liddell Hart Centre, Alanbrooke Papers, 3/B/XII, f. 957. The Pope's request was forwarded to London on 26 Jan. 1944; it is quoted in Chadwick, *Britain and the Vatican*, p. 290.

24 See Brooke's comment on the diary entry of 21 Sep. 1943 in Liddell Hart Centre, Alanbrooke Papers, 3/A/10, f. 790.

25 In his memoirs, *Intelligence at the Top* (New York: Doubleday, 1964), pp. 164–65, Eisenhower's chief of intelligence, Sir Kenneth Strong, expresses the view that it was the closeness of the Salerno landing to disaster which led Eisenhower to insist on control of the heavy bombers.

26 One of the great virtues of David Eisenhower, *Eisenhower at War*, is its emphasis on the key role of the Red Army.

27 Note Schörner's letter to his friend Himmler of June 18, 1944, urging big transfers to the West and not worrying about landings elsewhere in France, in Imperial War Museum, General Edouard Schörner Papers, Box E 117, AL 2831/2; Magenheimer, "Das Gesetz des Schwergewichts," pp. 18–25.

28 These deception operations have become the subject of a vast literature, much of it belonging in the category of fiction. Reliable and serious are the pieces by Thomas L. Cubbage in Michael I. Handel (ed.), *Strategic and Operational Deception in the Second World War* (London: Franklin Cass, 1987), pp. 114–74 and 327–46. The piece by Klaus-Jürgen Müller in ibid., pp. 301–26, explains, among other things, the failure of "Fortitude North." The memoirs of "Garbo," a central figure in "Fortitude South," Juan Pujol with Nigel West, *Operation Garbo* (New York: Pocket Books, 1985), are very much worth reading. Ronald Lewin argues that "Fortitude North" *was* partially successful and also believes that the notional British 9th and 10th Armies in the Middle East helped tie down German forces in the Balkans (Rohwer and Jäckel, *Funkaufklärung*, pp. 209, 225–26). There are important additional details in Hinsley, *British Intelligence*, 4: 237–44, 112–17 and other places on "Garbo," and chap. 14 on security in general; 5: 18ff, 51–52, 75ff, chap. 6, 185ff.

29 Forrest C. Pogue, *The European Theater of Operations: The Supreme Command* (Washington: GPO, 1954), p. 199.

30 The best account remains Alan F. Wilt, *The Atlantic Wall: Hitler's Defenses in the West, 1941–1944* (Ames, Iowa: Iowa State Univ. Press, 1975).

31 According to a report by the Japanese naval attaché in Berlin to Tokyo (No. 02014–44 of 6 June 1944), German air reconnaissance photos of 28 Apr. 1944 had revealed new large type pontoons which could be flooded. It was believed in the German navy that these might be floated to cliffs and used for temporary harbors (NA, RG 457, SRNA 1525). Salewski's study of the German naval high command in World War II shows that no serious conclusions were ever drawn (*Seekriegsleitung*, 2: 431). On the Mulberries, see Alfred B. Stanford, *Force Mulberry: The Planning and Installation of the Artificial Harbor off U.S. Normandy Beaches in World War II* (New York: Morrow, 1951). The whole concept and its being pushed forward vigorously was undoubtedly due in large part to Churchill's personal interest.

32 For a summary account of the three systems devised for supplying gasoline and other petroleum products for Overlord, see Roland G. Ruppenthal, *The European Theater of Operations: Logistical Support of the Armies* (Washington: GPO, 1953), 1: 322–25.

33 See Wilt, *The Atlantic Wall*, pp. 143, 206 n 13. The German belief in a forthcoming

landing in the area between Calais and Le Havre can be followed in the reports of the Japanese naval attaché in Berlin which were read by the Americans, see his reports of 7, 10, 14, 22, 24 July 1944, NA, RG 457, SRNA 1873, 1886, 1965, 2009, 2020–21. It is not until his No. 308 of 7 Aug. 1944 (SRNA 2097) that the Germans were reported as thinking a second Channel landing unlikely.

34 Eisenhower, *Eisenhower at War*, p. 220. See Ralph C. Greene and Oliver E. Alen, "What Happened off Devon," *American Heritage* 36, No. 2 (1985), 26–35; Edwin P. Hoyt, *The Invasion before Normandy: The Secret Battle of Slapton Sands* (New York: Stein Day, 1985). Much was made in the 1980s of the alleged concealment of this incident; in fact the major details had been published decades earlier in the army and navy official histories (Harrison, p. 270; Morison, *US Naval Operations*, 11: 66).

35 Note Roosevelt to Marshall, 2 June 1944, FDRL, PSF Box 5 Marshall.

36 Lamb, *Ghosts of Peace*, p. 233; Tuvia Ben-Moshe, "Winston Churchill and the 'Second Front': A Reappraisal," *JMH* 62 (1990), 503–38.

37 Of the many accounts, see Eisenhower, *Eisenhower at War*, pp. 231–34; Morison, *US Naval Operations*, 11: 69–70. Montgomery's presentation is in Hamilton, *Monty*, 2: 570–78. On British doubts, hesitations, and the waning strength behind those doubts, see Max Hastings, *Overlord: D-Day and the Battle for Normandy* (New York: Simon & Schuster, 1984), pp. 22–26.

38 See *Eisenhower Papers*, 3: 1894–95; Eisenhower, *Eisenhower at War*, pp. 239–42, 252–53; Morison, 11: 82 n 5. John Keegan's *Six Armies in Normandy*, chap. 2, is an especially good account of the American 101st Airborne Division's drop.

39 Dieter Ose, *Entscheidung im Westen, 1944: Der Oberbefehlshaber West und die Abwehr der alliierten Invasion* (Stuttgart: Deutsche Verlags-Anstalt, 1982), pp. 72–73, gives the figures as 1,873,000 men including 950,000 in the army, Waffen-SS and air force ground units, with about 1370 tanks.

40 On the Indian Legion and Hitler's later comments on it, see Heiber, *Hitlers Lagebesprechungen*, pp. 939–40.

41 Tokyo to Berlin Nos. 477–78 of 3 July 1944, NA, RG 457, SRDJ 66043–45.

42 The details can be followed in Wilt, *The Atlantic Wall*, and Ose, *Entscheidung im Western*.

43 A good map in Ose, p. 58.

44 There are important materials on D-Day in the Ismay files, Liddell Hart Centre, II/3/278/1, 2a. The British Army Operational Research Group report, "Casualties and Effects of Fire Support on the British Beaches in Normandy," of 21 Apr. 1945, in PRO, WO 106/4447, reviews the British effort; see WO 106/4468 for the German opposition. The Canadians had the good fortune at Juno beach that the Germans had withdrawn a division to send East and replaced it with a very weak unit (Keegan, *Six Armies in Normandy*, pp. 128–31). The best accounts of D-Day remain the American and British official histories by Pogue, Harrison, Ellis, Morison, and Roskill. Some interesting new material in Hamilton, *Monty*, 2; Lamb, *Montgomery*; Ose, *Entscheidung im Westen*; Hastings, *Overlord*; and Eisenhower, *Eisenhower at War*. On the serious impact of bad weather on air support as well as on the landing of supplies, see the historical record of Leigh-Mallory's headquarters in PRO, AIR 37/1057.

45 An account of the movement of the 2nd SS Panzer Division "Das Reich," infamous for the Oradour massacre, from southern France to Normandy, 450 miles in more than two weeks, is in Max Hastings, *Das Reich: The March of the 2nd SS Panzer Division Through France* (New York: Jove, 1983). The combat narrative of this book is dependable; its broader analysis of the SS flawed by Hastings's unfamiliarity with its structure and personnel policies (see p. 13).

46 On the German shock at what they considered the early fall of Cherbourg, see "Streng vertraulicher Informationsbericht," 28 June 1944, BA, ZSg. 115/8, f. 95; Heiber, *Hitlers*

Lagebesprechungen, p. 600; Dönitz's comments on 24–25 Aug. 1945, Salewski, *Seekriegsleitung*, 2: 645.

47 A summary in Gordon A. Harrison, *Cross-Channel Attack* (Washington: GPO, 1951), pp. 441–42.

48 Very instructive is Montgomery's letter to Brooke, M 501 of 13 June 1944, in Liddell Hart Centre, Alanbrooke Papers, 14/26/6. The postscript Montgomery added on the morning of the 14th shows the first signs of change as more German armored divisions move toward the British front. This letter clearly shows that Montgomery originally hoped to break through but then adapted to the new situation – pretending afterwards that he had planned this all along. A good map in Hamilton, *Monty*, 2: 651.

49 See Montgomery's M 502 in Liddell Hart Centre, quoted in ibid., pp. 663–64.

50 Montgomery to Brooke, M 511 of 14 July 1944, Liddell Hart Centre, Alanbrooke Papers, 14/28. The accompanying map shows the 7th Armored Division taking Falaise.

51 Charles J. Dick, "The Goodwood Concept – Situating the Appreciation," *Journal of the Royal United Services Institute for Defence Studies* 127 (March 1982), 22–28; Keegan, *Six Armies in Normandy*, chap. 5; Hastings, *Overlord*, pp. 230–43; Hinsley, *British Intelligence*, 3/2: Appendix 18.

52 For example, on June 11, 1944, Hitler ordered II SS Panzer Corps from the Eastern Front back to the West. Its movement took until June 28 (Keegan, p. 179).

53 In the period June 6 – July 23 both sides had suffered something over 110,000 casualties, but the Germans had received only 10,000 replacements (Pogue, *Supreme Command*, p. 194).

54 See Scheidt Papers, Institut für Zeitgeschichte, B 2, f. 299–300; Frau Junge (Traudl Humps) material, Institut für Zeitgeschichte, f. 86.

55 On Churchill's advocacy of using poison gas and the arguments over this issue, see Bernstein, "Churchill"; Harris and Paxman, *A Higher Form of Killing*, pp. 126–35; Gellermann, *Der Krieg*, pp. 168–72, 249–51. On July 13 Churchill asked Stalin for access to the German firing test range at Blizna, which the Red Army had overrun, but the Russians waited for two months before allowing British observers there (Hinsley, *British Intelligence*, 3/1: 446n). It should be noted that the Germans were also considering the use of gas at this time to attack the Allied beachhead but decided against it for fear of retaliation. See Müller, "Gaskriegsvorbereitungen," pp. 45–46; Oshima to Tokyo No. 822 of 12 Aug. 1944, NA, RG 457, SRDJ 67480.

56 For Hitler's views and speeches at this time, see Wilhelm, "Hitlers Ansprache," pp. 134, 162 n 24; *Rommel Papers*, pp. 475–78; "Streng vertraulicher Informationsbericht," 28 June 1944, BA, ZSg. 115/8, f. 93–95; Reichspropagandaamt Berlin, "Sondertagesparole des Reichspressechefs," 3 July 1944, BA, ZSg. 115/18, f. 40–42. Quite revealing, frank, and detailed are Oshima's reports to Tokyo Nos. 621 of 23 June and 626 of 24 June 1944, NA, RG 457, SRDJ 62519–20, 62688–94.

57 John J. Sullivan, "The Botched Air Support of Operation Cobra," *Parameters–U.S. Army War College Quarterly* 18, No. 1 (1988), 97–110, is the best account available.

58 General Heinrich Eberbach replaced Geyr von Schweppenburg as commander of Panzer Group West.

59 A key figure in the tactical air support operations was U.S. Air Force General Elwood R. (Pete) Quesada. There is a useful sketch of his career and role in John L. Frisbee (ed.), *Makers of the United States Air Force* (Washington: GPO, 1987), pp. 177–204. The Germans kept using up what fighter reinforcements they could bring forward in vain efforts to cope with the rapidly changing situation in the West, and therefore could never build up an adequate reserve for defense against the bomber fleets assailing Germany (Boog, *Luftwaffenführung*, p. 136).

60 On the German attack at Mortain, see Pogue, *Supreme Command*, pp. 206–9; Ose, *Einscheidung im Westen*, pp. 222–32. For the use of ultra in coping with the attack, see

Ronald Lewin, *Ultra Goes to War* (New York: McGraw-Hill, 1978), pp. 337–40; Adolph G. Rosengarten, Jr., "With Ultra from Omaha Beach to Weimar, Germany – A Personal View," *Military Affairs* 42, No. 3 (1978), p. 129.

61 On the Falaise pocket, see Pogue, *Supreme Command*, pp. 208–17; Ose, *Einscheidung im Westen*, pp. 232–59; Hastings, *Overlord*, pp. 293–319; Lamb, *Montgomery*, pp. 167–78; Hamilton, 2: 756–84; Russell F. Weigley, *Eisenhower's Lieutenants: The Campaigns of France and Germany, 1944–1945* (Bloomington, Ind.: Indiana Univ. Press, 1981), pp. 201–9; Eisenhower, *Eisenhower at War*, pp. 403–10. According to Kazimierz Mczarski, *Gespräche mit dem Henker* (Dusseldorf: Droste, 1978), pp. 353–54, von Kluge did not commit suicide but was shot by Jürgen Stroop.

62 This action is the origin of the famous picture of American infantry in battle dress marching through the city – a picture used on the American postage stamp honoring the army. See also Eisenhower, *Eisenhower at War*, pp. 414–16, 424–27.

63 Keegan, *Six Armies in Normandy*, pp. 283–98.

64 The best account is Alan F. Wilt, *The French Riviera Campaign of August 1944* (Carbondale, Ill.: Southern Illinois Univ. Press, 1981). See also Arthur L. Funk, *Hidden Ally: The French Resistance, Special Operations, and the Landings in Southern France, 1944* (Westport, Conn.: Greenwood Press, 1992).

65 To keep operations moving in Italy, Alexander was willing to accept Red Army units there (Alexander to Brooke, 18 July 1944, Liddell Hart Centre, Alanbrooke Papers, 14/10/6)

66 The exchanges are printed in Kimball, *Churchill and Roosevelt*, 3. See esp. R-577 on p. 232 (Loewenheim No. 401). See Eisenhower, *Eisenhower at War*, pp. 387–90, on the Brittany project.

67 Relevant documents in AA, Nachlass Renthe-Fink, Paket 5; Mitani (Vichy) to Tokyo Nos. 249 of 19 July and 265 of 6 Aug. 1944, NA, RG 457, SRDJ 65150–52, 66834–35; Tokyo Circular 5699 of 21 Sep. 1944, SRDJ 72609–10; Japanese military attaché Berlin to Tokyo No. 416 of 17 Oct. 1944 on the situation in Sigmaringen, SRA 12970–75. See also Bertram B. Gordon, *Collaborationism in France during the Second World War* (Ithaca, N.Y.: Cornell Univ. Press, 1980), chap. 11. Needless to say, when the Germans used "force" to remove the Vichy regime first to Belfort and then to Sigmaringen, there was no resistance. On a supposed effort by Pétain to contact the Allies, see Z 6331/6331/17, PRO, FO 371/42096 (this is the message referred to in Thomas, *Britain and Vichy*, p. 177).

68 See the reports of the Japanese military attaché in Vichy of 10 and 17 July 1944, NA, RG 457, SRA 10090–91, 12445–46.

69 The text is published in Heiber, *Hitlers Lagebesprechungen*, pp. 584–609. It is from a collection different from that on which Felix Gilbert, *Hitler Directs His War* (New York: Oxford Univ. Press, 1950), is based and therefore not to be found there. A summary is in Pogue, *Supreme Command*, pp. 201–3.

70 See Ose, *Entscheidung im Westen*, p. 252; Heiber, *Hitlers Lagebesprechungen*, p. 686 n 5. On the Channel Islands being held until May 1945, see Cruikshank, *The German Occupation of the Channel Islands*, chap. 12.

71 Salewski, *Seekriegsleitung*, 2: 432, 448, 484–89.

72 Hans-Georg von Studnitz, *Als Berlin brannte: Diarium der Jahre 1943–1945* (Stuttgart: Kohlhammer, 1963), 28 Sep. 1944.

73 Montgomery to Brooke, M/92 of 14 Aug. 1944, Liddell Hart Centre, Alanbrooke Papers, 14/30; L. F. Ellis, *Victory in the West*, Vol 1: *The Battle of Normandy* (London: HMSO, 1962), 1: 453.

74 This summary of the argument is supported by Lamb, *Montgomery*, p. 411, but not by Hamilton, *Monty*, 2. On the promotion, the text of Brooke's diary for 30 Aug. 1944 in Bryant, 2: 197, is rather different from that in the original at the Liddell Hart Centre. On Montgomery's effort to fire General Henry Crerar, the commander of Canadian 1st

Army, see Lamb, *Montgomery*, pp. 252–57; on his relations with the Poles, see, e.g., ibid., pp. 73–74.

75 See Eisenhower, *Eisenhower at War*, pp. 416–23, 430–34, 438–52, 477–79. Note Montgomery to Simpson for CIGS of 20 Sep. 1944, Liddell Hart Centre, Alanbrooke Papers, 14/32 (which stresses Montgomery's troubles with the British officers at SHAEF). It is impossible to document, but nevertheless appears likely, that both Eisenhower and the British officers who agreed with him were influenced by their knowledge of Montgomery's proclivity for slow and steady advances in prior years; the one time he had tried a fast move, in Sicily, it had both disrupted the Allied plan and failed of its object. On the supply problems, see also van Creveld, *Supplying War*, chap. 7.

76 Lamb, *Montgomery*, pp. 200ff, 257–62; Eisenhower, *Eisenhower at War*, pp. 445–46.

77 Lamb, pp. 212–26.

78 The account in ibid., chap. 8, is especially critical of Montgomery, Brereton (the commander of 1st Airborne Army), and Browning (the corps commander). The account in *Eisenhower at War*, pp. 441–45, 455–56, 459–77, suggests that at the end neither Montgomery nor Eisenhower really wanted to go forward with the operation. Murray, "Ultra," p. 55, stresses Montgomery's disregard of ultra information on the SS Panzer divisions near Arnhem. Hamilton, in *Monty*, 3: Part 2, considers the Arnhem operation a mistake that Eisenhower should have prevented.

79 WM(44) War Cabinet 91(44) of 17 July 1944, PRO, CAB 65/43.

80 WM(44) War Cabinet 115(44) of 4 Sep. 1944, ibid.

81 On the Soviet June offensive against Finland, see Ziemke, *Stalingrad to Berlin*, pp. 296–303; Erickson, *Road to Berlin*, pp. 204–5, 328–30; Glantz, *Soviet Military Deception*, pp. 351, 358–60.

82 On the situation in July 1944, see esp. the piece by Ernst Klink in Ernst Klink et al., *Operationsgebiet östliche Ostsee und der finnisch-baltische Raum* (Stuttgart: Deutsche Verlags-Anstalt, 1961), pp. 43ff. See also "Pressekonferenz der Reichsregierung," 2 July 1944, BA, ZSg. 115/9, f. 27, 32; Japanese military attaché Helsinki to Tokyo No. 273 of 29 July 1944, NA, RG 457, SRA 10859–60.

83 On Finland's leaving the war, see Ziemke, *Stalingrad to Berlin*, pp. 389–91; Berry, *American Foreign Policy and the Finnish Exception*, pp. 418–21; German Minister Stockholm to Berlin Nos. 1339 of 18 Aug. and 1402 of 30 Aug. 1944, AA, Gesandtschaft Helsinki, "Drahtberichte geheim 1944," fr. H063444, H063472; Oshima's No. 867 of 22 Aug. 1944, NA, RG 457, SRDJ 68699–702; Japanese military attaché Helsinki to Tokyo No. 334 of 1 Sep. 1944, SRA 11307–8; documents in BA/MA, PG 39690; "Pressekonferenz der Reichsregierung," 12 Sep. 1944, BA, ZSg. 115/10, f. 32; Henrick S. Nissen (ed.), *Scandinavia during the Second World War* (Minneapolis: Univ. of Minnesota Press, 1983), pp. 280–84 with helpful maps. Thede Palm, *The Finnish–Soviet Armistice Negotiations of 1944* (Stockholm: Almqvist & Wiksell, 1971), is important for the period up to the signing of the armistice; Tuomo Polvinen, "Zur Vorgeschichte des finnisch-sowjetischen Vertrages über Freundschaft, Zusammenarbeit und gegenseitigen Beistand während der Jahre 1944–1945," *Jahrbücher für Geschichte Osteuropas* 30, No. 2 (1982), 227–29, is useful for the subsequent negotiations. The Soviets agreed to pay the British-controlled International Nickel Co. compensation for its mines in the Petsamo area (Foreign Office note of 30 Sep. 1944, N 5768/132/56, PRO, FO 371/43175).

84 On operation "Tanne" to seize Suursaari (Hogland), see Ursula von Gersdorff's piece in *Operationsgebiet östliche Ostsee*, pp. 143–82; the essay by Admiral Otto Schulz of Oct. 1945, in C 8254/8254/18, PRO, FO 371/47019; and the most recent analysis in the PhD dissertation by Davis Grier, "Hitler's Baltic Strategy," University of North Carolina, 1991.

85 On the Soviet offensive in the north and the German withdrawal, see Ziemke, *Stalingrad to Berlin*, pp. 387–403; Ziemke, *Northern Theater*, chap. 14; Major James F. Gebhardt,

The Petsamo–Kirkenes Operation: Soviet Breakthrough and Pursuit, October 1944 (Fort Leavenworth, Kans.: Combat Studies Institute, 1990). On Rendulic's pre-1938 Nazi background, see the documents in NA, T-120, Cont. 2695, Serial 5705, fr. E 414436, 414650; Historische Kommission des Reichsführere SS, *Die Erhebung der österreichischen Nationalsozialisten im Juli 1934* (Vienna: Europa-Verlag, 1965), pp. 227–28. In Oct. 1943 the German general in Croatia quoted Rendulic as saying: "Oh, if I had 20 divisions, I would murder everyone in this country if possible!" ("Ach, wenn ich 20 Divisionen hätte, dann würde ich in diesem Lande alles morden, so gut es ginge!" Broucek, *Ein General im Zwielicht*, 3: 291). It will be obvious to the reader why Rendulic had such a fabulous career in Hitler's army.

86 Wilhelm, "Die Prognosen der Abteilung Fremde Heere Ost 1942–1945," pp. 59–63, summarizes the evidence on the German side; Glantz, *Soviet Military Deception*, pp. 360–79, brings together Soviet deception schemes and the evidence of the Germans falling for them.

87 Accounts in Ziemke, *Stalingrad to Berlin*, chap. 15; Erickson, *Road to Berlin*, chap. 5; still useful, Hermann Gackenholz, "Der Zusammenbruch der Heeresgruppe Mitte im Sommer 1944," *VjZ* 3 (1955), 317–33. Recent studies include Rolf Hinze, *Der Zusammenbruch der Heeresgruppe Mitte im Osten 1944* (Stuttgart: Motorbuch, 1980); Gerd Niepold, *Mittlere Ostfront Juni 1944: Darstellung, Beurteilung, Lehren* (Herford: Mittler, 1985).

88 Sato No. 1444 of 17 July 1944, NA, RG 457, SRDJ 64921. There is a picture in Ziemke, *Stalingrad to Berlin*, p. 330; another in Jacobsen and Dollinger, *Zweite Weltkrieg*, 3: 44–45. For the origins of the idea, see Volkogonov, *Stalin*, pp. 476–77.

89 See Ziemke, *Stalingrad to Berlin*, p. 327; transcript of Jodl Diary, 16 Sep. 1944, Imperial War Museum; very detailed account in Grier.

90 On the northern sector of the front, see Ziemke, *Stalingrad to Berlin*, pp. 327–29, 333–36, 338–43; Erickson, *Road to Berlin*, pp. 307–26.

91 On German army Chief of Staff Guderian's trip to Budapest on 31 Aug. 1944 to discuss the defense of Hungary, see Hennyey, *Ungarns Schicksal zwischen Ost und West*, p. 64. On Soviet deception operations before the operations toward Lwow and Lublin, see Glantz, *Soviet Military Deception*, pp. 379–409.

92 Two books on the Majdanek trial are useful: Heiner Lichtenstein, *Majdanek: Reportage eines Prozesses* (Frankfurt/M: Europäische Verlagsanstalt, 1979); Karl Sauer, *KZ Majdanek: Report über das Vernichtungslager und über den Majdanekprozess*, 3d ed. (Frankfurt/M: Röderberg-Verlag, 1979). A short account in English in Konnilyn G. Feig, *Hitler's Death Camps: The Sanity of Madness* (New York: Holmes & Meier, 1979), pp. 313–32.

93 On the uprising, see the still useful account by its commander, Tadeusz Bor-Komorowski, *The Secret Army* (New York: Macmillan, 1951); also Lukas, *Forgotten Holocaust*, chap. 7; Joanna K.M. Hanson, *The Civilian Population and the Warsaw Uprising of 1944* (Cambridge: Cambridge Univ. Press, 1982); Janusz K. Zawodny, *Nothing but Honor: The Story of the Warsaw Uprising, 1944* (London: Macmillan, 1978). For the German operations to crush the uprising, see Hans von Krannhals, *Der Warschauer Aufstand 1944* (Frankfurt/M: Bernard & Graefe, 1962).

94 Note that in early October the Polish Communist Party's line was changed with Stalin's approval or at his urging to one of fighting the AK rather than establishing a national front with it (Jaime Reynolds, "'Lublin' versus 'London' – The Party and the Underground Movement in Poland, 1944–1945," *JCH* 16 [1981], 628–34).

95 On the British effort, see the material in PRO, FO 371/39492, 39494–96, AIR 8/1156, 1169; Slessor No. 581 to RAF HQ 20 Sep. 1944, AIR 8/1170. On the U.S. effort, see Lukas, *Eagles East*, pp. 202–7; Roosevelt to Leahy, 29 Sep. 1944, and Leahy to Roosevelt, 30 Sep. 1944, FDRL, PSF Box 66, Poland Sept.-Dec. 1944; Diane T. Putney, *Ultra and the Army Air Forces in World War II: An Interview with Associate Justice of the U.S.*

Supreme Court Lewis F. Powell Jr. (Washington: GPO, 1987), pp. 44–45; Neil D. Orpen, *Airlift to Warsaw: The Rising of 1944* (Norman, Okla.: Univ. of Oklahoma Press, 1984).

96 See C 11440/1077/55, PRO, FO 371/39494.

97 See Harriman to Roosevelt, Nos. 3021, 3028 of 17 Aug. 1944, and Hull to Roosevelt 19 Aug. 1944, FRDL, PSF Box 66, Poland, Aug. 1944; Michael Burleigh, *Germany Turns Eastwards: A Study of "Ostforschung" in the Third Reich* (Cambridge: Cambridge Univ. Press, 1989), p. 235.

98 In 1983 a distinguished Soviet historian privately confirmed that the halt before Warsaw was political, not military, in origin.

99 Note the documents cited in n. 97, above, and Beaumont, *Comrades in Arms*, pp. 182–83.

100 An account by Anna Josko, "The Slovak Resistance Movement," in Victor S. Mamatey and Radomir Luza (eds.), *A History of the Czechoslovak Republic, 1918–1948* (Princeton, N.J.: Princeton Univ. Press, 1973), chap. 13. Still useful, Peter A. Toma, "Soviet Strategy in the Slovak Uprising of 1944," *Journal of Central European Affairs* 19 (1959), 290–98. The closer coordination between the uprising and the Soviets — and the availability and use of Red air force planes — did not make for a different outcome. See Erickson, *Road to Berlin*, pp. 290–307. A journalistic account, important for its interview material, is Wolfgang Venohr, *Aufstand für die Tschechoslowakei* (Hamburg: Christian Wegner, 1969).

101 Stafford, *Britain and European Resistance*, pp. 185–87; documents in PRO, FO 371/38941–44.

102 Ziemke, *Stalingrad to Berlin*, chap. 16; Erickson, *Road to Berlin*, pp. 346–69; Glantz, *Soviet Military Deception*, pp. 409–27. An account extensively using Romanian materials, Ilie Ceausescu, Florin Constantiniu and Michael E. Ionescu, *A Turning Point in World War II: 23 August 1944 in Romania* (New York: Columbia Univ. Press, 1985). The head of the German military mission in Romania, General Erik Hansen, has some interesting comments in Institut für Zeitgeschichte, ZS 1130. There is a helpful summary in Peter Gosztony, "Rumänien im August 1944," *Österreichische Militärische Zeitschrift* 18, No. 1 (1980), 48–54. The account in Hillgruber, *Hitler, König Carol*, pp. 209ff, can still be consulted.

103 Arnold to Roosevelt, 22 Sep. 1944, FDRL, PSF Box 105, War Dept., Arnold 1942–45.

104 Oshima to Tokyo No. 946 of 6 Sep. 1944, NA, RG 457, SRDJ 70124–28; "Pressekonferenz der Reichsregierung," 31 Aug. 1944, BA, ZSg. 115/9, f. 161.

105 See Wilson to Brooke, 24 Sep. 1944, Liddell Hart Centre, Alanbrooke Papers, 14/45.

106 Note the comment of Field Marshal von Weichs of Oct. 1944(?) that the Bulgarians seemed to fight better under Russian direction (BA/MA, N 19/3, F 311 1944).

107 Hoppe, *Bulgarien*, p. 183 and n 68; "Pressekonferenz der Reichsregierung," 10 Sep. 1944, BA, ZSg. 115/10, f. 24.

108 Hennyey, *Ungarns Schicksal zwischen Ost und West*, pp. 166–67; see also Donovan to Roosevelt, 16 Oct. 1944, FDRL, PSF Box 169, OSS Oct. 1944.

109 A detailed account in Macartney, *October Fifteenth*, 2: chap. 18. See also his "Ungarns Weg aus den Zweiten Weltkrieg," *VjZ* 14 (1966), 79–103.

110 See Szöllösi-Janze, *Die Pfeilkreuzlerbewegung in Ungarn*.

111 Ziemke, *Stalingrad to Berlin*, p. 364.

112 See Kurihara (Ankara) to Tokyo, 7 Aug. 1944, NA, RG 457, SRDJ 67235–36.

113 Notes by von Weichs on the evening conference of 23 Aug. 1944 at Hitler's headquarters, BA/MA, N 19/3, f. 207–1944.

114 Ziemke, *Stalingrad to Berlin*, pp. 365–78; Hondros, *Occupation and Resistance*, pp. 195ff.

115 The Germans held Memel until Jan. 22, 1945. On the successful Soviet deception of the Germans before this offensive, see Glantz, *Soviet Military Deception*, pp. 433–42.

116 See Grier, "Hitler's Baltic Strategy," passim.

117 For such a report, see Japanese naval attaché Berlin to Tokyo No. 339 of 17 Aug. 1944,

NA, RG 457, SRNA 2190–92. Note the meeting of Abe with Admiral Meisel on 29 Aug. 1944, BA/MA, RM 7/254, f. 247, 258–59.

118 The account in Fleischhauer, *Sonderfrieden*, pp. 228–64, stresses the contacts of the German opposition and the impact of the July 20 coup attempt. But see Ziemke, *Stalingrad to Berlin*, pp. 404–5. Most important are the Japanese diplomatic documents: Shigemitsu (Tokyo) to Oshima (Berlin), Nos. 594 of 24 Aug., 615 and 616 of 29 Aug., 662 of 31 Aug. 1944, NA, RG 457, SRDJ 68635, 69162–64, 69165–66, 62698; Oshima to Tokyo Nos. 881 of 25 Aug., 944 of 5 Sep., 961 of 7 Sep. 1944, SRDJ 68848–49, 70101–13, 70336; Shigemitsu to Sato (Moscow) Nos. 1160, 1161 of 30 Aug. 1944, SRDJ 69505–6, 69451–52; Sato to Shigemitsu No. 1788 of 2 Sep. 1944, SRDJ 69721–24. Cf. Stahmer to Ribbentrop No. 2323 of 25 Aug. 1944, AA, Handakten Ritter, Bd. 4–5, fr. 363343–44; *ADAP*, E, 8, No. 223 (this is a report on Oshima's conversations with Hitler and Ribbentrop on 4 Sep. 1944 and is the answer to the preceding document listed in this note; there is a serious transcription error on p. 429 where "unmöglich" [impossible] has been misread as "möglich" [possible]); Shigemitsu to Oshima No. 670 of 14 Sep. 1944, SRDJ 71205–8; Oshima to Shigemitsu No. 1054 of 26 Sep. 1944, SRDJ 72699–701; Oshima's No. 1266 of 10 Nov. 1944 on a conversation with Goebbels the night before, SRDJ 78178–79; Shigemitsu to Sato No. 1694 of 24 Nov. 1944, SRDJ 79853–55; Oshima to Shigemitsu No. 1367 of 2 Dec. 1944, SRDJ 81008–13. See also the U.S. Pacific Strategic Intelligence Section, "Japanese Estimates of Germany's Ability to Continue the Struggle," 22 Jan. 1945, NA, RG 457, SRH-066, f. 7–8. In the discussions, the Japanese were especially generous on the concessions to be made by the Germans.

119 "Magic Far Eastern Summary," Nos. 199 of 5 Oct. and 216 of 22 Oct. 1944, NA, RG 457, SRS 199, 216.

120 See Salewski, *Seekriegsleitung*, 2: 491ff.

13: TENSIONS IN BOTH ALLIANCES

1 There is a survey of these problems, with added detail, in Hathaway, *Ambiguous Partnership*, chaps. 1–2. A different picture in Terry H. Anderson, *The United States, Great Britain, and the Cold War* (Columbia, Mo.: Univ. of Missouri Press, 1981).

2 Danchev, *Very Special Relationship*, chaps. 5–6, provides many examples. The file on the replacement for Dill on his death is in PRO, PREM 478/2.

3 A good introduction in William H. McNeill, *America, Britain and Russia: Their Co-operation and Conflict, 1941–1946* (1953, reprinted New York: Johnson Reprint, 1970), pp. 129ff.

4 The issue is reviewed in the preceding chapter. The relevant exchanges between Churchill and Roosevelt have been published by Loewenheim (*Roosevelt and Churchill*) and Kimball (*Churchill and Roosevelt*).

5 The best survey remains William Roger Louis, *Imperialism at Bay: The United States and the Decolonization of the British Empire, 1941–1945* (New York: Oxford Univ. Press, 1978). See now also Kimball, *The Juggler*, chap. 7.

6 Note Stettinius to Hull, 15 Aug. 1944, FDRL, PSF 94, Phillips; Kenton J. Clymer, "The Education of William Phillips: Self-Determination and American Policy toward India," *Diplomatic History* 8 (1984), 13–35.

7 See the exchange in Loewenheim, *Roosevelt and Churchill*, pp. 526, 535 n 1; Kimball, *Churchill and Roosevelt*, 3: 176–77, 188–89. The monarchy issue also played a role to some extent in the problems of liberated Belgium.

8 Hathaway, *Ambiguous Partnership*, pp. 90–96.

9 EAM was the political leadership of ELAS, the largest resistance force.

10 Hathaway, pp. 93–111.

11 Ibid., p. 98.

12 Gietz, *Die neue Alte Welt*, pp. 141–78, is particularly good on this subject. Of considerable

interest is the report by Welles of 13 Aug. 1942 to Roosevelt on a talk with Alexis Léger, FDRL, PSF Box 96, State Welles, 1942.

13 See the references to Churchill's requests of 3 Sep. 1941 and 24 Apr. 1942 in Desmond Morton to Air Chief Marshal Sir Wilfred R. Freeman, Vice-Chief of the Air Staff, of 27 Apr. 1942, PRO, AIR 20/2782.

14 It would appear that General Eisenhower was the one senior American converted, at least for a while, to this approach (Arthur L. Funk, "Eisenhower and de Gaulle," paper at the American Historical Association meeting, 29 Dec. 1990).

15 A summary in Hathaway, *Ambiguous Partnership*, pp. 72–88.

16 The issue is touched on in ibid., pp. 80–84. The relevant exchanges between Roosevelt and Churchill are printed in Kimball, *Churchill and Roosevelt*, 3: 402–8, 418–21, 423–25, 427–28. A recent discussion in Philip Cockrell, "International Civil Aviation and United States Foreign Policy," *Proceedings of the South Carolina Historical Association 1991*, 29–46.

17 An introduction to the issue in Hathaway, chap. 2; a recent treatment in Kimball, *The Juggler*, chap. 3.

18 On the question of the Soviet–Polish border, note Jan Karski, *The Great Powers and Poland, 1919–1945: From Versailles to Yalta* (Lanham, Md.: University Press of America, 1985), p. 411.

19 See esp. Karski, chap. 31.

20 Until new material is opened in Warsaw, the best examination of this issue is Cienciala, "The Activities of Polish Communists," 129–45, which demonstrates that a new government for Poland was being recruited in late 1943 at the latest.

21 Karski, *The Great Powers and Poland*, chap. 32; Richard C. Lucas, *The Strange Allies: The United States and Poland, 1941–1945* (Knoxville: Univ. of Tennessee Press, 1978), chaps. 3–5. See the letter of 11 Mar. 1944 signed by many Americans who had supported aid to Russia before Pearl Harbor urging that the Soviet Union not antagonize the United States by running rough-shod over Poland (Lord Halifax's copy in AN 1461/1271/45, PRO, FO 371/38674A).

22 Klaus Schwabe, "Roosevelt und Jalta," Jürgen Heideking et al. (eds.), *Wege in die Zeitgeschichte* (Berlin: Walter de Gruyter, 1989), p. 466.

23 See the documents in PRO, AIR 20/2710–11. For fear of British aid to the Polish resistance, the Soviet Union also would not allow damaged British bombers to fly on to Russian airfields (AIR 8/1110). There is an account of the related issues in Karski, chap. 33. The military context of the Warsaw uprising is reviewed in the preceding chapter, but the impact of the events of Aug.-Sep. 1944 was so great that it has to be placed into the diplomatic context as well.

24 Joan Beaumont, "A Question of Diplomacy: British Military Mission in the U.S.S.R. 1941–1945," *Journal of the Royal United Services Institute for Defence Studies* 118 (1973), 74–81; James R. Deane, *The Strange Alliance* (New York: Viking, 1946), passim; Mason-Macfarlane Papers, Imperial War Museum, MM 31; documents in PRO, AIR 20/2606–9, 5401. Stalin did, however, suggest a military committee, see 30 Mission (Moscow) No. MIL 1519 of 2 July 1944, PRO, CAB 119/128.

25 Craven and Cate, *Army Air Forces*, 3: 476; Deane, pp. 132–33; Lukas, *Eagles East*, pp. 182–85; documents in PRO, AIR 20/796.

26 Note WM(44) War Cabinet 43(44) Conclusions, Confidential Annex, PRO, CAB 65/46; cf. R 7380/68/67, FO 371/43636.

27 Dallek, *Roosevelt and Foreign Policy*, pp. 468ff.

28 Donovan to Roosevelt, 23 and 24 Mar. 1944, FDRL, PSF Box 6, OSS. Note also the papers rejecting a proposal for a fake Hitler broadcast in June 1944 out of consideration for Soviet sensitivities, in PSF Box 125, J.F. Carter file.

29 F.C. Nano, "The First Soviet Double Cross: A Chapter in the Secret History of World

War II," *Journal of Central European Affairs* 12 (Oct. 1952), 236–58. A broad survey of the issues in Paul D. Quinlan, *Clash over Romania: British and American Policies toward Romania, 1938–1947*, American Romanian Academy of Arts and Sciences No. 2 (Oakland, Calif.: The Academy, 1977).

30 See R 4903/68/64, PRO, FO 371/43636. There is a detailed account in Woodward, *British Foreign Policy*, 3: chap. 38. See also Erickson, *Road to Berlin*, pp. 331ff.

31 Albert Resis, "The Churchill–Stalin Secret 'Percentages' Agreement on the Balkans, Moscow, October 1944," *American Historical Review* 85 (1981), 368–87, and "Spheres of Influence in Soviet Diplomacy," *Journal of Modern History* 53 (1981), 417–39; Vojtech Mastny, *Russia's Road to the Cold War: Diplomacy, Warfare, and the Politics of Communism, 1941–1945* (New York: Columbia Univ. Press, 1979), pp. 207–11.

32 This is the basic point of Peter J. Stavrakis, *Moscow and Greek Communism, 1944–1949* (Ithaca, N.Y.: Cornell Univ. Press, 1989). The policy followed by the Soviet Union in 1944–45 did not, of course, keep it from hoping for gains from the post-1945 turmoil in Greece.

33 Edward M. Bennett, *Franklin D. Roosevelt and the Search for Victory: American-Soviet Relations 1939–1945* (Washington, Del.: Scholarly Resources, 1990), pp. 131–38. See also Edgar Snow to Roosevelt, 28 Dec. 1944, FDRL, PSF Box 68, Russia 1945.

34 See the entry for May 1944 in the War Diary of M.I. 19 in PRO, WO 165/41. A rather dubious account in Olaf Groehler, "Zur Geschichte eines britischen Antikomitees: Reaktion der beherrschended Kreise Grossbritanniens und der USA auf die Gründung des Nationalkomitees 'Freies Deutschland' 1943," *Zeitschrift für Geschichtswissenschaft* 32 (1984), 125–33. Naturally the suspicions of the Western Allies over Soviet contacts with the Germans concerning a possible separate peace did nothing to improve relations; note the concerns in London in Aug. 1944 reflected in C 11893, 11895, 12686/190/18, FO 371/39088.

35 Thus the Americans allowed Victor Kravchenko to remain in the U.S. (Watson to Roosevelt, 18 May 1944, FDRL, PSF Box 66, Poland 1944, Jan.-July; Bennett, *American–Soviet Relations* p. 121); while the British turned down the request of Alexander Rado for asylum (N 11501/11501/38, PRO, FO 371/47991; N 16622/1622/38, FO 371/48006). On the long-term efffects of Soviet espionage on that country's relations with the West, see John L. Gaddis, "The Intelligence Revolution's Impact on Postwar Diplomacy," in Hitchcock (ed.), *The Intelligence Revolution*, pp. 251–74.

36 See Eden to Kerr for Stalin, No. 331 of 4 Nov. 1942, and Kerr to Eden No. 1444 of 6 Nov. 1942, C 10635, 10418/61/18, PRO, FO 371/30920; Woodward, *British Foreign Policy*, 2: 277, 278, 280.

37 The series "Geheime Erlasse, Berichte, Telegramme" in the files of the German embassy in Turkey provides numerous illustrations of these German efforts. On Roosevelt's concern about such matters, see FDRL, PSF Box 146, Earle, George H.

38 The most recent account in Robert C. Hilderbrand, *Dumbarton Oaks: The Origins of the United Nations and the Search for Postwar Security* (Chapel Hill, N.C.: Univ. of North Carolina Press, 1990). An excellent preliminary account in McNeill, *America, Britain and Russia*, pp. 501ff. The British record is summarized in Woodward, *British Foreign Policy*, 5: chap. 43. For British Foreign Office hopes for future cooperation with the Soviet Union, see Graham Ross, "Foreign Office Attitudes to the Soviet Union 1941–45," *JCH* 16 (1981), pp. 528–29, 532.

39 Dallek, *Roosevelt and Foreign Policy*, pp. 466–67.

40 See Bennett, *American–Soviet Relations*, pp. 127–29.

41 Gaddis, *US and Origins*, pp. 26–31.

42 WM(44) War Cabinet 157(44) of 27 Nov. 1944, Conclusions, Confidential Annex, PRO, CAB 65/47. It will be noted that, except for Roosevelt's belief that China should be treated as a great power, this corresponded closely with his views.

43 Mastny, *Russia's Road*, pp. 218ff; see also Stalin's speech of 6 Nov. 1944, *Current History* 8, No. 41 (1945),57–64.

44 McNeill, *America, Britain and Russia*, p. 450. There is a short account in ibid., pp. 449–51. See also Milward, *War, Economy and Society*, pp. 362–64; David Rees, *Harry Dexter White: A Study in Paradox* (New York: Coward, McCann & Geoghegan, 1973), pp. 221ff; John M. Blum (ed.), *From the Morgenthau Diaries*, Vol. 3: *Years of War, 1941–1945* (Boston: Houghton Mifflin, 1967), pp. 426–36; Alfred E. Eckles, *A Search for Solvency: Bretton Woods and the International Monetary System, 1941–1971* (Austin: Univ. of Texas Press, 1975), chaps. 1–7.

45 A striking example of Schacht's devices is described in Weinberg, *Foreign Policy 1933–36*, pp. 138–39.

46 There is a three-volume official history by George Woodbridge (New York: Columbia Univ. Press, 1950). Roosevelt appointed Herbert Lehman (who gave up the governorship of New York a month early) to be the first head of the agency; much of its work remains unexplored by scholars (see FDRL, Morgenthau Presidential Diary, 12 Nov. 1942, Vol. 5: 1192).

47 Herring, *Aid to Russia*, pp. 160–62; Gaddis, *US and Origins*, pp. 22–23.

48 A lovely example in Martin, *Deutschland und Japan*, facing p. 176. A sample from the other extreme is the German decision that a proxy marriage in Japan had to be postponed because the bride's records proving her German descent had been burned by enemy action (Berlin to German naval attaché Tokyo, HA 1588 of 29 Dec. 1944, NA, RG 457, SRGL 2028)

49 There is a very thoughtful discussion of the Axis lack of committees and other structures as well as the importance of the disparagement of the virtues of compromise and cooperation, in *DRuZW*, 6: 95–96.

50 This issue is discussed at length in the books by Schröder and Deakin (see Bibliographic Essay, p. 929). After the Italian surrender of 1943, the Germans seized many Italian archives and searched them for information on the efforts of Italy and Germany's Southeast European satellites to leave the war.

51 Schreiber, *Italienische Militärinternierte*, is the best treatment of this subject.

52 Weinberg, *Foreign Policy 1937–39*, pp. 281–82, 311. See also Steinberg, *All or Nothing*.

53 See *ADAP*, E, 5, No. 158, on Ribbentrop's visit to Rome in Feb. 1943. Bastianini gave a report to the Japanese ambassador in Rome, whose telegram to Tokyo No. 142 of 6 Mar. 1943 is in NA, RG 457, SRDJ 32542–44.

54 Oshima to Tokyo No. 1306 of 14 Nov. 1942, NA, RG 457, SRDJ 28266–67; Martin, *Deutschland und Japan*, doc. 28.

55 *ADAP*, E, 3, No. 278; German embassy Tokyo Nos. 683, 684 of 25 Feb. 1943, AA, St.S., "Japan," Bd. 11, fr. 398514–17; Wiehl, "Aufzeichnung betr. Austausch von Rüstungslieferungen mit Japan," 10 July 1943, ibid., Bd. 12, fr. 17301–4; Tokyo to Rome No. 610 of 27 Mar. 1942, NA, RG 457, SRA 03039; Japanese military attaché Berlin to Tokyo No. 673 of 24 Sep. 1943, SRA 06750–55.

56 *ADAP*, E, 6, No. 41; Rome to Tokyo No. 294 of 23 May 1943, NA, RG 457, SRDJ 37442–43; Tokyo to Berlin Circular No. 46 of 29 Jan. 1944, SRDJ 49742–43; Shigemitsu (Tokyo) to Oshima (Berlin) Nos. 612 of 28 Aug. and 618 of 29 Aug. 1944, SRDJ 69069–70, 69510–11.

57 On the Okamoto mission, see Martin, pp. 204–5. The German report on the May 19 conversation is in Ribbentrop to Stahmer No. 847 of 25 May 1943, AA, St.S., "Japan," Bd. 12, fr. 17248–52; Oshima's report No. 549 of 21 May 1943 is in NA, RG 457, SRDJ 37447–52. See also Martin, p. 181; *ADAP*, E, 6, No. 41.

58 On Oshima, see Carl Boyd, *The Extraordinary Envoy: General Hiroshi Oshima and Diplomacy in the Third Reichs, 1934–1939* (Washington: University Press of America, 1980); on the

Anti-Comintern Pact, see Weinberg, *Foreign Policy 1933–36*, pp. 342–48; Krebs, *Japans Deutschlandpolitik*, pp. 15ff.

59 The point is made by the sub-title of Johanna M. Meskill's book: *Hitler and Japan: The Hollow Alliance*.

14: THE HALT ON THE EUROPEAN FRONTS

1 On the financing of these and other similar regimes, see BA, R 2/271.

2 On the Brazilian army contingent, see McCann, *Brazilian–American Alliance*, chap. 12; on the air force contingent, see David M. Todd, "Flight of the Ostrich — The Brazilian Air Force in World War II," *Air Power History* 37, No. 4 (Winter 1990), 30–41.

3 Note the German navy study of Oct. 29, 1944 showing that, if Sweden joined Germany's enemies, Germany was now too weak to occupy her (OKM, Skl, 1. "Studie: Lagebetrachtung für den Fall eines Kriegseintritts Schwedens auf der Seite unserer Gegner," BA/MA, RM 7/163, f. 266–316, 355ff).

4 See the reports of 7, 13, 14 July 1944 in Boberach (ed.), *Meldungen aus dem Reich*, 17: 6630–36, 6636–40, 6645–51.

5 BA/MA, Nachlass Weichs, N 19/3, f. 205–1944. One possible supporter of any new regime, Field Marshal Rommel, had been injured shortly before. Until July 20, the British had assumed that the German military would dump Hitler at the right moment to get a better peace and that there would, therefore, be a central government in place through which Germany could be administered (Kettennacker, "Die alliierte Kontrolle," p. 57). The British clearly did not have a realistic picture of the devotion of the higher German military to the Hitler regime.

6 A collection of pictures from trials of individuals involved in the July 20 plot is in the Library of Congress, Prints and Photographs Division, Lot. No. 3675.

7 Steinert, *Hitler's War*, pp. 264–73.

8 Orlow, *History of the Nazi Party*, pp. 462ff.

9 The Japanese were naturally most concerned about the upheaval in Germany. Reports by Oshima are in his Nos. 722 and unnumbered, 20 July 1944, NA, RG 457, SRDJ 65115–16, 728 of 21 July, 65222–24, 738 and 741 of 25 July, 65739–47 and 65636–42 (a German report on this Oshima–Ribbentrop meeting of 23 July in *ADAP*, E, 8, No. 133), 779 of 2 Aug., 66941–46; Japanese military attaché reports: Berlin No. 304 of 26 July, SRA 10078, Madrid No. 304 of 26 July, SRA 12890–92; Japanese naval attaché reports Berlin Nos. 273 of 24 July, SRNA 2017, 293(?) of 3 Aug., SRNA 2070–72, report of 28 Aug., SRNA 2254–58. An American analysis of the Japanese materials is in CinC U.S. Fleet and CNO, Pacific Strategic Intelligence Section, "Japanese Estimates Regarding Germany's Ability to Continue the Struggle (August–December 1944)," 22 Jan. 1945, SRH-068.

10 See Donovan's memoranda on the plot for Roosevelt of 22 and 29 July 1944, FDRL, PSF Box 168, OSS Reports July 1944. Roosevelt, who was leaving to meet his Pacific commanders in Hawaii, noted on July 21 that he might have to come back if "German revolt gets worse! I fear though that it won't" (*FDR Letters*, 2: 1525).

11 Wolfgang Bleyer (ed.), "Pläne der faschistischen Führung zum totalen Krieg," *Zeitschrift für Geschichtswissenschaft* 27 (1969), 1312–29.

12 Peter Longerich (ed.), "Joseph Goebbels und der Totale Krieg: Eine unbekannte Denkschrift des Propagandaministers vom 18. Juli 1944," *VjZ* 35 (1987), 289–314.

13 A comprehensive study in David Yeltsin, "The Volkssturm," PhD diss., Univ. of North Carolina–Chapel Hill, 1989.

14 An introductory survey in Ursula von Gersdorff, *Frauen im Kriegsdienst 1914–1945* (Stuttgart: Deutsche Verlags-Anstalt, 1969), pp. 60–76, 138ff. See also Franz W. Seidler,

Blitzmädchen: die Geschichte der Helferinnen der deutschen Wehrmacht im 2. Weltkrieg (Munich: Bernard & Graefe, 1979).

15 On the Flakhelfer, see Ludwig Schätz, *Schüler-Soldaten: Die Geschichte der Luftwaffenhelfer im zweiten Weltkrieg* (Darmstadt: Thesen-Verlag, 1974), an introduction greatly in need of revision; and Roman Bleistein, "Hitlers jüngste Soldaten," *Stimmen der Zeit* 200, No. 1 (1982), 61–63, a summary of the existing literature.

16 Steinert, *Hitler's War*, p. 280. An interesting, though very pro-Nazi, account written right after the war by a true believer, of some of these young women who ended up in a Waffen-SS anti-aircraft unit near Prague, is in Jutta Rüdiger (ed.), *Zur Problematik von Soldatinnen: Der Kampfeinsatz von Flakhelferinnen im Zweiten Weltkrieg, Berichte und Dokumentationen* (Lindhorst: Askania, 1987).

17 Hans-Erich Volkmann, "Das Vlasov-Unternehmen zwischen Ideologie und Pragmatismus," *MGM* 12 (1972), 130; "Vertrauliche Informationen Nr. 206/44," 19 Sep. 1944, BA, Oberheitmann, ZSg. 109/51, f. 116, Nr. 253/44 of 14 Nov., f. 80, Nr. 260/44 of 22 Dec., f. 90; Oshima to Tokyo No. 1147 of 10 Oct. 1944, NA, RG 457, SRDJ 74486–88.

18 Volkmann, "Das Vlasov-Unternehmen," p. 149 n 107.

19 Dallin, *German Rule in Russia*, pp. 613ff; Oshima to Tokyo No. 1298 of 28 Nov. 1944, NA, RG 457. SRDJ 80493–94.

20 Japanese military attaché to Italy Nos. 145 of 10 June and 241 of 24 Oct. 1944, NA, RG 457, SRA 11659–62, 13089–91; Hidaka (Venice) to Tokyo No. 280 of 1 Sep. 1944, SRDJ 70053–61.

21 There is extensive documentation on the Manfred Weiss question in *ADAP*, E, 8. Most of the relevant documents are published in facsimile in Braham (ed.) *Destruction of Hungarian Jewry*, 2: chap. 8. The German pretence that these were wartime measures was quickly penetrated by the Hungarians when they saw that the contracts were for 25 years. Hitler's approval of the arrangement is referred to in Braham, 2, No. 428.

22 Boog, *Luftwaffenführung*, pp. 147–48.

23 The most important single work on this topic, that by Macartney, is entitled *October Fifteenth* because this was the date of Horthy's failed attempt to take Hungary out of the war. For Hitler's ideas about a Szálasi coup in late Sep. 1944, see Jodl Diary transcript for 23 Sep. 1944, Imperial War Museum. On the fighting, see Ziemke, *Stalingrad to Berlin*, pp. 378–86; Erickson, *Road to Berlin*, pp. 384–97; Glantz, *Soviet Military Deception*, pp. 440–67.

24 This is from Szálasi's report to Oshima on 4 Dec. right after seeing Hitler; see Oshima to Tokyo No. 1375 of 5 Dec. 1944, NA, RG 457, SRDJ 81524. The German reports on the two Hitler-Szálasi talks are in Andreas Hillgruber (ed.), *Staatsmänner und Diplomaten bei Hitler*, 2 vols. (Frankfurt/M: Bernard & Graefe, 1967–70), 2: 520–36; only the second one is printed in *ADAP*, E, 8, No. 313. Note that the German reports are dated 7 and 8 Dec. so that the discrepancy between Szálasi's comments to Oshima and the German record prepared by Schmidt cannot simply be resolved in favor of the German record. There are no useful details in the relevant portion of Schmidt's memoirs, *Statist auf diplomatischer Bühne* (Bonn: Athenäum, 1950), pp. 574–75. On German relations with the Szálasi government in general, see Szöllösi-Janze, *Die Pfeilkreuzlerbewegung in Ungarn*, pp. 301–23, 413ff.

25 Ziemke, *Stalingrad to Berlin*, pp. 340–42, 344, 416.

26 Ibid., pp. 408–9; Erickson, *Road to Berlin*, pp. 421–22.

27 Grier, "Hitler's Baltic Strategy"; Erickson, *Road to Berlin*, pp. 420–21; note Dönitz's comment of 24/25 Aug. 1944 in Salewski, *Seekriegsleitung*, 2: 648.

28 There is a detailed account of the planning for the great Soviet winter offensive in Erickson, *Road to Berlin*, pp. 422–30, but the map which accompanies this text is filled with errors in both the borders and the front lines shown. There is now a good account

with much better maps in Christopher Duffy, *Red Storm on the Reich: The Soviet March on Germany, 1945* (New York: Atheneum, 1991), chap. 3. The very effective Soviet deception projects for their offensive are described by David Glantz in Hitchcock (ed.), *The Intelligence Revolution*, pp. 132–86.

29 The most useful study of the impact of logistics on strategy in the West remains Ruppenthal's two volumes, *The European Theater of Operations*, in the U.S. Army in World War II series; see also van Creveld, *Supplying War*, chap. 7.

30 Ruppenthal, 2: 507.

31 Ibid., pp. 134–39. This account also covers the other truck supply routes.

32 Very helpful is the discussion in the memoirs of the British officer in charge of intelligence on Eisenhower's staff, Sir Kenneth Strong, *Intelligence at the Top: The Recollections of an Intelligence Officer* (Garden City, N.Y.: Doubleday, 1969), pp. 197ff.

33 See Churchill's Personal Minute 1159/4 of 3 Dec. 1944, PRO, WO 259/79.

34 Brooke to Montgomery, tel. 1450A/3 of 3 Oct. 1944, Liddell Hart Centre, Alanbrooke Papers 14/33.

35 There are some details in Ruppental, *European Theater of Operations*, 2: chap. 11; there is a biting and rather excessive critique in Martin van Creveld, *Fighting Power: German and U.S. Army Performance, 1939–1945* (Westport, Conn: Greenwood Press, 1982). The whole issue was greatly complicated by the fact that the commander of the rear area (Com Z), General J.C.H. Lee, was a rather controversial figure.

36 Note David Eisenhower's assertion (*Eisenhower at War*, p. 499) that in October the Germans outnumbered the Allies in combat troops. The Allied situation was not helped by the fact that Brooke was as negative in his evaluation of Tedder as he was of Eisenhower (note the full text of his diary for 12 Dec. 1944).

37 Jeffrey Ethell, *Mustang: A Documentary History of the P-51* (London: Jane's, 1981), pp. 97–99.

38 A short history of the ME 262 is in Eugene M. Emme, *Hitler's Blitzbomber*, Air University Documentary Research Study (Maxwell AFB, Alabama, 1951); a summary in Hermann Jung, *Die Ardennen-Offensive 1944/45* (Göttingen: Musterschmidt, 1971), pp. 68–72. Murray, *Luftwaffe*, pp. 238–39, comes to a conclusion very similar to that given here. In any case, Hitler had little faith in the Luftwaffe by the fall of 1944; from Sep. 17 to Oct. 28 its Chief of Staff was forbidden to attend the situation conference at headquarters!

39 For the Ardennes offensive, as the Germans called it, or the Battle of the Bulge as the Americans named it, see Hugh M. Cole, *The Ardennes: Battle of the Bulge* (Washington: GPO, 1965); Jung, *Die Ardennen-Offensive*; Lamb, Montgomery, chap. 12. The account in Eisenhower, *Eisenhower at War*, is most interesting.

40 Jung, pp. 31–34.

41 Ibid., chap. 5, gives a good account. A key piece of evidence is the diary of General Kreipe, Chief of Staff of the German air force, for 16 Sep. 1944, published in ibid., p. 218.

42 Weinberg, *World in the Balance*, pp. 53–74.

43 It can be seen that I do not share Jung's view (pp. 97–100) that Hitler had a serious political objective with the offensive.

44 Jung, chap. 6.

45 A brief summary in Weigley, *Eisenhower's Lieutenants*, pp. 475–76, 495–96. In detail, James J. Weingartner, *Crossroads of Death: The Story of the Malmedy Massacre and Trial* (Berkeley, Calif.: Univ. of California Press, 1973). Jung never mentions the event.

46 On this unit, the 150th SS Panzer Brigade, see Jung, pp. 126–28. In U.S. Army trials, 16 Germans were executed and 3 were acquitted; see First U.S. Army, *Report of Operations (August 1944–22 February 1945)* (Washington: GPO, 1945), 2: 51 and 4: 229. There was also a small German parachute unit which had no impact on the fighting (Jung, pp. 128–29, 146–47).

47 It is worth noting that Brooke and Montgomery, who despised most American generals, wanted to have Patton transferred to command the 9th Army north of the Ardennes (Brooke to Montgomery, 1 Dec. 1944, Liddell Hart Centre, Alanbrooke Papers 14/2/15; Simpson to Brooke, 3 Dec. 1944, Alanbrooke Papers 14/3). See also Paul G. Munch, "Patton's Staff and the Battle of the Bulge," *Military Review* 70, No. 5 (1990), 46–54.

48 A good account in Eisenhower, *Eisenhower at War*, pp. 567–73.

49 Montgomery to Brooke, M2 388 of 22 Dec. 1944, Liddell Hart Centre, Alanbrooke Papers, 14/36.

50 Montgomery to Simpson, 25 Dec. 1944, ibid., 14/2/36. The relevant passages have been omitted in Bryant, 2: 278–79.

51 A balanced assessment, rather favorable to Montgomery, in Eisenhower, *Eisenhower at War*, pp. 575ff.

52 Years later, on June 8, 1959, General Ismay, who had been Churchill's immediate military assistant and representative, wrote to General (then President) Eisenhower, "If only someone would muzzle, or better still chloroform Monty, I should be spared the constant danger of blood pressure. I have come to the conclusion that his love of publicity is a disease, like alcoholism or taking drugs, and that it sends him equally mad." Liddell Hart Centre, Ismay Papers IV/Eis/131.

53 Wyant, *Sandy Patch*, chap. 20, is the most recent account.

54 See Jung, *Die Ardennen-Offensive*, pp. 186–87, for a summary; Horst Boog, "1. Januar 1945: Operation 'Bodenplatte'," *Luftwaffe* 16, No. 1 (1975), 32–34, is more detailed.

55 Montgomery to Brooke, 7 Dec. 1944, Liddell Hart Centre, Alanbrooke Papers, 14/2/20. Other portions of this long letter are in Bryant, 2: 264–65.

56 Oshima to Tokyo No. 1298 of 16 Nov. 1944, NA, RG 457, SRDJ 78970–84.

57 The assertions in Guderian's son's 1974 correspondence with David Irving about this issue in Institut für Zeitgeschichte, Guderian Papers, are borne out by the Jodl Diary for 29 Dec. 1944 (Imperial War Museum, AL 930/3–4).

58 Ruppenthal, *The European Theater of Operations*, 2: 124.

59 On a primitive device beginning to catch snorkel equipped submarines, see Comnavea to Cominch and CNO, NCR 7498 of 24 Jan. 1945, NA, RG 457, SRMN 46, pp. 84–85.

60 A helpful survey in Salewski, *Seekriegsleitung*, 2: 496–528.

61 This is completely ignored in the account of John Ehrman, *Grand Strategy*, 6: 16–18.

62 The JU-290 could fly 3800 miles (Enzio Angelucci, *Rand McNally Encyclopedia of Military Aircraft, 1914–1980* [New York: Military Press, 1983], pp. 351, 356).

63 Jung, *Die Ardennen-Offensive*, pp. 53–54.

64 Willi A. Boelcke (ed.), *Deutschlands Rüstung im Zweiten Weltkrieg: Hitlers Konferenzen mit Albert Speer 1942–1945* Frankfurt/M: Athenaion, 1969), pp. 368–69; cf. Wolfgang Birkenfeld, *Der synthetische Treibstoff* (Göttingen: Musterschmidt, 1964).

65 Boelcke, *Deutschlands Rüstung*, p. 370.

66 On the oil offensive and ultra, see Murray, *Luftwaffe*, pp. 258ff. The Americans could confirm the correctness of their strategy by reading Japanese Ambassador Oshima's report on Speer's explanation of this difference and its significance (Oshima to Tokyo No. 814 of 11 Aug. 1944, NA, RG 457, SRDJ 67653–59).

67 See Boelcke, *Deutschlands Rüstung*, pp. 416–18. For a balanced asessment of Speer's views in the fall and winter of 1944, see Alfred C. Mierzejewski, "When Did Albert Speer Give Up?" *Historical Journal* 31 (1988), 391–97.

68 Murray, *Luftwaffe*, pp. 260–61.

69 See the excellent study by Mierzejewski, *Collapse of the German War Economy*.

70 Hastings, *Bomber Command*, pp. 397–405; Saward, *"Bomber" Harris*, chap. 22. Evidently the Chief of the Air Staff, Marshal of the RAF Sir Charles Portal, realized that Churchill was not about to relieve Harris, so there was nothing to be done, an extraordinary situation without parallel in either the British or the American conduct of the war.

71 Mierzejewski, *Collapse of the German War Economy*, pp. 105, 130. There is a picture in Jacobsen and Dollinger, *Zweite Weltkrieg*, 3: 145.

72 Mierzejewski, pp. 104–5, 128–30. This success of Bomber Command included the blocking of the key Rhine–Herne canal by dropping bridges into it.

73 Boelcke, *Deutschlands Rüstung*, pp. 337–39.

74 Kreipe Diary for 2 Nov. 1944 in Jung, *Die Ardennen-Offensive*, pp. 228–29. Kreipe had been Chief of Staff since Aug. 1944 (on him see Boog, *Luftwaffenführung*, pp. 299–301). Already on Sep. 23, 1944, the Japanese naval representatives in Germany had relayed to Tokyo their assessment that there would be no negotiated peace in Europe; an unconditional surrender on all fronts was most likely (Japanese naval attaché Berlin to Tokyo "N" Serial 255 of 23 Sep. 1944, NA, RG 457, SRNA 2559–62).

75 Arno Rose, *Radikaler Luftkampf: die Geschichte deutscher Rammjäger* (Stuttgart: Motorbuch, 1977), is of some interest but neither comprehensive nor scholarly.

76 The suicide mission idea appears to have originated with Speer, developing out of earlier projects to bomb the Rybinsk hydro-electric dam north of Moscow at a time when such targets were still barely within the range of German long-range bombers (Boelcke, *Deutschlands Rüstung*, 6/7Dec. 1943, p. 319; 22/23 May 1944, p. 371; 19–22 June 1944, pp. 389–90).

77 Japanese naval attaché No. 658 of 5 Nov. 1944, NA, RG 457, SRNA 3081–82, and Tokyo's reply No. 021 of 18 Nov. 1944, SRNA 3154–55; Japanese naval attaché No. 745 of 29 Nov. 1944, SRNA 3344–46.

78 By late Dec. 1944 the British troop diversion to Greece had reached 80,000. Brooke commented on this with disgust in his diary (Liddell Hart Centre, Alanbrooke Papers, 23–30 Dec. 1944), but never compared its impact on the war with the operation Anvil–Dragoon which he had opposed so vehemently. The realities in Greece surely validated Marshall's earlier concern about the syphoning effect of operations in the Eastern Mediterranean on Allied strength.

79 At Marshall's insistence, Dill was buried in Arlington National Cemetery, where President Truman dedicated the equestrian monument which marks his grave (Pogue, *Marshall*, 3: 481–83). Dill's position as head of the British Joint Services Mission was taken by Field Marshal Sir Henry Maitland Wilson; the latter never occupied the informal but central role in British–U.S. relations which Dill had held.

80 On Baffle, see PRO, WO 106/3286, 5693. There is an extraordinary resemblance to the 1942 project for a British–U.S. air force to assist the Russians on the southern portion of the Eastern Front, which had been agreed to by Stalin and then fell apart when it became clear that the Soviets wanted only the planes, not the units.

81 See note 24, above.

82 Note Alan J. Foster, "*The Times* and Appeasement: The Second Phase," *JCH* 16 (1981), 441–66.

15: THE FINAL ASSAULT ON GERMANY

1 Motter, *Persian Corridor*, p. 483. About another third each went the northern route and across the Pacific.

2 See the COMINCH U.S. Navy 17 Jan. 1945 "Summary of Radio Intelligence" comparison of the German Naval Attaché Tokyo report to Berlin on Japanese naval losses with American estimates, in NA, RG 457, SRNS 1010.

3 The reports of the German Naval Attaché Tokyo of 19 and 23 Jan. 1945 are in War Dept. G-2 "Magic Far Eastern Summary," Nos. 309 of 23 Jan., 310 of 24 Jan., 315 of 29 Jan. 1945, NA, RG 457.

4 Salewski, *Seekriegsleitung*, 2: 448–56.

5 Note Kaufmann, "Im Bunker der Reichskanzlei März 1945," Hamburg, Forschungsstelle für Geschichte des Nationalsozialismus, Krogmann Papers, 11 k 21.

6 A detailed report on July 20 with considerable information from a member of the conspiracy (perhaps Hans Bernd Gisevius) was sent by the Acting Director of the OSS to Roosevelt on 1 Feb. 1945, FDRL, PSF Box 171, OSS Reports, February 1945.

7 This is one of the major findings of the USSBS documented in its report, *The Effects of Strategic Bombing on German Morale*, 2 vols. (Washington: GPO, 1946–47).

8 See Steinert, *Hitler's War*, pp. 290–305, for a survey entitled: "The Last Winter of War." A very good U.S. Office of Naval Intelligence analysis of 27 Feb. 1945 is in NA, RG 319, ID File, ID No. 121653.

9 Note the letters of the German Minister of Finance, Graf Lutz Schwerin von Krosigk, to Goebbels in Feb. and Mar. 1945, in BA, R 2/24242. A memorandum by Admiral Assmann of 3 Feb. 1945, asserting that the war was certainly lost, argued for unconditional ending of hostilities in the West; another form of trying to split the Allies but with the assumption that all of Germany would be occupied. The difference would be that the Oder river rather than the Elbe would provide the demarcation line between the Western and Soviet zones of occupation (BA/MA, III M 502/4).

10 Oshima's reports to Tokyo Nos. 19 of 7 Jan., 24 of 8 Jan., 36 of 11 Jan. 1945, NA, RG 457, SRDJ 85803–15, 85746–50, 86207–8; but then see his No. 178 of 15 Feb. 1945, SRDJ 90893.

11 Joseph Goebbels, *Tagebücher 1945: Die letzten Aufzeichnungen* (Hamburg: Hoffman & Campe, 1977), 5 and 12 Mar. 1945, pp. 112–13, 204.

12 Hansjakob Stehle, "Deutsche Friedensfühler bei den Westmächten im Februar/März 1945," *VjZ* 30 (1982), 538–55; Joachim von Ribbentrop, *The Ribbentrop Memoirs*, trans. Oliver Watson (London: Weidenfeld & Nicolson, 1954), pp. 171–72; Gustav Hilger and Alfred G. Meyer, *The Incompatible Allies: A Memoir History of German–Soviet Relations, 1918–1941* (New York: Macmillan, 1953), p. 340; Reimer Hansen, "Ribbentrops Friedensfühler im Frühjahr 1945," *Geschichte in Wissenschaft und Unterricht* 18 (1967), 716–30; Werner von Schmieden, "Notiz betreffend den deutschen Friedensfühler in der Schweitz Anfang 1945," 30 June 1947, Institut für Zeitgeschichte, Z.S. 604; Werner Dankwort, "Infernalische Reise," AA, Dankwort Papers, f. 79–99; Fleischhauer, *Sonderfrieden*, pp. 267–75; Goebbels, *Tagebücher 1945*, pp. 280, 287, 290–91, 339. British documents on the soundings of Fritz Hesse in Stockholm are in C 1000/45/18, PRO, FO 371/46782, C 1321, 1322/45/18, FO 371/46783. Oshima reported on Ribbentrop's preference for and thoughts about peace with the U.S.S.R. in his Nos. 362–64 of 31 Mar. 1945, NA, RG 457, SRDJ 95939–40, 95941–54, 96104–6, and his No. 375 of 6 Apr. 1945, SRDJ 96751–56. See also Stockholm to Tokyo No. 181 of 23 Mar. 1945, SRDJ 95647–50.

13 On this topic, see documents in BA, R 2/11602, 11609; Japanese military attaché Berlin to Tokyo No. 915 of 19 Jan. 1945, NA, RG 457, SRA 15610–11; Volkmann, "Das Vlasov-Unternehmen," p. 152. Note also the 1945 budget for Sofindus, the secret German organization for penetrating the Spanish economy, in BA, R 2/17316c.

14 Müller, "Gaskriegsvorbereitungen," p. 46; Gellermann, *Der Krieg der nicht stattfand*, pp. 175–77.

15 In the absence of access to Soviet archives, these issues are very difficult to reconstruct. The two best attempts appear to be Alexander Fischer's *Sowjetische Deutschlandpolitik im Zweiten Weltkrieg 1941–1945* (Stuttgart: Deutsche Verlags-Anstalt, 1975), and the first chapter in Gregory W. Sandford, *From Hitler to Ulbricht: The Communist Reconstruction of East Germany, 1945–1946* (Princeton, N.J.: Princeton Univ. Press, 1983). An earlier study, Boris Meissner, *Russland, die Westmächte, und Deutschland: Die sowjetische Deutschlandpolitik 1943–1953* (Hamburg: Nölke, 1953), is still of interest.

16 An excellent account in Bruce R. Kuniholm, *The Origins of the Cold War in the Near East:*

Great Power Conflict and Diplomacy in Iran, Turkey, and Greece (Princeton, N.J.: Princeton Univ. Press, 1980). For a brief background on the Kars and Ardahan areas, see ibid., p. 258 n 124. A map illustrating Soviet territorial claims on Turkey is on p. 289. This map also shows the Greek Aegean port of Dedeagatch (Alexandroupolis) which Stalin suggested as a possible Soviet base during the Potsdam meeting. See also Önder, *Türkische Aussenpolitik*, pp. 242–45.

17 A summary in Paul R. Magocsi, *The Shaping of a National Identity: Subcarpathian Rus', 1848–1948* (Cambridge, Mass.: Harvard Univ. Press, 1978), pp. 252–55. There is a more detailed account in Frantisek Nemec and Vladimir Moudry, *The Soviet Seizure of Subcarpathian Ruthenia* (Toronto: William R. Anderson, 1955). According to a report by the American ambassador in Moscow of 6 Jan. 1945, the issue of Ruthenia was still open at that time (Stettinius to Roosevelt and enclosure, 8 Jan. 1945, FDRL, PSF Box 68, Russia 1945), but in fact it had been resolved on the spot. There is a somewhat different account in Mastny, *Russia's Road*, pp. 227–29.

18 Rather polemical but quite helpful, R.C. Raack, "Stalin Fixes the Oder-Neisse Line," *JCH* 25 (1990), 467–88.

19 Luza, *Transfer of the Sudeten Germans*, pp. 236, 240–41. The issue is reviewed in greater detail in Brandes, *Grossbritannien*.

20 This is a major theme of Terry's *Poland's Place in Europe*.

21 The American estimate was that at the time of the 1939 census about nine million Germans lived in the portion of pre-war Germany and Danzig that were to be incorporated into Poland. There is a helpful map in *FRUS, 1945, Conferences at Malta and Yalta*, facing p. 233. When the British Cabinet agreed to the Curzon Line and vast increases in Poland at Germany's expense in the west, Churchill made it clear that whatever territory was transferred should be cleared of its German inhabitants; WM(45) War Cabinet 7(45) Confidential Annex, 22 Jan. 1945, PRO, CAB 65/51.

22 See the document from FDRL cited in n. 17, above, and Cienciala, "The Activities of the Polish Communists."

23 On the British, see S.F.V. Dornison, *Civil Affairs and Military Government* (London: HMSO, 1966), and *Civil Affairs and Military Government: North West Europe, 1944–1946* (London: HMSO, 1961) in the British official history series. On the American side there is a vast literature because of earlier access to the archives; an excellent introduction is Earl F. Ziemke, *The U.S. Army in the Occupation of Germany, 1944–1946* (Washington: GPO, 1975). There is now also a major collection of documents from the archives of both countries, published under the auspices of the Federal Republic of Germany, entitled *Dokumente zur Deutschlandpolitik*, 1st series: *Vom 3. September 1939 bis 8. Mai 1945* (Frankfurt/M: Metzner, 1984–). Summaries of the perspectives of many countries may be found in Manfred Messerschmidt and Ekkhart Gulh (eds.), *Die Zukunft des Reiches: Gegner, Verbündete und Neutrale (1943–1945)* (Herford: Mittler, 1990).

24 The arguments within the British government are delineated in John E. Farquharson, "Hilfe für den Feind: Die britische Debatte um Nahrungslieferungen an Deutschland," *VjZ* (1989), 253–78. See also Ross, *Foreign Office Attitudes*, p. 527.

25 The memoirs of the chief British representative, Lord Strang, *Home and Abroad* (London: Deutsch, 1956) chap. 6, remain useful. See also Donald J. Nelson, *Wartime Origins of the Berlin Dilemma* (University, Alab.: Univ. of Alabama Press, 1978); William M. Franklin, "Zonal Boundaries and Access to Berlin," *World Politics* 16 (1963), 1–31; Tony Sharp, *The Wartime Alliance and the Zonal Division of Germany* (London: Oxford Univ. Press), 1975; Kettenacker, "Alliance," pp. 450–54, and *Krieg zur Friedenssicherung*, pp. 270–302. See the War Cabinet Post Hostilities Planning Staff's memorandum, "Dismemberment of Germany," 25 Aug. 1944, and related documents in PRO, CAB 119/134. On broader issues, see Anne Deighton, *Impossible Peace: The Division of Germany and the Origins of the Cold War* (Oxford: Clarendon Press, 1990), chaps. 1–2.

26 See Franklin, "Zonal Boundaries," p. 17. A good survey in Ziemke, *The U.S. Army*, pp. 115–26.

27 The map drawn by Roosevelt before the Cairo Conference has been reproduced in Ziemke, *The U.S. Army*, facing p. 116; it was earlier reproduced in Matloff, *Strategic Planning 1943–44*, facing p. 341, where its origin is stated. See also the memorandum for Admiral Wilson Brown recounting the issue as of 31 Aug. 1944 in FDRL, Map Room 167, Naval Aide, Germany; and Roosevelt's 20 Sep. 1944 map for a division of Germany after peace in PSF Safe File, Cont. 4, Germany.

28 On the origins of the Bremen enclave, see Gretchen Skidmore, "The American Occupation of the Bremen Enclave, 1945–47," MA thesis, Univ. of North Carolina–Chapel Hill, 1989; and documents in PRO, CAB 119/134–35. On Roosevelt's reversal of his insistence on the northwestern zone, see Matloff, *Strategic Planning 1943–44*, p. 511.

29 Ziemke, *The U.S. Army*, chaps. 1, 2, 6, 7.

30 John M. Blum (ed.), *From the Morgenthau Diaries*, 3 vols. (Boston: Houghton Mifflin, 1959–67) is very helpful; the original materials are in FDRL and make fascinating, if at times also a bit tedious, reading.

31 Warren F. Kimball, *Swords or Plowshares? The Morgenthau Plan for Defeated Germany, 1943–1946* (Philadelphia: Lippincott, 1976); McJimsey, *Harry Hopkins*, pp. 342–47.

32 The text of the document Morgenthau gave Roosevelt in the fall of 1944 is photographically reproduced at the front of Morgenthau's book, *Germany is Our Problem* (New York: Harper, 1945). On his plan for the book, see Morgenthau to Roosevelt, 23 Mar. 1943, and Roosevelt to Morgenthau, 28 Mar. 1943, FDRL, OF 198. A more careful look at the issues surrounding Morgenthau's proposals for Germany may also make it easier to understand his key role in pushing General Lucius D. Clay for the position of military governor of the American zone of occupation (see Jean E. Smith [ed.], *The Papers of General Lucius D. Clay: Germany 1945–1949*, 2 vols. [Bloomington, Ind.: Indiana Univ. Press, 1974], 1: xxxiii–iv).

33 See *FDR Letters*, 2: 1534–35; Morgenthau Diary 19 Aug. and 2 Sep. 1944, FDRL, Morgenthau Presidential Diary, 6: 1386–88, 1422–26.

34 Roosevelt's views of Germany and its future have not been examined with sufficient care. An excellent start for the period before 1933 is made in Michaela Hönicke, "Franklin D. Roosevelt's View of Germany before 1933: Formative Experiences for a Future President," MA thesis, University of North Carolina–Chapel Hill, 1989. Gietz's *Die neue Alte Welt*, chap. 8, is of considerable help though like most others he has failed to look at the map accompanying the Morgenthau Plan and thus has missed both its nature and the main reason why it was abandoned.

35 Dallek, *Roosevelt and Foreign Policy*, p. 468; Morgenthau Diary 9 Sep. 1944, FDRL, Morgenthau Presidential Diary, 6: 1431–32.

36 Ibid., 15 Sep. 1944, 6: 1444–45; Kimball, *Swords or Plowshares?* pp. 39–40. It should be noted that British leaders were hardly surprised by the proposal; see, e.g., the 53 page memorandum of John Wheeler-Bennett of 31 May 1943, "On What to Do with Germany," U 2703/2399/70, PRO, FO 371/35453. See also Churchill's enthusiastic report to the Cabinet—and the British Cabinet's great satisfaction—in WM(44) War Cabinet 123, Conclusions Confidential Annex of 18 Sep. 1944, CAB 65/47.

37 Ziemke, *U.S. Army and the Occupation of Germany*, pp. 106ff.

38 The maps which accompany the 12 July 1944 War Cabinet Chiefs of Staff Committee report, "Occupation of Germany: Allotment of Zones," assume that Germany would lose East Prussia, Upper Silesia, and the easternmost portion of Pomerania (PRO, CAB 119/134). Thinking begins to change during the winter of 1944–45, see C 15747, 16177/62/55, 14 and 24 Nov. 1944, FO 371/39436. By late Jan. 1945, when it was becoming obvious that the Soviet Union was installing the Lublin Poles in

liberated Poland, the British were considering going back to the earlier maps at least in theory rather than agree to what they recognized would be a transfer of 8–9 million rather than 5–6 million Germans (WM[45] War Cabinet 10 [45] Conclusions, Confidential Annex, 26 Jan. 1945, CAB 65/51). These shifts of opinion have to be connected with the plans for Germany, as opposed to a body of scholarship which has almost invariably assumed that everyone was always talking about the borders which were eventually adopted.

39 A useful introduction remains Anton W. DePorte, *De Gaulle's Foreign Policy 1944–1946* (Cambridge, Mass.: Harvard Univ. Press, 1968); now substantially up-dated by John W. Young, *France, the Cold War, and the Western Alliance, 1944–49: French Foreign Policy and Post-war Europe* (New York: St. Martin's, 1990), chaps. 1–2, which is based on extensive access to French archives..

40 The key work is still Marcel Vigneras, *Rearming the French* (Washington: GPO, 1957). The relationship of American equipment of French forces to the reestablishment of a major role for France in Europe awaits scholarly investigation.

41 Ziemke, *Stalingrad to Berlin*, pp. 383–86; Erickson, *Road to Berlin*, pp. 433–46.

42 Ziemke, *Stalingrad to Berlin*, pp. 432–37; Erickson, *Road to Berlin*, pp. 508–9. According to Albert Speer, *Spandauer Tagebücher*, (Frankfurt/M: Propyläen 1975), pp. 32–33, the offensive was also designed to rally all of the Balkans.

43 Ziemke, *Stalingrad to Berlin*, pp. 448–54.

44 On the Soviet January offensive, see ibid., chap. 19; Erickson, *Road to Berlin*, pp. 426–29, chap. 7; Glantz, *Soviet Military Deception*, pp. 471–99; Duffy, *Red Storm*, chaps. 5–8.

45 Erickson, *Road to Berlin*, pp. 428, 449.

46 The reports of Japanese observers are especially revealing; note Japanese military attaché Italy No. 297 of 25 Jan. 1945, NA, RG 457, SRA 15854–64; Oshima to Tokyo No. 130 of 4 Feb. 1945, SRDJ 89327–31. There is a semi-fictional account which captures the atmosphere extraordinarily well in Gerhard Kramer, *We Shall March Again*, trans. Anthony G. Powell (New York: Putnam's, 1955) (German ed. *Wir werden weiter marschieren* [Berlin: L. Blanvalet, 1952]). This book is in my opinion one of the best recreations of the atmosphere of war on the German side: the occupation of France, anti-partisan warfare in the East, and the great German retreats.

47 On the German fighting to break out of and to hold East Prussia, and the Soviet success in containing and eventually crushing the two German armies trapped there, see Erickson, *Road to Berlin*, pp. 468–70; Glantz, *Soviet Military Deception*, pp. 402–14; Duffy, *Red Storm*, chaps. 12–14, 17–18.

48 Ziemke, *Stalingrad to Berlin*, chap. 20; Erickson, *Road to Berlin*, pp. 463, 472–76, 517–26; Duffy, *Red Storm*, chaps. 9–12 (the Stargard offensive is described on pp. 181–85). Again the reports of the Japanese ambassador in Berlin are of interest, see his Nos. 198 of 19 Feb. and 207 of 21 Feb. 1945, NA, RG 457, SRDJ 91303–8, 91682–88.

49 Hopkins went to Europe ahead of Roosevelt to prepare some of the decisions (McJimsey, *Harry Hopkins*, pp. 342–47).

50 Lamb, *Montgomery*, chap. 13.

51 See Gaddis, *US and Origins*, pp. 157–65. An excellent summary of the literature and controversies, especially about Roosevelt's role, in Klaus Schwabe, "Roosevelt und Jalta," in Jürgen Heideking et al. (eds.), *Wege in die Zeitgeschichte* (Berlin—New York: de Gruyter, 1989), pp. 460–72. An early very thoughtful review of all the major conferences with the Russians in John Snell, *Illusion and Necessity: The Diplomacy of Global War, 1939–1945* (Boston: Houghton Mifflin, 1963), chap. 4.

52 It appears that Hopkins played a major role in getting Roosevelt to change his mind on the role of France, see McJimsey, *Harry Hopkins*, pp. 363–70.

53 Note Stettinius to Roosevelt, 18(?) Nov. 1944, FDRL, PSF Box 68, Russia 1944.

54 Churchill informed the Cabinet that this was a very good concession to make and a

doubtful Cabinet went along; War Cabinet 16(45) Conclusions, Confidential Annex, 8 Feb. 1945. See also Dallek, *Roosevelt and Foreign Policy*, pp. 466–67.

55 Gaddis, *US and Origins*, pp. 165–71; C. David Thompkins, *Senator Arthur H. Vandenberg: The Evolution of a Modern Republican, 1884–1945* (Lansing, Mich.: Michigan State Univ. Press, 1970), pp. 235–40.

56 See Fischer, *Sowjetische Deutschlandpolitik*, pp. 122–34; Ross, *Foreign Office and the Kremlin*, p. 55.

57 Gaddis, pp. 126–29.

58 Ibid., pp. 78–79; McNeill, *America, Britain, and Russia*, pp. 544–47; Ross, *Foreign Office and the Kremlin*, p. 52.

59 Cathal J. Nolan, "Americans in the Gulag: Detention of U.S. Citizens by Russia and the Onset of the Cold War, 1944–49," *JCH* 25 (1990), 523–45; Russell D. Buhite, "Soviet-American Relations and the Repatriation of Prisoners of War," *The Historian* 35 (1973), 394–97.

60 The best account is Mark Elliott, *Pawns of Yalta: Soviet Refugees and America's Role in their Repatriation* (Urbana, Ill.: Univ. of Illinois Press, 1982). The title of his Conclusion is: "The West–Inept; The East–Vindictive."

61 Ibid., pp. 64–69, 72–73. At the same time, Soviet representatives were allowed all over Western Europe to look for Soviet citizens.

62 Ibid., pp. 86, 90, 102–4, 201.

63 See Montgomery to Nye, 14 Feb. 1945, Liddell Hart Centre, Alanbrooke Papers, 14/6/14; Brooke Diary, 20 Feb., 26 Feb., 8 Mar., 20 Mar. 1945, Alanbrooke Papers; Marshall to Roosevelt, 6 and 20 Mar. 1945, FDRL, PSF Box 66, Poland 1945; Keith P. Sword, "Their Prospects Will not be Bright: British Response to the Problem of the Polish 'Recalcitrants' 1946–49," *JCH* 21 (1986), 267–96. On 28 Mar. 1945 the British Cabinet decided that those who had fought under British command and could not return to Poland could stay in England and be naturalized as long as this procedure was not applied to others – like Jews (WM[45] War Cabinet 37[45], 28 Mar. 1945, PRO, CAB 65/49).

64 Jaime Reynolds, "'Lublin' versus 'London' – The Party and the Underground Movement in Poland, 1944–1945," *JCH* 16 (1981), 640.

65 Anderson, *The United States*, pp. 28–31.

66 See War Cabinet 22(45), Confidential Annex, 19 Feb. 1945, PRO, CAB 65/51. By the next meeting on Feb. 21 the tone was more cautious; all depended on free elections in Poland.

67 Donald C. Watt, "Die Sowjetunion im Urteil des Foreign Office 1945–1949," in Gottfried Niedhart (ed.), *Der Westen und die Sowjetunion* (Paderborn: Schöningh, 1983), p. 241; Ross, *Foreign Office and the Kremlin*, p. 535; Pogue, *Marshall*, 3: 577. The refusal of the Soviet Union to abide by the agreement on Poland had already been registered in the War Cabinet at its 26th 1945 meeting on March 6 (PRO, CAB 65/51). On the arrest of the sixteen Polish leaders, see the report on Dr. Stylpukowski in Imperial War Museum, MM 25.

68 Önder, *Türkische Aussenpolitik* pp. 240–41. The Americans wanted the Japanese observation post in Ankara closed down. The Turks subsequently routed their intelligence assistance for Japan through Madrid, something the Americans quickly learned from their decoding operation (see Kurihara [Ankara] to Madrid No. 1, 15 Jan. 1945, NA, RG 457, SRDJ 86955–56).

69 Wittmann, *Schwedens Wirtschaftsbeziehungen*, p. 339.

70 See Japanese embassy Madrid Nos. 299 of 23 Mar. and 360 of 12 Apr. 1945, NA, RG 457, SRDJ 95503–5, 98425–27.

71 On Eisenhower's pressuring the Army Group commander, General Devers, see David

Eisenhower, *Eisenhower at War*, pp. 662–63; a recent account from the perspective of the U.S. 7th Army, Wyant, *Sandy Patch*, chap. 21.

72 "Veritable" is covered in the official histories; recent discussion in Eisenhower, *Eisenhower at War*, pp. 665ff.; Lamb, *Montgomery*, pp. 352–53. A good survey of "Veritable" and "Grenade" in Alan F. Wilt, *War from the Top: German and British Military Decision Making during World War II* (Bloomington, Ind.: Indiana Univ. Press, 1990), pp. 279–83.

73 Pogue, *Supreme Command*, p. 427.

74 Hastings, *Bomber Command*, pp. 411–12; Saward *"Bomber" Harris*, pp. 281ff; Diane D. Putney, *ULTRA and the Army Air Forces in World War II: An interview with Associate Justice of the U.S. Supreme Court Lewis F. Powell, Jr.* (Washington: GPO, 1987), pp. 55–58.

75 Saward, pp. 290–97.

76 Lamb, *Montgomery*, pp. 354ff; Pogue, *Supreme Command*, pp. 427ff.

77 Lothar Gruchmann, *Der Zweite Weltkrieg: Kriegführung und Politik* (Munich: Deutscher Taschenbuch Verlag, 1967), p. 424, refers to this as defending the "wrong" bank of the river.

78 There remains a major debate whether the airborne operation made any sense at all and was worth the losses incurred. Perhaps there is here a sad reversal of Arnhem: in the earlier case, intelligence on the *arrival* of German reserve formations close to the drop zone had been ignored; this time it was the *withdrawal* of German forces to the front around the Remagen bridgehead which was not taken into consideration. For a detailed report at the time, see Headquarters First Allied Airborne Army, "Report of Operation Varsity, 24 March 1945," sent to SHAEF by General Brereton on 19 May 1945 (PRO, AIR 20/4314).

79 Montgomery order M 563, copy to CIGS, Liddell Hart Centre, Alanbrooke Papers, 14/7/30. The Field Marshal was right on the mark; I recall seeing in the records of German forces fighting on the Eastern Front in the spring of 1945 a letter from the "Plenipotentiary of the Reichsführer SS for All Military Dog and Pigeon Matters," offering some companies of dog handlers without dogs for the next offensive operation in a wooded area. General Gotthard Heinrici, the Army Group Vistula Commander-in-Chief, had scrawled across the document: "Suitable for publication in a humor magazine" (Zur Veröffentlichung in einem Witzblatt geeignet).

80 Lamb, *Montgomery*, chap. 14.

81 See Stephen E. Ambrose, *Eisenhower and Berlin 1945: The Decision to Halt at the Elbe* (New York: Norton, 1967). It should be noted that Montgomery's order of Mar. 28 quoted above specified the line of the Elbe as the goal for 21st Army Group.

82 On Apr. 2 Montgomery wrote to Brooke that he had instructed 9th Army to cross the Weser by the following night, "and I do not think the Army will go much further than that." He planned to urge 12th Army Group to move forward but doubted that they would (Liddell Hart Centre, Alanbrooke Papers, 14/11/2). On April 16 Montgomery told Simpson, the Director of Military Operations in the War Department, on the phone that his troops were getting exhausted, and that operations toward Lübeck and Kiel "would probably go very slowly," and that he needed and was getting some American divisions to help him get there (Simpson for Brooke and Nye, 17 Apr. 1945, Alanbrooke Papers, 14/9/21). On Apr. 21 Montgomery wrote Brooke about his plans for a set piece crossing of the Elbe (Alanbrooke Papers, 14/11/26). See also Eisenhower, *Eisenhower at War*, pp. 756–57.

83 Churchill personal minute D 9515, 3 Apr. 1945, Liddell Hart Centre, Alanbrooke Papers, 14/9/7.

84 See Pogue, *Supreme Command*, chap. 22; Günther W. Gellermann, *Die Armee Wenck: Hitlers letzte Hoffnung* (Koblenz: Bernard & Graefe, 1984), pp. 20–26.

85 Pogue, *Supreme Command*, p. 452; Gruchmann, *Die Zweite Weltkrieg*, pp. 430–31; Ziemke,

Stalingrad to Berlin, p. 479 n 50; Erickson, *Road to Berlin*, pp. 552–53; Gellermann, *Armee Wenck*, chap. 4.

86 Pogue, *Supreme Command*, pp. 461–69.

87 Rodney G. Minott, *The Fortress that Never Was: The Myth of Hitler's Bavarian Stronghold* (New York: Holt, Rinehart and Winston, 1964); Joachim Brückner, *Kriegsende in Bayers 1945* (Freiburg: Rombach, 1987).

88 This is the thrust of David Eisenhower's analysis.

89 The best account is Bradley F. Smith and Elena Agarossi, *Operation Sunrise: The Secret Surrender* (New York: Basic Books, 1979). The British code-name was "Crossword;" not all the files on it are as yet open; note C 1575/45/18, PRO, FO 371/46783 (Vol. 2 retained in the Foreign Office).

90 Smith and Agarossi, *Operation Sunrise*, pp. 50–51.

91 Ibid., p. 203 n 23. The whole "Sunrise" episode reflects very badly on the judgement of Allen Dulles who allowed himself to be carried away – and over JCS orders – by prospects of a great coup.

92 A very good account, which also covers parts of the fighting in Italy, is Geoffrey Cox, *The Race for Trieste* (London: Kimber, 1977). For the push from the north, see also Wyant, *Sandy Patch*, chaps. 22–23.

93 See *FDR Letters*, 2: 1577–78.

94 Smith and Agaross (*Operation Sunrise*) allege that the Soviet Union had every reason to be concerned, but I find their logic entirely unconvincing. They deprecate Roosevelt's reference to the isolated German garrisons in the Baltic but overlook that the largest of these, that in Courland, surrendered even later than that in Italy. The President's view, in spite of the confused situation at the time, was clearer than theirs decades later.

95 See C 1549/45/18, PRO, FO 371/46784.

96 Note Smith and Agarossi, pp. 55–56, 85ff, 170.

97 Eisenhower, *Eisenhower at War*, p. 792. The Red Army operations in East Prussia are covered in Duffy, *Red Storm*, chaps. 15–16; the various sieges in chaps. 19–23.

98 Erickson, *Road to Berlin*, pp. 509–17; Glantz, *Soviet Military Deception*, pp. 514–20, 522–23.

99 On the Berlin operation, see Erickson, *Road to Berlin*, pp. 528ff; Ziemke, *Stalingrad to Berlin*, chap. 21; Glantz, pp. 521, 524–44; Tony Le Tissier, *The Battle for Berlin 1945* (New York: St. Martin's, 1988).

100 Marshall to Roosevelt, 2 Apr. 1945, FDRL, Map Room Box 171, Naval Aide, Probable Developments in the German Reich.

101 See Abe and Kojima "N" Serial 315 to Tokyo of 10 Apr. 1945 on a tea given by Ribbentrop on 4 Apr., NA, RG 457, SRNA 4624–26.

102 Müller, "Gaskriegsvorbereitungen," pp. 47–48; Pacific Strategic Intelligence Section, "Japanese Reaction to German Defeat," 21 May 1945, NA, RG 457, SRH-075; Rudolf Semmler, *Goebbels – The Man Next to Hitler*, intro. by D. McLachlan and notes by G. S. Wagner (London: Westhouse, 1947), 13 Apr. 1945, pp. 190–92. A new edition of the Semmler Diary would be most welcome.

103 The death of Roosevelt was considered similar to the death of the Empress Elizabeth of Russia, which led to the breakup of the coalition against the Prussia of Frederick the Great in the Seven Years War of 1756–63. When Kawahara Syun-itiro, counsellor of the Japanese embassy in Berlin, asked whether the Allies might not simply declare the war over when they had seized Berlin, he was told that this could not be done legally and was referred to the experience of the Kingdom of Hanover in 1866! (Oshima to Tokyo No. 427 of 18 Apr. 1945, NA, RG 457, SRDJ 98241–42.)

104 Ziemke, *Stalingrad to Berlin*, p.488. See also his *The Battle for Berlin: End of the Third Reich* (New York: Ballantine, 1968); Igor N. Venkov, "How the Berlin Garrison Surrendered 2 May 1945," *Army History*, PB-20–91–1 (Winter 1990/91), 20–25.

105 The texts have been repeatedly published; see *TMWC*, 41: 548–54, for both the political and the private wills; Goebbels *Tagebücher, 1945*, pp. 550–55, has the political will only. A set of the originals is in the U.S. National Archives together with the marriage license.

106 Why the Soviet government kept its knowledge secret, at times pretended to believe Hitler was still alive, and finally changed its policy by authorizing the publication of an autopsy and related materials in 1968 remain open questions. A revised edition of Lev Bezymenski's book, *Der Tod des Adolf Hitler: der sowjetische Beitrag über das Ende des Dritten Reiches und seines Diktators* (Munich: Herbig, 1982) still contains the subsequently corrected assertion that there was only one testicle visible. To what purpose this portion of the autopsy was distorted is also hard to explain.

107 British intelligence had Hugh R. Trevor-Roper check into the issue; his report, expanded into a book, *The Last Days of Hitler* (New York: Macmillan, 1947), remains important for its insights into the subject.

108 Fisk, *In Time of War*, pp. 461–62. The incident may be related to Irish permission for the German Legation in Dublin to fly the swastika flag while the British mission was not allowed to fly the Union Jack (ibid., p. 135).

109 The German military attaché in Madrid radioed to Berlin No. 585 on 30 Apr. 1945: "Press news here of Himmler's surrender and severe illness of the Fuehrer. Request instructions" (NA, RG 457, SRIB 2653).

110 Krebs had been appointed to replace Guderian. He had been assistant military attaché in Moscow and spoke Russian; he committed suicide.

111 Erickson, *Road to Berlin*, p. 622. The figure includes both sides and also civilian losses.

112 Vlasov himself was captured by the Americans, turned over to the Russians, and shot in 1946.

113 This issue has been referred to repeatedly in connection with the holding of Courland; as Salewski (*Seekriegsleitung*) has shown, it was also true in regard to the holding of Tunisia and the Crimea. The subject is developed in detail in the Grier, "Hitler's Baltic Strategy".

114 Speer, *Spandauer Tagebücher*, pp. 334–35. Dönitz was then probably the only person on earth who thought Hitler's testament legally binding on Germany. See also Speer's comments on the Dönitz memoirs in ibid., pp. 506–8; Bodo Herzog, "Der Kriegsverbrecher Karl Dönitz," *Jahrbuch des Instituts für Deutsche Geschichte* 15 (1986), 477–89.

115 The best work on the Dönitz regime is Marlis Steinert, *Die 23 Tage der Regierung Dönitz* (Vienna: Econ-Verlag, 1967).

116 See President Truman's account to Mrs. Roosevelt in Robert H. Ferrell (ed.), *Off the Record: The Private Papers of Harry S. Truman* (New York: Harper & Row, Penguin ed., 1980), pp. 20–22.

117 Ziemke, *Stalingrad to Berlin*, pp. 498–99.

118 Note Eisenhower, *Eisenhower at War*, pp. 793ff.

119 Those Germans in East Asia who continued fighting alongside the Japanese long after the official German surrender were tried in Shanghai after the war by the Americans. The relevant materials are in the National Records Center in Suitland, Maryland, in RG 338, U.S. v. Büro Ehrhardt.

120 Marlis Steinert, "The Allied Decision to Arrest the Dönitz Government," *Historical Journal* 31 (1988), 651–63. The British Foreign Office memorandum of 17 May 1945 urging the arrest is in C 2316, 2436/2308/18, PRO, FO 361/46914.

121 Montgomery to Brooke, M 578 of 6 May 1945, Liddell Hart Centre, Alanbrooke Papers, 14/11/45.

122 On Roosevelt's reasonably good health at Yalta, see James M. Burns, *Roosevelt: The Soldier of Freedom 1940–1945* (New York: Harcourt Brace Jovanovich, 1970), pp. 573–74; cf. Kimball, *The Juggler*, pp. 205–6 n 24. Churchill had said that in ten years of research

they could not have found a worse place to meet than Yalta (Sherwood, *Roosevelt and Hopkins*, p. 847).

123 Halifax No. 2104 to the Foreign Office for Oliver Lyttleton, 30 Mar. 1945, PRO, PREM 4/27/9.

124 Burns, *Roosevelt*, p. 599.

125 The relevant papers are in FDRL, PSF Box 82, Navy, Wilson Brown folder. See also William L. Langer, *Our Vichy Gamble* (New York: Knopf, 1947), p. viii.

126 Roosevelt had stressed this point in his foreign policy speech of the 1944 campaign.

127 Note the very positive report by the British ambassador, Lord Halifax, No. 2504 of 13 Apr. 1945, PRO, PREM 4/27/9. See also the report in H.G. Nichols (ed.), *Washington Dispatches 1941–1945* (Chicago: Univ. of Chicago Press, 1981), pp. 539–41.

128 The question is reviewed from Churchill's perspective in Gilbert, *Churchill*, 7: chap 67, and 8. The relevant documents have been published in *FRUS* and the Smith edition of Clay papers (see n 32 above).

129 Brooke Diary, 23 May 1945, Bryant, 2: 357.

130 See Kettenacker, "Alliance," pp. 451, 453–54.

131 Brooke Diary, 31 May 1945, Liddell Hart Centre, Alanbrooke Papers.

132 Ibid., 24 May 1945, Bryant, 2: 357–58.

133 Churchill, *Second World War*, 6: chap. 16.

134 A.A. Gunson, *The Anglo-French Collision in Lebanon and Syria, 1940–1945* (London: Macmillan, 1986), chaps. 8–9.

135 Sebald (Pacific Strategic Intelligence Section) to Rochefort, 28 June 1945, NA, RG 457, SRMN 39, f. 126. Other documents on this are in PRO, WO 106/5176. See also Hinsley, *British Intelligence*, 3/2: Appendix 28.

136 Herring, *Aid to Russia*, pp. 187–90.

137 Ibid., pp. 193ff; Beaumont, *Comrades in Arms*, pp. 196–99.

138 See Beaumont, pp. 199–201, for the troubled end of aid to Britain in 1945.

139 Truman note of 19 May 1945, Ferrell, *Off the Record*, p. 32.

140 Eisenhower, *Eisenhower at War*, pp. 761–63, 770. Robert H. Abzug, *Inside the Vicious Heart: Americans and the Liberation of Nazi Concentration Camps* (New York: Oxford Univ. Press, 1985), and Jon Bridgman, *The End of the Holocaust: The Liberation of the Camps* (Portland, Oreg.: Timber Press/Areopagitica Press, 1990), are helpful. On Ohrdruf, see Feig, *Hitler's Death Camps*, pp. 231–32.

141 For the terms and fate of the relevant section of the Treaty of Versailles, see *FRUS, The Paris Peace Conference 1919*, 13: 327–80; Johann W. Brügel, "Das Schicksal der Strafbestimmungen des Versailler Vertrags," *VjZ* 6 (1958), 263–70.

142 The Allies had warned the neutral countries against allowing war criminals to take refuge in them and were to have endless troubles—which continue after decades—in obtaining extradition of identified criminals who had settled there. Argentina decided to open its files on the matter in early 1992; Spain has not done so as yet.

143 Robert H. Jackson, *International Conference on Military Trials, London, 1945* (Washington: GPO, 1949); U.N. War Crimes Commission, *History of the United Nations War Crimes Commission* (London: HMSO, 1948).

144 See Sidney J. Alderman, "Negotiating on War Crimes Prosecutions, 1945," in Raymond Dennett and Joseph E. Johnson (eds.), *Negotiating with the Russians* (Boston: World Peace Foundation, 1951), pp. 49–98.

145 WM(45) War Cabinet 43(45), 12 Apr. 1945, PRO, CAB 65/50.

146 WM(45) War Cabinet 57(45), 3 May 1945, ibid.

147 Ziemke, *The U.S. Army*, pp. 416ff.

148 Kase (Bern) to Tokyo No. 329 of 27 Mar. 1945, NA, RG 457, SRDJ 95469 (a very rare comment on the translation of 31 Mar. suggests that the Minister may be putting his own

thoughts into the mouth of a German, SRDJ 95472); Kase No. 565 of 11 May 1945, SRDJ 113581–82.

149 "Magic Far East Summary," No. 14, 4 May 1945, NA, RG 457, SRS 381–410; Pacific Strategic Intelligence Center, "Japanese Reaction to German Defeat," 21 May 1945, SRH-075, f. 4–5, 7–11; Pacific Strategic Intelligence Center, "Japanese–Portuguese Relations and the 'Macao Problem',' " SRH-076, f. 11–12; Tokyo Circular No. 456 to Moscow, 2 May 1945, SRDJ 99502–3.

150 It is the only one for which the three major Allies have published their documents. The two volumes of U.S. documents appeared in 1960 (*FRUS: Conferences at Berlin (Potsdam) 1945*). Preliminary publications of Soviet documents were issued in 1965 and 1967; these are included in Alexander Fischer (ed.), *Teheran Jalta Potsdam: Die sowjetischen Protokolle von den Kriegskonferenzen der "Grossen Drei"* (Cologne: Verlag Wissenschaft & Politik, 1968), pp. 199–410. A fuller publication of Soviet documents appeared in 1984 as Vol. 6 of a series on international conferences during the war; a German edition was issued in 1986 as *Die Sowjet Union auf internationalen Konferenzen während des Grossen Vaterländischen Krieges 1941 bis 1945*, Vol. 6: *Die Potsdamer (Berliner) Konferenz* (Berlin: Straatsverlag der DDR, 1986). The British documents are in *Documents on British Policy Overseas*, ser. 1, vol. 1: *The Conference at Potsdam July–August 1945* (London: HMSO, 1984). See also Gilbert, *Churchill*, 8: chap. 5.

151 Note the entries in Truman's Diary for 19 and 21 May 1945: Ferrell, *Off the Record*, pp. 29, 34.

152 Truman Diary 17 July 1945, ibid., p. 53.

153 Harry S. Truman to Bess Truman, 18 July 1945, Robert H. Ferrell (ed.), *Dear Bess: The Letters from Harry Truman to Bess Truman 1910–1959* (New York: Norton, 1983), p. 519. See also his letter of 22 July (ibid., p. 521), referring to some disagreements, "but I have already what I came for."

154 Roosevelt memorandum for the Secretary of State, 20 Oct. 1944, *FRUS, The Conferences at Malta and Yalta 1945*, p. 158.

155 Ibid., p. 159; Memorandum of Conversation 15 Nov. 1944, ibid., p. 172; Memorandum for Stettinius, 4 Dec. 1944, ibid., p. 174.

156 Roosevelt to Secretary of State, 29 Sep. 1944, ibid., p. 155.

157 Stalin had raised the question of Italian colonies with Truman at their first meeting on July 17 (Ferrell, *Off the Record*, p. 53; Soviet Potsdam collection, 6: No. 2) (see n. 150).

158 On Hopkins's trip, see Anderson, *The United States*, pp. 67–68; McJimsey, *Harry Hopkins*, pp. 380–88.

159 Truman Diary, 18 July 1945, Ferrell, *Off the Record*, pp. 53–54.

160 Truman Diary, 25 July 1945, ibid., pp. 55–56.

161 Ibid., p. 56.

16: THE WAR IN THE PACIFIC

1 Note Dill to Mountbatten, 12 Oct. 1944, PRO, CAB 106/329, Dill file 30/15.

2 Holmes, *Double-Edged Secrets*, p. 204. On British fleet operations in the later and the final stages of the Pacific War, see Roskill, *War at Sea*, 3: 330–35, 341–54, 373–75; Merrill Bartless and Robert W. Love, "Anglo-American Naval Diplomacy and the British Pacific Fleet 1942–1945," *American Neptune* 42 (1982), 203–16.

3 On this scheme, see the documents in PRO, AIR 8/814, 1284–85, 1288.

4 Churchill's Personal Minute D 203/4 to General Ismay, PRO, PREM 3/160/5, and his Personal Minute D (c) 7/4, "War Against Japan," 12 Sep. 1944, PREM 3/160/6.

5 On the United Kingdom and Canada, see WM(44) No. 123 of 18 Sep. 1944, PRO, CAB 65/47; documents in AIR 8/1174 and AIR 20/2981; on Australia, see AIR 8/1175–76; on New Zealand, AIR 8/1178; on South Africa, AIR 8/1177. There was also discussion

of French forces, see Brooke Diary, 23 Nov. 1944, Liddell Hart Centre, Alanbrooke Papers, and Vigneras, *Rearming the French*, chap. 24. A useful early summary in COS(44) 408(0), Revised Final War Cabinet COS Committee, "British Commonwealth Forces for the Far East," 10 May 1944, PREM 3/160/2.

6 Note the treatment of what London read as a peace feeler from Japan; WM(44) War Cabinet 125, 25 Sep. 1944, PRO, CAB 65/43; Foreign Office memorandum, 25 Sep. 1944, F 4370/208/23, FO 371/41804. The latter document refers to Japanese anxiety for a German–Soviet peace "of which we have very much secret evidence," undoubtedly a reference to intercepts.

7 M. Hamlin Cannon, *Leyte: The Return to the Philippines* (Washington: GPO, 1954), p. 367, cites January 1945 with 257,766 men (including the army air force).

8 Lewin, *American Magic*, pp. 235–37; "Magic Far East Summary," Nos. 260, 5 Dec. 1944, and 315, 29 Jan. 1945, NA, RG 457, SRS 260, 315.

9 See Japanese military attaché Bukarest to Tokyo No. 257 of 1 Aug. 1944, NA, RG 457, SRA 10352–53; Japanese military attaché Madrid to Tokyo No. 360 of 6 Sep. 1944, SRA 12221–29.

10 Japanese military attaché Stockholm to Tokyo No. 932 of 15 Sep. 1944, NA, RG 457, SRA 13124; Tokyo to the Attaché in Stockholm No 983 of 12 Dec. 1944, SRA 14612.

11 Oshima to Tokyo No. 791 of 5 Aug. 1944, NA, RG 457, SRDJ 66962–63.

12 Shigemitsu (Tokyo) to Sato (Moscow) Nos. 1011 of 7 Aug., 1201–2 of 5 Sep. 1944, NA, RG 457, SRDJ 66977–78, 69901–2; Sato to Shigemitsu No. 1610 of 10 Aug. 1944, SRDJ 67672–74 (see also SRNS 0859).

13 Sato to Tokyo Nos. 1909 of 16 Sep., 1911–12 of 17 Sep., 1916 of 18 Sep. 1944, NA, RG 457, SRDJ 71392–97, 71328–31, 71469–72, 71621–23; Japanese military attaché Bern to Tokyo No. 066 of 22 Sep. 1944, SRA 12281–82.

14 Harbin to Tokyo G-123 in Shigemitsu to Moscow No. 1454 of 18 Oct. 1944, NA, RG 457, SRDJ 74873–77; Tokyo to Harbin G-108 of 18 Oct. 1944, SRDJ 75290–92; Shigemitsu to Sato Nos. 1522–24 of 24 Oct. 1944, SRDJ 76542–43, 76526, 76538–39; Sato to Tokyo Nos. 2272 of 7 Nov., 2318 of 13 Nov., 2347, 2354, and 2356 of 18 Nov., 2365 of 20 Nov. 1944, SRDJ 77783–84, 78745–49, 79112–13, 79116–19, 79128–30, 79298–303.

15 Boyle, *China and Japan*, pp. 313–14. The Americans observed Japanese–Chinese peace feelers through Magic, see NA, RG 457, SRH-062, f. 6.

16 Boyle, p. 323.

17 See Morishima (Lisbon) to Tokyo No. 261 of 11 Aug. 1944, NA, RG 457, SRDJ 68329–32; Shigemitsu to Lisbon No. 208 of 26 Aug. 1944, SRDJ 69387–88.

18 Still important, Inoguchi Rikihei and Nakajima Tadashi with Roger Pineau, *The Divine Wind: Japan's Kamikaze Force in World War II* (Annapolis, Md.: Naval Institute Press, 1958). See also Edwin P. Hoyt, *The Kamikazes* (New York: Arbor House, 1983); Marder, *Old Friends, New Enemies*, 2: 398–403. There are innumerable references to the kamikaze forces in the *Ugaki Diary*, beginning with p. 485.

19 See Overy, *Air War*, pp. 92–95; USSBS, *The Effects of Strategic Bombing on Japan's War Economy: Appendix ABC* (Washington: GPO, 1946), pp. 24–26.

20 USSBS, *Summary Report Pacific War* (Washington: GPO, 1946), pp. 70–71. It should be noted that the American air force and navy as well as the British navy were very much more impressed by the casualties and damage inflicted by the kamikaze than was Overy (p. 99).

21 Wenneker (Tokyo) to Berlin No. 75 gKdos. of 1 Sep. 1944, NA, RG 457, SRGL 1454.

22 To begin with Japanese headquarters appear to have believed in this mythical victory. Note the report of the German naval attaché in Tokyo of 21 Oct. 1944 quoted in "Magic Far East Summary," No. 218 of 24 Oct. 1944, NA, RG 457, SRS 218, f. 3–4. Admiral Dönitz instructed the attaché to congratulate the Japanese navy minister on this great

triumph. Very interesting are the entries in the *Ugaki Diary*, pp. 442–500, 523–24.

23 Summaries may be found in Dull, *Imperial Japanese Navy*, pp. 313–31; Costello, 503–19. More detail in Morison, *US Naval Operations*, 12.

24 Cannon, *Leyte*, chap. 5; James, *The Years of MacArthur*, pp. 542–65; Drea, *MacArthur's Ultra*, chap. 6.

25 Kenney, *General Kenney Reports*, chap. 21, is very helpful.

26 There is a detailed account from the perspective of the escort carriers in William T. Y'Blood, *The Little Giants: U.S. Escort Carriers against Japan* (Annapolis, Md.: Naval Institute Press, 1987), pp. 154ff. The account in Dull, *Imperial Japanese Navy*, rather minimizes the dangers of the situation for the Americans. Marder, *Old Friends, New Enemies*, 2: 380, argues that Kurita broke off the battle because his ships were running low on fuel.

27 Cannon, *Leyte*, chap. 17; Kenney, chap. 22; James, *The Years of MacArthur*, chap. 14; Ronald H. Spector, *Eagle against the Sun: The American War with Japan* (New York: Free Press, 1985), pp. 511–17.

28 Figures are in Cannon, pp. 367–69.

29 Accounts in Hans C. Adamson and George F. Kosco, *Halsey's Typhoons* (New York: Crown Publishers, 1967). chaps. 1–7; C. Raymond Calhoun, *Typhoon: The Other Enemy, The Third Fleet and the Pacific Storm of December 1944* (Annapolis, Md.: Naval Institute Press, 1981).

30 Kenney, pp. 493–500; James, *The Years of MacArthur*, pp. 604–10; Spector, *Eagle against the Sun*, pp. 517–20.

31 Jan. 8, 1945, American date.

32 Costello, *Pacific War*, p. 526; Craven and Cate, *Army Air Forces*, 5: xiv-xvi and chaps. 1–5; James L. Cate, *History of the Twentieth Air Force: Genesis* (USAAF Historical Study No. 112, Washington: HQ USAAF, 1945).

33 Note Donovan's report to Roosevelt of 17 Nov. 1944 on the situation in China, FDRL, PSF Box 170, OSS, Nov. 16–30, 1944. See also Christopher Thorne, *Allies of a Kind* (New York: Oxford Univ. Press, 1978), chap. 26.

34 Ch'i, *Nationalist China*, pp. 111–17.

35 The troubles among the British commanders, however, continued; see Brooke Diary, 2 Nov. 1944, Liddell Hart Centre, Alanbrooke Papers. The emphasis in Thorne, *Allies of a Kind*, on friction between the British and Americans has the unintended effect of minimizing the internal British frictions.

36 Allen, *Burma*, chap. 6. Charles Cruikshank, *SOE in the Far East* (Oxford: Oxford Univ. Press, 1983), certainly gives the impression that SOE's organization of Burmese irregulars (Force 136) to assist in the reconquest of Burma was that organization's sole significant contribution to the war effort.

37 Allen, *Burma*, chaps. 7–9. A fine source on operations in Burma is the series of letters exchanged between Brooke and Leese, Nov. 1944 – Sept. 1945, in PRO, WO 106/4789.

38 Relevant correspondence in Liddell Hart Centre, Alanbrooke Papers, 14/49. By Mar. 1945 the Burmese collaborators were also turning against Japan and negotiating with the British (Lebra, *Japanese-Trained Armies*, pp. 163–65).

39 But note the Japanese expectation of relief from the effects of the German Ardennes offensive; see the report of the German naval attaché Tokyo of 5 Jan. 1945, "Magic Far East Summary," No. 296 of 10 Jan. 1945, NA, RG 457, SRS 296, f. 7.

40 Correspondence of Lumsden with Brooke shows that MacArthur took Lumsden fully into his confidence (PRO, WO 216/96).

41 A very useful account in Robert Ross Smith, *Triumph in the Philippines* (Washington: GPO, 1963) in the U.S. Army official series. See now also Drea, *MacArthur's Ultra*, chap. 7.

42 James, *The Years of MacArthur*, pp. 691–701; Steinberg, *Philippine Collaboration*.

43 James, pp. 670–90, provides a good account of the fighting on Luzon, Apr. to Aug. 1945.

44 A summary in ibid., pp. 702–10. More information may be found in Peter Charlton, *The Unnecessary War: Island Campaign of the South-West Pacific 1944–1945* (South Melbourne: Macmillan of Australia, 1983); Gavin Long, *Six Years War*, pp. 404ff; Horner, *High Command*, pp. 399ff; Gailey, *Bougainville*, chap. 11. See also Gairdner to Ismay, 30 May 1945, PRO, WO 216/137.

45 A survey in James, pp. 714–17, 751–63; Gavin Long, chap. 15.

46 See Craven and Cate, *Army Air Forces*, 5: chap. 17, for preparations and support.

47 Richard H. Kohn and Joseph P. Harahan (eds.), *Strategic Air Warfare: An Interview with Generals Curtis LeMay, Leon W. Johnson, David A. Burchinal, and Jack J. Catton* (Washington: GPO, 1988), pp. 153ff. The table in Overy, *Air War*, p. 113, compares the major U.S., British, and German bombers; the B-29 had twice the range of other bombers used in the war.

48 Craven and Cate, *Army Air Forces*, 5: chap. 18.

49 Butow, *Tojo*, pp. 440–42.

50 Ethell, *Mustang*, pp. 114–15.

51 Note the report of the German naval attaché in Tokyo of 5 Jan. 1945, in "Magic Far East Summary," No. 296 of 10 Jan. 1945, NA, RG 457, SRS 296, f. 8.

52 General Harry Schmidt actually commanded the 5th Amphibious Corps; Smith was brought in to provide a parallel position to Admiral Kelly Turner, the naval director of the assault. As the text makes clear, I am not entirely convinced by the defense of the navy on the bombardment issue in Morison, *US Naval Operations*, 14: 72–74.

53 The account of the Iwo landing in Iseley and Crowl, *The U.S. Marines*, chap. 10, remains most useful. See also Costello, *Pacific War*, pp. 539–47; Craven and Cate, *Army Air Forces*, 5: chap. 19; George W. Garrand and Truman R. Stobridge, *History of U.S. Marine Corps Operations in World War II* (Washington: GPO, 1971), 4: 443–738. The warships could, however, come in close because of the steep drop-off.

54 Edmund L. Castillo, *The Seabees of World War II* (New York: Random House, 1963); *Building the Navy's Bases in World War II: History of the Bureau of Yards and Docks and the Civil Engineer Corps, 1940–1946*, 2 vols. (Washington: GPO, 1947).

55 On the air–sea rescue program, see Craven and Cate, *Army Air Forces*, 5: 598–607.

56 "Magic Far East Summary," No. 405, 29 Apr. 1945, NA, RG 457, SRS 405.

57 See Craven and Cate, 5: 144, 609ff.

58 Shillony, *Wartime Japan*, pp. 75–76, and the sources cited there.

59 The report of 29 Mar. 1945 is quoted in "Magic Far East Summary," No. 378, 2 Apr. 1945, NA, RG 457, SRS 378.

60 The report of 20 Apr. 1945 is quoted in "Magic Far East Summary," No. 402, 26 Apr. 1945, NA, RG 457, SRS 402.

61 Craven and Cate, *Army Air Forces*, 5: 614–27, survey the initial fire raids and their impact.

62 Forrestal memorandum for Roosevelt, 2 Jan. 1945, FDRL, Map Room Box 162, Naval Aide, General A2–3. The summaries of radio intelligence in the Pacific were soon after sent regularly to the British; see NA, RG 457, SRNS-1060, f. 3.

63 For "Olympic" and "Coronet" planning, see James, *The Years of MacArthur*, pp. 765–71; Matloff, *Strategic Planning 1943–1944*, pp. 535–37; Thorne, *Allies of a Kind*, chap. 25; K. Jack Bauer, "Die amerikanischen Pläne für eine Landung in Japan," *Marine-Rundschau* 59 (1962), 140–47. A portion of the "Olympic" plan is printed as Appendix A in Paul Manning, *Hirohito: The War Years* (New York: Dodd Mead, 1986). See also Marc Gallicchio, "After Nagasaki: General Marshall's Plan for Tactical Nuclear Weapons in Japan," *Prologue* 23 (winter 1991) 396–404. One version of MacArthur's plan for "Coronet" omitted the 10th Army but assumed vastly greater Allied participation than was in fact anticipated (James, pp. 770–71).

64 On the planning for British Commonwealth troop participation in "Coronet," see Brooke

Diary, 9 Apr. 1945, Liddell Hart Centre, Alanbrooke Papers; Ismay to Gairdner, 29 June 1945, PRO, CAB 127/51; Chiefs of Staff [45] 423(0), "British Participation in the War Against Japan," 30 June 1945, F 4056/69/23, FO 371/46440, and F 4236/69/23, in ibid.; documents in AIR 20/3959; Ehrman, *Grand Strategy*, 6: 257–71; Roskill, *War at Sea*, 3/2: 330ff. On the anticipated assignment of a French corps to "Coronet," see Vigneras, *Rearming the French*, chap. 24.

65 BAS Washington to War Office, "GO 872," 12 June 1945, PRO, WO 106/3463. On the issue of the boundary between the theaters of Mountbatten and MacArthur, see Mountbatten to Ismay, 19 Mar. 1945, CAB 127/26. Thorne appears to me to exaggerate the friction.

66 See Combined Chiefs of Staff, "679/1, Redeployment of United States and British Forces after the Defeat of Germany," 2 Apr. 1945, PRO, CAB 119/165. A later and more detailed schedule is in Marshall to Wilson, 16 May 1945, CAB 106/329.

67 F 2146/630/23, PRO, FO 371/46453.

68 On the internal British debates over strategy in the final stages of the war in the Pacific, see Ehrman, *Grand Strategy*, 6: chap. 8; a summary in Bryant, 2: 350–54, with excerpts from the Brooke diary reflecting the impact of the forthcoming parliamentary election on the campaign in Southeast Asia. Documents in PRO, PREM 3/160/3–7.

69 James, *The Years of MacArthur*, pp. 763–65, summarizes the evidence. In later years MacArthur simply lied about his position at the time. In 1955 the U.S. Department of Defense published a collection of the military recommendations in "The Entry of the Soviet Union into the War Against Japan: Military Plans, 1941–1945." See also Forrest C. Pogue, *George C. Marshall*, Vol. 4, *Statesman 1945–1959* (New York: Penguin, 1987): 15–16.

70 David M. Glantz, *August Storm: The Soviet 1945 Strategic Offensive in Manchuria* (Fort Leavenworth, Kans.: U.S. Army Command and General Staff College, Combat Studies Institute, 1983), pp. 1–3. Based primarily on published Soviet sources, this is currently the best account of the campaign in Manchuria.

71 Ibid., pp. 73–79.

72 Pacific Strategic Intelligence Section, "Russo-Japanese Relations," 18 June 1945, NA, RG 457, SRH-078, f. 3, 2 July 1945, SRH-079, f. 10–11, 21 July 1945, SRH-085, f. 18; Japanese naval attaché Bern to Tokyo No. 131 of 25 June 1945, SRNA 5035. The British Minister in Stockholm reported on May 12 that the Swedish Minister to Tokyo who had just returned from Japan "was immensely impressed during his journey across Siberia by the endless stream of railway transport containing troops and all kinds of war material which was rolling eastwards" (Mallet to London No. 862 of 12 May 1945, F 2874/630/23, PRO, FO 371/46453). A U.S. naval intelligence assessment of Sino-Soviet relations was so gutted in the declassification process as to suggest American reading of some Soviet radio traffic at that time (Pacific Strategic Intelligence Section, "Sino-Soviet Relations," 1 June 1945, NA, RG 457, SRH-077).

73 See the report of the Japanese Consul in Vladivostok No. 233 of 21 June 1945, NA, RG 457, SRDJ 103772. The other side of this was the repudiation by the Soviet Union of its prior promise to allow the United States bases for its strategic air force against Japan, a promise on the basis of which supply deliveries had already been made. This episode may eventually be illuminated by new evidence from the Soviet side; in the meantime, see Deane's reports N 22050 and 22261 of 16 Dec. 1944 and 4 Jan. 1945, FDRL, Map Room Box 33, MR 310, Japan 1, Russian Participation in the War against.

74 Pacific Strategic Intelligence Section, "Russo-Japanese Relations," 2 July 1945, NA, RG 457, SRH-079, f. 10; Tokyo to Moscow No. 827 of 24 June 1945, SRDJ 103857; Gordon, *Brothers against the Raj*, pp. 517–18, 538–41.

75 The Soviet note is printed in *New York Times*, 6 Apr. 1945. For the Japanese–Soviet negotiations *preceding* the denunciation, see the American intercepts of relevant Japanese

messages in NA, RG 457, SRDJ 79936–45, 82775–76, 80397–408, 82389–90, 82442–47, 81973–76, 84170–71, 85256–60, 85277–96, 86131–32, 87156–57, 88455–56, 90116–21, 90592–95, 90516, 90827, 91558, 91813–15, 114209–18, 91944–49, 92124, 92704–5, 94826–29, 95665–68, 95640, 95691–93, 96515–21, 96535; Pacific Strategic Intelligence Section, "Notes on the Crimea (Yalta) Conference," 23 Mar. 1945, SRH-070, and "Abrogation of the Soviet-Japanese Neutrality Pact," 23 Apr. 1945, SRH-071.

76 On Japanese–Soviet relations *after* the abrogation, see the American intercepts of Japanese messages in NA, RG 457, SRDJ 96557–61, 97356–58, 96662, 96655–61, 96767–70, 96813–14, 96821, 96824–27, 98648–49, 98730–33, 112408, 100037–38, 101457–67, 101598–604, 102417–25, 103946–47, 104593–600, 105372–73, 105315, 105374, 105386; Pacific Strategic Intelligence Section, "Russo-Japanese Relations," 18 June 1945, SRH-078, 2 July 1945, SRH-079, 14 July 1945, SRH-084.

77 Tokyo, Vice-Chief, Gen. Staff Circular 442 of 27 Jan. 1945, NA, RG 457, SRA 15777–80, to the military attaché Berlin No. 203 of 8 Mar. 1945, SRA 18003, to military attaché Lisbon, 12 Apr. 1945, SRA 17069–70.

78 See Lisbon to Tokyo No. 25 of 24 Jan. 1945, NA, RG 457, SRDJ 88708–17; Japanese military attaché Lisbon to Tokyo No. 326 of 24 Jan. 1945, SRA 15712–13; Tokyo to Macao No. 30 of 27 Apr. 1945, SRDJ 99087; Pacific Strategic Intelligence Center, "Japanese–Portuguese Relations and the 'Macao Problem'," 23 May 1945, SRH-076.

79 See the Tokyo circulars to the military attachés in Europe of 19 Jan. and 29 Mar. 1945, NA, RG 457, SRA 15554–60, SRA 16930–32. Cf. Japanese naval attaché Stockholm to Tokyo No. 298 of 5 June 1945, SRNA 4943–44; Japanese naval attaché Bern to Tokyo No. 124 of 13 June 1945, SRNA 4989–90 (I believe that a study of the work of the Japanese naval attaché in Switzerland would make interesting reading).

80 Tokyo Circulars 852 and 870 to Berlin, 6 and 12 Dec. 1944, NA, RG 457, SRDJ 81500–3, 82283–86; a survey of the Mar. 1945 coup in Kiyoko Kurusu Nitz, "Japanese Policy towards French Indo-China during the Second World War: The Road to *Meigo Sukusen* (9 March 1945)," *Journal of SE Asian Studies* 14 (1983), 328–350; Lebra, *Japanese-Trained Armies*, pp. 134–39. On Japanese planning for the coup already in 1944, see SRDJ 61784–88, 61777–79. For the broader context of the coup, see Stein Tonneson, *The Vietnamese Revolution of 1945: Roosevelt, Ho Chi Minh and de Gaulle in a World at War* (Newbury Park, Ca.: Sage, 1991).

81 The Circular No. 442 of the Vice Chief of the General Staff of 27 Jan. 1945 is in NA, RG 457, SRA 15777–80.

82 Vice Chief of the General Staff Circular No. 208 of 8 Mar. 1945, NA, RG 457, SRA 16716–20.

83 See NA, RG 457, SRH-089; "Magic Far East Summary," No. 252 of 15 June 1945, f. 3; SRH-066, f. 4–5.

84 Shillony, *Wartime Japan*, pp. 81–82.

85 Williams and Wallace, *Unit 731*, pp. 124–27; Webber, *Silent Siege*. The balloon attacks did force the closing down of the Hanford plutonium plant for three days in March (Webber, pp. 278–80), but the B-29s destroyed the plants where the balloons were made. The Japanese appear to have halted the project in April in part because they had received no reports on its effect, something due largely to censorship in the United States and Canada.

86 Stephan, *Hawaii under the Rising Sun*, p. 169.

87 Potter, *Bull Halsey*, pp. 345–46; Morison, *US Naval Operations*, 14: 332–33.

88 More details are given later in this chapter. See also NA, RG 457, SRH-103. There is very extensive material in the *Ugaki Diary*. For American counter-preparations, see Holmes, *Undersea Victory*, p. 467.

89 On the technical aspects of these projects, see Richard O'Neill, *Suicide Squads: Axis and Allied Special Attack Weapons of World War II* (London: Salamander Books, 1981). A reliable scholarly study of the whole topic remains to be written. There is an interesting British report of May 1946, A.I.2(g) Report No. 2389, "Oka (Baka): The Japanese Suicide Aircraft," PRO, AIR 20/8775. For references in the *Ugaki Diary* to the ohka, see pp. 547, 558–59, 582, 609, 636–37.

90 On the Cabinet crisis, see Shillony, *Wartime Japan*, pp. 76–81; Butow, *Japan's Decision*, chap. 3. Interesting, but filled with special pleading, is Leon V. Seagal, *Fighting to a Finish: The Politics of War Termination in the United States and Japan* (Ithaca, N.Y.: Cornell Univ. Press, 1988).

91 See Kase (Bern) to Tokyo Nos. 450 of 27 Apr., 579 of 14 May 1945, NA, RG 457, SRDJ 99090–2, 100258–71.

92 Tokyo Circulars 490 of 15 May, 493 of 17 May 1945, NA, RG 457, SRDJ 100076, 100271–72.

93 On the Stockholm rumors, see the exchanges in NA, RG 457, SRDJ 103550–53, 103821, 105267–68, 105405–6; for the efforts of Dulles to arrange a Japanese surrender through Japanese naval channels, see the documents in SRNA 4961–63, 5092–94, 5131, 5142–43, 5145–46, 5186, 5208; Butow, *Japan's Decision*, chap. 5. Martin S. Quigley, *Peace without Hiroshima: Secret Action at the Vatican in the Spring of 1945* (London, Md.: Madison Books, 1991). On the role of Friedrich Wilhelm Hack or Hauck, see Butow, pp. 104–9; John W.M. Chapman, "A Dance on Eggs: Intelligence and the Anti-Comintern," *JCH* 22 (1987), 333–72.

94 Note Pacific Strategic Intelligence Section, "Japanese Reaction to German Defeat," 21 May 1945, NA, RG 457, SRH-075, f. 14.

95 See *Kido Diary*, 8 June 1945, pp. 434–36. President Truman's statement that unconditional surrender did not mean wiping out the Japanese people was interpreted as propaganda to weaken the Japanese home front; Tokyo Circular 557 of 20 June 1945, NA, RG 457, SRDJ 103616–17.

96 Shillony, *Wartime Japan*, pp. 82–83. A survey of the internal situation during the last year of war in Alvin D. Coox, *Japan: The Final Agony* (New York: Ballantine, 1970).

97 On the Okinawa battle, see Costello, *Pacific War*, chap. 33; Morison, *US Naval Operations*, 14: Part 2; Roy E. Appleman et al., *Okinawa: The Last Battle* (Washington: GPO, 1948); James and William Belote, *Typhoon of Steel: The Battle for Okinawa* (New York: Harper & Row, 1970); Marder, *Old Friends, New Enemies*, 2: 428–29, 439ff; Thomas M. Huber, *Japan's Battle of Okinawa, April–June 1945* (Fort Leavenworth, Kans.: U.S. Army Command and General Staff College, Combat Studies Institute, Washington: GPO, 1990). A brilliant but terrifying account from the perspective of a marine in the fighting is in part 2 of Sledge, *With the Old Breed*.

98 Robert N. Colwell, "Intelligence and the Okinawa Battle," *Naval War College Review* 38, No. 2 (1985), 86–87.

99 Note German naval attaché Tokyo to Berlin report of 20 April 1945, quoted in "Magic Far East Summary," No. 402, 26 Apr. 1945, NA, RG 457, SRS 402, f, 1–2.

100 On this see now the *Ugaki Diary*, 5 Apr.–7 May 1945, pp. 572–76, 586; cf. Marder *Old Friends, New Enemies*, 2: 429–39.

101 The relevant documents were first published in U.S. Department of Defense, "The Entry of the Soviet Union into the War against Japan: Military Plans, 1941–1945," pp. 54–57, 80.

102 The text of the memorandum on this conference makes dramatic reading; it is in *FRUS, The Conference of Berlin (Potsdam) 1945*, 1: 903–10. See also Herbert Feis, *Japan Subdued: The Atomic Bomb and the End of the War in the Pacific* (Princeton, N.J.: Princeton Univ. Press, 1961), pp. 7–14; Bauer, "Amerikanische Pläne," pp. 140–41; Department of Defense, "The Entry of the Soviet Union," pp. 76–85; Pogue, *Marshall*, 4: 9, 18; Charles

F. Brower, IV, "Sophisticated Strategist: George A. Lincoln and the Defeat of Japan," *Diplomatic History* 15 (1991), 317–37; Brian L. Villa, "The U.S. Army, Unconditional Surrender, and the Potsdam Proclamation," *Journal of American History* 63 (1976), 66–92; Barton J. Bernstein, "Writing, Righting or Wronging the Historical Record: President Truman's Letter on His Atomic Bomb Decision," *Diplomatic History* 16 (1992), 163–73. It must be noted that many of the U.S. military planners had not been initiated into the secret of the A-bomb (a point overlooked in some of the literature), see Ray S. Cline, *Washington Command Post: The Operations Division* (Washington: GPO, 1951), pp. 347–48 n 55.

103 Bauer, "Amerikanische Pläne," p. 143.

104 British Combined Operations Observers (Pacific), "Report on Operation 'Olympic' and Japanese Counter-Measures," 4 Apr. 1945, PRO, WO 106/3528–29. For U.S. information on the planned use of suicide weapons, see "Magic Far East Summary," No. 506, 8 Aug. 1945, NA, RG 457, SRS-506, annex "F-22's Estimate of Japanese Intentions." On the basis for the accurate Japanese intelligence assessment of the American landing plan for Olympic, see Alvin D. Coox in Hitchcock (ed.), *The Intelligence Revolution*, pp. 197–201.

105 A summary in Ehrman, *Grand Strategy*, 6: 247–57. The Japanese military attaché in Lisbon expected a British operation against Malaya already in July; see Lisbon to Tokyo No. 586, 2 July 1945, NA, RG 457, SRA 18033. See also Marder, *Old Friends, New Enemies*, 2: 454–57.

106 Note the comments quoted in Bryant, 2: 353–54.

107 See the note by the Chief of the Air Staff for the Prime Minister of 4 July 1945 in PRO, CAB 120/291; Brooke to Montgomery, CIGS/2419846 of 20 July 1945, Liddell Hart Centre, Alanbrooke Papers 14/14/19.

108 This is one of the major assumptions of World War II Britain and the U.S. ignored in Barton J. Bernstein, "Roosevelt, Truman and the Atomic Bomb, 1941–1945: A Reinterpretation," *Political Science Quarterly* 90 (1975), 23–69.

109 Pogue, *Marshall*, 3: 507.

110 Bernstein, "Roosevelt," pp. 32–34, mentions the tenuous evidence that Roosevelt toyed with the idea of a demonstration explosion before combat use but concludes that the operating assumption was that of employment on enemy targets. It is a conclusion that appears to me to be correct, especially when contrasted with the President's absolute clarity on the non-use of chemical and biological weapons except in retaliation.

111 See Truman's comments in Ferrell, *Off the Record*, p. 304. A recent review of the literature, J. Samuel Walker, "The Decision to Use the Bomb: A Historiographical Update," *Diplomatic History* 14 (1990), 97–114, is interesting but badly flawed by the absence of discussion of the fighting on Okinawa and the internal Japanese discussion as known to the Americans from intercepts. On the origins of some of the early literature, see Barton J. Bernstein, "Seizing the Contested Terrain of Early Nuclear History: Stimson, Conant and their Allies Explain the Decision to Use the Atomic Bomb" *Diplomatic History* 17 (1993), 35–72.

112 Coox, "The Rise and Fall," p. 79. There is a detailed comparison of the American estimates with actual Japanese strength in Drea, *MacArthur's Ultra*, pp. 218–23; the Japanese forces were, if anything, even larger than the Americans thought.

113 A particularly helpful document is the reporting on these to General Marshall, "'Magic' Diplomatic Extracts July 1945: Selected Items Prepared by MIS, War Department, for the Attention of General George C. Marshall," NA, RG 457, SRH-040.

114 The earlier studies of this remain the most helpful: Butow, *Japan's Decision*; USSBS, *Japan's Struggle to End the War*; Feis, *Japan Subdued*.

115 Even in this project the Japanese were very reluctant to make concessions, see Tokyo Nos. 889 of 10 July, 890, 891 of 11 July 1945, NA, RG 457, SRDJ 105771–72, 105662–

64. See also John A. Harrison, "The U.S.S.R., Japan, and the End of the Great Pacific War," *Parameters* 14, No. 2 (Summer 1984), 76–87.

116 See the reports by Japanese Ambassador Sato from Moscow: Nos. 1330 of 5 July, NA, RG 457, SRDJ 105236–38; 1379 of 11 July, SRDJ 105707–14; 1381 of 12 July, SRDJ 105917–22; 1382 of 12 July, SRDJ 105923–27; 1386 of 13 July, SRDJ 105951–54; 1392 of 15 July, SRDJ 106079–83; 1416 of 18 July, SRDJ 106429; 1418 of 19 July, SRDJ 106473–74; 1427 of 20 July 1945, SRDJ 106558–77.

117 See Kase (Bern) Nos. 796 of 20 July and 802 of 21 July, NA, RG 457, SRDJ 106930–33, 106966–73; Okamoto (Stockholm) No. 489 of 21 July, SRDJ 106699–704.

118 Tokyo Nos. 893 of 12 July and 913 of 17 July 1945, NA, RG 457, SRDJ 105731–33, 106266–69.

119 The exchanges can be followed today – as they were followed by American leaders at the time – in Sato to Tokyo Nos. 1392 of 15 July and 1427 of 20 July, NA, RG 457, SRDJ 106079–83, 106564, on the one hand, and Tokyo's Nos. 913 of 17 July, 932 of 21 July, 944 of 25 July, SRDJ 106266–69, 106637–39, 107041–45.

120 A U.S. assessment of 27 July 1945 of the Japanese dispute about surrender is in "Magic Far East Summary, Naval Section," NA, RG 457, SRS 494.

121 Full text in *Public Papers of the Presidents of the United States: Harry S. Truman 1945* (Washington: GPO, 1961), pp. 43–48.

122 The account in Feis, *Japan Subdued*, chaps. 3–4, remains most helpful. See also Robert J. Maddox, *From War to Cold War: The Education of Harry S. Truman* (Boulder, Col.: Westview Press, 1988), chaps. 4, 7.

123 A good review in Ehrman, *Grand Strategy*, 6: 275–95; see also Pogue, *Marshall*, 4: 9, 17–23.

124 Ehrman, 6: 295–99.

125 Note Truman's diary entry for 25 July 1945 in Ferrell, *Off the Record*, pp. 55–56. The relevant section of Brooke's diary for 25 July has been omitted by Bryant; it refers to possible targets in the Soviet Union (Liddell Hart Centre, Alanbrooke Papers).

126 G. Patrick March, "Yanks in Siberia: U.S. Navy Weather Stations in Soviet East Asia, August 1945," *Pacific Historical Review* 57 (1988), 327–42, explains the great importance of weather reports for the invasion plans, the discussions of this issue at Yalta and Potsdam, and the establishment of two stations with Stalin's approval for a few months in Aug. 1945.

127 Mountbatten, who was present at Potsdam, was briefed; MacArthur was not present and hence not informed (Ehrman, *Grand Strategy*, 6: 255).

128 The Japanese were observing these negotiations with great concern: see Tokyo to Moscow No. 875 of 5 July, NA, RG 457, SRDJ 104922–23; Sato to Tokyo No. 1331 of 6 July, SRDJ 105239–40.

129 On the contacts in Switzerland, see Note 93, above; Bern to Tokyo No. 797 of 21 July, which contains a detailed review of the soundings, NA, RG 457, SRDJ 106748–58; Bern Nos. 798 of 20 July and 838 of 30 July, SRDJ 106925–29, 111612–14.

130 On the absence of second thoughts, see the Japanese Army General Staff Circular No. 352 of 4 Aug. 1945, NA, RG 457, SRA 18258–64.

131 Bernstein, "Roosevelt," pp. 52–55.

132 The USSBS calculated after the war that it would have taken 210 B-29s each carrying a 10–ton bomb load to produce the same damage and casualties at Hiroshima, and 120 at Nagasaki. In the case of the latter, hills limited the destructiveness of the bomb; in open terrain, 270 B-29s would have been needed to produce an effect similar to that of the potentially more powerful bomb dropped on Nagasaki (USSBS, *The Effects of Atomic Bombs on Hiroshima and Nagasaki* [Washington: GPO, 1946], p. 33).

133 There was some difference of opinion on what information should be put out, with the U.S. wanting to release more than the British. At that time, Field Marshal Wilson

anticipated that a second bomb would be dropped about five days after the first (see Wilson to Brooke, 6 Aug. 1945, PRO, CAB 127/47). There is no reference to the Hiroshima bomb in Brooke's diary.

134 Glantz, *August Storm*. For U.S. intelligence assistance to the Red Army, see NA, RG 457, SRH-198.

135 Edward J. Drea, "Misreading Intentions: Japanese Intelligence and the Soviet Invasion of Manchuria, 1945," *Military Affairs* 48, No. 2 (Apr. 1984), 66–73.

136 In addition to the accounts in Butow and Feis, there is now the translation of the *Kido Diary*, pp. 444ff. A recent article on the role of Hirohito argues that his part in putting down the 1936 military coup attempt in Tokyo was such an intervention, but there is a significant difference. In 1936, Hirohito responded to questions about the coup posed directly to him *without* a prior formal agreement or disagreement among his advisors. In other cases, questions had come to him after all his official advisors had reached agreement on a policy; in the 1945 situation, those who favored surrender and knew that Hirohito was on their side deliberately brought an evenly divided Council into the imperial presence to provoke an intervention by the Emperor. Peter Wetzler, "Kaiser Hirohito und der Krieg im Pazifik: Zur politischen Verantwortung des Tenno in der modernen japanischen Geschichte," *VjZ* 37 (1989), 611–44.

137 The issue is reviewed in detail in Barton J. Bernstein, "The Perils and Politics of Surrender: Ending the War with Japan and Avoiding the Third Atomic Bomb," *Pacific Historical Review* 46 (1977), 1–27. The one major omission is any reference to the prior uproar over the deal with Darlan.

138 *FRUS 1945*, 6: 631–32.

139 There is a useful preliminary account in William Craig, *The Fall of Japan* (New York: Dial Press, 1967), chap. 13.

140 Shillony, *Wartime Japan*, p. 88.

141 There is an excellent discussion of this issue in the Burma theater of war, which may serve as a sample, in Allen, *Burma*, pp. 529–52.

142 Peter N. Davies, *The Man Behind the Bridge*, pp. 198–200; Marder, *Old Friends, New Enemies*, 2: 575; cf. ibid., pp. 254–58.

143 The Japanese puppet government in China naturally now disappeared also; note Nanking to Tokyo Greater East Asia Ministry No. 525 of 11 Aug. 1945, NA, RG 457, SRDJ 108401–2.

144 The Japanese did try to keep the Allies from getting access to their codes by destroying secret documents and codes, see Japanese military attaché Stockholm to Lisbon, No number of 10 Aug. 1945, NA, RG 457, SRA 18298; Tokyo to Bern Circular 666 of 14 Aug., SRDJ 108553. They did not realize that these instructions, like the codes they were trying to protect, were being read by the Americans.

145 Theodore Cohen, *Remaking Japan: The American Occupation as New Deal* (New York: Free Press, 1987), chaps. 1–3.

146 See footnote, p. 883.

CONCLUSIONS

1 There is a good summary of the different statistics on German losses, and the problematic character of all of them, in Rüdiger Overmans, "Die Toten des Zweiten Weltkriegs in Deutschland: Bilanz der Forschung unter besonderer Berücksichtigung der Wehrmacht- und Vertreibungsverluste," in Wolfgang Michalka (ed.), *Der Zweite Weltkrieg*, pp. 858–73. Useful for its statistics but not its text, Martin K. Sorge, *The Other Price of Hitler's War: German Military and Civilian Losses Resulting from World War II* (Westport, Conn.: Greenwood, 1986).

2 A useful brief survey in Ulrich Herbert, *Fremdarbeiter: Politik und Praxis des*

"Ausländer-Einsatzes" in der Kriegswirtschaft des Dritten Reiches (Bonn: Dietz, 1985), pp. 341-45. The issues as they developed in American planning and the American zone are dealt with in Ziemke, *The U.S. Army.*

3 Eden's minute of 29 Nov. 1942: "I had always hoped that we could take a firm line at the Peace Conference that the bulk of the Jews should stay where they were in Europe. One hopes that the post-war Europe will not be a home of recurrent persecution, and there is anyway no room for these people in Palestine, even if every Arab were sent packing," from FO 371/31380 is quoted in Richard Langhorne (ed.), *Diplomacy and Intelligence during the Second World War* (Cambridge: Cambridge Univ. Press, 1985), p. 291 n 57.

4 The argument put forward retrospectively by Andreas Hillgruber in his 1986 book, *Zweierlei Untergang: Die Zerschlagung des Deutschen Reiches und das Ende des europäischen Judentums* (Berlin: Siedler) about the German army in the last year of the war fighting not only to enable the regime to continue murdering Jews but also to protect the Germans of the eastern provinces is a preposterous reversal of the realities. Had the Germans (like the Finns) pulled out of the war in September 1944, vast numbers of Germans who later lost their lives would have survived; had the German army "succeeded" in holding out even longer than it did, the first atomic bombs would have been dropped on German cities. An earlier end of the war would have saved German as well as Jewish lives (to say nothing of the lives of Allied soldiers and civilians).

5 Weinberg, *Foreign Policy 1937-1939*, pp. 270-71.

6 On the problems with American, British and Russian prisoners, see Russell D. Buhite, "Soviet-American Relations and the Repatriation of Prisoners of War, 1945," *The Historian* 35 (1973), 384-97. On German POWs, see Arthur L. Smith, *Heimkehr aus dem Zweiten Weltkrieg: Die Entlassung der deutschen Kriegsgefangenen* (Stuttgart: Deutsche Verlags-Anstalt, 1985). An important book missing from Smith's bibliography is George G. Lewis and John Mewha, *History of Prisoner of War Utilization by the United States Army 1776-1945* (Washington: GPO, 1955), most of which is devoted to World War II. On the charges about American mistreatment of German prisoners, see Günther Bischof and Stephen A. Ambrose (eds.), *Eisenhower and the German POWs: Facts against Falsehood* (Baton Rouge: Louisiana State Univ. Press, 1992); Arthur L. Smith, *Die "vermisse Million": Zum Schicksal deutscher Kriegsgefangener nach dem Zweiten Weltkrieg* (Munich: Oldenbourg, 1992). On the return of Japanese prisoners, see Morison, 15: 3-6.

7 On the Japanese army, the comments and references in Louis Allen, *Singapore 1941-1942* (London: Davis Poynter, 1977), chap. 12, "Afterthoughts," are especially interesting. See also Ienaga, *Pacific War*, p. 190. On the German army, the works of Omer Bartov are useful, as are studies by Manfred Messerschmidt and Jürgen Förster, but no one has as yet examined the contrast between World War I and World War II behavior. There is an interesting attempt to compare the German and the Italian military's conduct toward the Jews in Steinberg, *All or Nothing.*

8 There is a massive literature on Allied trials of German war criminals; a selective bibliography is included in the author's introduction to the AMS reprint of the Nürnberg *Trial of the Major War Criminals*; this should be supplemented by the entries in Jacob Robinson and Mrs. Philip Freedman, *The Holocaust and After: Sources and Literature in English* (Jerusalem: Israel Univ. Press, 1973). There is a comprehensive survey of the American effort in Frank M. Buscher, *The U.S. War Crimes Trial Program in Germany, 1946-1955* (New York: Praeger, 1989). There are no analogous works on the British, Russian, or French programs. For trials conducted by the Germans, see Adalbert Ruckerl, *The Investigation of Nazi Crimes: A Documentation*, trans. by Derel Rutter (Heidelberg: C.F. Müller, 1979).

9 For a helpful survey, see Philip R. Piccigallo, *The Japanese on Trial: Allied War Crimes Operations in the East, 1945-1951* (Austin: Univ. of Texas Press, 1979).

10 It should be noted that the International Red Cross behaved in a somewhat similar fashion: during the war it paid practically no attention to the vast murder programs carried out by the Germans all over Europe; afterwards it was most solicitous about the fate of German prisoners of war.

11 A summary in Willi A. Boelcke, *Die Kosten von Hitlers Krieg: Kriegsfinanzierung und finanzialles Kriegserbe in Deutschland 1933-1948* (Paderborn: Schöningh, 1985). An internal German Ministry of Finance study of the five years of war from Sep. 1939 to Sep. 1944 show that exactions from the occupied territories by very conservative estimates had been equal to the whole German pre-war rearmament costs and were then contributing about 20 percent of total German revenues (Generalbüro "Nr. 3400-32 GenB g," 6 Oct. 1944, BA, R 2/24250).

12 On William II's 27 July 1900 speech, see Bernd Sösemann, "Die sog. Hunnenrede Wilhelms II. Textkritische und interpretatorische Bemerkungen zur Ansprache des Kaisers vom 27. Juli 1900 in Bremerhaven," *Historische Zeitschrift* 222 (1976), 342-58.

13 The personal role of Adenauer in the fundamental *political* decisions to try to make, instead of trying to avoid, payments is well illustrated in Michael Wolffsohn, "Das deutsch-israelische Wiedergutmachungsabkommen von 1952 im internationalen Zusammenhang," *VjZ* 36 (1988), 691-731. On American seizure of German patents, see John Gimbel *Science, Technology, and Reparations: Exploitation and Plunder in Postwar Germany* (Stanford Ca.: Stanford Univ. Press, 1990).

14 Note Philippe Bourdrel, *L'Epuration sauvage, 1944-1945* (Paris: Perrin, 1988); Herbert R. Lottman, *The Purge* (New York: Morrow, 1986); Henry Rousso, *The Vichy Syndrome: History and Memory in France since 1944*, trans. Arthur Goldhammer (Cambridge, Mass.: Harvard Univ. Press, 1991). On Quisling, the book by Oddvar K. Hoidal is by far the best.

15 There is a helpful brief summary of the peace treaties with Italy, Finland, Bulgaria, Hungary and Romania in the U.S. State Department's publication, *Making the Peace Treaties 1941-1947* (Washington: GPO, 1947).

16 For an introduction, see Benjamin Rivlin, *The United Nations and the Italian Colonies* (New York: Carnegie Endowment for International Peace, 1950).

17 The killing of Mountbatten many years later cannot be fitted into this context; what it was supposed to do for Ireland will remain the secret of those who murdered him.

18 On the systematic Soviet removal of industry, see Edwin W. Pauley, *Report on Japanese Assets in Manchuria to the President of the United States, July, 1946* (Washington: GPO, 1946).

19 The impact of economic policy in the liberated area, which included much of China's major industrial and commercial centers, is stressed in Ch'i, *Nationalist's China*, p. 222.

20 The 7 Oct. 1944 speech of Thomas E. Dewey in Charleston, W.Va., may be found in *Vital Speeches* 11, No. 1 (15 Oct. 1944), 15; the former head of the WAC appointed by Dwight D. Eisenhower was Oveta C. Hobby.

21 On the tiny American stockpile of nuclear weapons after August 1945, see David A. Rosenberg, "U.S. Nuclear Stockpile, 1945 to 1950," *Bulletin of the Atomic Scientists* 38 (May 1982), 25-30.

22 There is an account of the battle in Morison, *US Naval Operations*, 12: 88-109, but the whole issue of self-deception by Japanese commanders awaits investigation.

23 For unusually interesting pictures of personalities in headquarters, see the two volumes of Paul P. Rogers, *The Good Years*, and *The Bitter Years: MacArthur and Sutherland* (New York: Praeger, 1990-91); Harry C. Butcher, *My Three Years with Eisenhower* (New York: Simon and Schuster, 1946); Hastings Ismay, *The Memoirs of General Lord Ismay* (New York: Viking, 1960).

24 *Commander in Chief: Franklin Delano Roosevelt, His Lieutenants and Their War* (New York: Harper & Row, 1987).

25 Alanbrooke Diary for 12 June 1945, Liddell Hart Centre.

26 Henry H. Arnold, *Global Mission* (New York: Harper, 1949).

Map 1. The invasion and partition of Poland, 1939

Within the map:

LATVIA

LITHUANIA

Baltic
Sea

Memel

HELA
PENINSULA

Kovno
(Kaunas)

Vilna

Mariampole

Minsk

Gdynia

Königsberg

**EAST
PRUSSIA**

Suwałki

Danzig

Tszew
(Dirschau)

Bydgoszcz
(Bromberg)

Białystok

Narev R.

Poznan

Kutno

Modlin

Warsaw

Brest

Pinsk

Łowicz

P   O   L   A   N   D

Łódź

Silesia

Częstochowa

Cracow

Lwow

**GREATER
GERMANY**

Cieszyn
(Teschen)

Drogobic
Borislav
Przemysł

SLOVAKIA

Ruthenia
(Carpatho-Ukraine)

ROMANIA

Bratislava

- P. Neumann -

Vienna

HUNGARY

German advances

Russian advances

Territory lost to
Slovakia and Lithuania

Limit of the German-Soviet
"Interessensphäre": Aug. 23rd 1939

German-Soviet Demarcation
line: Sept. 28th 1939

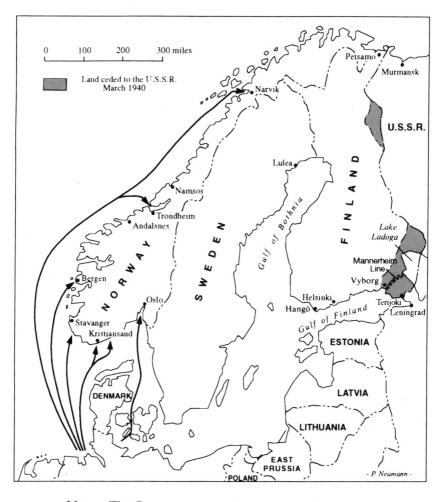

Map 2. The German invasion of Denmark and Norway, 1940

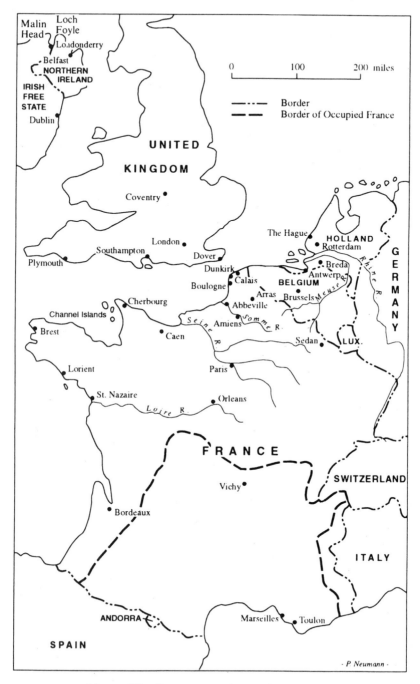

Map 3. The German campaign in the West, 1940

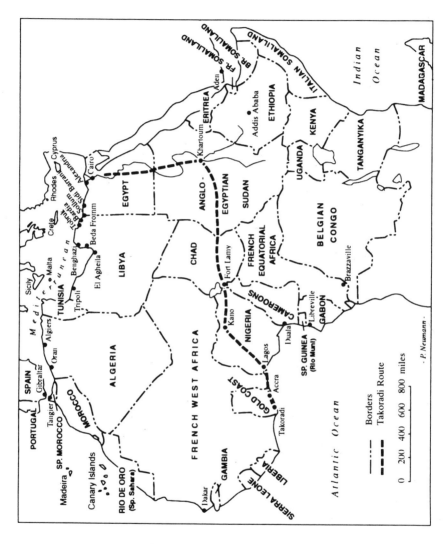

Map 4. The campaigns in East and North Africa, 1940–1941

- P. Neumann -

Borders
Takoradi Route

0   200   400   600   800 miles

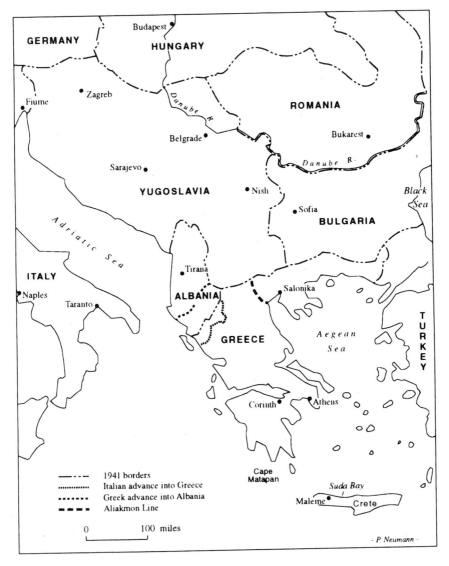

Map 5. The campaigns in the Balkans, 1940–1941

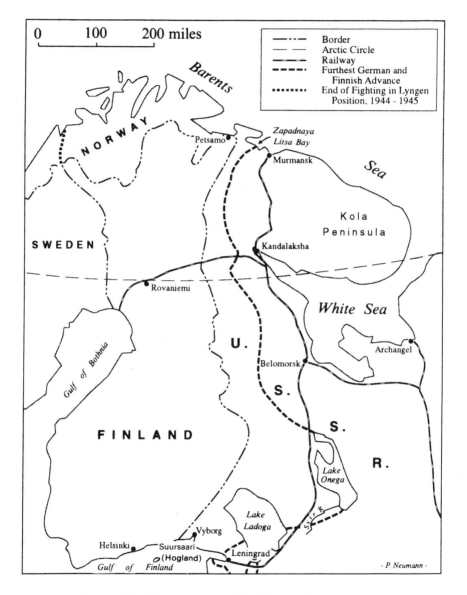

Map 6. The Finnish portion of the Eastern Front, 1941–1945

Map 7. The German invasion of the Soviet Union, 1941–1942

Map 8. The Eastern Front, 1943–1944

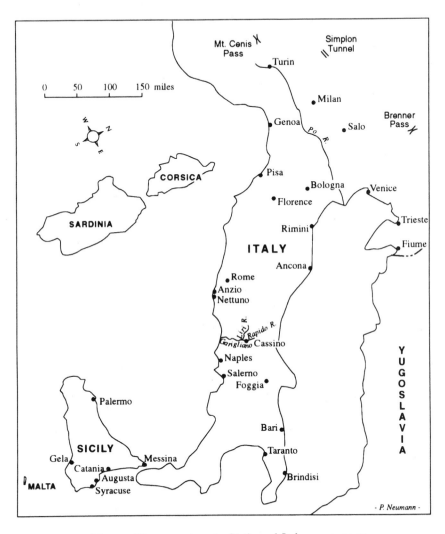

Map 9. The campaigns in Sicily and Italy, 1943–1945

Map 10. The campaigns in North Africa, 1942–1943

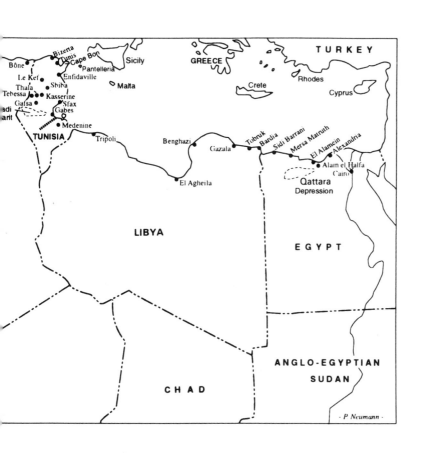

Bône
Bizerta
Tunis
Cape Bon
Sicily
GREECE
TURKEY
Le Kef
Pantelleria
Thala
Enfidaville
Shiba
Malta
Crete
Rhodes
Tebessa
Kasserine
Cyprus
Gafsa
Sfax
adi
Gabes
arit
Medenine
TUNISIA
Tripoli
Benghazi
Tobruk
Bardia
Sidi Barrani
Mersa Matruth
Gazala
El Alamein
Alexandria
Alam el Halfa
Cairo
El Agheila
Qattara
Depression
LIBYA
EGYPT
CHAD
ANGLO-EGYPTIAN
SUDAN
· P. Neumann ·

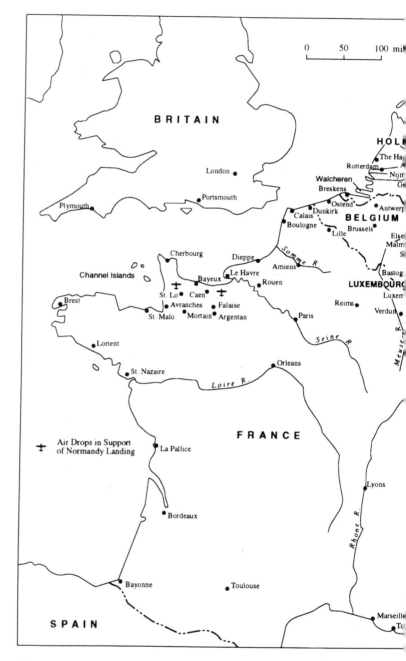

Map 11. The campaigns in the West, 1944–1945

Map 12. The Eastern Front, 1944–1945

Borders

Front 23 June 1944

Front 15 Dec. 1944

Front 15 Feb. 1945

ND

Helsinki · Leningrad

in

Narva

ESTONIA

Riga

LATVIA

ANIA · Vilna

Vitebsk

Orsha · Smolensk

Minsk · Mogilev

rodno

Rogachev

D

SOVIET

UNION

· Korosten

· Kiev

Moscow ·

Дnepr R.

NIA

· Ploesti

·

R.

· Constanta

Odessa

0   100   200 miles

- *P. Neumann* -

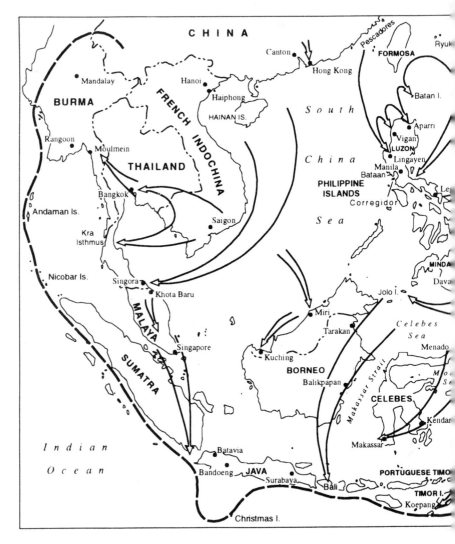

Map 13. The Japanese attack, 1941–1942

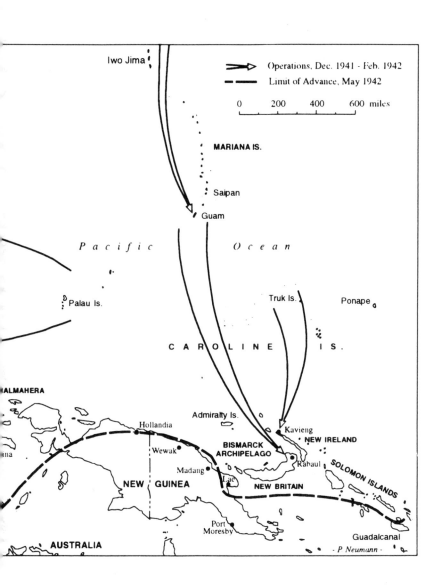

Iwo Jima

Operations, Dec. 1941 - Feb. 1942

Limit of Advance, May 1942

0   200   400   600 miles

MARIANA IS.

Saipan

Guam

P a c i f i c   *O c e a n*

Palau Is.

Truk Is.   Ponape

C A R O L I N E   I S .

HALMAHERA

Admiralty Is.

Hollandia

Kavieng

NEW IRELAND

Wewak   BISMARCK
ARCHIPELAGO

Madang   Rabaul

SOLOMON ISLANDS

Lae

NEW GUINEA   NEW BRITAIN

Port
Moresby

AUSTRALIA   Guadalcanal

- P. Neumann -

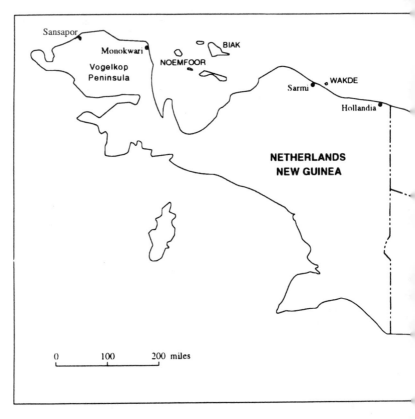

Map 14. The campaigns in New Guinea, 1942–1945

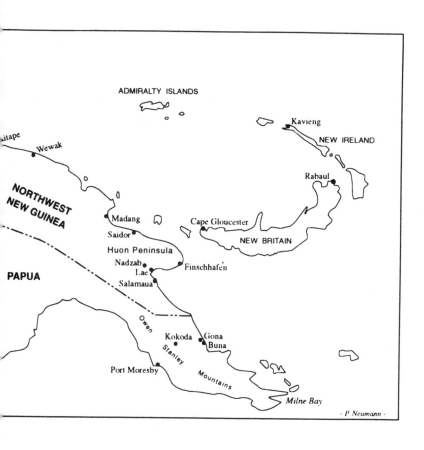

ADMIRALTY ISLANDS

Kavieng

NEW IRELAND

.itape

Wewak

NORTHWEST
NEW GUINEA

Rabaul

Madang

Cape Gloucester

Saidor

NEW BRITAIN

Huon Peninsula

PAPUA

Nadzab

Lae

Salamaua

Finschhafen

Owen

Kokoda

Gona

Buna

Stanley

Port Moresby

Mountains

Milne Bay

- P. Neumann -

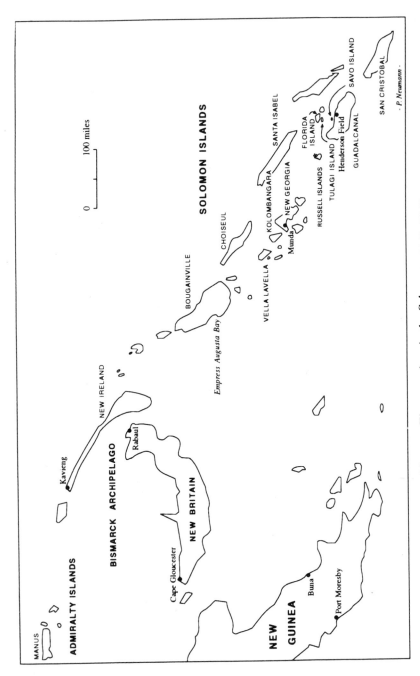

Map 15. The campaigns in the Solomons, 1942–1945

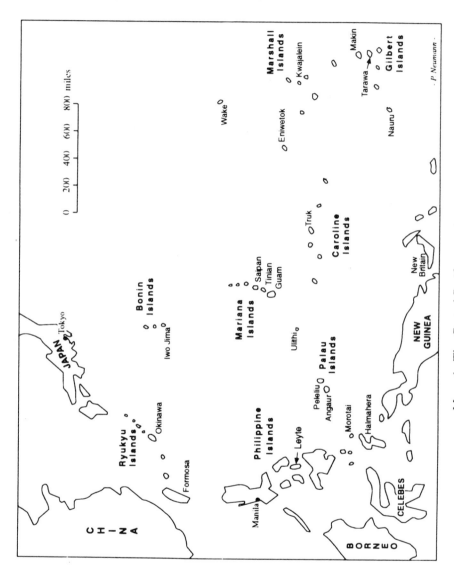

Map 16. The Central Pacific campaign, 1943–1945

1147

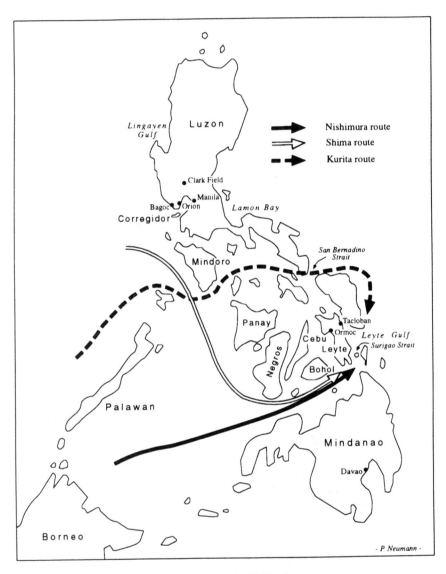

Map 17. The campaigns in the Philippines, 1944–1945

Map 18. The campaign in Malaya, 1941–1942

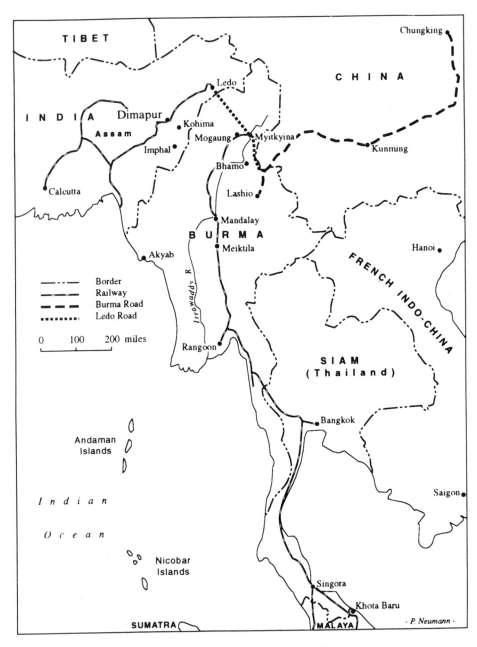

Map 19. The campaigns in Burma and India, 1942–1945

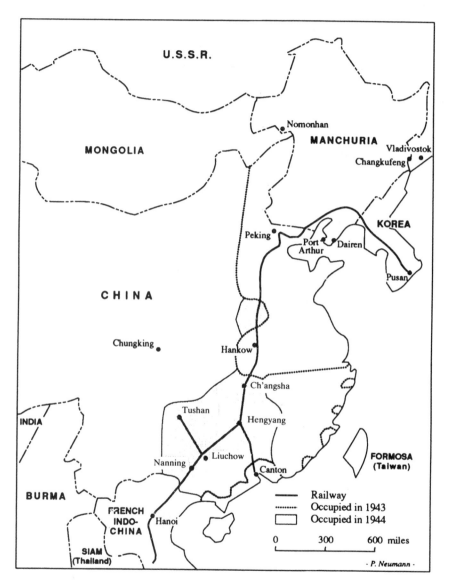

Map 20. The war in China, 1941–1945

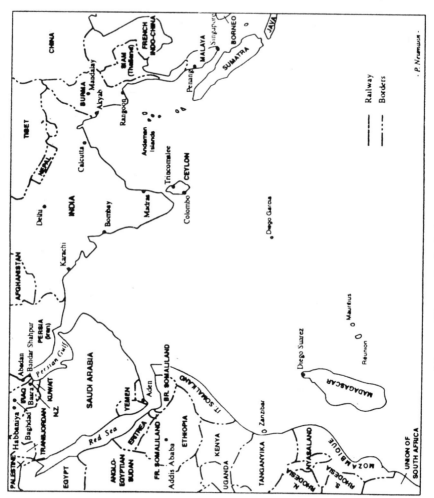

Map 21. The war in the Indian Ocean

Map 22. The campaign on Okinawa

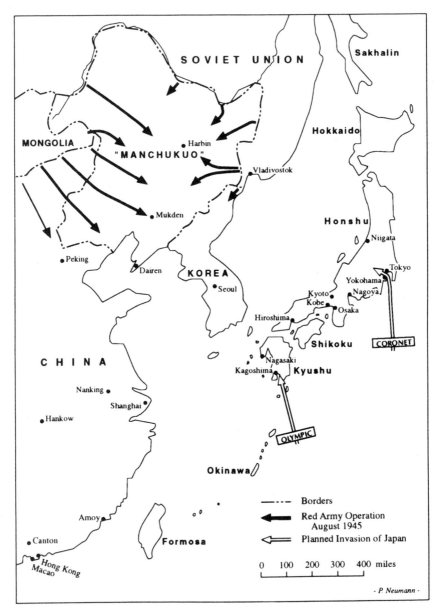

Map 23. The campaign in Manchuria and the invasion of Japan

INDEX